INGENIX.

ingenix *e*solutions

Electronic coding, billing & reimbursement products

Electronic coding, billing and reimbursement products.

Ingenix provides a robust suite of eSolutions to solve a wide variety of coding, billing and reimbursement issues. As the industry moves to electronic products, you can rely on Ingenix to help support you through the transition.

← **Web-based applications for all markets**

← **Dedicated support**

← **Environmentally responsible**

Key Features and Benefits

Using eSolutions is a step in the right direction when it comes to streamlining your coding, billing and reimbursement practices. Ingenix eSolutions can help you save time and increase your efficiency with accurate and on-time content.

- **Rely on a leader in health care.** Ingenix has been producing quality coding products for over 25 years. All of the expert content that goes into our books goes into our electronic resources.

- **Save time and money.** Ingenix eSolutions combine the content of over 37 code books and data files.

- **Go Green.** Eco-friendly electronic products are not only faster and easier to use than books, they require less storage space, less paper and leave a lighter carbon footprint.

- **Increase accuracy.** Electronic solutions are updated regularly so you know you're always working with the most current content available.

- **Get the training and support you need.** Convenient, online training and customized training programs are available to meet your specific needs.

- **Take baby steps.** Transition at your pace with code book and solution packages that let you keep your books while you learn how to become a whiz with your electronic products.

- **Get Started.** Visit **shopingenix.com/ eSolutions** for product listing.

SAVE UP TO 20%

with source code FB10E

 Visit **www.shopingenix.com** and enter the source code to save 20%.

 Call toll-free **1-800-INGENIX** (464-3649), option 1 and save 15%.

Ingenix | Information is the Lifeblood of Health Care | Call toll-free 1-800-INGENIX (464-3649), option 1.

100% Money Back Guarantee If our merchandise ever fails to meet your expectations, please contact our Customer Service Department toll-free at 1-800-INGENIX (464-3649), option 1, for an immediate response. Software: Credit will be granted for unopened packages only.

Also available from your medical bookstore or distributor.

FB10E

INGENIX®

Learning and Development Services

Information is what keeps an expert an expert.

Ingenix Learning and Development Services provides comprehensive education and training programs that provide opportunities for health care professionals to increase their knowledge, enhance their skills and keep pace with industry trends. The result is a more capable workforce that enables health care organizations to continually improve their services.

← **Convenient web-based eCourses**

← **Deep and diverse industry expertise**

← **Comprehensive coding curriculum**

SAVE UP TO 20%

with source code FB10G

 Visit **www.shopingenix.com** and enter the source code to save 20%.

 Call toll-free **1-800-INGENIX** (464-3649), option 1 and save 15%.

Key Features and Benefits

Ingenix coding and reimbursement eCourses provide a robust curriculum with a variety of courses that focus on urgent coding and claims review training needs. Easy tracking and documentation of training results, timely content updates and higher information retention rates make our online courses a powerful resource.

- **Satisfy your coding needs by creating your own coder.** Customized curriculum to meet your individual practice needs.

- **Keep up-to-date with coding and regulatory changes.** Ingenix experts develop new classes based on current guidelines and rules so you and your staff are always up-to-date and prepared in case of an audit.

- **Streamline your revenue cycle with knowledgeable coding professionals.** Quickly reap the benefits of knowledgeable coding professionals: fewer denied claims, faster reimbursements and increased revenue.

- **Save time and money.** Reduce overall training costs by eliminating travel expenses and reducing costs associated with instructor time and salary.

- **Keep your staff's credentials current and relevant.** Earn CEU credentials provided by the American Academy of Professional Coders and the American Health Information Management Association.

For our full curriculum, visit Learning and Development Services on www.shopingenix.com.

Ingenix | Information is the Lifeblood of Health Care | Call toll-free 1-800-INGENIX (464-3649), option 1.

100% Money Back Guarantee If our merchandise ever fails to meet your expectations, please contact our Customer Service Department toll-free at 1-800-INGENIX (464-3649), option 1, for an immediate response. Software: Credit will be granted for unopened packages only.

Also available from your medical bookstore or distributor.

INGENIX.

Coding *and* Payment Guide for the Physical Therapist

*An essential coding, billing, and reimbursement resource
for the physical therapist*

2010

American Physical Therapy Association

Ingenix Notice

Coding and Payment Guide for the Physical Therapist is designed to provide accurate and authoritative information in regard to the subject covered. Every reasonable effort has been made to ensure the accuracy of the information within these pages. However, the ultimate responsibility for accuracy lies with the user. Ingenix, its employees, agents, and staff, make no representation, guarantee, or warranty, express or implied, that this compilation is error-free or that the use of this publication will prevent differences of opinion or disputes with Medicare or other third-party payers, and will bear no responsibility or liability for the results or consequences of its use. If you identify a correction or wish to share information, please email the Ingenix customer service department at customerservice@ingenix.com or fax us at 801.982.4033.

American Medical Association Notice

CPT only © 2009 American Medical Association. All rights reserved.

Fee schedules, relative value units, conversion factors and/or related components are not assigned by the AMA, are not part of CPT, and the AMA is not recommending their use. The AMA does not directly or indirectly practice medicine or dispense medical services. The AMA assumes no liability for data contained or not contained herein.

CPT is a registered trademark of the American Medical Association.

The responsibility for the content of any "National Correct Coding Policy" included in this product is with the Centers for Medicare and Medicaid Services and no endorsement by the AMA is intended or should be implied. The AMA disclaims responsibility for any consequences or liability attributable to or related to any use, nonuse or interpretation of information contained in this product.

Our Commitment to Accuracy

Ingenix is committed to producing accurate and reliable materials.

To report corrections, please visit www.ingenixonline.com/accuracy or email accuracy@ingenix.com. You can also reach customer service by calling 1.800.INGENIX (464.3649), option 1.

Copyright

Acknowledgments

Kelly Armstrong, *Product Manager*
Karen Schmidt, BSN, *Technical Director*
Stacy Perry, *Manager, Desktop Publishing*
Lisa Singley, *Project Manager*
Deborah C. Hall, *Clinical/Technical Editor*
Karen H. Kachur, RN, CPC, *Clinical/Technical Editor*
Beth Ford, RHIT, CCS, *Clinical/Technical Editor*
Tracy Betzler, *Desktop Publishing Specialist*
Hope M. Dunn, *Desktop Publishing Specialist*
Toni R. Stewart, *Desktop Publishing Specialist*
Regina Heppes, *Editor*

American Physical Therapy Assosiation Contributors:

Helene M. Fearon, PT
Fearon & Roessler Physical Therapy, Phoenix, Arizona; Partner, Fearon & Levine Consulting, Ft. Lauderdale, Florida; AMA, CPT, HCPAC Co-Chair; AMA, CPT, Editorial Panelist
Paul A. Rockar Jr., PT, DPT, MS
CEO/Partner, Centers for Rehab Services, McKeesport, PA; Vice President, APTA Board of Directors
Stephen M. Levine, PT, DPT, MSHA
Partner, Fearon & Levine Consulting, Ft. Lauderdale, Florida; Past Speaker of the House of Delegates, APTA; AMA RUC HCPAC Representative

Technical Editors

Deborah C. Hall

Ms. Hall is a senior clinical/technical editor for Ingenix. Ms. Hall has more than 25 years of experience in the health care field. Her experience includes 10 years as office manager for large multi-specialty medical practices. Ms. Hall has written several multi-specialty newsletters and coding and reimbursement manuals, and served as a health care consultant. She has taught seminars on CPT/HCPCS and ICD-9-CM coding and physician fee schedules. She is an active member of the American Academy of Professional Coders.

Karen H. Kachur, RN, CPC

Ms. Kachur is a clinical/technical editor for Ingenix with expertise in CPT/HCPCS and ICD-9-CM coding, in addition to physician billing, compliance, and fraud and abuse. Prior to joining Ingenix, she worked for many years as a staff RN in a variety of clinical settings including medicine, surgery, intensive care, and psychiatry. In addition to her clinical background, Ms. Kachur served as assistant director of a hospital utilization management and quality assurance department and has extensive experience as a nurse reviewer for Blue Cross/Blue Shield. She is an active member of the American Academy of Professional Coders and the American College of Medical Coding Specialists.

Beth Ford, RHIT, CCS

Ms. Ford is a clinical/technical editor for Ingenix. She has extensive background in both physician and facility ICD-9-CM and CPT/HCPCS coding. Ms. Ford has served as a coding specialist, coding manager, coding trainer/educator and coding consultant, as well as a health information management director. She is an active member of the American Heath Information Management Association (AHIMA).

Contents

Introduction

Coding systems and claim forms are part of the reality of modern health care. This coding and payment book provides a comprehensive explanation of at the coding and reimbursement systems used by physical therapists. Organized by topics and by numerical code listings pertinent to physical therapy, it can be used as a coding as well as a compensation resource.

Coding systems grew out of the need for data collection. By having a standard notation for the procedures performed and for the diseases, injuries, and illnesses diagnosed, statisticians could identify effective treatments as well as broad practice patterns. Before long, these early coding systems emerged as the basis to pay claims. Coding systems and claim forms have evolved to become the basis of reimbursement for health care services. The correct application of codes and knowledge of payer policies correlates directly to payment.

The administrative simplification provisions of the Health Insurance Portability and Accountability Act (HIPAA) of 1996 required the standardization of the several hundred health care claim formats previously in existence, as well as the establishment of standardized code sets for medical data including diagnoses, drugs, procedures, equipment, and supplies. The goal of the national standards is to reduce the administrative encumbrances of the existing system, simplify the way medical claims are paid, reduce costs, and promote the growth of electronic business in the health care industry.

Coding Systems

Coding systems seek to answer two questions: what was wrong with the patient (i.e., the diagnosis or diagnoses) and what was done to treat the patient (i.e., the procedures or services rendered).

Under the aegis of the federal government, a three-tiered coding system emerged for physician offices and outpatient facilities. Current Procedural Terminology (CPT®) codes report medical procedures and services and comprises Level I of the system. A second level, known as HCPCS Level II codes, are mainly used to identify products, supplies, and services that are not included in the CPT codes. Dovetailing with each of these is the International Classification of Diseases, Ninth Revision, Clinical Modification (ICD-9-CM) classification system that reports the diagnosis of illnesses, diseases, and injuries. (A portion of ICD-9-CM also contains codes for inpatient procedures and is used exclusively by inpatient facilities.)

Further explanations of each of these coding systems follows.

ICD-9-CM Codes

The ICD-9-CM classification system is a method of translating medical terminology into codes. Codes within the system are either numeric or alphanumeric and are composed of three, four, or five characters. A decimal point follows all three-character codes when fourth and fifth characters are needed. Coding involves using a numeric or alphanumeric code to describe a disease or injury. For example, a frozen shoulder is classified to code 726.0.

Generally, the reason the patient seeks treatment should be sequenced first when multiple diagnoses are listed. Claims forms require that the appropriate ICD-9-CM code be reported rather than a description of the functional deficits.

Health care providers need to be aware of the necessity for specific diagnosis coding. Using only the first three digits of the ICD-9-CM diagnosis code when fourth and fifth digits are available will result in invalid coding, a delay in payment, and requests for additional information from the provider.

HCPCS Level I or CPT Codes

The Centers for Medicare and Medicaid Services (CMS), in conjunction with the American Medical Association (AMA), the American Dental Association (ADA) and several other professional groups developed, adopted, and implemented a coding system describing services rendered to patients. Known as HCPCS Level I, the CPT coding system is the most commonly used system to report procedures and services. Copyright of CPT codes and descriptions is held by the AMA. This system reports outpatient and provider services.

CPT codes predominantly describe medical services and procedures, and are adapted to provide a common billing language that providers and payers can use for payment purposes. The codes are required for billing by both private and public insurance carriers, managed care companies, and workers' compensation programs.

The AMA's CPT Editorial Panel reviews the coding system and adds, revises, and deletes codes and descriptions. The panel accepts information and feedback from providers about new codes and revisions to existing codes that could better reflect the provided service or procedure. The American Physical Therapy Association (APTA) is represented on the Health Care Professional Advisory Committee (HCPAC) for both the AMA CPT Editorial Panel and the AMA Relative Value Update Committee (RUC). The CPT HCPAC representative provides input for the development and revision of CPT codes, while the RUC HCPAC representative provides input into the establishment of relative values for the codes.

CPT category II codes are supplemental tracking codes that are primarily used when participating in the Physician Quality Reporting Initiative (PQRI) established by Medicare and are intended to aid in the collection of data about quality of care. At the present time, participation in this program is optional and physical therapists should not report these codes if they elect not to participate. Category II codes are alphanumeric, consisting of four digits followed by an "F" and should never be used in lieu of a category I CPT code. Category II codes have not been included in this edition of the *Coding and Payment Guide for the Physical Therapist* because the official PQRI measure specification document has not been released by CMS at time of printing. Therefore, we do not know which codes are associated with individual measures or which measures are pertinent to the physical therapist.

Category III of the CPT coding system contains temporary tracking codes for new and emerging technologies that are meant to aid in the collection of data on these new services and procedures. CPT category III codes consist of four numeric digits followed by a "T." Like category II codes, category III codes are released twice a year (January 1 and July I) and can be found on the AMA CPT website at http://www.ama-assn.org/go/cpt. RVUs are not assigned for category III codes and payment is made at the discretion of the payer. A service described by a CPT code may eventually become a category I code, as the efficacy and safety of the service is documented.

HCPCS Level II Codes

HCPCS Level II codes are commonly referred to as national codes or by the acronym HCPCS (Healthcare Common Procedure Coding System, pronounced "hik piks"). HCPCS codes are used for billing Medicare and Medicaid patients and are also used by some third-party payers.

HCPCS Level II codes, updated and published annually by the CMS, are intended to supplement the CPT coding system by including codes for durable medical equipment, prosthetics, orthotics, and supplies (DMEPOS); drugs; and biologicals. These Level II codes consist of one alphabetic character (A through V) followed by four numbers. In many instances, HCPCS Level II codes are developed as precursors to CPT codes.

Claim Forms

Institutional (facility) providers use the UB-04 claim form, also known as the CMS-1450, to file a Medicare Part A claim to Medicare contractors for service providers in hospital outpatient settings or in the electronic format using the 837i format. Noninstitutional providers and suppliers (private practices or other health care providers offices) utilize the CMS-1500 form or the 837p electronic format to submit claims to Medicare contractors for Medicare Part B-covered services. Medicare Part A coverage includes inpatient hospital, skilled nursing facilities (SNF), hospice, and home health. Part A providers also include rehabilitation agencies and comprehensive outpatient rehabilitation facilities (CORF). Medicare Part B coverage provides payment for medical supplies, physician services, and outpatient services delivered in a private practice setting.

Not all services rendered by a facility are inpatient services. Providers working in facilities routinely render services on an outpatient basis. Outpatient services are provided in settings that include rehabilitation centers, certified outpatient rehabilitation facilities, SNFs, and hospitals. Outpatient and partial hospitalization facility claims might be submitted on either a CMS-1500 or a UB-04 depending on the payer.

For professional component billing, most claims are filed using ICD-9-CM diagnosis code to indicate the reason for the service, CPT codes to identify the service provided, HCPCS Level II codes to report supplies on the CMS-1500 paper claim or the 837p electronic format.

Contents and Format of This Guide

The *Coding and Payment Guide for the Physical Therapist* contains chapters that address reimbursement, official Medicare regulatory information, and a glossary.

Reimbursement

The first section of the guide provides comprehensive information about the coding and reimbursement process. It contains four chapters: an introduction, "The Reimbursement Process," "Documentation—An Overview," and "Claims Processing." These chapters are predominantly narrative in nature; however, the claims processing chapter provides step-by-step explanations to complete the CMS-1500 and UB-04 claim forms and a crosswalk for electronic submissions.

Definitions, Guidelines, and Indexes

The second section provides definitions, guidelines, and alphabetic indexes for CPT, ICD-9-CM, and HCPCS Level II codes applicable to physical therapy.

CPT Definitions and Guidelines

Coding tips, definitions, CPT guidelines, and Medicare rules are presented in this section, which is organized numerically by CPT code. Codes may be listed individually, or in ranges. At the end of the CPT definitions and guidelines section is a CPT alphabetic index to help the coder find the correct CPT codes by using familiar terms.

Procedural information presented may include many components. The following is an example of the format.

97113	Therapeutic procedure, one or more areas, each 15 minutes; aquatic therapy with therapeutic exercises
	The therapist directs and/or performs therapeutic exercises with the patient/client in the aquatic environment. The code requires skilled intervention by the clinician and documentation must support medical necessity of the aquatic environment. This code can be billed in 15 minute units.

Coding Tip

When performing aquatic therapy, the physical therapist must be present providing one-to-one contact with the patient, but does not have to physically be in the pool.

ICD-9-CM

ICD-9-CM diagnostic codes listed are common diagnoses or reasons the procedure or service may be necessary. This list is inclusive to the specialty. In some cases, not every possible code is listed and the ICD-9-CM book should be referenced for other valid codes.

HCPCS Alphabetic Index

The guide contains a HCPCS alphabetic index to help the coder find the correct HCPCS codes by using familiar terms.

Medicare Official Regulatory Information

The full excerpts from the online CMS Manual System pertaining to physical therapy services are provided in this section. These references often do not identify the guideline with appropriate corresponding CPT or HCPCS Level II codes. Our experts have crosswalked the reference, wherever possible, to the applicable procedure or supply code. This crosswalk reference is listed under each applicable CPT or HCPCS code in the definitions, guidelines, and index section. The excerpts are listed in this section in numeric order.

Index
The final section consists of a comprehensive index that provides a list of pages on which each term is discussed, and a glossary of coding, billing, and clinical terms applicable to your specialty.

How to Use the Guide
By following logical steps when coding, providers will improve accuracy and experience fewer overlooked diagnoses and services. To locate codes in this book, follow these steps:

1. Carefully read the statement that describes the patient's diagnosis and the service provided. More than one diagnosis or service may have been documented.

2. To locate the code for the diagnosis, identify the main term for each diagnosis and any limitations or qualifiers accompanying the diagnosis. Then turn to the alphabetical ICD-9-CM index to find the code by locating the terms you've identified. The index at the back of the book may help you find the particular page on which the term is indexed.

3. Next, look to see whether the diagnosis code has an icon or a "☑" notation. If there is an icon, check the key for its meaning. The ☑ symbol indicates that a fifth digit is necessary to complete the code. The fifth-digit choices are defined in a boxed reference near the code. After checking for icons and fifth-digit requirements, review the code's description to make sure it accurately describes the patient's diagnosis.

4. Turn to the definitions and guidelines for diagnoses, and review and follow the instructions given for the diagnosis code.

5. To locate the correct procedure code or codes, turn to the alphabetic CPT book index. Locate the entry for the service or procedure performed. Turn to the definitions and guidelines for procedures, and review and follow the instruction for the service or procedure performed.

6. For the correct HCPCS Level II codes, find the key terms for the code description in the index of the HCPCS section to locate the appropriate code.

7. Finally, assign all codes. If you want any further clarification about medical terms, refer to the glossary.

Note: Due to space constraints, this product does not contain a complete list of all possible ICD-9-CM, CPT, or HCPCS Level II codes. Refer to an unabridged code book for any questions concerning more detailed coding.

The Reimbursement Process

Appropriate reimbursement for physical therapy services can sometimes be difficult because of the myriad of rules and paperwork involved. The following reimbursement guidelines help you understand the various requirements to get claims paid promptly and correctly.

Coverage Issues

First, you need to know which services are covered. Covered services are those payable by the insurer in accordance with the terms of the benefit-plan contract. Such services must be documented and medically necessary for payment to be made.

Typically, third-party payers define medically necessary services or supplies as:

- Services requiring the skills of a qualified provider
- Services established as safe and effective
- Services consistent with the symptoms or diagnosis
- Services necessary and consistent with generally accepted medical/professional standards
- Services furnished at the most appropriate, safe, and effective level

Documentation must be provided to support the medical necessity of a service, procedure, and/or other items. This documentation should show:

- What service or procedure was rendered
- To what extent the service or procedure was rendered
- Why the service, procedure, or other item was medically necessary

When providing physical therapy services, it is especially important for providers to thoroughly and individually document all care given to each patient at each visit, including the total treatment time and total direct contact time.

When in doubt, providers should consult with the specific payer or refer to Medicare national coverage determinations (NCD) or local coverage determinations (LCD). Local coverage determinations and national coverage determinations address the reasonable and necessary provisions of a service. LCDs include lists of conditions that support medical necessity, and often provide a corresponding ICD-9-CM code.

Verify that all services billed are medically necessary. If the provider feels that it is medically necessary for the patient to receive physical therapy interventions that are more or less than the current standard of practice, clearly document in the patient's record the rationale used for this decision. Physical and occupational therapy services are covered only for restorative therapy by Medicare, that is when there is the expectation to restore a patient's level of function that has been lost due to injury, disease, or illness, rather than to maintain a level of function. Maintenance care is not reimbursed by Medicare and many other third-party payers, but establishment and periodic reevaluation of a maintenance program is a covered service under Medicare.

Services, procedures, and/or other items that may not be considered medically necessary are:

- Services not furnished by a qualified provider
- Services that do not require the skills of a qualified provider
- Services not generally accepted as safe and effective for the condition being treated
- Services not proven to be safe and effective based on peer review or scientific literature
- Experimental or investigational services
- Services furnished at a duration, intensity, or frequency that is not medically appropriate
- Services not furnished in accordance with accepted standards of medical practice
- Services not furnished in a setting appropriate to the patient's medical needs and condition

Payer Types

Most providers have to deal with a number of different payers and plans, each with its own specific policies and methods of reimbursement. For that reason, it is important to become familiar with the guidelines for every payer and plan that your practice has contact with. Some insurance plans are administered by either federal or state government, including Medicare, Medicaid, and TRICARE. Private payers range from fee-for-services plans to health maintenance organizations (HMO).

Medicare

Administered by the federal government, Medicare provides health insurance benefits to those 65 years of age and older, and individuals of any age who are entitled to disability benefits under Social Security or Railroad Retirement programs. In addition, individuals with end-stage renal disease that requires hemodialysis or kidney transplants are also eligible for Medicare benefits. Consisting of four parts, Medicare Part A (for which all persons over 65 are qualified) covers hospitalization; Part B (which is optional, covers physician and other related health services); Medicare Advantage, also referred to as Medicare Part C, allows managed care plans including health maintenance organizations (HMO) and preferred provider organizations (PPO) to be a part of Medicare; and Medicare Part D is the subsidized prescription drug benefit. Fees for Medicare services delivered in the outpatient setting are based on the Medicare Physician Fee Schedule.

Medicaid

Medicaid is administered by the state governments under federal guidelines to provide health insurance for low-income or otherwise needy individuals. In addition to the broad guidelines established by the federal government, each state has the responsibility to administer its own program, including:

- Establishing eligibility standards
- Determining the type, amount, duration, and scope of services
- Setting payment rates for services

TRICARE

TRICARE provides health insurance to active and retired military personnel and dependents.

Blue Cross and Blue Shield

Blue Cross (hospital services) and Blue Shield (physician services) was the first prepaid health plan in the country. Although all "Blues" plans are independent, they are united by membership in the national Blue Cross and Blue Shield Association (BCBSA). In addition to its many private plans, the Blue Cross and Blue Shield system administers the four million-member Federal Employee Program (FEP), comprising all federal government employees, retirees, and dependents.

Preferred Provider Organizations

The most common form of managed care is the PPO. Preferred provider organizations (PPO) are generally contracted by an employer group or other plan to provide hospital and physician services at reduced rates. Although coverage is higher for preferred or participating providers, individuals have the option to seek services provided by nonparticipating providers. A variation of the PPO is the exclusive provider organization (EPO), where enrollees must receive care within the network and must assume responsibility for all out-of-network costs.

Health Maintenance Organizations

This type of plan has several variations, but basically, the subscriber pays a monthly fee for services, regardless of the type or amount of services provided. The primary care physician (PCP) acts as a gatekeeper to coordinate the individual's care and to make decisions regarding specialty referral and care. In a "group model" HMO, referrals for care outside of the large independent physician group must be arranged, care for emergency services must be preauthorized, and information about care provided in a life-threatening situation must be communicated to the plan within a specified period of time. On the other hand, the managed choice model HMO allows individuals to access care via the PCP or to go outside of the network to receive care without permission of the PCP, but at a lower level of benefits.

Point-of-Service Plans

Point-of-service plans (POS) permit covered individuals to receive services from participating or nonparticipating providers, but with a smaller co-pay when participating providers are used.

Independent Practice Association

This type of organization comprises providers that maintain separate practices and participate in the independent practice association (IPA) as a means to contract with HMOs or other health plans. The providers also generally treat patients who are not members of the HMO or other plans.

Indemnity Plans

Under indemnity plans, which are generally fee-for-service, the payer provides payment directly to the provider of service when benefits have been assigned by the patient. Many indemnity plans now include PPO attributes to help reduce costs.

Consumer-Directed Health Plans

Consumer choice health plans, also known as consumer-directed health plans, provide patients with more flexibility and accountability in managing their health care costs. Two of the most popular types of consumer choice health plans are the health savings account (HSA) and the health reimbursement account (HRA). These options are usually offered to patients who have a high deductible health plan (HDHP).

The HDHP features higher annual deductibles (many plans have at least a $1,000 deductible for individuals and $2,000 for family coverage) than other traditional health plans. The maximum out-of-pocket limit for HDHPs varies but can be as much as $5,000 for individuals and $10,000 for family enrollment. Often the patient has the choice of using in-network and out-of-network providers. Most plans require that the patient meet an annual deductible before the plan pays benefits, often with the exception of preventive care. Preventive care services are generally paid as first dollar coverage (paid at 100 percent and not subject to deductibles or coinsurance or subject to a small deductible or copayment).

Health Savings Account

By law, an HSA is available to members who are enrolled in an HDHP, are not Medicare enrolled, are not covered by another health plan, or are not claimed as a dependent on someone else's federal tax return. The health plan credits a portion of the health plan premium to the HSA. The credited amount is different for a self-only enrollment than for a self and family enrollment. Patients have the option to make additional tax-free contributions to this account, so long as total contributions do not exceed the limits established by law, usually the plan deductible. The funds can be used to pay for the plan deductible and/or qualified medical expenses that do not count toward the deductible. Features of an HSA include:

- Patient HSA contributions are tax-deductible

- Interest earned on an HSA account is tax-free

- Withdrawals for qualified medical expenses are tax free

- Unused funds and interest are carried over, without limit, from year to year

Health Reimbursement Accounts

Like an HSA, health reimbursement account (HRA) funds can be used to pay health plan deductibles and/or qualified medical expenses that do not count toward the deductible. The account may also be used to pay Medicare premiums. Employers usually contribute a portion of the premium amount into an HRA. Credits in an HRA are forfeited when a patient switches health plans. Features of an HRA include:

- Tax-free withdrawals for qualified medical expenses

- Carryover of unused credits, without limit, from year to year

- Credits in an HRA do not earn interest

While consumer-directed plans decrease the employer's cost of supplying health insurance, and often supplement a patient's coverage, they can be difficult for a provider to manage. Patients are often unsure of the types of coverage they have and the balances that are in the accounts. Providers should query payers regarding these types of accounts when verifying insurance coverage.

Patients need to know that, regardless of any type of coverage they may have, any balance that remains after all contractual agreements have been met, such as coinsurance, deductible, and copayments, are the responsibility of the patient. Patients also need to know that, regardless of coverage, copayments are due at the time service is rendered and that the patient may be reimbursed from the HSA or HRA account directly.

Third-Party Administrators and Administrative Services Organizations

Although neither insurers nor health plans, third-party administrators (TPA) and administrative service organizations (ASO) manage and pay claims for clients such as self-insured groups. The self-insured group then assumes the risk of providing the services and may contract directly with providers or use the services of a PPO.

Physician Hospital Organization

Hospitals and physician organizations may create a partial hospital organization (PHO) to assist in managed care contracting on behalf of the parties. Degrees of management, common ownership, and oversight vary depending on the model of the arrangement.

Payment Methodologies

Once covered services are known, the next issue to resolve is how you will be paid for those services. Over the last several years, there have been major changes to provider payment systems. The following will discuss the many varieties of payment methodologies used by Medicare and other third-party payers for outpatient and inpatient claims.

Diagnosis-related Groups

Diagnosis-related groups (DRG) apply to inpatient acute hospital or facility settings only, grouping multiple diagnoses together. Reimbursement is based on this grouping rather than on actual services rendered. Inpatient stays typically are reported by revenue codes to describe the treatments or procedures rendered.

Ambulatory Payment Classifications

Ambulatory payment classification (APC), Medicare's hospital outpatient prospective payment system, is a methodology for payments to hospitals for a wide range of facility services when performed on an outpatient or a partial hospitalization basis. It differs from DRGs used by hospitals for inpatient stays in that DRGs are driven by ICD-9-CM diagnostic groups, whereas APCs are grouped by the actual service provided. Procedural or CPT and supply or HCPCS Level II codes are organized into payment groups, with a fixed payment for each group that is geographically adjusted.

Some services have been exempted from APC payment methodology and will continue to be paid in accordance with the respective fee schedules for these specific services. These services include physical therapy, end-stage renal disease services, laboratory, durable medical equipment (DME), screening mammography, ambulance services, pulmonary rehabilitation, and clinical trials.

For more information on APCs, see our Ingenix publications identified in the front of this publication.

Usual, Customary, and Reasonable

Fee-for-service reimbursement based on reasonable and customary charges was the method that Medicare, as well as private payers, historically used to reimburse providers. Medicare's customary, prevailing, and reasonable (CPR) payment methodology was similar to the private sector's charge system of usual, customary, and reasonable (UCR).

This payment system is designed to pay providers based on their actual fees. An individual provider is paid the lowest of the actual fee for the service, the provider's customary charge (figured as the median of that provider's charges for the service over a defined time period), or the prevailing charge of all providers within the geographic area. Owing to the diversity in fees charged for the same services, this system allowed for a wide variance in payment for the same service. While some payers still use variations of the UCR method, most now follow Medicare's lead and employ relative value-based reimbursement methods, such as resource-based relative value scales (RBRVS). The RBRVS approach is explained more fully in the following sections.

Fee Schedules

Fee schedules are replacing the usual, customary, and reasonable payment methodology as the system of choice. Fee schedules eliminate the wide payment variation for similar services that occurs with the UCR method and allows both payers and providers to estimate the reimbursement they can expect to pay and receive. Use of fee schedules to maintain a fee-for-service system was considered critical by many medical professionals to protect providers' clinical and professional autonomy. A key factor in developing a fee schedule is the use of a relative value scale.

Relative Value Scales

A relative value scale (RVS) ranks services relative to each other and to a chosen base value. All services are assigned a number of relative value units (RVU), with more complex and/or time-consuming services having RVUs higher than the base value, and less complex and/or time-consuming services having RVUs lower than the base value. Values are then multiplied by a dollar conversion factor, resulting in the payment amount.

Conversion factors are national dollar amounts used to convert relative values into payment amounts. The Medicare conversion factor is published yearly in the *Federal Register* during the late fall and coincides with the Medicare physician fee schedule final rule.

Resource-Based Relative Value Scale

After much debate and analysis, Medicare decided its methodology of choice to replace the CPR approach. A payment schedule emerged, derived from an RVS based on the resources required to provide the services: work (time to provide service, technical skill and physical effort, mental effort and judgment, and stress associated with concern of risk to patient); the overhead expenses involved to maintain a practice; and the cost of malpractice insurance to protect the provider from liability. In an RBRVS, the services are ranked based on the relative costs of the resources required to provide those services, as opposed to the average fee for the service or average prevailing Medicare charge. The Medicare RBRVS, implemented in January 1992 and fully phased in by January 1996, was developed using the results of a Harvard University team that first identified and defined three distinct components affecting the value of each service or procedure:

Reimbursement

- Provider's work component reflecting the provider's time and skill

- Practice expense component reflecting the provider's rent, staff, supplies, equipment, and other overhead

- Malpractice insurance component reflecting the relative risk or liability associated with the service

RVUs are assigned to each component, and the sum of these comprises the total value of each service. CMS assigns a dollar amount to each CPT or HCPCS code by applying a conversion factor, determined annually by Congress, to the total value for each service. However, geographic practice cost indices (GPCI) must first be applied to each component prior to mutiplying the conversion factors that become the reimbursement rates found in the fee schedule. The conversion factor and RVU amounts are published annually in the *Federal Register.*

The GPCIs are figured into the three component values and added for a total geographically adjusted value for the service, which is then multiplied by the conversion factor to yield the locality-specific Medicare fee in the payment schedule.

Until 1999, only the work component was resource-based. The practice expense (PE) component was determined by historical provider charges. In 1999, Medicare began a four-year phase-in of resource-based practice expense, which is now complete. The practice expense unit is dependent upon the site of service; therefore, implementing a resource-based PE required that this particular component be subdivided into nonfacility and facility relative values. The nonfacility PE value reflects the cost of providing the service in the provider's office, patient's home, or residential care setting. The facility PE value reflects the cost of providing the service in a hospital, ambulatory surgery center (ASC), or skilled nursing facility (SNF). In all settings, outpatient physical therapy services are reimbursed based on the nonfacility RVUs.

Although the RBRVS was developed specifically for reimbursement of Medicare-covered services, more than 80 percent of non-Medicare payers now use RBRVS to establish fees and maximum allowable reimbursement rates.

RVUs are not assigned for the following types of services:

- Services that require carrier pricing or payment "by report," such as unlisted codes

- Services for which national values have not been instituted (carrier priced)

- Services that are not contained within the definition of physician services

The general RBRVS formula is:

Payment = (RVU work x GPCI work) + (RVU practice expense x GPCI practice expense) + (RVU malpractice x GPCI malpractice) x conversion factor

Under Medicare payment is rounded to the nearest cent, and the provider is paid 80 percent of the actual charge or the fee schedule amount, whichever is less. The patient is responsible for paying the remaining 20 percent and deductible amounts. As required by law, budget neutrality (BN) prohibits expenditures for the Medicare program to vary by more than $20 million. Due to changes brought about by the required five-year review of work RVUs, it was necessary to continue a budget neutrality adjustment for 2009 to offset the increases in the work RVUs.

The Medicare Improvements for Patients and Providers Act (MIPPA), PL 110-275, was enacted on July 15, 2008. This law prevented the statutory Medicare reduction in payments for physicians that would have gone into place July 1, 2008, and provided other future changes that directly impact physicians and other providers as well.

Each year, adjusted relative values are converted into dollar payment amounts by a conversion factor. In accordance with Medicare law, the formula for calculating the conversion factor is updated on an annual basis. For January 1, 2008, this formula would have resulted in a 10.1 percent cut in payment for Medicare services. The Medicare, Medicaid, and SCHIP Extension Act of 2007 changed the conversion factor update announced in the November 27, 2007, *Federal Register*, but only temporarily. Effective for claims with dates of service January 1, 2008, through June 30, 2008, the update to the conversion factor was to remain $38.0870. However, for claims with dates of service July 1, 2008 and after, the conversion factor was to revert back to the previous amount of $34.0682. Further, the passage of MIPPA not only averted the payment reduction that was to go into place, but updated the conversion factor by 1.1 percent for 2009 as well. The physician fee schedule (PFS) conversion factor (CF) is determined based on a complicated formula mandated by law. For 2009, a provision of the Medicare Improvements for Patients and Providers Act (MIPPA) of 2008 was implemented that prohibits the application of the BN adjustment to the work RVUs and instead, applies it to the CF. This change to the calculation maintains budget neutrality even though it results in an increase to the work RVUs by decreasing the CF. For 2010, the physician CF is $28.3895. However, Congress may elect to prevent the negative update. At press time, a bill to increase the conversion factor to $36.5047 is before the House and Senate. For 2011 and beyond, the conversion factor will be calculated as if this modification had never existed.

Fee calculators are available from APTA at APTA.org/reimbursement (member login required) and from CMS at http://www.cms.hhs.gov/pfslookup/02_PFSsearch.asp?agree=yes&next=Accept.

Capitation Plans

While not as prevalent as they once were, some capitated health plans remain. Capitation places a cap on the dollars spent on health care. Capitation contracts emphasize high-volume practices and/or primary care, generally where one provider is the gatekeeper for the patient's overall management. Payment is based on a certain amount of dollars per member and the amount does not vary according to the actual number of patients in the member population seen by the provider. Subsequently, health care in a capitated system depends on shared risk, or the ability to successfully manage a practice or a specialty clinic according to fees paid on a "per capita," or per person basis. This varies significantly from fee-for-service (FFS) health plans. Under capitation, incentive depends upon providing quality care in the most appropriate and lowest cost setting, whereas incentives in a FFS system depend on volume and the number of procedures actually performed. Terms important to capitation contracts include the following:

- **Risk pool.** A portion of the capitated payment set aside to cover certain expenses, such as the portion a primary care physician may set aside to pay for laboratory diagnostic services.

 © 2009 Ingenix

- **Stop-loss provision.** A member's age, sex, copayment, use patterns, and the scope of services covered by the plan are factors influencing the dollar amount in a capitated contract. The provider's financial risk increases with the number of services offered in the contract since reimbursement is set in advance and does not vary despite the intensity of services provided. The "stop-loss" provision of a capitated contract pays for the patient whose needs exceed the capitated rate.

- **Withhold.** The portion of the capitation rate that a health plan retains and repays to the provider if the health plan does not exceed its budget. Under this arrangement, the financial risk becomes a shared responsibility between the health plan and the provider.

Calculating Costs

It is recommended that fee schedules be based on the services rendered according to HCPCS or CPT listings and guidelines. Fees should be as independent of the diagnosis as possible because, although payers may link procedures to a diagnosis, fees for a given procedure are set without reference to a diagnosis.

After establishing a fee schedule, you may find occasions when a payer requires a code not on your schedule. In these instances, it is often best to base billing on a code from your fee schedule that most closely resembles the code in question. This is also true for those rare instances when no code exists for the service rendered. You can then add this information to your fee schedule.

A common question facing many health care providers is what can be charged for a given procedure. There are several ways to address this issue:

- **Cost-based charges.** In theory, your charges should reflect the cost of doing business, including the cost of making a reasonable profit. This is often easier said than done, however, as there is no one way to determine your costs. Nevertheless, if you have the business and accounting resources to make such a determination, it is best to base charges on the costs to provide services. You may choose to determine your fees using a publicly available fee schedule that already has been developed as a guideline, such as the RBRVS used by Medicare and many other payers.

- **Insurer-based charges.** Payers usually have a maximum payment amount. If you feel that your fees might be low, compare your billings with the amounts the insurer allows before any deductibles or patient co-payments. If the insurer consistently allows your charges in full, your charges may be below the allowed limit. Increasing your fees may make them more in line with fees charged by others in your community.

- **Community-based charges.** You may wish to base your charges on the fees appropriate for your geographic market area. The idea is that you charge what others in the community charge. Therefore, you will not lose revenue because your fees are too low or too high. It must be noted that this approach assumes that you are at least covering your costs, however they are defined. However, antitrust laws generally forbid the sharing of price (fee) information among providers and suppliers. Therefore, it is not appropriate to call other health care providers in your area or to conduct a fee survey. However, consultants and service firms may have geographic fee information available for sale.

Other Factors Influencing Medicare Payment

In addition to the above-stated payment methodologies, other issues also affect the manner in which you code and bill for your services.

A provision of the Balanced Budget Act (BBA) mandates that all claims for outpatient rehabilitation, including specific audiology services and comprehensive outpatient rehabilitation facility (CORF) services, have to be reported using a uniform coding system, and the coding systems chosen by CMS were HCPCS Level I and II. The BBA also mandated a prospective payment system for these services, and the Medicare physician fee schedule (MPFS) has become the method of payment for outpatient physical therapy (which includes outpatient speech-language pathology) services provided by the following:

- Comprehensive outpatient rehabilitation facilities

- Outpatient physical therapy providers (OPT), including physical therapists in private practice (PTPP)

- Outpatient rehabilitation facilities (ORF, also called rehabilitation agencies)

- Hospitals (when provided to outpatients and inpatients who are not in a covered Part A stay)

- Skilled nursing facilities (when provided to residents not in a covered Part A stay and to nonresidents receiving outpatient rehabilitation services from the SNF)

- Home health agencies (HHA) (for services provided to individuals who are not homebound or otherwise are not receiving services under a home health plan of care)

The MPFS is used as a method of payment for outpatient rehabilitation services furnished under arrangement with any of these providers. It is also used as the payment system for specific audiology and CORF services. Assignment is mandatory for CORFs.

The MPFS is not applicable to outpatient rehabilitation services when provided by critical access hospitals (CAH), which are paid on a reasonable-cost basis.

Medicare contractors process outpatient rehabilitation claims from hospitals, including CAHs, SNFs, CORFs, outpatient rehabilitation agencies, and outpatient physical therapy providers, for which they have received a tie in notice from the regional office. Carriers process claims from physicians, certain nonphysician practitioners (NPP), and physical and occupational therapists in private practice (PTPP and OTPP). A physician-directed clinic that reports services provided as incident to a physician's service also bills the carrier.

Facility rates are applicable to professional services performed in a facility other than the provider's office while nonfacility rates are applicable for services performed in the office. The nonfacility rate takes into account overhead and indirect expenses the provider incurs by operating his or her own facility and is somewhat higher than the facility rate. Physical therapy services are unique in that they are always paid based on the nonfacility rate.

Carriers pay the codes under the MPFS regardless of whether they may be considered rehabilitation services. However, FIs must determine whether to pay under outpatient rehabilitation rules or whether payment rules for other types of service may apply (e.g., outpatient prospective payment system [OPPS] for hospitals).

Payment for rehabilitation services provided to Part A inpatients of hospitals or SNFs is included in the respective prospective payment system (PPS) rate. Also for SNFs (but not hospitals), if the beneficiary has Part B, but not Part A coverage (e.g., Part A benefits are exhausted), the SNF must bill the FI for any rehabilitation service (except audiologic function services). The Balanced Budget Act of 1997 (BBA), contained a consolidated billing (CB) requirement for skilled nursing facilities. In accordance with this provision, a SNF is required to submit all Medicare claims for the services provided to its residents receive (with the exception of some specifically excluded services). This provision applies to services provided to a skilled nursing facility resident during the course of a covered Part A stay, with the exception of physical, occupational, and speech-language therapy (which are subject to CB regardless of whether the resident receiving them is in a covered Part A stay). Payment for rehabilitation services provided by home health agencies under a home health plan of care is included in the home health PPS rate.

The following table identifies the types of providers and where bills should be submitted.

Provider/Service Type	Bill to	Comments
Inpatient hospital Part A	FI	Included in PPS.
Inpatient SNF Part A	FI	Included in PPS.
Inpatient hospital Part B	FI	Hospital may obtain services under arrangements and bill, or rendering provider may bill.
Inpatient SNF Part B except for audiology function tests	FI	SNF must provide and bill, or obtain under arrangements and bill.
Inpatient SNF Part B audiology function tests only	FI	SNF may bill the FI or provider of service may bill the carrier.
Outpatient hospital	FI	Hospital may provide and bill or obtain under arrangements and bill, or rendering provider may bill.
Outpatient SNF	FI	SNF must provide and bill or obtain under arrangements and bill.
HHA billing for services rendered under a Part A or Part B home health plan of care	FI	Service is included in PPS rate. CMS determines whether payment is from Part A or Part B trust fund.
HHA billing for services not rendered under a Part A or Part B home health plan of care, but rendered under a therapy plan of care	FI	Service not under home health plan of care.
Other rehabilitation facility (ORF) with six-digit provider number assigned by CMS RO	FI	Paid MPFS for outpatient rehabilitation services effective January 1, 1999, and all other services except drugs effective July 1, 2000.

*A provision of the Medicare Improvement for Patients and Providers Act of 2008 included language recognizing private practice speech-language pathologists' ability to bill Medicare and will allow audiologists to participate in the Physician Quality Reporting Initiative.

Provider/Service Type	Bill to	Comments
CORF with six-digit provider number assigned by CMS RO	FI	Paid MPFS for outpatient rehabilitation services effective January 1, 1999, and all other services except drugs effective July 1, 2000.
Physician, NPPs, PTPPs, OTPPs, and, for diagnostic tests only, audiologists (service in hospital or SNF)	Carrier	Payment may not be made for therapy services to Part A inpatients of hospitals or SNFs, or for Part B SNF residents. Otherwise, carrier billing. Note that physician/ NPP/PTPP/OTPP employee of facility may assign benefits to the facility, enabling the facility to bill for physician/therapist to carrier.
Physician/NPP/PTPP/ OTPP/SLP* office, independent clinic or patient's home	Carrier	Paid via physician fee schedule.
Practicing audiologist for services defined as diagnostic tests only	Carrier	Some audiologists tests provided in hospitals are considered other diagnostic tests and are subject to HOPPS instead of MPFS for outpatient therapy fee schedule.
Critical access hospital — inpatient Part A	FI	Rehabilitation services are paid cost.
Critical access hospital — inpatient Part B	FI	Rehabilitation services are paid cost.
Critical access hospital — outpatient Part B	FI	Rehabilitation services are paid cost.

*A provision of the Medicare Improvement for Patients and Providers Act of 2008 included language recognizing private practice speech-language pathologists' ability to bill Medicare and will allow audiologists to participate in the Physician Quality Reporting Initiative.

Financial Limitation for Outpatient Therapy Services

Section 4541(c) of the Balanced Budget Act (BBA) requires application of financial limitations to all outpatient rehabilitation services other than those furnished by or under arrangement with a hospital. The financial limitation amounts, or therapy caps, for 2009 were $1810 for physical therapy and speech-language pathology combined, and a separate $1810 for occupational therapy. For 2010 the limits increase to $1860 for physical and occupational therapy combined and $1860 for occupational therapy. Limits apply to outpatient Part B therapy services from all settings except outpatient hospital (place of service code 22 on CMS-1500 claims) and hospital emergency department (place of service code 23 on CMS-1500 claims). There were exceptions to the therapy cap limitation through 2007 as legislated by the Tax Relief and Health Care Act of 2006, which extended the cap exceptions process through the calendar year. Passage of the Medicare, Medicaid, and SCHIP Extension Act of 2007 extended the cap exceptions process for services furnished through June 30, 2008. MIPPA (PL 110-275) enacted on July 15, 2008, further extended the exceptions process through 2009. For more information, see below.

The following modifiers are used to identify therapy services, whether or not the financial limitations are in effect, although the common working file (CWF) does track the financial limitation

© 2009 Ingenix

using the therapy modifiers. The following three modifiers refer only to those services provided under plans of care for physical therapy, occupational therapy, and speech-language pathology services, and should only be reported with codes on the list of applicable therapy codes.

GN   Services delivered under an outpatient speech-language pathology plan of care

GO   Services delivered under an outpatient occupational therapy plan of care

GP   Services delivered under an outpatient physical therapy plan of care

Since physical therapy, occupational therapy, and speech-language pathology services are the only services included in the limitations, these modifiers should not be used for any other services.

The financial limitations, also called therapy caps, apply to professional and facility services billed by SNFs for non-Part A stays, home health agency non-PPS claims, outpatient rehabilitation facility claims, and comprehensive outpatient rehabilitation facility claims. The therapy caps do not apply to services rendered in hospital outpatient departments. Specifically the applicable bill types are 022X, 023X, 034X, 074X and 075X. Services are accumulated for the financial limitation using the Medicare physician fee schedule allowed amount (before adjustment for beneficiary liability).

For SNFs, the financial limitation does apply to rehabilitation services furnished to those SNF residents in noncovered stays (bill type 022X) who are in a Medicare-certified section of the facility (e.g., a section that is either certified by Medicare alone, or is dually certified by Medicare as a SNF and by Medicaid as a nursing facility). For SNF residents, consolidated billing requires all outpatient rehabilitation services be billed to Part B by the SNF. If a resident has reached the financial limitation, and remains in the Medicare-certified section of the SNF, no further payment will be made to the SNF or any other entity. Therefore, SNF residents who are subject to consolidated billing may not obtain services from an outpatient hospital after the cap has been exceeded.

Therapy Cap Exceptions

The cap exception for therapy services based on the medical necessity of the service is in effect only when legislated by Congress.

The Deficit Reduction Act (DRA) of 2006 instructed CMS to develop a process to allow exceptions to the therapy caps in cases where continued therapy services are medically necessary. All covered services are eligible for exceptions when they are medically necessary. The Act allows an exception when the patient's condition is justified by documentation indicating that the patient requires continued skilled therapy (i.e., therapy beyond the amount payable under the therapy cap), to achieve the patient's prior functional status, or maximum expected functional status within a reasonable amount of time.

All services that require exceptions to caps are processed using the automatic process. "Automatic process exceptions" means that the claim processing for the exception is automatic, and not the exception itself. Automatic exceptions may be thought of as exceptions initially approved without review when the treating

provider determines that the patient needs an exception to the cap based on his or her clinical judgment. A patient may qualify for an automatic cap exception at any time during the episode when documented medically necessary services exceed the cap. The provider indicates that a request for automatic exception is being made by appending modifier KX Specific required documentation on file, to the appropriate procedure code. The use of modifier KX does not exempt services from manual or other medical review processes. Indeed, atypical use of the automatic exception process may invite contractor scrutiny. Particular care should be taken to ensure that the medical record documentation justifies the medical necessity and indicates the clinician's decisions concerning the exceptions. Specific documentation does not need to accompany the claim; however, it must be submitted to the contractor when requested for subsequent claim review. An additional documentation review (ADR) is sent to the provider specifying the records that the payer requests to be submitted. A summary that specifically addresses the justification for the therapy cap exception is recommended.

Modifier KX

Modifier KX plays a very important role in the therapy exceptions. CMS considers the use of modifier KX to be an attestation of the medical necessity of services billed. Modifier KX is appended to the CPT procedure code to indicate that an automatic exception applies.

KX   Requirements specified in the medical policy have been met

Modifier KX signifies not only that this determination has been made, but also that the provider's or supplier's medical records contain supporting documentation that indicate services are reasonable and medical necessity and justify the clinician's decisions.

Routine use of modifier KX for all patients with diagnosis codes on the automatic exception lists could show up on data analysis as aberrant and may invite inquiry with possible charges of fraud and abuse.

Append modifier KX only to those CPT procedure codes that are subject to the financial limitations, referred to here as therapy caps. Report modifier KX in addition to therapy modifiers GN, GO, or GP, which are currently required for therapy services. Refer to item 19 in the claims processing section of this book for additional information regarding the submission of multiple modifiers.

Exceptions to Services

Evaluations are to determine if the current status of the patient requires therapy services. Any subsequent treatment procedures for such beneficiaries would need to meet the cap exception requirements to be covered. The following are therapy evaluation procedures exempted from caps after the therapy caps are reached:

92506   **Evaluation of speech, language, voice, communication, and/or auditory processing**

92597   **Evaluation for use and/or fitting of voice prosthetic device to supplement oral speech**

92607   **Evaluation for prescription for speech-generating augmentative and alternative communication device, face-to-face with the patient; first hour**

92608	**each additional 30 minutes (List separately in addition to code for primary procedure)**
92610	**Evaluation of oral and pharyngeal swallowing function**
92611	**Motion fluoroscopic evaluation of swallowing function by cine or video recording**
92612	**Flexible fiberoptic endoscopic evaluation of swallowing by cine or video recording**
92614	**Flexible fiberoptic endoscopic evaluation, laryngeal sensory testing by cine or video recording**
92616	**Flexible fiberoptic endoscopic evaluation of swallowing and laryngeal sensory testing by cine or video recording**
96105	**Assessment of aphasia (includes assessment of expressive and receptive speech and language function, language comprehension, speech production ability, reading, spelling, writing, e.g. by Boston Diagnostic Aphasia Examination) with interpretation and report, per hour**
97001	**Physical therapy evaluation**
97002	**Physical therapy re-evaluation**
97003	**Occupational therapy evaluation**
97004	**Occupational therapy re-evaluation**

These codes will continue to be reported by facilities as outpatient therapy procedures using revenue codes 0424, 0434, and 0444 as appropriate. These codes must be reported with modifiers GN, GO, GP, indicating the type of therapist who performed the evaluation.

When reporting necessary evaluation CPT codes that are exempt from the caps, append modifier KX, Specific Required Documentation on File. This modifier alerts the contractor to override a denial for that service due to the cap.

Documentation should include:

- The complaint
- The condition that indicates why the evaluation was necessary
- The description of any complex situations that directly and substantially impact the patient's treatment.

Current Condition Exceptions
CMS identified conditions that will be exempted from the therapy caps. When a condition is the reason for the exception, that condition must be related to the therapy goals and must directly and significantly impact the rate of recovery. For example, if the condition underlying the reason for therapy is V43.64 Hip replacement, the treatment may have a goal to ambulate 60 feet with stand-by assistance. If additional sessions are required for gait training due to the severity of the patient's condition, an automatic exception to the cap would be allowed. It would be appropriate to append the modifier KX to the CPT procedure code. Conversely, it would not be appropriate to append modifier KX when the patient recovered from hip replacement last year and is being treated this year for a sprain that is not represented on the list as an exception.

Report the ICD-9-CM codes that describe a specific underlying condition or specific body part affected that resulted in the current therapy episode of care. Refer to the ICD-9-CM code book for coding instructions. If a diagnosis code is not listed here, then the disorder may still qualify for an exception by approval of a Medicare contractor based on the medical necessity of the specific service for the condition. The codes apply to all therapy disciplines, but should be used only when the code is applicable to the condition being actively treated. For example, an exception should not be claimed for a diagnosis of hip replacement when the service provided is for an unrelated dysphagia. If separate conditions are being treated by two physicians, Medicare contractors will accept as documentation either:

- Combined plan of care certified by one of the physicians/nonphysician practitioners (NPP)
- Two separate plans of care certified by the separate physicians/NPP

Complexities or Comorbidity Exceptions
Complexities are comorbidities or complications of circumstances that directly and significantly impact the rate of recovery for the condition being treated. They do not alone justify an exception but must be reported with another condition (which may or may not be listed an excepted condition) when **both are concurrently influencing** the length or intensity of treatment such that therapy caps are exceeded. A condition is considered a complexity **only** when applicable to the condition being actively treated. For example, an exception should not be claimed for a diagnosis of hip replacement when the service provided is for the treatment of an unrelated dysphagia. Both the condition being treated and the code for the complexity must be reported on the claim. The ICD-9-CM diagnosis codes in the following table describe the conditions (etiology or underlying medical conditions) that could result in excepted conditions (designated with "X") and complexities (designated with "*") that may cause medically necessary therapy services to qualify for the automatic process exception for each discipline—physical therapy, occupational therapy, and speech-language pathology-separately. When the field corresponding to the therapy discipline treating the patient and the diagnosis code is marked with a dash (–) services by that discipline are not appropriate for that diagnosis and, therefore, the services do not qualify for the exception.

These codes are grouped only to aid in referencing them.

ICD-9 Cluster	ICD-9 (Cluster) Description	PT	OT	SLP
V43.61–V43.69	Joint replacement	X	X	–
V45.4	Arthrodesis status	*	*	–
V45.81–V45.82, V45.89	Other postprocedural status	*	*	–
V49.1–V49.67	Upper limb amputation status	X	X	–
V49.71–V49.77	Lower limb amputation status	X	X	–
V54.10–V54.29	Aftercare for healing traumatic or pathologic fracture	X	X	–

X = Automatic (only ICD-9 needed on claim)
* = Complexity (requires another ICD-9 on claim)
– = Does not serve as qualifying ICD-9 on claim

ICD-9 Cluster	ICD-9 (Cluster) Description	PT	OT	SLP
V58.71–V58.78	Aftercare following surgery to specified body systems, not elsewhere classified	*	*	*
244.0–244.9	Acquired hypothyroidism	*	*	*
250.00–251.9	Diabetes mellitus and other disorders of pancreatic internal secretion	*	*	*
276.0–276.9	Disorders of fluid, electrolyte, and acid-base balance	*	*	*
278.00–278.01	Obesity and morbid obesity	*	*	*
280.0–289.9	Diseases of the blood and blood-forming organs	*	*	*
290.0–290.43	Dementias	*	*	*
294.0–294.9	Persistent mental disorders due to conditions classified elsewhere	*	*	*
295.00–299.91	Other psychoses	*	*	*
300.00–300.9	Anxiety, disassociative and somatoform disorders	*	*	*
310.0–310.9	Specific nonpsychotic mental disorders due to brain damage	*	*	*
311	Depressive disorder, not elsewhere classified	*	*	*
315.00–315.9	Specific delays in development	*	*	*
317	Mild mental retardation	*	*	*
320.0–326	Inflammatory diseases of the central nervous system	*	*	*
330.0–337.9	Hereditary and degenerative diseases of the central nervous system	X	X	X
340–345.91, 348.0–349.9	Other disorders of the central nervous system	X	X	X
353.0–359.9	Disorders of the peripheral nervous system	X	X	–
365.00–365.9	Glaucoma	*	*	*
369.00–369.9	Blindness and low vision	*	*	*
386.00–386.9	Vertiginous syndromes and other disorders of Vestibular system	*	*	*
389.00–389.9	Hearing loss	*	*	*
401.0–405.99	Hypertensive disease	*	*	*
410.00–414.9	Ischemic heart disease	*	*	*
415.0–417.9	Diseases of pulmonary circulation	*	*	*
420.0–429.9	Other forms of heart disease	*	*	*
430–438.9	Cerebrovascular disease	X	X	X
440.0–448.9	Diseases of arteries, arterioles, and capillaries	*	*	*
451.0–453.9, 456.0–459.9	Diseases of veins and lymphatics, and other diseases of circulatory system	*	*	*
465.0–466.19	Acute respiratory infections	*	*	*

X = Automatic (only ICD-9 needed on claim)
* = Complexity (requires another ICD-9 on claim)
– = Does not serve as qualifying ICD-9 on claim

ICD-9 Cluster	ICD-9 (Cluster) Description	PT	OT	SLP
478.30–478.5	Paralysis, polyps, or other diseases of vocal cords	*	*	*
480.0–486	Pneumonia	*	*	*
490–496	Chronic obstructive pulmonary disease and allied conditions	*	*	*
507.0–507.8	Pneumonitis due to solids and liquids	*	*	*
510.0–519.9	Other diseases of respiratory system	*	*	*
560.0–560.9	Intestinal obstruction without mention of hernia	*	*	*
578.0–578.9	Gastrointestinal hemorrhage	*	*	*
584.5–586	Renal failure and chronic kidney disease	*	*	*
590.00–599.9	Other diseases of urinary system	*	*	*
682.0–682.8	Other cellulitis and abscess	*	*	–
707.00–707.9	Chronic ulcer of skin	*	*	–
710.0–710.9	Diffuse diseases of connective tissue	*	*	*
711.00–711.99	Arthropathy associated with infections	*	*	–
712.10–713.8	Crystal arthropathies and arthropathy associated with other disorders classified elsewhere	*	*	–
714.0–714.9	Rheumatoid arthritis and other inflammatory Polyarthropathies	*	*	–
715.00–715.98	Osteoarthrosis and allied disorders (complexity except as listed below)	*	*	–
715.09	Osteoarthritis and allied disorders, multiple sites	X	X	–
715.11	Osteoarthritis, localized, primary, shoulder region	X	X	–
715.15	Osteoarthritis, localized, primary, pelvic region and thigh	X	X	–
715.16	Osteoarthritis, localized, primary, lower leg	X	X	–
715.91	Osteoarthritis, unspecified if gen. or local, shoulder	X	X	–
715.96	Osteoarthritis, unspecified if gen. or local, lower leg	X	X	–
716.00–716.99	Other and unspecified arthropathies	*	*	–
717.0–717.9	Internal derangement of knee	*	*	–
718.00–718.99	Other derangement of joint (complexity except as listed below)	*	*	–
718.49	Contracture of joint, multiple sites	X	X	–
719.00–719.99	Other and unspecified disorders of joint (complexity except as listed below)	*	*	–

X = Automatic (only ICD-9 needed on claim)
* = Complexity (requires another ICD-9 on claim)
– = Does not serve as qualifying ICD-9 on claim

Reimbursement

ICD-9 Cluster	ICD-9 (Cluster) Description	PT	OT	SLP
719.7	Difficulty walking	X	X	–
720.0–724.9	Dorsopathies	*	*	–
725–729.9	Rheumatism, excluding back (complexity except as listed below)	*	*	–
726.10–726.19	Rotator cuff disorder and allied syndromes	X	X	–
727.61–727.62	Rupture of tendon, nontraumatic	X	X	–
730.00–739.9	Osteopathies, chondropathies, and acquired musculoskeletal deformities (complexity except as listed below)	*	*	–
733.00	Osteoporosis	X	X	–
741.00–742.9, 745.0–748.9, 754.0–756.9	Congenital anomalies	*	*	*
780.31–780.39	Convulsions	*	*	*
780.71–780.79	Malaise and fatigue	*	*	*
780.93	Memory loss	*	*	*
781.0–781.99	Symptoms involving nervous and musculoskeletal system (complexity except as listed below)	*	*	*
781.2	Abnormality of gait	X	X	–
781.3	Lack of coordination	X	X	–
783.0–783.9	Symptoms concerning nutrition, metabolism, and development	*	*	*
784.3–784.69	Aphasia, voice and other speech disturbance, other symbolic dysfunction	*	*	X
785.4	Gangrene	*	*	–
786.00–786.9	Symptoms involving respiratory system and other chest symptoms	*	*	*
787.2	Dysphagia	*	*	X
800.00–828.1	Fractures (complexity except as listed below)	*	*	–
806.00–806.9	Fracture of vertebral column with spinal cord injury	X	X	–
810.11–810.13	Fracture of clavicle	X	X	–
811.00–811.19	Fracture of scapula	X	X	–
812.00–812.59	Fracture of humerus	X	X	–
813.00–813.93	Fracture of radius and ulna	X	X	–
820.00–820.9	Fracture of neck of femur	X	X	–
821.00–821.39	Fracture of other and unspecified parts of femur	X	X	–
828.0–828.1	Multiple fractures involving both lower limbs, lower with upper limb, and lower limb(s) with rib(s) and sternum	X	X	–
830.0–839.9	Dislocations	X	X	–
840.0–848.8	Sprains and strains of joints and adjacent muscles	*	*	–

X = Automatic (only ICD-9 needed on claim)
* = Complexity (requires another ICD-9 on claim)
– = Does not serve as qualifying ICD-9 on claim

ICD-9 Cluster	ICD-9 (Cluster) Description	PT	OT	SLP
851.00–854.19	Intracranial injury, excluding those with skull fracture	X	X	X
880.00–884.2	Open wound of upper limb	*	*	–
885.0–887.7	Traumatic amputation, thumb(s), finger(s), arm and hand (complete)(partial)	X	X	–
890.0–894.2	Open wound lower Limb	*	*	–
895.0–897.7	Traumatic amputation, toe(s), foot/feet, leg(s) (complete)(partial)	X	X	–
ICD-9 Cluster	ICD-9 (Cluster) Description	PT	OT	SLP
905.0–905.9	Late effects of musculoskeletal and connective tissue injuries	*	*	*
907.0–907.9	Late effects of injuries to the nervous system	*	*	*
941.00–949.5	Burns	*	*	*
952.00–952.9	Spinal cord injury without evidence of spinal bone injury	X	X	X
953.0–953.8	Injury to nerve roots and spinal plexus	X	X	*
959.01	Head injury, unspecified	X	X	X

X = Automatic (only ICD-9 needed on claim)
* = Complexity (requires another ICD-9 on claim)
– = Does not serve as qualifying ICD-9 on claim

Allowed Number of Units for Outpatient Therapy Services

One of the requirements of DRA is the implementation of clinically appropriate code edits to prevent improper payments for outpatient therapy services. The codes on the following chart may be billed, when covered, but only at or below the number of units indicated per day of treatment. If higher amounts of units are billed, the excessive units will be denied as not medically necessary. Denied claims may be appealed. An advance beneficiary notice (ABN) is appropriate in this situation. Bear in mind that this chart does not include all therapy codes. The following list applies to the codes in the table:

- Codes that are allowed one unit for allowed units may be billed no more than once per provider, per discipline, per date of service, per patient.

- Codes allowed 0 units may not be billed under a plan of care indicated by the discipline in that column. Some codes may be billed by one discipline (e.g., PT) and not by others (e.g., OT or SLP).

- When physicians/NPPs bill "always therapy" codes they must follow the policies of the type of therapy they are providing (e.g., use a plan of care, bill with the appropriate therapy modifier [GP, GO, GN], and bill the allowed units on the chart below for PT, OT or SLP depending on the plan). A physician/NPP shall not bill an always therapy code unless the service is provided under a therapy plan of care. Therefore, NA means "not applicable" in the chart below.

- When a "sometimes therapy" code is billed by a physician/NPP as a medical service, and not under a therapy plan of care, the therapy modifier should not be used, but the number of units billed must not exceed the number of units indicated in the chart below per patient, per provider/supplier, per day.

HCPCS Code	Code Description and Claim Line Outlier/Edit Details	Timed or Untimed	PT Allowed Units	OT Allowed Units	SLP Allowed Units	Physician/NPPNOT Under Therapy POC
92506	Speech/hearing evaluation	Untimed	0	0	1	NA
92597	Oral speech device evaluation	Untimed	0	1	1	NA
92607	Evaluation for speech device rx, 1hr	Timed	0	1	1	NA
92611	Motion fluoroscopy/ swallow with cine or video	Untimed	0	1	1	1
92612	Endoscope swallow test (fees)	Untimed	0	1	1	1
92614	Laryngoscopic sensory test	Untimed	0	1	1	1
92616	Fees w/laryngeal sense test	Untimed	0	1	1	1
95833	Limb muscle testing, manual	Untimed	1	1	0	1
95834	Limb muscle testing, manual	Untimed	1	1	0	1
96110	Developmental test, limited	Untimed	1	1	1	1
96111	Developmental test, extended	Untimed	1	1	1	1
97001	PT evaluation	Untimed	1	0	0	NA
97002	PT re-evaluation	Untimed	1	0	0	NA
97003	OT evaluation	Untimed	0	1	0	NA
97004	OT re-evaluation	Untimed	0	1	0	NA

Additional Considerations for Exception

In justifying exceptions for therapy caps, clinicians and contractors should not only consider the medical diagnoses and medical complications that might directly and significantly influence the amount of treatment required. Other variables that affect appropriate treatment shall also be considered. Factors that influence the need for treatment should be supportable by published research, clinical guidelines from professional sources, and/or clinical/common sense. See Pub. 100-02, *Medicare Benefit Policy Manual*, chapter 15, section 220.3, for subsections related to documentation for therapy services, and section 220.2, medical necessity for some factors that complicate treatment.

However, in cases where the beneficiary was treated in the same year for different episodes of the same condition, special attention should be paid to justifying the second episode as appropriate and necessary and not merely an extension of the first episode.

Note that the patient's lack of access to outpatient hospital therapy services alone does not justify excepted services. Residents of skilled nursing facilities prevented by consolidated

billing from accessing hospital services, debilitated patients for whom transportation to the hospital is a physical hardship or lack of therapy services at hospitals in the beneficiary's county may or may not qualify for continued services above the caps. The patient's condition and complexities might justify extended services, but their location does not.

Appeals Related to Disapproval of Cap Exceptions

DRA of 2005 allows that certain services that would not be covered due to caps, but are medically necessary, may be covered if they meet certain criteria. Therefore, when a service beyond the cap is determined to be medically necessary, it is covered and payable. But, when a service provided beyond the cap (outside the benefit) is determined to be NOT medically necessary, it is denied as a benefit category denial. Contractors may review claims with KX modifiers to determine whether the services are medically necessary, or for other reasons. Services that exceed therapy caps but do not meet Medicare criteria for medically necessary services are not payable even when clinicians recommend and furnish and these services.

Services without a Medicare benefit may be billed to Medicare with modifier GY Statutorily excluded, for the purpose of obtaining a denial that can be used with other insurers.

Applicable Outpatient Rehabilitation Codes

CMS (Medicare) identified the codes CPT and HCPCS Level II in the following list as therapy codes. Other third-party payers may follow these guidelines. Check with your payers to determine their policies.

Codes in regular type can be used by physical therapists when appropriate.

NOTE: Listing of the following codes does not imply that services are covered. When in effect, the financial limitations apply to services on the following list, except as noted

64550+	92616+	97010 %	97113	97606+ξ
90901+	95831+	97012	97116	97750
92506?	95832+	97016	97124	97755
92507?	95833+	97018	97139*◆	97760#?
92508	95834+	97022	97140	97761
92526	95851+	97024	97150	97762
92597	95852+	97026	97530	97799*
92605 %	95992+%	97028	97532+	G0281
92606 %	96105+	97032	97533	G0283
92607	96110+✓	97033	97535	G0329
92608	96111+✓	97034	97537	0019T+@
92609	96125	97035	97542	0183T+@ξ
92610+	97001	97036	97597+ξ	
92611+	97002	97039*◆	97598+ξ	
92612+	97003	97110	97602+≅	
92614+	97004	97112	97605+ξ	

*   The physician fee schedule abstract file does not contain a price for CPT codes 97039, 97139, or 97799 since the carrier prices them. Therefore, the FI must contact the carrier to obtain the appropriate fee schedule amount in order to make proper payment for these codes.

◆ Effective January 1, 2006, these codes will no longer be valued under the MPFS. They will be priced by the carriers.

? Effective January 1, 2006, the code descriptors for these services have been changed.

\# CPT code 97760 should not be reported with CPT code 97116 for the same extremity.

@ The physician fee schedule abstract file does not contain a price for CPT codes 0019T, 0029T, and 0183T since they are priced by the carrier. In addition, the carrier determines coverage for these codes. Therefore, the FI contacts the carrier to obtain the appropriate fee schedule amount.

% These HCPCS/CPT codes are bundled under the MPFS. They are bundled with any therapy codes. Regardless of whether they are billed alone or in conjunction with another therapy code, never make payment separately for these codes. If billed alone, HCPCS/CPT codes marked as "%" shall be denied using the existing MSN language. For remittance advice notices, use group code CO and claim adjustment reason code 97 that says: "Payment is included in the allowance for another service/procedure." Use reason code 97 to deny a procedure code that should have been bundled. Alternatively, reason code B15, which has the same intent, may also be used.

✓ If billed by an outpatient hospital department, these HCPCS codes are paid using the outpatient prospective payment system (OPPS).

— Underlined codes are "always therapy" services, regardless of who performs them. These codes always require therapy modifiers (GP, GO, GN).

ξ If billed by a hospital subject to OPPS for an outpatient service, these HCPCS codes—also indicated as "sometimes therapy" services—will be paid under the OPPS when the service is not performed by a qualified therapist and it is inappropriate to bill the service under a therapy plan of care. The requirements for other "sometimes therapy" codes, described below, apply.

+ These HCPCS/CPT codes sometimes represent therapy services. However, these codes always represent therapy services and require the use of a therapy modifier when performed by therapists.

There are some circumstances when these codes will not be considered representative of therapy services and therapy limits (when they are in effect) will not apply. Codes marked + are not therapy services when:

- It is not appropriate to bill the service under a therapy plan of care
- They are billed by practitioners/providers of services who are not therapists (i.e., physicians, clinical nurse specialists, nurse practitioners and psychologists), or they are billed to fiscal intermediaries by hospitals for outpatient services which are performed by nontherapists as noted in note "ξ" above.

While the "+" designates that a particular HCPCS/CPT code will not of itself always indicate that a therapy service was rendered, these codes always represent therapy services when rendered by therapists or by practitioners who

are not therapists in situations where the service provided is integral to an outpatient rehabilitation therapy plan of care. For these situations, these codes must always have a therapy modifier. For example, when the service is rendered by either a doctor of medicine or a nurse practitioner (acting within the scope of his or her license when performing such service), with the goal of rehabilitation, a modifier is required. When there is doubt about whether a service should be part of a therapy plan of care, the contractor shall make that determination.

"Outpatient rehabilitation therapy" refers to skilled therapy services, requiring the skills of qualified therapists, performed for restorative purposes and generally involving ongoing treatments as part of a therapy plan of care. In contrast, a nontherapy service is a service performed by nontherapist practitioners,

without an appropriate rehabilitative plan or goals (e.g., application of a surface (transcutaneous) neurostimulator); CPT code 64550, and biofeedback training by any modality CPT code 90901. When performed by therapists, these are "always" therapy services. Contractors have discretion to determine whether circumstances describe a therapy service or require a rehabilitation plan of care.

The underlined HCPCS codes on the above list do not have a + sign because they are considered "always therapy" codes and always require a therapy modifier. Therapy services, whether represented by "always therapy" codes, or + codes in the above list performed as outpatient rehabilitation therapy services, must follow all the policies for therapy services (e.g., *Medicare Claims Processing Manual*, Pub. 100-04, chapter 5; *Medicare Benefit Policy Manual*, Pub. 100-02, chapters 12 and 15).

Stark Self-Referral Regulations

In 1989, Congress enacted the Stark I law because of concern about potential kickbacks to physicians. The law, named after sponsor Rep. Fortney "Pete" Stark (D, Calif.), is designed to prevent physicians from referring Medicare patients for certain "designated health services" to clinical laboratories or other entities in which the physicians hold a financial stake, unless a particular exception applies.

The bill's passage came in the wake of increased business activities in the health care industry. Studies showed that physicians who had ownership in labs ordered tests more frequently than physicians who referred to independent laboratories.

The law was later expanded to include Medicaid services and 10 additional designated health services, such as physical and occupational therapy, radiology services (including MRI, CT, and ultrasound,) durable medical equipment and supplies, home health services, and outpatient prescription drugs. The expanded law is known as Stark II.

Because of the complexities of the law, Congress did not release rules to enforce Stark I until 1995. Also due to the complexities of regulating and monitoring physician referrals, CMS did not publish rules on Stark II until the final rule on January 4, 2001. These rules generated nearly 13,000 comments from doctors and other providers. The changes became effective January 4, 2002. In future years, the intent is to use a January 1 effective date to coincide with the effective date for new HCPCS or CPT codes. The full text of the January 4 rule can be obtained from the CMS website at http://hhs.cms.gov.

The majority of regulations were contained in phase I of the Stark legislation including ownership and compensation arrangement, definitions, employment agreements, and personal service contracts, and regulatory exceptions. Phase II, implemented July 26, 2004, focused on new regulatory definitions and exceptions as well as public comments pertaining to phase I.

CMS published the Phase II Stark II rule in the March 26 *Federal Register* with an effective date of July 26, 2004. A link to the rule is available at:

http://a257.g.akamaitech.net/7/257/2422/14mar20010800 /edocket.access.gpo.gov/2004/pdf/04-6668.pdf.

What's Prohibited

In general, the Stark II regulation is an attempt to clarify what are prohibited activities and to allow "particular and reasonable" exceptions to the regulations. It is important to remember that the prohibitions surrounding self-referrals apply specifically to Medicare and Medicaid patients. However, medical practices still must abide with the specific state statutes that apply to all patients, regardless of the insurer.

Under Stark II, a physician cannot refer Medicare or Medicaid patients to a health care entity in which a financial interest is held for the following services:

- Physical therapy services
- Occupational therapy services
- Radiology services and supplies
- Radiation therapy services and supplies
- Durable medical equipment and supplies
- Parenteral and enteral nutrients, equipment, and supplies
- Prosthetics, orthotics, and prosthetic devices, and supplies
- Home health services
- Outpatient prescription drugs
- Inpatient and outpatient hospital services
- Clinical lab tests

Exclusions for Medical Groups

Stark II does allow certain referrals to occur within a medical group practice. These exceptions include ancillary services performed in-office and referrals to physicians practicing within the same medical group.

Ancillary services (such as physical therapy, interpreting x-rays or echocardiograms) must be personally performed by the referring physician, another member of the physician group, or an in-office employee supervised by the physician. Physicians may refer patients to other doctors within their medical group.

In order to qualify for these exceptions, medical group practices must meet the following guidelines:

Under the rule, a medical group must demonstrate that:

- Billing, auditing, accounting, and financial statements originate from a centralized entity with overall responsibility for the group.
- Decision making is handled by a centralized unit that exercises responsibility and control over budget, salaries, compensation, assets, and liabilities.
- At least 75 percent of patient care is provided by group members. This includes owners and employees of the group, not independent contractors. In addition, at least 75 percent of group members' income must derive from practice within the group.

Durable Medical Equipment Supplied by Certified Providers
Physician-supplied home glucose monitors are allowed, and doctors who are certified DME providers may supply manual wheelchairs, crutches, canes, and walkers.

Stark II allows for compensation arrangements with independent contractors when referrals are made under specific circumstances. For example, if a group provides radiology services with its own equipment but pays a radiologist to interpret the images, the group can pay a flat fee for interpretations and then bill for professional and technical components.

PTs may either obtain a provider number and reassign payment to group practice or the physician may report the services under his or her own provider number.

Distributing Fees
In an effort to outlaw monetary rewards for referrals and the ordering of unnecessary tests, CMS designed the rules so that physicians cannot be rewarded directly or indirectly for a high volume of such referrals.

Since the rules defining a referral are intricate, this can become a complicated matter. For example, if a PT performs services on a patient, the fact that the PT is employed and/or supervised by a provider other than the one who ordered the services makes that service a referral under Stark II.

In this case, the compensation from those services performed by the PT cannot be allocated to physicians who recommended the PT services. However, these revenues can be allocated to group members via a "reasonable and verifiable" method that is derived from the volume of each physician's referrals.

Correct Coding Initiative
In an effort to save Medicare trust funds, CMS determined that it should:

- Reduce the number of unbundled services billed to Medicare
- Cut down on abusive coding practices
- Standardize coding on a national level

In August 1995, CMS awarded a contract to Administar Federal to define coding practices that would be the basis of national policy for claim payment. Using the CPT coding system, Administar developed correct coding combinations based on review of CPT descriptors, coding instructions, review of existing local and national edits, and review of Medicare billing history.

Administar developed a comprehensive narrative policy that outlines general and specific guidelines for the appropriate use of CPT codes for provider claims. This narrative policy was reviewed by physician specialty groups, the AMA, nonphysician specialty groups, and Medicare carrier medical directors.

Subsequently, upon receiving CMS approval, Administar developed a coding matrix to be embedded into the Medicare carriers' claims processing systems. This matrix, based on the correct coding policy, automatically identifies inappropriate CPT coding combinations and properly determines payment. Existing Medicare policy was not changed by the correct coding policy.

Currently the Correct Coding Initiative (CCI) edits are being administered by Correct Coding Solutions, LLC. In addition, it should be noted that many other non-Medicare payers have adopted the CCI as their method to determine unbundling of claims. Physical therapy services provided in SNFs, CORFs, rehabilitation agencies, and HHAs are subject to the CCI edits, which at one time were applicable only to physicians, PTPPs, and outpatient hospitals.

There are two basic types of code combinations:

- Column 1/column 2 correct coding edits (formerly called comprehensive/component code combinations)
- Mutually exclusive coding combinations

Reimbursement

All of the edits, whether they are column 1/column 2 correct coding edits or mutually exclusive edits, are composed of code pairs arranged in two columns. For both sets of edits, the column 2 code is not payable with the column 1 code unless the edit permits use of an appropriate modifier associated with CCI.

Column 1/Column 2 Correct Coding Edits

Although the column 1/ column 2 correct coding edits contain many edits where the column 2 code is a component of the column one comprehensive code there are also many code combinations where there is no comprehensive or component relationship, but the column 1 code and column 2 code should not be reported together for other reasons. The following is a summary of general coding policies applicable to code combinations pertinent to physical therapy services.

HCPCS/CPT Procedure Code Definition

The CPT procedure code definition, or descriptor, is based upon the procedure being consistent with current medical practice. In order to submit a CPT code to Medicare, the provider must have performed all the services in the code descriptor. Remember that payment is based on having performed all the services. If you have not performed all the services within the descriptor, then a less comprehensive code must be used. Providers must NOT submit codes describing components of a comprehensive code if the comprehensive code describes the services performed.

For example, it is not appropriate to report code combinations that report a procedure both "with" and "without" specific services. Along this same line, this policy states that a "partial" procedure is included in a "complete" or "total" procedure, "unilateral" is included in the "bilateral", and "single" is included in the "multiple" procedure.

CPT Book and CMS Coding Manual Instructions

CMS publishes coding instructions in its rules, manuals, and notices, which must be used when reporting services provided to Medicare patients.

The CPT book also contains instructions and guidelines that may appear in various places and are found at the beginning of each major section, at the beginning of subsections, and prior to or after a series of codes or individual codes. These instructions define items or provide explanations necessary to appropriately interpret and report the procedures or services and to define terms applicable to particular sections. CPT book instructions should be followed unless CMS provides different coding or reporting instructions.

Misuse of Column 2 with Column 1 Code

This represents the inappropriate interpretation of a CPT code definition, which is not to be used out of context. For this edit, CPT codes that describe procedures or services not usually performed with other procedures or services that may be interpreted to represent other services have been identified and paired with the column one CPT codes. In addition, code pairs have been identified that would not be reported together because another code more accurately describes the service provided.

Separate Procedure

When the HCPCS/CPT code descriptor includes the term "separate procedure," the code is not to be reported separately with a related procedure. CMS interprets this designation to prohibit the separate reporting of a separate procedure when performed with another procedure in an anatomically related region.

When a HCPCS/CPT code with the separate procedure designation is performed at a separate patient encounter on the same date of service or at the same patient encounter by a different approach, it may be reported in addition to another procedure. Modifier 59 Distinct procedural service, may be appended to the separate procedure HCPCS/CPT code to indicate that it qualifies as a separately reportable service.

More Extensive Procedure

When procedures are performed together that are basically the same, or performed on the same site but are qualified by an increased level of complexity, with the less extensive procedure included in the more extensive procedure.

Medical/Surgical Package

In general, most services have preprocedure and postprocedure work associated with them. When these services are performed at a single patient encounter, the preprocedure and postprocedure work does not change proportionately when multiple services are performed and the nature of the preprocedure and postprocedure work is reasonably consistent across the spectrum of procedures.

Mutually Exclusive Procedures

These codes represent services or procedures that would not or could not be performed at the same time, on the same patient, and by the same physician based on the CPT code descriptions or standard medical practice.

Under this edit, CPT codes that are mutually exclusive of one another based either on the CPT definition or the medical impossibility/improbability that the procedures could be performed at the same patient encounter have been identified as code pairs, which should not be reported together. Many of the edits in the mutually exclusive edit table permit CCI-associated modifiers to be reported. For example, the two procedures of a code pair edit may be performed at different anatomic sites or separate patient encounters on the same date of service.

Correct Coding Modifier Indicator

CMS authorized an indicator that specifies whether modifier 59 Distinct procedureal service, can be used to bypass the CCI edits. This is not, however, a method in which practices can circumvent the CCI edits and several coding combinations are denied regardless of the use of modifier 59.

If a provider files a claim for services included in the CCI edits and the services are identified on the indicator list as payable only for the column 1 service, the column 2 service will be denied by Medicare as being part of the comprehensive service. The use of modifier 59 (or any other modifier) will not bypass the denial of the service. The provider cannot collect payment from the patient or patient's secondary insurance for the denied component.

A list of the most recent CCI edits for physical therapy is located at the back of this publication. **These edits are subject to change during the year and quarterly email updates of the CCI edits related to physical therapy will be sent to you as part of this publication, if your email address has been provided to Ingenix.**

Medicare carrier bulletins should also be reviewed for changes affecting your coding practices.

Appeals for CCI Denials
Your Medicare carrier is unable to change the correct coding edits. Concerns regarding specific correct coding edits should be submitted in writing to:

National Correct Coding Initiative
Correct Coding Solutions LLC
P.O. Box 907
Carmel, IN 46082-0907
Attention: Niles R. Rosen, M.D., Medical Director and Linda S. Dietz, RHIA, CCS, CCS-P, Coding Specialist
Fax: 317.571.1745

However, if a claim or service was denied because modifier 59 was omitted, you may appeal the claim denial with the Medicare contractor or simply amend the claim by adding modifier 59 and refile it. You need to send your documentation with the appeal. By using the modifier, you are certifying that you have appropriate documentation in the patient's chart.

Medically Unlikely Edits

Effective January 1, 2007, in an effort to lower the Medicare fee-for-service paid claims error rate, CMS implemented edits referred to as the "medically unlikely edits" or MUEs. A medically unlikely edit for a HCPCS or CPT code is the maximum number of units of service allowable by the same provider for the same beneficiary, on the same date of service. Units of service that are in excess of an MUE are denied.

Edits were added in phases, with the initial MUEs focused on anatomic considerations. Currently, physical therapy codes affected include 97001–97004. CMS created modifier GD Units of service exceeds medically unlikely edit value and represents reasonable and necessary services, to override the MUE edits. However, CMS has also stated that since each line of a claim is adjudicated separately against the MUE for that code, the appropriate use of a CPT or HCPCS modifier on the same code on a separate line will allow the provider to indicate the medically reasonable and necessary units of that service in excess of an MUE. CPT modifiers such as 59 Distinct procedural service, or HCPCS Level II modifiers RT Right, LT Left, F1 Left hand second digit, and F2 Left hand third digit, are examples of modifiers that can be used to override the MUE when appropriate. It is important to remember that modifier 59 Distinct procedural service, should be used only when no other modifier describes the modifying circumstance.

Effective October 1, 2008, CMS began publishing a partial list of the medically unlikely edits (MUEs) and making them available to the public. The list contains approximately 2,600 of the 9,700 current MUEs. MUEs are intended to detect and discourage any questionable payments, and will not be published as the agency feels the efficacy of these edits would be compromised. MUEs are updated quarterly.

Medical Necessity

Medical necessity has been defined by CMS as the appropriateness of a diagnosis or treatment by a provider, based on the medical community's perception and understanding of the diagnosis and/or treatment plan. Section 1862 (a) (1) of the Social Security Act prohibits Medicare from covering items and services that "are not reasonable and necessary for the diagnosis or treatment of an illness, an injury, or to improve the function of a malformed body member."

To be considered medically necessary, items and services must be:

- Consistent with the symptoms or diagnosis of the illness or injury under treatment
- Necessary and consistent with generally accepted professional practice standards
- Not furnished primarily for the convenience of the patient, the physician, or the supplier
- Furnished at the most appropriate level that can be provided safely and effectively to the patient

If a service does not meet the above standards, it may be denied as not medically necessary. Unless the patient was previously notified of this fact and an advance beneficiary notice (ABN) has been completed, the patient may not be billed for these services.

Advance Beneficiary Notice

The Omnibus Budget Reconciliation Act (OBRA) of 1986 included a limitation of liability (or waiver) provision to the Social Security Act for both assigned and nonassigned claims. This provides beneficiaries with protection from liability when they, in good faith, receive services from a Medicare provider for which Medicare payment was subsequently denied as not reasonable and necessary.

While previous versions of the ABN were required only for denial reasons based on medical necessity, the revised version may also be used to provide voluntary notification of financial liability, which also eliminates the need for the NEMB for situations in which notification is provided.

When provided, the ABN must be verbally reviewed with the beneficiary or his/her representative and questions posed during that discussion answered prior to the form being signed. The form must be provided in advance to allow the beneficiary or representative time to consider options and make an informed choice. The ABN may be delivered by employees or subcontractors of the practice, and are not required when an emergent situation exists. After the form has been completely filled in, and the form is signed, a copy is given to the beneficiary or his or her representative. In all cases, the notifier must retain the original notice on file.

Approved ABNs are found on the CMS website at: http://www.cms.hhs.gov/BNI/02_ABNGABNL.asp#TopOfPage, where the notices can be downloaded. All ABNs must be reproduced on a single page—either letter or legal-size-with additional space allowed for each blank needing completion when a legal-size page is used. ABNs should be used as is, since it is a standardized OMB-approved notice. Some customization of the form may be allowed for those choosing to integrate the ABN into other automated business processes. Besides generic ABN, CMS will also provide alternate versions with certain blanks completed for those not wishing to do additional customization as permitted, including a version illustrating laboratory-specific use.

The form consists of 10 blanks, labeled from A through J. The CMS recommends removing the labels for the blanks prior to using. Blanks labeled A through F and H may be completed prior to delivering the notice, as appropriate. Entries may be typed or hand-written, but large enough (i.e., approximately 12-point font) to allow for easier reading. A 10-point font can be used in blanks when detailed information must be provided and is otherwise difficult to fit in the allowed space. The option box, blank G, must be completed by the beneficiary or his or her representative. Blank I should be a cursive signature, with printed annotation in order to be read, as needed.

Notifiers may put their logo at the top of the notice by typing, handwriting, preprinting, use of a label or other means. At a minimum, the name, address, and telephone number (including TTY when appropriate) of the notifier must appear, whether incorporated into the logo or not, in case the beneficiary has additional questions.

The first and last name and the middle initial of the beneficiary receiving the notice (if on the beneficiary's Medicare (HICN) card. Although optional, the beneficiary's identification number links the notice with the related claim when applicable. Do not use the beneficiary's Medicare number or HICN.

The body of the notice consists of the text below the header, the box to record the items and services, reasons coverage is not expected and estimated cost, and remaining text above the options box, and can be used for a single item or service or multiple items or services. When multiple items or services are at issue, each must be addressed either separately or, if they can be explained by one reason, or bundled into one cost.

In lieu of the default term "items and services" in blank D, the most appropriate of the following word choices below can be used by the notifier to prepare the ABN prior to delivery:

- Item
- Service
- Item or service
- Laboratory test
- Test
- Procedure
- Care
- Equipment
- Supply

Under the heading for blank E, "Reason Medicare May Not Pay" notifiers must explain, why they believe the care subject of the notice is not covered.

Like in the previous version of the ABN-L, there are three possible reasons for noncoverage preprinted on the ABN that are appropriate for blank E of the form. However, many other possible valid reasons may also be used, such as the following:

- "Medicare does not pay for these tests for your condition"
- "Medicare does not pay for these test as often as this (denied as too frequent)"
- "Medicare does not pay for experimental or research use tests"

These reasons are still appropriate for use in blank (E) of this ABN.

NOTE: In blank F, notifiers are required to enter a cost estimate for any items or services described in blank (D). In this field, as in blank D, there is flexibility in listing individual or total cost. The revised ABN will not be considered valid without a good faith attempt to estimate cost.

For blank G (options), CMS included additional guidance to reinforce critical aspects of the choice that a patient has to make. The three checkboxes represent the possible choices regarding the potentially noncovered care described in the body of the ABN. Only one checkbox may be checked, and if the beneficiary cannot or will not make a choice, the notice should be annotated.

When a beneficiary chooses to receive some, but not all, of the items or services subject of the notice, the items and services listed under blank D that he or she does not wish to receive may be crossed out, as long as this can be done in a way that also clearly indicates the reason and cost information in blanks E and F that correspond to that care. If this cannot be clearly stated, a new ABN must be used.

Blank H "Additional Information," is used to provide additional clarification that will be useful to beneficiaries and may include information such as the following

- Former ABN-L language, "[You should] notify your doctor who orders these laboratory tests you did not receive them"
- Providing context on Medicare payment policy applicable to a specific benefit
- Information on other insurance coverage for beneficiaries needing immediate reassurance of additional coverage

The ABN no longer includes an "other insurance" blank. Rather, the body of the notice indicates that the notifier may help the patient to access any other insurance, although this is not required by the Medicare program

The beneficiary or representative must sign the notice, with his or her own name, in blank I, "Signature," to allow maximum space for making the written entry. The signature denotes that he or she has received the notice and understands its contents. In blank J, the beneficiary or his or her representative must enter the date he or she signed the ABN.

Information regarding such restrictions and medical policies is published in the Medicare B carrier bulletins received by your practice. Services not payable due to not reasonable and necessary provisions must be billed to Medicare even though they will likely be denied. If the provider believes the services are not reasonable and necessary, bill for the services with modifiers GA, GY, or GZ as appropriate.

Generally, services necessitating a signed ABN are payable in some instances but not payable in others. By understanding these provisions, providers can protect their practice or company from financial liability for these denied services.

Nonparticipating providers who provide services to Medicare beneficiaries on a nonassigned basis that are subsequently determined not to be reasonable and necessary are required to refund any amounts collected from the beneficiary, unless one of the two following circumstances applies:

- The provider did not know and could not have reasonably been expected to know that Medicare would not pay for the service.

  There are several notification processes that the Medicare carrier considers in determining whether the provider should have known that Medicare would not cover a service. The most frequent notifications include general notice to all providers, such as the *Federal Register* or the carrier's Medicare newsletter, and notice to an individual provider, such as a letter or a previous denial of a similar service in a similar situation.

- The provider notified the patient in writing, prior to performing the service, that Medicare would likely deny the service and the reason why, and, after being so informed, the beneficiary agreed in writing to pay for the service (an example is shown on the following page). Acceptable evidence of prior notification to a Medicare beneficiary (or a person acting on the beneficiary's behalf) must include all of the following:

- The notice must be in writing, using approved notice language (refer to the sample ABN form on the following page).

- A copy of the agreement must be retained in the provider's files. Blanket waiver statements are not acceptable. As a courtesy, provide the beneficiary with a copy of the agreement.

- The notice must be signed and dated by the beneficiary (or a person acting on the beneficiary's behalf) prior to the service being provided.

- The notice must cite the specific service or services for which payment is likely to be denied.

- The notice must cite the provider's specific reason for believing Medicare payment will be denied. (The notice is not an acceptable waiver if it is no more than a statement to the effect that there is a possibility that Medicare may not pay for the service.) The following are examples of acceptable specific reasons:

The information in your case does not support the need for:

— this equipment

— this service

— this treatment

— this injection (not applicable to PT)

— this many injections (not applicable to PT)

— the level of service as shown on the claim

— similar services by more than one doctor/provider during the same time period

— similar services by more than one doctor/provider of the same specialty

— more than one visit a day

Medicare does not pay for:

— this number of home visits per month

— this many services within this period of time

— this many visits or treatments

— this laboratory test

— acupuncture

Providers and suppliers should not give notices to beneficiaries unless there is some genuine doubt regarding the likelihood of Medicare payment as evidenced by his or her stated reasons. Attempting to satisfy the requirement for an advance beneficiary notice by a signed statement to the effect that, should Medicare deny payment under section 1862(a)(1) of the Social Security Act, the beneficiary agrees to pay for the service, is not acceptable. Routine notices to beneficiaries simply stating that denial of payment by Medicare is possible or that the physician or supplier never knows whether Medicare will deny payment are also not considered acceptable evidence of advance notice. Giving notices for all claims or services is not an acceptable practice.

Reimbursement

*(A)*Notifier(s):
(B) Patient Name: *(C)* Identification Number:

ADVANCE BENEFICIARY NOTICE OF NONCOVERAGE (ABN)

NOTE: If Medicare doesn't pay for *(D)*_____ below, you may have to pay.

Medicare does not pay for everything, even some care that you or your health care provider have good reason to think you need. We expect Medicare may not pay for the *(D)*_____ below.

*(D)*_____	*(E)* Reason Medicare May Not Pay:	*(F)* Estimated Cost:

WHAT YOU NEED TO DO NOW:

- Read this notice, so you can make an informed decision about your care.
- Ask us any questions that you may have after you finish reading.
- Choose an option below about whether to receive the *(D)*_____ listed above.
  - **Note:** If you choose Option 1 or 2, we may help you to use any other insurance that you might have, but Medicare cannot require us to do this.

(G) OPTIONS: Check only one box. We cannot choose a box for you.

❏ **OPTION 1.** I want the *(D)*_____ listed above. You may ask to be paid now, but I also want Medicare billed for an official decision on payment, which is sent to me on a Medicare Summary Notice (MSN). I understand that if Medicare doesn't pay, I am responsible for payment, but **I can appeal to Medicare** by following the directions on the MSN. If Medicare does pay, you will refund any payments I made to you, less co-pays or deductibles.

❏ **OPTION 2.** I want the *(D)*_____ listed above, but do not bill Medicare. You may ask to be paid now as I am responsible for payment. **I cannot appeal if Medicare is not billed.**

❏ **OPTION 3.** I don't want the *(D)*_____ listed above. I understand with this choice I am **not** responsible for payment, and **I cannot appeal to see if Medicare would pay.**

(H) Additional Information:

This notice gives our opinion, not an official Medicare decision. If you have other questions on this notice or Medicare billing, call **1-800-MEDICARE** (1-800-633-4227/**TTY**: 1-877-486-2048).

Signing below means that you have received and understand this notice. You also receive a copy.

(I) Signature:	*(J)* Date:

According to the Paperwork Reduction Act of 1995, no persons are required to respond to a collection of information unless it displays a valid OMB control number. The valid OMB control number for this information collection is 0938-0566. The time required to complete this information collection is estimated to average 7 minutes per response, including the time to review instructions, search existing data resources, gather the data needed, and complete and review the information collection. If you have comments concerning the accuracy of the time estimate or suggestions for improving this form, please write to: CMS, 7500 Security Boulevard, Attn: PRA Reports Clearance Officer, Baltimore, Maryland 21244-1850.

Form CMS-R-131 (03/08)   Form Approved OMB No. 0938-0566

Some providers may wish to continue to use the notice of exclusions from Medicare benefits (NEMB) Form CMS-20007 instead of the ABN to inform beneficiaries that Medicare will not pay for certain items or services that are not Medicare benefits. The NEMB, which is used strictly on a voluntary basis, must be provided prior to the delivery of the services to allow beneficiaries to make informed consumer decisions about receiving items or services for which they must pay out of pocket and to be more active participants in their own health care treatment decisions.

The NEMB Form CMS-20007 is available online in English and Spanish at the CMS Beneficiary Notices Initiative (BNI) web page at: http://www.cms.hhs.gov/BNI/02_ABNGABNL.asp# TopOfPageHTU.

Reimbursement

NOTICE OF EXCLUSIONS FROM MEDICARE BENEFITS (NEMB)
There are items and services for which Medicare <u>will not pay</u>.

- Medicare does **not** pay for all of your health care costs. Medicare only pays for covered benefits. **Some items and services are not Medicare benefits and Medicare will not pay for them.**

- When you receive an item or service that is **not** a Medicare benefit, **you are responsible to pay for it,** personally or through any other insurance that you may have.

  The purpose of this notice is to help you make an informed choice about whether or not you want to receive these items or services, knowing that you will have to pay for them yourself. **Before you make a decision, you should read this entire notice carefully.**
  Ask us to explain, if you don't understand why Medicare won't pay.
  Ask us how much these items or services will cost you (**Estimated Cost: $_____**).

Medicare will not pay for: _____
_____;

☐ **1.** **Because it does not meet the definition of any Medicare benefit.**

☐ **2.** **Because of the following exclusion * from Medicare benefits:**

☐ Personal comfort items.
☐ Most shots (vaccinations).
☐ Hearing aids and hearing examinations.
☐ Most outpatient prescription drugs.
☐ Orthopedic shoes and foot supports (orthotics).
☐ Health care received outside of the USA.
☐ Services required as a result of war.
☐ Routine physicals and most tests for screening.
☐ Routine eye care, eyeglasses and examinations.
☐ Cosmetic surgery.
☐ Dental care and dentures (in most cases).
☐ Routine foot care and flat foot care.
☐ Services by immediate relatives.
☐ Services under a physician's private contract.
☐ Services paid for by a governmental entity that is not Medicare.
☐ Services for which the patient has no legal obligation to pay.
☐ Home health services furnished under a plan of care, if the agency does not submit the claim.
☐ Items and services excluded under the Assisted Suicide Funding Restriction Act of 1997.
☐ Items or services furnished in a competitive acquisition area by any entity that does not have a contract with the Department of Health and Human Services (except in a case of urgent need).
☐ Physicians' services performed by a physician assistant, midwife, psychologist, or nurse anesthetist, when furnished to an inpatient, unless they are furnished under arrangements by the hospital.
☐ Items and services furnished to an individual who is a resident of a skilled nursing facility (a SNF) or of a part of a facility that includes a SNF, unless they are furnished under arrangements by the SNF.
☐ Services of an assistant at surgery without prior approval from the peer review organization.
☐ Outpatient occupational and physical therapy services furnished incident to a physician's services.

* This is only a general summary of exclusions from Medicare benefits. It is not a legal document. The official Medicare program provisions are contained in relevant laws, regulations, and rulings.

Form No. CMS-20007   (January 2003)

© 2009 Ingenix

Modifiers for Noncovered Services

For all noncovered services, an appropriate modifier should be appended to the service based on the reason for the noncoverage, either as a statutory exclusion, not medically necessary, or whether an ABN was not completed.

In order for a service to be covered under Medicare, it must not be excluded by Title XVIII of the Social Security Act. Section 1862 (a) (1) of the Act lists the excluded items, which include, but are not limited to the following:

- Routine physical checkups
- Immunizations
- Cosmetic surgery
- Hearing aids
- Eyeglasses
- Routine foot care
- Most dental care

When one of these services is provided to a patient, the service will be denied by Medicare as statutorily excluded. When a claim is filed for the service, modifier GY should be appended to the code.

GY   Item or service statutorily excluded or does not meet the definition of any Medicare benefit

HCPCS Level II code A9270 Noncovered item or service, is an active code; however it should only be used by DME suppliers.

Not Medically Necessary

Another common reason for a service to be denied is because it is not considered medically necessary by the Medicare program.

CMS instructs payers that it considers a service to be reasonable and necessary if it is determined that the service is:

- Safe and effective
- Not experimental or investigational (exception: routine clinical trial services with dates of service on or after September 19, 2000, which meet the requirements of the clinical trials national coverage decision are considered reasonable and necessary)
- Appropriate, including the duration and frequency that is considered appropriate for the service, in terms of whether it is:
  — furnished in accordance with accepted standards of medical practice for the diagnosis or treatment of the patient's condition or to improve the function of a malformed body member
  — furnished in a setting appropriate to the patient's medical needs and condition
  — ordered and/or furnished by qualified personnel
  — one that meets, but does not exceed, the patient's medical need
  — at least as beneficial as an existing and available medically appropriate alternative

When a claim for a service is submitted that will more than likely be denied for this reason, and there is no ABN signed by the patient on file for the service, Modifier GZ should be appended to the procedure code for that service.

GZ   Item or service expected to be denied as not reasonable or necessary

A patient under the care of a physical therapist receives iontophoresis, CPT code 97033, which is designated as a noncovered service in accordance with a local carrier decision (LCD). The treatment has received this designation since there is no evidence from published, controlled clinical studies regarding the efficacy of the procedure as a physical medicine modality and as such, will be denied as not medically necessary. The provider needs to be aware that billing for iontophoresis will result in a denial of not medically necessary with provider liability. If the patient agrees and signs an ABN, the provider can collect payment from the patient for the service. If the patient does not sign an ABN, the provider becomes liable. In this situation, modifier GZ should be appended to the claim.

Modifier GA is used when the service is likely to be denied for reasons of medical necessity, but the practice did have the patient complete the necessary ABN.

In our example provided above, if the provider did have the patient sign an appropriately completed ABN for the upgraded DMEPOS item that the patient requested, then modifier GA would be appended to the code.

GA   Waiver of liability statement on file

The MPFS is released late in November on an annual basis and becomes effective January 1 of each year. This fee schedule also contains the CPT procedures that Medicare does not consider for payment or noncovered services.

Appealing Waiver of Liability Decisions

Providers may appeal a decision regarding whether or not an advance beneficiary notice should have been given before services were rendered. A request for review extends the time in which the provider has to refund any amounts that may have already been collected from the beneficiary. A provider may request a review based on the following information:

- A provider may state that the beneficiary was informed in advance that Medicare payment would not be made, and the beneficiary agreed to pay for the services.

  In this situation, the provider needs to furnish evidence to support his or her statement. This evidence consists of a notice to the beneficiary containing one of the following:

  — an appropriate waiver of liability
  — if a statement from the beneficiary cannot be obtained, an undisputed allegation by the provider that the beneficiary agreed (prior to the date the service was furnished) to pay for the service

- The provider may claim that he or she did not know and could not reasonably have been expected to know that the service was not covered.
- The provider supplies additional clinical documentation or information missing on the original claim that may support the necessity of the service.

If a provider requests a review within 30 days after receiving the denial notification, refunding the amount to the beneficiary may be delayed until the provider receives the results of the review. If the review determination is favorable, a refund is not necessary. If, however, the review is unfavorable, the law specifies that the provider must make the refund within 15 days of receiving the unfavorable review decision. A review requested after the 30-day limitation will not permit the provider to delay making the refund. The law also permits the provider to request a review of the determination at any time within six months of receiving the unfavorable review decision. Regardless of when a review is requested, the patient will be notified that the provider has requested a review and will receive a copy of the determination. Please refer to the appeal process section for more information.

Participation in Medicare Plans

Providers can elect to participate with Medicare. This may cause confusion regarding how participation affects payment amounts. If you participate, your Medicare fee schedule amounts are 5 percent higher. Also, regardless of the Medicare Part B services for which you are billing, participating providers have one stop billing for beneficiaries who have non-employment-related Medigap coverage and who assign both their Medicare and Medigap payments to participants. After Medicare has made payment, the claim is automatically sent to the Medigap insurer for payment of all coinsurance and deductible amounts due under the Medigap policy. The Medigap insurer must pay the participating provider directly.

Participating Providers

To become a participating provider, a participating physician or supplier agreement must be signed by the provider or supplier. Annually (usually mid-November), an enrollment package is sent to all providers explaining the legislative changes affecting the Medicare program (also known as open enrollment) for the upcoming year. Providers who have already signed a prior participating physician or supplier agreement do not need to sign another new agreement each year. Currently, a Medicare supplier disclosure report is mailed under separate cover and identifies the new reimbursement rates for the upcoming calendar year.

Once the carrier accepts the agreement, an annotated copy is sent back to the provider. The annotated copy identifies the effective date of the participation status. The agreement remains in effect every year thereafter, or until it is revoked during an open enrollment period (usually mid-November through December 31 of each year).

A participating provider or supplier may submit his or her regular charges for services on the claim form. However, as a participant, assignment must be accepted on all Medicare claims (see the section on claim form completion for more information on accepting assignment). Payment for covered services is sent directly to the provider once the carrier processes the claim. The provider or supplier cannot collect from anyone the difference between the billed amount on the claim and the Medicare-approved amount (this is called "balance billing"). Services denied as "not a benefit" or "not covered" may be billed to the patient if the patient was advised prior to the service being rendered (see the ABN section for more information). Note: The provider or supplier is responsible for refunding overpayments to the beneficiary.

Nonparticipating Providers

Nonparticipating providers can choose to have payment sent directly to the practice on some, none, or all of their Medicare claims. All nonparticipating providers are given the opportunity to change their participation status each year during the open enrollment period. The open enrollment period usually starts in the middle of November and runs through December 31 each year. During this period, all providers or suppliers are sent information on the reimbursement, charge limits, and regulation changes for the upcoming year.

Nonparticipating providers and suppliers submitting non-assigned claims for services payable on the physician fee schedule are limited in the amount they can charge the Medicare program and the patient. This limit is called the "charge limit" or "limiting charge." The limiting charge serves to protect Medicare beneficiaries from undue balance billing expenses.

Providers or suppliers who continually, knowingly, and willfully exceed the limiting charge can be assessed $10,000 for each limiting charge violation and face possible exclusion from the Medicare program.

Although the limiting charge exception report is no longer mailed to nonparticipating providers, practitioners, or suppliers, the limiting charges submitted by non-participating providers are still monitored by Medicare staff. In the absence of the limiting charge exception report, providers, other practitioners, and suppliers can use their remittance notices to calculate the limiting charge amounts.

Example: Take the approved amount times 115 percent to get the limiting charge amount (maximum amount that may be charged to the beneficiary).

Approved amount from remittance notice	$135.00
	x 115%
Limiting charge amount	$155.25

- The limiting charge amounts for most physician fee schedule services are listed on the disclosure reports and this constitutes "notice" of the Medicare charge limits of those services.

- The maximum amount that a nonparticipating provider or supplier is permitted to charge a Medicare beneficiary for unassigned services paid under the physician fee schedule, the limiting charge, is 115 percent of the Medicare-allowed charge.

- The submission of a non-assigned physician fee schedule service with a submitted/billed charge in excess of the Medicare limiting charge amount constitutes a violation of the charge limit.

- The limiting charge provision does not apply to submitted or billed charges of assigned services, but the provider can collect in total (from all Medicare payers) no more than the Medicare-approved charge for such services.

- For nonassigned services, the remittance form replaces the Limiting charge exception report.

- Refunds of overcharges are required, and the remittance form will serve as the provider's notice that a refund must be made.

© 2009 Ingenix

Reimbursement

- Providers who elect not to receive remittance statements for nonassigned claims are still required to make refunds of overcharges. Providers may, therefore, want to reconsider their decision not to receive remittance forms for nonassigned claims.

- Beneficiaries are notified on their EOMBs or Medicare summary notices (MSN) when their provider or supplier submits a nonassigned physician fee schedule service approved for payment but the fee billed to Medicare exceeds the limiting charge amount. The EOMB/MSN also informs beneficiaries how much the provider or supplier can legally bill for that service.

Supplemental Medicare Coverage

Medigap

CMS clarified the liability of Medicare supplemental payers with respect to the 1994 amendments on limiting charge activities. Limiting charge extends to supplemental payers on the beneficiary's behalf. The Social Security Act Amendments of 1994 (SSAA 1994) explicitly prohibit a nonparticipating provider who does not accept assignment from billing or collecting amounts above the applicable limiting charge, regardless of who would be responsible for payment.

Private Medicare supplemental (commonly referred to as Medigap) insurance is owned by approximately 43 percent of beneficiaries and is regulated under the Social Security Act.

The Omnibus Budget Reconciliation Act (OBRA) of 1990 revised the law to standardize Medigap plans into no more than 10 standardized plans. The National Association of Insurance Commissioners (NAIC) designed these plans, designated A–J. Of the 10 plans, four cover Part B extra charges or balance billing, up to any charge limit set by federal or state law. Therefore, any Medigap policy with balance billing protections issued since implementation of OBRA of 1990 would preclude payment of amounts in excess of the federal limiting charge.

If the insurer makes a payment to the provider and then discovers that the bill exceeded the applicable limiting charge, the insurer is legally entitled to an appropriate refund.

The statute directly authorizes the Medicare program to sanction the provider for failure to make a refund only if the refund is due the beneficiary. Medicare has some leverage, however, to persuade the provider to make a refund to an insurer. A provider that knowingly and willfully bills more than the limiting charge to the beneficiary, the insurer, or other party, on a repeated basis, is subject to sanctions.

Employee Retirement Income Security Act of 1974

Around 38 percent of beneficiaries have employer supplemental coverage under policies that are generally subject to the Employee Retirement Income Security Act (ERISA) of 1974, which is under the jurisdiction of the Department of Labor, and which generally places no requirements on plans with respect to the benefits provided. ERISA is the law that protects those enrolled in health, pension, and other types of benefit plans that are sponsored by employers in the private sector. These policies are not subject to the requirements of section 1882 of the Medicare

Act. Since CMS does not receive information regarding policies subject to ERISA, Medicare is unable to monitor compliance of supplemental payments made under these policies with Medicare's limiting charges.

A final regulation established minimum standards for processing claims and appeals effective for all claims filed on and after January 1, 2002. The regulation modified the benefits claims procedures of employee benefit plans and established new claims processing standards that will facilitate more timely determinations of benefits and reviews of claims that have been denied.

Time frames were established for claim decisions, with payment expected within a reasonable amount of time following plan approval. The time period starts once the claim is filed.

For postservice claims, in which the medical care has already been provided, decisions must be made no later than 30 days (with one extension of 15 days with notification to the claimant within the initial 30 days). Again, 180 days is allowed for an appeal of an adverse benefit determination, to which the plan has a maximum of 60 days to determine a resolution.

The standards for adverse benefit determinations require that claimants be notified with regards to the specific reasons for a denial of benefits. Plans are required to cite the guidelines, protocols and other criteria used to make the adverse benefit determination and provide it, free of change, if requested. Reviews of appeals for services denied as not medically necessary require a consultation with a health care professional with the training and expertise in the field. Medical experts consulted in connection with reviews must be individually identified upon request.

Additional information is available on the Department of Labor website at: www.dol.gov/ebsa.

For answers to frequently asked questions, see http://www.dol.gov/dolfaq/dolfaq.asp

Medicare Secondary Payer

Your office should implement procedures to determine if the beneficiary falls within the criteria for Medicare secondary payment. If possible, this determination should be made when the beneficiary is first seen.

When Medicare is the second payer, and the provider or supplier determines that the beneficiary has other insurance that may pay primary to Medicare, he or she should file a claim with the primary insurer on the beneficiary's behalf. The providers and suppliers are required by law to submit claims to other secondary payers including Medicare under these two circumstances:

- If the provider or supplier receives a determination on the claim directly from the primary payer, he or she is responsible for submitting a claim to Medicare for secondary payment.

- If a beneficiary forwards the primary payer information to the provider or supplier, the provider or supplier must submit the secondary claim to Medicare for the beneficiary in accordance with the mandatory claims filing requirements.

The provider may file a secondary payer claim with Medicare after the primary payer has paid. Keep in mind that these secondary claims must meet Medicare's guidelines for timely filing. In 2007, CMS developed HCPCS level II modifier M2, Medicare secondary payer.

Limiting Charge and MSP

The Social Security Act Amendments of 1994 (SSAA 1994) extended the limiting charge provision.

- **Nonassigned claims.** The statute prohibits nonparticipating providers or suppliers, who do not accept assignment, from billing or collecting amounts above the applicable limiting charge, regardless of whether Medicare is primary or secondary.

- **Assigned claims.** The limiting charge applies only when a nonparticipating provider or supplier does not take assignment on a Medicare claim. If the provider or supplier takes assignment on the Medicare claim (either as a result of a participation agreement to always take assignment, or as assignment for a specific claim), the limiting charge does not apply. The regulations in 42 CFR, section 411.31, which permit physicians and suppliers to bill and collect their full charges for services, continue to apply with regard to physicians and suppliers that take Medicare assignment for the Medicare claim. The SSAA 1994 restricted the charges only for services for which the nonparticipating provider or supplier does not take assignment for the Medicare claim. They did not impose the limiting charge on assigned claims, nor did they impose the obligations of Medicare assignment on provider or supplier claims to primary payers other than Medicare.

Calculating the Medicare Secondary Payment Amount

The method of calculating the Medicare secondary payment amount is the same whether the claim is assigned or unassigned.

Medicare may pay secondary benefits when a provider, supplier, or beneficiary submits a claim to a third party payer and it does not pay the entire charge. Medicare will not make a secondary payment if the provider or supplier accepts, or is obligated to accept, the third-party payer payment as full payment.

The provider/supplier cannot collect more than (1) the "obligated to accept" amount of the primary insurance or (2) the higher amount of either the Medicare physician fee schedule or the allowed amount of the primary payer when the beneficiary's Part B deductible has been met (see examples 1 and 2 below).

The following examples assume the provider or supplier is participating with Medicare. If the provider or supplier is non-participating, but accepting assignment, Medicare's approved amount will be based on the nonparticipating fee amount.

Example 1

Provider submits a claim for a covered procedure with an amount of $72

Actual charge by provider	$72.00
Amount allowed by primary payer	$65.00
Amount paid by primary payer	$52.00
Medicare par fee amount	$53.87
Medicare's 80 percent of par fee amount	$43.10

Medicare would approve a secondary payment in the amount of $13.

This fee is determined by performing the following calculations and using the lowest amount as Medicare's secondary payment amount:

First, calculate the difference between the actual charge by the provider or the amount the provider is obligated to accept and the amount paid by the primary payer:

Actual charge by provider	$72
Minus amount paid by primary payer	- 52
	$20

Second, calculate 80 percent of Medicare's Allowed amount:

Medicare allowed amount	$53.87
80 percent of allowed amount	$43.10

Third, calculate the difference between the Medicare fee schedule amount or the primary payer's allowable charge, whichever is higher, and the amount actually paid by the primary payer:

Allowed amount by primary payer	$65
Minus amount paid by primary payer	- 52
	$13

The lowest of the three calculations is Medicare's secondary payment: $13. Therefore, the maximum amount the provider could collect is $65 ($52 paid by primary and $13 paid by secondary). The provider would have to write off the $7 difference between the provider's actual charge and the amounts paid by the primary and secondary payers ($72 -$65 = $7).

Example 2

Same situation as in rxample 1, but using the obligated to accept amount of the primary insurance:

Actual charge by provider	$72
Amount allowed by primary payer	$65
Obligated to accept amount	$62
Amount paid by primary payer	$52
Medicare par fee amount	$53.87

Medicare would approve a secondary payment in the amount of $10. This is obtained by performing calculations similar to those in example 1, but using the obligated to accept amount as payment in full and subtracting the third-party payment ($62 - $52 = $10).

When the Medicare Part B deductible is unmet, the calculations are performed in the same manner, but the amount the health care provider is allowed to collect is based on Medicare's allowed amount.

Example 3

Provider submits a claim in which the individual's Part B deductible of $100 was unmet.

Actual charge by provider	$140
Amount allowed by primary payer	$120
Amount paid by primary payer	$ 96
Medicare par fee amount	$110
Actual charge by provider	$140
Minus amount paid by primary payer	- 96
	$ 44
Medicare allowed amount	$110
Minus deductible	-100
	$10
80 percent of allowed amount	$ 8
Allowed amount by primary payer	$120
Minus amount paid by primary payer	- 96
	$ 24

The lowest of the three calculations is Medicare's secondary payment: $8.

The beneficiary's Medicare deductible is credited with $100. The beneficiary is still obligated to pay the provider $6. The beneficiary's obligation is based on any remaining balance after the payments from the primary and secondary insurance up to the Medicare allowed amount ($110 - $96 - $8 = $6).

Sending a Refund to Medicare

If you receive payment from a primary insurer and you have received payment from Medicare for the same services, you have 60 days within receipt of a duplicate payment to send the refund to Medicare.

When sending a refund to Medicare, complete the refunds to Medicare form, and include:

* A copy of the EOB from the primary insurer
* The name and address of the employer or automobile or liability insurer
* The name of the primary insured (i.e., the beneficiary or beneficiary's spouse, or the party insured by the auto/liability insurer)

Medicare will void the claim and process an adjustment for any Medicare secondary payment that may be due.

Return any collected deductible and/or coinsurance to the beneficiary unless it is still due after Medicare has adjusted the claim to pay secondary, according to the primary group health plan or auto/liability insurer.

Following is a sample form that provides the information your Medicare carrier may be looking for when you are refunding an overpayment. Please note that your carrier may have a pre-printed form that should be used in lieu of a form you create yourself.

Sample Refunds to Medicare Form

Basic Information

(Please attach a copy of the Medicare remittance advice with this refund)

Provider Name: _____   Provider No: _____

Patient Name: _____

Medicare Number: _____   Internal Control # (Claim Number) _____

Date(s) of Service: _____   (through) _____

Refund Amount: $ _____   (including interest paid by Medicare)

Contact Person: _____   Telephone No _____

Reason for Refund (for multiple claims, specify reason for each on copies of remittance notice)

A. Incorrect Date of Service _____

B. Incorrect CPT Code(s) _____

C. Duplicate Payment _____

D. Incorrect HIC Number _____

E. Services Not Rendered _____

F. Incorrect Provider Number _____

G. Incorrect Assignment _____

H. Corrected/Changed Billing (attach a copy of the revised billing) _____

I. Other/Explanation _____

Medicare Secondary Payer

If the refund is related to Medicare secondary payer (MSP), please (X) below the type of MSP that applies. Attach a copy of the primary payer Notification of benefits or payment sheet. Include (below) the primary insurance company name, address, policy number, insured, and employer name.

Auto accident _____ injury date _____ injury diagnosis _____

Liability accident _____ injury date _____ injury diagnosis _____

Workers' compensation _____ injury date _____ injury diagnosis _____

Black lung

Primary Insurance

Disability (large group health plan-(LGHP)) Insurer _____

Employer group health plan-(EGHP) (Working Aged) Address _____

Insured _____

Employer _____ Policy Number _____

Reimbursement

Medicare and Quality Reporting

In 2007, the Centers for Medicare and Medicaid Services developed the Physician Quality Reporting Initiative (PQRI). The PQRI establishes a financial incentive for eligible professionals to participate in a voluntary quality reporting program. Eligible professionals, including physical therapists, who successfully report a designated set of quality measures on claims for defined reporting periods may earn a bonus payment, of 1.5 percent of total allowed charges for covered Medicare physician fee schedule services. Services that are not paid under the MPFS are, therefore, not eligible for the bonus payment includes laboratory services paid under the Clinical Laboratory (CLAB) fee schedule, durable medical equipment, and drugs and biologicals.

The physician quality reporting system, which was originally slated to run only through 2009, was extended through 2010 by implementation of the Medicare Improvements for Patients and Providers Act (MIPPA), enacted on July 15, 2008.

Reporting Quality Measures

For 2009 there were 153 quality measures. The final 2010 quality measures had not been released by CMS at press time. The quality measure data are reported using CPT category II codes and CPT category II modifiers or HCPCS Level II G codes and CPT category II modifiers, when there is no CPT category II code available.

HCPCS Level II codes G8006–G9139 are temporary codes developed by CMS for reporting quality measures. CMS states that these codes are to be used when there is no CPT category II code available or when the category II codes do not collect the type of information CMS wants.

CMS also established "measure groups," which are reported by submitting group-specific G codes to indicate intent (e.g., submit G8485 on first diabetic patient to begin reporting diabetes measures group). The individual measures within the selected group are then reported on the claim. At this time, there are no measure groups that are applicable to the physical therapist.

Reporting Quality Codes

To report the quality information a provider indicates the appropriate quality code (a CPT category II or HCPCS Level II code) or numerator for applicable patients. Patient eligibility is determined by the presence of a defined condition, as indicated by an ICD-9-CM code or a service or procedure as defined by a CPT or HCPCS Level II codes. These conditions or services are called the denominator. There are also CPT category II modifiers that indicate that a patient should be excluded from the measure for a specific reason. The numerators, denominators and applicable exclusion modifiers that are associated with the individual quality measure are defined in the quality measure specifications created by CMS.

There are two methods of submitting the PQRI data; claims-based or registry based. The claims-based reporting system enables the provider to report the quality measures on either the paper CMS-1500 claim or electronic 837p claim form. The registry-based reporting method allows providers to submit the quality measure codes electronically through an approved registry. The quality measure specifications and a list of the approved registries can be found at: www.cms.hhs.gov/pqri.

Quality codes are to be reported with a $0.00 amount as there is no charge associated with quality codes. If billing software does not accept a $0.00 charge, a small amount, such as one cent, can be substituted. Quality codes must be reported on the same claim as the related diagnosis and procedure code described in the measure specifications. Reporting quality codes (numerators) and diagnosis and procedure codes (denominators) together is required for analysis of the quality measure, calculation of individual provider performance, and determination of whether the provider has achieved the 80 percent minimum reporting threshold.

Reporting Options and Payment Thresholds

The legislation sets fourth the reporting thresholds that CMS must enforce. There are a number of reporting options that can be selected and the threshold that must be met in order to quality for the bonus payment is dependent upon the method selected.

Claim Based Reporting Option

When less then three measures are applicable to the providers practice, there is only one reporting option. The provider must report each measure for 80 percent or more of the applicable patients for the 12-month reporting period.

If three or more measures apply, there are two options that the provider can choose from. The first is to report three or more measures for 80 percent of eligible patients during the 12-month reporting period. The second and third are to report measure groups for the six month reporting period using either the 80 percent criteria or by reporting 100 percent of 15 consecutive eligible patients anytime within the six month period. Consecutive patients is defined by CMS as next in order. Patients are considered consecutive without regard to gender even though some measures in a group (preventive care measures) may apply only to male or female patients.

Registry-Based Reporting

When the provider elects to report the quality data using a registry there are six reporting options. The provider may elect to report data on at least three measures for 80 percent or more of eligible patient encounters during either the six- or 12-month reporting periods.

There are four registry reporting options that entail reporting measure groups using either the consecutive or 80 percent thresholds for either a six- or 12-month reporting period. Since these options involve the reporting of measure groups, which are not applicable to the physical therapist, we will not go into detail regarding these methods.

Measures Applicable to the Physical Therapist

The measures shown in the following table are applicable to the physical therapist.

Measure Number	Title
4	Screening for Future Fall Risk
124	HIT—Adoption/Use of Health Information Technology (Electronic Health Records)
126	HIT—Adoption/Use of e-Prescribing
127	Diabetic Foot and Ankle Care, Ulcer Prevention: Evaluation of Footwear

Measure Number	Title
128	Universal Weight Screening and Follow-Up
130	Universal Documentation and Verification of Current Medications in the Medical Record
131	Pain Assessment Prior to Initiation of Patient Treatment
132	Patient Co-Development of Treatment Plan/Plan of Care

Workers' Compensation

All states require workers' compensation benefits to provide medical and disability coverage for employees who are injured, contract an illness or disease, or become disabled as a result of their employment. In most states, employers voluntarily provide these benefits, but the criteria vary for mandatory coverage. Some states require employers to carry workers' compensation coverage only if a certain number of people are employed. Most programs require an initial accident or medical report, a periodic progress report, and a final report if the patient is temporarily disabled and unable to return to work.

The requirements to file a claim also vary from state to state. In some states the claim is sent directly to a court or the workers' compensation office, while others want it sent to the employer or directly to the insurance carrier. The amount paid is based on an allowable for that service, and the physician does not bill the patient for an unpaid balance. A practice accepting a workers' compensation case has agreed to accept the allowable as payment in full.

Workers' Compensation Checklist

The following questions can be used as a guide in determining what information should be obtained from your workers' compensation carrier in order to process claims efficiently.

- What coding system and year of version is used for diagnosis coding?

  ____ICD-9-CM   _____(year)

  ____Payer-developed system

- What coding system and year of version is used for procedure coding?

  ____CPT   _____(year)

  ____HCPCS Level II   _____(year)

  ____Payer-developed system

- Is there a limit to the number of visits a patient may receive? If so, what is the limit?

- Do you use a relative value scale? If yes, which scale? What is the current conversion factor used to compute payment?

- How are disputes/appeals handled?

- Must a special report be filed with workers' compensation cases? If so, how often?

- How often, if at all, does a patient have to be recertified for services to be covered?

- What type of utilization review method is used?

- Are there time requirements regarding when to file claims? If yes, what are they?

- Is a special claim form required?

Collection Policies

Does your practice have established collection policies and procedures? Whether your answer to this question is yes or no, it is important for you to recognize that having these procedures in place is crucial to your practice's financial—and legal—health.

The following tips are not all-inclusive, but they should help you refine your practice's existing policies or develop your own practice-specific guidelines in the form of a manual or some other written instructions.

When you attempt to collect on a debt or otherwise communicate in writing with a patient, here's what NOT to do:

- Do not use postcards. These can be read by anyone. The status of a patient's account is private, and you are violating the patient's privacy by making account information available to whomever has access to the mail.

- Do not mark the outside of envelopes with statements such as "past due." This announces to anyone who sees the envelope that the patient has not paid a bill, which again violates the patient's right to privacy.

- Do not send a bill with an incorrect balance. If there are adjustments that should be made to an account balance, be sure to do it before you send out a bill.

- Do not try to make your correspondence look like letters from attorneys or official court documents. This scare tactic may be helpful in getting your accounts paid, but you do not want to be accused of misrepresentation.

When contacting your patients via telephone regarding their accounts, use the following tips as guidelines in establishing practice-specific policies:

- Place your collection calls between the hours of 9 a.m. and 9 p.m.

- Do not refuse to identify yourself or use a fictitious name. This tactic is guaranteed to produce a negative response from the patient.

- Whenever possible, do not call patients at work. If a patient says not to call at work, then don't. Only call a patient at work as a last resort.

"Skiptracing," or the art of locating someone who may not want to be found, is another aspect of the collection process that can be a source of problems for your practice if you do not have established guidelines that personnel are required to follow. The following tips may help:

- Call friends and relatives for location information only. Call the emergency contact and/or the referral source listed in the medical record.

- Identify yourself and explain that you're trying to verify a patient's address and/or phone number. Do not say that you are calling in reference to a debt.

- Do not contact a source more than once unless they tell you to call back. These people do not owe your practice money, so try not to become a nuisance.

It is just as important to know when to stop trying to collect on a debt as it is to know how to go about collecting the payment. The following factors indicate when you should stop collection efforts:

- When the patient notifies you in writing that he or she refuses to pay the debt
- When the patient notifies you in writing to stop communicating with him or her
- When the patient notifies you, or you are otherwise informed, that the patient is represented by an attorney—all future communications should be through the attorney
- When the patient states that the reason for nonpayment is dissatisfaction with the medical care received or its outcome

In these cases, instruct your billing staff to suspend all collection efforts and ask the patient to put all concerns in writing. It is the provider's responsibility to review the medical record and communications from the patient to determine whether collection activity should continue or if the balance should be adjusted.

Here are some final points to remember:

- Never advise a third party of the facts of a patient's debt.
- Never say you are going to do something that you do not intend to do or cannot legally do. If you tell a patient you will sue, be prepared to do so.
- Do not share with other offices the names of patients who have delinquent accounts.
- Treat all patients fairly, regardless of their debt.
- Never lie or be deceptive.
- Never harass or use profanity.
- Never imply, by word or action, that your patient has committed a crime.
- Protect your practice by keeping detailed records of all written or verbal communications.

Establishing sound collection policies and procedures, and communicating these to the personnel in your practice, will go a long way toward ensuring that your practice is financially healthy, and that you won't find yourself on the receiving end of a harassment lawsuit.

Reimbursement

Documentation—An Overview

The role played by medical documentation has always been a supportive one. As the practice of medicine became more sophisticated and complex, the need to record specific clinical data has grown in importance. What certainly began as a simple written mechanism to jog the memory of a treating physician evolved into a more refined system to service others assisting in patient care. Tracking patient history emerged as a fundamental element in planning a course of treatment. When medical specialties evolved early in the last century, the patient record offered a means to provide pertinent data for referrals and consultations.

Still, until about 35 years ago, no clear standards existed for recording patient information. Medical documentation was seen, maintained, and used almost exclusively by physicians and medical staff. Patient care information was never submitted to insurance companies nor to government payers; only rarely did medical documentation become the focus of malpractice suits.

Marked changes to the Medicare program served to broaden the influence for medical documentation during the 1970s. For example, the Centers for Medicare and Medicaid Services (CMS), Medicare's federal administrator, authorized the program's regional carriers to review paid claims to determine whether the care was medically necessary, as mandated under the Social Security Act of 1996.

This type of review compares processed and paid claims against the documentation recorded at the time of service. The aim is to ensure that Medicare dollars are administered correctly and, once again, medical documentation must support the medical necessity of the service, to what extent the service was rendered, and why it was medically justified. For example, a physical therapist re-evaluates a patient after the prescribed treatment plan has been completed. The physical therapist determines that the patient would continue to benefit from further encounters for manual traction and therapeutic exercise. Depending upon the payer guidelines, this may require prior authorization from the primary care physician, or the payer.

Medicare does not pay for services that are "medically unnecessary" according to Medicare standards. Patients are not liable to pay for such services if the service is performed without prior notification from the physician. Medical necessity requires items and services to be:

- Consistent with symptoms or diagnosis of disease or injury
- Necessary and consistent with generally accepted professional medical standards (e.g., not experimental or investigational)
- Furnished at the most appropriate level that can be provided safely and effectively to the patient

Computer conversion of the review process has added a new twist: speed and a higher degree of accuracy. Claims adjudication, data analysis, and physician profiling revealed incongruities. A significant number of physicians and hospitals were found to have billed for services that were not provided or found to be medically unnecessary. Projected total estimates in the millions of dollars were publicized by CMS as findings of fraud and abuse. These findings led to the creation of the federal fraud

and abuse program coordinated by several federal organizations, including the Department of Health and Human Services (HHS) and its agencies, CMS, and the Office of Inspector General (OIG).

Commercial insurance companies were quick to follow suit. Similar to CMS, private payers monitor claims to uncover coding mistakes and to verify that the documentation supports the claims submitted. Although there are no national guidelines for proper documentation, the guidelines this chapter provides should ensure better quality of care and increase the chances of full and fair reimbursement.

General Guidelines for Documentation

Documentation is the recording of pertinent facts and observations about a patient's health history, including past and present illnesses, tests, treatments, and outcomes. The medical record chronologically documents the care of the patient to:

- Enable a health care professional to plan and evaluate the patient's treatment
- Enhance communication and promote continuity of care among health care professionals involved in the patient's care
- Facilitate claims review and payment
- Assist in utilization management and quality of care evaluations
- Reduce hassles related to medical review
- Provide clinical data for research and education
- Serve as a legal document to verify the care provided (e.g., as defense in the case of a professional liability claim)

Payers want to know that their health care dollars are well spent. Since they have a contractual obligation to beneficiaries, payers look for the documentation to validate that services are:

- Furnished by a qualified provider
- Appropriate for treating the patient's condition
- Medically necessary for the diagnosis
- Coded correctly

Coding Tip

To ensure the appropriate reimbursement for services, the provider should use documentation to demonstrate compliance with any third-party payer utilization guidelines.

Principles of Documentation

Documentation guidelines developed specifically for the physical therapist by the American Physical Therapy Association will be discussed in detail later in this chapter. To provide a basis for maintaining adequate medical record information, follow the principles of medical record documentation listed. The following organizations developed the documentation principles listed below:

- American Health Information Management Association (AHIMA)

- American Hospital Association (AHA)
- American Managed Care and Review Association (AMCRA)
- American Medical Association (AMA)
- American Medical Peer Review Association (AMPRA)
- Blue Cross and Blue Shield Association (BCBSA)
- Health Insurance Association of America (HIAA)

Medical Record Documentation

The following list outlines generic medical record documentation principals:

- The medical record should be complete and legible.
- The documentation of each patient encounter should include the date, the reason for the encounter, appropriate history and physical exam (when applicable). The documentation also should include a review of lab and x-ray data, as well as other ancillary services (where appropriate), an assessment, and plan for care (including discharge plan, if appropriate).
- Past and present diagnoses should be accessible to the treating or consulting health care professional.
- The reasons for and results of diagnostic tests and other ancillary services should be documented and included in the medical record.
- Relevant health risk factors should be identified.
- The patient's progress, including response to treatment, change in treatment, change in diagnosis, and patient noncompliance, should be documented.
- The written plan for care should include treatments and medications—specifying frequency and dosage, any referrals and consultations, patient and family education, and specific instructions for follow-up.
- The documentation should support the intensity of the patient evaluation and the treatment, including thought processes and the complexity of medical decision making.
- All entries to the medical record should be dated and authenticated.
- The codes reported on the health insurance claim form or billing statement should reflect the documentation in the medical record.

Documentation to Code and Bill

Many insurers rely on written evidence of the evaluation of the patient, care plan, and goals for improvement to determine and approve the medical necessity of care. Initial evaluation findings documenting the diagnosis form the basis for judging the reasonableness and necessity of care that was subsequently provided. Consequently, the more accurately the patient's evaluation and treatment are described, the easier it is to code the diagnoses and procedures properly.

ICD-9-CM Coding

ICD-9-CM codes relate to the medical diagnosis and are used to classify illnesses, injuries, and reasons for patient encounters with the health care system. Patients may have a single primary, or one primary and several secondary diagnoses. Diagnoses are sequenced by order of severity or importance. In addition to the

medical diagnosis, the physical therapist should identify the diagnosis for which the physical therapy is being provided (if different from the medical diagnosis).

Describing the onset of the problem and objectively documenting the patient's impairment are essential to ensuring accurate coding and description of the diagnosis. Confirming any diagnosis is based on objective measurements performed and values obtained during an assessment. The diagnostic description of the current problem for which the patient is being treated should be defined by:

- Patient's subjective complaint
- Problem's date of onset
- Objective test values confirming the diagnosis
- Outcomes expected after treatment

For more information tailored to physical therapy, see the ICD-9-CM Definitions and Guidelines chapter.

Coding Tip

At each visit, the therapist should record the medical condition being treated.

Procedure Coding

CPT and HCPCS Level II codes were developed specifically to define and describe services and procedures. They can be used by payers in combination with ICD-9-CM codes to analyze and describe practice patterns related to specific diagnoses and to project costs of procedures for diagnosis groups. Correct use of the procedure codes also depends on the accurate and specific documentation of the evaluation and treatment provided.

To substantiate the CPT codes used, documentation at a minimum should describe:

- Evaluation and treatment interventions performed
- Responses observed
- Time taken to provide the total visit as well as the time spent in performing direct contact procedures

For information tailored to physical therapy, see the CPT Definitions and Guidelines chapter.

Documentation of Time

Many of the services performed by physical therapist are represented by "timed" codes. This means that the CPT code for the service indicates that a service was performed for a specific amount of time. For example, CPT code 97116 should be reported once for each 15 minutes that a physical therapists provides gait training.

CMS guidelines to contractors indicate that the medical record documentation for physical therapy service must record time. The total amount of treatment time (including time providing untimed code services) and the amount of time spent providing direct contact services, represented by timed codes, should be documented.

If more than one timed CPT code is billed during a calendar day, then the total number of units that can be billed is constrained by the total treatment time. Medicare's expectation (based on the work values for these CPT codes) is that a therapist's direct one-on-one patient contact time will average 15 minutes in length for each unit. Therapy sessions should not be structured to consistently provide less than an average of 15 minutes of treatment for each timed unit.

Guidelines: Physical Therapy Documentation of Patient/Client Management

(From American Physical Therapy Association Board of Directors policy BOD G03-05-16-41, printed with permission of the American Physical Therapy Association.)

Preamble

The American Physical Therapy Association (APTA) is committed to meeting the physical therapy needs of society, to meeting the needs and interests of its members, and to developing and improving the art and science of physical therapy, including practice, education and research. To help meet these responsibilities, the APTA Board of Directors has approved the following guidelines for physical therapy documentation. It is recognized that these guidelines do not reflect all of the unique documentation requirements associated with the many specialty areas within the physical therapy profession. Applicable for both hand written and electronic documentation systems, these guidelines are intended to be used as a foundation for the development of more specific documentation guidelines in clinical areas, while at the same time providing guidance for the physical therapy profession across all practice settings. Documentation may also need to address additional regulatory or payer requirements.

Finally, be aware that these guidelines are intended to address documentation of patient/client management, not to describe the provision of physical therapy services. Other APTA documents, including APTA Standards of Practice for Physical Therapy, Code of Ethics and Guide for Professional Conduct, and the Guide to Physical Therapist Practice, address provision of physical therapy services and patient/client management.

APTA Position on Documentation

Documentation Authority for Physical Therapy Services (HOD 06-00-20-05 28)

It is the position of the American Physical Therapy Association that:

Physical therapy examination, evaluation, diagnosis, prognosis, and intervention shall be documented, dated, and authenticated by the physical therapist who performs the service. Intervention provided by the physical therapist or selected interventions provided by the physical therapist assistant is documented, dated, and authenticated by the physical therapist or, when permissible by law, the physical therapist assistant.

Other notations or flow charts are considered a component of the documented record but do not meet the requirements of documentation in or of themselves.

Students in physical therapist or physical therapist assistant programs may document when the record is additionally authenticated by the physical therapist or, when permissible by law, documentation by physical therapist assistant students may be authenticated by a physical therapist assistant.

Operational Definitions

Guidelines. APTA defines "guidelines" as approved, nonbinding statements of advice.

Authentication. The process used to verify that an entry is complete, accurate and final. Indications of authentication can include original written signatures and computer "signatures" on secured electronic record systems only.

The following describes the main documentation elements of patient/client management:

- Initial examination/evaluation
- Visit/encounter
- Reexamination
- Discharge or discontinuation summary

Initial Examination/Evaluation

Documentation of the initial encounter is typically called the "initial examination," "initial evaluation," or "initial examination/evaluation." Completion of the initial examination/evaluation is typically completed in one visit, but may occur over more than one visit. Documentation elements for the initial examination/evaluation include the following:

- **Examination.** Includes data obtained from the history, systems review, and tests and measures.
- **Evaluation.** Evaluation is a thought process that may not include formal documentation. It may include documentation of the assessment of the data collected in the examination and identification of problems pertinent to patient/client management.
- **Diagnosis.** Indicates level of impairment and functional limitation determined by the physical therapist. May be indicated by selecting one or more preferred practice patterns from the Guide to Physical Therapist Practice.
- **Prognosis.** Provides documentation of the predicted level of improvement that might be attained through intervention and the amount of time required to reach that level. Prognosis is typically not a separate documentation elements, but the components are included as part of the plan of care.
- **Plan of care.** Typically stated in general terms, includes goals, interventions planned, proposed frequency and duration, and discharge plans.

Visit/Encounter

Documentation of a visit or encounter, often called a progress note or daily note, documents sequential implementation of the plan of care established by the physical therapist, including changes in patient/client status and variations and progressions of specific interventions used. Also may include specific plans for the next visit or visits.

Reexamination

Documentation of reexamination includes data from repeated or new examination elements and is provided to evaluate progress and to modify or redirect intervention.

Discharge or Discontinuation Summary
Documentation is required following conclusion of the current episode in the physical therapy intervention sequence, to summarize progression toward goals and discharge plans.

I. General Guidelines
- Documentation is required for every visit/encounter.
- All documentation must comply with the applicable jurisdictional/regulatory requirements.
- All handwritten entries shall be made in ink and will include original signatures. Electronic entries are made with appropriate security and confidentiality provisions.
- Charting errors should be corrected by drawing a single line through the error and initialing and dating the chart or through the appropriate mechanism for electronic documentation that clearly indicates that a change was made without deletion of the original record.
- All documentation must include adequate identification of the patient/client and the physical therapist or physical therapist assistant:
  — The patient's/client's full name and identification number, if applicable, must be included on all official documents.
  — All entries must be dated and authenticated with the provider's full name and appropriate designation:
    – Documentation of examination, evaluation, diagnosis, prognosis, plan of care, and discharge summary must be authenticated by the physical therapist who provided the service.
    – Documentation of intervention in visit/encounter notes must be authenticated by the physical therapist or physical therapist assistant who provided the service.
    – Documentation by physical therapist or physical therapist assistant graduates or others physical therapist and physical therapist assistants pending receipt of an unrestricted license shall be authenticated by a licensed physical therapist, or, when permissible by law, documentation by physical therapist assistant graduates may be authenticated by a physical therapist assistant.
    – Documentation by students (SPT/SPTA) in physical therapist or physical therapist assistant programs must be additionally authenticated by the physical therapist or, when permissible by law, documentation by physical therapist assistant students may be authenticated by a physical therapist assistant.
- Documentation should include the referral mechanism by which physical therapy services are initiated. Examples include:
  — self-referral/direct access
  — request for consultation from another practitioner
- Documentation should include indication of no shows and cancellations.

Initial Examination/Evaluation

Examination (history, systems review, and tests and measures)

History
Documentation of history may include the following:
- General demographics
- Social history
- Employment/work (job/school/play)
- Growth and development
- Living environment
- General health status (self-report, family report, caregiver report)
- Social/health habits (past and current)
- Family history
- Medical/surgical history
- Current condition(s)/chief complaint(s)
- Functional status and activity level
- Medications
- Other clinical tests

Systems Review
Documentation of systems review may include gathering data for the following systems:
- Cardiovascular/pulmonary
  — blood pressure
  — edema
  — heart rate
  — respiratory rate
- Integumentary
  — pliability (texture)
  — presence of scar formation
  — skin color
  — skin integrity
- Musculoskeletal
  — gross range of motion
  — gross strength
  — gross symmetry
  — height
  — weight
- Neuromuscular
- Gross coordinated movement (e.g., balance, locomotion, transfers, and transitions)
- Motor function (motor control, motor learning)

Documentation of systems review may also address communication ability, affect, cognition, language, and learning style:
- Ability to make needs known

- Consciousness
- Expected emotional/behavioral responses
- Learning preferences (e.g., education needs, learning barriers)
- Orientation (person, place, time)

Tests and Measures

Documentation of tests and measures may include findings for the following categories:

- Aerobic capacity/endurance

  Examples of examination findings include:

  — aerobic capacity during functional activities

  — aerobic capacity during standardized exercise test protocols

  — cardiovascular signs and symptoms in response to increased oxygen demand with exercise or activity

  — pulmonary signs and symptoms in response to increased oxygen demand with exercise or activity

- Anthropometric characteristics

  Examples of examination findings include:

  — body composition

  — body dimensions

  — edema

- Arousal, attention, and cognition

  Examples of examination findings include:

  — arousal and attention

  — cognition

  — communication

  — consciousness

  — motivation

  — orientation to time, person, place, and situation

  — recall

- Assistive and adaptive devices

  Examples of examination findings include:

  — assistive or adaptive devices and equipment use during functional activities

  — components, alignment, fit, and ability to care for the assistive or adaptive devices and equipment

  — remediation of impairments, functional limitations, or disabilities with use of assistive or adaptive devices and equipment

  — safety during use of assistive or adaptive devices and equipment

- Circulation (arterial, venous, lymphatic)

  Examples of examination findings include:

  — cardiovascular signs

  — cardiovascular symptoms

  — physiological responses to position change

- Cranial and peripheral nerve integrity

  Examples of examination findings include:

  — electrophysiological integrity

  — motor distribution of the cranial nerves

  — motor distribution of the peripheral nerves

  — response to neural provocation

  — response to stimuli, including auditory, gustatory, olfactory, pharyngeal, vestibular, and visual

  — sensory distribution of the cranial nerves

  — sensory distribution of the peripheral nerves

- Environmental, home, and work (job/school/play) barriers

  Examples of examination findings include:

  — current and potential barriers

  — physical space and environment

- Ergonomics and body mechanics

  Examples of examination findings for ergonomics include:

  — dexterity and coordination during work

  — functional capacity and performance during work actions, tasks, or activities

  — safety in work environments

  — specific work conditions or activities

  — tools, devices, equipment, and work-stations related to work actions, tasks, or activities

  Examples of examination findings for body mechanics include:

  — body mechanics during self-care, home management, work, community, or leisure actions, tasks, or activities

- Gait, locomotion, and balance

  Examples of examination findings include:

  — balance during functional activities with or without the use of assistive, adaptive, orthotic, protection, supportive, or prosthetic devices or equipment

  — balance (dynamic and static) with or without the use of assistive, adaptive, orthotic, protective, supportive, or prosthetic devices or equipment

  — gait and locomotion during functional activities with or without the use of assistive, adaptive, orthotic, protective, supportive, or prosthetic devices or equipment

  — gait and locomotion with or without the use of assistive, adaptive, orthotic, protective, supportive, or prosthetic devices or equipment

  — safety during gait, locomotion, and balance

- Integumentary Integrity

  Examples of examination findings include:

  Associated skin:

  — activities, positioning, and postures that produce or relieve trauma to the skin

Documentation

— assistive, adaptive, orthotic, protective, supportive, or prosthetic devices and equipment that may produce or relieve trauma to the skin

— skin characteristics

Wound:

— activities, positioning, and postures that aggravate the wound or scar or that produce or relieve trauma

— burn

— signs of infection

— wound characteristics

— wound scar tissue characteristics

- Joint integrity and mobility

  Examples of examination findings include

  — joint integrity and mobility

  — joint play movements

  — specific body parts

- Motor function

  Examples of examination findings include:

  — dexterity, coordination, and agility

  — electrophysiological integrity

  — hand function

  — initiation, modification, and control of movement patterns and voluntary postures

- Muscle performance

  Examples of examination findings include:

  — electrophysiological integrity

  — muscle strength, power, and endurance

  — muscle strength, power, and endurance during functional activities

  — muscle tension

- Neuromotor development and sensory integration

  Examples of examination findings include:

  — acquisition and evolution of motor skills

  — oral motor function, phonation, and speech production

  — sensorimotor integration

- Orthotic, protective, and supportive devices

  Examples of examination findings include:

  — components, alignment, fit, and ability to care for the orthotic, protective, and supportive devices and equipment

  — orthotic, protective, and supportive devices and equipment use during functional activities

  — remediation of impairments, functional limitations, or disabilities with use of orthotic, protective, and supportive devices and equipment

  — safety during use of orthotic, protective, and supportive devices and equipment

- Pain

  Examples of examination findings include:

  — pain, soreness, and nociception

  — pain in specific body parts

- Posture

  Examples of examination findings include:

  — postural alignment and position (dynamic)

  — postural alignment and position (static)

  — specific body parts

- Prosthetic requirements

  Examples of examination findings include:

  — components, alignment, fit, and ability to care for prosthetic device

  — prosthetic device use during functional activities

  — remediation of impairments, functional limitations, or disabilities with use of the prosthetic device

  — residual limb or adjacent segment

  — safety during use of the prosthetic device

  — range of motion (including muscle length)

  Examples of examination findings include:

  — functional ROM

  — joint active and passive movement

  — muscle length, soft tissue extensibility, and flexibility

- Reflex integrity

  Examples of examination findings include:

  — deep reflexes

  — electrophysiological integrity

  — postural reflexes and reactions, including righting, equilibrium, and protective reactions

  — primitive reflexes and reactions

  — resistance to passive stretch

  — superficial reflexes and reactions

- Self-care and home management (including activities of daily living and instrumental activities of daily living)

  Examples of examination findings include:

  — ability to gain access to home environments

  — ability to perform self-care and home management activities with or without assistive, adaptive, orthotic, protective, supportive, or prosthetic devices and equipment

  — safety in self-care and home management activities and environments

- Sensory integrity

  Examples of examination findings include:

  — combined/cortical sensations

  — deep sensations

— electrophysiological integrity

- Ventilation and respiration

  Examples of examination findings include:

  — pulmonary signs of respiration/gas exchange

  — pulmonary signs of ventilatory function

  — pulmonary symptoms

- Work (job/school/play), community, and leisure integration or reintegration (including instrumental activities of daily living)

  Examples of examination findings include:

  — ability to assume or resume work (job/school/plan), community, and leisure activities with or without assistive, adaptive, orthotic, protective, supportive, or prosthetic devices and equipment

  — ability to gain access to work (job/school/play), community, and leisure environments

  — safety in work (job/school/play), community, and leisure activities and environments

Evaluation

Evaluation is a thought process that may not include formal documentation. However, the evaluation process may lead to documentation of impairments, functional limitations, and disabilities using formats such as:

- A problem list

- A statement of assessment of key factors (e.g., cognitive factors, comorbidities, social support) influencing the patient/client status.

Diagnosis

Documentation of a diagnosis determined by the physical therapist may include impairment and functional limitations. Examples include:

- Impaired joint mobility, motor function, muscle performance, and range of motion associated with localized inflammation (4E)

- Impaired motor function and sensory integrity associated with progressive disorders of the central nervous system (5E)

- Impaired aerobic capacity/endurance associated with cardiovascular pump dysfunction or failure (6D)

- Impaired integumentary integrity associated with partial-thickness skin involvement and scar formation (7C)

Prognosis

Documentation of the prognosis is typically included in the plan of care. See below.

Plan of Care

Documentation of the plan of care includes the following:

- Overall goals stated in measurable terms that indicate the predicted level of improvement in function

- A general statement of interventions to be used

- Proposed duration and frequency of service required to reach the goals

- Anticipated discharge plans

Visit/Encounter

Documentation of each visit/encounter shall include the following elements:

- Patient/client self-report (as appropriate)

- Identification of specific interventions provided, including frequency, intensity, and duration as appropriate. Examples include:

  — knee extension, three sets, ten repetitions, 10# weight

  — transfer training bed to chair with sliding board

  — equipment provided

- Changes in patient/client impairment, functional limitation, and disability status as they relate to the plan of care

- Response to interventions, including adverse reactions, if any

- Factors that modify frequency or intensity of intervention and progression goals, including patient/client adherence to patient/client-related instructions

- Communication/consultation with providers/patient/client/family/significant other

- Documentation to plan for ongoing provision of services for the next visit(s), which is suggested to include, but not be limited to:

  — the interventions with objectives

  — progression parameters

  — precautions, if indicated

Reexamination

Documentation of reexamination shall include the following elements:

- Documentation of selected components of examination to update patient's/client's impairment, function, and/or disability status

- Interpretation of findings and, when indicated, revision of goals

- When indicated, revision of plan of care, as directly correlated with goals as documented

Discharge/Discontinuation Summary

Documentation of discharge or discontinuation shall include the following elements:

- Current physical/functional status

- Degree of goals achieved and reasons for goals not being achieved

- Discharge/discontinuation plan related to the patient/client's continuing care. Examples include:

  — home program

  — referrals for additional services

  — recommendations for follow-up physical therapy care

  — family and caregiver training

  — equipment provided

Fraud and Abuse

Fraud and abuse is a concern for all payers. Medicare has established many guidelines and regulations in an attempt to thwart fraud and abuse amongst all types of providers. Non-Medicare payers often have guidelines that mirror Medicare's. The Office of Inspector General (OIG) also continues to drive this effort.

What is fraud?

CMS defines fraud as an intentional deception or misrepresentation made by an individual, knowing it to be false or not believing it to be true, and knowing that the deception could result in some unauthorized benefit to himself or herself or some other person. The violator may be a participating provider, a beneficiary, or some other person or business entity, including a Medicare employee.

Fraud in the Medicare program takes such forms as, but is not limited to:

- Misrepresenting dates and descriptions of the services provided
- Misrepresenting the identity of the beneficiary
- Misrepresenting the identify of the individual who furnished the services
- Incorrect reporting of diagnosis or procedures to maximize payments
- Billing that appears to be a deliberate application for duplicate payment for the same services or supplies. This includes billing the program twice, billing both Medicare and Medicaid, billing both Medicare and another insurer, or billing both Medicare and the beneficiary, all in an attempt to be paid twice
- Concealing business activities that are not in compliance with the provider agreement
- Soliciting, offering, or receiving a kickback, bribe, or rebate
- Patient's using another person's Medicare card in order to receive services
- Medicare employees who alter claims history to generate fraudulent payments
- Claiming costs for noncovered or nonchargeable services, supplies, or equipment (disguised as covered items)

What is abuse?

Abuse is an action that may directly or indirectly, result in unnecessary costs to the Medicare program, improper payment, or payment for services that fail to meet professionally recognized standards of care, or that are medically unnecessary.

Abuse involves payment for items or services when there is no legal entitlement to that payment; but the provider has not knowingly and intentionally misrepresented facts to obtain payment.

Examples of abuse include, but are not limited to:

- Billing for services that are not medically necessary
- Billing for services at a higher level than what is supported by documentation

Although these types of practices may initially be categorized as abusive in nature, under certain circumstances, they may develop into fraud. For instance, if a provider has received education regarding specific billing practices, but continues to bill improperly, this action may be considered intentional. Additionally, billing for services that the provider knew or should have known are not medically necessary may constitute fraud or abuse.

The rest of this section provides an overview of case development and penalties that may be applied.

What is the Medicare Anti-Fraud Unit?

The Medicare Anti-Fraud Unit combines the fraud functions from Part A and Part B into a single component. This unit is authorized to act independently of Medicare management in preventing, detecting, and investigating Medicare fraud. In summary, its objectives are to:

- Serve and protect the interests of all Medicare beneficiaries
- Protect and safeguard the Medicare Trust Fund against fraudulent activities by creating an environment in which it is difficult for health care fraud to exist
- Provide internal and external education and training to ensure the following:
  - There is a clear understanding of what constitutes fraud and abuse.
  - The Anti-Fraud Unit is widely known and easily accessible for referrals.
  - Appropriate investigation and follow-up communication occur.
  - The penalties that exist for fraud situations are clearly communicated.
- Enact the necessary and appropriate measures to ensure the potential for internal fraud is eliminated
- Cooperate with all requests from the OIG
- Be accurate, fair, consistent, and efficient in the review and the development of all Medicare fraud cases

Postings From the Office of Inspector General

The OIG website http://oig.hhs.gov supplies important information about fraud prevention and detection, fraud alerts, bulletins and inspection reports that will keep your practice apprised of issues that can raise red flags for investigations into fraud and abuse.

Receiving Complaints or Allegations

The Anti-Fraud Unit receives allegations of fraud or abuse by telephone or by mail, from beneficiaries, providers, Social Security offices, private insurers, other government agencies, or anonymous sources. Medicare staff, within the Anti-Fraud Unit or another department, may also discover potential fraud or abuse situations. The Anti-Fraud Unit will immediately investigate the allegation or situation to determine the facts, or may forward it to another department or agency that can better resolve the issue.

Review

The Anti-Fraud Unit, or other investigative department or agency, may use one of several review methods to substantiate allegations of fraud and abuse:

- Contacting the provider, complainant, and/or beneficiary whenever necessary to clarify all aspects of the alleged situation
- Contacting other Medicare carriers, government agencies, and/or private insurers for information on similar situations
- Selecting a representative sample of claims and obtaining and reviewing the supporting claim forms, medical records, hospital records, and any previous educational contact letters that relate to similar complaints
- Conducting telephone or written surveys with beneficiaries to verify that services were received
- Analyzing and comparing provider practice patterns to those of peer groups

Medical Opinion
When medical opinion is necessary, Medicare may refer the case to its medical director and/or an external medical consultant for a professional opinion.

Referral to the Office of Inspector General
If the Anti-Fraud Unit determines that Medicare fraud has occurred, it will refer the case to the OIG, which will then have jurisdiction. During its investigation, the OIG may request assistance from the Anti-Fraud Unit with certain aspects of the case. The OIG has authority to conduct its own investigation or to coordinate with other agencies, such as Medicaid, the U.S. postal inspector, the Federal Bureau of Investigation (FBI), local law enforcement, or private insurers.

Final Action by the OIG—Penalties Applied
After the OIG completes its investigation, one of the following actions will occur:

- Conviction of the offender through a federal, state, or county attorney's office, resulting in imprisonment and/or fines
- Assessment of a civil monetary penalty (CMP) by the secretary of HHS. The penalty may consist of a fine of up to $10,000 per each line item falsely or improperly claimed plus an assessment of up to three times the total amount that was falsely or improperly claimed
- Administrative sanctions may take different forms. These include but are not limited to:
  - revocation of the provider's assignment privileges
  - withholding Medicare payments
  - referral to state licensing authorities and medical boards that may result in the provider losing his or her license to practice medicine
  - exclusion of the provider from the Medicare program

The two categories of exclusions are mandatory and permissive.

Under mandatory exclusions, the OIG is required to exclude the provider from the Medicare program if the provider is convicted in a court of law of a crime related to the Medicare program, or related to patient abuse or neglect. The minimum exclusion term is five years.

Permissive exclusions may be imposed by the OIG by its own choice. These exclusions may be based on the findings of a court, licensing board, other agency, or the OIG's own findings. The

term of permissive exclusions may vary from one year to an indefinite term or the OIG may decline to take action on a case and refer it back to the Medicare Anti-Fraud Unit to collect any overpayment and/or educate the provider.

Overpayment
If an overpayment has occurred, Medicare will assess the provider with an actual and/or estimated overpayment based on review of a sample of claims. If a refund is due, the provider is notified in writing. The refund is due 30 days from the date of the notification letter, even if the provider requests a review.

Educational Contact
Whether a discovered problem requires repayment of money or not, Medicare will give the provider a written educational contact letter about the findings of the review, along with specific references to Medicare guidelines that concern the issue(s). Medicare will continue to review the provider's billing practices to ensure correction of the identified problem(s) and will keep copies of all educational correspondence on file for future reference.

Local Developments
The Medicare Anti-Fraud Unit continues to develop new claims data analysis capabilities to detect possible fraudulent practices. The unit is also an active participant in a health care fraud network. Greater cooperation and information sharing by current and new participants in the network has been fostered by the U.S. attorney general. In addition, the U.S. Attorney's Office will enact more monetary penalties against individuals and organizations who are found guilty of committing health care fraud, but who may or may not be convicted criminally.

Anti-Kickback Legislation
Anti-kickback legislation applies to nearly all health care providers—everyone from physicians to suppliers of medical equipment. In general, it prohibits them from giving or receiving (offering or soliciting) cash or other incentives for:

- Referrals of Medicare or Medicaid beneficiaries (or arranging such referrals)
- The buying, leasing, or ordering of goods or services payable by Medicare or Medicaid (or arranging for such purchases or leases); office space, pharmaceuticals, and clerical help are examples of such goods

The waiver of copayments/deductibles also may apply to providers. Under Medicare Part B, providers may waive copayments and deductibles for patients undergoing genuine financial hardship. However, providers who do so must adjust their bills to Medicare downward accordingly or risk a charge of fraud.

Providers who do not comply with this policy can be charged with making false statements and submitting false claims to the federal government. For more information regarding anti-kickback legislation, see the Reimbursement chapter.

Medicare Audits
CMS continues its campaign to fight the misuse of program funds as highlighted by audits conducted by the agency. The Balanced Budget Act provides guidelines to prevent the abuses.

Due to audits, CMS identified two problem areas responsible for the majority of the fraud and abuse charges: billing for services that were not medically necessary and upcoding services to secure a higher reimbursement than justified. See the claims processing chapter of this book for more information regarding Medicare audits.

Compliance

The detection of health care fraud has become a national priority for federal law enforcement; it is estimated that 10 percent of the nation's annual health care expenditures are due to fraud and abuse. Criminal penalties of up to 10 years in prison may be imposed and the health care provider could face up to 20 years and possible life imprisonment if the violation results in the death of a patient.

The OIG and Department of Justice (DOJ) have been given the power to enforce federal, state, or local laws designed to control fraud and abuse in health plans, and to conduct audits, investigations, inspections, and evaluations relating to the delivery of and payment for health care services. The civil monetary penalty for health care fraud and abuse is now up to $10,000 for each item or service involved. The law also may assess penalties against an individual to "not more than three times the amount" claimed for each such item or service.

Fraudulent or abusive coding practices may be identified and brought to the attention of law enforcement officials in a number of different ways, including the following:

- A contractor receives a complaint about suspected fraud and abuse activities.

- A whistle-blower files a civil case alleging fraud.

- A physician or other provider reports a peer for fraud and abuse.

Contractors also have special fraud units dedicated to investigating suspected instances of fraud and referring cases to the OIG. In addition, contractors have also established fraud and abuse hotlines for anonymous reporting of suspected instances of fraud and abuse. The Incentive Program for Fraud and Abuse Information was established as part of the Health Insurance Portability and Accountability Act (HIPAA) and rewards Medicare beneficiaries and others that report suspected fraud and abuse when the information provided leads to the recovery of Medicare funds. It is further estimated that four of five private insurers have also established anti-fraud programs.

The focused medical review (FMR) is another way carriers detect variations from the norm. With FMR, data analysis identifies trends of utilization and practice patterns. Contractor medical review resources are focused on providers, specialties, or specific types of services that are most likely to be medically unnecessary, unreasonable, or uncovered.

Once a problem provider is identified, an investigation is conducted and appropriate action taken.

CMS also established two additional programs for monitoring and reporting the accuracy of Medicare fee-for-service (FFS) payments: The Comprehensive Error Rate Testing (CERT) program and the Hospital Payment Monitoring Program (HPMP). The CERT program measures the error rate for claims submitted to carriers, durable medical equipment regional carriers (DMERC), and fiscal intermediaries (FI). The HPMP measures the error rate for the quality improvement organizations (QIO). Data from both of these programs is combined and used to analyze the national error rate.

The CERT methodology includes:

- Random selection of approximately 120,000 submitted claims

- Requesting medical records from the providers who submitted the claims

- Reviewing the claims and medical records for compliance with Medicare coverage, coding, and billing rules

This information is used to determine specific services that are experiencing high error rates and to identify individual providers for probe review. A probe review is composed of the review of a small number of claims from a particular provider for a specific service to see if the provider may be billing in error. If a probe review indicates corrective action is needed, the contractor will take the corrective action it deems most appropriate. All public reports produced by the CERT program as well as monthly newsletters, medical record request example letters, etc., are available through: www.CERTprovider.org.

Action Plan

Now you know the government's plan of action. Do you have one? Be proactive. Establish a plan that includes the following components:

- Coding and Documentation

    — Establish continuing education programs for CPT and ICD-9-CM coding to ensure the competency of the billing staff.

    — Prepare a coding policy manual to define the office policy in regards to ambiguous coding issues—cite sources.

    — Document services clearly, concisely, and completely to justify provided services or the choice of a particular code.

    — Arrange for an outside consultant to audit the coding and documentation practices and follow up on recommendations.

- Payer Correspondence

    — Carefully read all memos and newsletters sent out by contractors and other third-party payers and request more information or further training if you need assistance in coding or billing for services.

    — Keep all written correspondence from Medicare contractors and other payers. Insist that all recommendations be given in writing.

- Claims Review

    — Review claims on a regular basis to learn why claims are being rejected and then correct any problems before the government steps in.

    — If a mistake occurs and you receive an overpayment from Medicare, promptly refund it.

Documentation

Claims Processing

One of the most important documents for correct reimbursement is the insurance claim—whether submitted electronically or on a standardized paper claim form. Other information, such as operative reports, chart notes, and cover letters may establish medical necessity, but the claim sets the stage.

The term "claims processing" describes the course of submitting a claim to the payer and subsequent adjudication. Understanding how this process works allows providers and staff members to file claims properly and leads to maximum and timely reimbursement. In addition, this knowledge allows the provider's office to serve as a resource to patients in understanding the process.

With commercial insurance companies, submit the claim directly to the payer or provide the patient with the necessary information to submit the claim. If there is a signed agreement with a commercial payer or with a health maintenance organization (HMO) or preferred provider organization (PPO), the office may be required to send the claim directly to the insurer. Medicare requires that the office submit all Medicare claims directly to the Medicare contractor, whether participating or not in the Medicare program.

For paper claims, use standard claim forms (CMS-1500 and the UB-04 described in this chapter) when submitting charges, and be sure to complete the forms completely and accurately. For electronic claims, providers should use the 837p format, and institutional claims are filed using the 837i format.

What to Include on Claims

Patient Information
Before filing any claim, obtain clear, accurate information from the patient, and update the information regularly. Most offices verify the information at each visit. A uniform policy for multiple provider offices or clinics makes everyone accountable for current and correct patient data. If a claim is filed with missing or incorrect patient demographic information, it will more than likely be returned by the payer as unprocessable. Providers should be certain that they collect the necessary information and the information is verified frequently, advisably every time the patient presents for services.

In addition to items regarding the patient, demographic information should also be obtained for the person who is the subscriber of the insurance coverage, whether or not that coverage is primary, secondary, or tertiary. Information such as the subscriber's date of birth may inadvertently be uncollected or incorrect. A photocopy of the patient's health plan identification card should be made and kept on file.

Primary vs. Secondary Coverage
Households with dual incomes often have more than one insurer. Determine which is the primary and which is the secondary insurance company. For commercial plans, the subscriber's or insured's insurance company is always primary for the subscriber. In other words, the husband's insurance company is primary for him and the wife's insurance company is primary for her.

However, the primary insurance company for any dependents is determined by the insureds' birthdays, the primary insured being the individual whose birthday is first during the year. This is often referred to as the "birthday rule." For example, if the husband's birthday is October 14, 1960, and the wife's birthday is March 1, 1962, the wife is primary for their dependents because her birthday is first during the year (year of birth is ignored).

Medicare Secondary Payer
When the Medicare program was established, it was given the responsibility of paying health care expenses for eligible citizens. Then recognizing that many Medicare patients are also entitled to coverage under other insurance plans, Congress later expanded the Medicare secondary payer (MSP) program to include situations in which payment could reasonably be expected to be paid by other specific payers. Congress' intent was to force other payers to take primary responsibility for the payment of patient medical expenses when appropriate.

In general, Medicare is the secondary payer to the following insurance plans and programs under certain conditions:

- Patient's group health plan (GHP)
- Spouse's GHP or a family member's GHP
- Automobile insurance
- No-fault liability insurance
- Workers' compensation situations

When Medicare is the secondary payer, the provider must first submit the claim to the primary payer. The primary payer is then required to process and make primary payment on the claim in accordance with the coverage provisions of its contract (regardless of Medicare coverage or payment decisions). Once the primary payer has processed the claim, and if the primary payer does not pay in full for the services, Medicare secondary benefits may be paid. Too many times, offices assume that Medicare is primary, which is detrimental to a smooth claims filing process and cash flow. Failure to submit claims in the proper order will result in payment delays or denials, so it is important to determine the primary payer every time a patient is utilizing Medicare and another payer.

Assignment of Benefits and Release of Information
Consider adding an assignment of benefits statement to the patient information form. It should state that the patient has agreed to have insurance payments sent directly to the physician and that medical information can be released to the patient's insurance company. A signed copy of this assignment submitted with a claim helps ensure at least partial payment from most commercial insurers. Assignments also reduce collection expenses. An alternative, lifetime assignment of benefits should nearly eliminate the need to obtain a signature after each date of service; however, there are payers that require a current signature with each claim.

If the office participates with Medicare, an assignment of benefits and release of billing are necessary.

Determining Coverage

A patient's insurance coverage should be verified before any service is rendered with the common sense exception of emergency treatment. This policy should not apply exclusively to new patients. Established patients may have changed employers, married or divorced, or no longer be covered by the same policy that was in effect during the last visit. The law requires Medicaid patients to provide current proof of eligibility with each visit.

Preauthorization

Determining in advance the benefits and allowables provides the physician's office with reimbursement figures before the patient's visit. Under most circumstances, the office should be able to discuss the deductible, copayment, and balance over and above the allowable with the patient prior to providing costly services. Asking a few pointed questions of the patient and insurer will provide additional information regarding deductibles, for example:

- How much is the deductible and has it been met for the current year?
- What are the allowables for the quoted procedures?
- What percentage of the allowables will be paid?

Clean Claims

Claims submitted with all of the information necessary for processing are referred to as "clean" and are usually paid in a timely manner. Paying careful attention to what should appear on the claim form helps produce these clean claims. Common errors include the following:

- Failure to pay attention to communications from carriers (including Medicare and Medicaid transmittals)
- An incorrect patient identification number
- Patients' names and addresses that differ from the insurers' records
- Physician tax identification numbers, provider numbers, or Social Security numbers that are incorrect or missing
- No or insufficient information regarding primary or secondary coverage
- Missing authorized signatures—patient and/or physician
- Dates of service that are incorrect or don't coincide to the claims information sent by other providers (such as hospitals or nursing homes)
- Dates that lack the correct number of digits
- A fee column that is blank or not itemized and totaled
- Incomplete patient information
- Invalid CPT and ICD-9-CM codes, or diagnostic codes that are not linked to the correct services or procedures
- An illegible claim

Medicare Billing for Physical Therapists in Private Practice

Independent PTs billing Medicare for physical therapy services need to meet the following criteria:

- The physical therapist is in an unincorporated solo practice or unincorporated partnership that meets all state and local licensure laws; or is an individual practicing physical therapy as an employee of an unincorporated practice, professional corporation or other incorporated therapy practice. It does not include physical therapists working as (provider) employees.
- The physical therapist must be licensed or legally authorized to be in private practice in accordance to applicable state laws.
- Services must be provided in the physical therapist's office or in the home of the patient. "In the therapist's office" is defined as the location in which the practice is operated, where the physical therapist is legally authorized to provide services during the hours in which he or she engages in practice at that site.
- A physical therapist in private practice must maintain a private office even if he or she always provides services in the patient's home. When services are provided in private office space, that space must be owned, leased or rented by the practice for the exclusive purpose of operating the practice.
- Physical therapist assistants must be under the direct supervision of the PT as they provide services. (Direct supervision is defined as being in the office suite while the service is being provided to the patient.)
- Physical therapy aides assist the PT or PTA to perform tasks related to provision of services, but aides should never be the provider of the service. Both PTAs and aides must be employed by the PT, the partnership, or group to which the PT belongs or in the same private practice that employs the PT.
- Each physical therapist must enroll with the appropriate carrier as an individual. PTs also may reassign their individual provider number to the group practice for which they provide services.

The Health Insurance Portability and Accountability Act

The Health Insurance Portability and Accountability Act (HIPAA) of 1996 (104-191) is a complex, multifaceted law. HIPAA was passed in part as a means to improve the portability and availability of health insurance coverage for individuals and groups. While insurance reform (Title 1) is an important aspect of the law, it is the antifraud and abuse provisions that have the greatest impact on physician practices and daily operational activities. Other provisions promote the use of medical savings accounts, improving access to long-term care services and coverage, and simplification of health insurance administration.

Possibly the best approach is to be certain that your practice keeps abreast of any changes taking place as the different provisions of HIPAA are revised and updated. One of the best sources of information is the CMS website (or the Office of Civil Rights), which provides not only background information, but also keeps you up to date with current rules and CMS requirements. That address is http://www.cms.hhs.gov/hipaa.

Administrative Simplification Provisions

The administrative simplification provisions of HIPAA (Title II) require HHS to establish national standards for electronic health care transactions and national identifiers for providers, health plans, and employers. They also address the security and privacy of protected health information. Implementing these standards and encouraging the use of electronic data interchange (EDI) in health care will improve the efficiency of the nation's health care system, reduce the administrative burden on providers and health care plans, and save more than $30 billion over the next decade.

Under HIPAA, every health care provider will be able to use EDI standards for billing and other health care transactions, such as referrals and diagnosis reports. All health plans will be required to accept these standard electronic claims, and all health care providers using electronic transmittals will be required to use the EDI standards.

Guidelines specify that transactions involving the following types of information exchanges among health care plans, clearinghouses, and providers are subject to EDI standards:

- Health care claims and equivalent encounter information
- Health care payment and remittance advices
- Coordination of benefits
- Health care claim status
- Enrollment or disenrollment in a health plan
- Eligibility for a health plan
- Referral certification and authorization
- Health insurance plan premiums

The claims standard mandated by HIPAA is the ASC X12N 837, which is designed to accommodate claims billing data electronically. Implementation guides are available from the Washington Publishing Company on its website at http://www.wpc-edi.com.hipaa.

Passage of the Administrative Simplification Compliance Act (ASCA) required providers to submit electronic claims to Medicare, with the following exceptions:

- Providers with no capability for electronic claim submission
- Facility providers with fewer than 25 full-time employees
- Outpatient practices with fewer than 10 full-time employees

Electronic Claim Submission

Although not all providers are required to submit claims electronically, there are many distinct advantages to utilizing EDI, including:

- Quicker payment of electronic claims (13 days versus 27 days for paper claims)
- Reduced cost (e.g., lower postage, administrative and handling expenses)
- Lower error rate
- Online receipt or acknowledgment
- Standardized EDI format is accepted by all Medicare contractors as well as private payers.
- Electronic remittances are sent to a provider-preferred location
- Information about claim status and eligibility are available in 24 hours or less.
- While checks can take as long as a week to process, electronic funds transfer (EFT) can have accounts receivable

in provider's bank within two working days after payment is made.

Standards and Code Sets

CMS adopted the following standard medical data code sets:

- **Current Procedural Terminology (CPT).** CPT coding system, including modifiers, are required for reporting physician and other health care services
- **Alphanumeric HCPCS Level II.** Required for reporting not only physician and other health care services, but also for supplies, equipment, substances, and other items used for health care services
- **ICD-9-CM, volumes 1 and 2.** Required for reporting the following conditions: diseases, injuries, impairments, other health problems and their manifestations, and causes
- **ICD-9-CM, volume 3.** Required for reporting diagnostic, preventive, therapeutic, or management procedures or actions provided by hospitals.

CMS notes that the CDT and CPT code sets are proprietary and that there are royalty issues for electronic use, paid by insurers. Usually, outpatient services provided in settings that include rehabilitation agencies, certified outpatient rehabilitation facilities, skilled nursing facilities, and hospitals use the UB-04 claim form. Services provided in a private practice or health care provider's office use the CMS-1500 form or a similar variation.

There are also ASC X12N standards specified in the regulations for health care claims and encounters, eligibility for a health plan, referral certification and authorization, health care claim status, enrollment and disenrollment in a health plan, health care payment and remittance advice, health plan premium payments, and coordination of benefits.

National Privacy Standards

With publication of a final rule in December 2000, HHS established regulations that protect the privacy of an individual's health information. The regulations are applicable to all medical records and health information that can be individually identified that is transmitted or maintained in any form. The regulations also grant individuals the right to protect the disclosure of their health information and how it is used. Any improper use or disclosure of this information is subject to criminal and civil sanctions including civil monetary penalties, fines, and prison. Compliance for most covered entities was required by April 14, 2003, with the exception of small health plans that had an additional year to comply.

The final rule was published in the *Federal Register* on August 14, 2002, complete with revisions that not only protect an individual's confidential medical information, but also facilitate his or her access to care. One of the primary revisions made to the final rule was the elimination of the consent requirement with an acknowledgment of receipt of the privacy notice.

Highlights of the final rule and modifications are described below.

Marketing

A covered entity is required to obtain prior consent from the individual to use his or her protected health information for purposes of marketing with the exception of face-to-face encounters or communications that include a promotional gift of nominal value. Physicians and other covered entities discussing treatment options, health-related products, and additional health care plan coverage is not considered to be marketing.

Notice of Privacy
Entities are required to inform patients of their privacy rights and the privacy practices of the covered entity. Patients will be asked to acknowledge receipt of the privacy notice.

Uses and Disclosures Regarding FDA-Regulated Products and Activities
In the interest of public health and safety, entities are permitted to disclose PHI without authorization to a person subject to the jurisdiction of the Food and Drug Administration (FDA) for purposes such as reporting adverse effects, and defective or dangerous products.

Incidental Use and Disclosure
Incidental uses or disclosures that may occur are not considered to be in violation of the privacy rule, as long as reasonable safeguards and minimum necessary requirements are met. This means that waiting room sheets may be used in physician offices, and physicians may talk to patients in semiprivate rooms and with other staff members without violating the rule if the conversation was inadvertently overheard.

Authorization
Although patients have to provide permission for all non-routine use or disclosure of their protected medical information. Authorization must include core elements.

Minimum Necessary
All uses or disclosures for which the covered entity has received an authorization are exempt from the minimum necessary standard. Uses and disclosures are still in effect, however, for most other uses and disclosure.

Parents and Minors
With regards to the rights of parents and the health information pertaining to their minor children, the final rule has clarified that state and other applicable law will prevail.

Business Associates
Covered entities may disclose protected health information to business associates if the provider obtains assurances that the business associates will use the information for the purposes for which it was intended, and will safeguard the information from misuse. Some examples of business associates are:

- A consultant performing utilization reviews for a hospital

- An independent medical transcriptionist that provides transcription services for a physician practice

- Accounting firms providing independent audit services involving protected health information for hospitals

- Outside legal counsel to a hospital whose work includes access to protected health information

Research
Researchers will be able to use a single form to obtain informed consent for research and the authorization to use or disclose protected health information.

Limited Data Set
The rule allows for the development and distribution of limited data that does not include any identifiable health information.

Employment Record Exclusion
Employment records maintained by a covered entity are not considered to be PHI.

Group Health Plan Disclosure and Enrollment and Disenrollment Information
Group health plans, including HMOs acting in the capacity as a health plan, and health insurance issuers may disclose enrollment and disenrollment information to plan sponsors, such as employers.

Disclosure for Treatment, Payment, or Heath Care Operations
Protected health information may be disclosed for treatment, payment, and operation purposes.

Health Care Operations—Legal Ownership Changes
When a covered entity sells or merges with another, it is permitted to use and disclose PHI as part of the transaction.

Hybrid Entities
Entities performing covered and noncovered functions may use the hybrid entity provisions. A hybrid entity also has discretion in designating its health care components. Covered functions are defined as "those functions of a covered entity the performance of which makes the entity a health plan, health care provider, or health care clearinghouse."

Accounting of Disclosures
Exempt disclosures include those made pursuant to an authorization, incidental disclosures and those that are contained in a limited data set. Payment, treatment, and operations are exempt.

Content of the Accounting
The accounting of disclosures must include all disclosures of protected health information not specifically listed as excluded above that occurred within the six years prior to the date of the request. This does not include any disclosures from prior to the compliance date for your entity, so for most, the accounting will include only disclosures from April 14, 2003, and forward. Also, the patient may request an accounting for a shorter period of time than the six-year maximum. For each disclosure, the accounting must include the following:

- Date of the disclosure

- Name of the entity or person who received the PHI and, if known, that address of the recipient

- Brief description of the PHI that was disclosed

- Brief statement of the purpose of the disclosure—statement must provide the individual with a reasonable amount of information about the basis for the disclosure

In cases where a covered entity makes a disclosure for research purposes on 50 or more individuals pursuant to the guidelines for research disclosures, the entity may provide detailed information about the research study in the accounting, and state that the information may have been used for research purposes. In this case, if the individual wishes more detail on how his or her

Claims Processing

information was used in the research study, the entity must assist the individual in contacting the researcher to get that additional information.

Security Standards

Although the proposed HIPAA security standards for the protection of electronic health information were released in August of 1998, it took until February of 2003 for the release of the final security rule. This rule was effective in April 2005, although small health plans had until April 2006 to be in compliance. From the time of the proposed rule until the finalization, the terminology of the proposed rule was revised to make it more consistent with the language in the HIPAA privacy rule.

The security rule offers a broad scope of guidance with regards to how covered entities and their business associates should implement security, containing a description of the principles that should be incorporated as necessary depending on the specific circumstances of the covered entity. This results in leaving the specific details of the implementation of the security standards to the covered entity with the added responsibility of making modifications to the standards when circumstances change.

The scope of the security rule applies only to PHI that is in electronic format. This means that paper-to-paper faxes are not considered to be electronic, but computer faxes are. Telephone transmission of information also is not considered to be electronic. However, it is important to bear in mind that the privacy rule contains a security stipulation that requires covered entities and their business associates to implement appropriate administrative, technical, and physical safeguards to PHI in all forms.

In general, the security rule contains four main requirements:

- Ensure the confidentiality, integrity, and availability of all electronic PHI created, received, maintained, or transmitted by the covered entity
- Protect the information from any reasonably anticipated threats or hazards
- Protect the information from any reasonably anticipated prohibited use or disclosure
- Ensure compliance by the workforce

Other provisions require:

- Security awareness training for all employees
- A risk analysis to determine risks and vulnerabilities
- Policies and procedures that permit access to PHI on a need-to-know basis only
- Controls to determine who has logged into systems that contain electronic PHI
- Limit physical access to facilities containing electronic PHI
- Implement and enforce sanctions when failure to comply with security policies and procedures occurs

The enforcement of the security standards is delegated to the Health and Human Service's Office of Civil Rights (OCR), although the agency will collaborate with CMS on some issues.

Standard Unique Employer Identifier

HIPAA also required the establishment of a national standard for employer identification to be used by covered health care providers, health plans, and clearinghouses for electronic health transactions. For this purpose, the employer identification number (EIN), which is assigned by the Internal Revenue Service (IRS), was selected as a cost-effective choice.

Additional Requirements for Health Plans

Health plans must permit the use of EDI standard transactions when requested to do so. They may not delay or reject a transaction because it is an EDI standard transaction. They may not reject a standard transaction on the basis that it contains data elements not needed or used by the health plan. They may not offer incentives to steer providers toward direct data entry transactions.

A health plan that operates a health care clearinghouse, or requires a provider to use a health care clearinghouse to receive, process, or transmit a standard transaction may not charge fees or costs in excess of the fees or costs for normal telecommunications that the provider incurs when it directly transmits, or receives, a standard transaction to or from a health plan.

Processing the Claim

Once a payer receives the claim, the process of adjudication follows a well-established path. The claim may proceed unimpeded toward reimbursement. Or, along the way, the claim may be stopped and returned to your office for lack of information.

The Claims Adjudicator

Upon receipt, each claim is dated and possibly microfilmed or photocopied. Data are entered into the payer's computer system and if the claim is clean (no problems) it is paid. Claims must first pass through a series of edits to verify the patient's coverage and eligibility as well as check for medical necessity and noncovered services. If the claim requires additional information, also known as development, the insurer contacts the providers office or the patient.

Claims Correction

When a claims error is discovered that could result, or already has resulted, in inaccurate reimbursement, send a corrected claim. Clearly mark this claim as a "corrected billing—not a duplicate claim." Include a note describing the error, plus any additional documentation necessary to support your position. Do not keep overpayments; bring them to the attention of the insurance company with a refund. Medicare does not look favorably on practices holding claim overpayments and may prosecute.

Unprocessable Claims

CMS, through continuing efforts to reduce costs and administrative waste, changed the provider remittance advice and began to return unprocessable claims to providers. For some time, the denial of claims with incomplete or invalid information had resulted in claims surfacing inappropriately into the appeals process. This practice resulted in an inappropriate use of the appeals system that increased costs for processing claims.

What does "return as unprocessable" mean?

Returning a claim as unprocessable does not mean your Medicare carrier will physically return every claim you submit that contains incomplete or invalid information. The term "return as unprocessable" refers to the many processes used by your Medicare carrier today for notifying you that your claim cannot be processed, and that it must be corrected or resubmitted.

Some examples of the various reasons for returning claims as unprocessable include:

- Incomplete or invalid information is detected at the front-end of your Medicare carrier's claims processing system. The claim is returned to you either electronically or in a hardcopy or checklist type form with errors explained and how to correct them.

- Incomplete or invalid information is detected at the front end of the claims processing system and the claim is suspended and developed by your Medicare carrier. If corrections are submitted within a 45-day period, the claim is processed. Otherwise, the suspended portion is returned as unprocessable and you are notified by means of a remittance notice.

- Incomplete or invalid information is detected within the claims processing system and this claim is rejected through the remittance process by your Medicare carrier. You are notified of any error through the remittance notice, as well as information to correct it.

NOTE : An incomplete claim is missing required information, such as the national provider identifier (NPI). An invalid claim is one that contains complete and necessary information, but the information is illogical or incorrect, such as an incorrect NPI.

It is important to correct returned as unprocessable claims promptly. Until a processable claim is submitted, a provider has not met the mandatory claims submission law. Also, unprocessable claims are unappealable (no review or hearing is permitted). A new claim must be submitted.

Unprocessable claims will not physically be mailed back to you. Rather, they are noted on the remittance advice with a brief message identifying the problem. The provider must correct the mistake(s) and submit a new claim. The new claim can be submitted either electronically or on paper.

Generally, only assigned claims will be returned as unprocessable. Nonassigned claims will be developed through the usual process to protect the beneficiary's financial interest. If development letters are not answered, nonassigned claims will be denied.

The Appeals Process

There are times when, for a number of reasons, claims are paid inappropriately or inaccurately. In these instances, if is often worth the time and effort to appeal these claims. In fact, studies have shown that intital decisions are reversed in whole or in part for over 50 percent of reviewed claims.

In general, a request for a claim review or appeal may be requested by the provider, patient, or an authorized representative of the patient. For nonassigned Medicare claims, the provider may request a review only if the service was denied or reduced due to the medical necessity and the provider is held responsible for the denial or reduction in payment. The provider

may also request a review if given written authorization by the patient. A copy of the authorization must accompany the request.

Claim Resubmission

When a claim is denied, first consider resubmitting. Claims may be resubmitted only when the entire claim is denied. This most typically occurs when information on the claim is missing or when the payer requests additional information.

According to CMS, some of the most common scenarios in which a claim can be resubmitted include:

- Incorrect patient name, health insurance claim number (HICN), or sex
- Missing billing provider information
- Missing diagnosis
- Missing performing provider number
- Missing place of service code
- Missing or incorrect quantity of service billed
- Missing/incorrect provider identification number (PIN)

Appealing Medicare Claims

There are five levels in the Medicare appeals process:

- Redeterminations
- Reconsideration
- Administrative law judge (ALJ) hearings
- Departmental appeals board (DAB) review
- Federal Court

Redeterminations

The Medicare appeals process was revised based on provisions of the Benefits Improvement and Protection Act (BIPA) and Part B initial determinations. The request for review form, CMS-20027 (replacement for form CMS-1964) should be used but is not required. Providers may also elect to request a redetermination by a letter. When writing a letter to formally request a review of a denied claim, include pertinent information such as the patient's name, Medicare number, the date of service, and the services in question. Explain in detail why you think the services should be reviewed. Also, attach a copy of the EOMB for the services in question. You may also include any documentation that supports the review.

Medicare Fair Hearings

If you are not satisfied with the decision rendered on your review, the next step would be to request a fair hearing. Hearings must be requested within six months of the final review determination and for an amount of $100 or more (not including deductible and coinsurance). You may combine multiple claims to meet the threshold amount.

When requesting a fair hearing for Medicare claims, use form CMS-1965. A letter may also be used.

The three types of fair hearings that may be held are:

- **In-person hearing.** The claimant and/or representative is afforded the opportunity to present oral testimony supporting the claim and challenging the information the carrier used to deny the claim.

- **Telephone hearing.** Telephone hearings offer a convenient and less costly alternative to the in-person hearing. Oral testimony is presented and the opportunity exists for oral challenge. Be certain to submit new data well in advance of the hearing date in order to allow review time by the hearing officer.

- **On the record (OTR) decision.** OTR decisions are based on facts in the file. This includes any additional information obtained by, or furnished to, the hearing officer. The hearing office does not take testimony. The major advantage to this type of hearing is the speeds with which it can be heard and a decision made.

Qualified Independent Contractors

All redeterminations are subject to review by the QIC. This means that if an individual or entity is dissatisfied with the results of a redetermination, a request for reconsideration by a QIC can be made, regardless of the amount in controversy (AIC), as long as it is done within the 180-day time limit. The QIC has 60 days to notify the requestor of:

- The results of the reconsideration that support or reverse, in whole or partially, the initial determination, including the redetermination

- The inability of the QIC to complete the review within the 60-day time frame

- Dismissal by the QIC

Administrative Law Judge

When an individual is still not satisfied after the QIC's reconsideration or if the period of adjudication specified for the QIC to complete its reconsideration is over, an ALJ hearing may be requested. This hearing may be conducted in person, by video teleconference, or over the phone. In some situations, a CMS representative such as the QIC, carrier, or fiscal intermediary may participate in the hearing. The AIC requirement for requests prior to January 1, 2008, was $110. The AIC requirement increased to $120 for requests made on or after January 1, 2008. The AIC threshold amount will remain at $120 for 2009 as well.

A provision of the Medicare Prescription Drug, Improvement, and Modernization Act (MMA) of 2003, mandates that AIC threshold must be adjusted annually based on the increase in the medical care component of the consumer price index. If this adjusted amount is not a multiple of $10, the amount will be rounded to the nearest multiple of $10. The adjusted amount will be published in the *Federal Register*. This AIC threshold is required for hearing officer hearings and Part A redetermination decisions. For those hearing officer hearings and Part A redetermination decisions that are issued November 3 through December 31, the parties that appeal are to be notified of the AIC threshold required for an ALJ hearing on or before December 31, as well as the AIC threshold required beginning January 1. At this level of appeal, a Medicare employee is not making the determination. The request for hearing is made through the carrier's hearing officer. The hearing officer makes a final review of the case and decides whether a reversal of the original determination is warranted.

If the hearing officer reverses the decision, you will be notified and the appeal will go no further. If the hearing officer does not reverse the decision, the request and the case file will be forwarded to an ALJ.

Currently, reviews are performed by administrative law judges in the Office of Hearings and Appeals in the Social Security Administration (SSA). One of the judges or representative of the SSA will contact the requester to schedule the hearing and explain the protocol. It may take as long as a year to complete this level of review.

Expedited Access to Judicial Review

The MMA also provides for expedited access to judicial review (EAJR) in situations involving Medicare appeals. A party may request an EAJR only once with respect to a question of law or regulation for a specific matter in dispute. Requests for an EAJR must also meet the requirements for filing a civil action in a federal district court.

A review entity (defined as up to three reviewers who are ALJs or members of the departmental appeals board) must respond to a request for expedited access to judicial review in writing within 60 days after receiving the request. If the review entity fails to act within the 60-day deadline, the party can request judicial review. Expedited access to judicial review can be granted when the Medicare Appeals Council (MAC) does not have authority to decide questions of law or regulation relevant to matters in controversy and there is no material issue of fact in dispute.

Parties may request an expedited judicial review instead of an ALJ hearing or a MAC review in the following circumstances:

- A QIC made a reconsideration determination and the party filed a request for the following:
  - an ALJ hearing and final decision of the ALJ is issued
  - a MAC review and final decision of the MAC has not been issued
  - the appeal escalates from the contractor to the ALJ level after the review period expired and the contractor failed to issue final decision within the time allowed

- The requester is a party (persons or entities who were parties to the QIC's reconsideration determination and to the ALJ hearing, if applicable).

- The amount remaining in controversy meets the necessary requirements.

- When there is more than one party to the reconsideration, hearing, or MAC review, each must agree, in writing, with the EAJR request.

- No material issues of fact are in dispute. A party may request an expedited judicial review with an ALJ hearing or with MAC review. Or in the case where an appeal is already pending with the ALJ or MAC, file a written request for an EAJR where the appeal is being considered. When the request is received, the ALJ hearing office or MAC will then forward it to the review entity within five calendar days

Departmental Appeals Board Review

The departmental appeals board (DAB) contains a component responsible for Medicare claim appeals, called the Medicare Appeals Council. Before the interim final rule was published on March 8, 2005, MAC considered requests for review of Medicare

Claims Processing

cases under the procedures used by the SSA Appeals Council. New regulations contain some provisions regarding MAC proceedings, which are generally governed by SSA regulations. Written request for review must be made through the SSA within 60 days of the administrative law judge's decision and at least $500 must be in dispute. The request must specify the issues and findings of fact and conclusion of law, as well as the basis for contending that the findings and conclusion were incorrect. The SSA will contact the requestor regarding regulations and protocol.

At this level of appeal, retaining an experienced health care attorney should be considered, but it isn't mandatory. BIPA established a new standard for MAC review of an ALJ's action. The MAC is required to conduct its review of an ALJ decision and make a decision or remand the case to the ALJ within 90 days of a request for review. MAC is also required to review the case de novo. In addition, parties may request a MAC review if, within 90 days of timely filing a request for an ALJ hearing, the ALJ fails to issue a decision. MAC decisions constitute the final decision and can be appealed to a federal court.

U.S. District Court

A civil action must be filed in a federal district court within 60 days of the mailing of the appeals council's decision or the appeals council's denial to review an ALJ's decision. The amount remaining in controversy for requests made on or after January 1, 2007, increased to $1,130. For requests on and after January 1, 2008, the amount remaining in controversy was raised to $1,180. For 2009, the AIC was raised to $1,220. An attorney is mandatory, and the action must be filed in the federal district in which one lives or practices.

Expedited Review Process

Prepaid health care organization administrative review requirements require an expedited review for making and reconsidering determinations of benefits when an adverse determination could seriously jeopardize the life or health of the patient or the patient's ability to regain maximum function. This rule is also applicable to decisions to discontinue services, such as a discharge from a skilled nursing facility. The new regulations were established for Medicare beneficiaries who re-enrolled in health maintenance organizations, competitive medical plans, and health care prepayment plans to provide them with the opportunity to seek administrative review when the health plan is not providing a health service to which they believe they are entitled.

Although patients enrolled in prepaid health care organizations have the same appeal rights as those available to patients in fee-for-service plans, the standard 60-day time frame for issuing determinations was felt to be too long in time-sensitive situations when the patient's life or health was in jeopardy or if there was a threat to his or her ability to regain maximum function.

Health plans are required to conduct a review within a time period appropriate to the condition of the patient, but no longer than 72 hours after the time of the request. To speed things along even more, the patient or his or her representative could request an expedited review over the telephone and the health plan's decision could also be provided over the telephone, although a written follow-up must be issued within two working days.

Physicians are also permitted to request expedited reviews on behalf of the patient, and the health plan must accept the physician's decision that the situation meets the criteria for an expedited review—that is, a longer review period could place the patient in jeopardy. Only in limited situations will health plans be able to take more than 72 hours to issue determination. Health plans will be able to extend the 72-hour standard up to 10 additional working days if the extension of time benefits the patient, such as allowing for additional diagnostic tests or consultations with medical specialists, or if the patient requests the extension to provide the plan with additional information for making the decision.

If a health plan makes the decision not to expedite a determination and redirects that determination through the standard process, the patient could request an expedited reconsideration. If the health plan's decision is to uphold a decision that is adverse to the patient in whole or in part, the case must be forwarded to the Medicare reconsideration contractor within 24 hours of that decision for further review.

Provider Service Terminations

Medicare was also mandated to establish a process whereby a beneficiary could obtain an expedited determination if he or she received a notice from a provider that the provider plans to terminate all services or discharge the beneficiary.

This existed previously under statute for hospital discharges only. Notification requirements apply to skilled nursing facilities, home health agencies, comprehensive outpatient rehabilitation facilities, and hospice providers when the beneficiary's services are being terminated. The provider is required to deliver, no later than two days before the termination will take place, a standardized notice informing the beneficiary of the discharge date and how to file an appeal. A beneficiary has to submit a request for an expedited determination to the quality improvement organization (QIO) no later than noon of the day following receipt of the notice of termination. The beneficiary has to be available to respond to questions by the QIO and may submit evidence to be used in the decision-making process.

Within 72 hours, the QIO must notify the provider of a beneficiary's request for an expedited determination, determine the validity of the discharge notice, review pertinent medical records, reach a decision, and notify the appropriate parties. Once the beneficiary requests an expedited determination, the provider must send a detailed notification to the beneficiary that contains all of the reasons that services are no longer covered. This must be completed by close of business on the day of the QIO notification.

Providers are not allowed to bill a beneficiary for the disputed services during the expedited appeals process. A beneficiary who is dissatisfied with a QIO's expedited determination may request an expedited reconsideration by the appropriate QIC in writing or by telephone, no later than noon of the day following the initial notification of the QIO's determination. In the event that the QIC cannot accept the beneficiary's request, the beneficiary is required to submit the request by noon on the first day the QIC is available.

The beneficiary or his or her representative must be available to answer questions or supply information requested by the QIC. The beneficiary may also submit additional evidence for consideration by the QIC. If a beneficiary fails to file a timely request for an expedited QIC reconsideration, the beneficiary loses coverage protections, although the beneficiary may be able to request a standard appeal after the fact.

When the QIC receives an expedited determination request, it must notify the QIO that made the expedited determination, as well as the provider of services. The QIC must then render a decision within 72 hours and notify all parties involved.

Appealing to Commercial Payers: What Makes Commercial Payers Unique?

Appealing to a commercial payer is unique because there will not necessarily be a set procedure to follow. HMOs are required to provide specific directions to the medical providers and members on their appeals process. Health Net, for example, publishes the company policy in its handbook and on its website. Even the appeals form may be downloaded from the website. The appeal form outlines the step-by-step process and what can be expected along the way.

Other insurance companies will not provide this kind of guidance. In those cases, the only options are appealing by telephone or, better yet, in writing. A strong appeals letter is the best way to begin. A poorly written explanation of benefits (EOB) may be more than just a nuisance; it may also be a violation of federal and state law. Providers must attempt to receive a full explanation for any claim denial before appealing. ERISA regulations require insurers to include specific information in any denial notice. Further, self-funded plans bound by ERISA must include in any denial notice the reason for denial and include a specific reference to pertinent plan provisions on which the denial was based. Remember in appealing denied insurance claims, that attitude is just as important as facts. Develop a mindset that it is the insurance carrier's responsibility to prove the claim has been processed correctly. The right attitude will provide the perseverance necessary to continue the appeal process if the first appeal is denied.

Changes to the Medicare Claims Appeal Procedures
Printed with the pemission of the American Physical Therapy Association.

A. Summary
Section 521 of the Medicare, Medicaid, and SCHIP Benefits Improvement and Protection Act (BIPA) includes provisions to restructure the Medicare claims appeals process. In November 2002, the Centers for Medicare and Medicaid Services (CMS) published a proposed rule outlining the new procedural changes to the appeals process under BIPA. The proposed rule included:

- Uniform appeal procedures for both Part A and Part B claims
- Reduced decision-making time frames for most administrative appeals levels, as well as the right to escalate a case that is not decided on time to the next appeal level
- The establishment of Qualified Independent Contractors (QICs) to conduct reconsiderations of claims denials made by fiscal intermediaries, carriers, and quality improvement organizations
- Use of QIC panels, which include medical professionals, to reconsider all cases involving medical necessity issues

- A requirement for appeals-specific data collection by CMS

The Medicare Prescription Drug, Improvement, and Modernization Act (MMA) of 2003 also included structural changes to the Medicare appeals process. Among the new provisions are:

- Revised redetermination and reconsideration decision-making time frames
- A reduction in the minimum required number of QICs from 12 to 4
- A requirement to transfer the administrative law judge (ALJ) function from SSA to HHS
- Revised requirements for appeals decision notices
- A requirement for providers and suppliers to present evidence for an appeal no later than the QIC reconsideration level, unless there is good cause that prevented the timely introduction of the evidence
- The establishment of a process for the correction of minor errors or omissions without pursuing an appeal

These provisions are intended to reduce adjudication of fee-for-service Medicare appeals to 300 days or less from over 1,000 days to complete. The interim final rule summarized below established the regulations for implementing the Medicare claims appeals process from BIPA and the MMA.

Implementation: The new appeals procedures were implemented in two stages. First, as of May 1, 2005, all first level appeals carried out by fiscal intermediaries (generally Part A appeals) are subject to QIC reconsiderations. These appeals usually involve hospital services, skilled nursing facilities and home health agencies. Beginning on January 1, 2006, appeals redeterminations on Medicare Part B issues are reviewed by QICs, and the ALJ rules were in effect for all appeals that come through the QICs. Therefore, by January 1, 2006, the restructured Medicare appeals process was implemented in its entirety.

B. Quick Reference Timelines

Redeterminations
The provider, supplier or beneficiary has 120 days from the date the party receives the notice of an initial determination to file a redetermination request with the contractor (party is presumed to receive initial determination 5 days after initial determination is made).

Evidence Submitted with Redetermination Request
Evidence may be submitted at any time prior to the decision, however each new submission of evidence adds 14 days to the contractor's decision-making deadline.

Redetermination Timeline
The contractor has 60 days from the date the request is received to issue a redetermination decision (no expedited appeal option).

Reconsideration
An appellant must file a request for reconsideration with the QIC within 180 days of the date the party receives the redetermination notice (party is presumed to receive initial determination 5 days after initial determination is made).

Timeline for Reconsideration

The QIC has 60 days from the date the request for reconsideration is filed to make a decision. If the 60-day deadline will not be met, the QIC must notify the appellant. The appellant may then notify the QIC with an escalation request and the QIC has 5 days to complete the reconsideration or escalate the case to an ALJ.

ALJ Hearings

A party has 60 daysfrom the date of receipt of the QIC's reconsideration to file a written request for an ALJ hearing. In ALJ cases, the amount in controversy must be at least $100 (to be increased annually by the consumer price index).

Timeline for ALJ Decision

An ALJ must issue a written decision, dismissal, or remand to the QIC within 90 days from the date the party filed the request. If the appeal is escalated to the ALJ level because the QIC did not meet the deadline for issuing a reconsideration, the ALJ has 180 days from the date the escalation is received to issue a decision.

Submission of Evidence to the ALJ

Providers and suppliers are not permitted to submit additional evidence to the ALJ (evidence must be submitted prior to the QIC reconsideration) unless the evidence is accompanied by a written statement explaining why the evidence was not previously submitted to the QIC or prior decision-maker). Beneficiaries must submit any additional evidence to the ALJ within 10 days after receiving notice of the hearing.

Medicare Appeals Council (MAC) Review

The MAC has 90 days from receipt of the appellant's request to issue a decision based on a previous ALJ decision. If the appellant requested an escalated review because the ALJ did not meet the deadline for issuing a decision, the MAC has 180 days to issue a decision.

C. Potential Issues for Physical Therapists

1. Qualifications of the QICs

   Under the section 405.968(c) of new appeals rule, the qualified independent contractors (QIC) must have sufficient medical, legal and other expertise, including knowledge of the Medicare program. When a redetermination is made with respect to whether an item or service is reasonable and necessary, the QIC designates a panel of physicians or other appropriate health care professionals to consider the facts and circumstances of the redetermination. Under this provision, physicians have a specific carve out: in cases where a claim pertains to the furnishing of treatment by a physician, or the provision of items or services by a physician, the reviewing professional must be a physician. As with the provision for physician review of physician services, APTA believes that claims for physical therapy services provided by physical therapists should be reviewed by a licensed physical therapist. Physical therapists are the most qualified professionals to conduct medical review of physical therapy claims and make appropriate Medicare coverage determinations since they have unique experience, skills and training in this field.

2. Evidence Rules for Providers

   Under section 405.966 of the rule, suppliers and providers must submit all evidence at the redetermination or reconsideration level. Absent good cause, providers and suppliers will not be able to submit new evidence at the ALJ or MAC levels. This limitation applies only to providers and suppliers and not to beneficiaries—who will be permitted to submit new evidence at the ALJ and MAC levels. The limitation on the presentation of new evidence will also apply to beneficiaries represented by providers or suppliers to ensure that providers or suppliers do not circumvent this rule by offering to represent beneficiaries. CMS justifies this distinction in when new evidence may be presented by presuming that providers and suppliers have a better understanding of the appeals process and should know what materials to submit as evidence in an appeal. APTA questions this logic, as many providers do not seem well-informed about the Medicare appeals process. As the new regulations are supposed to provide providers and suppliers with similar appeals rights to beneficiaries, limiting when providers and suppliers may introduce new evidence may put these entities at a significant disadvantage when navigating their way through the new appeals rules.

3. Case Reopenings

   Under provisions of the new appeals process, beneficiaries, providers, suppliers and contractors may initiate a reopening of a final determination when the party determines that the decision resulted in an incorrect payment (either an overpayment or underpayment) based on clerical or computational error or new material evidence that was unavailable at the time of the decision. Providers will need to be aware that they have one year from the initial determination or redetermination or 4 years from the initial determination or redetermination with a showing of good cause (newly available material evidence that shows on its face that an obvious error was made at the time of decision). Contractors also have the same right to request a reopening within 1 year for incorrect payment decisions and 4 years for good cause. Changes in CMS policy, regulations or instructions are not a basis for reopening a redetermination or hearing decision under this section.

   One potential issue with this provision is that section 405.986 of the rule does not preclude contractors from conducting reopenings to effectuate local and national coverage decisions. This could mean that contractors would have 1 year to reopen a case affected by a local or national coverage decision that occurs within the year after the initial determination or redetermination. APTA is concerned this could lead to contractors reopening decisions when coverage is no longer extended to a certain treatment. Providers could then be forced to repay contractors for payments made while the treatment was part of the local or national coverage decision. APTA plans to submit comments on this provision of the rule for clarification and request revision if necessary.

 © 2009 Ingenix

D. Summary of Revised Appeals Procedures

On March 8, 2005, CMS published an Interim Final Rule on Changes to the Medicare Claims Procedures. The full text of the rule may be found at: http://www.cms.hhs.gov/quarterly providerupdates/downloads/CMS4064IFC.pdf

The Benefits Improvement and Protection Act passed in 2000, with CMS publishing a proposed rule in November 2002 seeking comments, and a final rule in November 2004. The changes to the appeal procedures will be implemented as part of the Medicare [Prescription Drug, Improvement, and] Modernization Act (MMA) Claims Appeals Procedures, which went into effect at the end of 2005. The following is a summary of the appeals rights under the BIPA and MMA published in the Federal Register on March 8, 2005.

1. Basis and Scope, Definitions, General Rules, and Parties to Initial Determinations, Redeterminations, Reconsiderations, Hearings and Reviews (section 405.900–section 405.906)

    This section of the proposed rule would extend to providers the same rights to administrative appeals of Medicare initial determinations as beneficiaries. Before implementation of this provision, providers could only appeal Medicare determinations when (1) the item or service was not covered because it constitutes custodial care or is not reasonable or necessary; and (2) the provider knows or reasonably could have been expected to know, that the item or service in question is not covered under Medicare. However, a provider or supplier can appeal a properly submitted claim only after the contractor has issued an initial determination on that claim. Thus, if a claim was improperly submitted, that rejection does not constitute an initial determination. Under the new rules, Medicare providers may file administrative appeals of initial determinations to the same extent of beneficiaries, allowing them to appeal all denials on their own accord.

2. Medicaid State Agencies (section 405.908)

    This provision acknowledges the right of a Medicaid State Agency to pursue an appeal on behalf of a beneficiary who is entitled to benefits under both Medicare and Medicaid. A Medicaid State Agency would not be considered a party unless it pursued a redetermination on behalf of a dually eligible beneficiary.

3. Appointed Representative (section 405.910)

    An appointed representative is an individual authorized by a party or under state law to act on a party's behalf in dealing with any of the levels of the appeals process, including initial determinations as well as appeals. The appointment must be in writing and signed by the party making the appointment and individual accepting the appointment. Such representation will last either the life of the initial appeal, or for appeals other than redeterminations, one year. However, a party may revoke the appointment at any time. This provision also clarifies that no award of attorney's fees may be made against the Medicare trust funds.

4. Assignment of Appeal Rights (section 405.912)

    A provider or supplier that furnished the item or service at issue in the appeal and wanted to take assignment of a beneficiary's appeal rights for a particular claim must waive any right to payment from the beneficiary in order to fully protect beneficiaries when their appeal rights are assigned. This does not prohibit the provider or supplier from recovery of any coinsurance or deductible or claiming payment in full where the beneficiary has signed an Advance Beneficiary Notice (ABN). The waiver of the right to collect payment by the assignee remains valid in the event of an unfavorable determination or decision. In addition, if the assignee fails to file an appeal of an unfavorable decision, or if an act or omission by the assignee is determined to be contrary to the financial interests of the beneficiary, the assignee will not be able to collect payment from the beneficiary.

    CMS will be developing a standardized form for assignment of appeal rights.

5. Initial Determinations (section 405.920–section 405.928)

    This provision of the statute establishes that an initial determination must be included for all claims (except for clean claims, which contain no defect or impropriety), and a notice of that determination must be mailed within 45 days after the carrier or fiscal intermediary receives the claim. The provisions maintain most of the existing policies concerning initial determinations, while also combining Part A and Part B rules. While the Social Security Administration (SSA) will continue to make Part A and Part B entitlement and enrollment determinations, HHS will be responsible for reviewing the entitlement and enrollment decisions at the ALJ level.

    This section also includes the notice requirements for initial determinations. Contractors must write the Medicare summary notice (MSN) in a manner than can be understood by the beneficiary. Under section 405.921 (a)(2) the contents of the notice must contain:

    —   The reasons for the determination, including whether a local medical review policy, local coverage determination or national coverage determination was applied

    —   The procedures for obtaining additional information concerning the determination, such as the specific provision of the policy, manual, law, or regulation used in making the determination

    —   Notification to the parties of their right to a redetermination if they are dissatisfied with the outcome of the initial determination

    —   Instructions on how to request a redetermination

    Under section 405.921 (b) the notice of initial determination sent to providers and suppliers must contain:

    —   The basis for any full or partial denial determination of services or items on the claim

    —   Information on the right to a redetermination if the provider or supplier is dissatisfied with the outcome of the initial determination

    —   All applicable claim adjustment reason and remark codes to explain the determination

— The source of the RA and who may be contacted if the provider or supplier requires further information

— All content requirements of the standard adopted for national use by covered entities under HIPAA

— Any other requirements specified by CMS

The initial determination provisions also add six items to the list of items that do not constitute an initial determination. Pursuant to section 405.926, those items are:

Determinations that a provider or supplier failed to submit a claim or failed to submit a timely claim despite being requested to do so by the beneficiary or the beneficiary's subrogee

Determinations with respect to whether an entity qualifies for an exception to the electronic claims submission requirement under part 424 of this chapter of the Code of Federal Regulations

Determination by the Secretary of sustained or high levels of payment errors in accordance with section 1983(f)(3)(A) of the Social Security Act

A contractor's prior determination related to coverage of physician services

Requests for anticipated payment under the home health prospective system under section 409.43 (c)(ii)(2) of this chapter

Claim submissions on forms or formats that are incomplete, invalid, or do not meet the requirements for a Medicare claim and returned or rejected to the provider or supplier

6. Redeterminations (section 405.940–section 405.958)

This provision of the new appeal regulations continues to allow parties to file their requests for a redetermination with the appropriate CMS contractor, as well as at a local CMS or SSA office. The date the redetermination request is considered filed is the date the contractor, SSA or CMS received the request. Under the new rules, all requests for redetermination must be made in writing (previously Part B requests could be made by telephone). CMS will allow an extension of the 120-day filing deadline for good cause shown. In these instances the contractor would consider the circumstances that kept the party from making the request on time, whether the contractor's actions misled the party, and whether any physical, mental, educational or language limitations prevented the party from filing a timely request.

For evidence submitted with the redetermination request, the party needs to explain why he or she disagrees with the contractor's initial determination and include any evidence the party believes should be considered by the contractor when making its redetermination. Providers and beneficiaries have the opportunity to submit evidence at any time during the redetermination process, but information should be submitted as quickly as possible.

The new MMA provisions made only minor changes to the time frame of the appeals requirements. Contractors have 60 days to issue a redetermination. To assist appellants who

might be unable to submit relevant documentation at the time of the redetermination request, the new provisions permit a 14-day extension to the decision-making process if a provider or beneficiary submits evidence after the request for redetermination. An appellant may submit new information as many times as necessary, and each submission will extend the deadline an additional 14 days.

The new rules state that a party may withdraw a redetermination request within 14 days of the original request. The provisions also include several reasons why a contractor may dismiss a request for redetermination, such as where the request for redetermination did not contain the minimum elements required for such a request under the statute. In addition, a contractor may dismiss the request upon the death of the party if there is no information in the record indicating that another party may be prejudiced by the dismissal. Dismissals of redetermination requests will be sent in writing to the parties. In cases where a redetermination request is dismissed, a party will have 6 months to submit information showing why the dismissal should be vacated and the redetermination restated. Finally, an appellant may request a QIC reconsideration of the dismissal within 60 days of the dismissal notice.

7. Redetermination, Notification and Subsequent Limitations on Evidence (section 405.954, section 405.956 and section 405.966)

When a contractor's redetermination reverses the initial determination, CMS will keep its current policy that proper notification would be achieved through the MSN or RA. The new provisions under the MMA affect cases where the redetermination affirmed the initial determination either in whole or in part. In these instances, the determination notice must contain:

— A clear statement indicating the extent to which the redetermination is favorable or unfavorable

— A summary of the facts

An explanation of how the pertinent laws, regulations, coverage rules, and CMS policies apply to the facts of the case

— A summary of the rationale for the redetermination

Notification to the parties of their right to reconsideration and time limits for requesting a reconsideration

A statement of the specific missing documentation that would need to be submitted with a request for a reconsideration

An explanation that if the specific supporting documentation required for a reconsideration is not submitted, that the evidence will not be considered by an ALJ at a hearing

Any other requirements specified by CMS

These requirements are similar to the existing provisions, but require contractors to specify the supporting documentation that would need to accompany a reconsideration request.

© 2009 Ingenix

Under the MMA, a provider or supplier may not, in any subsequent level of appeal, introduce evidence that was not presented at the reconsideration conducted by the QIC, unless there is good cause shown that precluded the introduction of that evidence at or before the reconsideration. Appellants who are beneficiaries do not have the same limitations, and may present new evidence at a reconsideration. However, the limitation prohibiting new evidence will also apply to beneficiaries represented by providers or suppliers to prevent providers and suppliers from circumventing the rules.

8. Reconsiderations (section 405.960–section 405.978)

The MMA implements new rules for the time frame for filing a reconsideration request. Appellants who wish to file a request for reconsideration must do so within 180 days of receipt of the redetermination notice or within additional time as the QIC might allow for good cause. Reconsiderations must be filed with the QIC. Reconsideration requests may be made by using the standard CMS form, or by a written request containing the beneficiary's name, HIC number, date of service at issue, and name and signature of the representative party. If the request does not contain this basic data, the QIC will dismiss the proposed reconsideration on the basis that it fails to be a valid request. The QIC has 60 days to complete the reconsideration, notify the parties that the reconsideration will not be complete by the deadline, or dismiss the reconsideration. If the QIC fails to complete the reconsideration within the 60-day deadline, appellants may request an escalation of the appeal to an ALJ. Once a QIC receives an escalation request, the QIC has 5 days to complete the reconsideration, or forward it to the ALJ.

Appellants may withdraw their requests for reconsideration within 14 days of making the request. The new rules also set for reasons why a QIC may dismiss a request for reconsideration, including if the person or entity making the request is not a proper party, or if the person or entity fails to meet the basic requirements needed for a valid request. Appellants may also request an ALJ review of a reconsideration if the request was filed within 60 days of the QIC's dismissal notice. In the case of the death of a party, the decision-maker will examine the following three circumstances to determine if dismissal of the request prejudices another party: (1) the beneficiary's surviving spouse or estate has no remaining financial interest in the case; (2) no other individual or entity with financial interest wishes to pursue the appeal; and (3) no other party to the redetermination filed a valid and timely reconsideration request.

The section of the new rule also describes the type of evidence that accompanies reconsideration requests and specifies that the failure to submit documentation listed in the redetermination notice at the reconsideration level generally prevents the introduction of that evidence a subsequent appeal levels. In cases where late submission of evidence is permitted (usually for beneficiaries), the late submission of documentation results in an automatic extension of the 14-day QIC decision-making time frame.

9. Conduct of a Reconsideration (section 405.968 and section 405.976)

A QIC reconsideration is an "independent, on-the-record review of an initial determination, including the redetermination." If an initial determination involved a finding on whether an item or service was reasonable or necessary for the diagnosis or treatment of an illness or injury, a QIC's reconsideration must be based on clinical experience and scientific evidence (to the extent applicable). QICs are bound by national coverage determinations. QICs must give substantial deference to LCDs LMRPs and CMS program guidance (i.e., a CMS manual instruction) and provide a reason if the policy should not be followed in this particular case.

Under the new rules, reconsiderations must be in writing and contain the following elements:

— A clear statement as to whether the reconsideration is favorable or unfavorable

— A summary of the facts

— An explanation of how the pertinent laws, regulations, coverage rules and CMS policies apply to the facts

— An explanation of the medical and scientific rationale for the reconsideration when the case involved determining whether an item or service was reasonably necessary for the diagnosis or treatment of an illness or injury

— A clear statement of the QIC's rationale for the decision

If the QIC's decision conflicts with an LCD, LMRP, or CMS guidance, the reconsideration notice needs to address how any missing documentation affects the reconsideration and the limitations on the presentation of evidence at the ALJ hearing level.

If an appellant files both a claim and a coverage appeal, both appeals will go forward on the same initial determination. In adjudicating the claim appeal, the decision-maker will apply the coverage policy that was in place on the date the item or service was provided, unless the appellant receives the favorable coverage decision prior to a decision being issued for a claim appeal. If the appellant receives the favorable coverage decision prior to a decision on the claim appeal, then the decision on the claim appeal will be made without the invalidated LCD. If an appellant receives a favorable decision in the coverage appeal after receiving an unfavorable decision in the claims appeal, then the appellant is entitled to have the claim appeal reopened and revised for good cause shown.

The new rules also include time frames for reconsideration decisions. A QIC has 60 days to issue a reconsideration, a dismissal or a notice that the QIC will not be able to complete the review by the deadline. The notice would also advise the appellant of the right to request an escalation of the appeal to an ALJ. If an escalation request is received prior to the end of the 60-day adjudication period, the QIC will proceed with its review of the reconsideration request and either (1) issue its reconsideration by the end of 65 days, or (2) send a response to the appellant that the review will not

Claims Processing

be completed by the 60-day deadline and escalate the request to the ALJ. Only the appellant will be notified of the reconsideration request, and the QIC will include in the notification whether the amount in controversy meets the threshold requirement for an ALJ hearing if the reconsideration is partially or fully unfavorable.

10. Reopening of Initial Determinations, Redeterminations, Reconsiderations, Hearings and Reviews (section 405.980–section 405.986)

A reopening is an action to change a final determination or decision that results in either an overpayment or underpayment (and different from an appeal), even though the decision was correct based on the evidence of record. Requests for adjustments to claims resulting from clerical errors (such as computational mistakes) must be handled through the reopening process. The MMA established the general rule that a reopening is a remedial action taken by a carrier, intermediary, QIC, ALJ, the Medicare Appeals Council (the MAC is an part of the Departmental Appeals Board of DHHS) or any other entity designated by CMS to change the final determination or decision made with respect to an initial determination, redetermination, reconsideration, hearing, or review, even though the determination or decision may have been correct based upon the evidence of record. A reopening is done at the level of the decision in question (i.e., a QIC opens a reconsideration). A party or a contractor can request a reopening on its own motion for any reason within one year from the date of the notice of the initial determination or redetermination. A party or contractor has a 4-year time frame for requesting or initiating a reopening for good cause (newly available material evidence that shows on its face that an obvious error was made at the time of decision). Reopenings are permitted at any time on claim determinations that have been procured through fraud or similar fault.

Section 405.986 of the rule does not preclude contractors from conducting reopenings to effectuate local and national coverage decisions. This could mean that contractors would have 1 year to reopen a case affected by a local or national coverage decision that occurs within the year after the initial determination or redetermination.

11. Expedited Access to Judicial Review (section 405.990)

Since the appeals process under the rule combines Part A and Part B claims, the process for expedited review of cases is also consolidated. Also, ALJs are now bound by all national coverage determinations. The MMA requires that a provider, supplier or beneficiary have access to judicial review when a review entity determines that the MAC (which functions under the Departmental Appeals Board) does not have the authority to decide the question or law or regulation relevant to the matters in controversy and that there is no material issue of fact in dispute. As it relates to this provision, the new rule requires expedited access to judicial review in these situations. A review entity is a decision-making body composed of 3 ALJ or members of the DAB, as determined by the Secretary. The MMA provides that a review entity's

determination is a final decision and not subject to review by the Secretary.

12. ALJ Hearings (section 405.1000–section 405.1064)

(a) Introduction: The procedures below implement provisions of both the BIPA and the MMA. The ALJ hearings procedures implemented with this rule are similar to the SSA disability appeals procedures.

(b) Escalation: One of the most significant changes under the MMA is the appellant's right to escalate a case to an ALJ if a QIC fails to make a timely reconsideration, or to the MAC if an ALJ hearing does not produce a timely decision on an appeal of a QIC reconsideration. The statute does not allow an appellant to proceed beyond the initial contractor level until the appellant receives a redetermination from that contractor (even if not issued within the statutory time frames). This is consistent with the statutory requirement for an appellant to complete all steps of the appeals process, except when an appellant invokes the expedited appeals process. Appellants must carefully consider the type of review that is best to resolve their case before deciding to escalate an appeal, as the type of proceedings and adjudicator varies with each step. For example, appellants who escalate a case from the ALJ level to the MAC will ordinarily not have the opportunity to present their case during an oral hearing, unless they received an oral hearing at the ALJ level before escalating their case to the MAC. An ALJ must issue a decision no later than 180 days after the date of the request for escalation is received by the ALJ hearing office. In situations where the case is close to completion the QIC, MAC or ALJ will have 5 days to complete the case after the adjudication period has expired before sending it on to the next level. If possible, the ALJ or QIC will issue its decision within the 5-day period.

(c) Conduct of ALJ Hearing—General Rules: Appellants may waive their right to an in-person hearing and request a decision based on the written record, or the opportunity to have the hearing by video teleconference (VTC) where available. This opportunity allows a hearing for beneficiaries who have trouble traveling even short distances and for providers who may not wish to travel to a more distant hearing site. A party that objects to either a VTC or telephone hearing may request an in-person hearing and will be granted one for good cause (such as the case presents complex or novel presentation issues that necessitate an in-person hearing).

(d) Actions That Are Reviewable by an ALJ: The new rule give the ALJ the authority to decide or review all final actions issued by a QIC, including dismissals for untimely filing and failure to exhaust administrative remedies. If the ALJ decides that the QIC's dismissal is improper, the ALJ will remand the case to the QIC for a substantive decision.

(e) Authorities That Are Binding on the ALJ: ALJs are bound by national coverage determinations, as well as CMS rulings that bind HHS components that adjudicate matters under CMS' jurisdiction. ALJs and the MAC should give deference to CMS manuals, LCDs and LMRPs, but can disregard the policy if the ALJ or the MAC provides a rationale should not be followed in this particular case.

(f) Aggregating Claims to Meet the Amount in Controversy: The new provisions changed the amount in controversy for an ALJ hearing to $100 for appeals of both Part A and Part B claims. In addition, two or more appeals are allowed to be aggregated when the appeals either involve the delivery of similar or related services to the same individual by one or more providers and suppliers, or there are common issues of law and fact arising from services furnished to two or more individuals by one or more providers or suppliers. The aggregation of eligible claims must occur within 60 days after receipt of all reconsiderations being appealed, and appellants must explain in writing the reason for requesting aggregation, including why they believe the claims contain common issues of law or fact or the delivery of similar or related services. Finally, the amount in controversy will be increased by the percentage increase in the medical care component of the consumer price index.

(g) The ALJ Hearing: These provisions provide that QICs, CMS, or CMS contractors may participate in the hearing process. Participation may include filing position papers with the ALJ, or providing testimony to clarify factual policy issues in a case. An ALJ will not have the authority to require CMS or a contractor to participate in a particular case, and cannot draw any inferences should the agency or contractor decide not to participate. In addition, the new rules allow CMS or its contractor to enter an appeal at the ALJ level as a party, unless an unrepresented beneficiary brings the appeal. In this circumstance, CMS or its contractor will have all the rights of a party, including the right to call witnesses, or cross-examine other witnesses, to submit additional evidence within the time frame specified by the ALJ, to seek MAC review of a decision adverse to CMS and to permit discovery. An ALJ is not required to send a notice of a hearing to a party who has not participated in the determinations below and whose liability status for the items or services in dispute has not been altered since the initial determination.

(h) Filing Requests for ALJ Hearing and MAC Review—Time and Place: Under the rule, an ALJ has 90 days to render a decision on a hearing from the date the request for a hearing was timely filed. The MAC also has 90 days from the date the hearing request is received to render a decision. An appellant has 60 days from the QIC's decision to make a request for a hearing with an ALJ.

13. Remand Authority (section 405.1034)

This section of the rule is intended to provide guidance concerning if and when an ALJ can remand a case to a contractor for further proceedings. The ALJ may remand a case to the QIC when the record provided to an ALJ lacks the technical information needed to resolve the case (or the ALJ may opt to retain jurisdiction). The ALJ will remand a case to the QIC when the ALJ decides that the QIC's dismissal of a request for reconsideration was improper.

14. When an ALJ Can Consolidate a Hearing (section 405.1044)

An ALJ may consolidate a hearing if one or more issues at the hearing are the same as those issues involved in another hearing before the same ALJ. The rules also permit an ALJ to grant or deny an appellant's request for consolidation based on factors such as the efficiency of consolidating the cases. The ALJ may also propose consolidation on his or her own, but cannot require an appellant to waive the adjudication deadline for any of the consolidated cases.

15. When an ALJ Can Dismiss a Request for a Hearing (section 405.1052)

An ALJ may dismiss a request for a hearing under the following conditions:

— If only one party requested the hearing and withdraws that request at any time before notice of the hearing decision is mailed

— Neither party that requested the hearing, nor the party's representative appears at the time and place the hearing was set without good cause

— The person or entity requesting a hearing has no right to it under section 405.1002

— The beneficiary whose claim is being appealed died while the request for hearing was pending and no other beneficiary with rights to pursue the request for hearing do so

— The ALJ dismisses a hearing request entirely or refuses to consider any one or more of the issues because a QIC, and ALJ or the MAC has made a previous decision on the same facts or claims for this appellant

— The appellant abandons the request for a hearing (i.e., the ALJ hearing office is unable to contact the appellant after making reasonable efforts to do so)

16. Content of an ALJ's Decision (section 405.1046)

The ALJ's decision must be written in a manner calculated to be understood by the beneficiary and must include the specific reasons for the decision, the procedures for obtaining additional information concerning the decision, and notification of the right to appeal the decisions and instructions on how to initiate such an appeal.

17. Appeals Involving Overpayments (section 405.1064)

When an appeal from the QIC involves an overpayment issue and the QIC used a statistical sample in reaching its reconsideration, the ALJ must base his or her decision on a review of the entire statistical sample used by the QIC.

18. Review by the MAC and Judicial Review (section 405.1100–section 405.1140)

The component of the Departmental Appeals Board that decides cases brought under this appeal rule is called the Medicare Appeals Council (MAC). A party to an ALJ hearing may request a MAC review if the party files a written request within 60 days of the ALJ's decision or dismissal. The new provisions direct the MAC to make a decision or remand a case to the ALJ within 90 days of a request for review for cases stemming from an ALJ's decision. Parties may request a review by the MAC if within 90 days of timely filing for an ALJ hearing, the ALJ has not issued a decision. For such escalation cases, the MAC has 180 days to issue a decision. CMS or any of its contractors may refer a case to the MAC if, in their view, the decision or dismissal contains an error of law affecting the outcome of the case, or if CMS participated in the appeal at the ALJ level and if in CMS's view the decision or dismissal is not supported by a preponderance of the evidence in the record.

Federal District Court Hearings

If at least $1,000 remains in controversy, judicial review before a federal district court judge can be considered. When appealing to this level, it is advisable that legal counsel be consulted.

The 10 Steps to the Appeals Process

1. File an appeal or complaint in writing. If the payer in question does not have a standard form that should be used, the following information should appear on the appeal letter:

   — Patient name

   — Policy number

   — Name and address of the provider

   — Date of the initial determination

   — Responsible party's name (insured)

   — Treatment dates

   — Dollar amount in question

2. Review the insured's evidence of coverage book or member handbook, which will include information on how to file an appeal within its deadlines. It will also indicate how soon you can expect a written acknowledgment. Further, it should explain the options at each stage of the appeals process.

3. Make sure you know the exact person, department, and address to whom the appeal should be sent. If you are concerned about meeting a specific deadline, send your appeal registered mail. This will provide proof that you filed on time.

4. Support your statements with facts and copies of the medical record, if applicable.

5. Be specific in what action you want the health plan to take.

6. Include in your appeal any supporting information you find, stating the source, the date, the page numbers, and any other details you believe are important to your case.

7. If you feel the need is urgent, ask for an expedited decision. In urgent situations, health plans must respond quickly, usually within 72 hours after receiving your appeal.

8. Base the claim's appeal not only on the billing guidelines, but also on the regulatory environment that the payer is required to follow.

9. Keep careful records of all interactions with the payer. Write down who said what, the date of the conversation, and the person's title and telephone number. Document everything.

10. Ask for decisions in writing. Always involve the patient and keep the patient informed of each step. Frequently, the patient's involvement may expedite a decision. Health plans want to keep their members happy.

Benefit Notices

Medicare Summary Notice

The Medicare summary notice (MSN) lists all claims filed during each month for each beneficiary. One type covers inpatient and outpatient facility services, another type includes all Part B physician and other services, and a third type covers durable medical equipment (DME). Each periodically carries messages pertinent to the beneficiary, such as the hotline for reporting fraud and abuse.

Remittance Advice/Explanation of Benefits

When a claim is paid, third-party payers, including Medicare, send an EOB or in the case of Medicare claims, an EOMB to both the provider and the patient informing them of their decisions. It is very important that the advice on these remittances be thoroughly reviewed as there are many messages that can tell you of problems with your claim.

The explanation of benefits (EOB) is the key to knowing what you were paid and why, but understanding what this document really means is sometimes not as easy as it sounds. An EOB has its own language: "applied to deductible," "above usual and customary," "patient co-pay," "allowable," and so on. Often hidden in this language is the explanation of what the patient is responsible for paying. Knowing how to read an EOB can help an office collect full reimbursement, including any balance owed by the patient.

Standard Remittance Remark Codes and Messages

There are three different classifications of codes:

- **Claim adjustment reason codes.** CAS Reason Codes show general reasons for claim financial adjustments such as denials, reductions, or increases in payments.

- **Remittance advice remark codes.** RA Remark Codes define service-specific Medicare remarks information.

- **Claim Status codes.** Medicare are used to convey appeal information and other claim-specific information that does not involve a financial adjustment.

Claim Adjustment Reason Codes

These reason codes report the reasons for any claim financial adjustments, such as denials, reductions, or increases in payment. Here are some of the most commonly seen standard claim adjustment (CAS) reason codes for claims:

1	Deductible amount.
2	Coinsurance amount.
3	Co-payment amount.
4	The procedure code is inconsistent with the modifier used, or a required modifier is missing.
5	The procedure code/bill type is inconsistent with the place of service.
6	The procedure/revenue code is inconsistent with the patient's age.
8	The procedure code is inconsistent with the provider type/specialty (taxonomy).
11	The diagnosis is inconsistent with the procedure.
12	The diagnosis is inconsistent with the provider type.

16 Claim/service lacks information which is needed for adjudication. At least one remark code must be provided (may be comprised of either the remittance advice remark code or NCPDP reject reason code).

18 Duplicate claim/service.

22 This care may be covered by another payer per coordination of benefits. *Last modified 4/1/2008.*

23 The impact of prior payer adjudication including payments and/or adjustments *Last modified 4/1/2008.*

24 Charges are covered under a capitation agreement/managed care plan. *Last modified 4/1/2008.*

50 These are noncovered services because this is not deemed a "medical necessity" by the payer.

56 Procedure/treatment has not been deemed "proven to be effective" by the payer. *Last modified 4/1/2008.*

59 Processed based on multiple or concurrent procedure rules. (For example multiple surgery or diagnostic imaging, concurrent anesthesia.) *Last modified 4/1/2008.*

60 Charges for outpatient services with this proximity to inpatient services are not covered.

85 Patient Interest Adjustment (Use Only Group code PR)
NOTE: Only use when the payment of interest is the responsibility of the patient.

96 Non-covered charge(s). At least one remark code must be provided (may be comprised of either the remittance advice remark code or NCPDP reject reason code).

97 The benefit for this service is included in the payment or allowance for another service/ procedure that has already been adjudicated. *Last modified 4/1/2008.*

100 Payment made to patient/insured/responsible party/employer.

125 Submission/billing error(s). At least one remark code must be provided (may be comprised of either the remittance advice remark code or NCPDP reject reason code).

150 Payer deems the information submitted does not support this level of service.

151 Payment adjusted because the payer deems the information submitted does not support this many/frequency of services.

152 Payer deems the information submitted does not support this length of service. *Last modified 4/1/2008.*

153 Payer deems the information submitted does not support this dosage. *Last modified 4/1/2008.*

154 Payer deems the information submitted does not support this day's supply. *Last modified 4/1/2008.*

206 National provider identifier—missing. *Last modified 4/1/2008.*

207 National provider identifier—invalid format *Last modified 4/1/2008.*

208 National provider identifier—not matched. *Last modified 4/1/2008.*

210 Payment adjusted because pre-certification/authorization not received in a timely fashion

213 Non-compliance with the physician self referral prohibition legislation or payer policy.

214 Workers' Compensation claim adjudicated as non-compensable. This payer not liable for claim or service/treatment. (**NOTE:** To be used for Workers' Compensation only)

215 Based on subrogation of a third party settlement

216 Based on the findings of a review organization

217 Based on payer reasonable and customary fees. No maximum allowable defined by legislated fee arrangement. (**NOTE:** To be used for Workers' Compensation only)

218 Based on entitlement to benefits (**NOTE:** To be used for Workers' Compensation only)

219 Based on extent of injury (**NOTE:** To be used for Workers' Compensation only)

220 The applicable fee schedule does not contain the billed code. Please resubmit a bill with the appropriate fee schedule code(s) that best describe the service(s) provided and supporting documentation if required. (**NOTE:** To be used for Workers' Compensation only)

221 Workers' compensation claim is under investigation. (**NOTE:** To be used for Workers' Compensation only. Claim pending final resolution)

B1 Non-covered visits.

B7 This provider was not certified/eligible to be paid for this procedure/service on this date of service.

B11 The claim/service has been transferred to the proper payer/processor for processing. Claim/service not covered by this payer/processor.

B12 Services not documented in patient's medical records.

B13 Previously paid. Payment for this claim/service may have been provided in a previous payment.

B14 Only one visit or consultation per physician per day is covered. *Last modified 4/1/2008.*

B15 This service/procedure requires that a qualifying service/procedure be received and covered. The qualifying other service/procedure has not been received/adjudicated. *Last modified 4/1/2008.*

B16 "New patient" qualifications were not met. *Last modified 4/1/2008.*

B22 This payment is adjusted based on the diagnosis.

Remittance Advice Remark Codes

Remark codes are used to relay service-specific Medicare informational messages that cannot be expressed with a reason code. These are some of the most common line level remark codes:

M2   Not paid separately when the patient is an inpatient.

M11   DME, orthotics and prosthetics must be billed to the DME carrier who services the patient's ZIP code.

M13   Only one initial visit is covered per specialty per medical group.

M15   Separately billed services/tests have been bundled as they are considered components of the same procedure. Separate payment is not allowed.

M20   Missing/incomplete/invalid HCPCS

M25   The information furnished does not substantiate the need for this level of service. If you believe the service should have been fully covered as billed, or if you did not know and could not reasonably have been expected to know that we would not pay for this level of service, or if you notified the patient in writing in advance that we would not pay for this level of service and he/she agreed in writing to pay, ask us to review your claim within 120 days of the date of this notice. If you do not request an appeal, we will, upon application from the patient, reimburse him/her for the amount you have collected from him/her for the in excess of any deductible and coinsurance amounts. We will recover the reimbursement from you as an overpayment.

M26   Information furnished does not substantiate the need for this level of service. If you have collected any amount from the patient for this level of service, any amount that exceeds the limiting charge for the less extensive service, the law requires you to refund that amount to the patient within 30 days of receiving this notice.

The requirements for refund are in 1824(l) of the Social Security Act and 2CFR411.408. The section specifies that physicians who knowingly and willfully fail to make appropriate refunds may be subject to civil monetary penalties and/or exclusion from the program. If you have any questions about this notice, please contact this office.

M39   **Alert:** The patient is not liable for payment for this service as the advance notice of noncoverage you provided the patient did not comply with program requirements.

M40   Claim must be assigned and must be filed by the practitioner's employer.

M51   Missing/incomplete/invalid procedure code(s).

M52   Missing/incomplete/invalid "from" date(s) of service.

M53   Missing/incomplete/invalid days or units of service.

M59   Missing/incomplete/invalid "to" date(s) of service.

M62   Missing/incomplete/invalid treatment authorization code.

M64   Missing/incomplete/invalid other diagnosis.

M67   Missing/incomplete/invalid other procedure code(s).

M69   Paid at the regular rate as you did not submit documentation to justify modiied procedure code.

M76   Missing/incomplete/invalid diagnosis or condition.

M77   Missing/incomplete/invalid place of service.

M79   Missing/incomplete/invalid charge.

M80   Not covered when performed during the same session/date as a previously processed service for the patient.

M81   You are required to code to the highest level of specificity.

M84   Medical code sets used must be the codes in effect at the time of service.

MA01 **Alert:** If you do not agree with what we approved for these services, you may appeal our decision. To make sure that we are fair to you, we require another individual that did not process your initial claim to conduct the appeal. However, in order to be eligible for an appeal, you must write to us within 120 days of the date you received this notice, unless you have a good reason for being late.

MA02 **Alert:** If you do not agree with this determination, you have the right to appeal. You must file a written request for an appeal within 180 days of the date you receive this notice.

MA04 Secondary payment cannot be considered without the identity of or payment information from the primary payer. The information was either not reported or was illegible.

MA07 **Alert:** The claim information has also been forwarded to Medicaid for review.

MA09 Claim submitted as unassigned but processed as assigned. You agreed to accept assignment for all claims.

MA10 **Alert:** The patient's payment was in excess of the amount owed. You must refund the overpayment to the patient.

MA18 **Alert:** The claim information is also being forwarded to the patient's supplemental insurer. Send any questions regarding supplemental benefits to them.

MA19 **Alert:** Information was not sent to the Medigap insurer due to incorrect/invalid information you submitted concerning that insurer. Please verify your information and submit your secondary claim directly to that insurer.

MA37 Missing/incomplete/invalid patient's address.

MA39 Missing/incomplete/invalid gender.

MA46 The new information was considered, however, additional payment cannot be issued. Please review the information listed for the explanation.

MA62 **Alert:** This is a telephone review decision.

MA67 Correction to a prior claim.

MA81 Missing/incomplete/invalid provider/supplier signature.

MA91 This determination is the result of the appeal you filed.

MA92 Missing plan information for other insurance.

© 2009 Ingenix

MA112 Missing/incomplete/invalid group practice information.

MA113 Incomplete/invalid taxpayer identification number (TIN) submitted by you per the Internal Revenue Service. Your claims cannot be processed without your correct TIN, and you may not bill the patient pending correction of your TIN There are no appeal rights for unprocessable claims, but you may resubmit this claim after you have notified this office of your correct TIN.

MA114 Missing/incomplete/invalid information on where the services were furnished.

MA130 Your claim contains incomplete and/or invalid information, and no appeal rights are afforded because the claim is unprocessable. Please submit a new claim with the complete/correct information.

N21 **Alert:** Your line item has been separated into multiple lines to expedite handling.

N22 This procedure code was added/changed because it more accurately describes the services rendered.

N23 **Alert:** Patient liability may be affected due to coordination of benefits with other carriers and/or maximum benefit provisions.

N29 Missing documentation/orders/notes/summary/report/chart.

N30 Patient ineligible for this service.

N31 Missing/incomplete/invalid prescribing provider identifier.

N56 Procedure code billed is not correct/valid for the services billed or the date of service billed.

N115 This decision was based on a local medical review policy (LMRP) or local coverage determination (LCD). An LMRP/LCD provides a guide to assist in determining whether a particular item or service is covered. A copy of this policy is available at http://www.cms.hhs.gov/mcd, or if you do not have web access, you may contact the contractor to request a copy of the LMRP/LCD.

N142 The original claim was denied. Resubmit a new claim, not a replacement claim.

N210 **Alert:** You may appeal this decision.

N211 **Alert:** You may not appeal this decision.

Claims Processing

Claim Status Codes

The following claim status codes are used by any payer using an electronic remittance advice (form 835):

0	Cannot provide further status electronically.
1	For more detailed information, see remittance advice.
2	More detailed information in letter.
3	Claim has been adjudicated and is awaiting payment cycle.
6	Balance due from the subscriber.
12	One or more originally submitted procedure codes have been combined.
15	One or more originally submitted procedure codes have been modified.
18	Entity received claim/encounter, but returned invalid status.
19	Entity acknowledges receipt of claim/encounter.
20	Accepted for processing.
21	Missing or invalid information. **NOTE:** At least one other status code is required to identify the missing or invalid information.
29	Subscriber and policy number/contract number mismatched.
30	Subscriber and subscriber ID mismatched.
31	Subscriber and policyholder name mismatched.
32	Subscriber and policy number/contract number not found.
33	Subscriber and subscriber id not found.
34	Subscriber and policyholder name not found.
35	Claim/encounter not found.
37	Predetermination is on file, awaiting completion of services.
38	Awaiting next periodic adjudication cycle.
40	Waiting for final approval.
41	Special handling required at payer site.
44	Charges pending provider audit.
45	Awaiting benefit determination.
46	Internal review/audit.
47	Internal review/audit—partial payment made.
49	Pending provider accreditation review.
50	Claim waiting for internal provider verification.
51	Investigating occupational illness/accident.
52	Investigating existence of other insurance coverage.
53	Claim being researched for insured ID/group policy number error.
54	Duplicate of a previously processed claim/line.
55	Claim assigned to an approver/analyst.
56	Awaiting eligibility determination.
65	Claim/line has been paid.
66	Payment reflects usual and customary charges.
67	Payment made in full.
78	Duplicate of an existing claim/line, awaiting processing.
84	Service not authorized.
86	Diagnosis and patient gender mismatch.
98	Charges applied to deductible.
107	Processed according to contract/plan provisions.
248	Accident date, state, description and cause.
249	Place of service.
670	Funds applied from a consumer spending account such as consumer-directed/driven health plan (CDHP), health savings account (HSA), and/or other similar accounts.
671	Funds may be available from a consumer spending account such as consumer-directed/ driven health plan (CDHP), health savings account (HSA), and or other similar accounts.

Group Codes

Group codes show financial liability for the amount of the adjustment or to identify a postinitial adjudication adjustment. The following are group codes that may be seen by a practice:

PR   Patient responsibility.

This group code signifies the amount that may be billed to the beneficiary or to another payer on the beneficiary's behalf. Providers may be subject to penalties if they bill a patient for charges not identified with the PR group code.

CO   Contractual obligations.

This group code includes any amounts for which the provider is financially liable, such as participation agreement violations, assignment amount violations, excess charges by a managed care plan provider, late filing penalties, Gramm-Rudman reductions, or medical necessity denials/reductions. The patient may not be billed for these amounts.

OA   Other adjustment.

This group code would only be used if neither PR nor CO applied.

CR   Correction to or reversal of a prior decision.

This group code applies whenever there is a change to a previously adjudicated claim. CR explains the reason for the correction.

CMS-1500

Purpose of CMS-1500 Claim Form

The CMS-1500 claim form was developed based on a format that was standard among private insurers and approved in 1983. It is the basic form prescribed by CMS for Medicare claims from physicians and suppliers, except for ambulance services. The CMS-1500 form has been adopted by the Office of Civilian Health and Medical Program of the Uniformed Services (TRICARE), and received the approval of the American Medical Association Council on Medical Services. The CMS-1500 is also the format of choice for third-party payers. Claims not containing the required information may be denied of rejected.

Claims Processing

If claims are not filed in a timely manner, cash flow will suffer. Eliminate, or at least try, to decrease potential problems. Consider the following:

- CMS regularly revises the information required on the claims form. Watch the *Federal Register* for these changes and make the necessary adjustments. For example, modify office computerized billing systems to meet claim form requirements. Gather any additional information CMS requires and enter it into patient demographic screens.

- Modify patient information sheets to accommodate additional data.

- Patients may be reluctant to provide such detailed information without understanding the claim requirements. Physicians should designate an office insurance specialist who can assist patients in completing the form and explain the need for extra information.

Payers are required to have the capability to receive claims electronically, according to HIPAA. Those who had to comply include all health plans, all payers, and all clearinghouses that process health data. Small health plans and workers' compensation are exempt at this time.

The legislation affects the following transactions:

- Health claims and equivalent encounter information (such as dental)
- Coordination of benefits (COB)
- Enrollment in a health plan
- Terminating participation in a health plan
- Health care payment and remittance advice
- Health plan premium payments
- First report of injury
- Health claim status
- Referral certification and authorization

How to Complete the CMS-1500 Form
The most recent revision to the CMS-1500 form is the 08/05, which replaced the 12/90 form effective April 2, 2007, and is the only form to be used for Medicare claims. At the current time, it is unknown when other third-party payers will require the use of the CMS-1500 (08/05). Most of the changes were made to the form to accommodate the implementation of the national provider identifier (NPI). Effective May 23, 2008, all identifiers submitted on the Form CMS-1500 are required to be in the form of an NPI.

CMS requires reporting of eight-digit birth dates (items 3, 9b, and 11a), and either six-digit or eight-digit dates in all other date fields (items 11b, 12, 14, 16, 18, 19, 24a, and 31). Providers of service and suppliers have the option of entering either six- or eight-digit dates in items 11b, 14, 16, 18, 19, or 24a; however, if a provider of service or supplier chooses to enter eight-digit dates for items 11b, 14, 16, 18, 19, or 24a, he or she must enter eight-digit dates for all these fields.

Items 19 and 23 have been limited to the amount and type of information reported in these fields. Only information listed in the specific instructions for items 19 and 23 can be reported in items 19 and 23. Item 19 can contain up to three conditions per claim, item 23 can contain only one condition. If a claim meets more

than three of the stated conditions in item 19, additional conditions must be reported on a separate CMS-1500 form. For item 23, any additional conditions must be reported on a separate CMS-1500 form.

Step-by-Step Claim Completion
The following section provides instructions for completing the CMS-1500 (08-05) form.

Items 1-13—Patient and Insured Information
Item 1: **This is a required item.** Show the type of health insurance coverage applicable to this claim by checking the appropriate box (e.g., if a Medicare claim is being filed, check the Medicare box).

Item 1a: **This is a required item.** Enter the insured's health insurance claim number (HICN) or dependent patient unique identification number, if applicable, as shown on the patient's ID card.

For workers' compensation claims, enter the employer's ID number.

Item 2: **This is a required item.** Enter the insured's last name, first name, and middle initial, if any, as shown on the patient's Medicare or insurance card.

If the patient has a last name suffix (e.g., Jr., Sr.), enter it after the last name, but before the first name. Titles (e.g., Sister, Capt., Dr.) and professional suffixes (e.g., PhD, MD, Esq.) should not be used. Commas should be used to separate the last name, first name, and middle initial. A hyphen may be used for hyphenated names. Do not use periods within the name.

Alert: Be certain the name appears as it does on the patient's card, as some patients go by their middle name or a nickname. Also, check the spelling; a simple transposition of letters can result in denial or suspension of the claim.

Item 3: **This is a required item.** Enter the patient's eight-digit birth date (MM | DD | CCYY). Place an "X" in the appropriate box indicating the patient's sex. If sex is unknown, leave blank.

Item 4: Enter the insured's full last name, first name, and middle initial. If the insured has a last name suffix (e.g., Jr., SR), enter it after the last name, but before the first name. Titles (e.g., Sister, Capt., Dr.) and professional suffixes (e.g., PhD, MD, Esq.) should not be used. Use commas to separate the last name, first name, and middle initial. A hyphen can be used for hyphenated names. Do not use periods within the name. For workers' compensation claims, enter the employer's name.

If the patient or their spouse has an insurance plan primary to Medicare, list the name of that insured here. When the insured and the patient are the same, enter the word SAME. Leave blank if Medicare is primary.

Item 5: **This is a required item.** Enter the patient's mailing address and telephone number, including area code. On the first line enter the street address; the second line, the city and state; the third line, the ZIP code and phone number.

Do not use commas, periods, or other punctuation in the address (e.g., 123 N Main Street 101 instead of 123 N. Main Street, #101). When entering a nine-digit ZIP code, include the hyphen. Do not use a hyphen or space as a separator within the telephone number.

837p Alert: The telephone field does not exist in the electronic Professional 4010A1.

Alert: Verify the demographic information. The patient's address may *not* be the same as the insured's, a common cause of delayed payment.

Alert: If this is a foreign address, contact the payer for specific reporting instructions.

Item 6: Check the appropriate box for patient's relationship to insured when item 4 is completed. This is a situational item. It must be completed if item 4 contains any information. Remember, the patient's relationship to the insured is not always "self."

Item 7: Enter the insured's address and telephone number. When the address is the same as the patient's, enter the word SAME. This is a situational item.

Do not use commas, periods, or other punctuation in the address (e.g., 123 N Main Street 101 instead of 123 N. Main Street, #101). When entering a nine-digit ZIP code, include the hyphen. Do not use a hyphen or space as a separator within the telephone number. For workers' compensation claims, enter the employer's address.

For Medicare claims, a nine-digit ZIP code is required.

Alert: Complete this item only when item 4 is completed.

837p Alert: The patient's telephone number does not exist in the electronic 837 Professional 4010A1.

Alert: If this is a foreign address, contact the payer for specific reporting instructions.

Item 8: **This is a required item.** Check the appropriate box for the patient's marital status and whether the patient is employed or a student.

Alert: This information relates to item 6.

If "spouse" is checked as the relationship to the insured, and then "single" is marked under patient status, chances are good that the payer's claim editing systems will suspend the claim until a correction is made.

837p Alert: Patient status does not exist in the electronic 837 Professional 4010A1.

Item 9: **This item is situational.** If item number 11d is marked, complete fields 9 and 9a-d, otherwise leave blank. When additional group health coverage exists, enter other insured's full last name, first name, and middle initial of the enrollee in another health plan if it is different from that shown in item number 2. If the insured uses a last name suffix (e.g., Jr., Sr.), enter it after the last name and before the first name. Titles (e.g., Sister, Capt., Dr.) and professional suffixes (e.g., PhD, MD, Esq.) should not be included with the name. Use commas to separate the last name, first

name, and middle initial. A hyphen can be used for hyphenated names. Do not use periods within the name.

Alert: Participating providers and suppliers must complete this section when the patient has Medigap benefits. If no Medigap benefits are assigned, leave blank. The item may be used in the future for supplemental insurance plans. Do not list other supplemental coverage in item 9 and its subdivisions at the time a Medicare claim is filed. Other supplemental claims are forwarded automatically to the private insurer if the private insurer contracts with the carrier to send Medicare claim information electronically. If there is no such contract, the patient must file his or her own supplemental claim.

Item 9a: **This item is situational.** Enter the policy or group number of the other insured.

For Medigap, enter the policy and/or group number of the Medigap insured preceded by MEDIGAP, MG, or MGAP. Item 9d must be completed, even when the provider enters a policy and/or group number in Item 9a.

Item 9b: **This item is situational.** Enter the eight-digit date of birth (MM|DD|CCYY) of the other insured and an X to indicate the sex of the other insured. Only one box can be marked. If gender is unknown, leave blank.

Item 9c: **This item is situational.** Enter the employer's name or school name. This must be completed when item 8 shows that the patient is employed and/or a student.

For Medigap, leave blank if the Medigap Payer ID is entered in Item 9d. Otherwise, enter the claims address for the Medigap insurer. Use an abbreviated street address, two-letter postal code, and ZIP code as shown on the insured's Medigap ID card.

837p Alert: Employer's name and school name do not exist in the electronic 837p Professional 4010A1.

Item 9d: **This item is situational.** Enter the other insured's insurance plan or program name.

For Medigap, enter the nine-digit PAYERID number of the Medigap insurer. When no PAYERID exists, enter the Medigap insurance program or plan name.

In order for Medicare payment data to be forwarded to a Medigap insurer via the claim-based crossover process, the participating provider of service or supplier must accurately complete all of the requested information in items 9, 9a, 9b, and 9d.

Medicare participating providers and suppliers should only enter the COBA Medigap claim-based ID in item 9d when they wish to have the beneficiary's claim cross over to a Medigap insurer. If the provider or supplier does NOT provide this information, Part B contractor or DMEAC will not be able to forward the claim information to the Medigap insurer prior to October 1, 2007 or to the Coordination of Benefits Contractor (COBC) for transfer to the Medicare insurer on or after October 1, 2007.

Item 10a: **This is a required item.** Enter an X in the correct box to indicate whether one or more of the services described in item number 24 are for a condition or injury that occurred on the job or as a result of an

Claims Processing

automobile or other accident. Only one box on each line can be marked. Primary insurance information must then be shown in item number 11.

Item 10b: **This is a required item.** Check "YES" or "NO" to indicate whether the encounter is due to an illness or injury that is related to an auto accident. The state postal code must be shown if "YES" is marked in 10b for "Auto Accident." Any item marked "YES" indicates there may be other applicable insurance coverage that would be primary, such as automobile liability insurance. Primary insurance information must then be shown in item number 11.

Item 10c: **This is a required item.** Check "YES" or "NO" to indicate whether the encounter is due to an illness or injury that is related to other accident involvement. Any item marked "YES" indicates there may be other applicable insurance coverage that would be primary, such as automobile liability insurance. Primary insurance information must then be shown in item number 11.

Alert: Identify primary insurance information in item 11.

Item 10d: **This item is situational.** Refer to the most current instructions from the applicable public or private payer regarding the use of this field. When required by payers to provide a sub-set of Condition Codes approved by the NUCC, enter the condition code in this field. For workers' compensation claims, condition codes are required when submitting a duplicate claim or an appeal. The original reference number must be indicated in item 22. Condition codes should **not** be used when submitting a revised or corrected claim.

For Medicaid claims, use this field exclusively for Medicaid (MCD) information. If the patient is entitled to Medicaid, enter the Medicaid number preceded by the letters MCD.

Item 11: **This is a required item.** Enter the insured's policy, group, or FECA number as it appears on the insured's health care identification card. If item number 4 is completed, then this field should be completed. For workers' compensation claims, the workers' compensation claim number as assigned by the payer should be entered.

Do not use a hyphen in the insurer's group number.

The FECA number is a nine-digit alphanumeric identifier assigned to a patient claiming work-related condition(s) under the Federal Employees Compensation Act 5 USC 8101.

For Medicare claims, this item is a required field. In completing this item, the physician/supplier is acknowledging that a good faith effort has been made to determine whether Medicare is the primary or secondary payer.

If there is insurance primary to Medicare, enter the insured's policy or group number and proceed to items 11a-11c, as well as items 4, 6, and 7. When there is no other insurance primary to Medicare, enter the word "NONE" in this field and proceed to 11b.

Circumstances under which Medicare payment may be secondary to other insurance include:

- Group health plan coverage
  - working aged
  - disability (large group health plan)
  - end-stage renal disease (ESRD)
- No fault and/or other liability
- Work-related illness/injury
  - workers' compensation
  - black lung
  - veterans' benefits

Item 11a: Enter the insured's eight-digit birth date (MM | DD | CCYY) and sex if different from that in item 3.

Item 11b: Enter the employer's name, if applicable. If there is a change in the insured's insurance status (e.g., retired), enter a six-digit (MM | DD | YY) or eight-digit (MM | DD | CCYY) retirement date preceded by the word "RETIRED."

Enter the employer's name or school name. This must be completed when item 8 shows that the patient is employed and/or a student.

837p Alert: Employer's name and school name do not exist in the electronic 837 Professional 4010A1.

Item 11c: Enter the insurance plan or program name of the insured. Some payers may require an identification number of the primary insurer rather than the name in this field.

For Medigap, enter the nine-digit PAYERID number of the primary insurer. If there is no PAYERID number, enter the complete primary payer's program or plan name.

If the primary payer's EOB does not contain the claims processing address, record the primary payer's claims processing address directly onto the EOB. This is required when there is insurance primary to Medicare indicated in Item 11.

Item 11d: **This item is situational.** "Is there another health benefit plan" indicates that the patient has insurance coverage other than the plan indicated in item number 1. When appropriate, enter an X in the correct box. If marked "YES," complete 9 and 9a–d. Only one box can be marked.

This item is not required by Medicare and should be left blank for Medicare claims.

Item 12: **This is a required item.** The patient or authorized representative must sign and enter a six-digit date (MM | DD | YY), eight-digit date (MM | DD | CCYY), or an alphanumeric date (e.g., January 1, 1998) unless the signature is on file. If the patient is physically or mentally unable to sign, a representative may sign on the patient's behalf. In this event, the statement's signature line must indicate the patient's name followed by the word "by" and the representative's name, address, and relationship to the patient, as well as stating the reason the patient cannot sign. The authorization is effective indefinitely unless the patient or the patient's representative revokes this arrangement.

Claims Processing

In lieu of signing the claim, the patient may sign a statement to be retained by the provider, physician, or supplier.

The patient's signature authorizes release of medical information necessary to process the claim. It also authorizes payment of benefits to the provider of service or supplier when the provider of service or supplier accepts assignment on the claim.

Signature on File

This can be "Signature on File" and/or a computer generated signature.

Signature by Mark (X)

When an illiterate or physically handicapped enrollee signs by mark, a witness must enter his or her name and address next to the mark.

Item 13: **This is a required item.** The signature in this item authorizes payment to the participating physician or supplier. The patient or his or her authorized representative signs this item or the signature must be on file as a separate authorization.

Enter "Signature on File," "SOF," or legal signature. If there is no signature on file, leave this item blank or enter "No Signature on File."

Alert: The assignment on file in the participating provider of service/supplier's office should be insurer specific. It may state the authorization applies to all occasions of service until it is revoked.

Items 14-33—Provider of Service or Supplier Information

Item 14: **This is a required item.** Enter an eight-digit (MM | DD | CCYY) or six-digit (MM | DD | YY) date of current illness, injury, or pregnancy.

Alert: Many payers require for chiropractic services, an eight-digit (MM | DD | CCYY) or six-digit (MM | DD | YY) date of the initiation of the course of treatment be entered, and an eight-digit (MM | DD | CCYY) or six-digit (MM | DD | YY) service date be entered in item 19.

Item 15: Enter the first date the patient had the same or a similar illness. Enter the date in the six-digit (MM | DD | YY) or eight-digit format (MM | DD | CCYY). Previous pregnancies are not a similar illness. Leave blank if unknown.

This item is not required by Medicare and should be left blank for Medicare claims.

Item 16: If the patient is employed and is unable to work in his or her current occupation, enter an eight-digit (MM | DD | CCYY) or six-digit (MM | DD | YY) date when the patient is unable to work. This is a situational item. Many workers' compensation payers and other personal injury protection (PIP) insurers require this item to be completed. It is not a required item for Medicare claims.

Alert: An entry in this item may indicate employment-related insurance coverage.

Item 17: Enter the name (first name, middle initial, last name) and credentials of the professional who referred,

ordered, or supervised the service(s) or supply(s) on the claim.

If multiple providers are involved, enter one provider using the following priority order:

1. Referring Provider
2. Ordering Provider
3. Supervising Provider

Do not use periods or commas within the name. A hyphen can be used for hyphenated names.

For Medicare, when a claim involves multiple referring and/or ordering physicians, a separate CMS-1500 form must be used for each referring/ordering physician.

Medicare defines "referring" and "ordering" as shown below:

A **referring physician** is a physician who requests an item or service for the patient for which payment may be made under the Medicare program.

An **ordering physician** is a physician or, when appropriate, a nonphysician practitioner who orders nonphysician services for the patient such as diagnostic laboratory tests, clinical laboratory tests, pharmaceutical services, durable medical equipment, and services incident to a physician's or nonphysician practitioner's service.

Item 17a: Report the other ID number of the referring, ordering, or supervising provider in the shaded area of this field. The qualifier indicating what the number represents should be reported to the immediate right of 17a.

For Medicare claims, this field is not reported; however, 17b must be reported when services are ordered or referred by a physician.

Item 17b: Enter the NPI of the referring/ordering physician listed in item 17.

For Medicare claims, all physicians who order services or refer beneficiaries must report this data.

Item 18: Enter an eight-digit (MM | DD | CCYY) or a six-digit (MM | DD | YY) hospital admission date followed by the discharge date (if discharge has occurred). If the patient has not been discharged, leave the date blank. This date is when a medical service is furnished as a result of, or subsequent to, a related hospitalization.

Item 19: This item is reserved for local use. Please refer to the most current instructions from the applicable public or private payer regarding the use of this field. Some payers ask for certain identifiers in this field. If identifiers are reported in this field, enter the appropriate qualifiers describing the identifier. Do not enter a space, hyphen, or other separator between the qualifier code and the number.

When reporting a second item of data, enter three blank spaces and the next qualifier and number/code/information.

For workers' compensation: This information is required based on Jurisdictional Workers' Compensation guidelines.

When reporting Supplemental Claim Information, use qualifier PWK for data, followed by the appropriate Report Type Code, the appropriate Transmission Type Code, and then the Attachment Control Number. No spaces should be entered between the qualifiers and the data.

The NUCC defines the following qualifiers, since they are the same as those used in the electronic 837 Professional 4010A1:

Report type code

PN   Physical therapy notes
PO   Prosthetics or orthotic certification
PZ   Physical therapy certification

Transmission type code

AA   Available on request at provider site
BM   By mail
EL   Electronically only (use to indicate that attachment is being transmitted electronically)
EM   E-mail
FX   By fax

Example: PWK77FX12363545465

For Medicare claims, the following guidelines apply: enter a six- or eight-digit date when the patient was last seen and the NPI of the attending physician when a physician providing routine foot care submits claims.

For physical therapy, occupational therapy, or speech-language pathology services, effective for claims with dates of service on or after June 6, 2005, the date the patient was last seen and the NPI of the ordering/referring/attending/certifying physician or provider is NOT required. However, should this information be submitted voluntarily, it is imperative that it be correct or it causes claim rejection or denial. Those therapy services provided "incident to" the services of a physician or nonphysician provider are still subject to the normal "incident to" policies.

Item 20: Complete this item when billing for purchased services entering an X in "yes." A "yes" check indicates that the service performed was by an entity other than the billing provider (e.g., services subject to Medicare's anti-markup rule). A "no" check or blank field indicates that no purchased services are included on the claim. When "yes" is annotated, enter the purchase price in item 32.

When entering the charge amount, enter the dollar amount to the left of the vertical line. Enter 00 for cents when the amount is a whole number. Do not use commas or decimal points when reporting dollar amounts. Negative dollar amounts are not allowed. Dollar signs should not be entered.

For Medicare claims, billing for multiple purchased diagnostic tests requires each test to be submitted on a separate CMS-1500. Multiple purchased tests may be submitted on the ASC X12 837 electronic format as long as appropriate line-level information is submitted when services are rendered at different service facility locations.

Item 21: **This is a required item.** Enter the patient's diagnosis/condition. No more than four ICD-9-CM codes should be listed. The highest level of code specificity should be used. Relate codes to item 24e by line number.

When entering the number, include a space (accommodated by the period) between the two sets of numbers. If entering a code with more than three beginning digits (e.g., E codes), enter the fourth digit above the period.

For Medicare claims, all physician and nonphysician specialties (i.e., PA, NP, CNS, CRNA) must use an ICD-9-CM code number and code to the highest level of specificity for the date of service with the exception of claims submitted by ambulance suppliers (specialty type 59). Enter up to four codes in priority order (primary, secondary condition). All narrative diagnoses for nonphysician specialties should be submitted on an attachment.

Item 22: List the original reference number for resubmitted claims. Please refer to the most current instructions from the applicable public or private payer regarding the use of this field (e.g., code).

When resubmitting a claim, enter the appropriate bill frequency code left justified in the left-hand side of the field, including:

7   Replacement of prior claim
8   Void/cancel of prior claim

This item number is not intended for use with original claims submissions.

For Medicare claims, leave blank as this field is not required by Medicare.

Item 23: Enter any of the following: prior authorization number or referral number as assigned by the payer for the current service, mammography precertification number, or Clinical Laboratory Improvement Amendment (CLIA) number. Do not enter hyphens or spaces within the number.

For workers' compensation, item 23 is required when a prior authorization, referral, concurrent review, or voluntary certification was received.

For Medicare claims, enter any of the following as applicable:

- A Quality Improvement Organization (QIO) prior authorization number for any procedure that requires QIO prior approval.
- An Investigational Device Exemption (IDE) number when an investigational device is used in an FDA-approved clinical trial. In addition, a Post Market Approval number should be reported here when applicable.
- For those physicians who perform care plan oversight services, the six-digit Medicare provider number or NPI of the home health agency or hospice when billing HCPCS code G0181 (HH) or G0182 (Hospice).
- A 10-digit CLIA certification number for laboratory services billed by any entity performing CLIA-covered services.

Alert: Item 23 can contain only one condition. Any additional conditions should be reported on a separate CMS-1500.

Item 24: The six service lines in section 24 of the CMS-1500 (08/05) have been divided horizontally so that both the NPI and legacy identifier may be submitted during the NPI transition and to accommodate the submission of supplemental information to support the billed service. The top portion in each of the six service lines is shaded and is the location for reporting supplemental information. It is not intended to allow the billing of 12 service lines.

For Medicaid rebates, NDC drug and quantity information is required and should be reported with the NDC code entered in the red shaded portion of the detail line item in positions 01-13. The NDC should be preceded with qualifier N4 and immediately followed by the 11-digit NDC code. NDC quantities are to be entered in positions 17-24 of the same red shaded area. Quantities entered will be preceded by the appropriate qualifier UN (units), F2 (international units), GR (gram), or ML (milliliter). Six bytes are available for quantity but for quantities less than six bytes, left justify and blank space should fill the remaining positions.

Item 24A: **This is a required item.** Enter date(s) of service, from and to. If there is only one date of service, enter the date under "From" and leave "To" blank or re-enter "From" date. If grouping services, the place of service, procedure code, charges, and individual provider for each line must be identical for that service line. Grouping is allowed only for services on consecutive days. The number of days must correspond to the number of units in 24G.

When required by payers to provide additional anesthesia services information (e.g., beginning and end times), narrative description of an unspecified code, NDC, VP-HIBCC codes, OZ-GTIN codes, contract rate, or tooth numbers and areas of the oral cavity, enter the applicable qualifier and number/code/information starting with the first space in the shaded line of this field. Do not enter a space, hyphen, or other separator between the qualifier and the number/code/information. The information may extend to 24G.

For Medicare claims this is a required field. A six- or eight-digit date for each procedure, service, or supply should be entered for this item. When a series of identical services are reported with "from" and "to" dates shown, enter the total number of days or units in column G.

Claims with a date of service extending more than one day but missing a valid "to" date will be returned as unprocessable.

Item 24B: **This is a required item.** Enter the appropriate place-of-service code(s) from the list in appendix 9. Identify the location, using a place-of-service code, for each item used or service performed.

Item 24C: This item number was originally titled "Type of Service" and "Type of Service" is no longer used so it has been eliminated. Check with trading partner to determine if this element (emergency indicator) is necessary. If required, enter Y for "YES" or leave blank if "NO" in the bottom, unshaded area of the field. The definition of emergency would be defined by federal or state regulations or programs, payer contracts, or as defined in the electronic 837 Professional 4010A1 implementation guide.

For Medicare claims, leave blank as this field is not required to be completed by Medicare providers.

Item 24D: **This is a required item.** Enter the procedures, services, or supplies using a CPT or HCPCS Level II code. When applicable, include modifiers with the code.

Enter the specific procedure code without a narrative description. Up to four, two-digit modifiers may be indicated on the claim.

For Medicare claims with an "unlisted procedure code" or a "not otherwise classified (NOC) code," include a narrative description in item 19 if a coherent description can be provided within the confines of the box; if not, an attachment must be submitted with the claim. Return any claims as unprocessable if an unlisted procedure code is indicated in item 24d but an accompanying narrative is not present in item 19 or on an attachment.

Item 24E: **This is a required item.** Enter the diagnosis code reference number (pointer) as shown in item 21 to relate the date of service and the procedures performed to the primary diagnosis. When multiple diagnoses are related to one service, the reference number for the primary diagnosis should be listed first; other applicable diagnosis reference numbers should follow. The reference number(s) should be a 1, 2, 3, 4, or multiple numbers as explained. ICD-9-CM diagnosis codes must be entered in item 21 only. Do not enter them in 24E.

For Medicare claims, providers should reference only one of the diagnoses in item 21 in those situations in which two or more diagnoses are required for a procedure code (e.g., pap smears).

Item 24F: **This is a required item.** Enter the charge for each listed service. Enter number right justified in the dollar area of the field. Do not use commas when reporting dollar amounts. Negative dollar amounts are not permitted. Dollars signs should not be entered. Enter 00 in the cents area if the amount is a whole number.

Item 24G: **This is a required item.** Enter the number of days or units. This field is most commonly used for multiple visits, units of supplies, anesthesia units or minutes, or oxygen volume. If only one service is performed, the numeral 1 must be entered.

Enter numbers right justified in the field. No leading zeros are required. If reporting a fraction of a unit, use the decimal point.

Medicare requires this field to contain at least one day or unit.

Item 24H: For Early and Periodic Screening, Diagnosis, and Treatment (EPSDT) related services.

Claims Processing

For Medicare claims, leave blank as this field is not required by Medicare.

Item 24I: Enter the qualifier identifying if the number is a non-NPI in the shaded area of this item. The other ID number of the rendering provider is reported in the shaded area of 24j.

The NUCC defines the following qualifiers, since they are the same as those used in the electronic 837 Professional 4010A1:

    0B   State License Number

    1B   Blue Shield Provider Number

    1C   Medicare Provider Number

    1D   Medicaid Provider Number

    1G   Provider UPIN Number

    1H   CHAMPUS Identification Number

    EI   Employer's Identification Number

    G2   Provider Commercial Number

    LU   Location NumberN5 Provider Plan Network Identification Number

    SY   Social Security Number (The social security number may not be used for Medicare.)

    X5   State Industrial Accident Provider Number

    ZZ   Provider Taxonomy

The aforementioned list contains provider identifiers, as well as the provider taxonomy code. The provider identifiers are assigned to the provider by a specific payer or by a third party in order to uniquely identify the provider. Taxonomy codes are designated by providers to identify his or her provider type, classification, and/or area of specialization. Both provider identifiers and provider taxonomy codes may be used in this field.

The rendering provider is the person or company (laboratory or other facility) who rendered or supervised the care. In the case where a substitute provider (locum tenens) was used, enter that provider's information here. Report the identification number in items 24I and 24J only when different from data recorded in items 33a and 33b.

For Medicare claims, enter the ID qualifier 1C in the shaded portion of this item.

Item 24J: **This is a required item.** The individual rendering the service is reported in 24J.The original fields for 24j and 24 k have been combined and renumbered as 24j. Enter the non-NPI ID number in the shaded area of the field. Enter the NPI number in the unshaded area of the field.

The rendering provider is the person or company (laboratory or other facility) who rendered or supervised the care. In the case where a substitute provider (locum tenens) was used, enter that provider's information here. Report the identification number in items 24I and 24J only when different from data recorded in items 33a and 33b.

For Medicare claims, enter the rendering provider's NPI in the lower, unshaded area. In the case of a service provided "incident to" the service of a physician or non-physician provider, when the person who ordered the service is not supervising, enter the NPI of the supervisor in the lower, unshaded area. As of May 23, 2008, the shaded portion of this item is no longer to be reported.

Item 25: **This is a required item.** Enter the federal tax ID number (employer identification number or social security number) of the billing provider identified in item 33. This is the tax ID number intended to be used for 1099 reporting purposes. Enter an X in the appropriate box to indicate which number is being reported. Only one box may be marked.

For Medicare claims, providers are not required to complete this item for crossover purposes since the Medicare contractor will retrieve the tax identification information from their internal provider file for inclusion on the COB outbound claim. However, tax ID information is used in the determination of accurate NPI reimbursement. Thus, reimbursement of claims submitted without this information will/may be delayed.

Item 26: **This item is situational.** Enter the patient's account number assigned by the service provider's or supplier's accounting system.

For Medicare claims, this item is optional to help the provider identify the patient. As a service, any account numbers entered here will be returned to the provider.

Item 27: **This is a required item.** Check the appropriate block to indicate whether the provider of service or supplier accepts assignment under the terms of the Medicare program

For Medicare claims, if Medigap is indicated in item 9 and Medigap payment authorization is given in item 13, the provider of service or supplier should also be a Medicare participating provider of service or supplier and accept assignment of Medicare benefits for all covered charges for all patients.

Item 28: **This is a required item.** Enter total charges for the services (i.e., total of all charges in item 24F). Enter number right justified in the dollar area of the field. Do not use commas when reporting dollar amounts. Negative dollar amounts are not allowed and dollar signs should not be entered. When the amount is a whole number, enter 00 in the cents area.

Item 29: **This is a required item.** Enter the total amount the patient and/or other payers paid on the covered services only.

Item 30: Enter the total amount due. Enter number right justified in the dollar area of the field. Do not use commas when reporting dollar amounts. Negative dollar amounts are not allowed and dollar signs should not be entered. When the amount is a whole number, enter 00 in the cents area.

837p Alert: Balance due does not exist in the electronic 837 Professional 4010A1.

Alert: For Medicare claims, leave blank as this field is not required by Medicare.

Item 31: **This is a required item.** Enter the legal signature of the practitioner or supplier, signature of the practitioner or supplier representative, "Signature on File," or "SOF." Enter either the six- or eight-digit date or alphanumeric date the form was signed.

837p Alert: Signature of physician or supplier including degrees or credential does not exist in the electronic 837 Professional 4010A1.

Alert: For Medicare claims, please note that in the case of a service that is provided incident to the service of a physician or nonphysician practitioner, when the ordering physician or nonphysician practitioner is directly supervising the service as in 42 CFR 410.32, the signature of the ordering physician or nonphysician practitioner shall be entered in item 31. When the ordering physician or nonphysician practitioner is not supervising the service, enter the signature of the physician or nonphysician practitioner providing the direct supervision in item 31.

Furthermore, although this is a required item, the claim can be processed if any of the following is true: A physician, supplier, or authorized person's signature is missing, but the signature is on file; an authorization is attached to the claim, or the signature item has "Signature on File" and/or a computer-generated signature.

Item 32: **This is a required item.** Enter the name, address, and ZIP code of the location where the services were rendered. Providers of service (namely physicians) must identify the supplier's name, address, ZIP code, and NPI number when billing for purchased diagnostic tests. When more than one supplier is used, a separate 1500 Claim Form should be used to bill for each supplier.

Enter the name and address information in the following format:

1st Line—Name

2nd Line—Address

3rd Line—City, State, and ZIP Code

Do not use commas, periods, or other punctuation in the address (e.g., 123 N Main Street 101 instead of 123 N. Main Street, #101). Enter a space between town name and state code; do not include a comma. When entering a nine-digit ZIP code, include the hyphen.

If a foreign address is provided, contact payer for specific reporting instructions.

For Medicare claims, the following applies:

Only one name, address, and ZIP code may be entered in this field. If additional entries are needed, separate CMS-1500 claim forms must be submitted.

For foreign claims, only the enrollee can file for Part B benefits rendered outside of the United States. These claims will not include a valid ZIP code. The contractor processing the foreign claim will follow instructions provided in chapter 1 of Pub.100-04

Claims Processing Manual for proper disposition of the claim.

Item 32a: Enter the NPI of the service facility.

For Medicare claims, if required by Medicare claims processing policy, enter the NPI of the service facility.

Item 32b: Enter the two-digit qualifier identifying the non-NPI number followed by the ID number. Do not enter a space, hyphen, or other separator between the qualifier and number.

The NUCC defines the following qualifiers, since they are the same as those used in the electronic 837 Professional 4010A1:

0B State License Number
1A Blue Cross Provider Number
1B Blue Shield Provider Number
1C Medicare Provider Number
1D Medicaid Provider Number
1G Provider UPIN Number
1H CHAMPUS Identification Number
G2 Provider Commercial Number
LU Location Number
N5 Provider Plan Network Identification Number
TJ Federal Taxpayer's Identification Number
X4 Clinical Laboratory Improvement Amendment Number
X5 State Industrial Accident Provider Number
ZZ Provider Taxonomy

The above list contains provider identifiers, as well as the provider taxonomy code. The provider identifiers are assigned to the provider by a specific payer or by a third party in order to uniquely identify the provider. Taxonomy codes are designated by providers to identify his or her provider type, classification, and/or area of specialization. Both provider identifiers and provider taxonomy codes may be used in this field.

For Medicare claims, leave blank as this field is not required by Medicare.

Item 33: **This is a required item.** Enter the provider's or supplier's billing name, address, ZIP code, and telephone number. The phone number is to be entered in the area to the right of the field title.

Enter the name and address information in the following format:

1st Line—Name

2nd Line—Address

3rd Line—City, State, and ZIP Code

This field identifies the provider who is requesting payment for services rendered and should always be completed.

Item 33a: **This is a required item.** Enter the NPI of the billing provider or group.

Item 33b: Enter the two-digit qualifier identifying the non-NPI number followed by the ID number. Do not enter a space, hyphen, or other separator between the qualifier and number.

The NUCC defines the following qualifiers, since they are the same as those used in the electronic 837 Professional 4010A1:

0B   State License Number
1A   Blue Cross Provider Number
1B   Blue Shield Provider Number
1C   Medicare Provider Number
1D   Medicaid Provider Number
1G   Provider UPIN Number
1H   CHAMPUS Identification Number
1J   Facility ID Number
B3   Preferred Provider Organization Number
BQ   Health Maintenance Organization Code Number
FH   Clinic Number
G2   Provider Commercial Number
G5   Provider Site Number
LU   Location Number
U3   Unique Supplier Identification Number (USIN)
X5   State Industrial Accident Provider Number
ZZ   Provider Taxonomy

The aforementioned list contains provider identifiers, as well as the provider taxonomy code. The provider identifiers are assigned to the provider by a specific payer or by a third party to uniquely identify the provider. Taxonomy codes are desiganted by providers to identify his or her provider type, classification, and/or area of specialization. Both provider identifiers and provider taxomony codes may be used in this field.

Medicare claims, enter the ID qualifier 1C followed by one blank space and then the PIN of the billing provider or group. Suppliers billing the DME MAC will use the National Supplier Clearinghouse (NSC) number in this item.

Information Regarding the Appropriate Method of Reporting Quality Indicators on the CMS 1500-Claim Form

The quality measure data is reported using CPT® category II codes and CPT category II modifiers or HCPCS Level II G codes when there is no CPT category II code available.

CPT category II codes are a set of supplemental tracking codes developed specifically for performance measurement. CPT category II codes are five-character codes with four digits followed by an F. CPT 2009 contains a partial list of category II codes used in the 153 PQRI measures and seven measures groups. HCPCS Level II codes G8006-G9139 are temporary codes developed by CMS for reporting quality measures. CMS has stated that these codes are to be used when there is no CPT category II code available. However, in most instances even when there is a CPT category II code available, CMS has allowed reporting of the HCPCS Level II G code.

The specific codes that apply to each measure are listed in the measure specifications with instructions for reporting the quality measure or exclusion circumstance.

The PQRI uses a claims-based reporting system. Quality codes may be reported on paper-based CMS-1500 claims or electronic 837p claims. Quality codes are to be reported with a $0.00 amount as there is no charge associated with quality codes. If billing software does not accept a $0.00 charge, a small amount, such as one cent, can be substituted. Quality codes must be reported on the same claim as the related diagnosis and procedure code described in the measure specifications.

Place-of-Service Codes

Place-of-service (POS) codes indicate where services were rendered (e.g., in a hospital, clinic, laboratory or any facility other than the patient's home or physician's office). POS codes are required in item 24b.

To standardize policies and procedures for the Medicare fee schedule, CMS approved the use of POS definitions and codes for billing purposes. Physicians are most likely to use POS codes 23 Department, hospital, and 22 Outpatient hospital), which should be used if services are provided in an urgent care center.

01   Pharmacy. A facility or location where drugs and other medically related items and services are sold, dispensed, or otherwise provided directly to patients.

02   Unassigned.

03   School. A facility whose primary purpose is education.

04   Homeless shelter. A facility or location whose primary purpose is to provide temporary housing to homeless individuals (e.g., emergency shelters, individual or family shelters).

05   Indian Health Service freestanding facility. A facility or location owned, operated by the Indian Health Service, which provides diagnostic, therapeutic (surgical and non-surgical) and rehabilitation services to American Indians and Alaskan natives who do not require hospitalization.

   NOTE: This POS is not applicable for the adjudication of Medicare claims. However, systems must recognize it for HIPAA.

06   Indian Health Service provider-based facility. A facility or location, owned and operated by the Indian Health Service, that provides diagnostic, therapeutic (surgical and nonsurgical), and rehabilitation services rendered by, or under the supervision of, physicians to American Indians and Alaskan natives admitted as inpatients or outpatients.

   NOTE: This POS is not applicable for the adjudication of Medicare claims. However, systems must recognize it for HIPAA.

07   Tribal 638 Free standing facility. A facility or location owned and operated by a federally recognized American Indian or Alaskan native tribe or tribal organization under a 638 agreement, which provides diagnostic, therapeutic (surgical and non-surgical), and rehabilitation services to tribal members who do not require hospitalization.

NOTE: This POS is not applicable for theadjudication of Medicare claims. However, systems must recognize it for HIPAA.

08   Tribal 638 provider-based facility. A facility or location owned and operated by a federally recognized American Indian or Alaska native tribe or tribal organization under a 638 agreement, which provides diagnostic, therapeutic (surgical and non-surgical), and rehabilitation services to tribal members admitted as inpatients or outpatients.

NOTE: This POS is not applicable for the adjudication of Medicare claims. However, systems must recognize it for HIPAA.

09–10   Prison-correctional facility. A prison, jail, reformatory, work farm, detention center, or any other similar facility maintained by either Federal, State or local authorities for the purpose of confinement or rehabilitation of adult or juvenile criminal offenders.

11   Office. Location, other than a hospital, skilled nursing facility (SNF), military treatment facility, community health center, state or local public health clinic, or intermediate care facility (ICF), where the health professional routinely provides health examinations, diagnosis, and treatment of illness or injury on an ambulatory basis.

Use this code if the physician is billing for laboratory services performed in the physician's office.

If the physician bills for a laboratory test furnished by another physician who maintains a laboratory in his or her office, use POS code 99. Also, item 20 must be completed for all laboratory services performed outside the physician's office.

This is a valid POS code for billing procedure codes for new patient office visits (99201–99205), established patient office visits (99211–99215), and consultations (99241–99245).

12   Home. Location, other than a hospital or other facility, where the patient receives health care in a private residence.

This is a valid POS code for billing procedure codes for home services for a new patient (99341–99345).

This is a valid POS code for billing supplies that are furnished to a patient by the physician.

13   Assisted living facility. A congregate residential facility with self-contained living units that provide assessment of each resident's needs and 24 hour onsite support, seven days a week, with the ability to deliver or arrange for services including some health care and other services.

14   Group home. This POS indicates a residential foster care setting for children and adolescents in the custody of the state that provides some social, health care, and educational support services and that promotes rehabilitation and reintegration of residents back into the community.

15   Mobile Unit. A facility/unit that moves from place-to-place equipped to provide preventive, screening, diagnostic, and/or treatment services.

16   Temporary lodging. (April 1, 2008) A short-term accommodation such as a hotel, camp ground, hostel, cruise ship, or resort where the patient receives care, and which is not identified by any other POS code.

17–19   Unassigned.

20   Urgent care facility. Location, distinct from a hospital emergency room, an office, or a clinic, whose purpose is to diagnose and treat illness or injury for unscheduled, ambulatory patients seeking immediate medical attention.

21   Inpatient hospital. A facility, other than a psychiatric facility, which primarily provides surgical and nonsurgical diagnostic, therapeutic, and rehabilitative services, by or under the supervision of physicians, to patients admitted for various medical conditions.

If an independent laboratory is billing for services, the place where the laboratory sample is taken is indicated. For example, if a test is taken at an independent laboratory, the code for independent laboratory (81) is used. If an independent laboratory bills for a test on a sample drawn from a hospital inpatient, the code for hospital inpatient (21) is used.

This is a valid POS code for billing procedure codes for hospital inpatient services involving initial hospital care (99221–99223), subsequent hospital care (99231–99233), hospital discharge services (99238), inpatient consultations (99251–99255), and critical care services (99291–99292).

22   Outpatient hospital. An area of a hospital that provides diagnostic, therapeutic (both surgical and nonsurgical), and rehabilitative services to sick or injured individuals who do not require inpatient hospitalization or institutionalization.

If services were rendered in the observation area of a hospital, use the appropriate level of E/M service code from the hospital observation services subsection of the CPT book with this POS code.

This is a valid POS code for billing procedure codes for initial hospital observation services (99218–99220), new patient office visits (99201–99205), established patient office visits (99211–99215), office consultations (99241–99245), and critical care services (99291–99292).

23   Emergency room—hospital. The hospital department where the patient receives emergency diagnosis and treatment of an illness or injury.

The procedure code ranges that may be appropriate for billing E/M services provided in an emergency department are 99281–99285 (item 24d). There is no distinction between new and established patients for emergency department services.

This is a valid POS code for billing procedure codes for emergency department services (99281–99288) and critical care services (99291–99292).

24   Ambulatory surgical center. A certified freestanding facility, other than a physician's office, where surgical

and diagnostic services are provided on an ambulatory basis.

25　Birthing center. A facility, other than a hospital's maternity facility or a physician's office, that provides a setting for labor, delivery, and immediate postpartum care as well as the immediate care of newborn infants.

26　Military treatment facility. A medical facility operated by one or more of the uniformed services. Military treatment facilities include certain former U.S. Public Health Service facilities now designated as uniformed service treatment facilities (USTF).

27–30　Unassigned.

31　Skilled nursing facility. A facility that provides mainly inpatient skilled nursing care and related services to patients who require medical, nursing or rehabilitative services but not at the level of care or treatment found in an inpatient hospital setting.

This POS code also can be used when billing for swing-bed visits.

This is a valid POS code for billing procedure codes for inpatient consultations (99251–99255), critical care services (99291–99292), comprehensive nursing facility services (99304–99306), and subsequent nursing facility services (99307–99310).

32　Nursing facility. A facility that provides residents with skilled nursing and related services for the rehabilitation of injured, disabled or sick persons or, on a regular basis, provides health care services to persons other than those who are mentally retarded above a custodial level of care.

This POS code also can be used when billing for intermediate or long-term care facility visits.

This is a valid POS code for billing procedure codes for initial inpatient consultations (99251–99255), critical care services (99291–99292), comprehensive nursing facility services (99304–99306), and subsequent nursing facility services (99307–99310).

33　Custodial care facility. A facility that provides room, board and other personal assistance services, generally on a long-term basis, but that does not provide the medical component of services.

The procedure code ranges for new patients (99321–99323) and established patients (99331–99333) may be appropriate for billing (Item 24d) E/M services provided in a custodial care facility.

This is a valid POS code for billing procedure codes for domiciliary or rest-home services for a new patient (99321–99323) or an established patient (99331–99333).

34　Hospice. A facility, other than a patient's home, to where palliative, supportive and other care is provided to terminally ill patients and their families to ease the severity of the illness.

This is a valid POS code for billing procedure codes for domiciliary or rest-home services for a new patient (99324–99328) or an established patient (99334–99337).

35–40　Unassigned.

41　Ambulance—Land. The land vehicle designed, equipped, and staffed for lifesaving and transporting the sick or injured.

42　Ambulance—air or water. An air or water vehicle designed, equipped, and staffed for lifesaving and transporting the sick or injured.

43–48　Unassigned.

49　Independent clinic. This is a location that is not a part of the hospital and not described by any other POS code that is operated and organized to provide preventive, diagnostic, therapeutic, rehabilitative, or palliative services to outpatients only.

50　Federally qualified health center. A facility in a medically underserved area that provides Medicare beneficiaries with preventive primary medical care under the general direction of a physician.

51　Inpatient psychiatric facility. A facility that provides inpatient psychiatric services for diagnosing and treating mental illness on a 24-hour basis, by or under the supervision of a physician.

This is a valid POS code for billing procedure codes for hospital inpatient services involving initial hospital care (99221–99223), subsequent hospital care (99231–99233), hospital discharge services (99238), and inpatient consultations (99251–99255).

52　Psychiatric facility partial hospitalization. A facility for diagnosing and treating mental illness that provides a planned therapeutic program for patients who do not require full-time hospitalization but who need broader programs than are possible from outpatient visits to a hospital-based or hospital-affiliated facility.

This is a valid POS code for billing procedure codes for new patient visits (99201–99205), established patient visits (99211–99215), office consultations (99241–99245), and inpatient consultations (99251–99255).

53　Community mental health center. A facility that provides the following services:

Outpatient services, including specialized outpatient services for children, the elderly, the chronically ill and residents of the CMHC's mental health services area who have been discharged from inpatient treatment at a mental health facility; 24-hour-a-day emergency care services, day treatment, other partial hospitalization services, or psychosocial rehabilitation services.

This is a valid POS code for billing procedure codes for new patient visits (99201–99205), established patient visits (99211–99215), office consultations (99241–99245), and inpatient consultations (99251–99255).

54　Intermediate care facility/mentally retarded. A facility that primarily provides health-related care and services above the level of custodial care to mentally retarded individuals but does not provide the level of care or treatment available in a hospital or SNF.

This is a valid POS code for billing procedure codes for initial inpatient consultations (99251–99255), initial nursing facility services (99304–99306), and subsequent nursing facility services (99307–99310).

55   Residential substance abuse treatment facility (RTC). A facility that provides treatment for substance (alcohol and drug) abuse to live-in residents who do not require acute medical care. Services include individual and group therapy and counseling, family counseling, laboratory tests, drugs and supplies, psychological testing, and room and board.

This is a valid POS code for billing procedure codes for domiciliary or rest-home services for a new patient (99324–99328) and subsequent services for an established patient (99334–99337).

56   Psychiatric residential treatment center. A facility or distinct part of a facility for psychiatric care that provides a total, 24-hour, therapeutically planned and professionally staffed group living and learning environment.

This is a valid POS code for billing procedure codes for inpatient consultations (99251–99255), initial nursing facility services (99304–99306), and subsequent nursing facility services (99307–99310).

57   Nonresidential substance abuse treatment facility. This POS denotes a location that provides alcohol and drug abuse treatment on an ambulatory basis. Services include individual and group therapy, counseling, family counseling, laboratory tests, drugs, supplies, and psychological testing.

58–59   Unassigned.

60   Mass immunization center. A location where providers administer pneumococcal pneumonia and influenza virus vaccinations and submit these services as electronic media claims, paper claims, or using the roster billing method. This generally takes place in a mass immunization setting, such as a public health center, pharmacy, or mall, but may include a physician office setting.

61   Comprehensive inpatient rehabilitation facility. A facility that provides comprehensive rehabilitation services under the supervision of a physician to physically disabled inpatients requiring physical, occupational, or speech pathology therapy, social or psychological services, or orthotic and prosthetic services.

This is a valid POS code for billing procedure codes for hospital inpatient services involving initial hospital care (99221–99223), and inpatient consultations (99251–99255).

62   Comprehensive outpatient rehabilitation facility. Facility that provides comprehensive rehabilitation services, under the supervision of a physician, to outpatients with physical disabilities. These services include physical and occupational therapy, and speech pathology services.

This is a valid POS code for billing procedure codes for new patient visits (99201–99205), established patient visits (99211–99215), office consultations (99241–99245).

63–64   Unassigned.

65   End-stage renal disease treatment facility. A facility other than a hospital that provides dialysis treatment, maintenance and/or training to patients or caregivers on an ambulatory or home-care basis.

This is a valid POS code for billing procedure codes for new patient visits (99201–99205), established patient visits (99211–99215), and office consultations (99241–99245).

66–70   Unassigned.

71   State or local public health clinic. A facility maintained by the state or local health departments that provides primary medical care to patients on an ambulatory basis under the general direction of a physician.

72   Rural health clinic. A certified facility located in a rural setting that provides primary medical care to patients on an ambulatory basis under the general direction of a physician.

73–80   Unassigned.

81   Independent laboratory. A laboratory certified to perform diagnostic and/or clinical tests independent of an institution or a physician's office.

Use this code if the physician is billing for a laboratory test furnished by an independent laboratory in his or her office.

Item 20 must be completed for all laboratory services performed outside the physician's office.

The POS code should be reported based on where the test is performed rather than where the specimen is drawn.

82–98   Unassigned.

99   Other place of service. A facility or service other than any of those mentioned above.

Use this code if the physician is billing for a laboratory test purchased from another physician who maintains a laboratory in his or her office.

Type of Service

For submitting a claim to the common working file (CWF), use the following table to assign the proper type of service (TOS). Some procedures may have more than one applicable TOS. The CWF rejects codes with incorrect TOS designations.

The only exceptions to this table are:

- Surgical services billed through December 31, 2007, with the ASC facility service modifier SG had to be reported as TOS F. Effective for services on or after January 1, 2008, modifier SG is no longer applicable for Medicare services and ASC providers must discontinue applying the SG modifier on ASC facility claims. The indicator "F" does not appear in the TOS table because its use depends upon claims submitted with POS 24 (ASC facility) from an ASC (specialty 49). This is effective for dates of service January 1, 2008, and after.

- Surgical services billed with an assistant-at-surgery modifier (80–82, AS) must be reported with TOS 8. The 8 indicator does not appear on the TOS table because its use is dependent upon the use of the appropriate modifier.

- Psychiatric treatment services that are subject to the outpatient mental health treatment limitation should be reported with TOS T.

- TOS H appears in the list of descriptors. However, it does not appear in the table. In CWF, "H" is used only as an indicator for hospice. You should not submit TOS H to CWF at this time.

- When transfusion medicine code appears on an outpatient claim that also contains a blood product, the service is paid under reasonable charge at 80 percent, and the coinsurance and deductible apply. When transfusion medicine codes are paid under the clinical laboratory fee schedule, pay at 100 percent, coinsurance and deductible are not applicable.

Type of Service Indicators

0	Whole blood
1	Medical care
2	Surgery
3	Consultation
4	Diagnostic radiology
5	Diagnostic laboratory
6	Therapeutic radiology
7	Anesthesia
8	Assistant at surgery
9	Other medical items or services
A	Used durable medical equipment
B	High-risk screening mammography
C	Low-risk screening mammography
D	Ambulance
E	Enteral/parenteral nutrients/supplies
F	Ambulatory surgical center (facility usage for surgical services)
G	Immunosuppressive drugs
H	Hospice
J	Diabetic shoes
K	Hearing items and services
L	End stage renal disease supplies
M	Monthly capitation payment for dialysis
N	Kidney donor
P	Lump sum purchase of DME, prosthetics, orthotics
Q	Vision items or services
R	Rental of durable medical equipment
S	Surgical dressings or other medical supplies
T	Outpatient mental health treatment limitation
U	Occupational therapy
V	Pneumococcal/flu vaccine
W	Physical therapy

Electronic Claim Completion

The 837 Electronic Claim Form

The growth in electronic data interchange within the health care community has been remarkable in recent years. It continues at a rapid pace to capture more of the health care claims processing business. Changes in federal and state requirements, as well as technological advancements by private payers will push us closer to an all-electronic claims system in the near future.

There are many advantages to submitting claims electronically including:

- Eliminating paperwork

- Reducing cost by not having to buy claim forms or postage

- Improved cash flow (average 14-day vs 72-day claim payment floor

Section 3 of the Administrative Simplification Compliance Act (ASCA), PL107-105, and the implementing regulation at 42 CFR, section 424.32, require most providers, with limited exceptions, to submit all initial claims for reimbursement under Medicare electronically, The exceptions to this electronic claim submission requirement are:

- Small providers (providers billing a Medicare FI that fewer than 25 full-time equivalent employees (FTE), and physicians, practitioners, or suppliers, with fewer than 10 FTEs that bills a Medicare carrier.

- Dentists

- Participants in a Medicare demonstration project in which paper claim filing is required

- Providers that conduct mass immunizations, such as flu injections

- Providers that submit claims when more than one other payer is responsible for payment prior to Medicare payment

- Providers that only furnish services outside of the United States

- Providers experiencing a disruption in electricity and communication connections that are beyond its control;

- Providers that can establish an unusual circumstance exists that precludes submission of claims electronically

The following claim denial codes are used by any payer using an electronic remittance advice (form 835).

M1	X-ray not taken within the past 12 months or near enough to the start of treatment.
M2	Not paid separately when the patient is an inpatient.
M3	Equipment is the same or similar to equipment already being used.
M4	This is the last monthly installment payment for this durable medical equipment.
M5	Monthly rental payments can continue until the earlier of the 15th month from the first rental month, or the month when the equipment is no longer needed.
M6	You must furnish and service this item for as long as the patient continues to need it. We can pay for maintenance and/or servicing for every 6 month

Claims Processing

period after the end of the 15th paid rental month or the end of the warranty period.

M7 No rental payments after the item is purchased, or after the total of issued rental payments equals the purchase price.

M8 We do not accept blood gas tests results when the test was conducted by a medical supplier or taken while the patient is on oxygen.

M9 This is the tenth rental month. You must offer the patient the choice of changing the rental to a purchase agreement.

M10 Equipment purchases are limited to the first or the tenth month of medical necessity.

M11 DME, orthotics and prosthetics must be billed to the DME carrier who services the patient's zip code.

M12 Diagnostic tests performed by a physician must indicate whether purchased services are included on the claim.

M13 Only one initial visit is covered per specialty per medical group.

M14 No separate payment for an injection administered during an office visit, and no payment for a full office visit if the patient only received an injection.

M15 Separately billed services/tests have been bundled as they are considered components of the same procedure. Separate payment is not allowed.

M16 Please see our web site, mailings, or bulletins for more details concerning this policy/procedure/decision.

M17 Payment approved as you did not know, and could not reasonably have been expected to know, that this would not normally have been covered for this patient. In the future, you will be liable for charges for the same service(s) under the same or similar conditions.

M18 Certain services may be approved for home use. Neither a hospital nor a Skilled Nursing Facility (SNF) is considered to be a patient's home.

M19 Missing oxygen certification/re-certification.

M20 Missing/incomplete/invalid HCPCS.

M21 Missing/incomplete/invalid place of residence for this service/item provided in a home.

M22 Missing/incomplete/invalid number of miles traveled.

M23 Missing invoice.

M24 Missing/incomplete/invalid number of doses per vial.

M25 Payment has been adjusted because the information furnished does not substantiate the need for this level of service. If you believe the service should have been fully covered as billed, or if you did not know and could not reasonably have been expected to know that we would not pay for this level of service, or if you notified the patient in writing in advance that we would not pay for this level of service and he/she agreed in writing to pay, ask us to review your claim within 120 days of the date of this notice. If you do not request a appeal, we will, upon application from

the patient, reimburse him/her for the amount you have collected from him/her in excess of any deductible and coinsurance amounts. We will recover the reimbursement from you as an overpayment.

M26 Payment has been adjusted because the information furnished does not substantiate the need for this level of service. If you have collected any amount from the patient for this level of service /any amount that exceeds the limiting charge for the less extensive service, the law requires you to refund that amount to the patient within 30 days of receiving this notice.

The requirements for refund are in 1824(I) of the Social Security Act and 42CFR411.408. The section specifies that physicians who knowingly and willfully fail to make appropriate refunds may be subject to civil monetary penalties and/or exclusion from the program. If you have any questions about this notice, please contact this office.

M27 The patient has been relieved of liability of payment of these items and services under the limitation of liability provision of the law. You, the provider, are ultimately liable for the patient's waived charges, including any charges for coinsurance, since the items or services were not reasonable and necessary or constituted custodial care, and you knew or could reasonably have been expected to know, that they were not covered.

You may appeal this determination. You may ask for an appeal regarding both the coverage determination and the issue of whether you exercised due care. The appeal request must be filed within 120 days of the date you receive this notice. You must make the request through this office.

M28 This does not qualify for payment under Part B when Part A coverage is exhausted or not otherwise available.

M29 Missing operative report.

M30 Missing pathology report.

M31 Missing radiology report.

M32 This is a conditional payment made pending a decision on this service by the patient's primary payer. This payment may be subject to refund upon your receipt of any additional payment for this service from another payer. You must contact this office immediately upon receipt of an additional payment for this service.

M36 This is the 11th rental month. We cannot pay for this until you indicate that the patient has been given the option of changing the rental to a purchase.

M37 Service not covered when the patient is under age 35.

M38 The patient is liable for the charges for this service as you informed the patient in writing before the service was furnished that we would not pay for it, and the patient agreed to pay.

M39 The patient is not liable for payment for this service as the advance notice of non-coverage you provided the patient did not comply with program requirements.

M40 Claim must be assigned and must be filed by the practitioner's employer.

M41 We do not pay for this as the patient has no legal obligation to pay for this.

M42 The medical necessity form must be personally signed by the attending physician.

M44 Missing/incomplete/invalid condition code.

M45 Missing/incomplete/invalid occurrence code(s).

M46 Missing/incomplete/invalid occurrence span code(s).

M47 Missing/incomplete/invalid internal or document control number.

M49 Missing/incomplete/invalid value code(s) or amount(s).

M50 Missing/incomplete/invalid revenue code(s).

M51 Missing/incomplete/invalid procedure code(s).

M52 Missing/incomplete/invalid "from" date(s) of service.

M53 Missing/incomplete/invalid days or units of service.

M54 Missing/incomplete/invalid total charges.

M55 We do not pay for self-administered anti-emetic drugs that are not administered with a covered oral anti-cancer drug.

M56 Missing/incomplete/invalid payer identifier.

M59 Missing/incomplete/invalid "to" date(s) of service.

M60 Missing Certificate of Medical Necessity.

M61 We cannot pay for this as the approval period for the FDA clinical trial has expired.

M62 Missing/incomplete/invalid treatment authorization code.

M64 Missing/incomplete/invalid other diagnosis.

M65 One interpreting physician charge can be submitted per claim when a purchased diagnostic test is indicated. Please submit a separate claim for each interpreting physician.

M66 Our records indicate that you billed diagnostic tests subject to price limitations and the procedure code submitted includes a professional component. Only the technical component is subject to price limitations. Please submit the technical and professional components of this service as separate line items.

M67 Missing/incomplete/invalid other procedure code(s).

M69 Paid at the regular rate as you did not submit documentation to justify the modified procedure code.

M70 Alert:NDC code submitted for this service was translated to a HCPCS code for processing, but please continue to submit the NDC on future claims for this item.

M71 Total payment reduced due to overlap of tests billed.

M73 The HPSA/Physician Scarcity bonus can only be paid on the professional component of this service. Rebill as separate professional and technical components.

M74 This service does not qualify for a HPSA/Physician Scarcity bonus payment.

M75 Allowed amount adjusted. Multiple automated multichannel tests performed on the same day combined for payment.

M76 Missing/incomplete/invalid diagnosis or condition.

M77 Missing/incomplete/invalid place of service.

M79 Missing/incomplete/invalid charge.

M80 Not covered when performed during the same session/date as a previously processed service for the patient.

M81 You are required to code to the highest level of specificity.

M82 Service is not covered when patient is under age 50.

M83 Service is not covered unless the patient is classified as at high risk.

M84 Medical code sets used must be the codes in effect at the time of service

M85 Subjected to review of physician evaluation and management services.

M86 Service denied because payment already made for same/similar procedure within set time frame.

M87 Claim/service(s) subjected to CFO-CAP prepayment review.

M89 Not covered more than once under age 40.

M90 Not covered more than once in a 12 month period.

M91 Lab procedures with different CLIA certification numbers must be billed on separate claims.

M93 Information supplied supports a break in therapy. A new capped rental period began with delivery of this equipment.

M94 Information supplied does not support a break in therapy. A new capped rental period will not begin.

M95 Services subjected to Home Health Initiative medical review/cost report audit.

M96 The technical component of a service furnished to an inpatient may only be billed by that inpatient facility. You must contact the inpatient facility for technical component reimbursement. If not already billed, you should bill us for the professional component only.

M97 Not paid to practitioner when provided to patient in this place of service. Payment included in the reimbursement issued the facility.

M99 Missing/incomplete/invalid Universal Product Number/Serial Number.

M100 We do not pay for an oral anti-emetic drug that is not administered for use immediately before, at, or within 48 hours of administration of a covered chemotherapy drug.

M102 Service not performed on equipment approved by the FDA for this purpose.

M103 Information supplied supports a break in therapy. However, the medical information we have for this patient does not support the need for this item as billed. We have approved payment for this item at a reduced level, and a new capped rental period will begin with the delivery of this equipment.

M105 Information supplied does not support a break in therapy. The medical information we have for this patient does not support the need for this item as billed. We have approved payment for this item at a reduced level, and a new capped rental period will not begin.

M107 Payment reduced as 90-day rolling average hematocrit for ESRD patient exceeded 36.5%.

M109 We have provided you with a bundled payment for a teleconsultation. You must send 25 percent of the teleconsultation payment to the referring practitioner.

M111 We do not pay for chiropractic manipulative treatment when the patient refuses to have an x-ray taken.

M112 The approved amount is based on the maximum allowance for this item under the DMEPOS Competitive Bidding Demonstration.

M113 Our records indicate that this patient began using this service(s) prior to the current round of the DMEPOS Competitive Bidding Demonstration. Therefore, the approved amount is based on the allowance in effect prior to this round of bidding for this item.

M114 This service was processed in accordance with rules and guidelines under the Competitive Bidding Demonstration Project. If you would like more information regarding this project, you may phone 1-888-289-0710.

M115 This item is denied when provided to this patient by a non-demonstration supplier.

M116 Paid under the Competitive Bidding Demonstration project. Project is ending, and future services may not be paid under this project.

M117 Not covered unless submitted via electronic claim.

M118 Letter to follow containing further information.

M119 Missing/incomplete/invalid/ deactivated/withdrawn National Drug Code (NDC).

M121 We pay for this service only when performed with a covered cryosurgical ablation.

M122 Missing/incomplete/invalid level of subluxation.

M123 Missing/incomplete/invalid name, strength, or dosage of the drug furnished.

M124 Missing indication of whether the patient owns the equipment that requires the part or supply.

M125 Missing/incomplete/invalid information on the period of time for which the service/supply/equipment will be needed.

M126 Missing/incomplete/invalid individual lab codes included in the test.

M127 Missing patient medical record for this service.

M130 Missing invoice or statement certifying the actual cost of the lens, less discounts, and/or the type of intraocular lens used.

M131 Missing physician financial relationship form.

M132 Missing pacemaker registration form.

M133 Claim did not identify who performed the purchased diagnostic test or the amount you were charged for the test.

M134 Performed by a facility/supplier in which the provider has a financial interest.

M135 Missing/incomplete/invalid plan of treatment.

M136 Missing/incomplete/invalid indication that the service was supervised or evaluated by a physician.

M137 Part B coinsurance under a demonstration project.

M138 Patient identified as a demonstration participant but the patient was not enrolled in the demonstration at the time services were rendered. Coverage is limited to demonstration participants.

M139 Denied services exceed the coverage limit for the demonstration.

M141 Missing physician certified plan of care.

M142 Missing American Diabetes Association Certificate of Recognition.

M143 We have no record that you are licensed to dispensed drugs in the State where located.

M144 Pre-/post-operative care payment is included in the allowance for the surgery/procedure.

MA01 **Alert:** If you do not agree with what we approved for these services, you may appeal our decision. To make sure that we are fair to you, we require another individual that did not process your initial claim to conduct the appeal. However, in order to be eligible for an appeal, you must write to us within 120 days of the date you received this notice, unless you have a good reason for being late.

MA02 **Alert:** If you do not agree with this determination, you have the right to appeal. You must file a written request for an appeal within 180 days of the date you receive this notice. Decisions made by a Quality Improvement Organization (QIO) must be appealed to that QIO within 60 days.

MA04 Secondary payment cannot be considered without the identity of or payment information from the primary payer. The information was either not reported or was illegible.

MA07 **Alert:** The claim information has also been forwarded to Medicaid for review.

MA08 **Alert:** You should also submit this claim to the patient's other insurer for potential payment of supplemental benefits. We did not forward the claim information as the supplemental coverage is not with a Medigap plan, or you do not participate in Medicare.

Claims Processing

MA09 Claim submitted as unassigned but processed as assigned. You agreed to accept assignment for all claims.

MA10 **Alert:** The patient's payment was in excess of the amount owed. You must refund the overpayment to the patient.

MA12 You have not established that you have the right under the law to bill for services furnished by the person(s) that furnished this (these) service(s).

MA13 **Alert:** You may be subject to penalties if you bill the patient for amounts not reported with the PR (patient responsibility) group code.

MA14 **Alert:** Patient is a member of an employer-sponsored prepaid health plan. Services from outside that health plan are not covered. However, as you were not previously notified of this, we are paying this time. In the future, we will not pay you for non-plan services.

MA15 **Alert:** Your claim has been separated to expedite handling. You will receive a separate notice for the other services reported.

MA16 The patient is covered by the Black Lung Program. Send this claim to the Department of Labor, Federal Black Lung Program, P.O. Box 828, Lanham-Seabrook MD 20703.

MA17 We are the primary payer and have paid at the primary rate. You must contact the patient's other insurer to refund any excess it may have paid due to its erroneous primary payment.

MA18 **Alert:** The claim information is also being forwarded to the patient's supplemental insurer. Send any questions regarding supplemental benefits to them.

MA19 **Alert:** Information was not sent to the Medigap insurer due to incorrect/invalid information you submitted concerning that insurer. Please verify your information and submit your secondary claim directly to that insurer.

MA20 Skilled Nursing Facility (SNF) stay not covered when care is primarily related to the use of an urethral catheter for convenience or the control of incontinence.

MA21 SSA records indicate mismatch with name and sex.

MA22 Payment of less than $1.00 suppressed.

MA23 Demand bill approved as result of medical review.

MA24 Christian Science Sanitarium/ Skilled Nursing Facility (SNF) bill in the same benefit period.

MA25 A patient may not elect to change a hospice provider more than once in a benefit period.

MA26 **Alert:** Our records indicate that you were previously informed of this rule.

MA27 Missing/incomplete/invalid entitlement number or name shown on the claim.

MA28 **Alert:** Receipt of this notice by a physician or supplier who did not accept assignment is for information only and does not make the physician or supplier a party to the determination. No additional rights to appeal this decision, above those rights already

provided for by regulation/instruction, are conferred by receipt of this notice.

MA30 Missing/incomplete/invalid type of bill.

MA31 Missing/incomplete/invalid beginning and ending dates of the period billed.

MA32 Missing/incomplete/invalid number of covered days during the billing period.

MA33 Missing/incomplete/invalid noncovered days during the billing period.

MA34 Missing/incomplete/invalid number of coinsurance days during the billing period.

MA35 Missing/incomplete/invalid number of lifetime reserve days.

MA36 Missing/incomplete/invalid patient name.

MA37 Missing/incomplete/invalid patient's address.

MA39 Missing/incomplete/invalid gender.

MA40 Missing/incomplete/invalid admission date.

MA41 Missing/incomplete/invalid admission type.

MA42 Missing/incomplete/invalid admission source.

MA43 Missing/incomplete/invalid patient status.

MA44 **Alert:** No appeal rights. Adjudicative decision based on law.

MA45 **Alert:** As previously advised, a portion or all of your payment is being held in a special account.

MA46 The new information was considered, however, additional payment cannot be issued. Please review the information listed for the explanation.

MA47 Our records show you have opted out of Medicare, agreeing with the patient not to bill Medicare for services/tests/supplies furnished. As result, we cannot pay this claim. The patient is responsible for payment.

MA48 Missing/incomplete/invalid name or address of responsible party or primary payer.

MA50 Missing/incomplete/invalid Investigational Device Exemption number for FDA-approved clinical trial services.

MA53 Missing/incomplete/invalid Competitive Bidding Demonstration Project identification.

MA54 Physician certification or election consent for hospice care not received timely.

MA55 Not covered as patient received medical health care services, automatically revoking his/her election to receive religious non-medical health care services.

MA56 Our records show you have opted out of Medicare, agreeing with the patient not to bill Medicare for services/tests/supplies furnished. As result, we cannot pay this claim. The patient is responsible for payment, but under Federal law, you cannot charge the patient more than the limiting charge amount.

MA57 Patient submitted written request to revoke his/her election for religious non-medical health care services.

Claims Processing

MA58 Missing/incomplete/invalid release of information indicator.

MA59 **Alert:** The patient overpaid you for these services. You must issue the patient a refund within 30 days for the difference between his/her payment and the total amount shown as patient responsibility on this notice.

MA60 Missing/incomplete/invalid patient relationship to insured.

MA61 Missing/incomplete/invalid social security number or health insurance claim number.

MA62 **Alert:** Telephone review decision.

MA63 Missing/incomplete/invalid principal diagnosis.

MA64 Our records indicate that we should be the third payer for this claim. We cannot process this claim until we have received payment information from the primary and secondary payers.

MA65 Missing/incomplete/invalid admitting diagnosis.

MA66 Missing/incomplete/invalid principal procedure code.

MA67 Correction to a prior claim.

MA68 **Alert:** We did not crossover this claim because the secondary insurance information on the claim was incomplete. Please supply complete information or use the PLANID of the insurer to assure correct and timely routing of the claim.

MA69 Missing/incomplete/invalid remarks.

MA70 Missing/incomplete/invalid provider representative signature.

MA71 Missing/incomplete/invalid provider representative signature date.

MA72 **Alert:** The patient overpaid you for these assigned services. You must issue the patient a refund within 30 days for the difference between his/her payment to you and the total of the amount shown as patient responsibility and as paid to the patient on this notice.

MA73 Informational remittance associated with a Medicare demonstration. No payment issued under fee-for-service Medicare as patient has elected managed care.

MA74 This payment replaces an earlier payment for this claim that was either lost, damaged or returned.

MA75 Missing/incomplete/invalid patient or authorized representative signature.

MA76 Missing/incomplete/invalid provider identifier for home health agency or hospice when physician is performing care plan oversight services.

MA77 **Alert:** The patient overpaid you. You must issue the patient a refund within 30 days for the difference between the patient's payment less the total of our and other payer payments and the amount shown as patient responsibility on this notice.

MA79 Billed in excess of interim rate.

MA80 Informational notice. No payment issued for this claim with this notice. Payment issued to the hospital by its intermediary for all services for this encounter under a demonstration project.

MA81 Missing/incomplete/invalid provider/supplier signature.

MA83 Did not indicate whether we are the primary or secondary payer.

MA84 Patient identified as participating in the National Emphysema Treatment Trial but our records indicate that this patient is either not a participant, or has not yet been approved for this phase of the study. Contact Johns Hopkins University, the study coordinator, to resolve if there was a discrepancy.

MA88 Missing/incomplete/invalid insured's address and/or telephone number for the primary payer.

MA89 Missing/incomplete/invalid patient's relationship to the insured for the primary payer.

MA90 Missing/incomplete/invalid employment status code for the primary insured.

MA91 This determination is the result of the appeal you filed.

MA92 Missing plan information for other insurance.

MA93 Non-PIP (Periodic Interim Payment) claim.

MA94 Did not enter the statement "Attending physician not hospice employee" on the claim form to certify that the rendering physician is not an employee of the hospice.

MA96 Claim rejected. Coded as a Medicare Managed Care Demonstration but patient is not enrolled in a Medicare managed care plan.

MA97 Missing/incomplete/invalid Medicare Managed Care Demonstration contract number or clinical trial registry number.

MA99 Missing/incomplete/invalid Medigap information.

MA100 Missing/incomplete/invalid date of current illness or symptoms

MA101 A Skilled Nursing Facility (SNF) is responsible for payment of outside providers who furnish these services/supplies to residents.

MA103 Hemophilia Add On.

MA106 PIP (Periodic Interim Payment) claim.

MA107 Paper claim contains more than three separate data items in field 19.

MA108 Paper claim contains more than one data item in field 23.

MA109 Claim processed in accordance with ambulatory surgical guidelines.

MA110 Missing/incomplete/invalid information on whether the diagnostic test(s) were performed by an outside entity or if no purchased tests are included on the claim.

MA111 Missing/incomplete/invalid purchase price of the test(s) and/or the performing laboratory's name and address.

MA112 Missing/incomplete/invalid group practice information.

MA113 Incomplete/invalid taxpayer identification number (TIN) submitted by you per the Internal Revenue Service. Your claims cannot be processed without your correct TIN, and you may not bill the patient pending correction of your TIN. There are no appeal rights for unprocessable claims, but you may resubmit this claim after you have notified this office of your correct TIN.

MA114 Missing/incomplete/invalid information on where the services were furnished.

MA115 Missing/incomplete/invalid physical location (name and address, or PIN) where the service(s) were rendered in a Health Professional Shortage Area (HPSA).

MA116 Did not complete the statement "Homebound" on the claim to validate whether laboratory services were performed at home or in an institution.

MA117 This claim has been assessed a $1.00 user fee.

MA118 Coinsurance and/or deductible amounts apply to a claim for services or supplies furnished to a Medicare-eligible veteran through a facility of the Department of Veterans Affairs. No Medicare payment issued.

MA120 Missing/incomplete/invalid CLIA certification number.

MA121 Missing/incomplete/invalid x-ray date.

MA122 Missing/incomplete/invalid initial treatment date.

MA123 Your center was not selected to participate in this study, therefore, we cannot pay for these services.

MA125 Per legislation governing this program, payment constitutes payment in full.

MA126 Pancreas transplant not covered unless kidney transplant performed.

MA128 Missing/incomplete/invalid FDA approval number.

MA130 Your claim contains incomplete and/or invalid information, and no appeal rights are afforded because the claim is unprocessable. Please submit a new claim with the complete/correct information.

MA131 Physician already paid for services in conjunction with this demonstration claim. You must have the physician withdraw that claim and refund the payment before we can process your claim.

MA132 Adjustment to the pre-demonstration rate.

MA133 Claim overlaps inpatient stay. Rebill only those services rendered outside the inpatient stay.

MA134 Missing/incomplete/invalid provider number of the facility where the patient resides.

N1 **Alert:** You may appeal this decision in writing within the required time limits following receipt of this notice by following the instructions included in your contract or plan benefit documents.

N2 This allowance has been made in accordance with the most appropriate course of treatment provision of the plan.

N3 Missing consent form.

N4 Missing/incomplete/invalid prior insurance carrier RA.

N5 RA received from previous payer. Claim not on file.

N6 Under FEHB law (U.S.C. 8904(b)), we cannot pay more for covered care than the amount Medicare would have allowed if the patient were enrolled in Medicare Part A and/or Medicare Part B.

N7 Processing of this claim/service has included consideration under Major Medical provisions.

N8 Crossover claim denied by previous payer and complete claim data not forwarded. Resubmit this claim to this payer to provide adequate data for adjudication.

N9 Adjustment represents the estimated amount a previous payer may pay.

N10 Payment based on the findings of a review organization/professional consult/manual adjudication/medical or dental advisor.

N11 Denial reversed because of medical review.

N12 Policy provides coverage supplemental to Medicare. As the member does not appear to be enrolled in the applicable part of Medicare, the member is responsible for payment of the portion of the charge that would have been covered by Medicare.

N13 Payment based on professional/technical component modifier(s).

N15 Services for a newborn must be billed separately.

N16 Family/member Out-of-Pocket maximum has been met. Payment based on a higher percentage.

N19 Procedure code incidental to primary procedure.

N20 Service not payable with other service rendered on the same date.

N21 **Alert:** Your line item has been separated into multiple lines to expedite handling.

N22 This procedure code was added/changed because it more accurately describes the services rendered.

N23 **Alert:** Patient liability may be affected due to coordination of benefits with other carriers and/or maximum benefit provisions.

N24 Missing/incomplete/invalid Electronic Funds Transfer (EFT) banking information.

N25 This company has been contracted by your benefit plan to provide administrative claims payment services only. This company does not assume financial risk or obligation with respect to claims processed on behalf of your benefit plan.

N26 Missing itemized bill/statement.

N27 Missing/incomplete/invalid treatment number.

N28 Consent form requirements not fulfilled.

N29 Missing documentation/orders/notes/summary/report/chart.

N30   Patient ineligible for this service.

N31   Missing/incomplete/invalid prescribing provider identifier.

N32   Claim must be submitted by the provider who rendered the service.

N33   No record of health check prior to initiation of treatment.

N34   Incorrect claim form/format for this service.

N35   Program integrity/utilization review decision.

N36   Claim must meet primary payer's processing requirements before we can consider payment.

N37   Missing/incomplete/invalid tooth number/letter.

N39   Procedure code is not compatible with tooth number/letter.

N40   Missing radiology film(s)/image(s).

N42   No record of mental health assessment.

N43   Bed hold or leave days exceeded.

N45   Payment based on authorized amount.

N46   Missing/incomplete/invalid admission hour.

N47   Claim conflicts with another inpatient stay.

N48   Claim information does not agree with information received from other insurance carrier.

N49   Court ordered coverage information needs validation.

N50   Missing/incomplete/invalid discharge information.

N51   Electronic interchange agreement not on file for provider/submitter.

N52   Patient not enrolled in the billing provider's managed care plan on the date of service.

N53   Missing/incomplete/invalid point of pick-up address.

N54   Claim information is inconsistent with pre-certified/authorized services.

N55   Procedures for billing with group/referring/performing providers were not followed.

N56   Procedure code billed is not correct/valid for the services billed or the date of service billed.

N57   Missing/incomplete/invalid prescribing date.

N58   Missing/incomplete/invalid patient liability amount.

N59   **Alert:** Please refer to your provider manual for additional program and provider information.

N61   Rebill services on separate claims.

N62   Inpatient admission spans multiple rate periods. Resubmit separate claims.

N63   Rebill services on separate claim lines.

N64   The "from" and "to" dates must be different.

N65   Procedure code or procedure rate count cannot be determined, or was not on file, for the date of service/provider.

N67   Professional provider services not paid separately. Included in facility payment under a demonstration project. Apply to that facility for payment, or resubmit your claim if: the facility notifies you the patient was excluded from this demonstration; or if you furnished these services in another location on the date of the patient's admission or discharge from a demonstration hospital. If services were furnished in a facility not involved in the demonstration on the same date the patient was discharged from or admitted to a demonstration facility, you must report the provider ID number for the non-demonstration facility on the new claim.

N68   Prior payment being canceled as we were subsequently notified this patient was covered by a demonstration project in this site of service. Professional services were included in the payment made to the facility. You must contact the facility for your payment. Prior payment made to you by the patient or another insurer for this claim must be refunded to the payer within 30 days.

N69   PPS (Prospective Payment System) code changed by claims processing system. Insufficient visits or therapies.

N70   Consolidated billing and payment applies.

N71   Your unassigned claim for a drug or biological, clinical diagnostic laboratory services or ambulance service was processed as an assigned claim. You are required by law to accept assignment for these types of claims.

N72   PPS (Prospective Payment System) code changed by medical reviewers. Not supported by clinical records.

N74   Resubmit with multiple claims, each claim covering services provided in only one calendar month.

N75   Missing/incomplete/invalid tooth surface information.

N76   Missing/incomplete/invalid number of riders.

N77   Missing/incomplete/invalid designated provider number.

N78   The necessary components of the child and teen checkup (EPSDT) were not completed.

N79   Service billed is not compatible with patient location information.

N80   Missing/incomplete/invalid prenatal screening information.

N81   Procedure billed is not compatible with tooth surface code.

N82   Provider must accept insurance payment as payment in full when a third party payer contract specifies full reimbursement.

N83   No appeal rights. Adjudicative decision based on the provisions of a demonstration project.

N84   **Alert:** Further installment payments forthcoming.

N85   **Alert:** This is the final installment payment.

N86   A failed trial of pelvic muscle exercise training is required in order for biofeedback training for the treatment of urinary incontinence to be covered.

N87   Home use of biofeedback therapy is not covered.

Claims Processing

N88   **Alert:** This payment is being made conditionally. An HHA episode of care notice has been filed for this patient. When a patient is treated under a HHA episode of care, consolidated billing requires that certain therapy services and supplies, such as this, be included in the HHA's payment. This payment will need to be recouped from you if we establish that the patient is concurrently receiving treatment under a HHA episode of care.

N89   **Alert:** Payment information for this claim has been forwarded to more than one other payer, but format limitations permit only one of the secondary payers to be identified in this remittance advice.

N90   Covered only when performed by the attending physician.

N91   Services not included in the appeal review.

N92   This facility is not certified for digital mammography.

N93   A separate claim must be submitted for each place of service. Services furnished at multiple sites may not be billed in the same claim.

N94   Claim/Service denied because a more specific taxonomy code is required for adjudication.

N95   This provider type/provider specialty may not bill this service.

N96   Patient must be refractory to conventional therapy (documented behavioral, pharmacologic and/or surgical corrective therapy) and be an appropriate surgical candidate such that implantation with anesthesia can occur.

N97   Patients with stress incontinence, urinary obstruction, and specific neurologic diseases (e.g., diabetes with peripheral nerve involvement) which are associated with secondary manifestations of the above three indications are excluded.

N98   Patient must have had a successful test stimulation in order to support subsequent implantation. Before a patient is eligible for permanent implantation, he/she must demonstrate a 50 percent or greater improvement through test stimulation. Improvement is measured through voiding diaries.

N99   Patient must be able to demonstrate adequate ability to record voiding diary data such that clinical results of the implant procedure can be properly evaluated.

N100   PPS (Prospect Payment System) code corrected during adjudication.

N102   This claim has been denied without reviewing the medical record because the requested records were not received or were not received timely.

N103   Social Security records indicate that this patient was a prisoner when the service was rendered. This payer does not cover items and services furnished to an individual while they are in State or local custody under a penal authority, unless under State or local law, the individual is personally liable for the cost of his or her health care while incarcerated and the State or local government pursues such debt in the same way and with the same vigor as any other debt.

N104   This claim/service is not payable under our claims jurisdiction area. You can identify the correct Medicare contractor to process this claim/service through the CMS website at www.cms.hhs.gov.

N105   This is a misdirected claim/service for an RRB beneficiary. Submit paper claims to the RRB carrier: Palmetto GBA, P.O. Box 10066, Augusta, GA 30999. Call 866-749-4301 for RRB EDI information for electronic claims processing.

N106   Payment for services furnished to Skilled Nursing Facility (SNF) inpatients (except for excluded services) can only be made to the SNF. You must request payment from the SNF rather than the patient for this service.

N107   Services furnished to Skilled Nursing Facility (SNF) inpatients must be billed on the inpatient claim. They cannot be billed separately as outpatient services.

N108   Missing/incomplete/invalid upgrade information.

N109   This claim was chosen for complex review and was denied after reviewing the medical records.

N110   This facility is not certified for film mammography.

N111   No appeal right except duplicate claim/service issue. This service was included in a claim that has been previously billed and adjudicated.

N112   This claim is excluded from your electronic remittance advice.

N113   Only one initial visit is covered per physician, group practice or provider.

N114   During the transition to the Ambulance Fee Schedule, payment is based on the lesser of a blended amount calculated using a percentage of the reasonable charge/cost and fee schedule amounts, or the submitted charge for the service. You will be notified yearly what the percentages for the blended payment calculation will be.

N115   This decision was based on a local medical review policy (LMRP) or Local Coverage Determination (LCD). An LMRP/LCD provides a guide to assist in determining whether a particular item or service is covered. A copy of this policy is available at http://www.cms.hhs.gov/mcd, or if you do not have web access, you may contact the contractor to request a copy of the LMRP/LCD.

N116   This payment is being made conditionally because the service was provided in the home, and it is possible that the patient is under a home health episode of care. When a patient is treated under a home health episode of care, consolidated billing requires that certain therapy services and supplies, such as this, be included in the home health agency's (HHA's) payment. This payment will need to be recouped from you if we establish that the patient is concurrently receiving treatment under an HHA episode of care.

N117   This service is paid only once in a patient's lifetime.

N118   This service is not paid if billed more than once every 28 days.

N119   This service is not paid if billed once every 28 days, and the patient has spent 5 or more consecutive days in any inpatient or Skilled /nursing Facility (SNF) within those 28 days.

N120   Payment is subject to home health prospective payment system partial episode payment adjustment. Patient was transferred/discharged/readmitted during payment episode.

N121   Medicare Part B does not pay for items or services provided by this type of practitioner for beneficiaries in a Medicare Part A covered Skilled Nursing Facility (SNF) stay.

N122   Add-on code cannot be billed by itself.

N123   This is a split service and represents a portion of the units from the originally submitted service.

N124   Payment has been denied for the/made only for a less extensive service/item because the information furnished does not substantiate the need for the (more extensive) service/item. The patient is liable for the charges for this service/item as you informed the patient in writing before the service/item was furnished that we would not pay for it, and the patient agreed to pay.

N125   Payment has been (denied for the/made only for a less extensive) service/item because the information furnished does not substantiate the need for the (more extensive) service/item. If you have collected any amount from the patient, you must refund that amount to the patient within 30 days of receiving this notice.

The requirements for a refund are in §1834(a)(18) of the Social Security Act (and in §§1834(j)(4) and 1879(h) by cross-reference to §1834(a)(18)). Section 1834(a)(18)(B) specifies that suppliers which knowingly and willfully fail to make appropriate refunds may be subject to civil money penalties and/or exclusion from the Medicare program. If you have any questions about this notice, please contact this office.

N126   Social Security Records indicate that this individual has been deported. This payer does not cover items and services furnished to individuals who have been deported.

N127   This is a misdirected claim/service for a United Mine Workers of America (UMWA) beneficiary. Please submit claims to them.

N128   This amount represents the prior to coverage portion of the allowance.

N129   Not eligible due to the patient's age.

N130   **Alert:** Consult plan benefit documents/guidelines for information about restrictions for this service.

N131   Total payments under multiple contracts cannot exceed the allowance for this service.

N132   **Alert:** Payments will cease for services rendered by this US Government debarred or excluded provider after the 30 day grace period as previously notified.

N133   **Alert:** Services for predetermination and services requesting payment are being processed separately.

N134   **Alert:** This represents your scheduled payment for this service. If treatment has been discontinued, please contact Customer Service.

N135   Record fees are the patient's responsibility and limited to the specified co-payment.

N136   **Alert:** To obtain information on the process to file an appeal in Arizona, call the Department's Consumer Assistance Office at (602) 912-8444 or (800) 325-2548.

N137   **Alert:** The provider acting on the Member's behalf, may file an appeal with the Payer. The provider, acting on the Member's behalf, may file a complaint with the State Insurance Regulatory Authority without first filing an appeal, if the coverage decision involves an urgent condition for which care has not been rendered. The address may be obtained from the State Insurance Regulatory Authority.

N138   **Alert:** In the event you disagree with the Dental Advisor's opinion and have additional information relative to the case, you may submit radiographs to the Dental Advisor Unit at the subscriber's dental insurance carrier for a second Independent Dental Advisor Review.

N139   **Alert:** Under the Code of Federal Regulations, Chapter 32, Section 199.13 a non-participating provider is not an appropriate appealing party. Therefore, if you disagree with the Dental Advisor's opinion, you may appeal the determination if appointed in writing, by the beneficiary, to act as his/her representative. Should you be appointed as a representative, submit a copy of this letter, a signed statement explaining the matter in which you disagree, and any radiographs and relevant information to the subscriber's Dental insurance carrier within 90 days from the date of this letter.

N140   **Alert:** You have not been designated as an authorized OCONUS provider therefore are not considered an appropriate appealing party. If the beneficiary has appointed you, in writing, to act as his/her representative and you disagree with the Dental Advisor's opinion, you may appeal by submitting a copy of this letter, a signed statement explaining the matter in which you disagree, and any relevant information to the subscriber's Dental insurance carrier within 90 days from the date of this letter.

N141   The patient was not residing in a long-term care facility during all or part of the service dates billed.

N142   The original claim was denied. Resubmit a new claim, not a replacement claim.

N143   The patient was not in a hospice program during all or part of the service dates billed.

N144   The rate changed during the dates of service billed.

N146   Missing screening document.

N147   Long term care case mix or per diem rate cannot be determined because the patient ID number is

Claims Processing

missing, incomplete, or invalid on the assignment request.

N148 Missing/incomplete/invalid date of last menstrual period.

N149 Rebill all applicable services on a single claim.

N150 Missing/incomplete/invalid model number.

N151 Telephone contact services will not be paid until the face-to-face contact requirement has been met.

N152 Missing/incomplete/invalid replacement claim information.

N153 Missing/incomplete/invalid room and board rate.

N154 **Alert:** This payment was delayed for correction of provider's mailing address.

N155 **Alert:** Our records do not indicate that other insurance is on file. Please submit other insurance information for our records.

N156 **Alert:** The patient is responsible for the difference between the approved treatment and the elective treatment.

N157 Transportation to/from this destination is not covered.

N158 Transportation in a vehicle other than an ambulance is not covered.

N159 Payment denied/reduced because mileage is not covered when the patient is not in the ambulance.

N160 The patient must choose an option before a payment can be made for this procedure/ equipment/ supply/ service.

N161 This drug/service/supply is covered only when the associated service is covered.

N162 **Alert:** Although your claim was paid, you have billed for a test/specialty not included in your Laboratory Certification. Your failure to correct the laboratory certification information will result in a denial of payment in the near future.

N163 Medical record does not support code billed per the code definition.

N167 Charges exceed the post-transplant coverage limit.

N170 A new/revised/renewed certificate of medical necessity is needed.

N171 Payment for repair or replacement is not covered or has exceeded the purchase price.

N172 The patient is not liable for the denied/adjusted charge(s) for receiving any updated service/item.

N173 No qualifying hospital stay dates were provided for this episode of care.

N174 This is not a covered service/procedure/ equipment/bed, however patient liability is limited to amounts shown in the adjustments under group "PR".

N175 Missing Review Organization Approval.

N176 Services provided aboard a ship are covered only when the ship is of United States registry and is in United States waters. In addition, a doctor licensed to

practice in the United States must provide the service.

N177 **Alert:** We did not send this claim to patient's other insurer. They have indicated no additional payment can be made.

N178 Missing pre-operative photos or visual field results.

N179 Additional information has been requested from the member. The charges will be reconsidered upon receipt of that information.

N180 This item or service does not meet the criteria for the category under which it was billed.

N181 Additional information is required from another provider involved in the care of this member. The charges will be reconsidered upon receipt of that information.

N182 This claim/service must be billed according to the schedule for this plan.

N183 **Alert:** This is a predetermination advisory message, when this service is submitted for payment additional documentation as specified in plan documents will be required to process benefits.

N184 Rebill technical and professional components separately.

N185 **Alert:** Do not resubmit this claim/service.

N186 Non-Availability Statement (NAS) required for this service. Contact the nearest Military Treatment Facility (MTF) for assistance.

N187 **Alert:** You may request a review in writing within the required time limits following receipt of this notice by following the instructions included in your contract or plan benefit documents.

N188 The approved level of care does not match the procedure code submitted.

N189 **Alert:** This service has been paid as a one-time exception to the plan's benefit restrictions.

N190 Missing contract indicator.

N191 The provider must update insurance information directly with payer.

N192 Patient is a Medicaid/Qualified Medicare Beneficiary.

N193 Specific federal/state/local program may cover this service through another payer.

N194 Technical component not paid if provider does not own the equipment used.

N195 The technical component must be billed separately.

N196 **Alert:** Patient eligible to apply for other coverage which may be primary.

N197 The subscriber must update insurance information directly with payer.

N198 Rendering provider must be affiliated with the pay-to provider.

N199 Additional payment/recoupment approved based on payer-initiated review/audit.

N200 The professional component must be billed separately.

N201 A mental health facility is responsible for payment of outside providers who furnish these services/supplies to residents.

N202 **Alert:** Additional information/explanation will be sent separately

N203 Missing/incomplete/invalid anesthesia time/units

N204 Services under review for possible pre-existing condition. Send medical records for prior 12 months

N205 Information provided was illegible

N206 The supporting documentation does not match the claim

N207 Missing/incomplete/invalid weight.

N208 Missing/incomplete/invalid DRG code

N209 Missing/invalid/incomplete taxpayer identification number (TIN)

N210 **Alert:** You may appeal this decision

N211 **Alert:** You may not appeal this decision

N212 Charges processed under a Point of Service benefit

N213 Missing/incomplete/invalid facility/discrete unit DRG/DRG exempt status information

N214 Missing/incomplete/invalid history of the related initial surgical procedure(s)

N215 **Alert:** A payer providing supplemental or secondary coverage shall not require a claims determination for this service from a primary payer as a condition of making its own claims determination.

N216 Patient is not enrolled in this portion of our benefit package

N217 We pay only one site of service per provider per claim

N218 You must furnish and service this item for as long as the patient continues to need it. We can pay for maintenance and/or servicing for the time period specified in the contract or coverage manual.

N219 Payment based on previous payer's allowed amount.

N220 **Alert:** See the payer's web site or contact the payer's Customer Service department to obtain forms and instructions for filing a provider dispute.

N221 Missing Admitting History and Physical report.

N222 Incomplete/invalid Admitting History and Physical report.

N223 Missing documentation of benefit to the patient during initial treatment period.

N224 Incomplete/invalid documentation of benefit to the patient during initial treatment period.

N225 Incomplete/invalid documentation/orders/notes/summary/report/chart.

N226 Incomplete/invalid American Diabetes Association Certificate of Recognition.

N227 Incomplete/invalid Certificate of Medical Necessity.

N228 Incomplete/invalid consent form.

N229 Incomplete/invalid contract indicator.

N230 Incomplete/invalid indication of whether the patient owns the equipment that requires the part or supply.

N231 Incomplete/invalid invoice or statement certifying the actual cost of the lens, less discounts, and/or the type of intraocular lens used.

N232 Incomplete/invalid itemized bill/statement.

N233 Incomplete/invalid operative note/report.

N234 Incomplete/invalid oxygen certification/re-certification.

N235 Incomplete/invalid pacemaker registration form.

N236 Incomplete/invalid pathology report.

N237 Incomplete/invalid patient medical record for this service.

N238 Incomplete/invalid physician certified plan of care

N239 Incomplete/invalid physician financial relationship form.

N240 Incomplete/invalid radiology report.

N241 Incomplete/invalid review organization approval.

N242 Incomplete/invalid radiology films(s)/image(s).

N243 Incomplete/invalid/not approved screening document.

N244 Incomplete/invalid pre-operative photos/visual field results.

N245 Incomplete/invalid plan information for other insurance

N246 State regulated patient payment limitations apply to this service.

N247 Missing/incomplete/invalid assistant surgeon taxonomy.

N248 Missing/incomplete/invalid assistant surgeon name.

N249 Missing/incomplete/invalid assistant surgeon primary identifier.

N250 Missing/incomplete/invalid assistant surgeon secondary identifier.

N251 Missing/incomplete/invalid attending provider taxonomy.

N252 Missing/incomplete/invalid attending provider name.

N253 Missing/incomplete/invalid attending provider primary identifier.

N254 Missing/incomplete/invalid attending provider secondary identifier.

N255 Missing/incomplete/invalid billing provider taxonomy.

N256 Missing/incomplete/invalid billing provider/supplier name.

N257 Missing/incomplete/invalid billing provider/supplier primary identifier.

N258 Missing/incomplete/invalid billing provider/supplier address.

N259 Missing/incomplete/invalid billing provider/supplier secondary identifier.

N260 Missing/incomplete/invalid billing provider/supplier contact information.

N261 Missing/incomplete/invalid operating provider name.

N262 Missing/incomplete/invalid operating provider primary identifier.

N263 Missing/incomplete/invalid operating provider secondary identifier.

N264 Missing/incomplete/invalid ordering provider name.

N265 Missing/incomplete/invalid ordering provider primary identifier.

N266 Missing/incomplete/invalid ordering provider address.

N267 Missing/incomplete/invalid ordering provider secondary identifier.

N268 Missing/incomplete/invalid ordering provider contact information.

N269 Missing/incomplete/invalid other provider name.

N270 Missing/incomplete/invalid other provider primary identifier.

N271 Missing/incomplete/invalid other provider secondary identifier.

N272 Missing/incomplete/invalid other payer attending provider identifier.

N273 Missing/incomplete/invalid other payer operating provider identifier.

N274 Missing/incomplete/invalid other payer other provider identifier.

N275 Missing/incomplete/invalid other payer purchased service provider identifier.

N276 Missing/incomplete/invalid other payer referring provider identifier.

N277 Missing/incomplete/invalid other payer rendering provider identifier.

N278 Missing/incomplete/invalid other payer service facility provider identifier.

N279 Missing/incomplete/invalid pay-to provider name.

N280 Missing/incomplete/invalid pay-to provider primary identifier.

N281 Missing/incomplete/invalid pay-to provider address.

N282 Missing/incomplete/invalid pay-to provider secondary identifier.

N283 Missing/incomplete/invalid purchased service provider identifier.

N284 Missing/incomplete/invalid referring provider taxonomy.

N285 Missing/incomplete/invalid referring provider name.

N286 Missing/incomplete/invalid referring provider primary identifier.

N287 Missing/incomplete/invalid referring provider secondary identifier.

N288 Missing/incomplete/invalid rendering provider taxonomy.

N289 Missing/incomplete/invalid rendering provider name.

N290 Missing/incomplete/invalid rendering provider primary identifier.

N291 Missing/incomplete/invalid rending provider secondary identifier.

N292 Missing/incomplete/invalid service facility name.

N293 Missing/incomplete/invalid service facility primary identifier.

N294 Missing/incomplete/invalid service facility primary address.

N295 Missing/incomplete/invalid service facility secondary identifier.

N296 Missing/incomplete/invalid supervising provider name.

N297 Missing/incomplete/invalid supervising provider primary identifier.

N298 Missing/incomplete/invalid supervising provider secondary identifier.

N299 Missing/incomplete/invalid occurrence date(s).

N300 Missing/incomplete/invalid occurrence span date(s).

N301 Missing/incomplete/invalid procedure date(s).

N302 Missing/incomplete/invalid other procedure date(s).

N303 Missing/incomplete/invalid principal procedure date.

N304 Missing/incomplete/invalid dispensed date.

N305 Missing/incomplete/invalid accident date.

N306 Missing/incomplete/invalid acute manifestation date.

N307 Missing/incomplete/invalid adjudication or payment date.

N308 Missing/incomplete/invalid appliance placement date.

N309 Missing/incomplete/invalid assessment date.

N310 Missing/incomplete/invalid assumed or relinquished care date.

N311 Missing/incomplete/invalid authorized to return to work date.

N312 Missing/incomplete/invalid begin therapy date.

N313 Missing/incomplete/invalid certification revision date.

N314 Missing/incomplete/invalid diagnosis date.

N315 Missing/incomplete/invalid disability from date.

N316 Missing/incomplete/invalid disability to date.

N317 Missing/incomplete/invalid discharge hour.

N318 Missing/incomplete/invalid discharge or end of care date.

N319 Missing/incomplete/invalid hearing or vision prescription date.

N320 Missing/incomplete/invalid Home Health Certification Period.

N321 Missing/incomplete/invalid last admission period.

N322 Missing/incomplete/invalid last certification date.

N323 Missing/incomplete/invalid last contact date.

N324 Missing/incomplete/invalid last seen/visit date.

N325 Missing/incomplete/invalid last worked date.

N326 Missing/incomplete/invalid last x-ray date.

N327 Missing/incomplete/invalid other insured birth date.

N328 Missing/incomplete/invalid Oxygen Saturation Test date.

N329 Missing/incomplete/invalid patient birth date.

N330 Missing/incomplete/invalid patient death date.

N331 Missing/incomplete/invalid physician order date.

N332 Missing/incomplete/invalid prior hospital discharge date.

N333 Missing/incomplete/invalid prior placement date.

N334 Missing/incomplete/invalid re-evaluation date

N335 Missing/incomplete/invalid referral date.

N336 Missing/incomplete/invalid replacement date.

N337 Missing/incomplete/invalid secondary diagnosis date.

N338 Missing/incomplete/invalid shipped date.

N339 Missing/incomplete/invalid similar illness or symptom date.

N340 Missing/incomplete/invalid subscriber birth date.

N341 Missing/incomplete/invalid surgery date.

N342 Missing/incomplete/invalid test performed date.

N343 Missing/incomplete/invalid Transcutaneous Electrical Nerve Stimulator (TENS) trial start date.

N344 Missing/incomplete/invalid Transcutaneous Electrical Nerve Stimulator (TENS) trial end date.

N345 Date range not valid with units submitted.

N346 Missing/incomplete/invalid oral cavity designation code.

N347 Your claim for a referred or purchased service cannot be paid because payment has already been made for this same service to another provider by a payment contractor representing the payer.

N348 You chose that this service/supply/drug would be rendered/supplied and billed by a different practitioner/supplier.

N349 The administration method and drug must be reported to adjudicate this service.

N350 Missing/incomplete/invalid description of service for a Not Otherwise Classified (NOC) code or an Unlisted/By report procedure.

N351 Service date outside of the approved treatment plan service dates.

N352 **Alert:** There are no scheduled payments for this service. Submit a claim for each patient visit.

N353 **Alert:** Benefits have been estimated, when the actual services have been rendered, additional payment will be considered based on the submitted claim.

N354 Incomplete/invalid invoice

N355 **Alert:** The law permits exceptions to the refund requirement in two cases: - If you did not know, and

could not have reasonably been expected to know, that we would not pay for this service; or - If you notified the patient in writing before providing the service that you believed that we were likely to deny the service, and the patient signed a statement agreeing to pay for the service.

If you come within either exception, or if you believe the carrier was wrong in its determination that we do not pay for this service, you should request appeal of this determination within 30 days of the date of this notice. Your request for review should include any additional information necessary to support your position.

If you request an appeal within 30 days of receiving this notice, you may delay refunding the amount to the patient until you receive the results of the review. If the review decision is favorable to you, you do not need to make any refund. If, however, the review is unfavorable, the law specifies that you must make the refund within 15 days of receiving the unfavorable review decision.

The law also permits you to request an appeal at any time within 120 days of the date you receive this notice. However, an appeal request that is received more than 30 days after the date of this notice, does not permit you to delay making the refund. Regardless of when a review is requested, the patient will be notified that you have requested one, and will receive a copy of the determination.

The patient has received a separate notice of this denial decision. The notice advises that he/she may be entitled to a refund of any amounts paid, if you should have known that we would not pay and did not tell him/her. It also instructs the patient to contact our office if he/she does not hear anything about a refund within 30 days

N356 This service is not covered when performed with, or subsequent to, a non-covered service.

N357 Time frame requirements between this service/procedure/supply and a related service/procedure/supply have not been met.

N358 **Alert:** This decision may be reviewed if additional documentation as described in the contract or plan benefit documents is submitted.

N359 Missing/incomplete/invalid height.

N360 **Alert:** Coordination of benefits has not been calculated when estimating benefits for this pre-determination. Submit payment information from the primary payer with the secondary claim.

N362 The number of Days or Units of Service exceeds our acceptable maximum.

N363 **Alert:** in the near future we are implementing new policies/procedures that would affect this determination.

N364 **Alert:** According to our agreement, you must waive the deductible and/or coinsurance amounts.

N365 This procedure code is not payable. It is for reporting/information purposes only.

N366 Requested information not provided. The claim will be reopened if the information previously requested is submitted within one year after the date of this denial notice.

N367 **Alert:** The claim information has been forwarded to a Consumer Spending Account processor for review; for example, flexible spending account or health savings account.

N368 You must appeal the determination of the previously adjudicated claim.

N369 **Alert:** Although this claim has been processed, it is deficient according to state legislation/regulation.

N370 Billing exceeds the rental months covered/approved by the payer.

N371 **Alert:** title of this equipment must be transferred to the patient.

N372 Only reasonable and necessary maintenance/service charges are covered.

N373 It has been determined that another payer paid the services as primary when they were not the primary payer. Therefore, we are refunding to the payer that paid as primary on your behalf.

N374 Primary Medicare Part A insurance has been exhausted and a Part B Remittance Advice is required.

N375 Missing/incomplete/invalid questionnaire/information required to determine dependent eligibility.

N376 Subscriber/patient is assigned to active military duty, therefore primary coverage may be TRICARE.

N377 Payment adjusted based on a processed replacement claim.

N378 Missing/incomplete/invalid prescription quantity.

N379 Claim level information does not match line level information.

N380 The original claim has been processed, submit a corrected claim.

N381 Consult our contractual agreement for restrictions/billing/payment information related to these charges.

N382 Missing/incomplete/invalid patient identifier.

N383 Services deemed cosmetic are not covered

N384 Records indicate that the referenced body part/tooth has been removed in a previous procedure.

N385 Notification of admission was not timely according to published plan procedures.

N386 This decision was based on a national coverage determination (NCD). An NCD provides a coverage determination as to whether a particular item or service is covered. A copy of this policy is available at http://www.cms.hhs.gov/mcd/search.asp. If you do not have web access, you may contact the contractor to request a copy of the NCD.

N387 You should submit this claim to the patient's other insurer for potential payment of supplemental benefits. We did not forward the claim information.

N388 Missing/incomplete/invalid prescription number

N389 Duplicate prescription number submitted.

N390 This service/report cannot be billed separately.

N391 Missing emergency department records.

N392 Incomplete/invalid emergency department records.

N393 Missing progress notes/report.

N394 Incomplete/invalid progress notes/report.

N395 Missing laboratory report.

N396 Incomplete/invalid laboratory report.

N397 Benefits are not available for incomplete service(s)/undelivered item(s).

N398 Missing elective consent form.

N399 Incomplete/invalid elective consent form.

N400 **Alert:** Electronically enabled providers should submit claims electronically.

N401 Missing periodontal charting.

N402 Incomplete/invalid periodontal charting.

N403 Missing facility certification.

N404 Incomplete/invalid facility certification.

N405 This service is only covered when the donor's insurer(s) do not provide coverage for the service.

N406 This service is only covered when the recipient's insurer(s) do not provide coverage for the service.

N407 You are not an approved submitter for this transmission format.

N408 This payer does not cover deductibles assessed by a previous payer.

N409 This service is related to an accidental injury and is not covered unless provided within a specific time frame from the date of the accident.

N410 This is not covered unless the prescription changes.

N418 Misrouted claim. See the payer's claim submission instructions.

N419 Claim payment was the result of a payer's retroactive adjustment due to a retroactive rate change.

N420 Claim payment was the result of a payer's retroactive adjustment due to a Coordination of Benefits or Third Party Liability Recovery.

N421 Claim payment was the result of a payer's retroactive adjustment due to a review organization decision.

N422 Claim payment was the result of a payer's retroactive adjustment due to a payer's contract incentive program.

N423 Claim payment was the result of a payer's retroactive adjustment due to a non standard program.

N424 Patient does not reside in the geographic area required for this type of payment.

N425 Statutorily excluded service(s).

N426 No coverage when self-administered.

N427 Payment for eyeglasses or contact lenses can be made only after cataract surgery.

N428   Service/procedure not covered when performed in this place of service.

N429   This is not covered since it is considered routine.

N430   Procedure code is inconsistent with the units billed.

N431   Service is not covered with this procedure.

N432   Adjustment based on a Recovery Audit.

N433   Resubmit this claim using only your National Provider Identifier (NPI).

N434   Missing/incomplete/invalid present on admission indicator.

N435   Exceeds number/frequency approved/allowed within time period without support documentation.

N436   The injury claim has not been accepted and a mandatory medical reimbursement has been made.

N437   **Alert:** If the injury claim is accepted, these charges will be reconsidered.

N438   This jurisdiction only accepts paper claims

N439   Missing anesthesia physical status report/indicators.

N440   Incomplete/invalid anesthesia physical status report/indicators.

N441   This missed appointment is not covered.

N442   Payment based on an alternate fee schedule.

N443   Missing/incomplete/invalid total time or begin/end time.

N444   **Alert:** This facility has not filed the Election for High Cost Outlier form with the Division of Workers' Compensation.

N445   Missing document for actual cost or paid amount.

N446   Incomplete/invalid document for actual cost or paid amount.

N447   Payment is based on a generic equivalent as required documentation was not provided.

N448   This drug/service/supply is not included in the fee schedule or contracted/legislated fee arrangement.

N449   Payment based on a comparable drug/service/supply.

N450   Covered only when performed by the primary treating physician or the designee.

N451   Missing admission summary report.

N452   Incomplete/invalid admission summary report.

N453   Missing consultation report.

N454   Incomplete/invalid consultation report.

N455   Missing physician order.

N456   Incomplete/invalid physician order.

N457   Missing diagnostic report.

N458   Incomplete/invalid diagnostic report.

N459   Missing discharge summary.

N460   Incomplete/invalid discharge summary.

N461   Missing nursing notes.

N462   Incomplete/invalid nursing notes.

N463   Missing support data for claim.

N464   Incomplete/invalid support data for claim.

N465   Missing physical therapy notes/report.

N466   Incomplete/invalid physical therapy notes/report.

N467   Missing report of tests and analysis report.

N468   Incomplete/invalid report of tests and analysis report.

N469   **Alert:** Claim/service(s) subject to appeal process, see section 935 of Medicare Prescription Drug, Improvement, and Modernization Act of 2003 (MMA).

N470   This payment will complete the mandatory medical reimbursement limit.

N471   Missing/incomplete/invalid HIPPS rate code.

N472   Payment for this service has been issued to another provider.

N473   Missing certification.

N474   Incomplete/invalid certification

N475   Missing completed referral form.

N476   Incomplete/invalid completed referral form

N477   Missing dental models.

N478   Incomplete/invalid dental models

N479   Missing explanation of benefits (coordination of benefits or Medicare secondary payer).

N480   Incomplete/invalid explanation of benefits (coordination of benefits or Medicare secondary payer).

N481   Missing models.

N482   Incomplete/invalid models

N483   Missing periodontal charts.

N484   Incomplete/invalid periodontal charts

N485   Missing physical therapy certification.

N486   Incomplete/invalid physical therapy certification.

N487   Missing prosthetics or orthotics certification.

N488   Incomplete/invalid prosthetics or orthotics certification

N489   Missing referral form.

N490   Incomplete/invalid referral form

N491   Missing/incomplete/invalid exclusionary rider condition.

N492   **Alert:** A network provider may bill the member for this service if the member requested the service and agreed in writing, prior to receiving the service, to be financially responsible for the billed charge.

N493   Missing doctor first report of injury.

N494   Incomplete/invalid doctor first report of injury.

N495   Missing supplemental medical report.

N496   Incomplete/invalid supplemental medical report.

N497   Missing medical permanent impairment or disability report.

N498   Incomplete/invalid medical permanent impairment or disability report.

N499 Missing medical legal report.

N500 Incomplete/invalid medical legal report.

N501 Missing vocational report.

N502 Incomplete/invalid vocational report.

N503 Missing work status report.

N504 Incomplete/invalid work status report.

N505 **Alert:** This response includes only services that could be estimated in real time. No estimate will be provided for the services that could not be estimated in real time.

N506 **Alert:** This is an estimate of the member's liability based on the information available at the time the estimate was processed. Actual coverage and member liability amounts will be determined when the claim is processed. This is not a pre-authorization or a guarantee of payment.

N507 Plan distance requirements have not been met.

N508 **Alert:** This real time claim adjudication response represents the member responsibility to the provider for services reported. The member will receive an explanation of benefits electronically or in the mail. Contact the insurer if there are any questions.

N509 **Alert:** A current inquiry shows the member's consumer spending account contains sufficient funds to cover the member liability for this claim/service. Actual payment from the consumer spending account will depend on the availability of funds and determination of eligible services at the time of payment processing.

N510 **Alert:** A current inquiry shows the member's consumer spending account does not contain sufficient funds to cover the member's liability for this claim/service. Actual payment from the consumer spending account will depend on the availability of funds and determination of eligible services at the time of payment processing.

N511 **Alert:** Information on the availability of consumer spending account funds to cover the member liability on this claim/service is not available at this time.

N512 Alert: This is the initial remit of a non-NCPDP claim originally submitted real-time without change to the adjudication.

N513 **Alert:** This is the initial remit of a non-NCPDP claim originally submitted real-time with a change to the adjudication.

N514 Consult plan benefit documents/guidelines for information about restrictions for this service.

N515 **Alert:** Submit this claim to the patient's other insurer for potential payment of supplemental benefits. We did not forward the claim information. (Use N387 instead).

Note: This RARC will be deactivated effective 10/01/2009.

N516 Records indicate a mismatch between the submitted NPI and EIN.
Start: 03/01/09

N517 Resubmit a new claim with the requested information.
Start: 03/01/09

N518 No separate payment for accessories when furnished for use with oxygen equipment.
Start: 03/01/09

N519 Invalid combination of HCPCS modifiers.
Start: 07/01/09

N520 **Alert:** Payment made from a Consumer Spending Account.
Start: 07/01/09

UB-04

Purpose of UB-04 Claim Form

Not all services rendered by a facility are inpatient services. Providers working in facilities routinely render services on an outpatient basis. Outpatient and partial hospitalization facility claims might be submitted on either a CMS-1500 or a UB-04 depending on the payer.

Usually outpatient services provided in settings that include rehabilitation agencies, certified outpatient rehabilitation facilities, skilled nursing facilities, and hospitals utilize the UB-04 claim form. Those services provided in a private practice or health care providers' office use the CMS-1500 form.

The data elements and design of the UB-04 and its electronic media format were determined by these committees:

* National Uniform Billing Committee (NUBC)

* State uniform billing committees (SUBC)

The NUBC membership comprises representatives of the following organizations:

* Centers for Medicare and Medicaid Services (CMS)

* Blue Cross/Blue Shield Association (BCBSA)

* Health Insurance Association of America (HIAA)

* Office of Civilian Health and Medical Programs of the Uniformed Services (TRICARE)

* Federation of American Hospitals (FAH)

* Healthcare Financial Management Association (HFMA)

* American Hospital Association (AHA)

* Individual hospitals

In determining the data elements to be included on the billing form, the NUBC and SUBCs attempted to balance the needs of the payers with the hospitals' and other providers' burden of providing information.

Most of the UB-04 form locators (FL) are required data elements for Medicare billing. Unassigned codes and spaces on the claim form are available to meet the future reporting needs of CMS, state and local regulatory agencies, and payer-specific requirements for hospital billing. The form and electronic media format are flexible to accommodate most third-party payers and hospitals and to promote uniform use of the claim.

CMS, the NUBC, and the SUBC regularly revise the FL requirements, revenue codes, and subcategory codes. Medicare changes that affect billing and the UB-04 form usually are administered through the online CMS Manual System.

How to Complete the UB-04 Form

What follows is a brief summary of the data fields included on the UB-04 claim form. To view a complete set of instructions, please refer to the complete text of the *UB-04 Data Specifications Manual* available from the NUBC at http://www.nubc.org.

FL 1 Provider Name, Address, Telephone Number, and Country Code

This field contains the name, complete mailing address, telephone number, and fax number of the provider submitting the bill.

FL 2 Pay-to Name and Address

This field contains the address to which payment should be sent if different from the information in FL 1. Not required. If submitted, the data will be ignored.

FL 3a Patient Control Number

Complete this field with the patient account number that allows for the retrieval of individual patient financial records.

FL 3b Medical/Health Record Number

In this field, report the patient's medical record number as assigned by the provider.

FL 4 Type of Bill

In this required field, the four-digit alphanumeric code gives three specific pieces of information after a leading zero. CMS will ignore the leading zero. CMS will continue to process three specific pieces of information. The second digit identifies the type of facility. The third classifies the type of care. The fourth indicates the sequence of this bill in this particular episode of care—referred to as a frequency code.

FL 5 Federal Tax Number

Enter the number assigned by the federal government for tax reporting purposes. Required field. The format is NN-NNNNNNN.

FL 6 Statement Covers Period

Use this field to report the beginning and end dates of service for the period reflected on the fill.

FL 7 Reserved for Assignment by the NUBC

FL 8 Patient Name/Identifier

This field is for the patient's last, middle initial, and first name as well as his or her identification number.

FL 9 Patient Address

The complete address of the patient including the ZIP code.

FL 10 Patient Birthdate

This field includes the patient's complete date of birth using the eight-digit format.

FL 11 Patient Sex

Use this field to identify the sex of the patient.

FL 12 Admission Date

Required field for inpatient and home health. The hospital enters the date the patient was admitted for inpatient care (MMDDYY). The HHA enters the same date of admission that was submitted on the RAP for the episode.

FL 13 Admission Hour

Not required. If submitted, the data will be ignored.

FL 14 Type of Admission/Visit

Enter the appropriate code for the priority of the admission or visit. Required for inpatient bills only.

FL 15 Point of Origin for Admission or Visit

This required field indicates the source of the referral for the visit or admission (e.g., physician, clinic, facility transfer, etc.).

Code Structure:

1   Non-Health Care Facility Point of Origin (Physician Referral)

Inpatient: The patient was admitted to this facility upon an order of a physician.

Usage note: Includes patients coming from home, a physician's office, or workplace.

Outpatient: The patient presents to this facility with an order from a physician for services or seeks scheduled services for which an order is not required (e.g., mammography). Includes non-emergent self referrals.

2   Clinic

Inpatient: The patient was admitted to this facility as a transfer from a freestanding or non-freestanding clinic.

Outpatient: The patient was referred to this facility for outpatient or referenced diagnostic services.

3   Reserved for national assignment.

4   Transfer from a Hospital (Different Facility)

Inpatient: The patient was admitted to this facility as a hospital transfer from an acute care facility where he or she was an inpatient or an outpatient.

Usage Note: Excludes Transfers from Hospital Inpatient in the Same Facility (See Code D).

Outpatient: The patient was referred to this facility for outpatient or referenced diagnostic services by a physician of a different acute care facility.

* For transfers from hospital inpatient in the same facility, see code D.

5   Transfer from a SNF or Intermediate Care Facility (ICF)

Inpatient: The patient was admitted to this facility as a transfer from a SNF or ICF where he or she was a resident.

Outpatient: The patient was referred to this facility for outpatient or referenced diagnostic services by a physician of the SNF or ICF where he or she was a resident.

6   Transfer from Another Health Care Facility

Inpatient: The patient was admitted to this facility as a transfer from another type of health care facility not defined elsewhere in this code list.

Outpatient: The patient was referred to this facility for services by (a physician of) another health care facility not defined elsewhere in this code list where he or she was an inpatient or outpatient.

7   Emergency Room (ER)

Inpatient: The patient was admitted to this facility after receiving services in this facility's emergency room department.

Usage Note: Excludes patients who came to the ER from another health care facility.

Outpatient: The patient received unscheduled services in this facility's emergency department and discharged without an inpatient admission. Includes self-referrals in emergency situations that require immediate medical attention.

8   Court/Law Enforcement

Inpatient: The patient was admitted to this facility upon the direction of a court of law, or upon the request of a law enforcement agency representative.

Usage Note: Includes transfers from incarceration facilities.

Outpatient: The patient was referred to this facility upon the direction of a court of law, or upon the request of a law enforcement agency representative for outpatient or referenced diagnostic services.

9   Information Not Available

Inpatient: The means by which the patient was admitted to this facility is not known.

Outpatient: For Medicare outpatient bills, this is not a valid code.

A   Reserved for national assignment.

B   Transfer From Another Home Health Agency

The patient was admitted to this home health agency as a transfer from another home health agency

C   Readmission to Same Home Health Agency

The patient was readmitted to this home health agency within the same home health episode period.

D   Transfer from hospital inpatient in the same facility resulting in a separate claim to the payer

The patient was admitted to this facility as a transfer from hospital inpatient within this facility resulting in a separate claim to the payer.

E   Transfer from Ambulatory Surgery Center

For Medicare bills, this is not a valid code.

F   Transfer from Hospice and is Under a Hospice Plan of Care or Enrolled in a Hospice Program

For Medicare bills, this is not a valid code.

G-Z   Reserved for national assignment.

FL 16 Discharge Hour

This field is for reporting the hour the patient is discharged from inpatient care. This is field is not required.

FL 17 Patient Discharge Status

Use this field to report the status of the patient upon discharge-required for institutional claims.

Code structure

01   Discharged to home or self care (routine discharge)

02   Discharged/transferred to a short-term general hospital for inpatient care.

03   Discharged/transferred to SNF with Medicare certification in anticipation of covered skilled care (effective 2/23/05). See Code 61 below.

04   Discharged/transferred to an Intermediate Care Facility (ICF)

05   Discharged/transferred to another type of institution not defined elsewhere in this code list (effective 2/23/05).

Usage Note: Cancer hospitals excluded from Medicare PPS and children's hospitals are examples of such other types of institutions.

Definition Change Effective 4/1/08: Discharged/Transferred to a Designated Cancer Center or Children's Hospital.

06   Discharged/transferred to home under care of organized home health service organization in anticipation of covered skills care (effective 2/23/05).

07   Left against medical advice or discontinued care

08   Reserved for national assignment

*09   Admitted as an inpatient to this hospital

10–19   Reserved for national assignment

20   Expired (or did not recover — Religious Non Medical Health Care Patient)

21–29   Reserved for national assignment

30   Still patient or expected to return for outpatient services

31–39   Reserved for National Assignment

40   Expired at home (Hospice claims only)

41   Expired in a medical facility, such as a hospital, SNF, ICF or freestanding hospice (Hospice claims only)

42   Expired - place unknown (Hospice claims only)

43   Discharged/transferred to a federal health care facility. (effective 10/1/03)

Usage note: Discharges and transfers to a government operated health care facility such as a department of defense hospital, a Veteran's Administration (VA) hospital or VA hospital or a VA nursing facility. To be used whenever the destination at discharge is a federal health care facility, whether the patient lives there or not.

44–49   Reserved for national assignment

50   Discharged/transferred to Hospice—home

51   Discharged/transferred to Hospice—medical facility

Code Structure

52–60   Reserved for national assignment

61   Discharged/transferred within this institution to a hospital based Medicare approved swing bed.

62   Discharged/transferred to an inpatient rehabilitation facility including distinct part units of a hospital

63   Discharged/transferred to long term care hospitals

64   Discharged/transferred to a nursing facility certified under Medicaid but not certified under Medicare

65   Discharged/transferred to a psychiatric hospital or psychiatric distinct part unit of a hospital.

66   Discharged/transferred to a Critical Access Hospital (CAH). (effective 1/1/06)

67–69   Reserved for national assignment

70   Discharge/transfer to another type of health care institution not defined elsewhere in the code list. (effective 4/1/08)

71–99   Reserved for national assignment

*In situations where a patient is admitted before midnight of the third day following the day of an outpatient diagnostic service or service related to the reason for the admission, the outpatient services are considered inpatient. Therefore, code 09 would apply only to services that began longer than three days earlier or were unrelated to the reason for admission, such as observation following outpatient surgery, which results in admission.

FLs 18-28 Condition Codes
Use these fields to report conditions or events related to the bill that may affect the processing of it.

FL 29 Accident State
Not used. Data entered will be ignored

FL 30 Reserved for Assignment by the NUBC

FLs 31-34 Occurrence Codes and Dates
The occurrence code and the date fields associated with it define a significant event associated with the bill that affecting processing by the payer (e.g. accident, employment related, etc.).

FLs 35-36 Occurrence Span Codes and Dates
This field is for reporting the beginning and end dates of the specific event related to the bill. Required for inpatient claims.

FL 37 Reserved for Assignment by the NUBC

FL 38 Responsible Party Name and Address
Not Required. For claims that involve payers of higher priority than Medicare.

FLs 39-41 Value Codes and Amounts
These field contain the codes and related dollar amounts to identify the monetary data for processing claims. This field is required by all payers.

FL 42 Revenue Code
These codes identify specific accommodation, unique billing calculations, and ancillary services. This field is required.

FL 43 Revenue Description
This field is used to report the abbreviated revenue code categories included in the bill. This field is not required.

FL 44 HCPCS/Rates/HIPPS Rate Codes
This field is used to report the appropriate HCPCS codes for ancillary services, the accommodation rate for bills for inpatient services, and the Health Insurance Prospective Payment System rate codes for specific patient groups that are the basis for payment under a prospective payment system. This field is required.

FL 45 Service Date
Indicates the date the outpatient service was provided and the date the bill was created using the six-digit format. This field is required.

FL 46 Service Units
In this field, units such as the pints of blood used, miles traveled, and the number of inpatient days are reported. This is a required field.

FL 47 Total Charges—Not Applicable for Electronic Billers
This field reports the total charges-covered and noncovered-related to the current billing period. This is a required field.

FL 48 Noncovered Charges
This field indicates charges that are noncovered by the payer as related to the revenue code.This is a required field.

FL 49 Reserved for Assignment by the NUBC

FL 50 Payer Identification
The name of the payer from which the provider expects payment is reported in this field.

FL 51A (Required), B (Situational), and C (Situational)—Health Plan ID
Report the national health plan identifier when one is established; otherwise report the "number" Medicare has assigned.

FLs 52A, B, and C—Release of Information Certification Indicator
Required. A "Y" code indicates that the provider has on file a signed statement permitting it to release data to other organizations in order to adjudicate the claim. Required when state or federal laws do not supersede the HIPAA privacy rule by requiring that a signature be collected. An "I" code indicates Informed Consent to Release Medical Information for Conditions or Diagnoses Regulated by Federal Statutes. Required when the provider has not collected a signature and state or federal laws do not supersede the HIPAA privacy rule by requiring a signature be collected.

Note: The back of Form CMS-1450 contains a certification that all necessary release statements are on file.

FL 53A, B, and C—Assignment of Benefits Certification Indicator
Not used. Data entered will be ignored.

FLs 54A, B, and C—Prior Payments

Situational. For all services other than inpatient hospital or SNF the provider must enter the sum of any amounts collected from the patient toward deductibles (cash and blood) and/or coinsurance on the patient (fourth/last line) of this column. In apportioning payments between cash and blood deductibles, the first three pints of blood are treated as noncovered by Medicare. Thus, for example, if total inpatient hospital charges were $350.00 including $50.00 for a deductible pint of blood, the hospital would apportion $300.00 to the Part A deductible and $50.00 to the blood deductible. Blood is treated the same way in both Part A and Part B.

FL 55A, B, and C—Estimated Amount Due From Patient

Not required.

FL 56—Billing Provider National Provider ID (NPI)

Required May 23, 2008. However, the CMS may require the NPI sooner than May 23, 2008.

FL 57—Other Provider ID (primary, secondary, and/or tertiary)

Situational. Use this field to report other provider identifiers as assigned by a health plan (as indicated in FL50 lines 1–3) prior to May 23, 2007.

FLs 58A, B, and C—Insured's Name

Required. On the same lettered line (A, B or C) that corresponds to the line on which Medicare payer information is shown in FLs 50–54, the provider must enter the patient's name as shown on the HI card or other Medicare notice. All additional entries across line A (FLs 59–66) pertain to the person named in Item 58A. The instructions that follow explain when to complete these items.

The provider must enter the name of the individual in whose name the insurance is carried if there are payer(s) of higher priority than Medicare and it is requesting payment because:

- Another payer paid some of the charges and Medicare is secondarily liable for the remainder
- Another payer denied the claim
- The provider is requesting conditional payment. If that person is the patient, the provider enters "patient." Payers of higher priority than Medicare include:
  — EGHPs for employed beneficiaries and spouses age 65 or over
  — EGHPs for beneficiaries entitled to benefits solely on the basis of ESRD during a period of up to l2 months
  — LGHPs for disabled beneficiaries
  — An auto-medical, no-fault, or liability insure
  — WC including BL

FL 59A, B, and C—Patient's Relationship to Insured

Required. If the provider is claiming payment under any of the circumstances described under FLs 58 A, B, or C, it must enter the code indicating the relationship of the patient to the identified insured, if this information is readily available.

Effective October 16, 2003

Code	Title
01	Spouse
18	Self
19	Child
20	Employee
21	Unknown
39	Organ Donor
40	Cadaver Donor
53	Life Partner
G8	Other Relationship

FLs 60A, B, and C—Insured's Unique ID (Certificate/Social Security Number/HI Claim/Identification Number (HICN))

Required. On the same lettered line (A, B, or C) that corresponds to the line on which Medicare payer information is shown in FLs 50–54, the provider enters the patient's HICN, i.e., if Medicare is the primary payer, it enters this information in FL 60A. It shows the number as it appears on the patient's HI Card, certificate of award, medicare summary notice, or as reported by the social security office.

If the provider is reporting any other insurance coverage higher in priority than Medicare (e.g., EGHP for the patient or the patient's spouse or during the first year of ESRD entitlement), it shows the involved claim number for that coverage on the appropriate line.

FL 61A, B, and C—Insurance Group Name

Situational (required if known). Where the provider is claiming payment under the circumstances described in FLs 58A, B, or C and a WC or an EGHP is involved, it enters the name of the group or plan through which that insurance is provided.

FL 62A, B, and C—Insurance Group Number

Situational (required if known). Where the provider is claiming payment under the circumstances described in FLs 58A, B, or C and a WC or an EGHP is involved, it enters the identification number, control number or code assigned by that health insurance carrier to identify the group under which the insured individual is covered.

FL 63 Treatment Authorization Code

The identification on the bill that indicates the treatment has been preauthorized by the payer. This field is situational.

FL 64 Document Control Number (DCN)

This number is assigned by the health plan to the bill for their internal control. This field is situational.

FL 65 Employer Name (of the Insured)

This field is for reporting the name of the employer through which health care coverage is provided. This field is situational.

FL 66 Diagnosis and Procedure Code Qualifier (ICD Version Indicator)

This qualifier is used to indicate the version of ICD-9-CM being used. A "9" is required in this field for the UB-04.

FL 67 Principal Diagnosis Code

The ICD-9-CM codes describing the principal diagnosis is reported in this field.

FLs 67 A-Q Other Diagnosis Codes

This field is for reporting all diagnosis codes in addition to the principal diagnosis that coexist, develop after admission, or impact the treatment of the patient or the length of stay.

FL 68 Reserved for Assignment by the NUBC

FL 69 Admitting Diagnosis

This field contains the diagnosis of the patient at the time of admission.

FL 70 -70C Patient's Reason for Visit

The ICD-9-CM codes that report the reason for the patient's outpatient visit is reported here.

FL 71 Prospective Payment System (PPS) Code

This code identifies the DRG based on the grouper software and is required only when the provider is under contract with a health plan.

FL 72 External Cause of Injury (ECI) Code

In the case of external causes of injuries, poisonings, or adverse affects, the appropriate ICD-9-CM diagnosis code is reported in this field.

FL 73 Reserved for Assignment by the NUBC

FL 74 Principal Procedure Code and Date

This field is used to report the principal ICD-9-CM procedure code covered by the bill and the related date.

FL 74 A-74E Other Procedure Codes and Dates

This field identifies all other procedures performed (other than the principal procedure) and the dates they were performed.

FL 75 Reserved for Assignment by the NUBC

FL 76 Attending Provider Names and Identifiers (Including NPI)

This field is for reporting the name and identifier of the provider with the responsibility for the care provided on the claim.

FL 77 Operating Physician Name and Identifiers (Including NPI)

Report the name and identification number of the physician responsible for performing surgical procedure in this field.

FLs 78-79 Other Provider Names and Identifiers (Including NPI)

This field is used for reporting the names and identification numbers of individuals that correspond to the provider type category.

FL 80 Remarks

This field is used to report additional information necessary to process the claim.

FL 81 Code-Code Field

This field is used to report codes that overflow other fields and for externally maintained codes NUBC has approved for the institutional data set.

Revenue Codes

What follows is a list of revenue codes applicable to services provided by physical therapists, occupational therapists, and speech-language pathologists.

042X   Physical Therapy

Revenue code 042X. This code for physical therapy indicates charges for therapeutic exercises, massage, and utilization of effective properties of light, heat, cold, water, electricity, and assistive devices. Recurring outpatient services billed under revenue category code 042X must be billed monthly or at the conclusion of treatment.

0420	Physical Therapy—General
0421	Physical Therapy—Visit Charge
0422	Physical Therapy—Hourly Charge
0423	Physical Therapy—Group Rate
0424	Physical Therapy—Evaluation or Re-evaluation
0429	Physical Therapy—Other Physical Therapy

043X   Occupational Therapy

Revenue code 043X. This occupational therapy code indicates charges for teaching manual skills and independence in personal care to stimulate the patient's mental and emotional activity. Recurring outpatient services billed under revenue category code 043X must be billed monthly or at the conclusion of treatment.

0430	Occupational Therapy—General
0431	Occupational Therapy—Visit Charge
0432	Occupational Therapy—Hourly Charge
0433	Occupational Therapy—Group Rate
0434	Occupational Therapy—Evaluation or Re-evaluation
0439	Occupational Therapy—Other Occupational Therapy

044X   Speech-Language Pathology

0440	Speech-Language Pathology—General
0441	Speech-Language Pathology—Visit Charge
0442	Speech-Language Pathology—Hourly Charge
0443	Speech-Language Pathology—Group Rate
0444	Speech-Language Pathology—Evaluation or Re-evaluation
0449	Speech-Language Pathology—Other Speech-Language Pathology

076X   Treatment or Observation Room

0761	Treatment or Observation Room—Treatment Room

Revenue code 0761. This code for treatment room charges may be used by the physical therapist for debridement procedures. Debridement procedures must be billed with the appropriate CPT code within the surgery range. A debridement CPT code cannot be billed with the physical therapy revenue code. The code must be shown with revenue code 0761 Treatment room. When the debridement is done by a physical therapist who is operating within the scope of his or her licensure, the NPI for the provider should be reported along with the health professional's name. (Remember to check with your contractor first to determine if physical therapists may be reimbursed for debridement services.)

094X   Other Therapeutic Services

(See also 095X, an extension of 094X.)

- 0940   Other Therapeutic Services—General
- 0941   Other Therapeutic Services—Recreational Therapy
- 0942   Other Therapeutic Services—Education/Training
- 0943   Other Therapeutic Services—Cardiac Rehabilitation

Revenue code 0943. This code for cardiac rehabilitation indicates charges for cardiac rehabilitation services. Recurring outpatient services billed under revenue code 0943 must be billed monthly or at the conclusion of the treatment.

- 0944   Other Therapeutic Services—Drug Rehabilitation
- 0945   Other Therapeutic Services—Alcohol Rehabilitation
- 0946   Other Therapeutic Services—Complex Medical Equipment Routine
- 0947   Other Therapeutic Services—Complex Medical Equipment Ancillary
- 0949   Other Therapeutic Services—Other Therapeutic Services

095X   Other Therapeutic Services—Extension of 094X

- 0950   Other Therapeutic Services—Reserved
- 0951   Other Therapeutic Services—Athletic Training
- 0952   Other Therapeutic Services—Kinesiotherapy

Modifiers for Outpatient Claims

When filing an outpatient claim on a UB-04, it is occasionally necessary to append either a CPT or HCPCS Level II modifier indicating that the service has been changed in some way or to specify the anatomical location of the service. These modifiers should be appended to the end of the procedure code in field 44 of the UB-04 form.

The following is a list of modifiers that can be used on the UB-04 when submitting outpatient physical therapy claims:

- 50   Bilateral Procedure
- 52   Reduced Services
- 59   Distinct Procedural Service
- F1   Left hand, second digit
- F2   Left hand, third digit
- F3   Left hand, fourth digit
- F4   Left hand, fifth digit
- F5   Right hand, thumb
- F6   Right hand, second digit
- F7   Right hand, third digit
- F8   Right hand, fourth digit
- F9   Right hand, fifth digit
- FA   Left hand, thumb
- LT   Left side
- RT   Right side
- T1   Left foot, second digit
- T2   Left foot, third digit
- T3   Left foot, fourth digit
- T4   Left foot, fifth digit
- T5   Right foot, great toe
- T6   Right foot, second digit
- T7   Right foot, third digit
- T8   Right foot, fourth digit
- T9   Right foot, fifth digit
- TA   Left foot, great toe

Claims Processing

CPT Definitions and Guidelines

The Physicians' Current Procedural Terminology (CPT®) coding system was developed and is updated annually by the American Medical Association (AMA). The AMA owns and maintains the CPT coding system and publishes its updates annually under copyright. CPT codes predominantly describe medical services and procedures performed by physicians and nonphysician professionals. The codes are classified as Level I of the Healthcare Common Procedure Coding System (HCPCS).

Typically, physical therapists should consider using CPT codes to describe their services. Government studies of patient care evaluate utilization of services by reviewing CPT codes. Because payers may question or deny payment for a CPT code, direct communication is often useful in educating payers about physical therapy services and practice standards. Accurate coding also can help an insurer determine coverage eligibility for services provided.

Appropriate Codes for Physical Therapists

The CPT book is divided into six major sections by type of service provided (evaluation and management, anesthesia, surgery, radiology, pathology and laboratory, and medicine). These sections are subdivided primarily by body system.

The physical therapist in general practice will find the most relevant codes in the physical medicine subsection of the medicine section (codes in the 97001–97799 range). Other services physical therapists provide, particularly those in specialty areas, are described under their appropriate body system within the medicine or surgery section.

For example, the neurological procedures most often performed by physical therapists including electromyography (EMG), are located in the neurology subsection of the medicine section, (95831–95999), while burn care codes (16000–16030) are located in the surgery section. None of the codes for these procedures are listed in the physical medicine subsection although they accurately describe services provided by a physical therapist.

Although codes within the physical medicine series (97001–97799) are most easily recognized by third-party payers as services provided by physical therapists they do not describe all physical therapy procedures. As noted above, some physical therapy services are described in other sections of the manual. You may be able to obtain reimbursement if you can provide a reasonable rationale directly to the payer for the service you are providing and support it with consistent, accurate documentation. However, payment policy may affect the reimbursement of these codes when reported by a physical therapist.

CPT Symbols

There are several symbols used in the CPT book:

- A bullet (●) before the code means that the code is new to the CPT coding system in the current year.

- A triangle (▲) before the code means that the code narrative has been revised in the current year.

- The symbols ►◄ enclose new or revised text other than that contained in the code descriptors.

- Codes with a plus (✦) symbol are "add-on" codes. Procedures described by "add-on" codes are always performed in addition to the primary procedure and should never be reported alone. This concept is applicable only to procedures or services performed by the same physician to describe any additional intraservice work associated with the primary procedure such as additional digits or lesions.

- The symbol ⊘ designates a code that is exempt from the use of modifier 51 when multiple procedures are performed even though they have not been designated as add-on codes.

- The number (#) symbol is new for 2010 and indicates that a code is out of numeric order or "resequenced." Beginning with the 2010 CPT book, the AMA will employ a new numbering methodology of resequencing. According to the AMA there are instances where a new code is needed within an existing grouping of codes and an unused code number is not available. In the instance where the existing codes will not be changed orhave minimal changes, the AMA will assign a code that is not in numeric sequence with the related codes. However, the code and description will appear in the CPT book with the other related codes.

  To facilitate the code sequence and maintain a sequential relationship according to the description of the codes theCPT codes in this grouping will be resequenced. Resequencing is the practice of displaying the codes outside of numerical order according to the description relationship.

Modifiers

A system of two-digit modifiers has been developed to allow the provider to indicate that the service or procedure has been altered by certain circumstances or to provide additional information about a procedure that was performed, or a service or supply that was provided. Fee schedules have been developed based on these modifiers. Some third-party payers, such as Medicare, require physical therapists to use modifiers in some circumstances, and others do not recognize the use of modifiers by physical therapists for coding or billing. Communication with the payer group ensures accurate coding. Addition of the modifier does not alter the basic description for the service, it merely qualifies the circumstances under which the service was provided. Circumstances that modify a service include the following:

- Procedures that have both a technical and professional component were performed

- More than one provider or setting was involved in the service

- Only part of a service was performed

- Unusual events occurred

For example, modifier 59 Distinct procedural service, could be used when billing for both 97022 Whirlpool, and 97597–97606 Wound debridement, to indicate that the two services were distinct from one another, or performed on different areas of the body.

Note that the CPT book uses the term "physician" when describing how a modifier is to be used. This does not limit the use of the modifiers to physicians; any practitioner, including the physical therapist, may use a modifier as long as the service or procedure to be modified can be performed within that practitioner's scope of work.

The following is a list of modifiers used most often by physical therapists:

22 **Increased procedural services.** When the work required to provide a service is substantially greater than typically required, it may be identified by adding modifier 22 to the usual procedure code. Documentation must support the substantial additional work and the reason for the additional work (i.e., increased intensity, time, technical difficulty of procedure, severity of patient's condition, physical and mental effort required).

   NOTE: This modifier should not be appended to an E/M service.

25 **Significant, separately identifiable evaluation and management service by the same physician on the same day of the procedure or other service.** It may be necessary to indicate that on the day a procedure or service identified by a CPT code was performed, the patient's condition required a significant, separately identifiable E/M service above and beyond the other service provided or beyond the usual preoperative and postoperative care associated with the procedure that was performed. A significant or separately identifiable E/M service is defined or substantiated by documentation that satisfies the reported (see Evaluation and Management Services Guidelines for instructions or determining level of E/M service). The E/M service may be prompted by the symptom or condition for which the procedure and/or service was provided. As such, different diagnoses are not required for reporting of the E/M service on the same date. This circumstance may be reported by adding modifier 25 to the appropriate level of E/M service.

   NOTE: This modifier is not used to report an E/M service that resulted in a decision to perform surgery. See modifier 57. For significant, separately identifiable non-E/M services, see modifier 59.

26 **Professional component.** Certain procedures are a combination of a physician component and a technical component. When the physician component is reported separately, the service may be identified by adding modifier 26 to the usual procedure number.

Coding Tip
Identifies that the professional component is being reported separately from the technical component for the diagnostic procedure performed. Payment is based solely on the professional component relative value of the procedure.

32 **Mandated services.** Services related to *mandated* consultation and/or related services (eg, third-party payer, governmental, legislative or regulatory requirement) may be identified by adding the modifier 32 to the basic procedure.

51 **Multiple procedures.** When multiple procedures, other than E/M services, physical medicine and rehabilitation services, or provision of supplies (e.g., vaccines), are performed at the same session by the same provider, the primary procedure or service may be reported as listed. The additional procedure(s) or service(s) may be identified by appending modifier 51 to the additional procedure or service code(s).

52 **Reduced services.** Under certain circumstances a service or procedure is partially reduced or eliminated at the provider's discretion. Under these circumstances the service provided can be identified by its usual procedure number and the addition of modifier 52, signifying that the service is reduced. This provides a means of reporting reduced services without disturbing the identification of the basic service.

59 **Distinct procedural service.** Under certain circumstances, it may be necessary to indicate that a procedure or service was distinct or independent from other non-E/M services performed on the same day. Modifier 59 is used to identify procedures or services, other than E/M services, that are not normally reported together but are appropriate under the circumstances. Documentation must support a different session, different procedure or surgery, different site or organ system, separate incision or excision, separate lesion, or separate injury (or area of injury in extensive injuries) not ordinarily encountered or performed on the same day by the same individual. However, when another already established modifier is appropriate it should be used rather than modifier 59. Only if no more descriptive modifier is available and the use of modifier 59 best explains the circumstances should modifier 59 be used.

   NOTE: Modifier 59 should not be appended to an E/M service. To report a separate and distinct E/M service with a non-E/M service performed on the same date, see modifier 25.

76 **Repeat procedure or service by same physician.** It may be necessary to indicate that a procedure or service was repeated subsequent to the original procedure or service. This circumstance may be reported by adding modifier 76 to the repeated procedure/service.

Coding Tip
Physical therapists in skilled nursing facilities might use modifier 76 for patients paid under Medicare Part B. These patients may receive services in both the morning and the afternoon of the same day, and modifier 76 would indicate that the services were not duplicative. (This applies only to untimed codes.)

HCPCS Level II modifiers may also be appended to CPT codes for services. Refer to the HCPCS Level II Definitions and Guidelines for a listing of the HCPCS Level II modifiers.

Unlisted Procedure Codes

Not all medical services or procedures are assigned CPT codes. The book does not contain codes for infrequently used, or all or new experimental procedures. Each code section contains codes set aside specifically for reporting unlisted procedures. Before choosing an unlisted procedure code, carefully review the CPT code list to ensure that a more specific code is not available. These codes are found at the end of the section or subsection of codes and most often end in either "99" or simply "9." For instance, the unlisted procedure codes in the physical medicine and rehabilitation subsection include:

97039   **Unlisted modality (specify type and time if constant attendance)**

97139   **Unlisted therapeutic procedure (specify)**

97799   **Unlisted physical medicine/rehabilitation service or procedure**

The CPT coding system does contain codes for some new and experimental procedures, see category III CPT codes for more information. Also, check for HCPCS Level II codes if these are acceptable to the third-party payer. Whenever an unlisted code is reported, it is necessary to include a descriptive narrative of the procedure performed. Some payers require that a description of the service or procedure be entered into item 19 of the CMS-1500 claim form since the 08-05 version can no longer accommodate a narrative in item 24. Otherwise, it may be necessary to attach a written summary describing the service. Check with specific payers for requirements. It is advisable to check with payers as to coverage issues concerning unlisted procedures.

Definitions and Guidelines: Procedures

General Guidelines

- Code the procedure as specifically as possible based on the documentation of the physiological system involved, the service performed, and anticipated outcome.

- Select the appropriate five-digit CPT code first, and add a modifier if applicable.

- Outpatient physical or occupational therapy procedures or services provided during the claim period should be itemized on the claim using standard CPT codes. Providers should contact their Medicare contractors to determine if there are any local coverage determinations (LCD), which will provide specific information regarding the coverage and reporting of specific services. Providers should contact their Medicare contractor as payment policies may differ.

- Use the following CPT codes for evaluations:

   97001   **Physical therapy evaluation**
   97002   **Physical therapy reevaluation**
   97003   **Occupational therapy evaluation**
   97004   **Occupational therapy reevaluation**

- If more than one service is provided in a single session (e.g., gait training [97116] and therapeutic exercise [97110]), each procedure should be coded separately. However, note that the number of units charged cannot exceed the total time spent with the patient.

- Any services coded and billed should be documented clearly in the patient's medical record (see the section on documentation).

- The total time of service provided to the patient should support the number of units billed.

- Evaluation and treatment, including use of modalities, should be coded accurately and match the documentation for the patient visit.

- Claims should be submitted as frequently as convenient in order to control cash flow.

- Payers require that physical therapy claims include diagnosis codes in addition to CPT codes. See chapter ICD-9-CM Definitions and Guidelines for more information on diagnostic coding guidelines.

- All bills for physical therapy should include:
   — date of service
   — name of provider (practice's legal name/individual's name and legal assignation)
   — appropriate service code (CPT, HCPCS Level II) and ICD-9-CM diagnosis code
   — number of units, if applicable
   — license number
   — name of primary or referring physician

- Prior authorization from the payer is often required when billing for any unusual services provided.

- Many third-party payers require reauthorization for therapy services every 30–90 days. (Check your payer policy.)

- Physical therapists should document and track for a particular payers successful use of codes related to services and diagnosis codes.

- Codes describing constant attendance modalities are based on 15-minute time increments. Most codes describing therapeutic procedures also are based on 15-minute time increments.

- Work hardening services (97545–97546) are based on hourly increments (i.e., two hours initially and each additional subsequent hour).

- Total time may be a question when more than one body area is being treated. If multiple procedures are appropriately performed concurrently, they should not be billed as done consecutively.

Coding Tip

For Medicare Part B patients, the Centers for Medicare and Medicaid Services (CMS) states that "only the services of the therapist can be billed and paid." However, the presence of a physical therapy student "in the room" does not make the service unbillable. In addition, CMS presents scenarios under which the therapist or physical therapist assistant under the therapist's supervision is considered to directly provide services, even though the student has some involvement.

According to the *Medicare Claims Processing Manual,* Pub. 100-04, chapter 5, section 100.10.1:

According to the *Medicare Benefit Policy Manual,* Pub 100-02, chapter 15, section 230.B.1, only the services of the therapist can be billed and paid under Medicare Part B. The services performed by a student are not reimbursed even if provided under line-of-sight supervision of the therapist; however, the presence of the student in the room does not make the service unbillable. Pay for the direct (one-to-one) patient contact services of the physician or therapist provided to Medicare Part B patients. Group therapy service performed by a therapist or physician may be billed when a student is also present in the room.

Therapists may bill and be paid for the provision of services in the following scenarios:

- The qualified practitioner is present and in the room for the entire session. The student participates in the delivery of the service when the qualified practitioner is directing the service, making the skilled judgment, and is responsible for the assessment and treatment.
- The qualified practitioner is present in the room guiding the student in service delivery when the therapy student and the therapy assistant student are participating in the provision of services, and the practitioner is not engaged in treating another patient or doing other tasks at the same time.
- The qualified practitioner is responsible for the services and as such, signs all documentation. (A student may, of course, also sign but it is not necessary since the Part B payment is for the clinician's service, not the student's services).

10021–69990 Surgical Services and Procedures

Use of these codes by PTs can be problematic because payers recognize that PTs do not perform surgical procedures. However, particularly for patients with burn wounds, some codes found in the surgical section of the CPT book do apply to PTs (16020, 16025, and 16030) and should be used when appropriate.

16000–16030 Burns, Local Treatment

Dressing and debridement of burns, codes 16020-16030, are often considered minor surgical procedures by third-party payers. Check in advance with the payer and follow payer-specific guidelines regarding the billing of minor surgical procedures.

16020	Dressings and/or debridement of partial-thickness burns, initial or subsequent; small (less than 5% total body surface area)
16025	medium (eg, whole face or whole extremity, or 5% to 10% total body surface area)
16030	large (eg, more than one extremity, or greater than 10% total body surface area)

Patients who suffer partial-thickness burns require frequent changes of bandages or dressings and debridement of tissues. Patients may or may not be placed under anesthesia. Devitalized tissue is removed, the wound is cleansed and a new dressing is applied. Report 16020 if without anesthesia, small; report 16025 without anesthesia, medium; and report 16030 if without anesthesia, large.

MED: 100-3, 270.5

Coding Tip

Before assigning a code from this section of the CPT book, see also codes 97597–97606.

20000–29999 Musculoskeletal System

The musculoskeletal section of the CPT book is generally arranged according to body region. Physical therapists most frequently use the strapping and splint application codes which are grouped together (29105–29280, 29505–29590), then arranged by general body region (e.g., upper body extremity, lower extremity).

29000–29799 Application of Casts and Strapping

The code for the initial treatment of a fracture or dislocation includes the application, maintenance, and removal of the first cast or traction. Codes 29700–29750 should only be used to:

- Report the application of a replacement cast or traction device
- Report the initial cast when no other restorative procedure or treatment is performed to stabilize the fracture or dislocation and to provide comfort to the patient
- Report removal and modifications of external fixation devices by other than the provider who applied the initial device

In general, casting supplies should be reported separately.

29105	Application of long arm splint (shoulder to hand)

The provider applies a splint from the shoulder to the hand. A long arm posterior splint is used to immobilize a number of injuries around the elbow and forearm. A cotton bandage is wrapped around the forearm from the midpalm region to midarm. Plaster strips or fiberglass splints are applied along the back of the arm and forearm, maintain the elbows and wrist in the desired position.

MED: 100-2, 15, 100

29125	Application of short arm splint (forearm to hand); static
29126	dynamic

The provider applies a splint from the forearm to the hand. A short arm splint is used to immobilize the wrist. Cotton padding is applied from midforearm to the midpalm region. Plaster strips or fiberglass splint material are applied along the palm side of the hand, extending to midforearm, maintain the wrist in the desired position. An Ace wrap is applied by the provider to hold the splint material in position.

Report 29125 if the splint is static, keeping the wrist totally immobilized. Report 29126 if the splint is dynamic, allowing some movement.

29130   Application of finger splint; static

29131   dynamic

The provider applies a finger splint. This type of splint is applied to immobilize the digits. A twin layer of cotton padding is applied by the provider to the digit, covering the last two joints of that digit. Plaster casting or fiberglass splint material is applied to the finger from just beyond the knuckle to the tip of the finger. Usually the finger is immobilized in a straight position. Report 29130 if the splint applied is static for full immobilization. Report 29131 if the splint applied is dynamic for some movement.

29200   Strapping; thorax

29240   shoulder (eg, Velpeau)

29260   elbow or wrist

29280   hand or finger

The provider performs strapping with tape on a patient of any age. In 29200, this technique was once more frequently used to compress the thorax, offering some support and limiting deep inhalation following fracture. This support does not promote healing, but provides palliative relief. A thoracic elastic or canvas binder is more commonly used. Report 29240 if the strapping is applied to the shoulder; report 29260 if strapping is applied to the elbow or wrist; and report 29280 if strapping is applied to the hand or finger.

MED: 100-2, 15, 100

Coding Tip

Code 29220 has been deleted. Code 29799 should be indicated on the claim when reporting strapping of the low back.

29505   Application of long leg splint (thigh to ankle or toes)

The provider applies a long leg splint from thigh to the ankle or toes. A long leg posterior splint is used to immobilize a number of injuries around the knee or ankle. The provider wraps cotton bandaging around the involved leg from the upper thigh to the ankle or toes. Plaster strips or fiberglass splint material are applied along the posterior aspect of the leg from the upper thigh to the ankle or toes. After the splint material dries, it is secured into place by an Ace wrap.

MED: 100-2, 15, 100

29515   Application of short leg splint (calf to foot)

The provider applies a short leg splint from calf to foot. A short leg splint is used to immobilize the ankle. The provider wraps cotton bandaging from just below the knee to the toes. Plaster strips or fiberglass splinting material are applied to the posterior of the calf, around the heel, and along the bottom of the foot to the toes. The splint material is

allowed to dry. The splint is secured into place with an Ace wrap.

MED: 100-2, 15, 100

29520   Strapping; hip

29530   knee

29540   ankle and/or foot

29550   toes

The provider uses tape to strap a lower extremity. In 29520, taping of the hip for immobilization is rarely used because of the hip muscles' superior strength to that of the tape. A hip spica taping procedure may be used to hold analgesic packs in place and to offer mild support to injured hip adductors or flexors. The patient stands with all weight on the unaffected leg. Six inch Ace wrap is usually used. The end of the wrap begins at the upper part of the thigh and immediately encircles the upper thigh and groin, crossing the starting point. When the starting end is reached the roll is taken completely around the waist and fixed firmly above the iliac crest. The wrap is carried around the thigh at groin level and up again around the waist. The end is secured with tape. Report 29520 if the site taped is the hip. Report 29530 if the site taped is the knee. Report 29540 if the site taped is the ankle or foot. Report 29550 if the site taped is the toes.

MED: 100-2, 15, 100

29580   Strapping; Unna boot

The provider applies an Unna boot to the leg of a patient. An Unna boot is typically used to treat or prevent venostasis dermatitis or ulcers of the lower leg.

It also is used to control postoperative edema like that resulting from an amputation. The provider prepares this semirigid dressing by first making a paste of zinc oxide, gelatin, and glycerin. This is applied to the skin of the leg. A spiral or figure eight bandage is wrapped evenly over the leg. Paste is then reapplied and further bandages are applied in the same fashion until the desired rigidity is obtained. Elastic bandages are often added to the dressings for reinforcement. The dressing is typically replaced at least once a week or more often as needed.

Coding Tip

Unna boot, a medicated dressing wrap usually used for ulcers caused by venous insufficiency, should be coded as 29580. The supplies are usually included in the practice expense for this code, and are not billed separately. If in doubt, check with the individual payer before billing the supplies separately.

✚ Add-On Code   ⊘ Modifer 51 Exempt   # Resequenced Code   ● New Codes   ▲ Changed Codes

● 29581 The health care practitioner applies a multilayer venous wound compression device to the area of the leg below the knee. Compression therapy is often used in the treatment of extensive venous ulcers. The device may consist of a multilayer bandaging system composed only of elastic bandages, or may be paired with a knitted, tubular, open-toed, and heelless elastic knee-length compression garment. In one method, after wound debridement and dressing, cotton gauze and cotton crepe bandages are applied to the lower leg. Next, a positioner is placed over the bandages and adjusted to the desired position. The compression device is slipped over the positioner, adjusted to ensure appropriate placement, and the positioner removed.

Coding Tip

This code is new for 2010. This code should not be reported in conjunction with strapping of the ankle and/or foot (29540) or Unna boot (29580). Depending on payer guidelines for the separate payment of supplies used when providing this procedure, it may be appropriate to separately report the supplies using one or more of the following HCPCS Level II codes that describe the supply: A6530–A6535, A6545, and A6549. Check with the specific payer to determine coverage.

29590 **Denis-Browne splint strapping**

The provider applies Denis-Browne splint strapping to an infant to correct equinovarus deformity. It is performed on infants no later than two to three weeks after birth. The deformed foot is taped to foot plates attached to a crossbar that is no wider than the infant's pelvis. The foot is retaped weekly to maintain a snug fit. This method involves three phases. Phase one requires at least five to six weeks and consists of progressive external rotation and abduction of the foot. The foot is maintained in this for about five months. Phase two consists of placing the foot in an open-toed shoe on the bar in the corrected position for an additional six months or until the infant begins walking. Phase three consists of wearing the shoe and bar at night and a below-knee brace during the day. The day brace has a 90 degree plantar flexion stop and a spring dorsiflexion assist. This is continued for as long as necessary and usually for a minimum of two to three years.

29799 **Unlisted procedure, casting or strapping**

Report this code when a casting or strapping procedure is performed, but is not described by a more specific CPT or HCPCS Level II code.

Coding Tip

A narrative report describing the service or procedure performed and the physician's order must be attached to the claim. A narrative description of the service should be indicated in item 19 of the CMS-1500 claim form.

61000–64999 Nervous System

This subsection includes procedures performed on the skull, meninges, brain, spine and spinal cord, and nerves. The codes are arranged according to the type of procedure and the area involved.

64550–64595 Nervous System-Neurostimulators (Peripheral Nerve)

64550 **Application of surface (transcutaneous) neurostimulator**

In 64550, the provider places electrode pads over the area to be stimulated and connects a transmitter box to the electrodes (e.g., TENS unit). Current is transmitted through the skin to sensory fibers which helps decrease the pain sensation at the brain level.

MED: 100-3, 10.2; 100-3, 130.5; 100-3, 130.6; 100-3, 160.2; 100-3, 160.7.1; 100-3, 230.1; 100-3, 250.1; 100-3, 250.4; 100-3, 270.4; 100-3, 280.13; 100-3, 40.50; 100-3, 45.25

Coding Tip

Application of surface neurostimulator includes instructing the patient on the purpose and operation of the unit, placement of the electrodes, and setting the parameters of the TENS unit. Code 64550 describes the application of the neurostimulator. If using the electrode as a treatment modality see codes 97014 (unattended) or 97032 (attended). Documentation must support the procedure identified on the claim. Some third-party payers provide specific guidelines for the coverage and reporting of this service. Contact specific payers to determine their policies.

90281–99607 Medicine

Within the medicine section, there are subsections for either the type of service being provided (e.g., biofeedback) or for the specialty providing the service (physical medicine and rehabilitation).

90901–90911 Biofeedback

Payment for coverage of biofeedback is determined by the payer. Because of this, a provider often must request prior authorization before providing this service.

Coding Tip

Under Medicare, use of biofeedback as part of a physical therapy plan of care is covered only when it is reasonable and necessary for the individual patient for muscle re-education of specific muscle groups or for treating pathological muscle abnormalities of spasticity, incapacitating muscle spasm, or weakness, and more conventional treatments (heat, cold, massage, exercise, support) have not been successful. As of July 1, 2001 (see the *Medicare National Coverage Determinations Manual*, Pub. 100-03, sec. 30.1.1), biofeedback is covered for the treatment of stress and/or urge incontinence in cognitively intact patients who have failed a documented trial of pelvic muscle exercise (PME) training. A failed trial of PME training is defined as no clinically significant improvement in urinary incontinence after completing up to four weeks of an ordered plan of pelvic muscle exercises to increase periurethral muscle strength. This therapy is not covered for treatment of ordinary muscle tension states or for psychosomatic conditions. Do not use codes 90875 or 90876; these codes are for individual psychophysiological therapy.

90901 **Biofeedback training by any modality**

Biofeedback trains patients to control their autonomic or involuntary nervous systems to help regulate vital signs such as heart rate, blood pressure, temperature, and muscle tension. Monitors of various types are used to indicate body responses, which the patient learns to control in serial sessions. The code applies to any of several modalities of biofeedback training.

MED: 100-3, 130.5; 100-3, 130.6; 100-3, 160.2; 100-3, 230.1; 100-3, 250.1; 100-3, 250.4; 100-3, 270.4; 100-3, 30.1; 100-3, 30.1.1

90911 **Biofeedback training, perineal muscles, anorectal or urethral sphincter, including EMG and/or manometry**

Biofeedback trains patients to control their autonomic or involuntary nervous systems to help regulate vital signs like heart rate, blood pressure, temperature, and muscle tension. The code applies to biofeedback training that uses the monitoring of the anus and/or rectum or urethra—including electromyography (measures muscle contractions) and manometry (measures pressure). This code is not timed.

MED: 100-3, 130.5; 100-3, 130.6; 100-3, 160.2; 100-3, 230.1; 100-3, 250.1; 100-3, 250.4; 100-3, 270.4; 100-3, 30.1; 100-3, 30.1.1

Coding Tip

Treatment of incontinence by pulsed magnetic neuromodulation should be reported using 53899.

92601–92633 Evaluative and Therapeutic Services

92605 **Evaluation for prescription of non-speech-generating augmentative and alternative communication device**

The assessment for the appropriate non-speech-generating augmentative and alternative communication (AAC) device is highly variable and dependent on the patient's age, ability, and motivation. Motor skills, hearing, vision, cognitive abilities, language comprehension, and general health are evaluated to determine the suitability of either a high-tech or low-tech device. Once these are evaluated, an appropriate AAC device is prescribed.

MED: 100-3, 50.2; 100-3, 50.3

Coding Tip

A therapeutic procedure may be reported on the same day as an evaluation or re-evaluation (97001–97002) when the medical record documentation supports the medical necessity of both services.

92607 **Evaluation for prescription for speech-generating augmentative and alternative communication device, face-to-face with the patient; first hour**

+ 92608 **each additional 30 minutes (List separately in addition to code for primary procedure)**

The patient is evaluated face to face by a specialist to determine the motor skills, hearing, cognitive abilities, comprehension, natural speech, esophageal and pharyngeal air flow, general health, and patient motivation for prescription of speech-generating augmentative and alternative communication (AAC) device. Once these are evaluated, an appropriate speech-generating device is prescribed. Report 92607 for the first hour and 92608 for each additional 30 minutes.

MED: 100-3, 50.1; 100-3, 50.2; 100-3, 50.3

92609 **Therapeutic services for the use of speech-generating device, including programming and modification**

This code includes therapeutic services associated with the use of speech generating devices. Services differ according to the device used. Electronic equipment may require routine maintenance, programming, or modification. Speech generating devices may require some patient therapeutic, rehabilitation, or occupational training.

MED: 100-2, 15, 230.3; 100-3, 50.1; 100-3, 50.2; 100-3, 50.3

92610 **Evaluation of oral and pharyngeal swallowing function**

The patient is evaluated to determine the oral and pharyngeal swallowing function. Assessment of the oral cavity includes the size, position, resting tone, range of motion and development of the tongue, lips, and palate. Palpation of the thyroid notch or cricoid arch with swallowing is used to determine elevation of the pharynx. Using a curved probe, sensation of the oral cavity may be assessed. An inventory of cranial nerves must also be included.

MED: 100-3, 50.3

92611 **Motion fluoroscopic evaluation of swallowing function by cine or video recording**

Motion fluoroscopic examinations are performed of the swallowing function by cine or video recording. The patient is seated upright in a normal eating posture. Small amounts of liquid barium and barium-coated foods of varying consistencies, textures, and flavors are administered allowing visualization of the swallowing function by fluoroscopy. The patient is given liquids, pastes, and solid foods that are visually followed from the oral cavity to the pharynx and the cervical esophagus. A portion of this test is usually repeated with the patient in a horizontal position.

MED: 100-2, 15, 230.3; 100-3, 50.3

Coding Tips

Most payers consider these procedures to be speech pathology services and coverage can vary depending on the patient's contractual agreement with the payer.

The majority of payers break speech pathology coverage into two categories—diagnosis, and evaluation and therapeutic services. In most instances, these services must be reasonable and necessary to the treatment of the individual's illness or injury or must be necessary to the establishment of a safe and effective maintenance program required in connection with a specific disease state.

Speech pathology is considered medically appropriate treatment for mental retardation when disorders such as aphasia or dysarthria are exhibited. The diagnosis and treatment of swallowing disorders (dysphagia) are also medically necessary regardless of the presence of a communication disability.

Coding Tip

A therapeutic procedure may be reported on the same day as an evaluation or re-evaluation (97001–97002) when the medical record documentation supports the medical necessity of both services.

92950–93799 Cardiovascular Services

Physical therapists specializing in the area of cardiopulmonary care administer maximum graded exercise tests, rehabilitate acutely ill patients in the intensive care unit, design exercise programs to restore endurance and function for patients with organ transplants, and enable patients with acute and chronic heart or lung problems to resume functional activities. Some of the programs require a team of specialists (cardiac rehabilitation, pulmonary rehabilitation). The patient may be seen for more than an hour a day, progressing in a multiple intervention program including exercise, bronchopulmonary hygiene, and education concerning cardiovascular fitness.

For treatment codes, the physical therapist should select a code based on the outcome of the care (e.g., therapeutic exercise (97110) for strengthening).

Under Medicare, physical therapy is not covered when furnished in connection with cardiac rehabilitation exercise program services (see the *Medicare National Coverage Determinations Manual* Pub. 100-03, sec. 20.10) unless there also is a diagnosed noncardiac condition requiring therapy (e.g., where a patient who is recuperating from an acute phase of heart disease had a stroke which requires physical therapy). While the cardiac rehabilitation exercise program may be considered by some a form of physical therapy, it is a specialized program with separately defined coverage and payment guidelines and is conducted and/or supervised by specially trained personnel whose services are performed under the direct supervision of a physician.

92950–92998 Therapeutic Services and Procedures

92950 Cardiopulmonary resuscitation (eg, in cardiac arrest)

Cardiopulmonary arrest occurs when the patient's heart and lungs suddenly stop. In a clinical setting, cardiopulmonary resuscitation, the attempt at restarting the heart and lungs, is usually directed by a provider or another health care provider who is certified in Advanced Cardiac Life Support (ACLS). The patient's lungs are ventilated by mouth-to-mouth breathing or by a bag and mask. The patient's circulation is assisted using external chest compression. An electronic defibrillator may be used to shock the heart into restarting. Medications used to restart the heart include epinephrine and lidocaine.

93000–93278 Cardiography

93015 Cardiovascular stress test using maximal or submaximal treadmill or bicycle exercise, continuous electrocardiographic monitoring and/or pharmacological stress; with physician supervision, with interpretation and report

A continuous recording of electrical activity of the heart is acquired under the supervision of a provider while the patient is exercising on a treadmill or bicycle and/or given medicines. The stress on the heart during the test is monitored. This code includes the test, provider supervision, and provider interpretation of the report.

MED: 100-3, 20.10; 100-3, 20.15

93016 Cardiovascular stress test using maximal or submaximal treadmill or bicycle exercise, continuous electrocardiographic monitoring, and/or pharmacological stress; physician supervision only, without interpretation and report

An assistant supervised by a physician makes a continuous recording of the electrical activity of a patient's heart while the patient is exercising on a treadmill or stationary bicycle with or without medication. This code applies only to the physician's supervision of the test.

93017 Cardiovascular stress test using maximal or submaximal treadmill or bicycle exercise, continuous electrocardiographic monitoring, and/or pharmacological stress; tracing only, without interpretation and report

An assistant supervised by a physician makes a continuous recording of the electrical activity of a patient's heart while the patient is exercising on a treadmill or stationary bicycle with or without medication. This code applies only to acquiring the test.

93018 Cardiovascular stress test using maximal or submaximal treadmill or bicycle exercise, continuous electrocardiographic monitoring, and/or pharmacological stress; interpretation and report only

Cardiovascular stress test using maximal or submaximal treadmill or bicycle exercise, continuous electrocardiographic monitoring, and/or pharmacological stress; interpretation and report only

94002–94799 Pulmonary Services

These codes include laboratory procedures and interpretation of test results. If a separate identifiable evaluation and management service is performed, the appropriate E/M service code should be reported in addition to 94002–94799.

94010–94799 Other Procedures

94010 **Spirometry, including graphic record, total and timed vital capacity, expiratory flow rate measurement(s) with or without maximal voluntary ventilation**

A spirometer in a pulmonary lab is used to measure functions of the lungs including amount of air in the lungs, rate of expiration, and the amount of air a patient respires. The provider interprets the results of the spirometry and a graphic record is obtained.

94150 **Vital capacity, total (separate procedure)**

This procedure measures the largest volume of air a patient can expire from his lungs. The patient amount of air inhaled and exhaled is measured and calculated with body size to determine the capacity of the lungs. This test is important for determining the threshold of capacity needed for vitality in patients with compromised respiration. For men, this is typically four to five liters; for women, this is normally three to four liters.

This is a separate procedure that by definition is usually a component of a more complex service and not identified separately. When performed alone or with other unrelated procedures/services, it may be reported. If performed alone, list the code; if performed with other unrelated procedures/services, list the code and append modifier 59.

94200 **Maximum breathing capacity, maximal voluntary ventilation**

This code applies to measuring maximum breathing capacity or maximal voluntary ventilation (the largest volume of air that a patient can inhale and exhale in 60 seconds). The patient inhales to the maximum vital capacity then exhales into a spirometer. The provider measures the maximal expiratory flow at 50 percent of expired vital capacity and at 75 percent of expired vital capacity.

94250 **Expired gas collection, quantitative, single procedure (separate procedure)**

Pulmonary function testing is performed in a pulmonary lab using helium, nitrogen open circuit, or another method to check lung functions to include residual capacity or residual volume, the volume of air remaining in the lung after a patient exhales. The provider interprets results. This code applies to collecting and, in a separately reportable procedure, evaluating expired air.

This is a separate procedure that by definition is usually a component of a more complex service and not identified separately. When performed alone or with other unrelated procedures/services, it may be reported. If performed alone, list the code; if performed with other unrelated procedures/services, list the code and append modifier 59.

94350 **Determination of maldistribution of inspired gas: multiple breath nitrogen washout curve including alveolar nitrogen or helium equilibration time**

Pulmonary function testing is performed in a pulmonary lab using helium, nitrogen open circuit, or another method to check lung functions to include residual capacity or residual volume, the volume of air remaining in the lung after a patient exhales. The provider interprets results. The code applies to the distribution of inspired gas using multiple breath nitrogen washout curves and including alveolar nitrogen or helium equilibration time.

94375 **Respiratory flow volume loop**

Pulmonary function testing is performed in a pulmonary lab using helium, nitrogen open circuit, or another method to check lung functions to include residual capacity or residual volume, the volume of air remaining in the lung after a patient exhales. The provider interprets results. The code applies to measuring the respiratory flow volume loop.

94620 **Pulmonary stress testing; simple (eg, 6-minute walk test, prolonged exercise test for bronchospasm with pre- and post-spirometry and oximetry)**

MED: 100-3, 240.7

94621 **complex (including measurements of CO_2 production, O_2 uptake, and electrocardiographic recordings)**

A pulmonary exercise stress test is done to test how much air moves in and out of the lungs during exercise and to determine where breathing problems are occurring, since they may be in the lungs, heart, or circulation. A simple exercise stress test is done with the patient riding a stationary bike (ergometer) or walking on a treadmill. Heart rate, breathing, and blood pressure are monitored before beginning the exercise. Basic ventilation studies are performed with a spirometer and recording device in a simple exercise test (94620) as the patient breathes through a mouthpiece and connecting tube while a nose clip prevents nasal breathing. The patient's oxygen level is monitored with pulse oximetry. Complex testing (94621) uses electrodes placed on the upper body to monitor the heart. Throughout the process, blood samples may be taken to measure oxygen uptake and carbon dioxide waste products in the blood during exercise.

MED: 100-3, 20.15

94640 **Pressurized or nonpressurized inhalation treatment for acute airway obstruction or for sputum induction for diagnostic purposes (eg, with an aerosol generator, nebulizer, metered dose inhaler or intermittent positive pressure breathing (IPPB) device)**

+ Add-On Code   ⊘ Modifer 51 Exempt   # Resequenced Code   ● New Codes   ▲ Changed Codes

Coding Tip

Append modifier 76 Repeat procedure or service by same physician, to codes 94640 and 94642 when more than one treatment is performed on the same date of service.

94642 Aerosol inhalation of pentamidine for pneumocystis carinii pneumonia treatment or prophylaxis

An antimicrobial medication called pentamidine is given in cases of pneumocystis carinii pneumonia treatment or prophylaxis in high risk groups. The patient breathes the aerosolized medication into his lungs.

94644 Continuous inhalation treatment with aerosol medication for acute airway obstruction; first hour

+ 94645 each additional hour (List separately in addition to code for primary procedure)

The patient breathes the aerosolized medication into the lungs for one or more hours.

Coding Tip

Code 94645 must be used in conjunction with code 94644. Code 94645 is an add-on code. As an "add-on" procedure, this service is not subject to multiple procedure rules. No reimbursement reduction or modifier 51 is applied. Add-on codes describe additional intraservice work associated with the primary procedure. They are performed by the same physician, on the same date of service as the primary service or procedure, and must never be reported as a stand-alone code.

94660 Continuous positive airway pressure ventilation (CPAP), initiation and management

MED: 100-4, 12, 30.6.12

94662 Continuous negative pressure ventilation (CNP), initiation and management

94664 Demonstration and/or evaluation of patient utilization of an aerosol generator, nebulizer, metered dose inhaler or IPPB device

Coding Tip

Report code 94664 only once per date of service.

94667 Manipulation chest wall, such as cupping, percussing and vibration to facilitate lung function; initial demonstration and/or evaluation

A provider manipulates the chest wall—cupping, vibration, and percussion—to help mobilize secretions and improve breathing for some lung disorders. The code applies to evaluation and/or demonstration.

MED: 100-3, 150.1; 100-3, 240.7

94668 Manipulation chest wall, such as cupping, percussing and vibration to facilitate lung function; subsequent

A provider manipulates the chest wall—cupping, vibration, and percussion—to help mobilize secretions and improve breathing for some lung disorders. The code applies to subsequent treatment.

MED: 100-3, 150.1; 100-3, 240.7

94680 Oxygen uptake, expired gas analysis; rest and exercise, direct, simple

Pulmonary testing supervised by a provider in a lab measures functions of the lungs. The code applies to collecting expired air and evaluating oxygen uptake using direct methods during rest and exercise.

94681 Oxygen uptake, expired gas analysis; including CO_2 output, percentage oxygen extracted

Pulmonary testing supervised by a provider in a lab measures functions of the lungs. The code applies to collecting expired air and evaluating oxygen uptake, carbon dioxide output, and percentage oxygen extracted.

94690 Oxygen uptake, expired gas analysis; rest, indirect (separate procedure)

Pulmonary testing supervised by a provider in a lab measures functions of the lungs. The code applies to collecting expired air and evaluating oxygen uptake using indirect methods during rest.

This is a separate procedure that by definition is usually a component of a more complex service and not identified separately. When performed alone or with other unrelated procedures/services, it may be reported. If performed alone, list the code; if performed with other unrelated procedures/services, list the code and append modifier 59.

94760 Noninvasive ear or pulse oximetry for oxygen saturation; single determination

A sensor is placed on either the ear lobe or finger to measure oxygen levels in the blood for a pulse oximetry. A light shines through the capillary bed for the measurement. The code applies to a single measurement.

MED: 100-4, 12, 30.6.12

94761 Noninvasive ear or pulse oximetry for oxygen saturation; multiple determinations (eg, during exercise)

A sensor is placed on either the ear lobe or finger to measure oxygen levels in the blood for a pulse oximetry. A light shines through the capillary bed for the measurement. The code applies to multiple measurements.

MED: Pub. 100-4, 12, 30.6.12

95803–96020 Neurology and Neuromuscular Procedures

Physical therapists in private practice may bill for the technical and professional component of certain diagnostic tests in the 95860–95937 code range, such as electromyograms and nerve conduction studies. The professional component is covered by Medicare as outpatient physical therapy when performed by a PT who meets the following criteria:

- The PT is certified by the American Board of Physical Therapist Specialties (ABPTS) as a clinical electrophysiologic-certified specialist.

- The PT is personally supervised by an ABPTS-certified PT. Only the certified PT may bill for the service.

Medicare will permit a PT without ABPTS certification to provide certain electromyography services if that PT was not ABPTS-certified as of July 1, 2001, and had been furnishing such diagnostic tests prior to May 1, 2001. The requirements vary depending on the CPT code billed.

Some third-party payers, such as Medicare, reimburse only for the technical portion of many procedures whose codes are in this subsection of the CPT book. It is important for each therapist to try to determine how insurers require physical therapists to bill services. Therapists should keep track of experiences with each insurance company and policy, providing data for future claims.

- Single fiber EMG testing is the innervation of one or more nerve cell(s) and some of the muscles stimulated. Code 95872 describes testing of each muscle studied. Normally, 20 pairs of nerves must be studied to significantly study each muscle. Each muscle is coded only once. However, if another muscle is studied, then the code is reported again.

- Nerve conduction studies describe the stimulation of nerves and recording from the connected muscle (motor) or the nerve itself (sensory). When the same nerve is stimulated multiple times or at multiple sites, use the code only once. When different nerves are studied, code each nerve separately.

- Analysis and programming of neurostimulators are reported using codes 95970–95982. Code assignment is based upon whether the stimulator system is simple or complex, intraoperative or subsequent, and the site affected by the stimulation (eg, peripheral, intracranial or spinal nerves).

- Somatosensory evoked potential testing is performed to access the proximal central nervous system. An average of 500–1,000 studies of each site is performed. Use each code only once even if two nerve studies are done per limb. These studies are also considered bilateral, so that if only one limb is studied, modifier 52 is appropriate.

- Modifier 51, multiple procedures, is not appropriate when reporting nerve conduction studies (95900–95904) performed on multiple nerves.

- The following codes can be used in addition to the standard evaluation. Note that, because these codes are outside the physical medicine series of codes, it is advisable for the physical therapist to obtain payment information or prior authorization from the payer before rendering the service.

  95831–95857 (muscle and range of motion testing)

  95860–95872 (electromyography)

  95900–95904 (nerve conduction tests)

- When electrical stimulation is used to aid bone healing, the bone stimulation code 20974 should be billed (if allowed by the carrier); the codes for nerve stimulation (CPT codes 64550–64595) are inappropriate for this service.

- Separate HCPCS Level II codes are used for TENS electrodes or batteries as allowed by payer guidelines.

- Electrical nerve stimulation: Submit claims for reasonable and necessary electrical stimulation to delay or prevent disuse atrophy, but only when your documentation indicates that the nerve supply (including brain, spinal cord, and peripheral nerves) to the muscle is intact, and other nonneurological reasons for disuse are causing atrophy.

- Electrotherapy for the treatment of facial nerve paralysis, such as Bell's palsy, is not a covered service by Medicare and most other third-party payers.

- Submit claims for functional electrical stimulation (FES) used to test the suitability of electrical nerve stimulation for improving the patient's functional ability when the PT notes document the loss of this ability or may be used to treat the problem. For example, FES could be used to test whether stimulating the dorsiflexors of the ankle would reduce toe drag during the swing-through phase of gait. Document the functional limitations for which FES is used.

95831–95857 Muscle and Range of Motion Testing

Coding Tip
A more appropriate code for a physical therapist to bill muscle testing, based on the procedure performed, may be code 97750 Physical performance test or measurement.

95831   **Muscle testing, manual (separate procedure) with report; extremity (excluding hand) or trunk**

Individual muscles or muscle groups are tested for strength. The code applies to manual testing of the arm, leg, or trunk.

This is a separate procedure that by definition is usually a component of a more complex service and not identified separately. When performed alone or with other unrelated procedures/services, it may be reported. If performed alone, list the code; if performed with other unrelated procedures/services, list the code and append modifier 59.

95832   **Muscle testing, manual (separate procedure) with report; hand with or without comparison with normal side**

Individual muscles or muscle groups are tested for strength. The code applies to manual testing of the hands.

This is a separate procedure that by definition is usually a component of a more complex service and not identified separately. When performed alone or with other unrelated procedures/services, it may be reported. If performed alone, list the code; if performed with other unrelated procedures/services, list the code and append modifier 59.

95833   **Muscle testing, manual (separate procedure) with report; total evaluation of body, excluding hands**

Individual muscles or muscle groups are tested for strength. The code applies to manual testing of the body, excluding the hands.

This is a separate procedure that by definition is usually a component of a more complex service and not identified separately. When performed alone or with other unrelated procedures/services, it may be reported. If performed alone, list the code; if performed with other unrelated procedures/services, list the code and append modifier 59.

95834   **Muscle testing, manual (separate procedure) with report; total evaluation of body, including hands**

Individual muscles or muscle groups are tested for strength. The code applies to manual testing of the body, including the hands.

This is a separate procedure that by definition is usually a component of a more complex service and not identified separately. When performed alone or

with other unrelated procedures/services, it may be reported. If performed alone, list the code; if performed with other unrelated procedures/services, list the code and append modifier 59.

95851   **Range of motion measurements and report (separate procedure); each extremity (excluding hand) or each trunk section (spine)**

Testing determines active and passive range of motion for extremities and joints. The code applies to manually testing each arm or leg or sections of the spine in a separately reported procedure.

This is a separate procedure that by definition is usually a component of a more complex service and not identified separately. When performed alone or with other unrelated procedures/services, it may be reported. If performed alone, list the code; if performed with other unrelated procedures/services, list the code and append modifier 59.

95852   **Range of motion measurements and report (separate procedure); hand, with or without comparison with normal side**

Testing determines active and passive range of motion for joints of the hand. The code applies to manually testing the hands.

This is a separate procedure that by definition is usually a component of a more complex service and not identified separately. When performed alone or with other unrelated procedures/services, it may be reported. If performed alone, list the code; if performed with other unrelated procedures/services, list the code and append modifier 59.

95860–95872 Electromyography

95860   **Needle electromyography; one extremity with or without related paraspinal areas**

95861   **two extremities with or without related paraspinal areas**

95863   **three extremities with or without related paraspinal areas**

95864   **four extremities with or without related paraspinal areas**

Needle electromyography (EMG) records the electrical properties of muscle using an oscilloscope. Recordings, which may be amplified and heard through a loudspeaker, are made during needle insertion, with the muscle at rest, and during contraction. Code 95860 should be used when one extremity (arm or leg) is tested, 95861 for tests of two extremities, 95863 for tests of three extremities and 95864 for tests of four extremities.

95866   **Needle electromyography; hemidiaphragm**

Needle electromyography (EMG) records the electrical properties of muscle using an oscilloscope. Recordings, which may be amplified and heard through a loudspeaker, are made during needle insertion, with the muscle at rest and during contraction. This code is specific to the nerves of the hemidiaphragm.

95867 Needle electromyography; cranial nerve supplied muscle(s), unilateral

95868 cranial nerve supplied muscles, bilateral

Needle electromyography (EMG) records the electrical properties of muscle using an oscilloscope. Recordings, which may be amplified and heard through a loudspeaker, are made during needle insertion, with the muscle at rest, and during contraction. These codes are specific to the twelve nerves that emerge from or enter the cranium. 95867 should be used for unilateral studies and 95868 for bilateral studies.

95869 Needle electromyography; thoracic paraspinal muscles (excluding T1 or T12)

95870 limited study of muscles in one extremity or non-limb (axial) muscles (unilateral or bilateral), other than thoracic paraspinal, cranial nerve supplied muscles, or sphincters

Needle electromyography (EMG) records the electrical properties of thoracic paraspinal muscles, excluding T1 or T12 (95869) using an oscilloscope. Recordings, which may be amplified and heard through a loudspeaker, are made during needle insertion, with the muscle at rest, and during contraction. Report 95870 for a limited study of muscles in one extremity or non-limb (axial) muscles other than thoracic paraspinal or cranial supplied muscles or sphincters.

95872 Needle electromyography using single fiber electrode, with quantitative measurement of jitter, blocking and/or fiber density, any/all sites of each muscle studied

Needle electromyography (EMG) records the electrical properties of muscle using an oscilloscope. Recordings, which may be amplified and heard through a loudspeaker, are made during needle insertion, with the muscle at rest, and during contraction. This procedure uses a single fiber electrode to obtain additional information on specific muscles, including quantitative measurement of jitter, blocking, and/or fiber density.

95873–95875 Guidance for Chemodenervation and Ischemic Muscle Testing

95875 Ischemic limb exercise test with serial specimen(s) acquisition for muscle(s) metabolite(s)

Needle electromyography (EMG) records the electrical properties of muscle using an oscilloscope. Recordings, which may be amplified and heard through a loudspeaker, are made during needle insertion, with the muscle at rest, and during contraction. This procedure tests electrical properties of ischemic limb during exercise and includes lactic acid determination.

95900–95904 Nerve Conduction Tests

⊘ **95900** Nerve conduction, amplitude and latency/velocity study, each nerve; motor, without F-wave study

⊘ **95903** motor, with F-wave study

⊘ **95904** sensory

Nerve testing uses sensors to measure and record nerve functions including: conduction, amplitude, and latency/velocity. Nerves are stimulated with electric shocks along the course of the muscle. The time required to initiation of contraction is measured and recorded. Measurements of distal latency, the time required to traverse the segment nearest the muscle, and conduction velocity, the time required for an impulse to travel a measured length of nerve, are also recorded. Code 95900 applies to motor testing without F-wave studies. Code 95903 applies to motor testing with F-wave studies; code 95904 if the test is of sensory response. Each nerve tested can be billed separately.

Coding Tip

The use of codes 95900–95904 for sensory nerve conduction threshold (SNCT) testing is not appropriate since this procedure fails to provide information on the nerve conduction, amplitude, latency, or velocity of the nerve response as described by these codes. HCPCS Level II code G0255 should be reported for this service, which is not covered by Medicare as not reasonable and necessary.

● **95905** Motor and/or sensory nerve conduction, using preconfigured electrode array(s), amplitude and latency/velocity study, each limb, includes F-wave study when performed, with interpretation and report

Nerve testing uses sensors to measure and record nerve functions including conduction, amplitude, and latency/velocity. Nerves are stimulated with electric shocks along the course of the muscle. The time required to initiate contraction is measured and recorded. Measurements of distal latency (the time required to traverse the segment nearest the muscle) and conduction velocity (the time required for an impulse to travel a measured length of nerve) are also recorded. Code 95905 reports motor and/or sensory nerve conduction tests performed using preconfigured electrode arrays. It includes F-wave study, when performed, as well as interpretation and report. Report 95905 only once for each limb studied.

Coding Tip

Code 95905 is new for 2010. It should be reported only once per extremity studied. This code is used to indicate nerve conduction studies performed with preconfigured electrodes that are customized to a particular anatomic site.

⊘ **95992** Canalith repositioning procedure(s) (eg, Epley maneuver, Semont maneuver), per day]

Benign paroxysmal positional vertigo (BPPV) is an inner ear problem caused by calcium crystals (otoconia) floating in the fluid of the inner ear that becomes lodged in the semicircular canals. With a change in position, these crystals may stimulate a portion of the inner ear, resulting in repeated short intense periods of dizziness and vertigo. The provider treats BPPV with a series of repositioning movements known as Epley or Semont maneuvers. The patient is methodically assisted in moving through planned positions during the maneuver in order to assist in the dislodging of these crystals in the ear canal, which may cause temporary dizziness and nausea. Report code 95992 once for each day of treatment.

Coding Tip
Because CMS bundles code 95992 with codes for which physical therapists do not bill, Medicare policy permits PTs to use code 97112 to bill for canalith repositioning services. Some private payers allow PTs to use 95992; check with your payer for individual policies.

Coding Tip
Codes 92531 and/or 92532 should not be reported in addition to 95992.

96000–96004 Motion Analysis

These codes are used to report services that are performed as part of a therapeutic or diagnostic patient evaluation and are provided in a dedicated motion analysis laboratory using sophisticated videotaping, computerized 3-D kinematics, and dynamic electromyography equipment.

96000 Comprehensive computer-based motion analysis by video-taping and 3-D kinematics;

96001   with dynamic plantar pressure measurements during walking

Human motion analysis has several applications including biomedical and athletic performance. To conduct a biomedical analysis, patient movements are recorded, digitized, copied on computer, and processed. For example, when calculating net joint moments, the joint center is calculated using a local coordinate system created from body markers. When tracking markers in 3D using video, two or more cameras are used to identify the markers. After all parameters are found (e.g., linear acceleration, angular acceleration, ground reaction forces) and gathered using stereo X-rays or MRI techniques, the resultant net joint forces and moments can be calculated. In 3-D kinematics, joint centers are digitized for the first few frames of the sequence recorded. Linear parameters of movement can be measured to assess horizontal and vertical motion. Also, angular parameters can measure the degrees of movement of the joints to analyze specific joint motion. In 96001, while taking dynamic plantar pressure measurements, data is collected using a pressure sensor platform positioned on a walkway. The patient walks along the walkway so pressure data can be analyzed in areas of the foot (i.e., the heel, metatarsal heads, and the hallux). The peak pressure is determined in all areas and the highest pressure of all sites (i.e., peak pressure foot) is measured. Report

96004 in addition to each of these codes for physician review and interpretation of results, which includes the physician's written report.

96002 Dynamic surface electromyography, during walking or other functional activities, 1-12 muscles

Electrodes placed on the muscle belly, parallel to the grain of the muscle fiber, detects an electrical signal that comes from active muscles (the patient is in motion during the test). The strength and pattern of the signal is seen on a computer screen and the data is collected in a software program that is able to run various analyses of the data to create useful reports regarding muscle function. For example, gait analysis allows the provider to analyze time normal activation patterns separately for stance and swing phases between conditions or against data base values. Report 96002 for a study of one to 12 muscles. Report 96004 in addition to this code for physician review and interpretation of results, which includes the physician's written report.

96003 Dynamic fine wire electromyography, during walking or other functional activities, 1 muscle

Electrodes placed in the muscle belly, parallel to the grain of the muscle fiber, detect an electrical signal that comes from active muscles (the patient is in motion during the test). The strength and pattern of the signal is seen on a computer screen and the data is collected in a software program that is able to run various analyses of the data to create useful reports regarding muscle function. For example, gait analysis allows the provider to analyze time normal activation patterns separately for stance and swing phases between conditions or against database values. Use 96003 to report dynamic fine wire electromyography for one muscle. Report 96004 in addition to this code for physician review and interpretation of results, which includes the physician's written report.

Coding Tip
Codes 95860–95864 and 95869–95872 should not be used to report motion analysis or reported with codes 96002–96003 for motion analysis.

96004 Physician review and interpretation of comprehensive computer based motion analysis, dynamic plantar pressure measurements, dynamic surface electromyography during walking or other functional activities, and dynamic fine wire electromyography, with written report

The provider reviews and interprets computer-based motion analysis, dynamic plantar pressure measurements, dynamic surface electromyography during walking or other functional activities, and dynamic fine wire electromyography performed using codes 96000, 96001, 96002, and 96003 to report the service.

+ Add-On Code   ⊘ Modifer 51 Exempt   # Resequenced Code   ● New Codes   ▲ Changed Codes

CPT Definitions & Guidelines

96101–96125 Central Nervous System Assessments/Tests

These codes are used to report services provided during testing of the cognitive function of the central nervous system.

Tests in this subsection include psychological testing, assessment of aphasia, developmental testing, neurobehavioral status examination and neuropsychological testing battery. These codes are billed per hour with the exception of code 96120.

Information obtained through the assessment is interpreted and a written report is generated. The interpretation and report are included in the service.

96105 **Assessment of aphasia (includes assessment of expressive and receptive speech and language function, language comprehension, speech production ability, reading, spelling, writing, eg, by Boston Diagnostic Aphasia Examination) with interpretation and report, per hour**

The provider administers tests to measure communication problems such as speech and writing in an aphasic patient. The code applies to each hour of testing.

MED: 100-1, 3, 30; 100-1, 3, 30.1; 100-1, 3, 30.2; 100-1, 3, 30.3; 100-2, 15, 160; 100-2, 15, 170; 100-2, 15, 80.2; 100-4, 12, 150; 100-4, 12, 160; 100-4, 12, 170; 100-4, 12, 170.1; 100-4, 12, 210; 100-4, 5, 20

96110 **Developmental testing; limited (eg, Developmental Screening Test II, Early Language Milestone Screen), with interpretation and report**

The provider measures cognitive, psychomotor and other abilities characteristic to development through written, oral, or combined format testing. The code applies to limited testing.

MED: 100-1, 3, 30; 100-1, 3, 30.1; 100-1, 3, 30.2; 100-1, 3, 30.3; 100-2, 15, 160; 100-2, 15, 170; 100-2, 15, 80.2; 100-4, 12, 150; 100-4, 12, 160; 100-4, 12, 170; 100-4, 12, 170.1; 100-4, 12, 210; 100-4, 5, 20

96125 **Standardized cognitive performance testing (eg, Ross Information Processing Assessment) per hour of a qualified health care professional's time, both face-to-face time administering tests to the patient and time interpreting these test results and preparing the report**

A qualified health care professional administers standardized cognitive performance testing to evaluate such factors as the patient's immediate, recent, and remote memory; temporal and spatial orientation; general information recall; problem-solving and abstract reasoning abilities; organizational skills; and auditory processing and retention. This code applies to each hour of testing and includes face-to-face time administering tests to the patient, as well as interpretation and preparation of the report.

97001–97799 Physical Medicine and Rehabilitation

The codes in this section are those most commonly used by physical therapists. Other appropriately qualified providers may report these codes depending on their scope of practice. Similarly, as evidenced by the range of codes listed in this book, physical therapists are not restricted to the use of only these physical medicine and rehabilitation codes to describe their services.

Supplies and Materials Guidelines

Codes for materials and supplies (e.g., prostheses, orthoses, educational items) can be billed in addition to the services themselves if (1) the payer permits providers to bill for supplies and materials, (2) the payer accepts HCPCS codes from providers, and (3) the item is not an inherent part of another service being billed, such as a topical agent, which is an inherent part of ultrasound.

Coding Tip
Under the RBRVS payment methodology, supplies that typically are used in the delivery of a service (such as electrodes) have been included in the calculation of the practice expense value for the code and should not be billed separately.

Separate HCPCS Level II modifiers must be used for patients who are renting (modifier RR) equipment.

When billing for supplies, try to be as specific as possible. In addition to the general supply and material CPT code (99070), there are HCPCS Level II A, E, and L codes that may describe the specific supply provided.

Fabrication of temporary prostheses, braces and splints: submit claims for reasonable and necessary fabrication of temporary prostheses, braces and splints, and any reasonable and necessary skilled training needed in their safe and effective use. Indicate the need for the device and training, documenting the patient's functional limitations.

97001–97006 Evaluation and Re-evaluation Services

These services can be performed in any setting that physical therapy services are available and reported through CPT codes (e.g., patient's home, physical therapist private practice or other outpatient facility, skilled nursing facility, hospital outpatient department). Be certain that correct place of service is indicated on claim form. See the claims processing chapter for more information regarding place of service codes.

97001 **Physical therapy evaluation**

Physical therapy evaluation is a dynamic process in which the physical therapist makes clinical judgments based on data gathered during examination. Examination includes taking a comprehensive history, performing a systems review and conducting tests and measures. Tests and measures may include but are not limited to tests of range of motion, motor function, muscle performance, joint integrity, neuromuscular status and review of orthotic or prosthetic devices. The PT will evaluate the examination findings, establish a physical therapy diagnosis, determine the prognosis, and develop a plan of care that includes anticipated goals and expected outcomes, interventions to be used, and anticipated discharge plans.

MED: 100-3, 20.10

97002   Physical therapy re-evaluation

The PT reexamines the patient/client to evaluate progress and to modify or redirect intervention and/or revise anticipated goals and expected outcomes. Reexamination may be indicated more than once during a plan of care. Tests and measures include but are not limited to those noted in 97001. The PT will modify the plan of care as is indicated and support medical necessity of skilled intervention.

MED: 100-3, 20.10

Coding Tip
A therapeutic procedure may be reported on the same day as an evaluation or re-evaluation (97001–97002) when the medical record documentation supports the medical necessity of both services.

97003   Occupational therapy evaluation

The provider evaluates the patient. Various movements required for activities of daily living are examined. Dexterity, range of movement, and other elements may also be studied.

MED: 100-3, 20.10

97004   Occupational therapy re-evaluation

The provider re-evaluates the patient to gauge progress of therapy. Various movements required for activities of daily living are examined. Dexterity, range of movement, and other elements may also be studied.

MED: 100-3, 20.10

Coding Tip
A therapeutic procedure may be reported on the same day as an evaluation or re-evaluation (97003–97004) when the medical record documentation supports the medical necessity of both services.

97005   Athletic training evaluation

The provider examines the patient, which includes taking a comprehensive history, systems review, and obtaining tests of range of motion, motor function, muscle performance, joint integrity, and neuromuscular status. The provider formulates an assessment, prognosis, and notes the anticipated intervention.

MED: 100-2, 15, 230.4; 100-4, 5, 10

97006   Athletic training re-evaluation

The provider re-examines the patient to obtain objective measures of progress toward stated goals. Tests include, but are not limited to, range of motion, motor function, muscle performance, joint integrity, and neuromuscular status. The provider modifies the

treatment plan as is indicated to support medical necessity of skilled intervention.

MED: 100-2, 15, 230.4; 100-4, 5, 10

Coding Tips
A therapeutic procedure may be reported on the same day as an evaluation or re-evaluation (97005–97006) when the medical record documentation supports the medical necessity of both services.

Codes 97005 and 97006 describe athletic training services and are not restricted to athletic trainers. However, consideration of payment may be subject to review or authorization of a third party. For physical therapy evaluations and re-evaluations performed by those licensed to do so, use codes 97001 and 97002.

97010–97039 Modalities

Modality is defined as any group of agents that may include thermal, acoustic, radiant, mechanical, or electrical energy to produce physiologic changes in tissues for therapeutic purposes. Codes included in this section do not include specific time increments as a requirement.

97010–97028 Supervised

The modalities identified by codes 97010–97028 require supervision by the provider but do not require direct patient contact (one-to-one).

According to the AMA (*CPT Coding Assistant*, August, 2002), codes from range 97010–97028 (application of a modality to one or more areas) are intended to be reported only one time per modality, per treatment session. If two separate treatment sessions are provided on the same date of service (e.g., a.m. and p.m.), then both may be reported but would require modifier 76 to indicate that the service-based code (with not time descriptors) is being reported for two speparate sessions on the same date. Check with third-party payers as their guidelines may differ.

97010   Application of a modality to one or more areas; hot or cold packs

The provider applies heat or cold to alleviate pain, decrease muscle spasms, prepare or cool down from exercise, or to promote tissue healing. The provider may apply a moist or dry hot pack, encased in sufficient padding to the area to be treated, monitoring progress. If a standard heating pad is applied, the control is given to the patient with instructions. The providers apply cold packs directly to the skin or over a towel, depending on the patient's tolerance to cold. This code may be billed only once regardless of the number of body areas or application times.

MED: 100-2, 15, 60.3; 100-2, 15, 230; 100-2, 15, 230.1; 100-2, 15, 230.2; 100-2, 15, 230.4; 100-4, 5, 10; 100-4, 5, 20

Coding Tip

Report code 97010 once only even when both cold and hot packs are provided during a single session. Medicare "bundles" the payment of hot and cold packs into all other services, meaning there is no separate payment for hot and cold packs. Several private payers, citing the Medicare example, also will not cover this modality separately. Check with your payer for coverage issues.

97012   Application of a modality to one or more areas; traction, mechanical

The provider applies traction to the area being treated. A head harness may be used for cervical traction with the patient supine or sitting, or the pelvis may be placed in a harness. The provider may use a traction machine, hydraulic or pneumatic device, or spring-loaded crank. This code may be billed only once regardless of the number of body areas or application times.

MED: 100-2, 15, 60.3; 100-2, 15, 230; 100-2, 15, 230.1; 100-2, 15, 230.2; 100-2, 15, 230.4; 100-4, 5, 10; 100-4, 5, 20

97014   Application of a modality to one or more areas; electrical stimulation (unattended)

The provider applies electrical stimulation to alleviate pain and enhance healing. The provider identifies the sites where electrode pads will be placed and applies them. Different types of unattended electrical stimulation exist, but they are all billed under this code. This code may be billed only once regardless of the number of body areas or application times.

MED: 100-2, 15, 60.3; 100-2, 15, 230

Coding Tips

Medicare requires that electrical stimulation for the treatment of wounds or other applications be reported using HCPCS Level II codes G0281–G0282 or G0283, respectively. Check with other third-party payers for their requirements.

Under the Medicare payment guidelines electrodes are included in the practice expense relative value units for this code and may not be billed separately.

97016   Application of a modality to one or more areas; vasopneumatic devices

The provider applies a vasopneumatic device to treat edema. A pressurized sleeve is applied. Girth measurements are taken pre and post treatment. This code may be billed only once regardless of the number of body areas or application times.

MED: 100-2, 15, 60.3; 100-2, 15, 230; 100-2, 15, 230.1; 100-2, 15, 230.2; 100-2, 15, 230.4; 100-4, 5, 10; 100-4, 5, 20

97018   Application of a modality to one or more areas; paraffin bath

The provider utilizes a paraffin bath to apply superficial heat to a part of an extremity. The part is repeatedly dipped into the paraffin forming a "glove." Use of paraffin is utilized to facilitate treatment of arthritis and other conditions that cause limitations in joint flexibility. Once the paraffin is applied and the patient instruction provided, the procedure requires supervision. This code may be billed only once regardless of the number of body areas or application times.

MED: 100-2, 15, 60.3; 100-2, 15, 230; 100-2, 15, 230.1; 100-2, 15, 230.2; 100-2, 15, 230.4; 100-4, 5, 10; 100-4, 5, 20

Coding Tip

For coverage guidelines for the treatment of lymphedema and chronic venous insufficiency see the Medicare national coverage decision 280.6 Pneumatic Compression Devices.

97022   Application of a modality to one or more areas; whirlpool

The provider uses a whirlpool to provide superficial heat and cold in an environment that facilitates range of motion and/or exercise. The provider decides the appropriate water temperature, provides safety instruction and supervises the treatment. This code may be billed only once regardless of the number of body areas or application times.

MED: 100-3, 130.5; 100-3, 130.6; 100-3, 150.5; 100-3, 160.2; 100-3, 20.10; 100-3, 250.1; 100-3, 250.4; 100-3, 270.4; 100-3, 40.5

Coding Tip

If the whirlpool is used as a wound care treatment, see code 97597, 97598, or 97602. Code 97022 may be reported with 97597 or 97598 only if used to treat a separately identifiable condition. Modifier 59 may be reported when reporting these codes together on the same day. For example, whirlpool therapy is used to treat an ankle sprain.

97024   Application of a modality to one or more areas; diathermy (eg, microwave)

The provider utilizes diathermy as a form of superficial heat for one or more body areas. After application and safety instructions have been provided, the provider supervises the treatment.

MED: 100-2, 15, 60.3; 100-2, 15, 230; 100-2, 15, 230.1; 100-2, 15, 230.2; 100-2, 15, 230.4; 100-4, 5, 10; 100-4, 5, 20

97026   Application of a modality to one or more areas; infrared

The provider utilizes infrared light as a form of superficial heat that will increase circulation to one or more localized areas. Once applied and safety instructions have been provided, the treatment is supervised.

MED: 100-2, 15, 60.3; 100-2, 15, 230; 100-2, 15, 230.1; 100-2, 15, 230.2; 100-2, 15, 230.4; 100-4, 5, 10; 100-4, 5, 20

97028 **Application of a modality to one or more areas; ultraviolet**

The provider utilizes ultraviolet light to treat dermatological problems. Once applied and safety instructions have been provided, the treatment is supervised. This code may be billed only once regardless of the number of body areas or application times.

MED: 100-2, 15, 60.3; 100-2, 15, 230; 100-2, 15, 230.1; 100-2, 15, 230.2; 100-2, 15, 230.4; 100-4, 5, 10; 100-4, 5, 20

97032–97039 Constant Attendance

The modalities identified by codes 97032–97039 require direct (one-to one) patient contact by the provider and include a time component.

97032 **Application of a modality to one or more areas; electrical stimulation (manual), each 15 minutes**

The provider applies electrical stimulation to one or more areas to promote muscle function, wound healing edema, and/or pain control using a handheld probe or other manual mechanism. This code requires constant attendance by the provider and may be billed in 15-minute units.

MED: 100-2, 15, 60.3; 100-2, 15, 230; 100-4, 5, 20

Coding Tip

Codes 97032–97039 are timed codes. According to CMS guidelines, at least eight minutes of direct contact with the patient must be provided for a single unit of service to be appropriately billed. Medical record documentation should indicate the total amount of time for the direct one-to-one patient contact provided by the physical therapist, as well as total treatment time (as defined by all timed and untimed codes). Check with other third-party payers for their guidelines.

97033 **Application of a modality to one or more areas; iontophoresis, each 15 minutes**

The provider utilizes electrical current to noninvasively administer medication to one or more areas. Iontophoresis is usually utilized for soft tissue inflammatory conditions and pain control. This code requires constant attendance by the provider and may be billed in 15-minute units.

MED: 100-2, 15, 60.3; 100-2, 15, 230; 100-2, 15, 230.2; 100-2, 15, 230.4; 100-4, 5, 10; 100-4, 5, 20

97034 **Application of a modality to one or more areas; contrast baths, each 15 minutes**

The provider uses hot and cold baths in a repeated, alternating fashion to stimulate the vasomotor response of a localized body part. This code requires constant attendance and may be billed in 15-minute units.

MED: 100-2, 15, 60.3; 100-2, 15, 230; 100-2, 15, 230.2; 100-2, 15, 230.4; 100-4, 5, 10; 100-4, 5, 20

97035 **Application of a modality to one or more areas; ultrasound, each 15 minutes**

The provider utilizes ultrasound to increase circulation to one or more areas. A coupling agent (such as a gel or water) must be used to facilitate the procedure. The delivery of corticosteroid medication via ultrasound is called phonophoresis and is reported using this code. The medication as a supply may or may not be paid by the payer. This code requires constant attendance and may be billed in 15-minute units.

MED: 100-2, 15, 60.3; 100-2, 15, 230; 100-2, 15, 230.1; 100-2, 15, 230.2

97036 **Application of a modality to one or more areas; Hubbard tank, each 15 minutes**

Hubbard tank is utilized when it is necessary to fully immerse the areas that require treatment into water. Care of wounds and burns may require use of the hubbard tank to facilitate tissue cleansing and debridement. This code requires constant attendance and may be billed in 15-minute units.

MED: 100-2, 15, 60.3; 100-2, 15, 230; 100-2, 15, 230.1; 100-2, 15, 230.2

Coding Tip

Code 97036 can be reported on the same date of service as code 97597, 97598, or 97602, if the Hubbard tank is used to treat an additional diagnosis separate from the wound debridement. If provided, report both codes with modifier 59. See code 97597, 97598, or 97602, if debridement is performed by water jet, sharp debridement, or wet-to-dry dressing. Documentation must support the use of this modifier, identifying the separate service.

97039 **Unlisted modality (specify type and time if constant attendance)**

MED: 100-2, 15, 60.3; 100-2, 15, 230; 100-2, 15, 230.1; 100-2, 15, 230.2; 100-2, 15, 230.4; 100-4, 5, 10; 100-4, 5, 20

Coding Tip

When using an unlisted code submit documentation explaining the service or procedure provided.

97110–97546 Therapeutic Procedures

Therapeutic Exercise Program

Documentation must support the skilled nature of the therapeutic procedures and/or the need for design and establishment of a maintenance exercise program. The goals should be to increase functional abilities in self-care, mobility, or patient safety. Document the goals and type of procedures provided and/or exercise program established and the major muscle groups treated.

Submit claims when the therapeutic exercise, because of documented medical complications, the condition of the patient or complexity of the exercise employed, must be rendered by or under the supervision of a PT. Include the patient's functional

CPT Definitions & Guidelines

losses and/or need for assistance in safely performing activities of daily living, including self-care and mobility in the home, in other living environments or in the workplace. Provide documentation that supports why skilled physical therapy is needed for the patient's medical condition and/or safety. This information usually is supported by documentation of the patient's evaluation and by establishment of a plan of care, which includes functional goals developed with input from the patient and, when appropriate, the patient's caregiver.

Submit claims that document establishment and design of a needed maintenance exercise program to fit the patient's level of activities of daily living (ADL), function and needed instruction to the patient, supportive personnel and/or family members to safely and effectively carry out the program.

Coding Tip

Medicare beneficiaries who are blind or visually impaired may be eligible for rehabilitation services to improve performance of activities of daily living including self-care and home management skills, as well as mobility skills when provided by an approved health professional such as a physical therapist. Visual impairment may range from total blindness to low vision and may be due to conditions such as glaucoma, retinitis pigmentosa, macular degeneration, or diabetes mellitus.

A physical therapist must have provided a complete evaluation of the patient's current level of functioning and implement a therapeutic plan of care that promotes safe independent living. Rehabilitation services provided to patients with primary visual impairments must be provided in accordance with a written plan of treatment that is established by a Medicare physician and implemented by approved Medicare providers or incident to physician services. It is expected that this service will be provided short-term, as maintenance therapy is not covered. Patients must have the potential for improvement and are expected to demonstrate significant improvement within a reasonable and fairly predictable amount of time. Covered services for beneficiaries with vision impairment include:

- Mobility
- Activities of daily living
- Other rehabilitation goals that are medically necessary

Applicable procedure codes could include the following:

97110   **Therapeutic procedure, one or more areas, each 15 minutes; therapeutic exercises to develop strength and endurance, range of motion and flexibility**

The provider, in direct contact with one patient while performing therapeutic exercises to one or more body areas to develop strength, range of motion, endurance, and flexibility. This code requires direct contact and may be billed in 15-minute units.

MED: 100-2, 15, 60.3; 100-2, 15, 230; 100-2, 15, 230.1; 100-2, 15, 230.2; 100-2, 15, 230.4; 100-4, 5, 10; 100-4, 5, 20

97112   **Therapeutic procedure, one or more areas, each 15 minutes; neuromuscular reeducation of movement, balance, coordination, kinesthetic sense, posture, and/or proprioception for sitting and/or standing activities**

The provider, in direct contact with one patient while performing activities to one or more body areas that facilitate reeducation of movement, balance, coordination, kinesthetic sense, posture and proprioception. This code requires direct contact and may be billed in 15-minute units.

MED: 100-2, 15, 60.3; 100-2, 15, 230; 100-2, 15, 230.1; 100-2, 15, 230.2; 100-2, 15, 230.4; 100-4, 5, 10; 100-4, 5, 20

Coding Tip

Physical therapists typically use code 97112 for canalith repositioning services, because CMS bundles code 95992 with codes for which PTs do not bill. Some private payers allow PTs to use code 95992; check with your payer for individual policies.

97113   **Therapeutic procedure, one or more areas, each 15 minutes; aquatic therapy with therapeutic exercises**

The provider, in direct contact with one patient while performing therapeutic exercises with the patient/client in the aquatic environment. The code requires skilled intervention by the provider and documentation must support medical necessity of the aquatic environment. This code may be billed in 15-minute units.

MED: 100-2, 15, 60.3; 100-2, 15, 230; 100-2, 15, 230.1; 100-2, 15, 230.2; 100-2, 15, 230.4; 100-4, 5, 10; 100-4, 5, 20

Coding Tip

When performing aquatic therapy, the physical therapist must be present, providing one-to-one contact with the patient, but does not have to physically be in the pool.

97116   **Therapeutic procedure, one or more areas, each 15 minutes; gait training (includes stair climbing)**

The provider trains the patient in specific activities that will facilitate ambulation and stair climbing with or without an assistive device. Proper gait sequencing, instruction in weight bearing, and safety instructions are included when appropriate. This code requires direct contact and may be billed in 15-minute units.

MED: 100-2, 15, 60.3; 100-2, 15, 230; 100-2, 15, 230.1; 100-2, 15, 230.2; 100-2, 15, 230.4; 100-4, 5, 10; 100-4, 5, 20

CPT Definitions
& Guidelines

97124 Therapeutic procedure, one or more areas, each 15 minutes; massage, including effleurage, petrissage and/or tapotement (stroking, compression, percussion)

The provider uses massage to provide muscle relaxation, increase localized circulation, soften scar tissue, or mobilize mucous secretions in the lung via tapotement and/or percussion. This code requires direct contact and may be billed in 15-minute units.

MED: 100-2, 15, 60.3; 100-2, 15, 230; 100-2, 15, 230.1; 100-2, 15, 230.2; 100-2, 15, 230.4; 100-4, 5, 10; 100-4, 5, 20

Coding Tip

The use of code 97124 Massage, by definition includes techniques such as effleurage, petrissage and/or tapotement; however, PTs often perform services that are more focused or complex than would fall under this definition. PTs should consider the use of 97140, Manual therapy, in these situations.

97139 Therapeutic procedure, one or more areas, each 15 minutes; unlisted therapeutic procedure (specify)

This code may be used if the provider performs a therapeutic procedure to one or more body areas that is not listed under the current codes. A narrative descriptor should be noted on the claim and documentation in the medical record should clearly support the procedure. This code may be billed in 15-minute units.

MED: 100-2, 15, 60.3; 100-2, 15, 230; 100-2, 15, 230.1; 100-2, 15, 230.2; 100-2, 15, 230.4; 100-4, 5, 10; 100-4, 5, 20

Coding Tip

Code 97139 requires direct contact by the provider.

97140 Manual therapy techniques (eg, mobilization/manipulation, manual lymphatic drainage, manual traction), one or more regions, each 15 minutes

The provider performs manual therapy techniques including soft tissue and joint mobilization, manipulation, manual traction and/or manual lymphatic drainage to one or more areas. This code requires direct contact with the patient and may be billed in 15-minute units.

MED: 100-2, 15, 60.3; 100-2, 15, 230; 100-2, 15, 230.1; 100-2, 15, 230.2; 100-2, 15, 230.4; 100-4, 5, 10; 100-4, 5, 20

Coding Tip

More than one of these techniques could be performed on a single date of service. The minutes are totaled and billed.

97150 Therapeutic procedure(s), group (2 or more individuals)

The provider provides a therapeutic procedure to two or more patients at the same time in either a land or aquatic environment. The need for skilled intervention must be documented.

MED: 100-2, 15, 60.3; 100-2, 15, 230; 100-2, 15, 230.1; 100-2, 15, 230.2; 100-4, 5, 20; 100-4, 5, 100.10

Coding Tip

Code 97150 requires the provider to have direct contact with the group. This code is untimed and billed only once per date of service, unless billed with a modifier. Supervised exercise by a nonqualified provided is not coded as 97150. This code should be reported for each individual member of the group.

Use of the Group Therapy Code

(*Printed with permission from the* American Physical Therapy Association)

The American Physical Therapy Association (APTA) supports the interpretation of the group therapy code for outpatient physical therapy services, as established by CMS and as clarified in the Carriers Manual Transmittal 1753. This longstanding policy states that outpatient physical therapy services provided simultaneously to two or more individuals by a practitioner constitutes group therapy services and should be billed as such. The individuals can be, but need not be, performing the same activity. The therapist involved in group therapy services must be in constant attendance and must provide skilled services to the group.

Furthermore, APTA supports the interpretation of the one-on-one codes as published by CMS.

Language describing the appropriate use of one-on-one codes and the group code first appeared in the *Federal Register* in 1994 (12-8-94, Vol. 59, No. 235, p 63451). This same language was republished in the *Federal Register* in 1996 (11-22-96, Vol. 61, No. 227, p 59542). CMS further clarified usage of the group code in Carriers Manual Transmittal 1753, dated May 17, 2002. The language, now published in the *Medicare Benefit Policy Manual*, Chapter 15, Section 230 states:

Group Therapy Services (Code 97150)
*   Pay for outpatient physical therapy services (which includes speech-language pathology services) and outpatient occupational therapy services provided simultaneously to two or more individuals by a practitioner as group therapy services. The individuals can be, but need not be performing the same activity. The physician or therapist involved in group therapy services must be in constant attendance, but one-on-one patient contact is not required.

APTA recognizes that in certain situations it may be possible to add the time spent with each individual patient and bill for these services with an appropriate one-on-one code when the one-on-one time requirements are met. This also may be the most efficient approach. However, APTA also supports the interpretation that would allow these professional services to be billed under the group code, which is an untimed code, all other requirements for professional services having been met.

The duration of the group session to which the code is applied should be sufficient to ensure that professional ("skilled") services are provided. Because the code is not a timed code, it can be used with other interventions provided on the same day of services, although modifiers may be required.

Last, APTA does not interpret CMS Transmittal 1753 as prohibiting payment for a supervised (unattended) modality and a one-on-one service being delivered to two patients in the same time interval.

97530 **Therapeutic activities, direct (one on one) patient contact by the provider (use of dynamic activities to improve functional performance), each 15 minutes**

The provider uses dynamic therapeutic activities designed to achieve improved functional performance (e.g., lifting, pulling, bending). This code requires direct contact and may be billed in 15-minute units.

MED: 100-2, 15, 60.3; 100-2, 15, 230; 100-2, 15, 230.1; 100-2, 15, 230.2; 100-2, 15, 230.4; 100-4, 5, 10; 100-4, 5, 20

97532 **Development of cognitive skills to improve attention, memory, problem solving, (includes compensatory training), direct (one-on-one) patient contact by the provider, each 15 minutes**

The provider instructs and trains the patient in a variety of tasks, in a manner that facilitates the development of cognitive reasoning. Cognitive skills training allows individuals with impairments related to diagnoses of brain injury, CVAs, and psychiatric disorders to live independently and function safely in their environment. This code may be billed in 15-minute units.

MED: 100-2, 15, 230; 100-2, 15, 230.1; 100-2, 15, 230.2; 100-2, 15, 230.4; 100-4, 5, 10

97533 **Sensory integrative techniques to enhance sensory processing and promote adaptive responses to environmental demands, direct (one-on-one) patient contact by the provider, each 15 minutes**

The provider uses a variety of techniques that engage the patient in a variety of activities that focus on enhancing sensory processing input and promote adaptive responses to environmental demands of one or more of the sensory systems (i.e., vestibular, proprioceptive, tactile [touch], visual or auditory). This code may be billed in 15-minute units.

MED: 100-2, 15, 230; 100-2, 15, 230.1; 100-2, 15, 230.2; 100-2, 15, 230.4; 100-4, 5, 10; 100-4, 5, 20

97535 **Self-care/home management training (eg, activities of daily living (ADL) and compensatory training, meal preparation, safety procedures, and instructions in use of assistive technology devices/adaptive equipment) direct one-on-one contact by provider, each 15 minutes**

The provider instructs and trains the patient in self-care and home management activities (e.g., ADL's use of adaptive equipment in the kitchen, bath, and/or car). Direct contact is required. This code may be billed in 15-minute units.

MED: 100-2, 15, 60.3; 100-2, 15, 230; 100-2, 15, 230.1; 100-2, 15, 230.2; 100-2, 15, 230.4; 100-4, 5, 10; 100-4, 5, 20

Transfer Training Documentation Tip

Describe the patient's current functional limitations in transfer ability that warrant skilled PT intervention. Include the special transfer training needed and rendered, and any training needed by supportive personnel and/or family members to safely and effectively carry it out. Transfer training may be approved only when your documentation supports a skilled need for evaluation, design, and effective monitoring and instruction of the special transfer technique for safety and completion of the task. If your documentation supports only repetitious carrying out of the transfer method, once established and monitored for safety and completion of the task, it will be considered noncovered care. Code choices could include 97530 (performance of daily activities such as lifting, throwing, reaching) or 97535 (managing activities in the living environment, such as safely using adaptive equipment in the kitchen/bath/car).

97537 **Community/work reintegration training (eg, shopping, transportation, money management, avocational activities and/or work environment/modification analysis, work task analysis, use of assistive technology device/adaptive equipment), direct one-on-one contact by provider, each 15 minutes**

The provider instructs and trains the patient/client in community reintegration activities (e.g., work task analysis and modification, safe accessing of transportation navigating through daily functions such as banking). This requires one-on-one contact with the provider and may be billed in 15-minute units.

MED: 100-2, 15, 60.3; 100-2, 15, 230; 100-2, 15, 230.1; 100-2, 15, 230.2; 100-2, 15, 230.4; 100-4, 5, 10; 100-4, 5, 20

97542 **Wheelchair management (eg, assessment, fitting, training), each 15 minutes**

The provider performs assessments, fitting and adjustments, and instructs and trains the patient in proper wheelchair skills (e.g., propulsion, safety techniques) in their home, facility, work, or community environment. This requires direct contact and may be billed in 15-minute units.

MED: 100-2, 15, 60.3; 100-2, 15, 230; 100-2, 15, 230.1; 100-2, 15, 230.2; 100-2, 15, 230.4; 100-4, 5, 10; 100-4, 5, 20

97545 Work hardening/conditioning; initial 2 hours

+ 97546 each additional hour (List separately in addition to code for primary procedure)

This code is used for a program where the injured worker is put through a series of conditioning exercises and job simulation tasks in preparation for return to work. Endurance, strength, and proper body mechanics are emphasized. The patient is also educated in problem solving skills related to job task performance and employing correct lifting and positioning techniques. Key components of work hardening include job simulation and targeted education related to safe return to work. Key components of work conditioning include exercise targeted to returning to functional work activities. Report 97546 for each additional hour after the initial two hours.

MED: 100-2, 15, 60.3; 100-2, 15, 230; 100-2, 15, 230.1; 100-2, 15, 230.2; 100-2, 15, 230.4; 100-4, 5, 10

Coding Tip

State workers' compensation payment policies often dictate how this code is used to describe work hardening or work conditioning interventions for the injured worker. Local codes may be in use by some payers.

97597–97606 Active Wound Care Management

Active wound care is performed to remove devitalized and/or necrotic tissues. The physical therapist must provide direct, one-to-one patient contact when billing these procedures.

97597 Removal of devitalized tissue from wound(s), selective debridement, without anesthesia (eg, high pressure waterjet with/without suction, sharp selective debridement with scissors, scalpel and forceps), with or without topical application(s), wound assessment, and instruction(s) for ongoing care, may include use of a whirlpool, per session; total wound(s) surface area less than or equal to 20 square centimeters

97598 total wound(s) surface area greater than 20 square centimeters

MED: 100-4, 5, 10

The provider performs wound care management by using selective debridement techniques to remove devitalized tissue without anesthesia. Selective techniques are those in which the provider has complete control over which tissue is removed and which is left behind. Selective techniques include high-pressure waterjet with or without suction, and sharp debridement techniques using scissors, a scalpel, or forceps. Another newer method of selective debridement is autolysis, which uses the body's own enzymes and moisture to rehydrate, soften, and finally liquefy hard eschar and slough. Autolytic debridement is accomplished using occlusive or semi-occlusive dressings that keep wound fluid in contact with the necrotic tissue. Types

of dressing applications used in autolytic debridement include hydrocolloids, hydrogels, and transparent films. Wound assessment, topical applications, instructions regarding ongoing care of the wound, and the possible use of a whirlpool for treatment are included in these codes. Report 97597 for a total wound surface area less than or equal to 20.0 sq. cm and 97598 for a total wound surface area greater than 20.0 sq. cm. Report the appropriate code per session.

Coding Tip

CPT code 97022 Whirlpool, should not be billed in conjunction with 97597 or 97598 if the whirlpool is for the purpose of treating the wound.

97602 Removal of devitalized tissue from wound(s), non-selective debridement, without anesthesia (eg, wet-to-moist dressings, enzymatic, abrasion), including topical application(s), wound assessment, and instruction(s) for ongoing care, per session

In 97602, the provider performs a nonselective debridement of devitalized tissue from a wound without anesthesia. Wet-to-moist dressings, enzymatic, abrasion, or another form of non-selective debridement is performed. This includes the application of dressing. Also included is assessment of the wound and instructions for aftercare. This code is reported per session.

Coding Tip

Code 97602 is a bundled service under Medicare. It reports treatment provided during a session, no matter how many wounds or body areas are treated during the session. Do not report codes 97597–97602 in addition to 11040–11044 (debridement).

MED: 100-3, 130.5; 100-3, 130.6; 100-3, 160.2; 100-3, 250.1; 100-3, 250.4; 100-3, 270.1; 100-3, 270.2; 100-3, 270.4; 100-3, 40.5

97605 Negative pressure wound therapy (eg, vacuum assisted drainage collection), including topical application(s), wound assessment, and instruction(s) for ongoing care, per session; total wound(s) surface area less than or equal to 50 square centimeters

97606 total wound(s) surface area greater than 50 square centimeters

The provider applies negative pressure wound therapy (NPWT) with vacuum assisted drainage collection to promote healing of a chronic non-healing wound, including diabetic or pressure (decubitus) ulcer. This procedure includes topical applications to the wound, wound assessment, and patient or caregiver instruction related to on-going care per session. Negative pressure wound therapy uses controlled application of subatmospheric pressure to a wound. The subatmospheric pressure is generated using an electrical pump. The electrical pump conveys intermittent or continuous subatmospheric pressure through connecting tubing to a specialized wound dressing. The specialized wound dressing includes a porous foam dressing that covers the entire wound surface and an airtight adhesive dressing that seals the wound and contains the subatmospheric pressure at the wound site. Negative pressure wound therapy promotes healing by increasing local vascularity and oxygenation of the wound bed, evacuating wound fluid thereby reducing edema, and removing exudates and bacteria. Drainage from the wound is collected in a canister. Report 97605 for a wound(s) with a total surface area less than or equal to 50.0 sq. cm. Report 97606 for a wound(s) with a total surface area greater than 50.0 sq. cm.

97750–97755 Tests and Measurements

Codes in this subsection require direct one-on-one patient contact as well as a separate written report.

97750   Physical performance test or measurement (eg, musculoskeletal, functional capacity), with written report, each 15 minutes

The provider performs a test of physical performance determining function of one or more body areas or measuring an aspect of physical performance; including functional capacity evaluations. A written report is part of this service. This code may be billed in 15-minute increments.

MED: 100-3, 20.10

Coding Tip

Third-party payers may limit reporting this code on the same day as a physical therapy evaluation or re-evaluation.

97755   Assistive technology assessment (eg, to restore, augment or compensate for existing function, optimize functional tasks and/or maximize environmental accessibility), direct one-on-one contact by provider, with written report, each 15 minutes

The provider performs an assessment for the suitability and benefits of acquiring any assistive technology device that will help restore, augment, or compensate for existing functional ability in the patient; or that will optimize functional tasks and/or maximize the patient's environmental accessibility and mobility. A written report is part of this service. This code requires direct one-on-one contact with the patient and may be billed in 15-minute units.

Coding Tip

Third-party payers may limit reporting this code on the same day as a physical therapy evaluation or re-evaluation.

Report codes 97535–97537 for training in use of assistive technology.

97760–97762 Orthotic Management and Prosthetic Management

97760   Orthotic(s) management and training (including assessment and fitting when not otherwise reported), upper extremity(s), lower extremity(s) and/or trunk, each 15 minutes

The clinician fits and/or trains the patient in the use of an orthotic device for one or more body parts. This includes assessment as to type of orthotic when appropriate. This does not include fabrication time, if appropriate, or cost of materials.

Coding Tips

A custom-fitted orthotic is a premanufactured orthotic that can be adjusted to fit the patient.

A custom-fabricated orthotic is made from basic materials on an individual basis by using actual measurements or positive molds of the patient. Generally, only the patient who was measured will be able to use a custom-fabricated orthotic.

Code 97760 Orthotic(s) management and training (including assessment and fitting when not otherwise reported), upper extremity(s), lower extremity(s), and/or trunk, each 15 minutes, was developed to include the training aspect of the management of a patient being assessed and fitted for an orthotic. If a HCPCS Level II code is reported and its description includes assessment and fitting, then documentation must also support the training aspect of the skilled services in order to also report CPT code 97760.

Coding Tip

Code 97760 should not be reported with code 97116 when performed on the same lower extremity. If, however, the two services are performed on lower and upper extremities, each code may be reported and modifier 59 should be assigned indicating that two distinct services were performed.

97761   Prosthetic training, upper and/or lower extremity(s), each 15 minutes

The clinician fits and/or trains the patient in the use of a prosthetic device for one or more body parts. This includes assessment for the appropriate type of prosthetic device. This does not include fabrication time, if applicable, or cost of materials.

97762   Checkout for orthotic/prosthetic use, established patient, each 15 minutes

The clinician evaluates the effectiveness, proper fit, and use of an existing orthotic or prosthetic device and makes recommendations for changes, as appropriate.

Coding Tip

Check with the payer about coding and billing procedures for orthotic supplies with respect to the distinction between fitting/training for the device and fabricating it.

97810–97814 Acupuncture

97810 Acupuncture, one or more needles, without electrical stimulation; initial 15 minutes of personal one-on-one contact with the patient

+ 97811 without electrical stimulation, each additional 15 minutes of personal one-on-one contact with the patient, with re-insertion of needle(s) (List separately in addition to code for primary procedure)

97813 with electrical stimulation, initial 15 minutes of personal one-on-one contact with the patient

+ 97814 with electrical stimulation, each additional 15 minutes of personal one-on-one contact with the patient, with re-insertion of needle(s) (List separately in addition to code for primary procedure)

The provider applies acupuncture therapy by inserting one or more fine needles into the patient as dictated by acupuncture meridians for the relief of pain. The needles are then twirled or manipulated by hand to generate therapeutic stimulation. Report 97810 for the initial 15 minutes of personal one-on-one contact with the patient and 97811 for each additional 15 minutes of personal one-on-one contact with reinsertion of the needle.

For 97813–97814, the needles are then energized by employing a micro-current for electrical stimulation. Report 97813 for the initial 15 minutes of personal one-on-one contact with the patient and 97814 for each additional 15 minutes of personal one-on-one contact with reinsertion of the needle.

Coding Tip

Dry needling of a joint or cyst should not be reported as acupuncture.

98960–98962 Education and Training for Patient Self-Management

Codes within this range are used to report education and training of a patient when prescribed by a physician but performed by a nonphysician provider. Guidelines indicate that a standardized curriculum must be utilized and may be modified to meet individual patient needs.

The focus of the training should be to teach the patient how to effectively manage his or her clinical condition. It may also include a patient's caregiver. The service can be provided to either a single patient (98960) or a group of patients (98961–98962).

98960 Education and training for patient self-management by a qualified, nonphysician health care professional using a standardized curriculum, face-to-face with the patient (could include caregiver/family) each 30 minutes; individual patient

98961 2-4 patients

98962 5-8 patients

The qualified, nonphysician health care professional provides education and training using a standard curriculum. This training is prescribed by a physician to enable the patient to concurrently self-manage established illnesses or diseases with health care providers. Report 98960 for education and training provided for an individual patient for each 30 minutes of service. Report 98961 for a group of two to four patients and 98962 for a group of five to eight patients.

98966–98968 Non-Face-to-Face Nonphysician Services

98966–98968 Telephone Services

These codes are used to report the telephone management of an established patient including the assessment of condition by a nonphysician provider.

98966 Telephone assessment and management services provided by a qualified nonphysician health care professional to an established patient, parent, or guardian not originating from a related assessment and management service provided within the previous seven days nor leading to an assessment and management service or procedure within the next 24 hours or soonest available appointment; 5 to 10 minutes of medical discussion

98967 11–20 minutes of medical discussion

98968 21–30 minutes of medical discussion

Telephone assessment and management services are those provided by telephone in a non-face-to-face encounter. Codes 98966–98968 report services provided by a qualified health care professional (nonphysician). These episodes of care may be initiated by an established patient or by the patient's guardian. These codes are not reported if the telephone service results in a decision to see the patient within 24 hours or at the next available urgent visit appointment; instead, the phone encounter is regarded as part of the preservice work of the subsequent face-to-face encounter. These codes are also not reported if the telephone call is in reference to a service performed and reported by the qualified health care professional that occurred within the past seven days or within the postoperative period of a previously completed procedure. Rather, the phone service is considered to be part of the previous service or procedure. This applies both to unsolicited patient follow-up services or services requested by the health care professional.

Coding Tip

Codes 98966–98968 are used to report nonphysician services only. When performed by a physician see codes 99441–99443. If the service ends in a decision to see the patient within 24 hours (or the next available urgent visit appointment), then the service is not reported separately. Correct code assignment is dependent upon the time of the medical discussion. Report code 98966 for telephone services requiring five to 10 minutes of medical discussion. Use code 98967 for those requiring 11 to 20 minutes and code 98968 for those requiring 21 to 30 minutes. Medical record documentation should include the nature and total time of the discussion. Coverage of this service varies. Check with third-party payers for their coverage guidelines.

CPT Definitions & Guidelines

98969 Online Medical Evaluation

An online medical evaluation is the assessment and management of condition by a nonphysician provider to an established patient or patient's family using Internet resources in response to a patient's on-line inquiry.

98969   On-line assessment and management service provided by a qualified nonphysician health care professional to an established patient, guardian, or health care provider not originating from a related assessment and management service provided within the previous 7 days, using the Internet or similar communication network

On-line medical assessment and management services are those provided to an established patient, guardian, or health care provider in response to a patient's on-line inquiry using Internet resources in a non-face-to-face encounter. Code 98969 reports services provided by a qualified health care professional (nonphysician). In order for these services to be reportable, the healthcare professional must provide a personal, timely response to the inquiry and the encounter must be permanently stored via electronic means or hard copy. A reportable service includes all communication related to the on-line encounter, such as phone calls, provision of prescriptions, and orders for laboratory services. This code is not reported if the on-line evaluation is in reference to a service performed and reported by the same health care professional that occurred within the past seven days or within the postoperative period of a previously completed procedure. Rather, the on-line service is considered to be part of the previous service or procedure. This applies both to unsolicited patient follow-up services or services requested by the health care professional.

Coding Tip
This code is used to report nonphysician services only. When performed by a physician see code 99444. This code is reported once per a seven-day period regardless of the number of communications (e.g., related telephone calls, additional on-line communications). Medical record documentation should include a permanent storage (electronic or hard paper copy) the nature and total time of the discussion. Coverage of this service varies. Check with third-party payers for their coverage guidelines.

99201–99499 Evaluation and Management

Most third-party payers do not accept evaluation and management codes when used to describe physical therapy evaluation services. Physical therapy evaluations and re-evaluations should be reported using codes 97001 and 97002, respectively.

99366–99368 Medical Team Conferences

Medical team conferences require the face-to-face participation of at least three participants of different disciplines providing direct care to the patient. The conference may also include the presence of the patient, patient's family or other guardian or caregiver. Medical team conference participants must have provided direct

face-to-face evaluation and/or treatment to the patient within 60 days previous to the conference. Documentation must include a record of participation in the conference, the information contributed by the provider and treatment recommendations provided from others. Only one provider from the same specialty may report a code for this service. If, by contractual agreement, a facility or other organization has agreed to provide a medical team conference, these services should not be billed separately. Team conference services provided by a physician with the patient or patient's family present are billed using the appropriate evaluation and management codes.

99366 Medical Team Conference, Direct (Face-to-Face) Contact with Patient and/or Family

99366   Medical team conference with interdisciplinary team of health care professionals, face-to-face with patient and/or family, 30 minutes or more, participation by nonphysician qualified health care professional

Coding Tip
Do not report this service when duration is less than 30 minutes. If the patient and/or the patient's family is not present, the nonphysician provider should see code 99368.

99367–99368 Medical Team Conference, Without Direct (Face-to-Face) Contact with Patient and/or Family

99368   Medical team conference with interdisciplinary team of health care professionals, patient and/or family not present, participation by nonphysician qualified health care professional

Coding Tip
Some payers may not provide coverage if the patient or patient's family is not present. Check with third-party payers for coverage guidelines. Do not report this service when duration is less than 30 minutes. When provided by a physician, code 99367 is reported.

MED: 100-1, 5, 70; 100-2, 15, 30; 100-4, 11, 40.1.3; 100-4, 12, 10; 100-4, 12, 30.6; 100-4, 12, 30.6.16; 100-4, 12, 70; 100-4, 13, 20; 100-4, 13, 90

Coding Tip
Medicare will not provide benefits for team conferences or telephone calls as these services are considered to be a part of the associated billable service and cannot be reported separately.

Category III Codes

Since the use of an unlisted code does not provide a method to collect specific data relating to emerging technology services and procedures, the AMA created category III CPT codes to report many of these services. Using these codes allows providers and payers to evaluate the efficacy of a procedure or service, as well as the utilization and outcome of said service. Although the category

III codes are temporary, the procedures and services they describe may receive category I status in the future based on progress toward meeting the requirement of a category I CPT code.

The existence of a category III CPT code does not guarantee coverage or payment of a service or procedure. Contact third-party payers to determine specific policies for reporting, coverage, and payment of an emerging technology.

Category III codes consist of four numbers followed by the letter "T." The codes are updated semiannually and for the most current listing see the AMA website at www.ama-assn.org/go/cpt.

0019T   **Extracorporeal shock wave involving musculoskeletal system, not otherwise specified, low energy**

0183T   **Low frequency, non-contact, non-thermal ultrasound, including topical application(s), when performed, wound assessment, and instruction(s) for ongoing care, per day**

CPT Index

A

Activities of Daily Living (ADL)
Training, 97535–97537

Acupuncture
One or More Needles
with Electrical Stimulation, 97813–97814
without Electrical Stimulation, 97810–97811

ADL
Activities of Daily Living, 97535–97537

Aerosol Inhalation
Inhalation Treatment, 94640, 94664
Pentamidine, 94642

Ankle
Strapping, 29540

Anorectal Procedure
Biofeedback, 90911

Aphasia Testing, 96105

Application
Neurostimulation, 64550

Aquatic Therapy
with Exercises, 97113

Arm, Lower
Splint, 29125–29126

Arm, Upper
Splint, 29105

AROM, 95851–95852, 97110, 97530

B

Bayley Scales of Infant Development
Developmental Testing, 96110

Biofeedback
Anorectal, 90911
Blood-flow, 90901
Blood Pressure, 90901
Brainwaves, 90901
EEG (Electroencephalogram), 90901
Electromyogram, 90901
Electro-Oculogram, 90901
EMG (with Anorectal), 90911
Eyelids, 90901
Nerve Conduction, 90901
Other (unlisted) biofeedback, 90901
Perineal Muscles, 90911
Urethral Sphincter, 90911

Blood Gases
by Pulse Oximetry, 94760

Bohler Splinting, 29515

Bronchospasm Evaluation, 94060
Pulmonology, Diagnostic, Spirometry, 94010, 94060

Burns
Allograft, 16020–16030
Debridement, 16020–16030
Dressing, 16020–16030

C

Canalith
Repositioning, 95992

Cardiac Rehabilitation, 93797–93798

Cardiology
Diagnostic
Stress Tests
Cardiovascular, 93015–93018
Therapeutic
Cardiopulmonary Resuscitation, 92950

Cardiopulmonary Resuscitation, 92950

Case Management Services
Team Conferences, 99361–99362
Telephone Calls, 99371–99373

Chest Wall
Manipulation, 94667–94668

Cognitive Skills Development, 97532

Cognitive Testing, 96125

Cold Pack Treatment, 97010

Communication Device
Non-speech-generating, 92605–92606
Speech-generating, 92607–92609

Community/Work Reintegration
Training, 97537

Computer Assisted Navigation
Medical
with Interdisciplinary Team, 99361–99373

Conference
Online 98969
Medical Team 99366–99368
Telephone 98966–98968

Continuous Positive Airway Pressure (CPAP), 94660
Intermittent Positive Pressure Breathing, 94660

Contrast Bath Therapy, 97034

CPAP (Continuous Positive Airway Pressure), 94660

CPR (Cardiopulmonary Resuscitation), 92950

D

Debridement
Burns, 16020–16030
Wound
Non-Selective, 97602
Selective, 97597–97598

Denis-Browne Splint, 29590

Developmental Testing
Evaluation
Limited, 96110

Diathermy, 97024

Dressings
Burns, 16020–16030

E

ECG, 93015–93018

Education
Patient
for Heart Failure, 4003F
Self-management by nonphysician, 98960–98962

EKG, 93015–93018

Elbow
Strapping, 29260

Electrical Stimulation
Physical Therapy
Attended, Manual, 97032
Unattended, 97014

Electromyography
Anus
Biofeedback, 90911
Fine Wire
Dynamic, 96004
Hemidiaphragm, 95866
Needle
Extremities, 95861–95864
Extremity, 95860
Face and Neck Muscles, 95867–95868
Other than Paraspinal, 95870
Single Fiber Electrode, 95872
Thoracic Paraspinal Muscles, 95869
Rectum
Biofeedback, 90911

CPT Index

CPT Index

Neurology—*continued*
Central Motor—*continued*
Somatosensory Testing,
95925–95927
Transcranial Motor Stimulation,
95928–95929
Visual Evoked Potential, CNS, 95930

Neuromuscular Junction Tests, 95937

Neuromuscular Reeducation, 97112
Intraoperative, Per Hour, 95920

Neurophysiologic Testing
Intraoperative, Per Hour, 95920

Neurostimulation
Application, 64550

O

Occupational Therapy
Evaluation, 97003–97004

Online Medical Evaluation 98969

Orthotics
Check-Out, 97762
Training and Fitting, 97760

Oximetry (Noninvasive)
Blood O2 Saturation
Ear or Pulse, 94760–94761

Oxygen Saturation
Ear Oximetry, 94760–94761
Pulse Oximetry, 94760–94761

P

Paraffin Bath Therapy, 97018

Peak Flow Rate, 94150

Pentamidine
Inhalation Treatment, 94640–94642,
94664

Performance Test
Performance Test Physical Therapy,
97750

**Physical Medicine/Therapy/
Occupational Therapy**
Activities of Daily Living, 97535
Aquatic Therapy
with Exercises, 97113
Athletic Training
Evaluation, 97005
Reevaluation, 97006
Cognitive Skills Development, 97532
Community/Work Reintegration,
97537
Evaluation, 97001–97002

**Physical Medicine/Therapy/
Occupational Therapy**—*continued*
Hydrotherapy
Hubbard Tank, 97036
Pool with Exercises, 97036, 97113
Joint Mobilization, 97140
Kinetic Therapy, 97530
Manipulation, 97140
Modalities
Contrast Baths, 97034
Diathermy Treatment, 97024
Electric Stimulation
Attended, Manual, 97032
Unattended, 97014
Hot or Cold Pack, 97010
Hydrotherapy (Hubbard Tank),
97036
Infrared Light Treatment, 97026
Iontophoresis, 97033
Paraffin Bath, 97018
Traction, 97012
Ultrasound, 97035
Ultraviolet Light, 97028
Unlisted Services and Procedures,
97039
Vasopneumatic Device, 97016
Whirlpool Therapy, 97022
Procedures
Aquatic Therapy, 97113
Gait Training, 97116
Group Therapeutic, 97150
Massage Therapy, 97124
Neuromuscular Reeducation, 97112
Physical Performance Test, 97750
Therapeutic Exercises, 97110-97113
Traction Therapy, 97140
Work Hardening, 97545–97546
Sensory Integration, 97533
Therapeutic Activities, 97530
Unlisted Services and Procedures,
97139, 97799
Wheelchair Management, 97542
Work Reintegration, 97537

Plantar Pressure Measurements
Dynamic, 96001, 96004

Pneumogram
Pediatric, 94772

Pool Therapy with Exercises, 97036,
97113

Pressure Breathing
Positive
Continuous (CPAP), 94660

Preventive Medicine
Respiratory Pattern Recording, 94772

PROM, 95851–95852, 97110, 97530

PT, 97001–97755

Pulmonology
Diagnostic
Bronchodilation, 94664
Bronchospasm Evaluation, 94060
Expired Gas Analysis, 94250
Oxygen and Carbon Dioxide,
94681
Oxygen Uptake, 94680
Oxygen Uptake, Indirect, 94690
Flow-Volume Loop, 94375
Inhalation Treatment, 94640
Maldistribution of Inspired Air,
94350
Maximum Breathing Capacity,
94200
Maximum Voluntary Ventilation,
94200
Nitrogen Washout Curve, 94350
Oximetry
Ear or Pulse, 94760–94761
Spirometry, 94010, 94060
with Bronchospasm Evaluation,
94060
Sputum Mobilization with Inhalants,
94664
Stress Test, 94621
Stress Test, Pulmonary, 94620
Vital Capacity, 94150
Therapeutic
Expired Gas Analysis, 94250
Therapeutic Inhalation
Continuous 94644-94645
Pentamidine, 94642
Inhalation Treatment, 94640,
94644-94645, 94664
Manipulation of Chest Wall,
94667–94668

Pulmonology
Pressure Ventilation
Positive CPAP, 94660

R

Range of Motion Test
Extremities, 95851
Hand, 95852
Rectum
Biofeedback, 90911
Trunk, 97530

Reflex Test
Blink, Reflex, 95933
H Reflex, 95934–95936

Rehabilitation
Cardiac, 93797–93798

Repositioning
Canalith, 95992

Respiratory Pattern Recording
Preventive
Infant, 94772

Resuscitation
Cardiopulmonary (CPR), 92950

ROM, 95851–95852, 97110, 97530

S

Self Care
Training, 97535

Shoulder
Strapping, 29240

Somatosensory Testing
Lower Limbs, 95926
Trunk or Head, 95927
Upper Limbs, 95925

Speech Evaluation
for Prosthesis, 92607–92608

Speech Prosthesis
Evaluation for Speech, 92607–92608
Maxillofacial
Evaluation of Speech Aid,
92607–92608

Spirometry, 94010, 94060

Splint
Arm
Long, 29105
Short, 29125–29126
Finger, 29130–29131
Foot, 29590
Leg
Long, 29505
Short, 29515

Strapping
Ankle, 29540
Back, 29799
Chest, 29200
Elbow, 29260
Finger, 29280
Foot, 29540, 29590
Hand, 29280
Hip, 29520
Knee, 29530
Shoulder, 29240
Thorax, 29200
Toes, 29550
Unna Boot, 29580
Wrist, 29260

Stress Tests
Cardiovascular, 93015–93018
Pulmonary, 94620–94621

Swallowing
Evaluation, 92610–92611

T

Team Conference
Case Management Services,
99361–99373

Telephone Services, 98966–98986

TENS, 64550, 97014, 97032

Testing
Neuropsychological
Intraoperative, 95920
Range of Motion
Extremities, 95851
Hand, 95852
Rectum
Biofeedback, 90911
Trunk, 97530
Standardized Cognitive Performance,
96125

Therapeutic Activities
Music
Per 15 Minutes, 97530

Thorax
Strapping, 29200

TNS, 64550

Toe
Strapping, 29550

Toes
Strapping, 29550

Traction Therapy
Manual, 97140
Mechanical, 97012

Training
Activities of Daily Living, 97535
Biofeedback, 90901–90911
Cognitive Skills, 97532
Community
Work Reintegration, 97537
Home Management, 97535
Management
Propulsion, 97542
Prosthetics, 97761
Seeing Impaired, 97799
Braille, or Moon, 97799
Lead Dog, Use of, 97799
Self Care, 97535
Sensory Integration, 97533
Walking (Physical Therapy), 97116
Wheelchair Management
Propulsion, 97542

U

Ultrasound
Physical Therapy, 97035

Ultraviolet Light Therapy
for Physical Medicine, 97028

Unlisted Services or Procedures
Physical Therapy, 97039, 97139,
97799

Unna Paste Boot, 29580

Urethral
Sphincter
Biofeedback Training, 90911

Urethral Sphincter
Biofeedback Training, 90911

V

Vasopneumatic Device Therapy, 97016

VEP, 95930

Vital Capacity Measurement, 94150

W

Wheelchair Management
Propulsion
Training, 97542

Whirlpool Therapy, 97022

Work Hardening, 97545–97546

Work Reintegration, 97545–97546

Wound
Debridement
Non-Selective, 97602
Selective, 97597–97598
Negative Pressure Therapy,
97605–97606

Wrist
Strapping, 29260

© 2009 Ingenix

ICD-9-CM Definitions and Guidelines

The International Classification of Diseases, Ninth Revision, Clinical Modification (ICD-9-CM) is a classification system in which diseases and injuries are arranged in groups of related cases for statistical purposes. Based on the World Health Organization's (WHO) International Classification of Diseases, the ICD system has been revised periodically to meet the needs of statistical data usage. In the United States, the system has been expanded and modified (-CM) to meet unique clinical purposes. Clinical uses include indexing medical records, facilitating medical care reviews, and completing reimbursement claims.

The responsibility for maintenance of the classification system is shared between the National Center for Health Statistics (NCHS) and the Centers for Medicare and Medicaid Services (CMS). These two organizations co-chair the ICD-9-CM Coordination and Maintenance Committee, which meets twice a year in a public forum to discuss revisions to the classification system. Final decisions concerning any revisions to the system are made by the director of NCHS and the administrator of CMS. Once determined, the final decisions are published in the *Federal Register* and become effective October 1 of each year.

The ICD-9-CM coding system is a method of translating medical terminology for diseases and procedures into codes. Codes within the system are either numeric or alphanumeric and are made up of three, four, or five characters. A decimal point follows all three-character codes when fourth and fifth characters are required. Coding involves using a numeric or alphanumeric code to describe a disease or injury. For example, frozen shoulder is translated into code 726.0.

Although hospitals and other health care facilities have used ICD-9-CM codes for many years, health care provider offices are also required to use ICD-9-CM codes for all Medicare billings. Thus, it is essential that coding staff, regardless of setting, become more knowledgeable, proficient, and accurate in their use of the ICD-9-CM diagnosis coding system. By improving coding skills, appropriate reimbursement, and efficient claims processing, coders limit audit liability and decrease the number of denied claims and requests for additional information.

This chapter provides information on the structure of ICD-9-CM. We have also identified coding tips and guidelines for the ICD-9-CM chapters that are pertinent to the physical therapy provider.

Coding Tip
Be sure that your ICD-9-CM coding system contains the most up-to-date information available. Changes take place October 1 of every year, and your code book must be current to ensure accurate coding.

The Structure of ICD-9-CM
The ICD-9-CM system contains two classifications, one for diseases and the other for procedures. It consists of three volumes:

- **Volume 1, Diseases** (tabular list)
- **Volume 2, Diseases** (alphabetic index)
- **Volume 3, Procedures** (tabular list and alphabetic index)

Volume 3, Procedures, is used primarily for inpatient coding. The health care provider office, outpatient clinics, or ambulatory surgery centers coding staff should use the Physicians' Current Procedural Terminology (CPT®) system for coding procedures. Therefore, volume 1 (tabular list) and volume 2 (alphabetic index) of ICD-9-CM are used in the health care provider office for assigning diagnosis codes. For this manual, physical therapy related index entries are listed.

The Structure of the Alphabetic Index
The alphabetic index of ICD-9-CM, commonly referred to as the index, is used in the first step in assigning a code. The index is divided into three sections: the "Alphabetic Index to Disease and Injury," the "Table of Drugs and Chemicals," and the "Alphabetic Index to External Causes of Injury and Poisoning." For this book, physical-therapy-related index entries are listed.

Alphabetic Index to Diseases and Injuries
Included in this section is an alphabetic list of diseases, injuries, symptoms, and other reasons for contact with the health care provider. This section also contains two tables that classify hypertension and neoplasms.

Table of Drugs and Chemicals
The drugs and chemicals that are the external causes of poisoning and other adverse effects are organized in table format. Specific drugs and chemical substances that the patient may have taken, or been given, are listed alphabetically. Each of these substances is assigned a code to identify the drug as a poisoning agent, resulting from incorrect substances given, incorrect dosages taken, overdose, or intoxication. The five columns titled, "External Cause," list E codes for external causes depending upon whether the circumstances involving the use of the drug were accidental, for therapeutic use, a suicide attempt, an assault, or undetermined.

Alphabetic Index to External Causes of Injury and Poisoning (E Codes)
This section is an alphabetic list of environmental events, circumstances, and other conditions that can cause injury and adverse effects.

Payer acceptance of E codes varies. Many payers will require an E code to determine if an injury is the result of an accident and, therefore, covered by another payer such as automobile insurance. Other payers will not process an E code. Check with your payers for their specific guidelines regarding the submission of E codes. An index for external causes of injury and poisoning can be found after the ICD-9-CM index.

The Structure of the Tabular List
The tabular list contains codes and their narrative descriptions. The three sections are the "Classification of Disease and Injuries," "Supplementary Classifications," and the appendices.

Section 1: Classification of Diseases and Injuries

The first section of the Tabular List contains 17 chapters. Ten chapters are devoted to major body systems. The other seven chapters describe specific types of conditions that affect the entire body. This classification contains only numeric codes, from 001.0 to 999.9.

Chapter	Chapter Title	Category Code Range
1.	Infectious and Parasitic Diseases	001–139
2.	Neoplasms	140–239
3.	Endocrine, Nutritional and Metabolic Diseases, and Immunity Disorders	240–279
4.	Diseases of the Blood and Blood forming Organs	280–289
5.	Mental Disorders	290–319
6.	Diseases of the Nervous System and Sense Organs	320–389
7.	Diseases of the Circulatory System	390–459
8.	Diseases of the Respiratory System	460–519
9.	Diseases of the Digestive System	520–579
10.	Diseases of the Genitourinary System	580–629
11.	Complications of Pregnancy, Childbirth and the Puerperium	630–679
12.	Diseases of the Skin and Subcutaneous Tissue	680–709
13.	Diseases of the Musculoskeletal System and Connective Tissue	710–739
14.	Congenital Anomalies	740–759
15.	Certain Conditions Originating in the Perinatal Period	760–779
16.	Symptoms, Signs and Conditions	780–799
17.	Injury and Poisoning	800–999

Each of the 17 chapters in the Classification of Diseases and Injuries is divided into the following:

- **Subchapters.** Subchapters are a group of closely related conditions. Separate titles describe the contents of each subchapter.

- **Category—three-digit codes.** Three-digit codes and their titles are called "category codes." Some three-digit codes are very specific and are not subdivided. These three-digit codes can stand alone to describe the condition being coded.

- **Subcategory—four-digit codes.** Most three-digit categories have been further subdivided with the addition of a decimal point followed by another digit. The fourth digit provides specificity or more information regarding such things as etiology, site, and manifestation. Four-digit codes are referred to as "subcategory codes" and take precedence over three-digit category codes.

- **Subclassification—five-digit codes.** Greater specificity has been added to the ICD-9-CM system with the expansion of four-digit subcategories to the fifth-digit subclassification

level. Five-digit codes are the most precise subdivisions in the ICD-9-CM system.

Section 2: Supplementary Classifications (V Codes and E Codes)

Classification of Factors Influencing Health Status and Contact with Health Services (V Codes). The codes in this classification, otherwise known as V codes, are alphanumeric and begin with the letter "V." These codes are used to describe circumstances, other than a disease or injury, that are the reason for an encounter with the health care delivery system or that have an influence on the patient's current condition.

Example

V70.0   **Routine general medical examination at a health care facility**

V codes are sequenced depending on the circumstance or problem being coded. Some V codes are sequenced first to describe the reason for the encounter, while others are sequenced second because they identify a circumstance that affects the patient's health status but is not in itself a current illness. Assignment of V codes will be discussed in depth in a separate section.

Classification of External Causes of Injury and Poisoning (E Codes). These codes are also alphanumeric and begin with the letter "E." They are used to describe circumstances and conditions that cause injury, poisoning, or other adverse side effects. They may be used in addition to codes in the main classification (001–999) to identify the external cause of an injury or condition. They may never be used alone and may never be listed as the first diagnosis.

Example

821.01   **Right femur shaft fracture**

E814.7   **Pedestrian struck by motorcycle**

Section 3: Appendices

Appendix A: Morphology of Neoplasms. This appendix is an adaptation of the International Classification of Diseases for Oncology (ICD-O), a coded nomenclature of the morphology of neoplasms. These codes are alphanumeric and begin with the letter "M." An example is code M8000/0 Neoplasm, benign.

Appendix B: Deleted effective October 2004.

Appendix C: Classification of Drugs by American Hospital Formulary Service List Number and Their ICD-9-CM Equivalents. The ICD-9-CM classification of adverse effects is keyed to the code structure of the Hospital Formulary of the American Hospital Formulary Service (AHFS). Published under the direction of the American Society of Hospital Pharmacists, the AHFS list is updated continuously to include newly released drugs.

Appendix D: Classification of Industrial Accidents According to Agency. This appendix is a classification of machines and other agents that might cause accidents in an industrial setting.

Appendix E: List of Three-Digit Categories. This appendix lists all three-digit categories of the Classification of Diseases and Injuries.

ICD-9-CM Definitions and Guidelines

At the beginning of your ICD-9-CM book you will find more guidelines regarding the conventions of the ICD-9-CM book. These conventions should be reviewed to give you a complete understanding to help you code accurately when using your unabridged ICD-9-CM code book.

General Coding Guidelines

Many types of source documents (e.g., medical records, encounter forms, superbills, operative reports, etc.) are used to identify a patient's diagnosis and the services provided to the patient. The source document furnishes information such as the diagnostic statement and the procedural statement.

Do not code the diagnosis if the condition is indicated as "suspected," "rule out," or "probable." Code only a condition that is known for certain at the time of the patient's visit. If a definite condition or problem is not documented at the conclusion of the patient's visit, the symptom should be coded.

When the statement in the record contains both the patient's complaints (e.g., shortness of breath, dizziness, frequent headache, and nosebleeds) and the physician's diagnoses explaining those symptoms (e.g., hypertension and obesity), code only the diagnoses.

Clearly document the reason for physical therapy treatment, particularly when using a medical diagnosis that is not readily related to the physical therapy service provided.

001–139 Infectious and Parasitic Diseases

Communicable diseases as well as diseases of unknown origin but possibly due to infectious organisms are covered in this chapter. Infections confined to a specific body system are classified to chapters covering the specific body site. Congenitally acquired infections, postoperative infections, and infections complicating pregnancy and delivery are classified elsewhere. An additional code from the "Infectious and Parasitic Disease" chapter may be used in combination with the codes from other chapters to further describe the nature of the infection.

Infective organisms classified to categories 001–139 include bacteria, chlamydia, fungi, helminths, mycoplasms, protozoans, rickettsias, and viruses. This chapter classifies infectious and parasitic diseases by anatomic site, by type of infectious organism or parasite, as well as by a combination of site and type of organism.

010–018 Tuberculosis

Infectious diseases caused primarily by the acid fast bacilli Mycobacterium tuberculosis, but also M. bovis, M. africanum, M. leprae, and other variants, are included in this subchapter. Infection occurs almost exclusively through the respiratory system by inhalation of the tubercule bacilli from an infected host. The disease spreads from the primary lesion in the lung to other parts of the body.

Tuberculosis is first coded according to site or type.

The Fifth-digit subclassification codes for this category are assigned according to the method of determining the positive diagnosis of tuberculosis.

Example

A diagnosis of tuberculosis of the kidney confirmed by bacterial culture of the sputum is coded 016.04. The same diagnosis confirmed by microscopic examination of the sputum is coded 016.03.

Late effects of tuberculosis are coded to category 137, which is discussed later in this chapter.

030–041 Other Bacterial Diseases

Leprosy, diphtheria, whooping cough, scarlet fever, streptococcal sore throat, meningitis, tetanus, septicemia, toxic shock syndrome, actinomycotic infections, and gas gangrene are grouped as other bacterial diseases in this subchapter.

Category 030 is used to indicate leprosy. A fourth digit is used to indicate the type or group of leprosy.

040.4 Other Specified Botulism

Botulism, an uncommon but serious neuromuscular poisoning caused by the toxin *Clostridium botulinum*, occurs in three forms. Food-borne botulism is a result of ingesting foods containing the botulism toxin and is reported with code 005.1 Wound botulism, caused by a toxin produced from a wound infected with *Clostridium botulinum,* is frequently the result of a traumatic injury or a deep puncture wound. Often caused by abscess formation due to self-injected illegal drugs, its manifestations include neurological symptoms with onset typically two weeks following the initial wound or trauma. Infant botulism is a result of consuming the spores of the botulinum bacteria and occurs most often in infants less than six months of age. The spores colonize in the large intestine, frequently resulting in constipation and progressing to neuromuscular paralysis. All forms of botulism can be fatal, with life-threatening impairment of respiratory function being one of the greatest complications.

Coding Tips

Codes 040.41 Infant botulism, and 040.42 Wound botulism, should be used for reporting specific botulism infections not classifiable to subcategory 005 Other food poisoning.

To report wound botulism or botulism classifiable to code 040.42, use an additional code to identify the complicated wound, by site.

042 Human Immunodeficiency Virus (HIV) Infection

Human immunodeficiency virus (HIV) disease is coded to this subchapter. HIV is a serious health concern and accurate coding of the disease is necessary for collecting important data concerning the manifestations and treatment of the disease. Manifestations of AIDS and HIV infection are often numerous and they should all be coded.

Code 042 should only be assigned when there has been a positive diagnosis of the infection as stated by the physician.

Coding Tips

Code 042 is sequenced first when a patient is seen for an HIV infection or complication due to the presence of the HIV infection. Additional codes are used to identify associated complications.

Code 042 is not sequenced first if the patient is seen for a condition unrelated to the HIV infection. Code 042 is assigned as a secondary diagnosis. For example: if a patient with HIV is seen for a fractured wrist, the fracture is sequenced first and the code for HIV is sequenced second.

An asymptomatic patient with a positive HIV test result is assigned code V08, Asymptomatic human immunodeficiency virus [HIV] infection status.

Once an asymptomatic patient develops HIV related symptoms, that patient must be assigned code 042 on every subsequent visit.

045–049 Poliomyelitis and Other Non-Arthropod-Borne Viral Diseases of Central Nervous System

Infections of the central nervous system due to viruses not transmitted by parasites, organisms, or infective agents (carriers) are classified to this section. These diseases include acute poliomyelitis, meningitis due to enterovirus, and other viral diseases such as viral encephalitis.

046 Slow Virus Infections and Prion Diseases of the Central Nervous System

Code category 046, which previously classified diseases caused by slow virus infections, has been revised and expanded to identify certain diseases now known to be caused by proteinaceous infection particles called prions. Prion diseases, also known as transmissible spongiform encephalopathies (TSEs), are a family of rare, progressive neurodegenerative disorders that affect both humans and animals. A prion is an abnormal, transmissible agent that induces abnormal folding of normal cellular prion proteins in the brain, leading to brain damage. Prion diseases are distinguished by certain clinical and pathological characteristics specific to each type of infection. Upon autopsy, noninflammatory lesions, vacuoles, amyloid protein deposits, and astrogliosis may be present in CNS and/or lymphoid tissue. Prion diseases infecting humans include:

- Creutzfeldt-Jakob disease (CJD) characteristic dementia, myoclonus, motor disturbances, characteristic EEG changes

- Variant Creutzfeldt-Jakob disease (vCJD) characteristic early onset psychiatric and sensory symptoms with delayed onset neurological abnormalities, related to bovine spongiform encephalopathy (BSE).

- Gerstmann-Sträussler-Scheinker syndrome (GSS) characteristic dysarthria, cerebellar ataxia, and dementia

- Fatal familial insomnia (FFI) progressive and severe sleep disorders, deterioration of mental and motor functions, dementia

Coding Tip

Mandatory coding is required to report the dementia without or with behavioral disturbances associated with either form of CJD. Code first the appropriate CJD, then assign either code 294.10 or 294.11 Dementia in diseases classified elsewhere without or with behavioral disturbances, respectively.

050–059 Viral Diseases Generally Accompanied by Exanthem

Viral diseases that commonly manifest with skin eruptions or rashes are classified to this subchapter. This includes such infections as smallpox, chickenpox, and fifth disease. Also classified in this subchapter are neurological complications that can result from these infections.

052.2 Postvaricella Myelitis

Myelitis, or inflammation of the spinal cord, can have numerous presentations and multiple underlying causes. Postvaricella myelitis is a neurological complication of chickenpox (varicella). Varicella is a common childhood infectious disease in which neurological complications are rare, occurring in less than 1 percent of patients and most often affecting children under the age of 15 years.

Coding Tip

Code 052.2 Postvaricella myelitis, was created in order to provide coders a means to uniquely identify this condition, also known as postchickenpox myelitis.

053.14 Herpes Zoster Myelitis
054.74 Herpes Simplex Myelitis

Myelitis attributable to herpes zoster or herpes simplex is a rare complication and most often occurs in an immunocompromised patient. Following an acute attack of chickenpox, the virus becomes dormant in cranial and spinal ganglia in a noninfectious state. The virus may later reactivate in a ganglion and cause a localized eruption of shingles (zoster) that may result in the neurologic sequela of myelitis, which typically develops days to weeks after the appearance of the rash. Symptoms most often begin unilaterally, and there may be abnormal but nonspecific MRI findings. Transverse myelitis due to herpes simplex may occur following acute infection with HSV or it may occur due to reactivation of the virus that infects the skin and neurones of the dorsal root ganglia, where it causes lifelong latent infection.

Coding Tip

Codes 053.14 Herpes zoster with other nervous system complications, herpes zoster myelitis, and 054.74 Herpes simplex with other specified complications, herpes simplex myelitis, are new codes designed to more precisely identify specific viral-related neurological complications. Appropriate code assignment is dependent upon the strain causing the infection. Herpes simplex viruses (types 1 and 2) are strains of the human herpes virus (HHV) family. Herpes simplex myelitis is more often associated with HSV-2.

058 Other Human Herpesviruses

Of those with human herpesviruses (HHV), the majority are infected with HHV-6 or HHV-7, primarily during childhood. These forms of HHVs are associated with various clinical manifestations such as fever, rash, and seizures. Immunocompromised hosts, such as transplant recipients or those with AIDS, are at increased risk for symptomatic primary disease or reactivation disease.

The sixth of the customary exanthems of childhood, roseola infantum is typically an acute benign disease manifested by a short-lived high fever followed by the appearance of a light pink maculopapular or erythematous rash. Cases of roseola infantum have been documented since the identification of the etiologic agent HHV-6 that lacks the characteristic rash, instead presenting as an acute febrile illness with associated gastrointestinal or respiratory manifestations.

Although the full range of clinical manifestations of HHV-6 is unclear, other recently recognized clinical signs include hepatitis, encephalitis, hemophagocytic syndrome, and adult mononucleosis like illness. HHV-7, which is closely related to both HHV-6 and cytomegalovirus (CMV), also can be the causative agent in a small number of roseola cases. Believed to affect more than 95 percent of the population, HHV-7 is the least pathogenic of the three viruses and is most often acquired prior to age five. As with other herpesviruses, the infection becomes latent in the host following the primary infection, which predisposes individuals to later reactivation.

Coding Tip
Code category 058 should be used to report specific herpesviruses not specifically classifiable elsewhere to type. Reported elsewhere in this chapter are cytomegalovirus/HHV-5 (078.5), Epstein-Barr/HHV-4 (075), and other forms of human herpesviruses (categories 052–054).

059 Other Poxvirus infections
Global travel and imported animals have increased the concern for exposure to poxvirus infections. Humans may be infected intentionally (e.g., smallpox vaccination) or unintentionally (e.g., secondary spread from a vaccine or infection from a dairy-associated wild type strain). Poxvirus infections are classifiable to these categories:

Orthopoxviruses: Cause systemic infections in humans, necessitating specific diagnosis, treatment, and infection control precautions. Orthopoxviruses include variola virus (agent of smallpox), monkeypox virus, vaccinia virus, and cowpox virus. Monkeypox virus and cowpox virus are not endemic within the United States but have the potential for importation via infected travelers or imported animals.

Parapoxviruses: Currently, all four parapox viruses (papular stomatitis virus, orf virus, pseudocowpox virus, and sealpox virus) are zoonotic in nature, and are endemic within the United States. Orf virus, associated with contact with sheep and goats, causes a sore mouth in humans. In general, these infections are self-limited but may cause severe infections in immunocompromised hosts.

Yatapoxviruses: Include yaba-like disease virus (YLDV), tanapox virus, and yaba monkey tumor virus, which are endemic to sub-Saharan Africa. Yatapoxviruses are endemic to monkeys, but accidental infections of humans have been reported. These viruses are a concern for travelers or handlers in animal research facilities.

Other poxviruses: These have yet to be formally classified (e.g., Cotia virus). Diagnostic tests for some poxvirus infections are not readily available, and clinicians may not be able to make a diagnosis beyond "poxvirus."

Coding Tip
Category 059 Other poxvirus infections, excludes cowpox (051.01) and other vaccinia and paravaccinia infections classified elsewhere. Generalized vaccinia (cutaneous and sometimes systemic reactions associated with vaccination) is reported with code 999.0, whereas vaccinia not from vaccine is reported with new code 051.02. It should be noted, infection due to vaccinia virus spread as an inadvertent inoculation of site other than the vaccination site is also reported with new code 051.02.

Example
Vaccinia of the eyelid requires two codes, 051.02 and 373.5 Other infective dermatitis of eyelid.

060–066 Arthropod-Bourne Viral Diseases
An arthropod-borne viral disease is transmitted to man through a parasite or insect, such as a mosquito, tick, or biting fly that carries the disease-causing organism and transfers it to humans. These viral infections cause different types of encephalitis, or inflammation of the brain, and a multitude of differentiated fevers, such as yellow fever, hemorrhagic fevers, and West Nile fever. These diseases are accompanied by a wide range of manifestations and may cause neurologic complications.

080–088 Rickettsioses and Other Arthropod-borne Diseases
Category 088 describes other arthropod-borne disease. Subclassification code 088.81 classifies Lyme disease, a multi-systemic disease causing arthritis of the large joints, myalgia, malaise, and development of neurological and cardiac abnormalities.

Coding Tip
If the documentation indicates arthritis due to or associated with Lyme disease, assign 088.81 and 711.8 as a secondary code. A fifth digit (0–9) must be assigned to code 711.8 indicating the affected joint.

090–099 Syphilis and Other Venereal Diseases
Syphilis is classified by type, early or late, and whether symptomatic, latent, or unspecified. Syphilis affecting the cardiovascular or nervous system is classified separately.

Examples
- Early syphilis, symptomatic with genital chancre is coded as 091.0.
- Latent early syphilis, unspecified, is coded as 092.9.
- Syphilis of the aortic valve is coded as 093.22.
- Tabes dorsalis, parenchymatous syphilis, is coded as 094.0.

Coding Tip
Venereal disease is classified by type, whether acute or chronic, and by site of complication.

Example
Acute gonococcal infection of the bladder is coded as 098.11. Chronic gonococcal infection of the seminal vesicles is coded as 098.34.

137–139 Late Effects of Infectious and Parasitic Diseases

Late effects of tuberculosis (137), acute poliomyelitis (138), and other infectious and parasitic diseases (139) are classified to this subchapter.

The acute infection is no longer present but the patient has a residual condition. A code from one of these three categories must be used in conjunction with the residual condition code.

Coding Tip

The codes in this subchapter are in effect "add-on" codes.

Example

Nephropathy resulting from past episode of tuberculosis of the kidney is coded as 583.89 and 137.2.

136.2 Specific Infections by Free-living Amebae

Diseases caused by the free-living ameboid protozoan *Acanthamoeba* include amoebic keratitis and encephalitis. Acanthamoeba keratitis is a rare but potentially blinding infection of the cornea, caused by (*Acanthamoeba*). Acanthamoeba keratitis primarily affects otherwise healthy persons who improperly store, handle, or disinfect their contact lenses (e.g., by using tap water or homemade solutions for cleaning). Symptoms are similar to other eye infections but targeted treatment is necessary to be effective. Complications include corneal scarring and loss of vision. Long-term therapy and management are often required.

Coding Tip

Assign additional code to identify the manifestation when reporting conditions classifiable to new code 136.21 Specific infection due to *Acanthamoeba*. More than one code may be necessary to fully describe and report the nature of the infection.

140–239 Neoplasms

According to the most widely accepted definition, a neoplasm is an abnormal mass of tissue, the growth of which exceeds and is uncoordinated with that of the normal tissues and persists in the same excessive manner after cessation of the stimulus that evoked the change.

For ICD-9-CM classification purposes, neoplasms are described in the following four ways:

- Behavior
- Site
- functional activity
- morphology

The behavior of a neoplasm refers to its biological behavior. ICD-9-CM recognizes four types: malignant, benign, uncertain, and unspecified. Site refers to the anatomic location of the neoplasm and is used as a subdivision for each of the four types of behaviors. Functional activity refers to the effects certain neoplasms have on tissues that are functionally active and is reported with a secondary code from another chapter of ICD-9-CM.

Example

A patient with a malignant neoplasm of the adrenal gland also experiences hyperactive catecholamine secretion. In this case, use code 194.0 to describe the neoplasm and code 255.6 to identify the hyperactive catecholamine production.

Morphology refers to the classification of neoplasms according to tissue type or cell origin. Tissues of the body can be divided broadly into either epithelial or connective tissue. In turn, each type of tissue can be subdivided and subcategorized further into very specific delineations based on the cell type of origin. The morphology of a neoplasm is reported using M codes, which are provided as a separate code listing in ICD-9-CM, appendix A.

Coding Tip

For the physical therapist, Medicare and most insurance carriers do not require the use of the Morphology codes.

The Neoplasm Table

The neoplasm table is divided into four categories: malignant, benign, uncertain behavior, and unspecified.

Malignant neoplasms, classified to categories 140–208, are tumors that behave in a life-threatening manner. Specifically, the behavior that makes certain neoplasms malignant is their ability to invade surrounding tissues as well as to metastasize. Malignant neoplasms are further differentiated into three types.

- Primary neoplasm identifies the originating site of the tumor
- Secondary neoplasm identifies the site to which a primary tumor has metastasized, or spread from the primary body site to a secondary site.
- Carcinoma in situ identifies tumors that are confined to their point of origin and have not invaded surrounding tissue.

Benign neoplasms, classified to categories 210–229, are tumors in which the dividing cells adhere to each other, with the resulting neoplastic mass remaining as a circumscribed lesion.

Uncertain behavior is the term used to describe neoplasms whose behavior cannot be determined at the time of discovery and continued study is necessary to accurately classify the neoplasm by behavior.

Unspecified behavior is assigned when the medical documentation does not specify the behavior of the neoplasm.

140–199 Malignant Neoplasms of Solid Tumor Type

Solid tumors have the capacity to spread to adjacent (direct extension metastasis) or distant sites in the body (embolic metastasis). The method of spreading is not reflected in the code assignment, only the fact that there has been metastasis is reflected.

When there has been direct extension and the site of origin cannot be determined (i.e., the neoplasm exists over two adjacent [contiguous] sites) ICD-9-CM classifies that neoplasm as other specified site, fourth digit of 8.

Code 199.2 identifies malignant neoplasm associated with transplant organ. Organ recipients are routinely placed on immunosuppressive drugs to prevent rejection of the transplanted organ, but this immunosuppression also renders them vulnerable to infection and disease, including malignancy. Additionally, a transplanted organ may contain malignant cells that were undetected prior to transplant. Multiple transplant operations may be a result of transplanted organ failure, rejection, or other complication such as neoplasm.

Coding Tip
Instructional notes are included with new code 199.2 Malignant neoplasm associated with transplanted organ, to "code first complication of transplanted organ (996.80–996.89)" and "use additional code for specific malignancy site." Multiple codes are required and are reported in a specific sequence.

200–208 Malignant Neoplasms of Lymphatic and Hematopoietic Tissue

Malignant neoplasms of the lymphatic and hematopoetic tissues are considered primary neoplasms and are not considered to spread to secondary sites. The malignant cells circulate to other areas but these are not considered secondary sites.

Some of the types of neoplasms that are included in this section are lymphosarcomas, Hodgkin's disease, lymphomas, malignant histocytosis, multiple myeloma, myeloid leukemia, acute leukemia, and chronic leukemia.

209 Neuroendocrine Tumors

Carcinoid tumors are a specific type of slow-growing neoplasm originating in the cells of the neuroendocrine system. The terms "carcinoid" and "neuroendocrine" may be used interchangeably in the clinical environment to describe specific types of neoplasm of neuroendocrine tissue. Carcinoid and oat cell tumors are currently the most commonly occurring neuroendocrine tumors in adults. Benign and malignant forms of neuroendocrine tumors can produce hormonal syndromes. Therefore, depending upon the system involved, the symptoms caused by neuroendocrine tumors include a diverse range of characteristic hormonal syndromes. The most common syndrome associated with carcinoid tumors is carcinoid syndrome in which an abnormally high concentration of serotonin secretion causes flushing, diarrhea, and heart disease. Carcinoid tumors occur most commonly in the respiratory and gastrointestinal tract and usually originate in hormone-producing cells in the linings of these organs. Gastrointestinal carcinoid tumors are classified according to the presumed embryonic site of origin: the foregut (bronchi and stomach), the midgut (small intestine and appendix), and the hindgut (colon and rectum).

Coding Tip
Neuroendocrine tumors are classified according to site and behavior. Instructional notes at category 209 advise that multiple codes may be required to report neuroendocrine malignancies and associated manifestations.

210–229 Benign Neoplasms

Benign neoplasms, classified to categories 210–229, are tumors in which the dividing cells adhere to each other, with the resulting neoplastic mass remaining as a circumscribed lesion.

Coding Tip
To correctly code a neoplasm, it is extremely important to wait for the pathology report to ensure an accurate diagnosis as well as CPT procedure code.

230–234 Carcinoma In Situ

Carcinoma in situ are neoplasms that have the potential for spreading to surrounding tissue but remain limited and have not extended beyond the basement membrane of the epithelial tissue. Other common terms used to describe carcinoma in situ are noninfiltrating, noninvasive, intraepithelial, preinvasive carcinoma, or cancer in situ.

235–238 Neoplasms of Uncertain Behavior

This subchapter classifies by site certain histomorphologically well-defined neoplasms, the subsequent behavior of which cannot be predicted from the present appearance without further study.

NOTE: Uncertain behavior is a histomorphological determination, as distinguished from "unspecified," which indicates lack of documentation to support a more specific code assignment.

This section is arranged by site or organ system and covers all major organ systems. Included in this subchapter are neurofibromatosis, polycythemia vera, and mast cell tumors.

Code 238.77 Post-transplant lymphoproliferative disorder (PTLD) identifies a disease of uncontrolled proliferation or production of B cell lymphocytes often following infection with the Epstein-Barr virus for post-transplant patients. Symptoms of PTLD are related to the site of tumor growth. The patient may present asymptomatically or with localized or systemic symptoms such as one or more nodal or extranodal tumors. Systemic presentations may range from an unexplained infectious syndrome or mononucleosis-like illness with or without lymphadenopathy to a disseminated sepsis syndrome. After cessation of immunosuppressant drug therapy, PTLD may spontaneously regress.

Coding Tip
Code 238.77 Post transplant lymphoproliferative disorder will likely be sequenced and reported as a secondary diagnosis, with the appropriate subcategory 996.8 as the first-listed diagnosis. However, the "code first" instruction listed at code 238.77 is without italicized print, designating that such codes are acceptable reported alone or as a secondary diagnosis depending on the circumstances of the admission/encounter.

239 Neoplasms of Unspecified Nature

This subchapter classifies by site neoplasms of unspecified morphology or behavior. This means that the medical record contains no further information that allows the coder to more accurately describe the condition or assign more specific codes to the condition. Neoplasm of unspecified nature indicates a lack of specific information in the documentation while neoplasm of uncertain behavior refers to incomplete assessment of the neoplasm. Other terms often documented in records with no further information include neoplasm, new growth, tumor, or growth.

Coding Tip
The term "mass" should not be regarded as a neoplasm. The alphabetic index main term "Mass" directs the coder to site- or organ-specific sections outside the neoplasm chapter for coding masses.

240–279 Endocrine, Nutritional and Metabolic Diseases, and Immunity Disorders

This chapter classifies diseases and disorders of the endocrine system, nutritional system, metabolic system, and the immune system.

Disorders of the endocrine system include a variety of specific glandular disorders that can affect any body system. Diseases of the endocrine system include hormonal disturbances that affect some of the body's most important physiological functions including reproduction, growth and development, and energy balance. Hormones are chemical substances secreted by endocrine glands to control and adjust the body's physiological functions.

Nutritional deficiencies include dietary and nutritional disorders such as protein-calorie malnutrition, vitamin deficiencies, and mineral deficiencies. Nutritional deficiencies due to problems relating to intestinal malabsorption normally are classified to category 579 in the digestive system chapter.

Metabolic disorders include disturbances in any of the chemical processes that take place in the human body. Metabolism is divided into two phases: anabolism, the constructive phase in which smaller molecules such as amino acids are converted into larger molecules such as proteins, and catabolism, the destructive phase in which the process is reversed. The result is growth and regeneration of tissue, elimination of waste products, energy production, and energy conservation (stored reserves).

Disorders of the immune system include conditions that compromise the patient's ability to respond to antigenic activity and fight off disease, especially infectious disease.

249 Secondary Diabetes Mellitus

Secondary diabetes develops due to damage or destruction of insulin-producing cells in the pancreas by the presence of chronic disease, drugs, trauma, hormonal disturbances, genetic disorders, and other conditions. Secondary diabetes mellitus presents with the same symptoms as diabetes mellitus as well as carrying the same risks as primary diabetes, including complications such as heart conditions, stroke, diabetic retinopathy, diabetic nephropathy, diabetic neuropathy, and sexual dysfunction. Treatment of secondary diabetes involves treating the underlying cause. When the underlying cause cannot be resolved or remains unidentified, the diabetes is treated similarly to primary diabetes, with consideration given to pre-existing comorbidities. In general, this treatment focuses on controlling the level of glucose (blood sugar) with a combination of diet and exercise, and may involve insulin therapy and antidiabetic agents.

Coding Tips
Category 249 Secondary diabetes mellitus includes 20 codes that parallel category 250. Similarly, all of the manifestation codes that apply to category 250 also apply to 249. In the same manner, instructional notes at

subcategories 249.4–249.8 direct the coder to "use additional code to identify manifestation." Multiple codes may be required to report secondary diabetes and associated conditions.

Sequencing of category 249 codes depends on the circumstances of the encounter, the documentation in the medical record, and official coding advice.

Category 249 includes drug-induced or chemical-induced diabetes mellitus. Use an additional E code to identify the causal drug or substance.

Report V58.67 to identify any associated insulin use.

250–259 Diseases of Other Endocrine Glands

This subchapter covers diabetes mellitus, disorders of the pancreas, parathyroid gland, pituitary gland, thymus gland, adrenal glands, ovarian dysfunction, testicular dysfunction, polyglandular dysfunction, and other endocrine disorders.

The most complex coding issue concerning this chapter is coding diabetes mellitus. Each subcategory of diabetes will be discussed separately since coding issues need to be addressed specifically.

250 Diabetes Mellitus

Coding Tip
The fifth-digit assignment for categories 249 and 250 indicates both types of diabetes and the status of disease control. The physician MUST document the type of diabetes in order to assign a fifth digit of "1" or "3," which indicates type I, [juvenile type]. The status of uncontrolled MUST also be stated by the physician in order to assign a fifth digit indicating uncontrolled status. When the physician specifically states that the patient has uncontrolled diabetes, then and only then can a fifth-digit assignment of 2 or 3 be made.

The second axis of coding for category 250 is the identification of complications present due to the diabetes.

Diabetes mellitus is a complex disease characterized by metabolic disturbances in the catabolism of carbohydrates, fat, and protein due to a relative (type II) or complete (type I) lack of insulin secretion or production by the beta cells of the pancreas, defects in the body's ability to respond to insulin, or both. The major part of the pancreas, called the exocrine pancreas, secretes digestive enzymes into the gastrointestinal tract. Distributed throughout the pancreas are clusters of endocrine cells that secrete insulin, glucagon, and somatostatin. These hormones all play a role in regulating energy production and metabolism in the body. Diabetes is a systemic disease and should be coded even when there is no documentation of active intervention during the patient encounter. When diabetes is not managed properly, it may lead to serious progressive and chronic systemic complications.

Type I patients have a completely inadequate, even absent insulin secretion from the beta cells within the islets of Langerhans and have virtually no endogenous circulating insulin. This type of diabetes is caused as a result of destruction of the pancreatic beta cells and is also known as juvenile diabetes. This form of diabetes is very difficult to regulate. These patients are thus dependent on exogenous insulin to metabolize the foods they eat, prevent ketosis, reduce hyperglucagonemia, and bring the elevated blood sugar level down.

Type II patients have some ability to secrete insulin and produce enough endogenous circulating insulin to prevent ketosis. Onset of type II diabetes is generally later in life. and this form has also been referred to as adult-onset diabetes. These patients may not produce sufficient amounts of insulin or may be unable to effectively utilize the insulin produced. This type of diabetes is being diagnosed more frequently in children, especially those with obesity problems that can cause the body's inability to respond to insulin or to produce enough insulin to metabolize the dietary intake. Age of onset is not a determining factor in coding diabetes.

NOTE: In some cases of type II diabetes, insulin is required because diet and/or oral hypoglycemic agents do not control hyperglycemia sufficiently. Also, it is not uncommon for hospitalized patients to be given insulin for better, more predictable control over the disease while the patient is being treated (whether for related or unrelated conditions). It is, therefore, very important that the physician document the specific form of diabetes that describes the patient's condition. The fact that a patient is receiving or dependent upon insulin is also not a determining factor for coding diabetes.

Coding Tip
Fifth-digit Assignment for Category 250

	Controlled	Uncontrolled	Unspecified Control
Type I	1	3	1
Type II	0	2	0
Unspecified Type	0	2	0

250.0 Diabetes Mellitus without Mention of Complication
This subcategory includes diabetes mellitus NOS and diabetes with no mention of complications. Both type I and type II diabetes can exist without complications. However, Type I diabetes most commonly has associated complications.

250.1 Diabetes with Ketoacidosis
Ketoacidosis is a form of metabolic acidosis characterized by raised levels of circulating ketone (acetone) bodies. Ketone bodies accumulate due to metabolization of fatty acids in place of carbohydrates. The carbohydrates are not being utilized due to a lack of insulin to metabolize them.

Coding Tip
Subcategory 250.1 is diabetic ketoacidosis (DKA) or diabetes acidosis without mention of coma. If coma is present, code to subcategory 250.3.

During periods of hyperosmolarity, coma and seizures are due primarily to the swelling of the brain. In type II diabetes, the pancreas secretes enough insulin to prevent ketosis. In type I diabetes, the pancreas fails completely, and ketone bodies start to accumulate. If the blood glucose levels are not brought down, the patient will develop diabetic ketoacidosis.

250.2 Diabetes with Hyperosmolarity
Diabetic coma that is due to very high glucose concentrations in the blood and an increased concentration of osmotically active particles (e.g., sodium and potassium), not ketone bodies, is coded to diabetes with hyperosmolarity.

Example
Hyperosmolar coma in a type II diabetic patient, stated as out of control, is coded as 250.22.

Coding Tip
Subcategory 250.2 is diabetes with hyperosmolarity with or without coma.

Hyperosmolar nonketonic coma is often potentiated by drug therapy in the elderly. Drugs such as diuretics (thiazides or furosemide), diazoxide, propranolol, cimetidine, glucocorticoids, and diphenylhydantoin have all been implicated. Follow the ICD-9-CM coding rules regarding poisonings and adverse effects when the condition is due to or potentiated by drug therapy.

Example
Hyperosmolarity coma in a type II diabetic due to cimetidine taken for a duodenal ulcer is coded as:

250.20	Diabetes with hyperosmolarity, type II, unspecified
532.90	Duodenal ulcer, unspecified
E943.0	Adverse reaction to antacids

250.3 Diabetes with Other Coma
When coma is due to a variety of metabolic conditions such as hypoglycemic coma, hyperglycemic coma with ketoacidosis, and hyperglycemic coma with lactic acidosis (and ketosis), code the condition to subcategory 250.3. Hypoglycemic coma is distinguished by rapid onset and abnormally low levels of blood glucose, usually after the administration of insulin or oral hypoglycemic agents. Hyperglycemic coma with ketoacidosis is distinguished by slow onset, respiratory problems, and blood and urine containing ketones. Coma due to lactic acidosis is more likely to develop in diabetics and is sometimes associated with ketoacidosis. It is characterized by profound metabolic acidosis with a blood pH below 7, low bicarbonate level, markedly increased anion gap, hypochloridemia, and blood lactate levels in excess of 5 mm.

This subcategory includes:

- Diabetic coma with ketoacidosis
- Diabetic hypoglycemic coma
- Insulin coma
- Kussmaul's coma

Coding Tip
Nondiabetic hypoglycemic coma is coded as 251.0.

Diabetic hyperosmolar coma is classified to subcategory 250.2.

Diabetic hypoglycemic coma and insulin coma are assigned to subcategory 250.3.

250.4 Diabetes with Renal Manifestations
Diabetes with renal manifestation presents as severe thickening of the capillary basement membrane of the kidney, which eventually impairs renal function. There are two basic types of diabetic nephropathy, diffuse and nodular, which may coexist.

With diffuse diabetic nephropathy, the entire glomerular mesangium (the suspensory structure of the renal glomerulus) thickens, causing glomerulosclerosis. With nodular diabetic nephropathy (also known as Kimmelstiel-Wilson syndrome and intercapillary glomerulosclerosis), fibrin caps, capsular drops, and adhesions form in one or several areas of the glomerulus, causing glomerulosclerosis. When clinical manifestations occur as a result of glomerulosclerosis, the condition is known as nephrotic syndrome. Serious diabetic nephropathy occurs in nearly 97 percent of all patients with diabetic renal disease.

Coding Tip
Use additional code to identify manifestation such as:

- Diabetic nephritis (583.81)
- Diabetic nephropathy NOS (583.81)
- Diabetic nephrosis (581.81)
- Ebstein's disease (581.81)
- Glomerulonephritis, chronic (582.81)
- Intercapillary glomerulosclerosis (581.81)
- Kimmelstiel-Wilson syndrome (581.81)
- Nephritis with nephrotic syndrome (581.81)
- Nephritis with nephropathy (583.81)
- Chronic kidney disease (585.1–585.9)

Nephritis is the first stage of renal disease that may progress to nephrosis leading to chronic kidney disease (CKD). Code only to the most severe stage exhibited by the patient's condition.

Example
Type I diabetes stated as uncontrolled with diabetic nephrosis is coded as 250.43 and 581.81.

250.5 Diabetes with Ophthalmic Manifestations
Ophthalmic disorders such as retinopathy and cataracts can result as complications of diabetes. Diabetic retinopathy is the most common ophthalmic complication and a leading cause of blindness in the United States. There are two basic types of diabetic retinopathy: nonproliferative (or simple) and proliferative. The term nonproliferative diabetic retinopathy (NDPR) is used to describe the earliest stages of the disease. Nonproliferative diabetic retinopathy is characterized by dilation, constriction, and tortuosity of the retinal veins and by microaneurysms that produce retinal hemorrhages. The next step in severity is termed proliferative at the disease's more advanced stages. Proliferative retinopathy is characterized by new blood vessels forming on the surface of the retina or within the vitreous cavity. The newly formed vessels are prone to bleeding and cause serious complications such as retinal detachment, vitreous hemorrhage, and blindness. Leakage of the retinal vessels can cause swelling of the retina which results in a condition known as diabetic macular edema (DME). When this edematous process occurs, the macula (central portion of the retina) swells and vision is impaired. This can condition can precipitate the loss of vision. DME is a common complication of diabetic retinopathy, and can occur an any stage of the disease.

Example
Type I diabetes stated as uncontrolled with mild nonproliferative diabetic retinopathy is coded as 250.53 and 362.03.

True diabetic cataracts are rare. Also known as sugar cataracts, they are characterized by sudden myopia associated with hyperglycemia and lens swelling. This is followed by a rapidly developing "snowstorm" or "snowflake" subcapsular cataract, which may clear partially or progress rapidly to a mature cataract. Most cataracts seen in diabetics are similar to those seen in nondiabetics, except that diabetics tend to develop them earlier in life for unknown reasons.

Coding Tip
Cataracts or retinopathies are classified to this subcategory only when the physician specifies that there is a cause and effect relationship with diabetes mellitus. Do not code cataracts as diabetic cataracts in the presence of diabetes mellitus unless the record supports a cause and effect relationship between the disease and the manifestation. Diabetics may develop senile cataracts that have no causal relationship to the diabetes.

Use additional codes to identify manifestations such as:

- Blindness (diabetic) (369.00–369.9)
- Diabetic cataract (366.41)
- Diabetic macular edema (DME) (362.07)
- Glaucoma (diabetic) (365.44)
- Iritis (364.42)
- Retinal edema (diabetic) (362.83)
- Retinopathy (diabetic) (362.01–362.06)

250.6 Diabetes with Neurological Manifestations
Common long-term complications of diabetes encompass several distinct syndromes that differ with respect to anatomical distribution, neurological deficits, and clinical course. Diabetic neuropathy can affect the peripheral nerves alone or in combination with the autonomic nerves. Involvement of just a single nerve trunk is called mononeuropathy. Mononeuropathies usually are acute, self-limiting disorders most often affecting the extraocular muscles, but they can affect any single nerve trunk.

Involvement of the nerves of the peripheral nervous system is called polyneuropathy or peripheral polyneuropathy. Diabetic neuropathy affecting the part of the nervous system that regulates involuntary vital functions, particularly in the gastrointestinal system, urogenital system, and cardiovascular system, are called autonomic neuropathies. Since the autonomic nervous system includes the peripheral nerves involved in regulating cardiovascular, respiratory, endocrine, and other autonomic body functions, the term "peripheral autonomic neuropathy" (polyneuropathy) often is used.

Other forms of diabetic neuropathy include amyotrophy, a rare and reversible syndrome of asymmetric pain, and weakness typically involving the muscles of the pelvic girdle and proximal thigh. Charcot's joint disease is a form of neuropathic joint disease characterized by chronic progressive degeneration of one or more joints.

 © 2009 Ingenix

Coding Tip

Use additional codes to identify associated manifestations such as:

- Charcôt joint disease (713.5)
- Diabetic amytrophy (353.5)
- Diabetic mononeuropathy (354.0–355.9)
- Diabetic neurogenic arthopathy (713.5)
- Diabetic peripheral autonomic neuropathy (337.1)
- Diabetic polyneuropathy (357.2)
- Diabetic impotence (607.84)
- Diabetic gastroparalysis (536.3)
- Diabetic gastroparesis (536.3)
- Neuropathic arthritis (713.5)
- Neuropathic ulcer (707.1x)

250.7 Diabetes with Peripheral Circulatory Disorders

Complications of diabetes that affect the blood vessels outside the heart and the lymphatic vessels are coded to this subcategory. Peripheral circulatory disorders usually are attributed to atherosclerosis and can generally be divided into two groups: macroangiopathy and microangiopathy. Macroangiopathy is a disease that affects the major arterial systems; microangiopathy is a disease that affects the capillary basement membranes and is a characteristic lesion of diabetes. Diabetics are two and a half times more likely than nondiabetics to develop atherosclerosis and arteriosclerosis, and they tend to develop the diseases earlier.

Coding Tip

Use additional codes to identify associated manifestations such as:

- Gangrene (785.4)
- Peripheral angiopathy (443.81)

Unless stated as a causal relationship with diabetes, the following circulatory diseases are not coded to subcategory 250.7 Arteriosclerotic heart disease, cardiomyopathy, cerebrovascular disease, and coronary artery disease.

250.8 Diabetes with Other Specified Manifestations

Complications or manifestations of diabetes affecting other body systems are classified to this subcategory. Included are complications such as bone changes, any associated ulceration, diabetic cachexia (malnutrition or Lancereaux's syndrome), lipidosis, and secondary glycogenosis.

Coding Tip

No additional code is required for the following manifestations:

- Diabetic hypoglycemia
- Hypoglycemic shock

Use additional codes to identify associated manifestations, such as:

- Glycogenosis (259.8)
- Lipidoses (272.7)
- Necrobiosis lipoidica diabeticorum (709.3)
- Oppenheim-Urbach disease (709.3)
- Osteomyelitis (731.8)
- Xanthoma (272.2)
- Any associated ulceration (707.10–707.9)
- Diabetic bone changes (731.8)

250.9 Diabetes with Unspecified Complications

Ill-defined or unspecified complications or manifestations of diabetes not elsewhere classifiable are included in this subcategory. This code should rarely be used.

Diabetes complicating pregnancy, delivery, or puerperium is classified to chapter 11. "Gestational Diabetes," which is an abnormal glucose tolerance during pregnancy is exhibited by patients previously not diagnosed as diabetic. This condition usually resolves after the pregnancy period. This condition is coded as 648.8x.

260–269 Nutritional Deficiencies

This subchapter covers nutritional deficiencies of specified vitamins, minerals, and protein-calorie malnutrition (PCM).

Coding Tip

Iron deficiencies of anemia are classified to chapter 4, "Diseases of the Blood and Blood Forming Organs (280–289)."

Some of the more well known vitamin deficiencies classified in this section are beriberi (265.0), a thiamin deficiency; pellagra (265.2), a niacin deficiency; scurvy (267), a vitamin C deficiency; and rickets (268.0), a vitamin D deficiency.

Coding Tip

When reporting code 268.1 Rickets, late effect, code first the nature of the late effect. Code 268.1 should be reported as an additional code to describe the underlying cause of the condition being treated.

270–279 Other Metabolic and Immunity Disorders

Included in this subchapter are categories of metabolic and immunity disorders, including obesity, gout, volume depletion, fluid and electrolyte imbalances, cystic fibrosis, disorders and disturbances of amino-acid transport and metabolism, lipoid metabolism, and mineral and carbohydrate metabolism.

Coding Tip
Abnormal findings without manifestation of disease are not sufficient evidence of disease and should not be coded unless the physician states the diagnosis.

Many of the disorders in metabolism result in associated mental retardation, which may be described by using an additional code.

Coders should pay careful attention to the includes notes for these categories. Many of the disorders are known by several eponyms and common names. ICD-9-CM has included many of these terms to assist the coder in assigning the correct code.

Gout is assigned to its own category (274) instead of being classified with other disorders of purine and pyrimidine metabolism (277.2).

Code 275.5 Hungry bone syndrome (HBS) identifies a state of severe or long-standing hypocalcemia, most commonly due to primary or secondary (including postsurgical) hypoparathyroidism. Elevated levels of parathyroid hormone and bone demineralization cause the bone to sequester calcium. This results in increased bone formation (density) and decreased bone resorption, characterized by a rapid fall in plasma calcium, phosphorus, and magnesium levels. The hypocalcemia may resolve within weeks, but in some cases the condition can persist for years. The resultant metabolic imbalance may precede osteoporosis and associated pathological fracture, tetany, or seizures. Other causal conditions for HBS include neoplasm or associated therapies, systemic metabolic acidosis, or other chronic disease (e.g., chronic renal disease).

Coding Tip
When reporting code 275.5, code also any causal conditions such as neoplasm, chronic disease, or certain postsurgical states (e.g., parathyroidectomy) documented in the medical record. Code also any other specified manifestations, as appropriate.

277 Other and Unspecified Disorders of Metabolism
Perioxisomal disorders (277.86) are rare congenital diseases whereby perioxisome metabolism fails and results in a wide range of conditions associated with developmental delay, mental retardation, autism, and physiological challenges. These disorders include Zellweger syndrome, X-linked andrenoleukodystrophy and adrenomyoloneuropathy.

Disorders of mitochondrial metabolism (277.87) are disorders that are a result of mitochondrial or nuclear DNA. Severity of condition relies upon a wide range of physiological and environmental factors. Mitochondrial defects are often associated with chronic neurodegenerative diseases such as Parkinson's disease, Alzheimer's disease and amyotrophic lateral sclerosis (ALS). Metabolic dysfunction inherent in the disease process may result in behavioral changes, seizures, glycemic control issues and a host of physiological challenges.

Coding Tip
When using a code from this category, assign an additional code to identify the associated conditions.

Overweight, obesity and other hyperalimentation (category 278), provides information about a person's weight, and is coded in accordance with the physician's documentation and guidelines for assigning secondary diagnoses. Specific information regarding severity of condition is reported by assigning additional codes from category V85 Body Mass Index.

320–389 Nervous System and Sense Organs
This chapter classifies diseases and disorders of the central and peripheral nervous systems and diseases of the eyes and ears.

320–326 Inflammatory Diseases of the Central Nervous System
Inflammatory diseases such as meningitis, encephalitis, cerebral abscesses, late effects of infections of the central nervous system, and other types of inflammations such as meningitis due to sarcoidosis, and lead poisoning (toxic) encephalitis are grouped together in this subchapter. However, many infections of the central nervous system that are considered communicable or transmissable are excluded from this section and are classified to chapter 1, "Infectious and Parasitic Diseases."

Bacterial meningitis (category 320) is the inflammation of the lining of the brain and/or spinal cord (meninges) due to a bacterial organism. Bacterial meningitis can be caused by a variety of pyogenic bacterial organisms, most commonly Haemophilus influenzae (type B), Streptococcus pneumoniae, Pneumococcus, Neisseria meningitidis, Staphylococcus aureus, Klebsiella, Pseudomonas, and Escherichia coli.

Coding Tip
Assign a fourth digit to indicate the organism causing the bacterial meningitis. If the medical documentation indicates aseptic, viral, or nonbacterial meningitis without further specification, see category 047. When meningitis is a manifestation of another disease process, code 320.7 and code the underlying disease first.

Example 1
Staphylococcal meningitis is coded as 320.3.

Example 2
Typhoid fever with meningitis is coded 002.0 Typhoid fever, and 320.7 Meningitis in other bacterial diseases classified elsewhere.

Example 3
Aseptic meningitis is coded as 047.9.

Example 4
Meningitis due to other specified bacteria (320.8) requires a fifth digit to further define the type of bacteria causing the meningitis as follows:

1   Anaerobic meningitis
2   Meningitis due to gram-negative bacteria, not elsewhere classified
9   Meningitis due to other specified bacteria

Meningitis due to other organisms (category 321) is the inflammation of the covering of the meninges due to organisms

© 2009 Ingenix

other than bacteria. These can be fungal organisms, viruses not classified elsewhere, or other nonbacterial organisms.

Coding Tip
Assign a fourth digit to indicate the organism causing the meningitis. Since meningitis classified to this category is a manifestation of another disease process, code the underlying disease first.

Example
Cryptococcal meningitis is coded as 117.5 Cryptococcosis, and 321.0 Cryptococcal meningitis.

323.0 Encephalitis, Myelitis, and Encephalomyelitis
Myelitis, or inflammation of the spinal cord, can have numerous presentations and multiple underlying causes. Transverse myelitis (TM) occurs across the width of the spinal cord and can damage or destroy the fatty insulating substance covering the nerve cell fibers (myelin).

Encephalitis, or inflammation of the brain, is a relatively uncommon condition, affecting approximately 1,500 people per year in the United States. The disease may be more severe in infants and the elderly. The majority of cases of encephalitis in the United States are caused by viruses, although other underlying causes include bacterial infections, immunization procedures, toxic substances, or postinfectious processes. There are two types of encephalitis: primary encephalitis (acute viral encephalitis) and secondary encephalitis (postinfective encephalitis). Primary encephalitis, also known as acute viral encephalitis, is a result of a direct viral infection of the brain and may be focal (located in only one area) or diffuse (located in different areas). Secondary, or postinfective encephalitis, can result from complications caused by a current infection. Secondary encephalitis resulting from a previous viral infection is known as acute disseminated encephalitis and frequently occurs two to three weeks after the initial infection. Acute and secondary encephalitis due to specific infectious processes are addressed in chapter 1 of ICD-9-CM.

In encephalomyelitis, the inflammation affects both the brain and the spinal cord. Also known as myeloencephalitis, etiologies may include viral or bacterial infections, immunization procedures, postinfectious processes, or toxic etiologies due to poisoning. Symptoms, diagnostic workup, and treatment are similar to those for encephalitis or myelitis.

Coding Tip
Encephalitis and encephalomyelitis in viral diseases classified elsewhere (323.01) and myelitis in viral diseases classified elsewhere (323.02) include these disease processes when due to viruses other than those specified in chapter 1 of ICD-9-CM.

Other encephalitis and encephalomyelitis due to infection classified elsewhere (323.41) and other myelitis due to infection classified elsewhere

(323.42) include these conditions that are due to infections, such as those caused by bacteria, other than those specified in chapter 1 of ICD-9-CM.

Encephalitis and encephalomyelitis following immunization procedures (323.51) and myelitis following immunization procedures (323.52) include these conditions occurring as a response to immunizations or vaccinations.

Infectious acute disseminated encephalomyelitis (ADEM) (323.61) is a secondary process resulting from a previous viral infection that typically occurs two to three weeks after the initial infection.

Other postinfectious encephalitis and encephalomyelitis (323.62) or postinfectious myelitis (323.63) include those diseases that manifest as a result of a postinfectious process.

Toxic encephalitis and encephalomyelitis (323.71) and toxic myelitis (323.72) may occur as a result of bodily absorption of toxic substances, including medicinal substances, carbon monoxide, lead, arsenic, or specific chemicals or gases.

Other causes of encephalitis and encephalomyelitis (323.81) or other causes of myelitis (323.82) include these conditions for which there is not a more specific code.

330–337 Hereditary and Degenerative Diseases of the Central Nervous System
Included in this subsection are degenerative diseases such as Alzheimers, Parkinson's disease, Huntington's Chorea, and peripheral autonomic neuropathy.

Alzheimer's disease (331.0) is a form of presenile dementia caused by the destruction of the subcortical white matter of the brain and characterized by increasing loss of intellectual functioning beginning with minor memory loss and eventually resulting in total loss of ability to function.

Coding Tips
When reporting codes classified to category 331 Other cerebral degenerations, assign an additional code to identify whether the associated dementia is with (294.11) or without behavioral disturbances (294.10).

331.5 Idiopathic Normal Pressure Hydrocephalus (INPH)
Normal pressure hydrocephalus (NPH) is a treatable disorder of gait impairment, subcortical dementia, and urinary urgency and incontinence associated with impaired cerebrospinal fluid (CSF) circulation and ventriculomegaly. NPH results from a disruption in the CSF circulation leading to gradual enlargement of the ventricles and emergence of symptoms. This syndrome, when secondary to disease processes such as subarachnoid hemorrhage, traumatic brain injury, cerebral infarction, and meningitis, is referred to as secondary NPH, or communicating hydrocephalus.

Coding Tip
Hydrocephalus in patients without known etiologies may be documented as idiopathic normal pressure hydrocephalus (INPH) which is reported with code 331.5. Congenital hydrocephalus associated with spina bifida (741.0) and congenital obstructive hydrocephalus (742.3) are classified to chapter 14, "Congenital Anomalies."

333 Other Extrapyramidal Disease and Abnormal Movement Disorders

This category contains codes which describe such conditions as athetoid cerebral palsy and dystonia.

Dystonia is defined as a condition in which muscle tone is abnormal and may be either excessive or inadequate. Involuntary movements and prolonged muscle contractions occur, with resultant abnormality in posture, tremors, and twisting body motions that may affect an isolated area or may involve the whole body. There are multiple forms, and dystonia may be genetic or acquired.

333.71 Athetoid Cerebral Palsy

Athetoid, or dyskinetic cerebral palsy is a form of acquired torsion dystonia that is manifested by abnormal, uncontrolled movements that are slow and writhing, usually affecting the extremities. The muscles of the tongue and face may also be affected, resulting in drooling or grimacing. Symptoms may be exacerbated during times of stress, and often disappear during sleep. Dysarthria may also be present.

333.79 Other Acquired Torsion Dystonia

Various underlying factors may contribute to acquired torsion dystonia. Underlying factors for other acquired forms of torsion dystonia may include trauma, infection, exposure to toxins, or certain environmental elements.

Coding Tip
If the acquired torsion dystonia is due to drugs, assign code 333.72.

337.01 Idiopathic Peripheral Autonomic Neuropathy

Code 337.01 reports carotid sinus syndrome (a.k.a., carotid sinus syncope [CSS], carotid sinus hypersensitivity [CSH]), which is an exaggerated vagal response of dizziness and syncope due to carotid sinus barorecepter stimulation. Specialized nerve cells called baroreceptors detect changes in pressure and tension in the large vessels of the body, such as the carotid arteries. The carotid sinus reflex plays an integral part in regulating normal blood pressure. This vagal response is a result of transient diminished cerebral perfusion resulting in dizziness or syncope. CSH attributes to 0.5-9.0 percent of patients with recurrent syncope, and is associated with an increased risk of falls, drop attacks, bodily injuries, and fractures in elderly patients. CSH is more common in males than in females, is predominantly a disease of elderly people, and is rarely identified in patients less than 50 years of age. Symptoms of CSS may include recurrent dizziness, syncope or near syncope, unexplained falls, symptoms associated with head turning or constriction of the neck, and possible amnesia related to the event. Physical signs observed with CSH include hypotension, bradycardia and asystole.

Coding Tip
Code 337.0 includes fifth-digit subclassification codes for unspecified (337.00) and other (337.09) idiopathic peripheral neuropathies, and a specific code to report carotid sinus syndrome (337.01).

Complex regional pain syndrome is reported with the appropriate code from subcategory 337.2 Reflex sympathetic dystrophy, by anatomic site (e.g., upper limb, lower limb, unspecified, or other specified site).

338 Pain, Not Elsewhere Classified

Until fiscal year 2007, there have been no specific codes to identify encounters for pain management, or for specific types of pain such as central or chronic pain syndrome or postoperative pain.

Coding Tip
Category 338 contains an instructional note to coders to use an additional code (307.89) to identify pain associated with psychological factors. It also contains an exclusions note for generalized and localized pain, as well as pain disorder exclusively attributed to psychological factors.

338.0 Central Pain Syndrome

Central pain syndrome is a neurological state caused by injury to or dysfunction of the central nervous system (CNS) and may have multiple etiologies, including stroke, multiple sclerosis, tumors, epilepsy, brain or spinal cord trauma, or Parkinson's disease. The CNS consists of the brain, brainstem, and spinal cord. Pain characteristics of the CNS may vary widely among affected individuals, in part because of the large number of potential causes. This syndrome may be restricted to certain areas, such as the hands or feet, or may affect a large portion of the body. The extent of pain is often related to the underlying cause of the CNS injury or damage. Pain is characteristically constant, may be moderate to severe in intensity, and is frequently made worse by touch, movement, emotions, and changes in temperature. Pain sensations vary, and may consist of "pins and needles" sensations; pressing, lacerating, or aching pain; and brief, excruciating bursts of sharp pain. Numbness or burning may occur in the pain-affected areas and are often most severe on the distant parts of the body, such as the hands or feet. Central pain syndrome often starts soon after the causative injury or damage, but may also be delayed by months or years, particularly if it is related to poststroke pain.

338.1 Acute Pain

Acute pain is a sensation generated in the nervous system that may be an alert to possible injury, as a response to trauma, or as a postoperative sequela. Analgesics are often prescribed to treat acute pain. Other treatment options may include application of heat or cold, massage, therapeutic touch, transcutaneous electrical nerve stimulation (TENS), relaxation techniques, guided imagery, hypnosis, music distraction, or cognitive therapies such as art and activity therapy.

Coding Tip
A fifth digit should be assigned to indicate the cause of the acute pain as follows:

338.11	Acute pain due to trauma
338.12	Acute post-thoracotomy pain
338.18	Other acute postoperative pain
338.19	Other acute pain

338.2 Chronic Pain

Chronic pain is a persistent condition in which the nervous system generates pain signals that may be ongoing for weeks to years. Although often as a result of past injuries, infections, or surgical interventions, chronic pain may also be due to ongoing causes, such as arthritis, cancer, or current infections. Some patients suffer chronic pain in the absence of past injury or signs of body damage. A variety of chronic pain conditions affect older adults, and complaints may include headache, low back pain, pain related to cancer or arthritis, and neurogenic or psychogenic pain.

Coding Tip
A fifth digit should be assigned to indicate the cause of the acute pain as follows:

338.21 Chronic pain due to trauma
338.22 Chronic post-thoracotomy pain
338.28 Other chronic postoperative pain
338.29 Other chronic pain

340–349 Other Disorders of the Central Nervous System

Other disorders include multiple sclerosis, hemiplegia and hemiparesis, epilepsy, and migraines.

Multiple sclerosis (340) is a chronic demyelinating disease affecting the white matter of the spinal cord and brain. Multiple sclerosis is characterized by the breaking down of the myelin fibers of the nervous system; patches of scarred nervous fibers develop at these sites. The etiology is unknown, but studies suggest the condition may be a cell-mediated autoimmune disease due to an inherited disorder of immune regulation. The disease affects adults between the age of 20 and 40 years and occurs more often in women.

341.20–341.22 Transverse Myelitis

Acute transverse myelitis (ATM) is a focal inflammatory condition of the spinal cord, resulting in motor, sensory, and autonomic dysfunction. "Transverse" indicates dysfunction at a specific level across the spinal cord, with altered function below this level and normal function above it. The cause of about 60 percent of TM cases is unknown, and so is referred to as idiopathic. Other cases can be linked to certain associated diseases. The most optimal treatment of ATM is dependent upon a timely and accurate diagnosis. Because acute transverse myelopathies are comparatively rare, delayed and incomplete work-ups often occur.

Coding Tip
Acute transverse myelitis, not otherwise specified, is reported with code 341.20. If occurring in conditions classified elsewhere, report with code 341.21. This code contains an instructional note to coders to code first the underlying condition. Idiopathic transverse myelitis is now uniquely identified by code 341.22.

Hemiplegia and hemiparesis (category 342) codes are to be used when hemiplegia (complete) (incomplete) is reported without further specification, or is stated to be old or long standing but of unspecified cause. The category is used also for multiple coding to identify these types of hemiplegia resulting from any cause. Hemiplegia and hemiparesis resulting from cerebrovascular disease is classified to category 438.

Coding Tip
Fifth-digit assignment identifies the affected side.

0 Affecting unspecified side
1 Affecting dominant side
2 Affecting nondominant side

Epilepsy (category 345) is a disorder characterized by recurrent transient disturbances of the cerebral function. An abnormal paroxysmal neuronal discharge in the brain usually results in convulsive seizures, but may result in loss of consciousness, abnormal behavior, sensory disturbances, or in any combination. Epilepsy may be secondary to prior trauma, hemorrhage, intoxication (toxins), chemical imbalances, anoxia, infections, neoplasms, or congenital defects.

The ICD-9-CM alphabetic index provides guidance regarding appropriate code assignment for single, recurrent, or repetitive seizures and seizure disorder. Accordingly, a single seizure is reported with code 780.39. Recurrent or repetitive seizures are reported with code 345.9x Epilepsy, unspecified. Report code 345.9x Epilepsy, unspecified, for seizure disorder, not otherwise specified, and recurrent seizures.

Coding Tips
Assign a fourth digit to indicate the type of epilepsy. If the type of epilepsy is not indicated by the physician in the medical record, assign code 345.9 Epilepsy, unspecified, with the appropriate fifth digit.

Assign a fifth digit to indicate whether the epilepsy is intractable, that is, whether the epileptic seizures are resistant to control by standard medical therapy or require higher dosages that carry an unacceptable level of adverse effects.

A fifth-digit assignment is not made with subcategories 345.2 Petit mal status, and 345.3 Grand mal status.

A series of seizures at intervals too brief to allow consciousness between attacks is known as status epilepticus and can result in death. Status epilepticus, not otherwise specified, is classified to code 345.3 Grand mal status. However, status epilepticus can occur in other specified forms of epilepsy.

Migraine (category 346) is a vascular-type headache usually located in the temporal lobe and unilateral in nature. These headaches are commonly associated with irritability, nausea, vomiting, and often photophobia. Preceding the attacks, the cranial arteries constrict resulting in the warning sensory symptoms.

Coding Tip
Fifth-digit subclassifications describe migraines with or without associated complications. Status migrainosus describes a severe, debilitating migraine lasting more than 72 hours. This is a relatively rare, but life threatening migraine complication that could result in a potentially fatal ischemic stroke. Except for its prolonged duration, the headache characteristics are the same as for typical migraine. Intractable migraine describes frequently occurring, continuous, unremitting, or other migraine recalcitrant to conventional medical therapy that often requires acute care to resolve.

Cataplexy and narcolepsy (category 347) are disabling neurological disorders that affect sleep and wakefulness cycles and control of muscle tone. Narcoleptic patients with suffer brief, recurrent, and uncontrollable episodes of REM cycle sleep during the day. Cataleptic patients experience sudden onset of muscle weakness with loss of strength and muscle tone in connection with aggressive or intense, spontaneous emotions. Narcolepsy may occur with or without catalepsy and may or may not be due to another identified, underlying disease.

350–359 Disorders of the Peripheral Nervous System

This subchapter classifies disorders of the peripheral nervous system based upon the specific nerve or nerve complex involvement, or condition, such as Bell's palsy, polyneuritis, polyneuropathy, muscular dystrophies and other myopathies, and myoneural disorders.

Subcategory 358.0 reports myasthenia gravis (MG), an autoimmune system disorder in which the body produces antibodies against its own acetylcholine receptors in the neuromuscular junction. Acetylcholine is a neurotransmitter. When acetylcholine binds to receptors, it causes associated ion channels to open, with the results that muscle contraction is initiated. Antibodies produced in MG block the acetylcholine binding sites, preventing acetylcholine from binding to its receptor and opening the ion channel. The neuromuscular junction has decreased numbers of available acetylcholine receptors, which in turn results in fewer interactions between acetylcholine and it's receptors, leading to decreased activation of electrical impulses. This accounts for the clinical features of weakness and fatigability.

Many of the conditions included in this subchapter are manifestations of other diseases and should be used in addition to the code for the underlying condition.

Coding Tip
Use an additional code to identify the organism causing the acute infective polyneuritis (357.0). Human immunodeficiency virus is becoming a common cause of acute or infective polyneuropathy and is coded 042 HIV disease, with code 357.0.

359.21–359.29 Myotonic Disorders

Myotonia, a neuromuscular disorder characterized by the slow relaxation of the muscles following contraction, may be inherited or acquired. Caused by an abnormality in the muscle membrane, it can affect all muscle groups. The most common form is myotonic muscular dystrophy (MMD, Steinart's disease), which is often manifested by weakness and wasting of the voluntary muscles generally noticed at the age of two to three years. Muscle stiffness, especially in the legs, may be brought on by sudden activity after rest. Muscle enlargement may occur and muscle strength may be increased. Myotonic chondrodystrophy is a rare genetic disorder characterized by joint contractures, bone dysplasia, myotonic myopathy, and growth delays resulting in dwarfism. Treatment options for the various myotonic disorders may include anticonvulsant drugs, physical therapy, and other rehabilitative measures designed to improve muscle function.

Coding Tip
To report drug-induced myotonia (359.24), an additional E code is required to identify the causative drug.

390–459 Disease of the Circulatory System

This chapter classifies disease and disorders that affect the heart, cerebrovascular diseases, arteries, veins and lymphatics.

401–405 Hypertensive Disease

Hypertension is a condition in which the arterial blood pressure is elevated above normal levels. The blood pressure range considered to be hypertensive varies, but most commonly a 140/90 mm Hg is considered hypertensive.

There are many diagnostic terms used to describe the types of hypertension. Referring to the "Includes" and "Excludes" notes will assist in accurate coding assignment. For example, essential hypertension (category 401) includes all the following diagnostic terms: high blood pressure, hyperpiesia, hyperpiesis, hypertension (arterial, essential, primary, or systemic), hypertensive vascular degeneration, and hypertensive vascular disease. The "Excludes" note indicates that a diagnosis of elevated blood pressure without a diagnosis of hypertension, pulmonary hypertension, or hypertension of vessels of the brain or eye are not coded to this category.

Coding Tips
Controlled hypertension usually indicates that the current treatment for existing hypertension is regulating the blood pressure adequately. Code assignment should be made according to type and nature only. ICD-9-CM does not include coding to indicate controlled or uncontrolled status. The diagnostic statement usually refers to an existing stage of hypertension under control by therapy.

Uncontrolled hypertension indicates that treatment is not adequately regulating blood pressure or the hypertension is not being treated. Again, code assignment should be made according to type and nature of the disease.

Transient hypertension is coded as elevated blood pressure (796.2) when no established diagnosis of hypertension has been made. Code to 642.3x for transient hypertension of pregnancy.

Hypertension crisis is coded to the type and nature of the hypertension with additional codes to identify associated conditions.

Essential hypertension (category 401) is also referred to as primary, idiopathic, or systolic hypertension, and is defined as hypertension occurring without apparent cause. The physician must document in the medical record whether the hypertension is malignant or benign to assign a fourth digit of 0 or 1 respectively. If the physician has made no entry in the medical record to support either designation then assign a fourth digit of 9 Unspecified.

NOTE: The need to refer to instructional notes is very important in coding hypertension. The hypertension table, a complete list of diagnoses associated with or due to hypertension, is located in the ICD-9-CM code book's alphabetic index under the main term "Hypertension."

Three terms "malignant," "benign," and "unspecified" serve as headings in the table to assist the coder in selecting the most specific code to describe the diagnosis.

Malignant. This type of hypertension is considered to be the most severe and difficult to treat. A diagnosis of malignant hypertension will be made by the physician if the patient's diastolic blood pressure is consistently greater than 140 and if other clinical features are present, such as cardiac and kidney involvement and neuroretinopathy. Progression of the disease is rapid.

Benign. This type of hypertension is considered to be relatively mild and usually is chronic or occurs over a prolonged period of time. Progression of the disease is slow.

Unspecified. This term is selected when the physician does not specify the type of hypertension as benign or malignant. If the physician has not specified the type, request clarification of the diagnosis.

Most hypertension codes can be found in the code range 401–405.

A patient may have an elevated blood pressure reading during an outpatient visit without having a known diagnosis of hypertension. In this situation, use code 796.2, which describes an elevated blood pressure reading that may be the result of emotional problems or stress. This diagnosis code can be found in the alphabetic index under the main term "Elevation" and subterms "blood pressure," "reading," and "no diagnosis of hypertension."

410–414 Ischemic Heart Disease

This subchapter of the ICD-9-CM classification system includes those conditions due to insufficient blood supply to the myocardium or heart muscle. Conditions classifiable to this section are acute myocardial infarction (category 410), other acute and subacute forms of ischemic heart disease (category 411), old myocardial infarction (412), angina pectoris (category 413), and other forms of chronic ischemic heart disease (category 414).

An acute myocardial infarction (AMI) results from an interruption of the blood supply to an area of the myocardium. Physicians associate the condition as part of acute ischemic heart disease,

which is classified to category 410. Category 410 has subcategories (use of a fourth digit) that identify the site of the myocardial infarction and fifth digits to indicate the episode of care involved with the myocardial infarction.

The terms of ST elevation (STEMI) and non-ST elevation (NSTEMI) mirror national standard guidelines for classifying patients with acute coronary syndrome. STEMI tends to occur in a wide range of anatomical sites. The non-Q-wave infarction tends to occur in mainly a subendocardial or mid-myocardial site, and does not display the usual Q-wave patterns seen in STEMIs. NSTEMI, however, can still produce minor, less-dramatic degrees of some ST or T wave abnormalities, but can be termed as "NSTEMI."

Old myocardial infarction, (412), is assigned for diagnosis of an old or healed myocardial infarction diagnosed by EKG but currently presenting no symptoms.

Angina pectoris, (category 413), is defined as severe constricting pain in the chest, often radiating down from the precordium to the left shoulder and down the arm, due to ischemia of the heart muscle. It is usually caused by coronary disease. The pain is usually precipitated by exertion, effort, or excitement. The subcategories of angina pectoris identify the specific type of angina such as angina decubitus, Prinzmetal angina, and angina NOS.

Other forms of ischemic heart disease (category 414) such as coronary atherosclerosis, aneurysm of the heart, coronary artery disease (CAD), and chronic ischemic heart disease are coded to category 414.

Remember, when coding coronary atherosclerosis, the fifth-digit assignment indicates the kind of coronary vessel affected by the atherosclerosis. Code 414.00 if the vessel type, whether native or graft, is unspecified. Use 414.01 if the medical record contains no history of coronary bypass graft and it is a native artery being affected. Code 414.02 is assigned for atherosclerosis of an autologous vein graft (i.e., saphenous vein). Code 414.03 is assigned when the atherosclerosis affects a nonautologous graft. Atherosclerosis of an internal mammary artery bypass graft is coded to 414.04. Assign 414.05 when the documentation does not specify the type of bypass graft involved, 414.06 when a native coronary artery of a transplanted heart is affected, and 414.07 for coronary atherosclerosis of a bypass graft of a transplanted heart.

414.2 Chronic Total Occlusion of Coronary Artery

Chronic total occlusion of a coronary artery is a complete blockage of the artery that has been present for an extended duration (typically longer than three months). In these cases, myocardial infarction may be avoided by a collateral flow process. Collateral flow, or vessels that "reroute" blood flow, do not function as efficiently and often result in limited activity due to cardiovascular symptoms. This vascular "rerouting" places stress on the vasculature of the heart and puts the patient at significant risk for myocardial infarction while increasing the risk of other morbidity and/or mortality. Due to the difficulty in passing a guidewire through a chronic total occlusion, treatment of this form of blockage is often more challenging than for other types of coronary stenosis.

Coding Tips

Use 414.2 to report chronic total occlusion of coronary artery. Acute coronary artery occlusion with myocardial infarction (410.00–410.92) or without myocardial infarction (411.81) is excluded from 414.2, and more appropriately reported elsewhere.

When reporting chronic total occlusion of coronary artery (414.2), code first the appropriate code for coronary atherosclerosis classifiable to codes in range 414.00–414.07.

414.3 Coronary Atherosclerosis Due to Lipid Rich Plaque

Lipid-rich atherosclerotic plaques are particularly unstable and vulnerable to rupture, increasing the risk of acute coronary events such as thrombosis, arrhythmia, and myocardial infarction. Atherosclerotic plaques containing lipid-rich cores have been identified as a cause of arterial filling defects during angiography procedures. In atherogenesis, plaque stability depends on multiple factors including plaque composition, size and location of the core, arterial wall stress, and relationship of plaque to blood flow. New imaging technologies are being studied as a way to identify vulnerable or high-risk plaques in their early stages and assist in determining the optimal course of treatment based on the nature and composition of the patient's coronary artery plaques. Since lipid-rich plaque is present in some coronary atherosclerotic diseased vessels (but perhaps not all vessels) the presence of this code is an indicator of disease severity.

Coding Tip

Lipid-rich plaque of coronary vessels cannot be present without coronary atherosclerosis. Therefore, the appropriate coronary atherosclerosis code from subcategory 414.0 should be sequenced first, followed by code 414.3, when documented as such.

420–429 Other Forms of Heart Disease

This subchapter covers inflammatory conditions of the pericardium, endocardium, and myocardium, as well as heart valve disorders, cardiomyopathies, congestive heart failure, diastolic and/or systolic heart failure, and nerve conduction disorders of the heart.

Congestive heart failure (428.0) (CHF) is a syndrome of impaired contraction, or power failure (in pumping of the heart), pressure volume overload, and impaired filling of the heart, in which the heart may be functioning normally otherwise.

Long QT syndrome (LQTS), 426.82 is associated with recurrent syncope, malignant arrythimas and sudden death. This conditions can present along with other congenital anomalies present, or in the absence of know congenital disorders. The arrythimic episode can either resolve or be come fatal when the next episode occurs. Death can occur in a matter of minutes as a result of these arrythmias.

430–438 Cerebrovascular Disease

This subchapter of ICD-9-CM classifies the acute, organic conditions of the cerebrovascular system. Conditions coded to this section are nontraumatic in origin and include hemorrhages, thromboses, embolisms, transient cerebral ischemia, other ill-defined cerebrovascular diseases, and the late effects of cerebrovascular disease.

Transient cerebral ischemia (435) is a temporary deficiency in blood flow to the structures of the brain due to occlusion or stenosis of cerebral arteries. Clinical manifestations resulting from the ischemia depend on the site of the ischemia. Codes from category 435 classify transient cerebral ischemia by syndromes that identify the aggregate of manifestations according to location of the ischemia.

A very common documented diagnosis is transient ischemic attack (TIA), which is coded to 435.9. The definition of TIA is a short episode of neurological dysfunction occurring before total occlusion of the vessel. These TIAs can be considered a precursor to cerebrovascular accident (CVA).

Coding Tip

Code 434.91 is assigned for the nonspecific diagnosis of stroke or CVA, not otherwise specified.

The default code for not otherwise specified stroke or CVA was moved from 436 Acute, but ill-defined cerebrovascular disease to a more appropriate category. Stroke is the localized death or infarction of brain tissue caused by nontraumatic occlusion or hemorrhage within the cerebral arteries. This condition is more appropriately coded to 434.91 Cerebral artery occlusion, unspecified, with cerebral infarction.

Late effects of cerebrovascular disease (438) category is to be used to indicate conditions in categories 430 through 437 as the cause of the late effect, which is classifiable elsewhere. The "late effect" includes conditions specified as such, or as sequelae, which may occur any time after the onset of the causal condition.

Coding Tip

Assigning a code from the 438 category is inappropriate in cases of past history of cerebrovascular disease that resulted in no neurological deficits. The appropriate code assignment would be V12.54 Transient ischemic attack (TIA), and cerebral infarction without residual deficits.

© 2009 Ingenix

440–449 Diseases of Arteries, Arterioles and Capillaries

This subchapter includes conditions affecting the arteries, arterioles, and capillaries such as atherosclerosis, aneurysms, dissections, peripheral vascular disease, embolisms and thrombosis, arteritis, stricture, and other specified conditions.

440.4 Chronic Total Arterial Occlusion of the Extremities

Chronic total occlusion of an extremity artery usually develops over a long period of time, although partial occlusion is initially present. Symptoms vary, but may include intermittent claudication when the lower extremity arteries are affected. The presence of a collateral blood supply can cause a wide variation in symptoms and may actually allow worsening of an occlusion even though symptoms may be relatively less. Since a total occlusion is more difficult to cross than a partial occlusion, treatment with angioplasty and/or stenting is significantly more complex.

Coding Tips

When reporting code 440.4, sequence first the underlying disease, atherosclerosis of arteries of extremities (440.20–440.29, 440.30–440.32).

Code 440.4 excludes acute occlusion of artery of extremity (444.21–444.22).

451–459 Diseases of the Veins and Lymphatics, and Other Diseases of Circulatory System

Phlebitis (category 451) is an inflammation of a vein. When the inflammation results in the formation of a thrombus, an aggregation of primarily platelets and fibrin, the condition is called thrombophlebitis. The primary axis of classification for this category is vessel involvement: superficial vessels of the lower extremities, deep vessels of the lower extremities, superficial vessels of the upper extremities, deep vessels of the upper extremities, or other sites.

Coding Tips

Classification of Veins of the Extremities

Vessel Type	Lower Extremity	Upper Extremity
Deep	Femoral	Brachial
	Femoropopliteal	Radial
	Popliteal	Ulnar
	Tibial	
Superficial	Greater saphenous	Antecubital
	Lesser saphenous	Basilic
		Cephalic

Use an additional E code to identify the drug, if the condition was drug-induced.

This category excludes thrombophlebitis that is due to or following an implant or catheter device (996.61–996.62) as well as infusion, perfusion, or transfusion (999.2).

In the absence of inflammation (phlebitis), thrombosis, and embolism of the veins are classified to the categories 452 and 453. Code 452 is specific to portal vein thrombosis and category 453 is assigned to other venous embolism and thrombosis.

Varicose veins (category 454) are dilated and sometimes painful veins of the legs. It is caused by interference with venous drainage or weakness of the walls. ICD-9-CM classifies varicose veins first by site, then by whether there is ulcer formation, inflammation, or both ulcer and inflammation.

Coding Tip

Varicose veins with hemorrhage, or rupture, are coded as with ulcer, with inflammation, with ulcer and inflammation, or without mention of inflammation or ulcer. The term "rupture" is a nonessential modifier and does not affect code assignment. Do not code the hemorrhage in addition to the varicose vein condition.

Hypotension (category 458) is abnormally low blood pressure. There are several different forms of hypotension and ICD-9-CM has created several subclassification categories to describe these conditions fully.

Orthostatic hypotension is a condition characterized by a fall in blood pressure upon standing with symptoms of dizziness, syncope, and blurred vision. This form of hypotension can be acquired, idiopathic in origin, or secondary to other disease processes. It may also be called postural hypotension. Assign code 458.0 for orthostatic hypotension.

Iatrogenic hypotension or postoperative hypotension is assigned code 458.29. This is abnormally low blood pressure due to medical or surgical treatment. Code 458.21 reports hypotension of hemodialysis, or intra-dialytic hypotension.

Coding Tip

Code 458.29 fully describes postoperative hypotension and does not require an additional code to indicate complication of surgical and medical care.

Postphlebitic syndrome (459.1) manifests itself by various conditions after a deep vein thrombosis has occurred. Postphlebitic syndrome may include edema, pain, stasis dermatitis, varicose veins, and ulcerations on the lower leg.

460–519 Respiratory System

This complex of organs is responsible for pulmonary ventilation and the exchange of oxygen and carbon dioxide between the lungs and the ambient air. The organs of the respiratory system also perform nonrespiratory functions such as warming and moisturizing the air passing into the lungs, providing air flow for the larynx and vocal cords for speech, and thermoregulation for homeostasis by releasing excess body heat. The lung also performs important metabolic and embolic filtering functions.

Coding Tip

Use an additional code to identify the infectious organism responsible for any condition classified to chapter 8 of ICD-9-CM, "Diseases of the Respiratory System." Normal floral of the respiratory system includes Streptococcus and Neisseria and should not be coded as additional, unless the documentation indicates that the levels of the organisms are elevated and constitute an infection.

ICD-9-CM Definitions and Guidelines

460–466 Acute Respiratory Infections

This subchapter includes infections of the respiratory tract, excluding pneumonia and influenza, and is organized by site.

Acute infective nasopharyngitis (460) or the common cold excludes allergic and chronic rhinitis, acute and chronic pharyngitis, and sore throat.

Acute pharyngitis (sore throat) (462) is an acute inflammatory disorder of the throat, which may be caused by a virus or bacteria. Frequently, acute pharyngitis is preceded by coryza (460) or other communicable disease.

Coding Tip

The "Excludes" note associated with code 462 is extensive. Infections specified as due to any of the following organisms are not classified to this category:

- Coxsackie virus (074.0)
- Gonococcus (098.6)
- Herpes simplex (054.79)
- Influenza (487.1)
- Septic (034.0)
- Streptococcal (034.0)

Sore throat associated with infectious mononucleosis is coded to 075.

Acute tonsillitis and acute adenoiditis is classified to code 463. This includes follicular, gangrenous, infective, pneumococcal, septic, staphylococcal, suppurative, ulcerative, and viral tonsillitis. Chronic tonsillitis is classified to category 474.

Category 465 acute upper respiratory infection (URI) of multiple or unspecified sites, classifies those upper respiratory infections such as acute laryngopharyngitis, multiple upper respiratory infection, and acute URI, NOS.

490–496 Chronic Obstructive Pulmonary Disease and Allied Conditions

Chronic obstructive pulmonary disease (COPD) is a term that causes confusion for many coders. COPD describes many disorders that cause persistent obstruction of the bronchial air flow. This general term, COPD, may refer to the following conditions:

Code	Conditions
491.20	Emphysematous chronic bronchitis, chronic obstructive bronchitis, bronchitis with chronic airway obstruction, bronchitis with emphysema
491.21	COPD with acute exacerbation, chronic obstructive bronchitis with acute exacerbation, decompensated COPD with exacerbation
491.22	COPD with acute bronchitis, acute and chronic obstructive bronchitis, emphysematous bronchitis with acute bronchitis, emphysema with acute and chronic bronchitis, obstructive diffuse pulmonary disease with acute bronchitis
491.8	Chronic tracheitis, chronic tracheobronchitis
493.2x	Chronic obstructive asthma, asthma with chronic obstructive pulmonary disease (COPD), chronic asthmatic bronchitis, chronic asthmatic bronchitis with acute exacerbation

Code	Conditions
495.9	Chronic obstructive lung disease with unspecified allergic alveolitis
496	Chronic airway obstruction NOS, nonspecific chronic lung disease, obstructive lung disease, COPD NOS, diffuse chronic obstructive lung disease with fibrosis

Chronic bronchitis combined with obstructive lung disease (491.2x) is defined as a persistent cough with sputum production occurring on most days for at least three months of the year for at least two years. Obstructive lung disease is defined as a chronic or recurrent reduction in expiratory airflow within the lung. Obstructive chronic bronchitis is characterized by an increased mass of mucous glands in the lung, resulting in an increase in the thickness of the bronchial mucosa. Its most common etiology is cigarette smoking, but it also may be caused by environmental pollution or inhalation of irritant chemicals.

Coding Tips

Assign a fifth digit "0" to indicate obstructive chronic bronchitis without mention of acute exacerbation, 491.20, and fifth digit "1" for obstructive chronic bronchitis with acute exacerbation, 491.21.

Acute exacerbation of chronic obstructive bronchitis is not the same as acute bronchitis, code 466.0. Do not assign 466.0 as an additional code or substitute code for 491.22. However, when the condition causing the acute exacerbation is known, it may be listed as an additional code.

Example

Acute exacerbation of chronic bronchitis due to acute influenzal upper respiratory infection is coded as 487.1 Influenza, and 491.21 Acute exacerbation of chronic obstructive bronchitis.

The term "emphysema" refers to any condition in which air is present in a small area of an organ or tissue, for example, subcutaneous emphysema, characterized by air in the subcutaneous tissue. Emphysema classified to category 492 refers to pulmonary emphysema only.

Asthma (category 493) is a narrowing of the airways due to increased responsiveness of the trachea and bronchi to various stimuli. Asthma is reversible, changing in severity either spontaneously or as a result of treatment. Asthma is associated with bronchospasm and pathologic features such as increased mucous secretion, mucosal edema and hyperemia, hypertrophy of bronchial smooth muscle, and acute inflammation.

Asthma has been classified as extrinsic, intrinsic, or unspecified. This differentiation is considered archaic by many clinicians because manifestations of both extrinsic and intrinsic disease commonly occur in the same patient.

Status asthmaticus is defined as severe episode of asthma that does not respond to normal therapeutic measures.

The following fifth-digit assignment is to be used with codes 493.0–493.2 and 493.9:

0	unspecified
1	with status asthmaticus
2	with (acute) exacerbation

Coding Tip
Bronchospasm is an integral part of the asthmatic episode and should not be coded separately.

Subcategory 493.8 Other forms of asthma, includes exercise induced bronchospasm and cough variant asthma.

Bronchiectasis (category 494) is acquired dilated bronchi as a result of destructive chronic lung infection due to foreign body aspiration, cystic fibrosis, or bronchial tumors. Bronchiectasis is also called acquired bronchiectasis or congenital bronchiectasis (although it is rarely congenital). Symptoms include chronic cough, coughing up blood, shortness of breath, weight loss, fatigue, clubbing of fingers, rales, wheezing, palpitations, headache, and paleness of skin coloration. Fifth-digit assignment is based upon whether or not the patient presents with acute exacerbation.

COPD (496) or chronic airway obstruction, not elsewhere classified, is defined as a nonspecific condition characterized by a chronic or recurrent reduction in expiratory airflow within the lung. COPD and chronic obstructive lung disease (COLD) are the two most common descriptive diagnostic terms assigned to this code category.

Coding Tip
COPD, Not elsewhere classified, 496, may not be used with any of the codes from categories 491–493. Also, this category excludes COPD with allergic alveolitis (495.0–495.9), and bronchiectasis (494).

510–519 Other Diseases of the Respiratory System

Diseases of the respiratory system, such as empyema, pleurisy, pneumothorax, respiratory failure, and others, are located in this subchapter.

Empyema (category 510) is the accumulation of pus within the pleural space. Use an additional code to identify the infectious organism from category 041.

Pleurisy (category 511) is the inflammation of the serous membrane of the lungs and lining of the thoracic cavity. Exudation develops in the cavity or on the surface of the membrane. This category excludes pleurisy mentioned with tuberculosis (012.0) and malignant pleural effusion (511.81). Pleurisy with pleural effusion (511.1) is the abnormal accumulation of fluid in the pleural space. Use an additional code to identify the bacterial organism.

Pleural effusion is a common manifestation of both systemic and intrathoracic disease.

Coding Tip
Pleural effusion (511.9) should not be coded with congestive heart failure (CHF). The pleural effusion is an integral part of the disease process.

Pneumothorax (category 512) is an accumulation of gas or air in the pleural space. The degree of lung collapse is determined by the amount of air or gas trapped in the intrapleural space. Postoperative pneumothorax is coded as 512.1. Traumatic pneumothorax is classified to 860.0–860.1 and 860.4–860.5.

Pulmonary collapse is the incomplete expansion of lobules (clusters of alveoli) or lung segments. Also called atelectasis, (518.0) this condition may result in partial or complete lung collapse, which impairs gas exchange, resulting in hypoxia. Pulmonary collapse may be due to obstructions, such as mucous plugs, neoplasms, and foreign bodies, or to external compression of the lungs from conditions such as pleural effusion, enlarged thoracic lymph nodes, and pneumothorax.

Acute respiratory failure (518.81) is the failure of oxygenation and/or ventilation that is severe enough to impair or threaten the functioning of vital organs. With failure of oxygenation, the tissues of the lung are not functioning properly. An example of failure of oxygenation would be an acute exacerbation of bronchial asthma in a patient with emphysema. With failure of ventilation, airflow in and out of the lungs is impaired, for example, by compression of the trachea caused by metastatic carcinoma of the thoracic lymph nodes.

Coding Tip
Acute respiratory distress is coded as 518.82.

Respiratory (cardiorespiratory) arrest is coded as 799.1.

Diagnosis of respiratory failure based on ABG values is not absolute and may be adjusted according to the patient's baseline blood gas levels. Since some COPD patients have chronically abnormal values, the diagnosis of respiratory failure is made based on further decompensation from the patient's baseline. Another method of determining respiratory failure is by looking for critical values on the ABG reports. Two of three values are considered diagnostic of respiratory failure: pO_2 less than 50, pCO_2 greater than 50, and pH less than 7.30.

However, sequencing may be dependent on the circumstances of admission or episode of care and the presence of any chapter-specific coding guidelines that take precedence.

Coding Tip
Code 518.81 Acute respiratory failure, may be sequenced as a principal or first-listed diagnosis when it is the condition chiefly responsible for admission or other service. The definition of principal diagnosis applies only to care provided in nonoutpatient settings. In the outpatient setting, the term "first-listed" diagnosis is used in lieu of the principal diagnosis. The first-listed condition in an outpatient setting may be defined as the diagnosis, condition, problem, or other reason for the encounter or visit as documented in the medical record to be chiefly responsible for the services provided.

Adult respiratory distress syndrome (ARDS) (518.5, 518.82) is an acute respiratory hypoxemic failure due to pulmonary interstitial and alveolar edema. Two code choices are available for ARDS, depending on assorted condition. When associated with trauma, this syndrome is also called "shock lung." ARDS is usually a result of surgery or traumatic injury (518.5) or acute inflammation (518.82).

Patients with chronic lung disease, such as asthma, bronchitis, and emphysema, often experience regular changes in arterial blood gases that are significant enough to be diagnosed as chronic respiratory failure (518.83). Treatment is directed toward the underlying disorder with the objective of reducing the severity and frequency of the ABG variations.

680–709 Skin and Subcutaneous Tissue

This chapter classifies diseases and disorders of the epidermis, dermis, subcutaneous tissue, nails, scar tissue, sebaceous glands, sweat glands, hair, and hair follicles.

680–686 Infections of the Skin and Subcutaneous Tissue

Certain infections and parasitic diseases of the skin and subcutaneous tissue such as herpes simplex and herpes zoster, viral warts, and molluscum contagiosum are classified to chapter 1. Refer to the alphabetic index for instructions concerning the correct classification of infectious conditions of the skin and subcutaneous tissue.

This subchapter classifies diseases and disorders such as boils, carbuncles, furuncles, cellulitis, abscess, lymphadenitis, local infections, and pilonidal cysts. Cellulitis that occurs in sites other than skin and subcutaneous tissue are not included in this subchapter.

Coding Tip
Use an additional code to identify the infective organism, typically Streptococcus or Staphylococcus, for conditions in this subchapter.

Carbuncle and furuncle (category 680) are infections caused by either aerobic or anaerobic bacterial organisms. A carbuncle is a collection of pus contained in a cavity or sac. A furuncle is a painful nodule formed by circumscribed inflammation of the skin and subcutaneous tissue, which encloses a central core.

Cellulitis (categories 681–682) is a diffuse infection of the dermis and subcutaneous tissues often caused by group A Streptococci or Staphylococcus aureus, but sometimes caused by other organisms. Cellulitis may be associated with an abscess, which is a collection of pus resulting from an acute or chronic localized infection with tissue destruction. Category 681 includes lymphangitis and abscess and is often associated with cellulitis of the skin affecting fingers and toes.

Coding Tips
When cellulitis occurs with chronic skin ulcer (category 707), code both conditions.

Example
Chronic decubitus ulcer of the heel with cellulitis, unspecified organism, is coded as 707.07 Pressure ulcer, 707.20 Unspecified stage, and 682.7. Sequencing is dependent upon circumstances of the episode of care.

When cellulitis occurs secondary to a superficial injury (e.g., frostbite or burn), two codes are required, sequenced according to the circumstances of the episode of care.

Example
Patient seen for care of staphylococcal cellulitis of a second-degree burn on the hand is coded as:

682.4	Cellulitis of the hand, except fingers and thumb
944.20	Burn, second degree of hand, unspecified site
041.10	Staphylococcus, unspecified

When cellulitis occurs as a complication of a postoperative wound, code the cellulitis as a postoperative infection (998.59) with an additional code for the cellulitis to specify the infection and a code to identify the infectious organism if known.

Example
Cellulitis caused by *Staphylococcus aureus* of an operative wound after an appendectomy is coded as 998.59 Postoperative infection, 682.2 Cellulitis of the trunk, and 041.11 Staphylococcus aureus.

690–698 Other Inflammatory Conditions of Skin and Subcutaneous Tissue

Other inflammatory conditions that affect the skin such as dermatitis, eczema, sunburn, rosacea, lupus erythematosus, psoriasis, and lichen are classified to this section.

Contact dermatitis (category 692) is classified by agent. The fourth digit specifies the agent such as detergents, solvents, medicines and drugs, food in contact with skin, solar radiation, plants, metals, cosmetics, and animal dander.

Coding Tip
Use the appropriate fourth digit to indicate the causative agent. An E code from the table of drugs and chemicals is optional except when identifying an adverse effect from a drug or chemical used properly in code range E930–E949.

Lupus erythematosus (695.4) is a chronic disease that causes inflammation of the connective tissue of the skin only. Occurring worldwide, this disease affects nine times as many women as men, usually those of childbearing age, and can lead to scarring and permanent disfigurement.

Coding Tip
This subcategory includes discoid lupus erythematosus, but excludes systemic lupus erythematosus (710.0).

Psoriasis (category 696) is a common skin disease characterized by patches of inflamed, red, usually very dry and itchy skin, covered by silvery scales and sometimes accompanied by painful swelling and stiffness of the joints (arthritis). With psoriasis, new cells produce 10 times faster than normal, but the rate at which old cells are shed is unchanged. Consequently, the stratum corneum becomes thickened with flaky, immature skin cells. Occurring predominantly over the elbows, knees, scalp and trunk, psoriasis tends to recur in attacks of varying severity. The disease tends to run in families, affects men and women equally, and usually appears between the ages of 10 and 30.

700–709 Other Diseases of Skin and Subcutaneous Tissue

Corns, calluses, scleroderma, keloid scars, ingrown nails, alopecia, hirsutism, disorders of the sweat glands and sebaceous glands, urticaria, actinic keratosis, and seborrheic keratosis are all classified to this section.

The National Pressure Ulcer Advisor Panel (NPUAP) has recently updated the definition and staging of pressure ulcers. A pressure ulcer is now defined as a "localized injury to the skin and/or underlying tissue, usually over a bony prominence, as a result of pressure, or pressure in combination with shear and/or friction." Clinicians ordinarily characterize pressure ulcers by location, shape, depth, and healing status. The depth of the lesion or stage of ulcer is the most important element in quality measurement:

- Unstageable/unspecified stage: Lesion inaccessible for evaluation due to nonremovable dressings, eschar, sterile blister, or suspected deep injury in evolution. Deep tissue injury may be difficult to detect in individuals with dark skin tones, and as such, evolution of the wound may progress rapidly. Suspected deep tissue injury may be characterized by purple or maroon discoloration of the skin with or without blistering. Affected tissue may be painful and variant in temperature and texture from surrounding normal tissue.

- Stage I: Nonblanching erythema (a reddened area on the skin)

- Stage II: Abrasion, blister, shallow open crater, or other partial-thickness skin loss

- Stage III: Full-thickness skin loss involving damage or necrosis into subcutaneous soft tissues

- Stage IV: Full-thickness skin loss with necrosis of soft tissues through to the muscle, tendons, or tissues around underlying bone

Subclassification 707.0 reports conditions also known as bedsores or pressure sores. These lesions initially affect superficial tissues and, depending on the state of patient's health and other circumstances, may progress to affect muscle and bone. Patients at risk for developing pressure ulcers include the bedridden, those who are unconscious or immobile such as stroke patients, or those with paralysis and limited motion. Intrinsic loss of pain and pressure sensations, disuse atrophy, malnutrition, anemia, and infection contribute to the formation and progression of decubitus ulcers. In the early stages, the condition is reversible, but left untended, the decubitus ulcer can become extensively infected, necrotic, and, ultimately, irreversible.

Coding Tip
Previous ICD-9-CM coding classified all stages together, with unique codes for pressure ulcers for the more common anatomic sites (707.05 for buttock, for example). This method of classification precluded the use of coded records to accurately reflect severity data for quality improvement initiatives. Assign the appropriate code for the site of ulcer from subcategory 707.0 with an additional code from subcategory 707.2 to specify the stage of the ulcer.

710–739 Musculoskeletal System and Connective Tissue

Diseases and disorders of the bones, muscles, cartilage, fascia, ligaments, synovia, tendons, and bursa are classified to this chapter.

Connective tissue disorders classified to chapter 13 are those primarily affecting the musculoskeletal system. Injuries and certain congenital disorders of the musculoskeletal system are classified elsewhere.

Many codes for the manifestation of musculoskeletal diseases due to specified infections and other diseases and disorders classified elsewhere are included in this chapter. Also included are many codes describing the residuals of previous diseases, disorders, and injuries classified as late effects. These codes often can be identified by the term "acquired" in the description.

710–719 Arthropathies and Related Disorders

Arthropathy is defined as any joint disease, including arthritis (inflammatory) and arthrosis (noninflammatory). This section excludes myelopathy disorders of the spinal cord, dorsopathy, and disorders of the spine.

Diffuse disease of connective tissue (category 710) is a group of diseases in which the primary lesion appears to be damage to collagen, a protein that is the major component of connective tissue. Collagen diseases, attributed largely to disorders of the immune complex mechanisms include dermatomyositis, systemic sclerosis, Sicca syndrome, polymyositis, collagen disease NOS, multifocal fibrosclerosis, and systemic lupus erythematosus. Many of these conditions, such as polyarteritis nodosa (a connective tissue disease that is a form of vasculitis) are classified to other chapters.

Coding Tip
Category 710 includes diffuse diseases of connective tissues, most of which are collagen diseases whose effects are not mainly confined to a single body system. For proper code assignment, follow the ICD-9-CM index carefully and read the includes and excludes notes pertaining to this category.

Use an additional code to identify manifestation.

Example
Sjogren's disease with lung involvement is coded as 710.2 and 517.8.

Arthropathies associated with infections (category 711) includes arthritis and other arthropathies associated with infectious organisms affecting the articular joints of bones and must be distinguished from infections of the bones classifiable to category 730.

Direct microbial contamination may cause a primary infection of the articular joints. The routes of infection include open fractures, surgical procedures, diagnostic needle aspirations and therapeutic drug injections. Direct microbial infections resulting from surgical, diagnostic, and therapeutic procedures are classified to categories 996–999.

Most of the arthropathies classified here are due to indirect (secondary) infections.

Pyogenic arthritis (711.0x) is acute, destructive bacterial infection in a joint, usually occurring as acute monoarticular (single joint) arthritis.

Associated conditions:

• Systemic or localized infections

• Intravenous drug abuse

• Recent trauma or surgery

• Pyogenic arthropathy

• Septicemia

• Osteomyelitis

Coding Tips

Subcategory 711.0 includes infections caused by organisms classified to category 041. Sequence a code from category 041 as a diagnosis code to identify the specific organism responsible for the arthritis or arthropathy.

Example

Arthritis due to Staphylococcus, unspecified, is coded as 711.00 and 041.10.

Not all pyogenic joint infections are classifiable to subcategory 711.0. Before assigning code 711.0x, carefully review the entries in the ICD-9-CM index under the main term "Arthritis, arthritic," subterm "due to or associated with." The alphabetic index will indicate when mandatory dual coding rules apply.

Example

Arthritis due to Gonococcus is coded as 098.50.

Other arthopathies due to bacterial infection are classified to subcategory 711.4. When coding arthopathies associated with other diseases, remember to code first the underlying disease.

Example

Arthritis due to diphtheria is coded as 032.89 Other specified diphtheria, and 711.40.

Arthropathy due to Reiter's disease is a syndrome consisting of a triad of non-specific (nongonococcal or simple) urethritis, conjunctivitis (or sometimes uveitis), and arthritis, and sometimes appears with mucotaneous lesions. Code first the Reiter's disease, 099.3, then the associated arthopathy, 711.1x.

Coding Tip

ICD-9-CM classifies etiology first, then manifestation, to remain compatible with the dual classification concept used in the international version of ICD-9.

Arthropathy in Behçet's syndrome (711.2x) is a multisystem disorder of unknown etiology and was named after the dermatologist who first described it. The arthritic component of the syndrome involves large and small joints with a nonspecific, self-limiting synovitis and, in more than two-thirds of the patients, commonly affects the knees and ankles. The arthritic changes resemble those of rheumatoid arthritis but are milder and lead only to shallow erosions of the articular cartilage in the more severe cases.

Coding Tip

Code the underlying condition first, Behcet's syndrome (136.1), then code the manifestation secondarily.

Arthropathy associated with other bacterial diseases (711.4x) can be caused by a wide variety of bacteria, excluding the pyogenic organisms identified under subcategory 711.0 and bacterial arthropathies classified elsewhere. This manifestation code includes arthropathy associated with other bacterial diseases, such as tuberculosis. Sequence the etiology code first, then the manifestation code.

Crystal arthropathies (category 712) includes chondrocalcinosis, arthritis, and synovitis, as well as pseudogout and calcium pyrophosphate dehydrate deposition (CPPD) disease. The crystals (apatite and hydroxyapatite, calcium pyrophosphate, calcium and dicalcium phosphate, calcium oxalate and lipid crystals) act as irritants due to their presence rather than their chemical composition. The mechanisms of initial precipitation are unknown, but predisposing conditions such as degradation of the cartilage matrix may be involved. Once the crystals have accumulated, they are taken up by phagocytic cells, initiating the inflammatory sequence. This in turn causes additional damage to the affected tissues.

Chondrocalcinosis refers to calcification of articular cartilage. Articular chondrocalcinosis also is known as pseudogout since the disease is characterized by calcified deposits in the cartilage but is free of the urate crystals found in gout. This category includes crystal (mineral) deposition arthropathies with the exception of gouty arthropathy, which is classified to 274.00–274.03. Code first the underlying disorder of mineral metabolism associated with the chondrocalcinosis.

Coding Tip

Assign a fourth digit to 712 as follows:

1	Chondrocalcinosis due to dicalcium phosphate crystals
2	Chondrocalcinosis due to pyrophosphate crystals
3	Chondrocalcinosis, unspecified
8	Other specified crystal arthropathies
9	Unspecified crystal arthropathy

Assign a fifth digit to specify the site:

0	Site unspecified
1	Shoulder region
2	Upper arm
3	Forearm
4	Hand
5	Pelvic region and thigh
6	Lower leg
7	Ankle and foot
8	Other specified sites
9	Multiple sites

Category 713 includes manifestation codes used to classify arthropathy associated with other disorders classified elsewhere. Assign the ICD-9-CM code that classifies the etiology first, then the manifestation code from category 713 secondarily.

Coding Tip
Assign a fourth digit to 713 as follows:

0 Associated with other endocrine and metabolic disorders
1 Associated with gastrointestinal conditions other than infections
2 Associated with hematological disorders
3 Associated with dermatological disorders
4 Associated with respiratory disorders
5 Associated with neurological disorders
6 Associated with hypersensitivity reaction
7 Associated with articular involvement
8 Associated with other conditions classifiable elsewhere

Rheumatoid arthritis (714.0) is a chronic, systemic, inflammatory disease of unknown etiology, characterized by a variable but prolonged course with exacerbations and remissions of joint pains and swelling. In early stages, the disease attacks the joints of the hands and feet. As the disease progresses, more joints become involved. Also known as primary progressive arthritis and proliferative arthritis, the disease often leads to progressive deformities, which may develop rapidly, and produce permanent disability.

Onset, distribution, degree of severity, and rate of progressions, as clinical manifestations of rheumatoid arthritis are highly variable. Joint disease is the major manifestation; systemic involvement (spleen, liver, eyes, etc.) is rare.

Coding Tip
Use an additional code to identify manifestations of rheumatoid arthritis (714.0) such as myopathy (359.6) and polyneuropathy (357.1).

Osteoarthrosis (category 715) is a degenerative, rather than inflammatory, disease of one or more joints. Also known as osteoarthritis and degenerative joint disease, osteoarthrosis is most conspicuous in the large joints and is initiated by local deterioration of the articular cartilage. It progressively destroys the cartilage, remodels the subchondral bone, and causes a secondary inflammation of the synovial membrane.

Coding Tip
Assignment of the fourth digit to codes in this category is based on whether the disease is generalized or localized and whether it is primary or secondary. In these subcategories, localized includes bilateral involvement of the same site.

Assign a fourth digit as follows:

0 Generalized
1 Localized, primary
2 Localized, secondary
3 Localized, not specified whether primary or secondary
8 Involving, or with mention of more than one site, but not specified as generalized
9 Unspecified whether generalized or localized

A fifth digit must also be assigned to specify the site.

0 Site unspecified

1 Shoulder region (not valid for 715.0, 715.8)
2 Upper arm (not valid for 715.0, 715.8)
3 Forearm (not valid for 715.0, 715.8)
4 Hand (not valid for 715.0, 715.8)
5 Pelvic region and thigh (not valid for 715.0, 715.8)
6 Lower leg (not valid for 715.0, 715.8)
7 Ankle and foot (not valid for 715.0, 715.8)
8 Other specified sites (not valid for 715.0, 715.8)
9 Multiple sites (not valid for 715.1, 715.2, 715.3, 715.9)

Example
Primary localized osteoarthritis of the hand is coded as 715.14 whether unilateral or bilateral, and is not considered generalized osteoarthritis because of the bilateral/regional nature of the condition.

Generalized disease is defined as osteoarthrosis involving many joints without any known pre-existing abnormality. There are three code choices for generalized arthritis or osteoarthrosis—unspecified site (715.00), the hand (715.04), or multiple sites (715.09).

Localized osteoarthrosis is a disease confined to a limited number of sites. The distinction between generalized and localized can be difficult for the clinician because the disease may be generalized, but detectable in only one or two of the larger weight-bearing joints such as the hip or knee. The physician must document localized or generalized, or the coder should assign the unspecified code, 715.9x Osteoarthrosis, unspecified whether generalized or localized.

Coding Tip
Often, the medical record indicates osteoarthritis of multiple sites without stating "generalized." Coders should assign 715.89 Osteoarthrosis involving, or with mention of more than one site, but not specified as generalized, multiple sites for this diagnosis.

Fifth digit "9" indicating multiple sites may not be used for osteoarthritis unspecified as generalized or localized. The term "localized" prohibits the use of the multiple site indication. Therefore, fifth-digit assignment for 715.9 is restricted to 0–8.

Primary osteoarthrosis is idiopathic or due to some constitutional or genetic factor. Secondary osteoarthrosis is due to some identifiable initiating factor. These factors include obesity, trauma, congenital malformations, superimposition of fibrosis and scarring from previous inflammatory disease or infection, foreign bodies, malalignment of joints, metabolic, or circulatory bone diseases and iatrogenic factors such as osteoarthrosis caused by continuous pressure on the joint surfaces during orthopedic treatment of congenital deformities. Secondary osteoarthroses should be paired with a second code describing the causative injury, disorder, or disease.

Traumatic arthropathy is classified in subcategory 716.1 and reports any joint disease that is a direct result of trauma, such as sprains, strains, and fractures.

Allergic arthritis (716.2x) is associated with a hypersensitive state acquired through exposure to an allergen.

Coding Tip

Loosening of orthopedic implants (including prostheses and other devices) due to an allergic or inflammatory reaction to chromium, cobalt, or nickel in the implant is classified as a postoperative complication. In such cases, use 996.66 or 996.67 to classify the postoperative complication, followed by 716.2X to further describe the nature of the complication.

Category 718 Other derangement of joint, includes such conditions as pathological and recurrent dislocation, joint contracture, and ankylosis of a joint.

Coding Tip

Assign a fourth digit for code 718 as follows:

0	Articular cartilage disorder
1	Loose body in joint
2	Pathological dislocation
3	Recurrent dislocation of joint
4	Contracture of joint
5	Ankylosis of joint
6	Unspecified intrapelvic protrusion of acetabulum
7	Developmental dislocation of joint
8	Other joint derangement, not elsewhere classified
9	Unspecified derangement of joint

Assign a fifth digit to specify the site as follows:

0	Site unspecified
1	Shoulder region
2	Upper arm
3	Forearm
4	Hand
5	Pelvic region and thigh
6	Lower leg
7	Ankle and foot
8	Other specified sites
9	Multiple sites

Valid fifth digits are listed in brackets underneath each code in ICD-9-CM.

Subcategory, 718.1, a loose body in the joint can be described as joint mice, rice bodies, or debris described as cartilaginous, osseous (bony), osteocartilaginous or fibrous in joints other than the knee.

A pathological dislocation, subcategory 718.2, of an articular joint is one caused by a disease process (e.g., neoplasm) rather than by a traumatic injury. This code should be accompanied by a second ICD-9-CM code identifying the etiology of the pathological dislocation.

A recurrent dislocation, subcategory 718.3, of a joint is chronic, subsequent, additional, and repeated dislocations or subluxations of a joint due to trauma. Use this code when the medical documentation indicates a chronic, old, habitual, or recurrent dislocation, regardless of whether the initial dislocation was open or closed.

Subcategory 718.4, Contracture of joint is characterized by restriction of joint motion due to contraction of the muscles that articulate the joint. The condition may be caused by tonic spasm, fibrosis, loss of musculature equilibrium, or disuse atrophy.

Joint ankylosis, subcategory 718.5, is an abnormal fusion of a joint. It results from fibrous or bone tissue bridging the joint space and restricting the motion of the joint.

Subcategory 718.8, Other joint derangement, not elsewhere classified, may be used as an additional code to classify instability of a joint secondary to removal of a prosthesis. Use code 909.3 when the instability is described as a late effect of the prosthesis removal. Try to use a more specific code if possible. If not, send medical documentation with the claim to clarify the diagnosis.

Category 719 is used to describe such conditions as joint effusion, pain in joint and other conditions that are not described elsewhere in the chapter more specifically. Difficulty in walking is coded as 719.7 and does not require a fifth-digit.

720–724 Dorsopathies

Dorsopathies classified to this section exclude curvature of the spine (category 737) and osteochondrosis of the spine (732.0, juvenile and 732.8, adult).

Code categories listed in this section include:

- Ankylosing spondylitis (720)
- Spondylosis (721)
- Intervertebral disc disorders (722)
- Other disorders of the cervical region (723)
- Other and unspecified disorders of the back (724)

Coding Tip

Assignment of a fourth digit to codes in category 721 is based on the presence or absence of myelopathy. For coding purposes, myelopathy includes any symptomatic impingement, compression, disruption, or disturbance of the spinal cord or blood supply of the spinal cord due to spondylosis.

Occipital neuralgia is a condition characterized by pain in the suboccipital region and is caused by nerve impingement or entrapment resulting from traumatic injury, arthritis, compression of the occipital nerve, or tumors of the dorsal roots of the second and third cervical nerves. Assign 723.8, Other syndromes affecting cervical region.

725–729 Rheumatism, Excluding the Back

Polymyalgia rheumatica (725) is a self-limiting disease of the elderly that often develops abruptly with joint and muscle pain and stiffness of the pelvis and shoulder girdle in association with fever, malaise, fatigue, weight loss, and anemia. The disease bears a close relationship with giant cell arteritis, and the two conditions often occur concomitantly.

Peripheral enthesopathies (category 726) and allied syndromes are disorders of peripheral ligamentous or muscular attachments. The term "enthesopathy" is an obscure medical term meaning disease of the ligamentous or muscular attachments of a joint. Included in this category are rotator cuff syndrome, iliotibial band syndrome of the hip and knee, and peroneal tendinitis.

Synovitis (727.0x) is the inflammation of a synovial membrane, especially the synovium that lines articular joints. In a normal joint, the smooth and reciprocally shaped cartilaginous opposing surfaces permit a fluid, frictionless, and painless articulation. Irregularities, disease, and damage to the articular surfaces lead to progressive degenerative changes resulting in pain and limitation of movement. The joint capsule is particularly sensitive to stretching and increased fluid pressure.

Tenosynovitis (727.0x) is the inflammation of a tendon and its synovial sheath. It is also known as tendosynovitis, tendovaginitis, tenontothecitis, tenontolemmitis, and vaginal or tendinous synovitis. At sites of friction, the tendon is enveloped by a sheath consisting of a visceral and parietal layer of synovial membrane and is lubricated by a synovial-like fluid containing hyaluronate. The synovial sheath is in turn covered by a dense, fibrous tissue sheath. Irregularities, disease, and damage to the tendon's attachment to the articular joints may lead to progressive degenerative changes with resultant limitation of movement and pain. The synovial membranes of tendon sheaths and bursae are capable of the same inflammatory reactions to abnormal conditions as the synovial membranes of joints.

Coding Tip
When the synovitis or tenosynovitis is due to diseases classified elsewhere, code first the underlying condition such as tuberculosis (015.0–015.9) in addition to 727.01.

A bunion (727.1) is a localized friction-type bursitis located at either the medial or dorsal aspect of the first metatarsophalangeal joint. Bunions of the medial aspect are usually associated with hallux valgus.

Ganglions and cysts of the synovium, tendon, and bursa (727.4x) are thin-walled cystic lesions of unknown etiology containing thick, clear, mucinous fluid, possibly due to mucoid degeneration. Arising in relation to periarticular tissues, joint capsules, and tendon sheaths, ganglions are limited to the hands and feet and are most common in the dorsum of the wrist.

A synovial cyst of the popliteal space (727.51), such as a Baker's cyst, is sometimes called a popliteal cyst. In children, Baker's cysts are common but usually are asymptomatic and regress spontaneously. In adults, Baker's cysts, in conjunction with synovial effusion due to rheumatoid arthritis or degenerative joint disease, may produce significant impairment. When a Baker's cyst interferes with normal knee function, surgical exploration and excision of the cyst is indicated. Baker's cysts usually communicate with the knee joint through a long and tortuous duct. This allows the cyst to become distended by synovial effusion and possibly extend down as far as the midcalf.

Subcategory 728.8 includes muscle weakness (728.87), excluding generalized weakness, which is coded to 780.79, and rhabdomyolysis (728.88). Rhabdomyolysis is a common disorder which may result from hereditary diseases, or by trauma or toxic insults to skeletal muscle. Rhabdomyolysis results from an injury damaging the integrity of the skeletal muscle, resulting in pain, weakness, tenderness, and contractures or even muscle necrosis and the release of potentially toxic muscle cell components into the circulation causing potential life-threatening complications to arise, including acute renal failure, hyperkalemia, and cardiac arrest.

Subcategory 729.9 classifies nontraumatic and posttraumatic seroma in addition to other and unspecified disorders of soft tissue. A nontraumatic hematoma is a localized collection of blood in a tissue or space due to the breakage in the wall of a blood vessel, which does not occur as a result of any obvious injury to

the affected area. A seroma is a localized accumulation of serum (fluid) within a tissue or space. Patients who suffer from a large traumatic hematoma may subsequently develop a seroma in the soft tissue of the affected area.

Coding Tip
When a nontraumatic compartment syndrome classifiable to subcategory 729.7 is associated with a postprocedural complication, it is necessary to assign two codes to report these conditions. Code first the postprocedural complication, followed by the appropriate code from subcategory 729.7. Note that compartment syndrome described as "postsurgical" is reported with code 998.89.

730–739 Osteopathies, Chondropathies, and Acquired Musculoskeletal Deformities

Osteoporosis (733.00–733.09) is a generalized bone disease characterized by decreased osteoblastic formation of matrix combined with increased osteoclastic resorption of bone, resulting in a marked decrease in bone mass. Osteoporosis often presents with osteopenia, which is a decrease in bone mineralization. Clinically, osteoporosis is classified into two major groups: primary and secondary. Primary osteoporosis implies that the condition is a fundamental disease entity itself and may be further broken down into involutional disease (e.g., postmenopausal or senile) and idiopathic disease (e.g., juvenile). Secondary osteoporosis attributes the condition to an underlying clinical disease, medical condition, or medication.

Coding Tip
When the osteoporosis is due to drug use, assign the appropriate drug code and E code in addition to the code for osteoporosis.

Pathological fractures (733.10–733.19) are fractures occurring at a site weakened by a pre-existing disease. They are often differentiated from traumatic fractures by clinically assessing the magnitude of the trauma or stress causing the fracture. A relatively minor trauma or stress can cause a pathological fracture in bones diseased by osteoporosis and other metabolic bone disease, disseminated bone disorders, inflammatory bone diseases, Paget's disease, neoplasms, or any other condition that can compromise bone strength and integrity. Other terms used to describe pathologic fractures are spontaneous and secondary fractures.

Code the underlying disease in addition to the appropriate code from subcategory 733.1. Sequencing of the codes depends on whether only the fracture or the fracture and the underlying disease were treated. Code the fracture first if the treatment was toward the fracture only. If treatment of the underlying disease was addressed then code the underlying disease first.

Coding Tip

Ensure appropriate reporting by assigning fifth digits identifying the site of pathological fractures:

0	Unspecified site
1	Humerus
2	Distal radius and ulna
3	Vertebrae
4	Neck of femur
5	Other specified part of femur
6	Tibia or fibula
9	Other specified site

Major osseous defects, a primary concern in many types of surgeries on the bones, occur as a result of extensive bone loss. Underlying causes are associated with conditions such as previous joint replacement, and may include osteomyelitis, osteoporosis, pathological fractures, trauma, or benign or malignant neoplasms. However, one of the most common causes is periprosthetic osteolysis from a prior joint replacement, which can affect patient outcome.

Coding Tip

Major osseous defects (731.3) should be reported secondary to the underlying disease, if known, such as:

170.0–170.9	Malignant neoplasm of bone
730.00–730.29	Osteomyelitis
733.00–733.09	Osteoporosis
733.40–733.49	Aseptic necrosis
996.45	Peri-prosthetic osteolysis

Subcategory 733.9 Other unspecified disorders of bone and cartilage includes fifth-digit subclassification codes for stress fractures. Stress fractures are caused by overuse or repetitive jarring which places intense stress on the bone. Stress fractures may occur as a result of overexertion; strenuous, repetitive motion; static positioning and load-bearing injuries; and sudden traumatic and cumulative trauma injuries. The most common sites for stress fractures are the metatarsals, lumbar spine, pelvis, femoral neck or shaft, tibia, and fibula.

Flat foot (734) is a condition in which one or more of the arches of the foot has flattened. The conditions included in this category are acquired pes planus and talipes planus.

Congenital flat foot, rigid flat foot, and spastic flat foot are all classified to category 754.

Acquired hallux valgus, hallux varus, hallux rigidus, hallux malleus, hammer toe, and claw toe are classified to category 735.

740–759 Congenital Anomalies

Congenital anomalies are certain physical traits that are present at the moment of birth. They include diseases, malformations, atresias, agenesis, hypoplastic or hyperplastic conditions, and any other condition that is a deviation from the norm. Congenital anomalies may be due to hereditary defects such as Down syndrome, to intrauterine events such as intrauterine pressure causing deformities, or teratogenic effects on the developing fetus that cause deformities such as in thalidomide phocomelia.

There are certain conditions that occur as either congenital or acquired. The medical record should contain documentation necessary to make the distinction between congenital and acquired. There is no age limit for assigning codes from the congenital anomaly chapter. For example, an individual with congenital spina bifida will be coded to this chapter regardless of age.

Anomalies that arise due to the birth process are considered injuries due to the birth process, not congenital anomalies, and are classified to category 767 Birth trauma, in chapter 15, "Conditions in the Perinatal Period."

Many congenital anomalies are patterns of multiple malformations that are considered to be pathogenetically related, meaning the cellular events and mechanical reactions occurring during the development of the disease are linked. These symptom complexes are called syndromes. When syndromes are not specifically indexed in ICD-9-CM, a code is assigned for each presenting manifestation of the syndrome that occurs as a set of symptoms or as multiple malformations.

This chapter classifies conditions present at birth including neurological problems, anomalies of the senses, heart anomalies, respiratory anomalies, and digestive system anomalies. The chapter is organized by organ system or anatomical site affected by the congenital anomaly. There are no subchapters, only categories present in this chapter.

Anencephalus (740.0) is a brain defect in which the cranial vault is absent, the cerebral hemispheres are completely missing or are just small masses attached to the base of the skull, or the size and shape of the brain are abnormal in other ways. Caused by a defect in the closure of the neural groove early in the first trimester of pregnancy, anencephalus is incurable and results in death soon after birth.

Spina bifida (category 741) is a defect of the neural tube characterized by defective closure of the bony encasement of the spinal cord. The spinal cord may or may not protrude through the skin. When the condition is associated with a hernial cyst containing meninges (meningocele), spinal cord (myelocele), or both (myelomeningocele), the condition is called spina bifida cystica. Most commonly seen in the lumbar, low thoracic or sacral region, spina bifida usually extends for three to six vertebral segments.

Congenital hydrocephalus (742.3) is a brain defect characterized by ventricular enlargement, increased cerebral spinal fluid, and, in most cases, increased intracranial pressure. Except for hydrocephalus secondary to choroid plexus papilloma, all forms of congenital hydrocephalus are obstructive and are either noncommunicating (intraventricular obstruction) or communicating (extraventricular obstruction).

Noncommunicating hydrocephalus may be due to obstruction of the fourth ventricle outlet, as seen in Dandy-Walker syndrome (741.0x) with spina bifida and arachnoiditis; lesions such as neoplasms, cysts, hematomas, or aneurysm of the vein of Galen; or congenital malformation of the aqueduct of Sylvius such as stenosis, gliosis, septal defects, or atresia. In addition, the obstruction in noncommunicating hydrocephalus may be secondary to exudate, hemorrhage, or parasites.

ICD-9-CM Definitions and Guidelines

Communicating hydrocephalus may be due to adhesions of the basilar cisterns or surface subarachnoid space following infection or hemorrhage, postdevelopmental adhesions, vitamin A deficiency, developmental failure or erythrocyte obstruction of the arachnoid villi, or Arnold-Chiari malformation (741.0x).

Cleft palate (749.0x) is the fissure or abnormal elongated opening of the palate. Cleft palate can occur either unilaterally or bilaterally and can be partial or involve the entire palate. The most common types of cleft palate are the complete left unilateral and partial midline cleft of the secondary palate. The dividing point between the primary and secondary palate is the incisive foramen. Fifth-digit assignment indicates laterality.

Spina bifida occulta (756.17) is the defective closure of the lumbosacral vertebral column lamina without hernial protrusion of the spinal cord or meninges.

Down syndrome (758.0) is a syndrome of congenital anomalies due to chromosomal abnormality, specifically, an extra chromosome, usually at 21 or 22. The condition also is known as mongolism and trisomy 21 or 22.

780–799 Symptoms, Signs, and Ill-defined Conditions

This chapter includes symptoms, signs, and abnormal results of laboratory or other investigative procedures, as well as ill-defined conditions for which there are no other, more specific diagnoses classifiable elsewhere.

Symptoms are subjective observations reported to the physician by the patient. These observations depart from the structure, function, or sensation that the patient normally experiences.

In general, codes from this chapter are used to report symptoms, signs, and ill-defined conditions that point with equal suspicion to two or more diagnoses or represent important problems in medical care that may affect management of the patient.

In addition, this chapter provides codes to classify abnormal findings that are reported without a corresponding definitive diagnosis. Codes for such findings can be located in the alphabetic index under such terms as "Abnormal, abnormality, abnormalities," "Decrease, decreased," "Elevation," and "Findings, abnormal, without diagnosis."

Codes from this chapter also are used to report:

- Symptoms and signs that existed on initial encounter but proved to be transient and whose causes could not be determined

- Provisional diagnoses for patients who fail to return for further investigation

- Cases referred elsewhere for further investigation before being diagnosed

- Cases in which a more definitive diagnosis was not available for other reasons

780–789 Symptoms

Some of the symptoms classified to this section include:

abdominal pain	hiccoughs
abnormal gait	hyperhidrosis

alteration of consciousness	incontinence
amnesia	involuntary movements
anorexia	jaundice
ascites	lack of coordination
cardiogenic shock	localized swelling
chest pain	loss of weight mass
chills	malaise and fatigue
chronic fatigue syndrome	nausea and vomiting
convulsions	ocular torticollis
cyanosis	pallor and flushing
dizziness and giddiness	palpitations
dyspnea	polydypsia
dysuria	rash
edema	shock without trauma
epistaxis	sleep disturbances
fever	stridor
fussy infant	syncope and collapse
gangrene	tetany
general pain	transient paralysis
hallucinations	weight gain, abnormal

Coding Tip

Idiopathic cyclical edema is edema of unknown cause, occurring episodically over a period of years, usually affecting women, usually worse during the premenstrual cycle, and is associated with increased aldosterone secretion. Assign 782.3 Edema, for this condition.

Functional quadriplegia (780.72) is the inability to move due to another condition (e.g., dementia, severe contractures, arthritis, etc.). Functionally, the patient is the same as a paralyzed person. The inability to move and perform routine daily tasks for themselves renders patients immobile. This state poses certain associated health risks such as pressure ulcers, contractures, and pneumonia. The amount and type of care required to attend to these patients is greater than that of a patient with similar state of health but who is more mobile or has a greater degree of physical function.

Coding Tip

New code 780.72 includes complete immobility due to severe physical disability or frailty.

This code helps provide essential assessment data to report the level of service of long-term nursing care provided. Multiple exclusions are listed to code 780.72 for specific types of quadriplegia and paralysis that are more appropriately classified elsewhere.

Failure to thrive (FTT) is a diagnosis most often assigned to pediatric patients who fail to gain weight in accordance with the standard weight gain chart. Organic FTT has many causes, such as an acute or chronic illness that interferes with nutritional intake, absorption, metabolism or excretion, or normal energy

ICD-9-CM Definitions and Guidelines

requirements. Nonorganic FTT is a symptom of neglect or abuse. Code 783.41 describes FTT in pediatric patients. Code 783.7 describes failure to thrive in adults.

790–796 Nonspecific Abnormal Findings

Abnormal findings (laboratory, x-ray, pathologic, and other diagnostic results) are not assigned and reported unless the physician indicates their clinical significance or a definitive diagnosis cannot be made. If the findings are outside the normal range and the physician has ordered other tests to evaluate the condition or prescribed treatment, it is appropriate to ask the physician whether the diagnosis should be added. Included in this section are categories that describe nonspecific findings on examination of blood (790), urine (791), other body substances (792), radiological and other examinations of body structure (793), function studies (794), immunological findings (795), and other abnormal findings (796).

797–799 Ill-defined and Unknown Causes of Morbidity and Mortality

All of these codes for ill-defined causes of mortality or morbidity should only be assigned if there is no further documentation in the record to substantiate a more definitive diagnosis. Coders should pay careful attention to the "Excludes" notes listed for each of the subcategories.

A few of the more common ill-defined causes of mortality and morbidity included in this section are sudden death, cause unknown (798.x), asphyxia (799.01), respiratory arrest (799.1), debility, unspecified (799.3), and cachexia (799.4).

800–999 Injury and Poisoning

Injuries, burns, poisoning, and adverse effects and complications of surgery and medical care are all covered in this one chapter of ICD-9-CM. E codes should be used to identify the cause and intent of the injury or poisoning.

800–829 Fractures

A fracture is a structural break in the continuity of a bone that occurs as the result of physical forces exerted on the rigid bone tissue beyond its ability to accommodate by resistance, elasticity, or bending. ICD-9-CM classifies fractures by anatomic site: skull (800–804), neck and trunk (805–809), upper limb (810–819), and lower limb (820–829).

Fractures may occur as a result of direct injury, such as a forceful blow to the bone by a heavy object, or indirect injury, such as indirect transmission of force through one or more joints (e.g., a stress fracture of the distal tibia caused by jogging).

Fractures may be defined as closed or open. A closed fracture is one in which the skin is intact at the site of the fracture. An open fracture is one in which there is a wound communicating from the skin surface to the fracture site. Open fractures may occur when an external object penetrates the skin to fracture the bone or when a bone or bone fragment penetrates the skin from within.

Coding Tip
Classify as closed any fractures not specified as open or closed.

Note that an open wound associated with a fracture does not necessarily indicate an open fracture.

Skull fracture (800–804) is a fracture of any of the bones of the cranial vault and facial bones, including nasal bones (category 802).

Rib fractures (category 807) are included in the neck and trunk sections 805–809.

Coding Tip
Fifth-digit assignment for subcategories 807.0 and 807.1 Fracture of rib closed and open, identify the number of ribs involved (e.g., 0 – unspecified, 1 – one rib, 2 – two ribs, etc.).

The subcategories for upper limb (810–819) and lower limb (820–829) fractures identify whether the fracture is open or closed. Fifth-digit assignment identifies the specific site of the fracture. Fifth-digit assignment may be either a common fifth-digit or a specific subclassification category.

Multiple fractures involving both upper limbs or upper limb with ribs or sternum are coded with category 819. Multiple fractures involving lower limbs, lower with upper limb, and lower limb with upper with rib and sternum, are coded in category 828.

Coding Tips
ICD-9-CM makes no provision for designating fractures that are of bilateral nature. For example: a bilateral closed fracture to the upper humerus of the same site is coded using the multiple fracture code 819.0 rather than 812.00 twice.

Multiple fractures of the same bone classified to different fourth-digit subcategories within the same three-digit category are coded individually by site.

Example
Closed fracture of the surgical neck of the upper end of the humerus with closed fracture of the greater tuberosity of the humerus is coded as 812.01 and 812.03.

Coding guidelines allow the use of acute fracture codes (800–829) while the patient is receiving active treatment for the fracture. Active treatment includes surgical treatment, emergency department encounter, and evaluation and treatment by a new physician. Aftercare codes classifiable to category V54 are assigned after active treatment of the fracture is complete, and for routine care of the fracture during the recovery or healing process including physical therapy services.

830–839 Dislocation

Dislocation is the traumatic displacement of the bones in any articulating joint severe enough to lose normal anatomic relationship. A dislocation (luxation) occurs when the bones completely lose contact with their articulating surfaces. A subluxation occurs when there is only a partial loss of contact.

© 2009 Ingenix

Coding Tip

Closed dislocation is described by terms such as complete, NOS, partial, simple, uncomplicated.

Open dislocation is described by terms such as compound, infected, and with foreign body.

Fourth- and fifth-digit assignments are still driven by whether the fracture is open or closed, and by site specificity.

Dislocations not specified as open or closed should be classified as closed.

840–848 Sprains and Strains of Joint and Adjacent Muscles

A sprain is a complete or incomplete tear in any one or more of the ligaments that surround and support a joint. A strain is an ill-defined injury caused by overuse or overextension of the muscles or tendons of a joint. A "charleyhorse" is an idiom for a strain of a muscle, usually one of the major muscles such as the quadriceps femoris or gastrocnemius. These categories also include muscle, tendon, ligament, or joint capsule ruptures.

Strains and sprains are classified according to site (e.g., wrist, foot, knee, leg, etc.) at the category level. Subcategory and subclassification further specify site or structure (e.g., joint or ligament).

870–897 Open Wounds

Open wounds are bites, avulsions, lacerations, puncture wounds, and traumatic amputations. Excluded injuries are burns, crushing injuries, puncture of internal organs, superficial injuries, and those incidental to dislocation, fracture, and intracranial injury.

Further subdivision of this category is by general body area: head, neck, trunk, upper limb, and lower limb.

Many types and sites of open wounds are excluded from this code range. Review the ICD-9-CM index under "Wound, open" for "see" and "see category" instructions, as well as the excludes note at the beginning of the code range in the Tabular List for proper code assignment.

Coding Tip

The description "complicated" used in the fourth-digit subdivisions includes those wounds with the mention of delayed healing, delayed treatment, foreign body, or major infection.

905–909 Late Effects of Injury, Poisoning, Toxic Effects, and Other External Causes

This category is to be used to indicate conditions classifiable to 800–999 (chapter 17, "Injury and Poisoning") as the cause of the late effects, which themselves are classified elsewhere. The "late effects" include those specified as such, or as sequelae, which may occur at any time after the acute injury.

Each section of chapter 17 has correlating "late effects" categories. For example, injuries classifiable to skull fracture (800–804) have "late effect" codes in the subcategory 905.0, Late effect of fracture of the skull and face bones.

Coding Tip

In coding late effects classifiable to sections 905–909, code first the residual condition, then list the late effect code from 905–909.

Example

Nonunion of a fracture of the coracoid process of the scapula is coded as:

733.82	Nonunion of a fracture
905.2	Late effect of fracture of the upper extremity

910–919 Superficial Injury

Superficial injuries are those described as abrasion, friction burn, blister, insect bite, superficial foreign body, such as a splinter, or superficial laceration.

Subdivisions are organized by site or body region. Superficial injury to the trunk (category 911) includes injury to the abdominal wall, anus, back, buttock, breast, chest wall, flank, groin, interscapular region, labium, penis, perineum, scrotum, testis, vagina, and vulva.

Contusion with intact skin surface (920–924) includes terms such as bruise and hematoma without fracture or open wound. Categories in this section are by site specificity.

Crushing injuries (925–929) excludes those described as associated with concussion or fracture, injuries to the internal organs, and intracranial injuries.

930–939 Effects of Foreign Body Entering Through Orifice

A foreign body entering any of the following areas of the body is classified to categories 930–939: external eye, ear, nose, pharynx and larynx, trachea, bronchus, lung, mouth, esophagus, stomach, intestine and colon, anus and rectum, and genitourinary system.

Excluded are foreign bodies such as those in an open wound, and any objects inadvertently left in an operative wound, or foreign body granuloma. Granuloma is a chronic inflammatory response initiated by infection that results in the formation of nodular, delimited aggregation of inflammatory cells.

940–949 Burns

Burns are injuries or destruction of tissue due to the effects of thermal energy, chemicals, electricity, or radiation. This section includes current unhealed burns from electricity, flame, hot object, lightening, radiation, chemicals, and scalds. Excluded are friction burns and sunburns that are classified elsewhere.

Burns are classified as the following:

- **First-degree burn** or erythema is injury limited to tissue damage to the outer layer of the epidermis.

- **Second-degree burn** is injury extending beyond the epidermis to partial thickness of the dermis.

- **Third-degree burn** is a full thickness skin loss. Third-degree burn with presence of necrotic tissue is termed deep necrosis and is further specified as with or without loss of body parts.

Categories 940–947 classify burns by degree and site. This section is subdivided by general anatomical site at the category level. Subcategory subdivision is according to either more specific site designation (scalp, shoulder, foot), causal agent (chemical), or degree of burn (first, second, third). "Excludes" notes direct coders to the appropriate site category for such areas as mouth (947 Internal organs) and scapula (943 Upper arm).

> **Coding Tip**
> Code burns to the highest degree possible. If a burn to the same site has both second- and third-degree burn, code the third-degree burn.

For multiple burn sites, sequence the code for the site with the highest degree of burn first.

Category 948 classifies burns according to the extent of body surface involved. This category is to be used when the site of the burn is unspecified or with categories 940–947 when the site is specified.

Examples
Patient presents to the emergency department with burns to 70 percent of the body; 50 percent of the body surface suffered third-degree burns and 20 percent second-degree burns. Assign code 948.75.

Patient presents to the emergency department with third-degree burns to the trunk and left leg and second-degree burn to the right leg, representing 70 percent of the body; 55 percent of the body surface suffered third-degree burns and 20 percent second-degree burns. Assign codes 942.30, 945.30, 945.20, and 948.75.

The percentage of body surface is calculated using the "rule of nines," which is a method of estimating the percent of body surface as listed below. This method is effective only for adults; the extent of burns in infants and small children should not be estimated using this method.

Body Area	Percent of Total Body Surface
Head and neck	9
Each arm	9
Each leg	18
Anterior trunk	18
Posterior trunk	18
Genitalia	1

Fourth-digit subdivision indicates the total percent of body surface involved in the burn injury regardless of degree.

Fifth-digit assignment indicates the percent of the body surface with third-degree burns as follows:

Fifth Digit	Percent of Body with Third-degree Burn
0	less than 10% or unspecified
1	10–19%
2	20–29%
3	30–39%
4	40–49%
5	50–59%
6	60–69%
7	70–79%
8	80–89%
9	90% or more of the body surface

> **Coding Tip**
> Because the fourth-digit assignment represents the percent of total body surface involved in the burn injury regardless of degree and the fifth digit represents the percent of body surface with third-degree burn, the fifth digit can never be greater than the fourth digit assigned.

Many clinicians use the term "fourth-degree" when referring to burns that extend through the subcutaneous tissue into the underlying muscle and bone. Classify burns termed fourth-degree to applicable ICD-9-CM categories specifying "deep necrosis of underlying tissue (deep third-degree)" with or without loss of body part.

960–979 Poisoning by Drugs, Medicinal, and Biological Substances

These categories include situations in which a patient suffers an adverse reaction, or poisoning, from a drug, medicine, or biological substance taken in error or a correct substance improperly administered.

Terms used to describe poisonings are:

- Wrong medication given or taken
- Wrong dosage given or taken
- Intoxication (except cumulative)
- Overdose
- Interaction of therapeutic drug (used correctly) and nonprescription drug (used correctly, not prescribed by a physician) or alcohol

Assign a code from categories 960–979 for each drug, medicine, or biological substance taken in error.

Use an additional code to specify the effects of the poisoning.

Use the E codes in the table of drugs and chemicals to identify the circumstances under which the poisoning occurred: accidental, suicide (attempt), assault, or undetermined. E codes identifying suicide or assault should never be used without specific physician documentation. Note that an E code from the therapeutic use column is never paired with a poisoning code.

> **Coding Tip**
> Coding poisonings by drugs, medicinal, and biological substances always requires at least three codes: code for the poisoning (960–979), code describing the effect, and E code describing the circumstances under which the poisoning occurred.
>
> **Example**
> Respiratory arrest due to an accidental overdose of Valium, marijuana, and ephedrine is coded as:
>
> | | |
> |---|---|
> | 969.4 | Poisoning by Valium |
> | 799.1 | Respiratory arrest |
> | E853.2 | Accidental poisoning by Valium |
> | 969.6 | Poisoning by marijuana |
> | E854.1 | Accidental poisoning by marijuana |
> | 971.2 | Poisoning by ephedrine |
> | E855.5 | Accidental poisoning by ephedrine |

The fact that a substance may have been administered by a physician, nurse, or other qualified clinician has no effect on the selection of a code for a poisoning or adverse effect of a correct

ICD-9-CM Definitions and Guidelines

substance properly administered. Verify with the physician when the chart documentation is unclear about whether the adverse reaction is regarded as a poisoning or an adverse effect.

If the drug is not specified, use 977.9 Unspecified drug or medicinal substance. To locate the appropriate E code refer to the drug table under the main entry "Drug." For drugs not otherwise classified use 977.8 Other specified drugs and medicinal substances.

Coding Tips
Acute conditions due to use of a drug in combination with alcohol, drug abuse, or dependence are classified as poisonings.

Assign the appropriate code from the 960–979 categories, code for the effects, code for substance dependence or abuse, and E code for the circumstances of the poisoning.

Chronic conditions occurring as a result of substance abuse or dependence are not classified as poisonings. Use codes from 303–305 to classify chronic abuse or dependence.

Late effects of poisoning due to drugs, medicinal, or biological substances are coded to subcategory 909.0. Code the residual first, then the late effect code, followed by the E code for poisoning.

Adverse effects of incorrectly administered drugs are not classified to this section.

NOTE: The interaction of a prescribed drug and an over the counter drug is coded as an adverse effect if both were used correctly and both prescribed by a physician. Adverse effects are described by the following terms:

• Allergic reaction

• Toxicity (cumulative effect of a drug)

• Hypersensitivity

• Idiosyncratic reaction

• Paradoxical reaction

• Synergistic reaction

To code adverse effects, code the condition and assign an E code from the therapeutic use column in the drug table. Do not assign a code from the 960–979 categories.

If the adverse effect is unspecified, or not elsewhere classifiable, assign the appropriate code from subcategory 995.2 Other and, unspecified effect of drug, medicinal, and biological substance.

Refer to the drug table under the main term "Drug" and choose the appropriate E code from the therapeutic use column. To locate drugs not listed as a main entry in the table refer to the AHFS listing in appendix C of the disease tabular section. Confirm the ICD-9-CM code listed in appendix C in the tabular list.

980–989 Toxic Effects of Substances Chiefly Nonmedicinal as to Source
This subchapter covers toxic effects of substances such as alcohol, petroleum products, corrosive aromatics, acids and alkalis, metal, noxious substances eaten as food, venoms, and detergents.

Use an additional code to specify the nature of the toxic effect.

Assign an E code from the Drug Table to identify the circumstances of the poisoning.

990–995 Other and Unspecified Effects of External Causes
This subchapter includes effects of radiation, reduced temperature, heat and light, pressure, and anaphylactic shock. Conditions such as frostbite, hypothermia, heat stoke and sun stroke are identified in this category. Follow the instructional notes within each category, since many other specified effects are classified elsewhere.

996–999 Complications of Surgical and Medical Care Not Elsewhere Classified
This subchapter includes complications of surgical and medical care that occur when the patient suffers additional pathology, injury, or other complications during, or as a result of, a procedure or medical treatment. These categories exclude complications due to pre-existing conditions and new conditions that are unrelated to the procedure or medical care.

When the index does not list a specific code for a given postoperative complication, assign the appropriate code from categories 996–999 as long as the complication is not listed in the "Excludes" notes for these categories.

Assigning a code for some postoperative complications, such as postoperative hyponatremia (276.1), depends solely on documentation in the medical record. If documentation supports the hyponatremia as a direct result of the procedure, assign codes 997.99 and 276.1.

When assigning a code from categories 996–999, an additional code from chapters 1–16 may be used to further specify the nature of the complication.

Other complications of procedure, NEC (category 998), includes postoperative shock, hemorrhage, accidental puncture or lacerations, disruption of wound, foreign body accidentally left in operative wound, and postoperative infection. These complications are termed nonmechanical complications.

The mechanical complication code subcategory 996.4 allows reporting of specific causes of failed hip or knee replacements. The type and cause of failure will determine the type of revision joint replacement procedure performed. The specific complication according to reason and site (prosthetic or periprosthetic) are specified within this subcategory, as well as fifth-digit options for unspecified (.0) and other (.7), (.9) factors.

Coding Tip
Report additional code 731.3 to identify any major osseous defects, if applicable, when code 996.45 is reported.

Supplementary Classifications

V01–V89 and E000–E999

V Codes
This chapter classifies the following situations that are not classifiable to categories 001–999, specifically:

- Encounters for health services
- Problems influencing a person's health status
- Other—facts needed for statistical tabulations

The encounter V codes are used to record a visit or classify a patient who is not acutely ill but needs a health service for a specific purpose, such as prophylactic immunization, routine examination, or counseling. Sequencing rules for V codes are addressed later in this chapter. These V codes are not procedure codes. If a procedure is performed as a result of the encounter, then an appropriate procedure code must be assigned. Policies may differ among payers, so it is advisable to check with the payer when using V codes.

The problem V codes describe circumstances that influence the person's health status but are not a current illness or injury, such as the status of a sprained ankle. Except in rare cases, the problem V codes are not reported as a principal diagnosis, nor do they stand alone. They do not describe the reason for the encounter, but rather provide an item of information about the state of the patient. These V codes are used only when the circumstance influences the patient's current condition or treatment.

Other V codes provide supplementary information that is important to record but is not representative of a problem or service. They identify outcome of delivery on the mother's record (secondary diagnosis only) and newborn infant (principal diagnosis only).

Terms commonly associated with V codes are "aftercare," "checking," "screening," "examination for," "history of," "follow-up," "problem with," "observation for," "Status Post," etc.

V codes often are not accepted as primary diagnosis codes, so clinicians should ensure they use a treatment and medical diagnosis code.

Unless instructed differently by the payer, if a diagnosis coded with a V code describes the primary reason for the encounter, sequence that code first on the claim. If a present illness or injury is influenced by a problem or circumstance that is not a part of the current illness or injury, sequence that V code second.

Carefully check the medical record for specific information regarding the patient's current and chronic health, as well as family and socioeconomic situation. Avoid using nonspecific codes when possible to prevent carrier delay or denial of claims submitted with V codes.

V codes are used in both inpatient and outpatient settings. V codes for encounters are more appropriate for outpatient and provider office visits.

V01–V06 Persons with Potential Health Hazards Related to Communicable Diseases

This subchapter contains service and problem V codes and are especially applicable for ambulatory care settings, including the emergency department. Encounters for vaccination, isolation, and prophylactic surgery are classified here.

Encounters for contact or exposure to communicable diseases (category V01) are to be used for patients who do not exhibit any signs or symptoms of the disease.

Carriers or suspected carriers of infectious disease are classified to category V02. This V code provides supplementary information about the patient that may affect the course or outcome of treatment.

Categories V03–V06 classify encounters for the reason of inoculation or vaccination as a prophylactic measure.

V07–V09 Persons with Need for Isolation, Other Potential Health Hazards and Prophylactic Measures

Encounters for the reasons of isolation and other prophylactic measures are classified to category V07. This category includes isolation, desensitization to allergens, postmenopausal hormone replacement therapy, and prophylactic fluoride treatments.

Code V08, asymptomatic human immunodeficiency virus (HIV) infection status, is to be used for patients who have the HIV virus (i.e., have tested positive) but have not ever manifested signs or symptoms of the disease.

Infection with drug-resistant micro-organism, category V09, is used to indicate that a patient has a form of infection resistant to drugs.

V10–V19 Persons with Potential Health Hazards Related to Personal and Family History

This subchapter contains personal and family history codes. Personal history codes often are reported to indicate the need for adjunctive surgery and treatment; family history codes often are used to indicate the need for prophylactic surgery and treatment. Family history codes are frequently used with screening codes to justify the test or procedure.

V20–V29 Persons Encountering Health Services in Circumstances Related to Reproduction and Development

This subchapter contains codes applicable to ambulatory settings, including the emergency department, to indicate supervision of uncomplicated pregnancy and perceived problems that, after evaluation, are determined to be normal states in development (e.g., onset of menses, teething). Codes to report outcome of delivery on the mother's record (used in addition to codes from the obstetric section of ICD-9-CM) also are included here.

V40–V49 Persons with a Condition Influencing Their Health Status

This subchapter contains codes for impairments and postoperative states that may influence treatment, especially in the ambulatory setting. Found here are codes to report artificial opening status, postsurgical states, and dependence on machines.

Do not use any code from this section as a principal diagnosis for inpatient admissions. Also, avoid indiscriminate reporting of conditions influencing health status as secondary codes. All secondary diagnoses in this code range are susceptible to the same tests of relevance and timeliness as defined by the Uniform Hospital Discharge Data Set (UHDDS) definition for "other diagnoses." The UHDDS defines "other diagnoses" as disease that coexists at the time of encounter and have a bearing on the management of the patient requiring any of the following: clinical evaluation, therapeutic treatment, diagnostic studies, or monitoring.

The subdivision of this section includes the following categories:

- Mental and behavioral problems (V40)
- Problems with special senses and other special functions (V41)
- Organ or tissue replacement by transplant (V42)
- Organ or tissue replaced by other means (V43)
- Artificial opening status (V44)
- Other postprocedural states (V45)
- Other dependence on machines and devices (V46)
- Other problems with internal organs (V47)
- Problems with head, neck, and trunk (V48)
- Other conditions influencing health status (V49)

Coding Tips

Many postmenopausal women encounter health care services for the purpose of being tested or screened for potential conditions related to menopause, although they do not exhibit any symptoms. Coding guidelines prohibit the assignment of diagnosis codes or symptom codes as a reason for the visit in cases where no pathology is determined after testing. Assign V49.81 Postmenopausal status (age-related) (natural).

Code V45.11 indicates a dialysis dependence status only, and is intended to be assigned as a secondary diagnosis code. If dialysis is the reason for the encounter, the appropriate code from category V56, Encounter for dialysis and dialysis catheter care, should be assigned as the first-listed diagnosis. To assign both codes together would be redundant. Instead, an additional code would be required to identify the associated condition (chronic kindey disease, end stage renal disease, etc.).

When reporting code V46.3 Wheelchair dependence, code first the cause of dependence, such as muscular dystrophy (359.1) or obesity (278.00, 278.01).

V50–V59 Persons Encountering Health Services for Specific Procedures and Aftercare

This subchapter contains codes to indicate reasons for care in patients who have already been treated for some disease or injury, but may need aftercare or adjunctive treatment to consolidate the treatment, deal with residual states, or prevent recurrence.

Encounters for plastic surgery are classified in two ways: procedures used for cosmetic surgery for conditions that are normal variations rather than the result of pathological states and procedures for the residual conditions of a healed injury or operation.

Also classified here are encounters for services such as chemotherapy, radiotherapy, rehabilitation and physical therapy, fittings and adjustments of devices, orthopedic aftercare, and dialysis.

The subdivision of this section includes the following categories:

- Elective surgery for purposes other than remedying health states (V50)
- Aftercare involving the use of plastic surgery (V51)
- Fitting and adjustment of prosthetic device or implant (V52)
- Fitting and adjustment of other device (V53)
- Other orthopedic aftercare (V54)
- Attention to artificial openings (V55)

- Encounter for dialysis and dialysis catheter care (V56)
- Care involving use of rehabilitation procedures (V57)
- Encounter for other and unspecified procedures and aftercare (V58)
  - radiation therapy
  - chemotherapy and immunotherapy
  - blood transfusion
  - attention to surgical sutures and dressings
  - aftercare following surgery
  - orthodontics
  - long-term drug use (current use) (see subcategory V67.5 for patients no longer using drugs)
  - fitting and adjustment for catheters
- Donors (V59)

Coding Tip

Aftercare codes are generally listed first on the claim, indicating the primary reason for the encounter. An additional diagnosis should be assigned to describe the resolving condition. Check with the payer ahead of time.

Example

A 72-year-old male, status post-total-hip replacement because of localized osteoarthritis is experiencing difficulty walking following the surgery. The patient is discharged with orders to receive physical therapy at home twice a week for gait training and strengthening. In this instance, code V54.81 Aftercare following joint replacement, is listed as the primary diagnosis. An instructional note below code V54.81 indicates that the appropriate code to identify the joint replacement site should be coded. For this reason, code V43.64 Joint replacement, hip, is assigned. Codes V57.1 Rehabilitative care, other physical therapy, 715.35 Osteoarthrosis, localized, not specified as primary or secondary, pelvic region and thigh, and 781.2 Abnormality of gait, should also be assigned.

V60–V68 Persons Encountering Health Services in Other Circumstances

This subchapter contains codes that add information to the medical record regarding family, household, administrative, follow-up, and psychosocial circumstances.

Included in this section is category V64 Persons encountering health services for specific procedures, not carried out. Code sequencing is dependent upon the reason the procedure was not performed.

Example

Patient was seen for the purpose of performing endoscopy for examination of a chronic bleeding ulcer. Procedure was cancelled due to patient having an acute URI. The coding for this scenario is:

531.40	Chronic gastric ulcer with hemorrhage no mention of obstruction
465.9	Acute URI, NOS
V64.1	Surgical procedure not carried out because of contraindication

Sequencing of V Codes

The V code sequencing table has been deleted from the *ICD-9-CM Official Guidelines for Coding and Reporting.* The October 2009 version is posted on the NCHS website at http://www.cdc.gov/nchs/data/icd9/icdguide09.pdf. The following list of V codes/categories has been designated as principal/first-listed diagnosis only, with the following exceptions:

- Multiple encounters occur on the same day and the medical records for the encounters are combined

- More than one V code meets the definition of principal diagnosis (e.g., a patient is admitted to home health care for both aftercare and rehabilitation and they equally meet the definition of principal diagnosis).

V20.X	Health supervision of infant or child
V22.0	Supervision of normal first pregnancy
V22.1	Supervision of other normal pregnancy
V24.X	Postpartum care and examination
V26.81	Encounter for assisted reproductive fertility procedure cycle
V26.82	Encounter for fertility preservation procedure
V30.X	Single liveborn
V31.X	Twin, mate liveborn
V32.X	Twin, mate stillborn
V33.X	Twin, unspecified
V34.X	Other multiple, mates all liveborn
V35.X	Other multiple, mates all stillborn
V36.X	Other multiple, mates live- and stillborn
V37.X	Other multiple, unspecified
V39.X	Unspecified
V46.12	Encounter for respirator dependence during power failure
V46.13	Encounter for weaning from respirator [ventilator]
V51.0	Encounter for breast reconstruction following mastectomy
V56.0	Extracorporeal dialysis
V57.X	Care involving use of rehabilitation procedures
V58.0	Radiotherapy
V58.11	Encounter for antineoplastic chemotherapy
V58.12	Encounter for antineoplastic immunotherapy
V59.X	Donors
V66.0	Convalescence and palliative care following surgery
V66.1	Convalescence and palliative care following radiotherapy
V66.2	Convalescence and palliative care following chemotherapy
V66.3	Convalescence and palliative care following psychotherapy and other treatment for mental disorder
V66.4	Convalescence and palliative care following treatment of fracture
V66.5	Convalescence and palliative care following other treatment
V66.6	Convalescence and palliative care following combined treatment
V66.9	Unspecified convalescence
V68.X	Encounters for administrative purposes
V70.0	Routine general medical examination at a health care facility
V70.1	General psychiatric examination, requested by the authority
V70.2	General psychiatric examination, other and unspecified
V70.3	Other medical examination for administrative purposes
V70.4	Examination for medicolegal reasons
V70.5	Health examination of defined subpopulations
V70.6	Health examination in population surveys
V70.8	Other specified general medical examinations
V70.9	Unspecified general medical examination
V71.X	Observation and evaluation for suspected conditions not found

E Codes

The "Supplementary Classification of External Causes of Injury and Poisoning" is commonly referred to as "E codes." E codes provide a classification of external causes that relate to the condition or injury being coded. E codes may indicate how an accident occurred, what caused an injury, whether a drug overdose was accidental, an adverse drug reaction, or the location of the injury occurrence.

Some major categories of E codes include:

- Transport accidents

- Poisoning and adverse effects of drugs, medicinal substances, and biologicals

- Accidental falls

- Accidents caused by fire and flames

- Accidents due to natural and environmental factors

- Late effects of accidents, assaults, or self injury

- Assaults or purposely inflicted injury

- Suicide or self-inflicted injury

- Terrorism

Coding Principles for E Codes

The following coding principles are used in assigning E codes:

- Look for the causes (fire, accident, fall, shooting, striking) in section 3 of the alphabetic index.

- For adverse reactions to medical or surgical care, look under the main term "Reaction" in the alphabetic index.

- When listing an E code on a claim, be sure to use the letter "E" with the code number.

Coding Tips

When coding the external cause of an injury or poisoning, remember that the alphabetic character "E" must precede the numeric code (e.g., E930.0.)

E codes are never used alone.

An E code is never used as a primary diagnosis.

- An E code may be used with any code in the range of 001–V89, which indicates an injury, poisoning, or adverse effect due to an external cause.

- Use the full range of E codes to completely describe the cause, the intent, and the place of occurrence, if applicable, for all injuries, poisonings, and adverse effects of drugs. Assign as many E codes as necessary to fully explain each cause. If only one E code can be recorded, assign the E code most related to the principal diagnosis.

- Late effect E codes exist for injuries and poisonings but not for adverse effects of drugs, misadventures, and surgical complications. A late effect E code from categories E929, E959, E969, E977, E989, or E999 should be assigned to report a late effect or sequela resulting from a previous injury or poisoning (905–909) and never to be used with an injury code.

Coding Tips

The first listed E code should correspond to the cause of the most serious diagnosis due to an assault, accident, or self-harm, following the order of hierarchy listed above.

When the cause of an injury or neglect is intentional child or adult abuse, the first listed E code should be assigned from categories E960–E968 Homicide and injury purposely inflicted by other persons (except category E967).

An E code from category E967 Child and adult battering and other maltreatment, should be added as an additional code to identify the perpetrator, if known.

In cases of neglect, when the intent is determined to be accidental, E904.0 Abandonment or neglect of infant and helpless person, should be the first listed E code.

Code E927 Overexertion and strenuous and repetitive movements or loads was expanded to allow for the fourth-digit subclassifications that identify the type of movement (mechanism) associated with an injury. Sudden traumatic injury and cumulative trauma injuries are separately identifiable. Code first the associated injury. E codes cannot be sequenced first or reported alone.

E codes are also used to identify place of occurrence of the external cause of injury and poisoning event. All place-of-occurrence codes are classified to category E849.

E codes for poisoning and adverse effects of drugs and chemicals as well as E codes for substance abuse are covered in previous chapters.

E codes provide information concerning intent (unintentional or accidental; or intentional, such as suicide or assault). If the intent (accident, self-harm, assault) of the cause of an injury or poisoning is unknown, questionable, probable, or suspected or unspecified, code the intent as undetermined (E980–E989).

When the intent of an injury or poisoning is known, but the cause is unknown, use codes E928.9 Unspecified accident; E958.9 Suicide and self-inflicted injury by unspecified means; and E968.9 Assault by unspecified means. These E codes should rarely be used, as the documentation in the medical record, in both the inpatient and outpatient settings, should normally provide sufficient detail to determine the cause of the injury.

ICD-9-CM Index

This ICD-9-CM chapter contains a comprehensive alphabetic listing of ICD-9-CM diagnosis codes for diagnosed conditions that could be treated by providers using this coding and payment guide. This book is based on official Centers for Medicare and Medicaid Services (CMS) material and uses the most up-to-date diagnosis coding information available.

This chapter is meant only as a quick reference for physical therapy services. It does not replace Ingenix ICD-9-CM code books.

Providers and hospitals are required by law to submit diagnosis codes for Medicare reimbursement. A passage in the Medicare Catastrophic Coverage Act of 1988 has required health care provider offices to include appropriate diagnosis codes when billing for services provided to Medicare beneficiaries since April 1, 1989. The repeal of the Act has not changed this requirement. CMS designated ICD-9-CM as the coding system health care providers must use.

This chapter concentrates on the most common diagnoses that are utilized by physical therapy services. Easy to use, it contains an alphabetic list of diagnoses, and has symbols (see the symbol key) to identify common coding principles. Understanding these principles will increase the efficiency and promptness of claim submission for Medicare and other third-party payers.

The codes in this book are effective October 1, 2009, to September 30, 2010.

ICD-9-CM Coding Conventions

The ICD-9-CM coding conventions, or rules, used in this book are outlined below. All ICD-9-CM coding rules can be found in the front of any ICD-9-CM code book.

The symbol ☑ is used to indicate when an additional subclassification digit is required to complete a code. This symbol refers the coder to corresponding boxed information that defines the appropriate additional digits.

Modifiers

The physician's diagnostic statement usually contains several medical terms. To translate the terms into diagnosis codes, choose only the condition as the main term. The other terms may be considered modifiers.

There are two types of modifiers, nonessential and essential:

- **Nonessential modifiers** are shown in parentheses after the term that they modify. Nonessential modifiers may be either present or absent in the diagnostic or procedure statement without affecting the code selection. These modifiers do not affect the code selection.

- **Essential modifiers** are indented under the main term. When there is only one essential modifier, it is listed next to the main term after a comma. Essential modifiers affect code assignment; therefore, they should be used in the coding process only if they are specified in the physician's diagnosis.

In the following example, found under the main term "Dislocation," subterm "ankle" the terms "scaphoid bone" and "closed" are nonessential modifiers while the term "open" is an essential modifier.

Dislocation (articulation) (closed) (displacement) (simple) (subluxation) 839.8
  ankle (scaphoid bone) (closed) 837.0
    open 837.1

Cross-References

Cross-references make locating a code easier. Two types of cross-references are used in this book: *see* and *see also*.

The "*see*" cross-reference directs the coder to look for another term elsewhere in the book. For example:

Effect, adverse
  Reduced temperature 991.9
    frostbite—*see* Frostbite

The "*see also*" cross-reference provides the coder with an alternative main term if the appropriate description is not found under the initial main term, such as:

Abscess
  Bone (subperiosteal) (*see also* Osteomyelitis) 730.0

Abbreviations

- **NEC (not elsewhere classifiable).** Not every condition has its own ICD-9-CM code. The NEC abbreviation is used with those categories of codes for which a more specific code is not available. The NEC code describes all other specified forms of a condition. For example:

Disorder (*see also* Disease)
  bone NEC 733.90

- **NOS (not otherwise specified).** Coders should use an NOS code only when they lack the information necessary for assigning a more specific code.

Coding Neoplasms

The index contains a neoplasm table in which the codes for each particular type of neoplasm are listed for the body part, system, or tissue type affected. The columns divide the codes into neoplasm type:malignant, benign, uncertain behavior, and unspecified with three distinct columns appearing under the malignant heading for primary, secondary, and carcinoma in situ.

Malignant neoplasms are uncontrolled new tissue growths or tumors that can progressively invade tissue in other parts of the body by spreading or metastasizing the disease producing cells from the initial site of malignancy. Primary defines the body site or tissue where the malignancy first began to grow and spread from there to other areas. Secondary malignancies are those sites that have been invaded by the cancer cells coming from another part of the body and are now exhibiting cancerous growth. Carcinoma in situ is confined to the epithelium of the vessels, glands, organs, or tissues in the body area where it originated and has not crossed the basement membrane to spread to the neighboring tissues.

Benign neoplasms are those found not to be cancerous in nature. The dividing cells adhere to each other in the tumor and remain a circumscribed lesion. Neoplasms of uncertain behavior are those whose subsequent behaviour cannot currently be predicted from the present appearance of the tumor and will require further study. Unspecified indicates simply a lack of documentation to support the selection of any more specific code.

Manifestation Codes

As in the following example, when two codes are required to indicate etiology and manifestation, the manifestation code appears in italics and brackets. The manifestation code is never a principal/primary diagnosis. The etiology code is always sequenced first.

Arthritis, arthritic (acute) (chronic) (subacute)
   due to or associated with
      diabetes 250.64 (*713.5*)

Diagnostic Coding and Reporting Guidelines for Outpatient Services (Hospital Based and Physician Office)

These coding guidelines for outpatient diagnoses have been approved for use by hospitals/providers in coding and reporting hospital-based outpatient services and provider-based office visits.

Information about the use of certain abbreviations, punctuation, symbols, and other conventions used in the ICD-9-CM tabular list (code numbers and titles), can be found in section IA of these guidelines, under "Conventions Used in the Tabular List." Information about the correct sequence to use in finding a code is also described in section I.

The terms encounter and visit are often used interchangeably in describing outpatient service contacts and, therefore, appear together in these guidelines without distinguishing one from the other.

Though the conventions and general guidelines apply to all settings, coding guidelines for outpatient and provider reporting of diagnoses will vary in a number of instances from those for inpatient diagnoses, recognizing that:

The Uniform Hospital Discharge Data Set (UHDDS) definition of principal diagnosis applies only to inpatients in acute, short-term, long-term care and psychiatric hospitals.

Coding guidelines for inconclusive diagnoses (probable, suspected, rule out, etc.) were developed for inpatient reporting and do not apply to outpatients.

A. Selection of first-listed condition

In the outpatient setting, the term first-listed diagnosis is used in lieu of principal diagnosis.

In determining the first-listed diagnosis the coding conventions of ICD-9-CM, as well as the general and disease specific guidelines take precedence over the outpatient guidelines.

Diagnoses often are not established at the time of the initial encounter/visit. It may take two or more visits before the diagnosis is confirmed.

The most critical rule involves beginning the search for the correct code assignment through the alphabetic index. Never begin searching initially in the tabular list as this will lead to coding errors.

1. **Outpatient Surgery**
   When a patient presents for outpatient surgery, code the reason for the surgery as the first-listed diagnosis (reason for the encounter), even if the surgery is not performed due to a contraindication.

2. **Observation Stay**
   When a patient is admitted for observation for a medical condition, assign a code for the medical condition as the first-listed diagnosis.

   When a patient presents for outpatient surgery and develops complications requiring admission to observation, code the reason for the surgery as the first reported diagnosis (reason for the encounter), followed by codes for the complications as secondary diagnoses.

B. **Codes from 001.0 through V84.8**
   The appropriate code or codes from 001.0 through V84.8 must be used to identify diagnoses, symptoms, conditions, problems, complaints, or other reason(s) for the encounter/visit.

C. **Accurate reporting of ICD-9-CM diagnosis codes**
   For accurate reporting of ICD-9-CM diagnosis codes, the documentation should describe the patient's condition, using terminology which includes specific diagnoses as well as symptoms, problems, or reasons for the encounter. There are ICD-9-CM codes to describe all of these.

D. **Selection of codes 001.0 through 999.9**
   The selection of codes 001.0 through 999.9 will frequently be used to describe the reason for the encounter. These codes are from the section of ICD-9-CM for the classification of diseases and injuries (e.g. infectious and parasitic diseases; neoplasms; symptoms, signs, and ill-defined conditions, etc.).

E. **Codes that describe symptoms and signs**
   Codes that describe symptoms and signs, as opposed to diagnoses, are acceptable for reporting purposes when a diagnosis has not been established (confirmed) by the provider. Chapter 16 of ICD-9-CM, Symptoms, Signs, and Ill-defined conditions (codes 780.0 - 799.9) contain many, but not all codes for symptoms.

F. **Encounters for circumstances other than a disease or injury**
   ICD-9-CM provides codes to deal with encounters for circumstances other than a disease or injury. The Supplementary Classification of factors Influencing Health Status and Contact with Health Services (V01.0–V86.1) is provided to deal with occasions when circumstances other than a disease or injury are recorded as diagnosis or problems. *See Section I.C. 18 for information on V-codes*

G. **Level of Detail in Coding**

☑ Additional Digit Required

1. ICD-9-CM codes with 3, 4, or 5 digits

ICD-9-CM is composed of codes with either 3, 4, or 5 digits. Codes with three digits are included in ICD-9-CM as the heading of a category of codes that may be further subdivided by the use of fourth and/or fifth digits, which provide greater specificity.

2. Use of full number of digits required for a code

A three-digit code is to be used only if it is not further subdivided. Where fourth-digit subcategories and/or fifth-digit subclassifications are provided, they must be assigned. A code is invalid if it has not been coded to the full number of digits required for that code.

See also discussion under Section I.b.3., General Coding Guidelines, Level of Detail in Coding.

H. ICD-9-CM code for the diagnosis, condition, problem, or other reason for encounter/visit

List first the ICD-9-CM code for the diagnosis, condition, problem, or other reason for encounter/visit shown in the medical record to be chiefly responsible for the services provided. List additional codes that describe any coexisting conditions. In some cases the first-listed diagnosis may be a symptom when a diagnosis has not been established (confirmed) by the physician.

I. Uncertain diagnosis

Do not code diagnoses documented as "probable", "suspected," "questionable," "rule out," or "working diagnosis" or other similar terms indicating uncertainty. Rather, code the condition(s) to the highest degree of certainty for that encounter/visit, such as symptoms, signs, abnormal test results, or other reason for the visit. **Please note:** This differs from the coding practices used by short-term, acute care, long-term care and psychiatric hospitals.

J. Chronic diseases

Chronic diseases treated on an ongoing basis may be coded and reported as many times as the patient receives treatment and care for the condition(s)

K. Code all documented conditions that coexist

Code all documented conditions that coexist at the time of the encounter/visit, and require or affect patient care treatment or management. Do not code conditions that were previously treated and no longer exist. However, history codes (V10-V19) may be used as secondary codes if the historical condition or family history has an impact on current care or influences treatment.

L. Patients receiving diagnostic services only

For patients receiving diagnostic services only during an encounter/visit, sequence first the diagnosis, condition, problem, or other reason for encounter/visit shown in the medical record to be chiefly responsible for the outpatient services provided during the encounter/visit. Codes for other diagnoses (e.g., chronic conditions) may be sequenced as additional diagnoses.

For encounters for routine laboratory/radiology testing in the absence of any signs, symptoms, or associated diagnosis,

assign V72.5 and V72.6. If routine testing is performed during the same encounter as a test to evaluate a sign, symptom, or diagnosis, it is appropriate to assign both the V code and the code describing the reason for the non-routine test.

For outpatient encounters for diagnostic tests that have been interpreted by a physician, and the final report is available at the time of coding, code any confirmed or definitive diagnosis(es) documented in the interpretation. Do not code related signs and symptoms as additional diagnoses.

Please note: This differs from the coding practice in the hospital inpatient setting regarding abnormal findings on test results.

M. Patients receiving therapeutic services only

For patients receiving therapeutic services only during an encounter/visit, sequence first the diagnosis, condition, problem, or other reason for encounter/visit shown in the medical record to be chiefly responsible for the outpatient services provided during the encounter/visit. Codes for other diagnoses (e.g., chronic conditions) may be sequenced as additional diagnoses.

The only exception to this rule is that when the primary reason for the admission/encounter is chemotherapy, radiation therapy, or rehabilitation, the appropriate V code for the service is listed first, and the diagnosis or problem for which the service is being performed listed second.

N. Patients receiving preoperative evaluations only

For patients receiving preoperative evaluations only, sequence first a code from category V72.8, Other specified examinations, to describe the pre-op consultations. Assign a code for the condition to describe the reason for the surgery as an additional diagnosis. Code also any findings related to the pre-op evaluation.

O. Ambulatory surgery

For ambulatory surgery, code the diagnosis for which the surgery was performed. If the postoperative diagnosis is known to be different from the preoperative diagnosis at the time the diagnosis is confirmed, select the postoperative diagnosis for coding, since it is the most definitive.

P. Routine outpatient prenatal visits

For routine outpatient prenatal visits when no complications are present, codes V22.0, Supervision of normal first pregnancy, or V22.1, Supervision of other normal pregnancy, should be used as the principal diagnosis. These codes should not be used in conjunction with chapter 11 codes.

ICD-9-CM Codes

Symbol Key

Please note that this section uses the following icon to indicate an additional digit is required for particular codes.

☑ Codes that require an additional digit.

A

Abarognosis 781.99
Abasia (-astasia) 307.9
  atactica 781.3
  choreic 781.3
  hysterical 300.11
  paroxysmal trepidant 781.3
  spastic 781.3
  trembling 781.3
  trepidans 781.3
Abetalipoproteinemia 272.5
Abionarce 780.79
Ablutomania 300.3
Abnormal, abnormality,
  abnormalities—*see also*
  Anomaly
  chest sounds 786.7
  development, developmental NEC
    759.9
    central nervous system 742.9
  electromyogram (EMG) 794.17
    ocular 794.14
  function studies
    oculomotor 794.14
    pulmonary 794.2
  gait 781.2
    hysterical 300.11
  head movement 781.0
  involuntary movement 781.0
  knee jerk 796.1
  loss of height 781.91
  movement 781.0
    disorder NEC 333.90
      specified NEC 333.99
    head 781.0
    involuntary 781.0
    specified type NEC 333.99
  muscle contraction, localized
    728.85
  percussion, chest 786.7
  plantar reflex 796.1
  posture NEC 781.92
  pulmonary
    test results 794.2
    ventilation, newborn 770.89
      hyperventilation 786.01
  reflex NEC 796.1
  scan
    lung 794.2
  shape
    head (*see also* Anomaly, skull)
      756.0
  size
    head (*see also* Anomaly, skull)
      756.0
  tracheal cartilage (congenital)
    748.3
  union
    cricoid cartilage and thyroid
      cartilage 748.3
    larynx and trachea 748.3
    thyroid cartilage and hyoid
      bone 748.3
  urination NEC 788.69
    urgency 788.63
  visually evoked potential (VEP)
    794.13
Abrachia 755.20
Abrachiatism 755.20

Abscess (acute) (chronic)
  (infectional) (lymphangitic)
  (metastatic) (multiple)
  (pyogenic) (septic) (with
  lymphangitis) (*see also* Cellulitis)
  682.9
  abdomen, abdominal
    wall 682.2
  ankle 682.6
  antecubital space 682.3
  arm (any part, above wrist) 682.3
  axilla, axillary (region) 682.3
  back (any part) 682.2
  brain (any part) 324.0
    cystic 324.0
    late effect—*see* category 326
    otogenic 324.0
  bursa 727.89
  buttock 682.5
  cartilage 733.99
  cerebellum, cerebellar 324.0
    late effect—*see* category 326
  cerebral (embolic) 324.0
    late effect—*see* category 326
  cervical (neck region) 682.1
  chest 510.9
    wall 682.2
    with fistula 510.0
  connective tissue NEC 682.9
  cranium 324.0
  digit NEC 681.9
  elbow 682.3
  epidural 324.9
    brain 324.0
    late effect—*see* category 326
    spinal cord 324.1
  epiglottis 478.79
  extradural 324.9
    brain 324.0
    late effect—*see* category 326
    spinal cord 324.1
  fascia 728.89
  femoral (region) 682.6
  finger (any) (intrathecal)
    (periosteal) (subcutaneous)
    (subcuticular) 681.00
  fistulous NEC 682.9
  flank 682.2
  foot (except toe) 682.7
  forearm 682.3
  glottis 478.79
  gluteal (region) 682.5
  groin 682.2
  hand (except finger or thumb)
    682.4
  head (except face) 682.8
  heel 682.7
  hip 682.6
  iliac (region) 682.2
  intracranial 324.0
    late effect—*see* category 326
  intraspinal 324.1
    late effect—*see* category 326
  joint (*see also* Arthritis, pyogenic)
    711.0☑

Abscess—*continued*

Note—Use the following fifth-digit
subclassification with categories 711-
712, 715-716:

 0 *site unspecified*
 1 *shoulder region*
 2 *upper arm*
 3 *forearm*
 4 *hand*
 5 *pelvic region and thigh*
 6 *lower leg*
 7 *ankle and foot*
 8 *other specified sites*
 9 *multiple sites*

  vertebral (tuberculous) (*see also*
    Tuberculosis) 015.0☑
    [730.88]

Note—Use the following fifth-digit
subclassification with categories 010-
018:

 0 *unspecified*
 1 *bacteriological or histological*
    examination not done
 2 *bacteriological or histological*
    examination unknown (at present)
 3 *tubercle bacilli found (in sputum)*
    by microscopy
 4 *tubercle bacilli not found (in*
    sputum) by microscopy, but found
    by bacterial culture
 5 *tubercle bacilli not found by*
    bacteriological examination, but
    tuberculosis confirmed
    histologically
 6 *tubercle bacilli not found by*
    bacteriological or histological
    examination, but tuberculosis
    confirmed by other methods
    [inoculation of animals]

      nontuberculous 724.8
  knee 682.6
    joint 711.06
  larynx 478.79
  leg, except foot 682.6
  loin (region) 682.2
  lung (miliary) (putrid) 513.0
  mediastinum 513.1
  mons pubis 682.2
  multiple sites NEC 682.9
  mural 682.2
  muscle 728.89
    psoas 567.31
  nail (chronic) (with lymphangitis)
    681.9
    finger 681.02
    toe 681.11
  nates 682.5
  navel 682.2
  neck (region) 682.1
  operative wound 998.59
  palmar (space) 682.4
  parietal region 682.8
  parumbilical 682.2
  pectoral (region) 682.2
  perineum, perineal (superficial)
    682.2
  peripleuritic 510.9
    with fistula 510.0
  peritoneum, peritoneal
    (perforated) (ruptured)
    567.22
    postoperative 998.59

Abscess—*continued*
  pernicious NEC 682.9
  phagedenic NEC 682.9
  phlegmonous NEC 682.9
  pleura 510.9
    with fistula 510.0
  popliteal 682.6
  postlaryngeal 478.79
  prepatellar 682.6
  regional NEC 682.9
  retrolaryngeal 478.79
  retroperineal 682.2
  rupture (spontaneous) NEC 682.9
  scalp (any part) 682.8
  shoulder 682.3
  side 682.2
  sinus (accessory) (chronic) (nasal)
    (*see also* Sinusitis) 473.9
    intracranial venous (any) 324.0
    late effect—*see* category 326
  skin NEC 682.9
  sloughing NEC 682.9
  specified site NEC 682.8
  spinal
    cord (any part) (staphy-lococcal)
      324.1
    epidural 324.1
  staphylococcal NEC 682.9
  stitch 998.59
  subarachnoid 324.9
    brain 324.0
    cerebral 324.0
    late effect—*see* category 326
    spinal cord 324.1
  subcutaneous NEC 682.9
  subdorsal 682.2
  subdural 324.9
    brain 324.0
    late effect—*see* category 326
    spinal cord 324.1
  subgaleal 682.8
  subpectoral 682.2
  subphrenic—*see also* Abscess,
    peritoneum
    postoperative 998.59
  subscapular 682.2
  subungual 681.9
  suppurative NEC 682.9
  supraclavicular (fossa) 682.3
  suprapubic 682.2
  temporosphenoidal 324.0
    late effect—*see* category 326
  tendon (sheath) 727.89
  thecal 728.89
  thigh (acquired) 682.6
  thorax 510.9
    with fistula 510.0
  thumb (intrathecal) (periosteal)
    (subcutaneous)
    (subcuticular) 681.00
  toe (any) (intrathecal) (periosteal)
    (subcutaneous)
    (subcuticular) 681.10
  trunk 682.2
  umbilicus NEC 682.2
  upper arm 682.3
  urachus 682.2
  web-space 682.4
  wrist 682.4
Absence (organ or part) (complete or
  partial)
  acoustic nerve 742.8
  arm (acquired) V49.60
    above elbow V49.66
    below elbow V49.65

Absence—*continued*
  arm—*continued*
    congenital (*see also* Deformity,
      reduction, upper limb)
      755.20
      upper (complete) (partial)
        (with absence of distal
        elements, incomplete)
        755.24
        complete absence of distal
          elements 755.21
        forearm (incomplete)
          755.23
  auditory canal (congenital)
    (external) 744.01
  auricle (ear) (with stenosis or atresia
    of auditory canal), congenital
    744.01
  bone (congenital) NEC 756.9
    skull 756.0
  bronchus (congenital) 748.3
  calvarium, calvaria (skull) 756.0
  carpal(s) (congenital) (complete)
    (partial) (with absence of
    distal elements, incomplete)
    (*see also* Deformity,
    reduction, upper limb)
    755.28
    with complete absence of distal
      elements 755.21
  caudal spine 756.13
  chin, congenital 744.89
  clavicle 755.51
  coccyx, congenital 756.13
  cold sense (*see also* Disturbance,
    sensation) 782.0
  cricoid cartilage 748.3
  ear, congenital 744.09
    auricle 744.01
    external 744.01
    inner 744.05
    middle, except ossicles 744.03
      ossicles 744.04
    ossicles 744.04
  epiglottis, congenital 748.3
  extremity (acquired)
    congenital (*see also* Deformity,
      reduction) 755.4
    lower V49.70
    upper V49.60
  face
    bones NEC 756.0
    specified part NEC 744.89
  femur, congenital (complete)
    (partial) (with absence of
    distal elements, incomplete)
    (*see also* Deformity,
    reduction, lower limb)
    755.34
    with
      complete absence of distal
        elements 755.31
      tibia and fibula (incomplete)
        755.33
  fibula, congenital (complete)
    (partial) (with absence of
    distal elements, incomplete)
    (*see also* Deformity,
    reduction, lower limb)
    755.37
    with
      complete absence of distal
        elements 755.31

Absence—*continued*
  fibula, congenital—*continued*
    with—*continued*
      tibia 755.35
      with
        complete absence of
          distal elements
          755.31
        femur (incomplete)
          755.33
        with complete
          absence of
          distal elements
          755.31
  finger (acquired) V49.62
    congenital (complete) (partial)
      (*see also* Deformity,
      reduction, upper limb)
      755.29
      meaning all fingers
        (complete) (partial)
        755.21
      transverse 755.21
  fissures of lungs (congenital) 748.5
  foot (acquired) V49.73
    congenital (complete) 755.31
  forearm (acquired) V49.65
    congenital (complete) (partial)
      (with absence of distal
      elements, incomplete)
      (*see also* Deformity,
      reduction, upper limb)
      755.25
    with
      complete absence of distal
        elements (hand and
        fingers) 755.21
      humerus (incomplete)
        755.23
  glottis 748.3
  hand (acquired) V49.63
    congenital (complete) (*see also*
      Deformity, reduction,
      upper limb) 755.21
  heat sense (*see also* Disturbance,
    sensation) 782.0
  humerus, congenital (complete)
    (partial) (with absence of
    distal elements, incomplete)
    (*see also* Deformity,
    reduction, upper limb)
    755.24
    with
      complete absence of distal
        elements 755.21
      radius and ulna (incomplete)
        755.23
  incus (acquired) 385.24
    congenital 744.04
  internal ear (congenital) 744.05
  joint, congenital NEC 755.8
  labyrinth, membranous 744.05
  larynx (congenital) 748.3
  leg (acquired) V49.70
    above knee V49.76
    below knee V49.75
    congenital (partial) (unilateral)
      (*see also* Deformity,
      reduction, lower limb)
      755.31

Absence—*continued*
  leg—*continued*
    congenital—*continued*
      lower (complete) (partial)
        (with absence of distal
        elements, incomplete)
        755.35
        with
          complete absence of
            distal elements
            (foot and toes)
            755.31
          thigh (incomplete)
            755.33
          with complete
            absence of
            distal elements
            755.31
  limb (acquired)
    congenital (complete) (partial)
      (*see also* Deformity,
      reduction) 755.4
      lower 755.30
        complete 755.31
        incomplete 755.32
        transverse 755.31
      upper 755.20
        complete 755.21
        incomplete 755.22
        transverse 755.21
    lower NEC V49.70
    upper NEC V49.60
  lumbar (congenital) (vertebra)
    756.13
    isthmus 756.11
    pars articularis 756.11
  lung (bilateral) (congenital)
    (fissure) (lobe) (unilateral)
    748.5
  metacarpal(s), congenital
    (complete) (partial) (with
    absence of distal elements,
    incomplete) (*see also*
    Deformity, reduction, upper
    limb) 755.28
    with all fingers, complete
      755.21
  metatarsal(s), congenital
    (complete) (partial) (with
    absence of distal elements,
    incomplete) (*see also*
    Deformity, reduction, lower
    limb) 755.38
    with complete absence of distal
      elements 755.31
  neck, part 744.89
  nerve 742.8
  nervous system, part NEC 742.8
  nose (congenital) 748.1
  nuclear 742.8
  organ
    of Corti (congenital) 744.05
    osseous meatus (ear) 744.03
  patella, congenital 755.64
  pelvic girdle (congenital) 755.69
  phalange(s), congenital 755.4
    lower limb (complete)
      (intercalary) (partial)
      (terminal) (*see also*
      Deformity, reduction, lower
      limb) 755.39
      meaning all toes (complete)
        (partial) 755.31
      transverse 755.31

Absence—*continued*
  phalange(s)—*continued*
    upper limb (complete)
      (intercalary) (partial)
      (terminal) (*see also*
      Deformity, reduction,
      upper limb) 755.29
      meaning all digits (complete)
        (partial) 755.21
      transverse 755.21
  radius, congenital (complete)
    (partial) (with absence of
    distal elements, incomplete)
    755.26
    with
      complete absence of distal
        elements 755.21
      ulna 755.25
      with
        complete absence of
          distal elements
          755.21
        humerus (incomplete)
          755.23
  ray, congenital 755.4
    lower limb (complete) (partial)
      (*see also* Deformity,
      reduction, lower limb)
      755.38
      meaning all rays 755.31
      transverse 755.31
    upper limb (complete) (partial)
      (*see also* Deformity,
      reduction, upper limb)
      755.28
      meaning all rays 755.21
      transverse 755.21
  rib (acquired) 738.3
  sacrum, congenital 756.13
  scapula 755.59
  shoulder girdle, congenital
    (complete) (partial) 755.59
  skull bone 756.0
    with
      anencephalus 740.0
      encephalocele 742.0
      hydrocephalus 742.3
        with spina bifida (*see also*
          Spina bifida)
          741.0☑

Note—Use the following fifth-digit
subclassification with category 741:
0 unspecified region
1 cervical region
2 dorsal [thoracic] region
3 lumbar region

      microcephalus 742.1
  spinal cord 742.59
  spine, congenital 756.13
  tarsal(s), congenital (complete)
    (partial) (with absence of
    distal elements, incomplete)
    (*see also* Deformity,
    reduction, lower limb)
    755.38
  thigh (acquired) 736.89
  thumb (acquired) V49.61
    congenital 755.29
  thyroid (gland) (surgical) 246.8
    cartilage, congenital 748.3

ICD-9-CM Index

Absence—continued
tibia, congenital (complete)
(partial) (with absence of
distal elements, incomplete)
(*see also* Deformity,
reduction, lower limb)
755.36
with
complete absence of distal
elements 755.31
fibula 755.35
with
complete absence of
distal elements
755.31
femur (incomplete)
755.33
with complete
absence of
distal elements
755.31
toe (acquired) V49.72
congenital (complete) (partial)
755.39
meaning all toes 755.31
transverse 755.31
great V49.71
trachea (cartilage) (congenital)
(rings) 748.3
ulna, congenital (complete)
(partial) (with absence of
distal elements, incomplete)
(*see also* Deformity,
reduction, upper limb)
755.27
with
complete absence of distal
elements 755.21
radius 755.25
with
complete absence of
distal elements
755.21
humerus (incomplete)
755.23
ventral horn cell 742.59
vertebra, congenital 756.13
Abstinence symptoms or
syndrome
drug 292.0
Acalculia 784.69
developmental 315.1
Acanthocytosis 272.5
Acanthrocytosis 272.5
Acataphasia 784.59
Acathisia 781.0
due to drugs 333.99
Accessory (congenital)
auditory ossicles 744.04
auricle (ear) 744.1
bone NEC 756.9
foot 755.67
carpal bones 755.56
digits 755.00
ear (auricle) (lobe) 744.1
face bone(s) 756.0
fingers 755.01
frontonasal process 756.0
lobule (ear) 744.1
lung (lobe) 748.69
navicular of carpus 755.56
nervous system, part NEC 742.8
nose 748.1
preauricular appendage 744.1

Accessory—continued
sesamoids 755.8
tarsal bones 755.67
thumb 755.01
toes 755.02
tragus 744.1
vertebra 756.19
vocal cords 748.3
Accident, accidental—see also
condition
cerebral (*see also* Disease,
cerebrovascular, acute)
434.91
cerebrovascular (current) (CVA)
(*see also* Disease,
cerebrovascular, acute)
434.91
healed or old V12.54
postoperative 997.02
craniovascular (*see also* Disease,
cerebrovascular, acute) 436
Accommodation
paralysis of 367.51
hysterical 300.11
Acheiria 755.21
Achillobursitis 726.71
Achillodynia 726.71
Achromia
unguium 703.8
Acmesthesia 782.0
Acontractile bladder 344.61
Aconuresis (*see also* Incontinence)
788.30
Acragnosis 781.99
Acroagnosis 781.99
Acroasphyxia, chronic 443.89
Acrobrachycephaly 756.0
Acrocephalopolysyndactyly
755.55
Acrocephalosyndactyly 755.55
Acrocephaly 756.0
Acrocyanosis 443.89
Acrodermatitis 686.8
enteropathica 686.8
Acrodysplasia 755.55
Acromelalgia 443.82
Acronyx 703.0
Acroparesthesia 443.89
simple (Schultz's type) 443.89
vasomotor (Nothnagel's type)
443.89
Acroscleriasis (*see also* Scleroderma)
710.1
Acroscleroderma (*see also*
Scleroderma) 710.1
Acrosclerosis (*see also* Scleroderma)
710.1
Acrosphacelus 785.4
Acrosphenosyndactylia 755.55
Acrosyndactyly (*see also*
Syndactylism) 755.10
Action, heart
irregular 427.9
psychogenic 306.2
Adactylia, adactyly (congenital)
755.4
lower limb (complete) (intercalary)
(partial) (terminal) (*see also*
Deformity, reduction, lower
limb) 755.39
meaning all digits (complete)
(partial) 755.31
transverse (complete) (partial)
755.31

Adactylia, adactyly—continued
upper limb (complete) (intercalary)
(partial) (terminal) (*see also*
Deformity, reduction, upper
limb) 755.29
meaning all digits (complete)
(partial) 755.21
transverse (complete) (partial)
755.21
Adaptation reaction (*see also*
Reaction, adjustment) 309.9
Adenoma (sessile) (M8140/0)—*see*
also Neoplasm, by site, benign
Adenomatosis (M8220/0)
pulmonary (M8250/1) 235.7
Adherent
scar (skin) NEC 709.2
tendon in scar 709.2
Adhesion(s), adhesive
(postinfectional) (postoperative)
congenital—*see also* Anomaly,
specified type NEC
fingers (*see also* Syndactylism,
fingers) 755.11
toes (*see also* Syndactylism,
toes) 755.13
epiglottis 478.79
joint (*see also* Ankylosis) 718.5☑
lung 511.0
meninges 349.2
congenital 742.8
spinal (any) 349.2
congenital 742.59
nerve NEC 355.9
spinal 355.9
root 724.9
cervical NEC 723.4
lumbar NEC 724.4
lumbosacral 724.4
thoracic 724.4
pleura, pleuritic 511.0
pleuropericardial 511.0
pulmonary 511.0
sciatic nerve 355.0
shoulder (joint) 726.0
spinal canal 349.2
nerve 355.9
root 724.9
cervical NEC 723.4
lumbar NEC 724.4
lumbosacral 724.4
thoracic 724.4
subscapular 726.2
tendonitis 726.90
shoulder 726.0
Admission (encounter)
for
adjustment (of)
artificial
arm (complete) (partial)
V52.0
leg (complete) (partial)
V52.1
device, unspecified type
V53.90
nervous system V53.09
prosthetic V52.9
specified type NEC
V52.8
special senses V53.09
substitution
auditory V53.09
nervous system V53.09
visual V53.09

Admission—continued
for—continued
adjustment (of)—continued
orthopedic (device) V53.7
brace V53.7
cast V53.7
shoes V53.7
prosthesis V52.9
arm (complete) (partial)
V52.0
leg (complete) (partial)
V52.1
specified type NEC V52.8
change of
dressing
wound V58.30
nonsurgical V58.30
surgical V58.31
examination (*see also*
Examination) V70.9
employment V70.5
exercise therapy V57.1
fitting (of)
artificial
arm (complete) (partial)
V52.0
leg (complete) (partial)
V52.1
device, unspecified type
V53.90
nervous system V53.09
special senses V53.09
substitution
auditory V53.09
nervous system V53.09
visual V53.09
orthopedic (device) V53.7
brace V53.7
cast V53.7
shoes V53.7
prosthesis V52.9
arm (complete) (partial)
V52.0
leg (complete) (partial)
V52.1
specified type NEC V52.8
follow-up examination (routine)
(following) V67.9
high-risk medication NEC
V67.51
treatment (for) V67.9
fracture V67.4
involving high-risk
medication NEC
V67.51
occupational therapy V57.21
physical therapy NEC V57.1
prophylactic
breathing exercises V57.0
rehabilitation V57.9
multiple types V57.89
occupational V57.21
orthoptic V57.4
orthotic V57.81
physical NEC V57.1
specified type NEC V57.89
speech V57.3
vocational V57.22
speech (-language) therapy
V57.3
therapy
breathing exercises V57.0
exercise (remedial) NEC
V57.1
breathing V57.0

☑ Additional Digit Required

Admission—*continued*
  for—*continued*
    therapy—*continued*
      long-term (current) drug use
        NEC V58.69
        antiplatelet V58.63
        antithrombotic V58.63
        aspirin V58.66
        insulin V58.67
        steroids V58.65
      occupational V57.21
      orthoptic V57.4
      physical NEC V57.1
      speech (-language) V57.3
      vocational V57.22
      vocational therapy V57.22
Aftercare V58.9
  amputation stump V54.89
  breathing exercise V57.0
    exercise (remedial) (therapeutic)
      V57.1
    breathing V57.0
  following surgery NEC V58.49
    of
      musculoskeletal system
        V58.78
      skin V58.77
      subcutaneous tissue V58.77
  gait training V57.1
    for use of artificial limb(s)
      V57.81
  involving
    gait training V57.1
      for use of artificial limb(s)
        V57.81
    orthoptic training V57.4
    orthotic training V57.81
    removal of
      dressings
        wound V58.30
          nonsurgical V58.30
          surgical V58.31
  occupational therapy V57.21
  orthoptic training V57.4
  orthotic training V57.81
  physical therapy NEC V57.1
    breathing exercises V57.0
  rehabilitation procedure V57.9
    breathing exercises V57.0
    multiple types V57.89
    occupational V57.21
    orthoptic V57.4
    orthotic V57.81
    physical therapy NEC V57.1
    remedial exercises V57.1
    specified type NEC V57.89
    speech V57.3
    therapeutic exercises V57.1
    vocational V57.22
  speech therapy V57.3
  vocational rehabilitation V57.22
Agenesis—*see also* Absence, by site,
    congenital
  acoustic nerve 742.8
  arm (complete) (partial) (*see also*
      Deformity, reduction, upper
      limb) 755.20
  auditory (canal) (external) 744.01
  auricle (ear) 744.01
  bronchus 748.3
  carpus NEC (*see also* Deformity,
      reduction, upper limb)
      755.28
  chin 744.89
  clavicle 755.51

Agenesis—*continued*
  coccyx 756.13
  cricoid cartilage 748.3
  ear NEC 744.09
    auricle 744.01
  epiglottis 748.3
  face
    bones NEC 756.0
    specified part NEC 744.89
  femur NEC (*see also* Absence,
      femur, congenital) 755.34
  fibula NEC (*see also* Absence, fibula,
      congenital) 755.37
  finger NEC (*see also* Absence,
      finger, congenital) 755.29
  foot (complete) (*see also* Deformity,
      reduction, lower limb)
      755.31
  glottis 748.3
  hand (complete) (*see also*
      Deformity, reduction, upper
      limb) 755.21
  humerus NEC (*see also* Absence,
      humerus, congenital) 755.24
  incus 744.04
  labyrinth, membranous 744.05
  larynx 748.3
  leg NEC (*see also* Deformity,
      reduction, lower limb)
      755.30
  limb (complete) (partial) (*see also*
      Deformity, reduction) 755.4
    lower NEC 755.30
    upper 755.20
  lung (bilateral) (fissures) (lobe)
      (unilateral) 748.5
  metacarpus NEC 755.28
  metatarsus NEC 755.38
  neck, part 744.89
  nerve 742.8
  nervous system, part NEC 742.8
  nose 748.1
  nuclear 742.8
  organ
    of Corti 744.05
  osseous meatus (ear) 744.03
  patella 755.64
  pelvic girdle (complete) (partial)
      755.69
  radioulnar NEC (*see also* Absence,
      forearm, congenital) 755.25
  radius NEC (*see also* Absence,
      radius, congenital) 755.26
  sacrum 756.13
  scapula 755.59
  shoulder girdle (complete) (partial)
      755.59
  skull (bone) 756.0
    with
      anencephalus 740.0
      encephalocele 742.0
      hydrocephalus 742.3
        with spina bifida (*see also*
          Spina bifida)
          741.0☑

Note—*Use the following fifth-digit*
subclassification with category 741:
  0 unspecified region
  1 cervical region
  2 dorsal [thoracic} region
  3 lumbar region

      microcephalus 742.1
  spinal cord 742.59

Agenesis—*continued*
  spine 756.13
    lumbar 756.13
      isthmus 756.11
      pars articularis 756.11
  tarsus NEC 755.38
  thyroid (gland) 243
    cartilage 748.3
  tibia NEC (*see also* Absence, tibia,
      congenital) 755.36
  tibiofibular NEC 755.35
  toe (complete) (partial) (*see also*
      Absence, toe, congenital)
      755.39
  trachea (cartilage) 748.3
  ulna NEC (*see also* Absence, ulna,
      congenital) 755.27
  vertebra 756.13
    lumbar 756.13
      isthmus 756.11
      pars articularis 756.11
Ageusia (*see also* Disturbance,
    sensation) 781.1
AIDS virus (disease) (illness) 042
AIDS-associated retrovirus
    (disease) (illness) 042
AIDS-associated virus (disease)
    (illness) 042
AIDS-like disease (illness)
    (syndrome) 042
AIDS-related complex 042
AIDS-related conditions 042
AIDS-related virus (disease) (illness)
    042
AIDS 042
Air
  anterior mediastinum 518.1
  hunger 786.09
    psychogenic 306.1
Akathisia, acathisia 781.0
  due to drugs 333.99
    neuroleptic-induced, acute 333.99
Akinesia algeria 352.6
Alalia 784.3
  developmental 315.31
    receptive-expressive 315.32
Albert's disease 726.71
Alcohol, alcoholic
  amnestic disorder, persisting 291.1
  anxiety 291.89
  cardiopathy 425.5
  delirium 291.0
    acute 291.0
    chronic 291.1
    tremens 291.0
    withdrawal 291.0
  insanity 291.9
  Korsakoff's, Korsakov's, Korsakow's
      291.1
  mania (acute) (chronic) 291.9
  mood 291.89
  psychosis (*see also* Psychosis,
      alcoholic) 291.9
    Korsakoff's, Korsakov's,
      Korsakow's 291.1
    polyneuritic 291.1
  withdrawal symptoms, syndrome
      NEC 291.81
    delirium 291.0

Allergy, allergic (reaction) 995.3
  alveolitis (extrinsic) 495.9
    due to
      Aspergillus clavatus 495.4
      cryptostroma corticale 495.6
      organisms (fungal,
        thermophilic
        actinomycete, other)
        growing in ventilation
        (air conditioning
        systems) 495.7
    specified type NEC 495.8
  drug, medicinal substance, and
      biological (any) (correct
      medicinal substance properly
      administered) (external)
      (internal) 995.2
  migraine 346.2☑
  pneumonia 518.3
Allocheiria, allochiria (*see also*
    Disturbance, sensation) 782.0
Alpers' disease 330.8
Aluminosis (of lung) 503
Alveolar capillary block
    syndrome 516.3
Alveolitis
  allergic (extrinsic) 495.9
    due to organisms (fungal,
        thermophilic
        actinomycete, other)
        growing in ventilation (air
        conditioning systems)
        495.7
    specified type NEC 495.8
    due to
      Aspergillus clavatus 495.4
      Cryptostroma corticale 495.6
  fibrosing (chronic) (cryptogenic)
      (lung) 516.3
    idiopathic 516.3
    rheumatoid 714.81
Alzheimer's
  dementia (senile)
    without behavioral disturbance
        331.0 [294.10]
    with behavioral disturbance
        331.0 [294.11]
  disease or sclerosis 331.0
Amelia 755.4
  lower limb 755.31
  upper limb 755.21
Amnesia (retrograde) 780.93
  auditory 784.69
    developmental 315.31
  hysterical or dissociative type
      300.12
  psychogenic 300.12
Amnestic (confabulatory) syndrome
    294.0
  alcohol induced 291.1
  drug-induced 292.83
  posttraumatic 294.0
Amputation
  arm
    bilateral
      any level 887.6
        complicated 887.7
    unilateral
      at or above elbow 887.2
        complicated 887.3
      below elbow 887.0
        complicated 887.2
      level not specified 887.4
        complicated 887.5

Amputation—*continued*
congenital
lower limb 755.31
upper limb 755.21
finger 886.0
complicated 886.1
foot
bilateral 896.2
complicated 896.3
unilateral 896.0
complicated 896.1
leg
bilateral
any level 897.6
complicated 897.7
unilateral
at or above knee 897.2
complicated 897.3
below knee 897.0
complicated 897.1
level not specified 897.4
complicated 897.5
stump (surgical) (posttraumatic)
abnormal, painful, or with
complication (late)
997.60
healed or old NEC—*see also*
Absence, by site, acquired
lower V49.70
upper V49.60
thumb 885.0
complicated 885.1
toe 895.0
complicated 895.1
traumatic (complete) (partial)
foot (except toe(s) only) 896.0
and other leg 897.6
complicated 897.7
both (bilateral) 896.2
complicated 896.3
leg 897.4
and other foot 897.6
complicated 897.7
both (bilateral) 897.6
complicated 897.7

Amputee (bilateral) (old)—*see also*
Absence, by site, acquired
V49.70
Amusia 784.69
developmental 315.39
Amyelia 742.59
Amyloid disease or degeneration
277.30
heart 277.39 *[425.7]*
Amyloidosis (familial) (general)
(generalized) (genetic)
(primary) (secondary) 277.30
heart 277.39 *[425.7]*
neuropathic (Portuguese) (Swiss)
277.39 *[357.4]*
pulmonary 277.39 *[517.8]*
secondary 277.39
with lung involvement 277.39
[517.8]
Amylophagia 307.52
Amyotonia 728.2
congenita 358.8
Amyotrophia, amyotrophy,
amyotrophic 728.2
diabetic 250.6☑ *[353.5]*

Amyotrophia, amyotrophy,
amyotrophic—*continued*
due to secondary diabetes 249.6☑
[353.5]

Note—Use the following fifth-digit
subclassification with category 250:
0 *type II [non-insulin dependent*
type] [NIDDM type] [adult-onset
type] or unspecified type, not
stated as uncontrolled
1 *type I [insulin dependent type]*
[IDDM type] [juvenile type], not
stated as uncontrolled
2 *type II [non-insulin dependent*
type] [NIDDM type] [adult-onset
type] or unspecified type,
uncontrolled
3 *type I [insulin dependent type]*
[IDDM] [juvenile type],
uncontrolled

lateral sclerosis (syndrome) 335.20
neuralgic 353.5
sclerosis (lateral) 335.20
spinal progressive 335.21
Analgesia (*see also* Anesthesia) 782.0
Analphalipoproteinemia 272.5
Anarthria 784.51
Anarthritic rheumatoid disease
446.5
Anasarca 782.3
cardiac (*see also* Failure, heart)
428.0
lung 514
pulmonary 514
Anesthesia, anesthetic 782.0
complication or reaction NEC
995.2
due to
correct substance properly
administered 995.2
functional 300.11
hysterical 300.11
local skin lesion 782.0
olfactory 781.1
skin 782.0
tactile 782.0
thermal 782.0
Aneurysm (anastomotic) (artery)
(cirsoid) (diffuse) (false)
(fusiform) (multiple) (ruptured)
(saccular) (varicose) 442.9
aorta, aortic (nonsyphilitic) 441.9
brain 437.3
arteriosclerotic 437.3
ruptured (*see also*
Hemorrhage,
subarachnoid) 430
arteriovenous 747.81
acquired 437.3
ruptured (*see also*
Hemorrhage, sub-
arachnoid) 430
ruptured (*see also*
Hemorrhage,
subarachnoid) 430
berry (congenital) (ruptured)
(*see also* Hemorrhage,
subarachnoid) 430
congenital 747.81
ruptured (*see also*
Hemorrhage,
subarachnoid) 430

Aneurysm—*continued*
brain—*continued*
meninges 437.3
ruptured (*see also*
Hemorrhage,
subarachnoid) 430
miliary (congenital) (ruptured)
(*see also* Hemorrhage,
subarachnoid) 430
mycotic 421.0
ruptured (*see also*
Hemorrhage,
subarachnoid) 430
ruptured (*See also* Hemorrhage,
subarachnoid) 430
cardiac (false) (*see also* Aneur-ysm,
heart) 414.10
carotid artery (common) (external)
442.81
internal (intracranial portion)
437.3
ruptured into brain (*see also*
Hemorrhage,
subarachnoid) 430
cavernous sinus (*see also* Aneurysm,
brain) 437.3
arteriovenous 747.81
ruptured (*see also*
Hemorrhage,
subarachnoid) 430
congenital 747.81
ruptured (*see also*
Hemorrhage,
subarachnoid) 430
circle of Willis (*see also* Aneurysm,
brain) 437.3
congenital 747.81
ruptured (*see also*
Hemorrhage,
subarachnoid) 430
ruptured (*see also* Hemorrhage,
subarachnoid) 430
congenital (peripheral) NEC 747.60
brain 747.81
ruptured (*see also*
Hemorrhage,
subarachnoid) 430
conus arteriosus (*see also*
Aneurysm, heart) 414.10
coronary (arteriosclerotic) (artery)
(vein) (*see also* Aneurysm,
heart) 414.11
heart (chronic or with a stated
duration of over 8 weeks)
(infectional) (wall) 414.10
interauricular septum (*see also*
Aneurysm, heart) 414.10
interventricular septum (*see also*
Aneurysm, heart) 414.10
jugular vein 453.89
miliary (congenital) (ruptured) (*see*
also Hemorrhage,
subarachnoid) 430
mitral (heart) (valve) 424.0
mural (arteriovenous) (heart) (*see*
also Aneurysm, heart) 414.10
mycotic, any site 421.0
without endocarditis—*see*
Aneurysm, by site
ruptured, brain (*see also*
Hemorrhage,
subarachnoid) 430
myocardium (*see also* Aneurysm,
heart) 414.10

Aneurysm—*continued*
pulmonary 417.1
valve (heart) (*see also*
Endocarditis, pulmonary)
424.3
ventricle (arteriovenous) (*see also*
Aneurysm, heart) 414.10
Angiitis 447.6
allergic granulomatous 446.4
necrotizing 446.0
Wegener's (necrotizing respiratory
granulomatosis) 446.4
Angina (attack) (cardiac) (chest)
(effort) (heart) (pectoris)
(syndrome) (vasomotor) 413.9
accelerated 411.1
crescendo 411.1
croupous 464.4
cruris 443.9
due to atherosclerosis NEC (*see*
also Arteriosclerosis,
extremities) 440.20
decubitus 413.0
equivalent 413.9
exudative, chronic 476.0
initial 411.1
membranous 464.4
nocturnal 413.0
preinfarctional 411.1
Prinzmetal's 413.1
progressive 411.1
psychogenic 306.2
stable NEC 413.9
trachealis 464.4
unstable 411.1
variant 413.1
Angiodysgensis spinalis 336.1
Angioneurosis 306.2
Angiopathia, angiopathy 459.9
diabetic (peripheral) 250.7☑
[443.81]
due to secondary diabetes 249.7☑
[443.81]

Note—Use the following fifth-digit
subclassification with category 250:
0 *type II [non-insulin dependent*
type] [NIDDM type] [adult-onset
type] or unspecified type, not
stated as uncontrolled
1 *type I [insulin dependent type]*
[IDDM type] [juvenile type], not
stated as uncontrolled
2 *type II [non-insulin dependent*
type] [NIDDM type] [adult-onset
type] or unspecified type,
uncontrolled
3 *type I [insulin dependent type]*
[IDDM] [juvenile type],
uncontrolled

peripheral 443.9
diabetic 250.7☑ *[443.81]*
due to secondary diabetes
249.7☑ *[443.81]*
specified type NEC 443.89
Angiospasm 443.9
brachial plexus 353.0
cervical plexus 353.2
nerve
arm 354.9
axillary 353.0
median 354.1
ulnar 354.2

Angiospasm—*continued*
  nerve—*continued*
    autonomic (*see also*
        Neuropathy, peripheral,
        autonomic) 337.9
      axillary 353.0
      leg 355.8
        plantar 355.6
      median 354.1
      peripheral NEC 355.9
      spinal NEC 355.9
      sympathetic (*see also*
        Neuropathy, peripheral,
        autonomic) 337.9
      ulnar 354.2
    peripheral NEC 443.9
    traumatic 443.9
      foot 443.9
      leg 443.9
    vessel 443.9
Angiospastic disease or edema
    443.9
Angulation
  coccyx (acquired) 738.6
    congenital 756.19
  femur (acquired) 736.39
    congenital 755.69
  sacrum (acquired) 738.5
    congenital 756.19
  spine (*see also* Curvature, spine)
    737.9
  tibia (acquired) 736.89
    congenital 755.69
  wrist (acquired) 736.09
    congenital 755.59
Angulus infectiosus 686.8
Ankylodactly (*see also* Syndactylism)
    755.10
Ankylosis (fibrous) (osseous) 718.50
  ankle 718.57
  any joint, produced by surgical
    fusion V45.4
  cricoarytenoid (cartilage) (joint)
    (larynx) 478.79
  elbow 718.52
  finger 718.54
  hip 718.55
  joint, produced by surgical fusion
    NEC V45.4
  knee 718.56
  lumbosacral (joint) 724.6
  multiple sites 718.59
  postoperative (status) V45.4
  sacroiliac (joint) 724.6
  shoulder 718.51
  specified site NEC 718.58
  spine NEC 724.9
  surgical V45.4
  wrist 718.53
Anomaly, anomalous (congenital)
    (unspecified type) 759.9
  acoustic nerve 742.9
  ankle (joint) 755.69
  arm 755.50
    reduction (*see also* Deformity,
      reduction, upper limb)
      755.20
  arytenoepiglottic folds 748.3
  auditory canal 744.3
    specified type NEC 744.29
      with hearing impairment
        744.02

Anomaly, anomalous—*continued*
  auricle
    ear 744.3
      causing impairment of
        hearing 744.02
  bone NEC 756.9
    ankle 755.69
    arm 755.50
    cranium 756.0
    face 756.0
    finger 755.50
    foot 755.67
    forearm 755.50
    frontal 756.0
    head 756.0
    hip 755.63
    leg 755.60
    lumbosacral 756.10
    nose 748.1
    pelvic girdle 755.60
    shoulder girdle 755.50
    skull 756.0
    toe 755.66
  brain 742.9
  branchial cleft NEC 744.49
    cyst 744.42
    fistula 744.41
    persistent 744.41
    sinus (external) (internal)
      744.41
  breast 757.6
  bronchus 748.3
  carpus 755.50
  cartilage, trachea 748.3
  cauda equina 742.59
  chin 744.9
    specified type NEC 744.89
  choroid 743.9
    plexus 742.9
  clavicle 755.51
  coccyx 756.10
  cricoid cartilage 748.3
  dura 742.9
    spinal cord 742.59
  ear 744.3
    causing impairment of hearing
      744.00
      specified type NEC 744.09
    external 744.3
      causing impairment of
        hearing 744.02
    inner (causing impairment of
      hearing) 744.05
    middle, except ossicles (causing
      impairment of hearing)
      744.03
      ossicles 744.04
    ossicles 744.04
    specified type NEC 744.29
      with hearing impair-ment
        744.09
  elbow (joint) 755.50
  epiglottis 748.3
  eyebrow 744.89
  face (any part) 744.9
    bone(s) 756.0
    specified type NEC 744.89
  femur 755.60
  fibula 755.60
  finger 755.50
    supernumerary 755.01
    webbed (*see also* Syndactylism,
      fingers) 755.11

Anomaly, anomalous—*continued*
  flexion (joint) 755.9
    hip or thigh (*see also*
      Dislocation, hip,
      congenital) 754.30
  foot 755.67
  forearm 755.50
  forehead (*see also* Anomaly, skull)
    756.0
  frontal bone (*see also* Anomaly,
    skull) 756.0
  glottis 748.3
  gyri 742.9
  hand 755.50
  head (*see also* Anomaly, skull)
    756.0
  heart 746.9
    fibroelastosis cordis 425.3
  heel 755.67
  hip (joint) 755.63
  humerus 755.50
  ilium 755.60
  intervertebral cartilage or disc
    756.10
  ischium 755.60
  joint 755.9
    hip
      dislocation (*see also*
        Dislocation, hip,
        congenital) 754.30
      predislocation (*see also*
        Subluxation,
        congenital, hip)
        754.32
      preluxation (*see also*
        Subluxation,
        congenital, hip)
        754.32
      subluxation (*see also*
        Subluxation,
        congenital, hip)
        754.32
    lumbosacral 756.10
      spondylolisthesis 756.12
      spondylosis 756.11
    multiple arthrogryposis 754.89
    sacroiliac 755.69
  Klippel-Feil (brevicollis) 756.16
  knee (joint) 755.64
  labyrinth, membranous (causing
    impairment of hearing)
    744.05
  larynx, laryngeal (muscle) 748.3
    web, webbed 748.2
  leg (lower) (upper) 755.60
    reduction NEC (*see also*
      Deformity, reduction,
      lower limb) 755.30
  limb, except reduction deformity
    755.9
    lower 755.60
      reduction deformity (*see also*
        Deformity, reduction,
        lower limb) 755.30
      specified type NEC 755.69
    upper 755.50
      reduction deformity (*see also*
        Deformity, reduction,
        upper limb) 755.20
      specified type NEC 755.59
  lower extremity 755.60
  lumbosacral (joint) (region) 756.10
  lung (fissure)(lobe) NEC 748.60
    agenesis 748.5
    specified type NEC 748.69

Anomaly, anomalous—*continued*
  Madelung's (radius) 755.54
  meningeal bands or folds,
    constriction of 742.8
  meninges 742.9
    spinal 742.59
  metacarpus 755.50
  metatarsus 755.67
  middle ear, except ossicles (causing
    impairment of hearing)
    744.03
    ossicles 744.04
  nasal sinus or septum 748.1
  neck (any part) 744.9
    specified type NEC 744.89
  nerve 742.9
    acoustic 742.9
      specified type NEC 742.8
    optic 742.9
      specified type NEC 742.8
    specified type NEC 742.8
  nervous system NEC 742.9
    brain 742.9
    specified type NEC 742.8
  neurological 742.9
  nonteratogenic NEC 754.89
  nose, nasal (bone) (cartilage)
    (septum) (sinus) 748.1
  optic
    nerve 742.9
  organ
    of Corti (causing impairment of
      hearing) 744.05
  osseous meatus (ear) 744.03
  patella 755.64
  pelvic girdle 755.60
    specified type NEC 755.69
  pelvis (bony) 755.60
  pharynx 750.9
    branchial cleft 744.41
  Pierre Robin 756.0
  preauricular sinus 744.46
  pulmonary 748.60
    specified type NEC 748.69
  radius 755.50
  rings, trachea 748.3
  rotation—*see also* Malrotation
    hip or thigh (*see also*
      Subluxation, congenital,
      hip) 754.32
  sacroiliac (joint) 755.69
  sacrum 756.10
  saddle
    back 754.2
  scapula 755.50
  sense organs 742.9
    specified type NEC 742.8
  septum
    nasal 748.1
  shoulder (girdle) (joint) 755.50
    specified type NEC 755.59
  skull (bone) 756.0
  specified type NEC
    ankle 755.69
    arm 755.59
    auditory canal 744.29
      causing impairment of
        hearing 744.02
    bone(s) 756.9
      arm 755.59
      face 756.0
      leg 755.69
      pelvic girdle 755.69
      shoulder girdle 755.59
      skull 756.0

Anomaly, anomalous—*continued*
specified type NEC—*continued*
bronchus 748.3
carpus 755.59
chin 744.89
clavicle 755.51
coccyx 756.19
cricoid cartilage 748.3
ear 744.29
auricle 744.29
causing impairment of
hearing 744.02
causing impairment of
hearing 744.09
inner (causing impairment of
hearing) 744.05
middle, except ossicles
744.03
ossicles 744.04
epiglottis 748.3
face 744.89
bone(s) 756.0
femur 755.69
fibula 755.69
finger 755.59
foot 755.67
glottis 748.3
hand 755.59
joint 755.8
knee 755.64
labyrinth, membranous 744.05
larynx 748.3
leg 755.69
limb, except reduction
deformity 755.8
lower 755.69
reduction deformity (*see
also* Deformity,
reduction, lower
limb) 755.30
upper 755.59
reduction deformity (*see
also* Deformity,
reduction, upper
limb) 755.20
lung (fissure) (lobe) 748.69
metacarpus 755.59
neck 744.89
nerve 742.8
acoustic 742.8
optic 742.8
nervous system 742.8
nose 748.1
organ NEC 759.89
of Corti 744.05
osseous meatus (ear) 744.03
patella 755.64
pelvic girdle 755.69
radius 755.59
sacrum 756.19
scapula 755.59
shoulder girdle 755.59
skull (bone(s)) 756.0
spinal cord 742.59
spine 756.19
tarsus 755.67
thyroid (gland) 759.2
cartilage 748.3
tibia 755.69
toe 755.66
trachea (cartilage) 748.3
ulna 755.59
vertebra 756.19
spine, spinal 756.10
column 756.10

Anomaly, anomalous—*continued*
spine, spinal—*continued*
cord 742.9
specified type NEC 742.59
meninges 742.59
nerve root 742.9
Sprengel's 755.52
tarsus 755.67
with complete absence of distal
elements 755.31
thigh 755.60
flexion (*see also* Subluxation,
congenital, hip) 754.32
thumb 755.50
supernumerary 755.01
thyroid (gland) 759.2
cartilage 748.3
tibia 755.60
toe 755.66
supernumerary 755.02
webbed (*see also* Synda-ctylism,
toes) 755.13
trachea, tracheal 748.3
cartilage 748.3
rings 748.3
ulna 755.50
union, trachea with larynx 748.3
upper extremity 755.50
valleculae 748.3
vertebra 756.10
wrist (joint) 755.50
Anonychia 757.5
acquired 703.8
Anorexia 783.0
hysterical 300.11
Anosmia (*see also* Disturbance,
sensation) 781.1
hysterical 300.11
psychogenic 306.7
Anosphrasia 781.1
Anotia 744.09
Anoxia 799.02
cerebral 348.1
during or resulting from a
procedure 997.01
Anterior—*see also* condition
spinal artery compression
syndrome 721.1
Anteversion
femur (neck), congenital 755.63
Anthracosilicosis (occupational)
500
Anthracosis (lung) (occupational)
500
Anthrax 022.9
with pneumonia 022.1 [484.5]
Anthropoid pelvis 755.69
Anxiety (neurosis) (reaction) (state)
300.00
alcohol-induced 291.89
drug-induced 292.89
due to or associated with physical
condition 293.84
generalized 300.02
hysteria 300.20
in
acute stress reaction 308.0
transient adjustment reaction
309.24
panic type 300.01
separation, abnormal 309.21
syndrome (organic) (transient)
293.84
Aortitis (nonsyphilitic) 447.6
arteriosclerotic 440.0

Apathy 799.25
Apert's syndrome
(acrocephalosyndactyly) 755.55
Aphagia 787.2
Aphalangia (congenital) 755.4
lower limb (complete) (intercalary)
(partial) (terminal) 755.39
meaning all digits (complete)
(partial) 755.31
transverse 755.31
upper limb (complete) (intercalary)
(partial) (terminal) 755.29
meaning all digits (complete)
(partial) 755.21
transverse 755.21
Aphasia (amnestic) (ataxic)
(auditory) (Broca's) (choreatic)
(classic) (expressive) (global)
(ideational) (ideokinetic)
(ideomotor) (jargon) (motor)
(nominal) (receptive) (semantic)
(sensory) (syntactic) (verbal)
(visual) (Wernicke's) 784.3
developmental 315.31
Aphthae, aphthous—*see also*
condition
ulcer (oral) (recurrent) 528.2
larynx 478.79
Aplasia—*see also* Agenesis
axialis extracorticalis (congenital)
330.0
bronchus 748.3
extracortical axial 330.0
labyrinth, membranous 744.05
limb (congenital) 755.4
lower NEC 755.30
upper NEC 755.20
lung (bilateral) (congenital)
(unilateral) 748.5
nervous system NEC 742.8
nuclear 742.8
Pelizaeus-Merzbacher 330.0
spinal cord 742.59
ventral horn cell 742.59
Apnea, apneic (spells) 786.03
psychogenic 306.1
sleep, unspecified 780.57
with
hypersomnia, unspecified
780.53
hyposomnia, unspecified
780.51
insomnia, unspecified 780.51
sleep disturbance NEC
780.57
central, in conditions classified
elsewhere 327.27
obstructive (adult) (pediatric)
327.23
organic 327.20
other 327.29
primary central 327.21
Apneumatosis newborn 770.4
Apodia 755.31
Apoplectiform convulsions (*see
also* Disease, cerebrovascular,
acute) 436
Apoplexia, apoplexy, apoplectic
(*see also* Disease,
cerebrovascular, acute 436
attack 436
basilar (*see also* Disease, cerebrovascular, acute) 436
brain (*see also* Disease, cerebrovascular, acute) 436

**Apoplexia, apoplexy,
apoplectic**—*continued*
bulbar (*see also* Disease, cerebrovascular, acute) 436
capillary (*see also* Disease,
cerebrovascular, acute) 436
cerebral (*see also* Disease, cerebrovascular acute) 436
chorea (*see also* Disease, cerebrovascular, acute) 436
congestive (*see also* Disease,
cerebrovascular, acute) 436
fit (*see also* Disease, cerebrovascular, acute) 436
healed or old V12.54
hemiplegia (*see also* Disease,
cerebrovascular, acute) 436
hemorrhagic (stroke) (*see also*
Hemorrhage, brain) 432.9
ingravescent (*see also* Disease,
cerebrovascular, acute) 436
meninges, hemorrhagic (*see also*
Hemorrhage subarachnoid)
430
progressive (*see also* Disease,
cerebrovascular, acute) 436
sanguineous (*see also* Disease,
cerebrovascular, acute) 436
seizure (*see also* Disease, cerebrovascular, acute) 436
serous (*see also* Disease, cerebrovascular, acute) 436
stroke (*see also* Disease,
cerebrovascular, acute) 436
Appendage
preauricular 744.1
Appetite
depraved 307.52
excessive 783.6
psychogenic 307.51
lack or loss (*see also* Anorexia)
783.0
nonorganic origin 307.59
perverted 307.52
hysterical 300.11
Apprehension, apprehensiveness
(abnormal) (state) 300.00
specified type NEC 300.09
Arc-welders' lung 503
ARC 042
Areflexia 796.1
Arrest, arrested
cardiac 427.5
complicating
anesthesia
correct substance properly
administered 427.5
cardiorespiratory (*see also* Arrest,
cardiac) 427.5
development or growth
bone 733.91
child 783.40
tracheal rings 748.3
epiphyseal 733.91
Arrhythmia (auricle) (cardiac)
(cordis) (gallop rhythm)
(juvenile) (nodal) (reflex) (sinus)
(supraventricular) (transitory)
(ventricle) 427.9
psychogenic 306.2
Arrillaga-Ayerza syndrome
(pulmonary artery sclerosis with
pulmonary hypertension) 416.0
Arterionephrosclerosis (*see also*
Hypertension, kidney) 403.90

☑ Additional Digit Required © 2009 Ingenix

Arteriosclerosis, arteriosclerotic
(artery) (deformans) (diffuse)
(disease) (endarteritis) (general)
(obliterans) (obliterative)
(occlusive) (senile) (with
calcification) 440.9
aorta 440.0
bypass graft
coronary artery 414.05
autologous artery
(gastroepiploic)
(internal mammary)
414.04
autologous vein 414.02
nonautologous biological
414.03
of transplanted heart 414.07
cardiorenal (see also Hypertension,
cardiorenal) 404.90
coronary (artery) 414.00
due to lipid rich plaque 414.3
native artery 414.01
extremities (native artery) NEC
440.20
claudication (intermittent)
440.21
and
gangrene 440.24
rest pain 440.22
and
gangrene 440.24
ulceration 440.23
ulceration 440.23
and gangrene 440.24
gangrene 440.24
rest pain 440.22
and
gangrene 440.24
ulceration 440.23
and gangrene 440.24
ulceration 440.23
and gangrene 440.24
heart (disease)—see also
Arteriosclerosis, coronary
valve 424.99
aortic 424.1
mitral 424.0
pulmonary 424.3
tricuspid 424.2
kidney (see also Hypertension,
kidney) 403.90
Mönckeberg's 440.20
medial NEC 440.20
nephrosclerosis (see also
Hypertension, kidney)
403.90
pulmonary (idiopathic) 416.0
renal (see also Hypertension,
kidney) 403.90
arterioles (see also Hypertension,
kidney) 403.90
specified artery NEC 440.8
with gangrene 440.8 [785.4]
with
gangrene 440.24
psychosis (see also Psychosis,
arteriosclerotic) 290.40
ulceration 440.23
Arteriospasm 443.9
Arteritis 447.6
cranial (left) (right) 446.5
giant cell 446.5
necrosing or necrotizing 446.0
nodosa 446.0
temporal 446.5

Arthophyte (see also Loose, body,
joint) 718.1☑

Note—Use the following fifth-digit
subclassification with categories 711-
712, 715-716, 718, 719.0-719.6,
719.8, 719.9:
0   site unspecified
1   shoulder region
2   upper arm
3   forearm
4   hand
5   pelvic region and thigh
6   lower leg
7   ankle and foot
8   other specified sites
9   multiple sites

Arthralgia (see also Pain, joint)
719.4☑
allergic (see also Pain, joint)
719.4☑
psychogenic 307.89
Arthritis, arthritic (acute) (chronic)
(subacute) 716.9☑
ankylosing (crippling) (spine) 720.0
atrophic 714.0
spine 720.9
back (see also Arthritis, spine)
721.90
Bechterew's (ankylosing
spondylitis) 720.0
cervical, cervicodorsal (see also
Spondylosis, cervical) 721.0
Charcôt's 094.0 [713.5]
diabetic 250.6☑ [713.5]
due to secondary diabetes
249.6☑ [713.5]

Note—Use the following fifth-digit
subclassification with category 250:
0   type II [non-insulin dependent
type] [NIDDM type] [adult-onset
type] or unspecified type, not
stated as uncontrolled
1   type I [insulin dependent type]
[IDDM type] [juvenile type], not
stated as uncontrolled
2   type II [non-insulin dependent
type] [NIDDM type] [adult-onset
type] or unspecified type,
uncontrolled
3   type I [insulin dependent type]
[IDDM] [juvenile type],
uncontrolled

syringomyelic 336.0 [713.5]
tabetic 094.0 [713.5]
coccyx 721.8
cricoarytenoid 478.79
deformans (see also Osteoarthrosis)
715.9☑
spine 721.90
with myelopathy 721.91
degenerative (see also
Osteoarthrosis) 715.9☑
idiopathic 715.09
polyarticular 715.09
spine 721.90
with myelopathy 721.91
dermatoarthritis, lipoid 272.8
[713.0]
due to or associated with
acromegaly 253.0 [713.0]
amyloidosis 277.39 [713.7]

Arthritis, arthritic—continued
due to or associated with—
continued
colitis, ulcerative (see also Colitis,
ulcerative) 556.9 [713.1]
cowpox 051.01 [711.5]
dermatoarthritis, lipoid 272.8
[713.0]
dermatological disorder NEC
709.9 [713.3]
diabetes 250.6☑ [713.5]
due to secondary diabetes
249.6☑ [713.5]
endocrine disorder NEC 259.9
[713.0]
enteritis NEC 009.1 [711.3]☑
regional (see also Enteritis,
regional) 555.9 [713.1]
erythema
multiforme 695.10 [713.3]
nodosum 695.2 [713.3]
gastrointestinal condition NEC
569.9 [713.1]
gout 274.00
hematological disorder NEC
289.9 [713.2]
hemochromatosis 275.0 [713.0]
hemoglobinopathy NEC (see
also Disease, hemoglobin)
282.7 [713.2]
hemophilia (see also
Hemophilia) 286.0
[713.2]
Henoch (-Schönlein) purpura
287.0 [713.6]
human parvovirus 079.83
[711.5]
parvovirus B19 079.83
[711.5]
hyperparathyroidism 252.0
[713.0]
hypersensitivity reaction NEC
995.3 [713.6]
hypogammaglobulinemia (see
also Hypogamma-
globulinemia) 279.00
[713.0]
hypothyroidism NEC 244.9
[713.0]
lipoid dermatoarthritis 272.8
[713.0]
Mediterranean fever, familial
277.31 [713.7]
metabolic disorder NEC 277.9
[713.0]
multiple myelomatosis
(M9730/3) 203.0☑
[713.2]
neurological disorder NEC 349.9
[713.5]
ochronosis 270.2 [713.0]
myotonic congenital,
recessive form 359.22
regional enteritis (see also
Enteritis, regional) 555.9
[713.1]
respiratory disorder NEC 519.9
[713.4]
sarcoidosis 135 [713.7]
serum sickness 999.5 [713.6]
syringomyelia 336.0 [713.5]
thalassemia 282.49 [713.2]
ulcerative colitis (see also Colitis,
ulcerative) 556.9 [713.1]

Arthritis, arthritic—continued
gouty 274.00
acute 274.01
hypertrophic (see also
Osteoarthrosis) 715.9☑
spine 721.90
with myelopathy 721.91
in caisson disease 993.3 [713.8]
infectious or infective (acute)
(chronic) (subacute) NEC
711.9☑

Note—Use the following fifth-digit
subclassification with categories 711-
712, 715-716, 718, 719.0-719.6,
719.8, 719.9:
0   site unspecified
1   shoulder region
2   upper arm
3   forearm
4   hand
5   pelvic region and thigh
6   lower leg
7   ankle and foot
8   other specified sites
9   multiple sites

spine 720.9
juvenile rheumatoid (chronic)
(polyarticular) 714.30
acute 714.31
monoarticular 714.33
pauciarticular 714.32
lumbar (see also Spondylosis,
lumbar) 721.3
neuropathic (Charcôt's) 094.0
[713.5]
diabetic 250.6☑ [713.5]
due to secondary diabetes 249.6☑
[713.5]

Note—Use the following fifth-digit
subclassification with category 250:
0   type II [non-insulin dependent
type] [NIDDM type] [adult-onset
type] or unspecified type, not
stated as uncontrolled
1   type I [insulin dependent type]
[IDDM type] [juvenile type], not
stated as uncontrolled
2   type II [non-insulin dependent
type] [NIDDM type] [adult-onset
type] or unspecified type,
uncontrolled
3   type I [insulin dependent type]
[IDDM] [juvenile type],
uncontrolled

nonsyphilitic NEC 349.9 [713.5]
syringomyelic 336.0 [713.5]
tabetic 094.0 [713.5]
nodosa (see also Osteoarthrosis)
715.9☑
spine 721.90
with myelopathy 721.91
nonpyogenic NEC 716.9☑
spine 721.90
with myelopathy 721.91
ochronotic 270.2 [713.0]
palindromic (see also Rheumatism,
palindromic) 719.3☑
postrheumatic, chronic (Jaccoud's)
714.4
primary progressive 714.0
spine 720.9

ICD-9-CM Index

Arthritis, arthritic—*continued*
proliferative 714.0
  spine 720.0
rheumatic 714.0
  chronic 714.0
    spine 720.9
rheumatoid (nodular) 714.0
  aortitis 714.89
  carditis 714.2
  heart disease 714.2
  juvenile (chronic) (polyarticular)
    714.30
    acute 714.31
    monoarticular 714.33
    pauciarticular 714.32
  spine 720.0
  with
    splenoadenomegaly and
      leukopenia 714.1
    visceral or systemic
      involvement 714.2
sacral, sacroiliac, sacrococcygeal
  (*see also* Spondylosis, sacral)
  721.3
senile or senescent (*see also*
  Osteoarthrosis) 715.9☑

*Note—Use the following fifth-digit
subclassification with categories 711-
712, 715-716, 718, 719.0-719.6,
719.8, 719.9:*

0 *site unspecified*
1 *shoulder region*
2 *upper arm*
3 *forearm*
4 *hand*
5 *pelvic region and thigh*
6 *lower leg*
7 *ankle and foot*
8 *other specified sites*
9 *multiple sites*

    spine 721.90
      with myelopathy 721.91
    serum (nontherapeutic)
      (therapeutic) 999.5 [713.6]
    spine 721.90
      atrophic 720.9
      degenerative 721.90
        with myelopathy 721.91
      hypertrophic (with deformity)
        721.90
        with myelopathy 721.91
      infectious or infective NEC
        720.9
      Marie-Strümpell 720.0
      nonpyogenic 721.90
        with myelopathy 721.91
      pyogenic 720.9
      rheumatoid 720.0
      traumatic (old) 721.7
      tuberculous (*see also*
        Tuberculosis) 015.0☑
        [720.81]
      with myelopathy 721.91
    syphilitic 094.0 [713.5]
      congenital 090.49 [713.5]
    syphilitica deformans (Charcôt)
      094.0 [713.5]
    thoracic (*see also* Spondylosis,
      thoracic) 721.2
    urica, uratic 274.00
    vertebral (*see also* Arthritis, spine)
      721.90
    von Bechterew's 720.0

Arthrodesis status V45.4
Arthrodynia (*see also* Pain, joint)
  719.4☑

*Note—Use the following fifth-digit
subclassification with categories 711-
712, 715-716, 718, 719.0-719.6,
719.8, 719.9:*

0 *site unspecified*
1 *shoulder region*
2 *upper arm*
3 *forearm*
4 *hand*
5 *pelvic region and thigh*
6 *lower leg*
7 *ankle and foot*
8 *other specified sites*
9 *multiple sites*

  psychogenic 307.89
Arthrodysplasia 755.9
Arthrofibrosis, joint (*see also*
  Ankylosis) 718.5☑
Arthrogryposis 728.3
  multiplex, congenita 754.89
Arthrolithiasis 274.00
Arthrokatadysis 715.35
Arthropathy (*see also* Arthritis)
  716.9☑

*Note—Use the following fifth-digit
subclassification with categories 711-
712, 715-716, 718, 719.0-719.6,
719.8, 719.9:*

0 *site unspecified*
1 *shoulder region*
2 *upper arm*
3 *forearm*
4 *hand*
5 *pelvic region and thigh*
6 *lower leg*
7 *ankle and foot*
8 *other specified sites*
9 *multiple sites*

  Charcôt's 094.0 [713.5]
    diabetic 250.6☑ [713.5]
    due to secondary diabetes
      249.6☑ [713.5]

*Note—The following fifth-digit
subclassification is for use with category
249:*

0 *not stated as controlled, or
   unspecified*
1 *uncontrolled*

  syringomyelic 336.0 [713.5]
  tabetic 094.0 [713.5]
  gouty 274.00
    acute 274.01
    chronic (without mention of
      tophus (tophi)) 274.02
      with tophus (tophi) 274.03
  neurogenic, neuropathic
    (Charcôt's) (tabetic) 094.0
    [713.5]
    diabetic 250.6☑ [713.5]
    due to secondary diabetes
      249.6☑ [713.5]

Arthropathy—*continued*

*Note—Use the following fifth-digit
subclassification with category 250:*

0 *type II [non-insulin dependent
   type] [NIDDM type] [adult-onset
   type] or unspecified type, not
   stated as uncontrolled*
1 *type I [insulin dependent type]
   [IDDM type] [juvenile type], not
   stated as uncontrolled*
2 *type II [non-insulin dependent
   type] [NIDDM type] [adult-onset
   type] or unspecified type,
   uncontrolled*
3 *type I [insulin dependent type]
   [IDDM] [juvenile type],
   uncontrolled*

    nonsyphilitic NEC 349.9 [713.5]
    syringomyelic 336.0 [713.5]
  postrheumatic, chronic (Jaccoud's)
    714.4
  syringomyelia 336.0 [713.5]
  tabes dorsalis 094.0 [713.5]
  tabetic 094.0 [713.5]
  uric acid 274.00
Arthrophytis 719.80
  ankle 719.87
  elbow 719.82
  foot 719.87
  hand 719.84
  hip 719.85
  knee 719.86
  multiple sites 719.89
  pelvic region 719.85
  shoulder (region) 719.81
  specified site NEC 719.88
  wrist 719.83
Arthrosis (deformans) (degenerative)
  (*see also* Osteoarthrosis)
  715.9☑

*Note—Use the following fifth-digit
subclassification with categories 711-
712, 715-716, 718, 719.0-719.6,
719.8, 719.9:*

0 *site unspecified*
1 *shoulder region*
2 *upper arm*
3 *forearm*
4 *hand*
5 *pelvic region and thigh*
6 *lower leg*
7 *ankle and foot*
8 *other specified sites*
9 *multiple sites*

  Charcôt's 094.0 [713.5]
  polyarticular 715.09
  spine (*see also* Spondylosis) 721.90
Arthus' phenomenon 995.21
  due to
    correct substance properly
      administered 995.21
Articular—*see also* condition
  spondylolisthesis 756.12
Astasia (-asbasia) 307.9
  hysterical 300.11
Asterixis 781.3
Asthenia, asthenic 780.79
  cardiac (*see also* Failure, heart)
    428.9
    psychogenic 306.2

Asthenia, asthenic—*continued*
  cardiovascular (*see also* Failure,
    heart) 428.9
    psychogenic 306.2
  heart (*see also* Failure, heart) 428.9
    psychogenic 306.2
  hysterical 300.11
  myocardial (*see also* Failure, heart)
    428.9
    psychogenic 306.2
  nervous 300.5
  neurocirculatory 306.2
  neurotic 300.5
    psychogenic 300.5
  psychoneurotic 300.5
  psychophysiologic 300.5
  reaction, psychoneurotic 300.5
  Stiller's 780.79
Asthenopia 368.13
  hysterical (muscular) 300.11
  psychogenic 306.7
Asthma, asthmatic (bronchial)
  (catarrh) (spasmodic) 493.9☑

*Note—Use the following fifth-digit
subclassification with category 493:*

0 *unspecified*
1 *with status asthmaticus*
2 *with (acute) exacerbation*

  cardiac (*see also* Failure, ventricular,
    left) 428.1
  cardiobronchial (*see also* Failure,
    ventricular, left) 428.1
  cardiorenal (*see also* Hypertension,
    cardiorenal) 404.90
  colliers' 500
  cough variant 493.82
  due to
    inhalation of fumes 506.3
  eosinophilic 518.3
  exercise induced bronchospasm
    493.81
  grinders' 502
  heart (*see also* Failure, ventricular,
    left) 428.1
  meat-wrappers' 506.9
  Millar's (laryngismus stridulus)
    478.75
  millstone makers' 502
  miners' 500
  Monday morning 504
  pneumoconiotic (occupational)
    NEC 505
  potters' 502
  psychogenic 316 [493.9]☑
  pulmonary eosinophilic 518.3
  red cedar 495.8
  Rostan's (*see also* Failure,
    ventricular, left) 428.1
  sandblasters' 502
  sequoiosis 495.8
  stonemasons' 502
  Wichmann's (laryngismus stridulus)
    478.75
  wood 495.8
Astroblastoma (M9430/3)
  nose 748.1
Astrocytoma (cystic) (M9400/3)
  nose 748.1
Astroglioma (M9400/3)
  nose 748.1
Asymmetrical breathing 786.09
Asymmetry—*see also* Distortion
  chest 786.9
Asynergia 781.3

Asynergy 781.3
Asystole (heart) (*see also* Arrest, cardiac) 427.5
Ataxia, ataxy, ataxic 781.3
  acute 781.3
  brain 331.89
  cerebellar 334.3
    hereditary (Marie's) 334.2
    in
      alcoholism 303.9☑ *[334.4]*

Note—Use the following fifth-digit subclassification with category 303:
0 *unspecified*
1 *continuous*
2 *episodic*
3 *in remission*

      myxedema (*see also* Myxedema) 244.9 *[334.4]*
      neoplastic disease NEC 239.9 *[334.4]*
  cerebral 331.89
  family, familial 334.2
    cerebral (Marie's) 334.2
    spinal (Friedreich's) 334.0
  Friedreich's (heredofamilial) (spinal) 334.0
  frontal lobe 781.3
  gait 781.2
    hysterical 300.11
  general 781.3
  hereditary NEC 334.2
    cerebellar 334.2
    spastic 334.1
    spinal 334.0
  heredofamilial (Marie's) 334.2
  hysterical 300.11
  locomotor (progressive) 094.0
    diabetic 250.6☑ *[337.1]*
      due to secondary diabetes 249.6☑ *[337.1]*

Note—Use the following fifth-digit subclassification with category 250:
0 *type II [non-insulin dependent type] [NIDDM type] [adult-onset type] or unspecified type, not stated as uncontrolled*
1 *type I [insulin dependent type] [IDDM type] [juvenile type], not stated as uncontrolled*
2 *type II [non-insulin dependent type] [NIDDM type] [adult-onset type] or unspecified type, uncontrolled*
3 *type I [insulin dependent type] [IDDM] [juvenile type], uncontrolled*

  Marie's (cerebellar) (heredofamilial) 334.2
  Sanger-Brown's 334.2
  spastic 094.0
    hereditary 334.1
  spinal
    hereditary 334.0
  telangiectasia 334.8
Ataxia-telangiectasia 334.8

Atelectasis (absorption collapse) (complete) (compression) (massive) (partial) (postinfective) (pressure collapse) (pulmonary) (relaxation) 518.0
  newborn (congenital) (partial) 770.5
    primary 770.4
  primary 770.4
Atelomyelia 742.59
Athetosis (acquired) 781.0
  bilateral 333.79
  congenital (bilateral) 333.6
  double 333.71
  unilateral 781.0
Atonia, atony, atonic
  abdominal wall 728.2
  bladder (sphincter) 596.4
    neurogenic NEC 596.54
      with cauda equina syndrome 344.61
  vesical 596.4
Atresia, atretic (congenital) 759.89
  auditory canal (external) 744.02
  bronchus 748.3
  canal, ear 744.02
  choana 748.0
  ear canal 744.02
  epiglottis 748.3
  glottis 748.3
  larynx 748.3
  lung 748.5
  nares (anterior) (posterior) 748.0
  nose, nostril 748.0
  osseous meatus (ear) 744.03
  trachea 748.3
At risk for falling V15.88
Atrophia—*see also* Atrophy
  unguium 703.8
Atrophy, atrophic
  Aran-Duchenne muscular 335.21
  arm 728.2
  arthrditis 714.0
    spine 720.9
  bone (senile) 733.99
    due to
      disuse 733.7
      infection 733.99
    posttraumatic 733.99
  brain (cortex) (progressive) 331.9
    Alzheimer's 331.0
    circumscribed (Pick's) 331.11
      with dementia
        without behavioral disturbance 331.11 *[294.10]*
        with behavioral disturbance 331.11 *[294.11]*
    senile 331.2
    with dementia 290.10
  cartilage (infectional) (joint) 733.99
  cast, plaster of Paris 728.2
  Charcôt-Marie-Tooth 356.1
  Cruveilhier's 335.21
  Déjérine-Thomas 333.0
  dacryosialadenopathy 710.2
  disuse
    bone 733.7
    muscle 728.2
  Duchenne-Aran 335.21
  emphysema, lung 492.8
  facioscapulohumeral (Landouzy-Déjérine) 359.1

Atrophy, atrophic—*continued*
  kidney (senile) (*see also* Sclerosis, renal) 587
    with hypertension (*see also* Hypertension, kidney) 403.90
  Landouzy-Déjérine 359.1
  laryngitis, infection 476.0
  larynx 478.79
  lung (senile) 518.89
    congenital 748.69
  muscle, muscular 728.2
    disuse 728.2
    Duchenne-Aran 335.21
    extremity (lower) (upper) 728.2
    familial spinal 335.11
    general 728.2
    idiopathic 728.2
    infantile spinal 335.0
    myelopathic (progressive) 335.10
    myotonic 359.21
    neuritic 356.1
    neuropathic (peroneal) (progressive) 356.1
    peroneal 356.1
    primary (idiopathic) 728.2
    progressive (familial) (hereditary) (pure) 335.21
      adult (spinal) 335.19
      infantile (spinal) 335.0
      juvenile (spinal) 335.11
      spinal 335.10
        adult 335.19
        Aran-Duchenne 335.10
        hereditary or familial 335.11
        infantile 335.0
    pseudohypertrophic 359.1
    spinal (progressive) 335.10
      adult 335.19
      Aran-Duchenne 335.21
      familial 335.11
      hereditary 335.11
      infantile 335.0
      juvenile 335.11
  myotatic 728.2
  myotonia 359.21
  nail 703.8
  nerve—*see also* Disorder, nerve
    accessory 352.4
    cranial 352.9
      first (olfactory) 352.0
      fifth (trigeminal) 350.8
      seventh (facial) 351.8
      ninth (glossopharyngeal) 352.2
      tenth (pneumogastric) (vagus) 352.3
      eleventh (accessory) 352.4
      twelfth (hypoglossal) 352.5
    facial 351.8
    glossopharyngeal 352.2
    hypoglossal 352.5
    olfactory 352.0
    peripheral 355.9
    pneumogastric 352.3
    trigeminal 350.8
    vagus (pneumogastric) 352.3
  nervous system, congenital 742.8
  neuritic (*see also* Disorder, nerve) 355.9
  neurogenic NEC 355.9
  olivopontocerebellar 333.0
  palsy, diffuse 335.20

Atrophy, atrophic—*continued*
  paralysis 355.9
  polyarthritis 714.0
  pseudohypertrophic 359.1
  scar NEC 709.2
  sclerosis, lobar (of brain) 331.0
    with dementia
      without behavioral disturbance 331.0 *[294.10]*
      with behavioral disturbance 331.0 *[294.11]*
  spinal (cord) 336.8
    acute 336.8
    muscular (chronic) 335.10
      adult 335.19
      familial 335.11
      juvenile 335.10
    paralysis 335.10
  spine (column) 733.99
  Sudeck's 733.7
  thenar, partial 354.0
  turbinate 733.99
  ulcer (*see also* Ulcer, skin) 707.9
  vertebra (senile) 733.99
  Werdnig-Hoffmann 335.0
Attack
  apoplectic (*see also* Disease, cerebrovascular, acute) 436
  benign shuddering 333.93
  cataleptic 300.11
  cerebral (*see also* Disease, cerebrovascular, acute) 436
  hemiplegia (*see also* Disease, cerebrovascular, acute) 436
  hysterical 300.11
  panic 300.01
  paralysis (*see also* Disease, cerebrovascular, acute) 436
  unconsciousness 780.2
    hysterical 300.11
Attention to
  dressing
    wound V58.30
      nonsurgical V58.30
      surgical V58.31
  surgical dressings V58.31
Auriculotemporal syndrome 350.8
Autonomic, autonomous
  bladder 596.54
    neurogenic NEC 596.54
      with cauda equina 344.61
  dysreflexia 337.3
  faciocephalalgia (*see also* Neuropathy, peripheral, autonomic) 337.9
  hysterical seizure 300.11
  imbalance (*see also* Neuropathy, peripheral, autonomic) 337.9

B

Baastrup's syndrome 721.5
Babinski-Nageotte syndrome 344.89
Backache (postural) 724.5
  psychogenic 307.89
  sacroiliac 724.6
Backknee (*see also* Genu, recurvatum) 736.5
Bacterid, bacteride (Andrews' pustular) 686.8
Bagassosis (occupational) 495.1

Bagratuni's syndrome (temporal arteritis) 446.5
Baker's
  cyst (knee) 727.51
Bal-'s disease or concentric sclerosis 341.1
Balbuties, balbutio 307.0
Ballooning posterior leaflet syndrome 424.0
Bamboo spine 720.0
Bar
  calcaneocuboid 755.67
  calcaneonavicular 755.67
  cubonavicular 755.67
  talocalcaneal 755.67
Barcoo disease or rot (*see also* Ulcer, skin) 707.9
Baritosis 503
Barium lung disease 503
Barlow's syndrome (meaning mitral valve prolapse) 424.0
Barré-Guillain syndrome 357.0
Barré-Liéou syndrome (posterior cervical sympathetic) 723.2
Barrel chest 738.3
Baseball finger 842.13
Bassen-Kornzweig syndrome (abetalipoproteinemia) 272.5
Batten's disease, retina 330.1 [362.71]
Batten-Mayou disease 330.1 [362.71]
Batten-Steinert syndrome 359.21
Battle exhaustion (*see also* Reaction, stress, acute) 308.9
Bauxite
  fibrosis (of lung) 503
  workers' disease 503
Beard's disease (neurasthenia) 300.5
Beat
  elbow 727.2
  hand 727.2
  knee 727.2
Beau's
  lines (transverse furrows on fingernails) 703.8
Bechterew's disease (ankylosing spondylitis) 720.0
Bechterew-Strümpell-Marie syndrome (ankylosing spondylitis) 720.0
Becker's
  disease
    idiopathic mural endomyocardial disease) 425.2
    myotonia congenita, recessive form 359.22
  dystrophy 359.22
Bed confinement status V49.84
Bedsore (*see also* Ulcer, pressure)707.00
  with gangrene 707.00 [785.4]
Bedwetting (*see also* Enuresis) 788.36
Beer-drinkers' heart (disease) 425.5
Bekhterev's disease (ankylosing spondylitis) 720.0
Bekhterev-Strümpell-Marie syndrome (ankylosing spondylitis) 720.0

Bell's
  palsy, paralysis 351.0
  spasm 351.0
Benedikt's syndrome (paralysis) 344.89
Bennett's
  fracture (closed) 815.01
Bent
  back (hysterical) 300.11
Bereavement V62.82
  as adjustment reaction 309.0
Berger's paresthesia (lower limb) 782.0
Bergeron's disease (hysteroepilepsy) 300.11
Beriberi (acute) (atrophic) (chronic) (dry) (subacute) (wet) 265.0
  heart (disease) 265.0 [425.7]
  neuritis 265.0 [357.4]
  with polyneuropathy 265.0 [357.4]
Bernard-Horner syndrome (*see also* Neuropathy, peripheral, autonomic) 337.9
Bernhardt's disease or paresthesia 355.1
Bernhardt-Roth disease or syndrome (paresthesia) 355.1
Bernheim's syndrome (*see also* Failure, heart) 428.0
Bertolotti's syndrome (sacralization of fifth lumbar vertebra) 756.15
Berylliosis (acute) (chronic) (lung) (occupational) 503
Bifid (congenital)—*see also* Imperfect, closure
  epiglottis 748.3
  nose 748.1
  patella 755.64
  toe 755.66
Bifurcation (congenital)—*see also* Imperfect, closure
  trachea 748.3
  vertebra 756.19
Bing-Horton syndrome (histamine cephalgia) 339.00
Binswanger's disease or dementia 290.12
Biparta, bipartite—*see also* Imperfect, closure
Birt-Hogg-Dube syndrome 759.89
Black
  lung disease 500
Blast
  injury 869.0
    brain (*see also* Concussion, brain) 850.9
Bleb(s) 709.8
  emphysematous (bullous) (diffuse) (lung) (ruptured) (solitary) 492.0
  lung (ruptured) 492.0
    congenital 770.5
  subpleural (emphysematous) 492.0
Blind
  bronchus (congenital) 748.3
Blindness (acquired) (congenital) (both eyes) 369.00
  with deafness V49.85
  concussion 950.9
  due to
    injury NEC 950.9
  emotional 300.11
  hysterical 300.11
  traumatic NEC 950.9
  word (developmental) 315.01

Block
  alveolar capillary 516.3
  atrioventricular (AV) (incomplete) (partial) 426.10
    first degree (incomplete) 426.11
    Mobitz (incomplete)
      type II 426.12
    second dcgree (Mobitz type I) 426.13
    Mobitz (type) II 426.12
  auriculoventricular (*see also* Block, atrioventricular) 426.10
  bundle branch (complete) (false) (incomplete) 426.50
    left (complete) (main stem) 426.3
    anterior fascicular 426.2
    hemiblock 426.2
    incomplete 426.2
    posterior fascicular 426.2
  fascicular (left anterior) (left posterior) 426.2
  foramen Magendie (acquired) 331.3
  heart 426.9
    first degree (atrioventricular) 426.11
  nodal 426.10
  spinal cord 336.9
Blood
  pressure
    high (*see also* Hypertension) 401.9
  spitting (*see also* Hemoptysis) 786.3
Blount's disease (tibia vara) 732.4
BMI (body mass index)
  adult
    25.0-25.9 V85.21
    26.0-26.9 V85.22
    27.0-27.9 V85.23
    28.0-28.9 V85.24
    29.0-29.9 V85.25
    30.0-30.9 V85.30
    31.0-31.9 V85.31
    32.0-32.9 V85.32
    33.0-33.9 V85.33
    34.0-34.9 V85.34
    35.0-35.9 V85.35
    36.0-36.9 V85.36
    37.0-37.9 V85.37
    38.0-38.9 V85.38
    39.0-39.9 V85.39
    40 and over V85.4
    between 19-24 V85.1
    less than 19 V85.0
  pediatric
    5th percentile to less than 85th percentile for age V85.52
    85th percentile to less than 95th percentile for age V85.53
    greater than or equal to 95th percentile for age V85.54
    less than 5th percentile for age V58.51
Boder-Sedgwick syndrome (ataxia-telangiectasia) 334.8

Body, bodies
  fibrin, pleura 511.0
  loose
    joint (*see also* Loose, body, joint) 718.1 ☑

Note—Use the following fifth-digit subclassification with categories 711-712, 715-716, 718, 719.0-719.6, 719.8, 719.9:
  0 *site unspecified*
  1 *shoulder region*
  2 *upper arm*
  3 *forearm*
  4 *hand*
  5 *pelvic region and thigh*
  6 *lower leg*
  7 *ankle and foot*
  8 *other specified sites*
  9 *multiple sites*

  sheath, tendon 727.82
  mass index (BMI)
    adult
      25.0-25.9 V85.21
      26.0-26.9 V85.22
      27.0-27.9 V85.23
      28.0-28.9 V85.24
      29.0-29.9 V85.25
      30.0-30.9 V85.30
      31.0-31.9 V85.31
      32.0-32.9 V85.32
      33.0-33.9 V85.33
      34.0-34.9 V85.34
      35.0-35.9 V85.35
      36.0-36.9 V85.36
      37.0-37.9 V85.37
      38.0-38.9 V85.38
      39.0-39.9 V85.39
      40 and over V85.4
      between 19-24 V85.1
      less than 19 V85.0
    pediatric
      5th percentile to less than 85th percentile for age V85.52
      85th percentile to less than 95th percentile for age V85.53
      greater than or equal to 95th percentile for age V85.54
      less than 5th percentile for age V58.51
  rice (joint) (*see also* Loose, body, joint) 718.1 ☑
  rocking 307.3
Boeck's
  disease (sarcoidosis) 135
  lupoid (miliary) 135
  sarcoid 135
Bonvale Dam fever 780.79
Bony block of joint 718.80
  ankle 718.87
  elbow 718.82
  foot 718.87
  hand 718.84
  hip 718.85
  knee 718.86
  multiple sites 718.89
  pelvic region 718.85
  shoulder (region) 718.81
  specified site NEC 718.88
  wrist 718.83
BOOP (bronchiolitis obliterans organized pneumonia) 516.8

Bouffée délirante 298.3
Boutonniere
deformity (finger) 736.21
hand (intrinsic) 736.21
Bowing
femur 736.89
congenital 754.42
fibula 736.89
congenital 754.43
forearm 736.09
away from midline (cubitus
valgus) 736.01
toward midline (cubitus varus)
736.02
leg(s), long bones, congenital
754.44
radius 736.09
away from midline (cubitus
valgus) 736.01
toward midline (cubitus varus)
736.02
tibia 736.89
congenital 754.43
Bowleg(s) 736.42
congenital 754.44
Brachycephaly 756.0
Bradycardia 427.89
reflex 337.09
Bradykinesia 781.0
Bradypnea 786.09
Brain—see also condition
syndrome (acute) (chronic)
(nonpsychotic) (organic)
(with neurotic reaction) (with
behavioral reaction) (see also
Syndrome, brain) 310.9
with
presenile brain disease
290.10
psychosis, psychotic reaction
(see also Psychosis,
organic) 294.9
Brandt's syndrome (acrodermatitis
enteropathica) 686.8
Breath
holding spells 786.9
shortness 786.05
Breathing
asymmetrical 786.09
bronchial 786.09
exercises V57.0
labored 786.09
periodic 786.09
high altitude 327.22
tic 307.20
Breathlessness 786.09
Brevicollis 756.16
Brissaud's
motor-verbal tic 307.23
Brock's syndrome (atelectasis due
to enlarged lymph nodes) 518.0
Broken
arches 734
congenital 755.67
Bronchiectasis (cylindrical) (diffuse)
(fusiform) (localized)
(moniliform) (postinfectious)
(recurrent) (saccular) 494.0
congenital 748.61
with acute exacerbation 494.1
Bronchiolitis (acute) (infectious)
(subacute) 466.19
catarrhal (acute) (subacute) 466.19
chemical 506.0
chronic 506.4

Bronchiolitis—continued
chronic (obliterative) 491.8
fibrosa obliterans 491.8
influenzal 487.1
obliterans 491.8
with organizing pneumonia
(BOOP) 516.8
obliterative (chronic) (diffuse)
(subacute) 491.8
due to fumes or vapors 506.4
respiratory syncytial virus 466.11
with
bronchospasm or obstruction
466.19
influenza, flu, or grippe 487.1
Bronchitis (diffuse) (hypostatic)
(infectious) (inflammatory)
(simple) 490
acute or subacute 466.0
chemical (due to fumes or
vapors) 506.0
due to
fumes or vapors 506.0
radiation 508.8
with
bronchiectasis 494.1
bronchospasm 466.0
obstruction 466.0
tracheitis 466.0
arachidic 934.1
aspiration 507.0
due to fumes or vapors 506.0
asthmatic (acute) 493.90
with
acute exacerbation 493.92
status asthmaticus 493.91
capillary 466.19
chronic 491.8
with bronchospasm or
obstruction 466.19
catarrhal 490
chronic 491.0
chemical (acute) (subacute) 506.0
chronic 506.4
due to fumes or vapors (acute)
(subacute) 506.0
chronic 506.4
chronic 491.9
catarrhal 491.0
chemical (due to fumes and
vapors) 506.4
due to
fumes or vapors (chemical)
(inhalation) 506.4
radiation 508.8
tobacco smoking 491.0
mucopurulent 491.1
obstructive 491.20
with exacerbation (acute)
491.21
purulent 491.1
simple 491.0
specified type NEC 491.8
with
tracheitis (chronic) 491.8
croupous 466.0
due to fumes or vapors
506.0
with bronchospasm or
obstruction 466.0
emphysematous 491.20
with exacerbation (acute)
491.21
exudative 466.0
fetid (chronic) (recurrent) 491.1

Bronchitis—continued
fibrinous, acute or subacute 466.0
with bronchospasm or
obstruction 466.0
grippal 487.1
influenzal 487.1
membranous, acute or subacute
466.0
with bronchospasm or
obstruction 466.0
moulders' 502
mucopurulent (chronic) (recurrent)
491.1
acute or subacute 466.0
non-obstructive 491.0
obliterans 491.8
obstructive (chronic) 491.20
with exacerbation (acute)
491.21
pituitous 491.1
plastic (inflammatory) 466.0
pneumococcal, acute or subacute
466.0
with bronchospasm or
obstruction 466.0
pseudomembranous 466.0
purulent (chronic) (recurrent)
491.1
acute or subacute 466.0
with bronchospasm or
obstruction 466.0
putrid 491.1
senile 491.9
septic, acute or subacute 466.0
with bronchospasm or
obstruction 466.0
smokers' 491.0
suffocative, acute or subacute
466.0
suppurative (chronic) 491.1
acute or subacute 466.0
ulcerative 491.8
viral, acute or subacute 466.0
with
influenza, flu, or grippe 487.1
obstruction airway, chronic
491.20
with exacerbation (acute)
491.21
tracheitis 490
acute or subacute 466.0
with bronchospasm or
obstruction 466.0
chronic 491.8
Bronchoalveolitis 485
Bronchogenic carcinoma 162.9
Broncholithiasis 518.89
Bronchomalacia 748.3
Bronchorrhagia 786.3
newborn 770.3
Bronchorrhea (chronic) (purulent)
491.0
acute 466.0
Bronchospasm 519.11
acute 519.11
exercise induced 493.81
with
bronchiolitis
due to respiratory syn-cytial
virus 466.11
chronic obstructive pulmonary
disease (COPD) 496
Brown-Séquard's paralysis
(syndrome) 344.89
Bruck's disease 733.99

Bruxism 306.8
sleep related 327.53
Bubbly lung syndrome 770.7
Bucket handle fracture (semilunar
cartilage) (see also **Tear,
meniscus**) 836.2
**Budgerigar-fanciers' disease or
lung** 495.2
Büdinger-Ludloff-Läwen disease
717.89
Buerger's disease (thromboangiitis
obliterans) 443.1
Bulging fontanels (congenital)
756.0
Bulimia 783.6
nonorganic origin 307.51
Bulla(e) 709.8
lung (emphysematous) (solitary)
492.0
Bundle
branch block (complete) (false)
(incomplete) 426.50
left (see also Block, bundle
branch, left) 426.3
hemiblock 426.2
Burn (acid) (cathode ray) (caustic)
(chemical) (electric heating
appliance) (electricity) (fire)
(flame) (hot liquid or object)
(irradiation) (lime) (radiation)
(steam) (thermal) (x-ray) 949.0
abdomen, abdominal (muscle)
(wall) 942.03
second degree 942.23
third degree 942.33
deep 942.43
with loss of body part
942.53
ankle 945.03
second degree 945.23
third degree 945.33
deep 945.43
with loss of body part
945.53
arm(s) 943.00
multiple sites, except hand(s) or
wrist(s) 943.09
second degree 943.29
third degree 943.39
deep 943.49
with loss of body part
943.59
second degree 943.30
third degree 943.30
deep 943.40
with loss of body part
943.50
upper 943.03
second degree 943.23
third degree 943.33
deep 943.43
with loss of body part
943.53
axilla 943.04
second degree 943.24
third degree 943.34
deep 943.44
with loss of body part
943.54
back 942.04
second degree 942.24
third degree 942.34
deep 942.44
with loss of body part
942.54

Burn—*continued*
breast(s) 942.01
second degree 942.21
third degree 942.31
deep 942.41
with loss of body part 942.51
cheek (cutaneous) 941.07
second degree 941.27
third degree 941.37
deep 941.47
chest wall (anterior) 942.02
second degree 942.22
third degree 942.32
deep 942.42
with loss of body part 942.52
chin 941.04
second degree 941.24
third degree 941.34
deep 941.44
ear (auricle) (canal) (drum) (external) 941.01
second degree 941.21
third degree 941.31
deep 941.41
elbow 943.02
second degree 943.22
third degree 943.32
deep 943.42
with loss of body part 943.52
eye(s) (and adnexa) (only) 940.9
with
face, head, or neck 941.02
second degree 941.22
third degree 941.32
deep 941.42
finger (nail) (subungual) 944.01
multiple (digits) 944.03
second degree 944.23
third degree 944.33
deep 944.43
with loss of body part 944.53
second degree 944.21
third degree 944.31
deep 944.41
with loss of body part 944.51
with
thumb 944.04
second degree 944.24
third degree 944.34
deep 944.44
with loss of body part 944.54
foot 945.02
second degree 945.22
third degree 945.32
deep 945.42
with loss of body part 945.52
forearm(s) 943.01
second degree 943.21
third degree 943.31
deep 943.41
with loss of body part 943.51
forehead 941.07
second degree 941.27
third degree 941.37
deep 941.47

Burn—*continued*
genitourinary organs
external 942.05
second degree 942.25
third degree 942.35
deep 942.45
with loss of body part 942.55
gum 947.0
hand(s) (phalanges) (and wrist) 944.00
back (dorsal surface) 944.06
second degree 944.26
third degree 944.36
deep 944.46
with loss of body part 944.56
multiple sites 944.08
second degree 944.28
third degree 944.38
deep 944.48
with loss of body part 944.58
second degree 944.20
third degree 944.30
deep 944.40
with loss of body part 944.50
head (and face) 941.00
multiple sites 941.09
second degree 941.29
third degree 941.39
deep 941.49
second degree 941.20
third degree 941.30
deep 941.40
knee 945.05
second degree 945.25
third degree 945.35
deep 945.45
with loss of body part 945.55
leg 945.00
lower 945.04
second degree 945.24
third degree 945.34
deep 945.44
with loss of body part 945.54
multiple sites 945.09
second degree 945.29
third degree 945.39
deep 945.49
with loss of body part 945.59
second degree 945.20
third degree 945.30
deep 945.40
with loss of body part 945.50
lip(s) 941.03
second degree 941.23
third degree 941.33
deep 941.43
mouth 947.0
neck 941.08
second degree 941.28
third degree 941.38
deep 941.48
nose (septum) 941.05
second degree 941.25
third degree 941.35
deep 941.45
oronasopharynx 947.0
palate 947.0

Burn—*continued*
palm(s) 944.05
second degree 944.25
third degree 944.35
deep 944.45
with loss of a body part 944.55
pharynx 947.0
salivary (ducts) (glands) 947.0
scalp 941.06
second degree 941.26
third degree 941.36
deep 941.46
scapular region 943.06
second degree 943.26
third degree 943.36
deep 943.46
with loss of body part 943.56
shoulder(s) 943.05
second degree 943.25
third degree 943.35
deep 943.45
with loss of body part 943.55
thigh 945.06
second degree 945.26
third degree 945.36
deep 945.46
with loss of body part 945.56
throat 947.0
thumb(s) (nail) (subungual) 944.02
second degree 944.22
third degree 944.32
deep 944.42
with loss of body part 944.52
toe (nail) (subungual) 945.01
second degree 945.21
third degree 945.31
deep 945.41
with loss of body part 945.51
tongue 947.0
tonsil 947.0
leg 945.00
trunk 942.00
second degree 942.20
third degree 942.30
deep 942.40
with loss of body part 942.50
uvula 947.0
wrist(s) 944.07
second degree 944.27
third degree 944.37
deep 944.47
with loss of body part 944.57
Burning
sensation (*see also* Disturbance, sensation) 782.0
Bursitis NEC 727.3
Achilles tendon 726.71
adhesive 726.90
shoulder 726.0
ankle 726.79
buttock 726.5
calcaneal 726.79
collateral ligament
fibular 726.63
tibial 726.62
Duplay's 726.2
elbow 726.33

Bursitis NEC—*continued*
finger 726.8
foot 726.79
hand 726.4
hip 726.5
infrapatellar 726.69
ischiogluteal 726.5
knee 726.60
occupational NEC 727.2
olecranon 726.33
pes anserinus 726.61
popliteal 727.51
prepatellar 726.65
radiohumeral 727.3
scapulohumeral 726.19
adhesive 726.0
shoulder 726.10
adhesive 726.0
subacromial 726.19
adhesive 726.0
subcoracoid 726.19
subdeltoid 726.19
adhesive 726.0
subpatellar 726.69
toe 726.79
trochanteric area 726.5
wrist 726.4
Buschke's disease or scleredema (adultorum) 710.1
Buttonhole hand (intrinsic) 736.21
Byssinosis (occupational) 504

C

Céstan's syndrome 344.89
Céstan-Chenais paralysis 344.89
Cachexia 799.4
due to malnutrition 799.4
nervous 300.5
Calcaneal spur 726.73
Calcaneonavicular bar 755.67
Calcicosis (occupational) 502
Calcification
aorta 440.0
bronchus 519.19
bursa 727.82
cartilage (postinfectional) 733.99
disc, intervertebral 722.90
cervical, cervicothoracic 722.91
lumbar, lumbosacral 722.93
thoracic, thoracolumbar 722.92
fascia 728.89
intervertebral cartilage or disc (postinfectional) 722.90
cervical, cervicothoracic 722.91
lumbar, lumbosacral 722.93
thoracic, thoracolumbar 722.92
intraspinal ligament 728.89
joint 719.80
ankle 719.87
elbow 719.82
foot 719.87
hand 719.84
hip 719.85
knee 719.86
multiple sites 719.89
pelvic region 719.85
shoulder (region) 719.81
specified site NEC 719.88
wrist 719.83
larynx (senile) 478.79
ligament 728.89
intraspinal 728.89
knee (medial collateral) 717.89

Calcification—continued
  lung 518.89
    active 518.89
    postinfectional 518.89
  massive (paraplegic) 728.10
  medial NEC (see also
    Arteriosclerosis, extremities)
    440.20
  muscle 728.10
    heterotopic, postoperative
      728.13
  periarticular 728.89
  pleura 511.0
    postinfectional 518.89
  Rider's bone 733.99
  semilunar cartilage 717.89
  tendon (sheath) 727.82
    with bursitis, synovitis or
      tenosynovitis 727.82
Calcinosis (generalized) (interstitial)
  (tumoral) (universalis) 275.49
  intervertebralis 275.49 [722.90]
  Raynaud's
    phenomenonsclerodactylytel
    angiectasis (CRST) 710.1
Calcium
  deposits—see also Calcification, by
    site
    in bursa 727.82
    in tendon (sheath) 727.82
      with bursitis, synovitis or
        tenosynovitis 727.82
Calculus, calculi, calculous 592.9
  bronchus 518.89
  lung 518.89
  pulmonary 518.89
Callositas, callosity (infected) 700
Callus (infected) 700
Camptocormia 300.11
Camptodactyly (congenital) 755.59
Canavan's disease 330.0
Cannabinosis 504
Caplan's syndrome 714.81
Caplan-Colinet syndrome 714.81
Capsulitis (joint) 726.90
  adhesive (shoulder) 726.0
  hip 726.5
  knee 726.60
  wrist 726.4
Caput
  crepitus 756.0
Carcinoid (tumor) (M8240/1) - see
  Tumor, carcinoid
Carcinoma (M8010/3)—see also
  Neoplasm, by site, malignant
  neuroendocrine
    high grade (M8240/3) 209.30
    malignant poorly differentiated
      (M8240/3) 209.30
Cardialgia (see also Pain, precordial)
  786.51
Cardiomegaly (see also Hypertrophy,
  cardiac) 429.3
  hypertensive (see also
    Hypertension, heart) 402.90
Cardiomyopathy (congestive)
  (constrictive) (familial)
  (infiltrative) (obstructive)
  (restrictive) (sporadic) 425.4
  alcoholic 425.5
  amyloid 277.39 [425.7]
  beriberi 265.0 [425.7]
  cobalt-beer 425.5
  congenital 425.3

Cardiomyopathy—continued
  due to
    amyloidosis 277.39 [425.7]
    beriberi 265.0 [425.7]
    cardiac glycogenosis 271.0
      [425.7]
    Friedreich's ataxia 334.0 [425.8]
    mucopolysaccharidosis 277.5
      [425.7]
    myotonia atrophica 359.21
      [425.8]
    progressive muscular dystrophy
      359.1 [425.8]
    sarcoidosis 135 [425.8]
  glycogen storage 271.0 [425.7]
  hypertrophic
    nonobstructive 425.4
    obstructive 425.1
  idiopathic (concentric) 425.4
  in
    sarcoidosis 135 [425.8]
  ischemic 414.8
  metabolic NEC 277.9 [425.7]
    amyloid 277.39 [425.7]
    thyrotoxic (see also
      Thyrotoxicosis) 242.9☑
      [425.7]

Note—Use the following fifth-digit
subclassification with category 242:
0 without mention of thyrotoxic crisis
   or storm
1 with mention of thyrotoxic crisis or
   storm

    thyrotoxicosis (see also
      Thyrotoxicosis) 242.9☑
      [425.7]
  nutritional 269.9 [425.7]
    beriberi 265.0 [425.7]
  obscure of Africa 425.2
  primary 425.4
  secondary 425.9
  stress induced 429.83
  takotsubo 429.83
  thyrotoxic (see also Thyrotoxicosis)
    242.9☑ [425.7]
  toxic NEC 425.9
  tuberculous (see also Tuberculosis)
    017.9☑ [425.8]
Cardioneurosis 306.2
Cardiopathia nigra 416.0
Cardiopathy (see also Disease, heart)
  429.9
  hypertensive (see also Hyper-
    tension, heart) 402.90
  idiopathic 425.4
  mucopolysaccharidosis 277.5
    [425.7]
Carditis (acute) (bacterial) (chronic)
  (subacute) 429.89
  hypertensive (see also Hyper-
    tension, heart) 402.90
  rheumatoid 714.2
Carotid body or sinus syndrome
  337.01
Carotidynia 337.01
Carpal tunnel syndrome 354.0
Carpopedal spasm (see also Tetany)
  781.7
Carpoptosis 736.05
Catalepsy 300.11
  hysterical 300.11
Cataphasia 307.0

Catarrh, catarrhal (inflammation)
  (see also condition) 460
  bronchial 490
    acute 466.0
    chronic 491.0
    subacute 466.0
  chest (see also Bronchitis) 490
  epidemic 487.1
  fibrinous acute 466.0
  larynx (see also Laryngitis, chronic)
    476.0
  lung (see also Bronchitis) 490
    acute 466.0
    chronic 491.0
  pneumococcal, acute 466.0
  pulmonary (see also Bronchitis) 490
    acute 466.0
    chronic 491.0
  tracheitis 464.10
    with obstruction 464.11
Catastrophe, cerebral (see also
  Disease, cerebrovascular, acute)
  436
Catatonia, catatonic (acute)
  781.99
  Churg-Strauss syndrome 446.4
  due to or associated with physical
    condition 293.89
Cauda equina—see also condition
  syndrome 344.60
Causalgia 355.9
  lower limb 355.71
  upper limb 354.4
Cavare's disease (familial periodic
  paralysis) 359.3
Cavovarus foot, congenital 754.59
Cavus foot (congenital) 754.71
  acquired 736.73
Cellulitis (diffuse) (with
  lymphangitis) (see also Abscess)
  682.9
  abdominal wall 682.2
  ankle 682.6
  arm (any part, above wrist) 682.3
  axilla 682.3
  back (any part) 682.2
  buttock 682.5
  cervical (neck region) 682.1
  chest wall 682.2
  chronic NEC 682.9
  digit 681.9
  drainage site (following operation)
    998.59
  finger (intrathecal) (periosteal)
    (subcutaneous)
    (subcuticular) 681.00
  flank 682.2
  foot (except toe) 682.7
  forearm 682.3
  gangrenous (see also Gangrene)
    785.4
  glottis 478.71
  gluteal (region) 682.5
  groin 682.2
  hand (except finger or thumb)
    682.4
  head (except face) NEC 682.8
  heel 682.7
  hip 682.6
  knee 682.6
  larynx 478.71
  leg, except foot 682.6
  multiple sites NEC 682.9
  neck (region) 682.1
  pectoral (region) 682.2

Cellulitis—continued
  perineal, perineum 682.2
  phlegmonous NEC 682.9
  scalp (any part) 682.8
  septic NEC 682.9
  shoulder 682.3
  specified sites NEC 682.8
  suppurative NEC 682.9
  thigh 682.6
  thumb (intrathecal) (periosteal)
    (subcutaneous)
    (subcuticular) 681.00
  toe (intrathecal) (periosteal)
    (subcutaneous)
    (subcuticular) 681.10
  trunk 682.2
  umbilical 682.2
  wrist 682.4
Cephalgia, cephalagia (see also
  Headache) 784.0
  histamine 339.00 ☑
  nonorganic origin 307.81
  psychogenic 307.81
  tension 307.81
Cerebromacular degeneration
  330.1
Cervical—see also condition
  auricle 744.43
Cervicalgia 723.1
Cervicoaural fistula 744.49
Chalicosis (occupational)
  (pulmonum) 502
Change(s) (of)—see also Removal of
  bone 733.90
    diabetic 250.8☑ [731.8]
    due to secondary diabetes
      249.8☑ [731.8]

Note—Use the following fifth-digit
subclassification with category 250:
0 type II [non-insulin dependent
   type] [NIDDM type] [adult-onset
   type] or unspecified type, not
   stated as uncontrolled
1 type I [insulin dependent type]
   [IDDM type] [juvenile type], not
   stated as uncontrolled
2 type II [non-insulin dependent
   type] [NIDDM type] [adult-onset
   type] or unspecified type,
   uncontrolled
3 type I [insulin dependent type]
   [IDDM] [juvenile type],
   uncontrolled

    in disease, unknown cause
      733.90
  cardiorenal (vascular) (see also
    Hyper-tension, cardiorenal)
    404.90
  coronary (see also Ischemia, heart)
    414.9
  degenerative
    spine or vertebra (see also
      Spondylosis) 721.90
  dressing
    wound V58.30
      nonsurgial V58.30
      surgical V58.31
  hip joint 718.95
  hyperplastic larynx 478.79
  joint (see also Derangement, joint)
    718.90
    sacroiliac 724.6
  peripheral nerve 355.9
  sacroiliac joint 724.6

Cellulitis—*continued*
sensory (*see also* Disturbance, sensation) 782.0
spinal cord 336.9
trophic 355.9
arm NEC 354.9
leg NEC 355.8
lower extremity NEC 355.8
upper extremity NEC 354.9
vasomotor 443.9
voice 784.49
psychogenic 306.1
Changing sleep-work schedule, affecting sleep 307.45
Charcôt's
arthropathy 094.0 [713.5]
joint (disease) 094.0 [713.5]
diabetic 250.6☑ [713.5]
due to secondary diabetes 249.6☑ [713.5]

Note—Use the following fifth-digit subclassification with category 250:
0 type II [non-insulin dependent type] [NIDDM type] [adult-onset type] or unspecified type, not stated as uncontrolled
1 type I [insulin dependent type] [IDDM type] [juvenile type], not stated as uncontrolled
2 type II [non-insulin dependent type] [NIDDM type] [adult-onset type] or unspecified type, uncontrolled
3 type I [insulin dependent type] [IDDM] [juvenile type], uncontrolled

syringomyelic 336.0 [713.5]
syndrome (intermitten claudication) 443.9
due to atherosclerosis 440.21
Charcôt-Marie-Tooth disease, paralysis, or syndrome 356.1
Charleyhorse (quadriceps) 843.8
Cheyne-Stokes respiration (periodic) 786.04
Chiropractic dislocation (*see also* Lesion, nonallopathic, by site) 739.9
Chondritis (purulent) 733.99
costal 733.6
Tietze's 733.6
patella, posttraumatic 717.7
posttraumatica patellae 717.7
Chondrodystrophy (familial) (hypoplastic) 756.4
myotonic (congenital) 359.23
Chondrolysis 733.99
Chondromalacia 733.92
epiglottis (congenital) 748.3
generalized 733.92
knee 717.7
larynx (congenital) 748.3
localized, except patella 733.92
patella, patellae 717.7
systemic 733.92
tibial plateau 733.92
trachea (congenital) 748.3
Chondropathia tuberosa 733.6
Chorea (gravis) (minor) (spasmodic) 333.5
apoplectic (*see also* Disease, cerebrovascular, acute) 436
chronic 333.4
habit 307.22

Chorea—*continued*
hereditary 333.4
Huntington's 333.4
posthemiplegic 344.89
progressive 333.4
chronic 333.4
hereditary 333.4
senile 333.5
Sydenham's 392.9
nonrheumatic 333.5
variabilis 307.23
Choreoathetosis (paroxysmal) 333.5
Chorionitis (*see also* Scleroderma) 710.1
Churg-Strauss syndrome 446.4
Cicatrix (adherent) (contracted) (painful) 709.2
bone 733.99
knee, semilunar cartilage 717.5
larynx 478.79
lung 518.89
muscle 728.89
skin 709.2
infected 686.8
postinfectional 709.2
specified site NEC 709.2
wrist, constricting (annular) 709.2
CIDP (chronic inflammatory demyelinating polyneuropathy) 357.81
Cirrhosis, cirrhotic 571.5
due to
cystic fibrosis 277.00
lung (chronic) (*see also* Fibrosis, lung) 515
pulmonary (*see also* Fibrosis, lung) 515
Ciuffini-Pancoast tumor (M8010/3) (carcinoma, pulmonary apex) 162.3
CJD (Creutzfeldt-Jakob disease) 046.19
variant (vCJD) 046.11
Clark's paralysis 343.9
Claude Bernard-Horner syndrome (*see also* Neuropathy, peripheral, autonomic) 337.9
Claude's syndrome 352.6
Claudication, intermittent 443.9
due to atherosclerosis 440.21
venous (axillary) 453.89
Clavus (infected) 700
Clawfoot (congenital) 754.71
acquired 736.74
Clawhand (acquired) 736.06
congenital 755.59
Clawtoe (congenital) 754.71
acquired 735.5
Clay eating 307.52
Cleft hand (congenital) 755.58
Cleft (congenital)—*see also* Imperfect, closure
branchial (persistent) 744.41
cyst 744.42
cricoid cartilage, posterior 748.3
nose 748.1
posterior, cricoid cartilage 748.3
thyroid cartilage (congenital) 748.3
Cleidocranial dysostosis 755.59
Cleptomania 312.32
Clergyman's sore throat 784.49
Climacteric (*see also* Menopause) 627.2
polyarthritis NEC 716.39

Clinodactyly 755.59
Clonus 781.0
Closure
congenital, nose 748.0
cranial sutures, premature 756.0
fontanelle, delayed 756.0
nose (congenital) 748.0
Club hand (congenital) 754.89
acquired 736.07
Clubbing of fingers 781.5
Clubfinger 736.29
acquired 736.29
congenital 754.89
Clubfoot (congenital) 754.70
acquired 736.71
equinovarus 754.51
paralytic 736.71
Clubnail (acquired) 703.8
Clumsiness 781.3
syndrome 315.4
Cluttering 307.0
Coal miners'
elbow 727.2
lung 500
Coal workers' lung or pneumoconiosis 500
Coalition
calcaneoscaphoid 755.67
calcaneus 755.67
tarsal 755.67
Coccydynia 724.79
Coccygodynia 724.79
Cocked-up toe 735.2
Coffee workers' lung 495.8
Cold 460
bronchus or chest—*see* Bronchitis
with grippe or influenza 487.1
deep 464.10
grippy 487.1
with influenza, flu, or grippe 487.1
Collagenosis (*see also* Collagen disease) 710.9
cardiovascular 425.4
Collapse 780.2
cardiorenal (*see also* Hypertension, cardiorenal) 404.90
hysterical 300.11
labyrinth, membranous (congenital) 744.05
lung (massive) (*see also* Atelectasis) 518.0
neurocirculatory 306.2
pulmonary (*see also* Atelectasis) 518.0
fetus or newborn 770.5
partial 770.5
primary 770.4
vascular (peripheral) 785.59
cerebral (*see also* Disease, cerebrovascular, acute) 436
vertebra 733.13
Colles' fracture (closed) (reversed) (separation) 813.41
Collet's syndrome 352.6
Collet-Sicard syndrome 352.6
Colliers'
asthma 500
lung 500
Coma 780.01
apoplectic (*see also* Disease, cerebrovascular, acute) 436
Combat fatigue (*see also* Reaction, stress, acute) 308.9

Commotion (current)
brain (without skull fracture) (*see also* Concussion, brain) 850.9
Compartment syndrome—*see* Syndrome, compartment
Complex
cardiorenal (*see also* Hyperten-sion, cardiorenal) 404.90
regional pain syndrome 355.9
type I 337.20
lower limb 337.22
specified site NEC 337.29
upper limb 337.21
type II
lower limb 355.71
upper limb 354.4
Complications
accidental puncture or laceration during a procedure 998.2
amputation stump (late) (surgical) 997.60
complication) 995.2
aortocoronary (bypass) graft 996.03
embolism 996.72
occlusion NEC 996.72
thrombus 996.72
blood vessel graft 996.1
aortocoronary 996.03
embolism 996.72
occlusion NEC 996.72
thrombus 996.72
bypass—*see also* Complica-tions, anastomosis
aortocoronary 996.03
embolism 996.72
occlusion NEC 996.72
thrombus 996.72
carotid artery 996.1
cardiac (*see also* Disease, heart) 429.9
device, implant, or graft NEC 996.72
infection or inflammation 996.61
valve prosthesis 996.71
infection or inflam-mation 996.61
cardiorenal (*see also* Hypertension, cardiorenal) 404.90
carotid artery bypass graft 996.1
coronary (artery) bypass (graft) NEC 996.03
embolism 996.72
infection or inflammation 996.61
occlusion NEC 996.72
specified type NEC 996.72
thrombus 996.72
due to (presence of) any device, implant, or graft classified to 996.0
arterial NEC 996.74
coronary NEC 996.03
embolism 996.72
occlusion NEC 996.72
specified type NEC 996.72
thrombus 996.72
cardiac NEC 996.72
defibrillator 996.72
pacemaker 996.72
coronary (artery) bypass (graft) NEC 996.03
embolism 996.72
occlusion NEC 996.72

Complications—continued
due to—continued
coronary—continued
thrombus 996.72
electrodes
heart 996.72
organ (immune or nonimmune cause) (partial) (total) 996.80
heart 996.83
heart—see also Disease, heart
transplant (immune or nonimmune cause) 996.83
infection and inflammation
due to (presence of) any device, implant or graft classified to 996.0-996.5 NEC 996.60
arterial NEC 996.62
coronary 996.61
artificial heart 996.61
cardiac 996.61
catheter NEC 996.69
portacath (port-a-cath) 999.31
umbilical venous 999.31
coronary artery bypass 996.61
electrodes
heart 996.61
heart assist device 996.61
heart valve 996.61
injection (procedure) 999.9
drug reaction (see also Reaction, drug) 995.2
mechanical
artificial heart 996.61
catheter NEC 996.59
dialysis (hemodialysis) 996.1
during a procedure 998.2
device NEC 996.59
balloon (counterpuls-ation), intra-aortic 996.1
counterpulsation, intra-aortic 996.1
prosthetic NEC 996.59
umbrella, vena cava 996.1
vascular 996.1
fistula, arteriovenous, surgically created 996.1
graft NEC 996.52
aortic (bifurcation) 996.1
blood vessel NEC 996.1
carotid artery bypass 996.1
organ (immune or nonimmune cause) 996.80
heart 996.83
vascular 996.1
implant NEC 996.59
vascular 996.1
respirator (ventilator) V46.14
shunt NEC 996.59
arteriovenous, surgically created 996.1
medical care NEC 999.9
nervous system NEC 997.00
respiratory NEC 997.39
nervous system
postoperative NEC 997.00
pacemaker (cardiac) 996.72
infection or inflammation 996.61

Complications—continued
respiratory 519.9
distress syndrome, adult, following trauma or surgery 518.5
insufficiency, acute, postoperative 518.5
seroma (intraoperative)(postoperative) (noninfected) 998.13
infected 998.51
surgical procedures 998.9
accidental puncture or laceration 998.2
amputation stump (late) 997.60
nervous system NEC 997.00
stitch abscess 998.59
wound infection 998.59
ventilator (respirator), mechanical V46.14

Compression
arm NEC 354.9
brachial plexus 353.0
brain (stem) 348.4
osteopathic 739.0
bronchus 519.19
cauda equina 344.60
with neurogenic bladder 344.61
cervical plexus 353.2
cranial nerve 352.9
fifth 350.8
seventh 351.8
laryngeal nerve, recurrent 478.79
leg NEC 355.8
lower extremity NEC 355.8
lumbosacral plexus 353.1
lung 518.89
lymphatic vessel 457.1
nerve NEC—see also Disorder, nerve
arm NEC 354.9
autonomic nervous system (see also Neuropathy, peripheral, autonomic) 337.9
axillary 353.0
cranial NEC 352.9
due to displacement of inter-vertebral disc 722.2
cervical 722.0
with myelopathy 722.71
lumbar, lumbosacral 722.10
with myelopathy 722.73
thoracic, thoracolumbar 722.11
with myelopathy 722.72
with myelopathy 722.70
iliohypogastric 355.79
ilioinguinal 355.79
leg NEC 355.8
lower extremity NEC 355.8
median (in carpal tunnel) 354.0
obturator 355.79
plantar 355.6
posterior tibial (in tarsal tunnel) 355.5
root (by scar tissue) NEC 724.9
cervical NEC 723.4
lumbar NEC 724.4
lumbosacral 724.4
thoracic 724.4
saphenous 355.79
sciatic (acute) 355.0
sympathetic 337.9
ulnar 354.2

Compression—continued
nerve NEC—continued
upper extremity NEC 354.9
spinal (cord) (old or nontraumatic) 336.9
nerve
root NEC 724.9
postoperative 722.80
cervical region 722.81
lumbar region 722.83
thoracic region 722.82
spondylogenic 721.91
cervical 721.1
lumbar, lumbosacral 721.42
thoracic 721.41
subcostal nerve (syndrome) 354.8
sympathetic nerve NEC 337.9
trachea 519.19
congenital 748.3
ulnar nerve (by scar tissue) 354.2
upper extremity NEC 354.9
Concavity, chest wall 738.3
Concussion (current) 850.9
brain or cerebral (without skull fracture) 850.9
without loss of consciousness 850.0
with
loss of consciousness 850.5
brief (less than one hour) 30 minutes or less 850.11
31-59 minutes 850.12
moderate (1-24 hours) 850.2
prolonged (more than 24 hours) (with complete recovery) (with return to pre-existing conscious level) 850.3
without return to pre-existing conscious level 850.4
mental confusion or disorientation (without loss of consciousness) 850.
cauda equina 952.4
conus medullaris (spine) 952.4
syndrome 310.2
without loss of consciousness 850.0
with
loss of consciousness 850.5
brief (less than one hour) 30 minutes or less 850.11
31-59 minutes 850.12
moderate (1-24 hours) 850.2
prolonged (more than 24 hours) (with com-plete recovery) (with return to pre-existing conscious level) 850.3
without return to pre-existing con-scious level 850.4
mental confusion or disorientation (without loss of consciousness) 850.0
Congestion, congestive
chest 786.9
glottis 476.0
heart (see also Failure, heart) 428.0

Congestion, congestive—continued
hypostatic (lung) 514
larynx 476.0
lung 786.9
active or acute (see also Pneumonia) 486
congenital 770.0
chronic 514
hypostatic 514
idiopathic, acute 518.5
passive 514
pleural 511.0
spinal cord 336.1
trachea 464.11
Constriction
anomalous, meningeal bands or folds 742.8
larynx 478.74
congenital 748.3
meningeal bands or folds, anomalous 742.8
Contraction, contracture, contracted
Achilles tendon (see also Short, tendon, Achilles) 727.81
axilla 729.90
Dupuytren's 728.6
face 729.9
fascia (lata) (postural) 728.89
Dupuytren's 728.6
palmar 728.6
plantar 728.71
finger NEC 736.29
congenital 755.59
joint (see also Contraction, joint) 718.44
flaccid, paralytic
joint (see also Contraction, joint) 718.4☑
muscle 728.85
hamstring 728.89
tendon 727.81
hip (see also Contraction, joint) 718.4☑
hysterical 300.11
joint (abduction) (acquired) (adduction) (flexion) (rotation) 718.40
ankle 718.47
congenital NEC 755.8
generalized or multiple 754.89
lower limb joints 754.89
hip (see also Subluxation, congenital, hip) 754.32
lower limb (including pelvic girdle) not involving hip 754.89
upper limb (including shoulder girdle) 755.59
elbow 718.42
foot 718.47
hand 718.44
hip 718.45
hysterical 300.11
knee 718.46
multiple sites 718.49
pelvic region 718.45
shoulder (region) 718.41
specified site NEC 718.48
wrist 718.43
ligament 728.89

Contraction, contracture, contracted—*continued*
muscle (postinfectional) (postural) NEC 728.85
  flaccid 728.85
  hysterical 300.11
  ischemic (Volkmann's) 958.6
  paralytic 728.85
  posttraumatic 958.6
  psychogenic 306.0
    specified as conversion reaction 300.11
myotonic 728.85
neck (*see also* Torticollis) 723.5
  psychogenic 306.0
palmar fascia 728.6
paralytic
  joint (*see also* Contraction, joint) 718.4☑

Note—Use the following fifth-digit subclassification with categories 711-712, 715-716, 718, 719.0-719.6, 719.8, 719.9:
0 *site unspecified*
1 *shoulder region*
2 *upper arm*
3 *forearm*
4 *hand*
5 *pelvic region and thigh*
6 *lower leg*
7 *ankle and foot*
8 *other specified sites*
9 *multiple sites*

    muscle 728.85
    plantar fascia 728.71
    spine (*see also* Curvature, spine) 737.9
    tendon (sheath) (*see also* Short, tendon) 727.81
    toe 735.8
    Volkmann's (ischemic) 958.6
Contusion (skin surface intact) 924.9
ankle 924.21
arm 923.9
  lower (with elbow) 923.10
cauda equina (spine) 952.4
conus medullaris (spine) 952.4
elbow 923.11
  with forearm 923.10
forearm (and elbow) 923.10
hand(s) (except fingers alone) 923.20
knee 924.11
popliteal space (*see also* Contusion, knee) 924.11
spinal cord—*see also* Injury, spinal, by site
  cauda equina 952.4
  conus medullaris 952.4
toe(s) (nail) (subungual) 924.3
wrist 923.21
  with hand(s), except finger(s) alone 923.20
Conus (any type) (congenital) 743.57
medullaris syndrome 336.8
Coordination disturbance 781.3
Cor
pulmonale (chronic) 416.9
Cowpox (abortive) 051.01
Coxa
valga (acquired) 736.31
  congenital 755.61
vara (acquired) 736.32
  congenital 755.62

Coxae malum senilis 715.25
Coxalgia (nontuberculous) 719.45
Coxalgic pelvis 736.30
Coxitis 716.65
Cramp(s) 729.82
extremity (lower) (upper) NEC 729.82
hysterical 300.11
linotypist's 300.89
  organic 333.84
muscle (extremity) (general) 729.82
  hysterical 300.11
occupational (hand) 300.89
  organic 333.84
psychogenic 307.89
sleep related, leg 327.52
telegraphers' 300.89
  organic 333.84
typists' 300.89
  organic 333.84
writers' 333.84
  organic 333.84
Craniocleidodysostosis 755.59
Craniofenestria (skull) 756.0
Cranioschisis 756.0
Craniostenosis 756.0
Craniosynostosis 756.0
Creaking joint 719.60
ankle 719.67
elbow 719.62
foot 719.67
hand 719.64
hip 719.65
knee 719.66
multiple sites 719.69
pelvic region 719.65
shoulder (region) 719.61
specified site NEC 719.68
wrist 719.63
Creeping
palsy 335.21
paralysis 335.21
Crepitus
caput 756.0
joint 719.60
  ankle 719.67
  elbow 719.62
  foot 719.67
  hand 719.64
  hip 719.65
  knee 719.66
  multiple sites 719.69
  pelvic region 719.65
  shoulder (region) 719.61
  specified site NEC 719.68
  wrist 719.63
Creutzfeldt-Jakob disease (CJD) (syndrome) 046.19
with dementia
  with behavioral disturbance 046.19 [294.11]
  without behavioral disturbance 046.19 [294.10]
familial 046.19
iatrogenic 046.19
specified NEC 046.19
sporadic 046.19
variant (vCJD) 046.11
  with dementia
    with behavioral disturbance 046.11 [294.11]
    without behavioral disturbance 046.11 [294.10]

Crisis
brain, cerebral (*see also* Disease, cerebro-vascular, acute) 436
emotional NEC 309.29
  acute reaction to stress 308.0
  adjustment reaction 309.9
  specific to childhood and adolescence 313.9
heart (*see also* Failure, heart) 428.9
oculogyric 378.87
psychogenic 306.7
Crocq's disease (acrocyanosis) 443.89
Crossfoot 754.50
Crouzon's disease (craniofacial dysostosis) 756.0
CRST syndrome (cutaneous systemic sclerosis) 710.1
Crural ulcer (*see also* Ulcer, lower extremity) 707.10
Crush, crushed, crushing (injury) 929.9
finger(s) 927.3
  with hand(s) 927.20
hand, except finger(s) alone (and wrist) 927.20
thumb(s) (and fingers) 927.3
wrist 927.21
  with hand(s), except fingers alone 927.20
Crutch paralysis 953.4
Cruveilhier's disease 335.21
Cubitus
valgus (acquired) 736.01
  congenital 755.59
varus (acquired) 736.02
  congenital 755.59
Curschmann (-Batten) (-Steinert) disease or syndrome 359.22
Curvature
Pott's (spinal) (*see also* Tuberculosis) 015.0☑ [737.43]

Note—Use the following fifth-digit subclassification with categories 010-018:
0 *unspecified*
1 *bacteriological or histological examination not done*
2 *bacteriological or histological examination unknown (at present)*
3 *tubercle bacilli found (in sputum) by microscopy*
4 *tubercle bacilli not found (in sputum) by microscopy, but found by bacterial culture*
5 *tubercle bacilli not found by bacteriological exam-ination, but tuberculosis confirmed histologically*
6 *tubercle bacilli not found by bacteriological or histological examination, but tuberculosis confirmed by other methods [inoculation of animals]*

  radius, idiopathic, progressive (congenital) 755.54
  spine (acquired) (angular) (idiopathic) (incorrect) (postural) 737.9
    congenital 754.2
    due to or associated with Charcôt-Marie-Tooth dis-ease 356.1 [737.40]
    mucopolysaccharidosis 277.5 [737.40]

Curvature—*continued*
spine—*continued*
  due to or associated with— *continued*
    neurofibromatosis 237.71 [737.40]
    osteitis
      deformans 731.0 [737.40]
      fibrosa cystica 252.0 [737.40]
    osteoporosis (*see also* Osteoporosis) 733.00 [737.40]
    poliomyelitis (*see also* Poliomyelitis) 138 [737.40]
    tuberculosis (Pott's curvature) (*see also* Tuberculosis) 015.0☑ [737.43]
  kyphoscoliotic (*see also* Kyphoscoliosis) 737.30
  kyphotic (*see also* Kyphosis) 737.10
  late effect of rickets 268.1 [737.40]
  Pott's 015.0☑ [737.40]
  scoliotic (*see also* Scoliosis) 737.30
  specified NEC 737.8
  tuberculous 015.0☑ [737.40]
Cyst (mucus) (retention) (serous) (simple)
air, lung 518.89
arytenoid 478.79
Baker's (knee) 727.51
branchial (cleft) 744.42
branchiogenic 744.42
bronchogenic (mediastinal) (sequestration) 518.89
  congenital 748.4
bursa, bursal 727.49
cauda equina 336.8
cervical lateral 744.42
congenital NEC 759.89
  epiglottis 748.3
  larynx 748.3
  lung 748.4
epiglottis 478.79
ganglion 727.43
intraligamentous 728.89
  knee 717.89
larynx 478.79
lung 518.89
  congenital 748.4
  giant bullous 492.0
meniscus knee 717.5
neuroenteric 742.59
paralabral
  hip 718.85
  shoulder 840.7
perineural (Tarlov's) 355.9
pleura 519.8
popliteal 727.51
preauricular 744.47
semilunar cartilage (knee) (multiple) 717.5
sympathetic nervous system 337.9
synovial 727.40
  popliteal space 727.51
Tarlov's 355.9
tendon (sheath) 727.42
vallecula, vallecular 478.79

☑ Additional Digit Required

Cystic—*see also* condition
  disease
    lung 518.89
      congenital 748.4
    semilunar cartilage 717.5
  fibrosis (pancreas) 277.00
    with
      meconium ileus 277.01
    lung 518.89
      congenital 748.4

D

Da Costa's syndrome
  (neurocirculatory asthenia)
  306.2
Dacryosialadenopathy, atrophic
  710.2
Dactylitis 686.9
Dactylosymphysis (*see also*
  Syndactylism) 755.10
Damage
  brain 348.9
    anoxic, hypoxic 348.1
      during or resulting from a
        procedure 997.01
    child NEC 343.9
    minimal (child) (*see also*
      Hyperkinesia) 314.9
  cardiorenal (vascular) (*see also*
    Hypertension, cardiorenal)
    404.90
  coronary (*see also* Ischemia, heart)
    414.9
  medication 995.20
Dangle foot 736.79
Darier-Roussy sarcoid 135
Davies' disease 425.0
Davies-Colley syndrome (slipping
  rib) 733.99
de Quervain's
  disease (tendon sheath) 727.04
Debility (general) (infantile)
  (postinfectional) 799.3
  nervous 300.5
Decalcification
  bone (*see also* Osteoporosis)
    733.00
Decompensation
  cardiorenal (*see also* Hyperten-sion,
    cardiorenal) 404.90
  respiratory 519.9
Decubital gangrene (*see also* Ulcer,
  pressure) 707.00 [785.4]
Decubiti (*see also* Ulcer, pressure)
  707.00
Decubitus (*see also* Ulcer, pressure)
  707.00
  with gangrene 707.00 [785.4]
  ankle 707.06
  back
    lower 707.03
    upper 707.02
  buttock 707.05
  coccyx 707.03
  elbow 707.01
  head 707.09
  heel 707.07
  hip 707.04
  other site 707.09
  sacrum 707.03
  shoulder blades 707.02
Deepening acetabulum 718.85

Defect, defective 759.9
  developmental—*see also* Anomaly,
    by site
  cauda equina 742.59
  extensor retinaculum 728.9
  learning, specific 315.2
  postural, spine 737.9
  speech NEC 784.59
    developmental 315.39
Deficiency, deficient
  limb V49.0
    lower V49.0
      congenital (*see also*
        Deficiency, lower limb,
        congenital) 755.30
    upper V49.0
      congenital (*see also*
        Deficiency, upper limb,
        congenital) 755.20
  lipoid (high-density) 272.5
  lipoprotein (familial) (high density)
    272.5
  lower limb V49.0
    congenital 755.30
      longitudinal (complete)
        (partial) (with distal
        deficiencies,
        incomplete) 755.32
        combined femoral, tibial,
          fibular (incomplete)
          755.33
        femoral 755.34
        fibular 755.37
        metatarsal(s) 755.38
        phalange(s) 755.39
          meaning all digits
            755.31
        tarsal(s) 755.38
        tibia 755.36
        tibiofibular 755.35
        with complete absence of
          distal elements
          755.31
      transverse 755.31
    congenital 755.30
      with complete absence of
        distal elements 755.31
  myocardial (*see also* Insufficiency
    myocardial) 428.0
  neck V48.1
  nose V48.8
  Short stature homeobox gene
    (SHOX)
    with
      dyschondrosteosis 756.89
      short stature (idiopathic)
        783.43
  thiamine, thiaminic (chloride)
    265.1
  tocopherol 269.1
  trunk V48.1
  upper limb V49.0
    congenital 755.20
      longitudinal (complete)
        (partial) (with distal
        deficiencies,
        incomplete) 755.22
        carpal(s) 755.28
        combined humeral, radial,
          ulnar (incomplete)
          755.23
        humeral 755.24
        metacarpal(s) 755.28

Deficiency, deficient—*continued*
  upper limb—*continued*
    congenital—*continued*
      longitudinal—*continued*
        phalange(s) 755.29
          meaning all digits
            755.21
        radial 755.26
        radioulnar 755.25
        ulnar 755.27
        transverse (complete)
          (partial) 755.21
      with complete absence of
        distal elements 755.21
Deflection
  radius 736.09
Defluvium
  unguium 703.8
Deformity 738.9
  ankle (joint) (acquired) 736.70
    abduction 718.47
    congenital 755.69
    contraction 718.47
    specified NEC 736.79
  aortic
    arch 747.21
      acquired 447.8
      acquired (*see also*
        Endocarditis, aortic)
        424.1
  arm (acquired) 736.89
    congenital 755.50
  artery (congenital) (peripheral)
    NEC (*see also* Deformity,
    vascular) 747.60
    coronary (congenital) 746.85
      acquired (*see also* Ischemia,
        heart) 414.9
  boutonniere (finger) 736.21
  brain (congenital) 742.9
  bronchus (congenital) 748.3
    acquired 519.19
  cerebral (congenital) 742.9
  chest (wall) (acquired) 738.3
    congenital 754.89
  choroid (congenital) 743.9
    plexus (congenital) 742.9
  clavicle (acquired) 738.8
    congenital 755.51
  coccyx (acquired) 738.6
    congenital 756.10
  coronary artery (congenital)
    746.85
    acquired (*see also* Ischemia,
      heart) 414.9
  cranium (acquired) 738.19
    congenital (*see also* Deformity,
      skull, congenital) 756.0
  cricoid cartilage (congenital) 748.3
    acquired 478.79
  dura (congenital) 742.9
    spinal 742.59
  elbow (joint) (acquired) 736.00
    congenital 755.50
    contraction 718.42
  epiglottis (congenital) 748.3
    acquired 478.79
  extremity (acquired) 736.9
    congenital, except reduction
      deformity 755.9
    lower 755.60
    upper 755.50
  eyebrow (congenital) 744.89
  femur (acquired) 736.89
    congenital 755.60

Deformity—*continued*
  finger (acquired) 736.20
    boutonniere type 736.21
    congenital 755.50
    flexion contracture 718.44
    swan neck 736.22
  flexion (joint) (acquired) 736.9
    congenital NEC 755.9
    hip or thigh (acquired) 736.39
      congenital (*see also*
        Subluxation, con-genital,
        hip) 754.32
  foot (acquired) 736.70
    cavovarus 736.75
      congenital 754.59
    congenital NEC 754.70
      specified type NEC 754.79
    valgus (acquired) 736.79
      congenital 754.60
        specified type NEC 754.69
    varus (acquired) 736.79
      congenital 754.50
        specified type NEC 754.59
  forearm (acquired) 736.00
    congenital 755.50
  forehead (acquired) 738.19
    congenital (*see also* Deformity,
      skull, congenital) 756.0
  frontal bone (acquired) 738.19
    congenital (*see also* Deformity,
      skull, congenital) 756.0
  gunstock 736.02
  hand (acquired) 736.00
    claw 736.06
    congenital 755.50
    minus (and plus) (intrinsic)
      736.09
    pill roller (intrinsic) 736.09
    plus (and minus) (intrinsic)
      736.09
    swan neck (intrinsic) 736.09
  head (acquired) 738.10
    congenital (*see also* Deformity,
      skull congenital) 756.0
  heel (acquired) 736.76
    congenital 755.67
  hip (joint) (acquired) 736.30
    congenital NEC 755.63
    flexion 718.45
      congenital (*see also*
        Subluxation,
        congenital, hip)
        754.32
  humerus (acquired) 736.89
    congenital 755.50
  ilium (acquired) 738.6
    congenital 755.60
  intervertebral cartilage or disc
    (acquired)—*see also*
    Displacement, intervertebral
    disc
    congenital 756.10
  ischium (acquired) 738.6
    congenital 755.60
  joint (acquired) NEC 738.8
    congenital 755.9
  Klippel-Feil (brevicollis) 756.16
  knee (acquired) NEC 736.6
    congenital 755.64
  larynx (muscle) (congenital) 748.3
    acquired 478.79
    web (glottic) (subglottic) 748.2
  leg (lower) (upper) (acquired) NEC
    736.89
    congenital 755.60

Deformity—*continued*
ligament (acquired) 728.9
limb (acquired) 736.9
  congenital, except reduction
    deformity 755.9
  lower 755.60
    reduction (*see also*
      Deformity,
      reduction, lower
      limb) 755.30
  upper 755.50
    reduction (*see also*
      Deformity,
      reduction, upper
      limb) 755.20
  specified NEC 736.89
lumbosacral (joint) (region)
  (congenital) 756.10
lung (congenital) 748.60
  acquired 518.89
  specified type NEC 748.69
Madelung's (radius) 755.54
meninges or membrane
  (congenital) 742.9
  spinal (cord) 742.59
metacarpus (acquired) 736.00
  congenital 755.50
metatarsus (acquired) 736.70
  congenital 754.70
middle ear, except ossicles
  (congenital) 744.03
  ossicles 744.04
muscle (acquired) 728.9
nervous system (congenital) 742.9
nose, nasal (cartilage) (acquired)
  738.0
  congenital 748.1
  septum 470
    congenital 748.1
  sinus (wall) (congenital) 748.1
organ of Corti (congenital) 744.05
patella (acquired) 736.6
  congenital 755.64
pelvis, pelvic (acquired) (bony)
  738.6
  congenital 755.60
Pierre Robin (congenital) 756.0
radius (acquired) 736.00
  congenital 755.50
reduction (extremity) (limb) 755.4
  lower limb 755.30
    longitudinal (complete)
      (partial) (with distal
      deficiencies,
      incomplete) 755.32
      combined femoral, tibial,
      fibular (incomplete)
      755.33
      femoral 755.34
      fibular 755.37
      metatarsal(s) 755.38
      phalange(s) 755.39
        meaning all digits
        755.31
      tarsal(s) 755.38
      tibia 755.36
      tibiofibular 755.35
      with complete absence of
        distal elements
        755.31
      transverse 755.31
      with complete absence of
        distal elements 755.31

Deformity—*continued*
reduction—*continued*
  upper limb 755.20
    longitudinal (complete)
      (partial) (with distal
      deficiencies,
      incomplete) 755.22
      carpal(s) 755.28
      combined humeral, radial,
      ulnar (incomplete)
      755.23
      humeral 755.24
      metacarpal(s) 755.28
      phalange(s) 755.29
        meaning all digits
        755.21
      radial 755.26
      radioulnar 755.25
      ulnar 755.27
      with complete absence of
        distal elements
        755.21
    transverse (complete)
      (partial) 755.21
    with complete absence of
      distal elements 755.21
rib (acquired) 738.3
rotation (joint) (acquired) 736.9
  congenital 755.9
  hip or thigh 736.39
    congenital (*see also*
      Subluxation,
      congenital, hip)
      754.32
sacroiliac joint (congenital) 755.69
sacrum (acquired) 738.5
  congenital 756.10
saddle
  back 737.8
scapula (acquired) 736.89
  congenital 755.50
septum (nasal) (acquired) 470
  congenital 748.1
shoulder (joint) (acquired) 736.89
  congenital 755.50
    specified type NEC 755.59
  contraction 718.41
skull (acquired) 738.19
  congenital 756.0
spinal
  cord (congenital) 742.9
    acquired 336.8
  nerve root (congenital) 742.9
    acquired 724.9
  spine (acquired) NEC 738.5
    congenital 756.10
    due to intrauterine
      malposition and
      pressure 754.2
    kyphoscoliotic (*see also*
      Kyphoscoliosis) 737.30
    kyphotic (*see also* Kyphosis)
      737.10
    lordotic (*see also* Lordosis)
      737.20
    scoliotic (*see also* Scoliosis)
      737.30
Sprengel's (congenital) 755.52
sternum (acquired) 738.3
swan neck (acquired)
  finger 736.22
  hand 736.09
thigh (acquired) 736.89
  congenital 755.60

Deformity—*continued*
thorax (acquired) (wall) 738.3
  congenital 754.89
thumb (acquired) 736.20
  congenital 755.50
thyroid (gland) (congenital) 759.2
  cartilage 748.3
    acquired 478.79
tibia (acquired) 736.89
  congenital 755.60
toe (acquired) 735.9
  congenital 755.66
  specified NEC 735.8
trachea (rings) (congenital) 748.3
  acquired 519.19
trunk (acquired) 738.3
ulna (acquired) 736.00
  congenital 755.50
wrist (joint) (acquired) 736.00
  congenital 755.50
  contraction 718.43
  valgus 736.03
    congenital 755.59
  varus 736.04
    congenital 755.59

Degeneration, degenerative
amyloid (any site) (general) 277.39
anterior cornua, spinal cord 336.8
anterior labral 840.8
aorta, aortic 440.0
  valve (heart) (*see also*
    Endocarditis, aortic) 424.1
artery, arterial (atheromatous)
  (calcareous)—*see also*
  Arteriosclerosis
  amyloid 277.39
  medial NEC (*see also*
    Arteriosclerosis,
    extremities) 440.20
articular cartilage NEC (*see also*
  Disorder, cartilage, articular)
  718.0☑

*Note—Use the following fifth-digit
subclassification with categories 711-
712, 715-716, 718, 719.0-719.6,
719.8, 719.9:*
0 site unspecified
1 shoulder region
2 upper arm
3 forearm
4 hand
5 pelvic region and thigh
6 lower leg
7 ankle and foot
8 other specified sites
9 multiple sites

  elbow 718.02
  knee 717.5
  patella 717.7
  shoulder 718.01
  spine (*see also* Spondylosis)
    721.90
basal nuclei or ganglia NEC 333.0
bone 733.90
brachial plexus 353.0
brain (cortical) (progressive) 331.9
  childhood 330.9
    specified type NEC 330.8
  familial NEC 331.89
  grey matter 330.8
  heredofamilial NEC 331.89

Degeneration, degenerative—
continued
brain—*continued*
  in
    alcoholism 303.9☑ [331.7]

*Note—Use the following fifth-digit
subclassification with category 303:*
0 unspecified
1 continuous
2 episodic
3 in remission

    beriberi 265.0 [331.7]
    cerebrovascular disease
      437.9 [331.7]
    congenital hydrocephalus
      742.3 [331.7]
      with spina bifida (*see also*
        Spina bifida)
        741.0☑ [331.7]

*Note—Use the following fifth-digit
subclassification with category 741:*
0 unspecified region
1 cervical region
2 dorsal [thoracic] region
3 lumbar region

    Fabry's disease 272.7 [330.2]
    Gaucher's disease 272.7
      [330.2]
    Hunter's disease or syndrome
      277.5 [330.3]
    lipidosis
      cerebral 330.1
      generalized 272.7 [330.2]
    mucopolysaccharidosis 277.5
      [330.3]
    myxedema (*see also*
      Myxedema) 244.9
      [331.7]
    neoplastic disease NEC
      (M8000/1) 239.9
      [331.7]
    Niemann-Pick disease 272.7
      [330.2]
    sphingolipidosis 272.7
      [330.2]
    vitamin B12 deficiency 266.2
      [331.7]
  motor centers 331.89
  senile 331.2
  specified type NEC 331.89
cardiorenal (*see also* Hypertension,
  cardiorenal) 404.90
cardiovascular (*see also* Disease,
  cardiovascular) 429.2
  renal (*see also* Hypertension,
    cardiorenal) 404.90
cerebellar NEC 334.9
  primary (hereditary) (sporadic)
    334.2
cerebromacular 330.1
cervical plexus 353.2
changes, spine or vertebra (*see also*
  Spondylosis) 721.90
collateral ligament (knee) (medial)
  717.82
  lateral 717.81
combined (spinal cord) (sub-acute)
  266.2 [336.2]
  due to vitamin B12 deficiency
    anemia (dietary) 281.1
    [336.2]

☑ Additional Digit Required

Degeneration, degenerative—
continued
  combined—*continued*
    with anemia (pernicious) 281.0
      [336.2]
      due to dietary deficiency
        281.1 *[336.2]*
    cortical (cerebellar)
      (parenchymatous) 334.2
      alcoholic 303.9☑ *[334.4]*

Note—Use the following fifth-digit
subclassification with category 303:

  0 unspecified
  1 continuous
  2 episodic
  3 in remission

  corticostriatal-spinal 334.8
  cruciate ligament (knee) (posterior)
    717.84
    anterior 717.83
  grey matter 330.8
  heart (brown) (calcareous) (fatty)
    (fibrous) (hyaline) (mural)
    (muscular) (pigmentary)
    (senile) (with arteriosclerosis)
    (*see also* Degeneration,
    myocardial) 429.1
    amyloid 277.39 *[425.7]*
    hypertensive (*see also*
      Hypertension, heart)
      402.90
    ischemic 414.9
  heredofamilial
    brain NEC 331.89
    spinal cord NEC 336.8
  hyaline (diffuse) (generalized)
    728.9
  internal semilunar cartilage 717.3
  intervertebral disc 722.6
    cervical, cervicothoracic 722.4
      with myelopathy 722.71
    lumbar, lumbosacral 722.52
      with myelopathy 722.73
    thoracic, thoracolumbar 722.51
      with myelopathy 722.72
    with myelopathy 722.70
  joint disease (*see also*
    Osteoarthrosis) 715.9☑

Note—Use the following fifth-digit
subclassification with categories 711-
712, 715-716, 718, 719.0-719.6,
719.8, 719.9:

  0 site unspecified
  1 shoulder region
  2 upper arm
  3 forearm
  4 hand
  5 pelvic region and thigh
  6 lower leg
  7 ankle and foot
  8 other specified sites
  9 multiple sites

  multiple sites 715.09
  spine (*see also* Spondylosis)
    721.90
  lateral column (posterior), spinal
    cord (*see also* Degeneration,
    combined) 266.2 *[336.2]*
  ligament
    collateral (knee) (medial) 717.82
      lateral 717.81

Degeneration, degenerative—
continued
  ligament—*continued*
    cruciate (knee) (posterior)
      717.84
      anterior 717.83
  lung 518.89
  Mönckeberg's (*see also*
    Arteriosclerosis, extremities)
    440.20
  membranous labyrinth, congenital
    (causing impairment of
    hearing) 744.05
  motor centers, senile 331.2
  muscle 728.9
    fatty 728.9
    fibrous 728.9
    hyaline 728.9
  muscular progressive 728.2
  myelin, central nervous system
    NEC 341.9
  myocardium, myocardial (brown)
    (calcareous) (fatty) (fibrous)
    (hyaline) (mural) (muscular)
    (pigmentary) (senile) (with
    arteriosclerosis) 429.1
    amyloid 277.39 *[425.7]*
    hypertensive (*see also*
      Hypertension, heart)
      402.90
    ischemic 414.8
  nervous system 349.89
    amyloid 277.39 *[357.4]*
    autonomic (*see also*
      Neuropathy, peripheral,
      autonomic) 337.9
    peripheral autonomic NEC (*see*
      also Neuropathy,
      peripheral,
      autonomic) 337.9
  olivopontocerebellar (familial)
    (hereditary) 333.0
  pallidal, pigmentary (progressive)
    333.0
  pigmentary (diffuse) (general)
    pallidal (progressive) 333.0
  posterolateral (spinal cord) (*see also*
    Degeneration, combined)
    266.2 *[336.2]*
  pulmonary valve (heart) (*see also*
    Endocarditis, pulmonary)
    424.3
  saccule, congenital (causing
    impairment of hearing)
    744.05
  senile 797
    brain 331.2
    motor centers 331.2
  spinal (cord) 336.8
    amyloid 277.39
    column 733.90
    combined (subacute) (*see also*
      Degeneration, combined)
      266.2 *[336.2]*
      with anemia (pernicious)
        281.0 *[336.2]*
    dorsolateral (*see also*
      Degeneration, combined)
      266.2 *[336.2]*
    familial NEC 336.8
    fatty 336.8
    funicular (*see also* Degeneration,
      com-bined) 266.2 *[336.2]*
    heredofamilial NEC 336.8

Degeneration, degenerative—
continued
  spinal (cord)—*continued*
    posterolateral (*see also*
      Degeneration, com-
      bined) 266.2 *[336.2]*
    spine 733.90
    strionigral 333.0
    turbinate 733.90
Deglutition
  paralysis 784.99
    hysterical 300.11
  pneumonia 507.0
Déjérine's disease 356.0
Déjérine-Sottas disease or
  neuropathy (hypertrophic)
  356.0
Déjérine-Thomas atrophy or
  syndrome 333.0
Delay, delayed
  closure—*see also* Fistula
    cranial suture 756.0
    fontanel 756.0
  development
    in childhood 783.40
      physiological 783.40
    intellectual NEC 315.9
    learning NEC 315.2
    reading 315.00
    speech 315.39
      associated with hyperkinesis
        314.1
    spelling 315.09
  milestone in childhood 783.42
Delirium, delirious 780.09
  acute (psychotic) 293.0
  alcoholic 291.0
    acute 291.0
    chronic 291.1
  alcoholicum 291.0
  chronic (*see also* Psychosis) 293.89
  exhaustion (*see also* Reaction,
    stress, acute) 308.9
  hysterical 300.11
  in
    presenile dementia 290.11
    senile dementia 290.3
  puerperal 293.9
  senile 290.3
  subacute (psychotic) 293.1
  tremens (impending) 291.0
  withdrawal
    alcoholic (acute) 291.0
      chronic 291.1
    drug 292.0
Dementia 294.8
  arteriosclerotic (simple type)
    (uncomplicated) 290.40
    depressed type 290.43
    paranoid type 290.42
    with
      acute confusional state
        290.41
      delirium 290.41
      delusional features 290.42
      depressive features 290.43
  Binswanger's 290.12
  degenerative 290.9
  dialysis 294.8
    transient 293.9
  due to or associated with
    condition(s) classified
    elsewhere
    Alzheimer's

Dementia —*continued*
  due to or associated with
    condition(s) classified
    elsewhere—*continued*
    Alzheimer's—*continued*
      without behavioral
        disturbance 331.0
        [294.10]
      with behavioral disturbance
        331.0 *[294.11]*
    Huntington's chorea
      without behavioral
        disturbance 333.4
        [294.10]
      with behavioral disturbance
        333.4 *[294.11]*
    Jakob-Creutzfeldt disease (CJD)
      with behavioral distur-bance
        046.19 *[294.11]*
      without behavioral
        disturbance 046.19
        [294.10]
      variant (vCJD) 046.11
        with dementia
          with behavioral
            disturbance
            046.11 *[294.11]*
        without behavioral
          disturbance 046.11
          [294.10]
    Parkinsonism
      without behavioral
        disturbance 331.82
        [294.10]
      with behavioral disturbance
        331.82 *[294.11]*
  old age 290.0
  presenile 290.10
    depressed type 290.13
    paranoid type 290.12
    simple type 290.10
    uncomplicated 290.10
    with
      acute confusional state
        290.11
      delirium 290.11
      delusional features 290.12
      depressive features 290.13
  senile 290.0
    depressed type 290.21
    exhaustion 290.0
    paranoid type 290.20
      acute confusional state 290.3
      delirium 290.3
      delusional features 290.20
      depressive features 290.21
  vascular 290.40
Demineralization, ankle (*see also*
  Osteoporosis) 733.00
Demyelination, demyelinization
  central nervous system 341.9
    specified NEC 341.8
  corpus callosum (central) 341.8
  global 340
Density
  increased, bone (dissem-inated)
    (generalized) (spotted)
    733.99
  lung (nodular) 518.89
Dependence
  with
    withdrawal symptoms
      drug 292.0
  on
    iron lung V46.11

Dependence—*continued*
  on—*continued*
    respirator (ventilator) V46.11
      encounter
        during
          mechanical failure
            V46.14
          power failure V46.12
      for weaning V46.13
    wheelchair V46.3
Deposit
  bone, in Boeck's sarcoid 135
Depraved appetite 307.52
Depression 311
  anaclitic 309.21
  arches 734
    congenital 754.61
  chest wall 738.3
  situational (acute) (brief) 309.0
    prolonged 309.1
  sternum 738.3
Deprivation
  sleep V69.4
Derangement
  ankle (internal) 718.97
    current injury (*see also*
      Dislocation, ankle) 837.0
    recurrent 718.37
  cartilage (articular) NEC (*see also*
    Disorder, cartilage, articular)
    718.0☑

*Note—Use the following fifth-digit
subclassification with categories 711-
712, 715-716, 718, 719.0-719.6,
719.8, 719.9:*

  0 site unspecified
  1 shoulder region
  2 upper arm
  3 forearm
  4 hand
  5 pelvic region and thigh
  6 lower leg
  7 ankle and foot
  8 other specified sites
  9 multiple sites

    knee 717.9
      recurrent 718.36
    recurrent 718.3☑
  collateral ligament (knee) (medial)
    (tibial) 717.82
    current injury 844.1
      lateral (fibular) 844.0
    lateral (fibular) 717.81
      current injury 844.0
  cruciate ligament (knee) (posterior)
    717.84
    anterior 717.83
      current injury 844.2
    current injury 844.2
  elbow (internal) 718.92
    recurrent 718.32
  hip (joint) (internal) (old) 718.95
    current injury (*see also*
      Dislocation, hip) 835.00
    recurrent 718.35
  joint (internal) 718.90
    ankle 718.97
    current injury—*see also*
      Dislocation, by site
      knee, meniscus or cartilage
        (*see also* Tear,
        meniscus) 836.2
    elbow 718.92

Derangement—*continued*
  joint—*continued*
    foot 718.97
    hand 718.94
    hip 718.95
    multiple sites 718.99
    pelvic region 718.95
    recurrent 718.30
      ankle 718.37
      elbow 718.32
      foot 718.37
      hand 718.34
      hip 718.35
      knee 718.36
      multiple sites 718.39
      pelvic region 718.35
      shoulder (region) 718.31
      specified site NEC 718.38
      wrist 718.33
    shoulder (region) 718.91
    specified site NEC 718.98
    spine NEC 724.9
    wrist 718.93
  knee (cartilage) (internal) 717.9
    current injury (*see also* Tear,
      meniscus) 836.2
    ligament 717.89
      capsular 717.85
      specified NEC 717.85
      recurrent 718.36
    low back NEC 724.9
    meniscus NEC (knee) 717.5
      current injury (*see also* Tear,
        meniscus) 836.2
      lateral 717.40
        anterior horn 717.42
        posterior horn 717.43
        specified NEC 717.49
      medial 717.3
        anterior horn 717.1
        posterior horn 717.2
      recurrent 718.3☑

*Note—Use the following fifth-digit
subclassification with categories 711-
712, 715-716, 718, 719.0-719.6,
719.8, 719.9:*

  0 site unspecified
  1 shoulder region
  2 upper arm
  3 forearm
  4 hand
  5 pelvic region and thigh
  6 lower leg
  7 ankle and foot
  8 other specified sites
  9 multiple sites

    mental (*see also* Psychosis) 298.9
    rotator cuff (recurrent) (tear)
      726.10
    sacroiliac (old) 724.6
    semilunar cartilage (knee) 717.5
      current injury 836.2
      lateral 836.1
      medial 836.0
      recurrent 718.3☑
    shoulder (internal) 718.91
      recurrent 718.31
    spine (recurrent) NEC 724.9
Dermatitis (allergic) (contact)
  (occupational) (venenata) 692.9
  gangrenosa, gangrenous
    (infantum) (*see also*
    Gangrene) 785.4

Dermatitis—*continued*
  hypostatic, hypostatica 454.1
    with ulcer 454.2
  infectious (staphylococcal)
    (streptococcal) 686.9
  purulent 686.00
  pyococcal 686.00
  pyocyaneus 686.09
  pyogenica 686.00
  septic (*see also* Septicemia) 686.00
  stasis 454.1
    due to
      postphlebitic syndrome
        459.12
        with ulcer 459.13
    ulcerated or with ulcer (varicose)
      454.2
  suppurative 686.00
  varicose 454.1
    with ulcer 454.2
  vegetans 686.8
Dermatoarthritis, lipoid 272.8
  [713.0]
Dermatomucomyositis 710.3
Dermatomyositis (acute) (chronic)
  710.3
Dermatosclerosis (*see also*
  Scleroderma) 710.1
Desert
  sore (*see also* Ulcer, skin) 707.9
Detachment
  knee, medial meniscus (old) 717.3
    current injury 836.0
Development
  arrested 783.40
    bone 733.91
    child 783.40
    tracheal rings (congenital) 748.3
  defective, congenital—*see also*
    Anomaly
    cauda equina 742.59
  delayed (*see also* Delay,
    development) 783.40
    arithmetical skills 315.1
    language (skills) 315.31
      and speech due to hearing
        loss 315.34
      expressive 315.31
      mixed receptive-expressive
        315.32
    learning skill, specified NEC
      315.2
    mixed skills 315.5
    motor coordination 315.4
    reading 315.00
    specified
      learning skill NEC 315.2
      type NEC, except learning
        315.8
    speech 315.39
      and language due to hearing
        loss 315.34
      associated with hyperkinesia
        314.1
      phonological 315.39
    spelling 315.09
  incomplete (fetus or newborn)
    764.9☑
    bronchial tree 748.3
  written expression 315.2
Devic's disease 341.0

Diabetes, diabetic (brittle)
  (congenital) (familial) (mellitus)
  (severe) (slight) (without
  complication) 250.0☑

*Note—Use the following fifth-digit
subclassification with category 250:*

  *0 type II [non-insulin dependent
    type] [NIDDM type] [adult-onset
    type] or unspecified type, not
    stated as uncontrolled*
  *1 type I [insulin dependent type]
    [IDDM type] [juvenile type], not
    stated as uncontrolled*
  *2 type II [non-insulin dependent
    type] [NIDDM type] [adult-onset
    type] or unspecified type,
    uncontrolled*
  *3 type I [insulin dependent type]
    [IDDM] [juvenile type],
    uncontrolled*

  amyotrophy 250.6☑ [353.5]
  angiopathy, peripheral 250.7☑
    [443.81]
    due to secondary diabetes
      249.7☑ [443.81]
      autonomic neuropathy
        (peripheral) 250.6☑
        [337.1]
        due to secondary diabetes
          249.6☑ [337.1]

*Note—The following fifth-digit
subclassification is for use with category
249:*

  *0 not stated as controlled, or
    unspecified*
  1 uncontrolled

    bone change 250.8☑ [731.8]
      due to secondary diabetes
        249.8☑ [731.8]
    dorsal sclerosis 250.6☑ [340]
      due to secondary diabetes
        249.6☑ [340]
    gangrene 250.7☑ [785.4]
      due to secondary diabetes
        249.7☑ [785.4]
    mononeuropathy 250.6☑ [355.9]
      due to secondary diabetes
        249.6☑ [355.9]
    neuralgia 250.6☑ [357.2]
      due to secondary diabetes
        249.6☑ [357.2]
    neuritis 250.6☑ [357.2]
      due to secondary diabetes
        249.6☑ [357.2]
    neurogenic arthropathy 250.6☑
      [713.5]
      due to secondary diabetes
        249.6☑ [713.5]
    neuropathy 250.6☑ [357.2]
      due to secondary diabetes
        249.6☑ [357.2]
      autonomic (peripheral) 250.6
        [337.1]
        due to secondary diabetes
          249.6 [337.1]
    osteomyelitis 250.8☑ [731.8]
      due to secondary diabetes
        249.8☑ [731.8]
    peripheral autonomic neuro-pathy
      250.6☑ [337.1]
      due to secondary diabetes
        249.6☑ [337.1]

Diabetes, diabetic—*continued*
  polyneuropathy 250.6 ☑ *[357.2]*
    due to secondary diabetes
      249.6 ☑ *[357.2]*
  ulcer (skin) 249.8 ☑ *[707.9]*
    steroid induced—*see also*
      Diabetes, secondary
  secondary (chemical-induced) (due
    to chronic condition) (due to
    infection) (drug-induced)
    249.0
  neuropathy 249.6 *[357.2]*
    autonomic (peripheral) 249.6
      [337.1]
  ulcer (skin) 250.8 ☑ *[707.9]*
    lower extremity 250.8 ☑
      [707.10]
      due to secondary diabetes
        249.8 ☑ *[707.10]*
    ankle 250.8 ☑ *[707.13]*
      due to secondary diabetes
        249.8 ☑ *[707.13]*
    calf 250.8 ☑ *[707.12]*
      due to secondary diabetes
        249.8 ☑ *[707.12]*
    foot 250.8 ☑ *[707.15]*
      due to secondary diabetes
        249.8 ☑ *[707.15]*
    heel 250.8 ☑ *[707.14]*
      due to secondary diabetes
        249.8 ☑ *[707.14]*
    knee 250.8 ☑ *[707.19]*
      due to secondary diabetes
        249.8 ☑ *[707.19]*
    specified site NEC 250.8 ☑
      [707.19]
      due to secondary diabetes
        249.8 ☑ *[707.19]*
    thigh 250.8 ☑ *[707.11]*
      due to secondary diabetes
        249.8 ☑ *[707.11]*
    toes 250.8 ☑ *[707.15]*
      due to secondary diabetes
        249.8 ☑ *[707.15]*
    specified site NEC 250.8 ☑
      [707.8]
      due to secondary diabetes
        249.8 ☑ *[707.8]*
  with
    gangrene 250.7 ☑ *[785.4]*
    osteomyelitis 250.8 ☑ *[731.8]*
Diaphragmalgia 786.52
Diaphragmitis 519.4
Diaphysitis 733.99
Diastasis
  cranial bones 733.99
    congenital 756.0
  muscle 728.84
  recti (abdomen) 728.84
Diastematomyelia 742.51
Diataxia, cerebral, infantile 343.0
Diathesis
  spasmophilic (*see also* Tetany)
    781.7
Difficulty
  feeding 783.3
    nonorganic (infant) NEC 307.59
  reading 315.00
    specific, spelling 315.09
  swallowing (*see also* Dysphagia)
    787.20
  walking 719.7
Diffused ganglion 727.42
Diplegia (upper limbs) 344.2
  congenital 343.0

Diplegia—*continued*
  facial 351.0
    congenital 352.6
  infantile or congenital (cerebral)
    (spastic) (spinal) 343.0
  lower limbs 344.1
Discitis 722.90
  cervical, cervicothoracic 722.91
  lumbar, lumbosacral 722.93
  thoracic, thoracolumbar 722.92
Discoid
  meniscus, congenital 717.5
  semilunar cartilage 717.5
Discoloration
  nails 703.8
Discomfort
  chest 786.59
Discrepancy
  leg length (acquired) 736.81
    congenital 755.30
Disease, diseased—*see also*
    Syndrome
  Albert's 726.71
  Alpers' 330.8
  amyloid (any site) 277.30
  anarthritic rheumatoid 446.5
  Andrews' (bacterid) 686.8
  angiospastic, angiospasmodic
    443.9
  anterior
    horn cell 335.9
      specified type NEC 335.8
  aortic (heart) (valve) (*see also*
    Endocarditis, aortic) 424.1
  aponeurosis 726.90
  arc-welders' lung 503
  arteriocardiorenal (*see also*
    Hypertension, cardiorenal)
    404.90
  ax(e)-grinders' 502
  Ayerza's (pulmonary artery sclerosis
    with pulmonary
    hypertension) 416.0
  Azorean (of the nervous system)
    334.8
  Büdinger-Ludloff-Läwen 717.89
  back bone NEC 733.90
  Bal-'s 341.1
  Barcoo (*see also* Ulcer, skin) 707.9
  barium lung 503
  Bechterew's (ankylosing
    spondylitis) 720.0
  Becker's
    idiopathic mural
      endomyocardial disease
      425.2
    myotonia congenita, recessive
      form 359.22
  Bekhterev's (ankylosing spondylitis)
    720.0
  Bergeron's (hysteroepilepsy)
    300.11
  black lung 500
  Blount's (tibia vara) 732.4
  Boeck's (sarcoidosis) 135
  bone 733.90
    specified type NEC 733.99
  brain 348.9
    Alzheimer's 331.0
    congenital 742.9
    inflammatory—*see also*
      Encephalitis
      late effect—*see* category 326

Disease, diseased—*continued*
  brain—*continued*
    Pick's 331.11
      with dementia
        without behavioral
          disturbance 331.11
          [294.10]
        with behavioral
          disturbance 331.11
          [294.11]
    senile 331.2
  bronchi 519.19
  bronchopulmonary 519.19
  cardiovascular (arteriosclerotic)
    429.2
    hypertensive (*see also*
      Hypertension, heart)
      402.90
      benign 402.10
      malignant 402.00
    renal (*see also* Hypertension,
      cardiorenal) 404.90
  cartilage NEC 733.90
    specified NEC 733.99
  Cavare's (familial periodic paralysis)
    359.3
  cellular tissue NEC 709.9
  central core 359.0
  cerebrovascular NEC 437.9
    acute 436
  Charcôt-Marie-Tooth 356.1
  Charcots' (joint) 094.0 *[713.5]*
  chest 519.9
  combined system (of spinal cord)
    266.2 *[336.2]*
    with anemia (pernicious) 281.0
      [336.2]
  cork-handlers' 495.3
  coronary (*see also* Ischemia, heart)
    414.9
  Cotugno's 724.3
  cranial nerve NEC 352.9
  Creutzfeldt-Jakob (CJD) 046.19
    with dementia
      without behavioral
        disturbance 046.19
        [294.10]
      with behavioral disturbance
        046.19 *[294.11]*
    familial 046.19
    iatrogenic 046.19
    specified NEC 046.19
    sporadic 046.19
    variant (vCJD) 046.11
      with dementia
        with behavioral
          disturbance 046.11
          [294.11]
        without behavioral
          disturbance 046.11
          [294.10]
  Crocq's (acrocyanosis) 443.89
  Crouzon's (craniofacial dysostosis)
    756.0
  Cruveilhier's 335.21
  Curschmann's 359.21
  cystic
    lung 518.89
      congenital 748.4
    semilunar cartilage 717.5
  cytomegalic inclusion (generalized)
    078.5
    with
      pneumonia 078.5 *[484.1]*
  Déjérine (-Sottas) 356.0

Disease, diseased—*continued*
  Davies' 425.0
  de Quervain's (tendon sheath)
    727.04
  demyelinating, demyelinizing
    (brain stem) (central nervous
    system) 341.9
    multiple sclerosis 340
    specified NEC 341.8
  Devic's 341.0
  diaphragm 519.4
  diatomaceous earth 502
  discogenic (*see also* Disease,
    intervertebral disc) 722.90
  Duchenne's 094.0
    muscular dystrophy 359.1
    paralysis 335.22
    pseudohypertrophy, muscles
      359.1
  Duchenne-Griesinger 359.1
  Duplay's 726.2
  Dupré's (meningism) 781.6
  Dupuytren's (muscle contracture)
    728.6
  fascia 728.9
    inflammatory 728.9
  Gerhardt's (erythromelalgia)
    443.82
  Gibney's (perispondylitis) 720.9
  Gilles de la Tourette's (motor-verbal
    tic) 307.23
  Hamman's (spontaneous
    mediastinal emphysema)
    518.1
  heart (organic) 429.9
    amyloid 277.39 *[425.7]*
    aortic (valve) (*see also*
      Endocarditis, aortic) 424.1
    beer drinkers' 425.5
    beriberi 265.0 *[425.7]*
    black 416.0
    congestive (*see also* Failure,
      heart) 428.0
    coronary 414.9
    due to
      amyloidosis 277.39 *[425.7]*
      beriberi 265.0 *[425.7]*
      cardiac glycogenosis 271.0
        [425.7]
      Friedreich's ataxia 334.0
        [425.8]
      mucopolysaccharidosis 277.5
        [425.7]
      myotonia atrophica 359.21
        [425.8]
      progressive muscular
        dystrophy 359.1
        [425.8]
      sarcoidosis 135 *[425.8]*
    functional 427.9
      psychogenic 306.2
    glycogen storage 271.0 *[425.7]*
    hypertensive (*see also*
      Hypertension, heart)
      402.90
      benign 402.10
      malignant 402.00
    hyperthyroid (*see also*
      Hyperthyroidism) 242.9 ☑
      [425.7]

Disease, diseased—*continued*
heart—*continued*
 ischemic (chronic) (*see also*
 Ischemia, heart) 414.9
 acute (*see also* Infarct,
 myocardium)
 without myocardial
 infarction 411.89
 with coronary (artery)
 occlusion 411.81
 asymptomatic 412
 diagnosed on ECG or other
 special investigation
 but currently
 presenting no
 symptoms 412
 kyphoscoliotic 416.1
 psychogenic (functional) 306.2
 pulmonary (chronic) 416.9
 specified NEC 416.8
 thyroid (gland) (*see also*
 Hyperthyroidism) 242.9☑
 [425.7]

*Note—Use the following fifth-digit
subclassification with category 242:*
 *0 without mention of thyrotoxic crisis
 or storm*
 *1 with mention of thyrotoxic crisis or
 storm*

 thyrotoxic (*see also* Thyrotoxicosis) 242.9☑ [425.7]
 tuberculous (*see also* Tuberculosis) 017.9☑ [425.8]

*Note—Use the following fifth-digit
subclassification with categories 010-
018:*
 0 unspecified
 *1 bacteriological or histological
 examination not done*
 *2 bacteriological or histological
 examination unknown (at present)*
 *3 tubercle bacilli found (in sputum)
 by microscopy*
 *4 tubercle bacilli not found (in
 sputum) by microscopy, but found
 by bacterial culture*
 *5 tubercle bacilli not found by
 bacteriological exam-ination, but
 tuberculosis confirmed
 histologically*
 *6 tubercle bacilli not found by
 bacteriological or histological
 examination, but tuberculosis
 confirmed by other methods
 [inoculation of animals]*

 acute pulmonary edema (*see
 also* Failure, ventricular,
 left) 428.1
 hypertensive 402.91
 benign 402.11
 with renal failure
 404.11
 malignant 402.01
 with renal failure
 404.01
 with renal failure
 404.91
 Heberden's 715.04
 Heerfordt's (uveoparotitis) 135
 Heidenhain's 290.10
 with dementia 290.10

Disease, diseased—*continued*
heredodegenerative NEC
 brain 331.89
 spinal cord 336.8
 hip (joint) NEC 719.95
 congenital 755.63
 suppurative 711.05
 HIV 042
 Horton's (temporal arteritis) 446.5
 host-versus-graft (immune or
 nonimmune cause) 279.50
 heart 996.83
 human immunodeficiency (virus)
 042
 Hunt's
 dyssynergia cerebellaris
 myoclonica 334.2
 Huntington's 333.4
 Hutchinson-Boeck (sarcoidosis) 135
 hyaline (diffuse) (generalized)
 728.9
 membrane (lung) (newborn)
 769
 hyperkinetic (*see also* Hyperkinesia)
 314.9
 hypertensive (*see also*
 Hypertension) 401.9
 internal semilunar cartilage, cystic
 717.5
 intervertebral disc 722.90
 cervical, cervicothoracic 722.91
 with myelopathy 722.71
 lumbar, lumbosacral 722.93
 with myelopathy 722.73
 thoracic, thoracolumbar 722.92
 with myelopathy 722.72
 with myelopathy 722.70
 Jüngling's (sarcoidosis) 135
 Jakob-Creutzfeldt (CJD) 046.19
 with dementia
 without behavioral
 disturbance 046.19
 [294.10]
 with behavioral disturbance
 046.19 [294.11]
 familial 046.19
 iatrogenic 046.19
 specified NEC 046.19
 sporadic 046.19
 variant (vCJD) 046.11
 with dementia
 with behavioral
 disturbance 046.11
 [294.11]
 without behavioral disturbance 046.11
 [294.10]
 Jansky-Bielschowsky 330.1
 joint NEC 719.9☑

*Note—Use the following fifth-digit
subclassification with categories 711-
712, 715-716, 718, 719.0-719.6,
719.8, 719.9:*
 0 site unspecified
 1 shoulder region
 2 upper arm
 3 forearm
 4 hand
 5 pelvic region and thigh
 6 lower leg
 7 ankle and foot
 8 other specified sites
 9 multiple sites

 ankle 719.97

Disease, diseased—*continued*
joint NEC—*continued*
 Charcôt 094.0 [713.5]
 degenerative (*see also*
 Osteoarthrosis) 715.9☑
 multiple 715.09
 spine (*see also* Spondylosis)
 721.90
 elbow 719.92
 foot 719.97
 hand 719.94
 hip 719.95
 hypertrophic (chronic)
 (degenerative) (*see also*
 Osteoarthrosis) 715.9☑
 spine (*see also* Spondylosis)
 721.90
 knee 719.96
 Luschka 721.90
 multiple sites 719.99
 pelvic region 719.95
 sacroiliac 724.6
 shoulder (region) 719.91
 specified site NEC 719.98
 spine NEC 724.9
 pseudarthrosis following
 fusion 733.82
 sacroiliac 724.6
 wrist 719.93
 Köhler's
 patellar 732.4
 Köhler-Pellegrini-Stieda
 (calcification, knee joint)
 726.62
 Kümmell's (-Verneuil) (spondylitis)
 721.7
 Kaschin-Beck (endemic
 polyarthritis) 716.00
 ankle 716.07
 arm 716.02
 lower (and wrist) 716.03
 upper (and elbow) 716.02
 foot (and ankle) 716.07
 forearm (and wrist) 716.03
 hand 716.04
 leg 716.06
 lower 716.06
 upper 716.05
 multiple sites 716.09
 pelvic region (hip) (thigh)
 716.05
 shoulder region 716.01
 specified site NEC 716.08
 Klinger's 446.4
 Klippel's 723.8
 Klippel-Feil (brevicollis) 756.16
 ligament 728.9
 locomotor system 334.9
 Lou Gehrig's 335.20
 Lucas-Championnière (fibrinous
 bronchitis) 466.0
 lumbosacral region 724.6
 lung NEC 518.89
 black 500
 cystic 518.89
 congenital 748.4
 fibroid (chronic) (*see also*
 Fibrosis, lung) 515
 in
 amyloidosis 277.39 [517.8]
 polymyositis 710.4 [517.8]
 sarcoidosis 135 [517.8]
 Sjögren's syndrome 710.2
 [517.8]

Disease, diseased—*continued*
lung NEC—*continued*
 in—*continued*
 systemic lupus
 erythematosus 710.0
 [517.8]
 systemic sclerosis 710.1
 [517.2]
 interstitial (chronic) 515
 acute 136.3
 nonspecific, chronic 496
 obstructive (chronic) (COPD)
 496
 diffuse (with fibrosis) 496
 with
 acute exacerbation NEC
 491.21
 alveolitis, allergic (*see also*
 Alveolitis, allergic)
 495.9
 bronchiectasis 494.0
 with acute
 exacerbation
 494.1
 bronchitis (chronic)
 491.20
 with exacerbation
 (acute) 491.21
 emphysema NEC 492.8
 polycystic 518.89
 congenital 748.4
 purulent (cavitary) 513.0
 restrictive 518.89
 rheumatoid 714.81
 diffuse interstitial 714.81
 specified NEC 518.89
 Möbius', Moebius' 346.2☑
 Mönckeberg's (*see also*
 Arteriosclerosis, extremities)
 440.20
 Münchmeyer's (exostosis luxurians)
 728.11
 Machado-Joseph 334.8
 maple bark 495.6
 Marchiafava (-Bignami) 341.8
 Marie-Strümpell (ankylosing
 spondylitis) 720.0
 Martin's 715.27
 mental (*see also* Psychosis) 298.9
 Merzbacher-Pelizaeus 330.0
 metal polishers' 502
 microvascular 413.9
 Mills' 335.29
 Minor's 336.1
 Mitchell's (erythromelalgia) 443.82
 Morton's (with metatarsalgia)
 355.6
 Morvan's 336.0
 motor neuron (bulbar) (mixed
 type) 335.20
 muscle 359.9
 inflammatory 728.9
 musculoskeletal system 729.90
 mushroom workers' 495.5
 myocardium, myocardial (*see also*
 Degeneration, myocardial)
 429.1
 hypertensive (*see also*
 Hypertension, heart
 402.90
 primary (idiopathic) 425.4
 myoneural 358.9
 nail 703.9
 specified type NEC 703.8
 nemaline body 359.0

☑ Additional Digit Required © 2009 Ingenix

Disease, diseased—*continued*
 nervous system (central) 349.9
  autonomic, peripheral (*see also*
    Neuropathy, peripheral,
    autonomic) 337.9
  congenital 742.9
  parasympathetic (*see also*
    Neuropathy, peripheral,
    autonomic) 337.9
  peripheral NEC 355.9
  prion NEC 046.79
  sympathetic (*see also*
    Neuropathy, peripheral,
    autonomic) 337.9
  vegetative (*see also* Neuropathy,
    peripheral, autonomic)
    337.9
 neurologic (central) NEC (*see also*
   Disease, nervous system)
   349.9
  peripheral NEC 355.9
 neuromuscular system NEC 358.9
 Oppenheim's 358.8
 Osgood's tibia (tubercle) 732.4
 Osgood-Schlatter 732.4
 Otto's 715.35
 pancreas 577.9
  fibrocystic 277.00
 Parkinson's 332.0
 Pelizaeus-Merzbacher 330.0
  with dementia
   without behavioral
     disturbance 330.0
     [294.10]
   with behavioral disturbance
     330.0 [294.11]
 Pellegrini-Stieda (calcification, knee
   joint) 726.62
 perineum
  male (inflammatory) 682.2
 periodic (familial) (Reimann's) NEC
   277.31
  paralysis 359.3
 periosteum 733.90
 peripheral
  arterial 443.9
  autonomic nervous system (*see
    also* Neuropathy,
    autonomic) 337.9
  nerve NEC (*see also*
    Neuropathy) 356.9
  vascular 443.9
   specified type NEC 443.89
 Perrin-Ferraton (snapping hip)
   719.65
 Pick's
  brain 331.11
   with dementia
    without behavioral
      disturbance 331.11
      [294.10]
    with behavioral
      disturbance 331.11
      [294.11]
  cerebral atrophy 331.11
   with dementia
    without behavioral
      disturbance 331.11
      [294.10]
    with behavioral
      disturbance 331.11
      [294.11]
 pigeon fanciers' or breeders' 495.2
 pituitary snuff-takers' 495.8

Disease, diseased—*continued*
 pleura (cavity) (*see also* Pleurisy)
   511.0
 policeman's 729.2
 polycystic (congenital) 759.89
  congenital 748.4
  lung or pulmonary 518.89
 Potain's (pulmonary edema) 514
 Pott's (*see also* Tuberculosis)
   015.0☑ [730.88]

Note—Use the following fifth-digit
subclassification with categories 010-
018:
 0 *unspecified*
 1 *bacteriological or histological*
   examination not done
 2 *bacteriological or histological*
   examination unknown (at present)
 3 *tubercle bacilli found (in sputum)*
   by microscopy
 4 *tubercle bacilli not found (in*
   sputum) by microscopy, but found
   by bacterial culture
 5 *tubercle bacilli not found by*
   bacteriological exam-ination, but
   tuberculosis confirmed
   histologically
 6 *tubercle bacilli not found by*
   bacteriological or histological
   examination, but tuberculosis
   confirmed by other methods
   [inoculation of animals]

 spinal curvature 015.0☑
   [737.43]
 spondylitis 015.0☑ [720.81]
 Poulet's 714.2
 Preiser's (osteoporosis) 733.09
 Profichet's 729.90
 psychiatric (*see also* Psychosis)
   298.9
 psychotic (*see also* Psychosis) 298.9
 pulmonary—*see also* Disease, lung
  amyloid 277.39 [517.8]
  diffuse obstructive (chronic) 496
   with
     exacerbation NEC (acute)
       491.21
  heart (chronic) 416.9
   specified NEC 416.8
  hypertensive (vascular) 416.0
   cardiovascular 416.0
  obstructive diffuse (chronic) 496
   decompensated 491.21
    with exacerbation 491.21
   with
     bronchitis (chronic)
       491.20
      with exacerbation
        (acute) 491.21
     exacerbation NEC (acute)
       491.21
  valve (*see also* Endocarditis,
    pulmonary) 424.3
 Putnam's (subacute combined
   sclerosis with pernicious
   anemia) 281.0 [336.2]
 Quervain's
  tendon sheath 727.04
 Raynaud's (paroxysmal digital
   cyanosis) 443.0
 Recklinghausen's (M9540/1)
   237.71
 Refsum's (heredopathia atactica
   polyneuritiformis) 356.3

Disease, diseased—*continued*
 respiratory (tract) 519.9
  acute or subacute (upper) NEC
    465.9
   due to fumes or vapors 506.3
  chronic 519.9
   arising in the perinatal period
     770.7
   due to fumes or vapors 506.4
  due to
   aspiration of liquids or solids
     508.9
   external agents NEC 508.9
    specified NEC 508.8
   fumes or vapors 506.9
    acute or subacute NEC
      506.3
    chronic 506.4
  fetus or newborn NEC 770.9
  obstructive 496
  specified type NEC 519.8
 retina, retinal NEC 362.9
  Batten's or Batten-Mayou 330.1
    [362.71]
 Roth (-Bernhardt) 355.1
 Rust's (tuberculous spondylitis) (*see
   also* Tuberculosis) 015.0☑
   [720.81]

Note—Use the following fifth-digit
subclassification with categories 010-
018:
 0 *unspecified*
 1 *bacteriological or histological*
   examination not done
 2 *bacteriological or histological*
   examination unknown (at present)
 3 *tubercle bacilli found (in sputum)*
   by microscopy
 4 *tubercle bacilli not found (in*
   sputum) by microscopy, but found
   by bacterial culture
 5 *tubercle bacilli not found by*
   bacteriological exam-ination, but
   tuberculosis confirmed
   histologically
 6 *tubercle bacilli not found by*
   bacteriological or histological
   examination, but tuberculosis
   confirmed by other methods
   [inoculation of animals]

 Sachs (-Tay) 330.1
 sacroiliac NEC 724.6
 Sandhoff's 330.1
 Schaumann's (sarcoidosis) 135
 Schilder (-Flatau) 341.1
 Schlatter's tibia (tubercle) 732.4
 Schlatter-Osgood 732.4
 Schmorl's 722.30
  cervical 722.39
  lumbar, lumbosacral 722.32
  specified region NEC 722.39
  thoracic, thoracolumbar 722.31
 Scholz's 330.0
 Schwalbe-Ziehen-Oppenheimer
   333.6
 Schwartz-Jampel 359.21
 Secretan's (posttraumatic edema)
   782.3
 semilunar cartilage, cystic 717.5
 Shaver's (bauxite pneumoconiosis)
   503
 silo fillers' 506.9
 Sinding-Larsen (juvenile
   osteopathia patellae) 732.4

Disease, diseased—*continued*
 Sjögren (-Gougerot) 710.2
  with lung involvement 710.2
    [517.8]
 skin NEC 709.9
 sleeping (*see also* Narcolepsy)
   347.00
 small vessel 443.9
 Spielmeyer-Stock 330.1
 Spielmeyer-Vogt 330.1
 spine, spinal 733.90
  combined system (*see also*
    Degeneration, combined)
    266.2 [336.2]
   with pernicious anemia
     281.0 [336.2]
  cord NEC 336.9
   congenital 742.9
  demyelinating NEC 341.8
  joint (*see also* Disease, joint,
    spine) 724.9
 spinocerebellar 334.9
  specified NEC 334.8
 Steinert's 359.21
 Stieda's (calcification, knee joint)
   726.62
 Still's (juvenile rheumatoid arthritis)
   714.30
  adult onset 714.2
 Stiller's (asthenia) 780.79
 stonemasons' 502
 Strümpell-Marie (ankylosing
   spondylitis) 720.0
 Thomsen's 359.22
 Unverricht (-Lundborg) 345.1
 vertebra, vertebral NEC 733.90
 Virchow's 733.99
 Vogt's (Cecile) 333.71
 Vogt-Spielmeyer 330.1
 Volhard-Fahr (malignant
   nephrosclerosis) 403.00
 Volkmann's
  acquired 958.6
 von Bechterew's (ankylosing
   spondylitis) 720.0
 von Eulenburg's (congenital
   paramyotonia) 359.29
 von Recklinghausen's (M9540/1)
   237.71
 Wardrop's (with lymphangitis)
   681.9
  finger 681.02
  toe 681.11
 wasting NEC 799.4
  paralysis 335.21
 Weir Mitchell's (erythromelalgia)
   443.82
 Werdnig-Hoffmann 335.0
 Wernicke's (superior hemorrhagic
   polioencephalitis) 265.1
 Wohlfart-Kugelberg-Welander
   335.11
 Woillez's (acute idiopathic
   pulmonary congestion)
   518.5
 Ziehen-Oppenheim 333.6
Disfigurement (due to scar) 709.2
 head V48.6
 limb V49.4
 neck V48.7
 trunk V48.7
Dislocatable hip, congenital (*see
  also* Dislocation, hip, congenital)
  754.30

Dislocation (articulation) (closed) (displacement) (simple) (subluxation) 839.8
  ankle (scaphoid bone) (closed) 837.0
    open 837.1
  astragalus (closed) 837.0
    open 837.1
  atlanto-axial (closed) 839.01
    open 839.11
  atlas (closed) 839.01
    open 839.11
  axis (closed) 839.02
    open 839.12
  Bell-Daly 723.8
  chiropractic (*see also* Lesion, nonallopathic) 739.9
  congenital NEC 755.8
    hip (*see also* Dislocation, hip, congenital) 754.30
    sacroiliac 755.69
    spine NEC 756.19
    vertebra 756.19
  elbow (closed) 832.00
    congenital 754.89
    recurrent 718.32
  femur
    distal end (closed) 836.50
      anterior 836.52
        open 836.62
      lateral 836.54
        open 836.64
      medial 836.53
        open 836.63
      open 836.60
      posterior 836.51
        open 836.61
    proximal end (closed) 835.00
      anterior (pubic) 835.03
      obturator 835.02
      posterior 835.01
  fibula
    distal end (closed) 837.0
      open 837.1
    proximal end (closed) 836.59
      open 836.69
  finger(s) (phalanx) (thumb) (closed) 834.00
    interphalangeal (joint) 834.02
    metacarpal (bone), distal end 834.01
      open 834.11
    metacarpophalangeal (joint) 834.01
      open 834.11
    recurrent 718.34
  foot (closed) 838.00
    open 838.10
    recurrent 718.37
  hip (closed) 835.00
    anterior 835.03
      obturator 835.02
    congenital (unilateral) 754.30
      bilateral 754.31
      with subluxation of other hip 754.35
    developmental 718.75
    posterior 835.01
    recurrent 718.35
  innominate (pubic juntion) (sacral junction) (closed) 839.69
    acetabulum (*see also* Dislocation, hip) 835.00

Dislocation—*continued*
  interphalangeal (joint)
    finger or hand (closed) 834.02
    foot or toe (closed) 838.06
      open 838.16
  joint NEC (closed) 839.8
    developmental 718.7☑

Note—*Use the following fifth-digit subclassification with categories 711-712, 715-716, 718, 719.0-719.6, 719.8, 719.9:*
0 *site unspecified*
1 *shoulder region*
2 *upper arm*
3 *forearm*
4 *hand*
5 *pelvic region and thigh*
6 *lower leg*
7 *ankle and foot*
8 *other specified sites*
9 *multiple sites*

  knee (closed) 836.50
    anterior 836.51
      open 836.61
    congenital (with genu recurvatum) 754.41
    habitual 718.36
    lateral 836.54
      open 836.64
    medial 836.53
      open 836.63
    old 718.36
    open 836.60
    posterior 836.52
      open 836.62
    recurrent 718.36
    rotatory 836.59
      open 836.69
  lumbar (vertebrae) (closed) 839.20
  lumbosacral (vertebrae) (closed) 839.20
    congenital 756.19
  metacarpal (bone)
    distal end (closed) 834.01
      open 834.11
    proximal end (closed) 833.05
  metacarpophalangeal (joint) (closed) 834.01
    open 834.11
  metatarsal (bone) (closed) 838.04
    open 838.14
  metatarsophalangeal (joint) (closed) 838.05
    open 838.15
  midtarsal (joint) (closed) 838.02
    open 838.12
  navicular (bone) foot (closed) 837.0
    open 837.1
  neck (*see also* Dislocation, vertebra, cervical) 839.00
  occiput from atlas (closed) 839.01
    open 839.11
  patella (closed) 836.3
    congenital 755.64
    open 836.4
  pathological NEC 718.20
    ankle 718.27
    elbow 718.22
    foot 718.27
    hand 718.24
    hip 718.25
    knee 718.26
    lumbosacral joint 724.6

Dislocation—*continued*
  pathological NEC—*continued*
    multiple sites 718.29
    pelvic region 718.25
    sacroiliac 724.6
    shoulder (region) 718.21
    specified site NEC 718.28
    spine 724.8
      sacroiliac 724.6
    wrist 718.23
  pelvis (closed) 839.69
    acetabulum (*see also* Dislocation, hip) 835.00
  phalanx
    foot or toe (closed) 838.09
      open 838.19
    hand or finger (*see also* Dislocation, finger) 834.00
  recurrent (*see also* Derangement, joint, recurrent) 718.3☑

Note—*Use the following fifth-digit subclassification with categories 711-712, 715-716, 718, 719.0-719.6, 719.8, 719.9:*
0 *site unspecified*
1 *shoulder region*
2 *upper arm*
3 *forearm*
4 *hand*
5 *pelvic region and thigh*
6 *lower leg*
7 *ankle and foot*
8 *other specified sites*
9 *multiple sites*

  elbow 718.32
  hip 718.35
  joint NEC 718.38
  knee 718.36
  lumbosacral (joint) 724.6
  patella 718.36
  sacroiliac 724.6
  shoulder 718.31
  sacroiliac (joint) (ligament) (closed) 839.42
    congenital 755.69
    recurrent 724.6
  scaphoid (bone)
    ankle or foot (closed) 837.0
      open 837.1
  shoulder (blade) (ligament) (closed) 831.00
    chronic 718.31
    recurrent 718.31
  spine (articular process) (*see also* Dislocation, vertebra) (closed) 839.40
    atlanto-axial (closed) 839.01
      open 839.11
      recurrent 723.8
    cervical, cervicodorsal, cervico-thoracic (closed) (*see also* Dislocation, vertebrae, cervical) 839.00
      open 839.10
      recurrent 723.8
    congenital 756.19
    recurrent 724.9
    sacroiliac 839.42
      recurrent 724.6
  tarsal (bone) (joint) 838.01
    open 838.11
  tarsometatarsal (joint) 838.03
    open 838.13

Dislocation—*continued*
  thigh
    distal end (*see also* Dislocation, femur, distal end) 836.50
    proximal end (*see also* Dislocation, hip) 835.00
  thumb(s) (*see also* Dislocation, finger) 834.00
  tibia
    distal end (closed) 837.0
      open 837.1
    proximal end (closed) 836.50
      anterior 836.51
        open 836.61
      lateral 836.54
        open 836.64
      medial 836.53
        open 836.63
      open 836.60
      posterior 836.52
        open 836.62
      rotatory 836.59
        open 836.69
  tibiofibular
    distal (closed) 837.0
      open 837.1
    superior (closed) 836.59
      open 836.69
  toe(s) (closed) 838.09
    open 838.19
  vertebra (articular process) (body) (closed) (traumatic) 839.40
    cervical, cervicodorsal or cervicothoracic (closed) 839.00
      first (atlas) 839.01
        open 839.11
      second (axis) 839.02
        open 839.12
      third 839.03
        open 839.13
      fourth 839.04
        open 839.14
      fifth 839.05
        open 839.15
      sixth 839.06
        open 839.16
      seventh 839.07
        open 839.17
      congenital 756.19
      multiple sites 839.08
        open 839.18
      open 839.10
    congenital 756.19
    dorsal 839.21
      recurrent 724.9
    lumbar, lumbosacral 839.20
    non-traumatic—*see* Displacement, intervertebral disc
    recurrent 724.9
  wrist (carpal bone) (scaphoid) (semilunar) (closed) 833.00
    metacarpal bone, proximal end 833.05
    recurrent 718.33
Disorder—*see also* Disease
  bone NEC 733.90
    specified NEC 733.99
  brachial plexus 353.0
  bursa 727.9
    shoulder region 726.10
  cardiac, functional 427.9
    psychogenic 306.2
  cardiovascular, psychogenic 306.2

☑ Additional Digit Required
© 2009 Ingenix

Disorder—*continued*
cartilage NEC 733.90
  articular 718.00
    ankle 718.07
    elbow 718.02
    foot 718.07
    hand 718.04
    hip 718.05
    multiple sites 718.09
    pelvic region 718.05
    shoulder region 718.01
    specified
      site NEC 718.08
      type NEC 733.99
    wrist 718.03
  cervical region NEC 723.9
  cervical root (nerve) NEC 353.2
  coccyx 724.70
    specified NEC 724.79
  cognitive 294.9
  coordination 781.3
  depressive NEC 311
  development, specific 315.9
    associated with hyperkinesia 314.1
    language 315.31
      and speech due to hearing loss 315.34
    learning 315.2
      arithmetical 315.1
      reading 315.00
    mixed 315.5
    motor coordination 315.4
    specified type NEC 315.8
    speech 315.39
  fascia 728.9
  identity
    childhood and adolescence 313.82
  impulse control (*see also* Disturbance, conduct, compulsive) 312.30
  intermittent explosive 312.34
  intervertebral disc 722.90
    cervical, cervicothoracic 722.91
    lumbar, lumbosacral 722.93
    thoracic, thoracolumbar 722.92
  introverted, of childhood and adolescence 313.22
  isolated explosive 312.35
  joint NEC 719.90
    ankle 719.97
    elbow 719.92
    foot 719.97
    hand 719.94
    hip 719.95
    knee 719.96
    multiple sites 719.99
    pelvic region 719.95
    psychogenic 306.0
    shoulder (region) 719.91
    specified site NEC 719.98
    wrist 719.93
  language (developmental) (expressive) 315.31
    mixed (receptive)(receptive-expressive) 315.32
  ligament 728.9
  ligamentous attachments, peripheral—*see also* Enthesopathy
    spine 720.1
  limb NEC 729.90
    psychogenic 306.0

Disorder—*continued*
lipoprotein deficiency (familial) 272.5
low back NEC 724.9
  psychogenic 306.0
lumbosacral
  plexus 353.1
  root (nerve) NEC 353.4
lymphoproliferative (chronic) NEC (M9970/1) 238.79
  post-transplant (PTLD) 238.77
male erectile 607.84
  nonorganic origin 302.72
mitral valve 424.0
motor tic 307.20
  chronic 307.22
movement NEC 333.90
  hysterical 300.11
  specified type NEC 333.99
  stereotypic 307.3
muscle 728.9
  psychogenic 306.0
  specified type NEC 728.3
muscular attachments, peripheral—*see also* Enthesopathy
  spine 720.1
musculoskeletal system NEC 729.90
  psychogenic 306.0
myoneural 358.9
  due to lead 358.2
  specified type NEC 358.8
  toxic 358.2
myotonic 359.29
neck region NEC 723.9
nerve 349.9
  accessory 352.4
  auriculotemporal 350.8
  axillary 353.0
  cranial 352.9
    eleventh 352.4
    fifth 350.9
    first 352.0
    multiple 352.6
    ninth 352.2
    seventh NEC 351.9
    tenth 352.3
    twelfth 352.5
  facial 351.9
    specified NEC 351.8
  femoral 355.2
  glossopharyngeal NEC 352.2
  hypoglossal 352.5
  iliohypogastric 355.79
  ilioinguinal 355.79
  intercostal 353.8
  lateral
    cutaneous of thigh 355.1
    popliteal 355.3
  lower limb NEC 355.8
  medial, popliteal 355.4
  median NEC 354.1
  obturator 355.79
  olfactory 352.0
  peroneal 355.3
  phrenic 354.8
  plantar 355.6
  pneumogastric 352.3
  posterior tibial 355.5
  radial 354.3
  recurrent laryngeal 352.3
  root 353.9
    specified NEC 353.8
  saphenous 355.79

Disorder—*continued*
  sciatic NEC 355.0
    specified NEC 355.9
      lower limb 355.79
      upper limb 354.8
    spinal 355.9
    sympathetic NEC 337.9
    trigeminal 350.9
      specified NEC 350.8
    ulnar 354.2
    upper limb NEC 354.9
    vagus 352.3
  nervous system NEC 349.9
    autonomic (peripheral) (*see also* Neuropathy, peripheral, autonomic) 337.9
    cranial 352.9
    parasympathetic (*see also* Neuropathy, peripheral, autonomic) 337.9
    sympathetic (*see also* Neuropathy, peripheral, autonomic) 337.9
    vegetative (*see also* Neuropathy, peripheral, autonomic) 337.9
  neurological NEC 781.99
    peripheral NEC 355.9
  neuromuscular NEC 358.9
    hereditary NEC 359.1
    specified NEC 358.8
    toxic 358.2
  obsessive-compulsive 300.3
  reflex 796.1
  respiration, respiratory NEC 519.9
    due to
      aspiration of liquids or solids 508.9
      inhalation of fumes or vapors 506.9
    psychogenic 306.1
  sacroiliac joint NEC 724.6
  sacrum 724.6
  schizoid, childhood or adolescence 313.22
  sense of smell 781.1
    psychogenic 306.7
  separation anxiety 309.21
  shyness, of childhood and adolescence 313.21
  skin NEC 709.9
  sleep 780.50
    circadian rhythm 327.30
      advanced sleep phase type 327.32
      alcohol induced 291.82
      delayed sleep phase type 327.31
      free running type 327.34
      irregular sleep-wake type 327.33
  social, of childhood and adolescence 313.22
  soft tissue 729.90
    specified type NEC 729.99
  speech NEC 784.59
  spine NEC 724.9
    ligamentous or muscular attachments, peripheral 720.1
  stress (*see also* Reaction, stress, acute) 308.9
    posttraumatic
      acute 308.3
      brief 308.3

Disorder—*continued*
  stress—*continued*
    posttraumatic—*continued*
      chronic 309.81
  substitution 300.11
  tendon 727.9
    shoulder region 726.10
  thoracic root (nerve) NEC 353.3
  tic 307.20
    chronic (motor or vocal) 307.22
    motor-verbal 307.23
    organic origin 333.1
  wakefulness (*see also* Hypersomnia) 780.54
    nonorganic origin (transient) 307.43
    persistent 307.44
Displacement, displaced
  brachial plexus (congenital) 742.8
  intervertebral disc
    lumbar, lumbosacral 722.10
      with myelopathy 722.73
    thoracic, thoracolumbar 722.11
      with myelopathy 722.72
  intervertebral disc (with neuritis, radiculitis, sciatica, or other pain) 722.2
    cervical, cervicodorsal, cervicothoracic 722.0
      with myelopathy 722.71
    due to trauma—*see* Dislocation, vertebra
    with myelopathy 722.70
  nail (congenital) 757.5
    acquired 703.8
  sacroiliac (congenital) (joint) 755.69
    old 724.6
  spine (congenital) 756.19
  trachea (congenital) 748.3
  xyphoid bone (process) 738.3
Disruption
  ligament(s)—*see also* Sprain
    knee
      old 717.89
        capsular 717.85
        collateral (medial) 717.82
          lateral 717.81
        cruciate (posterior) 717.84
          anterior 717.83
        specified site NEC 717.85
  phase-shift, of 24-hour sleep-wake cycle, unspecified 780.55
    nonorganic origin 307.45
  sleep-wake cycle (24-hour)
    unspecified 780.55
    circadian rhythm 327.33
    nonorganic origin 307.45
Dissection
  artery, arterial
    carotid 443.21
    iliac 443.22
    renal 443.23
    specified NEC 443.29
    vertebral 443.24
Dissociated personality NEC 300.15
Dissociative
  identity disorder 300.14
  reaction NEC 300.15
Dissolution, vertebra (*see also* Osteoporosis) 733.00

Distortion (congenital)
  ankle (joint) 755.69
  arm 755.59
  auditory canal 744.29
    causing impairment of hearing 744.02
  bronchus 748.3
  clavicle 755.51
  coccyx 756.19
  cricoid cartilage 748.3
  ear 744.29
    auricle 744.29
      causing impairment of hearing 744.02
      causing impairment of hearing 744.09
    external 744.29
      causing impairment of hearing 744.02
    inner 744.05
    middle, except ossicles 744.03
      ossicles 744.04
    ossicles 744.04
  epiglottis 748.3
  face bone(s) 756.0
  femur 755.69
  fibula 755.69
  finger(s) 755.59
  foot 755.67
  glottis 748.3
  hand bone(s) 755.59
  humerus 755.59
  knee (joint) 755.64
  larynx 748.3
  leg 755.69
  lumbar spine 756.19
  lumbosacral (joint) (region) 756.19
  lung (fissures) (lobe) 748.69
  nerve 742.8
  nose 748.1
  organ
    of Corti 744.05
  ossicles, ear 744.04
  patella 755.64
  radius 755.59
  sacroiliac joint 755.69
  sacrum 756.19
  scapula 755.59
  shoulder girdle 755.59
  skull bone(s) 756.0
  spinal cord 742.59
  spine 756.19
  thyroid (gland) 759.2
    cartilage 748.3
  tibia 755.69
  toe(s) 755.66
  trachea (cartilage) 748.3
  ulna 755.59
  vertebra 756.19
  wrist (bones) (joint) 755.59

Distress
  leg 729.5
  respiratory 786.09
    acute (adult) 518.82
    adult syndrome (following shock, surgery, or trauma) 518.5
    specified NEC 518.82
    syndrome (idiopathic) (newborn) 769

Disturbance—*see also* Disease
  coordination 781.3
  cranial nerve NEC 352.9
  gait 781.2
    hysterical 300.11

Disturbance—*continued*
  heart, functional (conditions classifiable to 426, 427, 428)
    psychogenic 306.2
  isolated explosive 312.35
  learning, specific NEC 315.2
  memory (*see also* Amnesia) 780.93
    mild, following organic brain damage 310.1
  mental (*see also* Disorder, mental) 300.9
    associated with diseases classified elsewhere 316
  motor 796.1
  nutritional 269.9
    nail 703.8
  ocular motion 378.87
    psychogenic 306.7
  oculogyric 378.87
    psychogenic 306.7
  oculomotor NEC 378.87
    psychogenic 306.7
  olfactory nerve 781.1
  reflex 796.1
  rhythm, heart 427.9
    psychogenic 306.2
  sensation (cold) (heat) (localization) (tactile discrimination localization) (texture) (vibratory) NEC 782.0
    hysterical 300.11
    skin 782.0
    smell 781.1
    taste 781.1
  sensory (*see also* Disturbance, sensation) 782.0
    innervation 782.0
  situational (transient) (*see also* Reaction, adjustment) 309.9
    acute 308.3
  sleep 780.50
    initiation or maintenance (*see also* Insomnia) 780.52
      nonorganic origin 307.41
    nonorganic origin 307.40
      specified type NEC 307.49
    specified NEC 780.59
      nonorganic origin 307.49
    wakefulness (*see also* Hypersomnia) 780.54
      nonorganic origin 307.43
  speech NEC 784.5
    developmental 315.39
      associated with hyperkinesis 314.1
  sympathetic (nerve) (*see also* Neuropathy, peripheral, autonomic) 337.9
  temperature sense 782.0
    hysterical 300.11
  touch (*see also* Disturbance, sensation) 782.0
  vasomotor 443.9
  vasospastic 443.9
  wakefulness (initiation or maintenance) (*see also* Hypersomnia) 780.54
    nonorganic origin 307.43

Disuse atrophy, bone 733.7
Ditthomska syndrome 307.81
Diuresis 788.42
Dizziness 780.4
  hysterical 300.11
  psychogenic 306.9

DOPS (diffuse obstructive pul-monary syndrome) 496
Double
  larynx 748.3
  vocal cords 748.3
Drainage
  stump (amputation) (surgical) 997.62
Dream state, hysterical 300.13
Dressler's syndrome (postmyocardial infarction) 411.0
Drift, ulnar 736.09
Droop
  facial 781.94
Drop
  finger 736.29
  foot 736.79
  toe 735.8
  wrist 736.05
Dropsy, dropsical (*see also* Edema) 782.3
  cardiac (*see also* Failure, heart) 428.0
  cardiorenal (*see also* Hyperension, cardiorenal) 404.90
  chest 511.9
  gangrenous (*see also* Gangrene) 785.4
  heart (*see also* Failure, heart) 428.0
  lung 514
Drug—*see also* condition
  adverse effect NEC, correct substance properly administered 995.20
  therapy (maintenance) status NEC V58.1
    long-term (current) use V58.69
      antiplatelet V58.63
      antithrombotic V58.63
      aspirin V58.66
      high risk medications NEC V58.69
      insulin V58.67
      opiate analgesic V58.69
      steroids V58.65
Duchenne's
  disease 094.0
    muscular dystrophy 359.1
    pseudohypertrophy, muscles 359.1
  paralysis 335.22
  syndrome 335.22
Duchenne-Aran myelopathic, muscular atrophy (non-progressive) (progressive) 335.21
Duchenne-Griesinger disease 359.1
Duplay's disease, periarthritis, or syndrome 726.2
Duplication—*see also* Accessory
  frontonasal process 756.0
  nose 748.1
  spinal cord (incomplete) 742.51
  vocal cords 748.3
Dupré's disease or syndrome (meningism) 781.6
Dupuytren's
  contraction 728.6
  disease (muscle contracture) 728.6
  fracture (closed) 824.4
    radius (closed) 813.42
  muscle contracture 728.6
Dust
  reticulation (occupational) 504

Dysarthria 784.51
  due to late effect of cerebrovascular disease (*see also* Late effect(s) (of) cerebrovascular disease) 438.13
Dysautonomia (*see also* Neuropathy, peripheral, autonomic) 337.9
  familial 742.8
Dysbasia 719.7
  angiosclerotica intermittens 443.9
    due to atherosclerosis 440.21
  hysterical 300.11
  lordotica (progressiva) 333.6
Dyscalculia 315.1
Dyschezia (*see also* Constipation) 564.00
Dysdiadochokinesia 781.3
Dysesthesia 782.0
  hysterical 300.11
Dysfunction
  associated with sleep stages or arousal from sleep 780.56
    nonorganic origin 307.47
  bladder NEC 596.59
  brain, minimal (*see also* Hyperkinesia) 314.9
  minimal brain (child) (*see also* Hyperkinesia) 314.9
  segmental (*see also* Dysfunc-tion, somatic) 739.9
  somatic 739.9
    abdomen 739.9
    acromioclavicular 739.7
    cervical 739.1
    cervicothoracic 739.1
    costochondral 739.8
    costovertebral 739.8
    extremities
      lower 739.6
      upper 739.7
    head 739.0
    hip 739.5
    lumbar, lumbosacral 739.3
    occipitocervical 739.0
    pelvic 739.5
    pubic 739.5
    rib cage 739.8
    sacral 739.4
    sacrococcygeal 739.4
    sacroiliac 739.4
    specified site NEC 739.9
    sternochondral 739.8
    sternoclavicular 739.7
    temporomandibular 739.0
    thoracic, thoracolumbar 739.2
  ventricular 429.9
    with congestive heart failure (*see also* Failure, heart) 428.0
  vesicourethral NEC 596.59
Dysgeusia 781.1
Dysgraphia 781.3
Dyskinesia 781.3
  hysterical 300.11
  neuroleptic-induced tardive 333.85
  orofacial 333.82
    due to drugs 333.85
  subacute, due to drugs 333.85
  tardive (oral) 333.85
Dyslalia 784.59
  developmental 315.39
Dyslexia 784.61
  developmental 315.02
Dysmetria 781.3
Dysorexia 783.0
  hysterical 300.11

Dysostosis
cleidocranial, cleidocranialis 755.59
craniofacial 756.0
mandibularis 756.0
mandibulofacial, incomplete 756.0
Dysphagia 784.59
cervical 787.29
functional 300.11
neurogenic 787.29
nervous 300.11
oral phase 787.21
oropharyngeal phase 787.22
pharyngeal phase 787.23
pharyngoesophageal phase 787.24
specified NEC 787.29
Dysphonia 784.49
clericorum 784.49
functional 300.11
hysterical 300.11
psychogenic 306.1
spastica 478.79
Dysplasia—see also Anomaly
brain 742.9
bronchopulmonary, fetus or
newborn 770.7
epithelial
epiglottis 478.79
hip (congenital) 755.63
with dislocation (see also
Dislocation, hip,
congenital) 754.30
joint 755.8
leg 755.69
lung 748.5
nervous system (general) 742.9
oculoauriculovertebral 756.0
periosteum 733.99
spinal cord 742.9
Dyspnea (nocturnal) (paroxysmal)
786.09
asthmatic (bronchial) (see also
Asthma) 493.9☑

Note—Use the following fifth-digit
subclassification with codes 493.0-
493.2, 493.9:
0   unspecified
1   with status asthmaticus
2   with (acute) exacerbation

cardiac (see also Failure,
ventricular, left) 428.1
cardiac (see also Failure, ventricular,
left) 428.1
functional 300.11
hyperventilation 786.01
hysterical 300.11
Monday morning 504
psychogenic 306.1
Dyspraxia 781.3
syndrome 315.4
Dysreflexia, autonomic 337.3
Dyssecretosis, mucoserous 710.2
Dyssomnia NEC 780.56
nonorganic origin 307.47
Dyssynergia
cerebellaris myoclonica 334.2
detrusor sphincter (bladder)
596.55
Dystasia, hereditary areflexic
334.3
Dystonia
acute
due to drugs 333.72
neuroleptic-induced acure
333.72

Dystonia—continued
deformans progressiva 333.6
lenticularis 333.6
musculorum deformans 333.6
torsion (idiopathic) 333.6
acquired 333.79
fragments (of) 333.89
genetic 333.6
symptomatic 333.79
Dystonic
movements 781.0
Dystrophy, dystrophia 783.9
Becker's type 359.22
brevicollis 756.16
cervical (sympathetic) NEC 337.09
Duchenne's 359.1
Erb's 359.1
Gowers' muscular 359.1
hereditary, progressive muscular
359.1
Landouzy-Déjérine 359.1
Leyden-Möbius 359.1
muscular 359.1
congenital (hereditary) 359.0
myotonic 359.22
distal 359.1
Duchenne's 359.1
Erb's 359.1
fascioscapulohumeral 359.1
Gowers' 359.1
hereditary (progressive) 359.1
Landouzy-Déjérine 359.1
limb-girdle 359.1
myotonic 359.21
progressive (hereditary) 359.1
Charcôt-Marie-Tooth 356.1
pseudohypertrophic (infantile)
359.1
myotonic 359.21
myotonica 359.21
nail 703.8
neurovascular (traumatic) (see also
Neuropathy, peri-pheral,
autonomic) 337.9
ocular 359.1
oculopharyngeal 359.1
pelvicrural atrophic 359.1
progressive ophthalmoplegic 359.1
reflex neuromuscular—see
Dystrophy, sympathetic
retina, retinal (hereditary) 362.70
in
Bassen-Kornzweig syndrome
272.5 [362.72]
cerebroretinal lipidosis 330.1
[362.71]
Refsum's disease 356.3
[362.72]
scapuloperoneal 359.1
skin NEC 709.9
sympathetic (posttraumatic)
(reflex) 337.20
lower limb 337.22
specified NEC 337.29
upper limb 337.21
unguium 703.8

E

Eaton-Lambert syndrome (see also
Neoplasm, by site, malignant)
199.1 [358.1]
Ecchordosis physaliphora 756.0
Ecthyma 686.8
gangrenosum 686.09

Ectopic, ectopia (congenital)
759.89
bone and cartilage in lung 748.69
Ectrodactyly 755.4
finger (see also Absence, finger,
congenital) 755.29
toe (see also Absence, toe,
congenital) 755.39
Ectromelia 755.4
lower limb 755.30
upper limb 755.20
Eczema (acute) (allergic) (chronic)
(erythematous) (fissum)
(occupational) (rubrum)
(squamous) 692.9
pustular 686.8
stasis (lower extremity) 454.1
ulcerated 454.2
Edema, edematous 782.3
angiospastic 443.9
cardiac (see also Failure, heart)
428.0
cardiovascular (see also Failure,
heart) 428.0
connective tissue 782.3
glottis, glottic, glottides
(obstructive) (passive) 478.6
heart (see also Failure, heart) 428.0
infectious 782.3
larynx (see also Edema, glottis)
478.6
legs 782.3
localized 782.3
lung 514
acute 518.4
chemical (due to fumes or
vapors) 506.1
due to
external agent(s) NEC
508.9
specified NEC 508.8
fumes and vapors
(chemical)
(inhalation) 506.1
radiation 508.0
with heart disease or failure
(see also Failure,
ventricular, left) 428.1
congestive 428.0
chemical (acute) 506.1
chronic 506.4
chronic 514
chemical (due to fumes or
vapors) 506.4
due to
external agent(s) NEC
508.9
specified NEC 508.8
fumes or vapors
(chemical)
(inhalation) 506.4
radiation 508.1
external agent 508.9
specified NEC 508.8
postoperative 518.4
terminal 514
lymphatic 457.1
pitting 782.3
spinal cord 336.1
stasis (see also Hypertension,
venous) 459.30
subglottic (see also Edema, glottis)
478.6
supraglottic (see also Edema,
glottis) 478.6

Edema, edematous—continued
toxic NEC 782.3
traumatic NEC 782.3
Effect, adverse NEC
biological, correct substance
properly administered (see
also Effect, adverse, drug)
995.20
drugs and medicinals NEC 995.20
correct substance properly
administered 995.20
medicinal substance, correct,
properly administered (see
also Effect, adverse, drugs)
995.20
other drug, medicinal and
biological substance 995.29
radiation (diagnostic) (fallout)
(infrared) (natural source)
(therapeutic) (tracer)
(ultraviolet) (x-ray) NEC 990
fibrosis of lungs 508.1
pneumonitis 508.0
with pulmonary manifestations
acute 508.0
chronic 508.1
Effort
intolerance 306.2
syndrome (aviators) (psychogenic)
306.2
Effusion
bronchial (see also Bronchitis) 490
joint 719.00
ankle 719.07
elbow 719.02
foot 719.07
hand 719.04
hip 719.05
knee 719.06
multiple sites 719.09
pelvic region 719.05
shoulder (region) 719.01
specified site NEC 719.08
wrist 719.03
pleura, pleurisy, pleuritic,
pleuropericardial 511.9
bacterial, nontuberculous 511.1
fetus or newborn 511.9
nontuberculous 511.9
bacterial 511.1
pneumococcal 511.1
staphylococcal 511.1
streptococcal 511.1
Eggshell nails 703.8
Ejaculation, semen
painful 608.89
psychogenic 306.59
Ekbom syndrome (restless legs)
333.94
Elastomyofibrosis 425.3
Elephant man syndrome 237.71
Elephantiasis (nonfilarial) 457.1
glandular 457.1
lymphangiectatic 457.1
lymphatic vessel 457.1
neuromatosa 237.71
scrotum 457.1
streptococcal 457.1
telangiectodes 457.1
Elevation
blood pressure (see also
Hypertension) 401.9
scapula, congenital 755.52

ICD-9-CM Index

Elongation, elongated
(congenital)—*see also* Distortion
petiolus (epiglottidis) 748.3
styloid bone (process) 733.99
Emancipation disorder 309.22
Embolism 444.9
artery 444.9
coronary (*see also* Infarct,
myocardium) 410.9☑

Note—Use the following fifth-digit
subclassification with category 410:
0   *episode unspecified*
1   *initial episode*
2   *subsequent episode without*
    recurrence

without myocardial infarction
411.81
coronary (artery or vein) (systemic)
(*see also* Infarct,
myocardium) 410.9☑
without myocardial infarction
411.81
intracranial (*see also* Embolism,
brain) 434.1☑
venous sinus (any) 325
late effect—*see* category 326
postoperative NEC 997.2
cerebral 997.02
pulmonary 415.11
septic 415.11
spinal cord (nonpyogenic) 336.1
pyogenic origin 324.1
late effect—*see* category 326
vein 453.9
antecubital
acute 453.81
chronic 453.71
axillary
acute 453.84
chronic 453.74
basilic
acute 453.81
chronic 453.71
brachial
acute 453.82
chronic 453.72
brachiocephalic (innominate)
acute 453.87
chronic 453.77
cephalic
acute 453.81
chronic 453.71
coronary (*see also* Infarct,
myocardium) 410.9☑
without myocardial infarction
411.81
internal jugular
acute 453.86
chronic 453.76
lower extremity (superficial)
453.6
deep 453.40
acute 453.40
calf 453.42
distal (lower leg)
453.42
femoral 453.41
iliac 453.41
lower leg 453.42
peroneal 453.42
popliteal 453.41
proximal (upper leg)
453.41

Embolism—*continued*
vein—*continued*
lower extremity—*continued*
deep—*continued*
acute—*continued*
thigh 453.41
tibial 453.42
chronic 453.50
calf 453.52
distal (lower leg)
453.52
femoral 453.51
iliac 453.51
lower leg 453.52
peroneal 453.52
popliteal 453.51
proximal (upper leg)
453.51
thigh 453.51
tibial 453.52
saphenous (greater) (lesser)
453.6
superficial 453.6
radial
acute 453.82
chronic 453.72
saphenous (greater) (lesser)
453.6
specified NEC (acute) 453.89
chronic 453.79
subclavian
acute 453.85
chronic 453.75
superior vena cava
acute 453.87
chronic 453.77
thoracic
acute 453.87
chronic 453.77
ulnar
acute 453.82
chronic 453.72
upper extremity 453.83
acute 453.83
deep 453.82
superficial 453.81
chronic 453.73
deep 453.72
superficial 453.71
vena cava
inferior 453.2
superior
acute 453.87
chronic 453.77
Emotogenic disease (*see also*
Disorder, psychogenic) 306.9
Emphysema (atrophic) (centriacinar)
(centrilobular) (chronic)
(diffuse) (essential)
(hypertrophic) (interlobular)
(lung) (obstructive) (panlobular)
(paracicatricial) (paracinar)
(postural) (pulmonary) (senile)
(subpleural) (traction)
(unilateral) (unilobular)
(vesicular) 492.8
bullous (giant) 492.0
compensatory 518.2
congenital 770.2
due to fumes or vapors 506.4
fetus or newborn (interstitial)
(mediastinal) (unilobular)
770.2
heart 416.9

Emphysema—*continued*
interstitial 518.1
congenital 770.2
fetus or newborn 770.2
mediastinal 518.1
fetus or newborn 770.2
newborn (interstitial) (mediastinal)
(unilobular) 770.2
obstructive diffuse with fibrosis
492.8
subcutaneous 958.7
nontraumatic 518.1
with bronchitis
chronic 491.20
with exacerbation (acute)
491.21
Employment examination
(certification) V70.5
Empyema (chest) (diaphragmatic)
(double) (encapsulated)
(general) (interlobar) (lung)
(medial) (necessitatis)
(perforating chest wall) (pleura)
(pneumococcal) (residual)
(sacculated) (streptococcal)
(supradiaphragmatic) 510.9
acute 510.9
with fistula 510.0
brain (any part) (*see also* Abcess,
brain) 324.0
ventricular (*see also* Abscess, brain)
324.0
with fistula 510.0
Encephalitis (bacterial) (chronic)
(hemorrhagic) (idiopathic)
(nonepidemic) (spurious)
(subacute) 323.9
due to
herpes 054.3
human herpesvirus 6 058.21
human herpesvirus 7 058.29
human herpesvirus NEC 058.29
human herpesvirus 6 058.21
human herpesvirus 7 058.29
human herpesvirus NEC 058.29
Encephalo-
myeloradiculoneuritis (acute)
357.0
Encephalopathy (acute) 348.30
congenital 742.9
demyelinating (callosal) 341.8
due to
dialysis 294.8
transient 293.9
drugs—(*see also* Table of Drugs
and Chemicals) 348.39
influenza (virus) 487.8
trauma (postconcussional)
310.2
current (*see also* Concussion,
brain) 850.9
vaccination 323.51
hypoxic—*see also* Damage, brain,
anoxic
Ischemic (HIE) 768.70
mild 768.71
moderage 768.72
severe 768.73
infantile cystic necrotizing
(congenital) 341.8
leukopolio 330.0
necrotizing
hemorrhagic (acute) 323.61

Encephalopathy—*continued*
necrotizing—*continued*
subacute 330.8
spongioform 046.19
viral, spongioform 046.19
postcontusional 310.2
posttraumatic 310.2
subacute
necrotizing 330.8
subcortical progressive (Schilder)
341.1
chronic (Binswanger's) 290.12
traumatic (postconcussional) 310.2
current (*see also* Concus-sion,
brain) 850.9
Wernicke's (superior hemorrhagic
polioencephalitis) 265.1
Encephalorrhagia (*see also*
Hemorrhage, brain) 432.9
healed or old V12.54
Endocarditis (chronic)
(indeterminate) (interstitial)
(marantic) (nonbacterial
thrombotic) (residual) (sclerotic)
(sclerous) (senile) (valvular)
424.90
aortic (heart) (nonrheumatic)
(valve) 424.1
arteriosclerotic 424.1
hypertensive 424.1
specified cause, except
rheumatic 424.1
atypical verrucous (Libman-Sacks)
710.0 [424.91]
congenital 425.3
due to
disseminated lupus
erythematosus 710.0
[424.91]
prosthetic cardiac valve 996.61
fetal 425.3
Libman-Sacks 710.0 [424.91]
mitral (chronic) (double) (fibroid)
(heart) (inactive) (valve)
(with chorea) 394.9
arteriosclerotic 424.0
hypertensive 424.0
nonrheumatic 424.0
pulmonary (chronic) (heart) (valve)
424.3
arteriosclerotic or due to
arteriosclerosis 424.3
hypertensive or due to
hypertension (benign)
424.3
tricuspid (chronic) (heart) (inactive)
(rheumatic) (valve) (with
chorea) 397.0
arteriosclerotic 424.2
hypertensive 424.2
nonrheumatic 424.2
specified cause, except
rheumatic 424.2
verrucous (acute) (any valve)
(chronic) (subacute) NEC
710.0 [424.91]
nonbacterial 710.0 [424.91]
nonrheumatic 710.0 [424.91]
Endomyofibrosis 425.0
Endophlebitis (*see also* Phlebitis)
451.9
Enthesopathy 726.39
ankle and tarsus 726.70
elbow region 726.30
specified NEC 726.39

☑ Additional Digit Required
© 2009 Ingenix

Enthesopathy—*continued*
hip 726.5
knee 726.60
peripheral NEC 726.8
shoulder region 726.10
adhesive 726.0
spinal 720.1
wrist and carpus 726.4
Epicondylitis (elbow) (lateral)
726.32
medial 726.31
Epilepsy, epileptic (idiopathic)
345.9☑

Note—use the following fifth-digit subclassification with categories 345.0, 345.1, 345.4-345.9:

0   without mention of intractable epilepsy

1   with intractable epilepsy

pharmacoresistant
(pharmacologically
resistant) poorly
controlled refractory
(medically) treatment
resistant
deterioration
without behavioral disturbance
345.9☑ [294.10]
with behavioral disturbance
345.9☑ [294.11]
laryngeal 786.2
localization related (focal) (partial)
and epileptic syndromes
with
complex partial seizures
345.4
simple partial seizures 345.5
myoclonus, myoclonic 345.1☑
progressive (familial) 345.1
partial (focalized) 345.5
without impairment of
consciousness 345.5
progresive myoclonic (familial)
345.1
sleep (*see also* Narcolepsy) 347.00
traumatic (injury unspecified)
907.0
twilight 293.0
Unverricht (-Lundborg) (familial
myoclonic) 333.2
Epiphyseal arrest 733.91
Episode
brain (*see also* Disease,
cerebrovascular, acute) 436
cerebral (*see also* Disease,
cerebrovascular, acute) 436
psychotic (*see also* Psychosis) 298.9
organic, transient 293.9
Erlacher-Blount syndrome (tibia
vara) 732.4
Erosion
bone 733.99
cartilage (joint) 733.99
vertebra 733.99
Erythermalgia (primary) 443.82
Eulenburg's disease (congenital
paramyotonia) 359.29
Eversion
foot NEC 736.79
congenital 755.67
Exaggerated lumbosacral angle
(with impinging spine) 756.12

Examination (general) (routine) (of)
(for) V70.9
follow-up (routine) (following)
V67.9
high-risk medication NEC
V67.51
following
treatment (for) V67.9
fracture V67.4

involving high-risk
medication NEC
V67.51
health (of)
armed forces personnel V70.5
defined subpopulation NEC
V70.5
inhabitants of institutions V70.5
occupational V70.5
pre-employment screening
V70.5
preschool children V70.5
prisoners V70.5
prostitutes V70.5
refugees V70.5
school children V70.5
students V70.5
medical (for) (of) V70.9
armed forces personnel V70.5
defined subpopulation NEC
V70.5
inhabitants of institutions V70.5
occupational V70.5
pre-employment V70.5
preschool children V70.5
prisoners V70.5
prostitutes V70.5
refugees V70.5
school children V70.5
students V70.5
Exercise
breathing V57.0
remedial NEC V57.1
therapeutic NEC V57.1
Exostosis 726.91
hip 726.5
luxurians 728.11
spine 721.8
wrist 726.4

F

Faciocephalalgia, autonomic (*see
also* Neuropathy, **peripheral,
autonomic**) 337.9
Facioscapulohumeral myopathy
359.1
Factor
psychic, associated with diseases
classified elsewhere 316
Fahr-Volhard disease (malignant
nephrosclerosis) 403.00
Failure, failed
cardiac (*see also* Failure, heart)
428.9
cardiorenal (chronic) 428.9
hypertensive (*see also*
Hypertension, cardiorenal)
404.93
cardiovascular (chronic) 428.9
congestive (*see also* Failure, heart)
428.0
coronary (*see also* Insufficiency,
coronary) 411.89

Failure, failed—*continued*
fusion (joint) (spinal) 996.49
heart (acute) (sudden) 428.9
arteriosclerotic 440.9
combined left-right sided 428.0
combined systolic and diastolic
428.40
acute 428.41
acute on chronic 428.43
chronic 428.42
compensated (*see also* Failure,
heart) 428.0
congestive (compensated)
(decompensated) (*see also*
Failure, heart) 428.0
hypertensive (*see also*
Hypertension, heart)
402.90
benign 402.11
malignant 402.01
with renal disease (*see also*
Hyper-tension,
cardio-renal) 404.91
with renal failure
404.93
decompensated (*see also* Failure,
heart) 428.0
diastolic 428.30
acute 428.31
acute on chronic 428.33
chronic 428.32
high output NEC 428.9
hypertensive (*see also*
Hypertension, heart)
402.91
benign 402.11
malignant 402.01
with renal disease (*see also*
Hypertension,
cardiorenal) 404.91
with renal failure 404.93
left (ventricular) (*see also* Failure,
ventricular, left) 428.1
with right-sided failure (*see
also* Failure, heart)
428.0
low output (syndrome) NEC
428.9
right (secondary to left heart
failure, conditions
classifiable to 428.1)
(ventricular) (*see also*
Failure, heart) 428.0
systolic 428.20
acute 428.21
acute on chronic 428.23
chronic 428.22
thyrotoxic (*see also*
Thyrotoxicosis) 242.9☑
[425.7]

*Note—Use the following fifth-digit
subclassification with category 242:*

*0   without mention of thyrotoxic crisis
or storm*

*1   with mention of thyrotoxic crisis or
storm*

with
acute pulmonary edema (*see
also* Failure, ventricular,
left) 428.1
with congestion (*see also*
Failure, heart) 428.0
decompensation (*see also*
Failure, heart) 428.0

Failure, failed—*continued*
hypertensive heart (*see also*
Hypertension, heart) 402.91
benign 402.11
malignant 402.01
initial alveolar expansion, newborn
770.4
myocardium, myocardial (*see also*
Failure, heart) 428.9
chronic (*see also* Failure, heart)
428.0
congestive (*see also* Failure,
heart) 428.0
renal 586
chronic 585
hypertensive or with
hypertension (*see also*
Hypertension, kidney)
403.91
hypertensive (*see also*
Hypertension, kidney)
403.91
with
hypertension (*see also*
Hypertension, kidney)
403.91
hypertensive heart disease
(conditions classifiable
to 402) 404.92
benign 404.12
with heart failure
404.13
malignant 404.02
with heart failure
404.03
with heart failure 404.93
respiration, respiratory 518.81
acute 518.81
acute and chronic 518.84
chronic 518.83
due to trauma, surgery or shock
518.5
segmentation—*see also* Fusion
fingers (*see also* Syndactylism,
fingers) 755.11
toes (*see also* Syndactylism,
toes) 755.13
senile (general) 797
with psychosis 290.20
to thrive
adult 783.7
transplant 996.80
organ (immune or non-immune
cause) 996.80
heart 996.83
ventricular (*see also* Failure, heart)
428.9
left 428.1
hypertensive (*see also*
Hypertension, heart)
402.91
benign 402.11
malignant 402.01
right (*see also* Failure, heart)
428.0
Fallen arches 734
False—*see also* condition
bursa 727.89
croup 478.75
joint 733.82
pregnancy 300.11
Farmers'
lung 495.0
Fasciculation 781.0

ICD-9-CM Index

Fasciitis 729.4
  eosinophilic 728.89
  plantar 728.71
Fatness 278.02
Feeding
  faulty (elderly) (infant) 783.3
  improper (elderly) (infant) 783.3
  problem (elderly) (infant) 783.3
    nonorganic origin 307.59
Feil-Klippel syndrome (brevicollis) 756.16
Felon (any digit) (with lymphangitis) 681.01
Felty's syndrome (rheumatoid arthritis with splenomegaly and leukopenia) 714.1
Femora vara 736.32
Fever
  West
    Nile (viral) 066.40
      with
        cranial nerve disorders 066.42
        encephalitis 066.41
        optic neuritis 066.42
        other complications 066.49
        other neurologic manifestations 066.42
        polyradiculitis 066.42
Fibrillation
  muscular 728.9
Fibrin
  ball or bodies, pleural (sac) 511.0
Fibrocellulitis progressiva ossificans 728.11
Fibrocystic
  disease 277.00
    lung 518.89
      congenital 748.4
    pancreas 277.00
Fibrodysplasia ossificans multiplex (progressiva) 728.11
Fibroelastosis (cordis) (endocardial) (endomyocardial) 425.3
Fibromatosis 728.79
  congenital generalized (CGF) 759.89
  Dupuytren's 728.6
  plantar fascia 728.71
Fibromyalgia 729.1
Fibromyositis (see also Myositis) 729.1
  scapulohumeral 726.2
Fibrosis, fibrotic
  alveolar (diffuse) 516.3
  bauxite (of lung) 503
  capillary—see also Arteriosclerosis
    lung (chronic) (see also Fibrosis, lung) 515
  cystic (of pancreas) 277.00
    with
      meconium ileus 277.01
  endomyocardial (African) 425.0
  graphite (of lung) 503
  interstitial pulmonary, newborn 770.7
  lung (atrophic) (capillary) (chronic) (confluent) (massive) (perialveolar) (peribronchial) 515
  diffuse (idiopathic) (interstitial) 516.3

Fibrosis, fibrotic—continued
  lung—continued
    due to
      bauxite 503
      fumes or vapors (chemical inhalation) 506.4
      graphite 503
    following radiation 508.1
    postinflammatory 515
    silicotic (massive) (occupational) 502
    with
      anthracosilicosis (occupational) 500
      anthracosis (occupational) 500
      asbestosis (occupational) 501
      bagassosis (occupational) 495.1
      bauxite 503
      berylliosis (occupational) 503
      byssinosis (occupational) 504
      calcicosis (occupational) 502
      chalicosis (occupational) 502
      dust reticulation (occupational) 504
      farmers' lung 495.0
      gannister disease (occupational) 502
      graphite 503
      pneumonoconiosis (occupational) 505
      pneumosiderosis (occupational) 503
      siderosis (occupational) 503
      silicosis (occupational) 502
  muscle NEC 728.2
  pancreas 577.8
    cystic 277.00
      with
        meconium ileus 277.01
  periarticular (see also Ankylosis) 718.5☑

Note—Use the following fifth-digit subclassification with categories 711-712, 715-716, 718, 719.0-719.6, 719.8, 719.9:
0 site unspecified
1 shoulder region
2 upper arm
3 forearm
4 hand
5 pelvic region and thigh
6 lower leg
7 ankle and foot
8 other specified sites
9 multiple sites

  perineural NEC 355.9
    foot 355.6
  pleura 511.0
  pulmonary (chronic) (see also Fibrosis, lung) 515
    alveolar capillary block 516.3
    interstitial
      diffuse (idiopathic) 516.3
      newborn 770.7
  skin NEC 709.2
  submucous NEC 709.2
Fibrositis (periarticular) (rheumatoid) 729.0
  humeroscapular region 726.2
  nodular, chronic
    Jaccoud's 714.4
    rheumatoid 714.4

Fibrositis—continued
  ossificans 728.11
  scapulohumeral 726.2
Fibrothorax 511.0
Findings, abnormal, without diagnosis (examination) (laboratory test) 796.4
  blood gas level 790.91
  culture, positive NEC 795.39
    HIV V08
    human immunodeficiency virus V08
    viral
      human immuno-deficiency V08
  electromyogram (EMG) 794.17
    ocular 794.14
  function study NEC 794.9
    oculomotor 794.14
    pulmonary 794.2
  oxygen saturation 790.91
  PO2-oxygen ratio 790.91
  scan NEC 794.9
    lung 794.2
  serological (for)
    human immunodeficiency virus (HIV) positive V08
Fish
  meal workers' lung 495.8
Fistula (sinus) 686.9
  abdominothoracic 510.0
  arteriovenous (acquired) 447.0
    brain 437.3
      congenital 747.81
        ruptured (see also Hemorrhage, subarachnoid) 430
    ruptured (see also Hemorrhage, subarachnoid) 430
  coronary 414.19
  heart 414.19
  surgically created (for dialysis) V45.11
  complication NEC 996.73
    mechanical 996.1
  aural 383.81
    congenital 744.49
  auricle 383.81
    congenital 744.49
  bone 733.99
  branchial (cleft) 744.41
  branchiogenous 744.41
  bronchial 510.0
  bronchocutaneous, bronchomediastinal, bronchopleural, bronchopleuromediastinal (infective) 510.0
  carotid-cavernous
    congenital 747.81
      with hemorrhage 430
  cervical, lateral (congenital) 744.41
  cervicoaural (congenital) 744.49
  chest (wall) 510.0
  coronary, arteriovenous 414.19
  costal region 510.0
  cutaneous 686.9
  diaphragm 510.0
    bronchovisceral 510.0
    pleuroperitoneal 510.0
    pulmonoperitoneal 510.0
  hepatopleural 510.0
  hepatopulmonary 510.0

Fistula—continued
  joint 719.89
    ankle 719.87
    elbow 719.82
    foot 719.87
    hand 719.84
    hip 719.85
    knee 719.86
    multiple sites 719.89
    pelvic region 719.85
    shoulder (region) 719.81
    specified site NEC 719.88
    wrist 719.83
  laryngotracheal 748.3
  larynx 478.79
  lung 510.0
  mediastinal 510.0
  mediastinobronchial 510.0
  mediastinocutaneous 510.0
  nasal 478.19
  nose 478.19
  pharynx 478.29
    branchial cleft (congenital) 744.41
  pleura, pleural, pleurocutaneous, pleuroperitoneal 510.0
  stomach 510.0
  preauricular (congenital) 744.46
  pulmonary 510.0
  pulmonoperitoneal 510.0
  skin 686.9
  thoracic 510.0
  thoracoabdominal 510.0
  thoracicogastric 510.0
  thoracicointestinal 510.0
  thoracoabdominal 510.0
  thoracogastric 510.0
Fistula (sinus) 686.9
  thorax 510.0
  trachea (congenital) (external) (internal) 748.3
Fit 780.39
  apoplectic (see also Disease, cerebrovascular, acute) 436
  hysterical 300.11
Fitting (of)
  artificial
    arm (complete) (partial) V52.0
    leg(s) (complete) (partial) V52.1
  device, unspecified type V53.90
    nervous system V53.09
    prosthetic V52.9
      specified type NEC V52.8
    special senses V53.09
    substitution
      auditory V53.09
      nervous system V53.09
      visual V53.09
  orthopedic (device) V53.7
    brace V53.7
    cast V53.7
    corset V53.7
    shoes V53.7
  prosthesis V52.9
    arm (complete) (partial) V52.0
    leg (complete) (partial) V52.1
    specified type NEC V52.8
Fixation
  larynx 478.79
Flaccid—see also condition
  foot 736.79
  forearm 736.09

Flail

joint (paralytic) 718.80
ankle 718.87
elbow 718.82
foot 718.87
hand 718.84
hip 718.85
knee 718.86
multiple sites 718.89
pelvic region 718.85
shoulder (region) 718.81
specified site NEC 718.88
wrist 718.83

Flat

chest, congenital 754.89
foot (acquired) (fixed type)
(painful) (postural) (spastic)
734
congenital 754.61
rocker bottom 754.61
vertical talus 754.61
rocker bottom (congenital)
754.61
vertical talus, congenital 754.61

Flatau-Schilder disease 341.1

Flattening

head, femur 736.39
hip 736.39
lip (congenital) 744.89

Flax dressers' disease 504

Flexibilitas cerea (see also
Catalepsy) 300.11

Flexion

contracture, joint (see also
Contraction, joint) 718.4☑

*Note—Use the following fifth-digit
subclassification with categories 711-
712, 715-716, 718, 719.0-719.6,
719.8, 719.9:*

0   *site unspecified*
1   *shoulder region*
2   *upper arm*
3   *forearm*
4   *hand*
5   *pelvic region and thigh*
6   *lower leg*
7   *ankle and foot*
8   *other specified sites*
9   *multiple sites*

deformity, joint (see also
Contraction, joint) 736.9☑
hip, congenital (see also
Subluxation, congenital,
hip) 754.32

Foix-Alajouanine syndrome 336.1

Follow-up (examination) (routine)
(following) V67.9
fracture V67.4
high-risk medication V67.51
treatment V67.9
fracture V67.4
involving high-risk medication
NEC V67.51

Food

asphyxia (from aspiration or
inhalation) (see also
Asphyxia, food) 933.1
choked on (see also Asphyxia, food)
933.1
refusal or rejection NEC 307.59
strangulation or suffocation (see
also Asphyxia, food) 933.1

Foreign body

entering through orifice (current)
(old)
air passage (upper) 933.0
lower 934.8
asphyxia due to (see also
Asphyxia, food) 933.1
bronchioles 934.8
bronchus (main) 934.1
inspiration (of) 933.1
larynx 933.1
lung 934.8
respiratory tract 934.9
specified part NEC 934.8
suffocation by (see also
Asphyxia, food) 933.1
trachea 934.0
wind pipe 934.0
granuloma (old) 728.82
bone 733.99
skin 709.4
soft tissue 709.4
subcutaneous tissue 709.4
bone (residual) 733.99
inhalation or inspiration (see also
Asphyxia, food) 933.1
old or residual
bone 733.99
skin 729.6
with granuloma 709.4
soft tissue 729.6
with granuloma 709.4
subcutaneous tissue 729.6
with granuloma 709.4
respiratory tree 934.9
specified site NEC 934.8
retained (old) (nonmagnetic) (in)
skin 729.6
with granuloma 709.4
soft tissue 729.6
with granuloma 709.4
subcutaneous tissue 729.6
with granuloma 709.4

Formication 782.0

Fothergill's

neuralgia (see also Neuralgia,
trigeminal) 350.1

Foville's syndrome 344.89

Fracture (abduction) (adduction)
(avulsion) (compression) (crush)
(dislocation) (oblique)
(separation) (closed) 829.0
acromion (process) (closed) 811.01
ankle (malleolus) (closed) 824.8
pathologic 733.16
arm (closed) 818.0
lower 813.80
Bennett's (closed) 815.01
bone (closed) NEC 829.0
pathologic NEC (see also
Fracture, pathologic)
733.10
stress NEC (see also Fracture,
stress) 733.95
buckle—see Fracture, torus
burst—see Fracture, traumatic, by
site
capitate (bone) (closed) 814.07
capitellum (humerus) (closed)
812.49
clavicle (interligamentous part)
(closed) 810.00
acromial end 810.03
Colles' (reversed) (closed) 813.41

Fracture—continued

coronoid process (ulna) (closed)
813.02
chronic—see Fracture, pathologic
cuneiform
wrist (closed) 814.03
Dupuytren's (ankle) (fibula)
(closed) 824.4
radius 813.42
elbow—see also Fracture, humerus,
lower end
olecranon (process) (closed)
813.01
supracondylar (closed) 812.41
femur, femoral (closed) 821.00
cervicotrochanteric 820.03
open 820.13
condyles, epicondyles 821.21
open 821.31
epiphysis (separation)
capital 820.01
open 820.11
head 820.01
open 820.11
lower 821.22
open 821.32
trochanteric 820.01
open 820.11
upper 820.01
open 820.11
head 820.09
open 820.19
lower end or extremity (distal
end) (closed) 821.20
condyles, epicondyles 821.21
open 821.31
epiphysis (separation) 821.22
open 821.32
multiple sites 821.29
open 821.39
open 821.30
specified site NEC 821.29
open 821.39
supracondylar 821.23
open 821.33
T-shaped 821.21
open 821.31
neck (closed) 820.8
base (cervicotrochanteric)
820.03
open 820.13
extracapsular 820.20
open 820.30
intertrochanteric (section)
820.21
open 820.31
intracapsular 820.00
open 820.10
intratrochanteric 820.21
open 820.31
midcervical 820.02
open 820.12
open 820.9
pathologic 733.14
specified part NEC 733.15
specified site NEC 820.09
open 820.19
transcervical 820.02
open 820.12
transtrochanteric 820.20
open 820.30
open 821.10
pathologic 733.14
specified part NEC 733.15

Fracture—continued

femur, femoral—continued
peritrochanteric (section)
820.20
open 820.30
shaft (lower third) (middle third)
(upper third) 821.01
open 821.11
subcapital 820.09
open 820.19
subtrochanteric (region)
(section) 820.22
open 820.32
supracondylar 821.23
open 821.33
T-shaped, into knee joint 821.21
open 821.31
transepiphyseal 820.01
open 820.11
trochanter (greater) (lesser) (see
also Fracture, femur, neck,
by site) 820.20
open 820.30
upper end 820.8
open 820.9
fibula (closed) 823.81
pathologic 733.16
shaft 823.21
with tibia 823.22
open 823.32
stress 733.93
upper end or extremity
(epiphysis) (head)
(proximal end) (styloid)
823.01
with tibia 823.02
finger(s), of one hand (closed) (see
also Fracture, phalanx, hand)
816.00
with
metacarpal bone(s), of same
hand 817.0
thumb of same hand 816.03
forearm (closed) NEC 813.80
lower end (distal end) (lower
epiphysis) 813.40
upper end (proximal end)
(upper epiphysis) 813.00
glenoid (cavity) (fossa) (scapula)
(closed) 811.03
hamate (closed) 814.08
hand, one (closed) 815.00
metacarpals 815.00
multiple, bones of one hand
817.0
phalanges (see also Fracture,
phalanx, hand) 816.00
hip (closed) (see also Fracture,
femur, neck) 820.8
open 820.9
pathologic 733.14
Hill-Sachs 812.09
humerus (closed) 812.20
anatomical neck 812.02
articular process (see also
Fracture humerus,
condyle(s)) 812.44
capitellum 812.49
condyle(s) 812.44
lateral (external) 812.42
medial (internal epicondyle)
812.43

Fracture—*continued*

humerus—*continued*

epiphysis

lower (*see also* Fracture, humerus, condyle(s)) 812.44

upper 812.09

external condyle 812.42

great tuberosity 812.03

head 812.09

internal epicondyle 812.43

lesser tuberosity 812.09

lower end or extremity (distal end) (*see also* Fracture, humerus, by site) 812.40

multiple sites NEC 812.49

specified site NEC 812.49

neck 812.01

pathologic 733.11

shaft 812.21

supracondylar 812.41

surgical neck 812.01

T-shaped 812.44

trochlea 812.49

upper end or extremity (proximal end) (*see also* Fracture, humerus, by site) 812.00

specified site NEC 812.09

insufficiency—*see* Fracture, pathologic, by site

knee

cap (closed) 822.0

open 822.1

limb

upper (multiple) (closed) NEC 818.0

lunate bone (closed) 814.02

malunion 733.81

march 733.95

fibula 733.93

metatarsals 733.94

tibia 733.93

metacarpus, metacarpal (bone(s)), of one hand (closed) 815.00

base 815.02

first metacarpal 815.01

thumb 815.01

multiple sites 815.09

neck 815.04

shaft 815.03

with phalanx, phalanges, hand (finger(s)) (thumb) of same hand 817.0

Monteggia's (closed) 813.03

Moore's—*see* Fracture, radius, lower end multangular bone (closed)

larger 814.05

smaller 814.06

navicular

carpal (wrist) (closed) 814.01

nonunion 733.82

olecranon (process) (ulna) (closed) 813.01

os

magnum (closed) 814.07

triquetrum (closed) 814.03

patella (closed) 822.0

open 822.1

pathologic (cause unknown) 733.10

ankle 733.16

femur (neck) 733.14

specified NEC 733.15

Fracture—*continued*

pathologic—*continued*

fibula 733.16

hip 733.14

humerus 733.11

radius 733.12

specified site NEC 733.19

tibia 733.16

ulna 733.12

vertebrae (collapse) 733.13

wrist 733.12

peritrochanteric (closed) 820.20

open 820.30

phalanx, phalanges, of one foot (closed) 826.0

open 826.1

hand (closed) 816.00

distal 816.02

middle 816.01

multiple sites NEC 816.03

proximal 816.01

with metacarpal bone(s) of same hand 817.0

pisiform (closed) 814.04

Quervain's (closed) 814.01

radius (alone) (closed) 813.81

lower end or extremity (distal end) (lower epiphysis) 813.42

torus 813.45

with ulna (lower end) 813.47

pathologic 733.12

shaft (closed) 813.21

with ulna (shaft) 813.23

upper end 813.07

epiphysis 813.05

head 813.05

multiple sites 813.07

neck 813.06

specified site NEC 813.07

with ulna (upper end) 813.0

with ulna NEC 813.83

scaphoid

wrist (closed) 814.01

scapula (closed) 811.00

acromial, acromion (process) 811.01

glenoid (cavity) (fossa) 811.03

neck 811.03

semilunar

bone, wrist (closed) 814.02

Smith's 813.41

sternum (closed) 807.2

stress 733.95

fibula 733.93

metatarsals 733.94

tibia 733.93

styloid process

metacarpal (closed) 815.02

supracondylar, elbow 812.41

thumb (and finger(s)) of one hand (closed) (*see also* Fracture, phalanx, hand) 816.00

with metacarpal bone(s) of same hand 817.0

tibia (closed) 823.80

pathologic 733.16

shaft 823.20

with fibula 823.22

open 823.32

stress 733.93

Fracture—*continued*

tibia—*continued*

upper end or extremity (condyle) (epiphysis) (head) (spine) (proximal end) (tuberosity) 823.00

open 823.10

with fibula 823.02

toe(s), of one foot (closed) 826.0

open 826.1

torus

fibula 823.41

with tibia 823.42

humerus 812.49

radius (alone) 813.45

with ulna 813.47

ulna (alone) 813.46

with radius 813.47

trapezium (closed) 814.05

trapezoid bone (closed) 814.06

triquetral (bone) (closed) 814.03

trochanter (greater) (lesser) (closed) (*see also* Fracture, femur, neck, by site) 820.20

open 820.30

ulna (alone) (closed) 813.82

coronoid process (closed) 813.02

lower end (distal end) (head) (lower epiphysis) (styloid process) 813.43

with radius (lower end) 813.44

olecranon process (closed) 813.01

pathologic 733.12

shaft 813.22

with radius (shaft) 813.23

torus 813.46

with radius 813.47

upper end (epiphysis) 813.04

multiple sites 813.04

specified site NEC 813.04

with radius (upper end) 813.08

with radius NEC 813.83

unciform (closed) 814.08

vertebra, vertebral (back) (body) (column) (neural arch) (pedicle) (spine) (spinous process) (transverse process) (closed) 805.8

chronic 733.13

collapsed 733.13

compression, not due to trauma 733.13

due to osteoporosis 733.13

nontraumatic 733.13

pathologic (any site) 733.13

stress (any site) 733.95

wrist (closed) 814.00

pathologic 733.12

Fragilitas

unguium 703.8

Fragility

nails 703.8

Frailty 797

Franceschetti's syndrome (mandibulofacial dysotosis) 756.0

Frequency (urinary) NEC 788.41

micturition 788.41

nocturnal 788.43

Frey's syndrome (auriculotemporal syndrome) 350.8

Friction

sounds, chest 786.7

Friedreich's

ataxia 334.0

combined systemic disease 334.0

disease 333.2

combined systemic 334.0

myoclonia 333.2

sclerosis (spinal cord) 334.0

Froin's syndrome 336.8

Frontal—*see also* condition

lobe syndrome 310.0

Frozen 991.9

shoulder 726.0

Fugue 780.99

hysterical (dissociative) 300.13

reaction to exceptional stress (transient) 308.1

Fuller's earth disease 502

Funnel

breast (acquired) 738.3

congenital 754.81

chest (acquired) 738.3

congenital 754.81

pelvis (acquired) 738.6

congenital 755.69

Furriers' lung 495.8

Furrowing nail(s) (transverse) 703.8

Fusion, fused (congenital)

astragaloscaphoid 755.67

auditory canal 744.02

choanal 748.0

cranial sutures, premature 756.0

ear ossicles 744.04

fingers (*see also* Syndactylism, fingers) 755.11

joint (acquired)—*see also* Ankylosis

congenital 755.8

larynx and trachea 748.3

limb 755.8

lower 755.69

upper 755.59

lobe, lung 748.5

lumbosacral (acquired) 724.6

congenital 756.15

surgical V45.4

nares (anterior) (posterior) 748.0

nose, nasal 748.0

nostril(s) 748.0

ossicles 756.9

auditory 744.04

sacroiliac (acquired) (joint) 724.6

congenital 755.69

surgical V45.4

skull, imperfect 756.0

spine (acquired) 724.9

arthrodesis status V45.4

congenital (vertebra) 756.15

postoperative status V45.4

talonavicular (bar) 755.67

toes (*see also* Syndactylism, toes) 755.13

G

Gait

abnormality 781.2

hysterical 300.11

ataxic 781.2

hysterical 300.11

disturbance 781.2

hysterical 300.11

paralytic 781.2

scissor 781.2

spastic 781.2

☑ Additional Digit Required

Gait—continued
staggering 781.2
hysterical 300.11
Gambling, pathological 312.31
Gampsodactylia (congenital)
754.71
Gamstorp's disease (adynamia
episodica hereditaria) 359.3
Ganglion 727.43
joint 727.41
tendon sheath (compound)
(diffuse) 727.42
Ganglionitis
fifth nerve (*see also* Neuralgia,
trigeminal) 350.1
gasserian 350.1
geniculate 351.1
Gangliosidosis 330.1
Gangrene, gangrenous (anemia)
(artery) (cellulitis) (dermatitis)
(dry) (infective) (moist)
(pemphigus) (septic) (skin)
(stasis) (ulcer) 785.4
with
arteriosclerosis (native artery)
440.24
diabetes (mellitus) 250.7☑
[785.4]
due to secondary diabetes
249.7☑ [785.4]
abdomen (wall) 785.4
auricle 785.4
connective tissue 785.4
cutaneous, spreading 785.4
decubital 707.00 [785.4]
diabetic (any site) 250.7☑ [785.4]
due to secondary diabetes
249.7☑ [785.4]

*Note—Use the following fifth-digit
subclassification with category 250:*
0   *type II [non-insulin dependent
type] [NIDDM type] [adult-onset
type] or unspecified type, not
stated as uncontrolled*
1   *type I [insulin dependent type]
[IDDM type] [juvenile type], not
stated as uncontrolled*
2   *type II [non-insulin dependent
type] [NIDDM type] [adult-onset
type] or unspecified type,
uncontrolled*
3   *type I [insulin dependent type]
[IDDM] [juvenile type],
uncontrolled*

dropsical 785.4
extremity (lower) (upper) 785.4
lung 513.0
Meleney's (cutaneous) 686.09
perineum 785.4
pneumonia 513.0
Pott's 440.24
presenile 443.1
pulmonary 513.0
Raynaud's (symmetric gangrene)
443.0 [785.4]
senile 440.24
spine 785.4
spreading cutaneous 785.4
symmetrical 443.0 [785.4]
umbilicus 785.4
Gannister disease (occupational)
502
Ganser's syndrome, hysterical
300.16

Gas 787.3
asphyxia, asphyxiation, inhalation,
poisoning, suffocation NEC
987.9
Gastralgia 536.8
psychogenic 307.89
Gayet's disease (superior
hemorrhagic polioencephalitis)
265.1
Gayet-Wernicke's syndrome
(superior hemorrhagic
polioencephalitis) 265.1
Genetic
susceptibility to
other disease V84.8
Genu
congenital 755.64
extrorsum (acquired) 736.42
congential 755.64
introrsum (acquired) 736.41
congenital 755.64
recurvatum (acquired) 736.5
congenital 754.40
with dislocation of knee
754.41
valgum (acquired) (knock-knee)
736.41
congenital 755.64
varum (acquired) (bowleg) 736.42
congenital 755.64
Gélineau's syndrome (*see also*
Narcolepsy) 347.00
**Gerstmann-Sträussler-Scheinker
syndrome** (GSS) 046.71
Gliosis (cerebral) 349.89
spinal 336.0
Globus 306.4
hystericus 300.11
Goldenhar's syndrome
(oculoauriculovertebral
dysplasia) 756.0
**Goldflam-Erb disease or
syndrome** 358.00
Golfer's elbow 726.32
**Gougerot (-Houwer) - Sjögren
syndrome** (keratoconjunctivitis
sicca) 710.2
Gout, gouty 274.9
with
specified manifestations NEC
274.89
tophi (tophus) 274.03
acute 274.01
arthritis 274.00
acute 274.01
arthropathy 274.00
acute 274.01
chronic (without mention of
tophus (tophi)) 274.02
with tophus (tophi) 274.03
attack 274.01
chronic 274.02
tophaceous 274.03
flare 274.01
joint 274.00
spondylitis 274.00
synovitis 274.00
tophi 274.03
Gowers'
muscular dystrophy 359.1
Graham Steell's murmur
(pulmonic regurgitation) (*see
also* Endocarditis, pulmonary)
424.3

Grain-handlers' disease or lung
495.8
Grand

*Note—use the following fifth-digit
subclassification with categories 345.0,
345.1, 345.4-345.9:*
0   *without mention of intractable
epilepsy*
1   *with intractable epilepsy*

mal (idiopathic) (*see also* Epilepsy)
345.1☑
hysteria of Charcôt 300.11
Granite workers' lung 502
Granuloma NEC 686.1
abdomen (wall) 568.89
skin (pyogenicum) 686.1
from residual foreign body
709.4
beryllium (skin) 709.4
lung 503
bone (*see also* Osteomyelitis)
730.1☑

*Note—Use the following fifth-digit
subclassification with category 730:*
0   *site unspecified*
1   *shoulder region*
2   *upper arm*
3   *forearm*
4   *hand*
5   *pelvic region and thigh*
6   *lower leg*
7   *ankle and foot*
8   *other specified sites*
9   *multiple sites*

from residual foreign body
733.99
foot NEC 686.1
foreign body (in soft tissue) NEC
728.82
bone 733.99
skin 709.4
subcutaneous tissue 709.4
larynx 478.79
lung (infectious) (*see also* Fibrosis,
lung) 515
operation wound 998.59
pyogenic, pyogenicum (skin) 686.1
sarcoid 135
septic (skin) 686.1
silica (skin) 709.4
skin (pyogenicum) 686.1
from foreign body or material
709.4
suppurative (skin) 686.1
telangiectaticum (skin) 686.1
umbilicus 686.1
Wegener's (necrotizing respiratory
granulomatosis) 446.4
Granulomatosis NEC 686.1
necrotizing, respiratory 446.4
Wegener's (necrotizing respiratory)
446.4
Graphite fibrosis (of lung) 503
Graphospasm 300.89
organic 333.84
Grating scapula 733.99
Greenfield's disease 330.0
Greig's syndrome (hypertelorism)
756.0
Grinders'
asthma 502
lung 502

Grippy cold 487.1
Grisel's disease 723.5
Grooved
nails (transverse) 703.8
Growing pains, children 781.99
GSS (Gerstmann-Sträussler-Scheinker
syndrome) 046.71
Guérin-Stern syndrome
(arthorgryposis multiplex
congenita) 754.89
**Gubler (-Millard) paralysis or
syndrome** 344.89
**Guillain-Barré disease or
syndrome** 357.0
Guinon's disease (motor-verbal tic)
307.23
Gunn's syndrome (jaw-winking
syndrome) 742.8

H

Haglund-Läwen-Fründ syndrome
717.89
Half vertebra 756.14
Hallermann-Streiff syndrome
756.0
**Hallervorden-Spatz disease or
syndrome** 333.0
Hallux 735.9☑
limitus 735.8
malleus (acquired) 735.3
rigidus (acquired) 735.2
congenital 755.66
valgus (acquired) 735.0
congenital 755.66
varus (acquired) 735.1
congenital 755.66
Hammer toe (acquired) 735.4
congenital 755.66
Headache 784.0
emotional 307.81
migraine 346.9☑
nonorganic origin 307.81
psychogenic 307.81
psychophysiologic 307.81
sick 346.9☑
tension 307.81
vascular 784.0
migraine type 346.9☑
vasomotor 346.9☑
Heberden's
disease or nodes 715.04
syndrome (angina pectoris) 413.9
Heerfordt's disease or syndrome
(uveoparotitis) 135
Heidenhain's disease 290.10
with dementia 290.10
Heloma 700
Hemarthrosis (nontraumatic)
719.10☑
ankle 719.17
elbow 719.12
foot 719.17
hand 719.14
hip 719.15
knee 719.16
multiple sites 719.19
pelvic region 719.15
shoulder (region) 719.11
specified site NEC 719.18
wrist 719.13
Hematite miners' lung 503

☑ Additional Digit Required

Hematoma (skin surface intact) (traumatic)—*see also* Contusion

Note—Use the following fifth-digit subclassification with categories 851-854:

0   *unspecified state of consciousness*
1   *with no loss of consciousness*
2   *with brief [less than one hour] loss of consciousness*
3   *with moderate [1-24 hours] loss of consciousness*
4   *with prolonged [more than 24 hours] loss of consciousness and return to pre-existing conscious level*
5   *with prolonged [more than 24 hours] loss of consciousness, without return to pre-existing conscious level*
    Use fifth-digit 5 to designate when a patient is unconscious and dies before regaining consciousness, regardless of the duration of the loss of consciousness
6   *with loss of consciousness of unspecified duration*
9   *with concussion, unspecified*

brain (traumatic) 853.0☑
    extradural or epidural 852.4☑
        nontraumatic 432.0
    nontraumatic (*see also* Hemorrhage, brain) 431
        epidural or extradural 432.0
        subarachnoid, arachnoid, or meningeal (*see also* Hemorrhage, subarachnoid) 430
        subdural (*see also* Hemorrhage, subdural) 432.1
    subarachnoid, arachnoid, or meningeal 852.0☑
        nontraumatic (*see also* Hemorrhage, subarachnoid) 430
    subdural 852.2☑
        nontraumatic (*see also* Hemorrhage, subdural) 432.1
extradural—*see also* Hematoma, brain, extradural
    nontraumatic 432.0
muscle (traumatic)—*see* Contusion, by site
    nontraumatic 729.92
soft tissue 729.92
spinal (cord) (meninges)—*see also* Injury, spinal, by site
    nontraumatic 336.1
subarachnoid—*see also* Hematoma, brain, subarachnoid
    nontraumatic (*see also* Hemorrhage, subarachnoid) 430
subdural—*see also* Hematoma, brain, subdural
    nontraumatic (*see also* Hemorrhage, subdural) 432.1
Hematomyelia 336.1
Hematomyelitis 323.9
    late effect—*see* category 326
Hematopneumothorax (*see also* Hemothorax) 511.89

Hematorachis, hematorrhachis 336.1
Hematothorax (*see also* Hemothorax) 511.89
Hemi-akinesia 781.8
Hemi-inattention 781.8
Hemianalgesia (*see also* Disturbance, sensation) 782.0
Hemianesthesia (*see also* Disturbance, sensation) 782.0
Hemiathetosis 781.0
Hemiatrophy 799.89
    cerebellar 334.8
    fascia 728.9
    leg 728.2
Hemiballism(us) 333.5
Hemiblock (cardiac) (heart) (left) 426.2
Hemichorea 333.5
Hemicrania 346.9☑

Note—Use the following fifth-digit subclassification with category 346:
0   *without mention of intractable migraine*
1   *without intractable migraine, so stated*

Hemiectromelia 755.4
Hemihypalgesia (*see also* Disturbance, sensation) 782.0
Hemihypertrophy (congenital) 759.89
    cranial 756.0
Hemihypesthesia (*see also* Disturbance, sensation) 782.0
Hemimelia 755.4
    lower limb 755.30
        paraxial (complete) (incomplete) (intercalary) (terminal) 755.32
            fibula 755.37
            tibia 755.36
        transverse (complete) (partial) 755.31
    upper limb 755.20
        paraxial (complete) (incomplete) (intercalary) (terminal) 755.22
            radial 755.26
            ulnar 755.27
        transverse (complete) (partial) 755.21
Hemiparesthesia (*see also* Disturbance, sensation) 782.0
Hemiplegia 342.9☑

Note—Use the following fifth-digit subclassification with category 342:
0   *affecting unspecified side*
1   *affecting dominant side*
2   *affecting nondominant side*

acute (*see also* Disease, cerebrovascular, acute) 436
alternans facialis 344.89
apoplectic (*see also* Disease, cerebrovascular, acute) 436
    late effect or residual
        affecting
            dominant side 438.21
            nondominant side 438.22
            unspecified side 438.20

Hemiplegia—*continued*
arteriosclerotic 437.0
    late effect or residual
        affecting
            dominant side 438.21
            nondominant side 438.22
            unspecified side 438.20
ascending (spinal) NEC 344.89
attack (*see also* Disease, cerebrovascular, acute) 436
brain, cerebral (current episode) 437.8
    congenital 343.1
congenital (cerebral) (spastic) (spinal) 343.1
conversion neurosis (hysterical) 300.11
due to
    arteriosclerosis 437.0
        late effect or residual
            affecting
                dominant side 438.21
                nondominant side 438.22
                unspecified side 438.20
    cerebrovascular lesion (*see also* Disease, cerebro-vascular, acute) 436
        late effect
            affecting
                dominant side 438.21
                nondominant side 438.22
                unspecified side 438.20
embolic (current) (*see also* Embolism, brain) 434.1☑

Note—Use the following fifth-digit subclassification with category 434:
0   *without mention of cerebral infarction*
1   *with cerebral infarction*

late effect
    affecting
        dominant side 438.21
        nondominant side 438.22
        unspecified side 438.20
infantile (postnatal) 343.4
late effect
    birth injury, intracranial or spinal 343.4
middle alternating NEC 344.89
seizure (current episode) (*see also* Disease, cerebro-vascular, acute) 436
spastic 342.1☑

Note—Use the following fifth-digit subclassification with category 342:
0   *affecting unspecified side*
1   *affecting dominant side*
2   *affecting nondominant side*

congenital or infantile 343.1
Hemispasm 781.0
    facial 781.0
Hemispatial neglect 781.8
Hemitremor 781.0
Hemivertebra 756.14

Hemorrhage, hemorrhagic
    (nontraumatic) 459.0
basilar (ganglion) (*see also* Hemorrhage, brain) 431
brain (miliary) (nontraumatic) 431
    due to
        rupture of aneurysm (congenital) (*see also* Hemorrhage, subarachnoid) 430
        mycotic 431
    iatrogenic 997.02
    postoperative 997.02
    stem 431
bronchus (cause unknown) (*see also* Hemorrhage, lung) 786.3
bulbar (*see also* Hemorrhage, brain) 431
bursa 727.89
cephalic (*see also* Hemorrhage, brain) 431
cerebellar (*see also* Hemorrhage, brain) 431
cerebellum (*see also* Hemorrhage, brain) 431
cerebral (*see also* Hemorrhage, brain) 431
cerebromeningeal (*see also* Hemorrhage, brain) 431
cerebrospinal (*see also* Hemorrhage, brain) 431
cerebrum (*see also* Hemorrhage, brain) 431
cortical (*see also* Hemorrhage, brain) 431
cranial 432.9
extradural (traumatic)—*see also* Hemorrhage, brain, traumatic, extradural
    nontraumatic 432.0
internal (organs) 459.0
    capsule (*see also* Hemorrhage, brain) 431
into
    bursa 727.89
    corpus luysii (*see also* Hemorrhage, brain) 431
intra-alveolar, newborn (lung) 770.3
intracerebral (*see also* Hemorrhage, brain) 431
intracranial NEC 432.9
intramedullary NEC 336.1
intrapontine (*see also* Hemorrhage, brain) 431
intraventricular (*see also* Hemorrhage, brain) 431
joint (nontraumatic) 719.10
    ankle 719.17
    elbow 719.12
    foot 719.17
    forearm 719.13
    hand 719.14
    hip 719.15
    knee 719.16
    lower leg 719.16
    multiple sites 719.19
    pelvic region 719.15
    shoulder (region) 719.11
    specified site NEC 719.18
    thigh 719.15
    upper arm 719.12
    wrist 719.13
knee (joint) 719.16

☑ Additional Digit Required   © 2009 Ingenix

Hemorrhage, hemorrhagic—
continued
 lenticular striate artery (see also
  Hemorrhage, brain) 431
 lung 786.3
  newborn 770.3
 mediastinum 786.3
 medulla (See also Hemorrhage,
  brain) 431
 membrane (brain) (see also
  Hemorrhage, subarachnoid)
  430
 meninges, meningeal (brain)
  (middle) (see also
  Hemorrhage, subarachnoid)
  430
 midbrain (see also Hemorrhage,
  brain) 431
 muscle 728.89
 respiratory tract (see also
  Hemorrhage, lung) 786.3
 spinal (cord) 336.1
  aneurysm (ruptured) 336.1
 subarachnoid (nontraumatic) 430
 subcortical (see also Hemorrhage,
  brain) 431
 subdural (nontraumatic) 432.1
  spinal 336.1
 subperiosteal 733.99
 subtentorial (see also Hemorrhage,
  subdural 432.1
 subungual 703.8
 ventricular (see also Hemorrhage,
  brain) 431
Hernia, hernial (acquired)
  (recurrent) 553.9
 fascia 728.89
 lumbar 553.8
  intervertebral disc 722.10
 lung (subcutaneous) 518.89
  congenital 748.69
 muscle (sheath) 728.89
Heterotopia, heterotopic—see also
  Malposition, congenital
 spinalis 742.59
Hiccough 786.8
 psychogenic 306.1
HIE (hypoxic-ischemic
  encephalopathy (HIE) 786.70
 mild 768.71
 moderage 768.72
 severe 768.73
High
 arch
  foot 755.67
 artery (arterial) tension (see also
  Hypertension) 401.9
 blood pressure (see also
  Hypertension) 401.9
 compliance bladder 596.4
 output failure (cardiac) (see also
  Failure, heart) 428.9
 risk
  patient taking drugs
   (prescribed) V67.51
Hilger's syndrome 337.09
History (personal) of
 arrest, sudden cardiac V12.53
 attack, transient ischemic (TIA)
  V12.54
 cardiovascular disease V12.50
  myocardial infarction 412
 circulatory system disease V12.50
  myocardial infarction 412

History—*continued*
 death, sudden, successfully
  resuscitated V12.53
 deficit
  prolonged reversible ischemic
   neurologic (PRIND)
   V12.54
  reversible ischemic neurologic
   (RIND) V12.54
 disease (of) V13.9
  circulatory system V12.50
   specified NEC V12.59
  respiratory system V12.6
 disorder (of) V13.9
  musculoskeletal NEC V13.59
 encephalitis V12.42
 falling V15.88
 fracture, healed
  pathologic V13.51
  stress V13.52
 traumatic V15.51
 malignant neoplasm (of) V10.9
  accessory sinus V10.22
  bronchus V10.11
  gum V10.02
  hypopharynx V10.02
  intrathoracic organs NEC
   V10.20
  larynx V10.21
  lip V10.02
  lung V10.11
  mediastinum V10.29
  middle ear V10.22
  mouth V10.02
   specified part NEC V10.02
  nasal cavities V10.22
  nasopharynx V10.02
  nose V10.22
  oropharynx V10.02
  pharynx V10.02
  pleura V10.29
  respiratory organs NEC V10.20
  salivary gland V10.02
  thymus V10.29
  tongue V10.01
 musculoskeletal disorder NEC
  V13.59
 myocardial infarction 412
 respiratory system disease V12.6
Human immunodeficiency virus
  (disease) (illness) 042
 infection V08
  with symptoms, symptomatic
   042
Humpback (acquired) 737.9
 congenital 756.19
Hunchback (acquired) 737.9
 congenital 756.19
Hunger 994.2
 air, psychogenic 306.1
Hungry bone syndrome 275.5
Hunt's
 syndrome (herpetic geniculate
  ganglionitis) 053.11
 dyssynergia cerebellaris
  myoclonica 334.2
Huntington's
 chorea 333.4
 disease 333.4
Hutchinson-Boeck disease or
  syndrome (sarcoidosis) 135
Hyaline
 degeneration (diffuse)
  (generalized) 728.9

Hyaline—*continued*
 membrane (disease) (lung)
  (newborn) 769
Hydrarthrosis (see also Effusion,
  joint) 719.0 ☑

Note—Use the following fifth-digit
subclassification with categories 711-
712, 715-716, 718, 719.0-719.6,
719.8, 719.9:

0	site unspecified
1	shoulder region
2	upper arm
3	forearm
4	hand
5	pelvic region and thigh
6	lower leg
7	ankle and foot
8	other specified sites
9	multiple sites

 intermittent (see also Rheumatism,
  palindromic) 719.3 ☑
Hydrocephalus (acquired) (external)
  (internal) (malignant)
  (noncommunicating)
  (obstructive) (recurrent) 331.4
 communicating 331.3
 foramen Magendie block
  (acquired) 331.3
 normal pressure 331.5
  idiopathic (INPH) 331.5
  secondary 331.3
 otitic 348.2
Hydrohematopneumothorax (see
  also Hemothorax) 511.89
Hydromyelia 742.53
Hydropneumohemothorax (see
  also Hemothorax) 511.89
Hydropneumothorax 511.89
 nontuberculous 511.89
  bacterial 511.1
  pneumococcal 511.1
  staphylococcal 511.1
  streptococcal 511.1
Hydrops 782.3
 articulorum intermittens (see also
  Rheumatism, palindromic)
  719.3 ☑
 cardiac (see also Failure, heart)
  428.0
 meningeal NEC 331.4
 pleura (see also Hydrothorax)
  511.89
Hydrorachis 742.53
Hydrothorax (double) (pleural)
  511.89
 nontuberculous 511.89
  bacterial 511.1
  pneumococcal 511.1
  staphylococcal 511.1
  streptococcal 511.1
Hygroma (congenital) (cystic)
  (M9173/0) 228.1
 prepatellar 727.3
Hypalgesia (see also Disturbance,
  sensation) 782.0
Hyperactive, hyperactivity 314.01
 bladder 596.51
 child 314.01
Hyperalgesia (see also Disturbance,
  sensation) 782.0
Hyperaphia 782.0
Hypercapnia 786.09

Hyperemia (acute) 780.99
 lung 514
 pulmonary 514
Hyperesthesia (body surface) (see
  also Disturbance, sensation)
  782.0
 larynx (reflex) 478.79
  hysterical 300.11
Hyperextension, joint 718.80
 ankle 718.87
 elbow 718.82
 foot 718.87
 hand 718.84
 hip 718.85
 knee 718.86
 multiple sites 718.89
 pelvic region 718.85
 shoulder (region) 718.81
 specified site NEC 718.88
 wrist 718.83
Hyperkinesia, hyperkinetic
  (disease) (reaction) (syndrome)
  314.9
 of childhood or adolescence NEC
  314.9
 with
  conduct disorder 314.2
  developmental delay 314.1
  simple disturbance of activity
   and attention 314.01
  specified manifestation NEC
   314.8
Hyperlucent lung, unilateral
  492.8
Hypermobility
 coccyx 724.71
 joint (acquired) 718.80
  ankle 718.87
  elbow 718.82
  foot 718.87
  hand 718.84
  hip 718.85
  knee 718.86
  multiple sites 718.89
  pelvic region 718.85
  shoulder (region) 718.81
  specified site NEC 718.88
  wrist 718.83
 meniscus (knee) 717.5
 scapula 718.81
 syndrome 728.5
 urethral 599.81
Hypernasality 784.49
Hyperosmia (see also Disturbance,
  sensation) 781.1
Hyperosteogenesis 733.99
Hyperostosis 733.99
 monomelic 733.99
 skull 733.3
  congenital 756.0
 vertebral 721.8
  ankylosing 721.6
Hyperoxia 987.8
Hyperpathia (see also Disturbance,
  sensation) 782.0
 psychogenic 307.80
Hyperplasia, hyperplastic
 bone 733.99
 fascialis ossificans (progressiva)
  728.11
 fascialis ossificans (progressiva)
  728.11

	Malignant	Benign	Unspecified
Hypertension, hypertensive (arterial) (arteriolar) (crisis) (degeneration) (disease) (essential) (fluctuating) (idiopathic) (intermittent) (labile) (low renin) (orthostatic) (paroxysmal) (primary) (systemic) (uncontrolled) (vascular)	401.0	401.1	401.9
with			
chronic kidney disease			
stage I through stage IV, or unspecified	403.00	403.10	403.90
stage V or end stage renal disease	403.01	403.11	403.91
heart involvement (conditions classifiable to 429.0-429.3, 429.8, 429.9 due to hypertension) (see also Hypertension, heart)	402.00	402.10	402.90
with kidney involvement—see Hypertension, cardiorenal			
renal (kidney) involvement (only conditions classifiable to 585) (excludes conditions classifiable to 584) (see also Hypertension, kidney)	403.00	403.10	403.90
with heart involvement—see Hypertension, cardiorenal			
failure (and sclerosis) (see also Hypertension, kidney)	403.01	403.11	403.91
sclerosis without failure (see also Hypertension, kidney)	403.00	403.10	403.90
accelerated (see also Hypertension, by type, malignant)	401.00	—	—
antepartum—see Hypertension, complicating pregnancy, childbirth, or the puerperium			
cardiorenal (disease)	404.00	404.10	404.90
with			
chronic kidney disease	403.01	403.11	403.91
stage I through stage IV, or unspecified	404.00	404.10	404.90
and heart failure	404.01	404.11	404.91
stage V or end stage renal disease	403.01	403.11	403.91
and heart failure	404.03	404.13	404.93
heart failure	404.01	404.11	404.91
and chronic kidney disease	404.01	404.11	404.91
stage I through stage IV, or unspecified	404.01	404.11	404.91
stage V or end stage renal disease	404.03	404.13	404.93
cardiovascular disease (arteriosclerotic) (sclerotic)	402.00	402.10	402.90
with			
heart failure	402.01	402.11	402.91
renal involvement (conditions classifiable to 403) (see also Hypertension, cardiorenal)	404.00	404.10	404.90
cardiovascular renal (disease) (sclerosis) (see also Hypertension, cardiorenal)	404.00	404.10	404.90
cerebrovascular disease NEC	437.2	437.2	437.2
complicating pregnancy, childbirth, or the puerperium	642.2 ☑	642.0 ☑	642.9 ☑
with			
albuminuria (and edema) (mild)	—	—	642.4 ☑
severe	—	—	642.5 ☑
chronic kidney disease	642.2 ☑	642.2 ☑	642.2 ☑
and heart disease	642.2 ☑	642.2 ☑	642.2 ☑
edema (mild)	—	—	642.4 ☑
severe	—	—	642.5 ☑
heart disease	642.2 ☑	642.2 ☑	642.2 ☑
and chronic kidney disease	642.2 ☑	642.2 ☑	642.2 ☑
renal disease	642.2 ☑	642.2 ☑	642.2 ☑
and heart disease	642.2 ☑	642.2 ☑	642.2 ☑
chronic	642.2 ☑	642.0 ☑	642.0 ☑
with pre-eclampsia or eclampsia	642.7 ☑	642.7 ☑	642.7 ☑
fetus or newborn	760.0	760.0	760.0
essential	—	642.0 ☑	642.0 ☑
with pre-eclampsia or eclampsia	—	642.7 ☑	642.7 ☑
fetus or newborn	760.0	760.0	760.0
fetus or newborn	760.0	760.0	760.0
gestational	—	—	642.3 ☑
pre-existing	642.2 ☑	642.0 ☑	642.0 ☑
with pre-eclampsia or eclampsia	642.7 ☑	642.7 ☑	642.7 ☑
fetus or newborn	760.0	760.0	760.0
secondary to renal disease	642.1 ☑	642.1 ☑	642.1 ☑
with pre-eclampsia or eclampsia	642.7 ☑	642.7 ☑	642.7 ☑
fetus or newborn	760.0	760.0	760.0
transient	—	—	642.3 ☑
due to			
aldosteronism, primary	405.09	405.19	405.99
brain tumor	405.09	405.19	405.99
bulbar poliomyelitis	405.09	405.19	405.99

☑ Additional Digit Required

	Malignant	Benign	Unspecified
Hypertension, hypertensive—*continued*			
due to—*continued*			
calculus			
kidney	405.09	405.19	405.99
ureter	405.09	405.19	405.99
coarctation, aorta	405.09	405.19	405.99
Cushing's disease	405.09	405.19	405.99
glomerulosclerosis (*see also* Hypertension, kidney)	403.00	403.10	403.90
periarteritis nodosa	405.09	405.19	405.99
pheochromocytoma	405.09	405.19	405.99
polycystic kidney(s)	405.09	405.19	405.99
polycythemia	405.09	405.19	405.99
porphyria	405.09	405.19	405.99
pyelonephritis	405.09	405.19	405.99
renal (artery)			
aneurysm	405.01	405.11	405.91
anomaly	405.01	405.11	405.91
embolism	405.01	405.11	405.91
fibromuscular hyperplasia	405.01	405.11	405.91
occlusion	405.01	405.11	405.91
stenosis	405.01	405.11	405.91
thrombosis	405.01	405.11	405.91
encephalopathy	437.2	437.2	437.2
gestational (transient) NEC	—	—	642.3 ☑
Goldblatt's	440.1	440.1	440.1
heart (disease) (conditions classifiable to 429.0-429.3, 429.8, 429.9 due to hypertension)	402.00	402.10	402.90
with heart failure	402.01	402.11	402.91
hypertensive kidney disease (conditions classifiable to 403) (*see also* Hypertension, cardiorenal)	404.00	404.10	404.90
renal sclerosis (*see also* Hypertension, cardiorenal)	404.00	404.10	404.90
intracranial, benign	—	348.2	—
intraocular	—	—	365.04
kidney	403.00	403.10	403.90
with			
chronic kidney disease			
stage I through stage IV, or unspecified	403.00	403.10	403.90
stage V or end stage renal disease	403.01	403.11	403.91
heart involvement (conditions classifiable to 429.0-429.3, 429.8, 429.9 due to hypertension) (*see also* Hypertension, cardiorenal)	404.00	404.10	404.90
hypertensive heart (disease) (conditions classifiable to 402) (*see also* Hypertension, cardiorenal)	404.00	404.10	404.90
lesser circulation	—	—	416.0
necrotizing	401.0	—	—
ocular	—	—	365.04
portal (due to chronic liver disease)	—	—	572.3
postoperative	—	—	997.91
psychogenic	—	—	306.2
puerperal, postpartum—*see* Hypertension, complicating pregnancy, childbirth, or the puerperium			
pulmonary (artery)	—	—	416.8
with cor pulmonale (chronic)	—	—	416.8
acute	—	—	415
idiopathic	—	—	416
primary	—	—	416
of newborn	—	—	747.83
secondary	—	—	416.8
renal (disease) (*see also* Hypertension, kidney)	403.00	403.10	403.90
renovascular NEC	405.01	405.11	405.91
secondary NEC	405.09	405.19	405.99
due to			
aldosteronism, primary	405.09	405.19	405.99
brain tumor	405.09	405.19	405.99
bulbar poliomyelitis	405.09	405.19	405.99
calculus			
kidney	405.09	405.19	405.99
ureter	405.09	405.19	405.99
coarctation, aorta	405.09	405.19	405.99

	Malignant	Benign	Unspecified
Hypertension, hypertensive—*continued*			
secondary NEC—*continued*			
due to—*continued*			
Cushing's disease	405.09	405.19	405.99
glomerulosclerosis (*see also* Hypertension, kidney)	403.00	403.10	403.90
periarteritis nodosa	405.09	405.19	405.99
pheochromocytoma	405.09	405.19	405.99
polycystic kidney(s)	405.09	405.19	405.99
polycythemia	405.09	405.19	405.99
porphyria	405.09	405.19	405.99
pyelonephritis	405.09	405.19	405.99
renal (artery)			
aneurysm	405.01	405.11	405.91
anomaly	405.01	405.11	405.91
embolism	405.01	405.11	405.91
fibromuscular hyperplasia	405.01	405.11	405.91
occlusion	405.01	405.11	405.91
stenosis	405.01	405.11	405.91
thrombosis	405.01	405.11	405.91
transient	—	—	796.2
of pregnancy	—	—	642.3 ☑
vascular degeneration	401.0	401.1	401.9
due to			
deep vein thrombosis (*see also* Syndrome, postphlebitic)			459.10
venous, chronic (asymptomatic) (idiopathic)	—	—	459.30
with			
complication, NEC	—	—	459.39
inflammation	—	—	459.32
with ulcer	—	—	459.33
ulcer	—	—	459.31
with inflammation	—	—	459.33

☑ Additional Digit Required
© 2009 Ingenix

ICD-9-CM Index

Hypertrophy, hypertrophic

arthritis (chronic) (see also
Osteoarthrosis) 715.9☑

*Note—Use the following fifth-digit
subclassification with categories 711-
712, 715-716, 718, 719.0-719.6,
719.8, 719.9:*

0 *site unspecified*
1 *shoulder region*
2 *upper arm*
3 *forearm*
4 *hand*
5 *pelvic region and thigh*
6 *lower leg*
7 *ankle and foot*
8 *other specified sites*
9 *multiple sites*

spine (see also Spondylosis)
721.90
arytenoid 478.79
bone 733.99
brain 348.89
cardiac (chronic) (idiopathic) 429.3
hypertensive (see also
Hypertension, heart)
402.90
falx, skull 733.99
foot (congenital) 755.67
ligament 728.9
spinal 724.8
lip (frenum) 528.5
congenital 744.81
medial meniscus, acquired 717.3
meniscus, knee, congenital 755.64
metatarsus 733.99
muscle 728.9
myocardium (see also Hypertrophy,
cardiac) 429.3
idiopathic 425.4
nail 703.8
pseudomuscular 359.1
scaphoid (tarsal) 733.99
spondylitis (spine) (see also
Spondylosis) 721.90
subaortic stenosis (idiopathic)
425.1
toe (congenital) 755.65
acquired 735.8
ventricle, ventricular (heart) (left)
(right)—see also
Hypertrophy, cardiac
due to hypertension (left) (right)
(see also Hypertension,
heart) 402.90
benign 402.10
malignant 402.00

Hypesthesia (see also Disturbance,
sensation) 782.0

Hypoplasia, hypoplasis 759.89

arm (see also Absence, arm,
congenital) 755.20
auditory canal 744.29
causing impairment of hearing
744.02
bone NEC 756.9
face 756.0
malar 756.0
skull (see also Hypoplasia, skull)
756.0
bronchus (tree) 748.3
carpus (see also Absence, carpal,
congenital) 755.28
clavicle 755.51
coccyx 756.19

Hypoplasia, hypoplasis—*continued*

cricoid cartilage 748.3
epiglottis 748.3
face 744.89
bone(s) 756.0
femur (see also Absence, femur,
congenital) 755.34
fibula (see also Absence, fibula,
congenital) 755.37
finger (see also Absence, finger,
congenital) 755.29
foot 755.31
glottis 748.3
hand 755.21
humerus (see also Absence,
humerus, congenital) 755.24
leg (see also Absence, limb,
congenital, lower) 755.30
limb 755.4
lower (see also Absence, limb,
congenital, lower) 755.30
upper (see also Absence, limb,
congenital, upper) 755.20
lung (lobe) 748.5
metacarpus (see also Absence,
metacarpal, congenital)
755.28
metatarsus (see also Absence,
metatarsal, congenital)
755.38
nervous system NEC 742.8
neural 742.8
organ
of Corti 744.05
osseous meatus (ear) 744.03
patella 755.64
pelvis, pelvic girdle 755.69
pulmonary 748.5
radioulnar (see also Absence,
radius, congenital, with ulna)
755.25
radius (see also Absence, radius,
congenital) 755.26
sacrum 756.19
scapula 755.59
shoulder girdle 755.59
skull (bone) 756.0
limb 755.4
lower (see also Absence, limb,
congenital, lower) 755.30
upper (see also Absence, limb,
congenital, upper) 755.20
lung (lobe) 748.5
metacarpus (see also Absence,
metacarpal, congenital)
755.28
metatarsus (see also Absence,
metatarsal, congenital)
755.38
nervous system NEC 742.8
neural 742.8
organ
of Corti 744.05
osseous meatus (ear) 744.03
patella 755.64
pelvis, pelvic girdle 755.69
pulmonary 748.5
radioulnar (see also Absence,
radius, congenital, with ulna)
755.25
radius (see also Absence, radius,
congenital) 755.26
sacrum 756.19
scapula 755.59
shoulder girdle 755.59

Hypoplasia, hypoplasis—*continued*

skull (bone) 756.0
spinal (cord) (ventral horn cell)
742.59
spine 756.19
tarsus (see also Absence, tarsal,
congenital) 755.38
tibiofibular (see also Absence, tibia,
congenital, with fibula)
755.35
toe (see also Absence, toe,
congenital) 755.39
trachea (cartilage) (rings) 748.3
ulna (see also Absence, ulna,
congenital) 755.27
vertebra 756.19

Hypopselaphesia 782.0
Hyporeflex 796.1
Hypostasis, pulmonary 514
Hypotension (arterial)
(constitutional) 458.9
orthostatic (chronic) 458.0
dysautonomic-dyskinetic
syndrome 333.0

Hypotonia, hypotonicity,
hypotony 781.3
benign congenital 358.8
bladder 596.4
congenital 779.89
benign 358.8
infantile muscular (benign) 359.0
muscle 728.9

Hypoventilation 786.09
Hypoxia (see also Anoxia) 799.02
cerebral 348.1
during or resulting from a
procedure 997.01
newborn 770.88
myocardial (see also Insufficiency,
coronary) 411.89

Hypoxic-ischemic
encephalopathy 786.70
mild 768.71
moderage 768.72
severe 768.73

I

Imbalance 781.2
autonomic (see also Neuropathy,
peripheral, autonomic) 337.9
hysterical (see also Hysteria) 300.10
posture 729.90
sympathetic (see also Neuropathy,
peripheral, autonomic) 337.9

Imbecile, imbecility 318.0
old age 290.9
senile 290.9

Immobile, immobility
complete
due to severe physical disability
or frality 780.72
syndrome (paraplegic) 728.3

Impaired, impairment (function)
arm V49.1
movement, involving
musculoskeletal system
V49.1
nervous system V49.2
back V48.3
leg V49.1
movement, involving
musculoskeletal system
V49.1
nervous system V49.2

Impaired, impairment—*continued*

leg —*continued*
movement, involving
musculoskeletal system
V49.1
nervous system V49.2
myocardium, myocardial (see also
Insufficiency, myocardial)
428.0
neuromusculoskeletal NEC V49.89
back V48.3
head V48.2
limb V49.2
neck V48.3
spine V48.3
trunk V48.3
spine V48.3

Impending
coronary syndrome 411.1
delirium tremens 291.0
myocardial infarction 411.1

Incompetence
pubocervical tissue 618.81
rectovaginal tissue 618.82

Incoordination
esophageal-pharyngeal (newborn)
787.24
muscular 781.3

Increase, increased
cold sense (see also Disturbance,
sensation) 782.0
heat sense (see also Distur-bance,
sensation) 782.0
intracranial pressure 781.99
pressure
intracranial 781.99

Induration, indurated
lung (black) (brown) (chronic)
(fibroid) (see also Fibrosis,
lung) 515
essential brown 275.0 [516.1]

Inequality, leg (acquired) (length)
736.81
congenital 755.30

Inertia
bladder 596.4
neurogenic 596.54
with cauda equina syndrome
344.61
vesical 596.4

Infarct, infarction
brain (stem) 434.91
healed or old without residuals
V12.54
iatrogenic 997.02
postoperative 997.02
cerebral (see also Infarct, brain)
434.91
aborted 434.91
impending (myocardium) 411.1
myocardium, myocardial (acute or
with a stated duration of 8
weeks or less) (with
hypertension) 410.9☑

*Note—Use the following fifth-digit
subclassification with category 410:*
0 *episode unspecified*
1 *initial episode*
2 *subsequent episode without
recurrence*

chronic (with symptoms after 8
weeks from date of
infarction) 414.8

Infarct, infarction—*continued*
myocardium, myocardial —
continued
diagnosed on ECG, but
presenting no symptoms
412
healed or old, currently
presenting no symptoms
412
impending 411.1
past (diagnosed on ECG or
other special
investigation, but
currently presenting no
symptoms) 412
with symptoms NEC 414.8
postprocedural 997.1
previous, currently presenting
no symptoms 412
Iwith symptoms after 8 weeks
from date of infarction
414.8
spinal (acute) (cord) (embolic)
(nonembolic) 336.1
Infection, infected, infective
(opportunistic) 136.9
acanthamoeba 136.21
acromioclavicular (joint) 711.91
ameba, amebic (histolytica) (*see
also* Amebiasis) 006.9
free-living 136.29
brain (*see also* Encephalitis) 323.9
late effect—*see* category 326
septic 324.0
branchial cyst 744.42
bronchus (*see also* Bronchitis) 490
buttocks (skin) 686.9
cartilage 733.99
cerebrospinal (*see also* Meningitis)
322.9
late effect—*see* category 326
cotia virus 059.8
due to or resulting from
surgery 998.59
Epstein-Barr virus 075
chronic 780.79 [139.8]
fascia 728.89
finger (skin) 686.9
abscess (with lymphangitis)
681.00
pulp 681.01
cellulitis (with lymphangitis)
681.00
distal closed space (with
lymphangitis) 681.00
nail 681.02
foot (skin) 686.9
HIV V08
with symptoms, symptomatic
042
human herpesvirus 7 058.82
human herpesvirus 8 058.89
human herpesvirus NEC 058.89
human immunodeficiency virus
V08
with symptoms, symptomatic
042
knee (skin) NEC 686.9
larynx NEC 478.79
leg (skin) NEC 686.9
local, skin (staphylococcal)
(streptococcal) NEC 686.9
ulcer (*see also* Ulcer, skin) 707.9
lung 518.89
basilar 518.89

Infection, infected, infective —
continued
local, skin —*continued*
chronic 518.89
metatarsophalangeal 711.97
monkeypox 059.01
muscle NEC 728.89
nail (chronic) (with lymphangitis)
681.9
finger 681.02
ingrowing 703.0
toe 681.11
operation wound 998.59
orthopoxvirus 059.00
specified NEC 059.09
parapoxvirus 059.10
specified NEC 059.19
postoperative wound 998.59
poxvirus 059.9
specified NEC 059.8
Pseudomonas NEC 041.7
pneumonia 482.1
respiratory 519.8
chronic 519.8
influenzal (acute) (upper) 487.1
lung 518.89
upper (acute) (infectious) NEC
465.9
influenzal 487.1
with flu, grippe, or influenza
487.1
septic
localized, skin (*see also* Abscess)
682.9
seroma 998.51
sinus (*see also* Sinusitis) 473.9
skin NEC 686.9
skin (local) (staphylococcal)
(streptococcal) NEC 686.9
ulcer (*see also* Ulcer, skin) 707.9
spinal cord NEC (*see also*
Encephalitis) 323.9
abscess 324.1
late effect—*see* category 326
late effect—*see* category 326
staphylococcal NEC 041.10
pneumonia 482.40
aureus 482.41
specified type NEC 482.49
stump (amputation)
(posttraumatic) (surgical)
997.62
subcutaneous tissue, local NEC
686.9
tendon (sheath) 727.89
thigh (skin) 686.9
thumb (skin) 686.9
abscess (with lymphangitis)
681.00
pulp 681.01
cellulitis (with lymphangitis)
681.00
nail 681.02
toe (skin) 686.9
abscess (with lymphangitis)
681.10
cellulitis (with lymphangitis)
681.10
nail 681.11
trachea, chronic 491.8
umbilicus (septic) 686.9
virus, viral 079.99
chest 519.8

Infection, infected, infective —
continued
wound (local) (posttraumatic) NEC
958.3
postoperative 998.59
surgical 998.59
**Inflammation, inflamed,
inflammatory** (with
exudation)
areolar tissue NEC 686.9
brain (*see also* Encephalitis) 323.9
late effect—*see* category 326
cerebral (*see also* Encephalitis)
323.9
late effect—*see* category 326
cerebrospinal (*see also* Meningitis)
322.9
late effect—*see* category 326
chest 519.9
connective tissue (diffuse) NEC
728.9
fascia 728.9
intervertebral disc 722.90
cervical, cervicothoracic 722.91
lumbar, lumbosacral 722.93
thoracic, thoracolumbar 722.92
joint NEC (*see also* Arthritis)
716.9☑

*Note—Use the following fifth-digit
subclassification with categories 711-
712, 715-716, 718, 719.0-719.6,
719.8, 719.9:*

0 *site unspecified*
1 *shoulder region*
2 *upper arm*
3 *forearm*
4 *hand*
5 *pelvic region and thigh*
6 *lower leg*
7 *ankle and foot*
8 *other specified sites*
9 *multiple sites*

sacroiliac 720.2
knee (joint) 716.66
leg NEC 686.9
lung (acute) (*see also* Pneumonia)
486
chronic (interstitial) 518.89
muscle 728.9
navel 686.9
nerve NEC 729.2
parotid region 686.9
perineum (female) (male) 686.9
respiratory, upper (*see also*
Infection, respiratory, upper)
465.9
due to
fumes or vapors (chemical)
(inhalation) 506.2
radiation 508.1
skin 686.9
spinal
cord (*see also* Encephalitis)
323.9
late effect—*see* category 326
spine (*see also* Spondylitis) 720.9
subcutaneous tissue NEC 686.9
tendon (sheath) NEC 726.90
thigh 686.9
umbilicus, umbilical 686.9
vein (*see also* Phlebitis) 451.9
thrombotic 451.9
Inflation, lung imperfect
(newborn) 770.5

Influenza, influenzal 487.1
A/H5N1 488.0
avian 488.0
abdominal 487.8
with
bronchitis 487.1
bronchopneumonia 487.0
cold (any type) 487.1
digestive manifestations 487.8
hemoptysis 487.1
involvement of
gastrointestinal tract 487.8
nervous system 487.8
laryngitis 487.1
manifestations NEC 487.8
respiratory 487.1
pneumonia 487.0
novel (2009) H1N1 488.1
novel A/H1N1 488.1
pharyngitis 487.1
pneumonia (any form
classifiable to 480-483,
485-486) 487.0
respiratory (upper) 487.1
Influenza-like disease 487.1
Ingrowing
nail (finger) (toe) (infected) 703.0
Injury 959.9
ankle (and foot) (and knee) (and
leg, except thigh) 959.7
blood vessel NEC 904.9
due to accidental puncture or
laceration during
procedure 998.2
brachial plexus 953.4
cauda equina 952.4
celiac ganglion or plexus 954.1
cortex (cerebral) (*see also* Injury,
intracranial) 854.0☑

*Note—Use the following fifth-digit
subclassification with categories 851-
854:*

0 *unspecified state of consciousness*
1 *with no loss of consciousness*
2 *with brief [less than one hour] loss
of consciousness*
3 *with moderate [1-24 hours] loss of
consciousness*
4 *with prolonged [more than 24
hours] loss of consciousness and
return to pre-existing conscious
level*
5 *with prolonged [more than 24
hours] loss of consciousness,
without return to pre-existing
conscious level*
*Use fifth-digit 5 to designate when a
patient is unconscious and dies
before regaining consciousness,
regardless of the duration of the
loss of consciousness*
6 *with loss of consciousness of
unspecified duration*
9 *with concussion, unspecified*

visual 950.3
cutaneous sensory nerve
lower limb 956.4
upper limb 955.5
deep tissue—*see* Contusion, by site
meaning pressure ulcer 707.25
elbow (and forearm) (and wrist)
959.3
finger(s) (nail) 959.5

☑ Additional Digit Required

Injury—continued
  foot (and ankle) (and knee) (and
    leg except thigh) 959.7
  forearm (and elbow) (and wrist)
    959.3
  hand(s) (except fingers) 959.4
  head NEC 959.01
    with
      loss of consciousness 850.5
  heel 959.7
  instrumental (during surgery)
    998.2
  joint NEC 959.9
    old or residual 718.80
      ankle 718.87
      elbow 718.82
      foot 718.87
      hand 718.84
      hip 718.85
      knee 718.86
      multiple sites 718.89
      pelvic region 718.85
      shoulder (region) 718.81
      specified site NEC 718.88
      wrist 718.83
  knee (and ankle) (and foot) (and
    leg, except thigh) 959.7
  leg except thigh (and ankle) (and
    foot) (and knee) 959.7
  lumbar (region) 959.19
    plexus 953.5
  lumbosacral (region) 959.19
    plexus 953.5
  mesenteric
    plexus, inferior 954.1
  musculocutaneous nerve 955.4
  nail
    finger 959.5
    toe 959.7
  nerve 957.9
    ankle and foot 956.9
    anterior crural, femoral 956.1
    arm (see also Injury, nerve,
      upper limb) 955.9
    axillary 955.0
    brachial plexus 953.4
    cervical sympathetic 954.0
    cranial 951.9
      second or optic 950.0
    cutaneous sensory
      lower limb 956.4
      upper limb 955.5
    digital (finger) 955.6
      toe 956.5
    femoral 956.1
    finger 955.9
    foot and ankle 956.9
    forearm 955.9
    hand and wrist 955.9
    head and neck, superficial 957.0
    involving several parts of body
      957.8
    leg (see also Injury, nerve, lower
      limb) 956.9
    lower limb 956.9
      multiple 956.8
      specified site NEC 956.5
    lumbar plexus 953.5
    lumbosacral plexus 953.5
    median 955.1
      forearm 955.1
      wrist and hand 955.1

Injury—continued
  nerve —continued
    multiple (in several parts of
      body) (sites not
      classifiable to the same
      three-digit category)
      957.8
    musculocutaneous 955.4
    musculospiral 955.3
      upper arm 955.3
    optic 950.0
    pelvic girdle 956.9
      multiple sites 956.8
      specified site NEC 956.5
    peripheral 957.9
      multiple (in several regions)
        (sites not classifiable to
        the same three-digit
        category) 957.8
      specified site NEC 957.1
    peroneal 956.3
      ankle and foot 956.3
      lower leg 956.3
    plantar 956.5
    plexus 957.9
      celiac 954.1
      mesenteric, inferior 954.1
      spinal 953.9
        brachial 953.4
        lumbosacral 953.5
        multiple sites 953.8
      sympathetic NEC 954.1
    radial 955.3
      wrist and hand 955.3
    sacral plexus 953.5
    sciatic 956.0
      thigh 956.0
    shoulder girdle 955.9
      multiple 955.8
      specified site NEC 955.7
    specified site NEC 957.1
    spinal 953.9
      root 953.9
        cervical 953.0
        dorsal 953.1
        lumbar 953.2
        multiple sites 953.8
        sacral 953.3
    splanchnic 954.1
    sympathetic NEC 954.1
      cervical 954.0
    thigh 956.9
    tibial 956.5
      ankle and foot 956.2
      lower leg 956.5
      posterior 956.2
    toe 956.9
    trunk, excluding shoulder and
      pelvic girdles 954.9
      specified site NEC 954.8
      sympathetic NEC 954.1
    ulnar 955.2
      forearm 955.2
      wrist (and hand) 955.2
    upper limb 955.9
      multiple 955.8
      specified site NEC 955.7
    wrist and hand 955.9
  nervous system, diffuse 957.8
  optic 950.9
    chiasm 950.1
    cortex 950.3
    nerve 950.0
    pathways 950.2

Injury—continued
  phalanges
    foot 959.7
    hand 959.5
  popliteal space 959.7
  sacral (region) 959.19
    plexus 953.5
  spinal (cord) 952.9
    cervical (C1-C4) 952.00
      C5-C7 level 952.05
        specified type NEC 952.09
        with
          anterior cord syndrome
            952.07
          central cord syndrome
            952.08
          complete lesion of cord
            952.06
          incomplete lesion NEC
            952.09
          posterior cord
            syndrome
            952.09
      specified type NEC 952.04
      with
        anterior cord syndrome
          952.02
        central cord syndrome
          952.03
        complete lesion of cord
          952.01
        incomplete lesion NEC
          952.04
        posterior cord syndrome
          952.04
    dorsal (D1-D6) (T1-T6)
      (thoracic) 952.10
      D7-D12 level (T7-T12)
      952.15
        specified type NEC 952.19
        with
          anterior cord syndrome
            952.17
          central cord syndrome
            952.18
          complete lesion of cord
            952.16
          incomplete lesion NEC
            952.19
          posterior cord
            syndrome
            952.19
      specified type NEC 952.14
      with
        anterior cord syndrome
          952.12
        central cord syndrome
          952.13
        complete lesion of cord
          952.11
        incomplete lesion NEC
          952.14
        posterior cord syndrome
          952.14
    lumbar 952.2
    multiple sites 952.8
    plexus 953.9
      brachial 953.4
      lumbosacral 953.5
      multiple sites 953.8
    sacral 952.3
    thoracic (see also Injury, spinal,
      dorsal) 952.10
  stellate ganglion 954.1

Injury—continued
  subungual
    fingers 959.5
    toes 959.7
  surgical complication (external or
    internal site) 998.2
  thumb(s) (nail) 959.5
  toe (nail) (any) 959.7
  visual 950.9
    cortex 950.3
  wrist (and elbow) (and forearm)
    959.3
INPH (idiopathic normal pressure
  hydrocephalus) 331.5
Inspiration
  food or foreign body (see also
    Asphyxia, food or foreign
    body) 933.1
  mucus (see also Asphyxia, mucus)
    933.1
Instability
  detrusor 596.59
  joint (posttraumatic) 718.80
    ankle 718.87
    elbow 718.82
    foot 718.87
    hand 718.84
    hip 718.85
    knee 718.86
    lumbosacral 724.6
    multiple sites 718.89
    pelvic region 718.85
    sacroiliac 724.6
    shoulder (region) 718.81
    specified site NEC 718.88
    wrist 718.83
  lumbosacral 724.6
  urethral 599.83
    correct substance properly
      administered 995.2
  effort 306.2
**Involuntary movement,
  abnormal** 781.0
Iron-miners' lung 503
Irregular, irregularity
  breathing 786.09
  respiratory 786.09
  sleep-wake rhythm (non-24-hour)
    327.39
    nonorganic origin 307.45
  vertebra 733.99
Irritability (nervous) 799.2
  bladder 596.8
    neurogenic 596.54
      with cauda equina syndrome
        344.61
  bronchial (see also Bronchitis) 490
  heart (psychogenic) 306.2
  myocardium 306.2
  sympathetic (nervous system) (see
    also Neuropathy, peripheral,
    autonomic) 337.9
  ventricular (heart) (psychogenic)
    306.2
Irritation
  axillary nerve 353.0
  brachial plexus 353.0
  bronchial (see also Bronchitis) 490
  cervical plexus 353.2
  lumbosacral plexus 353.1
  myocardium 306.2
  perineum 709.9
  peripheral

Irritation—*continued*
  peripheral—*continued*
    autonomic nervous system (*see also* Neuropathy, peripheral, autonomic) 337.9
    plantar nerve 355.6
    spinal (cord) (traumatic)—*see also* Injury, spinal, by site
    nerve—*see also* Disorder, nerve root NEC 724.9
    sympathetic nerve NEC (*see also* Neuropathy, peripheral, autonomic) 337.9
    ulnar nerve 354.2
Ischemia, ischemic 459.9
  bone NEC 733.40
  cardiac (*see also* Ischemia, heart) 414.9
  cardiomyopathy 414.8
  coronary (chronic) (*see also* Ischemia, heart) 414.9
  heart (chronic or with a stated duration of over 8 weeks) 414.9
    acute or with a stated duration of 8 weeks or less (*see also* Infarct, myocardium) 410.9☑

Note—Use the following fifth-digit subclassification with category 410:
  0 *episode unspecified*
  1 *initial episode*
  2 *subsequent episode without recurrence*

      without myocardial infarction 411.89
        with coronary (artery) occlusion 411.81
        subacute 411.89
      muscles, leg 728.89
      myocardium, myocardial (chronic or with a stated duration of over 8 weeks) 414.8
        acute (*see also* Infarct, myocardium) 410.9☑
Ischemia, ischemic 459.9
  myocardium, myocardial
    acute (*see also* Infarct, myocardium)
      without myocardial infarction 411.89
        with coronary (artery) occlusion 411.81
    spinal cord 336.1
    subendocardial (*see also* Insufficiency, coronary) 411.89
Ischialgia (*see also* Sciatica) 724.3

J

Jaccoud's nodular fibrositis, chronic (Jaccoud's syndrome) 714.4
Jackson's
  paralysis or syndrome 344.89
Jakob-Creutzfeldt disease (CJD) (syndrome) 046.19
  with dementia
    with behavioral disturbance 046.19 [294.11]

Jakob-Creutzfeldt disease—*continued*
  with dementia—*continued*
    without behavioral disturbance 046.19 [294.10]
  familial 046.19
  iatrogenic 046.19
  specified NEC 046.19
  sporadic 046.19
  variant (vCJD) 046.11
    with dementia
      with behavioral disturbance 046.11 [294.11]
      without behavioral disturbance 046.11 [294.10]
Jaw-blinking 374.43
  congenital 742.8
Jaw-winking phenomenon or syndrome 742.8
Jealousy
  childhood 313.3
  sibling 313.3
Jerks, myoclonic 333.2
Joint—*see also* condition
  Charcôt's 094.0 [713.5]
  false 733.82
Jumpers' knee 727.2
Jüngling's disease (sarcoidosis) 135

K

Kaolinosis 502
Kissing
  osteophytes 721.5
  spine 721.5
  vertebra 721.5
Kleptomania 312.32
Klinger's disease 446.4
Klippel's disease 723.8
Klippel-Feil disease or syndrome (brevicollis) 756.16
Klüver-Bucy (-Terzian) syndrome 310.0
Knock-knee (acquired) 736.41
  congenital 755.64
Köhler's disease (osteochondrosis) 732.5
  patellar 732.4
Köhler-Pellegrini-Stieda disease or syndrome (calcification, knee joint) 726.62
Koilonychia 703.8
Kümmell's disease or spondylitis 721.7
Kyphoscoliosis, kyphoscoliotic (acquired) (*see also* Scoliosis) 737.30
  congenital 756.19
  due to radiation 737.33
  heart (disease) 416.1
  idiopathic 737.30
    infantile
      progressive 737.32
      resolving 737.31
  late effect of rickets 268.1 [737.43]
  specified NEC 737.39
  thoracogenic 737.34
  tuberculous (*see also* Tuberculosis) 015.0☑ [737.43]

Kyphoscoliosis, kyphoscoliotic—*continued*

Note—Use the following fifth-digit subclassification with categories 010-018:
  0 *unspecified*
  1 *bacteriological or histological examination not done*
  2 *bacteriological or histological examination unknown (at present)*
  3 *tubercle bacilli found (in sputum) by microscopy*
  4 *tubercle bacilli not found (in sputum) by microscopy, but found by bacterial culture*
  5 *tubercle bacilli not found by bacteriological exam-ination, but tuberculosis confirmed histologically*
  6 *tubercle bacilli not found by bacteriological or histological examination, but tuberculosis confirmed by other methods [inoculation of animals]*

Kyphosis, kyphotic (acquired) (postural) 737.10
  adolescent postural 737.0
  congenital 756.19
  due to or associated with
    Charcôt-Marie-Tooth disease 356.1 [737.41]
    mucopolysaccharidosis 277.5 [737.41]
    neurofibromatosis 237.71 [737.41]
    osteitis
      deformans 731.0 [737.41]
      fibrosa cystica 252.0 [737.41]
    poliomyelitis (*see also* Poliomyelitis) 138 [737.41]
  radiation 737.11
  tuberculosis (*see also* Tuberculosis) 015.0☑ [737.41]
  Kümmell's 721.7
  late effect of rickets 268.1 [737.41]
  Morquio-Brailsford type (spinal) 277.5 [737.41]
  postlaminectomy 737.12
  specified cause NEC 737.19
  syphilitic, congenital 090.5 [737.41]
  tuberculous (*see also* Tuberculosis) 015.0☑ [737.41]

L

Labile
  vasomotor system 443.9
Labioglossal paralysis 335.22
Labored breathing (*see also* Hyperventilation) 786.09
Laceration—*see also* Wound, open, by site
  accidental, complicating surgery 998.2
  Achilles tendon 845.09
Laceration—*see also* Wound, open, by site
  meniscus (knee) (*see also* Tear, meniscus) 836.2
    old 717.5

Laceration—*continued*
  tendon 848.9
    Achilles 845.09
    lower limb NEC 844.9
Lack of
  coordination 781.3
  development—*see also* Hypoplasia
    physiological in childhood 783.40
  energy 780.79
  memory (*see also* Amnesia) 780.93
    mild, following organic brain damage 310.1
  physiologic development in childhood 783.40
  sleep V69.4
Lacunar skull 756.0
Lafora's disease 333.2
Lame back 724.5
Landouzy-Déjérine dystrophy (fascioscapulohumeral atrophy) 359.1
Landry's disease or paralysis 357.0
Landry-Guillain-Barré syndrome 357.0
Larsen's syndrome (flattened facies and multiple congenital dislocations) 755.8
Larsen-Johansson disease (juvenile osteopathia patellae) 732.4
Laryngeal—*see also* condition
  syncope 786.2
  congenital 748.3
Lassitude (*see also* Weakness) 780.79
Late—*see also* condition
  effect(s) (of)—*see also* condition
    abscess
      intracranial or intraspinal (con-ditions classifiable to 324)—*see* category 326
    adverse effect of drug, medicinal or biolo-gical substance 909.5
    amputation
      postoperative (late) 997.60
      traumatic (injury clas-sifiable to 885-887 and 895-897) 905.9
    burn (injury classifiable to 948-949) 906.9
      extremities NEC (injury classifiable to 943 or 945) 906.7
      hand or wrist (injury classifiable to 944) 906.6
      eye (injury classifiable to 940) 906.5
      face, head, and neck (injury classifiable to 941) 906.5
      specified site NEC (injury classifiable to 942 and 946-947) 906.8
    cerebrovascular disease (conditions classifiable to 430-437) 438.9
      specified type NEC 438.89
      with
        aphasia 438.11
        cognitive deficits 438.0
        dysarthria 438.13
        dysphagia 438.82

Late—*continued*
　effect(s) (of)—*continued*
　　cerebrovascular disease —
　　　continued
　　　with—*continued*
　　　　dysphasia 438.12
　　　　fluency disorder 438.14
　　　　hemiplegia/hemiparesis
　　　　　affecting
　　　　　　dominant side
　　　　　　　438.21
　　　　　　nondominant side
　　　　　　　438.22
　　　　　　unspecified side
　　　　　　　438.20
　　　　monoplegia of lower limb
　　　　　affecting
　　　　stuttering 438.14
　　cerebrovascular disease
　　　with
　　　　monoplegia of lower limb
　　　　　affecting
　　　　　　dominant side
　　　　　　　438.41
　　　　　　nondominant side
　　　　　　　438.42
　　　　　　unspecified side
　　　　　　　438.40
　　　　paralytic syndrome NEC
　　　　　affecting
　　　　　　bilateral 438.53
　　　　　　dominant side
　　　　　　　438.51
　　　　　　nondominant side
　　　　　　　438.52
　　　　　　unspecified side
　　　　　　　438.50
　　　　speech and language
　　　　　deficit 438.10
　　complication(s) of
　　　surgical and medical care
　　　　(conditions classifiable
　　　　to 996-999) 909.3
　　crushing (injury classifiable to
　　　925-929) 906.4
　　dislocation (injury classifiable to
　　　830-839) 905.6
　　encephalitis or
　　　encephalomyelitis
　　　(conditions classifiable to
　　　323)—*see* category 326
　　fracture (multiple) (injury
　　　classifiable to 828.0-828.1
　　　extremity
　　　　lower (injury classifiable to
　　　　　821-827) 905.4
　　　　　neck of femur (injury
　　　　　　classifiable to
　　　　　　820) 905.3
　　　　upper (injury classifiable
　　　　　to 810-819) 905.2
　　　face and skull (injury
　　　　classifiable to 800-804)
　　　　905.0
　　　skull and face (injury
　　　　classifiable to 800-804)
　　　　905.0
　　　spine and trunk (injury
　　　　classifiable to 805 and
　　　　807-809) 905.1
　　　　with spinal cord lesion
　　　　　(injury classifiable to
　　　　　806) 907.2

Late—*continued*
　effect(s) (of)—*continued*
　　infection
　　　pyogenic, intracranial—*see*
　　　　category 326
　　injury (injury classifiable to 959)
　　　908.9
　　　blood vessel 908.3
　　　　head and neck (injury
　　　　　classifiable to 900)
　　　　　908.3
　　　　intracranial (injury
　　　　　classifiable to
　　　　　850-854) 907.0
　　　　　with skull fracture
　　　　　　905.0
　　　intracranial (injury classifiable
　　　　to 850-854) 907.0
　　　　with skull fracture (injury
　　　　　classifiable to 800-
　　　　　801 and 803-804)
　　　　　905.0
　　　nerve NEC (injury classifiable
　　　　to 957) 907.9
　　　　cranial (injury classifiable
　　　　　to 950-951) 907.1
　　　　peripheral NEC (injury
　　　　　classifiable to 957)
　　　　　907.9
　　　　lower limb and pelvic
　　　　　girdle (injury
　　　　　classifiable to
　　　　　956) 907.5
　　　　upper limb and
　　　　　shoulder girdle
　　　　　(injury
　　　　　classifiable to
　　　　　955) 907.4
　　　　trunk (injury classifiable to
　　　　　954) 907.3
　　　spinal
　　　　cord (injury classi-fiable to
　　　　　806 and 952) 907.2
　　　tendon (tendon injury
　　　　classifiable to 840-848,
　　　　880-884 with .2, and
　　　　890-894 with .2) 905.8
　　meningitis
　　　bacterial (conditions
　　　　classifiable to 320)—
　　　　see category 326
　　　unspecified cause (conditions
　　　　classifiable to 322)—
　　　　see category 326
　　myelitis (*see also* Late, effect(s)
　　　(of), encephalitis)—*see*
　　　category 326
　　phlebitis or thrombophlebitis of
　　　intracranial venous sinuses
　　　(conditions classifiable to
　　　325)—*see* category 326
　　Lpoisoning due to drug,
　　　medicinal or biological
　　　substance (conditions
　　　classifiable to 960-979)
　　　909.0
　　radiation (conditions classifiable
　　　to 990) 909.2
　　sprain and strain without
　　　mention of tendon injury
　　　(injury classifiable to 840-
　　　848, except tendon
　　　injury) 905.7
　　　tendon involvement 905.8

Late—*continued*
　effect(s) (of)—*continued*
　　toxic effect of
　　　drug, medicinal or biological
　　　　substance (conditions
　　　　classifiable to 960-979)
　　　　909.0
　　　nonmedical substance
　　　　(conditions classifiable
　　　　to 980-989) 909.1
　　wound, open
　　　extremity (injury classifiable
　　　　to 880-884 and 890-
　　　　894, except .2) 906.1
　　　　tendon (injury classifiable
　　　　　to 880-884 with .2
　　　　　and 890-894
　　　　　with.2) 905.8
　　　head, neck, and trunk (injury
　　　　classifiable to 870-879)
　　　　906.0
Lax, laxity—*see also* Relaxation
　ligament 728.4
Lead miners' lung 503
Leakage
　spinal fluid at lumbar puncture site
　　997.09
Learning defect, specific NEC
　(strephosymbolia) 315.2
Left-sided neglect 781.8
Legionnaires' disease 482.84
Leigh's disease 330.8
Lengthening, leg 736.81
Leptomeningitis (chronic)
　(circumscribed) (hemorrhagic)
　(nonsuppurative) (*see also*
　Meningitis) 322.9
　late effect—*see* category 326
Lesion
　bone 733.90
　brachial plexus 353.0
　brain 348.89
　　congenital 742.9
　　　vascular (*see also* Lesion,
　　　　cerebro-vascular)
　　　　437.9
　　　　healed or old without
　　　　　residuals V12.54
　cauda equina 344.60
　　with neurogenic bladder 344.61
　cerebrovascular (*see also*
　　Disease, cerebro-vascular
　　NEC) 437.9
　　healed or old without
　　　residuals V12.54
　cervical root (nerve) NEC 353.2
　chorda tympani 351.8
　coronary artery (*see also* Ischemia,
　　heart) 414.9
　cranial nerve 352.9
　　eleventh 352.4
　　fifth 350.9
　　first 352.0
　　ninth 352.2
　　seventh 351.9
　　tenth 352.3
　　twelfth 352.5
　dermal (skin) 709.9
　gasserian ganglion 350.8
　glossopharyngeal nerve 352.2
　helix (ear) 709.9
　hypoglossal nerve 352.5
　iliohypogastric nerve 355.79
　ilioinguinal nerve 355.79

Lesion—*continued*
　joint 719.90
　　ankle 719.97
　　elbow 719.92
　　foot 719.97
　　hand 719.94
　　hip 719.95
　　knee 719.96
　　multiple sites 719.99
　　pelvic region 719.95
　　sacroiliac (old) 724.6
　　shoulder (region) 719.91
　　specified site NEC 719.98
　　wrist 719.93
　laryngeal nerve (recurrent) 352.3
　lumbosacral
　　plexus 353.1
　　root (nerve) NEC 353.4
　lung 518.89
　nerve (*see also* Disorder, nerve)
　　355.9
　nervous system 349.9
　　congenital 742.9
　nonallopathic NEC 739.9
　　in region (of)
　　　abdomen 739.9
　　　acromioclavicular 739.7
　　　cervical, cervicothoracic
　　　　739.1
　　　costochondral 739.8
　　　costovertebral 739.8
　　　extremity
　　　　lower 739.6
　　　　upper 739.7
　　　head 739.0
　　　hip 739.5
　　　lower extremity 739.6
　　　lumbar, lumbosacral 739.3
　　　occipitocervical 739.0
　　　pelvic 739.5
　　　pubic 739.5
　　　rib cage 739.8
　　　sacral, sacrococcygeal,
　　　　sacroiliac 739.4
　　　sternochondral 739.8
　　　sternoclavicular 739.7
　　　thoracic, thoracolumbar
　　　　739.2
　　　upper extremity 739.7
　obturator nerve 355.79
　osteolytic 733.90
　pulmonary 518.89
　　valve (*see also* Endocarditis,
　　　pulmonary) 424.3
　romanus 720.1
　sacroiliac (joint) 724.6
　saphenous nerve 355.79
　skin 709.9
　　suppurative 686.00
　spinal cord 336.9
　　congenital 742.9
　thoracic root (nerve) 353.3
　trigeminal nerve 350.9
　vagus nerve 352.3
Lethargy 780.79
Leukodystrophy (cerebral) (globoid
　cell) (metachromatic)
　(progressive) (sudanophilic)
　330.0
Leukoencephalopathy (*see also*
　Encephalitis) 323.9
　metachromatic 330.0
　reversible, posterior 348.5
Leukonychia (punctata) (striata)
　703.8

Leukopathia
unguium 703.8
Leukoplakia 702.8
larynx 478.79
Libman-Sacks disease or syndrome 710.0 *[424.91]*
Lichtheim's disease or syndrome (subacute combined sclerosis with pernicious anemia) 281.0 *[336.2]*
Likoff's syndrome (angina in menopausal women) 413.9
Limitation of joint motion (*see also* Stiffness, joint) 719.5 ☑

Note—Use the following fifth-digit subclassification with categories 711-712, 715-716, 718, 719.0-719.6, 719.8, 719.9:
0   site unspecified
1   shoulder region
2   upper arm
3   forearm
4   hand
5   pelvic region and thigh
6   lower leg
7   ankle and foot
8   other specified sites
9   multiple sites

mandible 524.52
sacroiliac 724.6
Lines
Beau's (transverse furrows on fingernails) 703.8
Harris' 733.91
Lipidosis 272.7
cerebral (infantile) (juvenile) (late) 330.1
cerebroretinal 330.1 *[362.71]*
sulfatide 330.0
Lipping
spine (*see also* Spondylosis) 721.90
vertebra (*see also* Spondylosis) 721.90
Listlessness 780.79
Lithosis (occupational) 502
Little
league elbow 718.82
Live flesh 781.0
Lobotomy syndrome 310.0
Lobster-claw hand 755.58
Locked-in state 344.81
Locking
joint (*see also* Derangement, joint) 718.90
Löffler's
eosinophilia or syndrome 518.3
pneumonia 518.3
syndrome (eosinophilic pneumonitis) 518.3
Löfgren's syndrome (sarcoidosis) 135
Long-term (current) drug use V58.69
antiplatelets/antithrombotics V58.63
aspirin V58.66
high-risk medications NEC V58.69
insulin V58.67
opiate analgesic V58.69
pain killers V58.69
anti-inflammatories, non-steroidal (NSAID) V58.64
aspirin V58.66
steroids V58.65

Longitudinal stripes or grooves, nails 703.8
Loose—*see also* condition
body
in tendon sheath 727.82
joint 718.10
ankle 718.17
elbow 718.12
foot 718.17
hand 718.14
hip 718.15
multiple sites 718.19
pelvic region 718.15
shoulder (region) 718.11
specified site NEC 718.18
wrist 718.13
cartilage (joint) (*see also* Loose, body, joint) 718.1 ☑

Note—Use the following fifth-digit subclassification with categories 711-712, 715-716, 718, 719.0-719.6, 719.8, 719.9:
0   site unspecified
1   shoulder region
2   upper arm
3   forearm
4   hand
5   pelvic region and thigh
6   lower leg
7   ankle and foot
8   other specified sites
9   multiple sites

facet (vertebral) 724.9
sesamoid, joint (*see also* Loose, body, joint) 718.1 ☑
Lordosis (acquired) (postural) 737.20
congenital 754.2
due to or associated with
Charcôt-Marie-Tooth disease 356.1 *[737.42]*
mucopolysaccharidosis 277.5 *[737.42]*
neurofibromatosis 237.71 *[737.42]*
osteitis
deformans 731.0 *[737.42]*
fibrosa cystica 252.0 *[737.42]*
osteoporosis (*see also* Osteoporosis) 733.00 *[737.42]*
poliomyelitis (*see also* Poliomyelitis) 138 *[737.42]*
tuberculosis (*see also* Tuberculosis) 015.0 ☑ *[737.42]*
late effect of rickets 268.1 *[737.42]*
postlaminectomy 737.21
postsurgical NEC 737.22
rachitic 268.1 *[737.42]*
specified NEC 737.29
tuberculous (*see also* Tuberculosis) 015.0 ☑ *[737.42]*

Lordosis—*continued*

Note—Use the following fifth-digit subclassification with categories 010-018:
0   unspecified
1   bacteriological or histological examination not done
2   bacteriological or histological examination unknown (at present)
3   tubercle bacilli found (in sputum) by microscopy
4   tubercle bacilli not found (in sputum) by microscopy, but found by bacterial culture
5   tubercle bacilli not found by bacteriological exam-ination, but tuberculosis confirmed histologically
6   tubercle bacilli not found by bacteriological or histological examination, but tuberculosis confirmed by other methods [inoculation of animals]

Lou Gehrig's disease 335.20
Louis-Bar syndrome (ataxia-telangiectasia) 334.8
Low
back syndrome 724.2
output syndrome (cardiac) (*see also* Failure, heart) 428.9
Lumbalgia 724.2
due to displacement, intervertebral disc 722.10
Lumbarization, vertebra 756.15
Lupus 710.0
disseminated 710.0
erythematosus (discoid) (local) 695.4
disseminated 710.0
systemic 710.0
with
encephalitis 710.0 *[323.81]*
lung involvement 710.0 *[517.8]*
nephritis 710.0 *[583.81]*
acute 710.0 *[580.81]*
chronic 710.0 *[582.81]*
pernio (Besnier) 135
Luschka's joint disease 721.90
Luxatio
coxae congenita (*see also* Dislocation, hip, congenital) 754.30
Lycanthropy (*see also* Psychosis) 298.9
Lymphedema
acquired (chronic) 457.1
chronic hereditary 757.0
secondary 457.1
surgical NEC 997.99
postmastectomy (syndrome) 457.0

M

Machado-Joseph disease 334.8
Macleod's syndrome (abnormal transradiancy, one lung) 492.8
Macrocephalia, macrocephaly 756.0
Macrocheilia (congenital) 744.81

Macrodactylia, macrodactylism (fingers) (thumbs) 755.57
toes 755.65
Macrohydrocephalus (*see also* Hydrocephalus) 331.4
Macrostomia (congenital) 744.83
Madelung's
deformity (radius) 755.54
Main en griffe (acquired) 736.06
congenital 755.59
Mal
perforant (*see also* Ulcer, lower extremity) 707.15
Maldevelopment—*see also* Anomaly, by site
brain 742.9
hip (joint) 755.63
congenital dislocation (*see also* Dislocation, hip, congenital) 754.30
mastoid process 756.0
middle ear, except ossicles 744.03
ossicles 744.04
ossicles, ear 744.04
spine 756.10
toe 755.66
Malformation (congenital)—*see also* Anomaly
cochlea 744.05
internal ear 744.05
joint NEC 755.9
specified type NEC 755.8
Mondini's (congenital) (malformation, cochlea) 744.05
nervous system (central) 742.9
sense organs NEC 742.9
specified type NEC 742.8
spinal cord 742.9
Malfunction—*see also* Dysfunction
arterial graft 996.1
vascular graft or shunt 996.1
Mallet, finger (acquired) 736.1
congenital 755.59
Malposition
congenital
auditory canal 744.29
causing impairment of hearing 744.02
auricle (ear) 744.29
causing impairment of hearing 744.02
cervical 744.43
brachial plexus 742.8
bronchus 748.3
clavicle 755.51
ear (auricle) (external) 744.29
ossicles 744.04
epiglottis 748.3
facial features 744.89
finger(s) 755.59
supernumerary 755.01
foot 755.67
glottis 748.3
hand 755.59
hip (joint) (*see also* Dislocation, hip, congenital) 754.30
joint NEC 755.8
larynx 748.3
limb 755.8
lower 755.69
upper 755.59
lung (lobe) 748.69
nerve 742.8
nervous system NEC 742.8

Malposition—*continued*
  congenital—*continued*
    nose, nasal (septum) 748.1
    patella 755.64
    scapula 755.59
    shoulder 755.59
    spinal cord 742.59
    spine 756.19
    symphysis pubis 755.69
    thyroid (gland) (tissue) 759.2
      cartilage 748.3
    toe(s) 755.66
      supernumerary 755.02
    trachea 748.3
Malposture 729.90
Malt workers' lung 495.4
Malum coxae senilis 715.25
Malunion, fracture 733.81
Maple bark-strippers' lung 495.6
March
  foot 733.94
Marchiafava (-Bignami) disease or syndrome 341.8
Marcus Gunn's syndrome (jaw-winking syndrome) 742.8
Marie's
  cerebellar ataxia 334.2
Marie-Charcôt-Tooth neuropathic atrophy, muscle 356.1
Marie-Strümpell arthritis or disease (ankylosing spondylitis) 720.0
Martin's disease 715.27
Masons' lung 502
Mass
  bone 733.90
  chest 786.6
  joint 719.60
    ankle 719.67
    elbow 719.62
    foot 719.67
    hand 719.64
    hip 719.65
    knee 719.66
    multiple sites 719.69
    pelvic region 719.65
    shoulder (region) 719.61
    specified site NEC 719.68
    wrist 719.63
  lung 786.6
  mediastinal 786.6
  substernal 786.6
Mastalgia 611.71
  psychogenic 307.89
Megalocephalus, megalo-cephaly NEC 756.0
Megalodactylia (fingers) (thumbs) 755.57
  toes 755.65
Megrim 346.9☑

Note—Use the following fifth-digit subclassification with category 346:

0 without mention of intractable migraine without mention of status migrainosus
1 with intractable migraine, so stated, without mention of status migrainosus
2 without mention of intractable migraine with status migrainosus
3 with intractable migraine, so stated, with status migrainosus

Meleney's
  gangrene (cutaneous) 686.09
  ulcer (chronic undermining) 686.09
Melkersson (-Rosenthal) syndrome 351.8
Melorheostosis (bone) (leri) 733.99
Meloschisis 744.83
Memory disturbance, loss or lack
  (see also Amnesia) 780.93
  mild, following organic brain damage 310.1
Meningism (see also Meningismus) 781.6
Meningismus (infectional) (pneumococcal) 781.6
  due to serum or vaccine 997.09 [321.8]
  influenzal NEC 487.8
Meningitis (basal) (basic) (basilar) (brain) (cerebral) (cervical) (congestive) (diffuse) (hemorrhagic) (infantile) (membranous) (metastatic) (nonspecific) (pontine) (progressive) (simple) (spinal) (subacute) (sympathetica) (toxic) 322.9
  due to
    preventive immunization, inoculation, or vaccination 997.09 [321.8]
    sarcoidosis 135 [321.4]
  sterile 997.09
Meningoencephalitis (see also Encephalitis) 323.9
  due to
    free-living amebae 136.29
      Naegleria (amebae) (gruberi) (organisms) 136.29
  late effect—see category 326
  toxic NEC 989.9 [323.71]
    due to
      carbon tetrachloride (vapor) 987.8 [323.71]
Meningoencephalomyelitis (see also Meningoenceph-alitis) 323.9
  late effect—see category 326
Meningomyelitis (see also Meningoencephalitis) 323.9
  late effect—see category 326
Meromelia 755.4
  lower limb 755.30
    intercalary 755.32
      femur 755.34
        tibiofibular (complete) (incomplete) 755.33
      fibula 755.37
      metatarsal(s) 755.38
      tarsal(s) 755.38
      tibia 755.36
      tibiofibular 755.35
    terminal (complete) (partial) (transverse) 755.31
      longitudinal 755.32
        metatarsal(s) 755.38
        phalange(s) 755.39
        tarsal(s) 755.38
      transverse 755.31
  upper limb 755.20
    intercalary 755.22
      carpal(s) 755.28

Meromelia—*continued*
  upper limb—*continued*
    intercalary—*continued*
      humeral 755.24
        radioulnar (complete) (incomplete) 755.23
      metacarpal(s) 755.28
      phalange(s) 755.29
      radial 755.26
      radioulnar 755.25
      ulnar 755.27
    terminal (complete) (partial) (transverse) 755.21
      longitudinal 755.22
        carpal(s) 755.28
        metacarpal(s) 755.28
        phalange(s) 755.29
      transverse 755.21
Merosmia 781.1
Merzbacher-Pelizaeus disease 330.0
Mesencephalitis (see also Encephalitis) 323.9
  late effect—see category 326
Metal
  polishers' disease 502
Metalliferous miners' lung 503
Metastasis, metastatic
  pneumonia 038.8 [484.8]
Metatarsalgia 726.70
  anterior 355.6
  Morton's 355.6
Metatarsus, metatarsal—see also condition
  abductus valgus (congenital) 754.60
  adductus varus (congenital) 754.53
  primus varus 754.52
  valgus (adductus) (congenital) 754.60
  varus (abductus) (congenital) 754.53
  primus 754.52
Metrorrhagia 626.6
  psychogenic 306.59
Meyenburg-Altherr-Uehlinger syndrome 733.99
Meynert's amentia (nonalcoholic) 294.0
  alcoholic 291.1
Mice, joint (see also Loose, body, joint) 718.1☑
Mice, joint

Note—Use the following fifth-digit subclassification with categories 711-712, 715-716, 718, 719.0-719.6, 719.8, 719.9:

0 site unspecified
1 shoulder region
2 upper arm
3 forearm
4 hand
5 pelvic region and thigh
6 lower leg
7 ankle and foot
8 other specified sites
9 multiple sites

Michotte's syndrome 721.5
Microangiopathy 443.9
  diabetic (peripheral) 250.7☑ [443.81]
  due to secondary diabetes 249.7☑ [443. 81]

Microangiopathy—*continued*

Note—Use the following fifth-digit subclassification with category 250:

0 type II [non-insulin dependent type] [NIDDM type] [adult-onset type] or unspecified type, not stated as uncontrolled
1 type I [insulin dependent type] [IDDM type] [juvenile type], not stated as uncontrolled
2 type II [non-insulin dependent type] [NIDDM type] [adult-onset type] or unspecified type, uncontrolled
3 type I [insulin dependent type] [IDDM] [juvenile type], uncontrolled

  peripheral 443.9
    diabetic 250.7☑ [443.81]
    due to secondary diabetes 249.7☑ [443.81]
Microcheilia 744.82
Microinfarct, heart (see also Insufficiency, coronary) 411.89
Microlithiasis, alveolar, pulmonary 516.2
Micromyelia (congenital) 742.59
Microstomia (congenital) 744.84
Microtia (congenital) (external ear) 744.23
Micturition
  frequency 788.41
  nocturnal 788.43
Middle
  lobe (right) syndrome 518.0
Miescher's disease 709.3
  cheilitis 351.8
Migraine (idiopathic) 346.9☑

Note—Use the following fifth-digit subclassification with category 346:

0 without mention of intractable migraine without mention of status migrainosus
1 with intractable migraine, so stated, without mention of status migrainosus
2 without mention of intractable migraine with status migrainosus
3 with intractable migraine, so stated, with status migrainosus

  with aura (acute-onset) (without headache) (prolonged) (typical) 346.0
  without aura 346.1
    chronic 346.7
    transformed 346.7
  atypical 346.8
  basilar 346.0
  chronic without aura 346.7
  classic(al) 346.0
  hemiplegic 346.3
    familial 346.3
    sporadic 346.3
  lower-half 339.00
  menstrual 346.4
  menstrually related 346.4
  ophthalmoplegic 346.2
  premenstrual 346.4
  pure menstrual 346.4
  retinal 346.0
  specified form NEC 346.8
  transformed without aura 346.7

Millar's asthma (laryngismus stridulus) 478.75
Millard-Gubler-Foville paralysis 344.89
Millard-Gubler paralysis or syndrome 344.89
Miller Fisher's syndrome 357.0
Mills' disease 335.29
Millstone makers' asthma or lung 502
Miners'—see also condition
  asthma 500
  elbow 727.2
  knee 727.2
  lung 500
Möbius'
  disease 346.2☑
  syndrome
    congenital oculofacial paralysis 352.6
    ophthalmoplegic migraine 346.2☑
Mönckeberg's arteriosclerosis, degeneration, disease, or sclerosis (see also Arteriosclerosis, extremities) 440.20
Monoarthritis 716.60
  ankle 716.67
  arm 716.62
    lower (and wrist) 716.63
    upper (and elbow) 716.62
  foot (and ankle) 716.67
  forearm (and wrist) 716.63
  hand 716.64
  leg 716.66
    lower 716.66
    upper 716.65
  pelvic region (hip) (thigh) 716.65
  shoulder (region) 716.61
  specified site NEC 716.68
Mononeuritis 355.9
  femoral nerve 355.2
  lateral
    cutaneous nerve of thigh 355.1
    popliteal nerve 355.3
  lower limb 355.8
    specified nerve NEC 355.79
  medial popliteal nerve 355.4
  median nerve 354.1
  multiplex 354.5
  plantar nerve 355.6
  posterior tibial nerve 355.5
  radial nerve 354.3
  sciatic nerve 355.0
  ulnar nerve 354.2
  upper limb 354.9
    specified nerve NEC 354.8
    lower limb 250.6☑ [355.8]
Mononeuropathy (see also Mononeuritis) 355.9
  diabetic NEC 250.6☑ [355.9]
    due to secondary diabetes 249.6☑ [355.9]
  lower limb 250.6☑ [355.8]
    due to secondary diabetes 249.6☑ [355.8]
  upper limb 250.6 [354.9]
    due to secondary diabetes 249.6☑ **Monomania** (see also Psychosis) 298.9

Monoplegia 344.5
  congenital or infantile (cerebral) (spastic) (spinal) 343.3
  infantile (cerebral) (spastic) (spinal) 343.3
  lower limb 344.30
    affecting
      dominant side 344.31
      nondominant side 344.32
  psychogenic 306.0
    specified as conversion reaction 300.11
  transient 781.4
  upper limb 344.40
    affecting
      dominant side 344.41
      nondominant side 344.42
Monteggia's fracture (closed) 813.03
Morbus
  coxae 719.95
Mortification (dry) (moist) (see also Gangrene) 785.4
Morton's
  disease 355.6
  foot 355.6
  metatarsalgia (syndrome) 355.6
  neuralgia 355.6
  neuroma 355.6
  syndrome (metatarsalgia) (neuralgia) 355.6
  toe 355.6
Morvan's disease 336.0
Moulders'
  bronchitis 502
Mounier-Kuhn syndrome 748.3
  with
    acute exacerbation 494.1
    bronchiectasis 494.0
      with acute exacerbation 494.1
  acquired 519.19
    with bronchiectasis 494.0
      with (acute) exacerbation 494.1
Mouse, joint (see also Loose, body, joint) 718.1☑
Movable
  coccyx 724.71
Movement
  abnormal (dystonic) (involuntary) 781.0
Multiple, multiplex—see also condition
  digits (congenital) 755.00
    fingers 755.01
    toes 755.02
  personality 300.14
Münchmeyer's disease or syndrome (exostosis luxurians) 728.11
Musculoneuralgia 729.1
Mushroom workers' (pickers') lung 495.5
Mushrooming hip 718.95
Mutism (see also Aphasia) 784.3
  elective (selective) 313.23
    adjustment reaction 309.83
  hysterical 300.11
Myalgia (intercostal) 729.1
  eosinophilia syndrome 710.5
  psychogenic 307.89

Myasthenia 358.00
  gravis 358.00
    with exacerbation (acute) 358.01
    in crisis 358.01
  pseudoparalytica 358.00
  syndrome
    in
      botulism 005.1 [358.1]
      diabetes mellitus 250.6☑ [358.1]
        due to secondary diabetes 249.6☑ [358.1]
      hypothyroidism (see also Hypothyroidism) 244.9 [358.1]
      malignant neoplasm NEC 199.1 [358.1]
      pernicious anemia 281.0 [358.1]
      thyrotoxicosis (see also Thyrotoxicosis) 242.9☑ [358.1]
Myasthenic 728.87
Myelatelia 742.59
Myelinosis, central pontine 341.8
Myelitis (ascending) (cerebellar) (childhood) (chronic) (descending) (diffuse) (disseminated) (pressure) (progressive) (spinal cord) (subacute) (see also Encephalitis) 323.9
  acute (transverse) 341.20
    idiopathic 341.22
    in conditions classified elsewhere 341.21
  due to
    infections classified elsewhere 136.9 [323.42]
    specified cause NEC 323.82
    vaccination (any) 323.52
    viral diseases classified elsewhere 323.02
  herpes simplex 054.74
  herpes zoster 053.14
  postchickenpox 052.2
  postimmunization 323.52
  postinfectious 136.9 [323.63]
  postvaccinal 323.52
  postvaricella 052.2
  toxic 989.9 [323.72]
  transverse 323.82
    acute 341.20
      idiopathic 341.22
      in conditions classified elsewhere 341.21
    idiopathic 341.22
Myelodysplasia (spinal cord) 742.59
Myelofibrosis 289.83
  with myeloid metaplasia 238.76
  idopathic (chronic) 238.76
  megakaryocytic 238.79
  primary 238.76
  secondary 289.83
Myeloleukodystrophy 330.0
Myelomalacia 336.8
Myelopathy (spinal cord) 336.9
  cervical 721.1
  diabetic 250.6☑ [336.3]
    due to secondary diabetes 249.6☑ [336.3]
  drug-induced 336.8
  due to or with

Myelopathy —continued
  due to or with—continued
    carbon tetrachloride 987.8 [323.72]
    degeneration or displacement, intervertebral disc 722.70
      cervical, cervicothoracic 722.71
      lumbar, lumbosacral 722.73
      thoracic, thoracolumbar 722.72
    intervertebral disc disorder 722.70
      cervical, cervicothoracic 722.71
      lumbar, lumbosacral 722.73
      thoracic, thoracolumbar 722.72
    neoplastic disease (see also Neoplasm, by site) 239.9 [336.3]
    pernicious anemia 281.0 [336.3]
    spondylosis 721.91
      cervical 721.1
      lumbar, lumbosacral 721.42
      thoracic 721.41
  lumbar, lumbosacral 721.42
  necrotic (subacute) 336.1
  proximal myotonic (PROMM) 359.21
  radiation-induced 336.8
  spondylogenic NEC 721.91
    cervical 721.1
    lumbar, lumbosacral 721.42
    thoracic 721.41
  thoracic 721.41
  transverse (see also Myelitis) 323.82
  vascular 336.1
Myeloradiculitis (see also Polyneuropathy) 357.0
Myeloradiculodysplasia (spinal) 742.59
Myelosclerosis 289.89
  disseminated, of nervous system 340
Myocardiopathy (congestive) (constrictive) (familial) (hypertrophic nonobstructive) (idiopathic) (infiltrative) (obstructive) (primary) (restrictive) (sporadic) 425.4
  alcoholic 425.5
  amyloid 277.39 [425.7]
  beriberi 265.0 [425.7]
  cobalt-beer 425.5
  due to
    amyloidosis 277.39 [425.7]
    beriberi 265.0 [425.7]
    cardiac glycogenosis 271.0 [425.7]
    Friedreich's ataxia 334.0 [425.8]
    influenza 487.8 [425.8]
    mucopolysaccharidosis 277.5 [425.7]
    myotonia atrophica 359.21 [425.8]
    progressive muscular dystrophy 359.1 [425.8]
    sarcoidosis 135 [425.8]
  glycogen storage 271.0 [425.7]
  hypertrophic obstructive 425.1
  metabolic NEC 277.9 [425.7]
  nutritional 269.9 [425.7]
  obscure (African) 425.2

Myocardiopathy—*continued*
  secondary 425.9
  thyrotoxic (*see also* Thyrotoxicosis)
    242.9☑ *[425.7]*

Note—Use the following fifth-digit subclassification with category 242:
  0 without mention of thyrotoxic crisis or storm
  1 with mention of thyrotoxic crisis or storm

  toxic NEC 425.9
Myocarditis (fibroid) (interstitial) (old) (progressive) (senile) (with arteriosclerosis) 429.0
  constrictive 425.4
  due to or in
    influenza 487.8 *[422.0]*
  hypertensive (*see also* Hypertension, heart) 402.90
  influenzal 487.8 *[422.0]*
Myocardosis (*see also* Cardiomyopathy) 425.4
Myoclonia (essential) 333.2
  epileptica 333.2
  Friedrich's 333.2
  massive 333.2
Myoclonic
  epilepsy, familial (progressive) 333.2
  jerks 333.2
Myoclonus (familial essential) (multifocal) (simplex) 333.2
  facial 351.8
  massive (infantile) 333.2
Myodiastasis 728.84
Myofascitis (acute) 729.1
  low back 724.2
Myofibromatosis
  infantile 759.88
Myofibrosis 728.2
  humeroscapular region 726.2
  scapulohumeral 726.2
Myofibrositis (*see also* Myositis) 729.1
  scapulohumeral 726.2
Myogelosis (occupational) 728.89
Myokymia—*see also* Myoclonus
  facial 351.8
Myomalacia 728.9
Myopathy 359.9
  alcoholic 359.4
  amyloid 277.39 *[359.6]*
  benign congenital 359.0
  central core 359.0
  centronuclear 359.0
  congenital (benign) 359.0
  distal 359.1
  due to drugs 359.4

Myopathy—*continued*
  endocrine 259.9 *[359.5]*
    specified type NEC 259.8 *[359.5]*
  facioscapulohumeral 359.1
  in
    Addison's disease 255.41 *[359.5]*
    amyloidosis 277.39 *[359.6]*
    cretinism 243 *[359.5]*
    Cushing's syndrome 255.0 *[359.5]*
    disseminated lupus erythematosus 710.0 *[359.6]*
    giant cell arteritis 446.5 *[359.6]*
    hyperadrenocorticism NEC 255.3 *[359.5]*
    hyperparathyroidism 252.0 *[359.5]*
    hypopituitarism 253.2 *[359.5]*
    hypothyroidism (*see also* Hypothyroidism) 244.9 *[359.5]*
    malignant neoplasm NEC (M8000/3) 199.1 *[359.5]*
    myxedema (*see also* Myxedema) 244.9 *[359.5]*
    polyarteritis nodosa 446.0 *[359.6]*
    rheumatoid arthritis 714.0 *[359.6]*
    sarcoidosis 135 *[359.6]*
    scleroderma 710.1 *[359.6]*
    Sjögren's disease 710.2 *[359.6]*
    thyrotoxicosis (*see also* Thyrotoxicosis) 242.9☑ *[359.5]*

Note—Use the following fifth-digit subclassification with category 242:
  0 without mention of thyrotoxic crisis or storm
  1 with mention of thyrotoxic crisis or storm

  inflammatory 359.79
    immune NEC 359.79
    specified NEC 359.79
  limb-girdle 359.1
  myotubular 359.0
  nemaline 359.0
  ocular 359.1
  oculopharyngeal 359.1
  rod body 359.0
  scapulohumeral 359.1
  toxic 359.4

Myositis 729.1
  due to posture 729.1
  fibrosa or fibrous (chronic) 728.2
    Volkmann's (complicating trauma) 958.6
  inclusion body (IBM) 359.71
  infective 728.0
  interstitial 728.81
  occupational 729.1
  ossificans 728.12
    circumscribed 728.12
    progressive 728.11
    traumatic 728.12
  progressive fibrosing 728.11
  purulent 728.0
  rheumatic 729.1
  rheumatoid 729.1
  suppurative 728.0
  traumatic (old) 729.1
Myospasia impulsiva 307.23
Myotonia (acquisita) (intermittens) 728.85
  atrophica 359.21
  congenita 359.22
    acetazolamide responsive 359.22
      dominant form 359.22
      recessive form 359.22
    drug-induced 359.24
  dystrophica 359.21
  fluctuans 359.29
  levior 359.29
  permanens 359.29
Myxedema (adult) (idiocy) (infantile) (juvenile) (thyroid gland) (*see also* Hypothyroidism) 244.9
  madness (acute) 293.0
    subacute 293.1

N

Naffziger's syndrome 353.0
Naga sore (*see also* Ulcer, skin) 707.9
Nager-de Reynier syndrome (dysostosis mandibularis) 756.0
Narcolepsy 347.00
  with cataplexy 347.01
Narcosis
  carbon dioxide (respiratory) 786.09
Narrowing
  joint space, hip 719.85
  larynx 478.74
Nasopharyngeal—*see also* condition
  torticollis 723.5
Necrosis, necrotic
  arteritis 446.0
  aseptic, bone 733.40
    femur (head) (neck) 733.42
      medial condyle 733.43
    humoral head 733.41

Necrosis, necrotic—*continued*
  aseptic, bone—*continued*
    medial femoral condyle 733.43
    specific site NEC 733.49
    talus 733.44
  avascular, bone NEC (*see also* Necrosis, aseptic, bone) 733.40
  bone (*see also* Osteomyelitis) 730.1☑

Note—Use the following fifth-digit subclassification with category 730:
  0 site unspecified
  1 shoulder region
  2 upper arm
  3 forearm
  4 hand
  5 pelvic region and thigh
  6 lower leg
  7 ankle and foot
  8 other specified sites
  9 multiple sites

Necrosis, necrotic
  aseptic or avascular 733.40
    femur (head) (neck) 733.42
      medial condyle 733.43
    humoral head 733.41
    medial femoral condyle 733.43
    specified site NEC 733.49
    talus 733.44
  ischemic 733.40
  fat, fatty (generalized) (*see also* Degeneration, fatty) 272.8
  femur (aseptic) (avascular) 733.42
    head 733.42
    medial condyle 733.43
    neck 733.42
  gangrenous 785.4
  glottis 478.79
  hip (aseptic) (avascular) 733.42
  ischemic 785.4
  larynx 478.79
  lung 513.0
  pneumonia 513.0
  pulmonary 513.0
  skin or subcutaneous tissue 709.8
    gangrenous 785.4
  spine, spinal (column) 730.18
    cord 336.1
Necrotizing angiitis 446.0
Neglect (child) (newborn) NEC 995.52
  hemispatial 781.8
  left-sided 781.8
  sensory 781.8
  visuospatial 781.8

	Malignant			Benign	Uncertain Behavior	Unspecified
	Primary	Secondary	Ca in situ			
Neoplasm, neoplastic	199.1	199.1	234.9	229.9	238.9	239.9

Notes - 1. *The list below gives the code numbers for neoplasms by anatomical site. For each site there are six possible code numbers according to whether the neoplasm in question is malignant, benign, in situ, of uncertain behavior, or of unspecified nature. The description of the neoplasm will often indicate which of the six columns is appropriate; e.g., malignant melanoma of skin, benign fibroadenoma of breast, carcinoma in situ of cervix uteri.*

Where such descriptors are not present, the remainder of the Index should be consulted where guidance is given to the appropriate column for each morphological (histological) variety listed; e.g., Mesonephroma - see Neoplasm, malignant; Embryoma - see also Neoplasm, uncertain behavior; Disease, Bowen's - see Neoplasm, skin, in situ. However, the guidance in the Index can be overridden if one of the descriptors mentioned above is present; e.g., malignant adenoma of colon is coded to 153.9 and not to 211.3 as the adjective malignant overrides the Index entry Adenoma - see also Neoplasm, benign.

2. *Sites marked with the sign* * *(e.g., face NEC*) should be classified to malignant neoplasm of skin of these sites if the variety of neoplasm is a squamous cell carcinoma or an epidermoid carcinoma, and to benign neoplasm of skin of these sites if the variety of neoplasm is a papilloma (any type).*

abdomen, abdominal	195.2	198.89	234.8	229.8	238.8	239.89
cavity	195.2	198.89	234.8	229.8	238.8	239.89
organ	195.2	198.89	234.8	229.8	238.8	239.89
viscera	195.2	198.89	234.8	229.8	238.8	239.89
wall	173.5	198.2	232.5	216.5	238.2	239.2
connective tissue	171.5	198.89	—	215.5	238.1	239.2
abdominopelvic	195.8	198.89	234.8	229.8	238.8	239.89
accessory sinus—*see* Neoplasm, sinus						
acoustic nerve	192.0	198.4	—	225.1	237.9	239.7
acromion (process)	170.4	198.5	—	213.4	238.0	239.2
adenoid (pharynx) (tissue)	147.1	198.89	230.0	210.7	235.1	239.0
adipose tissue (*see also* Neoplasm, connective tissue)	171.9	198.89	—	215.9	238.1	239.2
adnexa (uterine)	183.9	198.82	233.39	221.8	236.3	239.5
adrenal (cortex) (gland) (medulla)	194.0	198.7	234.8	227.0	237.2	239.7
ala nasi (external)	173.3	198.2	232.3	216.3	238.2	239.2
alimentary canal or tract NEC	159.9	197.8	230.9	211.9	235.5	239.0
alveolar	143.9	198.89	230.0	210.4	235.1	239.0
mucosa	143.9	198.89	230.0	210.4	235.1	239.0
lower	143.1	198.89	230.0	210.4	235.1	239.0
upper	143.0	198.89	230.0	210.4	235.1	239.0
ridge or process	170.1	198.5	—	213.1	238.0	239.2
carcinoma	143.9	—	—	—	—	—
lower	143.1	—	—	—	—	—
upper	143.0	—	—	—	—	—
lower	170.1	198.5	—	213.1	238.0	239.2
mucosa	143.9	198.89	230.0	210.4	235.1	239.0
lower	143.1	198.89	230.0	210.4	235.1	239.0
upper	143.0	198.89	230.0	210.4	235.1	239.0
upper	170.0	198.5	—	213.0	238.0	239.2
sulcus	145.1	198.89	230.0	210.4	235.1	239.0
alveolus	143.9	198.89	230.0	210.4	235.1	239.0
lower	143.1	198.89	230.0	210.4	235.1	239.0
upper	143.0	198.89	230.0	210.4	235.1	239.0
ampulla of Vater	156.2	197.8	230.8	211.5	235.3	239.0
ankle NEC*	195.5	198.89	232.7	229.8	238.8	239.89
anorectum, anorectal (junction)	154.8	197.5	230.7	211.4	235.2	239.0
antecubital fossa or space*	195.4	198.89	232.6	229.8	238.8	239.89
antrum (Highmore) (maxillary)	160.2	197.3	231.8	212.0	235.9	239.1
pyloric	151.2	197.8	230.2	211.1	235.2	239.0
tympanicum	160.1	197.3	231.8	212.0	235.9	239.1
anus, anal	154.3	197.5	230.6	211.4	235.5	239.0
canal	154.2	197.5	230.5	211.4	235.5	239.0
contiguous sites with rectosigmoid junction or rectum	154.8	—	—	—	—	—
margin	173.5	198.2	232.5	216.5	238.2	239.2
anus, anal						
skin	173.5	198.2	232.5	216.5	238.2	239.2
sphincter	154.2	197.5	230.5	211.4	235.5	239.0

☑ Additional Digit Required

© 2009 Ingenix

| | Malignant | | | | | |
	Primary	Secondary	Ca in situ	Benign	Uncertain Behavior	Unspecified
Neoplasm, neoplastic—*continued*						
aorta (thoracic)	171.4	198.89	—	215.4	238.1	239.2
abdominal	171.5	198.89	—	215.5	238.1	239.2
aortic body	194.6	198.89	—	227.6	237.3	239.7
aponeurosis	171.9	198.89	—	215.9	238.1	239.2
palmar	171.2	198.89	—	215.2	238.1	239.2
plantar	171.3	198.89	—	215.3	238.1	239.2
appendix	153.5	197.5	230.3	211.3	235.2	239.0
arachnoid (cerebral)	192.1	198.4	—	225.2	237.6	239.7
spinal	192.3	198.4	—	225.4	237.6	239.7
areola (female)	174.0	198.81	233.0	217	238.3	239.3
male	175.0	198.81	233.0	217	238.3	239.3
arm NEC*	195.4*	198.89	232.6	229.8	238.8	239.89
artery—*see* Neoplasm, connective tissue						
aryepiglottic fold	148.2	198.89	230.0	210.8	235.1	239.0
hypopharyngeal aspect	148.2	198.89	230.0	210.8	235.1	239.0
laryngeal aspect	161.1	197.3	231.0	212.1	235.6	239.1
marginal zone	148.2	198.89	230.0	210.8	235.1	239.0
arytenoid (cartilage)	161.3	197.3	231.0	212.1	235.6	239.1
fold—*see* Neoplasm, aryepiglottic						
atlas	170.2	198.5	—	213.2	238.0	239.2
atrium, cardiac	164.1	198.89	—	212.7	238.8	239.89
auditory						
canal (external) (skin)	173.2	198.2	232.2	216.2	238.2	239.2
internal	160.1	197.3	231.8	212.0	235.9	239.1
nerve	192.0	198.4	—	225.1	237.9	239.7
tube	160.1	197.3	231.8	212.0	235.9	239.1
Eustachian	160.1	197.3	231.8	212.0	235.9	239.1
opening	147.2	198.89	230.0	210.7	235.1	239.0
auricle, ear	173.2	198.2	232.2	216.2	238.2	239.2
cartilage	171.0	198.89	—	215.0	238.1	239.2
auricular canal (external)	173.2	198.2	232.2	216.2	238.2	239.2
internal	160.1	197.3	231.8	212.0	235.9	239.1
autonomic nerve or nervous system NEC	171.9	198.89	—	215.9	238.1	239.2
axilla, axillary	195.1	198.89	234.8	229.8	238.8	239.89
fold	173.5	198.2	232.5	216.5	238.2	239.2
back NEC*	195.8	198.89	232.5	229.8	238.8	239.89
Bartholin's gland	184.1	198.82	233.32	221.2	236.3	239.5
basal ganglia	191.0	198.3	—	225.0	237.5	239.6
basis pedunculi	191.7	198.3	—	225.0	237.5	239.6
bile or biliary (tract)	156.9	197.8	230.8	211.5	235.3	239.0
canaliculi (biliferi) (intrahepatic)	155.1	197.8	230.8	211.5	235.3	239.0
canals, interlobular	155.1	197.8	230.8	211.5	235.3	239.0
contiguous sites	156.8	—	—	—	—	—
duct or passage (common) (cystic) (extrahepatic)	156.1	197.8	230.8	211.5	235.3	239.0
contiguous sites with gallbladder	156.8	—	—	—	—	—
interlobular	155.1	197.8	230.8	211.5	235.3	239.0
intrahepatic	155.1	197.8	230.8	211.5	235.3	239.0
and extrahepatic	156.9	197.8	230.8	211.5	235.3	239.0
bladder (urinary)	188.9	198.1	233.7	223.3	236.7	239.4
contiguous sites	188.8	—	—	—	—	—
dome	188.1	198.1	233.7	223.3	236.7	239.4
neck	188.5	198.1	233.7	223.3	236.7	239.4
orifice	188.9	198.1	233.7	223.3	236.7	239.4
ureteric	188.6	198.1	233.7	223.3	236.7	239.4
urethral	188.5	198.1	233.7	223.3	236.7	239.4
sphincter	188.8	198.1	233.7	223.3	236.7	239.4

| | Malignant | | | | | |
	Primary	Secondary	Ca in situ	Benign	Uncertain Behavior	Unspecified
Neoplasm, neoplastic—*continued*						
bladder (urinary)—*continued*						
trigone	188.0	198.1	233.7	223.3	236.7	239.4
urachus	188.7	—	233.7	223.3	236.7	239.4
wall	188.9	198.1	233.7	223.3	236.7	239.4
anterior	188.3	198.1	233.7	223.3	236.7	239.4
lateral	188.2	198.1	233.7	223.3	236.7	239.4
posterior	188.4	198.1	233.7	223.3	236.7	239.4
blood vessel—*see* Neoplasm, connective tissue						
bone (periosteum)	170.9	198.5	—	213.9	238.0	239.2

Note - Carcinomas and adenocarcinomas, of any type other than intraosseous or odontogenic, of the sites listed under Neoplasm, bone should be considered as constituting metastatic spread from an unspecified primary site and coded to 198.5 for morbidity coding.

acetabulum	170.6	198.5	—	213.6	238.0	239.2
acromion (process)	170.4	198.5	—	213.4	238.0	239.2
ankle	170.8	198.5	—	213.8	238.0	239.2
arm NEC	170.4	198.5	—	213.4	238.0	239.2
astragalus	170.8	198.5	—	213.8	238.0	239.2
atlas	170.2	198.5	—	213.2	238.0	239.2
axis	170.2	198.5	—	213.2	238.0	239.2
back NEC	170.2	198.5	—	213.2	238.0	239.2
calcaneus	170.8	198.5	—	213.8	238.0	239.2
calvarium	170.0	198.5	—	213.0	238.0	239.2
carpus (any)	170.5	198.5	—	213.5	238.0	239.2
cartilage NEC	170.9	198.5	—	213.9	238.0	239.2
clavicle	170.3	198.5	—	213.3	238.0	239.2
clivus	170.0	198.5	—	213.0	238.0	239.2
coccygeal vertebra	170.6	198.5	—	213.6	238.0	239.2
coccyx	170.6	198.5	—	213.6	238.0	239.2
costal cartilage	170.3	198.5	—	213.3	238.0	239.2
costovertebral joint	170.3	198.5	—	213.3	238.0	239.2
cranial	170.0	198.5	—	213.0	238.0	239.2
cuboid	170.8	198.5	—	213.8	238.0	239.2
cuneiform	170.9	198.5	—	213.9	238.0	239.2
ankle	170.8	198.5	—	213.8	238.0	239.2
wrist	170.5	198.5	—	213.5	238.0	239.2
digital	170.9	198.5	—	213.9	238.0	239.2
finger	170.5	198.5	—	213.5	238.0	239.2
toe	170.8	198.5	—	213.8	238.0	239.2
elbow	170.4	198.5	—	213.4	238.0	239.2
ethmoid (labyrinth)	170.0	198.5	—	213.0	238.0	239.2
face	170.0	198.5	—	213.0	238.0	239.2
lower jaw	170.1	198.5	—	213.1	238.0	239.2
femur (any part)	170.7	198.5	—	213.7	238.0	239.2
fibula (any part)	170.7	198.5	—	213.7	238.0	239.2
bone						
finger (any)	170.5	198.5	—	213.5	238.0	239.2
foot	170.8	198.5	—	213.8	238.0	239.2
forearm	170.4	198.5	—	213.4	238.0	239.2
frontal	170.0	198.5	—	213.0	238.0	239.2
hand	170.5	198.5	—	213.5	238.0	239.2
heel	170.8	198.5	—	213.8	238.0	239.2
hip	170.6	198.5	—	213.6	238.0	239.2
humerus (any part)	170.4	198.5	—	213.4	238.0	239.2
hyoid	170.0	198.5	—	213.0	238.0	239.2
ilium	170.6	198.5	—	213.6	238.0	239.2
innominate	170.6	198.5	—	213.6	238.0	239.2
intervertebral cartilage or disc	170.2	198.5	—	213.2	238.0	239.2

☑ Additional Digit Required
© 2009 Ingenix

| | Malignant | | | | | |
	Primary	Secondary	Ca in situ	Benign	Uncertain Behavior	Unspecified
Neoplasm, neoplastic—*continued*						
bone—*continued*						
ischium	170.6	198.5	—	213.6	238.0	239.2
jaw (lower)	170.1	198.5	—	213.1	238.0	239.2
upper	170.0	198.5	—	213.0	238.0	239.2
knee	170.7	198.5	—	213.7	238.0	239.2
leg NEC	170.7	198.5	—	213.7	238.0	239.2
limb NEC	170.9	198.5	—	213.9	238.0	239.2
lower (long bones)	170.7	198.5	—	213.7	238.0	239.2
short bones	170.8	198.5	—	213.8	238.0	239.2
upper (long bones)	170.4	198.5	—	213.4	238.0	239.2
short bones	170.5	198.5	—	213.5	238.0	239.2
long	170.9	198.5	—	213.9	238.0	239.2
lower limbs NEC	170.7	198.5	—	213.7	238.0	239.2
upper limbs NEC	170.4	198.5	—	213.4	238.0	239.2
malar	170.0	198.5	—	213.0	238.0	239.2
mandible	170.1	198.5	—	213.1	238.0	239.2
marrow NEC	202.9 ☑	198.5	—	—	—	238.79
mastoid	170.0	198.5	—	213.0	238.0	239.2
maxilla, maxillary (superior)	170.0	198.5	—	213.0	238.0	239.2
inferior	170.1	198.5	—	213.1	238.0	239.2
metacarpus (any)	170.5	198.5	—	213.5	238.0	239.2
metatarsus (any)	170.8	198.5	—	213.8	238.0	239.2
navicular (ankle)	170.8	198.5	—	213.8	238.0	239.2
hand	170.5	198.5	—	213.5	238.0	239.2
nose, nasal	170.0	198.5	—	213.0	238.0	239.2
occipital	170.0	198.5	—	213.0	238.0	239.2
orbit	170.0	198.5	—	213.0	238.0	239.2
parietal	170.0	198.5	—	213.0	238.0	239.2
patella	170.8	198.5	—	213.8	238.0	239.2
pelvic	170.6	198.5	—	213.6	238.0	239.2
phalanges	170.9	198.5	—	213.9	238.0	239.2
foot	170.8	198.5	—	213.8	238.0	239.2
hand	170.5	198.5	—	213.5	238.0	239.2
pubic	170.6	198.5	—	213.6	238.0	239.2
radius (any part)	170.4	198.5	—	213.4	238.0	239.2
rib	170.3	198.5	—	213.3	238.0	239.2
sacral vertebra	170.6	198.5	—	213.6	238.0	239.2
sacrum	170.6	198.5	—	213.6	238.0	239.2
scaphoid (of hand)	170.5	198.5	—	213.5	238.0	239.2
of ankle	170.8	198.5	—	213.8	238.0	239.2
scapula (any part)	170.4	198.5	—	213.4	238.0	239.2
sella turcica	170.0	198.5	—	213.0	238.0	239.2
short	170.9	198.5	—	213.9	238.0	239.2
lower limb	170.8	198.5	—	213.8	238.0	239.2
upper limb	170.5	198.5	—	213.5	238.0	239.2
shoulder	170.4	198.5	—	213.4	238.0	239.2
skeleton, skeletal NEC	170.9	198.5	—	213.9	238.0	239.2
skull	170.0	198.5	—	213.0	238.0	239.2
sphenoid	170.0	198.5	—	213.0	238.0	239.2
spine, spinal (column)	170.2	198.5	—	213.2	238.0	239.2
coccyx	170.6	198.5	—	213.6	238.0	239.2
sacrum	170.6	198.5	—	213.6	238.0	239.2
sternum	170.3	198.5	—	213.3	238.0	239.2
tarsus (any)	170.8	198.5	—	213.8	238.0	239.2
temporal	170.0	198.5	—	213.0	238.0	239.2
thumb	170.5	198.5	—	213.5	238.0	239.2

	Malignant					
	Primary	Secondary	Ca in situ	Benign	Uncertain Behavior	Unspecified
Neoplasm, neoplastic—*continued*						
bone—*continued*						
tibia (any part)	170.7	198.5	—	213.7	238.0	239.2
toe (any)	170.8	198.5	—	213.8	238.0	239.2
trapezium	170.5	198.5	—	213.5	238.0	239.2
trapezoid	170.5	198.5	—	213.5	238.0	239.2
turbinate	170.0	198.5	—	213.0	238.0	239.2
ulna (any part)	170.4	198.5	—	213.4	238.0	239.2
unciform	170.5	198.5	—	213.5	238.0	239.2
vertebra (column)	170.2	198.5	—	213.2	238.0	239.2
coccyx	170.6	198.5	—	213.6	238.0	239.2
sacrum	170.6	198.5	—	213.6	238.0	239.2
vomer	170.0	198.5	—	213.0	238.0	239.2
wrist	170.5	198.5	—	213.5	238.0	239.2
xiphoid process	170.3	198.5	—	213.3	238.0	239.2
zygomatic	170.0	198.5	—	213.0	238.0	239.2
book-leaf (mouth)	145.8	198.89	230.0	210.4	235.1	239.0
bowel—*see* Neoplasm, intestine						
brachial plexus	171.2	198.89	—	215.2	238.1	239.2
brain NEC	191.9	198.3	—	225.0	237.5	239.6
basal ganglia	191.0	198.3	—	225.0	237.5	239.6
cerebellopontine angle	191.6	198.3	—	225.0	237.5	239.6
cerebellum NOS	191.6	198.3	—	225.0	237.5	239.6
cerebrum	191.0	198.3	—	225.0	237.5	239.6
choroid plexus	191.5	198.3	—	225.0	237.5	239.6
contiguous sites	191.8	—	—	—	—	—
corpus callosum	191.8	198.3	—	225.0	237.5	239.6
corpus striatum	191.0	198.3	—	225.0	237.5	239.6
cortex (cerebral)	191.0	198.3	—	225.0	237.5	239.6
frontal lobe	191.1	198.3	—	225.0	237.5	239.6
globus pallidus	191.0	198.3	—	225.0	237.5	239.6
hippocampus	191.2	198.3	—	225.0	237.5	239.6
hypothalamus	191.0	198.3	—	225.0	237.5	239.6
internal capsule	191.0	198.3	—	225.0	237.5	239.6
medulla oblongata	191.7	198.3	—	225.0	237.5	239.6
meninges	192.1	198.4	—	225.2	237.6	239.7
midbrain	191.7	198.3	—	225.0	237.5	239.6
occipital lobe	191.4	198.3	—	225.0	237.5	239.6
parietal lobe	191.3	198.3	—	225.0	237.5	239.6
peduncle	191.7	198.3	—	225.0	237.5	239.6
pons	191.7	198.3	—	225.0	237.5	239.6
stem	191.7	198.3	—	225.0	237.5	239.6
tapetum	191.8	198.3	—	225.0	237.5	239.6
temporal lobe	191.2	198.3	—	225.0	237.5	239.6
thalamus	191.0	198.3	—	225.0	237.5	239.6
uncus	191.2	198.3	—	225.0	237.5	239.6
ventricle (floor)	191.5	198.3	—	225.0	237.5	239.6
branchial (cleft) (vestiges)	146.8	198.89	230.0	210.6	235.1	239.0
breast (connective tissue) (female) (glandular tissue) (soft parts)	174.9	198.81	233.0	217	238.3	239.3
areola	174.0	198.81	233.0	217	238.3	239.3
male	175.0	198.81	233.0	217	238.3	239.3
axillary tail	174.6	198.81	233.0	217	238.3	239.3
central portion	174.1	198.81	233.0	217	238.3	239.3
contiguous sites	174.8	—	—	—	—	—
ectopic sites	174.8	198.81	233.0	217	238.3	239.3
inner	174.8	198.81	233.0	217	238.3	239.3

☑ Additional Digit Required © 2009 Ingenix

	Malignant			Benign	Uncertain Behavior	Unspecified
	Primary	Secondary	Ca in situ	Benign	Uncertain Behavior	Unspecified
Neoplasm, neoplastic—*continued*						
breast—*continued*						
lower	174.8	198.81	233.0	217	238.3	239.3
lower-inner quadrant	174.3	198.81	233.0	217	238.3	239.3
lower-outer quadrant	174.5	198.81	233.0	217	238.3	239.3
male	175.9	198.81	233.0	217	238.3	239.3
areola	175.0	198.81	233.0	217	238.3	239.3
ectopic tissue	175.9	198.81	233.0	217	238.3	239.3
nipple	175.0	198.81	233.0	217	238.3	239.3
mastectomy site (skin)	173.5	198.2	—	—	—	—
specified as breast tissue	174.8	198.81	—	—	—	—
midline	174.8	198.81	233.0	217	238.3	239.3
nipple	174.0	198.81	233.0	217	238.3	239.3
male	175.0	198.81	233.0	217	238.3	239.3
outer	174.8	198.81	233.0	217	238.3	239.3
skin	173.5	198.2	232.5	216.5	238.2	239.2
tail (axillary)	174.6	198.81	233.0	217	238.3	239.3
upper	174.8	198.81	233.0	217	238.3	239.3
upper-inner quadrant	174.2	198.81	233.0	217	238.3	239.3
upper-outer quadrant	174.4	198.81	233.0	217	238.3	239.3
broad ligament	183.3	198.82	233.39	221.0	236.3	239.5
bronchiogenic, bronchogenic (lung)	162.9	197.0	231.2	212.3	235.7	239.1
bronchiole	162.9	197.0	231.2	212.3	235.7	239.1
bronchus	162.9	197.0	231.2	212.3	235.7	239.1
carina	162.2	197.0	231.2	212.3	235.7	239.1
contiguous sites with lung or trachea	162.8	—	—	—	—	—
lower lobe of lung	162.5	197.0	231.2	212.3	235.7	239.1
main	162.2	197.0	231.2	212.3	235.7	239.1
middle lobe of lung	162.4	197.0	231.2	212.3	235.7	239.1
upper lobe of lung	162.3	197.0	231.2	212.3	235.7	239.1
brow	173.3	198.2	232.3	216.3	238.2	239.2
buccal (cavity)	145.9	198.89	230.0	210.4	235.1	239.0
commissure	145.0	198.89	230.0	210.4	235.1	239.0
groove (lower) (upper)	145.1	198.89	230.0	210.4	235.1	239.0
mucosa	145.0	198.89	230.0	210.4	235.1	239.0
sulcus (lower) (upper)	145.1	198.89	230.0	210.4	235.1	239.0
bulbourethral gland	189.3	198.1	233.9	223.81	236.99	239.5
bursa—*see* Neoplasm, connective tissue						
buttock NEC*	195.3	198.89	232.5	229.8	238.8	239.89
calf*	195.5	198.89	232.7	229.8	238.8	239.89
calvarium	170.0	198.5	—	213.0	238.0	239.2
calyx, renal	189.1	198.0	233.9	223.1	236.91	239.5
canal						
anal	154.2	197.5	230.5	211.4	235.5	239.0
auditory (external)	173.2	198.2	232.2	216.2	238.2	239.2
auricular (external)	173.2	198.2	232.2	216.2	238.2	239.2
canaliculi, biliary (biliferi) (intrahepatic)	155.1	197.8	230.8	211.5	235.3	239.0
canthus (eye) (inner) (outer)	173.1	198.2	232.1	216.1	238.2	239.2
capillary—*see* Neoplasm, connective tissue						
caput coli	153.4	197.5	230.3	211.3	235.2	239.0
cardia (gastric)	151.0	197.8	230.2	211.1	235.2	239.0
cardiac orifice (stomach)	151.0	197.8	230.2	211.1	235.2	239.0
cardio-esophageal junction	151.0	197.8	230.2	211.1	235.2	239.0
cardio-esophagus	151.0	197.8	230.2	211.1	235.2	239.0
carina (bronchus)	162.2	197.0	231.2	212.3	235.7	239.1
carotid (artery)	171.0	198.89	—	215.0	238.1	239.2
body	194.5	198.89	—	227.5	237.3	239.7

	Malignant				Uncertain Behavior	Unspecified
	Primary	Secondary	Ca in situ	Benign		
Neoplasm, neoplastic—*continued*						
carpus (any bone)	170.5	198.5	—	213.5	238.0	239.2
cartilage (articular) (joint) NEC—*see also* Neoplasm, bone	170.9	198.5	—	213.9	238.0	239.2
arytenoid	161.3	197.3	231.0	212.1	235.6	239.1
auricular	171.0	198.89	—	215.0	238.1	239.2
bronchi	162.2	197.3	—	212.3	235.7	239.1
connective tissue—*see* Neoplasm, connective tissue						
costal	170.3	198.5	—	213.3	238.0	239.2
cricoid	161.3	197.3	231.0	212.1	235.6	239.1
cuneiform	161.3	197.3	231.0	212.1	235.6	239.1
ear (external)	171.0	198.89	—	215.0	238.1	239.2
ensiform	170.3	198.5	—	213.3	238.0	239.2
epiglottis	161.1	197.3	231.0	212.1	235.6	239.1
anterior surface	146.4	198.89	230.0	210.6	235.1	239.0
eyelid	171.0	198.89	—	215.0	238.1	239.2
intervertebral	170.2	198.5	—	213.2	238.0	239.2
larynx, laryngeal	161.3	197.3	231.0	212.1	235.6	239.1
nose, nasal	160.0	197.3	231.8	212.0	235.9	239.1
pinna	171.0	198.89	—	215.0	238.1	239.2
rib	170.3	198.5	—	213.3	238.0	239.2
semilunar (knee)	170.7	198.5	—	213.7	238.0	239.2
thyroid	161.3	197.3	231.0	212.1	235.6	239.1
trachea	162.0	197.3	231.1	212.2	235.7	239.1
cauda equina	192.2	198.3	—	225.3	237.5	239.7
cavity						
buccal	145.9	198.89	230.0	210.4	235.1	239.0
nasal	160.0	197.3	231.8	212.0	235.9	239.1
oral	145.9	198.89	230.0	210.4	235.1	239.0
peritoneal	158.9	197.6	—	211.8	235.4	239.0
tympanic	160.1	197.3	231.8	212.0	235.9	239.1
cecum	153.4	197.5	230.3	211.3	235.2	239.0
central						
nervous system—*see* Neoplasm, nervous system						
white matter	191.0	198.3	—	225.0	237.5	239.6
cerebellopontine (angle)	191.6	198.3	—	225.0	237.5	239.6
cerebellum, cerebellar	191.6	198.3	—	225.0	237.5	239.6
cerebrum, cerebral (cortex) (hemisphere) (white matter)	191.0	198.3	—	225.0	237.5	239.6
meninges	192.1	198.4	—	225.2	237.6	239.7
peduncle	191.7	198.3	—	225.0	237.5	239.6
ventricle (any)	191.5	198.3	—	225.0	237.5	239.6
cervical region	195.0	198.89	234.8	229.8	238.8	239.89
cervix (cervical) (uteri) (uterus)	180.9	198.82	233.1	219.0	236.0	239.5
canal	180.0	198.82	233.1	219.0	236.0	239.5
contiguous sites	180.8	—	—	—	—	—
endocervix (canal) (gland)	180.0	198.82	233.1	219.0	236.0	239.5
exocervix	180.1	198.82	233.1	219.0	236.0	239.5
external os	180.1	198.82	233.1	219.0	236.0	239.5
internal os	180.0	198.82	233.1	219.0	236.0	239.5
nabothian gland	180.0	198.82	233.1	219.0	236.0	239.5
squamocolumnar junction	180.8	198.82	233.1	219.0	236.0	239.5
stump	180.8	198.82	233.1	219.0	236.0	239.5
cheek	195.0	198.89	234.8	229.8	238.8	239.89
external	173.3	198.2	232.3	216.3	238.2	239.2
inner aspect	145.0	198.89	230.0	210.4	235.1	239.0

☑ Additional Digit Required

ICD-9-CM Index

	Malignant					
	Primary	Secondary	Ca in situ	Benign	Uncertain Behavior	Unspecified
Neoplasm, neoplastic—*continued*						
cheek—*continued*	195.0	198.89	234.8	229.8	238.8	239.89
internal	145.0	198.89	230.0	210.4	235.1	239.0
mucosa	145.0	198.89	230.0	210.4	235.1	239.0
chest (wall) NEC	195.1	198.89	234.8	229.8	238.8	239.89
chiasma opticum	192.0	198.4	—	225.1	237.9	239.7
chin	173.3	198.2	232.3	216.3	238.2	239.2
choana	147.3	198.89	230.0	210.7	235.1	239.0
cholangiole	155.1	197.8	230.8	211.5	235.3	239.0
choledochal duct	156.1	197.8	230.8	211.5	235.3	239.0
choroid	190.6	198.4	234.0	224.6	238.8	239.89
plexus	191.5	198.3	—	225.0	237.5	239.6
ciliary body	190.0	198.4	234.0	224.0	238.8	239.89
clavicle	170.3	198.5	—	213.3	238.0	239.2
clitoris	184.3	198.82	233.32	221.2	236.3	239.5
clivus	170.0	198.5	—	213.0	238.0	239.2
cloacogenic zone	154.8	197.5	230.7	211.4	235.5	239.0
coccygeal						
body or glomus	194.6	198.89	—	227.6	237.3	239.7
vertebra	170.6	198.5	—	213.6	238.0	239.2
coccyx	170.6	198.5	—	213.6	238.0	239.2
colon—*see also* Neoplasm, intestine, large						
and rectum	154.0	197.5	230.4	211.4	235.2	239.0
column, spinal—*see* Neoplasm, spine						
columnella	173.3	198.2	232.3	216.3	238.2	239.2
commissure						
labial, lip	140.6	198.89	230.0	210.4	235.1	239.0
laryngeal	161.0	197.3	231.0	212.1	235.6	239.1
common (bile) duct	156.1	197.8	230.8	211.5	235.3	239.0
concha	173.2	198.2	232.2	216.2	238.2	239.2
nose	160.0	197.3	231.8	212.0	235.9	239.1
conjunctiva	190.3	198.4	234.0	224.3	238.8	239.89
connective tissue NEC	171.9	198.89	—	215.9	238.1	239.2

Note: For neoplasms of connective tissue (blood vessel, bursa, fascia, ligament, muscle, peripheral nerves, sympathetic and parasympathetic nerves and ganglia, synovia, tendon, etc.) or of morphological types that indicate connective tissue, code according to the list under Neoplasm, connective tissue; for sites that do not appear in this list, code to neoplasm of that site, for example:

liposarcoma, shoulder 171.2

leiomyosarcoma, stomach 151.9

neurofibroma, chest wall 215.4

Morphological types that indicate connective tissue appear in the proper place in the alphabetic index with the instruction "see Neoplasm, connective tissue..."

abdomen	171.5	198.89	—	215.5	238.1	239.2
abdominal wall	171.5	198.89	—	215.5	238.1	239.2
ankle	171.3	198.89	—	215.3	238.1	239.2
antecubital fossa or space	171.2	198.89	—	215.2	238.1	239.2
arm	171.2	198.89	—	215.2	238.1	239.2
auricle (ear)	171.0	198.89	—	215.0	238.1	239.2
axilla	171.4	198.89	—	215.4	238.1	239.2
back	171.7	198.89	—	215.7	238.1	239.2
breast (female) (*see also* Neoplasm, breast)	174.9	198.81	233.0	217	238.3	239.3
male	175.9	198.81	233.0	217	238.3	239.3
buttock	171.6	198.89	—	215.6	238.1	239.2
calf	171.3	198.89	—	215.3	238.1	239.2
cervical region	171.0	198.89	—	215.0	238.1	239.2
cheek	171.0	198.89	—	215.0	238.1	239.2
chest (wall)	171.4	198.89	—	215.4	238.1	239.2
chin	171.0	198.89	—	215.0	238.1	239.2
contiguous sites	171.8	—	—	—	—	—

	Malignant					
	Primary	Secondary	Ca in situ	Benign	Uncertain Behavior	Unspecified
Neoplasm, neoplastic—*continued*						
connective tissue NEC—*continued*						
diaphragm	171.4	198.89	—	215.4	238.1	239.2
ear (external)	171.0	198.89	—	215.0	238.1	239.2
elbow	171.2	198.89	—	215.2	238.1	239.2
extrarectal	171.6	198.89	—	215.6	238.1	239.2
extremity	171.8	198.89	—	215.8	238.1	239.2
lower	171.3	198.89	—	215.3	238.1	239.2
upper	171.2	198.89	—	215.2	238.1	239.2
eyelid	171.0	198.89	—	215.0	238.1	239.2
face	171.0	198.89	—	215.0	238.1	239.2
finger	171.2	198.89	—	215.2	238.1	239.2
flank	171.7	198.89	—	215.7	238.1	239.2
foot	171.3	198.89	—	215.3	238.1	239.2
forearm	171.2	198.89	—	215.2	238.1	239.2
forehead	171.0	198.89	—	215.0	238.1	239.2
gastric	171.5	198.89	—	215.5	238.1	—
gastrointestinal	171.5	198.89	—	215.5	238.1	—
gluteal region	171.6	198.89	—	215.6	238.1	239.2
great vessels NEC	171.4	198.89	—	215.4	238.1	239.2
groin	171.6	198.89	—	215.6	238.1	239.2
hand	171.2	198.89	—	215.2	238.1	239.2
head	171.0	198.89	—	215.0	238.1	239.2
heel	171.3	198.89	—	215.3	238.1	239.2
hip	171.3	198.89	—	215.3	238.1	239.2
hypochondrium	171.5	198.89	—	215.5	238.1	239.2
iliopsoas muscle	171.6	198.89	—	215.5	238.1	239.2
infraclavicular region	171.4	198.89	—	215.4	238.1	239.2
inguinal (canal) (region)	171.6	198.89	—	215.6	238.1	239.2
intrathoracic	171.4	198.89	—	215.4	238.1	239.2
intestine	171.5	198.89	—	215.5	238.1	—
ischorectal fossa	171.6	198.89	—	215.6	238.1	239.2
jaw	143.9	198.89	230.0	210.4	235.1	239.0
knee	171.3	198.89	—	215.3	238.1	239.2
leg	171.3	198.89	—	215.3	238.1	239.2
limb NEC	171.9	198.89	—	215.8	238.1	239.2
lower	171.3	198.89	—	215.3	238.1	239.2
upper	171.2	198.89	—	215.2	238.1	239.2
nates	171.6	198.89	—	215.6	238.1	239.2
neck	171.0	198.89	—	215.0	238.1	239.2
orbit	190.1	198.4	234.0	224.1	238.8	239.89
pararectal	171.6	198.89	—	215.6	238.1	239.2
para-urethral	171.6	198.89	—	215.6	238.1	239.2
paravaginal	171.6	198.89	—	215.6	238.1	239.2
pelvis (floor)	171.6	198.89	—	215.6	238.1	239.2
pelvo-abdominal	171.8	198.89	—	215.8	238.1	239.2
perineum	171.6	198.89	—	215.6	238.1	239.2
perirectal (tissue)	171.6	198.89	—	215.6	238.1	239.2
periurethral (tissue)	171.6	198.89	—	215.6	238.1	239.2
popliteal fossa or space	171.3	198.89	—	215.3	238.1	239.2
presacral	171.6	198.89	—	215.6	238.1	239.2
psoas muscle	171.5	198.89	—	215.5	238.1	239.2
pterygoid fossa	171.0	198.89	—	215.0	238.1	239.2
rectovaginal septum or wall	171.6	198.89	—	215.6	238.1	239.2
rectovesical	171.6	198.89	—	215.6	238.1	239.2
retroperitoneum	158.0	197.6	—	211.8	235.4	239.0
sacrococcygeal region	171.6	198.89	—	215.6	238.1	239.2

☑ Additional Digit Required

	Malignant					
	Primary	Secondary	Ca in situ	Benign	Uncertain Behavior	Unspecified
Neoplasm, neoplastic—*continued*						
connective tissue NEC—*continued*						
scalp	171.0	198.89	—	215.0	238.1	239.2
scapular region	171.4	198.89	—	215.4	238.1	239.2
shoulder	171.2	198.89	—	215.2	238.1	239.2
skin (dermis) NEC	173.9	198.2	232.9	216.9	238.2	239.2
stomach	171.5	198.89	—	215.5	238.1	—
submental	171.0	198.89	—	215.0	238.1	239.2
supraclavicular region	171.0	198.89	—	215.0	238.1	239.2
temple	171.0	198.89	—	215.0	238.1	239.2
temporal region	171.0	198.89	—	215.0	238.1	239.2
thigh	171.3	198.89	—	215.3	238.1	239.2
thoracic (duct) (wall)	171.4	198.89	—	215.4	238.1	239.2
thorax	171.4	198.89	—	215.4	238.1	239.2
thumb	171.2	198.89	—	215.2	238.1	239.2
toe	171.3	198.89	—	215.3	238.1	239.2
trunk	171.7	198.89	—	215.7	238.1	239.2
umbilicus	171.5	198.89	—	215.5	238.1	239.2
vesicorectal	171.6	198.89	—	215.6	238.1	239.2
wrist	171.2	198.89	—	215.2	238.1	239.2
conus medullaris	192.2	198.3	—	225.3	237.5	239.7
cord (true) (vocal)	161.0	197.3	231.0	212.1	235.6	239.1
false	161.1	197.3	231.0	212.1	235.6	239.1
spermatic	187.6	198.82	233.6	222.8	236.6	239.5
spinal (cervical) (lumbar) (thoracic)	192.2	198.3	—	225.3	237.5	239.7
cornea (limbus)	190.4	198.4	234.0	224.4	238.8	239.89
corpus						
albicans	183.0	198.6	233.39	220	236.2	239.5
callosum, brain	191.8	198.3	—	225.0	237.5	239.6
cavernosum	187.3	198.82	233.5	222.1	236.6	239.5
gastric	151.4	197.8	230.2	211.1	235.2	239.0
penis	187.3	198.82	233.5	222.1	236.6	239.5
striatum, cerebrum	191.0	198.3	—	225.0	237.5	239.6
uteri	182.0	198.82	233.2	219.1	236.0	239.5
isthmus	182.1	198.82	233.2	219.1	236.0	239.5
cortex						
adrenal	194.0	198.7	234.8	227.0	237.2	239.7
cerebral	191.0	198.3	—	225.0	237.5	239.6
costal cartilage	170.3	198.5	—	213.3	238.0	239.2
costovertebral joint	170.3	198.5	—	213.3	238.0	239.2
Cowper's gland	189.3	198.1	233.9	223.81	236.99	239.5
cranial (fossa, any)	191.9	198.3	—	225.0	237.5	239.6
meninges	192.1	198.4	—	225.2	237.6	239.7
nerve (any)	192.0	198.4	—	225.1	237.9	239.7
craniobuccal pouch	194.3	198.89	234.8	227.3	237.0	239.7
craniopharyngeal (duct) (pouch)	194.3	198.89	234.8	227.3	237.0	239.7
cricoid	148.0	198.89	230.0	210.8	235.1	239.0
cartilage	161.3	197.3	231.0	212.1	235.6	239.1
cricopharynx	148.0	198.89	230.0	210.8	235.1	239.0
crypt of Morgagni	154.8	197.5	230.7	211.4	235.2	239.0
crystalline lens	190.0	198.4	234.0	224.0	238.8	239.89
cul-de-sac (Douglas')	158.8	197.6	—	211.8	235.4	239.0
cuneiform cartilage	161.3	197.3	231.0	212.1	235.6	239.1
cutaneous—*see* Neoplasm, skin						
cutis—*see* Neoplasm, skin						
cystic (bile) duct (common)	156.1	197.8	230.8	211.5	235.3	239.0
dermis—*see* Neoplasm, skin						

	Malignant					
	Primary	**Secondary**	**Ca in situ**	**Benign**	**Uncertain Behavior**	**Unspecified**
Neoplasm, neoplastic—*continued*						
diaphragm	171.4	198.89	—	215.4	238.1	239.2
digestive organs, system, tube, or tract NEC	159.9	197.8	230.9	211.9	235.5	239.0
contiguous sites with peritoneum	159.8	—	—	—	—	—
disc, intervertebral	170.2	198.5	—	213.2	238.0	239.2
disease, generalized	199.0	199.0	234.9	229.9	238.9	199.0
disseminated	199.0	199.0	234.9	229.9	238.9	199.0
Douglas' cul-de-sac or pouch	158.8	197.6	—	211.8	235.4	239.0
duodenojejunal junction	152.8	197.4	230.7	211.2	235.2	239.0
duodenum	152.0	197.4	230.7	211.2	235.2	239.0
dura (cranial) (mater)	192.1	198.4	—	225.2	237.6	239.7
cerebral	192.1	198.4	—	225.2	237.6	239.7
spinal	192.3	198.4	—	225.4	237.6	239.7
ear (external)	173.2	198.2	232.2	216.2	238.2	239.2
auricle or auris	173.2	198.2	232.2	216.2	238.2	239.2
canal, external	173.2	198.2	232.2	216.2	238.2	239.2
cartilage	171.0	198.89	—	215.0	238.1	239.2
external meatus	173.2	198.2	232.2	216.2	238.2	239.2
inner	160.1	197.3	231.8	212.0	235.9	239.89
lobule	173.2	198.2	232.2	216.2	238.2	239.2
middle	160.1	197.3	231.8	212.0	235.9	239.89
contiguous sites with accessory sinuses or nasal cavities	160.8	—	—	—	—	—
skin	173.2	198.2	232.2	216.2	238.2	239.2
earlobe	173.2	198.2	232.2	216.2	238.2	239.2
ejaculatory duct	187.8	198.82	233.6	222.8	236.6	239.5
elbow NEC*	195.4	198.89	232.6	229.8	238.8	239.89
endocardium	164.1	198.89	—	212.7	238.8	239.89
endocervix (canal) (gland)	180.0	198.82	233.1	219.0	236.0	239.5
endocrine gland NEC	194.9	198.89	—	227.9	237.4	239.7
pluriglandular NEC	194.8	198.89	234.8	227.8	237.4	239.7
endometrium (gland) (stroma)	182.0	198.82	233.2	219.1	236.0	239.5
ensiform cartilage	170.3	198.5	—	213.3	238.0	239.2
enteric—*see* Neoplasm, intestine						
ependyma (brain)	191.5	198.3	—	225.0	237.5	239.6
epicardium	164.1	198.89	—	212.7	238.8	239.89
epididymis	187.5	198.82	233.6	222.3	236.6	239.5
epidural	192.9	198.4	—	225.9	237.9	239.7
epiglottis	161.1	197.3	231.0	212.1	235.6	239.1
anterior aspect or surface	146.4	198.89	230.0	210.6	235.1	239.0
cartilage	161.3	197.3	231.0	.212.1	235.6	239.1
free border (margin)	146.4	198.89	230.0	210.6	235.1	239.0
junctional region	146.5	198.89	230.0	210.6	235.1	239.0
posterior (laryngeal) surface	161.1	197.3	231.0	212.1	235.6	239.1
suprahyoid portion	161.1	197.3	231.0	212.1	235.6	239.1
esophagogastric junction	151.0	197.8	230.2	211.1	235.2	239.0
esophagus	150.9	197.8	230.1	211.0	235.5	239.0
abdominal	150.2	197.8	230.1	211.0	235.5	239.0
cervical	150.0	197.8	230.1	211.0	235.5	239.0
contiguous sites	150.8	—	—	—	—	—
distal (third)	150.5	197.8	230.1	211.0	235.5	239.0
lower (third)	150.5	197.8	230.1	211.0	235.5	239.0
middle (third)	150.4	197.8	230.1	211.0	235.5	239.0
proximal (third)	150.3	197.8	230.1	211.0	235.5	239.0
specified part NEC	150.8	197.8	230.1	211.0	235.5	239.0
thoracic	150.1	197.8	230.1	211.0	235.5	239.0
upper (third)	150.3	197.8	230.1	211.0	235.5	239.0

☑ Additional Digit Required
© 2009 Ingenix

Neoplasm, neoplastic—*continued*	Primary	Secondary	Ca in situ	Benign	Uncertain Behavior	Unspecified
		Malignant				
ethmoid (sinus)	160.3	197.3	231.8	212.0	235.9	239.1
bone or labyrinth	170.0	198.5	—	213.0	238.0	239.2
Eustachian tube	160.1	197.3	231.8	212.0	235.9	239.1
exocervix	180.1	198.82	233.1	219.0	236.0	239.5
external						
meatus (ear)	173.2	198.2	232.2	216.2	238.2	239.2
os, cervix uteri	180.1	198.82	233.1	219.0	236.0	239.5
extradural	192.9	198.4	—	225.9	237.9	239.7
extrahepatic (bile) duct	156.1	197.8	230.8	211.5	235.3	239.0
contiguous sites with gallbladder	156.8	—	—	—	—	—
extraocular muscle	190.1	198.4	234.0	224.1	238.8	239.89
extrarectal	195.3	198.89	234.8	229.8	238.8	239.89
extremity*	195.8	198.89	232.8	229.8	238.8	239.89
lower*	195.5	198.89	232.7	229.8	238.8	239.89
upper*	195.4	198.89	232.6	229.8	238.8	239.89
eye NEC	190.9	198.4	234.0	224.9	238.8	239.89
contiguous sites	190.8	—	—	—	—	—
specified sites NEC	190.8	198.4	234.0	224.8	238.8	239.89
eyeball	190.0	198.4	234.0	224.0	238.8	239.89
eyebrow	173.3	198.2	232.3	216.3	238.2	239.2
eyelid (lower) (skin) (upper)	173.1	198.2	232.1	216.1	238.2	239.2
cartilage	171.0	198.89	—	215.0	238.1	239.2
face NEC*	195.0	198.89	232.3	229.8	238.8	239.89
fallopian tube (accessory)	183.2	198.82	233.39	221.0	236.3	239.5
falx (cerebelli) (cerebri)	192.1	198.4	—	225.2	237.6	239.7
fascia—*see also* Neoplasm, connective tissue						
palmar	171.2	198.89	—	215.2	238.1	239.2
plantar	171.3	198.89	—	215.3	238.1	239.2
fatty tissue—*see* Neoplasm, connective tissue						
fauces, faucial NEC	146.9	198.89	230.0	210.6	235.1	239.0
pillars	146.2	198.89	230.0	210.6	235.1	239.0
tonsil	146.0	198.89	230.0	210.5	235.1	239.0
femur (any part)	170.7	198.5	—	213.7	238.0	239.2
fetal membrane	181	198.82	233.2	219.8	236.1	239.5
fibrous tissue—*see* Neoplasm, connective tissue						
fibula (any part)	170.7	198.5	—	213.7	238.0	239.2
filum terminale	192.2	198.3	—	225.3	237.5	239.7
finger NEC*	195.4	198.89	232.6	229.8	238.8	239.89
flank NEC*	195.8	198.89	232.5	229.8	238.8	239.89
follicle, nabothian	180.0	198.82	233.1	219.0	236.0	239.5
foot NEC*	195.5	198.89	232.7	229.8	238.8	239.89
forearm NEC*	195.4	198.89	232.6	229.8	238.8	239.89
forehead (skin)	173.3	198.2	232.3	216.3	238.2	239.2
foreskin	187.1	198.82	233.5	222.1	236.6	239.5
fornix						
pharyngeal	147.3	198.89	230.0	210.7	235.1	239.0
vagina	184.0	198.82	233.31	221.1	236.3	239.5
fossa (of)						
anterior (cranial)	191.9	198.3	—	225.0	237.5	239.6
cranial	191.9	198.3	—	225.0	237.5	239.6
ischiorectal	195.3	198.89	234.8	229.8	238.8	239.89
middle (cranial)	191.9	198.3	—	225.0	237.5	239.6
pituitary	194.3	198.89	234.8	227.3	237.0	239.7
posterior (cranial)	191.9	198.3	—	225.0	237.5	239.6
pterygoid	171.0	198.89	—	215.0	238.1	239.2
pyriform	148.1	198.89	230.0	210.8	235.1	239.0

| | Malignant | | | | | |
	Primary	Secondary	Ca in situ	Benign	Uncertain Behavior	Unspecified
Neoplasm, neoplastic—*continued*						
fossa (of)—*continued*						
Rosenmüller	147.2	198.89	230.0	210.7	235.1	239.0
tonsillar	146.1	198.89	230.0	210.6	235.1	239.0
fourchette	184.4	198.82	233.32	221.2	236.3	239.5
frenulum						
labii—*see* Neoplasm, lip, internal						
linguae	141.3	198.89	230.0	210.1	235.1	239.0
frontal						
bone	170.0	198.5	—	213.0	238.0	239.2
lobe, brain	191.1	198.3	—	225.0	237.5	239.6
pole	191.1	198.3	—	225.0	237.5	239.6
sinus	160.4	197.3	231.8	212.0	235.9	239.1
fundus						
stomach	151.3	197.8	230.2	211.1	235.2	239.0
uterus	182.0	198.82	233.2	219.1	236.0	239.5
gall duct (extrahepatic)	156.1	197.8	230.8	211.5	235.3	239.0
intrahepatic	155.1	197.8	230.8	211.5	235.3	239.0
gallbladder	156.0	197.8	230.8	211.5	235.3	239.0
contiguous sites with extrahepatic bile ducts	156.8	—	—	—	—	—
ganglia (*see also* Neoplasm, connective tissue)	171.9	198.89	—	215.9	238.1	239.2
basal	191.0	198.3	—	225.0	237.5	239.6
ganglion (*see also* Neoplasm, connective tissue)	171.9	198.89	—	215.9	238.1	239.2
cranial nerve	192.0	198.4	—	225.1	237.9	239.7
Gartner's duct	184.0	198.82	233.31	221.1	236.3	239.5
gastric—*see* Neoplasm, stomach						
gastrocolic	159.8	197.8	230.9	211.9	235.5	239.0
gastroesophageal junction	151.0	197.8	230.2	211.1	235.2	239.0
gastrointestinal (tract) NEC	159.9	197.8	230.9	211.9	235.5	239.0
generalized	199.0	199.0	234.9	229.9	238.9	199.0
genital organ or tract						
female NEC	184.9	198.82	233.39	221.9	236.3	239.5
contiguous sites	184.8	—	—	—	—	—
specified site NEC	184.8	198.82	233.39	221.8	236.3	239.5
male NEC	187.9	198.82	233.6	222.9	236.6	239.5
contiguous sites	187.8	—	—	—	—	—
specified site NEC	187.8	198.82	233.6	222.8	236.6	239.5
genitourinary tract						
female	184.9	198.82	233.39	221.9	236.3	239.5
male	187.9	198.82	233.6	222.9	236.6	239.5
gingiva (alveolar) (marginal)	143.9	198.89	230.0	210.4	235.1	239.0
lower	143.1	198.89	230.0	210.4	235.1	239.0
mandibular	143.1	198.89	230.0	210.4	235.1	239.0
maxillary	143.0	198.89	230.0	210.4	235.1	239.0
upper	143.0	198.89	230.0	210.4	235.1	239.0
gland, glandular (lymphatic) (system)—*see also* Neoplasm, lymph gland						
endocrine NEC	194.9	198.89	—	227.9	237.4	239.7
salivary—*see* Neoplasm, salivary, gland						
glans penis	187.2	198.82	233.5	222.1	236.6	239.5
globus pallidus	191.0	198.3	—	225.0	237.5	239.6
glomus						
coccygeal	194.6	198.89	—	227.6	237.3	239.7
jugularis	194.6	198.89	—	227.6	237.3	239.7
glosso-epiglottic fold(s)	146.4	198.89	230.0	210.6	235.1	239.0
glossopalatine fold	146.2	198.89	230.0	210.6	235.1	239.0
glossopharyngeal sulcus	146.1	198.89	230.0	210.6	235.1	239.0

☑ Additional Digit Required

ICD-9-CM Index

	Malignant					
	Primary	**Secondary**	**Ca in situ**	**Benign**	**Uncertain Behavior**	**Unspecified**
Neoplasm, neoplastic—*continued*						
glottis	161.0	197.3	231.0	212.1	235.6	239.1
gluteal region*	195.3	198.89	232.5	229.8	238.8	239.89
great vessels NEC	171.4	198.89	—	215.4	238.1	239.2
groin NEC	195.3	198.89	232.5	229.8	238.8	239.89
gum	143.9	198.89	230.0	210.4	235.1	239.0
contiguous sites	143.8	—	—	—	—	—
lower	143.1	198.89	230.0	210.4	235.1	239.0
upper	143.0	198.89	230.0	210.4	235.1	239.0
hand NEC*	195.4	198.89	232.6	229.8	238.8	239.89
head NEC*	195.0	198.89	232.4	229.8	238.8	239.89
heart	164.1	198.89	—	212.7	238.8	239.89
contiguous sites with mediastinum or thymus	164.8	—	—	—	—	—
heel NEC*	195.5	198.89	232.7	229.8	238.8	239.89
helix	173.2	198.2	232.2	216.2	238.2	239.2
hematopoietic, hemopoietic tissue NEC	202.8 ☑	198.89	—	—	—	238.79
hemisphere, cerebral	191.0	198.3	—	225.0	237.5	239.6
hemorrhoidal zone	154.2	197.5	230.5	211.4	235.5	239.0
hepatic	155.2	197.7	230.8	211.5	235.3	239.0
duct (bile)	156.1	197.8	230.8	211.5	235.3	239.0
flexure (colon)	153.0	197.5	230.3	211.3	235.2	239.0
primary	155.0	—	—	—	—	—
hilus of lung	162.2	197.0	231.2	212.3	235.7	239.1
hip NEC*	195.5	198.89	232.7	229.8	238.8	239.89
hippocampus, brain	191.2	198.3	—	225.0	237.5	239.6
humerus (any part)	170.4	198.5	—	213.4	238.0	239.2
hymen	184.0	198.82	233.31	221.1	236.3	239.5
hypopharynx, hypopharyngeal NEC	148.9	198.89	230.0	210.8	235.1	239.0
contiguous sites	148.8	—	—	—	—	—
postcricoid region	148.0	198.89	230.0	210.8	235.1	239.0
posterior wall	148.3	198.89	230.0	210.8	235.1	239.0
pyriform fossa (sinus)	148.1	198.89	230.0	210.8	235.1	239.0
specified site NEC	148.8	198.89	230.0	210.8	235.1	239.0
wall	148.9	198.89	230.0	210.8	235.1	239.0
posterior	148.3	198.89	230.0	210.8	235.1	239.0
hypophysis	194.3	198.89	234.8	227.3	237.0	239.7
hypothalamus	191.0	198.3	—	225.0	237.5	239.6
ileocecum, ileocecal (coil) (junction) (valve)	153.4	197.5	230.3	211.3	235.2	239.0
ileum	152.2	197.4	230.7	211.2	235.2	239.0
ilium	170.6	198.5	—	213.6	238.0	239.2
immunoproliferative NEC	203.8 ☑	—	—	—	—	—
infraclavicular (region)*	195.1	198.89	232.5	229.8	238.8	239.89
inguinal (region)*	195.3	198.89	232.5	229.8	238.8	239.89
insula	191.0	198.3	—	225.0	237.5	239.6
insular tissue (pancreas)	157.4	197.8	230.9	211.7	235.5	239.0
brain	191.0	198.3	—	225.0	237.5	239.6
interarytenoid fold	148.2	198.89	230.0	210.8	235.1	239.0
hypopharyngeal aspect	148.2	198.89	230.0	210.8	235.1	239.0
laryngeal aspect	161.1	197.3	231.0	212.1	235.6	239.1
marginal zone	148.2	198.89	230.0	210.8	235.1	239.0
interdental papillae	143.9	198.89	230.0	210.4	235.1	239.0
lower	143.1	198.89	230.0	210.4	235.1	239.0
upper	143.0	198.89	230.0	210.4	235.1	239.0
internal						
capsule	191.0	198.3	—	225.0	237.5	239.6
os (cervix)	180.0	198.82	233.1	219.0	236.0	239.5
intervertebral cartilage or disc	170.2	198.5	—	213.2	238.0	239.2

☑ Additional Digit Required

ICD-9-CM Index

| | Malignant | | | | | |
	Primary	Secondary	Ca in situ	Benign	Uncertain Behavior	Unspecified
Neoplasm, neoplastic—*continued*						
intestine, intestinal	159.0	197.8	230.7	211.9	235.2	239.0
large	153.9	197.5	230.3	211.3	235.2	239.0
appendix	153.5	197.5	230.3	211.3	235.2	239.0
caput coli	153.4	197.5	230.3	211.3	235.2	239.0
cecum	153.4	197.5	230.3	211.3	235.2	239.0
colon	153.9	197.5	230.3	211.3	235.2	239.0
and rectum	154.0	197.5	230.4	211.4	235.2	239.0
ascending	153.6	197.5	230.3	211.3	235.2	239.0
caput	153.4	197.5	230.3	211.3	235.2	239.0
contiguous sites	153.8	—	—	—	—	—
descending	153.2	197.5	230.3	211.3	235.2	239.0
distal	153.2	197.5	230.3	211.3	235.2	239.0
left	153.2	197.5	230.3	211.3	235.2	239.0
pelvic	153.3	197.5	230.3	211.3	235.2	239.0
right	153.6	197.5	230.3	211.3	235.2	239.0
sigmoid (flexure)	153.3	197.5	230.3	211.3	235.2	239.0
transverse	153.1	197.5	230.3	211.3	235.2	239.0
contiguous sites	153.8	—	—	—	—	—
hepatic flexure	153.0	197.5	230.3	211.3	235.2	239.0
ileocecum, ileocecal (coil) (valve)	153.4	197.5	230.3	211.3	235.2	239.0
sigmoid flexure (lower) (upper)	153.3	197.5	230.3	211.3	235.2	239.0
splenic flexure	153.7	197.5	230.3	211.3	235.2	239.0
small	152.9	197.4	230.7	211.2	235.2	239.0
contiguous sites	152.8	—	—	—	—	—
duodenum	152.0	197.4	230.7	211.2	235.2	239.0
ileum	152.2	197.4	230.7	211.2	235.2	239.0
jejunum	152.1	197.4	230.7	211.2	235.2	239.0
tract NEC	159.0	197.8	230.7	211.9	235.2	239.0
intra-abdominal	195.2	198.89	234.8	229.8	238.8	239.89
intracranial NEC	191.9	198.3	—	225.0	237.5	239.6
intrahepatic (bile) duct	155.1	197.8	230.8	211.5	235.3	239.0
intraocular	190.0	198.4	234.0	224.0	238.8	239.89
intraorbital	190.1	198.4	234.0	224.1	238.8	239.89
intrasellar	194.3	198.89	234.8	227.3	237.0	239.7
intrathoracic (cavity) (organs NEC)	195.1	198.89	234.8	229.8	238.8	239.89
contiguous sites with respiratory organs	165.8	—	—	—	—	—
iris	190.0	198.4	234.0	224.0	238.8	239.89
ischiorectal (fossa)	195.3	198.89	234.8	229.8	238.8	239.89
ischium	170.6	198.5	—	213.6	238.0	239.2
island of Reil	191.0	198.3	—	225.0	237.5	239.6
islands or islets of Langerhans	157.4	197.8	230.9	211.7	235.5	239.0
isthmus uteri	182.1	198.82	233.2	219.1	236.0	239.5
jaw	195.0	198.89	234.8	229.8	238.8	239.89
bone	170.1	198.5	—	213.1	238.0	239.2
carcinoma	143.9	—	—	—	—	—
lower	143.1	—	—	—	—	—
upper	143.0	—	—	—	—	—
lower	170.1	198.5	—	213.1	238.0	239.2
upper	170.0	198.5	—	213.0	238.0	239.2
carcinoma (any type) (lower) (upper)	195.0	—	—	—	—	—
skin	173.3	198.2	232.3	216.3	238.2	239.2
soft tissues	143.9	198.89	230.0	210.4	235.1	239.0
lower	143.1	198.89	230.0	210.4	235.1	239.0
upper	143.0	198.89	230.0	210.4	235.1	239.0
jejunum	152.1	197.4	230.7	211.2	235.2	239.0

☑ Additional Digit Required © 2009 Ingenix

	Malignant					
	Primary	Secondary	Ca in situ	Benign	Uncertain Behavior	Unspecified
Neoplasm, neoplastic—*continued*						
joint NEC (*see also* Neoplasm, bone)	170.9	198.5	—	213.9	238.0	239.2
acromioclavicular	170.4	198.5	—	213.4	238.0	239.2
bursa or synovial membrane—*see* Neoplasm, connective tissue						
costovertebral	170.3	198.5	—	213.3	238.0	239.2
sternocostal	170.3	198.5	—	213.3	238.0	239.2
temporomandibular	170.1	198.5	—	213.1	238.0	239.2
junction						
anorectal	154.8	197.5	230.7	211.4	235.5	239.0
cardioesophageal	151.0	197.8	230.2	211.1	235.2	239.0
esophagogastric	151.0	197.8	230.2	211.1	235.2	239.0
gastroesophageal	151.0	197.8	230.2	211.1	235.2	239.0
hard and soft palate	145.5	198.89	230.0	210.4	235.1	239.0
ileocecal	153.4	197.5	230.3	211.3	235.2	239.0
pelvirectal	154.0	197.5	230.4	211.4	235.2	239.0
pelviureteric	189.1	198.0	233.9	223.1	236.91	239.5
rectosigmoid	154.0	197.5	230.4	211.4	235.2	239.0
squamocolumnar, of cervix	180.8	198.82	233.1	219.0	236.0	239.5
kidney (parenchyma)	189.0	198.0	233.9	223.0	236.91	239.5
calyx	189.1	198.0	233.9	223.1	236.91	239.5
hilus	189.1	198.0	233.9	223.1	236.91	239.5
pelvis	189.1	198.0	233.9	223.1	236.91	239.5
knee NEC*	195.5	198.89	232.7	229.8	238.8	239.89
labia (skin)	184.4	198.82	233.32	221.2	236.3	239.5
majora	184.1	198.82	233.32	221.2	236.3	239.5
minora	184.2	198.82	233.32	221.2	236.3	239.5
labial—*see also* Neoplasm, lip						
sulcus (lower) (upper)	145.1	198.89	230.0	210.4	235.1	239.0
labium (skin)	184.4	198.82	233.32	221.2	236.3	239.5
majus	184.1	198.82	233.32	221.2	236.3	239.5
minus	184.2	198.82	233.32	221.2	236.3	239.5
lacrimal						
canaliculi	190.7	198.4	234.0	224.7	238.8	239.89
duct (nasal)	190.7	198.4	234.0	224.7	238.8	239.89
gland	190.2	198.4	234.0	224.2	238.8	239.89
punctum	190.7	198.4	234.0	224.7	238.8	239.89
sac	190.7	198.4	234.0	224.7	238.8	239.89
Langerhans, islands or islets	157.4	197.8	230.9	211.7	235.5	239.0
laryngopharynx	148.9	198.89	230.0	210.8	235.1	239.0
larynx, laryngeal NEC	161.9	197.3	231.0	212.1	235.6	239.1
aryepiglottic fold	161.1	197.3	231.0	212.1	235.6	239.1
cartilage (arytenoid) (cricoid) (cuneiform) (thyroid)	161.3	197.3	231.0	212.1	235.6	239.1
commissure (anterior) (posterior)	161.0	197.3	231.0	212.1	235.6	239.1
contiguous sites	161.8	—	—	—	—	—
extrinsic NEC	161.1	197.3	231.0	212.1	235.6	239.1
meaning hypopharynx	148.9	198.89	230.0	210.8	235.1	239.0
interarytenoid fold	161.1	197.3	231.0	212.1	235.6	239.1
intrinsic	161.0	197.3	231.0	212.1	235.6	239.1
ventricular band	161.1	197.3	231.0	212.1	235.6	239.1
leg NEC*	195.5	198.89	232.7	229.8	238.8	239.89
lens, crystalline	190.0	198.4	234.0	224.0	238.8	239.89
lid (lower) (upper)	173.1	198.2	232.1	216.1	238.2	239.2
ligament—*see also* Neoplasm, connective tissue						
broad	183.3	198.82	233.39	221.0	236.3	239.5
Mackenrodt's	183.8	198.82	233.39	221.8	236.3	239.5

	Malignant					
	Primary	Secondary	Ca in situ	Benign	Uncertain Behavior	Unspecified
Neoplasm, neoplastic—*continued*						
ligament—*continued*						
non-uterine—*see* Neoplasm, connective tissue						
round	183.5	198.82	—	221.0	236.3	239.5
sacro-uterine	183.4	198.82	—	221.0	236.3	239.5
uterine	183.4	198.82	—	221.0	236.3	239.5
utero-ovarian	183.8	198.82	233.39	221.8	236.3	239.5
uterosacral	183.4	198.82	—	221.0	236.3	239.5
limb*	195.8	198.89	232.8	229.8	238.8	239.89
lower*	195.5	198.89	232.7	229.8	238.8	239.89
upper*	195.4	198.89	232.6	229.8	238.8	239.89
limbus of cornea	190.4	198.4	234.0	224.4	238.8	239.89
lingual NEC (*see also* Neoplasm, tongue)	141.9	198.89	230.0	210.1	235.1	239.0
lingula, lung	162.3	197.0	231.2	212.3	235.7	239.1
lip (external) (lipstick area) (vermillion border)	140.9	198.89	230.0	210.0	235.1	239.0
buccal aspect—*see* Neoplasm, lip, internal						
commissure	140.6	198.89	230.0	210.4	235.1	239.0
contiguous sites	140.8	—	—	—	—	—
with oral cavity or pharynx	149.8	—	—	—	—	—
frenulum—*see* Neoplasm, lip, internal						
inner aspect—*see* Neoplasm, lip, internal						
internal (buccal) (frenulum) (mucosa) (oral)	140.5	198.89	230.0	210.0	235.1	239.0
lower	140.4	198.89	230.0	210.0	235.1	239.0
upper	140.3	198.89	230.0	210.0	235.1	239.0
lower	140.1	198.89	230.0	210.0	235.1	239.0
internal (buccal) (frenulum) (mucosa) (oral)	140.4	198.89	230.0	210.0	235.1	239.0
mucosa—*see* Neoplasm, lip, internal						
oral aspect—*see* Neoplasm, lip, internal						
skin (commissure) (lower) (upper)	173.0	198.2	232.0	216.0	238.2	239.2
upper	140.0	198.89	230.0	210.0	235.1	239.0
internal (buccal) (frenulum) (mucosa) (oral)	140.3	198.89	230.0	210.0	235.1	239.0
liver	155.2	197.7	230.8	211.5	235.3	239.0
primary	155.0	—	—	—	—	—
lobe						
azygos	162.3	197.0	231.2	212.3	235.7	239.1
frontal	191.1	198.3	—	225.0	237.5	239.6
lower	162.5	197.0	231.2	212.3	235.7	239.1
middle	162.4	197.0	231.2	212.3	235.7	239.1
occipital	191.4	198.3	—	225.0	237.5	239.6
parietal	191.3	198.3	—	225.0	237.5	239.6
temporal	191.2	198.3	—	225.0	237.5	239.6
upper	162.3	197.0	231.2	212.3	235.7	239.1
lumbosacral plexus	171.6	198.4	—	215.6	238.1	239.2
lung	162.9	197.0	231.2	212.3	235.7	239.1
azygos lobe	162.3	197.0	231.2	212.3	235.7	239.1
carina	162.2	197.0	231.2	212.3	235.7	239.1
contiguous sites with bronchus or trachea	162.8	—	—	—	—	—
hilus	162.2	197.0	231.2	212.3	235.7	239.1
lingula	162.3	197.0	231.2	212.3	235.7	239.1
lobe NEC	162.9	197.0	231.2	212.3	235.7	239.1
lower lobe	162.5	197.0	231.2	212.3	235.7	239.1
main bronchus	162.2	197.0	231.2	212.3	235.7	239.1
middle lobe	162.4	197.0	231.2	212.3	235.7	239.1
upper lobe	162.3	197.0	231.2	212.3	235.7	239.1
lymph, lymphatic						
channel NEC (*see also* Neoplasm, connective tissue)	171.9	198.89	—	215.9	238.1	239.2

☑ Additional Digit Required

© 2009 Ingenix

ICD-9-CM Index

	Malignant					
	Primary	Secondary	Ca in situ	Benign	Uncertain Behavior	Unspecified
Neoplasm, neoplastic—*continued*						
lymph, lymphatic—*continued*						
gland (secondary)	—	196.9	—	229.0	238.8	239.89
abdominal	—	196.2	—	229.0	238.8	239.89
aortic	—	196.2	—	229.0	238.8	239.89
arm	—	196.3	—	229.0	238.8	239.89
auricular (anterior) (posterior)	—	196.0	—	229.0	238.8	239.89
axilla, axillary	—	196.3	—	229.0	238.8	239.89
brachial	—	196.3	—	229.0	238.8	239.89
bronchial	—	196.1	—	229.0	238.8	239.89
bronchopulmonary	—	196.1	—	229.0	238.8	239.89
celiac	—	196.2	—	229.0	238.8	239.89
cervical	—	196.0	—	229.0	238.8	239.89
cervicofacial	—	196.0	—	229.0	238.8	239.89
Cloquet	—	196.5	—	229.0	238.8	239.89
colic	—	196.2	—	229.0	238.8	239.89
common duct	—	196.2	—	229.0	238.8	239.89
cubital	—	196.3	—	229.0	238.8	239.89
diaphragmatic	—	196.1	—	229.0	238.8	239.89
epigastric, inferior	—	196.6	—	229.0	238.8	239.89
epitrochlear	—	196.3	—	229.0	238.8	239.89
esophageal	—	196.1	—	229.0	238.8	239.89
face	—	196.0	—	229.0	238.8	239.89
femoral	—	196.5	—	229.0	238.8	239.89
gastric	—	196.2	—	229.0	238.8	239.89
groin	—	196.5	—	229.0	238.8	239.89
head	—	196.0	—	229.0	238.8	239.89
hepatic	—	196.2	—	229.0	238.8	239.89
hilar (pulmonary)	—	196.1	—	229.0	238.8	239.89
splenic	—	196.2	—	229.0	238.8	239.89
hypogastric	—	196.6	—	229.0	238.8	239.89
ileocolic	—	196.2	—	229.0	238.8	239.89
iliac	—	196.6	—	229.0	238.8	239.89
infraclavicular	—	196.3	—	229.0	238.8	239.89
inguina, inguinal	—	196.5	—	229.0	238.8	239.89
innominate	—	196.1	—	229.0	238.8	239.89
intercostal	—	196.1	—	229.0	238.8	239.89
intestinal	—	196.2	—	229.0	238.8	239.89
intra-abdominal	—	196.2	—	229.0	238.8	239.89
intrapelvic	—	196.6	—	229.0	238.8	239.89
intrathoracic	—	196.1	—	229.0	238.8	239.89
jugular	—	196.0	—	229.0	238.8	239.89
leg	—	196.5	—	229.0	238.8	239.89
limb						
lower	—	196.5	—	229.0	238.8	239.89
upper	—	196.3	—	229.0	238.8	239.89
lower limb	—	196.5	—	229.0	238.8	239.89
lumbar	—	196.2	—	229.0	238.8	239.89
mandibular	—	196.0	—	229.0	238.8	239.89
mediastinal	—	196.1	—	229.0	238.8	239.89
mesenteric (inferior) (superior)	—	196.2	—	229.0	238.8	239.89
midcolic	—	196.2	—	229.0	238.8	239.89
multiple sites in categories 196.0-196.6	—	196.8	—	229.0	238.8	239.89
neck	—	196.0	—	229.0	238.8	239.89
obturator	—	196.6	—	229.0	238.8	239.89
occipital	—	196.0	—	229.0	238.8	239.89
pancreatic	—	196.2	—	229.0	238.8	239.89

| | Malignant | | | | | |
	Primary	Secondary	Ca in situ	Benign	Uncertain Behavior	Unspecified
Neoplasm, neoplastic—*continued*						
lymph, lymphatic—*continued*						
gland (secondary)—*continued*	—	196.9	—	229.0	238.8	239.89
para-aortic	—	196.2	—	229.0	238.8	239.89
paracervical	—	196.6	—	229.0	238.8	239.89
parametrial	—	196.6	—	229.0	238.8	239.89
parasternal	—	196.1	—	229.0	238.8	239.89
parotid	—	196.0	—	229.0	238.8	239.89
pectoral	—	196.3	—	229.0	238.8	239.89
pelvic	—	196.6	—	229.0	238.8	239.89
peri-aortic	—	196.2	—	229.0	238.8	239.89
peripancreatic	—	196.2	—	229.0	238.8	239.89
popliteal	—	196.5	—	229.0	238.8	239.89
porta hepatis	—	196.2	—	229.0	238.8	239.89
portal	—	196.2	—	229.0	238.8	239.89
preauricular	—	196.0	—	229.0	238.8	239.89
prelaryngeal	—	196.0	—	229.0	238.8	239.89
presymphysial	—	196.6	—	229.0	238.8	239.89
pretracheal	—	196.0	—	229.0	238.8	239.89
primary (any site) NEC	202.9 ☑	—	—	—	—	—
pulmonary (hiler)	—	196.1	—	229.0	238.8	239.89
pyloric	—	196.2	—	229.0	238.8	239.89
retroperitoneal	—	196.2	—	229.0	238.8	239.89
retropharyngeal	—	196.0	—	229.0	238.8	239.89
Rosenmüller's	—	196.5	—	229.0	238.8	239.89
sacral	—	196.6	—	229.0	238.8	239.89
scalene	—	196.0	—	229.0	238.8	239.89
site NEC	—	196.9	—	229.0	238.8	239.89
splenic (hilar)	—	196.2	—	229.0	238.8	239.89
subclavicular	—	196.3	—	229.0	238.8	239.89
subinguinal	—	196.5	—	229.0	238.8	239.89
sublingual	—	196.0	—	229.0	238.8	239.89
submandibular	—	196.0	—	229.0	238.8	239.89
submaxillary	—	196.0	—	229.0	238.8	239.89
submental	—	196.0	—	229.0	238.8	239.89
subscapular	—	196.3	—	229.0	238.8	239.89
supraclavicular	—	196.0	—	229.0	238.8	239.89
thoracic	—	196.1	—	229.0	238.8	239.89
tibial	—	196.5	—	229.0	238.8	239.89
tracheal	—	196.1	—	229.0	238.8	239.89
tracheobronchial	—	196.1	—	229.0	238.8	239.89
upper limb	—	196.3	—	229.0	238.8	239.89
Virchow's	—	196.0	—	229.0	238.8	239.89
node—*see also* Neoplasm, lymph gland						
primary NEC	202.9 ☑	—	—	—	—	—
vessel (*see also* Neoplasm, connective tissue)	171.9	198.89	—	215.9	238.1	239.2
Mackenrodt's ligament	183.8	198.82	233.39	221.8	236.3	239.5
malar	170.0	198.5	—	213.0	238.0	239.2
region—*see* Neoplasm, cheek						
mammary gland—*see* Neoplasm, breast						
mandible	170.1	198.5	—	213.1	238.0	239.2
alveolar						
mucose	143.1	198.89	230.0	210.4	235.1	239.0
ridge or process	170.1	198.5	—	213.1	238.0	239.2
carcinoma	143.1	—	—	—	—	—
carcinoma	143.1	—	—	—	—	—
marrow (bone) NEC	202.9 ☑	198.5	—	—	—	238.79

ICD-9-CM Index

	Malignant					
	Primary	Secondary	Ca in situ	Benign	Uncertain Behavior	Unspecified
Neoplasm, neoplastic—*continued*						
mastectomy site (skin)	173.5	198.2	—	—	—	—
specified as breast tissue	174.8	198.81	—	—	—	—
mastoid (air cells) (antrum) (cavity)	160.1	197.3	231.8	212.0	235.9	239.1
bone or process	170.0	198.5	—	213.0	238.0	239.2
maxilla, maxillary (superior)	170.0	198.5	—	213.0	238.0	239.2
alveolar						
mucosa	143.0	198.89	230.0	210.4	235.1	239.0
ridge or process	170.0	198.5	—	213.0	238.0	239.2
carcinoma	143.0	—	—	—	—	—
antrum	160.2	197.3	231.8	212.0	235.9	239.1
carcinoma	143.0	—	—	—	—	—
inferior—*see* Neoplasm, mandible						
sinus	160.2	197.3	231.8	212.0	235.9	239.1
meatus						
external (ear)	173.2	198.2	232.2	216.2	238.2	239.2
Meckel's diverticulum	152.3	197.4	230.7	211.2	235.2	239.0
mediastinum, mediastinal	164.9	197.1	—	212.5	235.8	239.89
anterior	164.2	197.1	—	212.5	235.8	239.89
contiguous sites with heart and thymus	164.8	—	—	—	—	—
posterior	164.3	197.1	—	212.5	235.8	239.89
medulla						
adrenal	194.0	198.7	234.8	227.0	237.2	239.7
oblongata	191.7	198.3	—	225.0	237.5	239.6
meibomian gland	173.1	198.2	232.1	216.1	238.2	239.2
melanoma—*see* Melanoma						
meninges (brain) (cerebral) (cranial) (intracranial)	192.1	198.4	—	225.2	237.6	239.7
spinal (cord)	192.3	198.4	—	225.4	237.6	239.7
meniscus, knee joint (lateral) (medial)	170.7	198.5	—	213.7	238.0	239.2
mesentery, mesenteric	158.8	197.6	—	211.8	235.4	239.0
mesoappendix	158.8	197.6	—	211.8	235.4	239.0
mesocolon	158.8	197.6	—	211.8	235.4	239.0
mesopharynx—*see* Neoplasm, oropharynx						
mesosalpinx	183.3	198.82	233.39	221.0	236.3	239.5
mesovarium	183.3	198.82	233.39	221.0	236.3	239.5
metacarpus (any bone)	170.5	198.5	—	213.5	238.0	239.2
metastatic NEC—*see also* Neoplasm, by site, secondary	—	199.1	—	—	—	—
metatarsus (any bone)	170.8	198.5	—	213.8	238.0	239.2
midbrain	191.7	198.3	—	225.0	237.5	239.6
milk duct—*see* Neoplasm, breast						
mons						
pubis	184.4	198.82	233.32	221.2	236.3	239.5
veneris	184.4	198.82	233.32	221.2	236.3	239.5
motor tract	192.9	198.4	—	225.9	237.9	239.7
brain	191.9	198.3	—	225.0	237.5	239.6
spinal	192.2	198.3	—	225.3	237.5	239.7
mouth	145.9	198.89	230.0	210.4	235.1	239.0
contiguous sites	145.8	—	—	—	—	—
floor	144.9	198.89	230.0	210.3	235.1	239.0
anterior portion	144.0	198.89	230.0	210.3	235.1	239.0
contiguous sites	144.8	—	—	—	—	—
lateral portion	144.1	198.89	230.0	210.3	235.1	239.0
roof	145.5	198.89	230.0	210.4	235.1	239.0
specified part NEC	145.8	198.89	230.0	210.4	235.1	239.0
vestibule	145.1	198.89	230.0	210.4	235.1	239.0

	Malignant			Benign	Uncertain Behavior	Unspecified
	Primary	Secondary	Ca in situ			
Neoplasm, neoplastic—*continued*						
mucosa						
alveolar (ridge or process)	143.9	198.89	230.0	210.4	235.1	239.0
lower	143.1	198.89	230.0	210.4	235.1	239.0
upper	143.0	198.89	230.0	210.4	235.1	239.0
buccal	145.0	198.89	230.0	210.4	235.1	239.0
cheek	145.0	198.89	230.0	210.4	235.1	239.0
lip—*see* Neoplasm, lip, internal						
nasal	160.0	197.3	231.8	212.0	235.9	239.1
oral	145.0	198.89	230.0	210.4	235.1	239.0
Müllerian duct						
female	184.8	198.82	233.39	221.8	236.3	239.5
male	187.8	198.82	233.6	222.8	236.6	239.5
multiple sites NEC	199.0	199.0	234.9	229.9	238.9	199.0
muscle—*see also* Neoplasm, connective tissue						
extraocular	190.1	198.4	234.0	224.1	238.8	239.89
myocardium	164.1	198.89	—	212.7	238.8	239.89
myometrium	182.0	198.82	233.2	219.1	236.0	239.5
myopericardium	164.1	198.89	—	212.7	238.8	239.89
nabothian gland (follicle)	180.0	198.82	233.1	219.0	236.0	239.5
nail	173.9	198.2	232.9	216.9	238.2	239.2
finger	173.6	198.2	232.6	216.6	238.2	239.2
toe	173.7	198.2	232.7	216.7	238.2	239.2
nares, naris (anterior) (posterior)	160.0	197.3	231.8	212.0	235.9	239.1
nasal—*see* Neoplasm, nose						
nasolabial groove	173.3	198.2	232.3	216.3	238.2	239.2
nasolacrimal duct	190.7	198.4	234.0	224.7	238.8	239.89
nasopharynx, nasopharyngeal	147.9	198.89	230.0	210.7	235.1	239.0
contiguous sites	147.8	—	—	—	—	—
floor	147.3	198.89	230.0	210.7	235.1	239.0
roof	147.0	198.89	230.0	210.7	235.1	239.0
specified site NEC	147.8	198.89	230.0	210.7	235.1	239.0
wall	147.9	198.89	230.0	210.7	235.1	239.0
anterior	147.3	198.89	230.0	210.7	235.1	239.0
lateral	147.2	198.89	230.0	210.7	235.1	239.0
posterior	147.1	198.89	230.0	210.7	235.1	239.0
superior	147.0	198.89	230.0	210.7	235.1	239.0
nates	173.5	198.2	232.5	216.5	238.2	239.2
neck NEC*	195.0	198.89	234.8	229.8	238.8	239.89
nerve (autonomic) (ganglion) (parasympathetic) (peripheral) (sympathetic)—*see also* Neoplasm, connective tissue						
abducens	192.0	198.4	—	225.1	237.9	239.7
accessory (spinal)	192.0	198.4	—	225.1	237.9	239.7
acoustic	192.0	198.4	—	225.1	237.9	239.7
auditory	192.0	198.4	—	225.1	237.9	239.7
brachial	171.2	198.89	—	215.2	238.1	239.2
cranial (any)	192.0	198.4	—	225.1	237.9	239.7
facial	192.0	198.4	—	225.1	237.9	239.7
femoral	171.3	198.89	—	215.3	238.1	239.2
glossopharyngeal	192.0	198.4	—	225.1	237.9	239.7
hypoglossal	192.0	198.4	—	225.1	237.9	239.7
intercostal	171.4	198.89	—	215.4	238.1	239.2
lumbar	171.7	198.89	—	215.7	238.1	239.2
median	171.2	198.89	—	215.2	238.1	239.2
obturator	171.3	198.89	—	215.3	238.1	239.2
oculomotor	192.0	198.4	—	225.1	237.9	239.7

☑ Additional Digit Required

© 2009 Ingenix

ICD-9-CM Index

	Malignant					
	Primary	Secondary	Ca in situ	Benign	Uncertain Behavior	Unspecified
Neoplasm, neoplastic—*continued*						
nerve—*continued*						
olfactory	192.0	198.4	—	225.1	237.9	239.7
optic	192.0	198.4	—	225.1	237.9	239.7
peripheral NEC	171.9	198.89	—	215.9	238.1	239.2
radial	171.2	198.89	—	215.2	238.1	239.2
sacral	171.6	198.89	—	215.6	238.1	239.2
sciatic	171.3	198.89	—	215.3	238.1	239.2
spinal NEC	171.9	198.89	—	215.9	238.1	239.2
trigeminal	192.0	198.4	—	225.1	237.9	239.7
trochlear	192.0	198.4	—	225.1	237.9	239.7
ulnar	171.2	198.89	—	215.2	238.1	239.2
vagus	192.0	198.4	—	225.1	237.9	239.7
nervous system (central) NEC	192.9	198.4	—	225.9	237.9	239.7
autonomic NEC	171.9	198.89	—	215.9	238.1	239.2
brain—*see also* Neoplasm, brain						
membrane or meninges	192.1	198.4	—	225.2	237.6	239.7
contiguous sites	192.8	—	—	—	—	—
parasympathetic NEC	171.9	198.89	—	215.9	238.1	239.2
sympathetic NEC	171.9	198.89	—	215.9	238.1	239.2
nipple (female)	174.0	198.81	233.0	217	238.3	239.3
male	175.0	198.81	233.0	217	238.3	239.3
nose, nasal	195.0	198.89	234.8	229.8	238.8	239.89
ala (external)	173.3	198.2	232.3	216.3	238.2	239.2
bone	170.0	198.5	—	213.0	238.0	239.2
cartilage	160.0	197.3	231.8	212.0	235.9	239.1
cavity	160.0	197.3	231.8	212.0	235.9	239.1
contiguous sites with accessory sinuses or middle ear	160.8	—	—	—	—	—
choana	147.3	198.89	230.0	210.7	235.1	239.0
external (skin)	173.3	198.2	232.3	216.3	238.2	239.2
fossa	160.0	197.3	231.8	212.0	235.9	239.1
internal	160.0	197.3	231.8	212.0	235.9	239.1
mucosa	160.0	197.3	231.8	212.0	235.9	239.1
septum	160.0	197.3	231.8	212.0	235.9	239.1
posterior margin	147.3	198.89	230.0	210.7	235.1	239.0
sinus—*see* Neoplasm, sinus						
skin	173.3	198.2	232.3	216.3	238.2	239.2
turbinate (mucosa)	160.0	197.3	231.8	212.0	235.9	239.1
bone	170.0	198.5	—	213.0	238.0	239.2
vestibule	160.0	197.3	231.8	212.0	235.9	239.1
nostril	160.0	197.3	231.8	212.0	235.9	239.1
nucleus pulposus	170.2	198.5	—	213.2	238.0	239.2
occipital						
bone	170.0	198.5	—	213.0	238.0	239.2
lobe or pole, brain	191.4	198.3	—	225.0	237.5	239.6
odontogenic—*see* Neoplasm, jaw bone						
oesophagus—*see* Neoplasm, esophagus						
olfactory nerve or bulb	192.0	198.4	—	225.1	237.9	239.7
olive (brain)	191.7	198.3	—	225.0	237.5	239.6
omentum	158.8	197.6	—	211.8	235.4	239.0
operculum (brain)	191.0	198.3	—	225.0	237.5	239.6
optic nerve, chiasm, or tract	192.0	198.4	—	225.1	237.9	239.7
oral (cavity)	145.9	198.89	230.0	210.4	235.1	239.0
contiguous sites with lip or pharynx	149.8	—	—	—	—	—
ill-defined	149.9	198.89	230.0	210.4	235.1	239.0
mucosa	145.9	198.89	230.0	210.4	235.1	239.0

| | Malignant | | | | | |
	Primary	Secondary	Ca in situ	Benign	Uncertain Behavior	Unspecified
Neoplasm, neoplastic—*continued*						
orbit	190.1	198.4	234.0	224.1	238.8	239.89
bone	170.0	198.5	—	213.0	238.0	239.2
eye	190.1	198.4	234.0	224.1	238.8	239.89
soft parts	190.1	198.4	234.0	224.1	238.8	239.89
organ of Zuckerkandl	194.6	198.89	—	227.6	237.3	239.7
oropharynx	146.9	198.89	230.0	210.6	235.1	239.0
branchial cleft (vestige)	146.8	198.89	230.0	210.6	235.1	239.0
contiguous sites	146.8	—	—	—	—	—
junctional region	146.5	198.89	230.0	210.6	235.1	239.0
lateral wall	146.6	198.89	230.0	210.6	235.1	239.0
pillars of fauces	146.2	198.89	230.0	210.6	235.1	239.0
posterior wall	146.7	198.89	230.0	210.6	235.1	239.0
specified part NEC	146.8	198.89	230.0	210.6	235.1	239.0
vallecula	146.3	198.89	230.0	210.6	235.1	239.0
os						
external	180.1	198.82	233.1	219.0	236.0	239.5
internal	180.0	198.82	233.1	219.0	236.0	239.5
ovary	183.0	198.6	233.39	220	236.2	239.5
oviduct	183.2	198.82	233.39	221.0	236.3	239.5
palate	145.5	198.89	230.0	210.4	235.1	239.0
hard	145.2	198.89	230.0	210.4	235.1	239.0
junction of hard and soft palate	145.5	198.89	230.0	210.4	235.1	239.0
soft	145.3	198.89	230.0	210.4	235.1	239.0
nasopharyngeal surface	147.3	198.89	230.0	210.7	235.1	239.0
posterior surface	147.3	198.89	230.0	210.7	235.1	239.0
superior surface	147.3	198.89	230.0	210.7	235.1	239.0
palatoglossal arch	146.2	198.89	230.0	210.6	235.1	239.0
palatopharyngeal arch	146.2	198.89	230.0	210.6	235.1	239.0
pallium	191.0	198.3	—	225.0	237.5	239.6
palpebra	173.1	198.2	232.1	216.1	238.2	239.2
pancreas	157.9	197.8	230.9	211.6	235.5	239.0
body	157.1	197.8	230.9	211.6	235.5	239.0
contiguous sites	157.8	—	—	—	—	—
duct (of Santorini) (of Wirsung)	157.3	197.8	230.9	211.6	235.5	239.0
ectopic tissue	157.8	197.8	230.9	211.6	235.5	239.0
head	157.0	197.8	230.9	211.6	235.5	239.0
islet cells	157.4	197.8	230.9	211.7	235.5	239.0
neck	157.8	197.8	230.9	211.6	235.5	239.0
tail	157.2	197.8	230.9	211.6	235.5	239.0
para-aortic body	194.6	198.89	—	227.6	237.3	239.7
paraganglion NEC	194.6	198.89	—	227.6	237.3	239.7
parametrium	183.4	198.82	—	221.0	236.3	239.5
paranephric	158.0	197.6	—	211.8	235.4	239.0
pararectal	195.3	198.89	—	229.8	238.8	239.89
parasagittal (region)	195.0	198.89	234.8	229.8	238.8	239.89
parasellar	192.9	198.4	—	225.9	237.9	239.7
parathyroid (gland)	194.1	198.89	234.8	227.1	237.4	239.7
paraurethral	195.3	198.89	—	229.8	238.8	239.89
gland	189.4	198.1	233.9	223.89	236.99	239.5
paravaginal	195.3	198.89	—	229.8	238.8	239.89
parenchyma, kidney	189.0	198.0	233.9	223.0	236.91	239.5
parietal						
bone	170.0	198.5	—	213.0	238.0	239.2
lobe, brain	191.3	198.3	—	225.0	237.5	239.6
paroophoron	183.3	198.82	233.39	221.0	236.3	239.5
parotid (duct) (gland)	142.0	198.89	230.0	210.2	235.0	239.0

☑ Additional Digit Required

| | Malignant | | | | | |
	Primary	Secondary	Ca in situ	Benign	Uncertain Behavior	Unspecified
Neoplasm, neoplastic—*continued*						
parovarium	183.3	198.82	233.39	221.0	236.3	239.5
patella	170.8	198.5	—	213.8	238.0	239.2
peduncle, cerebral	191.7	198.3	—	225.0	237.5	239.6
pelvirectal junction	154.0	197.5	230.4	211.4	235.2	239.0
pelvis, pelvic	195.3	198.89	234.8	229.8	238.8	239.89
bone	170.6	198.5	—	213.6	238.0	239.2
floor	195.3	198.89	234.8	229.8	238.8	239.89
renal	189.1	198.0	233.9	223.1	236.91	239.5
viscera	195.3	198.89	234.8	229.8	238.8	239.89
wall	195.3	198.89	234.8	229.8	238.8	239.89
pelvo-abdominal	195.8	198.89	234.8	229.8	238.8	239.89
penis	187.4	198.82	233.5	222.1	236.6	239.5
body	187.3	198.82	233.5	222.1	236.6	239.5
corpus (cavernosum)	187.3	198.82	233.5	222.1	236.6	239.5
glans	187.2	198.82	233.5	222.1	236.6	239.5
skin NEC	187.4	198.82	233.5	222.1	236.6	239.5
periadrenal (tissue)	158.0	197.6	—	211.8	235.4	239.0
perianal (skin)	173.5	198.2	232.5	216.5	238.2	239.2
pericardium	164.1	198.89	—	212.7	238.8	239.89
perinephric	158.0	197.6	—	211.8	235.4	239.0
perineum	195.3	198.89	234.8	229.8	238.8	239.89
periodontal tissue NEC	143.9	198.89	230.0	210.4	235.1	239.0
periosteum—*see* Neoplasm, bone						
peripancreatic	158.0	197.6	—	211.8	235.4	239.0
peripheral nerve NEC	171.9	198.89	—	215.9	238.1	239.2
perirectal (tissue)	195.3	198.89	—	229.8	238.8	239.89
perirenal (tissue)	158.0	197.6	—	211.8	235.4	239.0
peritoneum, peritoneal (cavity)	158.9	197.6	—	211.8	235.4	239.0
contiguous sites	158.8	—	—	—	—	—
with digestive organs	159.8	—	—	—	—	—
parietal	158.8	197.6	—	211.8	235.4	239.0
pelvic	158.8	197.6	—	211.8	235.4	239.0
specified part NEC	158.8	197.6	—	211.8	235.4	239.0
peritonsillar (tissue)	195.0	198.89	234.8	229.8	238.8	239.89
periurethral tissue	195.3	198.89	—	229.8	238.8	239.89
phalanges	170.9	198.5	—	213.9	238.0	239.2
foot	170.8	198.5	—	213.8	238.0	239.2
hand	170.5	198.5	—	213.5	238.0	239.2
pharynx, pharyngeal	149.0	198.89	230.0	210.9	235.1	239.0
bursa	147.1	198.89	230.0	210.7	235.1	239.0
fornix	147.3	198.89	230.0	210.7	235.1	239.0
recess	147.2	198.89	230.0	210.7	235.1	239.0
region	149.0	198.89	230.0	210.9	235.1	239.0
tonsil	147.1	198.89	230.0	210.7	235.1	239.0
wall (lateral) (posterior)	149.0	198.89	230.0	210.9	235.1	239.0
pia mater (cerebral) (cranial)	192.1	198.4	—	225.2	237.6	239.7
spinal	192.3	198.4	—	225.4	237.6	239.7
pillars of fauces	146.2	198.89	230.0	210.6	235.1	239.0
pineal (body) (gland)	194.4	198.89	234.8	227.4	237.1	239.7
pinna (ear) NEC	173.2	198.2	232.2	216.2	238.2	239.2
cartilage	171.0	198.89	—	215.0	238.1	239.2
piriform fossa or sinus	148.1	198.89	230.0	210.8	235.1	239.0
pituitary (body) (fossa) (gland) (lobe)	194.3	198.89	234.8	227.3	237.0	239.7
placenta	181	198.82	233.2	219.8	236.1	239.5
pleura, pleural (cavity)	163.9	197.2	—	212.4	235.8	239.1
contiguous sites	163.8	—	—	—	—	—

☑ Additional Digit Required

	Malignant					
	Primary	**Secondary**	**Ca in situ**	**Benign**	**Uncertain Behavior**	**Unspecified**
Neoplasm, neoplastic—*continued*						
pleura, pleural (cavity)—*continued*						
parietal	163.0	197.2	—	212.4	235.8	239.1
visceral	163.1	197.2	—	212.4	235.8	239.1
plexus						
brachial	171.2	198.89	—	215.2	238.1	239.2
cervical	171.0	198.89	—	215.0	238.1	239.2
choroid	191.5	198.3	—	225.0	237.5	239.6
lumbosacral	171.6	198.89	—	215.6	238.1	239.2
sacral	171.6	198.89	—	215.6	238.1	239.2
pluri-endocrine	194.8	198.89	234.8	227.8	237.4	239.7
pole						
frontal	191.1	198.3	—	225.0	237.5	239.6
occipital	191.4	198.3	—	225.0	237.5	239.6
pons (varolii)	191.7	198.3	—	225.0	237.5	239.6
popliteal fossa or space*	195.5	198.89	234.8	229.8	238.8	239.89
postcricoid (region)	148.0	198.89	230.0	210.8	235.1	239.0
posterior fossa (cranial)	191.9	198.3	—	225.0	237.5	239.6
postnasal space	147.9	198.89	230.0	210.7	235.1	239.0
prepuce	187.1	198.82	233.5	222.1	236.6	239.5
prepylorus	151.1	197.8	230.2	211.1	235.2	239.0
presacral (region)	195.3	198.89	—	229.8	238.8	239.89
prostate (gland)	185	198.82	233.4	222.2	236.5	239.5
utricle	189.3	198.1	233.9	223.81	236.99	239.5
pterygoid fossa	171.0	198.89	—	215.0	238.1	239.2
pubic bone	170.6	198.5	—	213.6	238.0	239.2
pudenda, pudendum (female)	184.4	198.82	233.32	221.2	236.3	239.5
pulmonary	162.9	197.0	231.2	212.3	235.7	239.1
putamen	191.0	198.3	—	225.0	237.5	239.6
pyloric						
antrum	151.2	197.8	230.2	211.1	235.2	239.0
canal	151.1	197.8	230.2	211.1	235.2	239.0
pylorus	151.1	197.8	230.2	211.1	235.2	239.0
pyramid (brain)	191.7	198.3	—	225.0	237.5	239.6
pyriform fossa or sinus	148.1	198.89	230.0	210.8	235.1	239.0
radius (any part)	170.4	198.5	—	213.4	238.0	239.2
Rathke's pouch	194.3	198.89	234.8	227.3	237.0	239.7
rectosigmoid (colon) (junction)	154.0	197.5	230.4	211.4	235.2	239.0
contiguous sites with anus or rectum	154.8	—	—	—	—	—
rectouterine pouch	158.8	197.6	—	211.8	235.4	239.0
rectovaginal septum or wall	195.3	198.89	234.8	229.8	238.8	239.89
rectovesical septum	195.3	198.89	234.8	229.8	238.8	239.89
rectum (ampulla)	154.1	197.5	230.4	211.4	235.2	239.0
and colon	154.0	197.5	230.4	211.4	235.2	239.0
contiguous sites with anus or rectosigmoid junction	154.8	—	—	—	—	—
renal	189.0	198.0	233.9	223.0	236.91	239.5
calyx	189.1	198.0	233.9	223.1	236.91	239.5
hilus	189.1	198.0	233.9	223.1	236.91	239.5
parenchyma	189.0	198.0	233.9	223.0	236.91	239.5
pelvis	189.1	198.0	233.9	223.1	236.91	239.5
respiratory						
organs or system NEC	165.9	197.3	231.9	212.9	235.9	239.1
specified sites NEC	165.8	197.3	231.8	212.8	235.9	239.1
tract NEC	165.9	197.3	231.9	212.9	235.9	239.1
upper	165.0	197.3	231.9	212.9	235.9	239.1
retina	190.5	198.4	234.0	224.5	238.8	239.89

ICD-9-CM Index

☑ Additional Digit Required

| | Malignant | | | | | |
Neoplasm, neoplastic—*continued*	Primary	Secondary	Ca in situ	Benign	Uncertain Behavior	Unspecified
retrobulbar	190.1	198.4	—	224.1	238.8	239.89
retrocecal	158.0	197.6	—	211.8	235.4	239.0
retromolar (area) (triangle) (trigone)	145.6	198.89	230.0	210.4	235.1	239.0
retro-orbital	195.0	198.89	234.8	229.8	238.8	239.89
retroperitoneal (space) (tissue)	158.0	197.6	—	211.8	235.4	239.0
contiguous sites	158.8	—	—	—	—	—
retroperitoneum	158.0	197.6	—	211.8	235.4	239.0
contiguous sites	158.8	—	—	—	—	—
retropharyngeal	149.0	198.89	230.0	210.9	235.1	239.0
retrovesical (septum)	195.3	198.89	234.8	229.8	238.8	239.89
rhinencephalon	191.0	198.3	—	225.0	237.5	239.6
rib	170.3	198.5	—	213.3	238.0	239.2
Rosenmüller's fossa	147.2	198.89	230.0	210.7	235.1	239.0
round ligament	183.5	198.82	—	221.0	236.3	239.5
sacrococcyx, sacrococcygeal	170.6	198.5	—	213.6	238.0	239.2
region	195.3	198.89	234.8	229.8	238.8	239.89
sacrouterine ligament	183.4	198.82	—	221.0	236.3	239.5
sacrum, sacral (vertebra)	170.6	198.5	—	213.6	238.0	239.2
salivary gland or duct (major)	142.9	198.89	230.0	210.2	235.0	239.0
contiguous sites	142.8	—	—	—	—	—
minor NEC	145.9	198.89	230.0	210.4	235.1	239.0
parotid	142.0	198.89	230.0	210.2	235.0	239.0
pluriglandular	142.8	198.89	230.0	210.2	235.0	239.0
sublingual	142.2	198.89	230.0	210.2	235.0	239.0
submandibular	142.1	198.89	230.0	210.2	235.0	239.0
submaxillary	142.1	198.89	230.0	210.2	235.0	239.0
salpinx (uterine)	183.2	198.82	233.39	221.0	236.3	239.5
Santorini's duct	157.3	197.8	230.9	211.6	235.5	239.0
scalp	173.4	198.2	232.4	216.4	238.2	239.2
scapula (any part)	170.4	198.5	—	213.4	238.0	239.2
scapular region	195.1	198.89	234.8	229.8	238.8	239.89
scar NEC (*see also* Neoplasm, skin)	173.9	198.2	232.9	216.9	238.2	239.2
sciatic nerve	171.3	198.89	—	215.3	238.1	239.2
sclera	190.0	198.4	234.0	224.0	238.8	239.89
scrotum (skin)	187.7	198.82	233.6	222.4	236.6	239.5
sebaceous gland—*see* Neoplasm, skin						
sella turcica	194.3	198.89	234.8	227.3	237.0	239.7
bone	170.0	198.5	—	213.0	238.0	239.2
semilunar cartilage (knee)	170.7	198.5	—	213.7	238.0	239.2
seminal vesicle	187.8	198.82	233.6	222.8	236.6	239.5
septum						
nasal	160.0	197.3	231.8	212.0	235.9	239.1
posterior margin	147.3	198.89	230.0	210.7	235.1	239.0
rectovaginal	195.3	198.89	234.8	229.8	238.8	239.89
rectovesical	195.3	198.89	234.8	229.8	238.8	239.89
urethrovaginal	184.9	198.82	233.39	221.9	236.3	239.5
vesicovaginal	184.9	198.82	233.39	221.9	236.3	239.5
shoulder NEC*	195.4	198.89	232.6	229.8	238.8	239.89
sigmoid flexure (lower) (upper)	153.3	197.5	230.3	211.3	235.2	239.0
sinus (accessory)	160.9	197.3	231.8	212.0	235.9	239.1
bone (any)	170.0	198.5	—	213.0	238.0	239.2
contiguous sites with middle ear or nasal cavities	160.8	—	—	—	—	—
ethmoidal	160.3	197.3	231.8	212.0	235.9	239.1
frontal	160.4	197.3	231.8	212.0	235.9	239.1
maxillary	160.2	197.3	231.8	212.0	235.9	239.1
nasal, paranasal NEC	160.9	197.3	231.8	212.0	235.9	239.1

	Malignant			Benign	Uncertain Behavior	Unspecified
	Primary	Secondary	Ca in situ			

Neoplasm, neoplastic—*continued*

sinus (accessory)—*continued*

pyriform	148.1	198.89	230.0	210.8	235.1	239.0
sphenoidal	160.5	197.3	231.8	212.0	235.9	239.1
skeleton, skeletal NEC	170.9	198.5	—	213.9	238.0	239.2
Skene's gland	189.4	198.1	233.9	223.89	236.99	239.5
skin NEC	173.9	198.2	232.9	216.9	238.2	239.2
abdominal wall	173.5	198.2	232.5	216.5	238.2	239.2
ala nasi	173.3	198.2	232.3	216.3	238.2	239.2
ankle	173.7	198.2	232.7	216.7	238.2	239.2
antecubital space	173.6	198.2	232.6	216.6	238.2	239.2
anus	173.5	198.2	232.5	216.5	238.2	239.2
arm	173.6	198.2	232.6	216.6	238.2	239.2
auditory canal (external)	173.2	198.2	232.2	216.2	238.2	239.2
auricle (ear)	173.2	198.2	232.2	216.2	238.2	239.2
auricular canal (external)	173.2	198.2	232.2	216.2	238.2	239.2
axilla, axillary fold	173.5	198.2	232.5	216.5	238.2	239.2
back	173.5	198.2	232.5	216.5	238.2	239.2
breast	173.5	198.2	232.5	216.5	238.2	239.2
brow	173.3	198.2	232.3	216.3	238.2	239.2
buttock	173.5	198.2	232.5	216.5	238.2	239.2
calf	173.7	198.2	232.7	216.7	238.2	239.2
canthus (eye) (inner) (outer)	173.1	198.2	232.1	216.1	238.2	239.2
cervical region	173.4	198.2	232.4	216.4	238.2	239.2
cheek (external)	173.3	198.2	232.3	216.3	238.2	239.2
chest (wall)	173.5	198.2	232.5	216.5	238.2	239.2
chin	173.3	198.2	232.3	216.3	238.2	239.2
clavicular area	173.5	198.2	232.5	216.5	238.2	239.2
clitoris	184.3	198.82	233.32	221.2	236.3	239.5
columnella	173.3	198.2	232.3	216.3	238.2	239.2
concha	173.2	198.2	232.2	216.2	238.2	239.2
contiguous sites	173.8	—	—	—	—	—
ear (external)	173.2	198.2	232.2	216.2	238.2	239.2
elbow	173.6	198.2	232.6	216.6	238.2	239.2
eyebrow	173.3	198.2	232.3	216.3	238.2	239.2
eyelid	173.1	198.2	232.1	216.1	238.2	239.2
face NEC	173.3	198.2	232.3	216.3	238.2	239.2
female genital organs (external)	184.4	198.82	233.30	221.2	236.3	239.5
clitoris	184.3	198.82	233.32	221.2	236.3	239.5
labium NEC	184.4	198.82	233.32	221.2	236.3	239.5
majus	184.1	198.82	233.32	221.2	236.3	239.5
minus	184.2	198.82	233.32	221.2	236.3	239.5
pudendum	184.4	198.82	233.32	221.2	236.3	239.5
vulva	184.4	198.82	233.32	221.2	236.3	239.5
finger	173.6	198.2	232.6	216.6	238.2	239.2
flank	173.5	198.2	232.5	216.5	238.2	239.2
foot	173.7	198.2	232.7	216.7	238.2	239.2
forearm	173.6	198.2	232.6	216.6	238.2	239.2
forehead	173.3	198.2	232.3	216.3	238.2	239.2
glabella	173.3	198.2	232.3	216.3	238.2	239.2
gluteal region	173.5	198.2	232.5	216.5	238.2	239.2
groin	173.5	198.2	232.5	216.5	238.2	239.2
hand	173.6	198.2	232.6	216.6	238.2	239.2
head NEC	173.4	198.2	232.4	216.4	238.2	239.2
heel	173.7	198.2	232.7	216.7	238.2	239.2
helix	173.2	198.2	232.2	216.2	238.2	239.2
hip	173.7	198.2	232.7	216.7	238.2	239.2

☑ Additional Digit Required
© 2009 Ingenix

Neoplasm, neoplastic—continued	Malignant			Benign	Uncertain Behavior	Unspecified
	Primary	Secondary	Ca in situ			
skin NEC—*continued*						
infraclavicular region	173.5	198.2	232.5	216.5	238.2	239.2
inguinal region	173.5	198.2	232.5	216.5	238.2	239.2
jaw	173.3	198.2	232.3	216.3	238.2	239.2
knee	173.7	198.2	232.7	216.7	238.2	239.2
labia						
majora	184.1	198.82	233.32	221.2	236.3	239.5
minora	184.2	198.82	233.32	221.2	236.3	239.5
leg	173.7	198.2	232.7	216.7	238.2	239.2
lid (lower) (upper)	173.1	198.2	232.1	216.1	238.2	239.2
limb NEC	173.9	198.2	232.9	216.9	238.2	239.5
lower	173.7	198.2	232.7	216.7	238.2	239.2
upper	173.6	198.2	232.6	216.6	238.2	239.2
lip (lower) (upper)	173.0	198.2	232.0	216.0	238.2	239.2
male genital organs	187.9	198.82	233.6	222.9	236.6	239.5
penis	187.4	198.82	233.5	222.1	236.6	239.5
prepuce	187.1	198.82	233.5	222.1	236.6	239.5
scrotum	187.7	198.82	233.6	222.4	236.6	239.5
mastectomy site	173.5	198.2	—	—	—	—
specified as breast tissue	174.8	198.81	—	—	—	—
meatus, acoustic (external)	173.2	198.2	232.2	216.2	238.2	239.2
nates	173.5	198.2	232.5	216.5	238.2	239.0
neck	173.4	198.2	232.4	216.4	238.2	239.2
nose (external)	173.3	198.2	232.3	216.3	238.2	239.2
palm	173.6	198.2	232.6	216.6	238.2	239.2
palpebra	173.1	198.2	232.1	216.1	238.2	239.2
penis NEC	187.4	198.82	233.5	222.1	236.6	239.5
perianal	173.5	198.2	232.5	216.5	238.2	239.2
perineum	173.5	198.2	232.5	216.5	238.2	239.2
pinna	173.2	198.2	232.2	216.2	238.2	239.2
plantar	173.7	198.2	232.7	216.7	238.2	239.2
popliteal fossa or space	173.7	198.2	232.7	216.7	238.2	239.2
prepuce	187.1	198.82	233.5	222.1	236.6	239.5
pubes	173.5	198.2	232.5	216.5	238.2	239.2
sacrococcygeal region	173.5	198.2	232.5	216.5	238.2	239.2
scalp	173.4	198.2	232.4	216.4	238.2	239.2
scapular region	173.5	198.2	232.5	216.5	238.2	239.2
scrotum	187.7	198.82	233.6	222.4	236.6	239.5
shoulder	173.6	198.2	232.6	216.6	238.2	239.2
sole (foot)	173.7	198.2	232.7	216.7	238.2	239.2
specified sites NEC	173.8	198.2	232.8	216.8	232.8	239.2
submammary fold	173.5	198.2	232.5	216.5	238.2	239.2
supraclavicular region	173.4	198.2	232.4	216.4	238.2	239.2
temple	173.3	198.2	232.3	216.3	238.2	239.2
thigh	173.7	198.2	232.7	216.7	238.2	239.2
thoracic wall	173.5	198.2	232.5	216.5	238.2	239.2
thumb	173.6	198.2	232.6	216.6	238.2	239.2
toe	173.7	198.2	232.7	216.7	238.2	239.2
tragus	173.2	198.2	232.2	216.2	238.2	239.2
trunk	173.5	198.2	232.5	216.5	238.2	239.2
umbilicus	173.5	198.2	232.5	216.5	238.2	239.2
vulva	184.4	198.82	233.32	221.2	236.3	239.5
wrist	173.6	198.2	232.6	216.6	238.2	239.2
skull	170.0	198.5	—	213.0	238.0	239.2
soft parts or tissues—*see* Neoplasm, connective tissue						

☑ Additional Digit Required

	Malignant					
	Primary	Secondary	Ca in situ	Benign	Uncertain Behavior	Unspecified
Neoplasm, neoplastic—*continued*						
specified site NEC	195.8	198.89	234.8	229.8	238.8	239.89
spermatic cord	187.6	198.82	233.6	222.8	236.6	239.5
sphenoid	160.5	197.3	231.8	212.0	235.9	239.1
bone	170.0	198.5	—	213.0	238.0	239.2
sinus	160.5	197.3	231.8	212.0	235.9	239.1
sphincter						
anal	154.2	197.5	230.5	211.4	235.5	239.0
of Oddi	156.1	197.8	230.8	211.5	235.3	239.0
spine, spinal (column)	170.2	198.5	—	213.2	238.0	239.2
bulb	191.7	198.3	—	225.0	237.5	239.6
coccyx	170.6	198.5	—	213.6	238.0	239.2
cord (cervical) (lumbar) (sacral) (thoracic)	192.2	198.3	—	225.3	237.5	239.7
dura mater	192.3	198.4	—	225.4	237.6	239.7
lumbosacral	170.2	198.5	—	213.2	238.0	239.2
membrane	192.3	198.4	—	225.4	237.6	239.7
meninges	192.3	198.4	—	225.4	237.6	239.7
nerve (root)	171.9	198.89	—	215.9	238.1	239.2
pia mater	192.3	198.4	—	225.4	237.6	239.7
root	171.9	198.89	—	215.9	238.1	239.2
sacrum	170.6	198.5	—	213.6	238.0	239.2
spleen, splenic NEC	159.1	197.8	230.9	211.9	235.5	239.0
flexure (colon)	153.7	197.5	230.3	211.3	235.2	239.0
stem, brain	191.7	198.3	—	225.0	237.5	239.6
Stensen's duct	142.0	198.89	230.0	210.2	235.0	239.0
sternum	170.3	198.5	—	213.3	238.0	239.2
stomach	151.9	197.8	230.2	211.1	235.2	239.0
antrum (pyloric)	151.2	197.8	230.2	211.1	235.2	239.0
body	151.4	197.8	230.2	211.1	235.2	239.0
cardia	151.0	197.8	230.2	211.1	235.2	239.0
cardiac orifice	151.0	197.8	230.2	211.1	235.2	239.0
contiguous sites	151.8	—	—	—	—	—
corpus	151.4	197.8	230.2	211.1	235.2	239.0
fundus	151.3	197.8	230.2	211.1	235.2	239.0
greater curvature NEC	151.6	197.8	230.2	211.1	235.2	239.0
lesser curvature NEC	151.5	197.8	230.2	211.1	235.2	239.0
prepylorus	151.1	197.8	230.2	211.1	235.2	239.0
pylorus	151.1	197.8	230.2	211.1	235.2	239.0
wall NEC	151.9	197.8	230.2	211.1	235.2	239.0
anterior NEC	151.8	197.8	230.2	211.1	235.2	239.0
posterior NEC	151.8	197.8	230.2	211.1	235.2	239.0
stroma, endometrial	182.0	198.82	233.2	219.1	236.0	239.5
stump, cervical	180.8	198.82	233.1	219.0	236.0	239.5
subcutaneous (nodule) (tissue) NEC—*see* Neoplasm, connective tissue						
subdural	192.1	198.4	—	225.2	237.6	239.7
subglottis, subglottic	161.2	197.3	231.0	212.1	235.6	239.1
sublingual	144.9	198.89	230.0	210.3	235.1	239.0
gland or duct	142.2	198.89	230.0	210.2	235.0	239.0
submandibular gland	142.1	198.89	230.0	210.2	235.0	239.0
submaxillary gland or duct	142.1	198.89	230.0	210.2	235.0	239.0
submental	195.0	198.89	234.8	229.8	238.8	239.89
subpleural	162.9	197.0	—	212.3	235.7	239.1
substernal	164.2	197.1	—	212.5	235.8	239.89
sudoriferous, sudoriparous gland, site unspecified	173.9	198.2	232.9	216.9	238.2	239.2
specified site—*see* Neoplasm, skin						
supraclavicular region	195.0	198.89	234.8	229.8	238.8	239.89

☑ Additional Digit Required

| | Malignant | | | | | |
	Primary	Secondary	Ca in situ	Benign	Uncertain Behavior	Unspecified
Neoplasm, neoplastic—*continued*						
supraglottis	161.1	197.3	231.0	212.1	235.6	239.1
suprarenal (capsule) (cortex) (gland) (medulla)	194.0	198.7	234.8	227.0	237.2	239.7
suprasellar (region)	191.9	198.3	—	225.0	237.5	239.6
sweat gland (apocrine) (eccrine), site unspecified	173.9	198.2	232.9	216.9	238.2	239.2
specified site—*see* Neoplasm, skin						
sympathetic nerve or nervous system NEC	171.9	198.89	—	215.9	238.1	239.2
symphysis pubis	170.6	198.5	—	213.6	238.0	239.2
synovial membrane—*see* Neoplasm, connective tissue						
tapetum, brain	191.8	198.3	—	225.0	237.5	239.6
tarsus (any bone)	170.8	198.5	—	213.8	238.0	239.2
temple (skin)	173.3	198.2	232.3	216.3	238.2	239.2
temporal						
bone	170.0	198.5	—	213.0	238.0	239.2
lobe or pole	191.2	198.3	—	225.0	237.5	239.6
region	195.0	198.89	234.8	229.8	238.8	239.89
skin	173.3	198.2	232.3	216.3	238.2	239.2
tendon (sheath)—*see* Neoplasm, connective tissue						
tentorium (cerebelli)	192.1	198.4	—	225.2	237.6	239.7
testis, testes (descended) (scrotal)	186.9	198.82	233.6	222.0	236.4	239.5
ectopic	186.0	198.82	233.6	222.0	236.4	239.5
retained	186.0	198.82	233.6	222.0	236.4	239.5
undescended	186.0	198.82	233.6	222.0	236.4	239.5
thalamus	191.0	198.3	—	225.0	237.5	239.6
thigh NEC*	195.5	198.89	234.8	229.8	238.8	239.89
thorax, thoracic (cavity) (organs NEC)	195.1	198.89	234.8	229.8	238.8	239.89
duct	171.4	198.89	—	215.4	238.1	239.2
wall NEC	195.1	198.89	234.8	229.8	238.8	239.89
throat	149.0	198.89	230.0	210.9	235.1	239.0
thumb NEC*	195.4	198.89	232.6	229.8	238.8	239.89
thymus (gland)	164.0	198.89	—	212.6	235.8	239.89
contiguous sites with heart and mediastinum	164.8	—	—	—	—	—
thyroglossal duct	193	198.89	234.8	226	237.4	239.7
thyroid (gland)	193	198.89	234.8	226	237.4	239.7
cartilage	161.3	197.3	231.0	212.1	235.6	239.1
tibia (any part)	170.7	198.5	—	213.7	238.0	239.2
toe NEC*	195.5	198.89	232.7	229.8	238.8	239.89
tongue	141.9	198.89	230.0	210.1	235.1	239.0
anterior (two-thirds) NEC	141.4	198.89	230.0	210.1	235.1	239.0
dorsal surface	141.1	198.89	230.0	210.1	235.1	239.0
ventral surface	141.3	198.89	230.0	210.1	235.1	239.0
base (dorsal surface)	141.0	198.89	230.0	210.1	235.1	239.0
border (lateral)	141.2	198.89	230.0	210.1	235.1	239.0
contiguous sites	141.8	—	—	—	—	—
dorsal surface NEC	141.1	198.89	230.0	210.1	235.1	239.0
fixed part NEC	141.0	198.89	230.0	210.1	235.1	239.0
foreamen cecum	141.1	198.89	230.0	210.1	235.1	239.0
frenulum linguae	141.3	198.89	230.0	210.1	235.1	239.0
junctional zone	141.5	198.89	230.0	210.1	235.1	239.0
margin (lateral)	141.2	198.89	230.0	210.1	235.1	239.0
midline NEC	141.1	198.89	230.0	210.1	235.1	239.0
mobile part NEC	141.4	198.89	230.0	210.1	235.1	239.0
posterior (third)	141.0	198.89	230.0	210.1	235.1	239.0
root	141.0	198.89	230.0	210.1	235.1	239.0

☑ Additional Digit Required

	Malignant					
	Primary	Secondary	Ca in situ	Benign	Uncertain Behavior	Unspecified
Neoplasm, neoplastic—*continued*						
tongue—*continued*						
surface (dorsal)	141.1	198.89	230.0	210.1	235.1	239.0
base	141.0	198.89	230.0	210.1	235.1	239.0
ventral	141.3	198.89	230.0	210.1	235.1	239.0
tip	141.2	198.89	230.0	210.1	235.1	239.0
tonsil	141.6	198.89	230.0	210.1	235.1	239.0
tonsil	146.0	198.89	230.0	210.5	235.1	239.0
fauces, faucial	146.0	198.89	230.0	210.5	235.1	239.0
lingual	141.6	198.89	230.0	210.1	235.1	239.0
palatine	146.0	198.89	230.0	210.5	235.1	239.0
pharyngeal	147.1	198.89	230.0	210.7	235.1	239.0
pillar (anterior) (posterior)	146.2	198.89	230.0	210.6	235.1	239.0
tonsillar fossa	146.1	198.89	230.0	210.6	235.1	239.0
tooth socket NEC	143.9	198.89	230.0	210.4	235.1	239.0
trachea (cartilage) (mucosa)	162.0	197.3	231.1	212.2	235.7	239.1
contiguous sites with bronchus or lung	162.8	—	—	—	—	—
tracheobronchial	162.8	197.3	231.1	212.2	235.7	239.1
contiguous sites with lung	162.8	—	—	—	—	—
tragus	173.2	198.2	232.2	216.2	238.2	239.2
trunk NEC*	195.8	198.89	232.5	229.8	238.8	239.89
tubo-ovarian	183.8	198.82	233.32	221.8	236.3	239.5
tunica vaginalis	187.8	198.82	233.6	222.8	236.6	239.5
turbinate (bone)	170.0	198.5	—	213.0	238.0	239.2
nasal	160.0	197.3	231.8	212.0	235.9	239.1
tympanic cavity	160.1	197.3	231.8	212.0	235.9	239.1
ulna (any part)	170.4	198.5	—	213.4	238.0	239.2
umbilicus, umbilical	173.5	198.2	232.5	216.5	238.2	239.2
uncus, brain	191.2	198.3	—	225.0	237.5	239.6
unknown site or unspecified	199.1	199.1	234.9	229.9	238.9	239.9
urachus	188.7	198.1	233.7	223.3	236.7	239.4
ureter, ureteral	189.2	198.1	233.9	223.2	236.91	239.5
orifice (bladder)	188.6	198.1	233.7	223.3	236.7	239.4
ureter-bladder (junction)	188.6	198.1	233.7	223.3	236.7	239.4
urethra, urethral (gland)	189.3	198.1	233.9	223.81	236.99	239.5
orifice, internal	188.5	198.1	233.7	223.3	236.7	239.4
urethrovaginal (septum)	184.9	198.82	233.39	221.9	236.3	239.5
urinary organ or system NEC	189.9	198.1	233.9	223.9	236.99	239.5
bladder—*see* Neoplasm, bladder						
contiguous sites	189.8	—	—	—	—	—
specified sites NEC	189.8	198.1	233.9	223.89	236.99	239.5
utero-ovarian	183.8	198.82	233.39	221.8	236.3	239.5
ligament	183.3	198.82	—	221.0	236.3	239.5
uterosacral ligament	183.4	198.82	—	221.0	236.3	239.5
uterus, uteri, uterine	179	198.82	233.2	219.9	236.0	239.5
adnexa NEC	183.9	198.82	233.39	221.8	236.3	239.5
contiguous sites	183.8	—	—	—	—	—
body	182.0	198.82	233.2	219.1	236.0	239.5
contiguous sites	182.8	—	—	—	—	—
cervix	180.9	198.82	233.1	219.0	236.0	239.5
cornu	182.0	198.82	233.2	219.1	236.0	239.5
corpus	182.0	198.82	233.2	219.1	236.0	239.5
endocervix (canal) (gland)	180.0	198.82	233.1	219.0	236.0	239.5
endometrium	182.0	198.82	233.2	219.1	236.0	239.5
exocervix	180.1	198.82	233.1	219.0	236.0	239.5
external os	180.1	198.82	233.1	219.0	236.0	239.5
fundus	182.0	198.82	233.2	219.1	236.0	239.5

☑ Additional Digit Required
© 2009 Ingenix

Neoplasm, neoplastic—continued	Malignant			Benign	Uncertain Behavior	Unspecified
	Primary	Secondary	Ca in situ			
uterus, uteri, uterine—continued						
internal os	180.0	198.82	233.1	219.0	236.0	239.5
isthmus	182.1	198.82	233.2	219.1	236.0	239.5
ligament	183.4	198.82	—	221.0	236.3	239.5
broad	183.3	198.82	233.39	221.0	236.3	239.5
round	183.5	198.82	—	221.0	236.3	239.5
lower segment	182.1	198.82	233.2	219.1	236.0	239.5
myometrium	182.0	198.82	233.2	219.1	236.0	239.5
squamocolumnar junction	180.8	198.82	233.1	219.0	236.0	239.5
tube	183.2	198.82	233.39	221.0	236.3	239.5
utricle, prostatic	189.3	198.1	233.9	223.81	236.99	239.5
uveal tract	190.0	198.4	234.0	224.0	238.8	239.89
uvula	145.4	198.89	230.0	210.4	235.1	239.0
vagina, vaginal (fornix) (vault) (wall)	184.0	198.82	233.31	221.1	236.3	239.5
vaginovesical	184.9	198.82	233.31	221.9	236.3	239.5
septum	194.9	198.82	233.39	221.9	236.3	239.5
vallecula (epiglottis)	146.3	198.89	230.0	210.6	235.1	239.0
vascular—see Neoplasm, connective tissue						
vas deferens	187.6	198.82	233.6	222.8	236.6	239.5
Vater's ampulla	156.2	197.8	230.8	211.5	235.3	239.0
vein, venous—see Neoplasm, connective tissue						
vena cava (abdominal) (inferior)	171.5	198.89	—	215.5	238.1	239.2
superior	171.4	198.89	—	215.4	238.1	239.2
ventricle (cerebral) (floor) (fourth) (lateral) (third)	191.5	198.3	—	225.0	237.5	239.6
cardiac (left) (right)	164.1	198.89	—	212.7	238.8	239.89
ventricular band of larynx	161.1	197.3	231.0	212.1	235.6	239.1
ventriculus—see Neoplasm, stomach						
vermillion border—see Neoplasm, lip						
vermis, cerebellum	191.6	198.3	—	225.0	237.5	239.6
vertebra (column)	170.2	198.5	—	213.2	238.0	239.2
coccyx	170.6	198.5	—	213.6	238.0	239.2
sacrum	170.6	198.5	—	213.6	238.0	239.2
vesical—see Neoplasm, bladder						
vesicle, seminal	187.8	198.82	233.6	222.8	236.6	239.5
vesicocervical tissue	184.9	198.82	233.39	221.9	236.3	239.5
vesicorectal	195.3	198.89	234.8	229.8	238.8	239.89
vesicovaginal	184.9	198.82	233.39	221.9	236.3	239.5
septum	184.9	198.82	233.39	221.9	236.3	239.5
vessel (blood)—see Neoplasm, connective tissue						
vestibular gland, greater	184.1	198.82	233.32	221.2	236.3	239.5
vestibule						
mouth	145.1	198.89	230.0	210.4	235.1	239.0
nose	160.0	197.3	231.8	212.0	235.9	239.1
Virchow's gland	—	196.0	—	229.0	238.8	239.89
viscera NEC	195.8	198.89	234.8	229.8	238.8	239.89
vocal cords (true)	161.0	197.3	231.0	212.1	235.6	239.1
false	161.1	197.3	231.0	212.1	235.6	239.1
vomer	170.0	198.5	—	213.0	238.0	239.2
vulva	184.4	198.82	233.32	221.2	236.3	239.5
vulvovaginal gland	184.4	198.82	233.32	221.2	236.3	239.5
Waldeyer's ring	149.1	198.89	230.0	210.9	235.1	239.0
Wharton's duct	142.1	198.89	230.0	210.2	235.0	239.0
white matter (central) (cerebral)	191.0	198.3	—	225.0	237.5	239.6
windpipe	162.0	197.3	231.1	212.2	235.7	239.1
Wirsung's duct	157.3	197.8	230.9	211.6	235.5	239.0

	Malignant			Benign	Uncertain Behavior	Unspecified
	Primary	Secondary	Ca in situ			

Neoplasm, neoplastic—*continued*

wolffian (body) (duct)						
female	184.8	198.82	233.39	221.8	236.3	239.5
male	187.8	198.82	233.6	222.8	236.6	239.5
womb—*see* Neoplasm, uterus						
wrist NEC*	195.4	198.89	232.6	229.8	238.8	239.89
xiphoid process	170.3	198.5	—	213.3	238.0	239.2
Zuckerkandl's organ	194.6	198.89	—	227.6	237.3	239.7

Nervous (see also condition) 799.21
heart 306.2
Neuralgia, neuralgic (acute) (*see also* Neuritis) 729.2
accessory (nerve) 352.4
ankle 355.8
anterior crural 355.8
arm 723.4
axilia 353.0
brachial 723.4
ciliary 346.2☑

Note—Use the following fifth-digit subclassification with category 346:
0   without mention of intractable migraine without mention of status migrainosus
1   with intractable migraine, so stated, without mention of status migrainosus
2   without mention of intractable migraine with status migrainosus
3   with intractable migraine, so stated, with status migrainosus

cranial nerve—*see also* Disorder, nerve, cranial
   fifth or trigeminal (*see also* Neuralgia, trigeminal) 350.1
ear 388.71
   middle 352.1
facial 351.8
finger 354.9
flank 355.8
foot 355.8
forearm 354.9
Fothergill's (*see also* Neuralgia, trigeminal) 350.1
glossopharyngeal (nerve) 352.1
groin 355.8
hand 354.9
heel 355.8
Horton's 346.2☑
hypoglossal (nerve) 352.5
iliac region 355.8
infraorbital (*see also* Neuralgia, trigeminal) 350.1
inguinal 355.8
intercostal (nerve) 353.8
jaw 352.1
knee 355.8
loin 355.8
maxilla 352.1
median thenar 354.1
metatarsal 355.6
middle ear 352.1
migrainous 346.2☑

Neuralgia, neuralgic—*continued*

Note—Use the following fifth-digit subclassification with category 346:
0   without mention of intractable migraine without mention of status migrainosus
1   with intractable migraine, so stated, without mention of status migrainosus
2   without mention of intractable migraine with status migrainosus
3   with intractable migraine, so stated, with status migrainosus

Morton's 355.6
nose 352.0
occipital 723.8
perineum 355.8
pleura 511.0
pubic region 355.8
radial (nerve) 723.4
sacroiliac joint 724.3
sciatic (nerve) 724.3
shoulder 354.9
Sluder's 337.09
sphenopalatine (ganglion) 337.09
subscapular (nerve) 723.4
suprascapular (nerve) 723.4
thenar (median) 354.1
thigh 355.8
tongue 352.5
trifacial (nerve) (*see also* Neuralgia, trigeminal) 350.1
trigeminal (nerve) 350.1
ulnar (nerve) 723.4
vagus (nerve) 352.3
wrist 354.9
writers' 300.89
   organic 333.84
Neurasthenia 300.5
cardiac 306.2
heart 306.2
postfebrile 780.79
postviral 780.79
Neurilemmoma (M9560/0)—*see also* Neoplasm, connective tissue, benign
acoustic (nerve) 225.1
malignant (M9560/3)—*see also* Neoplasm, con-nective tissue, malignant
   acoustic (nerve) 192.0
Neuritis (*see also* Neuralgia) 729.2
accessory (nerve) 352.4
alcoholic 357.5
   with psychosis 291.1
amyloid, any site 277.39 *[357.4]*
anterior crural 355.8

Neuritis—*continued*
arm 723.4
ascending 355.2
brachial (nerve) NEC 723.4
   due to displacement, inter-vertebral disc 722.0
cervical 723.4
chest (wall) 353.8
costal region 353.8
cranial nerve—*see also* Disorder, nerve, cranial
   eleventh or accessory 352.4
   fifth or trigeminal (*see also* Neuralgia, trigeminal) 350.1
   first or olfactory 352.0
   ninth or glossopharyngeal 352.1
   seventh or facial 351.8
   tenth or vagus 352.3
   twelfth or hypoglossal 352.5
Déjérine-Sottas 356.0
diabetic 250.6☑ *[357.2]*
   due to secondary diabetes 249.6☑ *[357.2]*

Note—Use the following fifth-digit subclassification with category 250:
0   type II [non-insulin dependent type] [NIDDM type] [adult-onset type] or unspecified type, not stated as uncontrolled
1   type I [insulin dependent type] [IDDM type] [juvenile type], not stated as uncontrolled
2   type II [non-insulin dependent type] [NIDDM type] [adult-onset type] or unspecified type, uncontrolled
3   type I [insulin dependent type] [IDDM] [juvenile type], uncontrolled

diphtheritic 032.89 *[357.4]*
due to
   beriberi 265.0 *[357.4]*
   displacement, prolapse, protrusion, or rupture of intervertebral disc 722.2
      cervical 722.0
      lumbar, lumbosacral 722.10
      thoracic, thoracolumbar 722.11
   herniation, nucleus pulposus 722.2
      cervical 722.0
      lumbar, lumbosacral 722.10
      thoracic, thoracolumbar 722.11

Neuritis—*continued*
endemic 265.0 *[357.4]*
facial (nerve) 351.8
geniculate ganglion 351.1
glossopharyngeal (nerve) 352.1
gouty 274.89 *[357.4]*
hypoglossal (nerve) 352.5
ilioinguinal (nerve) 355.8
infectious (multiple) 357.0
intercostal (nerve) 353.8
interstitial hypertrophic progressive NEC 356.9
leg 355.8
lumbosacral NEC 724.4
median (nerve) 354.1
   thenar 354.1
multiple (acute) (infective) 356.9
   endemic 265.0 *[357.4]*
multiplex endemica 265.0 *[357.4]*
nerve root (*see also* Radiculitis) 729.2
olfactory (nerve) 352.0
optic (nerve) 377.30
   in myelitis 341.0
pelvic 355.8
pneumogastric (nerve) 352.3
progressive hypertrophic interstitial NEC 356.9
radial (nerve) 723.4
rheumatic (chronic) 729.2
sacral region 355.8
sciatic (nerve) 724.3
   due to displacement of intervertebral disc 722.10
spinal (nerve) 355.9
   root (*see also* Radiculitis) 729.2
subscapular (nerve) 723.4
suprascapular (nerve) 723.4
thenar (median) 354.1
thoracic NEC 724.4
toxic NEC 357.7
ulnar (nerve) 723.4
vagus (nerve) 352.3
Neurocirculatory asthenia 306.2
Neuroma (M9570/0)—*see also* Neoplasm, connective tissue, benign
acoustic (nerve) (M9560/0) 225.1
auditory nerve 225.1
digital 355.6
   toe 355.6
interdigital (toe) 355.6
intermetatarsal 355.6
Morton's 355.6
multiple 237.70
   type 1 237.71
   type 2 237.72
nonneoplastic 355.9
   arm NEC 354.9

☑ Additional Digit Required
© 2009 Ingenix

Neuroma —*continued*
  nonneoplastic—*continued*
    leg NEC 355.8
      lower extremity NEC 355.8
      upper extremity NEC 354.9
    optic (nerve) 225.1
    plantar 355.6
    surgical (nonneoplastic) 355.9
      arm NEC 354.9
      leg NEC 355.8
      lower extremity NEC 355.8
      upper extremity NEC 354.9
Neuromyalgia 729.1
Neuromyelitis 341.8
  ascending 357.0
  optica 341.0
Neuromyopathy NEC 358.9
Neuromyositis 729.1
Neuronitis 357.0
  ascending (acute) 355.2
Neuropathy, neuropathic (*see also* Disorder, nerve) 355.9
  alcoholic 357.5
    with psychosis 291.1
  arm NEC 354.9
  axillary nerve 353.0
  brachial plexus 353.0
  cervical plexus 353.2
  congenital sensory 356.2
  Déjérine-Sottas 356.0
  diabetic 250.6☑ [357.2]
    due to secondary diabetes 249.6☑ [357.2]

Note—Use the following fifth-digit subclassification with category 250:
  0 type II [non-insulin dependent type] [NIDDM type] [adult-onset type] or unspecified type, not stated as uncontrolled
  1 type I [insulin dependent type] [IDDM type] [juvenile type], not stated as uncontrolled
  2 type II [non-insulin dependent type] [NIDDM type] [adult-onset type] or unspecified type, uncontrolled
  3 type I [insulin dependent type] [IDDM] [juvenile type], uncontrolled

  entrapment 355.9
    iliohypogastric nerve 355.79
    ilioinguinal nerve 355.79
    lateral cutaneous nerve of thigh 355.1
    median nerve 354.0
    obturator nerve 355.79
    peroneal nerve 355.3
    posterior tibial nerve 355.5
    saphenous nerve 355.79
    ulnar nerve 354.2
  facial nerve 351.9
  hereditary 356.9
    peripheral 356.0
    sensory (radicular) 356.2
  hypertrophic
    Charcôt-Marie-Tooth 356.1
    Déjérine-Sottas 356.0
    interstitial 356.9
    Refsum 356.3
  intercostal nerve 354.8
  Jamaican (ginger) 357.7
  leg NEC 355.8
  lower extremity NEC 355.8
  lumbar plexus 353.1

Neuropathy, neuropathic—*continued*
  median nerve 354.1
  multiple (acute) (chronic) (*see also* Polyneuropathy) 356.9
  peripheral (nerve) (*see also* Polyneuropathy) 356.9
    arm NEC 354.9
    autonomic 337.9
      amyloid 277.39 [337.1]
      idiopathic 337.00
      in
        amyloidosis 277.39 [337.1]
        diabetes (mellitus) 250.6☑ [337.1]
          due to secondary diabetes 249.64 [337.1]

Note—Use the following fifth-digit subclassification with category 250:
  0 type II [non-insulin dependent type] [NIDDM type] [adult-onset type] or unspecified type, not stated as uncontrolled
  1 type I [insulin dependent type] [IDDM type] [juvenile type], not stated as uncontrolled
  2 type II [non-insulin dependent type] [NIDDM type] [adult-onset type] or unspecified type, uncontrolled
  3 type I [insulin dependent type] [IDDM] [juvenile type], uncontrolled

      diseases classified elsewhere 337.1
      gout 274.89 [337.1]
      hyperthyroidism 242.9☑ [337.1]
    due to
      antitetanus scrum 357.6
      arsenic 357.7
      drugs 357.6
      lead 357.7
      organophosphate compounds 357.7
      toxic agent NEC 357.7
    hereditary 356.0
    idiopathic 356.9
      progresive 356.4
      specified type NEC 356.8
    leg NEC 355.8
    lower extremity NEC 355.8
    upper extremity NEC 354.9
  plantar nerves 355.6
  progressive hypertrophic interstitial 356.9
  radicular NEC 729.2
    brachial 723.4
    cervical NEC 723.4
    hereditary sensory 356.2
    lumbar 724.4
    lumbosacral 724.4
    thoracic NEC 724.4
  sacral plexus 353.1
  sciatic 355.0
  spinal nerve NEC 355.9
    root (*see also* Radiculitis) 729.2
  toxic 357.7
  trigeminal sensory 350.8
  ulnar nerve 354.2
  upper extremity NEC 354.9
  uremic 585 [357.4]

Neuropathy, neuropathic—*continued*
  vitamin B12 266.2 [357.4]
    with anemia (pernicious) 281.0 [357.4]
      due to dietary deficiency 281.1 [357.4]
Neurophthisis—(*see also* Disorder, nerve peripheral) 356.9
  diabetic 250.6 [357.2]
    due to secondary diabetes 249.6☑ [357.2]
Nonunion
  fracture 733.82
  symphysis pubis, congenital 755.69
  top sacrum, congenital 756.19
Nosomania 298.9
Nostalgia 309.89
Notching nose, congenital (tip) 748.1
Nothnagel's
  vasomotor acroparesthesia 443.89
Numbness 782.0
Nuns' knee 727.2
Nursemaid's
  elbow 832.2
Nycturia 788.43

O

Obesity (constitutional) (exogenous) (familial) (nutritional) (simple) 278.00
  due to hyperalimentation 278.00
  severe 278.01
Obliteration
  lymphatic vessel 457.1
Obstruction, obstructed, obstructive
  airway NEC 519.8
    chronic 496
      with
        allergic alveolitis NEC 495.5
        bronchiectasis 494.0
          with acute exacer-bation 494.1
        bronchitis (chronic) (*see also* Bronchitis, with, obstruc-tion) 491.20
        emphysema NEC 492.8
      due to
        foreign body 934.9
        inhalation of fumes or vapors 506.9
        laryngospasm 478.75
      allergic alveolitis NEC 495.9
      bronchiectasis 494.0
        with acute exacer-bation 494.1
      bronchitis (chronic) (*see also* Bronchitis, with, obstruction) 491.20
      emphysema NEC 492.8
  aortic (heart) (valve) (*see also* Stenosis, aortic) 424.1
  aqueduct of Sylvius 331.4
  coronary (artery) (heart)—*see also* Arteriosclerosis, coronary
    acute (*see also* Infarct, myocardium) 410.9☑

Obstruction, obstructed, obstructive—*continued*

Note—Use the following fifth-digit subclassification with category 410:
  0 episode unspecified
  1 initial episode
  2 subsequent episode without recurrence

      without myocardial infarction 411.81
  glottis 478.79
  intestine (mechanical) (neurogenic) (paroxysmal) (postinfectional) (reflex) 560.9
    newborn
      due to
        meconium (plug) 777.1
          in mucoviscidosis 277.01
  larynx 478.79
    congenital 748.3
  lung 518.89
    airway, chronic 496
    chronic NEC 496
    disease, chronic 496
    emphysematous 492.8
    with
      bronchitis (chronic) 491.20
      emphysema NEC 492.8
  lymphatic 457.1
  meconium
    fetus or newborn 777.1
      in mucoviscidosis 277.01
  pulmonary
    valve (heart) (*see also* Endocarditis, pulmonary) 424.3
  respiratory 519.8
    chronic 496
  thoracic duct 457.1
  vascular graft or shunt 996.1
Occlusion
  aqueduct of Sylvius 331.4
  arteries of extremities, lower 444.22
    upper 444.21
      without thrombus or embolus (*see also* Arteriosclerosis, extremities) 440.20
  artery NEC (*see also* Embolism, artery) 444.9
    chronic total
      coronary 414.2
      extremity(ies) 440.4
    complete
      coronary 414.2
      extremity(ies) 440.4
    coronary (thrombotic) (*see also* Infarct, myocardium) 410.9☑

Note—Use the following fifth-digit subclassification with category 410:
  0 episode unspecified
  1 initial episode
  2 subsequent episode without recurrence

      acute 410.9☑
        without myocardial infarction 411.81
      healed or old 412

Occlusion—continued
choanal 748.0
coronary (artery) (thrombotic) (see also Infarct, myocardium) 410.9☑
acute 410.9☑
without myocardial infarction 411.81
complete 414.2
healed or old 412
total 414.2
extremity(ies)
chronic total 440.4
complete 440.4
total 440.4
lung 518.89
lymph or lymphatic channel 457.1
nose 478.1
congenital 748.0
peripheral arteries (lower extremity) 444.22
upper extremity 444.21
without thrombus or embolus (see also Arteriosclerosis, extremities 440.20
without thrombus or embolus (see also Arteriosclerosis, extremities) 440.20
stent
coronary 996.72
thoracic duct 457.1
ventricle (brain) NEC 331.4
Occupational
therapy V57.21
Ocular muscle—see also condition
myopathy 359.1
Oculoauriculovertebral dysplasia 756.0
Oculogyric
crisis or disturbance 378.87
psychogenic 306.7
Odynophagia 787.20
Old age 797
dementia (of) 290.0
Omphalitis (congenital) (newborn) 771.4
not of newborn 686.9
Onychauxis 703.8
Onychia (with lymphangitis) 681.9
finger 681.02
toe 681.11
Onychitis (with lymphangitis) 681.9
finger 681.02
toe 681.11
Onychocryptosis 703.0
Onychodystrophy 703.8
Onychogryphosis 703.8
Onychogryposis 703.8
Onycholysis 703.8
Onychomadesis 703.8
Onychomalacia 703.8
Onychoptosis 703.8
Onychorrhexis 703.8
Onychoschizia 703.8
Onychotrophia (see also Atrophy, nail) 703.8
Onyxis (finger) (toe) 703.0
Onyxitis (with lymphangitis) 681.9
finger 681.02
toe 681.11
Ophthalmia (see also Conjunctivitis) 372.30
migraine 346.8☑

Ophthalmia—continued

Note—Use the following fifth-digit subclassification with category 346:
0 without mention of intractable migraine
1 without intractable migraine, so stated

Ophthalmoneuromyelitis 341.0
Ophthalmoplegia (see also Strabismus) 378.9
ataxia-areflexia syndrome 357.0
diabetic 250.5 [378.86]
due to secondary diabetes 249.5☑ [378.86]
migraine 346.2☑
supranuclear, progressive 333.0
Opisthotonos, opisthotonus 781.0
Oppenheim's disease 358.8
Orthopnea 786.02
Orthoptic training V57.4
Osgood-Schlatter
disease 732.4
osteochondrosis 732.4
Ossification
cartilage (senile) 733.99
diaphragm 728.10
fascia 728.10
fontanel
defective or delayed 756.0
premature 756.0
larynx 478.79
ligament
posterior longitudinal 724.8
cervical 723.7
meninges (cerebral) 349.2
spinal 336.8
multiple, eccentric centers 733.99
muscle 728.10
heterotopic, postoperative 728.13
periarticular 728.89
tendon 727.82
Osteitis (see also Osteomyelitis) 730.2☑

Note—Use the following fifth-digit subclassification with category 730:
0 site unspecified
1 shoulder region
2 upper arm
3 forearm
4 hand
5 pelvic region and thigh
6 lower leg
7 ankle and foot
8 other specified sites
9 multiple sites

condensans (ilii) 733.5
deformans (Paget's) 731.0
due to or associated with malignant neoplasm (see also Neoplasm, bone, malignant) 170.9 [731.1]
pubis 733.5
tuberculosa
cystica (of Jüngling) 135
multiplex cystoides 135
Osteoarthritica spondylitis (spine) (see also Spondylosis) 721.90

Osteoarthritis (see also Osteoarthrosis) 715.9☑

Note—Use the following fifth-digit subclassification with categories 711-712, 715-716, 718, 719.0-719.6, 719.8, 719.9:
0 site unspecified
1 shoulder region
2 upper arm
3 forearm
4 hand
5 pelvic region and thigh
6 lower leg
7 ankle and foot
8 other specified sites
9 multiple sites

interspinalis (see also Spondylosis) 721.90
spine, spinal NEC (see also Spondylosis) 721.90
Osteoarthrosis (degenerative) (hypertrophic) (rheumatoid) 715.9☑

Note—Use the following fifth-digit subclassification with categories 711-712, 715-716, 718, 719.0-719.6, 719.8, 719.9:
0 site unspecified
1 shoulder region
2 upper arm
3 forearm
4 hand
5 pelvic region and thigh
6 lower leg
7 ankle and foot
8 other specified sites
9 multiple sites

generalized 715.09
multiple sites, not specified as generalized 715.89
polyarticular 715.09
spine (see also Spondylosis) 721.90
Osteochondromatosis (M9210/1) 238.0
synovial 727.82
Osteochondrosis 732.9
Blount's 732.4
deformans juvenilis (coxae) (hip) 732.1
tibia 732.4
juvenile, juvenilis 732.6
lower extremity, except foot 732.4
patella 732.4
primary patellar center (of Köhler) 732.4
tibia (epiphysis) (tuberosity) 732.4
Köhler's (disease) (navicular, ankle) 732.5
patellar 732.4
lower extremity (juvenile) 732.4
Osgood-Schlatter 732.4
patella (juvenile) 732.4
patellar center
primary (of Köhler) 732.4
secondary (of Sinding-Larsen) 732.4
Sinding-Larsen (secondary patellar center) 732.4
tibia (proximal) (tubercle) 732.4
Osteocopic pain 733.90

Osteodynia 733.90
Osteomyelitis (general) (infective) (localized) (neonatal) (purulent) (pyogenic) (septic) (staphylococcal) (streptococcal) (suppurative) (with periostitis) 730.2☑

Note—Use the following fifth-digit subclassification with category 730:
0 site unspecified
1 shoulder region
2 upper arm
3 forearm
4 hand
5 pelvic region and thigh
6 lower leg
7 ankle and foot
8 other specified sites
9 multiple sites

due to or associated with diabetes mellitus 250.8☑ [731.8]
due to secondary diabetes 249.8 [731.8]

Note—Use the following fifth-digit subclassification with category 250:
0 type II [non-insulin dependent type] [NIDDM type] [adult-onset type] or unspecified type, not stated as uncontrolled
1 type I [insulin dependent type] [IDDM type] [juvenile type], not stated as uncontrolled
2 type II [non-insulin dependent type] [NIDDM type] [adult-onset type] or unspecified type, uncontrolled
3 type I [insulin dependent type] [IDDM] [juvenile type], uncontrolled

Osteonecrosis 733.40
Osteopenia 733.90
borderline 733.90
Osteoporosis (generalized) 733.00
disuse 733.03
drug-induced 733.09
idiopathic 733.02
postmenopausal 733.01
posttraumatic 733.7
senile 733.01
specified type NEC 733.09
Otto's disease or pelvis 715.35
Outlet—see also condition
syndrome (thoracic) 353.0
Overbreathing (see also Hyperventilation) 786.01
Overeating 783.6
nonorganic origin 307.51
Overgrowth, bone NEC 733.99
Overinhibited child 313.0
Overlapping toe (acquired) 735.8
congenital (fifth toe) 755.66
Overriding
finger (acquired) 736.29
congenital 755.59
toe (acquired) 735.8
congenital 755.66
Overstrained 780.79
Overweight (see also Obesity) 278.02
Overwork 780.79
Oxycephaly, oxycephalic 756.0

ICD-9-CM Index

☑ Additional Digit Required

© 2009 Ingenix

P

P.R.I.N.D. 436
Pachyderma, pachydermia 701.8
  laryngitis 478.79
  larynx (verrucosa) 478.79
Pachyonychia (congenital) 757.5
  acquired 703.8
Pain(s)
  acute 338.19
    due to trauma 338.11
    postoperative 338.18
      post-thoracotomy 338.12
  anginoid (see also Pain, precordial) 786.51
  arch 729.5
  arm 729.5
  axillary 729.5
  back (postural) 724.5
    low 724.2
    psychogenic 307.89
  bone 733.90
  breast 611.71
    psychogenic 307.89
  cancer associated 338.36
  cartilage NEC 733.90
  cervicobrachial 723.3
  chest (central) 786.50
    atypical 786.59
    midsternal 786.51
    musculoskeletal 786.59
    noncardiac 786.59
    substernal 786.51
    wall (anterior) 786.52
  chronic 338.29
    associated with significant psychosocial dysfunction 338.4
    due to trauma 338.21
    postoperative 338.28
      post-thoracotomy 338.22
    syndrome 338.4
  coccyx 724.79
  costochondral 786.52
  diaphragm 786.52
  extremity (lower) (upper) 729.5
  face, facial 784.0
    atypical 350.2
    nerve 351.8
  female genital organ NEC 625.9
    psychogenic 307.89
  finger 729.5
  foot 729.5
  generalized 780.96
  genital organ
    psychogenic 307.89
  growing 781.99
  hand 729.5
  heart (see also Pain, precordial) 786.51
  infraorbital (see also Neuralgia, trigeminal) 350.1
  joint 719.40
    ankle 719.47
    elbow 719.42
    foot 719.47
    hand 719.44
    hip 719.45
    knee 719.46
    multiple sites 719.49
    pelvic region 719.45
    psychogenic 307.89
    shoulder (region) 719.41
    specified site NEC 719.48
    wrist 719.43
  leg 729.5

Pain(s)—continued
  limb 729.5
  low back 724.2
  lumbar region 724.2
  metacarpophalangeal (joint) 719.44
  metatarsophalangeal (joint) 719.47
  muscle 729.1
    intercostal 786.59
  musculoskeletal (see also Pain, by site) 729.1
  neck NEC 723.1
    psychogenic 307.89
  nerve NEC 729.2
  neuromuscular 729.1
  osteocopic 733.90
  ovary 625.9
    psychogenic 307.89
  over heart (see also Pain, precordial) 786.51
  pericardial (see also Pain, precordial) 786.51
  pleura, pleural, pleuritic 786.52
  postoperative 338.18
    acute 338.18
    chronic 228.22
  precordial (region) 786.51
    psychogenic 307.89
  psychogenic 307.80
    cardiovascular system 307.89
    gastrointestinal system 307.89
    genitourinary system 307.89
    heart 307.89
    musculoskeletal system 307.89
    respiratory system 307.89
  radicular (spinal) (see also Radiculitis) 729.2
  respiration 786.52
  retrosternal 786.51
  rheumatic NEC 729.0
    muscular 729.1
  rib 786.50
  root (spinal) (see also Radiculitis) 729.2
  sacroiliac 724.6
  sciatic 724.3
  scrotum 608.9
    psychogenic 307.89
  skin 782.0
  spinal root (see also Radiculitis) 729.2
  stomach 536.8
    psychogenic 307.89
  substernal 786.51
  testis 608.9
    psychogenic 307.89
  thoracic spine 724.1
    with radicular and visceral pain 724.4
  tibia 733.90
  toe 729.5
  trigeminal (see also Neuralgia, trigeminal) 350.1
  tumor associated 338.3
  uterus 625.9
    psychogenic 307.89
  vertebrogenic (syndrome) 724.5
  xiphoid 733.90
Painful—see also Pain
  arc syndrome 726.19
  respiration 786.52
  scar NEC 709.2

Palindromic arthritis (see also Rheumatism, palindromic) 719.3☑

Note—Use the following fifth-digit subclassification with categories 711-712, 715-716, 718, 719.0-719.6, 719.8, 719.9:
  0 site unspecified
  1 shoulder region
  2 upper arm
  3 forearm
  4 hand
  5 pelvic region and thigh
  6 lower leg
  7 ankle and foot
  8 other specified sites
  9 multiple sites

Palpitation (heart) 785.1
  psychogenic 306.2
Palsy (see also Paralysis) 344.9
  atrophic diffuse 335.20
  Bell's 351.0
  brachial plexus 353.0
  brain—see also Palsy, cerebral
    noncongenital or noninfantile 344.89
  bulbar (chronic) (progressive) 335.22
    pseudo NEC 335.23
  cerebral (congenital) (infantile) (spastic) 343.9
    athetoid 333.71
    diplegic 343.0
    hemiplegic 343.1
    monoplegic 343.3
    paraplegic 343.0
    quadriplegic 343.2
    tetraplegic 343.2
  cranial nerve—see also Disorder, nerve, cranial
    multiple 352.6
  creeping 335.21
  facial 351.0
  glossopharyngeal 352.2
  median nerve (tardy) 354.0
  peroneal nerve (acute) (tardy) 355.3
  progressive supranuclear 333.0
  pseudobulbar NEC 335.23
  radial nerve (acute) 354.3
  seventh nerve 351.0
  shaking (see also Parkinsonism) 332.0
  spastic (cerebral) (spinal) 343.9
    hemiplegic 343.1
  supranuclear NEC 356.8
    progressive 333.0
  ulnar nerve (tardy) 354.2
  wasting 335.21
Panaris (with lymphangitis) 681.9
  finger 681.02
  toe 681.11
Panaritium (with lymphangitis) 681.9
  finger 681.02
  toe 681.11
Panarteritis (nodosa) 446.0
Pancake heart 793.2
  with cor pulmonale (chronic) 416.9
Pancoast's syndrome or tumor (carcinoma, pulmonary apex) (M8010/3) 162.3

Pancoast-Tobias syndrome (M8010/3) (carcinoma, pulmonary apex) 162.3
Panic (attack) (state) 300.01
  reaction to exceptional stress (transient) 308.0
Panneuritis endemica 265.0 [357.4]
Panniculitis 729.30
  back 724.8
  neck 723.6
  sacral 724.8
Papilloma (M8050/0)—see also Neoplasm, by site, benign
  choroid plexus (M9390/0) 225.0
Parageusia 781.1
  psychogenic 306.7
Paralysis, paralytic (complete) (incomplete) 344.9
  abdomen and back muscles 355.9
  abdominal muscles 355.9
  abductor 355.9
    lower extremity 355.8
    upper extremity 354.9
  accessory nerve 352.4
  accommodation 367.51
    hysterical 300.11
  agitans 332.0
    arteriosclerotic 332.0
  alternating 344.89
    oculomotor 344.89
  amyotrophic 335.20
  ankle 355.8
  anterior serratus 355.9
  apoplectic (current episode) (see also Disease, cerebrovascular, acute) 436
  arm 344.40
    affecting
      dominant side 344.41
      nondominant side 344.42
  arm 344.40
    both 344.2
    hysterical 300.11
    psychogenic 306.0
      transient 781.4
      traumatic NEC (see also Injury, nerve, upper limb) 955.9
  ascending (spinal), acute 357.0
  associated, nuclear 344.89
  asthenic bulbar 358.00
  ataxic NEC 334.9
  athetoid 333.71
  atrophic 356.9
    muscle NEC 355.9
    progressive 335.21
  attack (see also Disease, cerebrovascular, acute) 436
  axillary 353.0
  Babinski-Nageotte's 344.89
  Bell's 351.0
  Benedikt's 344.89
  bladder (sphincter) 596.53
    neurogenic 596.54
      with cauda equina syndrome 344.61
    sensory 344.61
      with cauda equina 344.61
    spastic 344.61
      with cauda equina 344.61
  brachial plexus 353.0
  brain
    diplegia 344.2
    paraplegia 344.1

Paralysis, paralytic—*continued*
brain—*continued*
    triplegia 344.89
  Brown-Séquard's 344.89
  bulbar (chronic) (progessive) 335.22
    pseudo 335.23
    supranuclear 344.89
  bulbospinal 358.00
  Céstan-Chenais 344.89
  cardiac (*see also* Failure, heart) 428.9
  cerebrocerebellar 437.8
    diplegic infantile 343.0
  cervical
    plexus 353.2
    sympathetic NEC 337.09
  Charcöt-Marie-Tooth type 356.1
  Clark's 343.9
  compression
    arm NEC 354.9
    leg NEC 355.8
    lower extremity NEC 355.8
    upper extremity NEC 354.9
  cordis (*see also* Failure, heart) 428.9
  cranial or cerebral nerve (*see also* Disorder, nerve, cranial) 352.9
  creeping 335.21
  crossed leg 344.89
  crutch 953.4
  deglutition 784.99
    hysterical 300.11
  descending (spinal) NEC 335.9
  diaphragm (flaccid) 519.4
    due to accidental section of phrenic nerve during procedure 998.2
  Duchenne's 335.22
  extremity
    spastic (hereditary) 343.3
      noncongenital or noninfantile 344.1
    transient (cause unknown) 781.4
  facial (nerve) 351.0
    following operation NEC 998.2
  familial 359.3
    periodic 359.3
    spastic 334.1
  finger NEC 354.9
  foot NEC 355.8
  gait 781.2
  gastric nerve 352.3
  glossopharyngeal (nerve) 352.2
  glottis (*see also* Paralysis, vocal cord) 478.30
  gluteal 353.4
  Gubler (-Millard) 344.89
  hand 354.9
    hysterical 300.11
    psychogenic 306.0
  heart (*see also* Failure, heart) 428.9
  hyperkalemic periodic (familial) 359.3
  hypoglossal (nerve) 352.5
  hypokalemic periodic 359.3
  hysterical 300.11
  inferior nuclear 344.9
  interosseous 355.9
  ischemic, Volkmann's (complicating trauma) 958.6
  jake 357.7
  Jamaica ginger (jake) 357.7

Paralysis, paralytic—*continued*
labioglossal (laryngeal) (pharyngeal) 335.22
  Landry's 357.0
  laryngeal nerve (recurrent) (superior) (*see also* Paralysis, vocal cord) 478.30
  larynx (*see also* Paralysis, vocal cord) 478.30
  lateral 335.24
  leg 344.30
    affecting
      dominant side 344.31
      nondominant side 344.32
    both (*see also* Paraplegia) 344.1
    crossed 344.89
    hysterical 300.11
    psychogenic 306.0
    transient or transitory 781.4
      traumatic NEC (*see also* Injury, nerve, lower limb) 956.9
  limb NEC 344.5
  local 355.9
  lower limb—*see also* Paralysis, leg
    both (*see also* Paraplegia) 344.1
  lung 518.89
  median nerve 354.1
  medullary (tegmental) 344.89
  mesencephalic NEC 344.89
    tegmental 344.89
  middle alternating 344.89
  Millard-Gubler-Foville 344.89
  motor NEC 344.9
  muscle (flaccid) 359.9
    due to nerve lesion NEC 355.9
    ischemic (complicating trauma) (Volkmann's) 958.6
    pseudohypertrophic 359.1
  muscular (atrophic) 359.9
    progressive 335.21
  musculocutaneous nerve 354.9
  musculospiral 354.9
  nerve—*see also* Disorder, nerve
    accessory 352.4
    cranial or cerebral (*see also* Disorder, nerve, cranial) 352.9
    facial 351.0
    laryngeal (*see also* Paralysis, vocal cord) 478.30
    phrenic 354.8
    radial 354.3
    seventh or facial 351.0
      due to
        operation NEC 997.09
    traumatic NEC (*see also* Injury, nerve, by site) 957.9
    trigeminal 350.9
    ulnar 354.2
  normokalemic periodic 359.3
  oculofacial, congenital 352.6
  oculomotor (nerve) (partial) 378.51
    alternating 344.89
  olfactory nerve 352.0
  palatopharyngolaryngeal 352.6
  paratrigeminal 350.9
  periodic (familial) (hyperkalemic) (hypokalemic) (normokalemic) (secondary) 359.3
  peripheral
    nerve NEC 355.9
  peroneal (nerve) 355.3

Paralysis, paralytic—*continued*
phrenic nerve 354.8
  plantar nerves 355.6
  pneumogastric nerve 352.3
  popliteal nerve 355.3
  pressure (*see also* Neuropathy, entrapment) 355.9
  progressive 335.21
    atrophic 335.21
    bulbar 335.22
    multiple 335.20
  pseudobulbar 335.23
  pseudohypertrophic 359.1
    muscle 359.1
  psychogenic 306.0
  quadriceps 355.8
  radial nerve 354.3
  recurrent
    laryngeal nerve (*see also* Paralysis, vocal cord) 478.30
  respiratory (muscle) (system) (tract) 786.09
    center NEC 344.89
  Saturday night 354.3
  sciatic nerve 355.0
  seizure (cerebral) (current episode) (*see also* Disease, cerebrovascular, acute) 436
  senile NEC 344.9
  serratus magnus 355.9
  shaking (*see also* Parkinsonism) 332.0
  shock (*see also* Disease, cerebrovascular, acute) 436
  shoulder 354.9
  spastic 344.9
    familial 334.1
    hereditary 334.1
    infantile 343.9
    noncongenital or noninfantile, cerebral 344.9
  spinal (cord) NEC 344.1
    accessory nerve 352.4
    ascending acute 357.0
    congenital NEC 343.9
    hereditary 336.8
    late effect NEC 344.89
    nerve 355.9
    progressive 335.10
    spastic NEC 343.9
  sternomastoid 352.4
  stroke (current episode) (*see also* Disease, cerebrovascular, acute) 436
  subscapularis 354.8
  superior nuclear NEC 334.9
  supranuclear 356.8
  sympathetic
    cervical NEC 337.09
    nerve NEC (*see also* Neuropathy, peripheral, autonomic) 337.9
  syndrome 344.9
    specified NEC 344.89
  thigh 355.8
  thumb NEC 354.9
  Todd's (postepileptic transitory paralysis) 344.89
  toe 355.6
  transient
    arm or leg NEC 781.4
    traumatic NEC (*see also* Injury, nerve, by site) 957.9
  trapezius 352.4

Paralysis, paralytic—*continued*
traumatic, transient NEC (*see also* Injury, nerve, by site) 957.9
  trembling (*see also* Parkinsonism) 332.0
  triceps brachii 354.9
  trigeminal nerve 350.9
  ulnar nerve 354.2
  upper limb—*see also* Paralysis, arm
    both (*see also* Diplegia) 344.2
  uveoparotitic 135
  uvula 528.9
    hysterical 300.11
  vagus nerve 352.3
  vasomotor NEC 337.9
  vocal cord 478.30
    bilateral (partial) 478.33
      complete 478.34
    complete (bilateral) 478.34
    unilateral (partial) 478.31
      complete 478.32
  Volkmann's (complicating trauma) 958.6
  wasting 335.21
  Weber's 344.89
  wrist NEC 354.9
Paramyoclonus multiplex 333.29
Paramyotonia 359.29
  congenita 359.2
  (of von Eulenburg) 359.29
Paraparesis (*see also* paraplegia) 344.1
Paraplegia 344.1
  congenital or infantile (cerebral) (spastic) (spinal) 343.0
  familial spastic 334.1
  functional (hysterical) 300.11
  hysterical 300.11
  infantile 343.0
  late effect 344.1
  psychogenic 306.0
  spastic
    hereditary 334.1
    not infantile or congenital 344.1
Parasomnia 780.59
  nonorganic origin 307.47
Paraspasm facialis 351.8
Parencephalitis (*see also* Encephalitis) 323.9
  late effect—*see* category 326
Parergasia 298.9
Paresis (*see also* Paralysis) 344.9
  heart (*see also* Failure, heart) 428.9
  peripheral progressive 356.9
  pseudohypertrophic 359.1
  senile NEC 344.9
  transient, limb 781.4
Paresthesia (*see also* Disturbance, sensation) 782.0
  Berger's (paresthesia of lower limb) 782.0
  Bernhardt 355.1
  Magnan's 782.0
Parkinsonism (arteriosclerotic) (idiopathic) (primary) 332.0
  associated with orthostatic hypotension (idiopathic) (symptomatic) 333.0
  due to drugs 332.1
  neuroleptic-induced 332.1
  secondary 332.1
Paronychia (with lymphangitis) 681.9
  chronic 681.9
    finger 681.02

☑ Additional Digit Required

Paronychia—*continued*
  chronic—*continued*
    toe 681.11
    finger 681.02
    toe 681.11
Parsonage-Aldren-Turner
  syndrome 353.5
Parsonage-Turner syndrome
  353.5
Patellofemoral syndrome 719.46
Pavor nocturnus 307.46
Pectus
  carinatum (congenital) 754.82
    acquired 738.3
  excavatum (congenital) 754.81
    acquired 738.3
  recurvatum (congenital) 754.81
    acquired 738.3
Pelizaeus-Merzbacher
  disease 330.0
  sclerosis, diffuse cerebral 330.0
Pellagra (alcoholic or with
  alcoholism) 265.2
  with polyneuropathy 265.2 [357.4]
Pellegrini's disease (calcifi-cation,
  knee joint) 726.62
Pellegrini (-Stieda) disease or
  syndrome (calcification, knee
  joint) 726.62
Pelvis, pelvic—*see also* condition or
  type
  Robert's 755.69
Pemphigus 694.4
  gangrenous (*see also* Gangrene)
  785.4
Perforation, perforative
  (nontraumatic)
  by
    instrument (any) during a
      procedure, accidental
      998.2
  instrumental
    surgical (accidental) (blood
      vessel) (nerve) (organ)
      998.2
  surgical (accidental) (by
    instrument) (blood vessel)
    (nerve) (organ) 998.2
Periangiitis 446.0
Periarteritis (disseminated)
  (infectious) (necrotizing)
  (nodosa) 446.0
Periarthritis (joint) 726.90
  Duplay's 726.2
  humeroscapularis 726.2
  scapulohumeral 726.2
  shoulder 726.2
  wrist 726.4
Peribronchitis 491.9
Pericapsulitis, adhesive (shoulder)
  726.0
Pericarditis (granular) (with
  decompensation) (with effusion)
  423.9
  postinfarction 411.0
Pericellulitis (*see also* Cellulitis)
  682.9
Perichondritis
  bronchus 491.9
  larynx 478.71
    typhoid 002.0 [478.71]
Perineuritis NEC 729.2

Periodic—*see also* condition
  limb movement disorder 327.51
  paralysis (familial) 359.3
  somnolence (*see also* Narcolepsy)
    347.00
Perionychia (with lymphangitis)
  681.9
  finger 681.02
  toe 681.11
Periostitis (circumscribed) (diffuse)
  (infective) 730.3☑

Note—Use the following fifth-digit
subclassification with category 730:
  0 *site unspecified*
  1 *shoulder region*
  2 *upper arm*
  3 *forearm*
  4 *hand*
  5 *pelvic region and thigh*
  6 *lower leg*
  7 *ankle and foot*
  8 *other specified sites*
  9 *multiple sites*

  monomelic 733.99
Periphlebitis (*see also* Phlebitis)
  451.9
Peritendinitis (*see also*
  Tenosynovitis) 726.90
  adhesive (shoulder) 726.0
Perlèche 686.8
Persistence, persistent (congenital)
  759.89
  arteria stapedia 744.04
  branchial cleft 744.41
Personality
  change 310.1
  dual 300.14
  multiple 300.14
Perversion, perverted
  appetite 307.52
    hysterical 300.11
  sense of smell or taste 781.1
    psychogenic 306.7
Pes (congenital) (*see also* Talipes)
  754.70
  abductus (congenital) 754.60
    acquired 736.79
  acquired NEC 736.79
    planus 734
  adductus (congenital) 754.79
    acquired 736.79
  cavus 754.71
    acquired 736.73
  planovalgus (congenital) 754.69
    acquired 736.79
  planus (acquired) (any degree) 734
    congenital 754.61
  valgus (congenital) 754.61
    acquired 736.79
  varus (congenital) 754.50
    acquired 736.79
Petges-Cléjat or Petges-Clégat
  syndrome
  (poikilodermatomyositis) 710.3
Phagomania 307.52
Phantom limb (syndrome) 353.6
Pharyngeal—*see also* condition
  arch remnant 744.41
Phenomenon
  flashback (drug) 292.89
  jaw-winking 742.8
  L. E. cell 710.0
  lupus erythematosus cell 710.0

Phenomenon—*continued*
  Raynaud's (paroxysmal digital
    cyanosis) (secondary) 443.0
  Reilly's (*see also* Neuropathy,
    peripheral, autonomic) 337.9
  vasospastic 443.9
Phlebitis (infective) (pyemic)
  (septic) (suppurative) 451.9
  gouty 274.89 [451.9]
  intracranial sinus (any) (venous)
    325
    late effect—*see* category 326
  ulcer, ulcerative 451.9
  varicose (leg) (lower extremity) (*see*
    also Varicose, vein) 454.1
Phlegm, choked on 933.1
Phlegmon (*See also* Abscess) 682.9
  iliac 682.2
Phobia, phobic (reaction) 300.20
  obsessional 300.3
  state 300.20
Phocomelia 755.4
  lower limb 755.32
    complete 755.33
    distal 755.35
    proximal 755.34
  upper limb 755.22
    complete 755.23
    distal 755.25
    proximal 755.24
Physical therapy NEC V57.1
  breathing exercises V57.0
Pica 307.52
  hysterical 300.11
Pick's
  cerebral atrophy 331.11
    with dementia
      without behavioral
        disturbance 331.11
        [294.10]
      with behavioral disturbance
        331.11 [294.11]
  disease
    brain 331.11
    dementia in
      without behavioral
        disturbance 331.11
        [294.10]
      with behavioral
        disturbance 331.11
        [294.11]
Pierre Robin deformity or
  syndrome (congenital) 756.0
Pigeon
  breast or chest (acquired) 738.3
    congenital 754.82
  breeders' disease or lung 495.2
  fanciers' disease or lung 495.2
  toe 735.8
Pill roller hand (intrinsic) 736.09
Pink
  puffer 492.8
Pitchers' elbow 718.82
Pithecoid pelvis 755.69
Pitting (edema) (*see also* Edema)
  782.3
  lip 782.3
  nail 703.8
Pituitary snuff-takers' disease
  495.8
Plaster ulcer (*see also* Decubitus)
  707.00
Platybasia 756.0
Platyonychia (congenital) 757.5
  acquired 703.8

Platypelloid pelvis 738.6
  congenital 755.69
Platyspondylia 756.19
Pleuralgia 786.52
Pleurisy (acute) (adhesive) (chronic)
  (costal) (diaphragmatic)
  (double) (dry) (fetid) (fibrinous)
  (fibrous) (interlobar) (latent)
  (lung) (old) (plastic) (primary)
  (residual) (sicca) (sterile)
  (subacute) (unresolved) (with
  adherent pleura) 511.0
  encysted 511.89
  exudative (*see also* Pleurisy, with
    effusion) 511.9
    bacterial, nontuberculous 511.1
  fibrinopurulent 510.9
    with fistula 510.0
  fibropurulent 510.9
    with fistula 510.0
  hemorrhagic 511.8
  influenzal 487.1
  pneumococcal 511.0
    with effusion 511.1
  purulent 510.9
    with fistula 510.0
  septic 510.9
    with fistula 510.0
  serofibrinous (*see also* Pleurisy, with
    effusion) 511.9
  serofibrinousserofibrinous
    bacterial, nontuberculous 511.1
  seropurulent 510.9
    with fistula 510.0
  serous (*see also* Pleurisy, with
    effusion) 511.9
    bacterial, nontuberculous 511.1
  staphylococcal 511.0
    with effusion 511.1
  streptococcal 511.0
    with effusion 511.1
  suppurative 510.9
    with fistula 510.0
  with
    effusion (without mention of
      cause) 511.9
      bacterial, nontuber-culous
        511.1
      nontuberculous NEC 511.9
        bacterial 511.1
        pneumococcal 511.1
      specified type NEC 511.89
      staphylococcal 511.1
      streptococcal 511.1
  influenza, flu, or grippe 487.1
Pleurobronchopneumonia (*see*
  also Pneumonia, broncho-) 485
Pleurodynia 786.52
Pleuropneumonia (acute) (bilateral)
  (double) (septic) (*see also*
  Pneumonia) 486
  chronic (*see also* Fibrosis, lung) 515
Pleurorrhea (*see also* Hydrothorax)
  511.89
Plexitis, brachial 353.0
Plica
  knee 727.83
Plicae dysphonia ventricularis
  784.49
Plus (and minus) hand (intrinsic)
  736.09
Pneumatocele (lung) 518.89
  tension 492.0
Pneumatosis
  pulmonum 492.8

Pneumoconiosis (due to) (inhalation of) 505
aluminum 503
asbestos 501
bagasse 495.1
bauxite 503
beryllium 503
carbon electrode makers' 503
coal
  miners' (simple) 500
  workers' (simple) 500
cotton dust 504
diatomite fibrosis 502
dust NEC 504
  inorganic 503
  lime 502
  marble 502
  organic NEC 504
fumes or vapors (from silo) 506.9
graphite 503
hard metal 503
mica 502
moldy hay 495.0
rheumatoid 714.81
silica NEC 502
  and carbon 500
silicate NEC 502
talc 502
Pneumocystis carinii pneumonia 136.3
Pneumocystosis 136.3
  with pneumonia 136.3
Pneumohemothorax (see also Hemothorax) 511.89
Pneumohydrothorax (see also Hydrothorax) 511.89
Pneumomediastinum 518.1
  congenital 770.2
  fetus or newborn 770.2
Pneumonia (acute) (Alpenstich) (benign) (bilateral) (brain) (cerebral) (circumscribed) (congestive) (creeping) (delayed resolution) (double) (epidemic) (fever) (flash) (fulminant) (fungoid) (granulomatous) (hemor-rhagic) (incipient) (infantile) (infectious) (infiltration) (insular) (intermittent) (latent) (lobe) (migratory) (newborn) (organized) (overwhelming) (primary) (progressive) (pseudolobar) (purulent) (resolved) (secondary) (senile) (septic) (suppurative) (terminal) (true) (unresolved) (vesicular) 486
adenoviral 480.0
adynamic 514
allergic 518.3
anaerobes 482.81
anthrax 022.1 [484.5]
ascaris 127.0 [484.8]
aspiration 507.0
  due to
    aspiration of microorganisms
      bacterial 482.9
        specified type NEC 482.89
      specified organism NEC 483.8
        bacterial NEC 482.89
      viral 480.9

Pneumonia—continued
aspiration—continued
  due to—continued
    aspiration of microorganisms
      bacterial—continued
      viral—continued
        specified type NEC 480.8
    food (regurgitated) 507.0
    gastric secretions 507.0
    milk 507.0
    vomitus 507.0
  newborn 770.1
asthenic 514
atypical (disseminated, focal) (primary) 486
  with influenza 487.0
bacillus 482.9
  specified type NEC 482.89
bacterial 482.9
  specified type NEC 482.89
Bacteroides (fragilis) (oralis) (melaninogenicus) 482.81
bronchiolitis obliterans organized (BOOP) 516.8
broncho-, bronchial (confluent) (croupous) (diffuse) (disseminated) (hemorrhagic) (involving lobes) (lobar) (terminal) 485
allergic 518.3
aspiration (see also Pneumonia, aspiration) 507.0
bacterial 482.9
  specified type NEC 482.89
capillary 466.19
  with bronchospasm or obstruction 466.19
chronic (see also Fibrosis, lung) 515
congenital (infective) 770.0
diplococcal 481
Eaton's agent 483.0
broncho-, bronchial
  Escherichia coli (E. coli) 482.82
  Friedländer's bacillus 482.0
  Hemophilus influenzae 482.2
  hiberno-vernal 083.0 [484.8]
  hypostatic 514
  influenzal 487.0
  inhalation (see also Pneumonia, aspiration) 507.0
    due to fumes or vapors (chemical) 506.0
  Klebsiella 482.0
  lipid 507.1
    endogenous 516.8
  Mycoplasma (pneumoniae) 483.0
  pleuropneumonia-like organisms (PPLO) 483.0
  pneumococcal 481
  Proteus 482.83
  pseudomonas 482.1
  specified organism NEC 483.8
    bacterial NEC 482.89
  staphylococcal 482.40
    aureus 482.41
      methicillin
        resistant (MRSA) 482.42
        susceptible (MSSA) 482.41
    specified type NEC 482.49
  typhoid 002.0 [484.8]

Pneumonia—continued
broncho-, bronchial—continued
  viral, virus (see also Pneumonia, viral) 480.9
    with influenza 487.0
butyrivibrio (fibriosolvens) 482.81
capillary 466.19
  with bronchospasm or obstruction 466.19
  pneumoniae 483.1
Chlamydia, chlamydial 483.1
  specified type NEC 483.1
  trachomatis 483.1
cholesterol 516.8
chronic (see also Fibrosis, lung) 515
Clostridium (haemolyticum) (novyi) NEC 482.81
cytomegalic inclusion 078.5 [484.1]
deglutition (see also Pneumonia, aspiration) 507.0
desquamative interstitial 516.8
diplococcal, diplococcus (broncho-) (lobar) 481
due to
  adenovirus 480.0
  Bacterium anitratum 482.83
  Chlamydia, chlamydial 483.1
    pneumoniae 483.1
    specified type NEC 483.1
    trachomatis 483.1
  Diplococcus (pneumoniae) 481
  Eaton's agent 483.0
  Escherichia coli (E. coli) 482.82
  Friedländer's bacillus 482.0
  fumes or vapors (chemical) (inhalation) 506.0
  fungus NEC 117.9 [484.7]
  Hemophilus influenzae (H. influenzae) 482.2
  Herellea 482.83
  influenza 487.0
  Klebsiella pneumoniae 482.0
  Mycoplasma (pneumoniae) 483.0
  parainfluenza virus 480.2
  pleuropneumonia-like organism (PPLO) 483.0
  Pneumococcus 481
  Pneumocystis carinii 136.3
  Proteus 482.83
  pseudomonas 482.1
  respiratory syncytial virus 480.1
  rickettsia 083.9 [484.8]
  SARS-associated coronavirus 480.3
  specified
    bacteria NEC 482.89
    organism NEC 483.8
    virus NEC 480.8
  Staphylococcus 482.40
    aureus 482.41
    specified type NEC 482.49
  Streptococcus—see also Pneumonia, streptococcal
    pneumoniae 481
  virus (see also Pneumonia, viral) 480.9
Eaton's agent 483.0
eosinophilic 518.3
Escherichia coli (E. coli) 482.82
Eubacterium 482.81
fibroid (chronic)(see also Fibrosis, lung) 515
fibrous (see also Fibrosis, lung) 515

Pneumonia—continued
Friedländer's bacillus 482.0
Fusobacterium (nucleatum) 482.81
gangrenous 513.0
giant cell (see also Pneumonia, viral) 480.9
gram-negative bacteria NEC 482.83
  anaerobic 482.81
grippal 487.0
Hemophilus influenzae (bronchial) (lobar) 482.2
hypostatic (broncho-) (lobar) 514
in
  anthrax 022.1 [484.5]
  aspergillosis 117.3 [484.6]
  cytomegalic inclusion disease 078.5 [484.1]
  infectious disease NEC 136.9 [484.8]
  mycosis, systemic NEC 117.9 [484.7]
  pneumocystosis 136.3
  Q fever 083.0 [484.8]
  typhoid (fever) 002.0 [484.8]
  whooping cough (see also Whooping cough) 033.9 [484.3]
infective, acquired prenatally 770.0
influenzal (broncho) (lobar) (virus) 487.0
inhalation (see also Pneumonia, aspiration) 507.0
  fumes or vapors (chemical) 506.0
interstitial 516.8
  acute 136.3
  chronic (see also Fibrosis, lung) 515
  desquamative 516.8
  hypostatic 514
  lymphoid 516.8
  plasma cell 136.3
  pseudomonas 482.1
  with influenzal 487.0
Klebsiella pneumoniae 482.0
Löffler's 518.3
Legionnaires' 482.84
lipid, lipoid (exogenous) (interstitial) 507.1
  endogenous 516.8
lobar (diplococcal) (disseminated) (double) (interstitial) (pneumococcal, any type) 481
  bacterial 482.9
    specified type NEC 482.89
  chronic (see also Fibrosis, lung) 515
  Escherichia coli (E. coli) 482.82
  Friedländer's bacillus 482.0
  Hemophilus influenzae (H. influenzae) 482.2
  hypostatic 514
  influenzal 487.0
  Klebsiella 482.0
  Proteus 482.83
  pseudomonas 482.1
  specified organism NEC 483.8
    bacterial NEC 482.89
  staphylococcal 482.40
    aureus 482.41
      methicillin
        resistant (MRSA) 482.42

ICD-9-CM Index

Pneumonia—continued
lobar—continued
staphylococcal—continued
aureus—continued
methicillin—continued
susceptible (MSSA)
482.41
specified type NEC 482.49
viral, virus (see also Pneumonia,
viral) 480.9
with influenza 487.0
metastatic NEC 038.8 [484.8]
Mycoplasma (pneumoniae) 483.0
necrotic 513.0
nitrogen dioxide 506.9
orthostatic 514
parainfluenza virus 480.2
parenchymatous (see also Fibrosis,
lung) 515
passive 514
Peptococcus 482.81
Peptostreptococcus 482.81
plasma cell 136.3
pleuropneumonia-like organism
(PPLO) 483.0
pneumococcal (broncho) (lobar)
481
Pneumocystis (carinii) 136.3
postinfectional NEC 136.9 [484.8]
primary atypical 486
Proprionibacterium 482.81
Proteus 482.83
pseudomonas 482.1
radiation 508.0
respiratory syncytial virus 480.1
rheumatic 390 [517.1]
SARS-associated coronavirus 480.3
Serratia (marcescens) 482.83
specified
bacteria NEC 482.89
organism NEC 483.8
virus NEC 480.8
spirochetal 104.8 [484.8]
staphylococcal (broncho) (lobar)
482.40
aureus 482.41
methicillin
resistant 482.42
susceptible (MSSA)
482.41
specified type NEC 482.49
static, stasis 514
streptococcal (broncho) (lobar)
NEC 482.30
Group
A 482.31
B 482.32
specified NEC 482.39
pneumoniae 481
specified type NEC 482.39
Streptococcus pneumoniae 481
TWAR agent 483.1
Veillonella 482.81
viral, virus (broncho) (interstitial)
(lobar) 480.9
adenoviral 480.0
parainfluenza 480.2
respiratory syncytial 480.1
SARS-associated coronavirus
480.3
specified type NEC 480.8
with influenza, flu, or grippe
487.0
with influenza, flu, or grippe 487.0

Pneumonitis (acute) (primary) (see
also Pneumonia) 486
ventilation 495.7
allergic 495.9
specified type NEC 495.8
aspiration 507.0
due to fumes or gases 506.0
chemical 506.0
due to fumes or gases 506.0
cholesterol 516.8
chronic (see also Fibrosis, lung) 515
due to
fumes or vapors 506.0
inhalation
food (regurgitated), milk,
vomitus 507.0
saliva 507.0
toxoplasmosis (acquired) 130.4
congenital (active) 771.2
[484.8]
eosinophilic 518.3
fetal aspiration 770.18
hypersensitivity 495.9
interstitial (chronic) (see also
Fibrosis, lung) 515
lymphoid 516.8
lymphoid, interstitial 516.8
postanesthetic
correct substance properly
administered 507.0
radiation 508.0
ventilator-associated 997.31
wood-dust 495.8
Pneumopathy NEC 518.89
alveolar 516.9
specified NEC 516.8
due to dust NEC 504
parietoalveolar 516.9
specified condition NEC 516.8
Pneumopericardium—see also
Pericarditis
congenital 770.2
fetus or newborn 770.2
Pneumoperitoneum 568.89
fetus or newborn 770.2
Pneumopleurisy,
pneumopleuritis (see also
Pneumonia) 486
Pneumopyothorax (see also
Pyopneumothorax) 510.9
with fistula 510.0
Pneumorrhagia 786.3
newborn 770.3
Pneumosiderosis (occupational)
503
Pneumothorax (acute) (chronic)
512.8
congenital 770.2
fetus or newborn 770.2
spontaneous 512.8
fetus or newborn 770.2
Poikilodermatomyositis 710.3
Poise imperfect 729.90
Poker spine 720.0
Policeman's disease 729.2
Polioencephalitis (acute) (bulbar)
(see also Poliomyelitis, bulbar)
045.0☑

Note—Use the following fifth-digit
subclassification with category 045:
0   poliovirus, unspecified type
1   poliovirus, type I
2   poliovirus, type II
3   poliovirus, type III

Polioencephalitis—continued
inferior 335.22
influenzal 487.8
superior hemorrhagic (acute)
(Wernicke's) 265.1
Wernicke's (superior hemorrhagic)
265.1
Polioencephalopathy, superior
hemorrhagic 265.1
Poliomyelitis (acute) (anterior)
(epidemic) 045.9☑
chronic 335.21
Polyalgia 729.90
Polyangiitis (essential) 446.0
Polyarteritis (nodosa) (renal) 446.0
Polyarthralgia 719.49
psychogenic 306.0
Polyarthritis, polyarthropathy
NEC 716.59
inflammatory 714.9
specified type NEC 714.89
juvenile (chronic) 714.30
acute 714.31
rheumatic 714.0
Polychondritis (atrophic) (chronic)
(relapsing) 733.99
Polycystic (congenital) (disease)
759.89
lung 518.89
congenital 748.4
Polydactylism, polydactyly 755.00
fingers 755.01
toes 755.02
Polymyalgia 725
arteritica 446.5
rheumatica 725
Polymyositis (acute) (chronic)
(hemorrhagic) 710.4
ossificans (generalisata)
(progressiva) 728.19
Wagner's (dermatomyositis) 710.3
with involvement of
lung 710.4 [517.8]
skin 710.3
Polyneuritis, polyneuritic (see also
Polyneuropathy) 356.9
alcoholic 357.5
with psychosis 291.1
cranialis 352.6
diabetic 250.6☑ [357.2]
due to secondary diabetes
249.6☑ [357.2]

Note—Use the following fifth-digit
subclassification with category 250:
0   type II [non-insulin dependent
type] [NIDDM type] [adult-onset
type] or unspecified type, not
stated as uncontrolled
1   type I [insulin dependent type]
[IDDM type] [juvenile type], not
stated as uncontrolled
2   type II [non-insulin dependent
type] [NIDDM type] [adult-onset
type] or unspecified type,
uncontrolled
3   type I [insulin dependent type]
[IDDM] [juvenile type],
uncontrolled

due to lack of vitamin NEC 269.2
[357.4]
endemic 265.0 [357.4]
febrile 357.0
hereditary ataxic 356.3
idiopathic, acute 357.0

Polyneuritis, polyneuritic—
continued
infective (acute) 357.0
nutritional 269.9 [357.4]
postinfectious 357.0
Polyneuropathy (peripheral) 356.9
alcoholic 357.5
amyloid 277.39 [357.4]
arsenical 357.7
demyelinating, chronic
inflammatory (CIDP) 357.81
diabetic 250.6☑ [357.2]
due to
antitetanus serum 357.6
arsenic 357.7
drug or medicinal substance
357.6
correct substance properly
administered 357.6
lack of vitamin NEC 269.2
[357.4]
lead 357.7
organophosphate compounds
357.7
pellagra 265.2 [357.4]
porphyria 277.1 [357.4]
serum 357.6
toxic agent NEC 357.7
hereditary 356.0
idiopathic 356.9
progressive 356.4
in
amyloidosis 277.39 [357.4]
avitaminosis 269.2 [357.4]
specified NEC 269.1 [357.4]
beriberi 265.0 [357.4]
collagen vascular disease NEC
710.9 [357.1]
deficiency
B-complex NEC 266.2
[357.4]
vitamin B 266.1 [357.4]
vitamin B 266.9 [357.4]
diabetes 250.6☑ [357.2]

Note—Use the following fifth-digit
subclassification with category 250:
0   type II [non-insulin dependent
type] [NIDDM type] [adult-onset
type] or unspecified type, not
stated as uncontrolled
1   type I [insulin dependent type]
[IDDM type] [juvenile type], not
stated as uncontrolled
2   type II [non-insulin dependent
type] [NIDDM type] [adult-onset
type] or unspecified type,
uncontrolled
3   type I [insulin dependent type]
[IDDM] [juvenile type],
uncontrolled

diphtheria (see also Diphtheria)
032.89 [357.4]
disseminated lupus
erythematosus 710.0
[357.1]
hypoglycemia 251.2 [357.4]
malignant neoplasm (M8000/3)
NEC 199.1 [357.3]
pellagra 265.2 [357.4]
polyarteritis nodosa 446.0
[357.1]
porphyria 277.1 [357.4]
rheumatoid arthritis 714.0
[357.1]

Polyneuritis, polyneuritic—
continued
in—*continued*
sarcoidosis 135 *[357.4]*
uremia 585.9 *[357.4]*
lead 357.7
nutritional 269.9 *[357.4]*
specified NEC 269.8 *[357.4]*
progressive 356.4
sensory (hereditary) 356.2
specified NEC 356.8
Polyotia 744.1
Polyradiculitis (acute) 357.0
Polyradiculoneuropathy (acute)
(segmentally demyelinating)
357.0
Polyunguia (congenital) 757.5
acquired 703.8
Polyuria 788.42
Poor
sucking reflex (newborn) 796.1
Porencephaly (congenital)
(developmental) (true) 742.4
traumatic (post) 310.2
Postconcussional syndrome 310.2
Postcontusional syndrome 310.2
Postencephalitic—*see also*
condition
syndrome 310.8
Posthemiplegic chorea 344.89
Posthepatitis syndrome 780.79
Postinfluenzal syndrome 780.79
Postlaminectomy syndrome
722.80
cervical, cervicothoracic 722.81
kyphosis 737.12
lumbar, lumbosacral 722.83
thoracic, thoracolumbar 722.82
Postleukotomy syndrome 310.0
Postlobectomy syndrome 310.0
Postoperative—*see also* condition
confusion state 293.9
psychosis 293.9
**Posttraumatic brain syndrome,
nonpsychotic** 310.2
Postures, hysterical 300.11
Potain's disease (pulmonary edema)
514
Pott's
curvature (spinal) (*see also*
Tuberculosis) 015.0☑
[737.43]

Note—*Use the following fifth-digit
subclassification with categories 010-
018:*
0 *unspecified*
1 *bacteriological or histological
examination not done*
2 *bacteriological or histological
examination unknown (at present)*
3 *tubercle bacilli found (in sputum)
by microscopy*
4 *tubercle bacilli not found (in
sputum) by microscopy, but found
by bacterial culture*
5 *tubercle bacilli not found by
bacteriological exam-ination, but
tuberculosis confirmed
histologically*
6 *tubercle bacilli not found by
bacteriological or histological
examination, but tuberculosis
confirmed by other methods
[inoculation of animals]*

Pott's—*continued*
gangrene 440.24
spinal curvature (*see also*
Tuberculosis) 015.0☑
[737.43]
Potter's
asthma 502
lung 502
Pouch
bronchus 748.3
Poulet's disease 714.2
Preachers' voice 784.49
Preauricular appendage 744.1
Precordial pain 786.51
psychogenic 307.89
**Predislocation status of hip, at
birth** (*see also* Subluxation,
congenital, hip) 754.32
Pregnancy (single) (uterine) (without
sickness) V22.2
false 300.11
Preiser's disease (osteoporosis)
733.09
Preluxation of hip, congenital
(*see also* Subluxation,
congenital, hip) 754.32
Premature—*see also* condition
closure
cranial suture 756.0
fontanel 756.0
lungs 770.4
Presbycardia 797
hypertensive (*see also*
Hypertension, heart) 402.90
Presbyophrenia 310.1
Presenile—*see also* condition
dementia (*see also* Dementia,
presenile) 290.10
Prespondylolisthesis (congenital)
(lumbosacral) 756.11
Pressure
area, skin ulcer (*see also* Ulcer,
pressure) 707.00
atrophy, spine 733.99
brachial plexus 353.0
chest 786.59
increased
intracranial 781.99
lumbosacral plexus 353.1
necrosis (chronic) (skin) (*see also*
Decubitus) 707.00
paralysis (*see also* Neuropathy,
entrapment) 355.9
sore (chronic) (*see also* Ulcer,
pressure) 707.00
spinal cord 336.9
ulcer (chronic) (*see also* Ulcer,
pressure) 707.00
Prickling sensation (*see also*
Disturbance, sensation) 782.0
Primus varus (bilateral) (metatarsus)
754.52
PRIND (prolonged reversible ischemic
neurologic deficit) 434.91
history of (personal) V12.54
Prinzmetal's angina 413.1
Prinzmetal-Massumi syndrome
(anterior chest wall) 786.52
Problem (with) V49.9
communication V40.1
enuresis, child 307.6
eye NEC V41.1
fear reaction, child 313.0
feeding (elderly) (infant) 783.3
nonorganic 307.59

Problem—*continued*
head V48.9
disfigurement V48.6
mechanical V48.2
motor V48.2
movement of V48.2
sensory V48.4
specified condition NEC V48.8
jealousy, child 313.3
learning V40.0
limb V49.9
deficiency V49.0
disfigurement V49.4
mechanical V49.1
motor V49.2
movement, involving
musculoskeletal system
V49.1
nervous system V49.2
sensory V49.3
specified condition NEC V49.5
mastication V41.6
neck V48.9
deficiency V48.1
disfigurement V48.7
mechanical V48.3
motor V48.3
movement V48.3
sensory V48.5
specified condition NEC V48.8
neurological NEC 781.99
relationship, childhood 313.3
sleep disorder, child 307.40
sleep, lack of V69.4
speech V40.1
swallowing V41.6
trunk V48.9
deficiency V48.1
disfigurement V48.7
mechanical V48.3
motor V48.3
movement V48.3
sensory V48.5
specified condition NEC V48.8
voice production V41.4
Proctalgia 569.42
fugax 564.6
spasmodic 564.6
psychogenic 307.89
Proctospasm 564.6
Profichet's disease or syndrome
729.90
Prolapse, prolapsed
laryngeal muscles or ventricle
478.79
mitral valve 424.0
Prolonged, prolongation
PR interval 426.11
QT interval 794.31
syndrome 426.82
Prominence
nose (congenital) 748.1
PROMM (proximal myotonic
myotonia) 359.21
Pronation
ankle 736.79
foot 736.79
congenital 755.67
Prostration 780.79
nervous 300.5
Proteinosis
alveolar, lung or pulmonary 516.0
Protrusio acetabuli 718.65
Protrusion
acetabulum (into pelvis) 718.65

Pseudarthrosis, pseudoarthrosis
(bone) 733.82
joint following fusion V45.4
Pseudobursa 727.89
Pseudocroup 478.75
Pseudocyesis 300.11
Pseudocyst
lung 518.89
Pseudodementia 300.16
Pseudoemphysema 518.89
Pseudoencephalitis
superior (acute) hemorrhagic 265.1
Pseudohemianesthesia 782.0
**Pseudohypertrophic muscular
dystrophy** (Erb's) 359.1
Pseudohypertrophy, muscle 359.1
Pseudoinfluenza 487.1
Pseudoinsomnia 307.49
Pseudoparalysis
arm or leg 781.4
atonic, congenital 358.8
Pseudopsychosis 300.16
Pseudosclerosis (brain)
Jakob's 046.19
spastic 046.19
with dementia
without behavioral
disturbance 046.19
[294.10]
with behavioral disturbance
046.19 *[294.11]*
Pseudoseizure 780.39
psychiatric 300.11
Pseudotabes 799.89
diabetic 250.6☑ *[337.1]*
due to secondary diabetes
249.6☑ *[337.1]*

Note—*Use the following fifth-digit
subclassification with category 250:*
0 *type II [non-insulin dependent
type] [NIDDM type] [adult-onset
type] or unspecified type, not
stated as uncontrolled*
1 *type I [insulin dependent type]
[IDDM type] [juvenile type], not
stated as uncontrolled*
2 *type II [non-insulin dependent
type] [NIDDM type] [adult-onset
type] or unspecified type,
uncontrolled*
3 *type I [insulin dependent type]
[IDDM] [juvenile type],
uncontrolled*

Pseudotetany 781.7
hysterical 300.11
Pseudotrichinosis 710.3
Psoitis 728.89
Psoriasis 696.1
psychogenic 316 *[696.1]*
Psychalgia 307.80
Ptyalism 527.7
hysterical 300.11
Pulmolithiasis 518.89
Pulmonitis (unknown etiology) 486
Pulse
alternating 427.89
psychogenic 306.2
water-hammer (*see also*
Insufficiency, aortic) 424.1
Pulsus
alternans or trigeminy 427.89
psychogenic 306.2
Punch drunk 310.2

☑ Additional Digit Required
© 2009 Ingenix

Puncture (traumatic)—*see also*
    Wound, open, by site
    accidental, complicating surgery
    , 998.2
    by
        instrument (any) during a
            procedure, accidental
            998.2
Pustule 686.9
    nonmalignant 686.9
Putnam's disease (subacute
    combined sclerosis with
    pernicious anemia) 281.0
    [336.2]
Putnam-Dana syndrome (subacute
    combined sclerosis with
    pernicious anemia) 281.0
    [336.2]
Pyococcal dermatitis 686.00
Pyococcide, skin 686.00
Pyocyaneus dermatitis 686.09
Pyoderma, pyodermia 686.00
    gangrenosum 686.01
    specified type NEC 686.09
    vegetans 686.8
Pyodermatitis 686.00
    vegetans 686.8
Pyomyositis 728.0
    ossificans 728.19
Pyopneumothorax (infectional)
    510.9
    with fistula 510.0
Pyothorax 510.9
    with fistula 510.0
Pyramidopallidonigral syndrome
    332.0
Pyromania 312.33

Q

Quadriplegia 344.00
    C1-C4
        complete 344.01
        incomplete 344.02
    C5-C7
        complete 344.03
        incomplete 344.04
    congenital or infantile (cerebral)
        (spastic) (spinal) 343.2
    functional 780.72
    infantile (cerebral) (spastic) (spinal)
        343.2
    specified NEC 344.09
Quervain's disease 727.04

R

Radiculitis (pressure) (vertebrogenic)
    729.2
    accessory nerve 723.4
    anterior crural 724.4
    arm 723.4
    brachial 723.4
    cervical NEC 723.4
    leg 724.4
    lumbar NEC 724.4
    lumbosacral 724.4
    rheumatic 729.2
    thoracic (with visceral pain) 724.4
Radiculomyelitis 357.0
Radiculopathy (*see also* Radiculitis)
    729.2
Railroad neurosis 300.16
Railway spine 300.16

Rales 786.7
Ramsay Hunt syndrome (herpetic
    geniculate ganglionitis) 053.11
    meaning dyssynergia cerebellaris
        myoclonica 334.2
Rapid
    heart (beat) 785.0
        psychogenic 306.2
    respiration 786.06
        psychogenic 306.1
    time-zone change syndrome
        327.35
Rarefaction, bone 733.99
Raynaud's
    disease or syndrome (paroxysmal
        digital cyanosis) 443.0
    gangrene (symmetric) 443.0
        [785.4]
    phenomenon (paroxysmal digital
        cyanosis) (secondary) 443.0
RDS 769
Recklinghausen's disease
    (M9540/1) 237.71
Red cedar asthma 495.8
Reduced ventilatory or vital
    capacity 794.2
Reduction
    ventilatory capacity 794.2
    vital capacity 794.2
Reflex—*see also* condition
    neurogenic bladder NEC 596.54
        atonic 596.54
            with cauda equina syndrome
                344.61
    vasoconstriction 443.9
Refsum's disease or syndrome
    (heredopathia atactica
        polyneuritiformis) 356.3
Refusal of
    food 307.59
        hysterical 300.11
Regulation feeding (elderly)
    (infant) 783.3
Regurgitated
    food, choked on 933.1
    stomach contents, choked on
        933.1
Regurgitation
    aortic (valve) (*see also* Insuf-
        ficiency, aortic) 424.1
    pulmonary (heart) (valve) (*see also*
        Endocarditis, pulmonary)
        424.3
Rehabilitation V57.9
    multiple types V57.89
    occupational V57.21
    specified type NEC V57.89
    speech-language V57.3
    vocational V57.22
Reilly's syndrome or
    phenomenon (*see also*
    Neuropathy, peripheral,
    autonomic) 337.9
Rejection
    food, hysterical 300.11
    transplant 996.80
        organ (immune or nonimmune
            cause) 996.80
            heart 996.83
Relaxation
    anus (sphincter) 569.49
        due to hysteria 300.11
    arch (foot) 734
        congenital 754.61
    back ligaments 728.4

Relaxation—*continued*
    bladder (sphincter) 596.59
    diaphragm 519.4
    joint (capsule) (ligament)
        (paralytic) (*see also*
        Derangement, joint) 718.90
        congenital 755.8
    lumbosacral joint 724.6
    posture 729.90
    sacroiliac (joint) 724.6
    vesical 596.59
Remnant
    fingernail 703.8
    meniscus, knee 717.5
Replacement by artificial or
    mechanical device or
    prosthesis of (*see also* Fitting
    (of))
    intestine V43.89
    kidney V43.89
    liver V43.89
    lung V43.89
    organ NEC V43.89
    pancreas V43.89
    tissue NEC V43.89
Respiration
    asymmetrical 786.09
    bronchial 786.09
    Cheyne-Stokes (periodic
        respiration) 786.04
    disorder of 786.00
        psychogenic 306.1
        specified NEC 786.09
    failure 518.81
        acute 518.81
        acute and chronic 518.84
        chronic 518.83
    insufficiency 786.09
        acute 518.82
    Kussmaul (air hunger) 786.09
    painful 786.52
    periodic 786.09
    poor 786.09
    sighing 786.7
        psychogenic 306.1
    wheezing 786.07
Respiratory syncytial virus (RSV)
    079.6
    bronchiolitis 466.11
    pneumonia 480.1
Respiratory—*see also* condition
    distress 786.09
        acute 518.82
        syndrome (newborn) 769
            adult (following shock,
                surgery, or trauma)
                518.5
            specified NEC 518.82
    failure 518.81
        acute 518.81
        chronic 518.83
Restless leg (syndrome) 333.94
Retention, retained
    bladder NEC (*see also* Retention,
        urine) 788.20
    fecal (*see also* Constipation) 564.00
    foreign body—*see also* Foreign
        body, retained
    bone 733.99
    urine NEC 788.20
        bladder, incomplete emptying
        788.21
        specified NEC 788.29
    water (in tissue) (*see also* Edema)
        782.3

Reticulation, dust (occupational)
    504
Retraction
    finger 736.29
    head 781.0
    lung 518.89
    palmar fascia 728.6
    pleura (*see also* Pleurisy) 511.0
    sternum (congenital) 756.3
        acquired 738.3
        during respiration 786.9
    substernal 738.3
Rett's syndrome 330.8
Rhabdomyolysis (idiopathic) 728.88
Rheumatism, rheumatic (acute
    NEC) 729.0
    arthritis
        chronic 714.0
            spine 720.0
    back 724.9
    chronic NEC 729.0
    intercostal 729.0
        meaning Tietze's disease 733.6
    muscular 729.0
    myositis 729.1
    neck 724.9
    neuralgic 729.0
    neuritis (acute) (chronic) 729.2
    neuromuscular 729.0
    nonarticular 729.0
    palindromic 719.30
        ankle 719.37
        elbow 719.32
        foot 719.37
        hand 719.34
        hip 719.35
        knee 719.36
        multiple sites 719.39
        pelvic region 719.35
        shoulder (region) 719.31
        specified site NEC 719.38
        wrist 719.33
    pneumonia 390 *[517.1]*
    pneumonitis 390 *[517.1]*
    polyarthritis
        chronic 714.0
    psychogenic 306.0
    radiculitis 729.2
    sciatic 724.3
    spine 724.9
    subacute NEC 729.0
    torticollis 723.5
Rheumatoid—*see also* condition
    lungs 714.81
Rhinolalia (aperta) (clausa) (open)
    784.43
Rhizomelique,
    pseudopolyarthritic 446.5
Rhythm
    sleep, inversion 327.39
        nonorganic origin 307.45
Rice bodies (*see also* Loose, body,
    joint) 718.1☑

☑ Additional Digit Required
© 2009 Ingenix

ICD-9-CM Index

Sclerosis, sclerotic—*continued*
  lateral—*continued*
    descending 335.24
    primary 335.24
    spinal 335.24
  lobar, atrophic (of brain) 331.0
    with dementia
      without behavioral
        disturbance 331.0
        [294.10]
      with behavioral distur-bance
        331.0 *[294.11]*
  lung (*see also* Fibrosis, lung) 515
  Mönckeberg's (medial) (*see also* Arteriosclerosis, extremities) 440.20
  multiple (brain stem) (cerebral) (generalized) (spinal cord) 340
  peripheral arteries NEC (*see also* Arteriosclerosis, extremities) 440.20
  plaques 340
  primary lateral 335.24
  progressive systemic 710.1
  pulmonary (*see also* Fibrosis, lung) 515
    artery 416.0
    valve (heart) (*see also* Endocarditis, pulmonary) 424.3
  renal 587
    arteriolar (hyaline) (*see also* Hypertension, kidney) 403.90
    hyperplastic (*see also* Hypertension, kidney) 403.90
    hypertension (*see also* Hypertension, kidney) 403.90
    hypertensive heart disease (conditions classifiable to 402) (*see also* Hypertension, cardiorenal) 404.90
  Schilder's 341.1
  spinal (cord) (general) (progressive) (transverse) 336.8
    ascending 357.0
    combined—*see also* Degeneration, combined
      multiple 340
    disseminated 340
    hereditary (Friedreich's) (mixed form) 334.0
    lateral (amyotrophic) 335.24
    multiple 340
  subendocardial, congenital 425.3
  systemic (progressive) 710.1
    with lung involvement 710.1 *[517.2]*
Scoliosis (acquired) (postural) 737.30
  congenital 754.2
  due to or associated with
    Charcôt-Marie-Tooth disease 356.1 *[737.43]*
    mucopolysaccharidosis 277.5 *[737.43]*
    neurofibromatosis 237.71 *[737.43]*
    osteitis
      deformans 731.0 *[737.43]*
      fibrosa cystica 252.0 *[737.43]*

Scoliosis—*continued*
  due to or associated with—*continued*
    osteitis—*continued*
      osteoporosis (*see also* Osteoporosis) 733.00 *[737.43]*
    poliomyelitis 138 *[737.43]*
    radiation 737.33
    tuberculosis (*see also* Tuberculosis) 015.0☑ *[737.43]*

Note—Use the following fifth-digit subclassification with categories 010-018:
0 *unspecified*
1 *bacteriological or histological examination not done*
2 *bacteriological or histological examination unknown (at present)*
3 *tubercle bacilli found (in sputum) by microscopy*
4 *tubercle bacilli not found (in sputum) by microscopy, but found by bacterial culture*
5 *tubercle bacilli not found by bacteriological exam-ination, but tuberculosis confirmed histologically*
6 *tubercle bacilli not found by bacteriological or histological examination, but tuberculosis confirmed by other methods [inoculation of animals]*

  idiopathic 737.30
    infantile
      progressive 737.32
      resolving 737.31
  paralytic 737.39
  sciatic 724.3
  specified NEC 737.39
  thoracogenic 737.34
  tuberculous (*see also* Tuberculosis) 015.0☑ *[737.43]*
Secretan's disease or syndrome (posttraumatic edema) 782.3
Secretion
  urinary
    excessive 788.42
Segmentation, incomplete (congenital)—*see also* Fusion
  lumbosacral (joint) 756.15
  vertebra 756.15
    lumbosacral 756.15
Seizure(s) 780.39
  Disorder (*see also* Epilepsy) 345.9
  due to stroke 438.89
Sensation
  burning (*see also* Distur-bance, sensation) 782.0
  loss of (*see also* Disturbance, sensation) 782.0
  prickling (*see also* Disturbance, sensation) 782.0
  tingling (*see also* Disturbance, sensation) 782.0
Sense loss (touch) (*see also* Disturbance, sensation) 782.0
  smell 781.1
  taste 781.1
Sensibility disturbance NEC (cortical) (deep) (vibratory) (*see also* Disturbance, sensation) 782.0

Sensitivity, sensitization—*see also* Allergy
  carotid sinus 337.01
  child (excessive) 313.21
Sensory
  extinction 781.8
  neglect 781.8
Septic—*see also* condition
  arm (with lymphangitis) 682.3
  finger (with lymphangitis) 681.00
  foot (with lymphangitis) 682.7
  hand (with lymphangitis) 682.4
  leg (with lymphangitis) 682.6
  nail 681.9
    finger 681.02
    toe 681.11
  sore (*see also* Abscess) 682.9
  toe (with lymphangitis) 681.10
Septicemia, septicemic (generalized) (suppurative) 038.9
  postoperative 998.59
Sequestration
  lung (congenital) (extralobar) (intralobar) 748.5
Sequoiosis asthma 495.8
Seroma (postoperative) (non-infected) 998.13
  infected 998.51
Serotonin syndrome 333.99
Serum
  arthritis 999.5 *[713.6]*
Sesamoiditis 733.99
Shaking
  head (tremor) 781.0
  palsy or paralysis (*see also* Parkinsonism) 332.0
Shallowness, acetabulum 736.39
Shaver's disease or syndrome (bauxite pneumoconiosis) 503
Shedding
  nail 703.8
Shell
  shock (current) (*see also* Reaction, stress, acute) 308.9
    lasting state 300.16
Shifting
  sleep-work schedule (affecting sleep) 327.36
Shin splints 844.9
Shoemakers' chest 738.3
Short, shortening, shortness
  Achilles tendon (acquired) 727.81
  arm 736.89
    congenital 755.20
  back 737.9
  breath 786.05
  femur (acquired) 736.81
    congenital 755.34
  hamstrings 727.81
  hip (acquired) 736.39
    congenital 755.63
  leg (acquired) 736.81
    congenital 755.30
  metatarsus (congenital) 754.79
    acquired 736.79
  radius (acquired) 736.09
    congenital 755.26
  sleeper 307.49
  tendon 727.81
    Achilles (acquired) 727.81
      congenital 754.79
  thigh (acquired) 736.81
    congenital 755.34
  tibialis anticus 727.81

Sialosis 527.8
  rheumatic 710.2
Sicard's syndrome 352.6
Sicca syndrome (keratoconjunctivitis) 710.2
Siderosis (lung) (occupational) 503
Sighing respiration 786.7
Silicosis, silicotic (complicated) (occupational) (simple) 502
  fibrosis, lung (confluent) (massive) (occupational) 502
  non-nodular 503
  pulmonum 502
Silo fillers' disease 506.9
Sinding-Larsen disease (juvenile osteopathia patellae) 732.4
Sinus—*see also* Fistula
  branchial cleft (external) (internal) 744.41
  infected, skin NEC 686.9
  preauricular 744.46
  skin
    infected NEC 686.9
  tarsi syndrome 726.79
Sjögren (-Gougerot) syndrome or disease (keratoconjunctivitis sicca) 710.2
  with lung involvement 710.2 *[517.8]*
Slate-dressers' lung 502
Slate-miners' lung 502
Sleep
  deprivation V69.4
  disorder 780.50
    child 307.40
    nonorganic origin 307.40
      specified type NEC 307.49
  disturbance 780.50
    nonorganic origin 307.40
      specified type NEC 307.49
  drunkenness 307.47
  paroxysmal (*see also* Narcolepsy) 347.00
  rhythm inversion 327.39
    nonorganic origin 307.45
  walking 307.46
    hysterical 300.13
Sleeplessness (*see also* Insomnia) 780.52
  nonorganic origin 307.41
Slipped, slipping
  patella 717.89
  rib 733.99
  sacroiliac joint 724.6
  ulnar nerve, nontraumatic 354.2
  vertebra NEC (*see also* Spondylolisthesis) 756.12
Sloughing (multiple) (skin) 686.9
  fascia 728.9
  phagedena (*see also* Gangrene) 785.4
  ulcer (*see also* Ulcer, skin) 707.9
Sluder's neuralgia or syndrome 337.09
Smith's fracture (separation) (closed) 813.41
Smokers'
  bronchitis 491.0
  cough 491.0
Smothering spells 786.09
Snapping
  finger 727.05
  hip 719.65
  thumb 727.05
Snoring 786.09

Soft—*see also* condition
nails 703.8
Softening
brain (necrotic) (progressive) 434.9☑

Note—Use the following fifth-digit subclassification with categories 433 and 434:

0   *without mention of cerebral infarction*
1   *with cerebral infarction*

hemorrhagic (*see also* Hemorrhage, brain) 431
cartilage 733.92
nails 703.8
spinal cord 336.8
Soldier's
heart 306.2
Somatization reaction, somatic reaction (*see also* Disorder, psychosomatic) 306.9
Somnambulism 307.46
hysterical 300.13
Somnolence 780.09
nonorganic origin 307.43
Sore
desert (*see also* Ulcer, skin) 707.9
muscle 729.1
Naga (*see also* Ulcer, skin) 707.9
pressure (*see also* Ulcer, pressure) 707.00
with gangrene (*see also* Ulcer, pressure) 707.00 [785.4]
skin NEC 709.9
throat 462
clergyman's 784.49
influenzal 487.1
with influenza, flu, or grippe 487.1
tropical (*see also* Ulcer, skin) 707.9
veldt (*see also* Ulcer, skin) 707.9
Sounds
friction, pleural 786.7
succussion, chest 786.7
Spade-like hand (congenital) 754.89
Spading nail 703.8
Spasm, spastic, spasticity (*see also* condition) 781.0
anus, ani (sphincter) (reflex) 564.6
artery NEC 443.9
Bell's 351.0
carpopedal (*see also* Tetany) 781.7
compulsive 307.22
diaphragm (reflex) 786.8
psychogenic 306.1
facial 351.8
gait 781.2
glottis 478.75
hysterical 300.11
psychogenic 306.1
specified as conversion reaction 300.11
reflex through recurrent laryngeal nerve 478.75
habit 307.20
chronic 307.22
hysterical 300.11
larynx, laryngeal 478.75
hysterical 300.11
psychogenic 306.1
specified as conversion reaction 300.11
mobile 781.0

Spasm, spastic, spasticity — *continued*
muscle 728.85
back 724.8
psychogenic 306.0
nerve, trigeminal 350.1
nervous 306.0
nodding 307.3
orbicularis 781.0
peroneo-extensor (*see also* Flat, foot) 734
pharynx (reflex) 478.29
hysterical 300.11
psychogenic 306.1
specified as conversion reaction 300.11
psychogenic 306.0
rectum (sphincter) 564.6
sacroiliac 724.6
saltatory 781.0
throat 478.29
hysterical 300.11
psychogenic 306.1
specified as conversion reaction 300.11
tic 307.20
chronic 307.22
torsion 333.6
trigeminal nerve 350.1
vascular NEC 443.9
vasomotor NEC 443.9
Spasmophilia (*see also* Tetany) 781.7
Spasmus nutans 307.3
Spastic—*see also* Spasm
child 343.9
Spasticity—*see also* Spasm
cerebral, child 343.9
Speakers' throat 784.49
Speech
language therapy V57.3
Spells 780.39
breath-holding 786.9
Sphacelus (*see also* Gangrene) 785.4
Sphenopalatine ganglion neuralgia 337.09
Spider
finger 755.59
Spiegler-Fendt sarcoid 686.8
Spielmeyer-Stock disease 330.1
Spielmeyer-Vogt disease 330.1
Spina bifida (aperta) 741.9☑

Note—Use the following fifth-digit subclassification with category 741:

0   *unspecified region*
1   *cervical region*
2   *dorsal [thoracic] region*
3   *lumbar region*

occulta 756.17
Spitting blood (*see also* Hemoptysis) 786.3
Split, splitting
nails 703.8
Spondylarthritis (*see also* Spondylosis) 721.90
Spondylarthrosis (*see also* Spondylosis) 721.90
Spondylitis 720.9
ankylopoietica 720.0
ankylosing (chronic) 720.0
atrophic 720.9
ligamentous 720.9
chronic (traumatic) (*see also* Spondylosis) 721.90

Spondylitis—*continued*
deformans (chronic) (*see also* Spondylosis) 721.90
gouty 274.00
hypertrophic (*see also* Spondylosis) 721.90
infectious NEC 720.9
juvenile (adolescent) 720.0
Kümmell's 721.7
Marie-Strümpell (ankylosing) 720.0
muscularis 720.9
ossificans ligamentosa 721.6
osteoarthritica (*see also* Spondylosis) 721.90
posttraumatic 721.7
proliferative 720.0
rheumatoid 720.0
rhizomelica 720.0
sacroiliac NEC 720.2
senescent (*see also* Spondylosis) 721.90
senile (*see also* Spondylosis) 721.90
static (*see also* Spondylosis) 721.90
traumatic (chronic) (*see also* Spondylosis) 721.90
tuberculous (*see also* Tuberculosis) 015.0☑ [720.81]

Note—Use the following fifth-digit subclassification with categories 010-018:

0   *unspecified*
1   *bacteriological or histological examination not done*
2   *bacteriological or histological examination unknown (at present)*
3   *tubercle bacilli found (in sputum) by microscopy*
4   *tubercle bacilli not found (in sputum) by microscopy, but found by bacterial culture*
5   *tubercle bacilli not found by bacteriological exam-ination, but tuberculosis confirmed histologically*
6   *tubercle bacilli not found by bacteriological or histological examination, but tuberculosis confirmed by other methods [inoculation of animals]*

typhosa 002.0 [720.81]
Spondyloarthrosis (*see also* Spondylosis) 721.90
Spondylolisthesis (congenital) (lumbosacral) 756.12
Spondylolysis (congenital) 756.11
cervical 756.19
lumbosacral region 756.11
Spondylopathy
inflammatory 720.9
specified type NEC 720.89
traumatic 721.7
Spondylose rhizomelique 720.0
Spondylosis 721.90
cervical, cervicodorsal 721.0
with myelopathy 721.1
inflammatory 720.9
lumbar, lumbosacral 721.3
with myelopathy 721.42
sacral 721.3
with myelopathy 721.42
thoracic 721.2
with myelopathy 721.41
traumatic 721.7

Spondylosis—*continued*
with
myelopathy NEC 721.91
Spoon nail 703.8
Sprain, strain (joint) (ligament) (muscle) (tendon) 848.9
Achilles tendon 845.09
ankle 845.00
and foot 845.00
astragalus 845.00
calcaneofibular 845.02
carpometacarpal 842.11
cartilage
knee 844.9
with current tear (*see also* Tear, meniscus) 836.2
semilunar (knee) 844.8
with current tear (*see also* Tear, meniscus) 836.2
collateral, knee (medial) (tibial) 844.1
lateral (fibular) 844.0
recurrent or old 717.89
lateral 717.81
medial 717.82
coronary, knee 844.8
cruciate
knee 844.2
old 717.89
anterior 717.83
posterior 717.84
deltoid
ankle 845.01
elbow 841.9
and forearm 841.9
femur (proximal end) 843.9
distal end 844.9
fibula (proximal end) 844.9
distal end 845.00
fibulocalcaneal 845.02
finger(s) 842.10
foot 845.10
and ankle 845.00
forearm 841.9
and elbow 841.9
hand 842.10
hip 843.9
and thigh 843.9
humerus (proximal end) 840.9
distal end 841.9
iliofemoral 843.0
innominate
acetabulum 843.9
internal
collateral, ankle 845.01
semilunar cartilage 844.8
old 717.5
with current tear (*see also* Tear, meniscus) 836.2
finger 842.13
ischiocapsular 843.1
knee 844.9
and leg 844.9
old 717.5
collateral
lateral 717.81
medial 717.82
cruciate
anterior 717.83
posterior 717.84
lateral collateral, knee 844.0
old 717.81
leg 844.9
and knee 844.9
ligamentum teres femoris 843.8

ICD-9-CM Index

Sprain, strain—*continued*
  lumbar (spine) 847.2
  lumbosacral 846.0
    chronic or old 724.6
  medial collateral, knee 844.1
    old 717.82
  meniscus
    knee 844.8
      old 717.5
        with current tear (*see also*
          Tear, meniscus) 836.2
  metacarpal 842.10
    distal 842.12
    proximal 842.11
  metacarpophalangeal 842.12
  metatarsal 845.10
  midcarpal 842.19
  neck 847.0
  orbicular, hip 843.8
  patella(r) 844.8
    old 717.89
  phalanx
    finger 842.10
    toe 845.10
  radioulnar 841.9
  radius, radial (proximal end) 841.9
    and ulna 841.9
    distal end 842.00
  round ligament—*see also* Injury,
    internal, round ligament
  femur 843.8
  sacroiliac (region) 846.9
    chronic or old 724.6
  scaphoid bone, ankle 845.00
  semilunar cartilage (knee) 844.8
    old 717.5
      with current tear (*see also* Tear,
        meniscus) 836.2
  shoulder 840.9
  spine 847.9
    dorsal 847.1
    lumbar 847.2
    lumbosacral 846.0
      chronic or old 724.6
    sacroiliac (*see also* Sprain,
      sacroiliac) 846.9
      chronic or old 724.6
  talofibular 845.09
  tarsal 845.10
  teres
    ligamentum femoris 843.8
  thigh (proximal end) 843.9
    and hip 843.9
    distal end 844.9
  thumb 842.10
  tibia (proximal end) 844.9
    distal end 845.00
    distal 845.03
    superior 844.3
  toe(s) 845.10
  ulna, ulnar (proximal end) 841.9
    distal end 842.00
  wrist (cuneiform) (scaphoid)
    (semilunar) 842.00
Sprengel's deformity (congenital)
  755.52
Spring fever 309.23
Spur—*see also* Exostosis
  bone 726.91
    calcaneal 726.73
  calcaneal 726.73
  iliac crest 726.5
Sputum, abnormal (amount)
  (color) (excessive) (odor)
  (purulent) 786.4

Sputum, abnormal—*continued*
  bloody 786.3
Staggering gait 781.2
  hysterical 300.11
Stammering 307.0
Standstill
  cardiac (*see also* Arrest, cardiac)
    427.5
  ventricular (*see also* Arrest, cardiac)
    427.5
Stannosis 503
Staphyloderma (skin) 686.00
Starch eating 307.52
Stasis
  bronchus (*see also* Bronchitis) 490
  cardiac (*see also* Failure, heart)
    428.0
  dermatitis (*see also* Varix, with stasis
    dermatitis) 454.1
  eczema (*see also* Varix, with stasis
    dermatitis) 454.1
  edema (*see also* Hypertension,
    venous) 459.30
  pneumonia 514
  pulmonary 514
  ulcer
    without varicose veins 459.81
    with varicose veins 454.0
  urine NEC (*see also* Retention,
    urine) 788.20
  venous 459.81
Status (post)
  anginosus 413.9
  arthrodesis V45.4
  bed confinement V49.84
  chemotherapy V66.2
    current V58.69
  drug therapy or regimen V67.59
    high-risk medication NEC
      V67.51
  marmoratus 333.79
  organ replacement
    by artificial or mechanical device
      or prosthesis of
        intestine V43.89
        joint V43.60
          specified NEC V43.69
        kidney V43.89
        liver V43.89
        lung V43.89
        organ NEC V43.89
        pancreas V43.89
        tissue NEC V43.89
  postcommotio cerebri 310.2
  respirator V46.11
    heart V42.1
    lung V42.6
  ventilator V46.11
  wheelchair confinement V46.3
Steinert's disease 359.21
Stenosis (cicatricial)—*see also*
  Stricture
  aorta (ascending) 747.22
    arteriosclerotic 440.0
    calcified 440.0
  aortic (valve) 424.1
    specified cause, except
      rheumatic 424.1
  aqueduct of Sylvius (congenital)
    742.3
    acquired 331.4
  bronchus 519.19
  glottis 478.74
  hypertrophic subaortic (idiopathic)
    425.1

Stenosis—*continued*
  larynx 478.74
    congenital 748.3
  mitral (valve) (chronic) (inactive)
    394.0
    specified cause, except
      rheumatic 424.0
  myocardium, myocardial (*see also*
    Degeneration, myocardial)
    429.1
  hypertrophic subaortic
    (idiopathic) 425.1
  nares (anterior) (posterior) 478.19
    congenital 748.0
  pulmonary (artery) (congenital)
    747.3
    valve (*see also* Endocarditis,
      pulmonary) 424.3
  spinal 724.00
    cervical 723.0
    lumbar, lumbosacral 724.02
    nerve (root) NEC 724.9
    specified region NEC 724.09
    thoracic, thoracolumbar 724.01
  subaortic 746.81
    hypertrophic (idiopathic) 425.1
  trachea 519.19
    congenital 748.3
  tricuspid (valve) (*see also*
    Endocarditis, tricuspid) 397.0
    nonrheumatic 424.2
  vascular graft or shunt 996.1
Stereotypes NEC 307.3
Sternalgia (*see also* Angina) 413.9
Stieda's disease (calcification, knee
  joint) 726.62
Stiff
  back 724.8
  neck (*see also* Torticollis) 723.5
Stiffness, joint NEC 719.50
  ankle 719.57
  back 724.8
  elbow 719.52
  finger 719.54
  hip 719.55
  knee 719.56
  multiple sites 719.59
  sacroiliac 724.6
  shoulder 719.51
  specified site NEC 719.58
  spine 724.9
  surgical fusion V45.4
  wrist 719.53
Still's disease or syndrome 714.30
  adult onset 714.2
Still-Felty syndrome (rheumatoid
  arthritis with splenomegaly and
  leukopenia) 714.1
Stiller's disease (asthenia) 780.79
Stitch
  abscess 998.59
  in back 724.5
Stonecutters' lung 502
Stonemasons'
  asthma, disease, or lung 502
Stoppage
  heart (*see also* Arrest, cardiac)
    427.5
  urine NEC (*see also* Retention,
    urine) 788.20
Strümpell-Marie disease or spine
  (ankylosing spondylitis) 720.0
Strain—*see also* Sprain, by site
  postural 729.90

Strangulation, strangulated
  994.7
  food or foreign body (*see also*
    Asphyxia, food) 933.1
  mucus (*see also* Asphyxia, mucus)
    933.1
Strephosymbolia 315.01
Streptoderma 686.00
Stress
  reaction (gross) (*see also* Reaction,
    stress, acute) 308.9
Striations of nails 703.8
Stridor 786.1
  congenital (larynx) 748.3
Strippling of nails 703.8
Stroke (*see also* Disease,
  cerebrovascular, acute) 434.91
  apoplectic (*see also* Disease,
    cerebrovascular, acute) 436
  brain (*see also* infarct, brain)
    healed or old V12.54
  iatrogenic 997.02
  In evolution 434.91
  MEN (multiple endocrine
    neoplasia)
    type I 258.01
    type IIA 258.02
    type IIB 258.03
  paralytic (*see also* infarct, brain)
  postoperative 997.02
Students' elbow 727.2
Stupor 780.09
  mental (anergic) (delusional) 298.9
  psychogenic 298.8
  reaction to exceptional stress
    (transient) 308.2
Stuttering 307.0
  due to late effect of cerebrovascular
    disease (see also Late
    effect(s)((of) cerebrovascular
    disease) 438.14
Subcostal syndrome 098.86
  nerve compression 354.8
Subdelirium 293.1
Suberosis 495.3
Subluxation—*see also* Dislocation,
  by site
  congenital NEC—*see also*
    Malposition, congenital
  hip (unilateral) 754.32
    bilateral 754.33
      with dislocation of other hip
        754.35
  joint
    lower limb 755.69
    shoulder 755.59
    upper limb 755.59
  lower limb (joint) 755.69
  shoulder (joint) 755.59
  upper limb (joint) 755.59
Sunken
  acetabulum 718.85
  fontanels 756.0
Supernumerary (congenital)
  auditory ossicles 744.04
  carpal bones 755.56
  digit(s) 755.00
    finger 755.01
    toe 755.02
  ear (lobule) 744.1
  finger 755.01
  lobule (ear) 744.1
  ossicles, auditory 744.04
  spinal vertebra 756.19
  tarsal bones 755.67

Supernumerary—*continued*
  thumb 755.01
  toe 755.02
  vertebra 756.19
Suppuration, suppurative—*see*
    also condition
  brain 324.0
    late effect 326
  diffuse (skin) 686.00
  lung 513.0
  muscle 728.0
Supraspinatus syndrome 726.10
Susceptibility
  genetic
    to
      other disease V84.8
Sutton and Gull's disease
    (arteriolar nephrosclerosis) (*see*
    also Hypertension, kidney)
    403.90
Swallowed, swallowing
  difficulty (*see also* Dysphagia)
    787.20
Swan neck hand (intrinsic) 736.09
Swelling 782.3
  ankle 719.07
  arm 729.81
  chest 786.6
  extremity (lower) (upper) 729.81
  finger 729.81
  foot 729.81
  hand 729.81
  leg 729.81
  limb 729.81
  lung 786.6
  mediastinal 786.6
  muscle (limb) 729.81
  substernal 786.6
  toe 729.81
Swyer-James syndrome (unilateral
    hyperlucent lung) 492.8
Sympatheticotonia (*see also*
    Neuropathy, peripheral,
    autonomic) 337.9
Symphalangy (*see also*
    Syndactylism) 755.10
Symptoms, specified (general) NEC
    780.99
  bone NEC 733.90
  chest NEC 786.9
  joint NEC 719.60
    ankle 719.67
    elbow 719.62
    foot 719.67
    hand 719.64
    hip 719.65
    knee 719.66
    multiple sites 719.69
    pelvic region 719.65
    shoulder (region) 719.61
    specified site NEC 719.68
    wrist 719.63
  muscle NEC 728.9
  musculoskeletal NEC 781.99
  nervous system NEC 781.99
  respiratory system NEC 786.9
Synarthrosis 719.80
  ankle 719.87
  elbow 719.82
  foot 719.87
  hand 719.84
  hip 719.85
  knee 719.86
  multiple sites 719.89
  pelvic region 719.85

Synarthrosis—*continued*
  shoulder (region) 719.81
  specified site NEC 719.88
  wrist 719.83
Syndactylism, syndactyly (multiple
    sites) 755.10
  fingers (without fusion of bone)
    755.11
    with fusion of bone 755.12
  toes (without fusion of bone)
    755.13
    with fusion of bone 755.14
Syndrome—*see also* Disease
  approximate answers 300.16
  abdominal
    migraine 346.2☑
  abstinence
    drug 292.0
  acquired immune deficiency 042
  acquired immunodeficiency 042
  acrocephalosyndactylism 755.55
  acute chest 517.3
  acute coronary 411.1
  affective organic NEC 293.89
    drug-induced 292.84
  Alice in Wonderland 293.89
  alien hand 781.8
  alveolar capillary block 516.3
  Alzheimer's 331.0
  amnestic (confabulatory) 294.0
    alcoholic 291.1
    drug-induced 292.83
    posttraumatic 294.0
  amotivational 292.89
  amyotrophic lateral sclerosis
    335.20
  angina (*see also* Angina) 413.9
  anterior
    chest wall 786.52
    spinal artery 433.8☑

Note—*Use the following fifth-digit
subclassification with categories 433
and 434:*
  *0 without mention of cerebral
    infarction*
  1 with cerebral infarction

    compression 721.1
  anxiety (*see also* Anxiety) 300.00
    organic 293.84
  Apert's (acrocephalosyndactyly)
    755.55
  arm-shoulder (*see also* Neuropathy,
    peripheral, autonomic) 337.9
  Arrillaga-Ayerza (pulmonary artery
    sclerosis with pulmonary
    hypertension) 416.0
  asphyctic (*see also* Anxiety) 300.00
  ataxia-telangiectasia 334.8
  auriculotemporal 350.8
  Avellis' 344.89
  Ayerza (-Arrillaga) (pulmonary
    artery sclerosis with
    pulmonary hypertension)
    416.0
  Büdinger-Ludloff-Löwen 717.89
  Baastrup's 721.5
  Babinski-Nageotte 344.89
  Bagratuni's (temporal arteritis)
    446.5
  ballooning posterior leaflet 424.0
  Barlow's (mitral valve prolapse)
    424.0
  Barré-Guillain 357.0

Syndrome—*continued*
  Barré-Liéou (posterior cervical
    sympathetic) 723.2
  Bassen-Kornzweig
    (abetalipoproteinemia) 272.5
  Batten-Steinert 359.21
  Bechterew-Strümpell-Marie
    (ankylosing spondylitis)
    720.0
  Bekhterev-Strümpell-Marie
    (ankylosing spondylitis)
    720.0
  Benedikt's 344.89
  Bernard-Horner (*see also*
    Neuropathy, peripheral,
    autonomic) 337.9
  Bernhardt-Roth 355.1
  Bernheim's (*see also* Failure, heart)
    428.0
  Bertolotti's (sacralization of fifth
    lumbar vertebra) 756.15
  Besnier-Boeck-Schaumann
    (sarcoidosis) 135
  Bing-Horton's 339.00☑

Note—*Use the following fifth-digit
subclassification with category 346:*
  *0 without mention of intractable
    migraine without mention of status
    migrainosus*
  *1 with intractable migraine, so
    stated, without mention of status
    migrainosus*
  *2 without mention of intractable
    migraine with status migrainosus*
  *3 with intractable migraine, so
    stated, with status migrainosus*

  Birt-Hogg-Dubb 759.89
  black lung 500
  bladder neck (*see also*
    Incontinence, urine) 788.30
  Blount-Barber (tibia vara) 732.4
  blue
    bloater 491.20
      with exacerbation (acute)
        491.21
  Boder-Sedgwick (ataxia-
    telangiectasia) 334.8
  brachial plexus 353.0
  brain (acute) (chronic)
      (nonpsychotic) (organic)
      (with behavioral reaction)
      (with neurotic reaction)
      310.9
    postcontusional 310.2
    posttraumatic
      nonpsychotic 310.2
      psychotic 293.9
        acute 293.0
        chronic (*see also*
          Psychosis, organic)
          294.8
        subacute 293.1
    psycho-organic (*see also*
      Syndrome, psycho-
      organic) 310.9
    psychotic (*see also* Psychosis,
      organic) 294.9
    senile (*see also* Dementia, senile)
      290.0
    with
      presenile brain disease (*see
        also* Dementia,
        presenile) 290.10

Syndrome—*continued*
  brain—*continued*
    with—*continued*
      psychosis, psychotic reaction
        (*see also* Psychosis,
        organic) 294.9
  branchial arch 744.41
  Brandt's (acrodermatitis
    enteropathica) 686.8
  Brock's (atelectasis due to enlarged
    lymph nodes) 518.0
  Brown-Séquard 344.89
  bubbly lung 770.7
  bulbar 335.22
    lateral (*see also* Disease,
      cerebrovascular, acute)
      436
  Céstan's 344.89
  Céstan-Chenais 344.89
  Caplan (-Colinet) syndrome 714.81
  cardiac asthma (*see also* Failure,
    ventricular, left) 428.1
  cardiacos negros 416.0
  cardiorenal (*see also* Hypertension,
    cardiorenal) 404.90
  cardiorespiratory distress
    (idiopathic), newborn 769
  cardiovascular renal (*see also*
    Hypertension, cardiorenal)
    404.90
  carotid
    body or sinus 337.01
  carpal tunnel 354.0
  cauda equina 344.60
  causalgia 355.9
    lower limb 355.71
    upper limb 354.4
  cervical (root) (spine) NEC 723.8
    disc 722.71
    posterior, sympathetic 723.2
    rib 353.0
    sympathetic paralysis 337.09
  cervicobrachial (diffuse) 723.3
  cervicocranial 723.2
  cervicodorsal outlet 353.2
  Charcôt's (intermittent
    claudication) 443.9
    angina cruris 443.9
    due to atherosclerosis 440.21
  Charcôt-Marie-Tooth 356.1
  Charcôt-Weiss-Baker 337.01
  chest wall 786.52
  Churg-Strauss 446.4
  Claude Bernard-Horner (*see also*
    Neuropathy, peripheral,
    autonomic) 337.9
  Claude's 352.6
  clumsiness 315.4
  Collet (-Sicard) 352.6
  compartment(al) (anterior) (deep)
    (posterior) 958.8
    nontraumatic
      arm 729.71
      buttock 729.72
      fingers 729.71
      foot 729.72
      forearm 729.71
      hand 729.71
      hip 729.72
      leg 729.72
      lower extremity 729.72
      shoulder 729.71
      specified site NEC 729.79
      thigh 729.72
      toes 729.72

Syndrome—*continued*
  compartment(al)—*continued*
    nontraumatic—*continued*
      upper extremity 729.71
        wrist 729.71
    traumatic 958.90
      arm 958.91
      fingers 958.91
      foot 958.92
      forearm 958.91
      hand 958.91
      hip 958.92
      leg 958.92
      lower extremity 958.92
      shoulder 958.91
      specified site NEC 958.99
      thigh 958.92
      tibial 958.92
      toes 958.92
      upper extremity 958.91
      wrist 958.91
  compression 958.5
    cauda equina 344.60
      with neurogenic bladder
        344.61
  complex regional pain—*see also*
    Dystrophy, sympathetic
    type I—*see* Dystrophy,
      sympathetic
      (posttraumatic) (reflex)
    type II—*see* Causalgia
  concussion 310.2
  congenital
    facial diplegia 352.6
  conus medullaris 336.8
  cor pulmonale 416.9
  coronary insufficiency or
    intermediate 411.1
  costochondral junction 733.6
  costoclavicular 353.0
  craniovertebral 723.2
  Creutzfeldt-Jakob (CJD) 046.19
    with dementia
      without behavioral
        disturbance 046.19
        [294.10]
      with behavioral disturbance
        046.19 *[294.11]*
    variant 046.11
      with dementia
        with behavioral
          disturbance 046.11
          [294.11]
        without behavioral
          disturbance 046.11
          [294.10]
  cricopharyngeal 787.20
  crocodile tears 351.8
  croup 464.4
  CRST (cutaneous systemic sclerosis)
    710.1
  cubital tunnel 354.2
  Cuiffini-Pancoast (M8010/3)
    (carcinoma, pulmonary apex)
    162.3
  Curschmann (-Batten) (-Steinert)
    359.21
  Cyriax's (slipping rib) 733.99
  Déjérine-Thomas 333.0
  Da Costa's (neurocirculatory
    asthenia) 306.2
  Dana-Putnam (subacute combined
    sclerosis with pernicious
    anemia) 281.0 *[336.2]*

Syndrome—*continued*
  Danbolt (-Closs) (acrodermatitis
    enteropathica) 686.8
  Davies-Colley (slipping rib) 733.99
  delusional
    induced by drug 292.11
  demyelinating NEC 341.9
  diabetic amyotrophy 250.6☑
    [353.5]
    due to secondary diabetes
      249.6☑ *[353.5]*

Note—Use the following fifth-digit
subclassification with category 250:
0 type II [non-insulin dependent
   type] [NIDDM type] [adult-onset
   type] or unspecified type, not
   stated as uncontrolled
1 type I [insulin dependent type]
   [IDDM type] [juvenile type], not
   stated as uncontrolled
2 type II [non-insulin dependent
   type] [NIDDM type] [adult-onset
   type] or unspecified type,
   uncontrolled
3 type I [insulin dependent type]
   [IDDM] [juvenile type],
   uncontrolled

  diffuse cervicobrachial 723.3
  diffuse obstructive pulmonary 496
  Ditthomska 307.81
  dorsolateral medullary (*see also*
    Disease, cerebrovascular,
    acute) 436
  Dressler's (postmyocardial
    infarction) 411.0
  Duchenne's 335.22
  Duplay's 726.2
  Dupré's (meningism) 781.6
  dyspraxia 315.4
  Eaton-Lambert (*see also* Neoplasm,
    by site, malignant) 199.1
    [358.1]
  effort (aviators') (psychogenic)
    306.2
  Ekbom's (restless legs) 333.99
  Elephant man 237.71
  eosinophilia myalgia 710.5
  Erb (-Oppenheim)-Goldflam
    358.00
  Erlacher-Blount (tibia vara) 732.4
  exhaustion 300.5
  eyelid-malar-mandible 756.0
  facet 724.8
  falx (*see also* Hemorrhage, brain)
    431
  fatigue NEC 300.5
    chronic 780.71
  Feil-Klippel (brevicollis) 756.16
  Felty's (rheumatoid arthritis with
    splenomegaly and
    leukopenia) 714.1
  fibrositis (periarticular) 729.0
  first arch 756.0
  Fisher's 357.0
  flat back
    acquired 737.29
    postprocedural 738.5
  floppy
    infant 781.99
    valve (mitral) 424.0
  Foix-Alajouanine 336.1
  Foville's (peduncular) 344.89
  Franceschetti's (mandibulofacial
    dysostosis) 756.0

Syndrome—*continued*
  Frey's (auriculotemporal) 350.8
  Froin's 336.8
  frontal lobe 310.0
  ganglion (basal, brain) 333.90
    geniculi 351.1
  Ganser's, hysterical 300.16
  Gayet-Wernicke's (superior
    hemorrhagic
    polioencephalitis) 265.1
  Gerhardt's (vocal cord paralysis)
    478.30
  Gerstmann-Sträussler-Scheinker
    (GSS) 046.71
  Gilles de la Tourette's 307.23
  Gélineau's (*see also* Narcolepsy)
    347.00
  Goldenhar's
    (oculoauriculovertebral
    dysplasia) 756.0
  Goldflam-Erb 358.00
  Gougerot (-Houwer)-Sjögren
    (keratoconjunctivitis sicca)
    710.2
  Greig's (hypertelorism) 756.0
  GSS (Gerstmann-Sträussler-
    Scheinker) 046.71
  Guérin-Stern (arthrogryposis
    multiplex congenita) 754.89
  Gubler-Millard 344.89
  Guillain-Barré (-Strohl) 357.0
  Gunn's (jaw-winking syndrome)
    742.8
  gustatory sweating 350.8
  Haglund-Läwen-Fründ 717.89
  Hallermann-Streiff 756.0
  Hallervorden-Spatz 333.0
  Hamman's (spontaneous
    mediastinal emphysema)
    518.1
  Hamman-Rich (diffuse interstitial
    pulmonary fibrosis) 516.3
  Hare's (M8010/3) (carcinoma,
    pulmonary apex) 162.3
  Harkavy's 446.0
  Heberden's (angina pectoris) 413.9
  Hench-Rosenberg (palindromic
    arthritis) (*see also*
    Rheumatism, palindromic)
    719.3☑

Note—Use the following fifth-digit
subclassification with categories 711-
712, 715-716, 718, 719.0-719.6,
719.8, 719.9:
0 site unspecified
1 shoulder region
2 upper arm
3 forearm
4 hand
5 pelvic region and thigh
6 lower leg
7 ankle and foot
8 other specified sites
9 multiple sites

  Hilger's 337.0
  Hoffmann's 244.9 *[359.5]*
  Hoffmann-Werdnig 335.0
  Hoppe-Goldflam 358.00
  Horner's (*see also* Neuropathy,
    peripheral, autonomic) 337.9
  hungry bone 275.5
  Hunt's (herpetic geniculate
    ganglionitis) 053.11

Syndrome—*continued*
  Hunt's—*continued*
    dyssynergia cerebellaris
      myoclonica 334.2
  Hutchinson-Boeck (sarcoidosis) 135
  hypermobility 728.5
  hypersympathetic (*see also*
    Neuropathy, peripheral,
    autonomic) 337.9
  hyperventilation, psychogenic
    306.1
  idiopathic cardiorespiratory
    distress, newborn 769
  immobility (paraplegic) 728.3
  impending coronary 411.1
  impingement
    shoulder 726.2
    vertebral bodies 724.4
  incomplete
    mandibulofacial 756.0
  influenza-like 487.1
  intermediate coronary (artery)
    411.1
  interspinous ligament 724.8
  IRDS (idiopathic respiratory
    distress, newborn) 769
  Sirritable
    heart 306.2
    weakness 300.5
  Jaccoud's 714.4
  Jackson's 344.89
  Jakob-Creutzfeldt 046.19
    with dementia
      without behavioral
        disturbance 046.19
        [294.10]
      with behavioral disturbance
        046.19 *[294.11]*
    variant 046.11
      with dementia
        with behavioral
          disturbance 046.11
          [294.11]
        without behavioral
          disturbance 046.11
          [294.10]
  jaw-winking 742.8
  jet lag 307.45
  jugular foramen 352.6
  Köhler-Pellegrini-Stieda
    (calcification, knee joint)
    726.62
  Klüver-Bucy (-Terzian) 310.0
  Klippel-Feil (brevicollis) 756.16
  Korsakoff (-Wernicke)
    (nonalcoholic) 294.0
    alcoholic 291.1
  Korsakoff's (nonalcoholic) 294.0
    alcoholic 291.1
  Lévy-Roussy 334.3
  Löffler's (eosinophilic pneumonitis)
    518.3
  Löfgren's (sarcoidosis) 135
  Larsen's (flattened facies and
    multiple congenital
    dislocations) 755.8
  lateral
    cutaneous nerve of thigh 355.1
    medullary (*see also* Disease,
      cerebrovascular acute)
      436
  lazy
    posture 728.3

Syndrome—*continued*

Lichtheim's (subacute combined sclerosis with pernicious anemia) 281.0 *[336.2]*
Likoff's (angina in menopausal women) 413.9
lobotomy 310.0
Louis-Bar (ataxia-telangiectasia) 334.8
low
  back 724.2
    psychogenic 306.0
  output (cardiac) (*see also* Failure, heart) 428.9
lumbar vertebral 724.4
Möbius'
  congenital oculofacial paralysis 352.6
  ophthalmoplegic migraine 346.2☑

Note—Use the following fifth-digit subclassification with category 346:
0 *without mention of intractable migraine without mention of status migrainosus*
1 *with intractable migraine, so stated, without mention of status migrainosus*
2 *without mention of intractable migraine with status migrainosus*
3 *with intractable migraine, so stated, with status migrainosus*

Münchmeyer's (exostosis luxurians) 728.11
MacLeod's 492.8
magnesium-deficiency 781.7
malabsorption 579.9
  spinal fluid 331.3
mandibulofacial dysostosis 756.0
Marchiafava-Bignami 341.8
MEN (multiple endocrine neoplasia)
  type I 258.01
  type IIA 258.02
  type IIB 258.03
Marcus Gunn's (jaw-winking syndrome) 742.8
Martin's 715.27
massive aspiration of newborn 770.18
Meige (blepharospasm-oromandibular dystonia) 333.82
Melkersson (-Rosenthal) 351.8
Meyenburg-Altherr-Uehlinger 733.99
Michotte's 721.5
micrognathia-glossoptosis 756.0
middle
  lobe (lung) (right) 518.0
  radicular 353.0
Mikity-Wilson (pulmonary dysmaturity) 770.7
Millard-Gubler 344.89
Miller Fisher's 357.0
mitral
  valve prolapse 424.0
Morton's (foot) (metatarsalgia) (metatarsal neuralgia) (neuralgia) (neuroma) (toe) 355.6
Mounier-Kuhn 748.3
  with acute exacerbation 494.1

Syndrome—*continued*

multiple
  endocrine neoplasia (MEN)
    type I 258.01
    type IIA 258.02
    type IIB 258.03
myofascial pain NEC 729.1
Naffziger's 353.0
Nager-de Reynier (dysostosis mandibularis) 756.0
nonsense 300.16
Nothnagel's
  vasomotor acroparesthesia 443.89
  nucleus ambiguous-hypoglossal 352.6
OAV (oculoauriculovertebral dysplasia) 756.0
os trigonum 755.69
paralytic 344.9
  specified type NEC 344.89
Parkinson's (*see also* Parkinsonism) 332.0
parkinsonian (*see also* Parkinsonism) 332.0
Parsonage-Aldren-Turner 353.5
Parsonage-Turner 353.5
patella clunk 719.66
patellofemoral 719.46
Pellegrini-Stieda 726.62
Petges-Cléjat (poikilodermatomyositis) 710.3
Pfeiffer (acrocephalosyndactyly) 755.55
phantom limb 353.6
PIE (pulmonary infiltration with eosinophilia) 518.3
Pierre Robin 756.0
pink puffer 492.8
plantar fascia 728.71
plica knee 727.83
postconcussional 310.2
postcontusional 310.2
postencephalitic 310.8
posterior
  cervical sympathetic 723.2
  inferior cerebellar artery (*see also* Disease, cerebrovascular, acute) 436
posthepatitis 780.79
postinfarction 411.0
postinfluenza (asthenia) 780.79
postlaminectomy 722.80
  cervical, cervicothoracic 722.81
  lumbar, lumbosacral 722.83
  thoracic, thoracolumbar 722.82
postleukotomy 310.0
postlobotomy 310.0
postmyocardial infarction 411.0
postphlebitic (asymptomatic) 459.10
  with
    complications NEC 459.19
    inflammation 459.12
      and ulcer 459.13
    stasis dermatitis 459.12
      with ulcer 459.13
    ulcer 459.11
      with inflammation 459.13
postviral (asthenia) NEC 780.79
preinfarction 411.1
Prinzmetal-Massumi (anterior chest wall syndrome) 786.52
Profichet's 729.9

Syndrome—*continued*

progressive pallidal degeneration 333.0
pyramidopallidonigral 332.0
pyriformis 355.0
QT interval prolongation 426.82
radicular NEC 729.2
  lower limbs 724.4
  upper limbs 723.4
Ramsay Hunt's
  dyssynergia cerebellaris myoclonica 334.2
rapid time-zone change 307.45
Raynaud's (paroxysmal digital cyanosis) 443.0
RDS (respiratory distress syndrome, newborn) 769
Refsum's (heredopathia atactica polyneuritiformis) 356.3
Reilly's (*see also* Neuropathy, peripheral, autonomic) 337.9
respiratory distress (idiopathic) (newborn) 769
  adult (following shock, surgery, or trauma) 518.5
  specified NEC 518.82
restless leg 333.94
Rett's 330.8
Ridley's (*see also* Failure, ventricular, left) 428.1
Riley-Day (familial dysautonomia) 742.8
Robin's 756.0
Rosen-Castleman-Liebow (pulmonary proteinosis) 516.0
rotator cuff, shoulder 726.10
Roth's 355.1
Roussy-Lévy 334.3
sacralization-scoliosis-sciatica 756.15
sacroiliac 724.6
scalenus anticus (anterior) 353.0
scapulocostal 354.8
scapuloperoneal 359.1
scapulovertebral 723.4
Schaumann's (sarcoidosis) 135
Scheuthauer-Marie-Sainton (cleidocranialis dysostosis) 755.59
Schmidt's
  sphallo-pharyngo-laryngeal hemiplegia 352.6
  vagoaccessory 352.6
Scholz (-Bielschowsky-Henneberg) 330.0
Schwartz (-Jampel) 359.23
Secretan's (posttraumatic edema) 782.3
secretoinhibitor (keratoconjunctivitis sicca) 710.2
serotonin 333.99
Shaver's (bauxite pneumoconiosis) 503
shock (traumatic) 958.4
  lung 518.5
  neurogenic 308.9
  psychic 308.9
shoulder-arm (*see also* Neuropathy, peripheral, autonomic) 337.9
shoulder-girdle 723.4
shoulder-hand (*see also* Neuropathy, peripheral, autonomic) 337.9

Syndrome—*continued*

Shy-Drager (orthostatic hypotension with multisystem degeneration) 333.0
Sicard's 352.6
sicca (keratoconjunctivitis) 710.2
sinus tarsi 726.79
Sjögren (-Gougerot) (keratoconjunctivitis sicca) 710.2
  with lung involvement 710.2 *[517.8]*
Sluder's 337.0
South African cardiomyopathy 425.2
spasmodic
  winking 307.20
spinal cord injury—*see also* Injury, spinal, by site
  fluid malabsorption (acquired) 331.3
Steinbrocker's (*see also* Neuropathy, peripheral, autonomic) 337.9
Still's (juvenile rheumatoid arthritis) 714.30
Still-Felty (rheumatoid arthritis with splenomegaly and leukopenia) 714.1
stone heart (*see also* Failure, ventricular, left) 428.1
straight-back 756.19
stroke (*see also* Disease, cerebrovascular, acute) 436
subcostal 098.86
  nerve compression 354.8
Sudeck's 733.7
Sudeck-Leriche 733.7
superior
  cerebellar artery (*see also* Disease, cerebrovascular, acute) 436
  pulmonary sulcus (tumor) (M8010/3) 162.3
supraspinatus 726.10
Swyer-James (unilateral hyperlucent lung) 492.8
sympathetic
  cervical paralysis 337.09
syndactylic oxycephaly 755.55
Tapia's 352.6
tarsal tunnel 355.5
tegmental 344.89
temporal 383.02
  lobectomy behavior 310.0
tethered (spinal) cord 742.59
Thibierge-Weissenbach (cutaneous systemic sclerosis) 710.1
Thiele 724.6
thoracic outlet (compression) 353.0
Tietze's 733.6
time-zone (rapid) 307.45
Tobias' (carcinoma, pulmonary apex) (M8010/3) 162.3
toxic
  oil 710.5
Treacher Collins' (incomplete mandibulofacial dysostosis) 756.0
Unverricht (-Lundborg) 345.1
Unverricht-Wagner (dermatomyositis) 710.3
vagohypoglossal 352.6

☑ Additional Digit Required

Syndrome—*continued*
  vasomotor 443.9
  Vernet's 352.6
  vertebral
    artery 435.1
      compression 721.1
    lumbar 724.4
  vertebrogenic (pain) 724.5
  video display tube 723.8
  Villaret's 352.6
  Vogt's (corpus striatum) 333.71
  Volkmann's 958.6
  von Bechterew-Strümpell
    (ankylosing spondylitis)
    720.0
  Wagner (-Unverricht)
    (dermatomyositis) 710.3
  Weiss-Baker (carotid sinus syncope)
    337.01
Synesthesia (*see also* Disturbance,
  sensation) 782.0
Synostosis (congenital) 756.59
  astragaloscaphoid 755.67
  radioulnar 755.53
  talonavicular (bar) 755.67
  tarsal 755.67
Synovitis 727.00
  chronic crepitant, wrist 727.2
  gouty 274.00
  villonodular 719.20
    ankle 719.27
    elbow 719.22
    foot 719.27
    hand 719.24
    hip 719.25
    knee 719.26
    multiple sites 719.29
    pelvic region 719.25
    shoulder (region) 719.21
    specified site NEC 719.28
    wrist 719.23
Syphilis, syphilitic (acquired) 097.9
  arthropathy (neurogenic) (tabetic)
    094.0 [713.5]
  Charcôt's joint 094.0 [713.5]
Syringopontia 336.0
  lupus erythematosus 710.0

T

Türck's trachoma (chronic catarrhal
  laryngitis) 476.0
Tabes, tabetic
  arthropathy 094.0 [713.5]
  spasmodic 094.0
    not dorsal or dorsalis 343.9
  with
    Charcôt's joint 094.0 [713.5]
Taboparesis (remission) 094.1
  with
    Charcôt's joint 094.1 [713.5]
Tachycardia 785.0
  HV nodule re-entry (re-entrant)
    427.89
  junctional ectopic 427.0
  nonsustained 427.2
  paroxysmal 427.2
    atrial (PAT) 427.0
      psychogenic 316 [427.0]
    atrioventricular (AV) 427.0
      psychogenic 316 [427.0]
    psychogenic 316 [427.2]
    atrial 316 [427.0]
    supraventricular 316 [427.0]
    ventricular 316 [427.1]

Tachycardia—*continued*
  paroxysmal—*continued*
    supraventricular 427.0
      psychogenic 316 [427.0]
      psychogenic 316 [427.1]
    psychogenic 306.2
    sustained 427.2
      supraventricular 427.0
      ventricular 427.1
    ventricular (paroxysmal) 427.1
      psychogenic 316 [427.1]
Tachypnea 786.06
  hysterical 300.11
  newborn (idiopathic) (transitory)
    770.6
  psychogenic 306.1
  transitory, of newborn 770.6
Tag (hypertrophied skin) (infected)
  701.9
  preauricular 744.1
  skin 701.9
    preauricular 744.1
Talcosis 502
Talipes (congenital) 754.70
  acquired NEC 736.79
    planus 734
  asymmetric 754.79
    acquired 736.79
  calcaneovalgus 754.62
    acquired 736.76
  calcaneovarus 754.59
    acquired 736.76
  calcaneus 754.79
    acquired 736.76
  cavovarus 754.59
    acquired 736.75
  cavus 754.71
    acquired 736.73
  equinovalgus 754.69
    acquired 736.72
  equinovarus 754.51
    acquired 736.71
  equinus 754.79
    acquired, NEC 736.72
  percavus 754.71
    acquired 736.73
  planovalgus 754.69
    acquired 736.79
  planus (acquired) (any degree) 734
    congenital 754.61
  valgus 754.60
    acquired 736.79
  varus 754.50
    acquired 736.79
Talma's disease 728.85
Tangier disease (familial high-
  density lipoprotein deficiency)
  272.5
Tapia's syndrome 352.6
Tarlov's cyst 355.9
Tarsal tunnel syndrome 355.5
Tarsalgia 729.2
Tay-Sachs
  amaurotic familial idiocy 330.1
  disease 330.1
TBI (traumatic brain injury) (*see also*
  Injury, intracranial) 854.0
  with skull fracture—see Fracture,
    skull, by site
Tear, torn (traumatic)—*see also*
  Wound, open, by site
  meniscus (knee) (current injury)
    836.2
    bucket handle 836.0
      old 717.0

Tear, torn—*continued*
  meniscus—*continued*
    lateral 836.1
      anterior horn 836.1
        old 717.42
      bucket handle 836.1
        old 717.41
      old 717.40
      posterior horn 836.1
        old 717.43
      specified site NEC 836.1
        old 717.49
    medial 836.0
      anterior horn 836.0
        old 717.1
      bucket handle 836.0
        old 717.0
      old 717.3
      posterior horn 836.0
        old 717.2
    old NEC 717.5
  rotator cuff (traumatic) 840.4
    degenerative 726.10
    nontraumatic 727.61
  semilunar cartilage, knee (*see also*
    Tear, meniscus) 836.2
    old 717.5
  vessel, from catheter 998.2
Tenderness
  skin 782.0
Tendinitis, tendonitis (*see also*
  Tenosynovitis) 726.90
  Achilles 726.71
  adhesive 726.90
    shoulder 726.0
  calcific 727.82
    shoulder 726.11
  gluteal 726.5
  patellar 726.64
  peroneal 726.79
  pes anserinus 726.61
  psoas 726.5
  tibialis (anterior) (posterior) 726.72
  trochanteric 726.5
Tennis elbow 726.32
Tenosynovitis 727.00
  adhesive 726.90
    shoulder 726.0
  ankle 727.06
  bicipital (calcifying) 726.12
  buttock 727.09
  elbow 727.09
  finger 727.05
  foot 727.06
  hand 727.05
  hip 727.09
  knee 727.09
  radial styloid 727.04
  shoulder 726.10
    adhesive 726.0
  spine 720.1
  supraspinatus 726.10
  toe 727.06
  wrist 727.05
Tension
  arterial, high (*see also*
    Hypertension) 401.9
  headache 307.81
Therapy V57.9
  breathing V57.0
  exercise NEC V57.1
    breathing V57.0
  occupational V57.21
  orthoptic V57.4
  orthotic V57.81

Therapy—*continued*
  physical NEC V57.1
  speech -language V57.3
  vocational V57.22
Thermalgesia 782.0
Thermalgia 782.0
Thermanalgesia 782.0
Thermanesthesia 782.0
Thiaminic deficiency 265.1
Thibierge-Weissenbach
  syndrome (cutaneous systemic
  sclerosis) 710.1
Thickening
  bone 733.99
    extremity 733.99
  larynx 478.79
  nail 703.8
  periosteal 733.99
  pluera (*see also* Pleurisy) 511.0
  subepiglottic 478.79
Thiele syndrome 724.6
Thinning vertebra (*see also*
  Osteoporosis) 733.00
Thomsen's disease 359.2
Thoracic—*see also* condition
  outlet syndrome 353.0
Threshers' lung 495.0
Thromboangiitis 443.1
  obliterans (general) 443.1
Thrombophlebitis 451.9
  cerebral (sinus) (vein) 325
    late effect—see category 326
  intracranial venous sinus (any) 325
    late effect—see category 326
Thrombosis, thrombotic
  (marantic) (multiple)
  (progressive) (septic) (vein)
  (vessel) 453.9
  artery, arteries (postinfectional)
    444.9
    coronary (*see also* Infarct,
      myocardium) 410.9☑

---

*Note—Use the following fifth-digit
subclassification with category 410:*

0 episode unspecified
1 initial episode
*2 subsequent episode without
   recurrence*

---

    healed or specified as old 412
    without myocardial infarction
      411.81
  brain (artery) (stem) 434.0☑

---

*Note—Use the following fifth-digit
subclassification with categories 433
and 434:*

*0 without mention of cerebral
   infarction*
1 with cerebral infarction

---

    iatrogenic 997.02
    postoperative 997.02
  cardiac (*see also* Infarct,
    myocardium) 410.9☑
    healed or specified as old 412
  coronary (artery) (*see also* Infarct,
    myocardium) 410.9☑
    healed or specified as old 412
    without myocardial infarction
      411.81
  intramural (*see also* Infarct,
    myocardium) 410.9☑
    healed or specified as old 412

Thrombosis, thrombotic—
continued
leg (*see also* Thrombosis, lower
extremity) 453.6
deep 453.40
acute 453.40
lower (distal) 453.42
upper (proximal) 453.41
chronic 453.50
lower (distal) 453.52
upper (proximal) 453.51
lower extremity—*see* Thrombosis,
leg
lower extremity (superficial) 453.6
deep vessels 453.40
acute 453.40
calf 453.42
distal (lower leg) 453.42
femoral 453.41
iliac 453.41
lower leg 453.42
peroneal 453.42
popliteal 453.41
proximal (upper leg)
453.41
thigh 453.41
tibial 453.42
chronic 453.50
calf 453.52
distal (lower leg) 453.52
femoral 453.51
iliac 453.51
lower leg 453.52
peroneal 453.52
popliteal 453.51
proximal (upper leg)
453.51
thigh 453.51
tibial 453.52
saphenous vein (greater)
(lesser) 453.6
supervicial 453.6
mural (heart chamber) (*see also*
Infarct, myocardium)
410.9☑

*The following fifth-digit subclassification
is for use with category 410*
*0   episode of care unspecified
Use when the source document
does not contain sufficient
information for the assignment of
fifth-digit 1 or 2*
*1   initial episode of care
Use fifth-digit 1 to designate the
first episode of care (regardless of
facility site) for a newly diagnosed
myocardial infarction. The fifth-
digit 1 is assigned regardless of the
number of times a patient may be
transferred during the initial
episode of care.*
*2   subsequent episode of care
Use fifth digit 2 to designate an
episode of care following the initial
episode when the patient is
admitted for further observation,
evaluation or treatment for a
myocardial infarction that has
received initial treatment, but is still
less than 8 weeks old.*

healed or specified as old 412
spinal cord 336.1
pyogenic origin 324.1
late effect—*see* category 326

Thrombosis, thrombotic—
continued
upper extremity 453.83
acute 453.83
deep 453.82
superficial 453.81
chronic 453.73
deep 453.72
superficial 453.71
Thomsen's disease 359.22
Thumb—*see also* condition
gamekeeper's 842.12
Thyrotoxic
heart failure (*see also*
Thyrotoxicosis) 242.9☑
[425.7]

*Note—Use the following fifth-digit
subclassification with category 242:*
*0   without mention of thyrotoxic crisis
or storm*
*1   with mention of thyrotoxic crisis or
storm*

Thyrotoxicosis 242.9☑
heart 242.9☑ [425.7]
Tibia vara 732.4
Tic 307.20
breathing 307.20
compulsive 307.22
convulsive 307.20
degenerative (generalized)
(localized) 333.3
facial 351.8
douloureux (*see also* Neuralgia,
trigeminal) 350.1
atypical 350.2
habit 307.20
chronic (motor or vocal) 307.22
lid 307.20
motor-verbal 307.23
orbicularis 307.20
organic origin 333.3
psychogenic 307.20
compulsive 307.22
salaam 781.0
spasm 307.20
chronic (motor or vocal) 307.22
Tics and spasms, compulsive
307.22
Tietze's disease or syndrome
733.6
Tight, tightness
chest 786.59
fascia (lata) 728.9
tendon 727.81
Achilles (heel) 727.81
Tilting vertebra 737.9
Tin-miners' lung 503
Tingling sensation (*see also*
Disturbance, sensation) 782.0
Tiredness 780.79
Tobias' syndrome (carcinoma,
pulmonary apex) (M8010/3)
162.3
Tocopherol deficiency 269.1
Topagnosis 782.0
Taphi (gouty) 274.03
Torsion
tibia 736.89
Torticollis (intermittent) (spastic)
723.5
hysterical 300.11
psychogenic 306.0
specified as conversion reaction
300.11

Torticollis—*continued*
rheumatic 723.5
rheumatoid 714.0
spasmodic 333.83
Torus
fracture
fibula 823.41
humerus 812.49
radius (alone) 813.45
with ulna 813.47
ulna (alone) 813.46
with radius 813.47
Tourette's disease (motor-verbal
tic) 307.23
Tower skull 756.0
with exophthalmos 756.0
Toxemia 799.89
lung 518.89
pulmonary 518.89
Toxemica cerebropathia psychica
(nonalcoholic) 294.0
alcoholic 291.1
Toxic (poisoning)—*see also* condition
oil syndrome 710.5
Tracheitis (acute) (catarrhal)
(infantile) (membranous)
(plastic) (pneumococcal)
(septic) (suppurative) (viral)
464.10
chronic 491.8
with
bronchitis (chronic) 491.8
laryngitis (chronic) 476.1
edematous 464.11
influenzal 487.1
with
bronchitis 490
acute or subacute 466.0
chronic 491.8
laryngitis (acute) 464.20
chronic 476.1
with obstruction 464.21
obstruction 464.11
Tracheobronchitis (*see also*
Bronchitis) 490
acute or subacute 466.0
with bronchospasm or
obstruction 466.0
chronic 491.8
influenzal 487.1
senile 491.8
Tracheobronchomegaly
(congenital) 748.3
with bronchiectasis 494.0
with (acute) exacerbation 494.1
acquired 519.19
with bronchiectasis 494.0
Tracheocele (external) (internal)
519.19
congenital 748.3
Tracheomalacia 519.19
congenital 748.3
Tracheostenosis 519.19
congenital 748.3
Trachoma, trachomatous 076.9
Türck's (chronic catarrhal laryngitis)
476.0
Trachyphonia 784.49
Training
orthoptic V57.4
orthotic V57.81
Trance 780.09
hysterical 300.13
**Transitional, lumbosacral joint of
vertebra** 756.19

Transplant(ed)
complication—*see also*
Complications, due to
(presence of) any device,
implant, or graft classified to
996.0☑
organ (failure) (immune or
nonimmune cause)
(infection) (rejection)
996.87
heart 996.83
heart V42.1
lung V42.6
Treacher Collins' syndrome
(incomplete facial dysostosis)
756.0
Trembling paralysis (*see also*
Parkinsonism) 332.0
Tremor 781.0
essential (benign) 333.1
familial 333.1
hereditary 333.1
hysterical 300.11
intention 333.1
medication induced postural 333.1
muscle 728.85
Parkinson's (*see also* Parkinsonism)
332.0
psychogenic 306.0
specified as conversion reaction
300.11
specified type NEC 333.1
Trigger finger (acquired) 727.03
Trigonocephaly 756.0
Triplegia 344.89
congenital or infantile 343.8
Trismus 781.0
Trophoneurosis NEC 356.9
arm NEC 354.9
disseminated 710.1
leg NEC 355.8
lower extremity NEC 355.8
upper extremity NEC 354.9
Tubercle—*see also* Tuberculosis
epithelioid noncaseating 135
**Tuberculosis, tubercular,
tuberculous** (calcification)
(calcified) (caseous)
(chromogenic acid-fast bacilli)
(congenital) (degeneration)
(disease) (fibrocaseous) (fistula)
(gangrene) (interstitial) (isolated
circumscribed lesions) (necrosis)
(parenchymatous) (ulcerative)
011.9☑

☑ Additional Digit Required

Tuberculosis, tubercular, tuberculous—continued

Note—Use the following fifth-digit subclassification with categories 010-018:

0 *unspecified*
1 *bacteriological or histological examination not done*
2 *bacteriological or histological examination unknown (at present)*
3 *tubercle bacilli found (in sputum) by microscopy*
4 *tubercle bacilli not found (in sputum) by microscopy, but found by bacterial culture*
5 *tubercle bacilli not found by bacteriological exam-ination, but tuberculosis confirmed histologically*
6 *tubercle bacilli not found by bacteriological or histological examination, but tuberculosis confirmed by other methods [inoculation of animals]*

arthritis (chronic) (synovial) 015.9☑ *[711.40]*
  hip 015.1☑ *[711.45]*
  knee 015.2☑ *[711.46]*
  specified site NEC 015.8☑ *[711.48]*
  spine or vertebra (column) 015.0☑ *[720.81]*
cardiomyopathy 017.9☑ *[425.8]*
curvature, spine 015.0☑ *[737.40]*
heart 017.9☑ *[425.8]*
kyphoscoliosis 015.0☑ *[737.43]*
kyphosis 015.0☑ *[737.41]*
lordosis 015.0☑ *[737.42]*
scoliosis 015.0☑ *[737.43]*
spondylitis 015.0☑ *[720.81]*
synovitis 015.9☑ *[727.01]*
  hip 015.1☑ *[727.01]*
  knee 015.2☑ *[727.01]*
  spine or vertebra 015.0☑ *[727.01]*
tenosynovitis 015.9☑ *[727.01]*
  hip 015.1☑ *[727.01]*
  knee 015.2☑ *[727.01]*
  specified site NEC 015.8☑ *[727.01]*
  spine or vertebra 015.0☑ *[727.01]*
Tumor (M8000/1)—*see also* Neoplasm, by site, unspecified nature
carcinoid (M8240/1)—209.60
  benign 209.60
    appendix 209.51
    ascending colon 209.53
    bronchus 209.61
    cecum 209.52
    colon 209.50
    descending colon 209.55
    duodenum 209.41
    foregut 209.65
    hindgut 209.67
    ileum 209.43
    jejunum 209.42
    kidney 209.64
    large intestine 209.50
    lung 209.61
    midgut 209.66
    rectum 209.57

Tumor—continued

carcinoid—*continued*
  benign—*continued*
    sigmoid colon 209.56
    small intestine 209.40
    specified NEC 209.69
    stomach 209.63
    thymus 209.62
    transverse colon 209.54
  malignant (of) 209.20
    appendix 209.11
    ascending colon 209.13
    bronchus 209.21
    cecum 209.12
    colon 209.10
    descending colon 209.15
    duodenum 209.01
    foregut 209.25
    hindgut 209.27
    ileum 209.03
    jejunum 209.02
    kidney 209.24
    large intestine 209.10
    lung 209.21
    midgut 209.26
    rectum 209.17
    sigmoid colon 209.16
    small intestine 209.00
    specified NEC 209.29
    stomach 209.23
    thymus 209.22
    transverse colon 209.14
  neuroendocrine 209.60
    malignant poorly differentiated 209.30
Müllerian, mixed (M8950/3)—*see* Neoplasm, by site, malignant
Pancoast's (M8010/3) 162.3
phantom 300.11
superior sulcus (lung) (pulmonary) (syndrome) (M8010/3) 162.3
suprasulcus (M8010/3) 162.3
von Recklinghausen's (M9540/1) 237.71
Turricephaly 756.0
Twitch 781.0
Tylosis 700
Tympany
  chest 786.7

U

Ulcer, ulcerated, ulcerating, ulceration, ulcerative 707.9
abdomen (wall) (*see also* Ulcer, skin) 707.8
arm (*see also* Ulcer, skin) 707.8
bronchitis 491.8
buttock (*see also* Ulcer, skin) 707.8
  decubitus (*see also* Ulcer, decubitus) 707.00
chest (wall) (*see also* Ulcer, skin) 707.8
chin (pyogenic) (*see also* Ulcer, skin) 707.8
decubitus (unspecified site) 707.00
  with gangrene 707.00 *[785.4]*
  ankle 707.06
  back
    lower 707.03
    upper 707.02
  buttock 707.05
  coccyx 707.03

Ulcer, ulcerated, ulcerating, ulceration, ulcerative—continued

decubitus—*continued*
  elbow 707.01
  head 707.09
  heel 707.07
  hip 707.04
  other site 707.09
  sacrum 707.03
  shoulder blades 707.02
diabetes, diabetic (mellitus) 250.8☑ *[707.9]*
  due to secondary diabetes 249.8☑ *[707.9]*

Note—Use the following fifth-digit subclassification with category 250:

0 *type II [non-insulin dependent type] [NIDDM type] [adult-onset type] or unspecified type, not stated as uncontrolled*
1 *type I [insulin dependent type] [IDDM type] [juvenile type], not stated as uncontrolled*
2 *type II [non-insulin dependent type] [NIDDM type] [adult-onset type] or unspecified type, uncontrolled*
3 *type I [insulin dependent type] [IDDM] [juvenile type], uncontrolled*

  lower limb 250.8☑ *[707.10]*
    due to secondary diabetes 249.8☑ *[707.10]*
    ankle 250.8☑ *[707.13]*
      due to secondary diabetes 249.8☑ *[707.13]*
    calf 250.8☑ *[707.12]*
      due to secondary diabetes 249.8☑ *[707.12]*
    foot 250.8☑ *[707.15]*
      due to secondary diabetes 249.8☑ *[707.15]*
    heel 250.8☑ *[707.14]*
      due to secondary diabetes 249.8☑ *[707.14]*
    knee 250.8☑ *[707.19]*
      due to secondary diabetes 249.8☑ *[707.19]*
    specified site NEC 250.8☑ *[707.19]*
      due to secondary diabetes 249.8☑ *[707.19]*
    thigh 250.8☑ *[707.11]*
      due to secondary diabetes 249.8☑ *[707.11]*
    toes 250.8☑ *[707.15]*
      due to secondary diabetes 249.8☑ *[707.15]*
epiglottis 478.79
face (*see also* Ulcer, skin) 707.8
foot (indolent) (*see also* Ulcer, lower extremity) 707.15
  perforating 707.15
  trophic 707.15
  varicose 454.0
    inflamed or infected 454.2
gangrenous (*see also* Gangrene) 785.4
glottis 478.79
groin (*see also* Ulcer, skin) 707.8
hand (*see also* Ulcer, skin) 707.8

Ulcer, ulcerated, ulcerating, ulceration, ulcerative—continued

heel (*see also* Ulcer, lower extremity) 707.14
  decubitus (*see also* Ulcer, pressure) 707.07
hip (*see also* Ulcer, skin) 707.8
  decubitus (*see also* Ulcer, pressure) 707.04
ischemic 707.9
  lower extremity (*see also* Ulcer, lower extremity) 707.10
    ankle 707.13
    calf 707.12
    foot 707.15
    heel 707.14
    knee 707.19
    specified site NEC 707.19
    thigh 707.11
    toes 707.15
larynx (aphthous) (contact) 478.79
lower extremity (atrophic) (chronic) (neurogenic) (perforating) (pyogenic) (trophic) (tropical) 707.10
  with gangrene (*see also* Ulcer, lower extremity) 707.10 *[785.4]*
    arteriosclerotic 440.24
  ankle 707.13
    arteriosclerotic 440.23
      with gangrene 440.24
  calf 707.12
  decubitus 707.00
    with gangrene 707.00 *[785.4]*
    ankle 707.06
    buttock 707.05
    heel 707.07
    hip 707.04
  foot 707.15
  heel 707.14
  knee 707.19
  specified site NEC 707.19
  thigh 707.11
  toes 707.15
  varicose 454.0
    inflamed or infected 454.2
lung 518.89
Meleney's (chronic undermining) 686.09
neck (*see also* Ulcer, skin) 707.8
perforating NEC (*see also* Ulcer, peptic, with perforation) 533.5☑

Note—Use the following fifth-digit subclassification with categories 531-534:

0 *without mention of obstruction*
1 *with obstruction*

skin 707.9
perineum (*see also* Ulcer, skin) 707.8
plaster (*see also* Ulcer, decubitus) 707.00
pressure 707.00
  with
    abrasion, blister, partial thickness skin loss involving epidermis and/or dermis 707.22

Ulcer, ulcerated, ulcerating, ulceration, ulcerative—
continued
pressure—*continued*
with—*continued*
full thickness skin loss
involving damage or
necrosis of
subcutaneous tissue
707.23
gangrene 707.00 *[785.4]*
necrosis of soft tissues
through to underlying
muscle, tendon, or
bone 707.24
ankle 707.06
back
lower 707.03
upper 707.02
buttock 707.05
coccyx 707.03
elbow 707.01
head 707.09
healed—*omit code*
healing—code to Ulcer,
pressure, by stage
heel 707.07
hip 707.04
other site 707.09
sacrum 707.03
shoulder blades 707.02
stage
I (healing) 707.21
II (healing) 707.22
III (healing) 707.23
IV (healing) 707.24
unspecified (healing) 707.20
unstageable 707.25
sacrum (region) (*see also* Ulcer,
skin) 707.8
scalp (*see also* Ulcer, skin) 707.8
skin (atrophic) (chronic)
(neurogenic) (non-healing)
(perforating) (pyogenic)
(trophic) 707.9
decubitus (*see also* Ulcer,
pressure) 707.00
with gangrene 707.00
[785.4]
lower extremity (*see also* Ulcer,
lower extremity) 707.10
ankle 707.13
arteriosclerotic 440.23
with gangrene 440.24
calf 707.12
foot 707.15
heel 707.14
knee 707.19
specified site NEC 707.19
thigh 707.11
toes 707.15
with gangrene 707.10
[785.4]
arteriosclerotic 440.24
with gangrene 707.9 *[785.4]*
stasis (leg) (venous) 454.0
with varicose veins 454.0
without varicose veins 459.81
inflamed or infected 454.2
submental (*see also* Ulcer, skin)
707.8
tropical NEC (*see also* Ulcer, skin)
707.9
varicose (lower extremity, any part)
454.0

Ulcer, ulcerated, ulcerating, ulceration, ulcerative—
continued
varicose—*continued*
inflamed or infected 454.2
with gangrene 707.9 *[785.4]*
Unequal leg (acquired) (length)
736.81
congenital 755.30
Unguis incarnatus 703.0
Uninhibited bladder 596.54
with cauda equina syndrome
344.61
Union, abnormal—*see also* Fusion
divided tendon 727.89
larynx and trachea 748.3
Unsoundness of mind (*see also*
Psychosis) 298.9
Unstable
back NEC 724.9
lumbosacral joint (congenital)
756.19
acquired 724.6
sacroiliac 724.6
spine NEC 724.9
**Unverricht (-Lundborg) disease,
syndrome, or epilepsy** 333.2
Unverricht-Wagner syndrome
(dermatomyositis) 345.1

V

Vaginismus (reflex) 625.1
hysterical 300.11
Vagotonia 352.3
**van Bogaert-Nijssen (-Peiffer)
disease** 330.0
Vanishing lung 492.0
**Vapor asphyxia or suffocation
NEC** 987.9
Varicose
ulcer (lower extremity, any part)
454.0
inflamed or infected 454.2
vein (lower extremity) (ruptured)
(*see also* Varix) 454.9
inflamed or infected 454.1
with ulcer 454.2
ulcerated 454.0
inflamed or infected 454.2
vein (*see also* Varix)
with
complications NEC 454.8
edema 454.8
inflammation or infection
454.1
ulcerated 454.2
pain 454.8
stasis dermatitis 454.1
with ulcer 454.2
swelling 454.8
ulcer 454.0
inflamed or infected 454.2
Varix (lower extremity) (ruptured)
454.9
inflamed or infected 454.1
ulcerated 454.2
ulcerated 454.0
inflamed or infected 454.2
with
complications NEC 454.8
edema 454.8
inflammation or infection 454.1
with ulcer 454.2
pain 454.8

Varix—*continued*
with—*continued*
stasis dermatitis 454.1
with ulcer 454.2
swelling 454.8
ulcer 454.0
with inflammation or
infection 454.2
Vascular—*see also* condition
spasm 443.9
Vasculopathy
cardiac allograft 996.83
Vasodilation 443.9
Vasoplegia, splanchnic (*see also*
Neuropathy, peripheral,
autonomic) 337.9
Vasospasm 443.9
nerve
arm NEC 354.9
autonomic 337.9
brachial plexus 353.0
cervical plexus 353.2
leg NEC 355.8
lower extremity NEC 355.8
peripheral NEC 355.9
spinal NEC 355.9
sympathetic 337.9
upper extremity NEC 354.9
peripheral NEC 443.9
Vasovagal attack (paroxysmal)
780.2
psychogenic 306.2
vCJD (variant Creutzfeldt-Jakob
disease) 046.11
Veldt sore (*see also* Ulcer, skin) 707.9
Ventricle, ventricular—*see also*
condition
standstill (*see also* Arrest, cardiac)
427.5
Vernet's syndrome 352.6
Verrucous endocarditis (acute)
(any valve) (chronic) (subacute)
710.0 *[424.91]*
nonbacterial 710.0 *[424.91]*
Verse's disease (calcinosis
intervertebralis) 275.49
[722.90]
Vertigo 780.4
hysterical 300.11
laryngeal 786.2
Vesania (*see also* Psychosis) 298.9
Vestige, vestigial—*see also*
Persistence
branchial 744.41
Video display tube syndrome
723.8
Villaret's syndrome 352.6
Virchow's disease 733.99
Vitality, lack or want of 780.79
Vocational rehabilitation V57.22
**Vogt's (Cecile) disease or
syndrome** 333.71
Vogt-Spielmeyer disease
(amaurotic familial idiocy) 330.1
Voice
change (*see also* Dysphonia)
784.49
loss (*see also* Aphonia) 784.41
Volhard-Fahr disease (malignant
nephrosclerosis) 403.00
**Volkmann's ischemic contracture
or paralysis** (complicating
trauma) 958.6

**von Bechterew (-Strumpell)
disease or syndrome**
(ankylosing spondylitis) 720.0
von Eulenburg's disease
(congenital paramyotonia)
359.29
von Recklinghausen's
disease or syndrome (nerves) (skin)
(M9540/1) 237.71
tumor (M9540/1) 237.71
von Schroetter's syndrome
(intermittent venous
claudication) 453.89

W

Wagner (-Unverricht) syndrome
(dermatomyositis) 710.3
Wakefulness disorder (*see also*
Hypersomnia) 780.54
nonorganic origin 307.43
Walking
difficulty 719.7
sleep 307.46
hysterical 300.13
Wallenberg's syndrome (posterior
inferior cerebellar artery) (*see
also* Disease, cerebrovascular,
acute) 436
Wandering
acetabulum 736.39
War neurosis 300.16
Wardrop's disease (with
lymphangitis) 681.9
finger 681.02
toe 681.11
Wasting
muscular NEC 728.2
palsy, paralysis 335.21
pelvic muscle 618.83
Water-hammer pulse (*see also*
Insufficiency, aortic) 424.1
Water
on
chest 511.8
Weak, weakness (generalized)
780.79
arches (acquired) 734
congenital 754.61
bladder sphincter 596.59
facial 781.94
heart, cardiac (*see also* Failure,
heart) 428.9
muscle 728.87
myocardium (*see also* Failure,
heart) 428.9
pubocervical tissue 618.81
rectovaginal tissue 618.82
Web, webbed (congenital)—*see also*
Anomaly, specified type NEC
digits (*see also* Syndactylism)
755.10
fingers (*see also* Syndactylism,
fingers) 755.11
larynx (glottic) (subglottic) 748.2
toes (*see also* Syndactylism, toes)
755.13
Weber's paralysis or syndrome
344.89
Weber-Gubler syndrome 344.89
Weber-Leyden syndrome 344.89
**Wedge-shaped or wedging
vertebra** (*see also*
Osteoporosis) 733.00

☑ Additional Digit Required

Wegener's granulomatosis or syndrome 446.4

Weingarten's syndrome (tropical eosinophilia) 518.3

Weir Mitchell's disease (erythromelalgia) 443.82

Weiss-Baker syndrome (carotid sinus syncope) 337.01

Weissenbach-Thibierge syndrome (cutaneous systemic sclerosis) 710.1

Werdnig-Hoffmann syndrome (muscular atrophy) 335.0

Wernicke's encephalopathy, disease, or syndrome (superior hemorrhagic polioencephalitis) 265.1

Wernicke-Korsakoff syndrome or psychosis (nonalcoholic) 294.0
    alcoholic 291.1

West Nile
    encephalitis 066.41
    encephalomyelitis 066.41
    fever 066.40
        with
            cranial nerve disorders 066.42
            encephalitis 066.41
            optic neuritis 066.42
            other complications 066.49
            other neurologic manifestations 066.42
            polyradiculitis 066.42
            virus 066.40

Wet
    lung (syndrome)
        adult 518.5
        newborn 770.6

Wheelchair confinement status V46.3

Wheezing 786.07

Whitlow (with lymphangitis) 681.01

Whooping cough 033.9
    due to
        Bordetella
            bronchoseptica 033.8
                with pneumonia 033.8 [484.3]
            parapertussis 033.1
                with pneumonia 033.1 [484.3]
            pertussis 033.0
                with pneumonia 033.0 [484.3]
        specified organism NEC 033.8
            with pneumonia 033.8 [484.3]
    with pneumonia 033.9 [484.3]

Wichmann's asthma (laryngismus stridulus) 478.75

Wilson-Mikity syndrome 770.7

Winged scapula 736.89

Withdrawal symptoms, syndrome
    alcohol 291.81
        delirium (acute) 291.0
            chronic 291.1
    drug or narcotic 292.0

Withdrawing reaction, child or adolescent 313.22

Wohlfart-Kugelberg-Welander disease 335.11

Woillez's disease (acute idiopathic pulmonary congestion) 518.5

Wood asthma 495.8

Word
    blindness (congenital) (developmental) 315.01
    deafness (secondary to organic lesion) 784.69
    developmental 315.31

Worn out (see also Exhaustion) 780.79
    joint prosthesis (see also Complications, mechanical, device NEC, prosthetic NEC, joint) 996.46

Wound, open (by cutting or piercing instrument) (by firearms) (cut) (dissection) (incised) (laceration) (penetration) (perforating) (puncture) (with initial hemorrhage, not internal) 879.8
    amputation, traumatic
        arm
            bilateral
                any level 887.6
                    complicated 887.7
            unilateral
                at or above elbow 887.2
                    complicated 887.3
                below elbow 887.0
                    complicated 887.1
                level not specified 887.4
                    complicated 887.5
        finger 886.0
            complicated 886.1
        foot
            bilateral 896.2
                complicated 896.3
            unilateral 896.0
                complicated 896.1
        leg
            bilateral
                any level 897.6
                    complicated 897.7
            unilateral
                at or above knee 897.2
                    complicated 897.3
                below knee 897.0
                    complicated 897.1
                level not specified 897.4
                    complicated 897.5
        thumb 885.0
            complicated 885.1
        toe 895.0
            complicated 895.1
    ankle 891.0
        complicated 891.1
        with tendon involvement 891.2
    arm
        amputation, traumatic
            bilateral
                any level 887.6
                    complicated 887.7

Wound, open—continued
    arm—continued
        amputation, traumatic—continued
            unilateral
                at or above elbow 887.2
                    complicated 887.3
                below elbow 887.0
                    complicated 887.1
                level not specified 887.4
                    complicated 887.5
        upper 880.0☑
            complicated 880.1☑
            with tendon involvement 880.2☑

Note—Use the following fifth-digit subclassification with category 880:
0   shoulder region
1   scapular region
2   axillary region
3   upper arm
9   multiple sites

---

    calf 891.0
        complicated 891.1
    digit(s)
        hand 883.0
            complicated 883.1
            with tendon involvement 883.2
    elbow 881.01
        complicated 881.11
        with tendon involvement 881.21
    finger(s) (nail) (subungual) 883.0
        complicated 883.1
        with tendon involvement 883.2
    foot (any part except toe(s) alone) 892.0
        complicated 892.1
        with tendon involvement 892.2
    forarm 881.00
        complicated 881.10
        with tendon involvement 881.20
    hand (except finger(s) alone) 882.0
        complicated 882.1
        with tendon involvement 882.2
    heel 892.0
        complicated 892.1
    hip 890.0
        complicated 890.1
        with tendon involvement 890.2
    instep 892.0
        complicated 892.1
    knee 891.0
        complicated 891.1
        with tendon involvement 891.2
    leg (multiple) 891.0
        complicated 891.1
        lower 891.0
            complicated 891.1
            with tendon involvement 891.2
    limb
        multiple and unspecified
            lower 894.0
                complicated 894.1

Wound, open—continued
    limb—continued
        multiple and unspecified—continued
            lower—continued
                with tendon involvement 894.2
            upper 884.0
                complicated 884.1
                with tendon involvement 884.2
    nail
        finger(s) 883.0
            complicated 883.1
        thumb 883.0
            complicated 883.1
    popliteal space 891.0
        complicated 891.1
    shin 891.0
        complicated 891.1
    shoulder 880.0☑
        complicated 880.1☑
        with tendon involvement 880.2☑
    thigh 890.0
        complicated 890.1
        with tendon involvement 890.2
    thumb (nail) (subungual) 883.0
        complicated 883.1
        with tendon involvement 883.2
    wrist 881.02
        complicated 881.12
        with tendon involvement 881.22

Wright's syndrome (hyperabduction) 447.8
    pneumonia 390 [517.1]

Wrist—see also condition
    drop (acquired) 736.05

X

Xiphodynia 733.90
Xiphoidalgia 733.90
Xiphoiditis 733.99

Y

Yawning 786.09
    psychogenic 306.1

Z

Ziehen-Oppenheim disease 333.6
Zygodactyly (see also Syndactylism) 755.10

Alphabetic Index to External Causes of Injury and Poisoning (E Code)

This section contains the index to the codes which classify environmental events, circumstances, and other conditions as the cause of injury and other adverse effects. Where a code from the section Supplementary Classification of External Causes of Injury and Poisoning (E800–E999) is applicable, it is intended that the E code will be used in addition to a code from the main body of the classification, chapters 1 to 17.

The alphabetic index to the E codes is organized by main terms that describe the accident, circumstance, event, or specific agent that caused the injury or other adverse effect.

Note: Categories E001-E030 are provided to use to indicate the activity of the person seeking healthcare for an injury or health condition such as a fracture while climbing, which resulted from, or was contributed to, by the activity. These codes are for use for both acute injuries and conditions that are due to the long-term, cumulative affects of an injury. They are also appropriate for use with external cause codes for cause and intent if identifying the activity provides additional information about the event. These codes should be used in conjunction with other external cause codes for external cause status and place of occurrence.

Note: Transport accidents (E800–E848) include accidents involving:

> Aircraft and spacecraft (E840–E845)
>
> Watercraft (E830–E838)
>
> Motor vehicle (E810–E825)
>
> Railway (E800–E807)
>
> Other road vehicles (E826–E829)

For definitions and examples related to transport accidents, *see* volume 1 code categories E800–E848.

The fourth-digit subdivisions for use with categories E800–E848 to identify the injured person are found at the end of this section.

For identifying the place in which an accident or poisoning occurred (circumstances classifiable to categories E850–E869 and E880–E928), *see* the listing in this section under "Accident, occurring."

☑ Additional Digit Required

A

Accident (to) E928.9
  aircraft (in transit) (powered)
      E841☑
    at landing, take-off E840☑
    due to, caused by cataclysm—
        see categories E908☑,
        E909☑
    late effect of E929.1
    unpowered (see also Collision,
        aircraft, unpowered)
        E842☑
    while alighting, boarding
        E843☑
  amphibious vehicle
    on
      land—see Accident, motor
          vehicle
      water—see Accident,
          watercraft
  animal, ridden NEC E828☑
  animal-drawn vehicle NEC E827☑
  balloon (see also Collision, aircraft,
      unpowered) E842☑
  caused by, due to
    abrasive wheel (metalworking)
        E919.3
    animal NEC E906.9
      being ridden (in sport or
          transport) E828☑
    avalanche NEC E909.2
    band saw E919.4
    bench saw E919.4
    bore, earth-drilling or mining
        (land) (seabed) E919.1
    bulldozer E919.7
    cataclysmic
      earth surface movement or
          eruption E909.9
      storm E908.9
    chain
      hoist E919.2
        agricultural operations
            E919.0
        mining operations E919.1
      saw E920.1
    circular saw E919.4
    cold (excessive) (see also Cold,
        exposure to) E901.9
    combine E919.0
    conflagration—see
        Conflagration
    corrosive liquid, substance NEC
        E924.1
    cotton gin E919.8
    crane E919.2
      agricultural operations
          E919.0
      mining operations E919.1
    cutting or piercing instrument
        (see also Cut) E920.9
    dairy equipment E919.8
    derrick E919.2
      agricultural operations
          E919.0
      mining operations E919.1
    drill E920.1
      earth (land) (seabed) E919.1
      hand (powered) E920.1
        not powered E920.4
      metalworking E919.3
      woodworking E919.4
    earth(-)
      drilling machine E919.1
      moving machine E919.7

Accident (to)—*continued*
  caused by, due to—*continued*
    earth(-)—*continued*
      scraping machine E919.7
    electric
      current (see also Electric
          shock) E925.9
      motor—see also Accident,
          machine, by type of
          machine
        current (of)—see Electric
            shock
    elevator (building) (grain)
        E919.2
      agricultural operations
          E919.0
      mining operations E919.1
    environmental factors NEC
        E928.9
    excavating machine E919.7
    explosive material (see also
        Explosion) E923.9
    farm machine E919.0
    fire, flames—see also Fire
      conflagration—see
          Conflagration
    firearm missile—see Shooting
    forging (metalworking) machine
        E919.3
    forklift (truck) E919.2
      agricultural operations
          E919.0
      mining operations E919.1
    gas turbine E919.5
    harvester E919.0
    hay derrick, mower, or rake
        E919.0
    heat (excessive) (see also Heat)
        E900.9
    hoist (see also Accident, caused
        by, due to, lift) E919.2
      chain—see Accident, caused
          by, due to, chain
      shaft E919.1
    hot
      liquid E924.0
        caustic or corrosive
            E924.1
      object (not producing fire or
          flames) E924.8
      substance E924.9
        caustic or corrosive
            E924.1
        liquid (metal) NEC E924.0
        specified type NEC E924.8
    human bite E928.3
    ignition—see Ignition
    internal combustion engine
        E919.5
    landslide NEC E909.2
    lathe (metalworking) E919.3
      turnings E920.8
      woodworking E919.4
    lift, lifting (appliances) E919.2
      agricultural operations
          E919.0
      mining operations E919.1
      shaft E919.1
    lightning NEC E907
    machine, machinery—see also
        Accident, machine
      drilling, metal E919.3
      manufacturing, for
          manufacture of
          beverages E919.8

Accident (to)—*continued*
  caused by, due to—*continued*
    machine, machinery—*continued*
      manufacturing, for
          manufacture of—
          continued
        clothing E919.8
        foodstuffs E919.8
        paper E919.8
        textiles E919.8
      milling, metal E919.3
      moulding E919.4
      power press, metal E919.3
      printing E919.8
      rolling mill, metal E919.3
      sawing, metal E919.3
      specified type NEC E919.8
      spinning E919.8
      weaving E919.8
    natural factor NEC E928.9
    overhead plane E919.4
    plane E920.4
      overhead E919.4
    powered
      hand tool NEC E920.1
      saw E919.4
        hand E920.1
    printing machine E919.8
    pulley (block) E919.2
      agricultural operations
          E919.0
      mining operations E919.1
      transmission E919.6
    radial saw E919.4
    radiation—see Radiation
    reaper E919.0
    road scraper E919.7
      when in transport under its
          own power—see
          categories E810-
          E825☑
    roller coaster E919.8
    sander E919.4
    saw E920.4
      band E919.4
      bench E919.4
      chain E920.1
      circular E919.4
      hand E920.4
        powered E920.1
      powered, except hand
          E919.4
      radial E919.4
    sawing machine, metal E919.3
    shaft
      hoist E919.1
      lift E919.1
      transmission E919.6
    shears E920.4
      hand E920.4
        powered E920.1
      mechanical E919.3
    shovel E920.4
      steam E919.7
    spinning machine E919.8
    steam—see also Burning, steam
      engine E919.5
      shovel E919.7
    thresher E919.0
    thunderbolt NEC E907
    tractor E919.0
      when in transport under its
          own power—see
          categories E810-
          E825☑

Accident (to)—*continued*
  caused by, due to—*continued*
    transmission belt, cable, chain,
        gear, pinion, pulley, shaft
        E919.6
    turbine (gas) (water driven)
        E919.5
    under-cutter E919.1
    weaving machine E919.8
    winch E919.2
      agricultural operations
          E919.0
      mining operations E919.1
  diving E883.0
    with insufficient air supply
        E913.2
  glider (hang) (see also Collision,
      aircraft, unpowered) E842☑
  hovercraft
    on
      land—see Accident, motor
          vehicle
      water—see Accident,
          watercraft
  ice yacht (see also Accident, vehicle
      NEC) E848
  in
    medical, surgical procedure
      as, or due to misadventure—
          see Misadventure
      causing an abnormal reaction
          or later complication
          without mention of
          misadventure—see
          Reaction, abnormal
  kite carrying a person (see also
      Collision, involving aircraft,
      unpowered) E842☑
  land yacht (see also Accident,
      vehicle NEC) E848
  late effect of—see Late effect
  launching pad E845☑
  machine, machinery (see also
      Accident, caused by, due to,
      by specific type of machine)
      E919.9
    agricultural including animal-
        powered E919.0
    earth-drilling E919.1
    earth moving or scraping
        E919.7
    excavating E919.7
    involving transport under own
        power on highway or
        transport vehicle—see
        categories E810-E825☑,
        E840-E845☑
    lifting (appliances) E919.2
    metalworking E919.3
    mining E919.1
    prime movers, except electric
        motors E919.5
      electric motors—see
          Accident, machine, by
          specific type of
          machine
    recreational E919.8
    specified type NEC E919.8
    transmission E919.6
    watercraft (deck) (engine room)
        (galley) (laundry)
        (loading) E836☑
    woodworking or forming
        E919.4

☑ Additional Digit Required

Assault—continued
    drugs or medicinals E962.0
    gas(es) or vapors, except drugs
        and medicinals E962.2
    solid or liquid substances,
        except drugs and
        medicinals E962.1
    puncture, any part of body E966
    pushing
        before moving object, train,
          vehicle E968.5
        from high place E968.1
    rape E960.1
    scalding E968.3
    shooting—*see* Shooting, homicide
    sodomy E960.1
    stab, any part of body E966
    strangulation E963
    submersion E964
    suffocation E963
    transport vehicle E968.5
    violence NEC E968.9
    vitriol E961
        swallowed E962.1
    weapon E968.9
        blunt or thrown E968.2
        cutting or piercing E966
        firearm—*see* Shooting, homicide
    wound E968.9
        cutting E966
        gunshot—*see* Shooting,
          homicide
        knife E966
        piercing E966
        puncture E966
        stab E966
Attack by animal NEC E906.9

B

Bending, injury in E927.8

C

Collision (accidental)

*Note—In the case of collisions between
different types of vehicles, persons and
objects, priority in classification is in the
following order:*

  Aircraft
  Watercraft
  Motor vehicle
  Railway vehicle
  Pedal cycle
  Animal-drawn vehicle
  Animal being ridden
  *Streetcar or other nonmotor road
    vehicle*
  Other vehicle
  *Pedestrian or person using pedestrian
    conveyance*
  *Object (except where falling from or set
    in motion by vehicle etc. listed
    above)*

*In the listing below, the combinations are
listed only under the vehicle etc. having
priority. For definitions see Supplementary
Classification of External Causes of Injury
and Poisoning (E800-E999).*

    aircraft (with object or vehicle)
        (fixed) (movable) (moving)
        E841☑

Collision —continued
  aircraft—continued
    with
        person (while landing, taking
          off) (without accident
          to aircraft) E844☑
        powered (in transit) (with
          unpowered aircraft)
          E841☑
          while landing, taking off
            E840☑
        unpowered E842☑
        while landing, taking off E840☑
  animal being ridden (in sport or
      transport) E828☑
    and
        animal (being ridden)
          (herded) (unattended)
          E828☑
        nonmotor road vehicle,
          except pedal cycle or
          animal-drawn vehicle
          E828☑
        object (fallen) (fixed)
          (movable) (moving)
          not falling from or set
          in motion by vehicle of
          higher priority E828☑
        pedestrian (conveyance or
          vehicle) E828☑
  animal-drawn vehicle E827☑
    and
        animal (being ridden)
          (herded) (unattended)
          E827☑
        nonmotor road vehicle,
          except pedal cycle
          E827☑
        object (fallen) (fixed)
          (movable) (moving)
          not falling from or set
          in motion by vehicle of
          higher priority E827☑
  animal-drawn vehicle
    and
        pedestrian (conveyance or
          vehicle) E827☑
        streetcar E827☑
  motor vehicle (on public highway)
      (traffic accident) E812☑
    after leaving, running off, public
        highway (without
        antecedent collision)
        (without re-entry) E816☑
    with antecedent collision on
        public highway—*see*
        categories E810-
        E815☑
    with re-entrance collision
        with another motor
        vehicle E811☑
    and
        abutment (bridge) (overpass)
          E815☑
        animal (herded)
          (unattended) E815☑
        carrying person, property
          E813☑
        animal-drawn vehicle E813☑
        another motor vehicle
          (abandoned) (disabled)
          (parked) (stalled)
          (stopped) E812☑

Collision —continued
  motor vehicle—continued
    and—continued
        another motor vehicle—
          continued
          with, involving re-
            entrance (on same
            roadway) (across
            median strip)
            E811☑
        any object, person, or vehicle
          off the public highway
          resulting from a
          noncollision motor
          vehicle nontraffic
          accident E816☑
        avalanche, fallen or not
          moving E815☑
        falling E909.2
        stone E815☑
        tree E815☑
        guard post or guard rail
          E815☑
        inter-highway divider E815☑
        landslide, fallen or not
          moving E815☑
          moving E909☑
        machinery (road) E815☑
        nonmotor road vehicle NEC
          E813☑
        object (any object, person, or
          vehicle off the public
          highway resulting from
          a noncollision motor
          vehicle nontraffic
          accident) E815☑
        off, normally not on,
          public highway
          resulting from a
          noncollision motor
          vehicle traffic
          accident E816☑
        pedal cycle E813☑
        pedestrian (conveyance)
          E814☑
        person (using pedestrian
          conveyance) E814☑
        post or pole (lamp) (light)
          (signal) (telephone)
          (utility) E815☑
        railway rolling stock, train,
          vehicle E810☑
        safety island E815☑
        street car E813☑
        traffic signal, sign, or marker
          (temporary) E815☑
        tree E815☑
        tricycle E813☑
        wall of cut made for road
          E815☑
    due to cataclysm—*see*
        categories E908☑,
        E909☑
    not on public highway,
        nontraffic accident
        E822☑
        and
          animal (carrying person,
            property) (herded)
            (unattended)
            E822☑
          animal-drawn vehicle
            E822☑

Collision —continued
  motor vehicle—continued
    not on public highway,
        nontraffic accident—
        continued
        and—continued
          another motor vehicle
            (moving), except
            off-road motor
            vehicle E822☑
            stationary E823☑
          avalanche, fallen, not
            moving E823☑
            moving E909.2
          landslide, fallen, not
            moving E823☑
            moving E909.2
          nonmotor vehicle
            (moving) E822☑
            stationary E823☑
          object (fallen) (normally)
            (fixed) (movable
            but not in motion)
            (stationary) E823☑
          moving, except when
            falling from, set
            in motion by,
            aircraft or
            cataclysm
            E822☑
          pedal cycle (moving)
            E822☑
            stationary E823☑
          pedestrian (conveyance)
            E822☑
          person (using pedestrian
            conveyance)
            E822☑
          railway rolling stock, train,
            vehicle (moving)
            E822☑
            stationary E823☑
          road vehicle (any)
            (moving) E822☑
            stationary E823☑
          tricycle (moving) E822☑
            stationary E823☑
    off-road type motor vehicle (not on
        public highway) E821☑
    and
        animal (being ridden) (-
          drawn vehicle) E821☑
        another off-road motor
          vehicle, except snow
          vehicle E821☑
        other motor vehicle, not on
          public highway E821☑
        other object or vehicle NEC,
          fixed or movable, not
          set in motion by
          aircraft, motor vehicle
          on highway, or snow
          vehicle, motor driven
          E821☑
        pedal cycle E821☑
        pedestrian (conveyance)
          E821☑
        railway train E821☑
    on public highway—*see*
        Collision, motor vehicle

Collision —continued
pedal cycle E826☑
    and
        animal (carrying person,
            property) (herded)
            (unherded) E826☑
        animal-drawn vehicle E826☑
        another pedal cycle E826☑
        nonmotor road vehicle
            E826☑
        object (fallen) (fixed)
            (movable) (moving)
            not falling from or set
            in motion by aircraft,
            motor vehicle, or
            railway train NEC
            E826☑
        pedestrian (conveyance)
            E826☑
        person (using pedestrian
            conveyance) E826☑
        street car E826☑
pedestrian(s) (conveyance) E917.9
    with fall E886.9
        in sports E886.0
    and
        crowd, human stampede
            E917.1
            with subsequent fall
                E917.6
        furniture E917.3
            with subsequent fall
                E917.7
        machinery—see Accident,
            machine
        object (fallen) (moving) not
            falling from NEC, fixed
            or set in motion by any
            vehicle classifiable to
            E800-E848 E917.9
            with subsequent fall
                E917.6
            caused by a crowd E917.1
                with subsequent fall
                    E917.6
            furniture E917.3
                with subsequent fall
                    E917.7
            in
                running water E917.2
                    with drowning or
                        submersion—
                        see Submersion
                sports E917.0
                    with subsequent fall
                        E917.5
                stationary E917.4
                    with subsequent fall
                        E917.8
        vehicle, nonmotor, nonroad
            E848
    in
        running water E917.2
            with drowning or
                submersion—see
                Submersion
        sports E917.0
            with fall E886.0
    person(s) (using pedestrian
        conveyance) (see also
        Collision, pedestrian) E917.9

Collision —continued
railway (rolling stock) (train)
    (vehicle) (with (subsequent)
    derailment, explosion, fall or
    fire) E800☑
    with antecedent derailment
        E802☑
    and
        animal (carrying person)
            (herded) (unattended)
            E801☑
        another railway train or
            vehicle E800☑
        buffers E801☑
        fallen tree on railway E801☑
        farm machinery, nonmotor
            (in transport)
            (stationary) E801☑
        gates E801☑
        nonmotor vehicle E801☑
        object (fallen) (fixed)
            (movable) (moving)
            not falling from, set in
            motion by, aircraft or
            motor vehicle NEC
            E801☑
        pedal cycle E801☑
        pedestrian (conveyance)
            E805☑
        person (using pedestrian
            conveyance) E805☑
        platform E801☑
        rock on railway E801☑
        street car E801☑
snow vehicle, motor-driven (not on
    public highway) E820☑
    and
        animal (being ridden) (-
            drawn vehicle) E820☑
        another off-road motor
            vehicle E820☑
        other motor vehicle, not on
            public highway E820☑
        other object or vehicle NEC,
            fixed or movable, not
            set in motion by
            aircraft or motor
            vehicle on highway
            E820☑
        pedal cycle E820☑
        pedestrian (conveyance)
            E820☑
        railway train E820☑
    on public highway—see
        Collision, motor vehicle
street car(s) E829☑
    and
        animal, herded, not being
            ridden, unattended
            E829☑
        nonmotor road vehicle NEC
            E829☑
        object (fallen) (fixed)
            (movable) (moving)
            not falling from or set
            in motion by aircraft,
            animal-drawn vehicle,
            animal being ridden,
            motor vehicle, pedal
            cycle, or railway train
            E829☑
        pedestrian (conveyance)
            E829☑
        person (using pedestrian
            conveyance) E829☑

Collision —continued
vehicle
    animal-drawn—see Collision,
        animal-drawn vehicle
    motor—see Collision, motor
        vehicle
    nonmotor
        nonroad E848
        and
            another nonmotor,
                nonroad vehicle
                E848
            object (fallen) (fixed)
                (movable)
                (moving) not
                falling from or
                set in motion by
                aircraft, animal-
                drawn vehicle,
                animal being
                ridden, motor
                vehicle,
                nonmotor road
                vehicle, pedal
                cycle, railway
                train, or streetcar
                E848
        road, except animal being
            ridden, animal-drawn
            vehicle, or pedal cycle
            E829☑
        and
            animal, herded, not
                being ridden,
                unattended
                E829☑
            another nonmotor
                road vehicle,
                except animal
                being ridden,
                animal-drawn
                vehicle, or pedal
                cycle E829☑
            object (fallen) (fixed)
                (movable)
                (moving) not
                falling from or
                set in motion by,
                aircraft, animal-
                drawn vehicle,
                animal being
                ridden, motor
                vehicle, pedal
                cycle, or railway
                train E829☑
            pedestrian
                (conveyance)
                E829☑
            person (using
                pedestrian
                conveyance)
                E829☑
            vehicle, nonmotor,
                nonroad E829☑
    watercraft E838☑
    and
        person swimming or water
            skiing E838☑
    causing
        drowning, submersion
            E830☑
        injury except drowning,
            submersion E831☑

**Complication of medical or
    surgical procedure or
    treatment**
as an abnormal reaction—see
    Reaction, abnormal
delayed, without mention of
    misadventure—see Reaction,
    abnormal
due to misadventure—see
    Misadventure
Conflagration
building or structure, except
    private dwelling (barn)
    (church) (convalescent or
    residential home) (factory)
    (farm outbuilding) (hospital)
    (hotel) (institution)
    (educational) (domitory)
    (residential) (school) (shop)
    (store) (theater) E891.9
    with or causing (injury due to)
        accident or injury NEC
            E891.9
            specified circumstance
                NEC E891.8
    burns, burning E891.3
    carbon monoxide E891.2
    fumes E891.2
        polyvinylchloride (PVC) or
            similar material
            E891.1
    smoke E891.2
    causing explosion E891.0
    in terrorism E979.3
not in building or structure E892
private dwelling (apartment)
    (boarding house) (camping
    place) (caravan) (farmhouse)
    (home (private)) (house)
    (lodging house) (private
    garage) (rooming house)
    (tenement) E890.9
    with or causing (injury due to)
        accident or injury NEC
            E890.9
            specified circumstance
                NEC E890.8
    burns, burning E890.3
    carbon monoxide E890.2
    fumes E890.2
        polyvinylchloride (PVC) or
            similar material
            E890.1
    smoke E890.2
    causing explosion E890.0
Crash
aircraft (in transit) (powered)
    E841☑
    at landing, take-off E840☑
    in
        terrorism E979.1
        war operations E994
    on runway NEC E840☑
    stated as
        homicidal E968.8
        suicidal E958.6
        undetermined whether
            accidental or
            intentional E988.6
    unpowered E842☑
    glider E842☑
motor vehicle—see also Accident,
    motor vehicle
    homicidal E968.5
    suicidal E958.5

Crash—*continued*
  motor vehicle—*continued*
    undetermined whether
      accidental or intentional
      E988.5
Crushed (accidentally) E928.9
  between
    boat(s), ship(s), watercraft (and
      dock or pier) (without
      accident to watercraft)
      E838☑
    after accident to, or collision,
      watercraft E831☑
    objects (moving) (stationary and
      moving) E918
  by
    avalanche NEC E909.2
    boat, ship, watercraft after
      accident to, collision,
      watercraft E831☑
    cave-in E916
      with asphyxiation or
        suffocation (*see* also
        Suffocation, due to,
        cave-in) E913.3
    crowd, human stampede
      E917.1
    falling
      aircraft (*see* also Accident,
        aircraft) E841☑
        in
          terrorism E979.1
          war operations E994.8
      earth, material E916
        with asphyxiation or
          suffocation (*see* also
          Suffocation, due to,
          cave-in) E913.3
      object E916
        on ship, watercraft
          E838☑
          while loading, unloading
            watercraft E838☑
    landslide NEC E909.2
    lifeboat after abandoning ship
      E831☑
    machinery—*see* Accident,
      machine
    railway rolling stock, train,
      vehicle (part of) E805☑
    street car E829☑
    vehicle NEC—*see* Accident,
      vehicle NEC
  in
    machinery—*see* Accident,
      machine
    object E918
    transport accident—*see*
      categories E800-E848☑
  late effect of NEC E929.9

E

**Exertion, excessive physical, from
  prolonged activity** E927.2
Exhaustion
  due to excessive exertion E927.8

F

Fall, falling (accidental) E888.9
  building E916
    burning E891.8
      private E890.8

Fall, falling —*continued*
  down
    escalator E880.0
    ladder E881.0
      in boat, ship, watercraft
        E833☑
    staircase E880.9
    stairs, steps—*see* Fall, from,
      stairs
    earth (with asphyxia or suffocation
      (by pressure)) (*see* also Earth,
      falling) E913.3
  from, off
    aircraft (at landing, take-off) (in-
      transit) (while alighting,
      boarding) E843☑
      resulting from accident to
        aircraft—*see* categories
        E840-E842☑
    animal (in sport or transport)
      E828☑
    animal-drawn vehicle E827☑
    balcony E882
    bed E884.4
    bicycle E826☑
    boat, ship, watercraft (into
      water) E832☑
      after accident to, collision,
        fire on E830☑
        and subsequently struck
          by (part of) boat
          E831☑
      and subsequently struck by
        (part of) while
        alighting, boat E838☑
      burning, crushed, sinking
        E830☑
        and subsequently struck
          by (part of) boat
          E831☑
    bridge E882
    building E882
      burning (uncontrolled fire)
        E891.8
        in terrorism E979.3
      private E890.8
    bunk in boat, ship, watercraft
      E834☑
      due to accident to watercraft
        E831☑
    cable car (not on rails) E847
      on rails E829☑
    car—*see* Fall from motor vehicle
    chair E884.2
    cliff E884.1
    commode E884.6
  from, off
    curb (sidewalk) E880.1
    elevation aboard ship E834☑
      due to accident to ship
        E831☑
    embankment E884.9
    escalator E880.0
    fire escape E882
    flagpole E882
    furniture NEC E884.5
    gangplank (into water) (*see* also
      Fall, from, boat) E832☑
      to deck, dock E834☑
    hammock on ship E834☑
      due to accident to watercraft
        E831☑
    haystack E884.9
    heelies E885.1

Fall, falling —*continued*
  from, off—*continued*
    high place NEC E884.9
      stated as undetermined
        whether accidental or
        intentional—*see*
        Jumping, from, high
        place
    horse (in sport or transport)
      E828☑
    in-line skates E885.1
    ladder E881.0
      in boat, ship, watercraft
        E833☑
        due to accident to
          watercraft E831☑
    machinery—*see* also Accident,
      machine
      not in operation E884.9
    motor vehicle (in motion) (on
      public highway) E818☑
      not on public highway
        E825☑
        stationary, except while
          alighting, boarding,
          entering, leaving
          E884.9
        while alighting, boarding,
          entering, leaving
          E824☑
      stationary, except while
        alighting, boarding,
        entering, leaving
        E884.9
      while alighting, boarding,
        entering, leaving,
        except off-road type
        motor vehicle E817☑
      off-road type—*see* Fall,
        from, off-road type
        motor vehicle
    nonmotor road vehicle (while
      alighting, boarding) NEC
      E829☑
      stationary, except while
        alighting, boarding,
        entering, leaving
        E884.9
    off road type motor vehicle (not
      on public highway) NEC
      E821☑
      on public highway E818☑
        while alighting, boarding,
          entering, leaving
          E817☑
    snow vehicle—*see* Fall from
      snow vehicle, motor-
      driven
    one
      deck to another on ship
        E834☑
        due to accident to ship
          E831☑
      level to another NEC E884.9
        boat, ship, or watercraft
          E834☑
          due to accident to
            watercraft
            E831☑
    pedal cycle E826☑
    playground equipment E884.0

Fall, falling —*continued*
  from, off—*continued*
    railway rolling stock, train,
      vehicle (while alighting,
      boarding) E804☑
      with
        collision (*see* also
          Collision, railway)
          E800☑
        derailment (*see* also
          Derailment, railway)
          E802☑
        explosion (*see* also
          Explosion, railway
          engine) E803☑
      rigging (aboard ship) E834☑
        due to accident to watercraft
          E831☑
      roller skates E885.1
      scaffolding E881.1
      scooter (nonmotorized) E885.0
      sidewalk (curb) E880.1
        moving E885.9
      skate board E885.2
      skis E885.3
      snow vehicle, motor-driven (not
        on public highway)
        E820☑
        on public highway E818☑
          while alighting, boarding,
            entering, leaving
            E817☑
      snowboard E885.4
      stairs, steps E880.9
        boat, ship, watercraft E833☑
          due to accident to
            watercraft E831☑
        motor bus, motor vehicle—
          see Fall, from, motor
          vehicle, while
          alighting, boarding
        street car E829☑
      stationary vehicle NEC E884.9
      stepladder E881.0
      street car (while boarding,
        alighting) E829
        stationary, except while
          boarding or alighting
          E884.9☑
      structure NEC E882
        burning (uncontrolled fire)
          E891.8
          in terrorism E979.3
      table E884.9
      toilet E884.6
      tower E882
      tree E884.9
      turret E882
      vehicle NEC—*see* also Accident,
        vehicle NEC
        stationary E884.9
      viaduct E882
      wall E882
      wheelchair E884.3
      wheelies E885.1
      window E882
  in, on
    aircraft (at landing, take-off) (in-
      transit) E843☑
      resulting from accident to
        aircraft—*see* categories
        E840-E842☑

Fall, falling —*continued*
in, on—*continued*
  boat, ship, watercraft E835☑
    due to accident to watercraft
     E831☑
    one level to another NEC
     E834☑
    on ladder, stairs E833☑
  cutting or piercing instrument
    or machine E888.0
  deck (of boat, ship, watercraft)
    E835☑
    due to accident to watercraft
     E831☑
  escalator E880.0
  gangplank E835☑
  glass, broken E888.0
  knife E888.0
  ladder E881.0
    in boat, ship, watercraft
     E833☑
     due to accident to
      watercraft E831☑
  object
    edged, pointed or sharp
     E888.0
    other E888.1
  pitchfork E888.0
  railway rolling stock, train,
    vehicle (while alighting,
    boarding) E804☑
    with
     collision (see also
      Collision, railway)
      E800☑
     derailment (see also
      Derailment, railway)
      E802☑
     explosion (see also
      Explosion, railway
      engine) E803☑
  scaffolding E881.1
  scissors E888.0
  staircase, stairs, steps (see also
    Fall, from, stairs) E880.9
  street car E829☑
  water transport (see also Fall, in,
    boat) E835☑
into
  cavity E883.9
  dock E883.9
    from boat, ship, watercraft
     (see also Fall, from,
     boat) E832☑
  hold (of ship) E834☑
    due to accident to watercraft
     E831☑
  hole E883.9
  manhole E883.2
  moving part of machinery—see
    Accident, machine
  opening in surface NEC E883.9
  pit E883.9
  quarry E883.9
  shaft E883.9
  storm drain E883.2
  tank E883.9
  water (with drowning or
    submersion) E910.9
  well E883.1
late effect of NEC E929.3
object (see also Hit by, object,
  falling) E916
other E888.8

Fall, falling —*continued*
over
  animal E885.9
  cliff E884.1
  embankment E884.9
  small object E885.9
overboard (see also Fall, from, boat)
  E832☑
resulting in striking against object
  E888.1
  sharp E888.0
rock E916
same level NEC E888.9
  aircraft (any kind) E843☑
    resulting from accident to
     aircraft—see categories
     E840-E842☑
  boat, ship, watercraft E835☑
    due to accident to, collision,
     watercraft E831☑
  from
    collision, pushing, shoving,
     by or with other
     person(s) E886.9
     as, or caused by, a crowd
      E917.6
     in sports E886.0
  in-line skates E885.1
  roller skates E885.1
  scooter (nonmotorized)
    E885.0
  skateboard E885.2
  slipping, stumbling, tripping
    E885.9
  snowboard E885.4
snowslide E916
  as avalanche E909.2
stone E916
through
  hatch (on ship) E834☑
    due to accident to watercraft
     E831☑
  roof E882
  window E882
timber E916
while alighting from, boarding,
  entering, leaving
  aircraft (any kind) E843☑
  motor bus, motor vehicle—see
    Fall, from, motor vehicle,
    while alighting, boarding
  nonmotor road vehicle NEC
    E829☑
  railway train E804☑
  street car E829☑
Fallen on by
animal (horse) (not being ridden)
  E906.8
  being ridden (in sport or
    transport) E828☑
**Fell or jumped from high place,
  so stated**—see Jumping, from,
  high place
Felo-de-se (see also Suicide) E958.9
Fever
heat—see Heat
thermic—see Heat
Fight (hand) (fist) (foot) (see also
  Assault, fight) E960.0
Fire (accidental) (caused by great
  heat from appliance (electrical),
  hot object or hot substance)
  (secondary, resulting from
  explosion) E899
  conflagration—see Conflagration

Fire—*continued*
controlled, normal (in brazier,
  fireplace, furnace, or stove)
  (charcoal) (coal) (coke)
  (electric) (gas) (wood)
  bonfire E897
  brazier, not in building or
    structure E897
controlled, normal
  in building or structure, except
    private dwelling (barn)
    (church) (convalescent or
    residential home) (factory)
    (farm outbuilding)
    (hospital) (hotel)
    (institution (educational)
    (dormitory) (residential))
    (private garage) (school)
    (shop) (store) (theatre)
    E896
    in private dwelling (apartment)
    (boarding house)
    (camping place) (caravan)
    (farmhouse) (home
    (private)) (house) (lodging
    house) (rooming house)
    (tenement) E895
  not in building or structure E897
  trash E897
forest (uncontrolled) E892
grass (uncontrolled) E892
hay (uncontrolled) E892
homicide (attempt) E968.0
  late effect of E969
in, of, on, starting in E892
  aircraft (in transit) (powered)
    E841☑
    at landing, take-off E840☑
    stationary E892
    unpowered (balloon) (glider)
    E842☑
  balloon E842☑
  boat, ship, watercraft—see
    categories E830☑,
    E831☑, E837☑
  building or structure, except
    private dwelling (barn)
    (church) (convalescent or
    residential home) (factory)
    (farm outbuilding)
    (hospital) (hotel)
    (institution (educational)
    (dormitory) (residential))
    (school) (shop) (store)
    (theatre) (see also
    Conflagration, building or
    structure, except private
    dwelling) E891.9
  forest (uncontrolled) E892
  glider E842☑
  grass (uncontrolled) E892
  hay (uncontrolled) E892
  lumber (uncontrolled) E892
  machinery—see Accident,
    machine
  mine (uncontrolled) E892
  motor vehicle (in motion) (on
    public highway) E818☑
    not on public highway
     E825☑
    stationary E892
  prairie (uncontrolled) E892

Fire—*continued*
in, of, on, starting in—*continued*
  private dwelling (apartment)
    (boarding house)
    (camping place) (caravan)
    (farmhouse) (home
    (private)) (house) (lodging
    house) (private garage)
    (rooming house)
    (tenement) (see also
    Conflagration, private
    dwelling) E890.9
  railway rolling stock, train,
    vehicle (see also Explosion,
    railway engine) E803☑
    stationary E892
  room NEC E898.1
in, of, on, starting in
  street car (in motion) E829☑
    stationary E892
  terrorism (by fire-producing
    device) E979.3
    fittings or furniture (burning
     building) (uncontrolled
     fire) E979.3
    from nuclear explosion
     E979.5
  transport vehicle, stationary
    NEC E892
  tunnel (uncontrolled) E892
  war operations (by fire-
    producing device or
    conventional weapon)
    E990.9
    from nuclear explosion (see
     also War operations,
     injury due to, nuclear
     weapons) E996.2
    incendiary bomb
     E990.0petrol bomb
     E990.0
late effect of NEC E929.4
lumber (uncontrolled) E892
mine (uncontrolled) E892
prairie (uncontrolled) E892
self-inflicted (unspecified whether
  accidental or intentional)
  E988.1
  stated as intentional, purposeful
    E958.1
specified NEC E898.1
  with
    conflagration—see
     Conflagration
    ignition (of)
     clothing—see Ignition,
      clothes
     highly inflammable
      material (benzine)
      (fat) (gasoline)
      (kerosene) (paraffin)
      (petrol) E894
started by other person
  stated as
    with intent to injure or kill
     E968.0
    undetermined whether or
     not with intent to
     injure or kill E988.1
suicide (attempted) E958.1
  late effect of E959
tunnel (uncontrolled) E892

Fracture (circumstances unknown or unspecified) E887
  due to specified external means—*see* manner of accident
  late effect of NEC E929.3
  occurring in water transport NEC E835☑

H

Hit, hitting (accidental) by
  aircraft (propeller) (without accident to aircraft) E844☑
    unpowered E842☑
  avalanche E909.2
  being thrown against object in or part of
    motor vehicle (in motion) (on public highway) E818☑
      not on public highway E825☑
    nonmotor road vehicle NEC E829☑
    street car E829☑
  boat, ship, watercraft
    after fall from watercraft E838☑
    damaged, involved in accident E831☑
  boat, ship, watercraft
    while swimming, water skiing E838☑
  bullet (*see also* Shooting) E922.9
    from air gun E922.4
    in
      terrorism E979.4
      war operations E991.2
        rubber E991.0
  flare, Verey pistol (*see also* Shooting) E922.8
  hailstones E904.3
  landslide E909.2
  law-enforcing agent (on duty) E975
    with blunt object (baton) (night stick) (stave) (truncheon) E973
  machine—*see* Accident, machine
  missile
    firearm (*see also* shooting) E922.9
    in
      terrorism—*see* Terrorism, missile
      war operations—*see* War operations, missile
  motor vehicle (on public highway) (traffic accident) E814☑
    not on public highway, nontraffic accident E822☑
    nonmotor road vehicle NEC E829☑
  object
    falling E916
      from, in, on
        aircraft E844☑
          due to accident to aircraft—*see* categories E840-E842☑
          unpowered E842☑
        boat, ship, watercraft E838☑
          due to accident to watercraft E831☑

Hit, hitting—*continued*
  object—*continued*
    falling—*continued*
      from, in, on—*continued*
        building E916
          burning (uncontrolled fire) E891.8
            in terrorism E979.3
            private E890.8
        cataclysmic
          earth surface movement or eruption E909.9
          storm E908.9
        cave-in E916
          with asphyxiation or suffocation (*see also* Suffocation, due to, cave-in) E913.3
        earthquake E909.0
        motor vehicle (in motion) (on public highway) E818☑
          not on public highway E825☑
          stationary E916
        nonmotor road vehicle NEC E829☑
        pedal cycle E826☑
        railway rolling stock, train, vehicle E806☑
        street car E829☑
        structure, burning NEC E891.8
        vehicle, stationary E916
    moving NEC—*see* Striking against, object
    projected NEC—*see* Striking against, object
    set in motion by
      compressed air or gas, spring, striking, throwing—*see* Striking against, object
      explosion—*see* Explosion
    thrown into, on, or towards
      motor vehicle (in motion) (on public highway) E818☑
        not on public highway E825☑
      nonmotor road vehicle NEC E829☑
      pedal cycle E826☑
      street car E829☑
    off-road type motor vehicle (not on public highway) E821☑
    on public highway E814☑
  other person(s) E917.9
    with blunt or thrown object E917.9
      in sports E917.0
        with subsequent fall E917.5
    intentionally, homicidal E968.2
    as, or caused by, a crowd E917.1
      with subsequent fall E917.6
    in sports E917.0
  pedal cycle E826☑

Hit, hitting—*continued*
  police (on duty) E975
    with blunt object (baton) (nightstick) (stave) (truncheon) E973
  railway, rolling stock, train, vehicle (part of) E805☑
  shot—*see* Shooting
  snow vehicle, motor-driven (not on public highway) E820☑
    on public highway E814☑
  street car E829☑
  vehicle NEC—*see* Accident, vehicle NEC

I

Injury, injured (accidental(ly)) NEC E928.9
  by, caused by, from
    air rifle (BB gun) E922.4
    animal (not being ridden) NEC E906.9
      being ridden (in sport or transport) E828☑
    assault (*see also* Assault) E968.9
    avalanche E909.2
    bayonet (*see also* Bayonet wound) E920.3
    being thrown against some part of, or object in
      motor vehicle (in motion) (on public highway) E818☑
        not on public highway E825☑
      nonmotor road vehicle NEC E829☑
      off-road motor vehicle NEC E821☑
      railway train E806☑
      snow vehicle, motor-driven E820☑
      street car E829☑
    bending E927.8
    bite, human E928.3
    broken glass E920.8
    bullet—*see* Shooting
    cave-in (*see also* Suffocation, due to, cave-in) E913.3
      without asphyxiation or suffocation E916
    earth surface movement or eruption E909.9
      storm E908.9
    cloudburst E908.8
    component of firearm or air gun E928.7
    cutting or piercing instrument (*see also* Cut) E920.9
    cyclone E908.1
    earth surface movement or eruption E909.9
    earthquake E909.0
    electric current (*see also* Electric shock) E925.9
    explosion (*see also* Explosion) E923.9
      gun recoil E928.7
      mechanism of firearm or air gun E928.7
      recoil of firearm E938.7
    fire—*see* Fire
    flare, Verey pistol E922.8

Injury, injured—*continued*
  by, caused by, from—*continued*
    flood E908.2
    foreign body—*see* Foreign body
    hailstones E904.3
    hurricane E908.0
    landslide E909.2
    law-enforcing agent, police, in course of legal intervention—*see* Legal intervention
    lightning E907
    live rail or live wire—*see* Electric shock
    machinery—*see also* Accident, machine
      aircraft, without accident to aircraft E844☑
      boat, ship, watercraft (deck) (engine room) (galley) (laundry) (loading) E836☑
    missile
      explosive E923.8
      firearm—*see* Shooting
      in
        terrorism—*see* Terrorism, missile
        war operations—*see* War operations, missile
    moving part of motor vehicle (in motion) (on public highway) E818☑
      not on public highway, nontraffic accident E825☑
      while alighting, boarding, entering, leaving—*see* Fall, from, motor vehicle, while alighting, boarding
    nail E920.8
    needle (sewing) E920.4
      hypodermic E920.5
    noise E928.1
    object
      fallen on
        motor vehicle (in motion) (on public highway) E818☑
          not on public highway E825☑
      falling—*see* Hit by, object, falling
    paintball gun E922.5
    radiation—*see* Radiation
    railway rolling stock, train, vehicle (part of) E805☑
      door or window E806☑
    rotating propeller, aircraft E844☑
    rough landing of off-road type motor vehicle (after leaving ground or rough terrain) E821☑
      snow vehicle E820☑
    saber (*see also* Wound, saber) E920.3
    shot—*see* Shooting
    sound waves E928.1
    splinter or sliver, wood E920.8
    straining E927
    street car (door) E829☑
    suicide (attempt) E958.9
    sword E920.3

Injury, injured—*continued*
by, caused by, from—*continued*
terrorism—*see* Terrorism
third rail—*see* Electric shock
thunderbolt E907
tidal wave E909.4
caused by storm E908.0
tornado E908.1
torrential rain E908.2
twisting E927.8
vehicle NEC—*see* Accident, vehicle NEC
vibration E928.2
volcanic eruption E909.1
weapon burst, in war operations E993
weightlessness (in spacecraft, real or simulated) E928.0
wood splinter or sliver E920.8
due to
civil insurrection—*see* War operations
occurring after cessation of hostilities E998
terrorism—*see* Terrorism
war operations—*see* War operations
occurring after cessation of hostilities E998
homicidal (*see also* Assault) E968.9
in, on
civil insurrection—*see* War operations
fight E960.0
parachute descent (voluntary) (without accident to aircraft) E844☑
with accident to aircraft—*see* categories E840-E842☑
public highway E819☑
railway right of way E807☑
terrorism—*see* Terrorism
war operations—*see* War operations
inflicted (by)
in course of arrest (attempted), suppression of disturbance, maintenance of order, by law enforcing agents—*see* Legal intervention
law-enforcing agent (on duty)—*see* Legal intervention
other person
stated as
accidental E928.9
homicidal, intentional—*see* Assault
undetermined whether accidental or intentional—*see* Injury, stated as undetermined
police (on duty)—*see* Legal intervention
late effect of E929.9
lifting, injury in E927.8
purposely (inflicted) by other person(s)—*see* Assault
self-inflicted (unspecified whether accidental or intentional) E988.9

Injury, injured—*continued*
self-inflicted—*continued*
stated as
accidental E928.9
intentionally, purposely E958.9
specified cause NEC E928.8
stated as
undetermined whether accidentally or purposely inflicted (by) E988.9
cut (any part of body) E986
cutting or piercing instrument (classifiable to E920) E986
drowning E984
explosive(s) (missile) E985.5
falling from high place E987.9
manmade structure, except residential E987.1
natural site E987.2
residential premises E987.0
hanging E983.0
knife E986
late effect of E989
puncture (any part of body) E986
shooting—*see* Shooting, stated as undetermined whether accidental or intentional
specified means NEC E988.8
stab (any part of body) E986
strangulation—*see* Suffocation, stated as undetermined whether accidental or intentional
submersion E984
suffocation—*see* Suffocation, stated as undetermined whether accidental or intentional
to child due to criminal abortion E968.8

J

Jammed (accidentally)
between objects (moving) (stationary and moving) E918
in object E918
Jumped or fell from high place, so stated—*see* Jumping, from, high place, stated as in undetermined circumstances
Jumping
before train, vehicle or other moving object (unspecified whether accidental or intentional) E988.0
stated as
intentional, purposeful E958.0
suicidal (attempt) E958.0
from
aircraft
by parachute (voluntarily) (without accident to aircraft) E844☑
due to accident to aircraft—*see* categories E840-E842☑

Jumping
from—*continued*
boat, ship, watercraft (into water)
after accident to, fire on, watercraft E830☑
and subsequently struck by (part of) boat E831☑
burning, crushed, sinking E830☑
and subsequently struck by (part of) boat E831☑
voluntarily, without accident (to boat) with injury other than drowning or submersion E883.0
building—*see also* Jumping, from, high place
burning (uncontrolled fire) E891.8
in terrorism E979.3
private E890.8
cable car (not on rails) E847
on rails E829☑
high place
in accidental circum-stances or in sport—*see* categories E880-E884☑
stated as
with intent to injure self E957.9
man-made structures NEC E957.1
natural sites E957.2
residential premises E957.0
in undetermined circumstances E987.9
man-made structures NEC E987.1
natural sites E987.2
residential premises E987.0
suicidal (attempt) E957.9
man-made structures NEC E957.1
natural sites E957.1
residential premises E957.0
motor vehicle (in motion) (on public highway)—*see* Fall, from, motor vehicle
nonmotor road vehicle NEC E829☑
street car E829☑
structure—*see also* Jumping, from, high place
burning NEC (uncontrolled fire) E891.8
in terrorism E979.3
into water
with injury other than drowning or submersion E883.0
drowning or submersion—*see* Submersion
from, off, watercraft—*see* Jumping, from, boat

K

Kicked by

animal E906.8
person(s) (accidentally) E917.9
with intent to injure or kill E960.0
as, or caused by a crowd E917.1
with subsequent fall E917.6
in fight E960.0
in sports E917.0
with subsequent fall E917.5
Kicking against
object (moving) E917.9
in sports E917.0
with subsequent fall E917.5
stationary E917.4
with subsequent fall E917.5
with subsequent fall E917.8
person—*see* Striking against, person
Knocked down (accidentally) (by) NEC E928.9
animal (not being ridden) E906.8
being ridden (in sport or transport) E828☑
blast from explosion (*see also* Explosion) E923.9
crowd, human stampede E917.6
late effect of—*see* Late effect
person (accidentally) E917.9
in brawl, fight E960.0
in sports E917.5
transport vehicle—*see* vehicle involved under Hit by
while boxing E917.5

L

Late effect of
accident NEC (accident classifiable to E928.9) E929.9
specified NEC (accident classifiable to E9l0-E928.8) E929.8
assault E969
fall, accidental (accident classifiable to E880-E888) E929.3
fire, accident caused by (accident classifiable to E890-E899) E929.4
homicide, attempt (any means) E969
injury due to terrorism E999.1
injury undetermined whether accidentally or purposely inflicted (injury classifiable to E980-E988) E989
legal intervention (injury classifiable to E970-E976) E977
medical or surgical procedure, test or therapy
as, or resulting in, or from abnormal or delayed reaction or complication—*see* Reaction, abnormal
misadventure—*see* Misadventure
motor vehicle accident (accident classifiable to E810-E825) E929.0
natural or environmental factor, accident due to (accident classifiable to E900-E909) E929.5

☑ Additional Digit Required

© 2009 Ingenix

Late effect of—*continued*
poisoning, accidental (accident classifiable to E850-E858, E860-E869) E929.2
suicide, attempt (any means) E959
transport accident NEC (accident classifiable to E800-E807, E826-E838, E840-E848) E929.1
war operations, injury due to (injury classifiable to E990-E998) E999.0
Launching pad accident E845☑
Liquid (noncorrosive) in eye E914
corrosive E924.1
Loss of control
motor vehicle (on public highway) (without antecedent collision) E816☑
with
antecedent collision on public highway—*see* Collision, motor vehicle
involving any object, person or vehicle not on public highway E816☑
on public highway—*see* Collision, motor vehicle
not on public highway, nontraffic accident E825☑
with antecedent collision—*see* Collision, motor vehicle, not on public highway
off-road type motor vehicle (not on public highway) E821☑
on public highway—*see* Loss of control, motor vehicle
snow vehicle, motor-driven (not on public highway) E820☑
on public highway—*see* Loss of control, motor vehicle

M

Mangled (accidentally) NEC E928.9
Manhandling (in brawl, fight) E960.0
legal intervention E975
Medical procedure, complication of
delayed or as an abnormal reaction without mention of misadventure—*see* Reaction, abnormal
due to or as a result of misadventure—*see* Misadventure

O

Object
falling
from, in, on, hitting
aircraft E844☑
due to accident to aircraft—*see* categories E840-E842☑

Object—*continued*
falling—*continued*
from, in, on, hitting—*continued*
machinery—*see also* Accident, machine
not in operation E916
motor vehicle (in motion) (on public highway) E818☑
not on public highway E825☑
stationary E916
nonmotor road vehicle NEC E829☑
pedal cycle E826☑
person E916
railway rolling stock, train, vehicle E806☑
street car E829☑
watercraft E838☑
due to accident to watercraft E831☑
set in motion by
accidental explosion of pressure vessel—*see* category E921☑
firearm—*see* category E922☑
machine(ry)—*see* Accident, machine
transport vehicle—*see* categories E800-E848☑
thrown from, in, on, towards
aircraft E844☑
cable car (not on rails) E847
on rails E829☑
motor vehicle (in motion) (on public highway) E818☑
not on public highway E825☑
nonmotor road vehicle NEC E829☑
pedal cycle E826☑
street car E829☑
vehicle NEC—*see* Accident, vehicle NEC
Overexertion E927.9
from
lifting E927.8
maintaining prolonged positions E927.1
holding E927.1
sitting E927.1
standing E927.1
prolonged static position E927.1
pulling E927.8
pushing E927.8
sudden strenuous movement E927.0
Overturning (accidental)
animal-drawn vehicle E827☑
boat, ship, watercraft
causing
drowning, submersion E830☑
injury except drowning, submersion E831☑
machinery—*see* Accident, machine
motor vehicle (see also Loss of control, motor vehicle) E816☑
with antecedent collision on public highway—*see* Collision, motor vehicle

Overturning—*continued*
motor vehicle—*continued*
not on public highway, nontraffic accident E825☑
with antecedent collision—*see* Collision, motor vehicle, not on public highway
nonmotor road vehicle NEC E829☑
off-road type motor vehicle—*see* Loss of control, off-road type motor vehicle
pedal cycle E826☑
railway rolling stock, train, vehicle (see also Derailment, railway) E802☑
street car E829☑
vehicle NEC—*see* Accident, vehicle NEC

P

Parachuting (voluntary) (without accident to aircraft) E844☑
due to accident to aircraft—*see* categories E840-E842☑
Paralysis
divers' E902.2
lead or saturnine E866.0
from pesticide NEC E863.4
Pinched
between objects (moving) (stationary and moving) E918
in object E918
Pinned under
machine(ry)—*see* Accident, machine
Place of occurrence of accident—*see* Accident (to), occurring (at) (in)
Projected objects, striking against or struck by—*see* Striking against, object
Pulling, injury in E927.8
Pushing (injury in) (overexertion) E927.8
by other person(s) (accidental) E917.9
as, or caused by, a crowd, human stampede E917.1
with subsequent fall E917.6
before moving vehicle or object
stated as
intentional, homicidal E968.5
undetermined whether accidental or intentional E988.8
from
high place
in accidental circumstances—*see* categories E880-E884☑

Pushing—*continued*
by other person(s)—*continued*
from—*continued*
high place—*continued*
stated as
intentional, homicidal E968.1
undetermined whether accidental or intentional E987.9
man-made structure, except residential E987.1
natural site E987.2
residential E987.0
motor vehicle (see also Fall, from, motor vehicle) E818☑
stated as
intentional, homicidal E968.5
undetermined whether accidental or intentional E988.8
in sports E917.0
with fall E886.0
with fall E886.9
in sports E886.0

R

Reaction, abnormal to or following (medical or surgical procedure) E879.9
amputation (of limbs) E878.5
lumbar puncture E879.4
procedures other than surgical operation (see also Reaction, abnormal, by specific type of procedure) E879.9
specified procedure NEC E879.8
radiological procedure or therapy E879.2
Residual (effect)—*see* Late effect
Rock falling on or hitting (accidentally)
motor vehicle (in motion) (on public highway) E818☑
not on public highway E825☑
nonmotor road vehicle NEC E829☑
pedal cycle E826☑
person E916
railway rolling stock, train, vehicle E806☑
Running off, away
animal (being ridden) (in sport or transport) E828☑
not being ridden E906.8
animal-drawn vehicle E827☑
rails, railway (see also Derailment) E802☑

Running off, away—*continued*
roadway
  motor vehicle (without
    antecedent collision)
    E816☑
    nontraffic accident E825☑
    with antecedent
      collision—*see*
      Collision, motor
      vehicle, not on
      public highway
  with
    antecedent collision—*see*
      Collision motor
      vehicle
    subsequent collision
      involving any object,
      person or vehicle
      not on public highway
      E816☑
      on public highway
      E811☑
  nonmotor road vehicle NEC
    E829☑
  pedal cycle E826☑
Run over (accidentally) (by)
  animal (not being ridden) E906.8
    being ridden (in sport or
      transport) E828☑
  animal-drawn vehicle E827☑
  machinery—*see* Accident, machine
  motor vehicle (on public
    highway)—*see* Hit by, motor
    vehicle
  nonmotor road vehicle NEC
    E829☑
  railway train E805☑
  street car E829☑
  vehicle NEC E848

S

Sequelae (of)
  in
    terrorism E999.1
    war operations E999.0
Skydiving E844☑
Slipping (accidental)
  on
    deck (of boat, ship, watercraft)
      (icy) (oily) (wet) E835☑
    ice E885.9
    ladder of ship E833☑
      due to accident to watercraft
      E831☑
    mud E885.9
    oil E885.9
    snow E885.9
    stairs of ship E833☑
      due to accident to watercraft
      E831☑
    surface
      slippery E885☑
      wet E885☑**Stepped on**
  by
    animal (not being ridden)
      E906.8
      being ridden (in sport or
        transport) E828☑
    crowd E917.1
    person E917.9
      in sports E917.0
  in sports E917.0

Stepping on
  object (moving) E917.9
    in sports E917.0
      with subsequent fall E917.5
    stationary E917.4
      with subsequent fall E917.8
  person E917.9
    as, or caused by a crowd E917.1
      with subsequent fall E917.6
    in sports E917.0
Straining, injury in E927.8
Strenuous movements (in
  recreational or other activities)
  E927.8
Striking against
  bottom (when jumping or diving
    into water) E883.0
  object (moving) E917.9
    caused by crowd E917.1
      with subsequent fall E917.6
    furniture E917.3
      with subsequent fall E917.7
    in
      running water E917.2
        with drowning or
          submersion—*see*
          Submersion
    sports E917.0
      with subsequent fall
      E917.5
    stationary E917.4
      with subsequent fall E917.8
  person(s) E917.9
    with fall E886.9
      in sports E886.0
    as, or caused by, a crowd E917.1
      with subsequent fall E917.6
      in sports E917.0
        with fall E886.0
Struck by—*see also* Hit by
  bullet
    in
      terrorism E979.4
      war operations E991.2
        rubber E991.0
  lightning E907
  missile
    in terrorism—*see* Terrorism,
      missile
  object
    falling
      from, in, on
        building
          burning (uncontrolled
          fire)
            in terrorism E979.3
  thunderbolt E907
**Stumbling over animal, carpet,
  curb, rug or (small) object**
  (with fall) E885.9
  without fall—*see* Striking against,
    object
**Surgical procedure, complication
  of**
  delayed or as an abnormal reaction
    without mention of
    misadventure—*see* Reaction,
    abnormal
  due to or as a result of
    misadventure—*see*
    Misadventure

T

Tackle in sport E886.0
Terrorism (injury) (by) (in) E979.8
  air blast E979.2
  aircraft burned, destroyed,
    exploded, shot down E979.1
    used as a weapon E979.1
  anthrax E979.6
  asphyxia from
    chemical (weapons) E979.7
    fire, conflagration (caused by
      fire-producing device)
      E979.3
    from nuclear explosion
      E979.5
    gas or fumes E979.7
  bayonet E979.8
  biological agents E979.6
  blast (air) (effects) E979.2
    from nuclear explosion E979.5
    underwater E979.0
  bomb (antipersonnel) (mortar)
    (explosion) (fragments)
    E979.2
  bullet(s) (from carbine, machine
    gun, pistol, rifle, shotgun)
    E979.4
  burn from
    chemical E979.7
    fire, conflagration (caused by
      fire-producing device)
      E979.3
    from nuclear explosion
      E979.5
    gas E979.7
  burning aircraft E979.1
  chemical E979.7
  cholera E979.6
  conflagration E979.3
  crushed by falling aircraft E979.1
  depth-charge E979.0
  destruction of aircraft E979.1
  disability, as sequelae one year or
    more after injury E999.1
  drowning E979.8
  effect
    of nuclear weapon (direct)
      (secondary) E979.5
    secondary NEC E979.9
    sequelae E999.1
  explosion (artillery shell) (breech-
    block) (cannon block) E979.2
    aircraft E979.1
    bomb (antipersonnel) (mortar)
      E979.2
      nuclear (atom) (hydrogen)
        E979.5
    depth-charge E979.0
    grenade E979.2
    injury by fragments from E979.2
    land-mine E979.2
    marine weapon E979.0
    mine (land) E979.2
      at sea or in harbor E979.0
      marine E979.0
    missile (explosive) NEC E979.2
    munitions (dump) (factory)
      E979.2
    nuclear (weapon) E979.5
      other direct and secondary
        effects of E979.5
    sea-based artillery shell E979.0
    torpedo E979.0
  exposure to ionizing radiation from
    nuclear explosion E979.5

Terrorism—*continued*
  falling aircraft E979.1
  fire or fire-producing device E979.3
  firearms E979.4
  fireball effects from nuclear
    explosion E979.5
  fragments from artillery shell,
    bomb NEC, grenade, guided
    missile, land-mine, rocket,
    shell, shrapnel E979.2
  gas or fumes E979.7
  grenade (explosion) (fragments)
    E979.2
  guided missile (explosion)
    (fragments) E979.2
    nuclear E979.5
  heat from nuclear explosion E979.5
  hot substances E979.3
  hydrogen cyanide E979.7
  land-mine (explosion) (fragments)
    E979.2
  laser(s) E979.8
  late effect of E999.1
  lewisite E979.7
  lung irritant (chemical) (fumes)
    (gas) E979.7
  marine mine E979.0
  mine E979.2
    at sea E979.0
    in harbor E979.0
    land (explosion) (fragments)
      E979.2
    marine E979.0
  missile (explosion) (fragments)
    (guided) E979.2
    marine E979.0
    nuclear weapons E979.5
  mortar bomb (explosion)
    (fragments) E979.2
  mustard gas E979.7
  nerve gas E979.7
  nuclear weapons E979.5
  pellets (shotgun) E979.4
  petrol bomb E979.3
  piercing object E979.8
  phosgene E979.7
  poisoning (chemical) (fumes) (gas)
    E979.7
  radiation, ionizing from nuclear
    explosion E979.5
  rocket (explosion) (fragments)
    E979.2
  saber, sabre E979.8
  sarin E979.7
  screening smoke E979.7
  sequelae effect (of) E999.1
  shell (aircraft) (artillery) (cannon)
    (land-based) (explosion)
    (fragments) E979.2
    sea-based E979.0
  shooting E979.4
    bullet(s) E979.4
    pellet(s) (rifle) (shotgun) E979.4
  shrapnel E979.2
  smallpox E979.7
  stabbing object(s) E979.8
  submersion E979.8
  torpedo E979.0
  underwater blast E979.0
  vesicant (chemical) (fumes) (gas)
    E979.7
  weapon burst E979.2

ICD-9-CM Index

Thrown (accidentally)
  against object in or part of vehicle
    by motion of vehicle
      aircraft E844☑
      boat, ship, watercraft E838☑
      motor vehicle (on public
        highway) E818☑
      not on public highway
        E825☑
      off-road type (not on
        public highway)
        E821☑
        on public highway
          E818☑
      snow vehicle E820☑
        on public highway
          E818☑
      nonmotor road vehicle NEC
        E829☑
      railway rolling stock, train,
        vehicle E806☑
      street car E829☑
  from
    animal (being ridden) (in sport
      or transport) E828☑
    high place, homicide (attempt)
      E968.1
    machinery—see Accident,
      machine
    vehicle NEC—see Accident,
      vehicle NEC
  off—see Thrown, from
  overboard (by motion of boat,
    ship, watercraft) E832☑
    by accident to boat, ship,
      watercraft E830☑
Tornado (any injury) E908.1
Traffic accident NEC E819☑
Trampled by animal E906.8
  being ridden (in sport or transport)
    E828☑
Trapped (accidentally)
  between
    objects (moving) (stationary and
      moving) E918
  by
    door of
      elevator E918
      motor vehicle (on public
        highway) (while
        alighting, boarding)—
        see Fall, from, motor
        vehicle, while alighting
      railway train (underground)
        E806☑
      street car E829☑
      subway train E806☑
  in object E918
Trauma
  cumulative
    from
      repetitive
        impact E927.4
        motion or movements
          E927.3
      sudden from strenuous
        movement E927.0
Tree
  falling on or hitting E916
    motor vehicle (in motion) (on
      public highway) E818☑
      not on public highway
        E825☑
      nonmotor road vehicle NEC
        E829☑

Tree—continued
  falling on or hitting—continued
    pedal cycle E826☑
    person E916
    railway rolling stock, train,
      vehicle E806☑
    street car E829☑
**Tripping over animal, carpet,
  curb, rug, or small object**
  (with fall) E885☑
  without fall—see Striking against,
    object
Twisting, injury in E927.8

V

Violence, nonaccidental (see also
  Assault) E968.9
Volcanic eruption (any injury)
  E909.1
Vomitus in air passages (with
  asphyxia, obstruction or
  suffocation) E911

W

War operations (during hostilities)
  (injury) (by) (in) E995.9
  after cessation of hostilities, injury
    due to E998.9
  air blast E993.9
  aircraft burned, destroyed,
    exploded, shot down E994
    ☑
  asphyxia from
    chemical E997.2
    fire, conflagration (caused by
      fire producing device or
      conventional weapon)
      E990.9
      from nuclear explosion (see
        also War operations,
        injury due to, nuclear
        weapons) E996.8
      incendiary bomb E990.0
      petrol bomb E990.0
    fumes E997.2
    gas E997.2
  baton (nightstick) E995.1
  battle wound NEC E995.8
  bayonet E995.2
  biological warfare agents E997.1
  blast (air) (effects) E993.9
    from nuclear explosion (see also
      War operations, injury due
      to, nuclear weapons)
      E996.1
    underwater E992.9
  bomb (mortar) (explosion) E993.2
    after cessation of hostilities
      E998.1
    fragments, injury by E991.4
      antipersonnel E991.3
  bullet(s) (from carbine, machine
    gun, pistol, rifle, shotgun)
    E991.2
    rubber E991.0
  burn from
    chemical E997.2

War operations—continued
  burn from—continued
    fire, conflagration (caused by
      fire-producing device or
      conventional weapon)
      E990.9
    from
      conventional weapon
        E990.3
      flamethrower E990.1
      incendiary bomb E990.0
      incendiary bullet E990.2
      nuclear explosion E996.2
      petrol bomb E990.0
    gas E997.2
  burning aircraft E994.3
  chemical E997.2
  chlorine E997.2
  conventional warfare, specified
    form NEC E995.8
  crushing by falling aircraft E994.8
  depth charge E992.1
  destruction of aircraft E994.9
  detonation of own munitions
    (ammunition) (artillery)
    (mortars), unintentional
    E993.6
  disability as sequela one year or
    more after injury E999.0
  discharge of own munitions launch
    device (autocannons)
    (automatic grenade
    launchers) (missile launchers)
    (small arms), unintentional
    E993.7
  drowning E995.4
  effect nuclear weapon (see also War
    operations, injury due to,
    nuclear weapons) E996.9
  explosion (breech block) (cannon
    shell) E993.9
    after cessation of hostilities
      bomb placed in war E998.1
      mine placed in war E998.0
    aircraft E994.1
    due to
      enemy fire or explosives
        E994.0
      own onboard explosives
        E994.1
    artillery shell E993.2
    bomb (mortar) E993.2
      aerial E993.0
      atom (see also War
        operations, injury due
        to, nuclear weapons)
        E996.9
      hydrogen (see also War
        operations, injury due
        to, nuclear weapons)
        E996.9
    injury by fragments from
      E991.4
      antipersonnel E991.3
    nuclear w(see also War
      operations, injury due
      to, nuclear weapons)
      E996.9
    depth charge E992.1
    injury by fragments from E991.4
      antipersonnel E991.3
    marine weapon NEC E992.8

War operations—continued
  explosion—continued
    mine
      at sea or in harbor E992.2
      land E993.8
        injury by fragments from
          E991.4
      marine E992.2
    missile, guided E993.1
    mortar E993.2
    munitions (accidental) (being
      used in war) (dump)
      (factory) E993.9
    own E993.7
      ammunition (artillery)
        (mortars) E993.6
      launch device
        (autocannons)
        (automatic grenade
        launchers) (missile
        launchers) (small
        arms) E993.7
    nuclear (weapon) (see also War
      operations, injury due to,
      nuclear weapons) E996.9
    own weapons (accidental)
      E993.7
      injury by fragments from
        E991.9
      antipersonnel E991.3
    sea-based artillery shell E992.3
    specified NEC E993.8
    torpedo E992.0
  exposure to ionizing radiation from
    nuclear explosion (see also
    War operations, injury due
    to, nuclear weapons)E996.3
  falling aircraft E994.8
  fireball effects from nuclear
    explosion E996.2
  fire or fire-producing device E990.9
    flamethrower E990.1
    incendiary bomb E990.0
    incendiary bullet E990.2
    indirectly caused from
      conventional weapon
      E990.3
    petrol bomb E990.0
  fragments from
    antipersonnel bomb E991.3
    artillery shell E991.4
    bomb NEC E991.4
    grenade E991.4
    guided missile E991.4
    land mine E991.4
    rocket E991.4
    shell E991.4
    shrapnel E991.9
  fumes E997.2
  gas E997.2
  grenade (explosion) E993.8
    fragments, injury by E991.4
  guided missile (explosion) E993.1
    fragments, injury by E991.4
    nuclear (see also War
      operations, injury due to,
      nuclear weapons) E996.9
  heat from nuclear explosion E996.2
  injury due to
    aerial bomb E993.0
    air blast E993.9
    aircraft shot down E994.0
    artillery shell E993.2

ICD-9-CM Index

War operations—continued
  injury due to—continued
    blast E993.9
      wave E993.9
      wind E993.9
    bomb E993.8
    but occurring after cessation of
      hostilities
      explosion of bombs E998.1
      explosion of mines E998.0
      specified NEC E998.8
    conventional warfare E995.9
      specified form NEC E995.8
    depth charge E992.1
    destruction of aircraft E994.9
      due to
        air to air missile E994.0
        collision with other aircraft E994.2
        enemy fire or explosives E994.0
        on board explosion (explosives) E994.1
        on board fire E994.3
        rocket propelled grenade [RPG] E994.0
        small arms fire E994.0
        surface to air missile E994.0
      specified NEC E994.8
    dirty bomb (see also War operations, injury due to, nuclear weapons) E996.9
    drowning E995.4
    explosion (direct pressure) (indirect pressure) (due to) E993.9
      depth charge E992.1
      improvised explosive device [IED]
        person borne E993.3
        roadside E993.5
        specified NEC E993.5
        transport vehicle (air) (land) (water) borne E993.4
        vehicle (air) (land) (water) borne E993.4
      marine mines (in harbor) (at sea) E992.2
      marine weapons E992.9
        specified NEC E992.8
      sea based artillery shell E992.3
      specified NEC E993.8
      torpedo E992.0
      unintentional (of own)
        autocannons E993.7
        automatic grenade launchers E993.7
        launch device discharge E993.7
        missile launchers E993.7

War operations—continued
  injury due to—continued
    explosion—continued
      unintentional—continued
        munitions detonation (ammunition) (artillery) (mortars) E993.6
        small arms E993.7
    fragments (from) E991.9
      artillery E991.8
      artillery shells E991.4
      autocannons E991.8
      automatic grenade launchers [AGL] E991.8
      bombs E991.4
        antipersonnel E991.3
      detonation of unexploded ordnance [UXO] E991.4
      grenade E991.4
      guided missile E991.4
      improvised explosive device [IED]
        person borne E991.5
        roadside E991.7
        specified NEC E991.7
        transport vehicle (air) (land) (water) borne E991.6
        vehicle (air) (land) (water) borne E991.6
      land mine E991.4
      missile launchers E991.8
      mortars E991.8
      munitions (artillery shells) (bombs) (grenades) (rockets) (shells) E991.4
      rockets E991.4
      shells E991.4
      small arms E991.8
      specified NEC E991.9
      weapons (artillery) (autocannons) (mortars) (small arms) E991.8
    grenade E993.8
    guided missile E993.1
    hand to hand combat, unarmed E995.0
    improvised explosive device [IED]
      person borne E993.3
      roadside E993.5
      specified NEC E993.5
      transport vehicle (air) (land) (water) borne E993.4
      vehicle (air) (land) (water) borne E993.4
    inability to surface or obtain air E995.4
    land mine E993.8
    marine mines (in harbor) (at sea) E992.2

War operations—continued
  injury due to—continued
    marine weapons E992.9
      specified NEC E992.8
    mortar E993.2
    nuclear weapons E996.9
      beta burns E996.3
      blast debris E996.1
      blast pressure E996.0
      burns due to thermal radiation E996.2
      direct blast effect E996.0
      fallout exposure E996.3
      fireball effect E996.2
      flash burns E996.2
      heat effect E996.2
      indirect blast effect E996.1
      nuclear radiation effects E996.3
      radiation exposure (acute) E996.3
      radiation sickness E996.3
      secondary effects E996.3
      specified effects NEC E996.8
      thermal radiation effect E996.2
    piercing object E995.2
    restriction of airway, intentional E995.3
    sea based artillery shell E992.3
    shrapnel E991.9
    stave E995.1
    strangulation E995.3
    strike by blunt object (baton) (nightstick) (stave) E995.1
    submersion (accidental) (unintentional) E995.4
      intentional E995.3
    suffocation E995.3
      accidental E995.4
    torpedo E992.0
    underwater blast E992.9
    weapon of mass destruction [WMD] E997.3
  knife E995.2
  lacrimator (gas) (chemical) E997.2
  land mine (explosion) E993.8
    after cessation of hostilities E998.0
    fragments, injury by E991.4
  laser(s) E997.0
  late effect of E999.0
  lewisite E997.2
  lung irritant (chemical) (fumes) (gas) E997.2
  marine mine E992.2
  mine
    after cessation of hostilities E998.0
    at sea E992.2
    in harbor E992.2
    land (explosion) E993.8
      fragments, injury by E991.4
    marine E992.2

War operations—continued
  missile (guided) (explosion) E993.1
    fragments, injury by E991.4
    marine E992.8
    nuclear (see also War operations, injury due to, nuclear weapons) E996.9
  mortar bomb (explosion) E993.2
    fragments, injury by E991.4
  mustard gas E997.2
  nerve gas E997.2
  phosgene E997.2
  piercing object E995.2
  poisoning (chemical) (fumes) (gas) E997.2
  radiation, ionizing from nuclear explosion (see also War operations, injury due to, nuclear weapons) E996.3
  rocket (explosion) E993.8
    fragments, injury by E991.4
  saber, sabre E995.2
  screening smoke E997.8
  shell (aircraft) (artillery) (cannon) (land based) (explosion) E993.2
    fragments, injury by E991.4
    sea-based E992.3
  shooting E991.2
    after cessation of hostilities E998.8
    bullet(s) E991.2
      rubber E991.0
    pellet(s) (rifle) E991.1
    shrapnel E991.9
    submersion E995 S
    torpedo E992 S
  stave E995.2
  strike by blunt object (baton) (nightstick) (stave) E995.1
  submersion E995.4 s
    intentional E995.3
  sword E995.2
  torpedo E992.0 s
  unconventional warfare, except by nuclear weapon E997.9
    biological (warfare) E997.1
    gas, fumes, chemicals E997.2
    laser(s) E997.0
    specified type NEC E997.8
  underwater blast E992.9 s
  vesicant (chemical) (fumes) (gas) E997.2
  weapon burst E993.9 s

Washed
  away by flood — see Flood
  away by tidal wave — see Tidal wave
  off road by storm (transport vehicle) E908.9
  overboard E832 S

Weather exposure — see also Exposure
  cold E901.0
  hot E900.0

☑ Additional Digit Required

Railway Accidents (E800–E807)

The following fourth-digit subdivisions are for use with categories E800-E807 to identify the injured person:

.0 Railway employee

Any person who by virtue of his employment in connection with a railway, whether by the railway company or not, is at increased risk of involvement in a railway accident, such as:

> catering staff on train
>
> postal staff on train
>
> driver
>
> railway fireman
>
> guard
>
> shunter
>
> porter
>
> sleeping car attendant

.1 Passenger on railway

Any authorized person traveling on a train, except a railway employee

> **EXCLUDES** intending passenger waiting at station (.8)
> unauthorized rider on railway vehicle (.8)

.2 Pedestrian *See* definition (r), E-Codes-2

.3 Pedal cyclist *See* definition (p), E-Codes-2

.8 Other specified person Intending passenger waiting at station

> Unauthorized rider on railway vehicle

.9 Unspecified person

Motor Vehicle Traffic and Nontraffic Accidents (E810–E825)

The following fourth-digit subdivisions are for use with categories E810-E819 and E820-E825 to identify the injured person:

.0 Driver of motor vehicle other than motorcycle *See* definition (1), E-Codes-2

.1 Passenger in motor vehicle other than motorcycle *See* definition (1), E-Codes-2

.2 Motorcyclist *See* definition (1), E-Codes-2

.3 Passenger on motorcycle *See* definition (1), E-Codes-2

.4 Occupant of streetcar

.5 Rider of animal; occupant of animal-drawn vehicle

.6 Pedal cyclist *See* definition (p), E-Codes-2

.7 Pedestrian *See* definition (r), E-Codes-2

.8 Other specified person

> Occupant of vehicle other than above
>
> Person in railway train involved in accident
>
> Unauthorized rider of motor vehicle

.9 Unspecified person

Other Road Vehicle Accidents (E826–E829) (animal-drawn vehicle, streetcar, pedal cycle, and other nonmotor road vehicle accidents)

The following fourth-digit subdivisions are for use with categories E826-E829 to identify the injured person:

.0 Pedestrian *See* definition (r), E-Codes-2

.1 Pedal cyclist (does not apply to codes E827, E828, E829) *See* definition (p), E-Codes-2

.2 Rider of animal (does not apply to code E829)

.3 Occupant of animal-drawn vehicle (does not apply to codes E828, E829)

.4 Occupant of streetcar

.8 Other specified person

.9 Unspecified person

Water Transport Accidents (E830–E838)

The following fourth-digit subdivisions are for use with categories E830-E838 to identify the injured person:

.0 Occupant of small boat, unpowered

.1 Occupant of small boat, powered *See* definition (t), E-Codes-2

> **EXCLUDES** water skier (.4)

.2 Occupant of other watercraft—crew

Persons:

> engaged in operation of watercraft
>
> providing passenger services [cabin attendants, ship's physician, catering personnel]
>
> working on ship during voyage in other capacity [musician in band, operators of shops and beauty parlors]

.3 Occupant of other watercraft—other than crew

Passengers

> Occupant of lifeboat, other than crew, after abandoning ship

.4 Water skier

.5 Swimmer

.6 Dockers, stevedores

> Longshoreman employed on the dock in loading and unloading ships

.8 Other specified person

> Immigration and custom officials on board ship
>
> Persons: accompanying passenger or member of crew visiting boat
>
> Pilot (guiding ship into port)

.9 Unspecified person

HCPCS Level II Definitions and Guidelines

Introduction

One of the keys to gaining accurate reimbursement lies in understanding the multiple coding systems that are used to identify services and supplies. To be well versed in reimbursement practices, coders should be familiar not only with the American Medical Association's (AMA) Physicians' Current Procedural Terminology (CPT®) coding system (HCPCS Level I) but also with HCPCS Level II codes, which are becoming increasingly important to reimbursement as they are extended to a wider array of medical services.

HCPCS Level II—National Codes

HCPCS Level II codes commonly are referred to as national codes or by the acronym HCPCS (pronounced "hik-piks"), which stands for the Healthcare Common Procedure Coding System. HCPCS codes are used for billing Medicare and Medicaid patients and have been adopted by some third-party payers.

These codes, updated and published annually by the Centers for Medicare and Medicaid Services (CMS), are intended to supplement the CPT coding system by including codes for nonphysician services, administration of injectable drugs, durable medical equipment (DME), and office supplies.

When using HCPCS Level II codes, keep the following in mind:

- CMS does not use consistent terminology for unlisted services or procedures. The code descriptions may include any one of the following terms: unlisted, not otherwise classified (NOC), unspecified, unclassified, other and miscellaneous.

- If billing for specific supplies and materials, avoid CPT code 99070 (General supplies), and be as specific as possible unless the local carrier directs otherwise.

- Coding and billing should be based on the service provided. Documentation should describe the patient's problems and the service provided to enable the payer to determine reasonableness and necessity of care.

- Refer to the Online CMS Manual System (www.cms.hhs.gov/home/regsguidance.asp) or third-party payment policy to determine whether the care provided is a covered service.

- When both a CPT and HCPCS Level II code share nearly identical narratives, apply the CPT code. If the narratives are not identical, select the code with the narrative that better describes the service. Generally, for Medicare claims, the HCPCS Level II code is more specific and takes precedence over the CPT code.

Structure and Use of HCPCS Level II Codes

The main terms are in boldface type in the index. Main term entries include tests, services, supplies, orthotics, prostheses, medical equipment, drugs, therapies, and some medical and surgical procedures. Where possible, entries are listed under a common main term. In some instances, the common term is a noun; in others, the main term is a descriptor.

Searching the Index

The steps to follow for searching the index are:

1. Analyze the statement or description provided that designates the item to be coded.

2. Identify the main term.

3. Locate the main term in the index.

4. Check for relevant subterms under the main term. Verify the meaning of any unfamiliar abbreviations.

5. Note the codes found after the selected main term or subterm.

6. Locate the code in the alphanumeric list to ensure the specificity of the code. If a code range is provided, locate the code range and review all code narratives in that code range for specificity.

In some cases, an entry may be listed under more than one main term.

Never code directly from the index. Always verify the code choice in the alphanumeric list and the index.

HCPCS Level II Codes: Sections A–V

Level II codes consist of one alphabetic character (letters A through V) and four numbers. Similar to CPT codes, they also can have modifiers, which can be alphanumeric or two letters. National modifiers can be used with all levels of HCPCS codes.

The HCPCS coding system is arranged in 17 sections:

A codes	A0021–A9999	Transportation Services Including Ambulance, Medical/Surgical Supplies, and Administrative, Miscellameous, and Investigational
B codes	B4034–B9999	Enteral and Parenteral Therapy
C codes	C1300–C9999	Outpatient PSS
D codes	D0120–D9999	Dental Procedures
E codes	E0100–E8002	Durable Medical Equipment
G codes	G0008–G9140	Procedures/Professional Services (Temporary Codes)
H codes	H0001–H2037	Alcohol and Drug Abuse Treatment Services
J codes	J0120–J9999	Drugs Administered Other Than Oral Method, Chemotherapy Drugs (Exception: Oral Immunosuppressive Drugs)
K codes	K0001–K0899	Durable Medical Equipment for Medicare Administrative Contractors (DME MACs) (Temporary Codes)

L codes	L0112–L9900	Orthotic and Prosthetic Procedures, Devices
M codes	M0064–M0301	Medical Services
P codes	P2028–P9615	Pathology and Laboratory Services
Q codes	Q0035–Q9967	Miscellaneous Services (Temporary Codes)
R codes	R0070–R0076	Radiology Services
S codes	S0012–S9999	Commercial Payers (Temporary Codes)
T codes	T1000–T9999	Medicaid Services
V codes	V2020–V5364	Vision, Hearing and Speech-Language Pathology Services

Section Guidelines

Examine the instructions found at the beginning of each of the 17 sections. Instructions include the guidelines, notes, unlisted procedures, special reports and the modifiers that pertain to each section.

Use the alphabetic index to initially locate a code by looking for the type of service or procedure performed. The same rule applies: never code directly from the index. Always check the specific code in the appropriate section.

The Conventions: Symbols and Modifiers

Symbols used in the HCPCS Level II coding system may be presented in various ways, depending on the vendor. In this publication the pattern established by the AMA in the CPT code book is followed. For example, bullets and triangles signify new and revised codes, respectively.

When a code is new to the HCPCS Level II system, a bullet (●) appears to the left of the code. This symbol is consistent with the CPT coding system's symbol for new codes. The bullet represents a code never before seen in the HCPCS coding system.

Example
● **E1036 Multi-positional patient transfer system, extra-wide, with integrated seat, operated by caregiver, patient weight capacity up to and including 300 lbs**

A triangle (▲) is used (as in the CPT coding system) to indicate that a change in the narrative of a code has been made from the previous year's edition. The change made may be slight or significant, but it usually changes the application of the code.

Example
▲ **E1035 Multi-positional patient transfer system, extra-wide, with integrated seat, operated by caregiver, patient weight capacity greater than 300 lbs**

In certain circumstances, modifiers must be used to report the alteration of a procedure or service or to furnish additional information about the service, supply or procedure that was provided. In the HCPCS Level I (CPT) coding system, modifiers are two-digit suffixes that usually directly follow the five-digit procedure or service code.

In HCPCS Level II, modifiers are composed of two alpha or alphanumeric characters that range from AA to VP.

E0260-NU Hospital bed, semi-electric (head and foot adjustment), with any type side rails, with mattress

NU = identifies the hospital bed as new equipment

Although both alpha and numeric modifiers are common throughout the country, some regional carriers do not recognize their use due to software limitations. It may be necessary to provide a cover letter, an invoice or other specific documentation with the claim for clarification.

Modifiers for Reporting Physical Therapy Services
The following HCPCS Level II modifiers are commonly used by physical therapy providers.

A1	Dressing for one wound
A2	Dressing for two wounds
A3	Dressing for three wounds
A4	Dressing for four wounds
A5	Dressing for five wounds
A6	Dressing for six wounds
A7	Dressing for seven wounds
A8	Dressing for eight wounds
A9	Dressing for nine or more wounds
AV	Item furnished in conjunction with a prosthetic device, prosthetic or orthotic
AW	Item furnished in conjunction with a surgical dressing
BP	The beneficiary has been informed of the purchase and rental options and has elected to purchase the item
BR	The beneficiary has been informed of the purchase and rental options and has elected to rent the item
BU	The beneficiary has been informed of the purchase and rental options and after 30 days has not informed the supplier of his/her decision
CC	Procedure code change (use 'CC' when the procedure code submitted was changed either for administrative reasons or because an incorrect code was filed)
F1	Left hand, second digit
F2	Left hand, third digit
F3	Left hand, fourth digit
F4	Left hand, fifth digit
F5	Right hand, thumb
F6	Right hand, second digit
F7	Right hand, third digit
F8	Right hand, fourth digit

F9   Right hand, fifth digit

FA   Left hand, thumb

FB   Item provided without cost to provider, supplier or practitioner, or full credit received for replaced device (examples, but not limited to, covered under warranty, replaced due to defect, free samples)

FC   Partial credit received for replaced device

GA   Waiver of liability statement on file

GB   Claim being resubmitted for payment because it is no longer covered under a global payment demonstration

GK   Reasonable and necessary item/service associated with a GA or GZ modifier

GL   Medically unnecessary upgrade provided instead of non-upgraded item, no charge, no advance beneficiary notice (ABN)

GN   Services delivered under an outpatient speech language pathology plan of care

GO   Services delivered under an outpatient occupational therapy plan of care

GP   Services delivered under an outpatient physical therapy plan of care

GY   Item or service statutorily excluded, does not meet the definition of any Medicare benefit or, for non-Medicare insurers, is not a contract benefit

GZ   Item or service expected to be denied as not reasonable and necessary

HJ   Employee assistance program

J4   DMEPOS item subject to DMEPOS competitive bidding program that is furnished by a hospital upon discharge

K0   Lower extremity prosthesis functional level 0—does not have the ability or potential to ambulate or transfer safely with or without assistance and a prosthesis does not enhance their quality of life or mobility.

K1   Lower extremity prosthesis functional level 1—has the ability or potential to use a prosthesis for transfers or ambulation on level surfaces at fixed cadence. Typical of the limited and unlimited household ambulator.

K2   Lower extremity prosthesis functional level 2—has the ability or potential for ambulation with the ability to traverse low level environmental barriers such as curbs, stairs or uneven surfaces. Typical of the limited community ambulator.

K3   Lower extremity prosthesis functional level 3—has the ability or potential for ambulation with variable cadence. Typical of the community ambulator who has the ability to traverse most environmental barriers and may have vocational, therapeutic, or exercise activity that demands prosthetic utilization beyond simple locomotion.

K4   Lower extremity prosthesis functional level 4—has the ability or potential for prosthetic ambulation that exceeds the basic ambulation skills, exhibiting high impact, stress, or energy levels, typical of the prosthetic demands of the child, active adult, or athlete.

LT   Left side (used to identify procedures performed on the left side of the body)

M2   Medicare Secondary Payer (MSP)

RA   Replacement of a DME item

RP   Repair and replacement of a DME item

RT   Right side (used to identify procedures performed on the right side of the body)

ST   Related to trauma or injury

T1   Left foot, second digit

T2   Left foot, third digit

T3   Left foot, fourth digit

T4   Left foot, fifth digit

T5   Right foot, great toe

T6   Right foot, second digit

T7   Right foot, third digit

T8   Right foot, fourth digit

T9   Right foot, fifth digit

TA   Left foot, great toe

U1   Medicaid level of care 1, as defined by each state

U2   Medicaid level of care 2, as defined by each state

U3   Medicaid level of care 3, as defined by each state

U4   Medicaid level of care 4, as defined by each state

U5   Medicaid level of care 5, as defined by each state

U6   Medicaid level of care 6, as defined by each state

U7   Medicaid level of care 7, as defined by each state

U8   Medicaid level of care 8, as defined by each state

U9   Medicaid level of care 9, as defined by each state

UA   Medicaid level of care 10, as defined by each state

UB   Medicaid level of care 11, as defined by each state

UC   Medicaid level of care 12, as defined by each state

UD   Medicaid level of care 13, as defined by each state

HCPCS Level II Codes and the Physical Therapist

CMS permits physical therapists billing independently to code with either CPT or HCPCS Level II codes for services delivered to Medicare beneficiaries. However, more recently, there has been an effort to reduce duplication between CPT and HCPCS Level II codes, and physical therapists should use CPT codes when they are available, choosing HCPCS Level II codes when there is no appropriate CPT code.

A Codes: Medical and Surgical Supplies (A0021–A9999)

This section covers a wide variety of medical and surgical supplies, as well as some DME-related supplies and accessories. Medicare generally covers DME-related supplies, accessories, maintenance, and repair under the prosthetic devices provision.

A4265 Paraffin, per pound

> MED: Pub. 100-3, Section 280.1

Coding Tip
Portable paraffin bath units and supplies may be covered when the patient has undergone a successful trial period of paraffin therapy ordered by a provider and the patient's condition is expected to be relieved by long term use of this modality.

Additional Miscellaneous Supplies

- **A4290 Sacral nerve stimulation test lead, each**

  A4450 Tape, non-waterproof, per 18 sq in

  > MED: Pub. 100-2, Chapter 15, Section 120

  A4452 Tape, waterproof, per 18 sq in

  > MED: Pub. 100-2, Chapter 15, Section 120

  A4455 Adhesive remover or solvent (for tape, cement or other adhesive), per ounce

  > MED: Pub. 100-2, Chapter 15, Section 120

- **A4456 Adhesive remover, wipes, any type, each**

  A4461 Surgical dressing holder, nonreusable, each

  A4463 Surgical dressing holder, reusable, each

  A4465 Nonelastic binder for extremity

- **A4466 Garment, belt, sleeve or other covering, elastic or similar stretchable**

  A4490 Surgical stocking above knee length, each

  > MED: Pub. 100-2, Chapter 15, Section 100, 130; Pub. 100-3, Section 280.1

  A4495 Surgical stocking thigh length, each

  > MED: Pub. 100-2, Chapter 15, Section 100, 130; Pub. 100-3, Section 280.1

  A4500 Surgical stocking below knee length, each

  > MED: Pub. 100-2, Chapter 15, Section 100, 130; Pub. 100-3, Section 280.1

A4510 Surgical stocking full length, each

> MED: Pub. 100-2, Chapter 15, Section 100, 130; Pub. 100-3, Section 280.1

A4556 Electrodes (e.g., Apnea monitor), per pair

A4558 Conductive gel or paste, for use with electrical device (e.g., TENS, NMES), per ounce

A4559 Coupling gel or paste, for use with ultrasound device, per ounce

A4565 Slings

Coding Tip
The initial casting of the fracture is considered part of the fracture care, inherent in the fracture care code. The sling, however, is not included in the global package for fracture care. Some carriers will pay for this additional patient care item; some will not. If the provider ordered the sling secondary to high probability of patient self-harm with a flailing, casted limb, or if the patient is a child who requires immobilization of the casted limb to avert further injury, reimbursement may be considered by some carriers. Clear evidence of these situations must be reflected in the medical documentation and should be submitted with the claim. In any case, it would be prudent to secure an advance beneficiary notice (ABN) from the patient in case a medical necessity denial is received.

A4570 Splint

> MED: Pub. 100-2, Chapter 15, Section 100

A4580 Cast supplies (e.g., plaster)

> MED: Pub. 100-2, Chapter 15, Section 100

A4590 Special casting material (e.g., fiberglass)

A4595 Electrical stimulator supplies, 2 lead, per month, (e.g. TENS, NMES)

> MED: Pub. 100-3, Section 270.3

A4600 Sleeve for intermittent limb compression device, replacement only, each

A4630 Replacement batteries, medically necessary, transcutaneous electrical stimulator, owned by patient

A4635 Underarm pad, crutch, replacement, each

A4636 Replacement, handgrip, cane, crutch, or walker, each

A4637 Replacement, tip, cane, crutch, walker, each

A4649 Surgical supply; miscellaneous

Coding Tip
Determine if an alternative national HCPCS Level II code or a local HCPCS Level III code better describes the supply being reported. Code A4649 should be used only if a more specific code is unavailable.

A5113 Leg strap; latex, replacement only, per set

> MED: Pub. 100-2, Chapter 15, Section 120

● New Codes   ▲ Revised Codes   MED: Medicare Reference

A5114 Leg strap; foam or fabric, replacement only, per set

MED: Pub. 100-2, Chapter 15, Section 120

Dressings

Medicare claims fall under the jurisdiction of the durable medical equipment Medicare administrative contractor (DME MAC) unless otherwise noted.

A6000 Non-contact wound warming wound cover for use with the non-contact wound warming device and warming card

MED: Pub. 100-3, Section 270.2

Coding Tip

Noncontact normothermic wound therapy (NNWT) encourages wound healing by warming a wound to a preset temperature. The device consists of a noncontact wound cover that contains a flexible, battery-powered infrared heating card. Benefits are not available under Medicare for this therapy based on a national coverage decision.

A6021 Collagen dressing, sterile, pad size 16 sq in or less, each

MED: Pub. 100-2, Chapter 15, Section 100

A6022 Collagen dressing, sterile, pad size more than 16 sq in but less than or equal to 48 sq in, each

MED: Pub. 100-2, Chapter 15, Section 100

A6023 Collagen dressing, sterile, pad size more than 48 sq in, each

MED: Pub. 100-2, Chapter 15, Section 100

A6024 Collagen dressing wound filler, sterile, per 6 in

MED: Pub. 100-2, Chapter 15, Section 100

A6025 Gel sheet for dermal or epidermal application, (e.g., silicone, hydrogel, other), each

MED: Pub. 100-2, Chapter 15, Section 100

A6154 Wound pouch, each

MED: Pub. 100-2, Chapter 15, Section 100

A6196 Alginate or other fiber gelling dressing, wound cover, sterile, pad size 16 sq in or less, each dressing

MED: Pub. 100-2, Chapter 15, Section 100

A6197 Alginate or other fiber gelling dressing, wound cover, sterile, pad size more than 16 sq in but less than or equal to 48 sq in, each dressing

MED: Pub. 100-2, Chapter 15, Section 100

A6198 Alginate or other fiber gelling dressing, wound cover, sterile, pad size more than 48 sq in, each dressing

MED: Pub. 100-2, Chapter 15, Section 100

A6199 Alginate or other fiber gelling dressing, wound filler, sterile, per 6 inches

MED: Pub. 100-2, Chapter 15, Section 100

A6203 Composite dressing, sterile, pad size 16 sq in or less, with any size adhesive border, each dressing

MED: Pub. 100-2, Chapter 15, Section 100

A6204 Composite dressing, sterile, pad size more than 16 sq in but less than or equal to 48 sq in, with any size adhesive border, each dressing

MED: Pub. 100-2, Chapter 15, Section 100

A6205 Composite dressing, sterile, pad size more than 48 sq in, with any size adhesive border, each dressing

MED: Pub. 100-2, Chapter 15, Section 100

A6206 Contact layer, sterile, 16 sq in or less, each dressing

MED: Pub. 100-2, Chapter 15, Section 100

A6207 Contact layer, sterile, more than 16 sq in but less than or equal to 48 sq in, each dressing

MED: Pub. 100-2, Chapter 15, Section 100

A6208 Contact layer, sterile, more than 48 sq in, each dressing

MED: Pub. 100-2, Chapter 15, Section 100

A6209 Foam dressing, wound cover, sterile, pad size 16 sq in or less, without adhesive border, each dressing

MED: Pub. 100-2, Chapter 15, Section 100

A6210 Foam dressing, wound cover, sterile, pad size more than 16 sq in but less than or equal to 48 sq in, without adhesive border, each dressing

MED: Pub. 100-2, Chapter 15, Section 100

A6211 Foam dressing, wound cover, sterile, pad size more then 48 sq in, without adhesive border, each dressing

MED: Pub. 100-2, Chapter 15, Section 100

A6212 Foam dressing, wound cover, sterile, pad size 16 sq in or less, with any size adhesive border, each dressing

MED: Pub. 100-2, Chapter 15, Section 100

A6213 Foam dressing, wound cover, sterile, pad size more than 16 sq in but less than or equal to 48 sq in, with any size adhesive border, each dressing

MED: Pub. 100-2, Chapter 15, Section 100

A6214 Foam dressing, wound cover, sterile, pad size more than 48 sq in, with any size adhesive border, each dressing

MED: Pub. 100-2, Chapter 15, Section 100

A6215 Foam dressing, wound filler, sterile, per gram

MED: Pub. 100-2, Chapter 15, Section 100

A6216 Gauze, non-impregnated, non-sterile, pad size 16 sq in or less, without adhesive border, each dressing

MED: Pub. 100-2, Chapter 15, Section 100

A6217 Gauze, non-impregnated, non-sterile, pad size more than 16 sq in but less than or equal to 48 sq in, without adhesive border, each dressing

MED: Pub. 100-2, Chapter 15, Section 100

A6218 Gauze, non-impregnated, non-sterile, pad size more than 48 sq in, without adhesive border, each dressing

MED: Pub. 100-2, Chapter 15, Section 100

A6219 Gauze, non-impregnated, sterile, pad size 16 sq in or less, with any size adhesive border, each dressing

MED: Pub. 100-2, Chapter 15, Section 100

A6220 Gauze, non-impregnated, sterile, pad size more than 16 sq in but less than or equal to 48 sq in, with any size adhesive border, each dressing

MED: Pub. 100-2, Chapter 15, Section 100

A6221 Gauze, non-impregnated, sterile, pad size more than 48 sq in, with any size adhesive border, each dressing

MED: Pub. 100-2, Chapter 15, Section 100

A6222 Gauze, impregnated with other than water, normal saline, or hydrogel, sterile, pad size 16 sq in or less, without adhesive border, each dressing

MED: Pub. 100-2, Chapter 15, Section 100

A6223 Gauze, impregnated with other than water, normal saline, or hydrogel, sterile, pad size more than 16 sq in but less than or equal to 48 sq in, without adhesive border, each dressing

MED: Pub. 100-2, Chapter 15, Section 100

A6224 Gauze, impregnated with other than water, normal saline, or hydrogel, sterile, pad size more than 48 sq in, without adhesive border, each dressing

MED: Pub. 100-2, Chapter 15, Section 100

A6228 Gauze, impregnated, water or normal saline, sterile, pad size 16 sq in or less, without adhesive border, each dressing

MED: Pub. 100-2, Chapter 15, Section 100

A6229 Gauze, impregnated, water or normal saline, sterile, pad size more than 16 sq in but less than or equal to 48 sq in, without adhesive border, each dressing

MED: Pub. 100-2, Chapter 15, Section 100

A6230 Gauze, impregnated, water or normal saline, sterile, pad size more than 48 sq in, without adhesive border, each dressing

MED: Pub. 100-2, Chapter 15, Section 100

A6231 Gauze, impregnated, hydrogel, for direct wound contact, sterile, pad size 16 sq in or less, each dressing

MED: Pub. 100-2, Chapter 15, Section 100

A6232 Gauze, impregnated, hydrogel, for direct wound contact, sterile, pad size greater than 16 sq in, but less than or equal to 48 sq in, each dressing

MED: Pub. 100-2, Chapter 15, Section 100

A6233 Gauze, impregnated, hydrogel for direct wound contact, sterile, pad size more than 48 sq in, each dressing

MED: Pub. 100-2, Chapter 15, Section 100

A6234 Hydrocolloid dressing, wound cover, sterile, pad size 16 sq in or less, without adhesive border, each dressing

MED: Pub. 100-2, Chapter 15, Section 100

A6235 Hydrocolloid dressing, wound cover, sterile, pad size more than 16 sq in but less than or equal to 48 sq in, without adhesive border, each dressing

MED: Pub. 100-2, Chapter 15, Section 100

A6236 Hydrocolloid dressing, wound cover, sterile, pad size more than 48 sq in, without adhesive border, each dressing

MED: Pub. 100-2, Chapter 15, Section 100

A6237 Hydrocolloid dressing, wound cover, sterile, pad size 16 sq in or less, with any size adhesive border, each dressing

MED: Pub. 100-2, Chapter 15, Section 100

A6238 Hydrocolloid dressing, wound cover, sterile, pad size more than 16 sq in but less than or equal to 48 sq in, with any size adhesive border, each dressing

MED: Pub. 100-2, Chapter 15, Section 100

A6239 Hydrocolloid dressing, wound cover, sterile, pad size more than 48 sq in, with any size adhesive border, each dressing

MED: Pub. 100-2, Chapter 15, Section 100

A6240 Hydrocolloid dressing, wound filler, paste, sterile, per fluid ounce

MED: Pub. 100-2, Chapter 15, Section 100

A6241 Hydrocolloid dressing, wound filler, dry form, sterile, per gram

MED: Pub. 100-2, Chapter 15, Section 100

A6242 Hydrogel dressing, wound cover, sterile, pad size 16 sq in or less, without adhesive border, each dressing

MED: Pub. 100-2, Chapter 15, Section 100

● New Codes   ▲ Revised Codes   MED: Medicare Reference   © 2009 Ingenix

A6243 Hydrogel dressing, wound cover, sterile, pad size more than 16 sq in but less than or equal to 48 sq in, without adhesive border, each dressing

MED: Pub. 100-2, Chapter 15, Section 100

A6244 Hydrogel dressing, wound cover, sterile, pad size more than 48 sq in, without adhesive border, each dressing

MED: Pub. 100-2, Chapter 15, Section 100

A6245 Hydrogel dressing, wound cover, sterile, pad size 16 sq in or less, with any size adhesive border, each dressing

MED: Pub. 100-2, Chapter 15, Section 100

A6246 Hydrogel dressing, wound cover, sterile, pad size more than 16 sq in but less than or equal to 48 sq in, with any size adhesive border, each dressing

MED: Pub. 100-2, Chapter 15, Section 100

A6247 Hydrogel dressing, wound cover, sterile,pad size more than 48 sq in, with any size adhesive border, each dressing

MED: Pub. 100-2, Chapter 15, Section 100

A6248 Hydrogel dressing, wound filler, gel, sterile, per fluid ounce

MED: Pub. 100-2, Chapter 15, Section 100

A6250 Skin sealants, protectants, moisturizers, ointments, any type, any size

MED: Pub. 100-2, Chapter 15, Section 100

A6251 Specialty absorptive dressing, wound cover, sterile, pad size 16 sq in or less, without adhesive border, each dressing

MED: Pub. 100-2, Chapter 15, Section 100

A6252 Specialty absorptive dressing, wound cover, sterile, pad size more than 16 sq in but less than or equal to 48 sq in, without adhesive border, each dressing

MED: Pub. 100-2, Chapter 15, Section 100

A6253 Specialty absorptive dressing, wound cover, sterile, pad size more than 48 sq in, without adhesive border, each dressing

MED: Pub. 100-2, Chapter 15, Section 100

A6254 Specialty absorptive dressing, wound cover, sterile, pad size 16 sq in or less, with any size adhesive border, each dressing

MED: Pub. 100-2, Chapter 15, Section 100

A6255 Specialty absorptive dressing, wound cover, sterile, pad size more than 16 sq in but less than or equal to 48 sq in, with any size adhesive border, each dressing

MED: Pub. 100-2, Chapter 15, Section 100

A6256 Specialty absorptive dressing, wound cover, sterile, pad size more than 48 sq in, with any size adhesive border, each dressing

MED: Pub. 100-2, Chapter 15, Section 100

A6257 Transparent film, sterile, 16 sq in or less, each dressing

MED: Pub. 100-2, Chapter 15, Section 100

A6258 Transparent film, sterile, more than 16 sq in but less than or equal to 48 sq in, each dressing

MED: Pub. 100-2, Chapter 15, Section 100

A6259 Transparent film, sterile, more than 48 sq in, each dressing

MED: Pub. 100-2, Chapter 15, Section 100

A6266 Gauze, impregnated, other than water, normal saline, or zinc paste, sterile, any width, per linear yard

MED: Pub. 100-2, Chapter 15, Section 100

A6402 Gauze, non-impregnated, sterile, pad size 16 sq in or less, without adhesive border, each dressing

MED: Pub. 100-2, Chapter 15, Section 100

A6403 Gauze, non-impregnated, sterile, pad size more than 16 sq in less than or equal to 48 sq in, without adhesive border, each dressing

A6404 Gauze, non-impregnated, sterile, pad size more than 48 sq in, without adhesive border, each dressing

A6407 Packing strips, non-impregnated, sterile, up to two inches in width, per linear yard

A6441 Padding bandage, non-elastic, non-woven/non-knitted, width greater than or equal to three inches and less than five inches, per yard

A6442 Conforming bandage, non-elastic, knitted/woven, non-sterile, width less than three inches, per yard

A6443 Conforming bandage, non-elastic, knitted/woven, non-sterile, width greater than or equal to three inches and less than five inches, per yard

A6444 Conforming bandage, non-elastic, knitted/woven, non-sterile, width greater than or equal to five inches, per yard

A6445 Conforming bandage, non-elastic, knitted/woven, sterile, width less than three inches, per yard

A6446 Conforming bandage, non-elastic, knitted/woven, sterile, width greater than or equal to three inches and less than five inches, per yard

A6447 Conforming bandage, non-elastic, knitted/woven, sterile, width greater than or equal to five inches, per yard

A6448 Light compression bandage, elastic, knitted/woven, width less than three inches, per yard

A6449 Light compression bandage, elastic, knitted/woven, width greater than or equal to three inches and less than five inches, per yard

A6450 Light compression bandage, elastic, knitted/woven, width greater than or equal to five inches, per yard

A6451 Moderate compression bandage, elastic, knitted/woven, load resistance of 1.25 to 1.34 foot pounds at 50 percent maximum stretch, width greater than or equal to three inches and less than five inches, per yard

A6452 High compression bandage, elastic, knitted/woven, load resistance greater than or equal to 1.35 foot pounds at 50 percent maximum stretch, width greater than or equal to three inches and less than five inches, per yard

A6453 Self-adherent bandage, elastic, non-knitted/non-woven, width less than three inches, per yard

A6454 Self-adherent bandage, elastic, non-knitted/non-woven, width greater than or equal to three inches and less than five inches, per yard

A6455 Self-adherent bandage, elastic, non-knitted/non-woven, width greater than or equal to five inches, per yard

A6456 Zinc paste impregnated bandage, non-elastic, knitted/woven, width greater than or equal to three inches and less than five inches, per yard

A6457 Tubular dressing with or without elastic, any width, per linear yard

A6501 Compression burn garment, bodysuit (head to foot), custom fabricated

MED: Pub. 100-2, Chapter 15, Section 100

A6502 Compression burn garment, chin strap, custom fabricated

MED: Pub. 100-2, Chapter 15, Section 100

A6503 Compression burn garment, facial hood, custom fabricated

MED: Pub. 100-2, Chapter 15, Section 100

A6504 Compression burn garment, glove to wrist, custom fabricated

MED: Pub. 100-2, Chapter 15, Section 100

A6505 Compression burn garment, glove to elbow, custom fabricated

MED: Pub. 100-2, Chapter 15, Section 100

A6506 Compression burn garment, glove to axilla, custom fabricated

MED: Pub. 100-2, Chapter 15, Section 100

A6507 Compression burn garment, foot to knee length, custom fabricated

MED: Pub. 100-2, Chapter 15, Section 100

A6508 Compression burn garment, foot to thigh length, custom fabricated

MED: Pub. 100-2, Chapter 15, Section 100

A6509 Compression burn garment, upper trunk to waist including arm openings (vest), custom fabricated

MED: Pub. 100-2, Chapter 15, Section 100

A6510 Compression burn garment, trunk, including arms down to leg openings (leotard), custom fabricated

MED: Pub. 100-2, Chapter 15, Section 100

A6511 Compression burn garment, lower trunk including leg openings (panty), custom fabricated

MED: Pub. 100-2, Chapter 15, Section 100

A6512 Compression burn garment, not otherwise classified

MED: Pub. 100-2, Chapter 15, Section 100

A6513 Compression burn mask, face and/or neck, plastic or equal, custom fabricated

A6530 Gradient compression stocking, below knee, 18-30 mm Hg, each

A6531 Gradient compression stocking, below knee, 30-40 mm Hg, each

A6532 Gradient compression stocking, below knee, 40-50 mm Hg, each

A6533 Gradient compression stocking, thigh length, 18-30 mm Hg, each

A6534 Gradient compression stocking, thigh length, 30-40 mm Hg, each

A6535 Gradient compression stocking, thigh length, 40-50 mm Hg, each

A6536 Gradient compression stocking, full length/chap style, 18-30 mm Hg, each

A6537 Gradient compression stocking, full length/chap style, 30-40 mm Hg, each

A6538 Gradient compression stocking, full length/chap style, 40-50 mm Hg, each

A6539 Gradient compression stocking, waist length, 18-30 mm Hg, each

A6540 Gradient compression stocking, waist length, 30-40 mm Hg, each

A6541 Gradient compression stocking, waist length, 40-50 mm Hg, each

A6544 Gradient compression stocking, garter belt

A6545 Gradient compression wrap, non-elastic, below knee, 30-50 mm Hg, each

● New Codes   ▲ Revised Codes   MED: Medicare Reference   © 2009 Ingenix

A6550 Dressing set for negative pressure wound therapy electrical pump, stationary or portable, each

MED: Pub. 100-2, Chapter 15, Section 100

A9270 Noncovered item or service

MED: Pub. 100-2, Chapter 16, Section 20

A9281 Reaching/grabbing device, any type, any length, each

A9283 Foot pressure off-loading/supportive device, any type, each

A9300 Exercise equipment

MED: Pub. 100-2, Chapter 15, Section 110.1; Pub. 100-3, Section 280.1; Pub. 100-4, Chapter 20, Section 10.1

E Codes: Durable Medical Equipment (E0100–E9999)

Before an item can be considered DME, it must meet all of the following requirements:

- It must be able to withstand repeated use.

- It must be primarily and customarily used to serve a medical purpose.

- It must be generally not useful to a person in the absence of an illness or injury.

- It must be appropriate for use in the home.

All E codes fall under the jurisdiction of the DME MAC unless otherwise noted.

Canes

E0100 Cane, includes canes of all materials, adjustable or fixed, with tip

MED: Pub. 100-2, Chapter 15, Section 110.1; Pub. 100-3, Section 280.1, 280.2; Pub. 100-4, Chapter 20, Section 10.1

E0105 Cane, quad or three-prong, includes canes of all materials, adjustable or fixed, with tips

MED: Pub. 100-2, Chapter 15, Section 110.1; Pub. 100-3, Section 20.9, 280.1; Pub. 100-4, Chapter 20, Section 10.1

Crutches

E0110 Crutches, forearm, includes crutches of various materials, adjustable or fixed, pair, complete with tips and handgrips

MED: Pub. 100-2, Chapter 15, Section 110.1; Pub. 100-3, Section 280.1; Pub. 100-4, Chapter 20, Section 10.1

E0111 Crutch, forearm, includes crutches of various materials, adjustable or fixed, each, with tip and handgrip

MED: Pub. 100-2, Chapter 15, Section 110.1; Pub. 100-3, Section 280.1; Pub. 100-4, Chapter 20, Section 10.1

E0112 Crutches, underarm, wood, adjustable or fixed, pair, with pads, tips and handgrips

MED: Pub. 100-2, Chapter 15, Section 110.1; Pub. 100-3, Section 280.1; Pub. 100-4, Chapter 20, Section 10.1

E0113 Crutch, underarm, wood, adjustable or fixed, each, with pad, tip and handgrip

MED: Pub. 100-2, Chapter 15, Section 110.1; Pub. 100-3, Section 280.1; Pub. 100-4, Chapter 20, Section 10.1

E0114 Crutches, underarm, other than wood, adjustable or fixed, pair, with pads, tips and handgrips

MED: Pub. 100-2, Chapter 15, Section 110.1; Pub. 100-3, Section 280.1; Pub. 100-4, Chapter 20, Section 10.1

E0116 Crutch, underarm, other than wood, adjustable or fixed, each, with pad, tip and handgrip

MED: Pub. 100-2, Chapter 15, Section 110.1; Pub. 100-3, Section 280.1; Pub. 100-4, Chapter 20, Section 10.1

E0117 Crutch, underarm, articulating, spring assisted, each

E0118 Crutch substitute, lower leg platform, with or without wheels, each

Walkers

E0130 Walker, rigid (pickup), adjustable or fixed height

MED: Pub. 100-2, Chapter 15, Section 110.1; Pub. 100-3, Section 280.1; Pub. 100-4, Chapter 20, Section 10.1

E0135 Walker, folding (pickup), adjustable or fixed height

MED: Pub. 100-2, Chapter 15, Section 110.1; Pub. 100-3, Section 280.1; Pub. 100-4, Chapter 20, Section 10.1

E0140 Walker, with trunk support, adjustable or fixed height, any type

MED: Pub. 100-2, Chapter 15, Section 110.1; Pub. 100-3, Section 280.1; Pub. 100-4, Chapter 20, Section 10.1

E0141 Walker, rigid, wheeled, adjustable or fixed height

MED: Pub. 100-2, Chapter 15, Section 110.1; Pub. 100-3, Section 280.1; Pub. 100-4, Chapter 20, Section 10.1

E0143 Walker, folding, wheeled, adjustable or fixed height

MED: Pub. 100-2, Chapter 15, Section 110.1; Pub. 100-3, Section 280.1; Pub. 100-4, Chapter 20, Section 10.1

E0144 Walker, enclosed, four sided framed, rigid or folding, wheeled with posterior seat

MED: Pub. 100-2, Chapter 15, Section 110.1; Pub. 100-3, Section 280.1; Pub. 100-4, Chapter 20, Section 10.1

E0147 Walker, heavy duty, multiple braking system, variable wheel resistance

MED: Pub. 100-2, Chapter 15, Section 110.1; Pub. 100-3, Section 20.9; Pub. 100-4, Chapter 20, Section 10.1

E0148 Walker, heavy duty, without wheels, rigid or folding, any type, each

E0149 Walker, heavy duty, wheeled, rigid or folding, any type

E0153 Platform attachment, forearm crutch, each

E0154 Platform attachment, walker, each

E0155 Wheel attachment, rigid pick-up walker, per pair seat attachment, walker

E0156 Seat attachment, walker

E0157 Crutch attachment, walker, each

E0158 Leg extensions for walker, per set of four (4)

E0159 Brake attachment for wheeled walker, replacement, each

E0185 Gel or gel-like pressure pad for mattress, standard mattress length and width

MED: Pub. 100-3, Section 256, 280.1

E0190 Positioning cushion/pillow/wedge, any shape or size, includes all components and accessories

E0191 Heel or elbow protector, each

E0197 Air pressure pad for mattress, standard mattress length and width

MED: Pub. 100-3, Section 280.1

E0198 Water pressure pad for mattress, standard mattress length and width

MED: Pub. 100-3, Section 280.1

E0199 Dry pressure pad for mattress, standard mattress length and width

MED: Pub. 100-3, Section 280.1

Heat/Cold Application

E0200 Heat lamp, without stand (table model), includes bulb, or infrared element

MED: Pub. 100-2, Chapter 15, Section 110.1; Pub. 100-3, Section 280.1; Pub. 100-4, Chapter 20, Section 10.1

E0205 Heat lamp, with stand, includes bulb, or infrared element

MED: Pub. 100-2, Chapter 15, Section 110.1; Pub. 100-3, Section 280.1; Pub. 100-4, Chapter 20, Section 10.1

E0210 Electric heat pad, standard

MED: Pub. 100-3, Section 280.1

E0215 Electric heat pad, moist

MED: Pub. 100-3, Section 280.1

E0217 Water circulating heat pad with pump

E0218 Water circulating cold pad with pump

E0220 Hot water bottle

E0225 Hydrocollator unit, includes pads

MED: Pub. 100-2, Chapter 15, Section 230.3; Pub. 100-3, Section 280.1

E0230 Ice cap or collar

E0231 Non-contact wound warming device (temperature control unit, AC adapter and power cord) for use with warming card and wound cover

E0232 Warming card for use with the non-contact wound warming device and non-contact wound warming wound cover

Coding Tip
Noncontact normothermic wound therapy (NNWT) encourages wound healing by warming a wound to a preset temperature. The device consists of a noncontact wound cover that contains a flexible, battery-powered infrared heating card. Benefits are not available under Medicare for this therapy based on a national coverage determination or NCD.

E0235 Paraffin bath unit, portable (see medical supply code A4265 for paraffin)

MED: Pub. 100-2, Chapter 15, Section 230.3; Pub. 100-3, Section 280.1

Coding Tip
Portable paraffin bath units and supplies may be covered when the patient has undergone a successful trial period of paraffin therapy ordered by a provider and the patient's condition is expected to be relieved by long-term use of this modality.

E0236 Pump for water circulating pad

MED: Pub. 100-3, Section 280.1

E0238 Nonelectric heat pad, moist

MED: Pub. 100-3, Section 280.1

E0239 Hydrocollator unit, portable

MED: Pub. 100-2, Chapter 15, Section 230.3; Pub. 100-3, Section 280.1

Bath and Toilet Aids

E0240   Bath/shower chair, with or without wheels, any size

MED: Pub. 100-3, Section 280.1

E0247   Transfer bench for tub or toilet with or without commode opening

E0248   Transfer bench, heavy duty, for tub or toilet with or without commode opening

Hospital Beds and Accessories

E0277   Powered pressure-reducing air mattress

MED: Pub. 100-3, Section 280.1

E0280   Bed cradle, any type

E0371   Nonpowered advanced pressure reducing overlay for mattress, standard mattress length and width

E0372   Powered air overlay for mattress, standard mattress length and width

E0373   Nonpowered advanced pressure reducing mattress

Suction Pump/Room Vaporizers

E0606   Postural drainage board

Transcutaneous and/or Neuromuscular Electrical Nerve Stimulators—TENS

E0720   Transcutaneous electrical nerve stimulation (TENS) device, two lead, localized stimulation

MED: Pub. 100-3, Section 160.2, 160.3, 160.7.1, 256

E0730   Transcutaneous electrical nerve stimulation (TENS) device, four or more leads, for multiple nerve stimulation

MED: Pub. 100-3, Section 160.2, 160.3, 160.7.1, 256

E0731   Form-fitting conductive garment for delivery of TENS or NMES (with conductive fibers separated from the patient's skin by layers of fabric)

MED: Pub. 100-3, Section 270.3

E0744   Neuromuscular stimulator for scoliosis

E0745   Neuromuscular stimulator, electronic shock unit

MED: Pub. 100-3, Section 150.4, 160.12

E0746   Electromyography (EMG), biofeedback device

MED: Pub. 100-3, Section 30.1

E0747   Osteogenesis stimulator, electrical, noninvasive, other than spinal applications

MED: Pub. 100-3, Section 150.2, 160.11

E0748   Osteogenesis stimulator, electrical, noninvasive, spinal applications

MED: Pub. 100-3, Section 150.2, 160.11

E0762   Transcutaneous electrical joint stimulation device system, includes all accessories

E0764   Functional neuromuscular stimulator, transcutaneous stimulation of muscles of ambulation with computer control, used for walking by spinal cord injured, entire system, after completion of training program

E0769   Electrical stimulation or electromagnetic wound treatment device, not otherwise classified

E0770   Functional electrical stimulator, transcutaneous stimulation of nerve and/or muscle groups, any type, complete system, not otherwise specified

Traction

E0849   Traction equipment, cervical, free-standing stand/frame, pneumatic, applying traction force to other than mandible

E0855   Cervical traction equipment not requiring additional stand or frame

E0860   Traction equipment, overdoor, cervical

MED: Pub. 100-3, Section 280.1

E0944   Pelvic belt/harness/boot

E0945   Extremity belt/harness

▲ **E1035**   Multi-positional patient transfer system, with integrated seat, operated by care giver patient weight capacity up to and including 300 lbs

MED: Pub. 100-2, Chapter 15, Section 110; Pub. 100-4, Chapter 20, Section 10

● **E1036**   Multi-positional patient transfer system, extra-wide, with integrated seat, operated by caregiver, patient weight capacity greater than 300 lbs

E1037   Transport chair, pediatric size

E1038   Transport chair, adult size, patient weight capacity up to and including 300 pounds

E1039   Transport chair, adult size, heavy duty, patient weight capacity greater than 300 pounds

E1399   Durable medical equipment, miscellaneous

Other Orthopedic Devices

E1800   Dynamic adjustable elbow extension/flexion device, includes soft interface material

E1801   Static progressive stretch elbow device, extension and/or flexion, with or without range of motion adjustment, includes all components and accessories

E1802   Dynamic adjustable forearm pronation/supination device, includes soft interface material

E1806   Static progressive stretch wrist device, flexion and/or extension, with or without range of motion adjustment, includes all components and accessories

E1811 Static progressive stretch knee device, extension and/or flexion, with or without range of motion adjustment, includes all components and accessories

E1816 Static progressive stretch ankle device, flexion and/or extension, with or without range of motion adjustment, includes all components and accessories

E1818 Static progressive stretch forearm pronation/supination device, with or without range of motion adjustment, includes all components and accessories

E1820 Replacement soft interface material, dynamic adjustable extension/flexion device

E2402 Negative pressure wound therapy electrical pump, stationary or portable

E2500 Speech generating device, digitized speech, using pre-recorded messages, less than or equal to 8 minutes recording time

MED: Pub. 100-3, Section 50.1

E2502 Speech generating device, digitized speech, using pre-recorded messages, greater than 8 minutes but less than or equal to 20 minutes recording time

MED: Pub. 100-3, Section 50.1

E2504 Speech generating device, digitized speech, using pre-recorded messages, greater than 20 minutes but less than or equal to 40 minutes recording time

MED: Pub. 100-3, Section 50.1

E2506 Speech generating device, digitized speech, using pre-recorded messages, greater than 40 minutes recording time

MED: Pub. 100-3, Section 50.1

E2508 Speech generating device, synthesized speech, requiring message formulation by spelling and access by physical contact with the device

MED: Pub. 100-3, Section 50.1

E2510 Speech generating device, synthesized speech, permitting multiple methods of message formulation and multiple methods of device access

MED: Pub. 100-3, Section 50.1

E2511 Speech generating software program, for personal computer or personal digital assistant

MED: Pub. 100-3, Section 50.1

E2512 Accessory for speech generating device, mounting system

MED: Pub. 100-3, Section 50.1

E2599 Accessory for speech generating device, not otherwise classified

MED: Pub. 100-3, Section 50.1

E2611 General use wheelchair back cushion, width less than 22 inches, any height, including any type mounting hardware

E2612 General use wheelchair back cushion, width 22 inches or greater, any height, including any type mounting hardware

E2613 Positioning wheelchair back cushion, posterior, width less than 22 inches, any height, including any type mounting hardware

E2614 Positioning wheelchair back cushion, posterior, width 22 in. or greater, any height, including any type mounting hardware

E2615 Positioning wheelchair back cushion, posterior-lateral, width less than 22 inches, any height, including any type mounting hardware

E2616 Positioning wheelchair back cushion, posterior-lateral, width 22 inches or greater, any height, including any type mounting hardware

E2619 Replacement cover for wheelchair seat cushion or back cushion, each

E8000 Gait trainer, pediatric size, posterior support, includes all accessories and components

E8001 Gait trainer, pediatric size, upright support, includes all accessories and components

E8002 Gait trainer, pediatric size, anterior support, includes all accessories and components

G Codes: Procedures/Professional Services (G0255–G0329)

Temporary G codes are assigned to services and procedures that are under review before being included in the CPT coding system. Payment for these services is under the jurisdiction of the local carriers.

▲ **G0151** Services of a physical therapist in home health or hospice settings, each 15 minutes

▲ **G0152** Services of an occupational therapist in home health or hospice settings, each 15 minutes

▲ **G0153** Services of a speech and language pathologist in home health or hospice settings, each 15 minutes

G0255 Current perception threshold/sensory nerve conduction test (SNCT), per limb, any nerve

MED: Pub. 100-3, Section 220.7

G0281 Electrical stimulation, (unattended), to one or more areas, for chronic stage III and stage IV pressure ulcers, arterial ulcers, diabetic ulcers, and venous statsis ulcers not demonstrating measurable signs of healing after 30 days of conventional care, as part of a therapy plan of care

● New Codes ▲ Revised Codes MED: Medicare Reference

G0282 Electrical stimulation, (unattended), to one or more areas, for wound care other than described in G0281

G0283 Electrical stimulation (unattended), to one or more areas for indication(s) other than wound care, as part of a therapy plan of care

G0295 Electromagnetic therapy, to one or more areas, for wound care other than described in G0329 or for other uses

G0329 Electromagnetic therapy, to one or more areas for chronic Stage III and Stage IV pressure ulcers, arterial ulcers, diabetic ulcers and venous stasis ulcers not demonstrating measurable signs of healing after 30 days of conventional care as part of a therapy plan of care

Coding Tips

On November 18, 1997, the U.S. District Court in Massachusetts issued a preliminary injunction against CMS to the effect that CMS must cease enforcement of its national noncoverage determination (NCD) that prohibited any Medicare coverage of, or reimbursement for, electrical stimulation (ES) therapy for the treatment of wounds. As a result of the injunction, Medicare carriers and intermediaries were authorized to cover and reimburse ES therapy in those cases in which they determined that such therapy is reasonable and necessary.

After considerable study and review, the agency issued a decision memorandum on July 23, 2002, regarding electrical stimulation for the treatment of wounds. Another decision memorandum was issued on December 17, 2003, regarding electromagnetic stimulation for wound treatment. Effective July 1, 2004, Medicare will allow either one covered ES therapy or one covered electromagnetic therapy for wound treatment. Electrical stimulation and electromagnetic therapy for wound treatment will not be covered as an initial intervention (the NCD uses the term "modality"); however, the use of electrical and electromagnetic stimulation will be covered as an adjunctive therapy only after there are no measurable signs of healing for at least 30 days of treatment with standard therapy. These interventions are applicable only for chronic stage III and stage IV pressure ulcers, arterial ulcers, diabetic ulcers, and venous stasis ulcers. ES and electromagnetic stimulation are only covered when administered by a physician, physical therapist, or incident to a physician service. Wounds must be evaluated at least every 30 days by the treating physician during administration of ES or electromagnetic therapy; continued treatment is not covered if measurable signs of healing have not been demonstrated within any 30-day period. These treatment modalities must be discontinued when the wound bed has completed epithelialization.

For purposes of this NCD, the following wound stages are recognized. A chronic ulcer is defined as one that has not healed within 30 days of onset.

Stage I: Observable pressure-related alteration of intact skin that may include one or more of the following: skin temperature (warm or cool), consistency of tissue (firm, boggy), and sensation (pain, itching). The ulcer presents as an area of persistent redness in patients with light skin, or as an area with red, blue, or purple hues in those with darker skin.

Stage II: The ulcer is superficial and appears as an abrasion, blister, or shallow crater. There is partial skin loss that involves the dermis, epidermis, or both.

Stage III: The ulcer appears as a deep crater with or without undermining of adjacent tissue. There is full-thickness skin loss that involves damage to or

necrosis of subcutaneous tissue. It may extend to, but not through, the underlying fascia.

Stage IV: The ulcer presents with full-thickness skin loss. There is widespread destruction including tissue necrosis or damage to muscles, bones, or supporting structures such as tendons and joint capsules. Undermining of adjacent tissue and sinus tracts also may be present.

All other uses of ES and electromagnetic therapy not otherwise specified for wound treatment will be at the discretion of the local contractor.

K Codes: Temporary Codes (K0734–K0737)

Temporary K codes are developed by the DME MACs to report supplies and other products for which a national code has not yet been developed. Payment jurisdiction lies with the DME MACs unless otherwise specified.

K0734 Skin protection wheelchair seat cushion, adjustable, width less than 22 inches, any depth

K0735 Skin protection wheelchair seat cushion, adjustable width 22 inches or greater, any depth

K0736 Skin protection and positioning wheelchair seat cushion, adjustable, width less than 22 inches, any depth

K0737 Skin protection and positioning wheelchair seat cushion, adjustable, width 22 inches or greater, any depth

L Codes: Orthotic Procedures, Devices (L0120–L4398)

Braces; trusses; and artifical legs, arms, and eyes are covered when furnished incident to a physician's services or on a physician's order. A brace includes rigid and semirigid devices used for the purpose of supporting a weak or deformed body member or restricting or eliminating motion in a diseased or injured part of the body. Back braces include, but are not limited to, sacroiliac, sacrolumbar, dorsolumbar corsets, and belts. Stump stockings and harnesses (including replacements) are also covered when these appliances are essential to the effective use of an artificial limb. Adjustments to an artificial limb or other appliance required by wear or by a change in the patient's condition are covered when ordered by a physician. Adjustments, repairs, and replacements are covered so long as the device continues to be medically required.

Cervical

L0120 Cervical, flexible, nonadjustable (foam collar)

L0140 Cervical, semi-rigid, adjustable (plastic collar)

L0150 Cervical, semi-rigid, adjustable molded chin cup (plastic collar with mandibular/occipital piece)

L0160 Cervical, semi-rigid, wire frame occipital/mandibular support

L0170 Cervical, collar, molded to patient model

L0172 Cervical, collar, semi-rigid thermoplastic foam, two piece

L0174 Cervical, collar, semi-rigid, thermoplastic foam, two piece with thoracic extension

L0180 Cervical, multiple post collar, occipital/mandibular supports, adjustable

L0190 Cervical, multiple post collar, occipital/mandibular supports, adjustable cervical bars (SOMI, Guilford, Taylor types)

L0200 Cervical, multiple post collar, occipital/mandibular supports, adjustable cervical bars, and thoracic extension

Thoracic

L0220 Thoracic, rib belt, custom fabricated

L0450 TLSO, flexible, provides trunk support, upper thoracic region, produces intracavitary pressure to reduce load on the intervertebral disks with rigid stays or panel(s), includes shoulder straps and closures, prefabricated, includes fitting and adjustment

L0454 TLSO flexible, provides trunk support, extends from sacrococcygeal junction to above T-9 vertebra, restricts gross trunk motion in the sagittal plane, produces intracavitary pressure to reduce load on the intervertebral disks with rigid stays or panel(s), includes shoulder straps and closures, prefabricated, includes fitting and adjustment

L0456 TLSO, flexible, provides trunk support, thoracic region, rigid posterior panel and soft anterior apron, extends from the sacrococcygeal junction and terminates just inferior to the scapular spine, restricts gross trunk motion in the sagittal plane, produces intracavitary pressure to reduce load on the intervertebral disks, includes straps and closures, prefabricated, includes fitting and adjustment

L0458 TLSO, triplanar control, modular segmented spinal system, two rigid plastic shells, posterior extends from the sacrococcygeal junction and terminates just inferior to the scapular spine, anterior extends from the symphysis pubis to the xiphoid, soft liner, restricts gross trunk motion in the sagittal, coronal, and transverse planes, lateral strength is provided by overlapping plastic and stabilizing closures, includes straps and closures, prefabricated, includes fitting and adjustment

L0460 TLSO, triplanar control, modular segmented spinal system, two rigid plastic shells, posterior extends from the sacrococcygeal junction and terminates just inferior to the scapular spine, anterior extends from the symphysis pubis to the sternal notch, soft liner, restricts gross trunk motion in the sagittal, coronal, and transverse planes, lateral strength is provided by overlapping plastic and stabilizing closures, includes straps and closures, prefabricated, includes fitting and adjustment

L0462 TLSO, triplanar control, modular segmented spinal system, three rigid plastic shells, posterior extends from the sacrococcygeal junction and terminates just inferior to the scapular spine, anterior extends from the symphysis pubis to the sternal notch, soft liner, restricts gross trunk motion in the sagittal, coronal, and transverse planes, lateral strength is provided by overlapping plastic and stabilizing closures, includes straps and closures, prefabricated, includes fitting and adjustment

L0464 TLSO, triplanar control, modular segmented spinal system, four rigid plastic shells, posterior extends from sacrococcygeal junction and terminates just inferior to scapular spine, anterior extends from symphysis pubis to the sternal notch, soft liner, restricts gross trunk motion in sagittal, coronal, and transverse planes, lateral strength is provided by overlapping plastic and stabilizing closures, includes straps and closures, prefabricated, includes fitting and adjustment

L0466 TLSO, sagittal control, rigid posterior frame and flexible soft anterior apron with straps, closures and padding, restricts gross trunk motion in sagittal plane, produces intracavitary pressure to reduce load on intervertebral disks, includes fitting and shaping the frame, prefabricated, includes fitting and adjustment

L0468 TLSO, sagittal-coronal control, rigid posterior frame and flexible soft anterior apron with straps, closures and padding, extends from sacrococcygeal junction over scapulae, lateral strength provided by pelvic, thoracic, and lateral frame pieces, restricts gross trunk motion in sagittal, and coronal planes, produces intracavitary pressure to reduce load on intervertebral disks, includes fitting and shaping the frame, prefabricated, includes fitting and adjustment

L0470 TLSO, triplanar control, rigid posterior frame and flexible soft anterior apron with straps, closures and padding, extends from sacrococcygeal junction to scapula, lateral strength provided by pelvic, thoracic, and lateral frame pieces, rotational strength provided by subclavicular extensions, restricts gross trunk motion in sagittal, coronal, and transverse planes, produces intracavitary pressure to reduce load on the intervertebral disks, includes fitting and shaping the frame, prefabricated, includes fitting and adjustment

L0472 TLSO, triplanar control, hyperextension, rigid anterior and lateral frame extends from symphysis pubis to sternal notch with two anterior components (one pubic and one sternal), posterior and lateral pads with straps and closures, limits spinal flexion, restricts gross trunk motion in sagittal, coronal, and transverse planes, includes fitting and shaping the frame, prefabricated, includes fitting and adjustment

● New Codes   ▲ Revised Codes   MED: Medicare Reference   © 2009 Ingenix

L0488 TLSO, triplanar control, one piece rigid plastic shell with interface liner, multiple straps and closures, posterior extends from sacrococcygeal junction and terminates just inferior to scapular spine, anterior extends from symphysis pubis to sternal notch, anterior or posterior opening, restricts gross trunk motion in sagittal, coronal, and transverse planes, prefabricated, includes fitting and adjustment

L0490 TLSO, sagittal-coronal control, one piece rigid plastic shell, with overlapping reinforced anterior, with multiple straps and closures, posterior extends from sacrococcygeal junction and terminates at or before the T-9 vertebra, anterior extends from symphysis pubis to xiphoid, anterior opening, restricts gross trunk motion in sagittal and coronal planes, prefabricated, includes fitting and adjustment

L0491 TLSO, sagittal-coronal control, modular segmented spinal sytem, two rigid plastic shells, posterior extends from the sacrococcygeal junction and terminates just inferior to the scapular spine, anterior extends from the symphysis pubis to the xiphoid, soft liner, restricts gross trunk motion in the sagittal and coronal planes, lateral strength is provided by overlapping plastic and stabilizing closures, includes straps and closures, prefabricated, includes fitting and adjustment

L0492 TLSO, sagittal-coronal control, modular segmented spinal system, three rigid plastic shells, posterior extends from the sacrococcygeal junction and terminates just inferior to the scapular spine, anterior extends from the symphysis pubis to the xiphoid, soft liner, restricts gross trunk motion in the sagittal and coronal planes, lateral strength is provided by overlapping plastic and stabilizing closures, includes straps and closures, prefabricated, includes fitting and adjustment

L0621 Sacroiliac orthosis, flexible, provides pelvic-sacral support, reduces motion about the sacroiliac joint, includes straps, closures, may include pendulous abdomen design, prefabricated, includes fitting and adjustment

L0623 Sacroiliac orthosis, provides pelvic-sacral support, with rigid or semi-rigid panels over the sacrum and abdomen, reduces motion about the sacroiliac joint, includes straps, closures, may include pendulous abdomen design, prefabricated, includes fitting and adjustment

L0625 Lumbar orthosis, flexible, provides lumbar support, posterior extends from L-1 to below L-5 vertebra, produces intracavitary pressure to reduce load on the intervertebral discs, includes straps, closures, may include pendulous abdomen design, shoulder straps, stays, prefabricated, includes fitting and adjustment

L0626 Lumbar orthosis, sagittal control, with rigid posterior panel(s), posterior extends from L-1 to below L-5 vertebra, produces intracavitary pressure to reduce load on the intervertebral discs, includes straps, closures, may include padding, stays, shoulder straps, pendulous abdomen design, prefabricated, includes fitting and adjustment

L0627 Lumbar orthosis, sagittal control, with rigid anterior and posterior panels, posterior extends from L-1 to below L-5 vertebra, produces intracavitary pressure to reduce load on the intervertebral discs, includes straps, closures, may include padding, shoulder straps, pendulous abdomen design, prefabricated, includes fitting and adjustment

L0628 LSO, flexible, provides lumbo-sacral support, posterior extends from sacrococcygeal junction to T-9 vertebra, produces intracavitary pressure to reduce load on the intervertebral discs, includes straps, closures, may include stays, shoulder straps, pendulous abdomen design, prefabricated, includes fitting and adjustment

L0630 LSO, sagittal control, with rigid posterior panel(s), posterior extends from sacrococcygeal junction to T-9 vertebra, produces intracavitary pressure to reduce load on the intervertebral discs, includes straps, closures, may include padding, stays, shoulder straps, pendulous abdomen design, prefabricated, includes fitting and adjustment

L0631 LSO, sagittal control, with rigid anterior and posterior panels, posterior extends from sacrococcygeal junction to T-9 vertebra, produces intracavitary pressure to reduce load on the intervertebral discs, includes straps, closures, may include padding, shoulder straps, pendulous abdomen design, prefabricated, includes fitting and adjustment

L0633 LSO, sagittal-coronal control, with rigid posterior frame/panel(s), posterior extends from sacrococcygeal junction to T-9 vertebra, lateral strength provided by rigid lateral frame/panels, produces intracavitary pressure to reduce load on intervertebral discs, includes straps, closures, may include padding, stays, shoulder straps, pendulous abdomen design, prefabricated, includes fitting and adjustment

L0635 LSO, sagittal-coronal control, lumbar flexion, rigid posterior frame/panel(s), lateral articulating design to flex the lumbar spine, posterior extends from sacrococcygeal junction to T-9 vertebra, lateral strength provided by rigid lateral frame/panel(s), produces intracavitary pressure to reduce load on intervertebral discs, includes straps, closures, may include padding, anterior panel, pendulous abdomen design, prefabricated, includes fitting and adjustment

L0637 LSO, sagittal-coronal control, with rigid anterior and posterior frame/panels, posterior extends from sacrococcygeal junction to T-9 vertebra, lateral strength provided by rigid lateral frame/panels, produces intracavitary pressure to reduce load on intervertebral discs, includes straps, closures, may include padding, shoulder straps, pendulous abdomen design, prefabricated, includes fitting and adjustment

L0639 LSO, sagittal-coronal control, rigid shell(s)/panel(s), posterior extends from sacrococcygeal junction to T-9 vertebra, anterior extends from symphysis pubis to xyphoid, produces intracavitary pressure to reduce load on the intervertebral discs, overall strength is provided by overlapping rigid material and stabilizing closures, includes straps, closures, may include soft interface, pendulous abdomen design, prefabricated, includes fitting and adjustment

Halo Procedure

L0810 Halo procedure, cervical halo incorporated into jacket vest

L0820 Halo procedure, cervical halo incorporated into plaster body jacket

L0830 Halo procedure, cervical halo incorporated into Milwaukee type orthosis

L0861 Addition to halo procedure, replacement liner/interface material

Additions to Spinal Orthosis

L0970 TLSO, corset front

Coding Tip
TLSO guidelines: The orthosis must comprise a rigid plastic shell that encircles the trunk and provides a high degree of immobility. The vest-like orthoses that contain flexible components are not classified as TLSOs.

L0972 LSO, corset front

L0974 TLSO, full corset

L0976 LSO, full corset

L0999 Addition to spinal orthosis, not otherwise specified

Coding Tip
Determine if an alternative national HCPCS Level II code better describes the service being reported. Code L0999 should be used only if a more specific code is unavailable.

L1000 CTLSO (Milwaukee), inclusive of furnishing initial orthosis, including model

L1001 CTLSO, immobilizer, infant size, prefabricated, includes fitting and adjustment

L1005 Tension based scoliosis orthosis and accessory pads, includes fitting and adjustment

L1600–L2999 Orthotic Devices, Lower Limb

The procedures in L1600–L2999 are considered base or basic procedures and may be modified by listing procedures from the additions sections and adding them to the base procedures. For Medicare, file claims for codes in this section with DME MAC.

L1600 HO, abduction control of hip joints, flexible, Frejka type with cover, prefabricated, includes fitting and adjustment

L1610 HO, abduction control of hip joints, flexible, (Frejka cover only), prefabricated, includes fitting and adjustment

L1620 HO, abduction control of hip joints, flexible, (Pavlik harness), prefabricated, includes fitting and adjustment

L1650 HO, abduction control of hip joints, static, adjustable (Ilfled type), prefabricated, includes fitting and adjustment

L1652 HO, bilateral thigh cuffs with adjustable abductor spreader bar, adult size, prefabricated, includes fitting and adjustment, any type

L1660 HO, abduction control of hip joints, static, plastic, prefabricated, includes fitting and adjustment

L1686 HO, abduction control of hip joint, postoperative hip abduction type, prefabricated, includes fitting and adjustments

L1690 Combination, bilateral, lumbo-sacral, hip, femur orthosis providing adduction and internal rotation control, prefabricated, includes fitting and adjustment

L1810 KO, elastic with joints, prefabricated, includes fitting and adjustment

L1820 KO, elastic with condylar pads and joints, with or without patellar control, prefabricated, includes fitting and adjustment

L1830 KO, immobilizer, canvas longitudinal, prefabricated, includes fitting and adjustment

L1831 KO, locking knee joint(s), positional orthosis, prefabricated, includes fitting and adjustment

L1832 KO, adjustable knee joints (unicentric or polycentric), positional orthosis, rigid support, prefabricated, includes fitting and adjustment

L1836 KO, rigid, without joint(s), includes soft interface material, prefabricated, includes fitting and adjustment

L1843 KO, single upright, thigh and calf, with adjustable flexion and extension joint (unicentric or polycentric), medial-lateral and rotation control, with or without varus/valgus adjustment, prefabricated, includes fitting and adjustment

L1845 KO, double upright, thigh and calf, with adjustable flexion and extension joint (unicentric or polycentric), medial-lateral and rotation control, with or without varus/valgus adjustment, prefabricated, includes fitting and adjustment

L1847 KO, double upright with adjustable joint, with inflatable air support chamber(s), prefabricated, includes fitting and adjustment

L1850 KO, Swedish type, prefabricated, includes fitting and adjustment

L1902 AFO, ankle gauntlet, prefabricated, includes fitting and adjustment

L1906 AFO, multiligamentus ankle support, prefabricated, includes fitting and adjustment

L1910 AFO, posterior, single bar, clasp attachment to shoe counter, prefabricated, includes fitting and adjustment

L1930 AFO, plastic or other material, prefabricated, includes fitting and adjustment

L1932 AFO, rigid anterior tibial section, total carbon fiber or equal material, prefabricated, includes fitting and adjustment

L1951 AFO, spiral, (Institute of Rehabilitative Medicine type), plastic or other material, prefabricated, includes fitting and adjustment

L1971 AFO, plastic or other material with ankle joint, prefabricated, includes fitting and adjustment

L2005 KAFO, any material, single or double upright, stance control, automatic Lock and swing phase release, mechanical activation, includes ankle joint, any type, custom fabricated

L2035 KAFO, full plastic, static (pediatric size), without free motion ankle, prefabricated, includes fitting and adjustment

L2112 AFO, fracture orthosis, tibial fracture orthosis, soft, prefabricated, includes fitting and adjustment

L2114 AFO, fracture orthosis, tibial fracture orthosis, semi-rigid, prefabricated, includes fitting and adjustment

L2116 AFO, fracture orthosis, tibial fracture orthosis, rigid, prefabricated, includes fitting and adjustment

L2132 KAFO, fracture orthosis, femoral fracture cast orthosis, soft, prefabricated, includes fitting and adjustment

L2134 KAFO, fracture orthosis, femoral fracture cast orthosis, semi-rigid, prefabricated, includes fitting and adjustment

L2136 KAFO, fracture orthosis, femoral fracture cast orthosis, rigid, prefabricated, includes fitting and adjustment

---

Coding Tips

A custom-fitted orthotic is a premanufactured orthotic that can be adjusted to fit the patient.

A custom-fabricated orthotic is made from basic materials on an individual basis by using actual measurements or positive molds of the patient.

Generally, only the patient who was measured will be able to use a custom-fabricated orthotic.

Code 97760 Orthotic(s) management and training (including assessment and fitting when not otherwise reported), upper extremity(s), lower extremity(s), and/or trunk, each 15 minutes, was developed to include the training aspect of the management of a patient being assessed and fitted for an orthotic. If a HCPCS Level II code is reported and its description includes assessment and fitting, then documentation must also support the training aspect of the skilled services in order to also report CPT code 97760.

L2232 Addition to lower extremity orthosis, rocker bottom for total contact ankle foot orthosis, for custom fabricated orthosis only

L3000–L3649 Orthotic Shoes
For Medicare, file claims for codes in this section with DME MAC.

L3430 Heel, counter, plastic reinforced

L3440 Heel, counter, leather reinforced

L3450 Heel, SACH cushion type

L3455 Heel, new leather, standard

L3460 Heel, new rubber, standard

L3465 Heel, Thomas with wedge

L3470 Heel, Thomas extended to ball

L3480 Heel, pad and depression for spur

MED: MCM 2323

L3485 Heel, pad, removable for spur

MED: MCM 2323

L3650–L3999 Orthotic Devices, Upper Limb
The procedures from L3650–L3956 are considered base or basic procedures and may be modified by listing procedures from the additions sections and adding them to the base procedure. For Medicare, file claims for codes in this section with DME MAC.

L3650 SO, figure of eight design abduction restrainer, prefabricated, includes fitting and adjustment

L3660 SO, figure of eight design abduction restrainer, canvas and webbing, prefabricated, includes fitting and adjustment

L3670 SO, acromio/clavicular (canvas and webbing type), prefabricated, includes fitting and adjustment

L3675 SO, vest type abduction restrainer, canvas webbing type, or equal, prefabricated, includes fitting and adjustment

L3677 SO, hard plastic, shoulder stabilizer, pre-fabricated, includes fitting and adjustment

MED: Pub. 100-2, Chapter 15, Section 120

L3710 EO, elastic with metal joints, prefabricated, includes fitting and adjustment

L3760 EO, with adjustable position locking joint(s), prefabricated, includes fitting and adjustments, any type

L3762 EO, rigid, without joints, includes soft interface material, prefabricated, includes fitting and adjustment

L3806 WHFO, includes one or more nontorsion joint(s), turnbuckles, elastic bands/springs, may include soft interface material, straps, custom fabricated, includes fitting and adjustment

L3807 WHFO, without joint(s), prefabricated, includes fitting and adjustments, any type

L3808 WHFO, rigid without joints, may include soft interface material; straps, custom fabricated, includes fitting and adjustment

L3908 WHO, wrist extension control cock-up, nonmolded, prefabricated, includes fitting and adjustment

L3912 HFO, flexion glove with elastic finger control, prefabricated, includes fitting and adjustment

L3914 WHO, wrist extension cock-up, prefabricated, includes fitting and adjustment

L3915 WHO, includes one or more nontorsion joint(s), elastic bands, turnbuckles, may include soft interface, straps, prefabricated, includes fitting and adjustment

L3917 HO, metacarpal fracture orthosis, prefabricated, includes fitting and adjustment

L3923 HFO, without joints, may include soft interface, straps, prefabricated, includes fitting and adjustment

L3925 FO, proximal interphalangeal (PIP)/distal interphalangeal (DIP), nontorsion joint/spring, extension/flexion, may include soft interface material, prefabricated, includes fitting and adjustment

L3929 HFO, includes one or more nontorsion joint(s), turnbuckles, elastic bands/springs, may include soft interface material, straps, prefabricated, includes fitting and adjustment

L3931 WHFO, includes one or more nontorsion joint(s), turnbuckles, elastic bands/springs, may include soft interface material, straps, prefabricated, includes fitting and adjustment

L3956 Addition of joint to upper extremity orthosis, any material; per joint

L3960 SEWHO, abduction positioning, airplane design, prefabricated, includes fitting and adjustment

L3962 SEWHO, abduction positioning, Erb's palsy design, prefabricated, includes fitting and adjustment

L3964 SEO, mobile arm support attached to wheelchair, balanced, adjustable, prefabricated, includes fitting and adjustment

L3965 SEO, mobile arm support attached to wheelchair, balanced, adjustable Rancho type, prefabricated, includes fitting and adjustment

L3966 SEO, mobile arm support attached to wheelchair, balanced, reclining, prefabricated, includes fitting and adjustment

L3968 SEO, mobile arm support attached to wheelchair, balanced, friction arm support (friction dampening to proximal and distal joints), prefabricated, includes fitting and adjustment

L3969 SEO, mobile arm support, monosuspension arm and hand support, overhead elbow forearm hand sling support, yoke type arm suspension support, prefabricated, includes fitting and adjustment

L3980 Upper extremity fracture orthosis, humeral, prefabricated, includes fitting and adjustment

L3982 Upper extremity fracture orthosis, radius/ulnar, prefabricated, includes fitting and adjustment

L3984 Upper extremity fracture orthosis, wrist, prefabricated, includes fitting and adjustment

Orthotic Supplies, Miscellaneous

L4000 Replace girdle for spinal orthosis (CTLSO or SO)

L4002 Replacement strap, any orthosis, includes all components, any length, any type

L4350 Ankle control orthosis, stirrup style, rigid, includes any type interface (e.g., pneumatic, gel), prefabricated, includes fitting and adjustment

L4360 Walking boot, pneumatic, and/or vacuum, with or without joints, with or without interface material, prefabricated, includes fitting and adjustment

L4370 Pneumatic full leg splint, prefabricated, includes fitting and adjustment

L4380 Pneumatic knee splint, prefabricated, includes fitting and adjustment

L4386 Walking boot, nonpneumatic, with or without joints, with or without interface material, prefabricated, includes fitting and adjustment

L4392 Replacement soft interface material, static AFO

L4394 Replace soft interface material, foot drop splint

L4396 Static ankle foot orthosis, including soft interface material, adjustable for fit, for positioning, pressure reduction, may be used for minimal ambulation, prefabricated, includes fitting and adjustment

L4398 Foot drop splint, recumbent positioning device, prefabricated, includes fitting and adjustment

Q Codes: Temporary Q0000–Q9999

CMS assigns Q codes to procedures, services, and supplies on a temporary basis. When a permanent code is assigned, the Q code is deleted and cross-referenced.

This section contains national codes assigned by CMS on a temporary basis. This list contains current codes.

Q codes fall under the jurisdiction of the local carrier unless they represent an incidental service or are otherwise specified.

Q4049   Finger splint, static

Q4051   Splint supplies, miscellaneous (includes thermoplastics, strapping, fasteners, padding and other supplies)

Coding Tips

Since Q codes are under the jurisdiction of local Medicare carriers, coverage and coding guidelines may vary.

Check your Medicare carrier's coding guidelines and coverage issues before reporting services using these codes.

S Codes: Temporary National Codes (Non-Medicare) (S5000–S9999)

Blue Cross/Blue Shield and other commercial payers develop S codes to report drugs, services, and supplies. These codes may not be used to bill services paid under any Medicare payment system. Medicare does not reimburse for services under S codes.

S8450   Splint, prefabricated, digit (specify digit by use of modifier)

S8451   Splint, prefabricated, wrist or ankle

S8452   Splint, prefabricated, elbow

S8948   Application of a modality (requiring constant provider attendance) to one or more areas; low-level laser; each 15 minutes

S8990   Physical or manipulative therapy performed for maintenance rather than restoration

S9131   Physical therapy; in the home, per diem

S9476   Vestibular rehabilitation program, non-physician provider, per diem

Coding Tip

S codes are not valid for reporting services performed on Medicare patients. Before reporting services with S codes to commercial insurance carriers, verify with your carrier that the selected code is covered.

HCPCS Level II Index

A

Absorptive dressing, A6251-A6256

Adhesive
    pads, A6203-A6205, A6212-A6214,
        A6219-A6221, A6237-A6239,
        A6245-A6247, A6254-A6256
    remover, A4455
    tape, A4450-A4452

Alginate dressing, A6196-A6199
    Algiderm, A6196-A6199
    Algosteril, A6196-A6199

Apnea monitor
    electrodes, A4556

Arm sling, A4565

B

Bandage
    compression
        high, A6452
        light, A6448-A6450
        medium, A6451
    conforming, A6442-A6447
    holder/binder
        non-reusble, A4461
        reusable, A4463
    Orthoflex elastic plaster bandages,
        A4580
    padding, A6441
    self-adherent, A6453-A6455
    Specialist Plaster bandages, A4580
    tubular, A6457
    zinc paste, A6456

Baseball finger splint, A4570

Bath aids, E0240-E0248

Battery
    TENS, A4630

Bed, hospital
    accessories, E0277-E0373

Binder
    extremity, nonelastic, A4465

Board, drainage, E0606

Burn
    garment, A6501-A6512
    mask, A6513

C

Cane, E0100-E0105
    accessory, A4636-A4637

Cast
    materials, special, A4590
    plaster, A4580
    supplies, A4580-A4590
        Delta-Cast—Elite—Casting Material,
            A4590
        Delta-Lite—Conformable Casting
            Tape, A4590
        Delta-Lite—C-Splint—Fibreglass
            Immobilizer, A4590
        Delta-Lite—Fibreglass Casting Tape,
            A4590
        Flashcast—Elite—Casting Material,
            A4590
        Orthoflex—Elastic Plaster Bandages,
            A4580
        Orthoplast—Splints (and
            Orthoplast—II Splints), A4590
        Specialist—Plaster Bandages, A4580
        Specialist—Plaster Roll Immobilizer,
            A4580
        Specialist—Plaster Splints, A4580

Cleaning solvent, Nu-Hope
    4 oz bottle, A4455
    16 oz bottle, A4455

Collagen
    wound dressing, A6021-A6024

Composite dressing, A6200-A6205

Compression
    burn garment, A6501-A6512
    burn mask, A6513
    gradient stocking, A6530-A6549

Compression bandage
    high, A6452
    light, A6448-A6450
    medium, A6451

Conductive
    paste or gel, A4558

Conforming bandage, A6442-A6447

Contact layer, A6206-A6208

Cover, wound
    alginate dressing, A6196-A6198
    foam dressing, A6209-A6214
    hydrocolloid dressing, A6234-A6239
    hydrogel dressing, A6242-A6247
    specialty absorptive dressing,
        A6251-A6256

Crutches, E0110-E0118
    accessories, A4635-A4637,
        E0153-E0157

Curasorb, alginate dressing,
    A6196-A6199

Cushion, wheelchair seat, K0734-K0737

D

Delta-Cast—Elite—Casting Material,
    A4590

Delta-Lite—Conformable Casting Tape,
    A4590

Delta-Lite—C-Splint—Fibreglass
    Immobilizer, A4590

Delta-Lite—Fibreglass Casting Tape,
    A4590

Dorsiwedge—Night Splint, A4570

Dressing —see also **Bandage**
    alginate, A6196-A6199
    collagen, A6021-A6024
    composite, A6200-A6205
    contact layer, A6206-A6208
    film, A6257-A6259
    foam, A6209-A6215
    gauze, A6216-A6233, A6266-A6402
    holder/binder
        non-reusble, A4461
        reusable, A4463
    hydrocolloid, A6234-A6241
    hydrogel, A6242-A6248
    specialty absorptive, A6251-A6256
    tape, A4450-A4452
    transparent film, A6257-A6259

Dropper, A4649

Durable medical equipment,
    miscellaneous, E1399

E

Electrical stimulator
    complete system, E0770
    replacement batteries, A4630
    supplies, A4595

Electrodes, per pair, A4556

Exercise
    equipment, A9300

Skin
   sealant, protectant, moisturizer, A6250,
      K0734-K0737

Sling, A4565

Sorbsan, alginate dressing,
   A6196-A6198

Specialist
   health/postoperative shoe, A9270
   J-splint, A4580
   plaster bandages, A4580
   plaster roll immobilizer, A4580
   plaster splint, A4580
   toe insert, A9270

Specialty absorptive dressing,
   A6251-A6256

Splint, A4570
   ankle, S8451
   digit, S8450
   elbow, S8452
   finger, Q4049
   foot drop, L4394, L4398
   full leg, L4370
   knee, L4380
   prefabricated, L4370-L4380, L4398,
      S8450-S8452
   replacement material, L4394
   supplies, Q4051
   wrist, S8451

Stimulators
   electric, supplies, A4595
   electrical, E0720-E0730, E0762,
      E0769-E0770
   neuromuscular, E0744-E0745, E0764
   osteogenesis, E0747-E0748

Surgical
   dressing holder A4461-A4463
   stocking, A4490-A4510
   supplies, miscellaneous, A4649

T

Tape
   non-waterproof, A4450
   waterproof, A4452

TENS, A4595, E0720-E0731

Therapy electromagnetic, G0295,
   G0329

Thinning solvent, NuHope, 2 oz bottle,
   A4455

Tibia
   Toad finger splint, A4570

Tip (cane, crutch, walker) replacement,
   A4637

Toe
   Specialist—Toe Insert for
      Specialist—Closed-Back Cast Boot
      and Specialist—Health/Post
      Operative Shoe, A9270

Toilet aids, E0247-E0248

Traction/transfer, E0849-E1035

Transparent film (for dressing),
   A6257-A6259

U

Universal
   remover for adhesives, A4455

Urinary
   incontinence supplies, A5113-A5114

W

Walker, E0130-E0149
   accessories, A4636-A4637,
      E0154-E0159

Wheelchair seat cushion, K0734-K0737

Wound
   cover
      alginate dressing, A6196-A6198
      foam dressing, A6209-A6214
      hydrocolloid dressing, A6234-A6239
      hydrogel dressing, A6242-A6247
      specialty absorptive dressing,
         A6251-A6256
      warming device
         non-contact warming cover,
            A6000
   filler
      alginate, A6199
      collagen, A6024
      foam, A6215
      hydrocolloid, A6240-A6241
      hydrogel, A6248
   packing strips, A6407
   pouch, A6154
   therapy
      negative pressure
         supplies, A6550

HCPCS Index

Medicare Regulatory Information

The Centers for Medicare and Medicaid Services restructured its paper-based manual system as a web-based system on October 1, 2003. Called the online CMS manual system, it combines all of the various program instructions into internet-only manuals (IOMs), which are used by all CMS programs and contractors. Complete versions of all of the manuals can be found at http://www.cms.hhs.gov/manuals.

Effective with implementation of the IOMs, the former method of publishing program memoranda (PMs) to communicate program instructions was replaced by the following four templates:

- One-time notification
- Manual revisions
- Business requirements
- Confidential requirements

The web-based system has been organized by functional area (e.g., eligibility, entitlement, claims processing, benefit policy, program integrity) in an effort to eliminate redundancy within the manuals, simplify updating, and make CMS program instructions available more quickly. The web-based system contains the functional areas included below:

Pub. 100	Introduction
Pub. 100-1	Medicare General Information, Eligibility, and Entitlement Manual
Pub. 100-2	Medicare Benefit Policy Manual
Pub. 100-3	Medicare National Coverage Determinations Manual
Pub. 100-4	Medicare Claims Processing Manual
Pub. 100-5	Medicare Secondary Payer Manual
Pub. 100-6	Medicare Financial Management Manual
Pub. 100-7	State Operations Manual
Pub. 100-8	Medicare Program Integrity Manual
Pub. 100-9	Medicare Contractor Beneficiary and Provider Communications Manual
Pub. 100-10	Quality Improvement Organization Manual
Pub. 100-11	Reserved
Pub. 100-12	State Medicaid Manual (under development)
Pub. 100-13	Medicaid State Children's Health Insurance Program (under development)
Pub. 100-14	Medicare ESRD Network Organizations Manual
Pub. 100-15	State Buy-In Manual
Pub. 100-16	Medicare Managed Care Manual
Pub. 100-17	CMS/Business Partners Systems Security Manual
Pub. 100-18	Reserved
Pub. 100-19	Demonstrations
Pub. 100-20	One-Time Notification
Pub. 100-21	Recurring Update Notification

A brief description of the Medicare manuals primarily used for this publication follows:

The **National Coverage Determinations Manual** (NCD), is organized according to categories such as diagnostic services, supplies, and medical procedures. The table of contents lists each category and subject within that category. Revision transmittals identify any new or background material, recap the changes, and provide an effective date for the change.

When complete, the manual will contain two chapters. Chapter 1 currently includes a description of CMS's national coverage determinations. When available, chapter 2 will contain a list of HCPCS codes related to each coverage determination. The manual is organized in accordance with CPT category sequences.

The **Medicare Benefit Policy Manual** contains Medicare general coverage instructions that are not national coverage determinations. As a general rule, in the past these instructions have been found in chapter II of the **Medicare Carriers Manual**, the **Medicare Intermediary Manual**, other provider manuals, and program memoranda.

The **Medicare Claims Processing Manual** contains instructions for processing claims for contractors and providers.

The **Medicare Program Integrity Manual** communicates the priorities and standards for the Medicare integrity programs.

PUB. 100 REFERENCES

Pub. 100-1, Chapter 3, Section 30
Outpatient Mental Health Treatment Limitation
Regardless of the actual expenses a beneficiary incurs for treatment of mental, psychoneurotic, and personality disorders while the beneficiary is not an inpatient of a hospital at the time such expenses are incurred, the amount of those expenses that may be recognized for Part B deductible and payment purposes is limited to 62.5 percent of the Medicare allowed amount for these services. The limitation is called the outpatient mental health treatment limitation. Since Part B deductible also applies the program pays for about half of the allowed amount recognized for mental health therapy services.

Expenses for diagnostic services (e.g., psychiatric testing and evaluation to diagnose the patient's illness) are not subject to this limitation. This limitation applies only to therapeutic services and to services performed to evaluate the progress of a course of treatment for a diagnosed condition.

Pub. 100-1, Chapter 3, Section 30.1
Application of Mental Health Limitation - Status of Patient
The limitation is applicable to expenses incurred in connection with the treatment of an individual who is not an inpatient of a hospital. Thus, the limitation applies to mental health services furnished to a person in a physician's office, in the patient's home, in a skilled nursing facility, as an outpatient, and so forth. The term "hospital" in this context means an institution which is primarily engaged in providing to inpatients, by or under the supervision of a physician(s):

- Diagnostic and therapeutic services for medical diagnosis, and treatment, and care of injured, disabled, or sick persons;
- Rehabilitation services for injured, disabled, or sick persons; or
- Psychiatric services for the diagnosis and treatment of mentally ill patients.

Pub. 100-1, Chapter 3, Section 30.2
Disorders Subject to Mental Health Limitation
The term "mental, psychoneurotic, and personality disorders" is defined as the specific psychiatric conditions described in the American Psychiatric Association's *Diagnostic and Statistical Manual of Mental Disorders*, Third Edition - Revised (DSM-III-R).

If the treatment services rendered are for both a psychiatric condition and one or more nonpsychiatric conditions, the charges are separated to apply the limitation only to the mental health charge. Normally HCPCS code and diagnoses are used. Where HCPCS code is not available on the claim, revenue code is used.

If the service is primarily on the basis of a diagnosis of Alzheimer's Disease (coded 331.0 in the International Classification of Diseases, 9th Revision) or Alzheimer's or other disorders (coded 290.XX in DSM-III-R), treatment typically represents medical management of the patient's condition (rather than psychiatric treatment) and is not subject to the limitation.

Pub. 100-1, Chapter 3, Section 30.3

Diagnostic Services

The mental health limitation does not apply to tests and evaluations performed to establish or confirm the patient's diagnosis. Diagnostic services include psychiatric or psychological tests and interpretations, diagnostic consultations, and initial evaluations. However, testing services performed to evaluate a patient's progress during treatment are considered part of treatment and are subject to the limitation.

Pub. 100-1, Chapter 5, Section 70

Physician Defined

Physician means doctor of medicine, doctor of osteopathy (including osteopathic practitioner), doctor of dental surgery or dental medicine (within the limitations in subsection Sec.70.2), doctor of podiatric medicine (within the limitations in subsection Sec.70.3), or doctor of optometry (within the limitations of subsection Sec.70.5), and, with respect to certain specified treatment, a doctor of chiropractic legally authorized to practice by a State in which he/she performs this function. The services performed by a physician within these definitions are subject to any limitations imposed by the State on the scope of practice. The issuance by a State of a license to practice medicine constitutes legal authorization. Temporary State licenses also constitute legal authorization to practice medicine. If State law authorizes local political subdivisions to establish higher standards for medical practitioners than those set by the State licensing board, the local standards determine whether a particular physician has legal authorization. If State licensing law limits the scope of practice of a particular type of medical practitioner, only the services within the limitations are covered. The issuance by a State of a license to practice medicine constitutes legal authorization. Temporary State licenses also constitute legal authorization to practice medicine. If State law authorizes local political subdivisions to establish higher standards for medical practitioners than those set by the State licensing board, the local standards determine whether a particular physician has legal authorization. If State licensing law limits the scope of practice of a particular type of medical practitioner, only the services within the limitations are covered. NOTE:The term physician does not include such practitioners as a Christian Science practitioner or naturopath.

Pub. 100-2, Chapter 15, Section 30

Physician Services

B3-2020, B3-4142

A. General

Physician services are the professional services performed by a physician or physicians for a patient including diagnosis, therapy, surgery, consultation, and care plan oversight. The physician must render the service for the service to be covered. (See Publication 100-1, the Medicare General Information, Eligibility, and Entitlement Manual, Chapter 5, Sec.70, for definition of physician.) A service may be considered to be a physician's service where the physician either examines the patient in person or is able to visualize some aspect of the patient's condition without the interposition of a third person's judgment. Direct visualization would be possible by means of x-rays, electrocardiogram and electroencephalogram tapes, tissue samples, etc. For example, the interpretation by a physician of an actual electrocardiogram or electroencephalogram reading that has been transmitted via telephone (i.e., electronically rather than by means of a verbal description) is a covered service. Professional services of the physician are covered if provided within the United States, and may be performed in a home, office, institution, or at the scene of an accident. A patient's home, for this purpose, is anywhere the patient makes his or her residence, e.g., home for the aged, a nursing home, a relative's home.

B. Telephone Services

Services by means of a telephone call between a physician and a beneficiary, or between a physician and a member of a beneficiary's family, are covered under Medicare, but carriers may not make separate payment for these services under the program. The physician work resulting from telephone calls is considered to be an integral part of the prework and postwork of other physician services, and the fee schedule amount for the latter services already includes payment for the telephone calls. See the Medicare Benefit Policy Manual, Chapter 15, "Covered Medical and Other Health Services," Sec.270, for coverage of telehealth services.

C. Consultations

A consultation may be paid when the consulting physician initiates treatment on the same day as the consultation. It is only after a transfer of care has occurred that evaluation and management (E&M) services may not be billed as consultations; they must be billed as subsequent office/outpatient visits. Therefore, if covered, a consultation is reimbursable when it is a professional service furnished a patient by a second physician at the request of the attending physician. Such a consultation includes the history and examination of the patient as well as the written report, which is furnished to the attending physician for inclusion in the patient's permanent medical record. These reports must be prepared and submitted to the provider for retention when they involve patients of institutions responsible for maintaining such records, and submitted to the attending physician's office for other patients. To reimburse laboratory consultations, the services must: Be requested by the patient's attending physician; Relate to a test result that lies outside of the clinically significant normal or expected/ established range relative to the condition of the patient; Result in a written narrative report included in the patient's medical record; andRequire medical judgment by the consultant physician. A consultation must involve a medical judgment that ordinarily requires a physician. Where a nonphysician laboratory specialist could furnish the

information, the service of the physician is not a consultation payable under Part B. The following indicators can ordinarily distinguish attending physician's claims:Therapeutic services are included on the bill in addition to an examination;The patient's history is before the examiner while the claim is reviewed and the billing physician has previously rendered other services to the patient; orInformation in the file indicates that the patient was not referred. The attending physician may remove himself from the care of the patient and turn the patient over to the person who performed a consultation service. In this situation, the initial examination would be a consultation if the above requirements were met at that time.

D. Patient-Initiated Second Opinions

Patient-initiated second opinions that relate to the medical need for surgery or for major nonsurgical diagnostic and therapeutic procedures (e.g., invasive diagnostic techniques such as cardiac catheterization and gastroscopy) are covered under Medicare. In the event that the recommendation of the first and second physician differs regarding the need for surgery (or other major procedure), a third opinion is also covered. Second and third opinions are covered even though the surgery or other procedure, if performed, is determined not covered. Payment may be made for the history and examination of the patient, and for other covered diagnostic services required to properly evaluate the patient's need for a procedure and to render a professional opinion. In some cases, the results of tests done by the first physician may be available to the second physician.

E. Concurrent Care

Concurrent care exists where more than one physician renders services more extensive than consultative services during a period of time. The reasonable and necessary services of each physician rendering concurrent care could be covered where each is required to play an active role in the patient's treatment, for example, because of the existence of more than one medical condition requiring diverse specialized medical services. In order to determine whether concurrent physicians' services are reasonable and necessary, the carrier must decide the following:

1. Whether the patient's condition warrants the services of more than one physician on an attending (rather than consultative) basis, and

2. Whether the individual services provided by each physician are reasonable and necessary.

In resolving the first question, the carrier should consider the specialties of the physicians as well as the patient's diagnosis, as concurrent care is usually (although not always) initiated because of the existence of more than one medical condition requiring diverse specialized medical or surgical services. The specialties of the physicians are an indication of the necessity for concurrent services, but the patient's condition and the inherent reasonableness and necessity of the services, as determined by the carrier's medical staff in accordance with locality norms, must also be considered. For example, although cardiology is a sub-specialty of internal medicine, the treatment of both diabetes and of a serious heart condition might require the concurrent services of two physicians, each practicing in internal medicine but specializing in different sub-specialties.

While it would not be highly unusual for concurrent care performed by physicians in different specialties (e.g., a surgeon and an internist) or by physicians in different sub-specialties of the same specialty (e.g., an allergist and a cardiologist) to be found medically necessary, the need for such care by physicians in the same specialty or sub-specialty (e.g., two internists or two cardiologists) would occur infrequently since in most cases both physicians would possess the skills and knowledge necessary to treat the patient. However, circumstances could arise which would necessitate such care. For example, a patient may require the services of two physicians in the same specialty or sub-specialty when one physician has further limited his or her practice to some unusual aspect of that specialty, e.g., tropical medicine. Similarly, concurrent services provided by a family physician and an internist may or may not be found to be reasonable and necessary, depending on the circumstances of the specific case. If it is determined that the services of one of the physicians are not warranted by the patient's condition, payment may be made only for the other physician's (or physicians') services.

Once it is determined that the patient requires the active services of more than one physician, the individual services must be examined for medical necessity, just as where a single physician provides the care. For example, even if it is determined that the patient requires the concurrent services of both a cardiologist and a surgeon, payment may not be made for any services rendered by either physician which, for that condition, exceed normal frequency or duration unless there are special circumstances requiring the additional care.

The carrier must also assure that the services of one physician do not duplicate those provided by another, e.g., where the family physician visits during the post-operative period primarily as a courtesy to the patient.

Hospital admission services performed by two physicians for the same beneficiary on the same day could represent reasonable and necessary services, provided, as stated above, that the patient's condition necessitates treatment by both physicians. The level of difficulty of the service provided may vary between the physicians, depending on the severity of the complaint each one is treating and that physician's prior contact with the patient. For example, the admission services performed by a physician who has been treating a patient over a period of time for a chronic condition would not be as involved as the services performed by a physician who has had no prior contact with the patient and who has been called in to diagnose and treat a major acute condition.

Carriers should have sufficient means for identifying concurrent care situations. A correct coverage determination can be made on a concurrent care case only where the claim is sufficiently documented for the carrier to determine the role each physician played in the patient's care (i.e., the condition or conditions for which the physician treated the patient). If, in any case, the role of each physician involved is not clear, the carrier should request clarification.

F. Completion of Claims Forms

Separate charges for the services of a physician in completing a Form CMS-1500, a statement in lieu of a Form CMS-1500, or an itemized bill are not covered. Payment for completion of the Form CMS-1500 claim form is considered included in the fee schedule amount.

G. Care Plan Oversight Services

Care plan oversight is supervision of patients under care of home health agencies or hospices that require complex and multidisciplinary care modalities involving regular physician development and/or revision of care plans, review of subsequent reports of patient status, review of laboratory and other studies, communication with other health professionals not employed in the same practice who are involved in the patient's care, integration of new information into the care plan, and/or adjustment of medical therapy.

Such services are covered for home health and hospice patients, but are not covered for patients of skilled nursing facilities (SNFs), nursing home facilities, or hospitals. These services are covered only if all the following requirements are met:

1. The beneficiary must require complex or multi-disciplinary care modalities requiring ongoing physician involvement in the patient's plan of care;

2. The care plan oversight (CPO) services should be furnished during the period in which the beneficiary was receiving Medicare covered HHA or hospice services;

3. The physician who bills CPO must be the same physician who signed the home health or hospice plan of care;

4. The physician furnished at least 30 minutes of care plan oversight within the calendar month for which payment is claimed. Time spent by a physician's nurse or the time spent consulting with one's nurse is not countable toward the 30-minute threshold. Low-intensity services included as part of other evaluation and management services are not included as part of the 30 minutes required for coverage;

5. The work included in hospital discharge day management (codes 99238-99239) and discharge from observation (code 99217) is not countable toward the 30 minutes per month required for work on the same day as discharge but only for those services separately documented as occurring after the patient is actually physically discharged from the hospital;

6. The physician provided a covered physician service that required a face-to-face encounter with the beneficiary within the six months immediately preceding the first care plan oversight service. Only evaluation and management services are acceptable prerequisite face-to-face encounters for CPO. EKG, lab, and surgical services are not sufficient face-to-face services for CPO;

7. The care plan oversight billed by the physician was not routine post-operative care provided in the global surgical period of a surgical procedure billed by the physician;

8. If the beneficiary is receiving home health agency services, the physician did not have a significant financial or contractual interest in the home health agency. A physician who is an employee of a hospice, including a volunteer medical director, should not bill CPO services. Payment for the services of a physician employed by the hospice is included in the payment to the hospice;

9. The physician who bills the care plan oversight services is the physician who furnished them;

10. Services provided incident to a physician's service do not qualify as CPO and do not count toward the 30-minute requirement;

11. The physician is not billing for the Medicare end stage renal disease (ESRD) capitation payment for the same beneficiary during the same month; and

12. The physician billing for CPO must document in the patient's record the services furnished and the date and length of time associated with those services.

Pub. 100-2, Chapter 15, Section 60.3
Incident to Physician's Service in Clinic
B3-2050.3

Services and supplies incident to a physician's service in a physician directed clinic or group association are generally the same as those described above.

A physician directed clinic is one where:

1. A physician (or a number of physicians) is present to perform medical (rather than administrative) services at all times the clinic is open;

2. Each patient is under the care of a clinic physician; and

3. The nonphysician services are under medical supervision.

In highly organized clinics, particularly those that are departmentalized, direct physician supervision may be the responsibility of several physicians as opposed to an individual attending physician. In this situation, medical management of all services provided in the clinic is assured. The physician ordering a particular service need not be the physician

who is supervising the service. Therefore, services performed by auxiliary personnel and other aides are covered even though they are performed in another department of the clinic. Supplies provided by the clinic during the course of treatment are also covered. When the auxiliary personnel perform services outside the clinic premises, the services are covered only if performed under the direct supervision of a clinic physician. If the clinic refers a patient for auxiliary services performed by personnel who are not supervised by clinic physicians, such services are not incident to a physician's servic

Pub. 100-2, Chapter 15, Section 80.2
Psychological Tests and Neuropsychological Tests

Medicare Part B coverage of psychological tests and neuropsychological tests is authorized under section 1861(s)(3) of the Social Security Act. Payment for psychological and neuropsychological tests is authorized under section 1842(b)(2)(A) of the Social Security Act. The payment amounts for the new psychological and neuropsychological tests (CPT codes 96102, 96103, 96119 and 96120) that are effective January 1, 2006, and are billed for tests administered by a technician or a computer reflect a site of service payment differential for the facility and non-facility settings.

Additionally, there is no authorization for payment for diagnostic tests when performed on an "incident to" basis.

Under the diagnostic tests provision, all diagnostic tests are assigned a certain level of supervision. Generally, regulations governing the diagnostic tests provision require that only physicians can provide the assigned level of supervision for diagnostic tests.

However, there is a regulatory exception to the supervision requirement for diagnostic psychological and neuropsychological tests in terms of who can provide the supervision.

That is, regulations allow a clinical psychologist (CP) or a physician to perform the general supervision assigned to diagnostic psychological and neuropsychological tests.

In addition, nonphysician practitioners such as nurse practitioners (NPs), clinical nurse specialists (CNSs) and physician assistants (PAs) who personally perform diagnostic psychological and neuropsychological tests are excluded from having to perform these tests under the general supervision of a physician or a CP. Rather, NPs and CNSs must perform such tests under the requirements of their respective benefit instead of the requirements for diagnostic psychological and neuropsychological tests. Accordingly, NPs and CNSs must perform tests in collaboration (as defined under Medicare law at section 1861(aa)(6) of the Act) with a physician. PAs perform tests under the general supervision of a physician as required for services furnished under the PA benefit.

Furthermore, physical therapists (PTs), occupational therapists (OTs) and speech language pathologists (SLPs) are authorized to bill three test codes as "sometimes therapy" codes. Specifically, CPT codes 96105, 96110 and 96111 may be performed by these therapists. However, when PTs, OTs and SLPs perform these three tests, they must be performed under the general supervision of a physician or a CP.

Who May Bill for Diagnostic Psychological and Neuropsychological Tests

- CPs - see qualifications under chapter 15, section 160 of the Benefits Policy Manual, Pub. 100-02.
- NPs - to the extent authorized under State scope of practice. See qualifications under chapter 15, section 200 of the Benefits Policy Manual, Pub. 100-02.
- CNSs - to the extent authorized under State scope of practice. See qualifications under chapter 15, section 210 of the Benefits Policy Manual, Pub. 100-02.
- PAs - to the extent authorized under State scope of practice. See qualifications under chapter 15, section 190 of the Benefits Policy Manual, Pub. 100-02.
- Independently Practicing Psychologists (IPPs)
- PTs, OTs and SLPs - see qualifications under chapter 15, sections 220-230.6 of the Benefits Policy Manual, Pub. 100-02.

Psychological and neuropsychological tests performed by a psychologist (who is not a CP) practicing independently of an institution, agency, or physician's office are covered when a physician orders such tests. An IPP is any psychologist who is licensed or certified to practice psychology in the State or jurisdiction where furnishing services or, if the jurisdiction does not issue licenses, if provided by any practicing psychologist. (It is CMS' understanding that all States, the District of Columbia, and Puerto Rico license psychologists, but that some trust territories do not. Examples of psychologists, other than CPs, whose psychological and neuropsychological tests are covered under the diagnostic tests provision include, but are not limited to, educational psychologists and counseling psychologists.)

The carrier must secure from the appropriate State agency a current listing of psychologists holding the required credentials to determine whether the tests of a particular IPP are covered under Part B in States that have statutory licensure or certification. In States or territories that lack statutory licensing or certification, the carrier checks individual qualifications before provider numbers are issued. Possible reference sources are the national directory of membership of the American Psychological Association, which provides data about the educational background of individuals and indicates which members are board-certified, the records and directories of the State or territorial psychological association, and the National Register of Health Service Providers. If qualification is dependent on a doctoral degree from a currently accredited program, the carrier verifies the date of accreditation of the school involved, since such accreditation is not retroactive. If the listed reference sources do not provide enough information (e.g., the psychologist is not a member of one of these sources), the carrier contacts the psychologist personally for the required information. Generally, carriers maintain a continuing list of psychologists whose qualifications have been verified.

NOTE: When diagnostic psychological tests are performed by a psychologist who is not practicing independently, but is on the staff of an institution, agency, or clinic, that entity bills for the psychological tests.

The carrier considers psychologists as practicing independently when:

- They render services on their own responsibility, free of the administrative and professional control of an employer such as a physician, institution or agency;
- The persons they treat are their own patients; and
- They have the right to bill directly, collect and retain the fee for their services.

A psychologist practicing in an office located in an institution may be considered an independently practicing psychologist when both of the following conditions exist:

- The office is confined to a separately-identified part of the facility which is used solely as the psychologist's office and cannot be construed as extending throughout the entire institution; and
- The psychologist conducts a private practice, i.e., services are rendered to patients from outside the institution as well as to institutional patients.

Payment for Diagnostic Psychological and Neuropsychological Tests Expenses for diagnostic psychological and neuropsychological tests are not subject to the outpatient mental health treatment limitation, that is, the payment limitation on treatment services for mental, psychoneurotic and personality disorders as authorized under Section 1833(c) of the Act. The payment amount for the new psychological and neuropsychological tests (CPT codes 96102, 96103, 96119 and 96120) that are billed for tests performed by a technician or a computer reflect a site of service payment differential for the facility and non-facility settings. CPs, NPs, CNSs and PAs are required by law to accept assigned payment for psychological and neuropsychological tests. However, while IPPs are not required by law to accept assigned payment for these tests, they must report the name and address of the physician who ordered the test on the claim form when billing for tests.

CPT Codes for Diagnostic Psychological and Neuropsychological Tests The range of CPT codes used to report psychological and neuropsychological tests is 96101-96120. CPT codes 96101, 96102, 96103, 96105, 96110, and 96111 are appropriate for use when billing for psychological tests. CPT codes 96116, 96118, 96119 and 96120 are appropriate for use when billing for neuropsychological tests.

All of the tests under this CPT code range 96101-96120 are indicated as active codes under the physician fee schedule database and are covered if medically necessary.

Payment and Billing Guidelines for Psychological and Neuropsychological Tests The technician and computer CPT codes for psychological and neuropsychological tests include practice expense, malpractice expense and professional work relative value units.

Accordingly, CPT psychological test code 96101 should not be paid when billed for the same tests or services performed under psychological test codes 96102 or 96103. CPT neuropsychological test code 96118 should not be paid when billed for the same tests or services performed under neuropsychological test codes 96119 or 96120. However, CPT codes 96101 and 96118 can be paid separately on the rare occasion when billed on the same date of service for different and separate tests from 96102, 96103, 96119 and 96120.

Under the physician fee schedule, there is no payment for services performed by students or trainees. Accordingly, Medicare does not pay for services represented by CPT codes 96102 and 96119 when performed by a student or a trainee. However, the presence of a student or a trainee while the test is being administered does not prevent a physician, CP, IPP, NP, CNS or PA from performing and being paid for the psychological test under 96102 or the neuropsychological test under 96119.

Pub. 100-2, Chapter 15, Section 100
Surgical Dressings, Splints, Casts, and Other Devices Used for Reductions of Fractures and Dislocations
B3-2079, A3-3110.3, HO-228.3

Surgical dressings are limited to primary and secondary dressings required for the treatment of a wound caused by, or treated by, a surgical procedure that has been performed by a physician or other health care professional to the extent permissible under State law. In addition, surgical dressings required after debridement of a wound are also covered, irrespective of the type of debridement, as long as the debridement was reasonable and necessary and was performed by a health care professional acting within the scope of his/her legal authority when performing this function. Surgical dressings are covered for as long as they are medically necessary.

Primary dressings are therapeutic or protective coverings applied directly to wounds or lesions either on the skin or caused by an opening to the skin. Secondary dressing materials that serve a therapeutic or protective function and that are needed to secure a primary dressing are also covered. Items such as adhesive tape, roll gauze, bandages, and disposable compression material are examples of secondary dressings. Elastic stockings,

support hose, foot coverings, leotards, knee supports, surgical leggings, gauntlets, and pressure garments for the arms and hands are examples of items that are not ordinarily covered as surgical dressings. Some items, such as transparent film, may be used as a primary or secondary dressing.

If a physician, certified nurse midwife, physician assistant, nurse practitioner, or clinical nurse specialist applies surgical dressings as part of a professional service that is billed to Medicare, the surgical dressings are considered incident to the professional services of the health care practitioner. (See Sec. 60.1, 180, 190, 200, and 210.) When surgical dressings are not covered incident to the services of a health care practitioner and are obtained by the patient from a supplier (e.g., a drugstore, physician, or other health care practitioner that qualifies as a supplier) on an order from a physician or other health care professional authorized under State law or regulation to make such an order, the surgical dressings are covered separately under Part B.

Splints and casts, and other devices used for reductions of fractures and dislocations are covered under Part B of Medicare. This includes dental splints.

Pub. 100-2, Chapter 15, Section 110
Durable Medical Equipment - General
B3-2100, A3-3113, HO-235, HHA-220

Expenses incurred by a beneficiary for the rental or purchases of durable medical equipment (DME) are reimbursable if the following three requirements are met:

- The equipment meets the definition of DME (Sec.110.1);
- The equipment is necessary and reasonable for the treatment of the patient's illness or injury or to improve the functioning of his or her malformed body member (Sec.110.1); and
- The equipment is used in the patient's home. The decision whether to rent or purchase an item of equipment generally resides with the beneficiary, but the decision on how to pay rests with CMS. For some DME, program payment policy calls for lump sum payments and in others for periodic payment. Where covered DME is furnished to a beneficiary by a supplier of services other than a provider of services, the DMERC makes the reimbursement. If a provider of services furnishes the equipment, the intermediary makes the reimbursement. The payment method is identified in the annual fee schedule update furnished by CMS. The CMS issues quarterly updates to a fee schedule file that contains rates by HCPCS code and also identifies the classification of the HCPCS code within the following categories. Category Code Definition IN Inexpensive and Other Routinely Purchased Items FS Frequently Serviced Items CR Capped Rental Items OX Oxygen and Oxygen Equipment OS Ostomy, Tracheostomy & Urological Items SD Surgical Dressings PO Prosthetics & Orthotics SU Supplies TE Transcutaneous Electrical Nerve Stimulators The DMERCs, carriers, and intermediaries, where appropriate, use the CMS files to determine payment rules. See the Medicare Claims Processing Manual, Chapter 20, "Durable Medical Equipment, Surgical Dressings and Casts, Orthotics and Artificial Limbs, and Prosthetic Devices," for a detailed description of payment rules for each classification. Payment may also be made for repairs, maintenance, and delivery of equipment and for expendable and nonreusable items essential to the effective use of the equipment subject to the conditions in Sec.110.2. See the Medicare Benefit Policy Manual, Chapter 11, "End Stage Renal Disease," for hemodialysis equipment and supplies.

Pub. 100-2, Chapter 15, Section 110.1
Definition of Durable Medical Equipment
B3-2100.1, A3-3113.1, HO-235.1, HHA-220.1, B3-2100.2, A3-3113.2, HO-235.2, HHA-220.2

- Durable medical equipment is equipment which:
- Can withstand repeated use;
- Is primarily and customarily used to serve a medical purpose;
- Generally is not useful to a person in the absence of an illness or injury; and
- Is appropriate for use in the home.

All requirements of the definition must be met before an item can be considered to be durable medical equipment. The following describes the underlying policies for determining whether an item meets the definition of DME and may be covered.

A. Durability

An item is considered durable if it can withstand repeated use, i.e., the type of item that could normally be rented. Medical supplies of an expendable nature, such as incontinent pads, lambs wool pads, catheters, ace bandages, elastic stockings, surgical facemasks, irrigating kits, sheets, and bags are not considered "durable" within the meaning of the definition. There are other items that, although durable in nature, may fall into other coverage categories such as supplies, braces, prosthetic devices, artificial arms, legs, and eyes.

B. Medical Equipment

Medical equipment is equipment primarily and customarily used for medical purposes and is not generally useful in the absence of illness or injury. In most instances, no development will be needed to determine whether a specific item of equipment is medical in nature. However, some cases will require development to determine whether the item constitutes medical equipment. This development would include the advice of local medical organizations (hospitals, medical schools, medical societies) and specialists in the field of physical medicine and rehabilitation. If the equipment is new on the market, it may be necessary, prior to seeking professional advice, to obtain information from the supplier or manufacturer explaining the design, purpose, effectiveness and method of using the equipment in the home as well as the results of any tests or clinical studies that have been conducted.

1. Equipment Presumptively
   MedicalItems such as hospital beds, wheelchairs, hemodialysis equipment, iron lungs, respirators, intermittent positive pressure breathing machines, medical regulators, oxygen tents, crutches, canes, trapeze bars, walkers, inhalators, nebulizers, commodes, suction machines, and traction equipment presumptively constitute medical equipment. (Although hemodialysis equipment is covered as a prosthetic device (Sec.120), it also meets the definition of DME, and reimbursement for the rental or purchase of such equipment for use in the beneficiary's home will be made only under the provisions for payment applicable to DME. See the Medicare Benefit Policy Manual, Chapter 11, "End Stage Renal Disease," Sec.30.1, for coverage of home use of hemodialysis.) NOTE: There is a wide variety in types of respirators and suction machines. The DMERC's medical staff should determine whether the apparatus specified in the claim is appropriate for home use.

2. Equipment Presumptively Nonmedical
   Equipment which is primarily and customarily used for a nonmedical purpose may not be considered "medical" equipment for which payment can be made under the medical insurance program. This is true even though the item has some remote medically related use. For example, in the case of a cardiac patient, an air conditioner might possibly be used to lower room temperature to reduce fluid loss in the patient and to restore an environment conducive to maintenance of the proper fluid balance. Nevertheless, because the primary and customary use of an air conditioner is a nonmedical one, the air conditioner cannot be deemed to be medical equipment for which payment can be made. Other devices and equipment used for environmental control or to enhance the environmental setting in which the beneficiary is placed are not considered covered DME. These include, for example, room heaters, humidifiers, dehumidifiers, and electric air cleaners. Equipment which basically serves comfort or convenience functions or is primarily for the convenience of a person caring for the patient, such as elevators, stairway elevators, and posture chairs, do not constitute medical equipment. Similarly, physical fitness equipment (such as an exercycle), first-aid or precautionary-type equipment (such as preset portable oxygen units), self-help devices (such as safety grab bars), and training equipment (such as Braille training texts) are considered nonmedical in nature.

3. Special Exception Items
   Specified items of equipment may be covered under certain conditions even though they do not meet the definition of DME because they are not primarily and customarily used to serve a medical purpose and/or are generally useful in the absence of illness or injury. These items would be covered when it is clearly established that they serve a therapeutic purpose in an individual case and would include:

   a. Gel pads and pressure and water mattresses (which generally serve a preventive purpose) when prescribed for a patient who had bed sores or there is medical evidence indicating that they are highly susceptible to such ulceration; and

   b. Heat lamps for a medical rather than a soothing or cosmetic purpose, e.g., where the need for heat therapy has been established.

In establishing medical necessity for the above items, the evidence must show that the item is included in the physician's course of treatment and a physician is supervising its use.

NOTE: The above items represent special exceptions and no extension of coverage to other items should be inferred

C. Necessary and Reasonable

Although an item may be classified as DME, it may not be covered in every instance. Coverage in a particular case is subject to the requirement that the equipment be necessary and reasonable for treatment of an illness or injury, or to improve the functioning of a malformed body member. These considerations will bar payment for equipment which cannot reasonably be expected to perform a therapeutic function in an individual case or will permit only partial therapeutic function in an individual case or will permit only partial payment when the type of equipment furnished substantially exceeds that required for the treatment of the illness or injury involved. See the Medicare Claims Processing Manual, Chapter 1, "General Billing Requirements;" Sec.60, regarding the rules for providing advance beneficiary notices (ABNs) that advise beneficiaries, before items or services actually are furnished, when Medicare is likely to deny payment for them. ABNs allow beneficiaries to make an informed consumer decision about receiving items or services for which they may have to pay out-of-pocket and to be more active participants in their own health care treatment decisions.

1. Necessity for the Equipment
   Equipment is necessary when it can be expected to make a meaningful contribution to the treatment of the patient's illness or injury or to the improvement of his or her malformed body member. In most cases the physician's prescription for the equipment and other medical information available to the DMERC will be sufficient to establish that the equipment serves this purpose.

2. Reasonableness of the Equipment
   Even though an item of DME may serve a useful medical purpose, the DMERC or intermediary must also consider to what extent, if any, it would be reasonable for the Medicare program to pay for the item prescribed. The following considerations should enter into the determination of reasonableness:

   1. Would the expense of the item to the program be clearly disproportionate to the therapeutic benefits which could ordinarily be derived from use of the equipment?

   2. Is the item substantially more costly than a medically appropriate and realistically feasible alternative pattern of care?

   3. Does the item serve essentially the same purpose as equipment already available to the beneficiary?

3. Payment Consistent With What is Necessary and Reasonable
   Where a claim is filed for equipment containing features of an aesthetic nature or features of a medical nature which are not required by the patient's condition or where there exists a reasonably feasible and medically appropriate alternative pattern of care which is less costly than the equipment furnished, the amount payable is based on the rate for the equipment or alternative treatment which meets the patient's medical needs. The acceptance of an assignment binds the supplier-assignee to accept the payment for the medically required equipment or service as the full charge and the supplier-assignee cannot charge the beneficiary the differential attributable to the equipment actually furnished.

4. Establishing the Period of Medical Necessity
   Generally, the period of time an item of durable medical equipment will be considered to be medically necessary is based on the physician's estimate of the time that his or her patient will need the equipment. See the Medicare Program Integrity Manual, Chapters 5 and 6, for medical review guideline

D. Definition of a Beneficiary's Home

For purposes of rental and purchase of DME a beneficiary's home may be his/her own dwelling, an apartment, a relative's home, a home for the aged, or some other type of institution. However, an institution may not be considered a beneficiary's home if it:

- Meets at least the basic requirement in the definition of a hospital, i.e., it is primarily engaged in providing by or under the supervision of physicians, to inpatients, diagnostic and therapeutic services for medical diagnosis, treatment, and care of injured, disabled, and sick persons, or rehabilitation services for the rehabilitation of injured, disabled, or sick persons; or

- Meets at least the basic requirement in the definition of a skilled nursing facility, i.e., it is primarily engaged in providing to inpatients skilled nursing care and related services for patients who require medical or nursing care, or rehabilitation services for the rehabilitation of injured, disabled, or sick persons.

Thus, if an individual is a patient in an institution or distinct part of an institution which provides the services described in the bullets above, the individual is not entitled to have separate Part B payment made for rental or purchase of DME. This is because such an institution may not be considered the individual's home. The same concept applies even if the patient resides in a bed or portion of the institution not certified for Medicare.

If the patient is at home for part of a month and, for part of the same month is in an institution that cannot qualify as his or her home, or is outside the U.S., monthly payments may be made for the entire month. Similarly, if DME is returned to the provider before the end of a payment month because the beneficiary died in that month or because the equipment became unnecessary in that month, payment may be made for the entire month.

Pub. 100-2, Chapter 15, Section 120
Prosthetic Devices
B3-2130, A3-3110.4, HO-228.4, A3-3111, HO-229

A. General
Prosthetic devices (other than dental) which replace all or part of an internal body organ (including contiguous tissue), or replace all or part of the function of a permanently inoperative or malfunctioning internal body organ are covered when furnished on a physician's order. This does not require a determination that there is no possibility that the patient's condition may improve sometime in the future. If the medical record, including the judgment of the attending physician, indicates the condition is of long and indefinite duration, the test of permanence is considered met. (Such a device may also be covered under Sec.60.I as a supply when furnished incident to a physician's service.)

Examples of prosthetic devices include artificial limbs, parenteral and enteral (PEN) nutrition, cardiac pacemakers, prosthetic lenses (see subsection B), breast prostheses (including a surgical brassiere) for postmastectomy patients, maxillofacial devices, and devices which replace all or part of the ear or nose. A urinary collection and retention system with or without a tube is a prosthetic device replacing bladder function in case of permanent urinary incontinence. The foley catheter is also considered a prosthetic device when ordered for a patient with permanent urinary incontinence. However, chucks, diapers, rubber sheets, etc., are supplies that are not covered under this provision. Although hemodialysis equipment is a prosthetic device, payment for the rental or purchase of such equipment in the home is made only for use under the provisions for payment applicable to durable medical equipment.

An exception is that if payment cannot be made on an inpatient's behalf under Part A, hemodialysis equipment, supplies, and services required by such patient could be covered under Part B as a prosthetic device, which replaces the function of a kidney. See the Medicare Benefit Policy Manual, Chapter 11, "End Stage Renal Disease," for payment for hemodialysis equipment used in the home. See the Medicare Benefit Policy Manual, Chapter 1, "Inpatient Hospital Services," Sec.10, for additional instructions on hospitalization for renal dialysis.

NOTE: Medicare does not cover a prosthetic device dispensed to a patient prior to the time at which the patient undergoes the procedure that makes necessary the use of the device. For example, the carrier does not make a separate Part B payment for an intraocular lens (IOL) or pacemaker that a physician, during an office visit prior to the actual surgery, dispenses to the patient for his or her use. Dispensing a prosthetic device in this manner raises health and safety issues. Moreover, the need for the device cannot be clearly established until the procedure that makes its use possible is successfully performed. Therefore, dispensing a prosthetic device in this manner is not considered reasonable and necessary for the treatment of the patient's condition.

Colostomy (and other ostomy) bags and necessary accouterments required for attachment are covered as prosthetic devices. This coverage also includes irrigation and flushing equipment and other items and supplies directly related to ostomy care, whether the attachment of a bag is required. Accessories and/or supplies which are used directly with an enteral or parenteral device to achieve the therapeutic benefit of the prosthesis or to assure the proper functioning of the device may also be covered under the prosthetic device benefit subject to the additional guidelines in the Medicare National Coverage Determinations Manual.

Covered items include catheters, filters, extension tubing, infusion bottles, pumps (either food or infusion), intravenous (I.V.) pole, needles, syringes, dressings, tape, Heparin Sodium (parenteral only), volumetric monitors (parenteral only), and parenteral and enteral nutrient solutions. Baby food and other regular grocery products that can be blenderized and used with the enteral system are not covered. Note that some of these items, e.g., a food pump and an I.V. pole, qualify as DME. Although coverage of the enteral and parenteral nutritional therapy systems is provided on the basis of the prosthetic device benefit, the payment rules relating to lump sum or monthly payment for DME apply to such items.

The coverage of prosthetic devices includes replacement of and repairs to such devices as explained in subsection D.

Finally, the Benefits Improvement and Protection Act of 2000 amended Sec.1834(h)(1) of the Act by adding a provision (1834 (h)(1)(G)(i)) that requires Medicare payment to be made for the replacement of prosthetic devices which are artificial limbs, or for the replacement of any part of such devices, without regard to continuous use or useful lifetime restrictions if an ordering physician determines that the replacement device, or replacement part of such a device, is necessary.

Payment may be made for the replacement of a prosthetic device that is an artificial limb, or replacement part of a device if the ordering physician determines that the replacement device or part is necessary because of any of the following:

1. A change in the physiological condition of the patient;

2. An irreparable change in the condition of the device, or in a part of the device; or

3. The condition of the device, or the part of the device, requires repairs and the cost of such repairs would be more than 60 percent of the cost of a replacement device, or, as the case may be, of the part being replaced.

This provision is effective for items replaced on or after April 1, 2001. It supersedes any rule that that provided a 5-year or other replacement rule with regard to prosthetic devices.

B. Prosthetic Lenses
The term "internal body organ" includes the lens of an eye. Prostheses replacing the lens of an eye include post-surgical lenses customarily used during convalescence from eye surgery in which the lens of the eye was removed. In addition, permanent lenses are also covered when required by an individual lacking the organic lens of the eye because of surgical removal or congenital absence. Prosthetic lenses obtained on or after the beneficiary's date of entitlement to supplementary medical insurance benefits may be covered even though the surgical removal of the crystalline lens occurred before entitlement.

1. Prosthetic Cataract Lenses
   One of the following prosthetic lenses or combinations of prosthetic lenses furnished by a physician (see Sec.30.4 for coverage of prosthetic lenses prescribed by a doctor of optometry) may be covered when determined to be reasonable and necessary to restore essentially the vision provided by the crystalline lens of the eye:

   • Prosthetic bifocal lenses in frames;

   • Prosthetic lenses in frames for far vision, and prosthetic lenses in frames for near vision; or

   • When a prosthetic contact lens(es) for far vision is prescribed (including cases of binocular and monocular aphakia), make payment for the contact lens(es) and prosthetic lenses in frames for near vision to be worn at the same time as the contact lens(es), and prosthetic lenses in frames to be worn when the contacts have been removed.

Lenses which have ultraviolet absorbing or reflecting properties may be covered, in lieu of payment for regular (untinted) lenses, if it has been determined that such lenses are medically reasonable and necessary for the individual patient.

Medicare does not cover cataract sunglasses obtained in addition to the regular (untinted) prosthetic lenses since the sunglasses duplicate the restoration of vision function performed by the regular prosthetic lenses.

2. Payment for Intraocular Lenses (IOLs) Furnished in Ambulatory Surgical Centers (ASCs) Effective for services furnished on or after March 12, 1990, payment for intraocular lenses (IOLs) inserted during or subsequent to cataract surgery in a Medicare certified ASC is included with the payment for facility services that are furnished in connection with the covered surgery.

   Refer to the Medicare Claims Processing Manual, Chapter 14, "Ambulatory Surgical Centers," for more information.

3. Limitation on Coverage of Conventional Lenses One pair of conventional eyeglasses or conventional contact lenses furnished after each cataract surgery with insertion of an IOL is covered.

C. Dentures
Dentures are excluded from coverage. However, when a denture or a portion of the denture is an integral part (built-in) of a covered prosthesis (e.g., an obturator to fill an opening in the palate), it is covered as part of that prosthesis.

D. Supplies, Repairs, Adjustments, and Replacement
Supplies are covered that are necessary for the effective use of a prosthetic device (e.g., the batteries needed to operate an artificial larynx). Adjustment of prosthetic devices required by wear or by a change in the patient's condition is covered when ordered by a physician. General provisions relating to the repair and replacement of durable medical equipment in Sec.110.2 for the repair and replacement of prosthetic devices are applicable. (See the Medicare Benefit Policy Manual, Chapter 16, "General Exclusions from Coverage," Sec.40.4, for payment for devices replaced under a warranty.) Replacement of conventional eyeglasses or contact lenses furnished in accordance with Sec.120.B.3 is not covered. Necessary supplies, adjustments, repairs, and replacements are covered even when the device had been in use before the user enrolled in Part B of the program, so long as the device continues to be medically required.

Pub. 100-2, Chapter 15, Section 130
Leg, Arm, Back, and Neck Braces, Trusses, and Artificial Legs, Arms, and Eyes
B3-2133, A3-3110.5, HO-228.5, AB-01-06 dated 1/18/01

These appliances are covered under Part B when furnished incident to physicians' services or on a physician's order. A brace includes rigid and semi-rigid devices which are used for the purpose of supporting a weak or deformed body member or restricting or eliminating motion in a diseased or injured part of the body. Elastic stockings, garter belts, and similar devices do not come within the scope of the definition of a brace. Back braces include, but are not limited to, special corsets, e.g., sacroiliac, sacrolumbar, dorsolumbar corsets, and belts. A terminal device (e.g., hand or hook) is covered under this provision whether an artificial limb is required by the patient. Stump stockings and harnesses (including replacements) are also covered when these appliances are essential to the effective use of the artificial limb.

Adjustments to an artificial limb or other appliance required by wear or by a change in the patient's condition are covered when ordered by a physician.

Adjustments, repairs and replacements are covered even when the item had been in use before the user enrolled in Part B of the program so long as the device continues to be medically required.

Pub. 100-2, Chapter 15, Section 230.1
Practice of Physical Therapy
A. General
Physical therapy services are those services provided within the scope of practice of physical therapists and necessary for the diagnosis and treatment of impairments, functional limitations, disabilities or changes in physical function and health status. (See Pub. 100-03, the Medicare National Coverage Determinations Manual, for specific conditions or services.) For descriptions of aquatic therapy in a community center pool see section 220C of this chapter.

B. Qualified Physical Therapist Defined
Reference: 42CFR484.4

The new personnel qualifications for physical therapists were discussed in the 2008 Physician Fee Schedule. See the Federal Register of November 27, 2007, for the full text. See also the correction notice for this rule, published in the Federal Register on January 15, 2008.

The regulation provides that a qualified physical therapist (PT) is a person who is licensed, if applicable, as a PT by the state in which he or she is practicing unless licensure does not apply, has graduated from an accredited PT education program and passed a national examination approved by the state in which PT services are provided. The phrase, "by the state in which practicing" includes any authorization to practice provided by the same state in which the service is provided, including temporary licensure, regardless of the location of the entity billing the services. The curriculum accreditation is provided by the Commission on Accreditation in Physical Therapy Education (CAPTE) or, for those who graduated before CAPTE, curriculum approval was provided by the American Physical Therapy Association (APTA). For internationally educated PTs, curricula are approved by a credentials evaluation organization either approved by the APTA or identified in 8 CFR 212.15(e) as it relates to PTs. For example, in 2007, 8 CFR 212.15(e) approved the credentials evaluation provided by the Federation of State Boards of Physical Therapy (FSBPT) and the Foreign Credentialing Commission on Physical Therapy (FCCPT). The requirements above apply to all PTs effective January 1, 2010, if they have not met any of the following requirements prior to January 1, 2010.

Physical therapists whose current license was obtained on or prior to December 31, 2009, qualify to provide PT services to Medicare beneficiaries if they:

- graduated from a CAPTE approved program in PT on or before December 31, 2009 (examination is not required); or,

- graduated on or before December 31, 2009, from a PT program outside the U.S. that is determined to be substantially equivalent to a U.S. program by a credentials evaluating organization approved by either the APTA or identified in 8 CFR 212.15(e) and also passed an examination for PTs approved by the state in which practicing.

Or, PTs whose current license was obtained before January 1, 2008, may meet the requirements in place on that date (i.e., graduation from a curriculum approved by either the APTA, the Committee on Allied Health Education and Accreditation of the American Medical Association, or both).

Or, PTs meet the requirements who are currently licensed and were licensed or qualified as a PT on or before December 31, 1977, and had 2 years appropriate experience as a PT, and passed a proficiency examination conducted, approved, or sponsored by the U.S. Public Health Service.

Or, PTs meet the requirements if they are currently licensed and before January 1, 1966, they were:

- admitted to membership by the APTA; or

- admitted to registration by the American Registry of Physical Therapists; or

- graduated from a 4-year PT curriculum approved by a State Department of Education; or

- licensed or registered and prior to January 1, 1970, they had 15 years of fulltime experience in PT under the order and direction of attending and referring doctors of medicine or osteopathy.

Or, PTs meet requirements if they are currently licensed and they were trained outside the U.S. before January 1, 2008, and after 1928 graduated from a PT curriculum approved in the country in which the curriculum was located, if that country had an organization that was a member of the World Confederation for Physical Therapy, and that PT qualified as a member of the organization.

For outpatient PT services that are provided incident to the services of physicians/NPPs, the requirement for PT licensure does not apply; all other personnel qualifications do apply. The qualified personnel providing PT services incident to the services of a physician/NPP must be trained in an accredited PT curriculum. For example, a person who, on or before December 31, 2009, graduated from a PT curriculum accredited by CAPTE, but who has not passed the national examination or obtained a license, could provide Medicare outpatient PT therapy services incident to the services of a physician/NPP if the physician assumes responsibility for the services according to the incident to policies. On or after January 1, 2010, although licensure does not apply, both education and examination requirements that are effective January 1, 2010, apply to qualified personnel who provide PT services incident to the services of a physician/NPP.

C. Services of Physical Therapy Support Personnel

Reference: 42CFR 484.4

Personnel Qualifications. The new personnel qualifications for physical therapist assistants (PTA) were discussed in the 2008 Physician Fee Schedule. See the Federal Register of November 27, 2007, for the full text. See also the correction notice for this rule, published in the Federal Register on January 15, 2008.

The regulation provides that a qualified PTA is a person who is licensed as a PTA unless licensure does not apply, is registered or certified, if applicable, is registered by the state in which practicing, and graduated from an approved curriculum for PTAs, and passed a national examination for PTAs. The phrase, "by the state in which practicing" includes any authorization to practice provided by the same state in which the service is provided, including temporary licensure, regardless of the location or the entity billing for the services. Approval for the curriculum is provided by CAPTE or, if internationally or military trained PTAs apply, approval will be through a credentialing body for the curriculum for PTAs identified by either the American Physical Therapy Association or identified in 8 CFR 212.15(e). A national examination for PTAs is, for example the one furnished by the Federation of State Boards of Physical Therapy. These requirements above apply to all PTAs effective January 1, 2010, if they have not met any of the following requirements prior to January 1, 2010.

Those PTAs also qualify who, on or before December 31, 2009, are licensed, registered or certified as a PTA and met one of the two following requirements:

1. Is licensed or otherwise regulated in the state in which practicing; or

2. In states that have no licensure or other regulations, or where licensure does not apply, PTAs have:

- graduated on or before December 31, 2009, from a 2-year college-level program approved by the APTA or CAPTE; and

- effective January 1, 2010, those PTAs must have both graduated from a CAPTE approved curriculum and passed a national examination for PTAs; or

PTAs may also qualify if they are licensed, registered or certified as a PTA, if applicable and meet requirements in effect before January 1, 2008, that is,

- they have graduated before January 1, 2008, from a 2 year college level program approved by the APTA; or

- on or before December 31, 1977, they were licensed or qualified as a PTA and passed a proficiency examination conducted, approved, or sponsored by the U.S. Public Health Service.

Services. The services of PTAs used when providing covered therapy benefits are included as part of the covered service. These services are billed by the supervising physical therapist. PTAs may not provide evaluation services, make clinical judgments or decisions or take responsibility for the service. They act at the direction and under the supervision of the treating physical therapist and in accordance with state laws.

A physical therapist must supervise PTAs. The level and frequency of supervision differs by setting (and by state or local law). General supervision is required for PTAs in all settings except private practice (which requires direct supervision) unless state practice requirements are more stringent, in which case state or local requirements must be followed. See specific settings for details. For example, in clinics, rehabilitation services, either on or off the organization's premises, those services are supervised by a qualified physical therapist who makes an onsite supervisory visit at least once every 30 days or more frequently if required by state or local laws or regulation.

The services of a PTA shall not be billed as services incident to a physician/NPP's service, because they do not meet the qualifications of a therapist.

The cost of supplies (e.g., theraband, hand putty, electrodes) used in furnishing covered therapy care is included in the payment for the HCPCS codes billed by the physical therapist, and are, therefore, not separately billable. Separate coverage and billing provisions apply to items that meet the definition of brace in Sec.130.

Services provided by aides, even if under the supervision of a therapist, are not therapy services and are not covered by Medicare. Although an aide may help the therapist by providing unskilled services, those services that are unskilled are not covered by Medicare and shall be denied as not reasonable and necessary if they are billed as therapy services.

D. Application of Medicare Guidelines to PT Services

This subsection will be used in the future to illustrate the application of the above guidelines to some of the physical therapy modalities and procedures utilized in the treatment of patient

Pub. 100-2, Chapter 15, Section 230.2

Practice of Occupational Therapy

(Rev. 88, Issued: 05-07-08, Effective: 01-01-08, Implementation: 06-09-08)

A. General

Occupational therapy services are those services provided within the scope of practice of occupational therapists and necessary for the diagnosis and treatment of impairments, functional disabilities or changes in physical function and health status. (See Pub. 100-03, the Medicare National Coverage Determinations Manual, for specific conditions or services.)

Occupational therapy is medically prescribed treatment concerned with improving or restoring functions which have been impaired by illness or injury or, where function has been permanently lost or reduced by illness or injury, to improve the individual's ability to perform those tasks required for independent functioning. Such therapy may involve:

The evaluation, and reevaluation as required, of a patient's level of function by administering diagnostic and prognostic tests;

The selection and teaching of task-oriented therapeutic activities designed to restore physical function; e.g., use of woodworking activities on an inclined table to restore shoulder, elbow, and wrist range of motion lost as a result of burns;

The planning, implementing, and supervising of individualized therapeutic activity programs as part of an overall "active treatment" program for a patient with a diagnosed psychiatric illness; e.g., the use of sewing activities which require following a pattern to reduce confusion and restore reality orientation in a schizophrenic patient;

The planning and implementing of therapeutic tasks and activities to restore sensoryintegrative function; e.g., providing motor and tactile activities to increase sensory input and improve response for a stroke patient with functional loss resulting in a distorted body image;

The teaching of compensatory technique to improve the level of independence in the activities of daily living, for example:

- Teaching a patient who has lost the use of an arm how to pare potatoes and chop vegetables with one hand;

- Teaching an upper extremity amputee how to functionally utilize a prosthesis;

- Teaching a stroke patient new techniques to enable the patient to perform feeding, dressing, and other activities as independently as possible; or

- Teaching a patient with a hip fracture/hip replacement techniques of standing tolerance and balance to enable the patient to perform such functional activities as dressing and homemaking tasks.

The designing, fabricating, and fitting of orthotics and self-help devices; e.g., making a hand splint for a patient with rheumatoid arthritis to maintain the hand in a functional position or constructing a device which would enable an individual to hold a utensil and feed independently; or Vocational and prevocational assessment and training, subject to the limitations specified in item B below.

Only a qualified occupational therapist has the knowledge, training, and experience required to evaluate and, as necessary, reevaluate a patient's level of function, determine whether an occupational therapy program could reasonably be expected to improve, restore, or compensate for lost function and, where appropriate, recommend to the physician/NPP a plan of treatment.

B. Qualified Occupational Therapist Defined
Reference: 42CFR484.4 The new personnel qualifications for occupational therapists (OT) were discussed in the 2008 Physician Fee Schedule. See the Federal Register of November 27, 2007, for the full text. See also the correction notice for this rule, published in the Federal Register on January 15, 2008.

The regulation provides that a qualified OT is an individual who is licensed, if licensure applies, or otherwise regulated, if applicable, as an OT by the state in which practicing, and graduated from an accredited education program for OTs, and is eligible to take or has passed the examination for OTs administered by the National Board for Certification in Occupational Therapy, Inc. (NBCOT). The phrase, "by the state in which practicing" includes any authorization to practice provided by the same state in which the service is provided, including temporary licensure, regardless of the location of the entity billing the services. The education program for U.S. trained OTs is accredited by the Accreditation Council for Occupational Therapy Education (ACOTE). The requirements above apply to all OTs effective January 1, 2010, if they have not met any of the following requirements prior to January 1, 2010.

The OTs may also qualify if on or before December 31, 2009:

- they are licensed or otherwise regulated as an OT in the state in which practicing (regardless of the qualifications they met to obtain that licensure or regulation); or

- when licensure or other regulation does not apply, OTs have graduated from an OT education program accredited by ACOTE and are eligible to take, or have successfully completed the NBCOT examination for OTs.

Also, those OTs who met the Medicare requirements for OTs that were in 42CFR484.4 prior to January 1, 2008, qualify to provide OT services for Medicare beneficiaries if:

- on or before January 1, 2008, they graduated an OT program approved jointly by the American Medical Association and the AOTA, or

- they are eligible for the National Registration Examination of AOTA or the National Board for Certification in OT.

Also, they qualify who on or before December 31, 1977, had 2 years of appropriate experience as an occupational therapist, and had achieved a satisfactory grade on a proficiency examination conducted, approved, or sponsored by the U.S. Public Health Service.

Those educated outside the U.S. may meet the same qualifications for domestic trained OTs. For example, they qualify if they were licensed or otherwise regulated by the state in which practicing on or before December 31, 2009. Or they are qualified if they:

- graduated from an OT education program accredited as substantially equivalent to a U.S. OT education program by ACOTE, the World Federation of Occupational Therapists, or a credentialing body approved by AOTA; and

- passed the NBCOT examination for OT; and

- Effective January 1, 2010, are licensed or otherwise regulated, if applicable as an OT by the state in which practicing.

For outpatient OT services that are provided incident to the services of physicians/NPPs, the requirement for OT licensure does not apply; all other personnel qualifications do apply. The qualified personnel providing OT services incident to the services of a physician/NPP must be trained in an accredited OT curriculum. For example, a person who, on or before December 31, 2009, graduated from an OT curriculum accredited by ACOTE and is eligible to take or has successfully completed the entry-level certification examination for OTs developed and administered by NBCOT, could provide Medicare outpatient OT services incident to the services of a physician/NPP if the physician assumes responsibility for the services according to the incident to policies. On or after January 1, 2010, although licensure does not apply, both education and examination requirements that are effective January 1, 2010, apply to qualified personnel who provide OT services incident to the services of a physician/NPP.

C. Services of Occupational Therapy Support Personnel
Reference: 42CFR 484.4

The new personnel qualifications for occupational therapy assistants were discussed in the 2008 Physician Fee Schedule. See the Federal Register of November 27, 2007, for the full text. See also the correction notice for this rule, published in the Federal Register on January 15, 2008.

The regulation provides that an occupational therapy assistant is a person who is licensed, unless licensure does not apply, or otherwise regulated, if applicable, as an OTA by the state in which practicing, and graduated from an OTA education program accredited by ACOTE and is eligible to take or has successfully completed the NBCOT examination for OTAs. The phrase, "by the state in which practicing" includes any authorization to practice provided by the same state in which the service is provided, including temporary licensure, regardless of the location of the entity billing the services.

If the requirements above are not met, an OTA may qualify if, on or before December 31, 2009, the OTA is licensed or otherwise regulated as an OTA, if applicable, by the state in which practicing, or meets any qualifications defined by the state in which practicing.

Or, where licensure or other state regulation does not apply, OTAs may qualify if they have, on or before December 31, 2009:

- completed certification requirements to practice as an OTA established by a credentialing organization approved by AOTA; and

- after January 1, 2010, they have also completed an education program accredited by ACOTE and passed the NBCOT examination for OTAs.

OTAs who qualified under the policies in effect prior to January 1, 2008, continue to qualify to provide OT directed and supervised OTA services to Medicare beneficiaries.

Therefore, OTAs qualify who after December 31, 1977, and on or before December 31, 2007:

- completed certification requirements to practice as an OTA established by a credentialing organization approved by AOTA; or

- completed the requirements to practice as an OTA applicable in the state in which practicing.

Those OTAs who were educated outside the U.S. may meet the same requirements as domestically trained OTAs. Or, if educated outside the U.S. on or after January 1, 2008, they must have graduated from an OTA program accredited as substantially equivalent to OTA entry level education in the U.S. by ACOTE, its successor organization, or the World Federation of Occupational Therapists or a credentialing body approved by AOTA. In addition, they must have passed an exam for OTAs administered by NBCOT.

Services. The services of OTAs used when providing covered therapy benefits are included as part of the covered service. These services are billed by the supervising occupational therapist. OTAs may not provide evaluation services, make clinical judgments or decisions or take responsibility for the service. They act at the direction and under the supervision of the treating occupational therapist and in accordance with state laws.

An occupational therapist must supervise OTAs. The level and frequency of supervision differs by setting (and by state or local law). General supervision is required for OTAs in all settings except private practice (which requires direct supervision) unless state practice requirements are more stringent, in which case state or local requirements must be followed. See specific settings for details. For example, in clinics, rehabilitation agencies, and public health agencies, 42CFR485.713 indicates that when an OTA provides services, either on or off the organization's premises, those services are supervised by a qualified occupational therapist who makes an onsite supervisory visit at least once every 30 days or more frequently if required by state or local laws or regulation.

The services of an OTA shall not be billed as services incident to a physician/NPP's service, because they do not meet the qualifications of a therapist.

The cost of supplies (e.g., looms, ceramic tiles, or leather) used in furnishing covered therapy care is included in the payment for the HCPCS codes billed by the occupational therapist and are, therefore, not separately billable. Separate coverage and billing provisions apply to items that meet the definition of brace in Sec.130 of this manual.

Services provided by aides, even if under the supervision of a therapist, are not therapy services in the outpatient setting and are not covered by Medicare. Although an aide may help the therapist by providing unskilled services, those services that are unskilled are not covered by Medicare and shall be denied as not reasonable and necessary if they are billed as therapy services.

D. Application of Medicare Guidelines to Occupational Therapy Services
Occupational therapy may be required for a patient with a specific diagnosed psychiatric illness. If such services are required, they are covered assuming the coverage criteria are met. However, where an individual's motivational needs are not related to a specific diagnosed psychiatric illness, the meeting of such needs does not usually require an individualized therapeutic program. Such needs can be met through general activity programs or the efforts of other professional personnel involved in the care of the patient. Patient motivation is an appropriate and inherent function of all health disciplines, which is interwoven with other functions performed by such personnel for the patient. Accordingly, since the special skills of an occupational therapist are not required, an occupational therapy program for individuals who do not have a specific diagnosed psychiatric illness is not to be considered reasonable and necessary for the treatment of an illness or injury. Services furnished under such a program are not covered.

Occupational therapy may include vocational and prevocational assessment and training. When services provided by an occupational therapist are related solely to specific employment opportunities, work skills, or work settings, they are not reasonable or necessary for the diagnosis or treatment of an illness or injury and are not covered. However, carriers and intermediaries exercise care in applying this exclusion, because the assessment of level of function and the teaching of compensatory techniques to improve the level of function, especially in activities of daily living, are services which occupational therapists provide for both vocational and nonvocational purposes. For example, an assessment of sitting and standing tolerance might be nonvocational for a mother of young children or a retired individual living alone, but could also be a vocational test for a sales clerk. Training an amputee in the use of prosthesis for telephoning is necessary for everyday activities as well as for employment purposes. Major changes in life style may be mandatory for an individual with a substantial disability. The techniques of adjustment cannot be considered exclusively vocational or nonvocational.

Pub. 100-2, Chapter 15, Section 230.3
Practice of Speech-Language Pathology
A. General
Speech-language pathology services are those services provided within the scope of practice of speech-language pathologists and necessary for the diagnosis and treatment of speech and language disorders, which result in communication disabilities and for the diagnosis and treatment of swallowing disorders (dysphagia), regardless of the presence of a communication disability. (See Pub. 100-03, chapter 1, Sec.170.3)

B. Qualified Speech-Language Pathologist Defined
A qualified speech-language pathologist for program coverage purposes meets one of the following requirements:

- The education and experience requirements for a Certificate of Clinical Competence in (speech-language pathology) granted by the American Speech-Language Hearing Association; or

- Meets the educational requirements for certification and is in the process of accumulating the supervised experience required for certification.

For outpatient speech-language pathology services that are provided incident to the services of physicians/NPPs, the requirement for speech-language pathology licensure does not apply; all other personnel qualifications do apply. Therefore, qualified personnel providing speech-language pathology services incident to the services of a physician/NPP must meet the above qualifications.

C. Services of Speech-Language Pathology Support Personnel
Services of speech-language pathology assistants are not recognized for Medicare coverage. Services provided by speech-language pathology assistants, even if they are licensed to provide services in their states, will be considered unskilled services and denied as not reasonable and necessary if they are billed as therapy services.

Services provided by aides, even if under the supervision of a therapist, are not therapy services and are not covered by Medicare. Although an aide may help the therapist by providing unskilled services, those services are not covered by Medicare and shall be denied as not reasonable and necessary if they are billed as therapy services.

D. Application of Medicare Guidelines to Speech-Language Pathology Services
1. Evaluation Services
   Speech-language pathology evaluation services are covered if they are reasonable and necessary and not excluded as routine screening by Sec.1862(a)(7) of the Act. The speechlanguage pathologist employs a variety of formal and informal speech, language, and dysphagia assessment tests to ascertain the type, causal factor(s), and severity of the speech and language or swallowing disorders. Reevaluation of patients for whom speech, language and swallowing were previously contraindicated is covered only if the patient exhibits a change in medical condition. However, monthly reevaluations; e.g., a Western Aphasia Battery, for a patient undergoing a rehabilitative speech-language pathology program, are considered a part of the treatment session and shall not be covered as a separate evaluation for billing purposes. Although hearing screening by the speechlanguage pathologist may be part of an evaluation, it is not billable as a separate service.

2. Therapeutic Services
   The following are examples of common medical disorders and resulting communication deficits, which may necessitate active rehabilitative therapy. This list is not all-inclusive:

   - Cerebrovascular disease such as cerebral vascular accidents presenting with dysphagia, aphasia/dysphasia, apraxia, and dysarthria;

   - Neurological disease such as Parkinsonism or

   - Multiple Sclerosis with dysarthria, dysphagia, inadequate respiratory volume/control, or voice disorder; or

   - Laryngeal carcinoma requiring laryngectomy resulting in aphonia.

3. Impairments of the Auditory System
   The terms, aural rehabilitation, auditory rehabilitation, auditory processing, lipreading and speech reading are among the terms used to describe covered services related to perception and comprehension of sound through the auditory system. See Pub. 100-04, chapter 12, section 30.3 for billing instructions. For example:

   - Auditory processing evaluation and treatment may be covered and medically necessary. Examples include but are not limited to services for certain neurological impairments or the absence of natural auditory stimulation that results in impaired ability to process sound. Certain auditory processing

disorders require diagnostic audiological tests in addition to speech-language pathology evaluation and treatment.

- Evaluation and treatment for disorders of the auditory system may be covered and medically necessary, for example, when it has been determined by a speechlanguage pathologist in collaboration with an audiologist that the hearing impaired beneficiary's current amplification options (hearing aid, other amplification device or cochlear implant) will not sufficiently meet the patient's functional communication needs. Audiologists and speech-language pathologists both evaluate beneficiaries for disorders of the auditory system using different skills and techniques, but only speech-language pathologists may provide treatment.

Assessment for the need for rehabilitation of the auditory system (but not the vestibular system) may be done by a speech language pathologist. Examples include but are not limited to: evaluation of comprehension and production of language in oral, signed or written modalities, speech and voice production, listening skills, speech reading, communications strategies, and the impact of the hearing loss on the patient/client and family.

Examples of rehabilitation include but are not limited to treatment that focuses on comprehension, and production of language in oral, signed or written modalities; speech and voice production, auditory training, speech reading, multimodal (e.g., visual, auditory-visual, and tactile) training, communication strategies, education and counseling. In determining the necessity for treatment, the beneficiary's performance in both clinical and natural environment should be considered.

4. Dysphagia
Dysphagia, or difficulty in swallowing, can cause food to enter the airway, resulting in coughing, choking, pulmonary problems, aspiration or inadequate nutrition and hydration with resultant weight loss, failure to thrive, pneumonia and death. It is most often due to complex neurological and/or structural impairments including head and neck trauma, cerebrovascular accident, neuromuscular degenerative diseases, head and neck cancer, dementias, and encephalopathies. For these reasons, it is important that only qualified professionals with specific training and experience in this disorder provide evaluation and treatment.

The speech-language pathologist performs clinical and instrumental assessments and analyzes and integrates the diagnostic information to determine candidacy for intervention as well as appropriate compensations and rehabilitative therapy techniques.

The equipment that is used in the examination may be fixed, mobile or portable.

Professional guidelines recommend that the service be provided in a team setting with a physician/NPP who provides supervision of the radiological examination and interpretation of medical conditions revealed in it.

Swallowing assessment and rehabilitation are highly specialized services. The professional rendering care must have education, experience and demonstrated competencies. Competencies include but are not limited to: identifying abnormal upper aerodigestive tract structure and function; conducting an oral, pharyngeal, laryngeal and respiratory function examination as it relates to the functional assessment of swallowing; recommending methods of oral intake and risk precautions; and developing a treatment plan employing appropriate compensations and therapy techniques.

Pub. 100-2, Chapter 15, Section 230.4
Services Furnished by a Physical or Occupational Therapist in Private Practice
A. General
In order to qualify to bill Medicare directly as a therapist, each individual must be enrolled as a private practitioner and employed in one of the following practice types: an unincorporated solo practice, unincorporated partnership, unincorporated group practice, physician/NPP group or groups that are not professional corporations, if allowed by state and local law. Physician/NPP group practices may employ physical therapists in private practice (PTPP) and/or occupational therapists in private practice (OTPP) if state and local law permits this employee relationship.

For purposes of this provision, a physician/NPP group practice is defined as one or more physicians/NPPs enrolled with Medicare who may bill as one entity. For further details on issues concerning enrollment, see the provider enrollment Web site at www.cms.hhs.gov/providers/enrollment.

Private practice also includes therapists who are practicing therapy as employees of another supplier, of a professional corporation or other incorporated therapy practice. Private practice does not include individuals when they are working as employees of an institutional provider.

Services should be furnished in the therapist's or group's office or in the patient's home. The office is defined as the location(s) where the practice is operated, in the state(s) where the therapist (and practice, if applicable) is legally authorized to furnish services, during the hours that the therapist engages in the practice at that location. If services are furnished in a private practice office space, that space shall be owned, leased, or rented by the practice and used for the exclusive purpose of operating the practice. For descriptions of aquatic therapy in a community center pool see section 220C of this chapter.

Therapists in private practice must be approved as meeting certain requirements, but do not execute a formal provider agreement with the Secretary.

If therapists who have their own Medicare Personal Identification number (PIN) or National Provider Identifier (NPI) are employed by therapist groups, physician/NPP groups, or groups that are not professional organizations, the requirement that therapy space be owned, leased, or rented may be satisfied by the group that employs the therapist. Each physical or occupational therapist employed by a group should enroll as a PT or OT in private practice.

When therapists with a Medicare PIN/NPI provide services in the physician's/NPP's office in which they are employed, and bill using their PIN/NPI for each therapy service, then the direct supervision requirement for PTAs and OTAs apply.

When the PT or OT who has a Medicare PIN/ NPI is employed in a physician's/NPP's office the services are ordinarily billed as services of the PT or OT, with the PT or OT identified on the claim as the supplier of services. However, services of the PT or OT who has a Medicare PIN/NPI may also be billed by the physician/NPP as services incident to the physician's/NPP's service. (See Sec.230.5 for rules related to PTA and OTA services incident to a physician.) In that case, the physician/NPP is the supplier of service, the Unique Provider Identification Number (UPIN) or NPI of the physician/NPP (ordering or supervising, as indicated) is reported on the claim with the service and all the rules for incident to services (Sec.230.5) must be followed.

B. Private Practice Defined
Reference: Federal Register November, 1998, pages 58863-58869; 42CFR 410.38(b)

The carrier considers a therapist to be in private practice if the therapist maintains office space at his or her own expense and furnishes services only in that space or the patient's home. Or, a therapist is employed by another supplier and furnishes services in facilities provided at the expense of that supplier.

The therapist need not be in full-time private practice but must be engaged in private practice on a regular basis; i.e., the therapist is recognized as a private practitioner and for that purpose has access to the necessary equipment to provide an adequate program of therapy.

The physical or occupational therapy services must be provided either by or under the direct supervision of the therapist in private practice. Each physical or occupational therapist in a practice should be enrolled as a Medicare provider. If a physical or occupational therapist is not enrolled, the services of that therapist must be directly supervised by an enrolled physical or occupational therapist. Direct supervision requires that the supervising private practice therapist be present in the office suite at the time the service is performed. These direct supervision requirements apply only in the private practice setting and only for physical therapists and occupational therapists and their assistants. In other outpatient settings, supervision rules differ. The services of support personnel must be included in the therapist's bill. The supporting personnel, including other therapists, must be W-2 or 1099 employees of the therapist in private practice or other qualified employer.

Coverage of outpatient physical therapy and occupational therapy under Part B includes the services of a qualified therapist in private practice when furnished in the therapist's office or the beneficiary's home. For this purpose, "home" includes an institution that is used as a home, but not a hospital, CAH or SNF, (Federal Register Nov. 2, 1998, pg 58869). Place of Service (POS) includes:

- 03/School, only if residential,
- 04/Homeless Shelter,
- 12/Home, other than a facility that is a private residence,
- 14/Group Home, 33/Custodial Care Facility.

C. Assignment
Reference: Nov. 2, 1998 Federal Register, pg. 58863

See also Pub. 100-04 chapter 1, Sec.30.2.

When physicians, NPPs, PTPPs or OTPPs obtain provider numbers, they have the option of accepting assignment (participating) or not accepting assignment (nonparticipating). In contrast, providers, such as outpatient hospitals, SNFs, rehabilitation agencies, and CORFs, do not have the option. For these providers, assignment is mandatory.

If physicians/NPPs, PTPPs or OTPPs accept assignment (are participating), they must accept the Medicare Physician Fee Schedule amount as payment. Medicare pays 80% and the patient is responsible for 20%. In contrast, if they do not accept assignment, Medicare will only pay 95% of the fee schedule amount. However, when these services are not furnished on an assignment-related basis, the limiting charge applies. (See Sec.1848(g)(2)(c) of the Act.)

NOTE: Services furnished by a therapist in the therapist's office under arrangements with hospitals in rural communities and public health agencies (or services provided in the beneficiary's home under arrangements with a provider of outpatient physical or occupational therapy services) are not covered under this provision. See section 230.6.

Pub. 100-2, Chapter 16, Section 20
Services Not Reasonable and Necessary
A3-3151, HO-260.1, B3-2303, AB-00-52 - 6/00

Items and services which are not reasonable and necessary for the diagnosis or treatment of illness or injury or to improve the functioning of a malformed body member are not covered, e.g., payment cannot be made for the rental of a special hospital bed to be used by the patient in their home unless it was a reasonable and necessary part of the patient's treatment. See also Sec.80.

A health care item or service for the purpose of causing, or assisting to cause, the death of any individual (assisted suicide) is not covered. This prohibition does not apply to the provision of an item or service for the purpose of alleviating pain or discomfort, even if such use may increase the risk of death, so long as the item or service is not furnished for the specific purpose of causing death.

Pub. 100-2, Chapter 16, Section 90
Routine Services and Appliances
A3-3157, HO-260.7, B3-2320, R-1797A3 - 5/00

Routine physical checkups; eyeglasses, contact lenses, and eye examinations for the purpose of prescribing, fitting, or changing eyeglasses; eye refractions by whatever practitioner and for whatever purpose performed; hearing aids and examinations for hearing aids; and immunizations are not covered.

The routine physical checkup exclusion applies to (a) examinations performed without relationship to treatment or diagnosis for a specific illness, symptom, complaint, or injury; and (b) examinations required by third parties such as insurance companies business establishments, or Government agencies.

If the claim is for a diagnostic test or examination performed solely for the purpose of establishing a claim under title IV of Public Law 91-173, "Black Lung Benefits," the service is not covered under Medicare and the claimant should be advised to contact their Social Security office regarding the filing of a claim for reimbursement under the "Black Lung" program.

The exclusions apply to eyeglasses or contact lenses, and eye examinations for the purpose of prescribing, fitting, or changing eyeglasses or contact lenses for refractive errors. The exclusions do not apply to physicians' services (and services incident to a physicians' service) performed in conjunction with an eye disease, as for example, glaucoma or cataracts, or to post-surgical prosthetic lenses which are customarily used during convalescence from eye surgery in which the lens of the eye was removed, or to permanent prosthetic lenses required by an individual lacking the organic lens of the eye whether by surgical removal or congenital disease. Such prosthetic lens is a replacement for an internal body organ - the lens of the eye. (See the Medicare Benefit Policy Manual, Chapter 15, "Covered Medical and Other Health Services," Sec.120). Expenses for all refractive procedures, whether performed by an ophthalmologist (or any other physician) or an optometrist and without regard to the reason for performance of the refraction, are excluded from coverage.

A. Immunizations
Vaccinations or inoculations are excluded as immunizations unless they are either

- Directly related to the treatment of an injury or direct exposure to a disease or condition, such as antirabies treatment, tetanus antitoxin or booster vaccine, botulin antitoxin, antivenin sera, or immune globulin. (In the absence of injury or direct exposure, preventive immunization (vaccination or inoculation) against such diseases as smallpox, polio, diphtheria, etc., is not covered.); or
- Specifically covered by statute, as described in the Medicare Benefit Policy Manual, Chapter 15, "Covered Medical and Other Health Services," Sec.50.

B. Antigens
Prior to the Omnibus Reconciliation Act of 1980, a physician who prepared an antigen for a patient could not be reimbursed for that service unless the physician also administered the antigen to the patient. Effective January 1, 1981, payment may be made for a reasonable supply of antigens that have been prepared for a particular patient even though they have not been administered to the patient by the same physician who prepared them if:

- The antigens are prepared by a physician who is a doctor of medicine or osteopathy, and
- The physician who prepared the antigens has examined the patient and has determined a plan of treatment and a dosage regimen.

A reasonable supply of antigens is considered to be not more than a 12-week supply of antigens that has been prepared for a particular patient at any one time. The purpose of the reasonable supply limitation is to assure that the antigens retain their potency and effectiveness over the period in which they are to be administered to the patient. (See the Medicare Benefit Policy Manual, Chapter 15, "Covered Medical and Other Health Services," Sec.50.4.4.2)

Pub. 100-3, Section 10.2
NCD for Transcutaneous Electrical Nerve Stimulation (TENS) for Acute Post-Operative Pain (10.2)
The use of TENS for the relief of acute post-operative pain is covered under Medicare. TENS may be covered whether used as an adjunct to the use of drugs, or as an alternative to drugs, in the treatment of acute pain resulting from surgery.

TENS devices, whether durable or disposable, may be used in furnishing this service. When used for the purpose of treating acute post-operative pain, TENS devices are considered supplies. As such they may be hospital supplies furnished inpatients covered under Part A, or supplies incident to a physician's service when furnished in connection with surgery done on an outpatient basis, and covered under Part B.

It is expected that TENS, when used for acute post-operative pain, will be necessary for relatively short periods of time, usually 30 days or less. In cases when TENS is used for longer periods, contractors should attempt to ascertain whether TENS is no longer being used for acute pain but rather for chronic pain, in which case the TENS device may be covered as durable medical equipment as described in 280.13.

Pub. 100-3, Section 20.10
NCD for Cardiac Rehabilitation Programs (20.10)
A. General
Phase II cardiac rehabilitation, as described by the U.S. Public Health Service, is a comprehensive, long-term program including medical evaluation, prescribed exercise, cardiac risk factor modification, education, and counseling. Phase II refers to outpatient, medically supervised programs that are typically initiated 1-3 weeks after hospital discharge and provide appropriate electrocardiographic monitoring.

B. Nationally Covered Indications
Effective for services performed on or after March 22, 2006, Medicare coverage of cardiac rehabilitation programs is considered reasonable and necessary only for patients who: (1) have a documented diagnosis of acute myocardial infarction within the preceding 12 months; or (2) have had coronary bypass surgery; or (3) have stable angina pectoris; or (4) have had heart valve repair/replacement; or (5) have had percutaneous transluminal coronary angioplasty (PTCA) or coronary stenting; or (6) have had a heart or heart-lung transplant.

1. Program Requirements
   a. Duration

      Services provided in connection with a cardiac rehabilitation exercise program may be considered reasonable and necessary for up to 36 sessions. Patients generally receive 2 to 3 sessions per week for 12 to 18 weeks. Coverage of additional sessions is discussed in section D below.

   b. Components

      Cardiac rehabilitation programs must be comprehensive and to be comprehensive they must include a medical evaluation, a program to modify cardiac risk factors (e.g., nutritional counseling), prescribed exercise, education, and counseling.

   c. Facility

      The facility must have available for immediate use the necessary cardio-pulmonary, emergency, diagnostic, and therapeutic life-saving equipment accepted by the medical community as medically necessary, e.g., oxygen, cardiopulmonary resuscitation equipment, or defibrillator.

   d. Staff

      The program must be staffed by personnel necessary to conduct the program safely and effectively, who are trained in both basic and advanced life support techniques and in exercise therapy for coronary disease. The program must be under the direct supervision of a physician, as defined in 42 CFR Sec.410.26(a)(2) (defined through cross reference to 42 CFR Sec.410.32(b)(3)(ii), or 42 CFR Sec.410.27(f)).

C. Nationally Non-Covered Indications
Except as provided in section D., all other indications are not covered.

D. Other
The contractor has the discretion to cover cardiac rehabilitation services beyond 18 weeks. Coverage must not exceed a total of 72 sessions for 36 weeks.

(This NCD last reviewed March 2006.)

Pub. 100-3, Section 30.1
NCD for Biofeedback Therapy (30.1)
Biofeedback therapy is covered under Medicare only when it is reasonable and necessary for the individual patient for muscle re-education of specific muscle groups or for treating pathological muscle abnormalities of spasticity, incapacitating muscle spasm, or weakness, and more conventional treatments (heat, cold, massage, exercise, support) have not been successful. This therapy is not covered for treatment of ordinary muscle tension states or for psychosomatic conditions. (See the Medicare Benefit Policy Manual, Chapter 15, for general coverage requirements about physical therapy requirements.)

Pub. 100-3, Section 30.1.1
NCD for Biofeedback Therapy for the Treatment of Urinary Incontinence (30.1.1)
This policy applies to biofeedback therapy rendered by a practitioner in an office or other facility setting.

Biofeedback is covered for the treatment of stress and/or urge incontinence in cognitively intact patients who have failed a documented trial of pelvic muscle exercise (PME)training. Biofeedback is not a treatment, per se, but a tool to help patients learn how to perform PME. Biofeedback-assisted PME incorporates the use of an electronic or mechanical device to relay visual and/or auditory evidence of pelvic floor muscle tone, in order to improve awareness of pelvic floor musculature and to assist patients in the performance of PME.

A failed trial of PME training is defined as no clinically significant improvement in urinary incontinence after completing 4 weeks of an ordered plan of pelvic muscle exercises to increase periurethral muscle strength.

Contractors may decide whether or not to cover biofeedback as an initial treatment modality.

Home use of biofeedback therapy is not covered.

Pub. 100-3, Section 40.5
NCD for Treatment of Obesity (40.5)
B. Nationally Covered Indications

Certain designated surgical services for the treatment of obesity are covered for Medicare beneficiaries who have a BMI >=35, have at least one co-morbidity related to obesity and have been previously unsuccessful with the medical treatment of obesity. See Sec.100.1.

C. Nationally Noncovered Indications

1. Treatments for obesity alone remain non-covered.

2. Supplemented fasting is not covered under the Medicare program as a general treatment for obesity (see section D. below for discretionary local coverage).

D. Other
Where weight loss is necessary before surgery in order to ameliorate the complications posed by obesity when it coexists with pathological conditions such as cardiac and respiratory diseases, diabetes, or hypertension (and other more conservative techniques to achieve this end are not regarded as appropriate), supplemented fasting with adequate monitoring of the patient is eligible for coverage on a case-by-case basis or pursuant to a local coverage determination. The risks associated with the achievement of rapid weight loss must be carefully balanced against the risk posed by the condition requiring surgical treatment.

(This NCD last reviewed February 2006.)

Pub. 100-3, Section 150.1
NCD for Manipulation (150.1)
A. Manipulation of the Rib Cage.
Manual manipulation of the rib cage contributes to the treatment of respiratory conditions such as bronchitis, emphysema, and asthma as part of a regimen which includes other elements of therapy, and is covered only under such circumstances.

B. Manipulation of the Head.
Manipulation of the occipitocervical or temporomandibular regions of the head when indicated for conditions affecting those portions of the head and neck is a covered service.

Pub. 100-3, Section 150.5
NCD for Diathermy Treatment (150.5)
High energy pulsed wave diathermy machines have been found to produce some degree of therapeutic benefit for essentially the same conditions and to the same extent as standard diathermy. Accordingly, where the contractor's medical staff has determined that the pulsed wave diathermy apparatus used is one which is considered therapeutically effective, the treatments are considered a covered service, but only for those conditions for which standard diathermy is medically indicated and only when rendered by a physician or incident to a physician's professional services.

Pub. 100-3, Section 160.2
NCD for Treatment of Motor Function Disorders with Electric Nerve Stimulation (160.2)
Where electric nerve stimulation is employed to treat motor function disorders, no reimbursement may be made for the stimulator or for the services related to its implantation since this treatment cannot be considered reasonable and necessary.

Note: For Medicare coverage of deep brain stimulation for essential tremor and Parkinson's disease, see Sec.160.24 of the NCD Manual.

Pub. 100-3, Section 160.7
NCD for Electrical Nerve Stimulators (160.7)
Two general classifications of electrical nerve stimulators are employed to treat chronic intractable pain: peripheral nerve stimulators and central nervous system stimulators.

A. Implanted Peripheral Nerve Stimulators
Payment may be made under the prosthetic device benefit for implanted peripheral nerve stimulators. Use of this stimulator involves implantation of electrodes around a selected peripheral nerve. The stimulating electrode is connected by an insulated lead to a receiver unit which is implanted under the skin at a depth not greater than 1/2 inch. Stimulation is induced by a generator connected to an antenna unit which is attached to the skin surface over the receiver unit. Implantation of electrodes requires surgery and usually necessitates an operating room.

Note: Peripheral nerve stimulators may also be employed to assess a patient's suitability for continued treatment with an electric nerve stimulator. As explained in Sec.160.7.1, such use of the stimulator is covered as part of the total diagnostic service furnished to the beneficiary rather than as a prosthesis.

B. Central Nervous System Stimulators (Dorsal Column and Depth Brain Stimulators)

The implantation of central nervous system stimulators may be covered as therapies for the relief of chronic intractable pain, subject to the following conditions:

1. Types of Implantations

   There are two types of implantations covered by this instruction:

   Dorsal Column (Spinal Cord) Neurostimulation - The surgical implantation of neurostimulator electrodes within the dura mater (endodural) or the percutaneous insertion of electrodes in the epidural space is covered.

   Depth Brain Neurostimulation - The stereotactic implantation of electrodes in the deep brain (e.g., thalamus and periaqueductal gray matter) is covered.

2. Conditions for Coverage

   No payment may be made for the implantation of dorsal column or depth brain stimulators or services and supplies related to such implantation, unless all of the conditions listed below have been met:

   The implantation of the stimulator is used only as a late resort (if not a last resort) for patients with chronic intractable pain;

   With respect to item a, other treatment modalities (pharmacological, surgical, physical, or psychological therapies) have been tried and did not prove satisfactory, or are judged to be unsuitable or contraindicated for the given patient;

   Patients have undergone careful screening, evaluation and diagnosis by a multidisciplinary team prior to implantation. (Such screening must include psychological, as well as physical evaluation);

   All the facilities, equipment, and professional and support personnel required for the proper diagnosis, treatment training, and followup of the patient (including that required to satisfy item c) must be available; and

   Demonstration of pain relief with a temporarily implanted electrode precedes permanent implantation.

   Contractors may find it helpful to work with QIOs to obtain the information needed to apply these conditions to claims.

Pub. 100-3, Section 160.7.1

NCD for Assessing Patient's Suitability for Electrical Nerve Stimulation Therapy (160.7.1)

Indications and Limitations of Coverage

CIM 35-46

Electrical nerve stimulation is an accepted modality for assessing a patient's suitability for ongoing treatment with a transcutaneous or an implanted nerve stimulator.

Accordingly, program payment may be made for the following techniques when used to determine the potential therapeutic usefulness of an electrical nerve stimulator:

A. Transcutaneous Electrical Nerve Stimulation(TENS)

This technique involves attachment of a transcutaneous nerve stimulator to the surface of the skin over the peripheral nerve to be stimulated. It is used by the patient on a trial basis and its effectiveness in modulating pain is monitored by the physician, or physical therapist. Generally, the physician or physical therapist is able to determine whether the patient is likely to derive a significant therapeutic benefit from continuous use of a transcutaneous stimulator within a trial period of 1 month; in a few cases this determination may take longer to make. Document the medical necessity for such services which are furnished beyond the first month. (See Sec.160.13 for an explanation of coverage of medically necessary supplies for the effective use of TENS.)

If TENS significantly alleviates pain, it may be considered as primary treatment; if it produces no relief or greater discomfort than the original pain electrical nerve stimulation therapy is ruled out. However, where TENS produces incomplete relief, further evaluation with percutaneous electrical nerve stimulation may be considered to determine whether an implanted peripheral nerve stimulator would provide significant relief from pain.

Usually, the physician or physical therapist providing the services will furnish the equipment necessary for assessment. Where the physician or physical therapist advises the patient to rent the TENS from a supplier during the trial period rather than supplying it himself/herself, program payment may be made for rental of the TENS as well as for the services of the physician or physical therapist who is evaluating its use. However, the combined program payment which is made for the physician's or physical therapist's services and the rental of the stimulator from a supplier should not exceed the amount which would be payable for the total service, including the stimulator, furnished by the physician or physical therapist alone.

B. Percutaneous Electrical Nerve Stimulation (PENS)

This diagnostic procedure which involves stimulation of peripheral nerves by a needle electrode inserted through the skin is performed only in a physician's office, clinic, or hospital outpatient department. Therefore, it is covered only when performed by a physician or incident to physician's service. If pain is effectively controlled by percutaneous stimulation, implantation of electrodes is warranted.

As in the case of TENS (described in subsection A), generally the physician should be able to determine whether the patient is likely to derive a significant therapeutic benefit from continuing use of an implanted nerve stimulator within a trial period of 1 month. In a few cases, this determination may take longer to make. The medical necessity for such diagnostic services which are furnished beyond the first month must be documented.

NOTE: Electrical nerve stimulators do not prevent pain but only alleviate pain as it occurs. A patient can be taught how to employ the stimulator, and once this is done, can use it safely and effectively without direct physician supervision. Consequently, it is inappropriate for a patient to visit his/her physician, physical therapist, or an outpatient clinic on a continuing basis for treatment of pain with electrical nerve stimulation. Once it is determined that electrical nerve stimulation should be continued as therapy and the patient has been trained to use the stimulator, it is expected that a stimulator will be implanted or the patient will employ the TENS on a continual basis in his/her home. Electrical nerve stimulation treatments furnished by a physician in his/her office, by a physical therapist or outpatient clinic are excluded from coverage by Sec.1862(a)(1) of the Act. (See Sec.160.7 for an explanation of coverage of the therapeutic use of implanted peripheral nerve stimulators under the prosthetic devices benefit. See Sec.280.13 for an explanation of coverage of the therapeutic use of TENS under the durable medical equipment benefit.)

Pub. 100-3, Section 160.8

NCD for Electroencephalographic (EEG) Monitoring During Surgical Procedures Involving the Cerebral Vasculature (160.8)

CIM 35-57

Electroencephalographic (EEG) monitoring is a safe and reliable technique for the assessment of gross cerebral blood flow during general anesthesia and is covered under Medicare. Very characteristic changes in the EEG occur when cerebral perfusion is inadequate for ce rebral function. EEG monitoring as an indirect measure of cerebral perfusion requires the expertise of an electroencephalographer, a neurologist trained in EEG, or an advanced EEG technician for its proper interpretation.

The EEG monitoring may be covered routinely in carotid endarterectomies and in other neurological procedures where cerebral perfusion could be reduced. Such other procedures might include aneurysm surgery where hypotensive anesthesia is used or other cerebral vascular procedures where cerebral blood flow may be interrupted.

Pub. 100-3, Section 160.10

NCD for Evoked Response Tests (160.10)

Evoked response tests, including brain stem evoked response and visual evoked response tests, are generally accepted as safe and effective diagnostic tools. Program payment may be made for these procedures.

Pub. 100-3, Section 160.12

NCD for Neuromuscular Electrical Stimulaton (NMES) (160.12)

Indications and Limitations of Coverage

Treatment of Muscle Atrophy

Coverage of NMES to treat muscle atrophy is limited to the treatment of disuse atrophy where nerve supply to the muscle is intact, including brain, spinal cord and peripheral nerves, and other non-neurological reasons for disuse atrophy. Some examples would be casting or splinting of a limb, contracture due to scarring of soft tissue as in burn lesions, and hip replacement surgery (until orthotic training begins). (See Sec.160.13 of the NCD Manual for an explanation of coverage of medically necessary supplies for the effective use of NMES.)

Use for Walking in Patients with Spinal Cord Injury (SCI)

The type of NMES that is use to enhance the ability to walk of SCI patients is commonly referred to as functional electrical stimulation (FES). These devices are surface units that use electrical impulses to activate paralyzed or weak muscles in precise sequence. Coverage for the use of NMES/FES is limited to SCI patients for walking, who have completed a training program which consists of at least 32 physical therapy sessions with the device over a period of three months. The trial period of physical therapy will enable the physician treating the patient for his or her spinal cord injury to properly evaluate the person's ability to use these devices frequently and for the long term. Physical therapy necessary to perform this training must be directly performed by the physical therapist as part of a one-on-one training program.

The goal of physical therapy must be to train SCI patients on the use of NMES/FES devices to achieve walking, not to reverse or retard muscle atrophy.

Coverage for NMES/FES for walking will be covered in SCI patients with all of the following characteristics:

- Persons with intact lower motor unite (L1 and below) (both muscle and peripheral nerve);

- Persons with muscle and joint stability for weight bearing at upper and lower extremities that can demonstrate balance and control to maintain an upright support posture independently;

- Persons that demonstrate brisk muscle contraction to NMES and have sensory perception electrical stimulation sufficient for muscle contraction;

- Persons that possess high motivation, commitment and cognitive ability to use such devices for walking;

- Persons that can transfer independently and can demonstrate independent standing tolerance for at least 3 minutes;
- Persons that can demonstrate hand and finger function to manipulate controls;
- Persons with at least 6-month post recovery spinal cord injury and restorative surgery;
- Persons with hip and knee degenerative disease and no history of long bone fracture secondary to osteoporosis; and
- Persons who have demonstrated a willingness to use the device long-term.

NMES/FES for walking will not be covered in SCI patient with any of the following:

- Persons with cardiac pacemakers;
- Severe scoliosis or severe osteoporosis;
- Skin disease or cancer at area of stimulation;
- Irreversible contracture; or
- Autonomic dysflexia.

The only settings where therapists with the sufficient skills to provide these services are employed, are inpatient hospitals; outpatient hospitals; comprehensive outpatient rehabilitation facilities; and outpatient rehabilitation facilities. The physical therapy necessary to perform this training must be part of a one-on-one training program.

Additional therapy after the purchase of the DME would be limited by our general policies in converge of skilled physical therapy.

Pub. 100-3, Section 240.7

NCD for Postural Drainage Procedures and Pulmonary Exercises (240.7)

In most cases, postural drainage procedures and pulmonary exercises can be carried out safely and effectively by nursing personnel. However, in some cases patients may have acute or severe pulmonary conditions involving complex situations in which these procedures or exercises require the knowledge and skills of a physical therapist or a respiratory therapist. Therefore, if the attending physician determines as part of his/her plan of treatment that for the safe and effective administration of such services the procedures or exercises in question need to be performed by a physical therapist, the services of such a therapist constitute covered physical therapy when provided as an inpatient hospital service, extended care service, home health service, or outpatient physical therapy service.

NOTE: Physical therapy furnished in the outpatient department of a hospital is covered under the outpatient physical therapy benefit.

If the attending physician determines that the services should be performed by a respiratory therapist, the services of such a therapist constitute covered respiratory therapy when provided as an inpatient hospital service, outpatient hospital service, or extended care service, assuming that such services are furnished to the skilled nursing facility by a hospital with which the facility has a transfer agreement. Since the services of a respiratory therapist are not covered under the home health benefit, payment may not be made under the home health benefit for visits by a respiratory therapist to a patient's home to provide such services. Postural drainage procedures and pulmonary exercises are also covered when furnished by a physical therapist or a respiratory therapist as incident to a physician's professional service.

Pub. 100-3, Section 270.1

NCD for Electrical Stimulation (ES) and Electromagnetic Therapy for the Treatment of Wounds (270.1)

A. Nationally Covered Indications

The use of ES and electromagnetic therapy for the treatment of wounds are considered adjunctive therapies, and will only be covered for chronic Stage III or Stage IV pressure ulcers, arterial ulcers, diabetic ulcers, and venous stasis ulcers. Chronic ulcers are defined as ulcers that have not healed within 30 days of occurrence. ES or electromagnetic therapy will be covered only after appropriate standard wound therapy has been tried for at least 30 days and there are no measurable signs of improved healing. This 30-day period may begin while the wound is acute.

Standard wound care includes: optimization of nutritional status, debridement by any means to remove devitalized tissue, maintenance of a clean, moist bed of granulation tissue with appropriate moist dressings, and necessary treatment to resolve any infection that may be present. Standard wound care based on the specific type of wound includes: frequent repositioning of a patient with pressure ulcers (usually every 2 hours), offloading of pressure and good glucose control for diabetic ulcers, establishment of adequate circulation for arterial ulcers, and the use of a compression system for patients with venous ulcers.

Measurable signs of improved healing include: a decrease in wound size (either surface area or volume), decrease in amount of exudates, and decrease in amount of necrotic tissue. ES or electromagnetic therapy must be discontinued when the wound demonstrates 100% epitheliliazed wound bed.

ES and electromagnetic therapy services can only be covered when performed by a physician, physical therapist, or incident to a physician service. Evaluation of the wound is an integral part of wound therapy. When a physician, physical therapist, or a clinician incident to a physician, performs ES or electromagnetic therapy, the practitioner must evaluate the wound and contact the treating physician if the wound worsens. If ES or electromagnetic therapy is being used, wounds must be evaluated at least monthly by the treating physician.

B. Nationally Noncovered Indications

1. ES and electromagnetic therapy will not be covered as an initial treatment modality.

2. Continued treatment with ES or electromagnetic therapy is not covered if measurable signs of healing have not been demonstrated within any 30-day period of treatment.

3. Unsupervised use of ES or electromagnetic therapy for wound therapy will not be covered, as this use has not been found to be medically reasonable and necessary.

C. Other

All other uses of ES and electromagnetic therapy not otherwise specified for the treatment of wounds remain at local contractor discretion.

(This NCD last reviewed March 2004.)

Pub. 100-3, Section 270.2

NCD for Noncontact Normothermic Wound Therapy (NNWT) (270.2)

There is insufficient scientific or clinical evidence to consider this device as reasonable and necessary for the treatment of wounds within the meaning of Sec.1862(a)(1)(A) of the Social Security Act and will not be covered by Medicare.

Pub. 100-3, Section 270.4

NCD for Treatment of Decubitus Ulcers (270.4)

An accepted procedure for healing decubitus ulcers is to remove dead tissue from the lesions and to keep them clean to promote the growth of new tissue. This may be accomplished by hydrotherapy (whirlpool) treatments. Hydrotherapy (whirlpool) treatment for decubitus ulcers is a covered service under Medicare for patients when treatment is reasonable and necessary. Some other methods of treating decubitus ulcers, the safety and effectiveness of which have not been established, are not covered under the Medicare program. Some examples of these types of treatments are: ultraviolet light, low intensity direct current, topical application of oxygen, and topical dressings with Balsam of Peru in castor oil.

Pub. 100-3, Section 270.5

NCD for Porcine Skin and Gradient Pressure Dressings (270.5)

Porcine (pig) skin dressings are covered, if reasonable and necessary for the individual patient as an occlusive dressing for burns, donor sites of a homograft, and decubiti and other ulcers.

Pub. 100-3, Section 280.1

Durable Medical Equipment Reference List
(Effective May 5, 2005)

(Rev. 37, Issued: 06-03-05; Effective: 05-05-05; Implementation: 07-05-05)

The durable medical equipment (DME) list that follows is designed to facilitate the contractor's processing of DME claims. This section is designed as a quick reference tool for determining the coverage status of certain pieces of DME and especially for those items commonly referred to by both brand and generic names. The information contained herein is applicable (where appropriate) to all DME national coverage determinations (NCDs) discussed in the DME portion of this manual. The list is organized into two columns. The first column lists alphabetically various generic categories of equipment on which NCDs have been made by the Centers for Medicare & Medicaid Services (CMS); the second column notes the coverage status.

In the case of equipment categories that have been determined by CMS to be covered under the DME benefit, the list outlines the conditions of coverage that must be met if payment is to be allowed for the rental or purchase of the DME by a particular patient, or cross-refers to another section of the manual where the applicable coverage criteria are described in more detail. With respect to equipment categories that cannot be covered as DME, the list includes a brief explanation of why the equipment is not covered. This DME list will be updated periodically to reflect any additional NCDs that CMS may make with regard to other categories of equipment.

When the contractor receives a claim for an item of equipment which does not appear to fall logically into any of the generic categories listed, the contractor has the authority and responsibility for deciding whether those items are covered under the DME benefit.

These decisions must be made by each contractor based on the advice of its medical consultants, taking into account:

The Medicare Claims Processing Manual, Chapter 20, "Durable Medical Equipment, Prosthetics and Orthotics, and Supplies (DMEPOS)."

Whether the item has been approved for marketing by the Food and Drug Administration (FDA) and is otherwise generally considered to be safe and effective for the purpose intended; and

Whether the item is reasonable and necessary for the individual patient. The term DME is defined as equipment which:

Can withstand repeated use; i.e., could normally be rented and used by successive patients;

Is primarily and customarily used to serve a medical purpose;

Generally is not useful to a person in the absence of illness or injury; and,

Is appropriate for use in a patient's home.

Durable Medical Equipment Reference List

Air Cleaners	Deny--environmental control equipment; not primarily medical in nature (§1861(n) of the Act).
Air Conditioners	Deny--environmental control equipment; not primarily medical in nature (§1861 (n) of the Act).
Air-Fluidized Bed s	(See Air-Fluidized Bed s, §280.8 of the NCD Manual.)
Alternating Pressure Pads, Mattresses and Lambs Wool Pads	Covered if patient has, or is highly susceptible to, decubitus ulcers and the patient's physician specifies that he/she has specified that he will be supervising the course of treatment.
Audible/Visible Signal/ Pacemaker Monitors	(See Self-Contained Pacemaker Monitors.)
Augmentative Communication Device s	(See Speech Generating Devices, §50.1 of the NCD Manual.)
Bathtub Lifts	Deny--convenience item; not primarily medical in nature (§1861(n) of the Act).
Bathtub Seats	Deny--comfort or convenience item; hygienic equipment; not primarily medical in nature (§1861(n) of the Act).
Bead Bed s	(See §280.8 of the NCD Manual.)
Bed Baths (home type)	Deny--hygienic equipment; not primarily medical in nature (§1861(n) of the Act).
Bed Lifter s (bed elevators)	Deny--not primarily medical in nature (§1861(n) of the Act).
Bedboards	Deny--not primarily medical in nature (§1861(n) of the Act).
Bed Pans (autoclavable hospital type)	Covered if patient is bed confined.
Bed Side Rails	(See Hospital Beds, §280.7 of the NCD Manual.)
Beds-Lounge s (power or manual)	Deny--not a hospital bed; comfort or convenience item; not primarily medical in nature (§1861(n) of the Act).
Beds--Oscillating	Deny--institutional equipment; inappropriate for home use.
Bidet Toilet Seat s	(See Toilet Seats.)
Blood Glucose Analyzer s - - Reflectance Colorimeter	Deny--unsuitable for home use (see §40.2 of the NCD Manual).
Blood Glucose Monitor s	Covered if patient meets certain conditions (see §40.2 of the NCD Manual).
Braille Teaching Texts	Deny--educational equipment; not primarily medical in nature (§1861(n) of the Act).
Canes	Covered if patient meets Mobility Assistive Equipment clinical criteria (see §280.3 of the NCD Manual).
Carafes	Deny--convenience item; not primarily medical in nature (§1861(n) of the Act).
Catheters	Deny--nonreusable disposable supply (§1861(n) of the Act). (See The Medicare Claims Processing Manual, Chapter 20, DMEPOS).
Commodes	Covered if patient is confined to bed or room.NOTE: The term "room confined" means that the patient's condition is such that leaving the room is medically contraindicated. The accessibility of bathroom facilities generally would not be a factor in this determination. However, confinement of a patient to a home in a case where there are no toilet facilities in the home may be equated to room confinement. Moreover, payment may also be made if a patient's medical condition confines him to a floor of the home and there is no bathroom located on that floor.

Communications	(See §50.1 of the NCD Manual "Speech Generating Devices")
Continuous Passive Motion Devices	Continuous passive motion devices are devices Covered for patients who have received a total knee replacement. To qualify for coverage, use of the device must commence within 2 days following surgery. In addition, coverage is limited to that portion of the 3-week period following surgery during which the device is used in the patient's home. There is insufficient evidence to justify coverage of these devices for longer periods of time or for other applications.
Continuous Positive Airway Pressure (CPAP) Devices	(See §240.4 of the NCD Manual.)
Crutches	Covered if patient meets Mobility Assistive Equipment clinical criteria (see section 280.3 of the NCD Manual).
Cushion Lift Power Seat s	(See Seat Lifts.)
Dehumidifiers (room or central heating system type)	Deny--environmental control equipment; not primarily medical in nature (§1861(n) of the Act).
Diathermy Machines (standard pulses wave types)	Deny--inappropriate for home use (see §150.5 of the NCD Manual).
Digital Electronic Pacemaker Monitor s	(See Self-Contained Pacemaker Monitor s .)
Disposable Sheets and Bags	Deny--nonreusable disposable supplies (§1861(n) of the Act).
Elastic Stockings	Deny--nonreusable supply; not rental-type items (§1861(n) of the Act). (See §270.5 of the NCD Manual.)
Electric Air Cleaners	Deny--(See Air Cleaners.) (§1861(n) of the Act).
Electric Hospital Beds	(See Hospital Beds 280.7 of the NCD Manual.)
Electrical Stimulation for Wounds	Deny--inappropriate for home use. (See §270.1 of the NCD Manual.)
Electrostatic Machines	Deny--(See Air Cleaners and Air Conditioners.) (§1861(n) of the Act).
Elevators	Deny--convenience item; not primarily medical in nature (§1861(n) of the Act).
Emesis Basins	Deny--convenience item; not primarily medical in nature (§1861(n) of the Act).
Esophageal Dilators	Deny--physician instrument; inappropriate for patient use.
Exercise Equipment	Deny--not primarily medical in nature (§1861(n) of the Act).
Fabric Supports	Deny--nonreusable supplies; not rental-type items (§1861(n) of the Act).
Face Masks (oxygen)	Covered if oxygen is covered. (See §240.2 of the NCD Manual.)
Face Masks (surgical)	Deny--nonreusable disposable items (§1861(n) of the Act).
Flowmeters	(See Medical Oxygen Regulators.) (See §240.2 of the NCD Manual.)
Fluidic Breathing Assisters	(See Intermittent Positive Pressure Breathing Machines.)
Fomentation Devices	(See Heating Pads.)
Gel Flotation Pads and Mattresses	(See Alternating Pressure Pads and Mattresses.)
Grab Bars	Deny--self-help device; not primarily medical in nature (§1861(n) of the Act).
Heat and Massage Foam Cushion Pads	Deny--not primarily medical in nature; personal comfort item (§§1861(n) and 1862(a)(6) of the Act).
Heating and Cooling Plants	Deny--environmental control equipment not primarily medical in nature (§1861(n) of the Act).
Heating Pads	Covered if the contractor's medical staff determines patient's medical condition is one for which the application of heat in the form of a heating pad is therapeutically effective.

Medicare Information

Heat Lamps	Covered if the contractor's medical staff determines patient's medical condition is one for which the application of heat in the form of a heat lamp is therapeutically effective.
Hospital Beds	(See §280.7 of the NCD Manual.)
Hot Packs	(See Heating Pads.)
Humidifiers (oxygen)	(See Oxygen Humidifiers.)
Humidifiers (room or central heating system types)	Deny--environmental control equipment; not medical in nature (§1861(n) of the Act).
Hydraulic Lifts	(See Patient Lifts.)
Incontinent Pads	Deny--nonreusable supply; hygienic item (§1861(n) of the Act).
Infusion Pumps	For external and implantable pumps, see §40.2 of the NCD Manual. If the pump is used with an enteral or parenteral nutritional therapy system. (See §180.2 of the NCD Manual for special coverage rules.)
Injectors (hypodermic jet	Deny--not covered self-administered drug supply;pressure powered devices (§1861(s)(2)(A) of the Act) for injection of insulin.
Intermittent Positive Pressure Breathing Machines	Covered if patient's ability to breathe is severely impaired.
Iron Lungs	(See Ventilators.)
Irrigating Kit s	Deny--nonreusable supply; hygienic equipment (§1861(n) of the Act).
Lambs Wool Pads	(See Alternating Pressure Pads, Mattresses, and Lamb s Wool Pads.)
Leotards	Deny--(See Pressure Leotards.) (§1861(n) of the Act).
Lymphedema Pumps	Covered--(See Pneumatic Compression Devices, §280.6 of the NCD Manual.)
Massage Devices	Deny--personal comfort items; not primarily medical in nature (§§1861(n) and 1862(a)(6) of the Act).
Mattresses	Covered only where hospital bed is medically necessary. (Separate Charge for replacement mattress should not be allowed where hospital bed with mattress is rented.) (See §280.7 of the NCD Manual.)
Medical Oxygen Regulators	Covered if patient's ability to breathe is severely impaired. (See §240.2 of the NCD Manual.)
Mobile Geriatric Chairs	Covered if patient meets Mobility Assistive Equipment clinical criteria (see §280.3 of the NCD Manual).
Motorized Wheelchairs	Covered if patient meets Mobility Assistive Equipment clinical criteria (see §280.3 of the NCD manual).
Muscle Stimulators	Covered for certain conditions. (See §250.4 of the NCD Manual.)
Nebulizers	Covered if patient's ability to breathe is severely impaired.
Oscillating Beds	Deny--institutional equipment - inappropriate for home use.
Overbed Tables	Deny--convenience item; not primarily medical in nature (§1861(n) of the Act).
Oxygen	Covered if the oxygen has been prescribed for use in connection with medically necessary DME . (See §240.2 of the NCD Manual.)
Oxygen Humidifiers	Covered if the oxygen has been prescribed for use in connection with medically necessary DME for purposes of moisturizing oxygen. (See §240.2 of the NCD Manual.)
Oxygen Regulators (Medical)	(See Medical Oxygen Regulators.)
Oxygen Tents	(See §240.2 of the NCD Manual.)
Paraffin Bath Units (Portable)	(See Portable Paraffin Bath Units.)
Paraffin Bath Units (Standard)	Deny--institutional equipment; inappropriate for home use.

Parallel Bars	Deny--support exercise equipment; primarily for institutional use; in the home setting other devices (e.g., walkers) satisfy the patient's need.
Patient Lifts	Covered if contractor's medical staff determines patient's condition is such that periodic movement is necessary to effect improvement or to arrest or retard deterioration in his condition.
Percussors	Covered for mobilizing respiratory tract secretions in patients with chronic obstructive lung disease, chronic bronchitis, or emphysema, when patient or operator of powered percussor receives appropriate training by a physician or therapist, and no one competent to administer manual therapy is available.
Portable Oxygen Systems	1. Regulated Covered (adjustable Covered under conditions specified in a flow rate). Refer all claims to medical staff for this determination.2. Preset Deny (flow rate Deny emergency, first-aid, or not adjustable) precautionary equipment; essentially not therapeutic in nature.
Portable Paraffin Bath Units	Covered when the patient has undergone a successful trial period of paraffin therapy ordered by a physician and the patient's condition is expected to be relieved by long term use of this modality.
Portable Room Heaters	Deny--environmental control equipment; not primarily medical in nature (§1861(n) of the Act).
Portable Whirlpool Pumps	Deny--not primarily medical in nature; personal comfort items (§§1861(n) and 1862(a)(6) of the Act).
Postural Drainage Boards	Covered if patient has a chronic pulmonary condition.
Preset Portable Oxygen Units	Deny--emergency, first-aid, or precautionary equipment; essentially not therapeutic in nature.
Pressure Leotards	Deny--non-reusable supply, not rental-type item (§1861(n) of the Act).
Pulse Tachometer s	Deny--not reasonable or necessary for monitoring pulse of homebound patient with or without a cardiac pacemaker.
Quad-Canes	Covered if patient meets Mobility Assistive Equipment clinical criteria (see §280.3 of the NCD Manual).
Raised Toilet Seats	Deny--convenience item; hygienic equipment; not primarily medical in nature (§1861(n) of the Act).
Reflectance Colorimeters	(See Blood Glucose Analyzers.)
Respirators	(See Ventilators.)
Rolling Chairs	Covered if patient meets Mobility Assistive Equipment clinical criteria (see §280.3 of the NCD Manual). Coverage is limited to those roll-about chairs having casters of at least 5 inches in diameter and specifically designed to meet the needs of ill, injured, or otherwise impaired individuals. Coverage is denied for the wide range of chairs with smaller casters as are found in general use in homes, offices, and institutions for many purposes not related to the care/treatment of ill/injured persons. This type is not primarily medical in nature. (§1861(n) of the Act.)
Safety Rollers	Covered if patient meets Mobility Assistive Equipment clinical criteria (see §280.3 of the NCD Manual).
Sauna Baths	Deny--not primarily medical in nature; personal comfort items (§§1861(n) and 1862(a)(6) of the Act).
Seat Lifts	Covered under the conditions specified in §280.4 of the NCD Manual. Refer all to medical staff for this determination.
Self Contained Pacemaker Monitors	Covered when prescribed by a physician for a patient with a cardiac pacemaker. (See §§20.8.1 and 280.2 of the NCD Manual.)
Sitz Baths	Covered if the contractor's medical staff determines patient has an infection or injury of the perineal area and the item has been prescribed by the patient's physician as a part of his planned regimen of treatment in the patient's home.
Spare Tanks of Oxygen	Deny--convenience or precautionary supply.

Medicare Information

Medicare Information

Speech Teaching Machines	Deny--education equipment; not primarily medical in nature (§1861(n) of the Act).
Stairway Elevators	Deny--(See Elevators.) (§1861(n) of the Act).
Standing Tables	Deny--convenience item; not primarily medical in nature (§1861(n) of the Act).
Steam Packs	These packs are Covered under the same condition s as heating pad s . (See Heating Pads.)
Suction Machins	Covered if the contractor's medical staff determines that the machine specified in the claim is medically required and appropriate for home use without technical or professional supervision.
Support Hose	Deny (See Fabric Supports.) (§1861(n) of the Act).
Surgical Leggings	Deny--non-reusable supply; not rental-type item (§1861(n) of the Act).
Telephone Alert Systems	Deny--these are emergency communications systems and do not serve a diagnostic or therapeutic purpose.
Toilet Seats	Deny--not medical equipment (§1861(n) of the Act).
Traction Equipment	Covered if patient has orthopedic impairment requiring traction equipment that prevents ambulation during the period of use (Consider covering devices usable during ambulation; e.g., cervical traction collar, under the brace provision).
Trapeze Bars	Covered if patient is bed confined and the patient needs a trapeze bar to sit up because of respiratory condition, to change body position for other medical reasons, or to get in and out of bed.
Treadmill Exercisers	Deny--exercise equipment; not primarily medical in nature (§1861(n) of the Act).
Ultraviolet Cabinets	Covered for selected patients with generalized intractable psoriasis. Using appropriate consultation, the contractor should determine whether medical and other factors justify treatment at home rather than at alternative sites, e.g., outpatient department of a hospital.
Urinals autoclavable	Covered if patient is bed confined hospital type.
Vaporizers	Covered if patient has a respiratory illness.
Ventilators	Covered for treatment of neuromuscular diseases, thoracic restrictive diseases, and chronic respiratory failure consequent to chronic obstructive pulmonary disease. Includes both positive and negative pressure types. (See §240.5 of the NCD Manual.)
Walkers	Covered if patient meets Mobility Assistive Equipment clinical criteria (see §280.3 of the NCD Manual).
Water and Pressure Pads and Mattresses	(See Alternating Pressure Pads, Mattresses and Lamb Wool Pads.)
Wheelchairs (manual)	Covered if patient meets Mobility Assistive Equipment clinical criteria (see §280.3 of the NCD Manual).
Wheelchairs (power operated)	Covered if patient meets Mobility Assistive Equipment clinical criteria (see §280.3 of the NCD Manual).
Wheelchairs (scooter/POV)	Covered if patient meets Mobility Assistive Equipment clinical criteria (see §280.3 of the NCD Manual).
Wheelchairs (specially-sized)	Covered if patient meets Mobility Assistive Equipment clinical criteria (see §280.3 of the NCD Manual).
Whirlpool Bath Equipment	Covered if patient is homebound and has a (standard)condition for which the whirlpool bath can be expected to provide substantial therapeutic benefit justifying its cost. Where patient is not homebound but has such a condition, payment is restricted to the cost of providing the services elsewhere; e.g., an outpatient department of a participating hospital, if that alternative is less costly. In all cases, refer claim to medical staff for a determination.
Whirlpool Pumps	Deny--(See Portable Whirlpool Pumps.) (§1861(n) of the Act).
White Canes	Deny--(See §280.2 of the NCD Manual.) (Not considered Mobility Assistive Equipment)

Pub. 100-3, Section 280.2

White Cane For Use By A Blind Person

A white cane for use by a blind person is more an identifying and self-help device rather than an item which makes a meaningful contribution in the treatment of an illness or injury.

Pub. 100-3, Section 280.13

NCD for Transcutaneous Electrical Nerve Stimulators (TENS) (280.13)

(Rev. 1, 10-03-03)

CIM 60-20

The TENS is a type of electrical nerve stimulator that is employed to treat chronic intractable pain. This stimulator is attached to the surface of the patient's skin over the peripheral nerve to be stimulated. It may be applied in a variety of settings (in the patient's home, a physician's office, or in an outpatient clinic). Payment for TENS may be made under the durable medical equipment benefit. (See §160.13 for an explanation of coverage of medically necessary supplies for the effective use of TENS and §10.2 for an explanation of coverage of TENS for acute post-operative pain.)

Pub. 100-4, Chapter 2, Section 70

Payment Conditions for Radiology Services

B3-15022

See chapter 13, for claims processing instructions for radiology.

Pub. 100-4, Chapter 5, Section 10

Part B Outpatient Rehabilitation and Comprehensive OutpatientRehabilitation Facility (CORF) Services - General

Part B Outpatient Rehabilitation and Comprehensive Outpatient Rehabilitation Facility (CORF) Services - General

Language in this section is defined or described in Pub. 100-02, chapter 15, sections 220 and 230.

Section 4541(a)(2) of the Balanced Budget Act (BBA) (P.L. 105-33), which added Sec.1834(k)(5) to the Social Security Act (the Act), required that all claims for outpatient rehabilitation, certain audiology services and comprehensive outpatient rehabilitation facility (CORF) services, be reported using a uniform coding system. The CMS chose HCPCS (Healthcare Common Procedure Coding System) as the coding system to be used for the reporting of these services. This coding requirement is effective for all claims for outpatient rehabilitation services including certain audiology services and CORF services submitted on or after April 1, 1998.

The BBA also required payment under a prospective payment system for outpatient rehabilitation services including audiology and CORF services. Effective for claims with dates of service on or after January 1, 1999, the Medicare Physician Fee Schedule (MPFS) became the method of payment for outpatient therapy services furnished by:

- Comprehensive outpatient rehabilitation facilities (CORFs);
- Outpatient physical therapy providers (OPTs);
- Other rehabilitation facilities (ORFs);
- Hospitals (to outpatients and inpatients who are not in a covered Part A stay);
- Skilled nursing facilities (SNFs) (to residents not in a covered Part A stay and to nonresidents who receive outpatient rehabilitation services from the SNF); and
- Home health agencies (HHAs) (to individuals who are not homebound or otherwise are not receiving services under a home health plan of care (POC)).

NOTE: No provider or supplier other than the SNF will be paid for therapy services during the time the beneficiary is in a covered SNF Part A stay. For information regarding SNF consolidated billing see chapter 6, section 10 of this manual.

Similarly, under the HH prospective payment system, HHAs are responsible to provide, either directly or under arrangements, all outpatient rehabilitation therapy services to beneficiaries receiving services under a home health POC. No other provider or supplier will be paid for these services during the time the beneficiary is in a covered Part A stay. For information regarding HH consolidated billing see chapter10, section 20 of this manual. Section 143 of the Medicare Improvements for Patients and Provider's Act of 2008 (MIPPA) authorizes the Centers for Medicare & Medicaid Services (CMS) to enroll speech-language pathologists (SLP) as suppliers of Medicare services and for SLPs to begin billing Medicare for outpatient speech-language pathology services furnished in private practice beginning July 1, 2009. Enrollment will allow SLPs in private practice to bill Medicare and receive direct payment for their services. Previously, the Medicare program could only pay SLP services if an institution, physician or nonphysician practitioner billed them.

In Chapter 23, as part of the CY 2009 Medicare Physician Fee Schedule Database, the descriptor for PC/TC indicator "7", as applied to certain HCPCS/CPT codes, is described as specific to the services of privately practicing therapists. Payment may not be made if the service is provided to either a hospital outpatient or a hospital inpatient by a physical therapist, occupational therapist, or speech-language pathologist in private practice.

The MPFS is used as a method of payment for outpatient rehabilitation services furnished under arrangement with any of these providers.

In addition, the MPFS is used as the payment system for audiology and CORF services identified by the HCPCS codes in Sec.20. Assignment is mandatory.

The Medicare allowed charge for the services is the lower of the actual charge or the MPFS amount. The Medicare payment for the services is 80 percent of the allowed charge after the Part B deductible is met. Coinsurance is made at 20 percent of the lower of the actual charge or the MPFS amount. The general coinsurance rule (20 percent of the actual charges) does not apply when making payment under the MPFS. This is a final payment.

The MPFS does not apply to outpatient rehabilitation services furnished by critical access hospitals (CAHs). CAHs are to be paid on a reasonable cost basis.

Contractors process outpatient rehabilitation claims from hospitals, including CAHs, SNFs, HHAs, CORFs, outpatient rehabilitation agencies, and outpatient physical therapy providers for which they have received a tie in notice from the RO. These provider types submit their claims to the contractors using the 837 Institutional electronic claim format or the UB-04 paper form when permissible. Contractors also process claims from physicians, certain nonphysician practitioners (NPPs), therapists in private practices (TPPs), (which are limited to physical and occupational therapists, and speech-language pathologists in private practices), and physician-directed clinics that bill for services furnished incident to a physician's service (see chapter 15 in Pub. 100-02, Medicare Benefit Policy Manual for a definition of "incident to"). These provider types submit their claims to the contractor using the 837 Professional electronic claim format or the CMS-1500 paper form when permissible.

There are different fee rates for nonfacility and facility services. Chapter 23 describes the differences in these two rates. (See fields 28 and 29 of the record therein described).

Facility rates apply to professional services performed in a facility other than the professional's office. Nonfacility rates apply when the service is performed in the professional's office. The nonfacility rate (that is paid when the provider performs the services in its own facility) accommodates overhead and indirect expenses the provider incurs by operating its own facility. Thus it is somewhat higher than the facility rate.

Contractors pay the nonfacility rate on institutional claims for services performed in the provider's facility. Contractors may pay professional claims using the facility or nonfacility rate depending upon where the service is performed (place of service on the claim), and the provider specialty.

Contractors pay the codes in Sec.20 under the MPFS on professional claims regardless of whether they may be considered rehabilitation services. However, contractors must use this list for institutional claims to determine whether to pay under outpatient rehabilitation rules or whether payment rules for other types of service may apply, e.g., OPPS for hospitals, reasonable costs for CAHs.

Note that because a service is considered an outpatient rehabilitation service does not automatically imply payment for that service. Additional criteria, including coverage, plan of care and physician certification must also be met. These criteria are described in Pub. 100-02, Medicare Benefit Policy Manual, chapters 1 and 15.

Payment for rehabilitation services provided to Part A inpatients of hospitals or SNFs is included in the respective PPS rate. Also, for SNFs (but not hospitals), if the beneficiary has Part B, but not Part A coverage (e.g., Part A benefits are exhausted), the SNF must bill for any rehabilitation service (but not audiologic function services).

Audiologists in private practice using a professional claim may bill directly for services rendered to Part B Medicare entitled beneficiaries residing in a SNF, but not in a SNF Part A covered stay. Payment is made based on the MPFS, whether on an institutional or professional claim. For beneficiaries not in a covered Part A SNF stay, who are sometimes referred to as beneficiaries in a Part B SNF stay, audiologic function tests are payable under Part B when billed by the SNF on an institutional claim as type of bill 22X, or when billed directly by the provider or supplier of the service on a professional claim. For tests that include both a professional component and technical component, the SNF may elect to bill the technical component on an institutional claim, but is not required to bill the service. (The professional component of a service is the direct patient care provided by the physician or audiologist, e.g., the interpretation of a test when the test is valued by the American Medical Association to include interpretation in the professional component.)

Payment for rehabilitation therapy services provided by home health agencies under a home health plan of care is included in the home health PPS rate. HHAs may submit bill type 34X and be paid under the MPFS if there are no home health services billed under a home health plan of care at the same time, and there is a valid rehabilitation POC (e.g., the patient is not homebound).

An institutional employer (other than a SNF) of the TPPs, or physician performing outpatient services, (e.g., hospital, CORF, etc.), or a clinic billing on behalf of the physician or therapist may bill the contractor on a professional claim.

The MPFS is the basis of payment for outpatient rehabilitation services furnished by TPPs, physicians, and certain nonphysician practitioners or for diagnostic tests provided incident to the services of such physicians or nonphysician practitioners. (See Pub. 100-02, Medicare Benefit Policy Manual, chapter 15, for a definition of "incident to, therapist, therapy and related instructions.") Such services are billed to the contractor on the professional claim format. Assignment is mandatory.

The following table identifies the provider and supplier types, and identifies which claim format they may use to submit bills to the contractor.

"Provider/Supplier Service" Type	Format	Bill Type	Comment
Inpatient hospital Part A	Institutional	11X	Included in PPS
Inpatient SNF Part A	Institutional	21X	Included in PPS
Inpatient hospital Part B	Institutional	12X	Hospital may obtain services under arrangements and bill, or rendering provider may bill.
Inpatient SNF Part B except for audiology function tests.	Institutional	22X	SNF must provide and bill, or obtain under arrangements and bill.
Inpatient SNF Part B audiology function tests only.	Institutional	22X	SNF may bill the contractor using the institutional claim format or the supplier of services may bill the contractor using the professional claim form.
Outpatient hospital	Institutional	13X	Hospital may provide and bill or obtain under arrangements and bill, or rendering provider may bill.
Outpatient SNF	Institutional	23X	SNF must provide and bill or obtain under arrangements and bill.
HHA billing for services rendered under a Part A or Part B home health plan of care.	Institutional	32X	Service is included in PPS rate. CMS determines whether payment is from Part A or Part B trust fund.
HHA billing for services not rendered under a Part A or Part B home health plan of care, but rendered under a therapy plan of care.	Institutional	34X	Service not under home health plan of care.
Other Rehabilitation Facility (ORF)	Institutional	74X	Paid MPFS for outpatient rehabilitation services effective January 1, 1999, and all other services except drugs effective July 1, 2000. Starting April 1, 2002, drugs are paid 95% of the AWP. For claims with dates of service on or after July 1, 2003, drugs and biologicals do not apply in an OPT setting. Therefore, FIs are to advise their OPTs not to bill for them.
Comprehensive Outpatient Rehabilitation Facility (CORF)	Institutional	75X	Paid MPFS for outpatient rehabilitation services effective January 1, 1999, and all other services except drugs effective July 1, 2000. Starting April 1, 2002, drugs are paid 95% of the AWP.

"Provider/Supplier Service" Type	Format	Bill Type	Comment
Physician, NPPs, TPPs, and, for diagnostic tests only, audiologists (service in hospital or SNF)	Professional	See Chapter 26 for place of service, and type of service coding.	Payment may not be made for therapy services to Part A inpatients of hospitals or SNFs, or for Part B SNF residents.\n\nOtherwise, suppliers bill to the contractor using the professional claim format.\n\nNote that services of a physician/ NPP/TPP employee of a facility may be billed by the facility to a contractor.
Physician/NPP/TPPs office, independent clinic or patient's home	Professional	See Chapter 26 for place of service, and type of service coding.	Paid via Physician fee schedule.
Practicing audiologist for services defined as diagnostic tests only	Professional	See Chapter 26 for place of service, and type of service coding.	Some audiologists tests provided in hospitals are considered other diagnostic tests and are subject to OPPS instead of MPFS for outpatient therapy fee schedule.
Critical Access Hospital - inpatient Part A	Institutional	11X	Rehabilitation services are paid cost.
Critical Access Hospital - inpatient Part B	Institutional	85X	Rehabilitation services are paid cost.
Critical Access Hospital – outpatient Part B	Institutional	85X	Rehabilitation services are paid cost.

Complete Claim form completion requirements are contained in chapters 25 and 26.

For a list of the outpatient rehabilitation HCPCS codes see Sec.20.

If a contractor receives an institutional claim for one of these HCPCS codes with dates of service on or after July 1, 2003, that does not appear on the supplemental file it currently uses to pay the therapy claims, it contacts its professional claims area to obtain the non-facility price in order to pay the claim.

NOTE: The list of codes in Sec.20 contains commonly utilized codes for outpatient rehabilitation services. Contractors may consider other codes on institutional claims for payment under the MPFS as outpatient rehabilitation services to the extent that such codes are determined to be medically reasonable and necessary and could be performed within the scope of practice of the therapist providing the service.

Pub. 100-4 , Chapter 5, Section 20
HCPCS Coding Requirement

A. Uniform Coding
Section 1834(k)(5) of the Act requires that all claims for outpatient rehabilitation therapy services and all comprehensive outpatient rehabilitation facility (CORF) services be reported using a uniform coding system. The current Healthcare Common Procedure Coding System/Current Procedural Terminology is used for the reporting of these services. The uniform coding requirement in the Act is specific to payment for all CORF services and outpatient rehabilitation therapy services - including physical therapy, occupational therapy, and speech-language pathology - that is provided and billed to carriers and fiscal intermediaries (FIs). The Medicare physician fee schedule (MPFS) is used to make payment for these therapy services at the nonfacility rate.

Effective for claims submitted on or after April 1, 1998, providers that had not previously reported HCPCS/CPT for outpatient rehabilitation and CORF services began using HCPCS to report these services. This requirement does not apply to outpatient rehabilitation services provided by:

- Critical access hospitals, which are paid on a cost basis, not MPFS;
- RHCs, and FQHCs for which therapy is included in the all-inclusive rate; or
- Providers that do not furnish therapy services.

The following "providers of services" must bill the FI for outpatient rehabilitation services using HCPCS codes:

- Hospitals (to outpatients and inpatients who are not in a covered Part A1 stay);

- Skilled nursing facilities (SNFs) (to residents not in a covered Part A1 stay and to nonresidents who receive outpatient rehabilitation services from the SNF);
- Home health agencies (HHAs) (to individuals who are not homebound or otherwise are not receiving services under a home health plan of care2 (POC);
- Comprehensive outpatient rehabilitation facilities (CORFs); and
- Providers of outpatient physical therapy and speech-language pathology services (OPTs), also known as rehabilitation agencies (previously termed outpatient physical therapy facilities in this instruction).

Note 1. The requirements for hospitals and SNFs apply to inpatient Part B and outpatient services only. Inpatient Part A services are bundled into the respective prospective payment system payment; no separate payment is made.

Note 2. For HHAs, HCPCS/CPT coding for outpatient rehabilitation services is required only when the HHA provides such service to individuals that are not homebound and, therefore, not under a home health plan of care.

The following practitioners must bill the carriers for outpatient rehabilitation therapy services using HCPCS/CPT codes:

- Physical therapists in private practice (PTPPs),
- Occupational therapists in private practice (OTPPs),
- Physicians, including MDs, DOs, podiatrists and optometrists, and
- Certain nonphysician practitioners (NPPs), acting within their State scope of practice, e.g., nurse practitioners and clinical nurse specialists.

Providers billing to intermediaries shall report:

- The date the therapy plan of care was either established or last reviewed (see Sec.220.1.3B) in Occurrence Code 17, 29, or 30.
- The first day of treatment in Occurrence Code 35, 44, or 45.

B. Applicable Outpatient Rehabilitation HCPCS Codes
The CMS identifies the following codes as therapy services, regardless of the presence of a financial limitation. Therapy services include only physical therapy, occupational therapy and speech-language pathology services. Therapist means only a physical therapist, occupational therapist or speech-language pathologist. Therapy modifiers are GP for physical therapy, GO for occupational therapy, and GN for speech-language pathology. Check the notes below the chart for details about each code.

When in effect, any financial limitation will also apply to services represented by the following codes, except as noted below.

NOTE: Listing of the following codes does not imply that services are covered or applicable to all provider settings.

64550+	90901+	92506¿	92507¿	92508	92526
92597	92605****	92606****	92607	92608	92609
92610+	92611+	92612+	92614+	92616+	95831+
95832+	95833+	95834+	95851+	95852+	95992****
96105+	96110+				

Pub. 100-4, Chapter 5, Section 100.10
Group Therapy Services (Code 97150)
Policies for group therapy services for CORF are the same as group therapy services for other Part B outpatient services. See Pub 100-02, chapter 15, section 230.

Pub. 100-4, Chapter 12, Section 30.6.14
Home Care and Domiciliary Care Visits (Codes 99324- 99350)
Physician Visits to Patients Residing in Various Places of Service
The American Medical Association's Current Procedural Terminology (CPT) 2006 new patient codes 99324 - 99328 and established patient codes 99334 - 99337(new codes beginning January 2006), for Domiciliary, Rest Home (e.g., Boarding Home), or Custodial Care Services, are used to report evaluation and management (E/M) services to residents residing in a facility which provides room, board, and other personal assistance services, generally on a long-term basis. These CPT codes are used to report E/M services in facilities assigned places of service (POS) codes 13 (Assisted Living Facility), 14 (Group Home), 33 (Custodial Care Facility) and 55 (Residential Substance Abuse Facility). Assisted living facilities may also be known as adult living facilities.

Physicians and qualified nonphysician practitioners (NPPs) furnishing E/M services to residents in a living arrangement described by one of the POS listed above must use the level of service code in the CPT code range 99324 - 99337 to report the service they provide. The CPT codes 99321 - 99333 for Domiciliary, Rest Home (e.g., Boarding Home), or Custodial Care Services are deleted beginning January, 2006.

Beginning in 2006, reasonable and medically necessary, face-to-face, prolonged services, represented by CPT codes 99354 - 99355, may be reported with the appropriate companion E/M codes when a physician or qualified NPP, provides a prolonged service involving direct (face-to-face) patient contact that is beyond the usual E/M visit service for a Domiciliary, Rest Home (e.g., Boarding Home) or Custodial Care Service. All the requirements for prolonged services at Sec.30.6.15.1 must be met.

The CPT codes 99341 through 99350, Home Services codes, are used to report E/M services furnished to a patient residing in his or her own private residence (e.g., private home, apartment, town home) and not residing in any type of congregate/shared facility living arrangement including assisted living facilities and group homes. The Home Services codes apply only to the specific 2-digit POS 12 (Home). Home Services codes may not be used for billing E/M services provided in settings other than in the private residence of an individual as described above.

Beginning in 2006, E/M services provided to patients residing in a Skilled Nursing Facility (SNF) or a Nursing Facility (NF) must be reported using the appropriate CPT level of service code within the range identified for Initial Nursing Facility Care (new CPT codes 99304 - 99306) and Subsequent Nursing Facility Care (new CPT codes 99307 - 99310). Use the CPT code, Other Nursing Facility Services (new CPT code 99318), for an annual nursing facility assessment. Use CPT codes 99315 - 99316 for SNF/NF discharge services. The CPT codes 99301 - 99303 and 99311 - 99313 are deleted beginning January, 2006. The Home Services codes should not be used for these places of service.

The CPT SNF/NF code definition includes intermediate care facilities (ICFs) and long term care facilities (LTCFs). These codes are limited to the specific 2-digit POS 31 (SNF), 32 (Nursing Facility), 54 (Intermediate Care Facility/Mentally Retarded) and 56 (Psychiatric Residential Treatment Center).

The CPT nursing facility codes should be used with POS 31 (SNF) if the patient is in a Part A SNF stay and POS 32 (nursing facility) if the patient does not have Part A SNF benefits. There is no longer a different payment amount for a Part A or Part B benefit period in these POS settings.

Pub. 100-4, Chapter 12, Section 30.6.14.1
Home Services (Codes 99341 - 99350)
B3-15515, B3-15066

A. Requirement for Physician Presence
Home services codes 99341-99350 are paid when they are billed to report evaluation and management services provided in a private residence. A home visit cannot be billed by a physician unless the physician was actually present in the beneficiary's home.

B. Homebound Status
Under the home health benefit the beneficiary must be confined to the home for services to be covered. For home services provided by a physician using these codes, the beneficiary does not need to be confined to the home. The medical record must document the medical necessity of the home visit made in lieu of an office or outpatient visit.

C. Fee Schedule Payment for Services to Homebound Patients under General Supervision
Payment may be made in some medically underserved areas where there is a lack of medical personnel and home health services for injections, EKGs, and venipunctures that are performed for homebound patients under general physician supervision by nurses and paramedical employees of physicians or physician-directed clinics. Section 10 provides additional information on the provision of services to homebound Medicare patients.

Pub. 100-4, Chapter 12, Section 150
Clinical Social Worker (CSW) Services
B3-2152, B3-17000 See Medicare Benefit Policy Manual, Chapter 15, for coverage requirements.

Assignment of benefits is required.

Payment is at 75 percent of the physician fee schedule.

CSWs are identified on the provider file by specialty code 80 and provider type 56.

Medicare applies the outpatient mental health limitation to all covered therapeutic services furnished by qualified CSWs. Refer to 210, below, for a discussion of the outpatient mental health limitation. The modifier "AJ" must be applied on CSN services.

Pub. 100-4, Chapter 12, Section 160
Independent Psychologist Services
B3-2150, B3-2070.2 See the Medicare Benefit Policy Manual, Chapter 15, for coverage requirements.

There are a number of types of psychologists. Educational psychologists engage in identifying and treating education-related issues. In contrast, counseling psychologists provide services that include a broader realm including phobias, familial issues, etc.

Psychometrists are psychologists who have been trained to administer and interpret tests.

However, clinical psychologists are defined as a provider of diagnostic and therapeutic services. Because of the differences in services provided, services provided by psychologists who do not provide clinical services are subject to different billing guidelines. One service often provided by nonclinical psychologist is diagnostic testing.

NOTE:Diagnostic psychological testing services performed by persons who meet these requirements are covered as other diagnostic tests. When, however, the psychologist is not practicing independently, but is on the staff of an institution, agency, or clinic, that entity bills for the diagnostic services.

Expenses for such testing are not subject to the payment limitation on treatment for mental, psychoneurotic, and personality disorders. Independent psychologists are not required by law to accept assignment when performing psychological tests. However, regardless of whether the psychologist accepts assignment, he or she must report on the claim form the name and address of the physician who ordered the test.

Glossary

* Starred definitions printed with permission from the *Guide to Physical Therapist Practice*, 2nd ed. <u>Phys Ther</u>, 2001; 81:9-744

abduction
Pulling away from a central reference line, such as moving away from the midline of the body.

aberrant
Deviation or departure from the normal or usual course, condition, or pattern.

ablation
Removal or destruction of tissue by cutting, electrical energy, chemical substances, or excessive heat application.

abrasion
Removal of layers of the skin occurring as a superficial injury, or a procedure for removal of problematic skin or skin lesions.

abscess
Circumscribed collection of pus resulting from bacteria, frequently associated with swelling and other signs of inflammation.

absorbable sutures
Strands prepared from collagen or a synthetic polymer and capable of being absorbed by tissue over time.

abuse
In medical reimbursement, an incident that is inconsistent with accepted medical, business, or fiscal practices and directly or indirectly results in unnecessary costs to the Medicare program, improper reimbursement, or reimbursement for services that do not meet professionally recognized standards of care or which are medically unnecessary. Examples of abuse include excessive charges, improper billing practices, billing Medicare as primary instead of other third-party payers that are primary, and increasing charges for Medicare beneficiaries but not to other patients.

Achilles tendon
The tendon attached to the back of the heel bone (calcaneus) that flexes the foot downward.

acquired
Produced by outside influences and not by genetics or birth defect.

acromioplasty
Repair of the part of the shoulder blade that connects to the deltoid muscles and clavicle.

activities of daily living
Self-care activities often used to determine a patient's level of function such as bathing, dressing, using a toilet, transferring in and out of bed or a chair, continence, eating, and walking.

acute
Sudden, severe. Documentation and reporting of an acute condition is important to establishing medical necessity.

acute lymphadenitis
Sudden, severe inflammation, infection, and swelling in lymphatic tissue.

add-on code
CPT code representing a procedure performed in addition to the primary procedure and designated with a + in the CPT book. Add-on codes are never reported for stand-alone services but are reported secondarily in addition to the primary procedure.

adduction
Pulling toward a central reference line, such as toward the midline of the body.

adhesion
Abnormal fibrous connection between two structures, soft tissue or bony structures, that may occur as the result of surgery, infection, or trauma.

advance beneficiary notice
Written communication with a Medicare beneficiary given before Part B services are rendered, informing the patient that the provider believes that Medicare will not pay for some or all of the services to be rendered. Form CMS-R-131-G is a general form that may be used for all services. Form CMS-R-131-L is for use only when laboratory services are rendered.

algoneurodystrophy
Neuropathy of the peripheral nervous system.

alignment
Establishment of a straight line or harmonious relationship between structures.

alloplastic
Inert, nonbiological material, such as plastic or metal, implanted into tissues to construct, augment, or reconstruct a body part, or synthetic materials applied immediately following an excisional procedure to enable the wound to generate new skin without the additional autografting procedures.

alternative delivery system
Any health care delivery system other than traditional fee-for-service.

amputation
Removal of all or part of a limb or digit through the shaft or body of a bone.

aneurysmal bone cyst
Solitary bone lesion that bulges into the periosteum, marked by a calcified rim.

angiodysplasia
Vascular abnormalities, with or without bleeding.

angioplasty
Reconstruction or repair of a diseased or damaged blood vessel.

ankylosis
Abnormal union or fusion of bones in a joint, which is normally moveable.

Glossary

anterior — Situated in the front area or toward the belly surface of the body; an anatomical reference point used to show the position and relationship of one body structure to another.

anterolateral — Situated in the front and off to one side.

anteromedial — Situated in the front and to the side of the central point or midline.

anteroposterior — Front to back.

anticoagulant — Substance that reduces or eradicates the blood's ability to clot.

appeal — Specific request made to a payer for reconsideration of a denial or adverse coverage or payment decision and potential restriction of benefit reimbursement.

appliance — Device providing function to a body part.

arthrocentesis — Puncture and aspiration of fluid from a joint for diagnostic or therapeutic purposes or injection of anesthetics or corticosteroids.

arthrodesis — Surgical fixation or fusion of a joint to reduce pain and improve stability, performed openly or arthroscopically.

arthrogram — X-ray of a joint after the injection of contrast material.

arthrography — Radiographic study of a joint and its internal structures. Air or contrast medium is injected into the joint just before the images are taken.

arthroplasty — Surgical reconstruction of a joint to improve function and reduce pain; may involve partial or total joint replacement.

arthrotomy — Surgical incision into a joint that may include exploration, drainage, or removal of a foreign body.

aseptic necrosis — Death of bone tissue resulting from a disruption in the vascular supply, caused by a noninfectious disease process, such as a fracture or the administration of immunosuppressive drugs.

aspirate — To withdraw fluid or air from a body cavity by suction.

assessment — Process of collecting and studying information and data, such as test values, signs, and symptoms.

assigned claim — Claim from a physician or supplier who has agreed to accept the Medicare allowable amount as payment in full for the services rendered. Reimbursement is made directly to the provider of the service.

assignment of benefits — Authorization from the patient allowing the third-party payer to pay the provider directly for medical services. Under Medicare, an assignment is an agreement by the hospital or physician to accept Medicare's payment as the full payment and not to bill the patient for any amounts over the allowance amount, except for deductible and/or coinsurance amounts or noncovered services.

assistive devices — Variety of implements or equipment used to aid patients in performing actions, activities, movements, or tasks.

atony — Absence of normal muscle tone and strength.

atrophy — Reduction in size or activity in an anatomic structure, due to wasting away from disease or other factors.

autograft — Any tissue harvested from one anatomical site of a person and grafted to another anatomical site of the same person. Most commonly, blood vessels, skin, tendons, fascia, and bone are used as autografts.

avulsion — Forcible tearing away of a part, by surgical means or traumatic injury.

axon — Extension from a neuron that carries impulses to receiving terminal branches.

balance billing — Arrangement prohibited in Medicare regulations and some payer contracts whereby a provider bills the patient for charges not reimbursed by the payer.

Bell's palsy — Facial paralysis or weakness resulting from facial nerve damage. The muscles on one side of the face are affected, causing the face to sag on the side involved. Bell's palsy usually occurs abruptly and often resolves spontaneously within a few weeks.

beneficiary — Person entitled to receive Medicare or other payer benefits who maintains a health insurance policy claim number.

bicipital tenosynovitis — Inflammatory condition affecting the bicipital tendon.

brachial plexus lesions — Acquired defect in tissues along the network of nerves in the shoulder, causing corresponding motor and sensory dysfunction.

bundled — Inclusive grouping of codes related to a procedure when submitting a claim.

bursa — Cavity or sac containing fluid that occurs between articulating surfaces and serves to reduce friction from moving parts.

bursectomy — Surgical excision of a bursa, a fluid-filled cavity or sac that reduces friction between neighboring, moving parts.

bursitis — Inflammation of a bursa.

calcifying tendinitis — Inflammation and hardening of tissue due to calcium salt deposits, occurring in the tendons and areas of tendonomuscular attachment.

cancellous bone — Bone found mostly in the midshaft of long bones that is spongy and porous with a lattice-like construction.

capsulectomy — Surgical excision of a joint capsule made of cartilage, fibrous, or fatty tissue.

capsulorrhaphy — Suturing or repair of a joint capsule.

capsulotomy — Incision of a joint capsule.

carcinoma in situ — Malignancy that arises from the cells of the vessel, gland, or organ of origin that remains confined to that site or has not invaded neighboring tissue.

carpal tunnel syndrome — Swelling and inflammation in the tendons or bursa surrounding the median nerve caused by repetitive activity. The resulting compression on the nerve causes pain, numbness, and tingling especially to the palm, index, middle finger, and thumb.

case management — Ongoing review of cases by professionals to assure the most appropriate utilization of services

cauda equina — Spinal roots occupying the lower end of the vertebral canal and descending from the distal end of the spinal cord, named for their appearance resembling that of the tail of a horse.

causalgia — Condition due to an injury of a peripheral nerve causing burning pain and possible trophic skin changes.

cellulitis — Sudden, severe, suppurative inflammation and edema in subcutaneous tissue or muscle, most often caused by bacterial infection secondary to a cutaneous lesion.

Centers for Medicare and Medicaid Services — Federal agency that oversees the administration of the public health programs such as Medicare, Medicaid, and State Children's Insurance Program.

cervicalgia — Pain localized to the cervical region, generally referring to the posterior or lateral regions of the neck.

cervicobrachial syndrome — Neuropathy of the brachial plexus causing pain leading from the neck and radiating down the arm.

cheilectomy — Chiseling off an irregular bony edge from a joint cavity, usually performed because the body edge interferes with motion of the joint.

cineplastic amputation — Amputation in which muscles and tendons of the remaining portion of the extremity are arranged so that they may be utilized for motor functions. Following this type of amputation, a specially constructed prosthetic device allows the individual to execute more complex movements because the muscles and tendons are able to communicate independent movements to the device.

classification of surgical wounds — Surgical wounds fall into four categories that determine treatment methods and outcomes: 1) Clean wound: No inflammation or contamination; treatment performed with no break in sterile technique; no alimentary, respiratory, or genitourinary tracts involved in the surgery; infection rate = up to five percent. 2) Clean-contaminated wound: No inflammation; treatment performed with minor break in surgical technique; no unusual contamination resulting when alimentary, respiratory, genitourinary, or oropharyngeal cavity is entered; infection rate = up to 11 percent. 3) Contaminated wound: Less than four hours old with acute, nonpurulent inflammation; treatment performed with major break in surgical technique; gross contamination resulting from the gastrointestinal tract; infection rate = up to 20 percent. 4) Dirty and infected wound: More than four hours old with existing infection, inflammation, abscess, and nonsterile conditions due to perforated viscus, fecal contamination, necrotic tissue, or foreign body; infection rate = up to 40 percent.

claudication — Lameness, pain, and weakness occurring in the arms or legs during exercise due to muscles not receiving the needed oxygen and nutrients.

closed dislocation — Simple displacement of a body part without an open wound.

closed fracture — Break in a bone without a concomitant opening in the skin.

closed reduction — Treatment of a fracture by manipulating it into proper alignment without opening the skin.

closed treatment — Realignment of a fracture or dislocation without surgically opening the skin to reach the site. Treatment methods employed include with or without manipulation, and with or without traction.

CMS Manual System	Web-based manuals organized by functional area that contains all program instructions in the *National Coverage Determinations Manual*, the *Medicare Benefit Policy Manual*, Pub. 100, one-time notifications, and manual revision notices.
comminuted fracture	Any type of fracture in which the bone is splintered or crushed, resulting in multiple bone fragments.
compliance officer	Individual in charge of compliance activities within the business. Should have sufficient authority, funding, and staff to perform necessary activities, including planning, implementing, and monitoring the compliance program.
compliance plan	Plan of established methods to eliminate errors in coding, billing, and other issues through auditing and monitoring, training, or other corrective actions. Such a plan also provides an avenue for employees and others to report problems.
conditional payment	Medicare payment requested by the provider for a claim for which Medicare is the secondary payer, but the provider anticipates a lengthy processing delay (more than 120 days) by the primary payer due to third-party liability. Once payment is received from the true primary payer, a refund or request for reconsideration must be issued to Medicare within 60 days.
condyle	Rounded end of a bone that forms an articulation.
connective tissue	Body tissue made from fibroblasts, collagen, and elastic fibrils that connects, supports, and holds together other tissues and cells and includes cartilage, collagenous, fibrous, elastic, and osseous tissue.
Consolidated Omnibus Budget Reconciliation Act (COBRA)	Federal law that allows and requires past employees to be covered under company health insurance plans for a set premium, allowing individuals to remain insured when their current plan or position has been terminated.
consultation	Advice or an opinion regarding diagnosis and treatment of a patient rendered by a medical professional at the request of the primary care provider.
coordination of benefits	Agreement that prevents double payment for services when the member is covered by two or more sources. The agreement dictates which organization is primarily and secondarily responsible for payment.
cordotomy	Surgical interruption of the spinal cord, usually for the relief of intractable pain.
CORF	Comprehensive outpatient rehabilitation facility. Facility that provides services that include physician's services related to administrative functions; physical, occupational, speech and respiratory therapies; social and psychological services; and prosthetic and orthotic devices. A service is covered as a CORF service if it is also covered as an inpatient hospital service provided to a hospital patient. CORF services require a plan of treatment within a maximum of 60-day intervals for rereviews.
Current Procedural Terminology	Definitive procedural coding system developed by the American Medical Association that lists descriptive terms and identifying codes to provide a uniform language that describes medical, surgical, and diagnostic services for nationwide communication among physicians, patients, and third parties.
Correct Coding Initiative	Official list of codes from the Centers for Medicare and Medicaid Services' (CMS) National Correct Coding Policy Manual for Part B Medicare Carriers that identifies services considered either an integral part of a comprehensive code or mutually exclusive of it.
covered services	Diagnostic or treatment services that are considered medically necessary and met coverage and program guidelines.
coxa valga	Hip joint deformity in which there is a lateral deviation.
coxa vara	Hip joint deformity in which there is a medial deviation.
CPT codes	Codes maintained and copyrighted by the AMA and selected for use under HIPAA for noninstitutional and nondental professional transactions.
CPT modifier	Two-character code used to indicate that a service was altered in some way from the stated CPT or HCPCS Level II description, but not enough to change the basic definition of the service.
debridement	Removal of dead or contaminated tissue and foreign matter from a wound.
deductible	Predetermined dollar amount of covered billed charges that the patient must pay toward the cost of care.
dehiscence	Complication of healing in which the surgical wound ruptures or bursts open, superficially or through multiple layers.
denervation	Resection or removal of a nerve.

denial	Refusal by an insurance plan to pay for services, procedures, or supplies. A denial may be made due to coverage limitations, medical necessity issues, or failure to follow appropriate prior authorization or claim submission guidelines.	**examination**	Comprehensive visual and tactile screening and specific testing leading to diagnosis or, as appropriate, to a referral to another practitioner.
diagnosis	Determination or confirmation of a condition, disease, or syndrome and its implications.	**expected outcomes**	Intended results of patient/client management, which indicate the changes in impairments, functional limitations, and disabilities and the changes in health, wellness, and fitness needs that are expected as the result of implementing the plan of care.
diplegia	Paralytic loss or impairment of motor function affecting like parts on both sides of the body (e.g., both arms or both legs).	**extravasation**	Escape of fluid from a vessel into the surrounding tissue.
distal	Located farther away from a specified reference point.	**exudate**	Fluid or other material, such as debris from cells, that has escaped blood vessel circulation and is deposited in or on tissues and usually occurs due to inflammation.
dorsal	Pertaining to the back or posterior aspect.		
dorsiflexion	Position of being bent toward the extensor side of a limb.	**face to face**	Interaction between two parties, usually provider and patient, that occurs in the physical presence of each other.
Dupuytren's contracture	Shortening of the palmar fascia resulting in flexion deformity of a finger.	**flexion**	Act of bending or being bent.
DuToit staple capsulorrhaphy	Reattachment of the capsule of the shoulder and glenoid labrum to the glenoid lip using staples to anchor the avulsed capsule and glenoid labrum.	**flexor**	Muscle/tendon that bends or flexes a limb or part as opposed to extending it.
dynamic	Manifesting motion in response to force.	**focused medical review**	The process of targeting and directing medical review efforts on Medicare claims where the greatest risk of inappropriate program payment exists. The goal is to reduce the number of noncovered claims or unnecessary services. CMS analyzes national data such as internal billing, utilization and payment data and provides its findings to the fiscal intermediary (FI). Local medical review policies are developed identifying aberrances, abuse, and overutilized services. Providers are responsible for knowing national Medicare coverage and billing guidelines and local medical review policies, and for determining whether the services provided to Medicare beneficiaries are covered by Medicare.
effusion	Escape of fluid from within a body cavity.		
electronic data interchange	Transference of claims, certifications, quality assurance reviews, and utilization data via computer in X12 format. May refer to any electronic exchange of formatted data.		
epicondyle	Bony protrusion at the distal end of the humerus (elbow).		
epicondylitis	Inflammation of the humeral epicondyle and the tissues adjoining it.		
epithelial tissue	Cells arranged in sheets that cover internal and external body surfaces that can absorb, protect, and/or secrete and includes the protective covering for external surfaces (skin), absorptive linings for internal surfaces such as the intestine, and secreting structures such as salivary or sweat glands.	**fourth and fifth digits**	Digits used in the ICD-9-CM coding system to provide more specific information about the diagnosis or procedure being coded. Certain ICD-9-CM codes require a fourth and fifth digit in order to be complete.
eschar	Leathery slough produced by burns.		
escharotomy	Surgical incision into the scab or crust resulting from a severe burn in order to relieve constriction and allow blood flow to the distal unburned tissue.	**fracture types**	There are three basic degrees of fracture: type I: a small crack in the bone without displacement; type II: a fracture in which the bone is slightly displaced; type III: a fracture in which there are more than three broken pieces of bone that cannot fit together.
evaluation	Dynamic process in which the physical, occupational, sports, or other therapist makes clinical judgments based on data gathered during the examination.		

fraud
Intentional deception or misrepresentation or statement that is known to be false and could result in unauthorized benefit to patient, provider or other persons.

function
Special, normal, or proper action of any part or organ, including activities identified by an individual as essential to supporting physical and psychological well-being, as well as to creating a personal sense of meaningful living.

functional assessment
Measurement or quantification of those activities identified by an individual as essential to support physical, social, and psychological well-being and to create a personal sense of meaningful living.

functional training
Education and training of patients/clients in activities of daily living (ADL) and instrumental activities of daily living (IADL) that are intended to improve the ability to perform physical actions, tasks, or activities in an efficient, typically expected, or competent manner.

gait
Manner in which a person walks.

gait analysis
Correlation of clinical findings and biomedical measures to determine the cause of a patient's postural and movement impairments when walking.

gait training
Procedural intervention to restore normal stance, balance, arm and leg swing, speed, and sequence of muscle contractions for walking. May also include teaching the patient to use an assistive device.

Galeazzi fracture
Break of the radius proximal to the wrist with a distal ulnar dislocation.

ganglion
Fluid-filled, benign cyst appearing on a tendon sheath or aponeurosis, frequently found in the hand, wrist, or foot and connecting to an underlying joint.

gangrene
Death of tissue, usually resulting from a loss of vascular supply, followed by a bacterial attack or onset of disease.

GPCI
Geographic practice cost indexes. Cost indexes used to adjust for differences among geographic areas. Under the resource-based relative value scale, there are three GPCIs for each locality, one for work, practice expense, and malpractice.

granulation tissue
Loose collection of fibroblasts, inflammatory cells, and new vessels in an edematous fleshy projection that forms at the base of open wounds over which new skin forms, unless excessive granulation tissue, or proud flesh, rises above the wound surface.

health care provider
Entity that administers diagnostic and therapeutic services.

HIPAA
Health Insurance Portability and Accountability Act of 1996. Federal law that allows persons to qualify immediately for comparable health insurance coverage when they change their employment relationships.

ICD-10
International Classification of Diseases, Tenth Revision. Classification of diseases by alphanumeric code, used by the World Health Organization.

ICD-10-CM
International Classification of Diseases, Tenth Edition, Clinical Modification. Diagnostic coding system developed to replace ICD-9-CM in the United States. It is a clinical modification of the World Health Organization's ICD-10, already in use in much of the world, and used for mortality reporting in the United States. The implementation date for ICD-10-CM has not yet been set.

ICD-10-PCS
New procedural coding system developed under contract with the Centers for Medicare and Medicaid Services (CMS) by 3M HIS.

ICD-9-CM
International Classification of Diseases, Ninth Edition, Clinical Modification. Clinical modification of the international statistical coding system used to report, compile, and compare health care data, using numeric and alphanumeric codes to help plan, deliver, reimburse, and quantify medical care in the United States.

impairment
Loss or abnormality of anatomical, physiological, mental, or psychological structure or function. Secondary impairment originates from other, preexisting impairments.

intervention
Purposeful interaction of the physical therapist with the patient and, when appropriate, with other individuals involved in patient care, using various physical therapy procedures and techniques to produce changes in the condition.

iontophoresis	Method of localized transdermal medication delivery using a low-level electrical current applied to a drug solution in a patch. The drug ions are propelled through the skin into underlying tissue. Iontophoresis is used to alleviate joint or muscle pain in sports medicine. It is also the method used for introducing pilocarpine in the sweat test for cystic fibrosis and as a treatment for hyperhidrosis.
kinetics	Motion or movement.
K-wires	Steel wires for skeletal fixation of fractured bones, inserted through soft tissue and bones.
kyphosis	Abnormal posterior convex curvature of the spine, usually in the thoracic region, resembling a hunchback.
Kyphoscoliosis	Combined posterior convexity and lateral curvature of the spine.
level of specificity	Diagnosis coding specificity (i.e., a three-digit disease code is assigned only when there are no four-digit codes within that category, a four-digit code is assigned only when there is no fifth-digit subclassification within that category, or a fifth digit is assigned for any category for which a fifth-digit subclassification is provided).
limitation of liability	Signed waiver a provider must obtain from the patient before performing a service that appears on a list of services Medicare classifies as medically unnecessary. The waiver notifies the patient in advance that the service may be denied coverage and that the patient is responsible for payment.
limiting charge	Maximum amount a nonparticipating physician or provider can charge for services to a Medicare patient.
linking codes	To establish medical necessity, CPT and HCPCS Level II codes must be supported by the ICD-9-CM diagnosis and injury codes submitted on the claim form and supported by the documentation.
lumbosacral plexus lesions	Acquired defect in tissue along the network of nerves in the lower back, causing corresponding motor and sensory dysfunction.
mallet finger	Congenital or acquired flexion deformity of the terminal interphalangeal joint that causes bowing of the fingertip and an inability to extend the fingertip.
malunion	Fracture that has united in a faulty position due to inadequate reduction of the original fracture, insufficient holding of a previously well-reduced fracture, contracture of the soft tissues, or comminuted or osteoporotic bone causing a slow disintegration of the fracture.
manipulation	Skillful treatment by hand to reduce fractures and dislocations, or provide therapy through forceful passive movement of a joint beyond its active limit of motion.
manual therapy techniques	Skilled hand movements intended to improve tissue extensibility; increase range of motion; induce relaxation; mobilize or manipulate soft tissue and joints; modulate pain; and reduce soft tissue swellling, inflammation, or restriction.
medical necessity	Medically appropriate and necessary to meet basic health needs; consistent with the diagnosis or condition and rendered in a cost-effective manner; and consistent with national medical practice guidelines regarding type, frequency, and duration of treatment.
medical review	Review by a Medicare fiscal intermediary, carrier and/or quality improvement organization (QIO) of services and items provided by physicians, other health care practitioners, and providers of health care services under Medicare. The review determines if the items and services are reasonable and necessary and meet Medicare coverage requirements, whether the quality meets professionally recognized standards of health care, and whether the services are medically appropriate in an inpatient, outpatient, or other setting as supported by documentation.
Medicare Fee Schedule	Fee schedule based upon physician work, expense, and malpractice designed to slow the rise in cost for services and standardize payment to physicians regardless of specialty or location of service with geographic adjustments.

Glossary

Medicare secondary payer	Specified circumstance when other third-party payers have the primary responsibility for payment of services and Medicare is the secondary payer. Medicare is secondary to workers' compensation and automobile, medical no-fault, and liability insurance, EGHPs, LGHPs, and certain employer health plans covering aged and disabled beneficiaries. The MSP program prohibits Medicare payment for items or services if payment has been made or can reasonably be expected to be made by another payer, as described above.
Medigap	Individual health insurance offered by a private entity to those persons entitled to Medicare benefits and is specifically designed to supplement Medicare benefits. It fills in some of the gaps in Medicare coverage by providing payment for some of the charges, deductibles, coinsurance amounts, or other limitations imposed by Medicare.
meralgia paresthetica	Neurologic disorder due to constriction of the lateral femoral cutaneous nerve as it exits the pelvis, manifested by tingling, lack of sensation, and burning pain of the outer thigh. It is often associated with obesity, diabetes, pregnancy, or restrictive clothing.
Minerva jacket	Spinal cast or brace that includes a sternal plate, dorsal plate, bonnet, and mandible piece attached to the superstructure of the sternal plate for cervical or high thoracic stability.
mobilization	Therapy that consists of small passive movements, usually applied as a series of gentle stretches in a smooth, rhythmic fashion to the individual vertebrae. The movements are applied at various locations on each of the affected vertebrae, and at various angles, directed at relieving restriction in movement at any particular level of the spine. Mobilization stretches stiff joints to restore range. It also relieves pain. For example, it is especially effective with arthritic joints. Report mobilization with CPT code 97140.
modality	Form of imaging. These include x-ray, fluoroscopy, ultrasound, nuclear medicine, duplex Doppler, CT, and MRI.
modifier	Two-character code attached to a HCPCS code as a suffix to identify circumstances that alter or enhance the description of a service or supply.
mononeuritis	Inflammation of one nerve.
mononeuritis multiplex	Peripheral neuropathy involving isolated damage to at least two separate nerves.
monoplegia	Loss or impairment of motor function in one arm or one leg.
Monteggia's fracture	Break in the proximal half of the ulnar shaft accompanied by a dislocation of the radial head.
motor control	Ability of the central nervous system to control or direct the neuromotor system in purposeful movement and postural adjustment by selective allocation of muscle tension across appropriate joint segments.
motor function	Ability to learn or demonstrate skillful and efficient assumption, maintenance, modification, and control of voluntary postures and movement patterns.
motor learning	Processes associated with practice or experience leading to relatively permanent changes in the capability for producing skilled action.
multiplane external fixation device	Stabilization device that uses more than one external fixation system to stabilize a fracture.
myasthenia gravis	Autoimmune neuromuscular disorder caused by antibodies to the acetylcholine receptors at the neuromuscular junction, interfering with proper binding of the neurotransmitter from the neuron to the target muscle, causing muscle weakness, fatigue, and exhaustion, without pain or atrophy.
myopathy	Any disease process within muscle tissue.
myositis	Inflammation of a muscle with voluntary movement.
myositis ossificans	Inflammatory disease of muscles due to bony deposits or conversion of muscle tissue to bony tissue.
national coverage policy	Statement of Medicare coverage decisions that applies to all practitioners in states and regions. These policies indicate whether and under what circumstances procedures, services, and supplies are covered.
neuralgia	Sharp, shooting pains extending along one or more nerve pathways. Underlying causes may include nerve injury, diabetes, or viral complications.
neurectomy	Excision of all or a portion of a nerve.
neuritis	Inflammation of a nerve or group of nerves, often manifested by loss of function and reflexes, pain, and numbness or tingling.

© 2008 Ingenix

osteoarthrosis — Most common form of a noninflammatory degenerative joint disease with degenerating articular cartilage, bone enlargement, and synovial membrane changes.

osteochondritis dissecans — Inflammation of the bone and cartilage that results in splinters or pieces of cartilage breaking off in the joint.

osteochondropathy — Any condition in which the bone and cartilage are affected, or in which endochondral ossification occurs.

osteochondrosis — Disease manifested by degeneration or necrosis of the growth plate or ossification centers of bones in children, followed by regenerating and reossification.

osteomyelitis — Inflammation of bone that may remain localized or spread to the marrow, cortex, or periosteum, in response to an infecting organism, usually bacterial and pyogenic.

osteophytes — Bony outgrowth.

out of plan — In health care contracting, services of a provider who is not a member of the preferred provider network.

outpatient physical therapy service — Physical therapy service provided to an outpatient of a hospital, clinic, CORF, rehabilitation agency, or public health agency. The attending physician must establish a plan of physical therapy or periodically review a plan developed by a qualified physical therapist. The term outpatient physical therapy services also includes physical therapy services provided by a physical therapist in office or at the patient's home and speech-language pathology services.

palmar flexion — Bending of the hand with the fingers toward the palm.

palmaris longus tendon — Tendon located in the hand that flexes the wrist joint.

participating provider — In health care contracting, provider who has contracted with the health plan to deliver medical services to covered persons.

patient education — Method or process of teaching a patient about his or her health and how to manage or treat any conditions or diagnoses the patient may have.

peer review — Evaluation of the quality of the total health care provided by medical staff with equivalent training, such as physician-to-physician or nurse-to-nurse evaluation.

periosteum — Double-layered connective membrane on the outer surface of bone.

peroneal muscular atrophy — Weakness and reduction in size of the muscles in the hands and lower limbs.

phonophoresis — Use of ultrasound to increase the diffusion of a drug into the skin.

physical agents — Broad group of procedures using various forms of energy that are applied to tissues in a systematic manner and that are intended to increase connective tissue extensibility; increase the healing rate of open wounds and soft tissue; modulate pain; reduce or eliminate soft tissue swelling, inflammation, or restriction associated with musculoskeletal injury or circulatory dysfunction; remodel scar tissue; or treat skin conditions. These agents may include athermal, cryotherapy, hydrotherapy, light, sound, and thermotherapy agents.

physical therapy/ physiotherapy — Physical therapy is examination, evaluation, diagnosis, prognosis, and intervention provided by physical therapists/physiotherapists. Physical therapy includes diagnosis and management of movement dysfunction and enhancement of physical and functional abilities; restoration, maintenance, and promotion of optimal physical function, optimal fitness and wellness, and optimal quality of life as it relates to movement and health; and prevention of the onset, symptoms, and progression of impairments, functional limitations, and disabilities that may result from diseases, disorders, conditions, or injuries. The terms physical therapy and physiotherapy are synonymous.

plica syndrome — Pain and swelling of the knee joint and often a snapping sensation upon bending, due to a fold in the lining of the joint resulting from injury or overuse.

polyneuropathy — Disease process of severe inflammation of multiple nerves.

preexisting condition — Symptom that causes a person to seek diagnosis, care, or treatment for which medical advice or treatment was recommended or received by a physician within a certain time period before the effective date of medical insurance coverage. The preexisting condition waiting period is the time the beneficiary must wait after buying health insurance before coverage begins for a condition that existed before coverage was obtained.

principal diagnosis	Condition established after study to be chiefly responsible for occasioning the admission of the patient to the hospital for care.	**relative value unit**	Value assigned a procedure based on difficulty and time consumed. Used for computing reimbursement under a relative value study.
principal procedure	Procedure performed for definitive treatment rather than for diagnostic or exploratory purposes, or that was necessary to treat a complication. Usually related to the principal diagnosis.	**Risser jacket**	Extended body cast with hinges and buckles that covers the neck, extends down to one knee, and sometimes includes an arm to the elbow. This is applied in cases of scoliosis.
qui tam actions	Legal action against an individual or entity believed to be involved in fraud against the government. Under the False Claims Act, any individual who has such knowledge can file a lawsuit in his or her own name and in the name of the United States government. An employee usually brings these types of lawsuits for actions he or she believes constitute fraud or abuse on the part of the employer.	**rule of nines**	Rapid measurement system used to calculate the total body surface area (TBSA) involved in burns, based upon dividing the total area into segments as multiples of 9 percent. The perineum or external genitals are 1 percent; each arm is 9 percent; the front and back of the trunk, and each leg are separately counted as 18 percent; and the head is another 9 percent in adults. For infants and children, the head is 18 percent involvement and the legs are 14 percent each, due to the larger surface area of a child's head in proportion to the body.
radiculitis	Pain along an inflamed nerve, with inflammation of the root of the associated spinal nerve.		
range of motion	Action of a body part throughout its extent of natural movement, measured in degrees of a circle.	**second-degree burn**	Deep partial-thickness burn with destruction of the epidermis, the upper portion of the dermis, possibly some deeper dermal tissues, and blistering of the skin with fluid exudate.
Raynaud's syndrome	Constriction of the arteries of the digits caused by cold or emotion. Temperature drops in extremities as much as 30 degrees Fahrenheit, and skin turns white with red and blue mottling. Caused by nerve or arterial damage and can be prompted by stress.	**self-disclosure**	Admitting or providing information that an individual or entity has performed an act that is improper or illegal.
		self-funding	Health care program in which employers fund benefit plans from their own resources without purchasing insurance. May be self-administered, or the employer may contract with an outside administrator.
RBRVS	Resource-based relative value scale. Fee schedule introduced by CMS to reimburse physician Medicare fees based on the amount of time and resources expended in treating patients with adjustments for overhead costs and geographical differences.	**sensory integration**	Ability to integrate information that is derived from the environment and that relates to movement.
reduction	Restoration to normal position or alignment.	**separate procedures**	Services commonly carried out as a fundamental part of a total service, and as such usually do not warrant a separate identification. They are noted in the CPT book with the parenthetical phrase (separate procedure) at the end of the description, and are payable only when they are performed alone.
referral	Approval from the primary care physician to see a specialist or receive certain services. May be required for coverage purposes before a patient receives care from anyone except the primary physician.		
reinnervation	Restoration of nerve function.	**spasmodic torticollis**	Neck muscle spasms and cervical dystonia, resulting in the head becoming inclined toward the affected side and the face toward the opposite side.
relative value scale	Ranking of all physician services based on the intensity of the procedure or service being performed. Relative value unit (RVU) is a specific value assigned to a procedure that is multiplied by a dollar conversion factor to determine a monetary value for the procedure.	**spica**	Figure-eight wrapped bandage, usually at the shoulder or hip.

spina bifida	Lack of closure in the vertebral column with protrusion of the spinal cord through the defect, often in the lumbosacral area. This condition can be recognized by the presence of alpha-fetoproteins in the amniotic fluid and may present alone or in conjunction with other anomalies, and with or without hydrocephalus. Spina bifida is reported with a code from ICD-9-CM category 741, with a mandatory fifth digit specifying the location of the lesion.	**tarsal tunnel syndrome**	Entrapment or compression of the posterior tibial nerve, causing tingling, pain, and numbness in the sole of the foot.
		tenosynovectomy	Excision of a tendon sheath.
		tenosynovitis	Inflammation of a tendon sheath due to infection or disease.
		tenotomy	Cutting into a tendon.
		therapeutic exercise	Systematic performance or execution of planned physical movements, postures, or activities intended to enable the patient to remediate or prevent impairments, enhance function, reduce risk, optimize overall health, and enhance fitness and well-being.
spinal stenosis	Narrowing of the canal (vertebral or nerve root) or intervertebral foramina of the lumbar spine.		
spondylolisthesis	Forward displacement of one vertebra slipping over another, usually in the fourth or fifth lumbar area.	**third-degree burn**	Full-thickness burn with total destruction of the epidermis and dermis, while deeper underlying tissue may also be affected, including the loss of body parts (e.g., nose, ear, extremity).
sternocleidomastoid	Large superficial muscle that passes obliquely across the anterolateral neck, originating at the sternum and clavicle and inserting at the mastoid process of the temporal bone.		
		torticollis	Twisted, unnatural position of the neck due to contracted cervical muscles that pull the head to one side.
subluxation	Partial or complete dislocation.	**traction**	Drawing out or holding tension on an area by applying a direct therapeutic pulling force.
superbill	Multipurpose sheet used for all patient encounters that typically contains a check-off list of ICD-9-CM diagnosis codes, evaluation and management codes, and procedure and HCPCS Level II codes in the outpatient setting.		
		transverse	Crosswise at right angles to the long axis of a structure or part.
		traumatic amputation	Removal of a part or limb from accidental injury.
supination	Lying on the back; turning the palm toward the front or upward; raising the medial margin of the foot by an inverting and adducting movement.	**turnbuckle jacket**	Spinal cast of plaster and hinges applied from the chin and base of the skull down past one thigh, sometimes including one arm, used in the correction of spinal curvature.
symphysis	Joint that unifies two opposed bones by a junction of bony surfaces to a plate of fibrocartilage.		
		unbundling	Separately packaging costs or services that might otherwise be billed together including billing separately for health care services that should be combined according to the industry standards or commonly accepted coding practices.
synchondrosis	Two bones joined by hyaline cartilage or fibrocartilage. Typically, the bones fuse as they mature.		
syndactyly	Fusion or webbing of two or more digits.		
synostosis	Unnatural fusion of bones that are normally separate or articulate with each other, due to growth of bony tissue between them.	**uniplane external fixation device**	Type of stabilization device that uses one external fixation system to stabilize a fracture.
		unspecified	Term in ICD-9-CM that indicates more information is necessary to code the term to further specificity. In these cases, the fourth digit of the code is always 9.
synovia	Clear fluid lubricant of joints, bursae, and tendon sheaths, secreted by the synovial membrane.		
synovitis	Inflammation of the synovial membrane that lines a synovial joint, resulting in pain and swelling.	**usual, customary, and reasonable**	Fees charged for medical services that are considered normal, common, and in line with the prevailing fees in a given geographical area.
tarsal bones	Seven bones that make up the ankle and heel consisting of the posterior talus and calcaneus, the anterior cuboid, navicular, and three cuneiform (medial, intermediate, and lateral) bones.		

Glossary

CPT codes only © 2008 American Medical Association. All Rights Reserved.

utilization review	Formal assessment of the medical necessity, efficiency, and/or appropriateness of health care services and treatment plans on a prospective, concurrent, or retrospective basis.	**work conditioning**	Work-related, intensive, goal-oriented treatment program specifically designed to restore an individual's systemic, neuromusculoskeletal (strength, endurance, movement, flexibility, and motor control), and cardiopulmonary functions to restore the client's physical capacity and function so the client can return to work.
V code	Part of ICD-9-CM codes, V codes describe circumstances that influence a patient's health status and identify reasons for medical encounters resulting from circumstances other than a disease or injury already classified in the main part of ICD-9-CM.	**work hardening**	Highly structured, goal-oriented, individualized treatment program designed to return the person to work by using real or simulated work activities to restore physical, behavioral, and vocational functions.
vertebral interspace	Non-bony space between two adjacent vertebral bodies that contains the cushioning intervertebral disk.		
whistleblower	Individual who discloses misconduct by a provider and may be eligible for monetary returns if the misconduct involves financial misconduct as determined on a case-by-case basis.		

Glossary

Correct Coding Initiative

0183T 97602❖

16020 01951-01952, 11000, 11040, 11100, 11719, 16000❖, 36000, 36400-36410, 36420-36430, 36440, 36600, 36640, 37202, 43752, 51701-51703, 62310-62319, 64400-64435, 64445-64450, 64470, 64475, 64479, 64483, 64505-64530, 69990, 93000-93010, 93040-93042, 93318, 94002, 94200, 94250, 94680-94690, 94770, 95812-95816, 95819, 95822, 95829, 95955, 96360, 96365, 96372, 96374-96376, 97022, 97597-97598❖, 97602-97606❖, 99148-99150, J2001

16025 01951-01952, 11000, 11040, 11100, 16020❖, 36000, 36400-36410, 36420-36430, 36440, 36600, 36640, 37202, 43752, 51701-51703, 62310-62319, 64400-64435, 64445-64450, 64470, 64475, 64479, 64483, 64505-64530, 69990, 93000-93010, 93040-93042, 93318, 94002, 94200, 94250, 94680-94690, 94770, 95812-95816, 95819, 95822, 95829, 95955, 96360, 96365, 96372, 96374-96376, 97022, 97597-97598❖, 97602-97606❖, 99148-99150, J2001

16030 01951-01952, 11000, 11040, 11100, 16020-16025❖, 36000, 36400-36410, 36420-36430, 36440, 36600, 36640, 37202, 43752, 51701-51703, 62310-62319, 64400-64435, 64445-64450, 64470, 64475, 64479, 64483, 64505-64530, 69990, 93000-93010, 93040-93042, 93318, 94002, 94200, 94250, 94680-94690, 94770, 95812-95816, 95819, 95822, 95829, 95955, 96360, 96365, 96372, 96374-96376, 97022, 97597-97598❖, 97602-97606❖, 99148-99150, J2001

29105 12001-12002, 12035, 29075, 29125, 29705, 36000, 36400-36410, 36420-36430, 36440, 36600, 36640, 37202, 43752, 51701-51703, 62310-62319, 64400-64435, 64445-64450, 64470, 64475, 64479, 64483, 64505-64530, 69990, 93000-93010, 93040-93042, 93318, 94002, 94200, 94250, 94680-94690, 94770, 95812-95816, 95819, 95822, 95829, 95955, 96360, 96365, 96372, 96374-96376, 99148-99150, G0168

29125 12001-12002, 12032, 12042-12044, 13121, 13132, 29130, 29260, 36000, 36400-36410, 36420-36430, 36440, 36600, 36640, 37202, 43752, 51701-51703, 62310-62319, 64400-64435, 64445-64450, 64470, 64475, 64479, 64483, 64505-64530, 69990, 93000-93010, 93040-93042, 93318, 94002, 94200, 94250, 94680-94690, 94770, 95812-95816, 95819, 95822, 95829, 95955, 96360, 96365, 96372, 96374-96376, 99148-99150, G0168

29126 36000, 36400-36410, 36420-36430, 36440, 36600, 36640, 37202, 43752, 51701-51703, 62310-62319, 64400-64435, 64445-64450, 64470, 64475, 64479, 64483, 64505-64530, 69990, 93000-93010, 93040-93042, 93318, 94002, 94200, 94250, 94680-94690, 94770, 95812-95816, 95819, 95822, 95829, 95955, 96360, 96365, 96372, 96374-96376, 99148-99150

29130 36000, 36400-36410, 36420-36430, 36440, 36600, 36640, 37202, 43752, 51701-51703, 62310-62319, 64400-64435, 64445-64450, 64470, 64475, 64479, 64483, 64505-64530, 69990, 93000-93010, 93040-93042, 93318, 94002, 94200, 94250, 94680-94690, 94770, 95812-95816, 95819, 95822, 95829, 95955, 96360, 96365, 96372, 96374-96376, 99148-99150

29131 36000, 36400-36410, 36420-36430, 36440, 36600, 36640, 37202, 43752, 51701-51703, 62310-62319, 64400-64435, 64445-64450, 64470, 64475, 64479, 64483, 64505-64530, 69990, 93000-93010, 93040-93042, 93318, 94002, 94200, 94250, 94680-94690, 94770, 95812-95816, 95819, 95822, 95829, 95955, 96360, 96365, 96372, 96374-96376, 99148-99150

29200 36000, 36400-36410, 36420-36430, 36440, 36600, 36640, 37202, 43752, 51701-51703, 62310-62319, 64400-64435, 64445-64450, 64470, 64475, 64479, 64483, 64505-64530, 69990, 93000-93010, 93040-93042, 93318, 94002, 94200, 94250, 94680-94690, 94770, 95812-95816, 95819, 95822, 95829, 95955, 96360, 96365, 96372, 96374-96376, 99148-99150

29240 36000, 36400-36410, 36420-36430, 36440, 36600, 36640, 37202, 43752, 51701-51703, 62310-62319, 64400-64435, 64445-64450, 64470, 64475, 64479, 64483, 64505-64530, 69990, 93000-93010, 93040-93042, 93318, 94002, 94200, 94250, 94680-94690, 94770, 95812-95816, 95819, 95822, 95829, 95955, 96360, 96365, 96372, 96374-96376, 99148-99150

29260 36000, 36400-36410, 36420-36430, 36440, 36600, 36640, 37202, 43752, 51701-51703, 62310-62319, 64400-64435, 64445-64450, 64470, 64475, 64479, 64483, 64505-64530, 69990, 93000-93010, 93040-93042, 93318, 94002, 94200, 94250, 94680-94690, 94770, 95812-95816, 95819, 95822, 95829, 95955, 96360, 96365, 96372, 96374-96376, 99148-99150

29280 36000, 36400-36410, 36420-36430, 36440, 36600, 36640, 37202, 43752, 51701-51703, 62310-62319, 64400-64435, 64445-64450, 64470, 64475, 64479, 64483, 64505-64530, 69990, 93000-93010, 93040-93042, 93318, 94002, 94200, 94250, 94680-94690, 94770, 95812-95816, 95819, 95822, 95829, 95955, 96360, 96365, 96372, 96374-96376, 99148-99150

29505 29445❖, 29515, 29540, 36000, 36400-36410, 36420-36430, 36440, 36600, 36640, 37202, 43752, 51701-51703, 62310-62319, 64400-64435, 64445-64450, 64470, 64475, 64479, 64483, 64505-64530, 69990, 93000-93010, 93040-93042, 93318, 94002, 94200, 94250, 94680-94690, 94770, 95812-95816, 95819, 95822, 95829, 95955, 96360, 96365, 96372, 96374-96376, 99148-99150

29515	11055-11056, 29445✧, 29540-29580, 36000, 36400-36410, 36420-36430, 36440, 36600, 36640, 37202, 43752, 51701-51703, 62310-62319, 64400-64435, 64445-64449, 64470, 64475, 64479, 64483, 64505-64530, 69990, 93000-93010, 93040-93042, 93318, 94002, 94200, 94250, 94680-94690, 94770, 95812-95816, 95819, 95822, 95829, 95955, 96360, 96365, 96372, 96374-96376, 99148-99150
29520	29445✧, 36000, 36400-36410, 36420-36430, 36440, 36600, 36640, 37202, 43752, 51701-51703, 62310-62319, 64400-64435, 64445-64450, 64470, 64475, 64479, 64483, 64505-64530, 69990, 93000-93010, 93040-93042, 93318, 94002, 94200, 94250, 94680-94690, 94770, 95812-95816, 95819, 95822, 95829, 95955, 96360, 96365, 96372, 96374-96376, 99148-99150
29530	12002, 29445✧, 36000, 36400-36410, 36420-36430, 36440, 36600, 36640, 37202, 43752, 51701-51703, 62310-62319, 64400-64435, 64445-64450, 64470, 64475, 64479, 64483, 64505-64530, 69990, 93000-93010, 93040-93042, 93318, 94002, 94200, 94250, 94680-94690, 94770, 95812-95816, 95819, 95822, 95829, 95955, 96360, 96365, 96372, 96374-96376, 99148-99150
29540	11900, 12004, 29445✧, 29550, 36000, 36400-36410, 36420-36430, 36440, 36600, 36640, 37202, 43752, 51701-51703, 62310-62319, 64400-64435, 64445-64449, 64470, 64475, 64479, 64483, 64505-64530, 69990, 93000-93010, 93040-93042, 93318, 94002, 94200, 94250, 94680-94690, 94770, 95812-95816, 95819, 95822, 95829, 95955, 96360, 96365, 96372, 96374-96376, 99148-99150
29550	11719, 11900, 36000, 36400-36410, 36420-36430, 36440, 36600, 36640, 37202, 43752, 51701-51703, 62310-62319, 64400-64435, 64445-64450, 64470, 64475, 64479, 64483, 64505-64530, 69990, 93000-93010, 93040-93042, 93318, 94002, 94200, 94250, 94680-94690, 94770, 95812-95816, 95819, 95822, 95829, 95955, 96360, 96365, 96372, 96374-96376, 99148-99150, G0127
29580	15852, 29540-29550, 29700, 36000, 36400-36410, 36420-36430, 36440, 36600, 36640, 37202, 43752, 51701-51703, 62310-62319, 64400-64435, 64445-64449, 64470, 64475, 64479, 64483, 64505-64530, 69990, 87070, 87076-87077, 93000-93010, 93040-93042, 93318, 94002, 94200, 94250, 94680-94690, 94770, 95812-95816, 95819, 95822, 95829, 95955, 96360, 96365, 96372, 96374-96376, 99148-99150
29590	29540, 29580, 36000, 36400-36410, 36420-36430, 36440, 36600, 36640, 37202, 43752, 51701-51703, 62310-62319, 64400-64435, 64445-64449, 64470, 64475, 64479, 64483, 64505-64530, 69990, 93000-93010, 93040-93042, 93318, 94002, 94200, 94250, 94680-94690, 94770, 95812-95816, 95819, 95822, 95829, 95955, 96360, 96365, 96372, 96374-96376, 99148-99150
64550	36000, 36400-36410, 36420-36430, 36440, 36600, 51701-51703, 61850✧, 61860✧, 61870-61880✧, 69990, 93000-93010, 93040-93042, 93318, 94002, 94200, 94250, 94680-94690, 94770, 95812-95816, 95819, 95829, 95955, 96360, 96365, 96372, 96374-96376, 99148-99150
90901	51701-51703, 51784-51785, 51795, 64550, 90804-90819, 90821-90824, 90826-90829, 90845-90853, 90857, 90865, 90880, 91122, 96360, 96365, 96372, 96374-96376, 99148-99150
90911	51701-51703, 51784-51785, 51795, 64550, 90804-90819, 90821-90824, 90826-90829, 90845-90853, 90857, 90865, 90880, 90901, 91122, 95860-95864, 95867-95872, 96360, 96365, 96372, 96374-96376, 97032, 97110-97112, 97530, 97535, 97750, 99148-99150
92607	92506✧, 92507-92508, 92597✧, 92609, 97755
92608	97755
92609	92506-92508, 97755
92610	92511
92611	76120-76125, 92511, 92610
92950	36000, 36410, 51701-51703, 92961✧, 96360, 96365, 96372, 96374-96376, 99148-99150
93015	0178T-0179T, 0180T, 36000, 36410, 93000-93010, 93016-93018, 93040-93042, 94760-94761, 96360, 96365, 96372, 96374-96376
93016	0178T-0179T, 0180T, 36000, 36410, 93000-93010, 93040-93042, 94760-94761, 96360, 96365, 96372, 96374-96376
93017	0178T-0179T, 0180T, 36000, 36410, 93000-93010, 93040-93042, 96360, 96365, 96372, 96374-96376
93018	0178T-0179T, 0180T, 36000, 36410, 93000-93010, 93040-93042, 93278, 94760-94761, 96372, 96374-96376, 96413
94010	00520, 94200, 94375, 95070-95071✧
94350	00520
94375	00520
94620	00520, 0178T-0179T, 0180T, 93000-93010, 93015-93018, 93040-93042, 94010, 94060, 94200, 94250, 94680-94690, 94760-94770, J1644
94621	00520, 0178T-0179T, 0180T, 93000-93010, 93015-93018, 93040-93042, 94010, 94060, 94200, 94250, 94620, 94680-94690, 94770
94640	89220, 94664
94642	00520
94644	94640, 94642✧
94662	94660✧
94664	00520
94667	00520
94668	00520, 94667✧
94680	94250, 94681-94690, J1644
94681	94250, 94690, J1644
94690	J1644
94760	94762
94761	94760, 94762
95831	95851, 97140
95832	95852, 97140
95833	95831-95832, 95851, 97140
95834	95831-95833, 95851-95852, 97140
95860	95869-95870, 95873-95874
95861	95860, 95869-95870, 95873-95874
95863	95860-95861, 95869-95870, 95873-95874, 95920
95864	95860-95863, 95869-95870, 95873-95874, 95920
95866	90901, 95867✧, 95870✧, 95873-95874, 95920

95867	95869-95870, 95873-95874
95868	92265, 95866❖, 95867, 95869-95870, 95873-95874
95869	90901, 95870, 95873-95874, 95920
95870	95873-95874
95875	36000, 36410, 95860, 95869, 96360, 96365, 96372, 96374-96376
95903	95900, 95920
96000	97116, 97750
96001	96000, 97116, 97750
96002	95860-95866, 95869-95872, 97116, 97750
96003	95860-95866, 95869-95872, 97116, 97750
96004	95860-95866, 95869-95872, 97116, 97750
96105	96110-96111❖, 96125
96110	96125
97001	62310-62319, 64400-64435, 64445-64450, 64470-64484, 64505-64530, 95831-95834, 95851-95852, 96150-96154, 97750, 97755, 97762, 97802-97804, 99201-99255❖, 99291-99292❖, 99304-99310❖, 99315-99318❖, 99324-99328❖, 99334-99337❖, 99341-99350❖, 99354-99357❖, 99455-99463❖, 99465-99466❖, 99468-99480❖, 99605-99606, G0270-G0271
97002	62310-62319, 64400-64435, 64445-64450, 64470-64484, 64505-64530, 95831-95834, 95851-95852, 96150-96154, 97001❖, 97750, 97755, 97762, 97802-97804, 99201-99255❖, 99291-99292❖, 99304-99310❖, 99315-99318❖, 99324-99328❖, 99334-99337❖, 99341-99350❖, 99354-99357❖, 99455-99463❖, 99465-99466❖, 99468-99480❖, 99605-99606, G0270-G0271
97003	62310-62319, 64400-64435, 64445-64450, 64470-64484, 64505-64530, 95831-95834, 95851-95852, 96150-96154, 97750, 97755, 97762, 97802-97804, 99201-99255❖, 99291-99292❖, 99304-99310❖, 99315-99318❖, 99324-99328❖, 99334-99337❖, 99341-99350❖, 99354-99357❖, 99455-99463❖, 99465-99466❖, 99468-99480❖, 99605-99606, G0270-G0271
97004	62310-62319, 64400-64435, 64445-64450, 64470-64484, 64505-64530, 95831-95834, 95851-95852, 96150-96154, 97003❖, 97750, 97755, 97762, 97802-97804, 99201-99255❖, 99291-99292❖, 99304-99310❖, 99315-99318❖, 99324-99328❖, 99334-99337❖, 99341-99350❖, 99354-99357❖, 99455-99463❖, 99465-99466❖, 99468-99480❖, 99605-99606, G0270-G0271
97012	62310-62319, 64400-64435, 64445-64450, 64470-64484, 64505-64530, 97002, 97004, 97018, 97140❖, 99186❖
97016	62310-62319, 64400-64435, 64445-64450, 64470-64484, 64505-64530, 97002, 97004, 97018, 97026, 99186❖
97018	62310-62319, 64400-64435, 64445-64450, 64470-64484, 64505-64530, 97002, 97004, 97022❖, 99186
97022	62310-62319, 64400-64435, 64445-64450, 64470-64484, 64505-64530, 97002, 97004, 97602, 99186
97024	62310-62319, 64400-64435, 64445-64450, 64470-64484, 64505-64530, 97002, 97004, 97018, 97026, 99186
97026	62310-62319, 64400-64435, 64445-64450, 64470-64484, 64505-64530, 97002, 97004, 97018❖, 97022❖, 99186
97028	62310-62319, 64400-64435, 64445-64450, 64470-64484, 64505-64530, 96910-96913❖, 97002, 97004, 97018, 97022❖, 97026, 99186
97032	62310-62319, 64400-64435, 64445-64450, 64470-64484, 64505-64550, 97002, 97004
97033	62310-62319, 64400-64435, 64445-64448, 64450, 64470-64484, 64505-64530, 97002, 97004
97034	62310-62319, 64400-64435, 64445-64450, 64470-64484, 64505-64530, 97002, 97004
97035	0183T❖, 62310-62319, 64400-64435, 64445-64450, 64470-64484, 64505-64530, 97002, 97004
97036	62310-62319, 64400-64435, 64445-64450, 64470-64484, 64505-64530, 97002, 97004
97039	62310-62319, 64400-64435, 64445-64450, 64470-64484, 64505-64530, 97002, 97004
97110	62310-62319, 64400-64435, 64445-64450, 64470-64484, 64505-64530, 93040-93042, 97002, 97004, 99186
97112	62310-62319, 64400-64435, 64445-64450, 64470-64484, 64505-64530, 97002, 97004, 97022, 97036, 99186
97113	62310-62319, 64400-64435, 64445-64450, 64470-64484, 64505-64530, 97002, 97004, 97022, 97036, 97110
97116	62310-62319, 64400-64435, 64445-64450, 64470-64484, 64505-64530, 97002, 97004, 99186
97124	62310-62319, 64400-64435, 64445-64450, 64470-64484, 64505-64530, 97002, 97004, 99186
97139	62310-62319, 64400-64435, 64445-64450, 64470-64484, 64505-64530, 97002, 97004
97140	62310-62319, 64400-64435, 64445-64450, 64470-64484, 64505-64530, 95851-95852, 97002, 97004, 97018, 97124, 97530❖, 97750, 99186
97150	62310-62319, 64400-64435, 64445-64450, 64470-64484, 64505-64530, 95831, 95834, 95851, 97002, 97004, 97110-97113❖, 97116❖, 97124, 97140❖, 97530❖, 97532-97537, 97542, 97760-97761
97530	62310-62319, 64400-64435, 64445-64450, 64470-64484, 64505-64530, 95831-95834, 95851-95852, 97002, 97004, 97113, 97116, 97532-97537, 97542, 97750, 99186
97532	62310-62319, 64400-64435, 64445-64450, 64470-64484, 64505-64530, 97002, 97004
97533	62310-62319, 64400-64435, 64445-64450, 64470-64484, 64505-64530, 97002, 97004
97535	62310-62319, 64400-64435, 64445-64450, 64470-64484, 64505-64530, 97002, 97004, 97802-97804, G0270-G0271
97537	97002, 97004, 97802-97804, G0270-G0271
97542	97002, 97004
97545	97002, 97004, 97140

CCI

97597   00100-00104, 00120-00126, 00140-00148, 00160-00164, 00170-00176, 00190-00192, 00210, 00212-00218, 00220-00222, 00300, 00320-00322, 00350-00352, 00400-00406, 00410, 00450-00454, 00470-00474, 00500, 00520-00529, 00530-00537, 00540-00542, 00546-00548, 00550, 00560-00566, 00580, 00600-00604, 00620-00626, 00630-00635, 00670, 00700-00702, 00730, 00740, 00750-00756, 00770, 00790-00796, 00800-00802, 00810, 00820, 00830-00832, 00840-00848, 00860-00868, 00870-00873, 00880-00882, 00902-00908, 00910-00918, 00920, 00922-00928, 00930-00938, 00940-00944, 00948, 00950-00952, 01112, 01120-01150, 01160, 01170, 01180-01202, 01210-01234, 01250-01260, 01270-01274, 01320, 01340, 01360, 01380-01404, 01420, 01430-01432, 01440-01444, 01462-01464, 01470-01474, 01480-01486, 01490, 01500-01502, 01520-01522, 01610, 01620-01622, 01630-01638, 01650-01656, 01670, 01680-01682, 01710-01716, 01730-01732, 01740-01744, 01756-01758, 01760, 01770-01772, 01780-01782, 01810, 01820, 01830-01832, 0183T✦, 01840-01844, 01850-01852, 01860, 01916, 01920, 01922-01926, 01930, 01935-01936, 01951-01952, 01960-01961, 01963, 01967, 01996, 11000✦, 11720-11721✦, 11900-11901, 29580, 64400-64435, 64445-64450, 64470, 64475, 64479, 64483, 69990, 96372, 96374-96376, 97002, 97022, 97602-97606✦

97598   00100-00104, 00120-00126, 00140-00148, 00160-00164, 00170-00176, 00190-00192, 00210, 00212-00218, 00220-00222, 00300, 00320-00322, 00350-00352, 00400-00406, 00410, 00450-00454, 00470-00474, 00500, 00520-00529, 00530-00537, 00540-00542, 00546-00548, 00550, 00560-00566, 00580, 00600-00604, 00620-00626, 00630-00635, 00670, 00700-00702, 00730, 00740, 00750-00756, 00770, 00790-00796, 00800-00802, 00810, 00820, 00830-00832, 00840-00848, 00860-00868, 00870-00873, 00880-00882, 00902-00908, 00910-00918, 00920, 00922-00928, 00930-00938, 00940-00944, 00948, 00950-00952, 01112, 01120-01150, 01160, 01170, 01180-01202, 01210-01234, 01250-01260, 01270-01274, 01320, 01340, 01360, 01380-01404, 01420, 01430-01432, 01440-01444, 01462-01464, 01470-01474, 01480-01486, 01490, 01500-01502, 01520-01522, 01610, 01620-01622, 01630-01638, 01650-01656, 01670, 01680-01682, 01710-01716, 01730-01732, 01740-01744, 01756-01758, 01760, 01770-01772, 01780-01782, 01810, 01820, 01830-01832, 0183T✦, 01840-01844, 01850-01852, 01860, 01916, 01920, 01922-01926, 01930, 01935-01936, 01951-01952, 01960-01961, 01963, 01967, 01996, 11000✦, 11720-11721✦, 11900-11901, 29580, 64400-64435, 64445-64450, 64470, 64475, 64479, 64483, 69990, 96372, 96374-96376, 97002, 97022, 97597, 97602-97606✦

97602   00100-00104, 00120-00126, 00140-00148, 00160-00164, 00170-00176, 00190-00192, 00210, 00212-00218, 00220-00222, 00300, 00320-00326, 00350-00352, 00400-00406, 00410, 00450-00454, 00470-00474, 00500, 00520-00529, 00530-00539, 00540-00542, 00546-00548, 00550, 00560-00566, 00580, 00600-00604, 00620-00626, 00630-00635, 00640, 00670, 00700-00702, 00730, 00740, 00750-00756, 00770, 00790-00797, 00800-00802, 00810, 00820, 00830-00836, 00840-00848, 00851, 00860-00868, 00870-00873, 00880-00882, 00902-00908, 00910-00918, 00920-00928, 00930-00938, 00940-00944, 00948, 00950-00952, 01112, 01120-01150, 01160, 01170-01173, 01180-01202, 01210-01234, 01250-01260, 01270-01274, 01320, 01340, 01360, 01380-01404, 01420, 01430-01432, 01440-01444, 01462-01464, 01470-01474, 01480-01486, 01490, 01500-01502, 01520-01522, 01610, 01620-01622, 01630-01638, 01650-01656, 01670, 01680-01682, 01710-01716, 01730-01732, 01740-01744, 01756-01758, 01760, 01770-01772, 01780-01782, 01810, 01820-01829, 01830-01832, 01840-01844, 01850-01852, 01860, 01916, 01920, 01922-01926, 01930-01933, 01951-01952, 01958, 01960-01963, 01965-01967, 01990-01992, 01996, 11000✦, 11720-11721✦, 11900-11901, 29580, 64400-64435, 64445-64450, 64470, 64475, 64479, 64483, 69990, 96372, 96374-96376, 97002

97605   00100-00104, 00120-00126, 00140-00148, 00160-00164, 00170-00176, 00190-00192, 00210, 00212-00218, 00220-00222, 00300, 00320-00326, 00350-00352, 00400-00406, 00410, 00450-00454, 00470-00474, 00500, 00520-00529, 00530-00539, 00540-00542, 00546-00548, 00550, 00560-00566, 00580, 00600-00604, 00620-00626, 00630-00635, 00640, 00670, 00700-00702, 00730, 00740, 00750-00756, 00770, 00790-00797, 00800-00802, 00810, 00820, 00830-00836, 00840-00848, 00851, 00860-00868, 00870-00873, 00880-00882, 00902-00908, 00910-00918, 00920-00928, 00930-00938, 00940-00944, 00948, 00950-00952, 01112, 01120-01150, 01160, 01170-01173, 01180-01202, 01210-01234, 01250-01260, 01270-01274, 01320, 01340, 01360, 01380-01404, 01420, 01430-01432, 01440-01444, 01462-01464, 01470-01474, 01480-01486, 01490, 01500-01502, 01520-01522, 01610, 01620-01622, 01630-01638, 01650-01656, 01670, 01680-01682, 01710-01716, 01730-01732, 01740-01744, 01756-01758, 01760, 01770-01772, 01780-01782, 01810, 01820-01829, 01830-01832, 0183T✦, 01840-01844, 01850-01852, 01860, 01916, 01920, 01922-01926, 01930-01936, 01951-01952, 01958, 01960-01963, 01965-01967, 01990-01992, 01996, 11000✦, 11720-11721✦, 11900-11901, 64400-64435, 64445-64450, 64470, 64475, 64479, 64483, 69990, 96372, 96374-96376, 97002, 97602✦

CCI

✦ Mutually Exclusive   CPT codes only © 2009 American Medical Association. All Rights Reserved.   © 2009 Ingenix

97606   00100-00104, 00120-00126, 00140-00148, 00160-00164,
00170-00176, 00190-00192, 00210, 00212-00218,
00220-00222, 00300, 00320-00326, 00350-00352,
00400-00406, 00410, 00450-00454, 00470-00474,
00500, 00520-00529, 00530-00539, 00540-00542,
00546-00548, 00550, 00560-00566, 00580,
00600-00604, 00620-00626, 00630-00635, 00640,
00670, 00700-00702, 00730, 00740, 00750-00756,
00770, 00790-00797, 00800-00802, 00810, 00820,
00830-00836, 00840-00848, 00851, 00860-00868,
00870-00873, 00880-00882, 00902-00908, 00910-00918,
00920-00928, 00930-00938, 00940-00944, 00948,
00950-00952, 01112, 01120-01150, 01160,
01170-01173, 01180-01202, 01210-01234, 01250-01260,
01270-01274, 01320, 01340, 01360, 01380-01404,
01420, 01430-01432, 01440-01444, 01462-01464,
01470-01474, 01480-01486, 01490, 01500-01502,
01520-01522, 01610, 01620-01622, 01630-01638,
01650-01656, 01670, 01680-01682, 01710-01716,
01730-01732, 01740-01744, 01756-01758, 01760,
01770-01772, 01780-01782, 01810, 01820-01829,
01830-01832, 0183T✦, 01840-01844, 01850-01852,
01860, 01916, 01920, 01922-01926, 01930-01936,
01951-01952, 01958, 01960-01963, 01965-01967,
01990-01992, 01996, 11000✦, 11720-11721✦,
11900-11901, 64400-64435, 64445-64450, 64470,
64475, 64479, 64483, 69990, 96372, 96374-96376,
97002, 97602✦, 97605

97750   95831-95834, 95851-95852, 97150

97755   97035, 97110-97112, 97140, 97530, 97532-97537,
97542-97545, 97750, 97760-97761, 97762✦

97760   29044-29085, 29105-29450, 29505-29580, 29700-29710,
29720-29750, 62310-62319, 64400-64435, 64445-64450,
64470-64484, 64505-64530, 97002, 97004, 97016,
97110-97112, 97116, 97124, 97140, 97762✦

97761   62310-62319, 64400-64435, 64445-64450, 64470-64484,
64505-64530, 97002, 97004, 97016, 97110-97112,
97116, 97124, 97140, 97760, 97762✦

CCI

Index

A

ABG 151, 152
ABN 21, 25, 26, 55, 292
abnormal findings 142, 159, 160
action plan 44
acupuncture 21, 124, 127
acute poliomyelitis 134, 136
acute respiratory infections 150
add-on code 110
adjudication 35, 45, 49, 51, 53, 57, 58, 59, 61, 64, 73, 74
ADL 119, 121, 127
advance beneficiary notice 21, 22, 25, 55, 292
alginate dressing 309, 310, 311
Alzheimer's 142, 143, 175, 181, 191, 193, 262, 266
APC 7
appeals 19, 27, 32, 49, 50, 51, 52, 53, 54, 55, 56, 57, 58, 59, 60
application 1, 42, 62, 104, 105, 106, 114, 116, 117, 118, 122, 127, 129, 144, 290, 293, 298, 299, 307, 326
APTA 1, 37, 54, 120, 121
aquatic therapy 2, 119, 127, 129
ARDS 151
arthritis 117, 135, 141, 145, 152, 153, 154, 155, 156, 157, 170, 172, 179, 180, 181, 195, 202, 211, 212, 217, 219, 255, 259, 261, 263, 265, 267, 268, 271
arthropathy 153, 154, 155, 180, 186, 192, 269
assignment of benefits 45
asthma 150, 151, 152, 180, 186, 199, 205, 218, 260, 261, 262, 263, 265, 266, 273

B

Bell's palsy 111
benign neoplasm 220
Blue Cross and Blue Shield 6, 36

C

calculating costs 9
cane 292, 297, 309, 310, 311, 328
capitation 8, 9, 61, 77
cardiac rehabilitation 99, 108, 127, 128
cardiopulmonary resuscitation 108, 127
cardiovascular services 108
cardiovascular stress test 108
cast supplies 292
casts 104
category III codes 125, 126
CCI 17, 18, 19
cellulitis 152, 172, 185, 186, 205, 212, 257
cerebrovascular disease 141, 145, 148, 190, 208, 214, 215
CHF 148, 151
chronic obstructive pulmonary disease (COPD) 150, 151, 183, 194, 328
claims 95, 96
CMS 1, 2, 8, 9, 10, 11, 12, 15, 16, 17, 18, 19, 25, 27, 35, 36, 42, 43, 44, 46, 47, 49, 50, 51, 53, 54, 55, 56, 57, 58, 59, 60, 64, 65, 73, 93, 94, 104, 120, 131, 169, 289, 292, 301, 306, 307

CMS-1500 2, 45, 47, 64, 65, 93
coding systems 1, 9, 289
collection policies 32, 33
complications 118, 132, 134, 135, 138, 139, 140, 141, 143, 157, 160, 163, 167, 186, 187, 202, 268, 270, 272, 273
concussion 161, 182, 186, 187, 200, 206, 212, 267
congenital anomalies 132, 148, 158, 159
congestive heart failure 148, 151, 198
constant attendance 103, 118, 120
convulsions 159, 178
COPD 150, 151
Correct Coding Initiative (CCI) 17, 19, 345
coverage issues 5, 103, 117, 307
CPAP 110, 127, 129, 326
CPR 7, 127, 130
CPT index 127
custom-fitted orthotic 123, 305
CVA 148, 174

D

decubitus ulcers 326
definitions and guidelines 2, 3, 36, 103, 131, 289
Denis-Browne splint strapping 106
dermatitis 105, 149, 152, 192, 205, 261, 265, 268, 272
developmental screening test II 115
diabetes 119, 138, 139, 140, 141, 179, 192, 193, 205, 218, 253, 254, 259, 271
diathermy 117, 127, 129, 326
dislocation 104, 128, 156, 160, 161, 177, 186, 192, 195, 196, 197, 199, 203, 205, 215, 216, 265
disuse atrophy 111, 156, 198
DME 62, 140, 297, 327
dressings 77, 104, 105, 122, 127, 165, 175, 181, 293
durable medical equipment (DME) 7, 16, 17, 25, 60, 62, 77, 140, 289, 293, 297, 299, 326, 327

E

E code 131, 149, 160, 166, 167, 274, 289
ear oximetry 129
EEG 111, 127
EKG 127, 147
electrical stimulation 111, 117, 124, 127, 299, 300
electrodes 106, 114, 187, 292, 309
electromyography 101, 107, 111, 112, 113, 114, 127, 128, 299
electronic remittance advice 77
electrotherapy 111
embolism 148, 149, 186, 200, 210
encephalitis 134, 135, 142, 143, 193, 216, 273
EOB 29, 53, 60
epilepsy 144, 145, 201, 219, 272
evaluation and management 74, 101, 109, 125
exercise therapy 174
explanation of benefits (EOB) 53, 60

F

flat foot **158**
foam dressing **123, 309, 311**
foreign body **151, 161, 205, 213, 253, 261, 265, 281**
fraud and abuse **11, 35, 42, 44, 60**
FTT **159, 160**
F-wave **113**

G

gout **141, 253**
gradient compression stocking **296**
group therapy **76, 120**
guidelines for physical therapy **37**

H

HCPCS Level II codes **2, 96**
HCPCS Level II index **289, 309**
health maintenance organizations (HMO) **5, 6, 45, 52**
health reimbursement accounts (HRA) **6**
health savings account (HSA) **6**
heel pad **305**
hemiplegia **145, 178, 181, 206, 262**
herpes zoster **134, 152, 218**
HIV **133, 134, 146, 164, 194, 202, 212**
home management training **121**
hot water bottle **298**
Huntington's chorea **143, 191**
hydrocephalus **158, 173, 175, 190, 207**
hydrocollator unit **298**
hydrocolloid dressing **294, 309, 310, 311**
hydrogel dressing **294, 295, 309, 310, 311**
hypertension **131, 133, 146, 178, 181, 208, 209, 210, 211**
hypotension **149, 211, 256, 268**

I

ICD-9-CM **98**
ICD-9-CM alphabetic index **274**
ICD-9-CM codes **1**
ICD-9-CM index **131, 169**
ice cap or collar **298**
IDDM **176, 179, 180, 181, 185, 186, 192, 205, 217, 252, 253, 254, 259, 260, 267, 271**
immunity disorder **132, 138, 141**
incident to **9, 119, 301**
independent practice association **6**
index **3**
infectious and parasitic diseases **132, 133, 136**
injury **98**
insurance **30**
intermittent positive pressure breathing (IPPB) **109**

L

lectromyography **128**
limiting charge **26, 28, 62**
LSO **303**
lupus **152**

M

malignant neoplasm **136, 220**
malnutrition **138, 141**
manifestation codes **154, 170**
manual therapy techniques **120**
MCM 2323 **305**
Medicaid **5, 11, 16, 42, 43, 46, 53, 55, 93, 131, 289, 291**
medical necessity **5, 11, 19, 25, 35, 36, 45, 49, 50, 53, 61, 292**
medigap **26, 27, 62**
meningitis **133, 142**
metabolic diseases **132, 138**
migraine **145, 175, 205, 217, 254, 266**
miscellaneous supplies **292**
motion analysis **114, 128**
multiple sclerosis **144, 193**
muscle testing **111, 112, 128**
muscular dystrophy **185, 193, 198, 205**
musculoskeletal system **104, 132, 153**
myasthenia gravis **146**

N

neoplasm **136, 137, 199, 207, 218, 220, 221, 222, 223, 224, 225, 226, 227, 228, 229, 230, 231, 232, 233, 234, 235, 236, 237, 238, 239, 240, 241, 242, 243, 244, 245, 246, 247, 248, 249, 250, 251, 252, 255**
neoplasm table **136**
nerve conduction **111, 113, 127, 128, 148**
nervous system **41, 106, 111, 115, 132, 134, 140, 142, 143, 144, 146, 226, 241, 249**
neurology **101, 111, 128, 129**
NIDDM **176**
non-participating providers **26**

O

Office of Inspector General (OIG) **35, 42, 43, 44**
open wounds **161**
orthotic **39, 40, 76, 123, 174, 269, 290, 304, 305, 306**
orthotic supplies **306**
osteoarthrosis **155, 165, 179, 191, 194**
osteomyelitis **141, 154, 158, 192, 193, 205, 219, 254**
osteoporosis **157, 188, 191, 195, 197, 216, 254, 263, 269**
other rehabilitation facility (ORF) **10**
outpatient rehabilitation CPT and HCPCS II codes **15**

P

paraffin bath **117, 129, 292, 298, 327**
Parkinson's disease **142, 143**
participating providers **6, 26**
patient information **35, 45, 46, 65**
phlebitis **149, 200, 212, 215, 257**
physical medicine and rehabilitation **115**
physical performance test **112, 123, 129**
physical therapy **2, 5, 7, 8, 9, 11, 12**
Physician Quality Reporting Initiative (PQRI)
   appropriate method of reporting quality indicators on the 1500 claim form **73**
pneumonia **76, 110, 150, 175, 187, 191, 193, 205, 212, 216, 217, 219, 258, 259, 265, 273**
pneumothorax **151, 259**

 © 2009 Ingenix

Index